The Park Chung Hee Era

THE PARK CHUNG HEE ERA

The Transformation of South Korea

Edited by

BYUNG-KOOK KIM

EZRA F. VOGEL

HARVARD UNIVERSITY PRESS
Cambridge, Massachusetts
London, England
2011

Library of Congress Cataloging-in-Publication Data

The Park Chung Hee era : the transformation of
South Korea / edited by Byung-Kook Kim and Ezra F. Vogel.
p.   cm.
Includes bibliographical references and index.
ISBN 978-0-674-05820-0 (alk. paper)
1. Korea (South)—Politics and government—1960–1988.
2. Park, Chung Hee, 1917–1979.
3. Comparative government—Case studies.
I. Kim, Pyong-guk, 1959 Mar. 18–   II. Vogel, Ezra F.
DS922.35.P336   2011
951.9504'3092—dc22   2010038046

Contents

Introduction:

The Case for Political History

Byung-Kook Kim

FEW PERIODS HAVE CHANGED South Korean history more than the Park era that began in May 1961 with a military coup d'état. The nature of leadership, the political parties and political opposition, the bureaucracy, the armed forces, relations between workers and farmers and their government, the *chaebol* industrial conglomerates, foreign policy—all were transformed. Meanwhile, economically South Korea grew out of poverty into an industrial powerhouse in one generation, albeit with massive political, social, and economic costs. And after the Park era suddenly ended in 1979, the reactions to what had taken place transformed the country once more.

The eighteen-year Park era has proved to be one of the most, if not *the* most, controversial topics for the Korean public, politicians, and scholars both at home and abroad. How much was the economic takeoff fueled by changes in the political and social fabric? To what degree was Park Chung Hee personally responsible for the transformation—both political and economic—across multiple sectors? Why did South Korea's political regime drift toward "hard" authoritarianism while its economy modernized at a hyper pace? Were these changes causally related? Why was his era marked by both dazzling policy successes and spectacular failures? How much were South Korea's successes and failures explained by its historically antecedent conditions? As one of a handful of newly industrializing countries (NICs) that succeeded in economically catching up with early developers and militarily building up a system of deterrence, but at huge costs, South Korea is a crucial case in understanding the politics of modernization.

This volume revisits South Korea's developmental era, but it distinguishes itself from other works on the nation's rebirth after 1961 by placing its analytic focus on political history. We have chosen *political* history for three reasons. First, although South Korea's macroeconomic indicators show a country continually undergoing a spectacular industrial transformation, its trajectory of modernization was anything but stable. The macroeconomic indicators covered up a deep sense of insecurity and vulnerability pervading South Korea. The high-payoff, high-risk strategy of subsidizing growth through bureaucratically distributed policy loans burdened banks with huge nonperforming loans, thus entrapping the economy in a cycle of boom and bust and presenting the South Korean leadership with hard policy choices in 1972 and 1979. The volatile swings in this U.S. ally's global, regional, and peninsular strategy aggravated or ameliorated South Korea's security dilemmas in 1961, 1964, 1969, and 1976, which triggered its policymakers' need to reassess competing budgetary priorities between military and economic programs. Most critical, Park Chung Hee was at first supposed to step down in 1971 and, after a constitutional revision to allow his third presidential term, in 1975. Whether he would do so was to have profound impacts on South Korea's regime character and, hence, its strategy of modernization. The choice made at each of these critical junctures, determining South Korea's subsequent path of economic growth, was heavily shaped by politics.

Second, we focus on political history because at many of the critical junctures, for South Korea to succeed at the state building, military security improvements, and market formation upon which its prospect for hypergrowth depended, the resolution of problems and issues could only come from its top political authorities' attempt at juggling the competing claims of geopolitics, geoeconomics, and domestic politics. To explain South Korea's power realignments between state ministries away from its intrinsically conservative Ministry of Finance (MoF) in 1962, 1965, and 1973, or toward the MoF in 1969, 1972, and 1979, we must examine how political leaders controlled state bureaucrats. State ministries, if left alone, only produce a deadlock of interests or a gradual adjustment of interests.[1] To explain the *chaebol* conglomerates' risk-taking behavior, one must look into what kind of incentives they had that made taking risks a rational strategy from their perspective and why those incentives were dangled in front of them in the first place. Such inquiries require an analysis of Park Chung Hee and his top aides' political goals, calculations, and strategies.

The primacy of politics is shown even more directly in the social and political realms. To explain the farmers' zigzagging behavior between "pro-Park" and "anti-Park" votes in 1963, 1967, 1971, and 1978, we must analyze Park's similarly zigzagging strategy of modernization between the Green Revolution and the agricultural squeeze, his transformation of rural state institutions into a political machine, and his awakening of politically contagious regionalist sentiments in all corners of South Korea. Likewise, explaining why labor failed to challenge his strategy of trickle-down growth requires an analysis of the top-down reorganization of labor unions in 1961, as well as Park's massive and persistent crackdown on dissident *chaeya* activists, which prevented leftists from establishing an enduring base of support in society. The decision to normalize relations with Japan and dispatch combat troops to South Vietnam in 1965 with an eye to securing the seed money for strategic industrial projects also constituted a political act of risk taking.

Third, we go back to political *history* because both economic theories and developmental state literatures are less effective in explaining the motives behind, as opposed to the outcomes of, Park's policy decisions. To begin with, many of his policy choices collided head on with prevailing economic ideas. Responding to a slowdown in growth rates in 1969, 1972, 1974, and 1979, South Korea adopted unorthodox measures, relieving stagflationary pressures quickly by imposing shock therapy—interest hikes, debt rescheduling, "industrial rationalization," devaluation, wage cuts, and, in 1972, even freezing payments of private *sach'ae* (curb-market) loans—on society, but then using this relief of market pressures only as grounds for another massive injection of government-subsidized bank loans to finance a new round of hypergrowth. This obsession with economic growth and the leadership's ability to carry out its shock therapy despite political risks and economic dangers can only be understood by turning to an analysis of Park's vision of *puguk kangbyŏng* (rich nation, strong army) and his strategy to leverage structural pressures to achieve that vision and, with it, satisfy his will to power.

Obviously, using political history does not require us to reject efforts at theory building. On the contrary, theories help us identify analytic and historical puzzles and issues, as well as map out our line of inquiry. However, it is also true that many of the complexities, ambiguities, and uncertainties in South Korea's historical trajectory of modernization have been lost in efforts at theory building. The chapters in this volume restore those lost stories and, in the process, provide us with an opportunity to assess both the strengths and the weaknesses of prevailing views and discover ways to modify those ideas. Placing theories in the context of political history, our chapters agree on three crucial analytic points.

First, South Korea's political actors defy any easy typology and transcend many dichotomous conceptualizations of prevailing theories. The chapters will argue that, for us to understand the role of these actors in the politics of modernization, we frequently need to combine what theories originally conceptualized as mutually exclusive concepts. The state was predatory and yet technocratic. The *chaebol* did receive special favors as "cronies" of Park and his ruling coalition but also, with dedication and entrepreneurial skill, pioneered new growth industries at immense risks. The military was politicized, defending its political master during crisis, but was also a professionalized actor successfully deterring Pyŏng-yang's invasion. Both the ruling and the opposition political parties were internally pulled apart by factional struggle and externally constrained by police surveillance, and yet their struggles for presidential succession seriously constrained Park's political options. The dissident *chaeya* was organizationally weak, but contentious—and sometime even capable of reshaping national agendas. The Park regime also boasted resilience, only to be shaken up by spontaneously organized political protests from below, to which it responded with increased repression. The "hegemonic" United States usually could not bring its weaker South Korean client-state to its knees when the two nations' interests diverged. Even in the realm of security, U.S. deterrence assumed dual political meanings, one against Pyŏng-yang's threats of war and another against South Korea's demand for retaliation after North Korean guerrilla attacks or against Park's nuclear ambitions. The chapters in this volume urge us to imagine actors that lie in between the opposite concepts of predatory and technocratic states, politicized and professionalized armed forces, weak and strong political parties, resilient and fragile regimes, and hegemonic and client powers.

Second, many of the variables identified as major drivers of South Korea's modernization—from its "Weberian developmental state"[2] to state-business "networks,"[3] to "Asian values" and U.S. aid policy, even to Park Chung Hee's leadership—were continually evolving entities, with many of their elements newly created, nurtured, and/or readjusted as part of a series of policy learning and institutional experiments during Park's political rule. The institutions as described by theorists of developmental states and networks were more an idealized end product of the eighteen years of Park's political rule than the actual state of political and economic relations at any one point in his era. The "Weberian" developmental state, the "radical" *chaeya*, the "modern" military, the "regionalist" political parties, the "ideologically contentious" labor forces, and the authoritarian "garrison state" we encounter in prevailing theories on South Korea's politics of modernization were more products of Park's political rule than a set of structures enabling or constraining his role as a modernizer during much of his developmental era. The chapters in this volume urge us to look at these actors as existing in a relationship of co-evolution, continually reshaping each other's political roles, identities, and strategies through their actions and counteractions.

Third, as a corollary of our evolutionary perspective, the chapters argue that intentions look more complex, options more numerous, and consequences more uncertain than what has been argued by other theorists. Many of Park's decisions at critical junctures of South Korea's trajectory of modernization could have gone very differently, given certain costs and uncertain benefits. He did not decide out of ignorance. On the contrary, Park knew the domestic political costs, economic obstacles, and foreign policy risks and yet he stuck with many of the decisions he made in the name of *puguk kangbyŏng*, with varying outcomes. The modernizer put South Korea on a path to hypergrowth by 1965 and kept it on that track through economic crises in 1969, 1972, and 1974 with a mix of shock therapy and subsidies. In the last year of his rule, however, Park saw his growth machine become paralyzed under the weight of its internal contradictions. He had successfully managed political crises in 1965, 1969, 1972, and 1975 with a combination of threats and appeasements, but in 1979 Park looked like a different man, no longer mixing carrots and sticks in his dealings with the opposition, which only aggravated regime instability. Similarly, Park dexterously brought the United States and Japan into a transnational coalition in support of his program of economic growth and military build-up in 1965 by normalizing relations with Japan and dispatching combat troops to South Vietnam, but after Richard M. Nixon's Guam Doctrine of 1969, his attempts at slowing down, if not reversing, U.S. military withdrawal only hurt national, regime, and personal interests by developing into a triple foreign policy crisis around human rights abuses, "Koreagate," and military withdrawal. These varying outcomes of his strategy of state building, market formation, and military security urge us to put Park and his intentions at the center of analysis.

Political Regime

Building a typology of political regimes, a central task in political science research, at first appears simple. South Korea under Park Chung Hee showed traits of what Juan J. Linz once identified as those of an authoritarian regime: "[a] political syste[m] with limited, not responsible, political pluralism; without elaborate and guiding ideology (but with distinctive mentalities); without intensive nor extensive political mobilization (except

[at] some points in their developments); and in which a leader (or occasionally a small group) exercises power within formally ill defined limits but actually quite predictable ones."[4]

By this definition, South Korea's developmental era qualifies as a period of authoritarian rule. Even before Park Chung Hee launched his *yushin* constitution in 1972 in order to prolong his rule indefinitely, South Korea's legislative and judiciary branches had too few constitutional prerogatives to ensure political pluralism; political parties and factions lacked not only vision and programs but also dense grassroots organizations for mobilization; and dissident activists *(chaeya),* labor organizers, and rural village leaders were still struggling to put their houses in order through much of his rule after having been torn apart under his military junta (1961–1963). Moreover, as Park's rhetoric of "Fatherland," "modernization," "catchup," "can do" spirit, and "administrative democracy" shows, his Third Republic (1963–1972) possessed an unsystematically articulated but still distinctive set of authoritarian norms and values that enabled society to grasp, however imperfectly and indirectly, what he stood for and what he opposed.

As Byung-Kook Kim analyzes in Chapter 5, Park—sitting on top of a "two-pronged structure of institutional power," with intelligence agents looking after his political interests and economic planners orchestrating a coordinated action across ministries—set national agendas, devised strategies, and organized institutional mechanisms without checks and balances not only from legislators, judges, *chaeya* activists, labor organizers, and farmers but also from within South Korea's executive branch. The coercive security arm of his rule was controlled through a "divide-and-conquer strategy," to quote Joo Hong Kim (Chapter 6), whereas his economic bureaucracy was made an instrument of Park's goals and strategies by putting his "alter ego" *(punsin)* head pilot agencies in charge of mobilizing what Byung-Kook Kim in Chapter 7 calls "rationalized but patrimonial" state ministries. In a similar spirit, Hyug Baeg Im perceives Park as a South Korean version of Niccolò Machiavelli's "prince," transforming structural crises into an opportunity for *yushin* in 1972 by tapping his immense political resources. The launching of *yushin* is presented as his choice, forced on both ruling and opposition parties as a fait accompli.

To be sure, Park's grip on political power was much weaker during his junta days and his late *yushin* years (1978–1979). As Yong-Sup Han reports in Chapter 1, Park was both a master and a captive of power struggles plaguing his military junta, which kept on fragmenting into factions along generational, regional, and school ties and by military services. As Hyung-A Kim describes in Chapter 3, Park, wary of his military rivals, turned to political and economic shock therapy in May 1961, June 1962, and March 1963 with an eye to protecting his power, with dire consequences for his state bureaucracy's developmental capabilities. Such a cycle of power struggles and shock therapy ended only after Park weeded out the last of his rivals in March 1963 and, more important, when he won a tight presidential race in October. His grip on political power began slipping away—but only after 1978 when Yi Ch'öl-sŭng's New Democratic Party (NDP) beat Park in National Assembly elections. A fatal split developed between "soft-liner" Kim Chae-gyu's Korea Central Intelligence Agency (KCIA) and "hard-liner" Ch'a Chi-ch'ŏl's Presidential Security Service (PSS) over how to deal with emboldened NDP opposition leaders, which Joo Hong Kim in Chapter 6 and Myung-Lim Park in Chapter 13 see as explaining Park Chung Hee's demise in October 1979.

However, these developments represented a variation of Park's grip on power, not his regime's authoritarian character. His control over political goals, agendas, and strategies, and his ability to contain the negative consequences of his decisions, waxed and waned depending on power structures and factional struggles within his inner circles, but, regardless of an increase or a decline in his grip on power, the political regime Park led remained authoritarian throughout his eighteen years of rule. Nonetheless, there are two problems with Linz's concept of authoritarianism.

First, there is the issue of whether the presence or absence of elections affects regime dynamics in visible ways even in an authoritarian context, so that this factor needs be taken as a key criterion in our typology of political regimes, no matter how far short elections fell from being a fair contest for power. The relationship between elections and political regimes is an issue because Park's Third Republic (1963–1972) exhibited many of Linz's features of authoritarianism, but it still regularly held presidential elections, albeit of a limited pluralistic kind marred by bureaucratically organized money politics and McCarthyist Red scares, before opting for a system of indirect presidential elections in 1972 to ensure lifelong rule. Jorge I. Domínguez in Chapter 20 argues that Park Chung Hee's 1972 political move transformed his regime from an "above-median performer" into a "below-median performer" in political governance, relying more on repression than on co-optation to maintain political order and social stability. The presence of elections, however imperfect they were as a mechanism of political representation and political accountability, is diagnosed as having helped Park to legitimate his authoritarian Third Republic. Electoral politics of even an illiberal character and restricted but still available institutions of consultation accompanying it, such as legislatures, political parties, and corporatist interest groups, help authoritarian rulers like Park, as Domínguez comments, "diversify the tool kit for ruling and policy-making . . . reduce the cost of rulership . . . sustain a broad base of support . . . [and] harness economic and social forces toward [their] goals while employing a minimum level of military force."

Echoing Domínguez's appraisal, Hyug Bae Im looks at Park's purge of limited but still contentious electoral competition in 1972 through the inauguration of his *yushin* regime as a decision of paramount importance, qualitatively altering regime dynamics. Finding Linz's sweeping typology of authoritarianism too limiting, Im distinguishes much of Park's directly elected presidential terms (1963–1971) as a case of "soft authoritarianism," and his subsequent period of rule as a "garrison state." With his legitimacy weakened by his own act of palace coup, Byung-Kook Kim argues in Chapter 5, Park ruled directly through his praetorian guards rather than indirectly through a circle of independently based party bosses. Such a change within his authoritarian regime also transformed society. As Myung-Lim Park describes, *chaeya* activists radicalized into a *panch'aeje* (anti-system) force and opposition party leaders turned "intransigent" in tandem with Park's greater use of repression. Gregory W. Noble in Chapter 21 also reports that South Korea took a path of industrial modernization different from that of Taiwan with the launching of *yushin*. Previously, the two had taken similar paths under common capital and technological requirements determined by the industrial sector. With his garrison state in place, Park was able to temporarily transcend these sectoral constraints to tackle ever more ambitious economic projects in the hope of legitimating his rule and strengthening his power.

Linz's concept thus needs be supplemented by a typology of authoritarian regimes if it is to help in clarifying their role in the politics of modernization. As Domínguez persuasively argues, there are diverse ways to design political institutions of authoritarian rule. Moreover, how institutional choices are aligned has a serious impact on political order and social stability by affecting regime capabilities for political control, co-optation, and repression. In an effort to distinguish authoritarian regimes by their diverging internal institutional designs, some differentiate "soft" from "hard" authoritarian regimes,[5] whereas others categorize their varying character into predatory[6] versus technocratic,[7] político versus técnico,[8] or state corporatist versus state monist types.[9] Such dichotomous typologies, however, miss many of the ambiguities of existing authoritarian regimes, especially those with a proven record of political stability or socioeconomic modernization, as in much of Park Chung Hee's rule. It cannot be otherwise, because success comes through dexterously mixing what look like mutually exclusive and unmixable concepts. Like Joel D. Aberbach,

Robert D. Putnam, and Bert A. Rockman, who, seeking to capture this mixture of seemingly opposite roles, speak of "pure hybrids" leading the bureaucratization of politics and the politicization of bureaucracy in Western democracies,[10] Roderic Ai Camp once spoke of "political technocrats" to describe Mexico's new hybrid ruling elite.[11]

The chapters in this book have a similar understanding of Park Chung Hee's political regime, describing its Blue House Secretariat as resting on a two-pronged leadership of mutually exclusive but functionally complementary economic bureaucrats and military praetorian guards (see Chapter 5), its economic state apparatus as lying between predatory and technocratic role types (Chapter 7), its ruling political party as highly centralized in organization but with potentially powerful centrifugal forces of factionalism (Chapters 5, 6, and 8), its power elite as recruiting much of its leaders from South Korea's professional but patrimonial military and civilian state bureaucracy (Chapters 6 and 7), and its mechanisms of policymaking as showing traits of both "institutionalization and personalization," to quote Paul D. Hutchcroft's Chapter 19. In other words, to explain how and why South Korea dramatically altered its course of modernization after 1961, we must go beyond Linz's concept of authoritarian regimes and analyze their varying internal institutional arrangements in nondichotomous ways.

Developmental State

Developmental state theories, Hyung-A Kim writes in Chapter 3, explain South Korea's hypergrowth "primarily in terms of its possession of a professional 'Weberian' state imbued with the ethos of 'plan rationality' . . . [but this] is a myth." As argued by many of our authors, developmental state theories have five issues wrong.

First, given their understanding of South Korean policymaking processes as basically "technocratic," developmental state theories analytically focus on state bureaucrats rather than on those bureaucrats' political master, Park Chung Hee, to explain policy preferences, goals, and strategies. The lack of documented historical data is certainly one cause of the neglect of Park's political role, but this problem does not invalidate our criticism. The system of political rule undergirding hypergrowth was thoroughly bureaucratic, with security guards and economic technocrats dominating ideologically shallow and organizationally weak political parties and interest groups, but its driver, wielding discretionary powers without checks or balances, was Park Chung Hee. Following Hyung-A Kim's lead, Byung-Kook Kim puts Peter Evans's notion of "embedded auton-omy" on its head in describing South Korea's developmental state in Chap-ter 7. The state possessed a Weberian sense of corporate coherence only because Park lined up ministries—and, by extension, their social con-stituencies and political allies—into an internally segmented hierarchy of "core," "strategic sectoral," and "auxiliary" groups with varying institu-tional privileges and vulnerabilities. To construct such a bureaucracy ex-ternally insulated from party politics and internally disciplined into a clear rank order, with his newly established Economic Planning Board (EPB) as its core, Park had to constantly intervene in bureaucratic politics to tilt power away from strategic sectoral and auxiliary ministries—and, in case of 1964–1967, even the MoF, another core agency in his bureaucratic scheme. South Korea's "Weberian" corporate coherence was a fundamen-tally political artifact, historically created, maintained, and driven by Park Chung Hee.

Second, as Evans argued, South Korea's developmental state was "em-bedded in a concrete set of social ties," which enabled a continual negotia-tion of goals and policies between state and *chaebol* actors, but it was Park who set the terms of the negotiation. The policy decisions responsible for putting South Korea on a path of hypergrowth, from its introduction of a reverse interest rate system in 1964, to a freeze of interest payments on pri-vate "curb-market" loans in 1972, to a promulgation of heavy and chemi-cal industrialization (HCI) in 1973, to an integrated stabilization policy in 1979, were all decided by Park in the face of resistance from one or an-other group of state ministries (see Chapter 7). Likewise, in Chapter 12 Young Jo Lee sees South Korea's plunge into *Saemaŭl Undong* (the New Village Movement) with massive price supports for rice and barley in 1975 as primarily driven by Park. His shadow was even larger in South Korea's foreign policy initiatives to back up developmental policies. As retold by Min Yong Lee in Chapter 14, Park offered to dispatch military troops to South Vietnam as early as 1961, only to see John F. Kennedy respond neg-atively. When his successor, Lyndon B. Johnson, altered U.S. policy and courted Park for troop dispatch in 1964, Park swiftly lined up Demo-cratic Republican Party (DRP) politicians behind military intervention in South Vietnam. The normalization of diplomatic relations with Japan in 1965, Jung-Hoon Lee similarly argues in Chapter 15, was possible only because Park Chung Hee stuck his neck out. The resources secured through both troop dispatch and diplomatic normalization with Japan be-came Park's seed money to subsidize industrial programs, including his pet project, the launching of an integrated steel mill.

Third, with Park at the top of a hierarchically organized state bureau-cracy and in control of institutional channels of negotiation with ministries, *chaebol* companies ended up directly engaging in asymmetric political exchange with Park and his Blue House Secretariat rather than working through bureaucratic hierarchies on most critical decisions. Contradicting developmental state theories, *chaebol* groups were junior partners of Park, but not of state bureaucrats. And this was a partnership between what Eun Mee Kim and Gil-Sung Park's Chapter 9 calls "visionaries," enabling each other to achieve vital interests—hypergrowth for Park and corporate expansion for *chaebol* owners—through "mutual guarantees" of political support and economic risk-taking, respectively. With an eye to prevent mutual guarantees from degenerating into moral hazards, Park developed three rules: partner with *chaebol* groups with a proven track record of entrepreneurship, build a structure of oligopolistic competition, and let failing *chaebol* companies go under once relief measures are exhausted. There was also a rule that *chaebol* should never seek political power either on their own or as an ally of Park Chung Hee's potential political rivals. They were severely punished when their political loyalty was in question.[12]

As recounted by Nae-Young Lee in Chapter 10, in South Korea's automobile industry, even the support of Park Chung Hee's right-hand men—Kim Chong-p'il and Yi Hu-rak—could not prevent Saenara from going bankrupt in 1963 or protect Sinjin Motors' monopoly on auto assembly from Hyundai Motors' and Asia Motor's challenges in 1967–1968, respectively. The auto industry was a "graveyard of would-be *chaebol* groups." Sinjin took over Saenara in 1965, then formed a 50:50 joint venture with General Motors in 1972, only to sell its shares to a state development bank in 1976, while Asia Motors was taken over by a latecomer, Kia Motors, in 1976. Only Hyundai Motors grew into an independent multinational, "producing autos with [its] own national brand name under an economically sustainable cycle of model changes, and in collaboration with a dense network of nationally owned but foreign technology–licensed suppliers as well as an extensive global distributive system of sales and services."

Fourth, as a corollary of the primacy of politics in South Korea's formation of a state that is both coherent and embedded in a set of political relationships of asymmetric exchange with *chaebol* industrialists, "technocratic rationality" is a concept with limited utility in describing that state's preferences, goals, and strategies. Much of its macroeconomic policies were, in fact, anything *but* technocratic. The military junta's shock therapy, coupled with its *churyu* (mainstream) faction's clandestine drive to raise political funds, derailed South Korea's fragile economy (see Chapter 3). The high-risk post-1964 strategy of getting *chaebol* groups to diversify into new frontiers of industrial growth through bureaucratically distributed subsidized loans burdened banks with huge nonperforming loans, which made policymakers hypersensitive to any signs of an interest rate hike, lest their highly leveraged *chaebol* partners fail under mounting interest payments and threaten creditors as well. To keep both *chaebol* groups and banks afloat, South Korea strove to keep its growth rate high, even with shock therapy that compromised private property rights, as its freeze of interest payments on curb-market loans in 1972 showed (Chapter 7). The phenomenal growth rate of 9.3 percent under Park, then, does not by itself demonstrate his state's technocratic character. On the contrary, it is more likely to have resulted from his fear of corporate and financial distress, which he knew could develop into an irreparable systemic crisis, once he had instituted a reverse interest rate system with deposit rates set higher than loan rates in 1965 at the cost of a massive accumulation of nonperforming loans.

The history of industrial policy under Park Chung Hee additionally urges us to adopt a political rather than a technocratic perspective. The state continually required a larger scale of production, a higher local content, a more infrequent change of models, a greater share of exports, as well as a tighter network of vertical integration *(kyeyŏlhwa)* with small-size parts-and-components producers in South Korea's auto industry as its conditions for policy support, until it de facto ended up demanding its infant assemblers' transformation into global players in 1973. The 1973 plan was "unrealistic . . . a dangerous gamble, if not wishful thinking," to quote Nae-Young Lee. Likewise, Sang-young Rhyu and Seok-jin Lew's Chapter 11 describes the consistently negative reactions of international donors and lenders, from U.S. policymakers to World Bank economists to Western European and Japanese bankers, to Park Chung Hee's proposal to build an integrated steel mill. "That it was Japan's 1969 provision of reparation funds rather than commercial loans that eventually got South Korea to launch its steel project," Rhyu and Lew write, "attested to the centrality of Park and his ambition, not his developmental state's technocratic prowess."

Fifth, if Park did not follow technocratic rationality in formulating goals and strategies, South Korea's hypergrowth during his highly personalized and yet bureaucratized rule becomes an even greater historical and theoretic puzzle. Many of our authors identify the South Korean developmental state's political and organizational capabilities to swiftly change gears to correct ideologically driven economic strategies rather than its possession of a technocratic ethos. "Experts," Park once recollected, "only try to discourage me by identifying risks and obstacles. Had I listened to their advice, I would have ended up doing nothing." When his aides called for scaling back investment projects to a more feasible level, Park answered:

"We should even be prepared to replace our original investor with a new one if the original investor fails" (see Chapter 5). Consequently, macroeconomic policy ended up zigzagging between hypergrowth policy and shock therapy as banks amassed nonperforming loans and *chaebol* groups suffered from surplus capacity (Chapter 7). The ownership of automakers changed (Chapter 10), while South Korea's larger *chaebol* community saw a continuous change in its membership under the pressures of surplus capacity (Chapter 9).

To understand South Korea's ability to generate hypergrowth, it is necessary to move our focus of analysis from any one particular policy, which is likely to be technocratically "irrational," toward relationships between separate sets of policies. It was only because Park corrected technocratically "irrational" hypergrowth measures with similarly unorthodox shock measures and replaced failing *chaebol* producers with new rising stars that South Korea was able to continue its hypergrowth in spite of its cycle of boom and bust. Individually, many of Park's policy decisions looked technocratically "irrational." Collectively, through periodic policy swings and *chaebol* restructuring, his decisions acquired a distinctive rationality of their own in that they enabled South Korea to expand, adjust, and expand again—all at a hyper pace, albeit with great costs. And those swings were possible because Park could swiftly redirect state ministries—and, by extension, their social clients—toward hypergrowth or shock therapy, depending on economic conditions.

External Political-Security Influences

Dependency theory[13] would predict that South Korea would be kept in poor peripheral condition by the world's dominant capitalist powers, and yet the opposite occurred. Instead of being a classic case of third world underdevelopment, with widespread poverty, chronic fiscal and trade deficits, inflationary pressures, and severe political instability, South Korea surprised everyone, including its own people, with an explosive show of energy for modernization after May 1961. Its economy took off with the help of global markets, flying in the face of dependency theorists. The way South Korea harnessed world markets for its goal of modernization, however, also diverged from patterns of dependent development.[14] Instead of a triple alliance anchored in multinational companies, there emerged a duo, with the *chaebol* growing into national champions through diversification and conglomeration under massive state support. The reliance on the *chaebol* rather than on the multinationals made South Korea choose commercial bank loans and technology licensing over direct foreign investment as its primary instrument of industrialization, with profound implications for its larger political economy.

The rise of a state-*chaebol* partnership does not imply that external factors mattered little for South Korea's modernization. On the contrary, many of its sources of growth came from abroad. The economy, which was initially too small and too poor in factor endowment, was capable of breaking supply-and-demand bottlenecks only with foreign support. The way the external factors mattered, however, diverged from explanations posited in dependency or dependent development theories—and, for that matter, developmental state theories, which focus on global *economic* forces. External economic contributors to South Korea's hypergrowth include an increasingly liberalized world trade regime, inexorable forces of product life cycle, Japan's integration of late-late developers into a "flying geese"–like transnational production network, and the growth of international lenders and investors. By contrast, many of our authors argue that military security figured more directly and pervasively in South Korea's modernization.

First, structurally, South Korea's security vulnerabilities encouraged its construction of an extremely centralized state, with its head making up an imperial presidency. As reported by Chung-in Moon and Byung-joon Jun in Chapter 4, its armed forces transformed into a defender of national security, a guardian of regime stability, *and* a modernizer of society, as it organizationally absorbed "technocratic" U.S. security ideas on top of its historically inherited Japanese "militarist" ethos, after Washington militarily intervened in the Korean War (1950–1953). The armed forces were South Korea's "most modernized, educated, and administratively experienced elite group" into much of the 1960s, to quote Yong-Sup Han. As a result, power decisively tilted toward Park and remained solidly in his hands when he weeded out rivals from his military junta through a series of purges (Chapters 1 and 3), placed military units under tight surveillance (Chapter 6), and divided and conquered his guardians of power by building a multi-layered and multi-centered security network, with KCIA agents, PSS guards, and Army Security Command soldiers looking over one another's surveillance work (Chapter 5). From this position of dominance, Park could take risky political, economic, and foreign policy options for his vision of *puguk kangbyŏng*. The armed forces were his political safety net, defending him in the event of political, economic, and foreign policy failure.

Second, ideationally, military security also shaped South Korea's trajectory of modernization through its impact on Park's political priorities.

Upon seizing power in 1961, he publicly declared anticommunism to be South Korea's *kuksi* (national essence), thus aligning his junta irreversibly with postwar conservatism and, by extension, foreclosing "leftist" options in modernization (Chapter 1). To militarily, economically, and politically catch up with Pyŏngyang, Park dispatched combat troops to South Vietnam and normalized diplomatic relations with Japan in 1965, with an eye toward constructing a regional security network (Chapters 14 and 15); put heavy and chemical industrialization high on South Korea's list of priorities to develop a modern defense industry, despite dire consequences for distributive equality and market stability (Chapter 7); and remolded his "soft" authoritarian regime into a "garrison state" *(yushin)* in 1972 as a measure to counter Kim Il Sung of North Korea's monolithic *yuil* regime (Chapter 8). More important, Park saw himself in the image of Meiji Japan's modernizers (1868–1912), who, a century earlier, embarked on economic modernization to contain and defeat security threats. Park's slogan of *pukuk kangbyŏng* echoed Meiji Japan's *fukoku kyohei* (Chapter 4) and his *yushin* regime the Meiji name of *ishin* (Chapter 8).

Third, military security also mattered in South Korea's modernization by providing policy instruments and leverage. With top U.S. policymakers as brokers, interested in bringing South Korea and Japan into a triple alliance with America, Park pursued diplomatic normalization without an explicit Japanese apology for colonial exploitation, in return for Japan's provision of reparation funds. These funds became seed money for an integrated steel mill judged too risky by commercial lenders (Chapter 11). The Vietnam War occasioned another asymmetric deal, with Park dispatching combat troops to support U.S. war operations in return for his superpower ally's pledge of greater military and economic assistance (Chapter 14). The *milwŏl* (honeymoon) Park enjoyed with Lyndon B. Johnson as a result of these foreign policy decisions, moreover, had the effect of strengthening Park's negotiating position on unrelated policy issues. Sharply departing from its traditional emphasis on stabilization, the United States did not stop Chang Ki-yŏng from setting deposit interest rates above loan rates in 1965 (Chapter 7). The reversal of deposit and loan rates enabled Park to put *chaebol* groups on a hypergrowth path. Nonperforming loans increased, but investment also climbed, *chaebol* groups grew into national champions, and production capacity expanded. Park even transformed Richard M. Nixon's 1969 Guam Doctrine of U.S. military disengagement and the U.S. 1968 failure to retaliate against North Korean military provocations into an opportunity to launch a force modernization program (Chapter 14).

That military security mattered in South Korea's modernization by shaping its power structures, ideas, and tool kit of policy instruments is clear. What is more uncertain is how these external pressures interacted with its domestic political actors, structures, and processes, and whether there existed any distinctive patterns in those interactions. In the case of external factors influencing South Korea's path of modernization, this book distinguishes impacts originating from its two most critical patrons: the United States and Japan. At the level of political regime, Taehyun Kim and Chang Jae Baik report in Chapter 2, U.S. policymakers preempted "socialist options" when they vetoed Park Chung Hee's heretical idea of freezing large bank deposits and forcing their depositors to buy the stock of a newly established state company with those funds in June 1962. The funds were to be spent on highly risky HCI projects. Moreover, by requiring Park's promise to transfer power to a civilian leadership through elections as a condition for the United States' acceptance of his military coup as a fait accompli in May 1961 (Chapter 1), and by delaying aid delivery, issuing diplomatic protests, pressuring for a purge of right-hand man Kim Chong-p'il's radical hard-liners, as well as supporting civilian opposition leaders including Yun Po-sŏn, in the middle of a political crisis to get Park to deliver on his earlier promise of holding presidential elections in October 1963 (Chapter 2), U.S. policymakers also vetoed his continual extension of military rule.

In spite of such crucial instances of U.S. intervention on the side of democratization, however, the patron state's role was too complex and sometimes even contradictory to say that it was unambiguously a promoter of democratization. Through the United States' structural role as a military guarantor of South Korea's security and a patron of its national interests in global marketplaces, the United States de facto ended up supporting Park's authoritarian rule when it kept silent in the face of violations of civil rights and political liberty. And it was mostly silent until Park compromised the principle of electoral competition by launching his *yushin* regime in 1972 (Chapter 13). Even then, it was only after the United States completed its troop withdrawal from South Vietnam in 1972 and Jimmy Carter won the U.S. presidential election in 1976 that U.S. policymakers began publicly demanding that Park lift his emergency powers. Trying to keep up the pressure on Hanoi to speed up the Paris peace negotiations, Nixon asked Park to postpone his plan for troop withdrawal from Saigon, which had the effect of discouraging Nixon from openly opposing Park's *yushin* in 1972 (Chapters 8 and 14). By contrast, having campaigned for withdrawing U.S. ground troops from South Korea in 1976, and making this pledge a reality by 1977, Yong-Jick Kim argues in Chapter 16, Carter thought he was less constrained by military interests in pressuring Park to democratize.

To complicate the story even more, the United States' military strategy was frequently as decisive as, if not more critical than, its conscious efforts at democratization in shaping South Korea's choice of political institutions. At one level, political stability was anchored in the United States' presence as a regional stabilizer in East Asia and as a deterrent of North Korean military threats. Any questioning of this role triggered severe South Korean domestic instability, with sometimes serious impacts on South Korea's political regime. To make South Korean politics even more volatile and uncertain, most of the changes in the U.S. security role were driven by U.S. domestic political forces outside South Korea's control, including Nixon's unilaterally declared Guam Doctrine of 1969, political rapprochement with China in 1972, the U.S. House investigation into Pak Tong-sǒn's Korea lobby after 1974, and Carter's policy to withdraw U.S. ground troops from South Korea in 1977. These security shocks drove Park into declaring his *yushin* regime in 1972 and further strengthening his emergency powers after 1974. Carter fought back, preempting the worst forms of human rights violations and in some instances forcing a release of political prisoners. More generally, however, in this game of regime change and survival, Carter's activist human rights policy failed to bring about a political opening (Chapter 16). Rather, it triggered a regime crisis in 1979 by emboldening both pro-Park and anti-Park forces to take intransigent positions against each other on the issue of political regime (Chapters 5, 6, and 13).

The portrait of the United States drawn in this volume is far from that of a hegemon. From the days of Park's military junta to his *yushin* regime, and across the issue-areas of political regime, military modernization, human rights, and U.S. troop withdrawal, the United States was as much an object of manipulation as a driver of South Korean domestic politics, providing Park with a rationale for lifelong rule during his *yushin* era. Moreover, in many of its instances of intervention against authoritarian rule, the United States saw outcomes diverging sharply from its intentions. Also, the United States affected its client state's domestic politics more directly and pervasively through its change of regional security policy than through its adoption of activist human rights policy. The United States' role as a promoter of democracy was constrained by the centrality of military security in its national interests, which enabled Park to present his coup as a fait accompli in 1961, restrain U.S. criticisms of his soft authoritarianism through a dispatch of combat troops to South Vietnam in 1965–

1972, and resist Carter's human rights policy during much of the *yushin* years. The United States, in fact, was never a unitary actor with one voice. The U.S. military establishment put deterrence before and above democracy, enabling Park to minimize the political damage from his resistance to U.S. pressure (Chapters 1, 8, 14, and 16). The only instance of "clear U.S. victory" occurred in 1971, when South Korea embarked on developing nuclear weapons to make up for the United States' declining military presence. As Sung Gul Hong writes in Chapter 17, with U.S. policymakers threatening a "dramatic change of the entire political, economic, and security relationship, Park gave up his reprocessing program" in 1975.

Despite crucial American and Japanese inputs in South Korea's economic growth, then, U.S.–South Korean political relations were anything but stable, friendly, and respectful of one another's interests during most of Park's rule. Most developmental state theories and network analysts lose sight of these conflicts in their efforts at generalization, thus making South Korea's task of modernization look easier than it actually was. South Korea and the United States had to work hard to prevent political conflicts from disrupting their economic relations.

External Economic-Ideational Influences

After a series of economic policy blunders shook his military junta's grip on the political order in 1962, Park realized the powers of the market and began searching for new ideas to harness those powers as an engine of growth. And with rival generals purged and his political leadership legitimized by an electoral victory in 1963, Park began heeding—however selectively and partially—U.S. advice for market liberalization, without worrying too much about his political capability to steer South Korea through that risky and dangerous economic sea. The United States' role in restraining Park's dirigiste instincts, however, should not be overemphasized. Park after 1962 was an only partly reformed economic thinker, with his obsession for bureaucratic control and his "can do" spirit somewhat tamed by major policy failures, but nevertheless still very much alive. The fixation on HCI (Chapter 7), rural mobilization (Chapter 12), and administrative democracy (Chapters 4 and 8) resurfaced in 1972 after years of preparation.[15] At the same time, as events in 1979 showed, he remained ready to swiftly make a U-turn in the direction of market-friendly shock therapy, lest the excesses of his dirigiste policies irreparably damage South Korea's comparative advantage in the international marketplace.

The economic takeoff in 1965 is particularly illustrative of Park's hybridization of foreign ideas. First, he transformed his U.S. ally's orthodox proposal for stabilization into an unorthodox program of hypergrowth by setting deposit interest rates above loan rates. Second, normalizing relations with Japan with the help of a garrison decree, he also began building a developmental state after the model of Meiji Japan. Such a diffusion of liberal U.S. ideas and dirigiste Japanese developmental state paradigms resulted in a set of seemingly incongruous institutions, with planning bureaucrats projecting a liberal stance Korean-style and industry bureaucrats emulating Japanese industrial policy in un-Japanese ways. Where and how these two ideational and organizational forces would come into balance was to decisively shape South Korea's direction of economic development (Chapter 7).

However, whether South Korea heeded U.S. advice on macro policy guidelines or used Japan as its benchmark in its design of micro industrial policy, foreign ideas were adopted only partially and selectively through syncretic learning processes. State bureaucrats constantly innovated and adapted in order to make foreign practices congruent with their own political master's priorities; to fit in with their ministries' organizational ethos, mission, and abilities; and to accommodate business interests. Adaptation became a way of life under Park, giving his initially foreign-originating ideas and practices a distinctively "South Korean" style. As Chung-in Moon and Byung-joon Jun show in Chapter 4, bureaucrats drew up industry laws by copying Japanese laws verbatim. They also thought and spoke in Japan's language of industrial policy, shaping *chaebol* behavior through *haengjŏng chido* (administrative guidance) and managing surplus capacity issues by *sanŏp haprihwa* (industrial rationalization measures). The way they formulated and implemented industrial policy, however, diverged critically from Japan's consensual and gradualist style. Given South Korea's imperial presidency, rational but patrimonial state bureaucracy, and infant *chaebol* community, big issues like entry into strategic industries were decided by Park and *chaebol* conglomerates (Chapter 9), policy coordination was orchestrated top-down by a pilot agency through a systematic chain of command (Chapter 7), and industrial rationalization was typically pursued as part of sudden and brief shock therapy (Chapters 7, 9, and 10).

Japanese ideas were equally profound for big business. The concept of a *chaebol* as a business organization, with a headquarters controlling a diverse array of subsidiaries through a system of cross shareholdings, and pulling resources together groupwide for common group interests, originated from interwar Japan's *zaibatsu*. Emboldened by this idea of constructing a corporate empire, many of South Korea's *chaebol* visionaries, including automakers (Chapter 10), licensed Japanese technology to enter new frontiers of industrial growth. Moreover, like state bureaucrats adapting Japanese industrial policy to South Korea's political soil of an imperial presidency, *chaebol* producers built up their technological capabilities through innovation. Even the crisis-ridden auto industry experienced a breakthrough when Hyundai Motors acquired the ability to assemble its own Pony model with technology licenses contracted separately from several foreign sources. The "car design," Nae-Young Lee writes, "came from Italy; its internal combustion engine from England; and [its] engine block design, transmission, and axles from Japan." South Korea's sole integrated steel producer was under even greater Japanese influence. Financed by Japanese reparation funds and built with Japanese technology under the support of the "bureaucrats, bankers, big business, and Liberal Democratic Party bosses of 'Japan, Inc.,'" Sang-young Rhyu and Seok-jin Lew report, the Pohang Iron and Steel Company (POSCO) strove to "catch up with Nippon Steel" by emulating its Japanese technology licensors' "corporate strategy, managerial practices, and company unionism." The way POSCO did so was, however, profoundly un-Japanese—with Pak T'ae-jun, Park Chung Hee's alter ego inside POSCO, getting POSCO to emulate the Japanese steel producers' consensual management models in a top-down manner in his capacity as "political entrepreneur, mediator of interests, facilitator of dialogue, and business strategist" (Chapter 11).

These adaptations of liberal U.S. ideas and dirigiste Japanese practices into distinctively illiberal macro shock therapy and politically driven micro industrial policy had an amplifying effect on South Korea's national energy for modernization, because of their timing. The world economic order was then creating a window of opportunity for late developers like South Korea in four critical ways. First, tariff barriers in developed countries were being dramatically lowered through the launching of the "Kennedy Round" of the General Agreement on Tariffs and Trade (GATT), which lowered the costs of South Korea's entry into world marketplaces. Second, however, nontariff trade barriers, including financial subsidies, were left alone until the next Tokyo and Uruguay rounds of trade liberalization, which had the effect of giving South Korea two decades to build its comparative advantage through industrial policy. Third, an extensive expansion of international commercial banking also took place throughout the 1960s, without which South Korea's strategy of financing growth through loans could not have worked. Fourth, Japan was then lining up its neighbors into a new regional division of labor after the image of "flying geese," with its multinational corporations relocating their declining business operations throughout East Asia via technology licensing and direct investment.[16] The normalization of diplomatic relations, followed by South Korea's ideational and institutional innovations, helped Park Chung Hee achieve his strategy of carving out a second-tier position in this flying geese model of regional economic integration through technology licensing.

Unfortunately for Park, however, his coalition was not alone in learning from foreign ideas. As Myung-Lim Park writes in Chapter 13, *chaeya* activists began transforming into an intransigent opposition force after Chŏn T'ae-il, a tailor and union organizer in one of Ch'ŏn'gyech'ŏn's sweatshops, dramatically took his life in protest against repressive labor practices in 1970. Suddenly awakened to South Korea's grim reality of social inequality by Chŏn T'ae-il's public suicide, *chaeya* dissidents took on the role of social reformers on top of their mid-1960s' role of anti-Japanese nationalists and democratic activists forged during South Korea's 1965 normalization of relations with Japan (Chapter 15) and its 1969 lifting of the two-term constitutional restriction on presidential terms, respectively. These efforts to add a third, reformist identity spread Marxist, Leninist, and Maoist revolutionary writings throughout South Korea's *chaeya*. But because much of their transformation was driven by historical events rather than by some preconceived theoretical or ideological worldview, and because postwar anticommunist sentiments still had a strong grip on society, *chaeya* dissidents ended up innovating in the promotion of foreign ideas as actively as did their political opponents, Park and his ruling coalition. The outcome was *minjungjuŭi*, which looked to the "people" for leadership in the struggle against South Korea's politically oppressive, economically exploitative, and internationally subservient "ruling clique" (Chapter 13).

Among diverse *chaeya* groups, it was Christian activists that proved to be most threatening to Park and his ruling coalition. Myung-Lim Park calls their impact "transformative," empowering *chaeya* activists with their "Christian notion of 'natural rights,'" which saw the "right to a minimum standard of living as an integral part of human rights." The church supported *chaeya* activists in multiple ways—as a political "sanctuary" from security forces, as a "fund-raiser" for dissident activities, as a "countermedia" of radical ideas, as an agenda setter in social issues, as an organizer of militant trade unions, as a "force of conscience" pressuring National Democratic Party politicians into confrontation against Park Chung Hee, and as a mobilizer of U.S. religious groups into a transnational clergy-intelligentsia coalition behind human rights (Chapter 13). These transnational ties were instrumental in getting the U.S. Congress to hold hearings on South Korean human rights abuses in 1974 (Chapter 16).

At the same time, it is important not to look at South Korea's intelligentsia as a unitary actor, with *chaeya* activists in leadership roles. The intelligentsia was never united ideologically; its conservative members, serving as personal advisors, presidential staff, cabinet ministers, and party leaders, participated as proactively in Park Chung Hee's modernization projects as others did in South Korea's robust political opposition movements. The conservative wing of South Korea's intelligentsia was present in most of its critical junctures of historical development, manning Kim Chong-p'il's "brain-trust" to draw up shock therapy in 1961 (Chapter 3), assisting in Park's rediscovery of traditional culture as a source of conservative modernization ideology in 1971 (Chapter 4), advocating price support for barley and rice between 1968 and 1971 (Chapter 12), joining Yi Hu-rak's *P'ungnyŏn saŏp* (Good Harvest Project) to prepare for *yushin* in 1972 (Chapter 8), and envisioning South Korea's development of an independently designed, assembled, and marketed small-size *kukminch'a* (citizen car) model in 1973 (Chapter 10). They were criticized by *chaeya* activists as a state-patronized and -controlled *(ŏyong)* political force. The reality was, however, much more complicated. Rather than being the forces of good and evil, and conscience *(yangsim)* versus state patronization *(ŏyong)*, *chaeya* activists and their conservative rivals diverged in worldviews.

Civil Society

The existing literature based on developmental state and network theories deals with popular forces even more inadequately than South Korea's bureaucracy, *chaebol*, and political parties. Typically, popular forces are seen as a mere objects of control sacrificed for economic growth and military security, as in the case of industrial workers and farmers; or as a brave voice of conscience, making democratization an inevitable outcome despite overwhelming state power, as in the case of the *chaeya* activists. The kind of hypergrowth South Korea achieved, with its prime impetus coming from exports and HCI, however, would have been impossible had state bureaucrats only wielded sticks, as many researchers have argued. Nor does an ideologically charged dichotomization of Park's supporters and opponents into passively mobilized parochial rural subjects and politically engaged urban citizen opponents help explain the many puzzles of Park Chung Hee's political rule: how it lasted eighteen years despite a seemingly endless series of political, economic, and security crises; why he fought hard for rural subsidies and built costly *Saemaŭl Undong* (New Village

Movement) projects, if farmers were already available for manipulation; and what accounted for his charisma among rural voters.

To explain such conundrums, this book takes both top-down and bottom-up views, looking into Park's use of carrots and sticks, organizations and symbols, as well as personal charisma and formal institutions for the political mobilization of popular forces. We strongly advise against assuming any zero-sum relationship between Park's use of carrots and sticks. The junta pledged in 1961 to liquidate "usurious debts" in the countryside, while disbanding all rural organizations by a decree (Chapter 3). Likewise, the *yushin* era witnessed a dramatic increase in both carrots and sticks for South Korean farmers, as Park tried to keep them away from *chaeya* dissidents as well as from historically more contentious urban voters. Distinguishing carrots from sticks, in fact, was very problematic in many instances of political intervention, as in Park's *Saemaŭl Undong*, because carrots could instantly become sticks with their threat of being taken away. The Ministry of Home Affairs, presiding over 14,000 subcounty offices *(myŏn),* the lowest and smallest administrative unit in South Korea, and the National Agricultural Cooperative Federation (NACF), boasting over 90 percent of South Korean farmers as its members, similarly constituted a double-edged institution that threatened with carrots (Chapter 12).

As argued by Young Jo Lee, in this game of rural mobilization, South Korean farmers were anything but parochial subjects, immersed in political conformism. Contrary to the prevailing views of *yŏch'onyado* (the countryside for the government, the city for the opposition), he draws an image of South Korean farmers resembling James C. Scott's "rational peasant," voting for or against Park depending on his agricultural policy's distributive implications, when there was no presidential aspirant from their native regions. Park Chung Hee also became a "rational mobilizer" after losing many Chŏlla voters in his 1967 presidential campaign. Making a U-turn from his policy of agricultural squeeze, Park supported barley and rice prices with subsidies, and put his *Saemaŭl Undong* on an entirely different scale by politically and economically supporting the Ministry of Agriculture and Forestry's Grain Management Fund, Fertilizer Fund, and high-yield rice development programs, in addition to rural public construction works in 1975.

This book also corrects South Korea's dominant views on *chaeya* dissidents in three major ways. First, contrary to the radical, if not revolutionary, image built up through struggles against Chun Doo-hwan (1980–1988) after the Kwangju massacre, the dissident intelligentsia championed anything but radical—let alone, immutable—ideas. The *chaeya* segment showed a particularly high level of ideological volatility, whereas its opposing rivals, regime participants, continued identifying their role as instruments of dirigiste modernization. The *chaeya* progressively radicalized, shedding their originally conservative anticommunist identity under the multiple shocks of the normalization of relations with Japan (Chapter 15), military intervention in South Vietnam (Chapter 14), political crackdown, and *yushin* (Chapter 8). Their organizationally dispersed and clandestinely operated network strengthened too as an army of student activists led "street struggles" *(kat'u)* and religious groups organized workers into labor unions after Park launched his *yushin* regime (Chapter 13).

Second, there is the question of power. By any standard, *chaeya* activists, with or without the support of opposition politicians and journalists, were unambiguously dwarfed by Park's ruling coalition in terms of power resources. Yet they were capable of dragging his *yushin* regime into a series of dangerous confrontations with the United States and, in the case of 1979, triggering a crisis, whose implosion into regime disintegration was kept at bay only through a regular, systematic, and coordinated exercise of emergency powers (Chapters 5, 6, and 16). At the same time, even in these instances of strong *chaeya* challenges, Park proved much stronger, putting down *chaeya* protests with a show of blunt force before the activists could incite other societal actors to join them. As events in 1979 show, it was a *combination* of radical opposition party protests, labor and urban unrest, United States hostility, unruly factional struggles among KCIA and PSS praetorian guards, and, most critically, Park Chung Hee's visible loss of political acumen and discipline in taming his opposition and controlling factionalism within his ruling coalition that brought about his sudden demise.

The *chaeya* were thus strong enough to block Park's institutionalization of authoritarian rule, but not strong enough to bring down his patrimonial yet rationalized regime. Or, conversely, Park Chung Hee was strong enough to withstand *chaeya* protests, but not strong enough to weed out *chaeya* activists. On the contrary, the stronger his "hard power" grew through changing South Korea's constitutional rules of the game, the stronger his *chaeya* opponents became in "soft power," by becoming flag bearers of justice, spokesmen for the popular forces, and martyrs of democratic struggles.[17] The abilities of Park and *chaeya* dissidents jointly rose, albeit in an asymmetric way.

This asymmetric growth of state and *chaeya* powers in part explains the many twists and turns of South Korea's developmental trajectory. Although South Korea boasted of its history of overthrowing Syngman Rhee (1948–1960) through a "student revolution" and launching a parliamentary system of democratic rule under Chang Myŏn (1960–1961), at the time of Park's military coup, civil society was still very weak, enabling Park to crack down on all forms of political opposition without any societal resistance in 1961 (Chapters 1, 2, and 3). The swift change toward what looked like the opposite direction of past trends or of the current situation continued into Park Chung Hee's "civilian" Third Republic and *yushin* years. The normalization of relations with Japan triggered an explosion of student protests in 1965, but once martial law was declared and diplomatic normalization was presented as a fait accompli, political order was quickly reestablished (Chapter 15). The same was true with *chaeya* protests during Park's *yushin* regime. They disappeared from sight as unexpectedly as they exploded without warning, making politics highly volatile, uncertain, and hence full of tension (Chapters 8 and 13). The spread of public hostility against Park also could be arrested and even reversed into a show of support in times of external shock, as with the assassination of his wife, Yuk Yŏng-su, in 1974 and South Vietnam's fall in 1975 (Chapter 16). This same volatility implied Park's political vulnerability, as well. Even after a seemingly successful crackdown on opposition activities, he had to keep repressive measures in place because he knew *chaeya* activists would soon fight back again.

The asymmetric growth or vulnerability of both state and *chaeya* power still cannot fully explain South Korea's political trajectory. On the contrary, at many critical points, there occurred perplexing policy choices that seemed to be politically hurting rather than serving Park, which makes his preferences an analytic issue in our book. The regime could have mixed sticks with carrots in its dealings with *chaeya* dissidents, as it did with labor and farmer organizations, but it did not. As Jorge I. Domínguez concludes (Chapter 20), more often it looked like the regime was pursuing a strategy of minimizing rather than maximizing its societal political base, triggering a sharp decline of real wages with painful shock therapy in 1964, 1965, 1972, and 1979 (Chapter 7); supporting industrial growth through economically squeezing farmers in 1964–1968 (Chapter 12); and causing a severe nationalist backlash with its normalization treaty with Japan in 1965 (Chapter 15). Apparently Park Chung Hee risked his political fortune for the high but uncertain benefits of policy reform. Why did he do so? This question leads to an analysis of Park the man.

Leadership

At each of South Korea's critical junctures stood Park Chung Hee. Despite the profound lack of archival sources, our researchers discover deep traces

of his presence in every aspect of South Korean politics. Trying to explain
and understand South Korea's choices in political, economic, and security
realms causes most of the chapters here to raise questions regarding Park's
vision, interests, and personality, because it was Park who chose policy options. To make his leadership even more perplexing, he went against common sense in most of his moments of critical decision making, taking huge
risks in the hope of what looked like an unlikely political and economic
bonanza. As his risky strategy of modernization frequently made Park use
shock therapy, from the arrest of *chaebol* owners under charges of illicit
wealth accumulation in 1961 (Chapter 9), to the emergency decree freezing payments of interest on informal private curb-market loans in 1972
(Chapter 7), to the use of garrison decrees and martial law to quell mounting political challenges from *chaeya* dissidents, opposition politicians, and
new emerging social forces (Chapters 5, 6, and 15), not only his preference
for a high risk, high payoff, and high cost strategy of modernization, but
also his ability to remain on that track of modernization despite myriad
political and economic crises—many of which he brought on himself by
aggressively pursuing his high risk, high payoff, and high cost strategy—
for eighteen years demand an explanation. These two questions of preference and ability ask many of our chapters to confront the issues of structure and agency.

Arising from our analysis of Park Chung Hee is a man with a very complex personality, which can be grasped only by combining analytic opposites. First, a soldier of imperial Japan before 1945 and an artillery officer in South Korea's rapidly modernizing armed forces after 1948, Park
looked like another bureaucrat, colorless in style and pragmatic in outlook. Beneath this appearance, however, hid his revolutionary ideological vision of "rich nation, strong army" (Chapter 4). Second, as a son of
a poor peasant, he also looked like a materialist only interested in *kyŏng-
chae chaeiljuŭi* (economy first) when presiding over monthly, weekly, and
even daily meetings on industrial and construction projects. The way he
commanded those meetings was, however, more Nietzschian, trying to instill in people his "can do" spirit *(hamyŏn tŏenda)* that idealized the power
of the human will (Chapters 7, 9, and 10). Third, in a similarly paradoxical way, Park saw Meiji Japan's *genros* of low samurai class origins as
his role models, but he ruled in most un-Japanese ways, preferring top-
down rather than collective leadership and command rather than consensus building (Chapters 5 and 7). Fourth, Park was a populist with a deep
contempt for South Korea's traditional elites, whom he held responsible
for the *Chosŏn* dynasty's colonial subjugation in 1910, but he was also an

elitist with a dirigiste vision of modernization, critical of his people's alleged passivity, opportunism, indolence, and defeatism.[18]

Ironies continued even in Park's political projects. As a born-again conservative with a history of leftist activities in his early years, he had to prove his anticommunism, which he did by containing North Korean threats throughout his rule. Yet, in some crucial moments of political change, Park looked like a distant ideological cousin of his North Korean rival. Some observers have spoken of Park's emulation of Kim Il Sung's establishment of Red Guards and Red Young Guards among workers and peasants when Park launched an armed reserve force of 2.5 million men in 1968 after a failed North Korean commando attack on his Blue House.[19] Park also launched his *yushin* regime in a mirror image of Kim Il Sung's *yuil* regime, with power centralized in his imperial presidency, in order to economically and militarily catch up with North Korea and negotiate inter-Korea reconciliation from a position of strength in a highly uncertain era of détente (Chapter 8). The Democratic Republican Party's original vision of developing into a party driven by a professionally staffed central secretariat likewise originated from his right-hand man Kim Chong-p'il's admiration of Taiwan's "Leninist" Kuomintang.

Such a complex juxtaposition of seemingly opposite political qualities results in what Ezra F. Vogel calls "transformative leadership" in Chapter 18. Vogel puts Park Chung Hee in the category of the twentieth century's great modernizers, with the likes of Mustafa Kemal Atatürk, Lee Kuan Yew, and Deng Xiaoping. Many of Park Chung Hee's personal qualities, from a spirit of "deep patriotism" to a "sense of direction," to a keen understanding of geopolitics, to a strategic mind capable of nurturing political power, Vogel argues, constituted the ingredients of a great nation-builder. These qualities were also found in Atatürk, Lee, and Deng. However, in Vogel's eyes, Park was also distinctive in two crucial ways. First, having seized power through a military coup rather than with the support of a mass political movement, Park was less prepared than Atatürk, Lee, and Deng for national leadership. The Democratic Republican Party, established top-down by Kim Chong-p'il's intelligence agents in 1962, was institutionally too weak to protect Park during crises. The coup leader, moreover, was the opposite of a seasoned politician, unable to effectively communicate with forces outside of South Korea's armed forces. Second, because South Korea had experienced a democratic system of governance before Park seized power, he was judged by much tougher political standards than Atatürk, Lee, and Deng and saw his legitimacy challenged even after ensuring growth and security.

Analysis at the level of agency, then, produces two contradictory images. On the one hand, Park appears as an individual with the qualities of a modernizer, a strategic thinker capable of transforming ideologically driven goals into a set of bureaucratically implementable action plans, with a keen understanding of how to grow power. On the other hand, his leadership looks more like that of a faction leader than of a political leader in command of a broad yet cohesive coalition. This shortcoming cannot be explained by his lack of constituency. Park was an authoritarian leader with a deep distaste for electoral politics, an open admiration of technocratic ideals, and an idealization of collective interests, but he did command loyal societal followers. When campaigning, Park spoke openly of weeding out messy, corrupt, and wasteful politics from policymaking processes under his vision of administrative democracy, and he triumphed in most of his campaigns by a sizable margin of votes. The exception was 1963, when Park transformed his military junta into a democratically elected regime by beating Yun Po-sŏn in a tight race, and 1978, when the New Democratic Party polled 1.1 percent more votes in National Assembly elections. This usually large reservoir of societal support was what Park called his unorganized "silent majority" (see our concluding chapter).

Why did Park Chung Hee fail to transform his "silent majority" into an institutionalized support base? The answer partly lies in Paul D. Hutchcroft's analysis of "structure," as opposed to Vogel's focus on agency. Conceptualizing South Korea's state-society relations as the "reverse image" of that prevailing in "kleptocratic" Ferdinand Marcos's Philippines, where a "strikingly decentralized and porous state [was] continually raided by a hegemonic oligarchy" and "representative institutions [empowered] local caciques," Hutchcroft zeroes in on the destruction of the *Chosŏn* dynasty's ruling *yangban*-landlord class under a series of sociopolitical shocks, including land reform followed immediately by the Korean War (1950–1953). The *yangban* destruction had the effect of eliminating the societal elite that could have acted as a countervailing force against the state. Moreover, that state was a more "institutionalized bureaucracy" with the potential for rationalization, whereas the Philippines's was "thoroughly patrimonial." As analyzed by Hutchcroft, it was these historical antecedents of a strong state and weak society that enabled Park to mobilize society in the direction of his modernization strategy.

Such a structural analysis does not invalidate the centrality of agency. On the contrary, it speaks for the importance of agency. With South Korea's lack of countervailing social forces, political authorities in charge of its patrimonial and yet rationalized state bureaucracy act as a swing factor, triggering economic growth or decay depending on their leader's preferences, interests, and strategies. The country suddenly geared for hypergrowth because there were no societal forces capable of stopping Park Chung Hee from imposing his high risk, high payoff, and high cost strategy of modernization. Conversely, had it been governed by a "Korean Marcos" with all the limitations of the Filipino Marcos, Hutchcroft counterfactually argues, such a leader would have raided institutions for his own advantage without any effective checks and balances from society (Chapter 19). From Hutchcroft's perspective, then, any attempt at explaining Park's failure to institutionalize his "silent majority" by structural variables would lead back to the question of his political preferences, ideas, and strategies.

Jorge I. Domínguez provides an insightful analytic framework for deciphering complex agency-structure relations. Comparing and contrasting Park Chung Hee's rule with Latin America's four major cases of authoritarian modernization, Domínguez explains Park's strategy of rulership in terms of what is a classic dilemma confronting political leaders who seize power through an act of force: whether to remain a "single towering political leader" or to act as an institutional builder "diversifying the tool kit for ruling and policymaking" beyond politically counterproductive repression. Included in this wider tool kit are succession rules, an elite-sponsored political party, a regime-licensed state-corporatist interest representation system, and a co-optative political machine. With those tools emerges a more durable authoritarian regime. As seen by Domínguez, there were two Parks. The pre-*yushin* Park relied more on institutions than did his post-*yushin* successor. The single most critical variable Domínguez lists as responsible for this "political decay" is the South Korean leader who "cared more for [his] personal power than for the construction of a broader-based authoritarian regime." Society's low resistance to Park's coup in 1961, coupled with his Third Republic's dazzling economic success, which also became a spectacular political success in his 1967 landslide electoral victory, structurally made his authoritarian regime the "'most likely to succeed' politically" among Domínguez's country cases, but it did not do so because of Park Chung Hee's will to stay in power without constitutional restrictions on presidential terms. That will prompted the undoing of many of his more effective political-institutional mechanisms of rulership crafted during his Third Republic (Chapter 20), which had the effect of preempting much of his social supporters' evolution into organized political actors, with restricted but still crucial institutional linkages to his ruling political party, state bureaucracy, and corporatist interest groups.

The Domínguez thesis looks even more plausible when it is put against the institutional and policy continuities the *yushin* era had with the three years immediately prior to Park Chung Hee's formal inauguration of *yushin*. The ruling political party had already weakened dramatically when Park dethroned Kim Chong-p'il from his role of "crown prince" with the introduction of a third presidential term in 1969 and purged Kim Chong-p'il's rival "Gang of Four" in control of political fund-raising and local party apparatus in 1971 (Chapter 8). By contrast, beginning in 1969, his Blue House presidential Secretariat sharply upgraded its economic policy-making capacity by recruiting Kim Chŏng-ryŏm, Chang Tŏk-chin, and O Wŏn-ch'ŏl from South Korea's state bureaucracy (Chapter 5). The economic bureaucracy also began introducing tighter regulatory control on banks (Chapter 7), increased its practice of copying Japan's special industrial laws with an eye to developing new industrial policy instruments for heavy and chemical industries (Chapter 4); further restricted labor rights through legally requiring state mediation of industrial disputes;[20] and attempted to forge farmers into a stabilizing force against contentious urban groups through price support and *Saemaŭl Undong* (Chapter 12). Structurally, in other words, South Korea's political system was moving toward a *yushin*-like regime, with power concentrated in its top political leader and implemented through a rapidly growing bureaucracy, without legislative checks and balances, three years before a regime with the name of *yushin* actually emerged. That Park moved toward his *yushin* incrementally but consistently across a broad period of three years attests to his will to power.

As a corollary of these agent-driven structural changes, Park also already possessed what were, in effect, if not in name, extralegal emergency powers even before his *yushin* formally established draconian emergency powers. The rescue of faltering *chaebol* industrialists with funds extracted from private curb-market lenders through an emergency decree in 1972 is a case in point. Also, even without the *yushin*, Park was capable of readily restructuring power relations within his ruling coalition. With his praetorian guards of the Korea Central Intelligence Agency, the Army Security Command, and the Presidential Security Service maintaining tight surveillance over second-tier political elites and his Blue House effectively controlling flows of political funds within the DRP, the Park of the 1969–1972 period could freely break apart both the "mainstream" and the "anti-mainstream" factions of his party. Kim Chong-p'il was disgraced in 1969, Kim Hyŏng-uk discharged in 1969, and Kim Sŏng-gon purged in 1971. A few months after the promulgation of *yushin*, Park also forced Yi Hu-rak to retire and arrested Yun P'il-yong on the charge of plotting a military coup, thereby eliminating all second-tier leaders who might have had any ambition to succeed him. The power structure that contained an extremely weak second-tier group of next-generation leaders, which many students of South Korean politics have claimed was a defining characteristic of Park Chung Hee's *yushin* regime, actually emerged between 1969 and 1972 rather than after 1972.

By now, the reader should be aware of the limitations of "rationalist" theories. The decision to simultaneously launch the *yushin* regime and pursue an HCI drive ultimately made Park's chances for lifelong rule very low, because in pursuit of these two goals he politically alienated much of South Korea's general public. Moreover, he was fully aware of this danger, defiantly rejecting societal demands for liberalization with an ominous soliloquy of "Spit on my grave!" *(Naemudŏme ch'imŭl paet'ŏra)*[21] and keeping his *yushin* regime afloat through a total of nine declarations of emergency measures during his last seven years of rule. His prior fixation with steel and petrochemical projects during his junta years, when per capita GNP barely surpassed one hundred dollars, also attests to his commitment to HCI projects, which cannot be explained merely in terms of a rationalist framework.

For Park Chung Hee, the *yushin* regime and its HCI strategy constituted an instrument to realize his ideological vision of "rich nation, strong army" and his nationalist self-identity as a Meiji samurai taking personal risks so that his country could catch up with North Korea and then Japan and the West. Without taking seriously his "can do" rhetoric and his Meiji discourse of *yushin* (restoration), it is not possible to explain how a calculating man like Park could have taken highly risky decisions both politically and economically and ended up with his assorted "successes" and "failures." In the chapters that follow, we consider not only the conflict and collaboration among the state, society, and foreign actors but also the interplay of Park's idealism, realism, and passion to provide a more complete picture of Park and his era.

PART I

BORN IN A CRISIS

CHAPTER ONE

The May Sixteenth Military Coup

Yong-Sup Han

THE SOUTH KOREAN ARMED FORCES' intervention in politics on May 16, 1961, was historically "inevitable." With the democratically elected Chang Myŏn government (1960–1961) paralyzed by internal factional rivalries, society had been waiting for a new political elite that could pull it out of economic poverty, political instability, and social stagnation. The armed forces answered by launching a coup, and the military succeeded in seizing power because of this generalized public discontent. Or so it is thought in much of the literature on South Korean politics. However, upon a closer examination, nothing looks inevitable. On the contrary, if there were any powerful forces at work, they were working against, rather than for, Park's ambition. Yet the outcome was his political triumph. History appears to be more open-ended than driven by some inexorable force to a predetermined course of events.

First, Park was at best a second-tier leader within the South Korean armed forces, without the charisma to claim the loyalty of the military as an institution. Second, the coup coalition he led to power was a heterogeneous group of soldiers, internally fragmented along regional, generational, school, and service ties, which obstructed Park's political tasks, ranging from those of coup planning, to the actual launching of military intervention, to the post-coup consolidation of power. Third, there were powerful forces outside the armed forces, especially the United States, which could exploit the internal divisions within the complex coup coalition to oppose Park's game plan at each stage. Fourth, the danger of hostile external forces teaming up with internal rivals within the coup coalition to obstruct Park was especially great during the first stage, when the planning for the coup proceeded almost openly despite his efforts to control the flow of information. To be sure, the success of the coup despite the information leaks shows the weakness of the civilian oversight of the military under Chang Myŏn, thus creating the conditions that permitted military intervention, but it is also true that the coup attempt could have been defeated at that early stage if its potential opponents had taken the leaked information seriously and cracked down on the key coup leaders.

Yet Park succeeded in launching the coup on May 16 and completing the first phase of power consolidation two months later with the purge of Chang To-yŏng and his followers in the armed forces. To explain Park's rise to power against all odds, Chapter 1 looks at Park's ability to make the best of what he had or did not have. His second-tier military leadership position became an asset when he chose the strategy of reaching down into the ranks of colonels and lieutenant colonels as a support base and then working up the ladders of the hierarchy within the coalition in two steps, first recruiting Chang To-yŏng and other senior generals to positions of top leadership to legitimize the coup, and then purging them, deeming them forces of counterrevolution, to clear the way to the top for himself. Likewise, the heterogeneous and complex composition of his coalition came to work to his advantage, once he recognized that the same heterogeneity and complexity weakened his rivals' political base as much as his own and that their fears of a failed coup were likely to prevent them from openly challenging his role as a coordinator during the planning stage and his purge of rivals during the power consolidation stage. Consequently, Park thought he could get away with his strategy of divide and conquer in consolidating his bases of power, and he did. Moreover, Park also understood that the United States would pursue a strategy of wait-and-see rather than veto the coup if he accommodated the superpower's vital interests, including an unambiguous anticommunism. In other words, the military coup succeeded because Park was a strategic thinker with a keen understanding of how to use and grow power.

Park Chung Hee's Odyssey

Park Chung Hee was born in November 1917 into a poor farming family in North Kyŏngsang Province. As a young man, he briefly worked as a schoolteacher after graduating from Taegu Teachers College. He joined Japan's Manchukuo army in 1940, enrolling in the Manchurian Xinjing Officers School, where he met other ambitious young Koreans, many of whom were to become co-conspirators in his 1961 plot. After graduating in March 1942, he entered the third grade of the Japanese Military Academy (JMA) in Tokyo and graduated in the 1944 class of foreign students. After graduation, Park was dispatched to the Eighth Manchurian Infantry Corps as a second lieutenant. When Korea was liberated from Japanese rule, he made his way to Beijing, where Korean soldiers from various units became part of the Korean resistance army *(kwangbokkun)* before returning to Korea. At that time he was the Second Company commander of its Chup'yŏngjin Battalion of the Third Detached Force. In September 1946, Park entered the Chosŏn Defense Guard School *(Chosŏn kyŏngbi sagwan hakkyo)*, later renamed the Korea Military Academy (KMA), and became a member of its second graduating class.

Park's career in the newly created South Korean army was a turbulent one. After graduation from the KMA, he was assigned to the U.S.-Korean force that was to put down the Yŏsu-Sunch'ŏn rebellion of October 1948. The rebellion was staged by leftist elements within the army in defiance of the government's order to suppress a communist uprising on Cheju Island. Before Park could report for duty, however, he was arrested when his name came up in connection with investigations into communist cells within the Korean army. Although there was no evidence that any of these cells was directly involved in the rebellion, Park himself was a card-carrying member of the South Korea Workers' Party before 1948, making him a target of a crackdown by the military security police. He was initially sentenced to death for his connections to the workers' party and for allegedly providing arms to the insurgents of the rebellion.[1] The sentence was then reduced to twenty years of imprisonment. But Park was released soon thereafter, after providing information on the party's clandestine activities.[2] His direct superior at the time, Major General Paek Sŏn-yŏp, a graduate of the Manchurian Fengtian Officers School, the predecessor institution to the Xinjing Officers School, and Brigadier General Chang To-yŏng cleared him of the charges. After Park left prison, he was assigned to the post of director of operations and intelligence at army headquarters as a civilian.

The outbreak of the Korean War (1950–1953) saved him. Fourteen months after his discharge and only three days after the outbreak of war, Park was reinstated in Suwŏn as a major on the recommendation of General Chang To-yŏng to then–chief of staff Lieutenant General Chŏng Il-gwŏn, who was himself an earlier graduate of the Japanese Military Academy. Given the intense left-right ideological strife plaguing the country, and the eventual eradication of leftist forces in South Korea, it is remarkable that Park not only went free but was able to resume his military career. His reinstatement perhaps attests to the high personal esteem that he enjoyed among his superiors, enough to make them risk their own careers to vouch for him in the ideologically charged times. Factionalism within the South Korean military helped as well, encouraging the graduates of the Manchurian Xinjing and Fengtian Officers School as well as of the Japanese Military Academy to look after Park in an effort to win followers in their struggle against other factions or even among themselves. Most important, Park had proved his ideological loyalty to South Korea and to the officer corps, first by betraying his leftist comrades during the Yŏsu-Sunch'ŏn rebellion and then by fleeing south with the army headquarters' Intelligence Bureau during the early days of the war, when North Korea's military victory seemed certain.

Once returned to the military, Park—like many others in his age group —was rapidly promoted up the ranks from major to colonel in the spring of 1951. Park was perceived as a competent officer because he had predicted a North Korean invasion as early as December 1949. During the war, Park was awarded the Order of Military Merit Ch'ungmu in December 1950 for his bravery in the Mid-East Battle of that year, the Order of Military Merit Hwarang in December 1951 as the commandant of the Army Intelligence School, and the Order of Military Merit Ch'ungmu in May 1953 as the artillery commander of the Second Corps.[3] Park's career was also helped by the shortage of qualified officers in the South Korean army, which went through a massive organizational expansion during the war. After he became brigadier general his promotions slowed, but at this critical juncture, General Paek Sŏn-yŏp, then the army chief of staff, once again helped Park by clearing his record of any leftist activities. But Park's troubles did not abate. In 1956, when he was in command of the army's Fifth Division, some of his subordinates defected to the North as a protest against the blatant rigging of the presidential election by President Syngman Rhee (1948–1960). That same year, fifty-nine soldiers of his division died in an avalanche. In 1957, when he commanded the army's Seventh Division, a massive fire broke out in his logistics depot. Such problems would have ended most officers' military careers, but as in 1948 and 1950, Park survived with the help of his superiors. In 1958 Paek Sŏn-yŏp once again intervened on Park's behalf, helping him to get promoted to the rank of major general when his past communist record again became an issue for the army's promotion board. It was from this rank that Park planned and launched his military coup.

Climbing up through Factional Strife

In the 1950s the South Korean army was divided into three groups, based on regional background. The Northwest Group, natives of the P'yŏngan Provinces, was led by Paek Sŏn-yŏp and later Chang To-yŏng; the Northeast Group, from the Hamgyŏng Provinces, by Chŏng Il-gwŏn and later Yi Yong-mun; and the Mid-South Group, from the middle-south provinces, by Yi Hyŏng-gŭn. There were also cleavages based on school ties. The graduates of the Japanese Military Academy competed against those from the Fengtian and Xinjing Officers School. When Song Yo-ch'an became army chief of staff in 1960, the influence of the JMA graduates surpassed that of the Manchurian faction, which strongly opposed Song not only because of factional ties but also because of his support for President Rhee in the rigged election of 1960.[4] After the April 19 Student Revolution that followed that election, members of the Mid-South Group, along with graduates of the fifth KMA class, weeded out Song Yo-ch'an's faction, only to be purged themselves a year later by the coup that Park—a graduate of the Xinjing Officers School—carried off with the assistance of younger graduates of the KMA.[5] The senior officers of the 1961 coup coalition came from the Northwest Group and had received their military education at the Fengtian and Xinjing Officers School. The two leaders of this Northwest-Manchurian faction, Paek Sŏn-yŏp and Chang To-yŏng, had been patrons of Park throughout the 1950s. As the leader of the coalition, Park, though from the southeast, recruited many senior officers from this faction as major shareholders in the coup. In addition to sharing common school ties, Park had bonds with many in the faction through the KMA. Generals Yun T'ae-il, Pak Im-hang, Kim Tong-ha, and Pang Wŏn-ch'ŏl were from the academy's first graduating class; Yi Chu-il was from the second; and Ch'oe Chu-jong from the third. Marine corps brigadier general Kim Yun-gŭn graduated in the KMA's sixth class. These officers joined Park to make up the core of the coalition's leaders, destined to become members of the postcoup Supreme Council for Nation Reconstruction (SCNR).[6] Kim Yun-gŭn mobilized his marine corps to cross the Han River on the morning of the coup. The support of other generals—Chŏng Il-gwŏn, Sin Hyŏn-jun, and Paek Sŏn-yŏp, all graduates of the Manchurian Fengtian Officers School—could be counted on once forces had crossed the river.

Despite the participation of generals of similar rank, it was Park who controlled the initiative from the very beginning stage of planning for the coup, because he had the loyalty of the lieutenant colonels and colonels

in command of battalions and regiments lower down in the military hierarchy. To organize this mid-level officer-led nucleus, Park fully utilized the
personal ties he had built up throughout his military career. As a company
commander at the KMA, he won the trust and loyalty of the cadets with
his taciturn yet forceful personality, self-discipline, generosity, and patriotism. In particular, Park built close ties with four promising cadets in
the fifth KMA graduating class—Ch'ae Myŏng-sin, Kim Chae-ch'un, Pak
Ch'i-ok, and Mun Chae-jun—who were to lead their troops as vanguards
of the coup coalition at dawn on May 16. When Park worked in the intelligence division at army headquarters as a civilian, he had also forged
ties with leading young officers of the eighth KMA class, including Kim
Chong-p'il, his later close ally, and Sŏk Chŏng-sŏn, Yi Yŏng-gŭn, and
Chŏn Chae-gu, who were to become coup planners and, afterward, founders of the Korea Central Intelligence Agency (KCIA) that worked to consolidate Park's power. With his promotion to the rank of brigadier general,
Park began to bring together many of these trustworthy followers into his
military unit, while at the same time cultivating the trust of new faces as
well, such as Yi Nak-sŏn, Yi Wŏn-yŏp, Hong Chong-ch'ŏl, Ku Cha-ch'un,
Kim Kye-wŏn, Pak T'ae-jun, Yun P'il-yong, and Han Pyŏng-gi. By acting
as a bridge that linked the senior group of Northwest-Manchurian officers
with the junior group of the fifth and eighth KMA graduating classes, Park
put himself at the center of the coalition. Rather than being the first among
equals, Park was indispensable to the planning, creating a cohesive organization out of different components.

Park appears to have toyed with the idea of a military coup as early as
1956, when Rhee was re-elected through a rigged presidential election.[7] As
he later recollected, the plotting became more serious in January 1960
with the approach of another presidential election.[8] When student activists launched a revolution on April 19, 1960, in protest against the rigging
of this election, the increasingly corrupt and dictatorial government of
Syngman Rhee responded with force, killing 183 demonstrators on April
19 alone. The bloody crackdown bankrupted the Liberal Party, forcing
Rhee to go into exile in Hawaii. The student revolution prevented Park
from going further down the road to a military coup. As he later lamented,
he lost the initiative to the students and had to wait for another civilian
government to falter before he could have his chance.

Park's chance came in 1961, when it became increasingly evident to
many that the leaders of the Second Republic (1960–1961), who had come
to power two months after the fall of Syngman Rhee, were incompetent
and corrupt. The internally fragmented civilian regime of Chang Myŏn betrayed people's hopes for a clean and effective government.[9] Many thought

that the civilian government could not handle the political, social, and economic crises then gripping the country. Some feared that the national woes would invite leftist-communist subversion.[10] South Korean society was waiting for effective leadership, and Park and his fellow officers exploited the power vacuum created by the April 19 Student Revolution with their superior intelligence, organizational capabilities, and political skill.

Advent of the Military as a Leading Institution

The once-fledgling armed forces of South Korea had then transformed into a 600,000-strong, thoroughly modern, and formidable fighting force, thanks to the Korean War.[11] Training hundreds of thousands of men for combat, providing the soldiers with supplies, and planning and executing troop deployment required enormous logistical capabilities. In carrying out these tasks, the South Korean military gained modern administrative and managerial know-how, allowing the 1961 coup leaders to boast that their level of managerial skill was "ten years ahead of the private sector."[12] The coup makers even claimed the military to be the most democratic institution in South Korea, with its leaders of humble origin extensively trained in the United States under myriad military transfer programs[13] and its organization acting as the melting pot for men of diverse social and economic backgrounds. In the poverty-stricken country, devastated by colonial exploitation, the military constituted one of the very few avenues open to young men seeking opportunities to advance. The armed forces also functioned as a social safety net for many of the unemployed and underemployed.

In particular, the training programs in the United States helped officers to define their role comprehensively to include not only military defense but also nation building. Certainly, the comprehensive definition of the military role was not new to many of the Fengtian and Xinjing graduates, including Park. The Japanese imperial army had defined the mission of the armed forces as nation building too. Now the South Korean armed forces, with their new U.S. military training and education, could combine the Japanese militarist ethos with the American spirit of technical efficiency to expand its mission from defending the country against communist aggression to that of helping it build itself into a modern nation. From this it was only a short step for the armed forces to entertain the idea of military intervention in the country's political and economic affairs as a legitimate and necessary part of its mission. Moreover, the armed forces became increasingly contemptuous of both ruling and opposition political parties that remained trapped in partisan gridlock. In particular, the junior officer corps became rebellious, critical of superior officers who had been corrupted by politicians. Removed from the political fray because of their lower rank, the junior officers could project an image of ideological purity and incorruptibility. For South Koreans, longtime witnesses to the corrosive effects of faction-driven, inefficient, and corrupt civilian party politics, the junior officers gradually gained in esteem as an alternative group of elites to lead the nation.

Adding to the junior officers' discontent was the serious imbalance in the South Korean military promotion system. Because the armed forces had expanded to over 600,000 men in a mere five years after its establishment, there developed a huge gap in the time required for promotion between different graduating classes of the KMA. The higher the rank in 1948, the faster the subsequent promotion. For the early starters, the rapid organizational expansion of the armed forces during the Korean War meant a great opportunity to climb the ranks. Once they rose and filled in higher posts, they necessarily prevented their subordinates from climbing up the ladder as rapidly as they had. For example, whereas the fifth KMA class became colonels in eight years after their graduation,[14] the eighth KMA graduating class had to spend eight years to be promoted from the rank of major to colonel. The promotional imbalance caused serious discontent among lieutenant colonels and colonels by the late 1950s. They were to become core members of the 1961 coup.

The situation was thus ripe for military intervention in politics, with both "push" and "pull" factors driving military factions to challenge the civilian political leadership. For this professional but politicized military to seize power and lead society, however, there had to be a leader who could forge myriad military factions into a coalition and imbue it with a sense of purpose and destiny with his vision, charisma, strategic mind, and organizational capabilities. That leader was Park Chung Hee.

At the same time, it is important not to exaggerate Park's basis of support within the armed forces at the time of military coup. The opposite seemed more likely, with the mainstream of the South Korean military withholding support for, if not opposing, the 1961 coup. Nor did Park appear as the natural leader of the entire South Korean military. As with any institution of its size, the South Korean armed forces had its share of internal strife between rival factions. At the time of the coup, Park was the deputy commander of the Second Army, not favorably positioned to mobilize troops in the event of a military clash. Rather, it was more the dynamics of power between different factions within the South Korean military than his own resources that enabled Park to engineer the coup and then to consolidate power within the junta. The key to his success was a strategy of divide-and-rule that neutralized the rivals despite their seemingly greater strength within the army.

From Military Reform to National Revolution

Ironically, it was the April 19 Student Revolution of 1960 that brought the armed forces onto the center stage of politics. The student revolution not only spread the spirit of reform to the South Korean military, but also entrusted it with the task of restoring order after Syngman Rhee stepped down from his office on April 26. The army, as the executor of martial law, had to confront the challenge of governance directly. Suddenly thrown into a volatile political arena, and directly engaging societal forces in reforms, military officers were eventually led to form their own ideas about what was happening in the country. The younger officers, in particular, gathered into groups to exchange information and views. These ad hoc meetings provided conditions favorable for a military coup by becoming the catalyst for the wide dissemination of radical ideas and reformist views regarding problems plaguing the military as well as the country.

The issue of corruption had been simmering for a long time. Under Rhee, the ruling Liberal Party raised political funds through illegal means to bribe opposition party politicians to gain their support. In the military, too, the generals fabricated inventory reports to dispose of military property and assets not only for their own personal gain, but also for the raising of political funds.[15] Politicization of the military had also become a serious issue, because Rhee used its top leadership for the rigging of elections. Senior officers regularly ordered their subordinates to vote for Syngman Rhee and his Liberal Party through open ballots and mock ballots. During the Rhee regime, some fifty officers were arrested for "intervention in politics" when they disobeyed the order to get their regiments to vote for the ruling party. After Rhee's overthrow, young colonels and lieutenant colonels began to demand that the military's top leadership take responsibility for their role in the vote rigging of the 1956 and 1960 presidential elections. The reformist campaign gained momentum when Major General Park Chung Hee joined the young officers and demanded that the army chief of staff, Song Yo-ch'an, resign for having meddled in the 1960 presidential election. On a personal level, Park's move was an act of betrayal, for Song had saved Park's career on various occasions during the 1950s and had helped Park receive his promotion to the rank of major general in 1958. Politically, however, it was a brilliant move, pushing Park onto the center stage of military reform politics and transforming him overnight into a leader of national stature. Park could side unambiguously with the forces of reform because as a second-tier general, excluded from powerful posts and political crony networks during the 1950s, he was clean on the corruption issue. The issue of his earlier leftist record remained, but he could also fight back with his impeccable record of anticommunism in the Korean War. Untainted by corruption, Park was favorably positioned to transform the societywide anticorruption reform movements into his vehicle to challenge others of his rank and to build up his own military faction. In the process Park found his supporters, allies, and confidants among the people with whom he had cultivated trust during the 1950s. In Seoul, members of the eighth graduating class of the KMA—lieutenant colonels Kim Hyŏng-uk, Kil Chae-ho, Ok Ch'ang-ho, Sin Yun-ch'ang, Sŏk Ch'ang-hŭi, Ch'oe Chun-myŏng, O Sang-gyun, and Kim Chong-p'il—with whom Park had cultivated close ties ever since his three years at the army headquarters' Intelligence Bureau, secretly gathered to support Park's appeal for the resignation of the army chief of staff. Their activity was leaked to the military security forces, ending in the arrest of the men on charges of conspiracy. Nevertheless, the damage had been done and Song Yo-ch'an stepped down from his office on May 19, 1960, as the anticorruption campaign began to gain support inside as well as outside the military.

Song's removal proved to be only the beginning of intense political conflict within the military. The new army chief of staff was Ch'oe Yŏng-hŭi, an old-timer as vulnerable to the charge of corruption and politicization as his predecessor. On August 19, the lieutenant colonels visited newly inaugurated prime minister Chang Myŏn to set the criteria for the appointment of the next army chief of staff and defense minister. Their bold move verged on insubordination. On September 10, Kim Chong-p'il and Kim Hyŏng-uk, aided by their KMA classmates, tried to pay a visit to the defense minister, Hyŏn Sŏk-ho, to ask what policy measures he would take to root out corruption. Not only was their request for the meeting denied, but the two were arrested for insubordination. That night, the other leaders of the anticorruption movements met in downtown Seoul to discuss concrete measures to advance the cause of the anticorruption campaign on their own initiative, because they thought it futile to appeal to either the national political leadership or the military establishment. This was the beginning of preparations for a military coup.

In the eyes of the anticorruption camp, Prime Minister Chang Myŏn's Democratic Party was as hostile to the idea of reform as Syngman Rhee's now-dismantled Liberal Party. The lieutenant colonels began to think that the only way to reform the military establishment was not by working through the hierarchy of the armed forces, but by pressuring for change from outside by challenging the national political leadership and initiating political reform. The problem of corruption within the military was perceived as structural in nature, inextricably linked to the larger structure of political, economic, and social domination of the nation. The leaders of the military clean-up campaign began to shift their goal from initiating an internal military reform to launching a military coup to carry out a full-fledged national reform. Sometime in May 1960, the colonels and lieutenant colonels of the eighth graduating class of the KMA had gotten the green light from Park to prepare for a military coup.[16] Park then was the commander of the Logistics Headquarters in Pusan, geographically too far away from Seoul to occupy and control the capital. Moreover, he had only a lightly armed battalion or two under his personal command. To seize power, he needed to assemble a coalition of forces, which he thought could be done by getting the eighth KMA graduating class to link up different regiments through horizontal networks. Having reached the ranks of lieutenant colonel and colonel, graduates of the eighth KMA class commanded combat battalions and regiments. The question was how to bring these functionally strategic but geographically dispersed mid-ranking officers into one cohesive coalition to carry out a coup. It was necessary to break into the military hierarchy and divert the loyalty of the mid-ranking officers away from their immediate boss. Park calculated that the informal group loyalty based on school ties would outweigh the formal discipline of military hierarchy.

Park used his own school ties with generals of the Manchurian faction to put together the coup's leadership. He approached Major General Kim Tong-ha of the marine corps, one year his senior at the Manchurian Xinjing Officers School, about launching a coup. Park also got Yi Chu-il, another Xinjing Officers School graduate, to persuade Brigadier General Yun T'ae-il of the Thirty-Sixth Division to join the group. Park secured support from the editor in chief of the *Pusan Daily News* for the purposes of propaganda. Park also tested the intentions of the Second Army commander, Chang To-yŏng, by arguing the need for a military intervention.[17] Given the political instability of the time, the lieutenant colonels, colonels, and generals of the coalition were able to appeal directly to higher authorities for a military coup and to express their discontent with the state of political and military affairs openly without getting punished for insubordination. The open plotting was possible not only because the Military Security Command responsible for monitoring officers' activities and maintaining military discipline was seriously demoralized due to its implication in illegal activities during the Rhee regime but also because South Korea was in the midst of a veritable civil revolution after the April 19 student uprising. All sectors of society took turns in expressing their frustration and grievances through demonstrations and riots. The Chang Myŏn government was losing control of South Korean politics, and that fractured political force was evident in the demoralization of the security command.

The officers began to plan for a coup and organize in earnest in October 1960, with the core members assigned to strategic roles. Kim Chong-p'il became their general secretary while Kim Hyŏng-uk and Chŏng Mun-sun coordinated intelligence. The office of personnel went to O Ch'i-sŏng, that of economic affairs to Kim Tong-hwan, and that of legal matters to Kil Chae-ho. Ok Ch'ang-ho, Sin Yun-ch'ang, and U Hyŏng-ryong were put in charge of operations.

On November 9, the nine core members held a second meeting at Major General Park Chung Hee's house in Seoul. As luck would have it, he had been transferred from Pusan to Seoul to become the director general of operations at army headquarters, enabling him to attend the preparatory meetings regularly. To be sure, the new post did not bestow Park with any operational command over combat troops, still making him dependent on the lieutenant colonels and colonels of the eighth KMA graduating class in building horizontal networks among would-be coup makers. At the critical meeting in November, the core members decided to use the anticorruption movement as the pretext for the coup. The strategy was chosen because two of their comrades, Kil Chae-ho and Ok Ch'ang-ho, had been arrested for involvement in the movement. As part of their effort to widen the coalition, O Ch'i-sŏng succeeded in winning the support of an artillery unit in the Sixth Corps and of the Army War College. While the colonels and lieutenant colonels concentrated their efforts on recruiting young officers and establishing revolutionary cells within and outside Seoul, Park continued cultivating the trust of generals.

Game Plan

The core group formulated four guiding principles for the coup:

- The goal is to liberate people from political corruption and economic poverty through a "maximum-effect dose of medicine"—revolution, recognizing the reality that the country had lost the momentum to reform peacefully the military establishment.

- The revolutionaries shall risk their lives to achieve "great righteousness."
- The task of organizing the revolutionary organ shall proceed in top secrecy.
- The decision to undertake the coup is based on an objective analysis of the nation's reality and the people's hopes.[18]

With the articulation of these rather fuzzy four principles, the core group started to organize its central and local organs to stage the coup. From November 1960 until May 1961, Park focused on persuading more generals in command of combat and noncombat troops on the front lines with North Korea as well as in the rear area to join the coup coalition. In November, Brigadier General Chang Kyŏng-sun, of army headquarters, and Han Ung-jin, of the Intelligence School in Yŏngch'ŏn (who set aside his own plan for a coup), came on board. With the goal of preventing a crackdown on the organization of the coup, which by then had become an open secret, Park tried to persuade officers at the Counter-Intelligence Command to sign on. To equip his coup coalition with guns and tanks, Park also tried to win over the army's Ninth Division, the major armored division located in the vicinity of Seoul. Both efforts failed, however. But to the relief of the coup makers, neither the Counter-Intelligence Command nor the Ninth Division reported the conspiracy to higher authorities.

Toward the end of 1960, Park began other talks parallel to the ongoing meetings with the core group, in order to broaden his support base among younger officers. He purposely put himself in the position of coordinating activities of the different segments of the coalition. The participants communicated and coordinated only through Park, making him the de facto leader. The loose network gave Park freedom to maneuver and flexibility to adjust swiftly to changes in the political environment. Once the coup succeeded in May 1961, the same structure—with a built-in system of checks and balances among the mid-ranking core members and between the colonels and the generals and with the hub occupied by Park—would be of great assistance to Park in consolidating power around him. One member of a parallel group whom Park brought in to the heterogeneous coalition was Major General Yi Chu-il. Park met Yi in Taegu at the end of 1960 to draw up three separate guiding principles of the coup:

- Once the coup was launched, the two would ask Lieutenant General Chang To-yŏng, army chief of staff, to become the chairman of the Revolutionary Council in order to get the entire military establishment behind the coup. The implementation of coup plans would fall under the purview of Park Chung Hee, who would take up the position of commander of the Revolutionary Army.

- Park would take charge of organizing the central organ of the Revolutionary Army by recruiting field army generals, while Yi would be responsible for assembling support groups in the rear area.
- Colonel Pak Ki-sŏk would assist Yi in the organization of the Revolutionary Army in Taegu.

On April 10, 1961, Park boldly revealed the coup plan to Chang To-yŏng. The reaction of Chang was perplexing. The army chief of staff turned down Park's request to head the coalition, but he did not report the conspiracy to Prime Minister Chang Myŏn. Nor did he move to preempt the coup by ordering the Counter-Intelligence Command and the Security Command to arrest the conspirators. Moreover, although Chang turned down the leadership position, Park came out of the meeting with the impression that Chang had given tacit support for the coup, through elusive gestures and equivocal expressions. Perhaps the two miscommunicated, but it is more likely that the army chief of staff could see that the coup planners had already developed too much momentum for him to stop them. Besides, he could later side with Park if the coup looked promising. Whatever Chang To-yŏng's motive was, his indecisiveness allowed Park to persuade others to join the coalition by portraying Chang To-yŏng as the "invisible hand" behind the military coup. The strategy was to use Chang to provide the stamp of legitimacy and the unity of the military behind the plan, something only the army chief of staff could give.

Park also frequently visited the army's Fifth Division commander Ch'ae Myŏng-sin and obtained his full support by May 1960. In December 1960, he secured support from the generals at the Second Army Headquarters in Taegu. Later, in April 1961, Park visited Kwangju to recruit Colonel Yi Wŏn-yŏp, the commandant of the Army Aviation School, to spread the revolutionary communiqué on the day of the military coup. According to the plan, the coup headquarters was to be located at the Sixth District Command in Seoul. Lieutenant Colonel Pak Wŏn-bin was put in charge of organizing coup units there.

In March 1961, the core group of lieutenant colonels and colonels refined their plot at the Ch'ungmu-jang Restaurant in Seoul. They agreed on five major points:

- The core group of the military coup would consist of the eighth and ninth graduating classes of the KMA.
- Only those "qualified" officers, without records of personal corruption or politicization, would be recruited into the coup coalition.

- The list of the officers who have agreed to join the coup will not be made known among the coup makers until the end of March 1961.
- In April, they would convene a meeting for all members of the coup coalition.
- Colonel O Ch'i-sŏng would be in charge of communications among the eighth KMA graduating class and Lieutenant Colonel Kang Sang-uk in charge of communication among the ninth KMA graduating class.

In designing their plan, the coup makers, mindful of possible undesirable consequences for national security, decided not to mobilize units on the front lines. They chose the first anniversary of the April 19 Student Revolution as D-day for the coup, because they expected severe political unrest to break out near that day to protest against the incompetence of Chang Myŏn, thus justifying the military move as an attempt not only to restore order but also to inherit and carry out the democratic spirit of the year before. As a back-up plan, they set mid-May as another D-day in case the mid-April plan did not materialize. Park was in charge of mobilizing regular and reserve forces stationed in the rear area. At the Sixth District Command, where lieutenant colonels Pak Wŏn-bin and Ok Ch'ang-ho were to take charge of military operations on the day of the coup, were the forces of the Thirtieth and Thirty-Third Army Divisions as well as the special military forces charged with the defense of Seoul. Getting these forces to capture strategically important posts in the capital was crucial for the plan's success, and by the end of March their support had been secured.

Park also obtained financial support in the amount of 7.5 million hwan —76.5 percent of the total budget for the coup—from civilian business-people, including Kim Chong-rak (Kim Chong-p'il's elder brother).[19] Yi Hak-su, with a small print company, was in charge of printing the propaganda leaflets in cooperation with Chang T'ae-hwa, who gathered intelligence. Park used his own connections to small-sized entrepreneurs to raise financial resources for the coup.

But contrary to the expectation of political unrest, the first anniversary of the April 19 Student Revolution passed without major protest, forcing the coup leaders to reschedule D-day to May 12. This, too, was abruptly aborted when the plan was accidentally leaked to the military security forces and reported to Prime Minister Chang Myŏn and Defense Minister Hyŏn Sŏk-ho. The coup was postponed to 3:00 AM on May 16, 1961.

The Chang Myŏn government failed to initiate an investigation to counter the coup makers, because army chief of staff Chang To-yŏng questioned the reliability of the security report when the prime minister asked him about it. Chang Myŏn trusted Chang To-yŏng deeply as a fellow Roman Catholic, and Chang To-yŏng's words stopped Chang Myŏn from ordering an investigation. The fact that there had been rumors of a military coup by one or another faction of the South Korean armed forces since early 1961 also helped Park, since Chang Myŏn thought the security report on the May 12 coup was another false alarm. Nonetheless, the incident provoked Lieutenant General Yi Han-lim (of the First Army) and other generals not recruited for the coup to keep a close eye on Park's moves.

On May 16, Park went to the Sixth District Army Headquarters to coordinate the coup himself after finding out that the plan had once again been leaked. The military police were already in the process of rounding up the coup makers in the Sixth District Army at the order of army chief of staff Chang To-yŏng after receiving a Counter-Intelligence Command report that a mutiny was being plotted by officers of the Thirtieth Division under the command of the Sixth District Army. Park hurriedly tried to reverse the situation. Concealing his anxiety, Park gave a moving speech before the recalcitrant troops, saying, "We have been waiting for the civilian government to bring back order to the country. The Prime Minister and the Ministers, however, are mired in corruption, leading the country to the verge of collapse. We shall rise up against the government to save the country. We can accomplish our goals without bloodshed. Let us join in this Revolutionary Army to save the country."[20]

The speech was a great success. Even the military police units sent out to arrest the mutineers ended up joining the coup. The military's distrust of the Chang Myŏn government was by then irreversible, enabling Park to win the support of many of the officer corps with his example of courage. Once he got control of the Sixth District Army, he left it to Colonel Kim Chae-ch'un to use it to organize the vanguard forces to occupy Seoul. Subsequently Park went to the Special Forces Command and the Marine Corps to order them personally to cross the Han River and seize the Blue House, the seat of presidential power. Before his departure for the Special Forces Command, Park also sent a letter to army chief of staff Chang To-yŏng, making it clear that Chang would not be free of responsibility should the military coup fail. This was a politically calculated move to implicate the army chief of staff in the coup so that he would not go further in mobilizing a countercoup coalition. In spite of the earlier pledge of support, the actual mobilization of the Special Forces on D-day also ran into difficulty and was delayed for an hour, making the marine corps under Kim Yun-gŭn the first military unit to cross the Han River at dawn on May 16.

The marines' crossing of the river was facilitated by the fact that the artillery brigade of the Sixth Corps had taken over army headquarters an hour earlier and was in control of the downtown north of the Han. The marine corps and paratroopers of the Special Forces Command could therefore cross the river from the south with few casualties. There was some exchange of fire with the military police units guarding the bridge to the downtown area, but by 4:15 AM the coup coalition succeeded in seizing the buildings that housed the three branches of the government. The coalition also occupied the Korean Broadcasting Company and from there issued the revolutionary manifesto to the nation:

> The military authorities, thus far avoiding conflict, can no longer restrain themselves, and have taken a concerted operation at the dawn of this day to completely take over the three branches of the Government . . . and to form the Military Revolutionary Committee . . . The armed services have staged this uprising because:

1. We believe that the fate of the nation and the people cannot be entrusted to the corrupt and incompetent [Chang Myŏn] regime and its politicians.
2. We believe that the time has come [for the armed forces] to give direction to our nation, which has gone dangerously astray.[21]

The Military Revolutionary Committee then issued a six-point political platform:

1. Oppose Communism and reorganize and strengthen anti-Communist readiness, which has been so far asserted only rhetorically.
2. Respect the United Nations Charter, faithfully carry out international obligations, and strengthen ties with the United States and other free-world allies.
3. Root out corruption and the accumulated evils in this nation and its society, instill moral principles and national spirit among the people, and encourage a new and fresh outlook.
4. Speedily solve the misery of the masses, who are reduced to despair, and concentrate on the construction of an independent national economy.
5. Increase the national capacity to achieve national unification, the unanimous goal of all Korean people, and to oppose Communism.
6. Transfer power to new [generations of] conscientious politicians as soon as our mission has been completed, and return to our original [military] duties.

The communiqué was issued in the name of Lieutenant General Chang To-yŏng, now presented as the chairman of the Military Revolutionary Committee, but without his prior approval.[22]

The coup leaders succeeded in occupying Seoul on May 16, 1961. The consolidation of the power and the stabilization of the ruling junta, however, were far from guaranteed. The Revolutionary Army had four more hurdles to overcome before it could claim success. First, President Yun Po-sŏn had to accept the military coup as a fait accompli and entrust the task of governance to the Military Revolutionary Committee. His resignation in protest against the coup could cause a diplomatic crisis, given the role of the president as head of state. Second, General Carter B. Magruder, serving as the commander of the United States Forces in Korea (USFK) and of the United Nations Command (UNC), with operational control of the South Korean armed forces, had to accept the irreversibility of the coup. Otherwise, latent rivals to Park in the military establishment could be lured into resisting Park's claim to power. Third, after the occupation of Seoul on May 16, Lieutenant General Yi Han-lim, who had been a classmate of Park at the Manchurian Xinjing Officers School and the Japanese Imperial Military Academy and who was now commander of the First Army, stationed at the front lines, threatened to organize a countercoup despite the twenty heavily armed combat divisions who were on the side of the coalition. Fourth, Park had to defeat potential rivals and challengers from within the military junta, especially Chang To-yŏng, in order to transform the junta into an organization loyal only to himself.

Under the parliamentary system of government established after the April 19 Student Revolution, Chang Myŏn was the commander in chief of the South Korean armed forces. Rather than standing up against the coup makers on the crucial day of May 16, Chang Myŏn fled to a Catholic convent at the news of the coup, depriving the government of the opportunity to strike Park at his most vulnerable moment. President Yun Po-sŏn, a leader of the Old Faction and a longtime rival of Chang Myŏn, of the New Faction, accepted the coup and decided to stay on as head of state. By remaining as the president, Yun Po-sŏn not only legitimized the military coup but countered his old enemy. There is no evidence that the junta launched the coup with the expectation that the deep rivalry between Yun Po-sŏn and Chang Myŏn would enable it to fragment the civilian opposition, but it was this split in the civilian political leadership that swiftly shifted the balance of power toward the coup makers.

Park also made rapid progress in purging potential anticoup forces from within the military. After hearing of the coup, Commander Yi Han-lim of the First Army, based in Wŏnju, ordered the Reserve First Corps of the First Army to prepare for the suppression of the coup. Yi Han-lim eventually backed down, because mobilizing the Reserve First Corps would leave the front lines open to possible North Korean attack. With the arrest of Yi Han-lim on May 18, the Revolutionary Army quelled all resistance within the military.

The situation continued to tip quickly in favor of Park. The KMA cadets held a public march in the streets of Seoul in support of the coup, thus strengthening Park's claim that he had the backing of the armed forces as an institution.[23] Prime Minister Chang Myŏn reappeared after three days of hiding to announce the resignation of the cabinet. That same day, the coup makers formed the Supreme Council for National Reconstruction (SCNR) as the military junta, with executive, legislative, and judicial powers.[24] Lieutenant General Chang To-yŏng became its chairman, while Park assumed the post of vice chairman. The key generals of the coalition chaired the committees of the SCNR. The colonels and lieutenant colonels who initiated the coup became the heads of subcommittees.

In the evening of May 16, Kim Chong-p'il called on his KMA classmates to help him organize the Korea Central Intelligence Agency (KCIA), with the goal of providing policy advice to Park and the SCNR and to collect intelligence on pro-communist and anticoup forces. The colonels and lieutenant colonels he summoned were intelligence officers who had worked with Park before and during the Korean War, including Ch'oe Yŏng-t'aek, Sŏk Chŏng-sŏn, Yi Yŏng-gŭn, and Ko Che-hun. Kim Chong-p'il also recruited his civilian comrades, including Kim Yong-t'ae, Chang T'ae-hwa, and Sin Chik-su, as bureau chiefs. The KCIA was legally created on June 10, 1961. By getting the young colonels to head the SCNR subcommittees and organize the KCIA, Park came to control the two most powerful sources of political influence. The SCNR announced the appointment of General Kim Chong-o as the new army chief of staff and former army chief of staff Song Yo-ch'an as the defense minister. These appointments were made by Park and his followers and not by Chang To-yŏng, who was rapidly reduced to a figurehead. Colonel Mun Chae-jun became the commander of the military police. Likewise, Lieutenant General Pak Im-hang was promoted from his post as Fifth Corps commander to be the commander of the First Army to replace Yi Han-lim. Park now had control of the strategic units stationed near the capital.

Consolidating Military Rule

Once Park stabilized the military situation, his eyes turned to the issues of how to secure U.S. government support (see Chapter 2), remove rival leaders from the junta (see Chapter 3), and purge "corrupt" civilian politicians with the goal of winning public support as well as preempting civilian-led opposition. The purge started with Chang To-yŏng on July 3. Park had used Chang as a protective shield during the early days of the junta to buy time, to prevent both South Koreans and the U.S. government from probing into Park's past leftist activities, and to claim that the entire military establishment was behind the coup. Park, who had survived several difficult moments during his lifetime, knew not only how to win the trust of others but also when to betray them to consolidate his power. With the United States moving to build close ties with him, he knew he could purge Chang To-yŏng without risking his leadership.

In his relationship with political parties and societal forces, Park developed three strategies. First, he used the public relations apparatus at his disposal to plant in the public's mind an image of the junta as an able, patriotic force dedicated to rebuilding the nation. Second, he weakened civilian politicians through divide-and-rule tactics. Third, he bet on economic development to win over the hearts of ordinary people.

As part of the first strategy, Park mobilized the intellectuals and the national media to the fullest extent. The media campaign had a common theme, portraying the junta as being the opposite of "corrupt" and "incompetent" civilian politicians. To this end, the SCNR organized civilian demonstrations in support of the coup and pressured college professors to write newspaper articles in its support. Yi Pyŏng-do, a leading historian of the time, wrote in the *Korea Times*: "The May Sixteenth Military Revolution saved the nation from the cliffs of national crisis, which could have turned the country over to the hands of the Communists."[25] On May 23, the junta issued a sweeping eight-point decree to put censorship of the press in place, prohibiting the publication of any reports that could "agitate counterrevolutionary sentiment." In June 1962, Park followed with a new media policy designed to purge antimilitary newspapers. He also forced the entire state bureaucracy and schools to disseminate the revolutionary goals and principles of the SCNR. Anyone who opposed the revolution would be purged as a communist sympathizer and an enemy of national reconstruction.

In order to weaken civilian politicians, the coup makers imposed martial law until they were confident that the United States and the South Korean people would support the junta. Martial law, promulgated on the day of the coup, was lifted on May 27, 1961, after General Magruder and the U.S. government announced that they would accept the coup. On May 16, Park had also banned all political activities, dissolved the National Assembly, and arrested most of the civilian politicians on the charge of being proxies of Kim Il Sung and communism. The divide-and-rule strategy toward civilian politicians was evident when Park and his allies lifted the ban on political activities for those politicians and political groups that either were too weak to challenge the junta or had recently switched sides to support it, while continuing the ban for others that might cause it trouble. In particular, the major party politicians critical of military rule were banned from engaging in political activities until March 1962. Even then, still unsure of the junta's ability to win the coming elections, Park had the junta promulgate the Political Purification Law of March 1962. The law made President Yun Po-sŏn resign in protest, thus bringing the Old Faction of the now-dismantled Democratic Party to join Chang Myŏn's New Faction in the opposition. The "cleanup" law enabled the military junta to indict 1,336 politicians on charges of corruption, so that Park could have an early start in preparing for the coming elections.

With the power to decide who could and could not reenter politics, the junta used the issue of the restoration of electoral competition and civilian rule and the accompanying process of candidate screening as an instrument not only to fuel jealousies and rivalries among the already internally fragmented civilian politicians but also to build a new ruling military-civilian coalition for the coming Third Republic (1963–1972). As part of the junta's tactics, Chang Myŏn and most of his New Faction were prohibited from engaging in political activities, whereas Yun Po-sŏn of the Old Faction and Hŏ Chŏng of the earlier interim government (April-August 1960) were allowed to organize the Democratic Politics Party, or Minjŏng-dang, and the People's Party, or Kungminŭi-dang, respectively. The three leaders of the civilian camp, partly manipulated by the KCIA and partly driven by their own deeply rooted factional divide going back to the formative years of the Democratic Party, chose to go their separate ways rather than unite their forces to oppose Park in the upcoming elections.

To discredit the civilian politicians as an incompetent force, moreover, the junta moved rapidly on the economic front. Having defined one of its roles to be the rescue of South Koreans from their absolute poverty, the junta thought it imperative that it show visible progress in economic development. On May 19, 1961, the Military Revolutionary Committee changed its name to the Supreme Council for National Reconstruction to underscore its economic commitment. The junta members followed up with the reorganization of government structures and the introduction of modern management ideas and techniques, the topic of later chapters.

WHY DID the May 16 coup succeed under Park Chung Hee's leadership? The first set of variables were those external to the South Korean armed forces that pulled Park and his followers into politics. The "pull factors" consisted of the failure of the Chang Myŏn government to tame the contentious voice of reform in the post-April 19 Student Revolution period and restore order; the pervasive corruption that cost the Chang Myŏn government its political credibility among the people; and the factionalism within the Democratic Party that deprived society of the opportunity to develop a force of reform to unite the nation and to develop the South Korean economy. There also existed "push factors" inside the South Korean military that drove Park and his followers to intervene in politics as a way of solving the internal issues of the armed forces. Among these push factors was the transformation of the South Korean military into the country's most modernized, educated, and administratively experienced elite group, equipped with both a nationalist ethos and a U.S.-based spirit of technocracy that gave it the confidence to intervene in politics. The availability of a strategically minded and ethically uncompromised leader, Park Chung Hee, enabled the forging of a loosely organized cross-regional and cross-generational coalition to awaken in the armed forces a sense of mission to rebuild the nation, the result of which was to get the officer corps interested in politics. Most critically, the chronic corruption and promotion problems plaguing the South Korean military drove discontented young colonels and lieutenant colonels to rise up against their superiors in the military and their patrons in the ruling political party.

This combination of factors explains the military's entry into politics in May 1961, but it does not explain the success of the revolutionary government in its consolidation of power after the military coup. The military junta had to prove that it was different from civilian politicians, and therefore articulated its goal of achieving economic development as quickly as possible.

The coup also succeeded because Park was a strategic thinker with a keen understanding of power. The formidable KCIA, organized by Kim Chong-p'il, Park's trusted lieutenant, exercised power frequently outside legal supervision to monitor countercoup activities and to conduct covert political operations to suppress or manipulate civilian politicians. The agency also became a think tank for Park on issues such as inter-Korea relations, foreign affairs, and even economic policy.

Finally, the success of the coup owed much to Park's ability to quell and control factionalism within the military. There occurred a series of purges in the name of suppressing counterrevolutionary forces during the junta years. The July 1961 purge of Chang To-yŏng and his followers from the fifth KMA graduating class eliminated the Northwest faction as a rival to Park's Southeast faction. The last of the purges to occur in March 1963 was to remove Pak Im-hang, Kim Tong-ha, and their followers in the mid-

dle of a political crisis over the issue of power transfer to a civilian government. And with it, Park weeded out the generals who had a legitimate
claim to sharing power, given their active participation in the coup of May
16, 1961, and became the supreme leader within the South Korean armed
forces without rivals.

CHAPTER TWO

Taming and Tamed by
the United States

Taehyun Kim and Chang Jae Baik

.

THE UNITED STATES had an overwhelming presence in South Korea in
the years leading up to 1961. It was the United States that liberated
the Korean Peninsula from Japanese colonialism in 1945, ruled its southern half directly for three years as a military government, and helped to
create a strong anticommunist regime. The United States defended South
Korea from military takeover by the communist North during the Korean War (1950–1953). As a legacy of the armed conflict, a large U.S. military presence near the demilitarized zone was maintained by the Americans, who also exercised operational control over the South Korean armed
forces. Even in 1960, after major parts of U.S. military forces were withdrawn from South Korea, the power and presence of the United States remained predominant. Most of the South Korean budget was made up of
the counterpart fund[1] originating from U.S. aid, in addition to the large
sum spent directly on the South Korean military through the Military Assistance Program. American advisors were present throughout the South
Korean military, and over five hundred officials at the United States Operations Mission (USOM) managed aid money and hence the budgetary allocation of counterpart funds, thus overseeing and shaping South Korea's
major social and economic policies for all practical purposes. On many occasions, moreover, South Korea lacked the expertise necessary for modern
government and frequently relied on American advisors to strengthen state
capabilities.

Yet the United States could not prevent Park Chung Hee from launching a military coup that toppled democratically elected Chang Myŏn on May 16, 1961. Once the United States accepted the coup as a fait accompli, it succeeded in persuading Park to accept the principle of an eventual transfer of power to the civilians, but failed to set the timing and conditions of the power transfer. On the contrary, it was Park who had the upper hand, delaying the elections to sometime in 1963 to buy time and lay down the institutional infrastructure of selective political coercion and mobilization to back his presidential candidacy as a military-turned-civilian leader. Even in the economic realm, where the United States appeared to have the resources to make or break Park, the client more often outmaneuvered the patron than was checked and balanced by it. The two agreed on the primacy of economic development in fighting the communist threat, but disagreed profoundly on how to bring about economic growth. Under political pressure to demonstrate to the public that the military junta had the capacity to deliver the growth it had promised, but also with an eye to strengthen the financial base of his faction within the junta at the cost of his rivals, Park entrusted economic policy to the hands of the Korea Central Intelligence Agency (KCIA), with close associate Kim Chong-p'il in charge, and tried to jump-start the economy through a series of shock therapies. Meanwhile, the USOM was calling for opposite policies for financial stabilization. Park also effectively resisted U.S. pressure to reduce the size of the South Korean armed forces through the end of the junta years.

Chapter 2 argues that the failure of the United States in transforming its political, military, and economic resources into power is owed mainly to three factors. First, the primacy of U.S. military interests in South Korea and the security dilemmas of defending the southern half of the Korean Peninsula in the communist-dominated Asian continent prevented the United States from flexing its muscle to the point of undermining Park's ability to govern what was already a volatile and uncertain political situation. When Park's political survival was at stake, the United States believed it necessary to tone down its political pressure and, if possible, compromise with the military junta. Second, given the complexity of U.S. interests in South Korea, ranging from military deterrence to democratization to economic development, there were always multiple agencies of the U.S. government competing against each other to shape U.S. policy there. The United States was not a unitary actor. On the contrary, interagency rivalry was the norm, preventing Park's bigger ally from confronting him with a unified policy. Third, in order to achieve the goals of military deterrence, democratization, and economic development, the United States needed Park's cooperation, the result of which was to temper U.S. pressure.

U.S. Preferences and Interests

In the late1950s, U.S. policy toward South Korea began shifting from an exclusively military focus[2] to a more political and economic one. Military containment remained at the center of U.S. policy, justifying the stationing of large numbers of U.S. troops in South Korea, the ratification of a Mutual Defense Treaty with the South, and assistance to modernize its armed forces, but views on how to ensure military containment became more complex as U.S. policymakers increasingly realized that the task was as much political and economic as it was military. This evaluation was based on the Soviet Union's impressive economic growth throughout the 1950s, the quick postwar reconstruction of North Korea, and the continued economic stagnation and political turmoil in the South. The Soviet model of development looked more attractive to less-developed states than the Western one, prompting the United States to redefine the Soviet danger to be more political. The combined strength of the United States Forces in Korea (USFK) and the South Korean armed forces, together with a firm U.S. commitment to the defense of the South, was deemed sufficient to deter any North Korean resumption of hostilities with or without Chinese military support.

The North Korean threat, instead, was psychological and political, making the South look like a hopeless case of poverty, social anomie, and political instability that was destined to lose in the inter-Korea competition to become the sole legitimate government of the entire Korean peoples. In 1961, North Korea's per capita GNP stood at $160, twice that of the South, and the gap in economic performance was rising. To undercut the South's confidence further, its political stability proved to be fragile. In 1956, the popularity of Syngman Rhee did not translate into the election of his designated successor, Yi Ki-bung, to the office of vice president, causing the Liberal Party to panic over its ability to survive the transition to a post-Rhee era. Moreover, Cho Pong-am of the leftist Progressive Party won over 2 million votes (24 percent of the valid votes), making the entire conservative camp worry about the revival of leftist forces.

The U.S. decision to give its policy of military deterrence a more political and economic character was also triggered by tight resource constraints. When Dwight D. Eisenhower ordered a review of U.S. policy toward South Korea in 1957, the country was then its largest aid beneficiary in the third world. The United States hoped to reduce aid to the South as its trade surplus declined and then turned into deficit, but the reduction of aid seemed possible only if the South could begin to generate economic growth. It was in this context that the United States came to review the colossal size of the South Korean armed forces, whose needs posed an unbearable burden on the war-devastated economy. In January 1957, the U.S. National Security Council (NSC) prepared four alternative programs, with the goal of reducing the size of the South's military without undermining its deterrence capabilities, through weaponry-upgrade programs for both the South Koreans and the USFK.[3] After six months of deliberation, program NSC 5702/2 was adopted. It called for the conversion of four of the twenty South Korean army divisions into reserves and the provision of dual conventional-nuclear weapons to the USFK. Reflecting the newly recognized importance of political stability and economic development, NSC 5702/2 added two points to the list of U.S. objectives: (a) "Encouraging [South Korea] in the further development of stable democratic institutions and of cooperative relations with the other free nations in Asia" and (b) "Enabling [the South] to achieve a maximum rate of economic development compatible with a reasonable degree of stability and present levels of essential consumption."[4] The U.S. shift of focus became more evident in NSC 6018, adopted after the election of John F. Kennedy. The document embraced the takeoff theory of economic development, based on Keynesian economics, of the economist and deputy special assistant to the president for national security affairs, Walt W. Rostow.[5] NSC 6018 also reflected the dramatic overthrow of Syngman Rhee by a student-led revolution in April 1960. The growing apprehension that poverty, authoritarian rule, and corruption could lead to chronic political instability gave greater legitimacy to those in U.S. policy circles who advocated a shift from a military to a political and economic emphasis. NSC 6018 redefined the long-range objective of America's South Korea policy as seeking to build "a unified Korea with a self-supporting, *growing* economy, possessing a free, independent and representative government *responding effectively to popular aspirations and dealing effectively with social problems,* oriented toward the United States and other countries of the Free World, and capable of maintaining internal security and offering strong resistance in the event of external attack" (emphasis added).[6]

By February 1961, the continuing political instability in post-Rhee South Korea came to command the attention of top officials in Washington, including NSC staff members led by Walt Rostow. Hugh D. Farley, the assistant director of the USOM in South Korea until February 1961, initiated an interagency review of U.S. policy with the submission of a report to the White House in early March. Farley argued that the conjunction of three circumstances made "it imperative that the U.S. Government recognize the gravity of the situation and act promptly to remedy it." He cited: (a) deep-rooted corruption in South Korean society and the resulting lack of public confidence in the government and political leaders; (b) rapidly deteriorating political dynamics in South Korea that undermined the governing capabilities of the post-Rhee Democratic Party leadership; and (c) the indecisive and inadequate leadership of the USOM.[7] USOM, a powerful organization manned by as many as five hundred staff members to operate U.S. aid programs, was deemed inept and perhaps as corrupt as the South Korean government in performing its mission of overseeing the economic reconstruction of South Korea. U.S. aid financed over 90 percent of the South Korean government budget as late as 1961, and the ineffectiveness of USOM meant that the South Koreans were losing an opportunity to catch up economically with the North and to benefit from a government with greater political legitimacy. Farley predicted that a major political crisis could break out in the coming months, particularly around the first anniversary of the April 19 Student Revolution that had overthrown Syngman Rhee. Farley did not rule out the possibility of a military takeover. On the contrary, he thought a coup likely, unless the United States acted promptly and decisively.

The U.S. embassy in South Korea and the U.S. Central Intelligence Agency disregarded Farley's warnings. The two thought the possibility of a coup was remote, because any such thoughts would be "deterred by the knowledge that the United States would oppose such a project."[8] However, they shared the view that the situation was gloomy, predicting that "South Korea [was] basically so weak economically and unsteady politically that internal crisis or threat of crisis [would] be the norm, not the exception, over the years ahead."[9] In a memo to Rostow in March 1961, Robert W. Komer of the NSC staff argued:

> Look at the basic problems of the ROK: (a) a poor country with few resources and skills; (b) saddled with staggering task of supporting a far larger military establishment than it really [is] able to (or than is needed); (c) corruption feeding on inexperience in democratic government; and (d) a rising nationalism and expectancy frustrated by what the ROK increasingly believe is U.S. disinclination to accord them full equality, push for unification, or change overwhelming military emphasis in ROK. Underlying ills and needs are *economic*. Major thrust of U.S. effort over next decade must be: (a) substantial cutback in ROK military establishment, with diversion of U.S. funds thus released to crash economic development. Defense of ROK could be met by ROK plus U.S. forces in Korea and reminders to [the Soviet] Bloc of U.S. intent instantly to protect from outside Korea; (b) buildup of ROK economy, stressing public sector, creation of light labor-intensive industry, and full utilization of main ROK resources—people.[10] (original emphasis)

Rostow informed Kennedy of the controversy surrounding the Farley report, and pointed out that the fundamental problem was "to get our massive aid to [South] Korea shifted around in a way which would not merely keep [it] from going down . . . but would begin to get [South] Korea moving forward."[11] At the NSC meeting of May 5, Kennedy approved the establishment of a Task Force on Korea, headed by assistant secretary of state for Far Eastern affairs Walter P. McConaughy (ambassador to Korea until that April), to prepare a new policy toward South Korea. While the report was under preparation, a military coup led by Major General Park Chung Hee with some 3,600 troops took place at dawn on May 16.

The Coup

The United States was aware of the existence of potential coup groups as early as April 1961.[12] No evidence, however, supports the suspicion that the United States was so disappointed with the Chang Myŏn government that it worked on a covert operation to overthrow it.[13] Yet it is also true that with the exception of the confusing days of May 16 and 17, when General Carter B. Magruder, chief of both UN and U.S. forces in South Korea, tried to persuade President Yun Po-sŏn to resist the coup by mobilizing troops, Washington hesitated to put down the military junta that had overthrown a democratically elected government or to restore the Chang Myŏn regime. In the first official document issued by the State Department on the day of the coup, a telegram to the U.S. embassy in South Korea, undersecretary of state Chester B. Bowles, acting for secretary of state Dean Rusk, ordered the embassy to take a "wait and see" attitude instead of identifying the United States "with the fate of what may be a lost cabinet."[14]

When Prime Minister Chang Myŏn announced his resignation together with that of his cabinet members on May 18, the State Department welcomed Chang's action in a press release, anticipating that the move would end the political turmoil.[15] The *New York Times* ran an editorial urging the acceptance of the coup as a fait accompli.[16] U.S. officials were aware of Park's communist activities during the chaotic days after Korea's liberation in 1945, but believed he had fully converted to South Korean conservatism. The USFK thought that the people were indifferent, if not sympathetic, to the junta's takeover. Indeed, it seems that within a few days of the coup, the U.S. government was willing to accept what had occurred and to work with coup leaders. As early as May 25, the State Department drafted a telegram acknowledging the receipt of the "official" message from Lieutenant General Chang To-yŏng, chairman of the Military Revolutionary Committee and the army chief of staff, that explained the objectives of the coup.[17] Yet in subsequent days Washington deliberately delayed any public announcement recognizing the military junta as the new government of South Korea, so that the United States could increase its leverage in the coming negotiations with the coup leaders on the issue of restoration of civilian rule. Chang To-yŏng, soon to become chairman of the Supreme Council for National Reconstruction and prime minister, sought to visit Washington to see Kennedy in an attempt to solidify U.S. acceptance of the coup and, through it, his position within the junta. The meeting would have conferred legitimacy on Chang To-yŏng, but he received cold responses from the U.S. embassy in Seoul as well as from its superiors in Washington. Park Chung Hee got even worse treatment in the early days of the coup. At the embassy in Seoul, U.S. deputy chief of missions Marshall Green consulted mainly with Chang To-yŏng and Lieutenant General-in-reserve Kim Hong-il, the minister of foreign affairs, on the issues of day-to-day government, although it was soon revealed that Park held the real power in spite of his formally supplementary role as the vice chairman of the SCNR.

There were other reasons for the delay in establishing working relations with the junta. In addition to the goal of strengthening U.S. leverage over the military, the United States had to deal with the problematic situation of the transition, during which Yun Po-sŏn remained president. Although the office of the president was mostly a symbolic one, with Yun serving as the formal head of state, his presence gave a semblance of legal continuity and meant that there was no urgency for the United States to recognize the junta as the "new" government of South Korea. The United States had time to accept the coup leaders on U.S. terms. Moreover, it was not certain who would emerge as the winner in the fierce power struggles within the junta. Not only was there no need to risk U.S. influence by betting on a particular faction, but by withholding U.S. support, the superpower patron could "tame" the emerging leadership, whether it turned out to be Park, Chang To-yŏng, or some unknown third force. Delay was the best tactic for the strong when the future was uncertain.

In addition, the coup leaders irritated U.S. officials in Seoul and Washington in several instances. After the junta's arrest of Lieutenant General Yi Han-lim, the commander of the First Army, on May 18, for counter-coup activities, it moved two divisions under the First Army from the front lines to the capital without the prior approval of General Magruder, in violation of the Taejŏn Agreement of July 12, 1950, which gave operational control of the South Korean military to the chief of the UN Command, or UNC (he was, in addition, the commander of the USFK). Chang To-yŏng also abruptly announced his plan to visit Washington for a meeting with

Kennedy without consulting the U.S. embassy. Apparently the coup leaders were convinced that the United States had no choice but to accept their actions, and even tried to intimidate U.S. officials with the argument that the "only alternative to the continuation of [the] junta [is] a Communist takeover."[18] Therefore, in order to put the junta on the defensive and set the conditions of its military rule, the United States believed that taking "a position of friendly reserve [was] infinitely preferable to expressions of complete confidence and support," especially during the early uncertain days of the military coup.[19]

The first meeting between Green and Park occurred on June 9. On the State Department's instructions, Green stated that "the United States saw the Supreme Council for National Reconstruction 'as an established government, with which it [was] prepared to work in good faith on [a] friendly and cooperative basis'; welcomed the six objectives of the May 16 message from Chang To-yŏng and accepted them in good faith; and hoped for a fruitful relationship serving [the] 'Korean people and our common interests and objectives.'" After the meeting, Green reported to Washington that "the military leaders were often disregarding American advice, but were somewhat influenced by it." He suggested that it was "premature to move too close to them, since some reserve would offer greater bargaining leverage."[20]

Meanwhile, in Washington, the report of the Task Force on Korea was completed on June 5 and discussed and approved as NSC Action 2430 on June 13.[21] The document affirmed U.S. intentions to deal with the new military regime on a friendly and cooperative basis, continue economic and military support, and back the junta-initiated national development plan, if the military junta was intent on planning and implementing it. The report also recommended that the United States receive the chairman of the SCNR in Washington for a meeting with President Kennedy, provided that the SCNR was serious about formulating and implementing a national development plan, ready to consider the eventual return to civilian rule, and recognized the USFK-UNC's authority to exercise operational control over the South Korean armed forces.

It was not until mid-July, however, that the United States had the opportunity to make a deal with the junta on the three issues of economic development, civilian rule, and military operational control, because (supposed) authority and (actual) power did not coincide within the new leadership. Until the two became aligned through the purges of Park's rivals from the junta and then his election to the presidency, the United States did not have an authoritative counterpart on the South Korean side with whom to deal. The coup leaders first had to put their house in order. The opportunity for deal making came on July 3, nine days after the new ambassador, Samuel Berger, had taken office. That day Chang To-yŏng was purged and Park took over the SCNR chairmanship, finally surfacing from the closed-door politics of the junta. Park soon found Berger to be a challenging but constructive and reliable counterpart in negotiating the terms of political rapprochement.

What Berger had found upon his arrival in South Korea was a series of sweeping, revolutionary reforms led by a group of young, enthusiastic, but inexperienced colonels. Some of the measures were distasteful to Berger, involving countless arrests without warrants and the trial of Park's political foes on trumped-up charges. Others looked economically reckless, often contradicting basic market principles. The military junta, led by Park, did not conceal its nationalistic tendencies, which could easily have turned anti-American or embraced the ideology of nonalignment then popular in many parts of the third world. Still, Berger found positive elements, such as "energy, earnestness, determination and imagination" among the coup leaders, attributes that could potentially lead the country out of its poverty.[22] Berger's complex attitude reflected American ambivalence toward Park and his junta. On the one hand, U.S. policymakers deplored his arbitrary military rule and pressed for the restoration of democracy. On the other hand, concerned over the geopolitical requirements of maintaining a united front against the two countries' cold war enemy as well as encouraged by the reformist character of the junta in many areas, they were restrained in the exercise of their power to promote democratization.

Berger's mission was to ensure political stability and an eventual transition to a democratic government, but at the same time to help the junta harness the population's nationalistic fervor as the engine for economic development. On July 16, 1961, Berger paid a visit to Park and stressed the importance of taking steps toward a return to civilian rule. Now in control of the junta, Park accommodated most of Berger's demands, including a promise of transfer to civilian rule within a fixed time frame. From that point on, Park's relationship with Washington became relatively cordial. On August 12 Park publicly pledged the transfer of power back to a civilian government by the middle of 1963. In September, Berger delivered his part of the deal by arranging the U.S. invitation to Park for a "working visit" to Washington. Park went in November, receiving hospitalities beyond his expectations.

After Park's visit to Washington, Berger sent a letter to secretary of state Dean Rusk and praised his visitor highly:

Chairman Park Chung Hee has established himself in [the] Republic's mind as a forceful, fair and intelligent leader who can be trusted with power, trusted to keep the revolution on the path of decency and moderation, and trusted to abide by the pledge he gave on August 12 to return to civilian government after the election in May 1963. Park, therefore, represents a most important link between the government and the people, and a most important stabilizing element in the situation. . . . The public support given [to] the military government by the United States and the friendly reception of Park during his visit to the United States have, however, been perhaps the decisive factors in stabilizing the situation. One Korean put it to me in a sentence, "Since the United States is impressed with Park, we Koreans value him more."[23]

The U.S. recognition of Park's leadership not only gave him the opportunity to consolidate power in the immediate post–Chang To-yŏng period, but also provided him with two more years of power to experiment with new ways of economic development and national reconstruction with the goal of winning the support of the common people in the elections of 1963. Park bought the time he sought to forge his image as a nation rebuilder in return for complying with the U.S. demand that he return the country to civilian rule within a set period of time.

Transition Politics, 1962–1963

After the U.S. acceptance of the coup and its legitimation of the SCNR through the Park-Kennedy summit in November 1961, South Korea entered a new and crucial chapter in its postwar history, with Park already working to leave a lasting legacy on the South Korean polity. The Republic began a new phase of historical development, profoundly shaped by Park's ability to hold on to U.S. support and the United States' ability to steer Park into the restoration of civilian electoral politics.

Although Park came to consult Berger on major political decisions after November 1961,[24] Washington still had reservations about the intentions of the junta and especially about its mainstream *(churyu)* faction led by Park and his nephew-in-law Kim Chong-p'il, who did not hesitate to make reckless decisions without notifying the United States when the moves were perceived as strengthening the SCNR or increasing Park's chances of winning the coming elections of 1963. The SCNR put anti-mainstream *(pijuryu)* military officers on trial as counterrevolutionaries to continue transforming the South Korean armed forces into an organization loyal only to Park. As mentioned in Chapter 1, the junta also enacted the Political Purification Law to suppress civilian opposition. Included in the radical moves that brought U.S. opposition was also the trial and conviction of the ousted prime minister, Chang Myŏn.

These conflicts revealed that U.S.–South Korean relations during the formative years of the Third Republic were far from smooth. On the contrary, the coup leaders frequently acted independently on their own timetable to consolidate their power, while U.S. officials exerted pressure to keep them as responsive to U.S. influence as possible.

Politics: Return to Civilian Government

U.S.–South Korean relations during 1962–1963 were characterized by the United States' efforts to twist the arm of a hesitant, if not resistant, Park to return to civilian rule. At the center of the U.S.–South Korean conflict was Kim Chong-p'il, of the eighth Korea Military Academy (KMA) graduating class. Serving as the director of the KCIA and commanding the loyalty of many of his classmates in his position as the chairman of various SCNR subcommittees, Kim Chong-p'il was not only Park's relative but his henchman. As the United States suspected, Kim Chong-p'il was behind most of the junta's unsavory moves, and the United States tried to constrain his power and roles.

The sources of U.S. concern were threefold. First, Kim wielded too much power as director of the KCIA, whose jurisdiction included not only the protection of the state from external security threats but also the maintenance of internal order. Second, the concentration of power in Kim Chong-p'il ironically aggravated the junta's factionalism, historically a major destabilizing factor in South Korean politics, because by encouraging the eighth KMA graduating class and the natives of Kyŏngsang and Ch'ungch'ŏng provinces to coalesce around the Park-Kim axis, it prompted the fifth KMA graduating class—sometimes alone and at other times in collaboration with the older Hamgyŏng generals whose educational background lay in Manchuria during the colonial era—to form an anti-mainstream faction in response to the threat of being squeezed out of power. Third, and most important, Kim Chong-p'il and his followers were suspected of being radical, extreme nationalists, or even leftist in political orientation.

In June and July 1962, South Korean politics were thrown into a deep crisis after the KCIA-led mainstream rushed into an ill-fated currency conversion and clandestinely engaged in stock market speculation to raise funds for heavy and chemical industrialization (HCI), particularly a huge project at Ulsan, and for the organization of a political party in anticipation of the coming 1963 elections. The two fiascos triggered an intense power struggle within the junta. While waging a war against his junta opponents, Kim Chong-p'il was also dragged into conflict with Berger. In a telegram to the State Department, Berger expressed his frustration by reporting rumors that Kim was "out to get 'certain Americans'" and that Park had written South Korea's ambassador to the United States, Chŏng Il-gwŏn, to ask that he request Berger's recall. Berger could not substantiate the rumors, but he personally "believed that [the] idea of declaring [himself] PNG [persona non grata] [had] been considered."[25] Rusk advised Berger not to take the problem personally, but proposed that Kim could be "removed from [the] picture gracefully, say as Ambassador to Japan."[26]

Kim Chong-p'il brought matters to a head by trying to meet President Kennedy during his visit to Washington in October 1962.[27] Berger, while generally opposed to Kim's visit, found in it an opportunity "to expose him directly to Washington views and influence" and let him "be impressed with [the] limits within which the military government must remain if our support was to be maintained."[28] To Kim Chong-p'il's disappointment, he could see neither President Kennedy nor Vice President Lyndon B. Johnson, but he did meet with secretary of state Rusk, secretary of defense Robert McNamara, and attorney general Robert Kennedy in the middle of the Cuban missile crisis. In a series of conversations, the Americans emphasized the importance of holding fair and free elections within the promised timetable and improving relations between South Korea and Japan, an improvement that the United States had long sought and now thought possible after the ousting of the staunchly anti-Japanese Syngman Rhee. While Kim Chong-p'il used his visit to upgrade his public image as a next-generation statesman in domestic South Korean politics, he failed to convince his Washington audience that he was the person whom the United States had to deal with. Nor were the Americans able to moderate his actions in the coming months.

Initially, the return to civilian rule progressed on the agreed schedule. A new constitution was prepared with the participation of two American scholars and was put to a national referendum in December 1962. The public response to the proposed reestablishment of a presidential system was overwhelmingly positive. Later that month, Park announced that the presidential election would be held in the spring of 1963, followed by the general election for the National Assembly in the fall. But a crisis broke out when Kim Chong-p'il unveiled the clandestinely prepared organization of the Democratic Republican Party (DRP) as the coup makers' vehicle to win the coming elections. The anti-mainstream military faction struck hard against Kim, calling for his purge, because they were excluded from the key positions in the DRP. Civilian politicians joined in as well, because they had been legally prohibited from organizing political parties since the day of the military coup. With martial law lifted and political activity allowed as of December 1962 in order to prepare for the transition to civilian rule, Kim retired from the army in early January with the rank of brigadier general and resigned from the KCIA as well in order to serve as the public head of the DRP.

Because the DRP was generally designed to exclude or limit the power of the anti-mainstream factions within the junta and to provide Park and Kim Chong-p'il with a monopoly on power, a group of senior generals, commonly referred to as the Hamgyŏng faction because of its provincial origin, openly challenged the Park-Kim mainstream line and demanded Kim's resignation from the office of DRP chairman. The factional struggle was so serious that there was rampant speculation of an impending armed struggle among the military factions. Park contemplated the use of force to quell the division within his ranks.[29]

Berger seized the opportunity to put pressure on Park to get rid of Kim. Upon the ambassador's request, Washington suspended indefinitely the delivery of already approved development loans on February 7, 1963. Berger also accepted a luncheon invitation from Yun Po-sŏn, who had resigned from the presidency in March 1962 and was now preparing to launch a Democratic Politics Party to lead the civilian opposition movements. On February 17, defense minister Pak Pyŏng-gwŏn and the chiefs of staff of all four armed services—the army, air force, navy, and marines—met with Park to deliver an ultimatum that Kim Chong-p'il must withdraw from the DRP and leave the country at once.[30] Disillusioned by the factional dispute, but also planning to strike back with greater force after the worst of the crisis had passed, Park surprised the country not only by getting Kim to resign from the DRP chairmanship but also by announcing the next day that he would not run for the presidency, provided that the civilian opposition met nine conditions, including promising not to retaliate politically against the military junta and its members for the overthrow of Chang Myŏn. Kim Chong-p'il subsequently resigned from all public posts, and went into "exile" in February as a roving ambassador.

On February 13, Berger had written the State Department that the "United States Government must within next few days make [a] fundamental decision on [its] attitude toward Chairman Park, his government and their plans for election and transition to civilian government." On the next day, in a telegram to Berger, the State Department showed its readiness to give up on Park and accept Hŏ Chŏng—the head of the 1960 interim government after Syngman Rhee was forced out—as an alternative to lead South Korea in the difficult transition to civilian rule. The U.S. embassy immediately gave public support to Park's proposal of February 18 to withdraw from the presidential race in the upcoming election as "the best hope for political and economic stability."[31]

In mid-March, the political situation took an expected turn. The KCIA allegedly uncovered a series of coup plots and arrested a group of senior generals, mostly from the Hamgyŏng faction. The arrests weeded out the last remaining faction that claimed a share of power as original members of the military coup. In addition, the mainstream faction mobilized soldiers on active duty to demonstrate publicly in downtown Seoul for an extension of military rule. On the evening of March 15, Park privately informed Berger of his plan to extend military rule for another four years through a national referendum. The ensuing actions by the U.S. government proved to be one of its most overt and active interventions in South Korean politics.

Upon receiving Berger's report of Park's plan, Rusk authorized Berger to inform Park that the U.S. government, among others, could "not possibly approve and might be compelled openly to oppose continuation of military government for four more years."[32] Park's plan for the extension of military rule was reported to President Kennedy, whereupon the president had the Department of State and the White House draw up a letter of protest to Park.[33] On April 8 Park backed down partway, announcing that he would delay but not scrap the idea of holding a national referendum and that he would allow the resumption of political activities. The United States accepted Park's proposal, although it was worded as a compromise. Nonetheless, Berger believed that "the strong stand by the United States was an important factor in this conclusion."[34] Having defused the political crisis, U.S. attention quickly moved on to the social and economic crisis caused by the spring famine in the countryside.

In July the political situation turned more favorable for Park. Kim Chae-ch'un, a moderate in the military junta and from the fifth graduating class of the KMA, was forced to resign from the directorship of the KCIA once he had completed the task of leading the campaign to weed out the Hamgyŏng faction the past March. The removal of the Hamgyŏng faction ironically made Kim Chae-ch'un and his fifth KMA graduating class expendable. Using a classic divide-and-rule approach, Park replaced Kim Chae-ch'un with Kim Hyŏng-uk, a member of Kim Chong-p'il's clique. Berger's worries returned. He evaluated Kim Chong-p'il's followers in the military junta as having "a will to power and a willingness to be ruthless," inclined to "frequent rejection of U.S. advice on political matters and [tending] to originate and support unsound economic policies." The Kim Chong-p'il faction was also seen to be tainted by a "touchy ultra-nationalism and barely concealed anti-Americanism" and as assisted by a "group of political advisors with pro-Communist backgrounds who [have] extraordinary influence."[35] The U.S. ambassador was disturbed by Kim Chong-p'il's followers, "who believed U.S. [policymakers would] have to go along with anything which they [might] do," making Berger take "pains to prove them wrong."[36]

With Kim Chong-p'il's faction back in power, Park announced his entry into the coming presidential election, now scheduled for October 15. The election was held as planned, and the result was surprising. Park's margin of victory over Yun Po-sŏn was merely 150,000 votes (1.4 percent of the total), and Yun received more votes from the military than did Park. The close race had the effect of proving that the election process was generally free of fraud, unlike during that of the Rhee regime, and of legitimizing Park's continued rule. The State Department recognized that the election was held "in [an] orderly manner."[37] The general elections in November ran contrary to the U.S. embassy's prediction of an opposition comeback, and provided the DRP with an overwhelming majority in the National Assembly (110 out of 175 seats). Although the winner-take-all simple-plurality system of single-member districts, coupled with the skewed allocation of additional "party-list" seats to the political party with the most votes, helped immensely in giving the DRP its large majority, the fact that the DRP received the single largest chunk of votes among the political parties was more than enough to demoralize the civilian opposition and legitimize Park's military-turned-civilian ruling coalition.[38] The worst days of political instability seemed to be over, although the expected return of Kim Chong-p'il from his "exile" worried the United States.[39]

Economy: Development Plan

Immediately after the coup, the military junta had launched a long-term economic development plan, the first of its kind in the nation's history, which eventually led to the so-called Miracle on the Han River. The state-led development policy was designed not only to legitimize Park's political rule but also to help the coup leaders, including Park, gain recognition from the United States as nation rebuilders. Given the enormous power and presence of the United States in the political economy of South Korea during the 1960s, it can readily be inferred that the United States was deeply involved in the making of the first Five-Year Economic Development Plan (FYEDP) and especially the reforms required to implement it.

Yet it is wrong to assume that the U.S. role in economic planning was always constructive. Sometimes it was; at other times it was not. What is beyond doubt, however, is that Park's political ascendancy in the early 1960s coincided with or was closely preceded by the change in U.S. aid policy. The interest in economic issues rose simultaneously on both sides of the Pacific as the allies tried to tackle the same challenge of making the Republic a self-sustaining polity. The heightened U.S. interest in economic growth was well reflected in a memorandum drawn up by Robert Komer, an NSC staffer, in the immediate aftermath of the Korean task force report of June 5, 1961. In the memo, sent to the special assistant to the president for national security affairs, McGeorge Bundy, on June 12, under the title "Relative Priority of Military vs. Reconstruction Focus in Korea," Komer argued that "one of the basic reasons why [the United States] had accomplished so little in [South] Korea since 1953 [has been the] predominantly military focus" of U.S. policy. He continued:

We have spent more money on MAP [the Military Assistance Program] 1953–60 than on the domestic economy. This mal-focus arose largely from the fiction that there was only a truce on the "38th parallel" and that hostilities might reopen at any time. As a result, we did little more than keep the economy afloat, while focusing our main effort on maintaining very substantial ROK forces. . . . Given all these deterrent[s], the risk of the ROK being attacked again is far less than that of its being subverted because of internal weakness. The North Koreans are already beginning to play the siren song of reunification, and it may have increasing appeal in a weak and disunited south. If South Korea goes, it will go this route and not that of local war.[40]

Komer's proposal was that "a gradual cut in ROK [military] forces to around 14 and ultimately 12 divisions would still give the [Allied forces] quite a deterrent, and free substantial resources to meet the real problems facing [the United States] in the ROK."[41]

The shift in U.S. aid policy had been in the making since the late 1950s, and it came as part of the larger change occurring in U.S. global aid policy. First, the authority to process and release aid money was transferred from the UN Command to the U.S. ambassador, reflecting the growing U.S. intention to use aid for nonmilitary purposes. In particular, the United States began trying to link the release of aid money to the implementation of economic reform and development planning by the aid recipient, as reflected in the "Dillon Letter" of October 1960. The objective was to generate self-sustaining economic growth so that the United States could progressively reduce its burden of economic support and reverse its trend of trade deficit. This turn in aid policy met with an unexpected political backlash in South Korea, where the tight control by the United States over the use of aid money was criticized as violating South Korea's national sovereignty. Moreover, the reduction of U.S. aid worsened South Korea's economic plight. But despite these negative consequences, the change in U.S. aid policy persuaded even the ineffective Chang Myŏn government to prepare an economic development plan that was to become a cornerstone of the military junta's first FYEDP.

Shortly after the coup, the United States formed a new country team on South Korea and appointed Ambassador Berger to lead it. Having been trained in economics, Berger understood the discipline "better than most ambassadors" and oversaw the refocus of South Korea aid policy.[42] The organization of USOM was to be overhauled by its newly appointed director, James Killen. Under his leadership the USOM cut its personnel by half and became more efficient. Initially, the new country team was optimistic about its economic mission. Berger was encouraged by a series of reforms being undertaken by the junta parallel to its aid donor's own reforms. Deeply impressed by the junta's pursuit of economic reform with "energy, earnestness, determination and imagination," Berger reported:

> [It] is . . . a genuine revolution from the top trying to introduce sweeping reforms of a most fundamental kind. Projects of reform long talked about or under actual consideration by previous governments are becoming realities in banking and credit policy, foreign trade, increased public works for unemployed, agriculture, trade union organization, education, public administration, social welfare . . . and other fields. Others while well-intentioned have been too hastily developed or are poorly implemented. Some of these latter have already undergone correction, for government, at least in some cases, is prepared to admit and correct mistakes.[43]

Nevertheless, it was not until 1965 that the United States began to provide full-fledged support for South Korea's economic development program with long-term investment funds. A number of factors discouraged such support earlier. First, as Komer complained in his memo to Bundy, the idea of shifting U.S. aid policy from military to economic programs and freeing South Korean resources for the task of economic development through a reduction in the South Korean armed forces encountered strong resistance from the U.S. military establishment, particularly its Joint Chiefs of Staff. Second, the State Department and the ambassador became increasingly wary of the intentions of the junta, particularly of the young, hardcore element led by Kim Chong-p'il, as its members engaged in economically reckless shock therapies. Washington expressed its concern as early as 1961. Robert Johnson, an NSC staffer who was part of the South Korean task force, wrote:

> In the case of the old Chang Myŏn regime we were more confident about its good intentions than about its political capabilities. In the case of the new military regime we are somewhat more confident about capabilities, at least

to initiate reform measures, and less confident of intentions. Thus the strategy outlined in the report is one designed to elicit indications of the purposes of the new group and its willingness to act and to give the ambassador considerable discretion in determining when performance merits responsive action on our part.[44]

Third, many of the economic plans and initiatives drawn up by the military junta were met with skepticism in Washington, thus preventing Berger from backing Park with resources. The first FYEDP announced in January 1962 was regarded by Washington as rash and infeasible. The plan called for constructing a self-reliant economy through inward-looking import-substitution industrialization and identified the creation of heavy and chemical industries as the engine for growth. The first FYEDP also set an annual growth rate of more than 7 percent as the target goal. The objectives were set without due consideration of South Korea's short supply of capital and technology. Nor did the plan take into account the political uncertainty and instability that prevented big business from undertaking long-term investments.[45]

The economic projects, initiatives, and scandals of 1962 further deepened U.S. worries over the soundness of the military government's economic policy. While inflation soared, the military junta kept pursuing expansionary monetary policy and looked for foreign investors in ambitious projects such as the Ulsan Industrial Complex. The failure to secure foreign investors led the junta not to a critical review of the developmental strategy, but to a series of dangerous schemes to mobilize domestic capital that only resulted in economic disaster by mid-1962. In the beginning, the junta tried the conventional method of interest rate manipulation to increase national savings. When the policy brought inflation rather than investment, the junta took the more adventurous path of manipulating the stock market not only to secure capital for industrialization but also, as we have seen, to finance the organization of what later became the DRP. The stock market not only crashed within six months, but also brought a crisis of confidence in the junta when the press reported that the KCIA was behind the massive fraudulent rigging of stock prices.

On June 10, 1962, the SCNR passed its Emergency Measure on Currency Reform, which changed the currency unit from hwan to won by a conversion ratio of 10 to 1. The measure blocked individuals from withdrawing money above administratively set upper ceilings. The excess money was to be frozen and used for state-designated investment projects. Six days later, the SCNR legislated another emergency law, which forced individuals to "purchase" stock in the Korea Industrial Development Corporation (KIDC), a newly established state developmental company, with their frozen funds.[46] The funds channeled to KIDC through the money-stock swap were to be spent on HCI. This shock therapy was tried in order to force money that South Koreans and ethnic Chinese residents had supposedly hoarded in their closets into banks and then into ambitious industrialization projects. The measure only discredited the military junta when it was revealed that there was no hoarded money on the scale imagined by Kim Chong-p'il's mainstream faction. Park was forced to rescind both emergency measures when the United States accused him of transforming South Korea into a socialist economy. But the damage was done. The shock therapy shook up the monetary system and aggravated inflation, bringing the weak South Korean economy to the brink of collapse.

Most of these unorthodox economic actions were undertaken without consulting the United States. The currency conversion was deliberately kept secret from the U.S. embassy until 48 hours before it was implemented. Washington was upset by this incident, and deputy assistant secretary of state Edward Rice called in the South Korean ambassador to the United States, Chŏng Il-gwŏn, to complain that the South Korean government "unfortunately seemed to have taken the path of non-consultation. If the United States was to be helpful," Rice added, "it must know what was being planned. 'If U.S. efforts are to be nullified, [the United States] must reassess assistance policy.'"[47] The American officers in Seoul also emphasized the need for consultation.[48] In addition to the lack of consultation, what made U.S. officials particularly unhappy was the nature of the emergency measures of June 10 and 16, 1962. The U.S. embassy held Kim Chong-p'il and other "nationalist" officers of the KCIA responsible for the currency conversion and the establishment of the KIDC. Some saw the incident as a conspiracy by subversive elements to transform South Korea into an anticapitalist statist—if not outright socialist—economy.[49]

The two emergency measures constituted a turning point in Washington's assessment of the intentions of the military junta, particularly the plans of Kim Chong-p'il. With this came a change in U.S. policy toward South Korean economic development. Henceforth the United States stopped emphasizing the Rostovian model of development and instead tilted even more toward stabilization. Both Killen and Berger tried to discourage the implementation of the overly ambitious HCI plan. In putting pressure on Park, the most effective and frequently used instrument was the threat of withholding aid. Because U.S. aid constituted not only the seed money for the ambitious HCI plan but also a much needed relief fund for economic turmoil and bad harvests, the threat of withholding aid proved to be effective in making Park rescind the two emergency measures. The threat did not always work, however. In July 1963 Berger asked Washington to withhold "$15 million support assistance on grounds of inadequate implementation of stabilization measures until and unless adequate corrective action is taken."[50] The move made Park correct overly inflationary financing in the short run, but it was not until mid-1964 that he tackled stabilization in earnest. Even then, the "rationalization" program was manipulated to accelerate economic growth—not stabilize the economy (see Chapter 7).

Nonetheless, the dismal performance of the South Korean economy in 1962, coupled with the U.S. refusal to supply capital for HCI projects, persuaded Park to revise the first FYEDP. The pressures of trade and fiscal deficits demanded the lowering of the target growth rate. Throughout the tenure of Killen and Berger, U.S. pressure for stabilization remained high, which provoked strong resentment from South Korean officials. Upon Killen's departure in August 1964, *Hankook Ilbo*, a daily newspaper owned by Chang Ki-yŏng, then the deputy prime minister and minister of the Economic Planning Board (EPB), ran an editorial saying that "if the U.S. is not to repeat her mistake in Vietnam, it is hoped that it will not overlook the fact that many economic tasks remain in this land—problems which are more important than the financial stabilization program that U.S. aid officials in South Korea . . . have emphasized so often."[51]

Military: Force Reduction

The U.S. proposal (NSC 5702/2) to convert four of the twenty active South Korean army divisions into reserve units in 1957 had met strong resistance from Syngman Rhee. The U.S. military also resisted by remaining passive on the sidelines, de facto refusing to pressure South Korea for arms reduction. Consequently Rhee reduced the active army by only two divisions. In return for his concessions, Rhee got a U.S. pledge to deploy conventional-nuclear dual-purpose weapons and to assist in the modernization of the South Korean armed forces' conventional weapons system. With the advent of the Chang Myŏn government in 1960, economic growth became the top item on the national agenda. Within a few months of his inauguration, the prime minister initiated the reduction of the South Korean armed forces by 100,000 troops. This time, the U.S. military openly resisted.

By contrast, the new Kennedy administration, and particularly its NSC staff, showed strong interest in lowering the level of South Korean forces.

The memo drawn by Komer for Bundy and Rostow on March 15, 1961, constituted one such endeavor to release South Korean resources to be used to improve economic development.[52] Yet the task force report, issued on June 5, did not fully reflect the concerns of the NSC staff, including Komer. At the NSC meeting of June 13, defense secretary McNamara and chairman of the Joint Chiefs of Staff Lyman Lemnitzer teamed up against the idea of force reduction. Kennedy took the middle road, proposing to take measures to "increase to any measurable extent the contribution of the armed forces to civilian work" before reducing the size of the South Korean military.[53] While the issue of force reduction was put off for further review by the relevant agencies at the NSC, Ambassador Berger and newly appointed UN forces commander Guy S. Meloy, Jr., disputed over how to divide U.S. aid for the South Korean budget between economic and military programs. Reflecting the White House's changing strategic thinking and being an economist himself, Berger pushed for a greater emphasis on economic development, whereas Meloy argued that South Korea's present 600,000-man force level was "sacred." The South Korean military was unhappy with Berger's perspective as well, and threatened to cut its forces unilaterally, if Berger continued to demand a greater allocation of aid money to the economic side of the budget. The South Koreans made this move with the expectation that the U.S. military would not agree to such a force reduction. On the contrary, Meloy reported the South Korean armed forces' resentment of U.S. demands and his dispute with Berger on the issue to the higher authorities in Washington.[54]

The issue of South Korean force reduction was raised repeatedly at NSC meetings throughout the first half of 1962. The Joint Chiefs of Staff opposed it, as expected. They argued that because South Korea constituted an essential component of the U.S. forward defense strategy in Northeast Asia, any reduction of its armed forces needed to take into account power configurations not only on the Korean Peninsula but also in the wider Northeast Asian region. Specifically, the Joint Chiefs of Staff argued that a reduction in the South Korean force level would increase military risk regionwide, lower U.S. influence in Asia, decrease U.S. capabilities to keep an armed conflict on the Korean Peninsula at the level of non-nuclear limited war, force the United States to take up a greater share of the collective security burden through the augmentation of its own military forces' capabilities, and complicate the logistics of troop mobilization by dramatically shortening the time required to assemble and fly in U.S. forces outside of the Korean Peninsula into South Korea in the event of war. In the eyes of the Joint Chiefs, it could not be "emphasized too strongly that current US/

ROK force levels in [South] Korea are the minimum acceptable for assuring the long-term security of Northeast Asia."[55]

In an April 1962 report, by contrast, the U.S. CIA gave a mixed assessment. While agreeing that the communist threat to South Korea was likely to take the form of political warfare and subversion rather than military invasion, the CIA noted the danger of political instability if the South Korean armed forces were significantly reduced. The report stated: "As long as the Communist powers believe that the U.S. will defend South Korea, they will almost certainly not launch an overt military invasion. Accordingly, a reduction of strength of the South Korean armed forces, by anything up to about one-third of present numbers, would probably not in itself increase the likelihood of invasion from the north. It would, however, produce considerable political unrest within the country, which would probably be great enough to endanger any government initiating the measure."[56]

Another study, conducted by retired air force general John Cary at the Defense Department's request, opposed the force reduction from a political perspective similar to the views of the CIA. The Cary report concluded: "the defense policy of the U.S. for the security of South Korea should not now undergo drastic revision and . . . the armed forces of the Republic of Korea should remain at approximately the level now programmed."[57] The published version of the report did not explain the reasoning behind its policy recommendation, but from Komer's comments it is possible to infer that Cary's primary concern was political rather than military. As seen by Komer, "the [Cary] report opposes such a cut at present, primarily because it would upset Park's regime and secondarily because it would have adverse repercussions on U.S. allies throughout East Asia, who would see in it a reduced U.S. interest in their defense as well." Komer objected to both rationales. In his view, Park preferred that the United States provide assistance to South Korea's economic development rather than to the modernization of its armed forces, because Park's legitimacy depended on his ability to bring about economic growth.[58] Moreover, U.S. credibility was not on the line, because much of the force reduction involved the South Korean military. Turning the Cary report on its head, Komer argued that if the cut would not upset the Park regime, many of the arguments in the report justified the reduction of the South Korean force level.[59]

Ambassador Berger came up with a compromise, proposing to reduce the South Korean armed forces by 30,000–40,000 men annually during the years 1963 and 1964 and to review the possibility of further reductions later. At the same time, Berger proposed to keep the South Korean military budget and U.S. Military Assistance Program at their current levels despite the force reduction. The issue came to an impasse and no decision was made under Kennedy. After Johnson took office in 1963, he ordered a further review. In 1964 the State Department came up with a plan to reduce the South Korean armed forces to the level of 500,000 men with force modernization, to which the Defense Department agreed with great reluctance. Ironically, after all this bureaucratic infighting in Washington, the modernization program took place, but the force reduction did not. After South Korean combat troops began participating in the Vietnam War, force reduction was removed from the agenda.

U.S. Power and Park's Political Choices

The South Korean dependence on the United States for military deterrence and economic survival provided the U.S. ambassador, the USFK-UNC commanders, and the USOM director with enormous power, prestige, and leverage to influence South Korean societal actors as well as government agencies. The United States wielded its power in at least three ways. First, there existed the myriad of routinized and institutionalized channels of U.S. influence built into budgetary processes and policymaking mechanisms that enabled American aid officials to influence the implementation of South Korean economic policy. At the top of this transnational policy network was the USOM director, who was an economic advisor to the prime minister during the Chang Myŏn regime and the U.S. counterpart to the EPB minister in a bilateral coordinating committee during Park's rule. The UN Command was always consulted on military appointments, including that of the chief of staff of the South Korean army. A council headed jointly by the USOM and the EPB also oversaw economic development during the military government, because much of the funding came from the counterpart funds.

Second, the United States de facto commanded veto power when it did not approve of particular South Korean policies and political moves. To be sure, Americans were generally reluctant to intervene overtly, particularly in political matters, because they feared a nationalist backlash and needed Park's cooperation in achieving their objectives. Once Park agreed on the principle of the restoration of civilian rule by mid-1963, the United States was willing to let Park prepare for the elections even when this involved political repression. Conversely, when the fundamental understanding between the two allies was seen to have been breached, as when the KCIA infringed upon market principles with the launching of the KIDC with the money "frozen" by an emergency measure in mid-1962, or when Park announced the extension of military rule in early 1963, the United States was explicit in opposing South Korean authorities and pressed for their compliance by threatening to withhold U.S. aid.

Third, the overwhelming power and presence of the United States had the effect of editing the South Korean political agenda and strategy by setting certain limits on what local actors could and could not do. In contemplating his coup, Park asked Yi Tong-wŏn, an Oxford-trained political scientist, how the United States would react. Yi replied with confidence, "The United States must support it so long as you proclaim anti-communism as its goal."[60] Apparently Park followed this advice, declaring anticommunism and adherence to the United Nations Charter and respect for and faithful fulfillment of all international treaties and agreements as the first two principles of his six-point revolutionary manifesto on the day of the military coup. The two points were included not only to ensure the support of the South Korean conservative camp, but also to preempt U.S. resistance. In spite of his nationalist inclinations and deep-rooted distrust of U.S. intentions, Park could not consider nonalignment as an option. In a similar spirit of avoiding conflict with the United States through the accommodation of vital U.S. interests, Park invited two U.S. law professors to help the military junta draft a new constitution in 1962 in order to "ease American concerns."[61] U.S. officials were well aware of the power they had over the South Korean government, sometimes to the detriment of their ability to adjust flexibly to changes in the country's politics. In denying the possibility of a military coup in March 1961 because coup makers would be deterred by U.S. opposition, for example, Ambassador McConaughy illustrated the degree to which the United States was thought to influence South Korean politics without actually exercising its power.[62]

At the same time, it is important not to exaggerate U.S. power. Because South Korea's important role in U.S. global security strategy remained unchanged as an outpost of the "free world" to contain communist expansion in East Asia, the United States could not impose its will on its client state. This reality became even more evident as the U.S. redefined its containment policy from narrowly military deterrence to the preemption of social and political subversion, because the preemption of subversion required economic development, whose success depended even more on the cooperation of the South Korean political authorities. The agenda of economic growth strengthened South Korean leverage as much as it gave the United States an instrument with which to reshape the preferences of South Korean political authorities.

Given the leverage of the weak stemming from the enduring cold war geopolitics of East Asia and the shifting U.S. strategy of containment, it was ironically not U.S. policy initiatives but volatile South Korean domestic politics that shaped U.S.–South Korean relations. The U.S. long-term policy objectives in South Korea were revised after the April 19 Student Revolution in 1960 and the May 16 military coup in 1961, not the other way around. The pattern of U.S. officials reacting to South Korean political changes rather than leading them was visible even after the worst part of the country's political instability ended, and it came to characterize U.S. policy throughout the 1961–1963 period. Even though U.S. power and presence in South Korea were overwhelming, the United States was limited in shaping South Korean history. During the period of military rule, it was the indigenous dynamics of South Korean society that shaped the direction of South Korean political development. The U.S. role was a more limited one that affected the direction and speed of the political evolution unleashed by domestic political forces.

Apart from these general limitations on U.S. power, a careful reading of U.S. diplomatic documents reveals a varying pattern in the way power was wielded by the United States. The superpower used power most directly and overtly in the area of economic policy. The South Korean refusal or failure to consult the United States on the currency conversion and monetary policy predictably drew U.S. threats of aid reduction and delay. The Americans believed that they could effectively intervene in the making of economic policy, given the massive economic aid they provided. Moreover, economic conflict is not the type of issue over which countries fight to the death, thus making U.S. officials more willing to confront Park. Ironically, the U.S. readiness to oppose the junta sometimes led Park to bypass U.S. officials. When finance minister Ch'ŏn Pyŏng-gyu, upon learning of the currency conversion plan, argued for consultation with the United States, for example, Park opposed the idea because he knew that the United States would oppose the plan.[63]

By contrast, the United States was much subtler and constrained in its exercise of power when the military junta's political power was at stake, preferring to counsel or advise rather than to confront its leadership openly. In a reply to Berger's complaint against Kim Chong-p'il's recklessness, Rusk took the position that "just as [the United States] should not support any individual qua individual, [it] should not overtly so oppose anyone. However [the United States] can make it clear . . . that a director of espionage and secret police should not at the same time be a principal policy maker and second-ranking leader of [a] modern state."[64] The U.S. officials in the field were concerned that "undue" American interference in

South Korean politics could damage long-term U.S. interests by spreading anti-American sentiments among South Koreans. The only exception to the U.S. preference for incremental accommodation and low-profile negotiation on the issues of power occurred in March-April 1963, when U.S. officials, in a de facto alliance with South Korean civilian opposition politicians, openly opposed Park's proposal to extend military rule.

Obstacles to effective U.S. intervention in South Korean economic as well as security policies arose more from interagency rivalries in the United States than from the South Korean military junta. The United States was not a unitary actor in its dealings with its client state. Although Berger enjoyed unusually wide discretion as an ambassador, his room to maneuver was often constrained by the U.S. military even in economic realms, because what resources he could secure for developmental purposes depended on his ability to extract resources from the U.S. military.[65] His dispute with General Meloy over the distribution of aid between military and economic programs was public knowledge in both Washington and Seoul. The internal split in the U.S. government sometimes provided the weak with an opportunity to neutralize U.S. attempts at policy change. The South Korean armed forces' opposition to force reduction is a case in point.

The junta years thus cannot be framed in terms of a dichotomous win-lose or strong-weak framework. Rather, it is more accurate to describe the two countries' political authorities as being locked in a frustrating game of hide-and-seek and mutual hostage. Knowing that the United States would oppose his scheme to mobilize capital through the currency conversion program and the KIDC money–stock swap arrangement, Park kept U.S. officials in the dark until the last days of preparation, only to back down at the U.S. threat to withhold aid. Despite McConaughy's confidence in the deterrence effect of U.S. ideological opposition to military intervention in politics, a military coup took place only two months after his disregard of reports it was brewing, demonstrating that the United States did not necessarily have control over political events in South Korea. Further, in a mirror image of U.S. veto power against Park's capital mobilization scheme, the South Korean armed forces under Park's leadership could and did move history in the opposite direction of U.S. policy—albeit in covert ways, given the regime's weak position. Contradicting realist theories that explain the outcome in terms of relative power capabilities, the military junta found some bargaining leverage in the U.S. interest in normalizing South Korea–Japan relations, in interagency rivalries between the U.S. State and Defense departments, and in U.S. dependence on South Korea to protect its central ally in Asia, Japan, from communist military threats.

The military junta often tried to limit Berger's influence by mobilizing the support of the U.S. military—as when Chang To-yŏng attempted to arrange a "summit" with Kennedy with the help of General Maxwell Taylor. In a similar way, Kim Chong-p'il sought help from General James A. Van Fleet in improving his standing in the United States.[66] Most critically, as U.S. officials repeatedly found out, the military junta frequently acted on the belief that "the United States would have to go along with anything" to avoid a communist takeover.[67] The Park-Kim axis tried to force its desires on U.S. policymakers by presenting its actions as a fait accompli, forcing the United States to concede because the only alternative seemed to be political instability and military risk. The brinkmanship sometimes worked, as in the case of the May 16 coup. Other times, as in the case of the 1962 currency conversion, it failed dismally. Still other times, as in the case of the 1963 dispute over the extension of military rule, it made both Park and the United States a winner, each achieving its top priority goal while letting the other also realize its top agenda through the zigzags of political events. In evaluating the extent of U.S. influence, one therefore needs to keep in mind the context within which the United States tried to exercise its power and the strategy of local actors in responding to it. It is true that without U.S. pressure, military rule might have been extended for four years in 1963.[68] But it is also true that the United States ended up accommodating Park's conditions regarding transition to civilian rule and accepted his presidency in 1963.

CHAPTER THREE

State Building: The Military Junta's Path to Modernity through Administrative Reforms

Hyung-A Kim

DEVELOPMENTAL STATE THEORIES explain South Korea's successful transformation into a modern industrial economy primarily in terms of its possession of a professional "Weberian" state imbued with the ethos of "plan rationality," mobilizing resources top-down in a highly concerted way to minimize costs and maximize benefits, and insulating policy processes from political forces and social interests so that the ethos of plan rationality prevails and drives policymaking. This is a myth. A study of the military junta years (1961–1963), when the South Korean state was recreated as a developmental state, reveals that the role of the state was more complex and uncertain than developmental state theories would have it.

First, the South Korean state was not a static but a dynamic set of institutional arrangements that continuously transformed during the years of the junta. There did not exist in May 1961 a proto-developmental state waiting for a new political leadership to awaken its technocratic potential and harness its latent institutional capabilities for the modernization of the country. On the contrary, the state Park Chung Hee inherited was a politically demoralized and technically backward institution—albeit with a few isolated pockets of innovation. The developmental state was not a given, but a human artifact that was to emerge out of Park and his inner circle's political risk-taking, policy experiments, and transnational networking with the United States and Japan. The speed with which Park was able to gain control of the instruments of state power and remold them into a developmental apparatus after his coup was an important factor in his success.[1] In the two and a half years of military rule, Park and his followers swiftly laid the groundwork for the governmental framework that would prove to be so effective in spearheading the nation's rapid economic development. Scarcely six months after the coup, the initially skeptical U.S. ambassador Samuel D. Berger was impressed enough by Park's leadership to write in his report to the secretary of state, Dean Rusk, that "this genuine revolution from the top [is] breathlessly implementing across the board the much talked about reforms of the past: banking and credit policy, tax, foreign trade, increased public works for the unemployed, agriculture, education, public administration, and welfare."[2] The multiple administrative reforms were steered by two institutions, the Supreme Council of National Reconstruction (SCNR) and the Korea Central Intelligence Agency (KCIA). In particular, the KCIA was instrumental in establishing the powers and functions of the junta's key economic institutions—the Economic Planning Board (EPB), the Ministry of Finance (MoF), and the Ministry of Commerce and Industry (MCI)[3]—as well as strengthening the political arm of Park's rule, including the Ministry of Home Affairs (MHA) and the police. The architect of the South Korean developmental state was the KCIA, not economic technocrats.

Second, given the primacy of politics, the history of state building and policy reform during the military junta was rocky, taking sharp twists and turns in economically dysfunctional directions as struggles for power heated up in the volatile junta. The birth of the developmental state was anything but technocratic. Despite their effectiveness, the administrative reforms carried out by Park and his junta derived from no blueprint or master plan prepared at the outset of the coup with clear objectives and well-defined steps to harness the state apparatus for political stability and economic growth. There was hardly a "grand design." On the contrary, the junta's programs were preoccupied with the issue of political control rather than with the question of how to use a strengthened control mechanism for other goals, including economic growth. The obsession with political control led Park not only to establish the KCIA but also to entrust many policymaking responsibilities to the intelligence agency. The centrality of the KCIA in the policymaking process meant that South Korean politics were characterized by repressive and punitive measures and South Korean economics by dysfunctional shock therapies. Under martial law, the dissolution of the National Assembly and local government councils and the disbanding of political parties and social organizations were the norm rather than the exception, while economic policy was based on the assumption that the junta could force savings on society and redirect the economy by administrative fiat.

Third, in parallel with the misguided efforts using various shock therapies, there also emerged powerful currents of political learning. The failures of the junta's experiments taught Park that he had much to learn about the intrinsic limitations of his initial control-oriented strategy and that he needed to find a balance between state power and market forces to generate economic growth. Fortunately for Park, the military junta, and the country, he was not afraid to acknowledge his mistakes, learn from them, switch policy directions, and redefine policy goals when performance lagged behind target objectives. He gradually shifted the locus of power in economic policymaking from the KCIA to technocrats in the state bureaucracy in order to implement the newly redefined policy goals. For someone trying to undertake a revolution, Park was surprisingly free of ideological hang-ups.

Park could only learn of the need to shift power to the state bureaucracy and technocratize economic policy, however, when he had successfully steered the internally fragmented junta through the treacherous waters of post-coup power politics to consolidate his basis of power. Politics had to be put in order first before Park put his policy learning to use. Here he was also a quick study. Despite his seeming vulnerability as ostensibly second in charge of the coup, and with only a narrow power base, Park held undisputed leadership in the post-coup period while power dynamics shifted constantly. The most critical part of this story was his complex relationship with Kim Chong-p'il, his right-hand man.[4] Indeed, it is difficult to imagine how Park could have so quickly taken control of the government and carried out fundamental administrative reforms had he not secured the support of Kim Chong-p'il. Kim was widely regarded as a "co-owner" of the military coup of 1961. Founder and first director of the KCIA, he became the crown prince, wielding power rivaling that of Park.

Once Park consolidated power with the help of Kim Chong-p'il in the politics of purges by early 1963, however, Kim had to be brought down from the position of crown prince, not only in the interest of Park's further consolidation of power, but also for the sake of the transition to a more technocratic growth strategy. Park reduced Kim's dominance when his role became the single most explosive threat to the stability of the SCNR and to Park's power. Park used the rivals of Kim Chong-p'il to force Kim to step down from the chairmanship of the Democratic Republican Party and then "retire." This maneuver in turn proved to be an opportunity to crack down on those rivals. The manner in which Park handled these relationships is an example of his ability to tap the talents of others to consolidate his power and to play politics of the most dispassionate and efficient kind to tame the ambitions of his allies, advisors, and supporters.

The Supreme Council for National Reconstruction

The question of power was paramount, not only determining the prospects for Park's survival as a political leader but also shaping his preferences for the direction of state building and economic policy. The issue he faced in the immediate aftermath of the military coup was how to project the image of the armed forces' unified institutional support for him while he weeded out potential rivals to his leadership from the military and constructed a system of checks and balances within the junta. The question of how to recruit scarce civilian talent for rebuilding the South Korean state into a capable instrument of the military junta also occupied Park throughout the two and a half years of military rule. In the process of resolving these questions and issues of power, he ended up establishing an internally fractured, multilayered structure of governance.

Formally, it was the junta, renamed from the Military Revolutionary Committee to the Supreme Council for National Reconstruction (Kukka chaegŏn ch'oego hoeŭi) three days after the coup, that was the seat of power. As the supreme political authority replacing the three branches of government, the SCNR was composed of the thirty highest-ranking military personnel, including the chiefs of all the branches of the armed forces. The inclusion of the highest-ranking military personnel was a way to keep firm control over the military and a close eye on any possible countercoup within the armed forces, as well as to project the armed forces' unity behind the coup. The SCNR initially consisted of fourteen subcommittees, which were reduced to seven by July 1961. Although the membership changed five times between May 1961 and February 1963 because of a series of purges and retirements, the SCNR remained the highest political authority, with the power to enact laws, examine the budget, and oversee national administration. In addition, it had special powers to direct and control the cabinet over matters relating to national administration, planning, and policy.[5] The cabinet could advise the SCNR, but the power to appoint the cabinet was vested in the SCNR. The SCNR also had the power to appoint the Planning Council for National Reconstruction (PCNR). It had five committees made up of civilians but was headed by a military officer. On May 20, 1961, the SCNR established a fourteen-member cabinet of active military officers and placed it under Lieutenant

General Chang To-yŏng, who wore four hats as the prime minister, defense minister, SCNR chairman, and army chief of staff. The launching of the cabinet triggered intense power struggles, which were to end in the downfall of Chang. Having won U.S. acceptance of the coup and having defeated General Yi Han-lim's countercoup efforts, Park took away two of the positions that had given Chang authority over the military—army chief of staff and minister of defense—within two weeks of his appointment as prime minister by getting the SCNR to enact the Law Regarding Extraordinary Measures for National Reconstruction on June 6, which barred the SCNR chairman (Chang To-yŏng) from holding any office other than that of prime minister. Next, on June 12, the vice chairman of the SCNR, Major General Park Chung Hee, was appointed chairman of the SCNR Standing Committee in accordance with the Supreme Council for National Reconstruction Law (SCNRL) promulgated on June 10. The law stipulated that "the Vice Chairman of the SCNR shall also be Chairman of the SCNR Standing Committee," thus further subverting Chang's power base.[6] The clause had been drafted by Lieutenant Colonel Yi Sŏkche, chairman of SCNR's Subcommittee on Legislation and Justice and one of Park's protégés. Yi had also played a central role in drafting and enacting the Law Regarding Extraordinary Measures for National Reconstruction under instructions to "eliminate" Chang To-yŏng.[7]

On July 3, Chang was arrested on the charge of conspiring to carry out a countercoup, along with a mixed group of forty-four generals, colonels, and other officers.[8] The purge of Chang, generally seen as a power struggle between the Southern factions, which included primarily the provinces of Kyŏngsang and Ch'ungch'ŏng, and the Northern faction, mostly from P'yŏngan province, also led to the fall of the fifth graduating KMA class as a next-generation contender for the position of crown prince within the military junta against Kim Chong-p'il and his young colonels of the eighth KMA class.

On the same day, the SCNR engaged in another round of legal change— this time in the opposite direction, allowing Park to assume the chairmanship of both the SCNR and its powerful standing committee. The SCNR also appointed the new minister of defense, Song Yo-ch'an, as prime minister. At the same time, the SCNR overhauled the cabinet on July 22, establishing an overarching ministry, the Economic Planning Board, as a lead agency to steer South Korean economic development with an impressive arsenal of budgetary, foreign capital, and planning powers. Once Park made himself the undisputed leader of the junta, he moved to transform the SCNR into a cohesive organization capable of mobilizing power for reform more effectively. Park made the chairman of each of the now seven subcommittees a member of the SCNR standing committee, with himself as chair after July 2. The seven subcommittees were Legislation and Justice, Home Affairs, Foreign Affairs and National Defense, Finance and Economy, Education and Society, Transportation and Communications, and Management and Planning.

The structure of power Park had built was "upside-down."[9] On the one hand, senior high-ranking officers in the reserves and on active duty were drafted by Park to serve as cabinet ministers in order to project an image of the South Korean armed forces' unified institutional support behind the coup and to legitimize Park's leadership. Their role was conceived as primarily one of professional-administrative management by the core group of the military junta, including Park. On the other hand, the core group of mid-ranking officers loyal to Park and Kim Chong-p'il placed its members in the SCNR because of their lower ranking in the military hierarchy, but thought of itself as the real owner of the coup because it had been the lieutenant colonels and colonels who had actually mobilized troops and occupied Seoul on May 16, 1961. Moreover, with this self-image, the core group had made the SCNR the supreme body with the power to appoint the cabinet. The ministers were without political decision-making power, required to work with, through, and sometimes around the SCNR members, who were their military subordinates but also their political superiors. In this dual power structure, the young SCNR officers on active duty had the power to overrule the cabinet ministers in areas that included personnel administration, budget, and policy formulation.

In its efforts to amass power, the SCNR drafted whoever it believed was needed to implement its state-led reform programs, resulting in the participation of a diverse array of civilian professionals and experts in various SCNR programs, ranging from economic planning and rural development to constitutional revision to party organization. These civilians participated as advisors rather than as decision makers, even when they had decision-making government posts.

The two-tier structure of governance with its locus of power placed in the mid-ranking officers who staffed the SCNR appeared to work—at least in the second half of 1961. The assistant secretary of state for Far Eastern affairs, Walter P. McConaughy, in his "Revised Progress Report on Follow-Up Actions Responsive to Recommendations of Korea Task Force Report" of September 8, 1961, reported that the military junta had made real advances since the coup in May, including the maintenance of a unified exchange rate at 1,300 *hwan* per dollar, the reorganization of South Korea's fragmented and inefficient electric power industry into a single public corporation, the establishment of improved credit facilities, the elimination of dirigiste banking regulations and price controls, the release of South Korea's leading businessmen placed under house arrest on charges of illicit wealth accumulation during the Rhee regime, and actions to engender business confidence and to stimulate the economy.[10]

Korea Central Intelligence Agency

At the center of policy reform and bureaucratic restructuring was the KCIA. The primary task of its director, Kim Chong-p'il,[11] was the consolidation of Park's grip on power in and outside the SCNR and cabinet. Modeled after, but also going beyond, the U.S. Central Intelligence Agency and the Japanese Investigation Bureau, the KCIA was designed not only to collect intelligence on external threats to national security but also to eliminate all obstacles in the execution of the "revolutionary tasks" of Park's junta. Only thirty-five years old in 1961, tall and handsome, Kim Chong-p'il had a charismatic personality and great revolutionary zeal. He was known among U.S. officials for being "extraordinarily intelligent" and full of energy. At the same time, the United States deplored his "identification of revolution with himself."[12] As Berger reported to his superiors, Kim was not just an intelligence chief. He was at the "core of [the] revolution as planner, leader and administrator."[13]

Once Park and Kim Chong-p'il seized power in May 1961, their central instrument of power consolidation became the KCIA, founded on June 10.[14] According to Law no. 619, the KCIA had the power "to control and supervise both international and domestic intelligence activities, and the criminal investigation undertaken by all government intelligence agencies, including that of the military."[15] The powers of the KCIA had also been strengthened by the Law Regarding the Extraordinary Measures for National Reconstruction. Promulgated on June 6, this was the first law the coup leaders enacted. Designed to "regularize, legalize, and explain" the new system of military rule,[16] it stipulated that if any articles of the South Korean Constitution were contrary to the articles of the emergency measures law, the latter would prevail.[17]

These extraordinary legal measures were drafted by three members of the eighth KMA graduating class: Sŏk Chŏng-sŏn, Yi Yŏng-gŭn, and Kim Pyŏng-hak. Sin Chik-su, a civilian lawyer, revised the initial draft of Law no. 619 and subsequently became an advisor to Park, while also acting as an advisor to the KCIA. Kim Chong-p'il filled in all the key positions of the KCIA with members of his clique, hand-picking the director, deputy director, and chiefs of each of the agency's six bureaus and six divisions.[18]

On May 20, 1961, Kim Chong-p'il had briefed the members of the Military Revolutionary Committee (MRC) on the organization and functions of the KCIA. Kim also explained to the coup leaders that the KCIA and the headquarters of the National Reconstruction Movement were to be managed directly by the MRC. The briefing showed that Kim Chong-p'il was recognized de facto as the planner and implementer of the junta's reform drive. In fact, Kim publicly announced that he was the master planner of the SCNR laws and the architect of the SCNR's governing structure.[19] Moreover, even before the adoption of the KCIA law, much of its organization had already been established and placed under the direction of Kim Chong-p'il.

According to Ch'oe Yŏng-t'aek, the National Police were the first institution to report to the KCIA.[20] On May 22, the KCIA took over the Chang Myŏn government's intelligence agency, officially known as the Research Committee on Central Intelligence, headed by Yi Hu-rak, who later became Park's chief of staff. Yi boasted of close ties to the American CIA.

It was the overwhelming powers of the KCIA that allowed Kim Chong-p'il to remove Lieutenant General Chang To-yŏng from the SCNR chairmanship to make way for Park's rise to the top. The carefully orchestrated purge of Chang and his followers less than fifty days after the coup showed Kim Chong-p'il at the height of his power, in control of both the SCNR and the cabinet, as well as other public and private institutions. The initiative to control civilian institutions also began with purges. The Ministry of Home Affairs, which sat on top of myriad administrative organs of political control, including the police, saw a massive purge of civil servants at the provincial and local levels as Kim attempted to get control of the state bureaucracy and to exert his influence over the military junta's economic and social programs through that control. There was also a Joint Investigation Team, led by the SCNR's Inspection Committee on Irregularities in the Public Service, which tried to establish discipline across state ministries. Some 20,000 civil servants were dismissed by June 17, 1961, as a result of the team's activities.

Then, in accordance with the SCNR's newly announced thirteen-point guidelines for the reduction of civil servants, those "aged over fifty" were included in this massive purge. By July 20, the military junta planned to reduce the number of civil servants to 200,000 by forcing the retirement of 40,989 "excess" bureaucrats.[21] The campaign was not based on any objective assessment of bureaucratic manpower. On the contrary, the objective was to establish discipline in the civil service with a show of arbitrary power, as well as to satisfy public demand for a cut in state expenditures. As Park openly declared the need to rejuvenate the country with generational change, the purge aimed to change the leadership in the state bureaucracy. The younger generation was presumably more loyal to the military junta, because their promotion had been made possible by the purges.

Kim Chong-p'il's modus operandi ultimately led to the remodeling of the state bureaucracy into a military-style organization. Less than two weeks after the coup, Lieutenant General Han Sin, as the home affairs minister, publicly issued guidelines to all civil servants to "obey unconditionally" all official orders and to complete their assigned tasks within designated timelines. The eight-point guidelines also prohibited public servants from smoking foreign cigarettes as well as from frequenting "drinking bars."[22]

The same shock therapy of purges and arrests was applied to societal groups. Only a week after the coup, the KCIA led the SCNR's comprehensive "clean-up campaign" by arresting 51 "illicit profiteers" and "tax evaders," 4,200 "hoodlums," and 2,100 "communist sympathizers."[23] Around the same time, the SCNR dissolved all political parties and social organizations (Decree no. 6) and banned indoor and outdoor political assemblies. The subsequently held courts martial even meted out sentences ranging from three to twelve months in prison for dancing in unlicensed dance halls (Decree no. 1).[24] In its day-to-day enforcement of these measures, the MHA mobilized the police as its official watchdog, the effect of which was to strengthen police powers and functions, especially as tools to weed out the opposition and to back the implementation of the military government's reform program. The MHA was able to do so because the KCIA stood in the background as its supporter. The KCIA was able to project power because its initiatives were endorsed by the Park–Kim Chong-p'il *churyu* (mainstream faction) in control of the armed forces.

The KCIA also performed the role of recruiting some of the best talent in and outside of the state apparatus for the mainstream faction's task of state building and economic modernization. Kim Chŏng-ryŏm,[25] O Wŏn-ch'ŏl,[26] and Kim Hak-ryŏl[27] were the stars among the civilian experts recruited in 1961. Like most other civilian recruits, they were in their early thirties with promising career experience in their chosen fields. Except for Kim Hak-ryŏl, a career bureaucrat, Kim Chŏng-ryŏm and O Wŏn-ch'ŏl were appointed to posts in the state bureaucracy through the *tŭkch'ae* (special appointment) system that operated outside the *haengsi* (administrative entrance examination) system. Newly recruited from outside the bureaucracy, both Kim and O were bound to their political master, SCNR chairman Park.

To be sure, the junta also sought to rejuvenate the *haengsi* system in 1961 by dramatically increasing the number of successful examinees with an eye to recruiting the best of the younger generation in their early twenties, with college and graduate degrees, into the state bureaucracy at the mid-level, and through the establishment of a new Ministry of Government Affairs (MGA) to promote on the basis of merit rather than on the existing tradition of seniority.[28] However, because it took time for the young *haengsi* bureaucrats to climb up the ladder of hierarchy, it was the "specially appointed" *t'ǔkch'ae* from the Bank of Korea, private firms, and academia, coupled with a handful of career bureaucrats like Kim Hak-ryǒl, who were to make up the core of the new technocracy for much of the 1960s. These professional managers moved freely from one economic ministry to another, each time increasing their rank until they were appointed as a senior presidential staff member or a minister. Kim Chǒng-ryǒm, a brilliant fiscal manager, was the star among the stars, serving as the MoF vice minister and the MCI minister during much of the 1962–1968 period.[29] He was to become the longest-serving chief of staff (1968–1978) under Park.

The KCIA's effort to take control of the business community, however, was harder and took longer because that community had the resources to deliver the economic growth that the Park–Kim Chong-p'il team coveted. Moreover, getting the business community to move in the direction desired by the junta required complex legal measures and technically precise policy actions. The attempt at control began with the SCNR's establishment of a seven-member Committee for the Prosecution of Illicit Profiteering, with Major General Yi Chu-il as its chairman, on May 28, 1961. Park, like many other coup leaders, initially regarded the *chaebol* (large family-owned business conglomerates) as being nothing more than "rapacious wolves" who deserved to be "punished severely . . . in the name of our nation,"[30] for their exploitation of monopolistic market powers to win licenses, bank loans, and U.S. aid under the Rhee government.[31] After the enactment of the Special Measure for the Control of Illicit Profiteering, more than a dozen leading businessmen, including Chǒng Chae-ho, Yi Chǒng-lim, and Namgung Ryǒn, were arrested by the KCIA as "illicit profiteers and tax evaders," and were subsequently ordered to relinquish their illegal profits and to pay all outstanding taxes in arrears plus fines within six months.[32] By setting a demanding schedule for the payments, which, if implemented, would have driven many of the *chaebol* into de facto bankruptcy and led to the confiscation of their entire assets, the SCNR hoped to get an upper hand in the upcoming negotiations with the *chaebol* on the political and economic terms of their participation in economic development.

It was Yi Pyǒng-ch'ǒl, the owner-manager of South Korea's largest *chaebol,* Samsung, who put into motion the negotiations. Yi had escaped arrest because he was in Tokyo at the time of the coup. The day before his return to Seoul, Yi Pyŏng-ch'ŏl "volunteered" to donate his entire fortune to the SCNR's national reconstruction program. As he recollected, he expected to go to jail, like all the other arrested illicit profiteers and tax evaders, upon his arrival at Kimpo Airport.[33] He was indeed arrested, but was put under only house arrest. On July 14 he and other *chaebol* owner-managers were released after signing a pledge to "voluntarily donate" their entire assets to the SCNR when required for "national construction."[34] Once they were released, however, the business leaders backtracked, wavered, pleaded, and even resisted. Their central issue was the terms of their tax assessments and fines. The business community argued that they had "few liquid assets and therefore [were] in no position to pay [fines] in so short a time."[35] Many complained that they did not even have enough money to run their businesses and cover the operational costs of manufacturing goods. U.S. ambassador Berger wryly observed that the *chaebol* were "on strike," holding the sluggish domestic economy hostage in their attempt to negotiate more favorable terms for their fines and tax assessments. Outraged by the business community's resistance, some members of the SCNR, especially the young colonels of the eighth KMA graduating class, even suggested the execution of the "illicit profiteers."[36] Park loathed the *chaebol* as well. In talking with Berger, he stated that "Govt [*sic*] had gone more than half way to compromise [on the] original [tax] assessments and still they were not satisfied. When they were in jail, [the] businessmen recognized that revolution saved [South] Korea from chaos and communism and had promised to fight, bleed and die for [South] Korea and the revolution, and even turn over their whole fortunes. Once they were out of jail it was [the] same old story: they were using every dodge to evade repayment of illegal gains and they [are] now using [the] American Embassy to bail them out."[37]

Berger seems to have been at pains to explain to Park the disastrous consequences of what he termed "unsatisfactory relations between [the South Korean government] and several dozen key industrialists who dominate Korean industry and were [the] only ones with present capacity to manage and revive these industries." Berger insisted that Park alter his strategy, because "if [the business] strike goes on for only a few months, it is going to cost [the] country many times [the] $35 million dollars" that the military junta assessed as the total amount of the tax to be paid by the *chaebol.* The potential cost in lost production and wages required that Park reach an agreement with big business. At the same time, Berger warned the business community "not to press their monopolistic position too far" and to work out a compromise with the junta. Otherwise, Berger concluded, the stand-off "might well end in nationalization."[38]

In July 1961, under an SCNR directive, the thirteen leading business-men, including Yi Pyŏng-ch'ŏl, established the Federation of Korean Business Leaders (Han'guk kyŏngjein hyŏphoe).[39] The first act of FKI was to agree with the SCNR that they build their SCNR-planned and -assigned factories first, and then pay their fines and arrears in taxes by donating parts of the shares in their newly built companies to the SCNR.[40] Apparently Berger's advice to Park had been effective. The junta both lengthened the timeline for the payments and opted to receive the taxes in shares. By doing so, the SCNR got the *chaebol* commitment to invest in the military junta's pet industrial projects. Six industries—cement, synthetic fiber, electricity, fertilizer, iron, and oil—were targeted as the engines of economic growth in the first Five-Year Economic Development Plan (FYEDP). Except for oil refining, which was to be managed directly by the state, the responsibility for building the other five industries was divided among the thirteen FKI members. For the *chaebol,* the compromise provided new opportunities for corporate growth as the executor of the military junta's industrial projects. The issue of illicit profiteering and tax evasion thus occasioned the forging of a new military-*chaebol* coalition for economic growth and corporate expansion.

The relationship between the military junta and *chaebol* quickly deteriorated, however, when the KCIA arrested many members of the SCNR Committee for the Prosecution of Illicit Profiteering, on the charge of giving favorable treatment to certain *chaebol* owner-managers from the northern provinces. The arrest of the subcommittee members was part of Kim Chong-p'il's move to cut off the channels of political funding for the northern faction of the same regional origin within the SCNR. The northern faction dominated the subcommittee, supplying three of its six members. Its chairman, Major General Yi Chu-il, was also from the Hamgyŏng region and served concurrently as the SCNR vice chairman.

The incident revealed not only the emerging political cleavage between the Park–Kim Chong-p'il mainstream faction of the Kyŏngsang and Ch'ungch'ŏng provinces, on the one hand, and the generals of the northern provinces, on the other, but also the rivalry of *chaebol* owner-managers along the same north-south regional divide. The ensuing military trial tipped the balance of power further toward the Park-Kim mainstream. The *chaebol* owners from the Hamgyŏng region, such as Sŏl Kyŏng-dong, Yi Yang-gu, and Kim Yŏn-jun, were found guilty of bribing the investigators and as a result were denied government support for their industrial projects. By contrast, the *chaebol* owners from the south, including Yi Pyŏng-ch'ŏl and Chŏng Chae-ho, received a huge reduction in their original fines.[41] As the process wore on, Colonel Yu Wŏn-sik, a member of the Committee for the Prosecution of Illicit Profiteering and also a central player in the SCNR Subcommittee on Commerce and Industry, became the spokesman for the mainstream faction. Although Kim Chong-p'il failed in his attempt to remove Yi Chu-il because of Park's unswerving trust in the general,[42] Kim succeeded in demoralizing and weakening the northern faction and filled in the power vacuum that resulted with even more of his KMA classmates. At a minimum, the crackdown made every member of the SCNR fear the KCIA, thus getting Kim Chong-p'il closer to his goal of becoming Park's heir.[43]

A by-product of the consolidation of power around the KCIA at the expense of the SCNR was policy disarray. The authority of the cabinet ministers had been undermined by the SCNR's claim of executive, legislative, and judicial powers, and now there developed a tension among SCNR members as the KCIA took control of many of the SCNR's reform programs. Even the recruitment of civilian and academic advisors to the SCNR for the task of assisting with its 1961–1962 National Reconstruction Movement was dominated by the KCIA. Moreover, the intelligence agency frequently excluded the SCNR from important reform programs.

The KCIA was able to seize ever-larger policy roles because it had its own brain trust known as the Policy Research Institute, almost identical to the SCNR's Planning Committee, to advise Kim Chong-p'il on the issues of politics, economics, society and culture, law, and reconstruction. Whereas the SCNR Planning Committee recruited a large number of prominent university professors, including Yu Chin-o, Ch'oe Ho-jin, Pak Chong-hong, and Yi Man-gap, the KCIA Policy Research Institute drafted mid-career and even younger professionals and academics, including Kim Chŏng-ryŏm, Pak Kwan-suk, Yun Ch'ŏn-ju, Kim Sŏng-hŭi, and Yi Chong-gŭk, in addition to an even larger group of prominent figures such as Ch'oe Kyu-ha, a career diplomat.[44] The KCIA, given Park's trust in it, the cohesiveness of the eighth KMA graduating class who worked for it, its colossal internal resources, and its strategically minded leader, Kim Chong-p'il, quickly squeezed out the SCNR Planning Committee and took control of the military junta's policy planning. The SCNR Planning Committee came to be seen as a redundant agency and was soon dismantled.[45]

In the course of administrative reforms and policy changes, the KCIA's dominance brought Park many political problems, including strong pressure from Ambassador Berger to reduce the KCIA's role, not to mention Kim Chong-p'il's influence. Yet Park continued to rely heavily on Kim Chong-p'il and his KCIA for sweeping reforms. Park did so because no other coup maker had the vision, strategy, and organizational capabilities of Kim Chong-p'il. Also, a generation younger, Kim Chong-p'il did not pose a threat to Park's leadership at that time.

According to Yi Sŏk-je, the chairman of the SCNR Subcommittee on Legislation and Justice, the military government's administrative reform program was initially prepared by a group of young pro–Kim Chong-p'il colonels, including himself. In early 1961, as part of their preparation for the coup, the officers had begun to collect policy ideas to bring about a comprehensive reform of government administration, including the introduction of an emergency constitution, the drafting of the SCNR laws, and the trial of illicit profiteers and tax evaders.[46] The objective was to legislate a massive number of reform bills within the first hundred days of military rule at lightning speed in order to differentiate the "efficient" military from the faction-ridden, incompetent Chang Myŏn government and to build public support with the image of a "can do" government. In the first hundred days after the coup, the Park-Kim mainstream faction introduced a dozen extraordinary measures, including martial law (May 16), the Press Purification Measure (May 23), the Plan for the Liquidation of Usurious Debts in the Countryside (May 25), the Law Regarding the Extraordinary Measures for National Reconstruction (June 6), the Supreme Council for National Reconstruction Law (June 7), the Act of Establishing the Central Intelligence Agency (June 10), the Act on Disposition of Illicit Fortunes (June 14), the Emergency Economic Measures for Industrial Recovery (July 18), and the Outline of a Five-Year Economic Development Plan, as well as the establishment of the Economic Planning Board (July 22).

Some of these reform measures, such as martial law, the SCNR law, and the KCIA law, had been prepared by the coup makers before their seizure of power. Others, like the EPB and the currency reform law, were developed in cooperation with reform-minded bureaucrats after the takeover of state power and state institutions. The military junta's way of "revolution" was more one of muddling through, adding to its own desires the attractive ideas and strategies of the state bureaucracy, big business, and the intelligentsia. The junta, not having had a master plan when it overthrew Chang Myŏn, made reforms as its members learned the complexities of governance and development. Equally important, they learned only what they wanted to learn: arts and techniques to take control of the institutions of power. What to do with those mechanisms of control was left vague or, more accurately, was to be decided by power struggles, experiments, and learning, especially in the areas of economic development and administrative efficiency. As Yi Sŏk-je recalled in 1995, the history of the military government itself was a "continuation of trial and error,"[47] because many reform programs contradicted one another or were ill-conceived, resulting in policy fiascos, although they were motivated by the same interest in power consolidation.

Eventually, however, lagging policy performance threatened the junta's credibility as a "can do" political force and jeopardized its performance-based instrumental legitimacy, making learning how to make effective policy a matter of survival for coup leaders. The junta discovered that its programs contradicted each other even during the first three months of reform. For example, the implementation of the first FYEDP required the cooperation of the *chaebol*, but the campaign of historical rectification caused the arrest of most of the *chaebol* owners as illicit profiteers and tax evaders. The businessmen's cooperation in the first FYEDP projects was secured only when the junta backed down and reduced the fines and accepted more flexible and lenient payment conditions. The inner circles of the KCIA did not learn enough, however, because when they were under intense pressure to raise political funds or to demonstrate their "can do" spirit through a spectacular showdown with their industrial rivals, as they thought they were in June 1962, they again imposed economically risky policy and drove the South Korean economy to the verge of collapse. Only after this humiliating policy failure did Park make the KCIA withdraw from the economic and fiscal realm and focus on politics.

Economic Bureaucracy

Contrary to the later image of Park the modernizer, the military junta's record of economic policy was anything but developmentalist. Power struggles within the faction-ridden SCNR, the crippling of the cabinet's authority by the "upside-down" power structures of the military junta, and the KCIA's use of economic policy as an instrument of power consolidation rather than of economic growth all ended up marginalizing the role of the economic ministries and their technocratic rationality. It was only when the KCIA's economic role was thoroughly discredited (June 1962), all the potential rivals of Park were weeded out from the SCNR (March 1963), *and* Park was legitimated electorally (October 1963) that Park was able to follow the tenets of technocratic rationality in economic policy-making. Until the threats to his power were resolved through purges and elections, Park remained a político, not a técnico, in his approach to the issues of the day, making decisions almost solely on the basis of how his choices affected his power.

Nonetheless, it was also true that the years of military rule laid down the institutional infrastructure for a developmental state through a series of organizational experiments. It might be said that the military junta failed at the level of articulating a strategy of development, but succeeded at the level of putting in place the institutions of power that would later contribute to the economic takeoff, once there emerged an effective strategy. The most important organizational experiment was the establishment of the Economic Planning Board (EPB) in July 1961. The EPB was a product of two forces: the reformist bureaucrats in the Ministries of Reconstruction (MoR) and Finance (MoF) and the Park–Kim Chong-p'il mainstream faction in the SCNR. The MoR-MoF reformers were then searching for a patron and co-owner for their idea of creating a superministry to prevent the sorts of planning failures that had occurred under the Rhee regime, whereas the SCNR was in need of an institution that could translate its broad goals into a concrete set of feasible targets and strategies and speed up the process of developing new policy approaches. The SCNR knew it needed more than military organizational skills and experience to turn the South Korean economy around. The need to recruit civilian talent was especially pressing in view of the formulation and implementation of the first Five-Year Economic Development Plan that was to be the centerpiece of the junta's budgetary, monetary, fiscal, and industrial policy. As a superministry, the EPB took on the responsibility of economic planning. To give the board authority for the implementation of its plans, the EPB absorbed budgetary powers, foreign capital licensing authority, and statistics functions from the MoF's Budget Bureau and the MHA's Bureau of Statistics. Kim Yu-t'aek, then minister of finance and former chairman of the Bank of Korea, became the first minister of the EPB on July 22, 1961, just a month after his appointment as finance minister.[48]

Although a strong ability to lead was not one of Kim Yu-t'aek's attributes, he understood the complexity of economic issues from his career as a banker and a diplomat.[49] By making Kim Yu-t'aek one of the two civilian ministers appointed to the junta's cabinet, the Park-Kim mainstream faction hoped to show its seriousness in reaching out to civilian experts for the implementation of the first FYEDP. But the question of power inevitably dominated technocratic rationales, making Kim Yu-t'aek not much different from the other cabinet ministers in that he was limited to strictly managerial tasks, implementing goals formulated elsewhere. In fact, it was Park who ordered three young economists—Kim Sŏng-bŏm (thirty-seven years old), Chŏng So-yŏng (twenty-nine years old, with a PhD in economics), and Paek Yong-ch'an (thirty-two years old)—to draft the first FYEDP even before the EPB was organized. The team completed the plan in less than sixty days, providing a blueprint for ac-

tion for the Economic Planning Board upon its establishment on July
22. This five-year plan was popularly known as the May 1961 Plan, or
more formally as the Comprehensive Five-Year Economic Development
Plan.[50]

The May 1961 Plan sought to double South Korea's gross national
product within a decade by maintaining economic growth at an annual average rate of 7.1 percent. Given the country's 1960 growth rate of 2.3 percent, the plan was criticized as overly ambitious both within the SCNR
and by the U.S. State Department. The United States referred to the plan as
a "shopping list" for U.S. assistance when Park explained its goals in his
official visit to Washington in November 1961.

The first FYEDP was based on the principle of what Park then defined as
"guided capitalism." The driver in guided capitalism was to be the state,
and the objective of state-led economic and industrial management was
defined as guaranteeing the "equalization of income and public benefit
from the economy." To Park and many other coup leaders, the greatest
challenge in implementing the plan stemmed from the lack of an institutional mechanism to oversee the process of capital mobilization, resource
allocation, and policy coordination within the state. Their efforts at reform consequently focused on the establishment of a state bureaucracy
powerful enough to resist the "overwhelming pressure on legislative and
administrative organs [by the *chaebol*] to get laws favorable to them."
Park believed that the *chaebol*'s past activities "clashed head-on with free
economic activities" and constituted "a betrayal of democratic principles." His concept of guided capitalism was designed to end any further
obstruction by *chaebol* leaders.[51]

Once Kim Yu-t'aek completed his mission of readying the first FYEDP
for implementation in March 1962, Park had Song Yo-ch'an serve as minister of the EPB. In spite of Song's ignominious retirement from the army in
the middle of the anticorruption campaign led by Park and his young colonels immediately after the April 19 Student Revolution in 1960, Park
thought Song to be the man for the job given his reputation for "strong
drive." Park had already tested Song by appointing him to the post of
prime minister between July 1961 and March 1962. Having confirmed
Song's ability to implement Park's directives on administrative reform with
a sense of loyalty, military efficiency, and fortitude as prime minister, Park
chose him as the implementor of the ideas prepared by Kim Yu-t'aek.
Song's style of leadership made him many enemies among the military
coup makers,[52] but as a U.S. embassy telegram dated August 12, 1961,
shows, he got things done, thus winning respect from U.S. officials. The
telegram reported positively on the introduction of training programs

based on ones used by the military into the South Korean civil service under Song's leadership:

> Prime Minister Song . . . is working his ministries 18-hour days to drive through programs and decisions . . . He has instituted methods used by [the] military, i.e., staff studies defining the problem, discussing the issues, and coming up with alternate recommendations for top level decision. He has established task forces and date deadlines for completion . . . Job analyses and work assignments are being reviewed at breath-taking speed and civil servants are being given firm instructions on how to handle routine paper work with maximum efficiency and within a fixed time period. Offenders are being disciplined and even fired.[53]

Despite Song's contribution, it is important to emphasize that he was the implementor, not the original formulator, of these goals, ideas, and strategies. The vision of establishing a state bureaucracy modeled after the South Korean hybrid military organization with the American ethos of technocracy and the Japanese tradition of discipline through sweeping top-down reforms of a fundamental kind was the vision of Park—not Song. Song succeeded because he was the implementor of Park's ideas. The SCNR chairman expected his cabinet ministers, including prime minister and later EPB minister Song, to lead the state in the fashion of a military organization. Capitalizing on Song's military credentials as former army chief of staff just before the coup, Park entrusted Song with the task of building the EPB into a military-style organization, using military concepts and ideas in its day-to-day language and copying the ministry staff organization in its structure.

In the process of transforming the EPB and other state ministries into military-style organizations, Park overlooked the complexity of creating a civilian superministry in charge of formidable developmental tasks that required the cooperation of societal forces, some of whom held veto power. The economy could not be run according to military practice. Issues were complex, roadblock players were many, and policymaking required economic and fiscal management expertise. Although Song exposed the concept of staff, task forces, job specifications, and deadlines to the civilian bureaucracy, he lacked ideas on what to do once the infrastructure was set up. In any case, at that time the KCIA had usurped the role of economic policymaker. Consequently, Kim Yu-t'aek was brought back as the EPB minister in July 1962 for the second time, less than four months after his departure, when the KCIA-led currency conversion reform plunged the junta into crisis.

The fiasco began when the Ministry of Finance, under Park and Kim Chong-p'il's secret instructions, officially announced the KCIA-prepared currency conversion reform in June 1962. The conversion of South Korea's currency from *hwan* to *won* at a ratio of 10:1 was simultaneously announced with an emergency banking measure that froze saving accounts with large deposits. The goal was to channel the frozen money into the military junta's heavy and chemical industrialization projects by forcing depositors to purchase stock in the Korea Industrial Development Corporation. The whole operation was initiated by the KCIA, with Colonel Yu Wŏn-sik, a member of the SCNR's Finance and Economics Subcommittee, acting as the front man. With the exception of Yu, the SCNR was kept in the dark, although the planning for currency conversion began as early as December 1961, if not earlier, when Major General Chŏng Nae-hyŏk, on his way to Europe to seek economic cooperation, visited Great Britain in his capacity as the minister of commerce and industry to negotiate the printing of the new currency.[54]

The currency conversion reform was poorly conceived and executed. Even the United States, which was supplying 90 percent of the South Korean budget as late as 1961, was not consulted, infuriating U.S. policymakers and aid officials. Deputy assistant secretary of state Edward Rice officially warned the South Korean ambassador to the United States, Chŏng Il-gwŏn, that "if U.S. efforts are to be nullified, [the United States] must reassess [its] assistance policy."[55] The primary aim of the reform was to raise domestic capital by freezing large bank accounts. The KCIA was tempted into the idea of currency conversion by the rumor that ethnic Chinese residents in South Korea had stashed away large amounts of money in bank accounts opened in the names of third parties.

Park and Kim Chong-p'il quickly became aware of their miscalculation when it was found that not many people in South Korea, including its Chinese residents, had much cash on hand. By mid-1962 it was also clear that the actual growth rate was below the target of the first FYEDP, prompting Park to review the goals and assumptions of the plan. A U-turn from the KCIA's strategy of shock therapies quickly set in. Under U.S. threats to cut aid and in the middle of financial turmoil, the junta rescinded the freeze on the bank accounts. Also, Park personally ordered EPB planning director Chŏng Chae-sŏk to revise the first FYEDP in December 1962, the result of which was the announcement of a revised plan in mid-1964 that significantly lowered South Korea's projected growth rate to 5 percent, with the goal of restraining inflationary pressures caused by an excessive push for rapid industrialization.[56] The colossal failure of the currency conversion reform, coupled with the disappointing early results of the first FYEDP, triggered the KCIA's disengagement from the junta's economic reforms.

The policy fiasco thus led to a significant change in the structure of power, as well as discrediting the radical nationalist ideas held by Kim Chong-p'il and the KCIA. The incident prompted the opponents of Kim Chong-p'il in the SCNR as well as the U.S. embassy to urge Park to downgrade the role of Kim Chong-p'il and curtail the activities of the KCIA.[57] The failure taught Park the lesson that some of Kim Chong-p'il's policy ideas could threaten economic growth, backfire on South Korea–U.S. relations, and thereby threaten his power. Henceforth Park began to rely more on civilian technocrats not only for policy implementation but for policy formulation. For the sake of his own power and credibility, Park needed to keep Kim Chong-p'il under check. As the KCIA withdrew from economic issues and focused on the political realm, the economic bureaucracy began to take charge of economic reforms.

The direct beneficiary of the KCIA's disgrace was the Ministry of Finance. Having been profoundly weakened through the frequent change of its minister during the first year of military rule,[58] the MoF's power grew rapidly after mid-1962 as its Financial Management Bureau (FMB) took over where the KCIA had left off in the management of economic reform. In 1962 the appointment of two career financial experts, Kim Se-ryŏn and Kim Chŏng-ryŏm, as the finance minister and vice minister, respectively, was one consequence of the failed currency reform. The appointment of Kim Chŏng-ryŏm to the post of MoF vice minister was part of Park's efforts to place the most trusted of the civilian aides recruited in the immediate aftermath of the coup to positions of power within the economic bureaucracy. The shift of power put the economic ministries under the control of a tightly knit "patrimonial" force of civilian experts loyal only to Park. As will be shown below, Kim Hak-ryŏl was promoted to EPB vice minister in 1962, while O Wŏn-ch'ŏl moved up to the Ministry of Commerce and Industry (MCI). These constituted the most spectacular examples of Park's efforts to create a professional and yet patrimonial hybrid state bureaucracy, but they were joined by many other figures in the EPB, MoF, MCI, and the Blue House in this goal.[59] Their forward deployment represents Park's engagement of civilian experts in reform processes to supplement the military ethos of discipline and control with technical expertise: the mix of these two ingredients laid the groundwork for an effective economic bureaucracy. Ironically, these civilian aides' efforts to create a powerful professional and yet patrimonial state bureaucracy in the post–currency conversion period were critically assisted by the institutional infrastructure established by the Kim Chong-p'il–led radicals who had previously driven economic policy. Thanks to Kim's ambition to fundamentally reshape the structures of power in South Korean society, the MoF had been in control of the five major nationwide commercial banks since their nationalization immediately after the May 1961 coup. To establish pockets of expertise within the state and ensure their political independence from the faction-ridden SCNR, Park refrained from appointing military officers as the banks' governors. Instead he turned to civilians to lead both the MoF and the EPB, in sharp contrast to large parastatal institutions under the direction of other state ministries, including the Ministry of Commerce and Industry (MCI) and the Ministry of Agriculture and Forestry (MAF), where Park recruited former generals and sometimes colonels on active duty to maintain support from the armed forces for himself. Park had thus learned by mid-1962 that he needed to rely on professional civil servants in the elite ministries for financial and banking management. The practice of ensuring civilian leadership of key economic ministries, while at the same time using other ministries and state institutions to build a loyal following within the military establishment, was to become institutionalized after Park's inauguration as president in 1963.

After the failed currency reform, the *chaebol* had to go through the MoF, especially its Financial Management Bureau, rather than deal with the KCIA or the commercial banks. The Financial Management Bureau became the headquarters for South Korea's bank loan arrangements, both domestic and foreign, to carry out credit allocation effectively and speedily. The introduction of government guarantees on the payment of foreign commercial loans in July 1962 also contributed to the rise of the FMB to the status of "prince" among ministries and institutions. The authority of the FMB quickly came to be seen by many high-ranking policymakers and business leaders as the "FMB Republic," and the Bank of Korea as a "branch office" of the MoF. The extraordinary powers of the FMB also strengthened the status of the MoF and made it a de facto coordinator until the EPB began to assume its leadership role as a superministry in mid-1964.

The evolution of the MCI during the military junta followed a different track. The ministry underwent a radical overhaul in organization with the appointment of Major General Chŏng Nae-hyŏk as its minister in May 1961. Chŏng turned the MCI upside-down by undertaking a massive top-down military-style restructuring of both line and staff organization, dismissing many of the senior bureaucrats and recruiting a new breed of highly qualified experts from the outside. Both of the assistant vice ministers and three of the four bureau directors he appointed were experts with training in engineering and the natural sciences, creating a new working environment with an emphasis on efficiency and productivity. The technocrats recruited during Chŏng's tenure included O Wŏn-ch'ŏl, who was to become the senior economic secretary responsible for leading heavy and chemical industrialization in the 1970s, and Ch'oe Hyŏng-sŏp, the founder in 1966 of the Korean Institute of Science and Technology, which became the hub of technological development in South Korea.[60] Whereas the elite MoF relied on its internal experts and the new EPB recruited its personnel from other ministries, the MCI was reborn through an infusion of new blood from society.

Moreover, unlike the MoF and the EPB, the MCI was headed by a major general, which made the ministry more receptive to the innovative ideas developed by the South Korean armed forces since the Korean War. Chŏng led the MCI in a strictly military style. The MCI minister made every MCI bureaucrat above the rank of section chief undertake a compulsory "thought training" program for a week at the Korea Military Graduate School and take a written test upon completion of the program. The performance was assessed by Chŏng's military aides. A marine colonel in full gear, wearing a pistol, watched over the MCI bureaucrats' day-to-day conduct, including after working hours, with the power to dismiss anyone found to be unworthy of revolutionary tasks. Even going to a bar could risk one's job. Chŏng also appointed many young military officers to lead or staff state-owned and MCI-controlled industry organizations. In his memoirs, Chŏng recalls that he appointed "capable officers" from the army, navy, air force, and marine corps as heads of all MCI-controlled industry organizations. He believed that military officers assigned to these new positions were more capable than civilians in carrying out his agenda, such as the maintenance of probity and the reformulation of industry goals in accordance with the "soldier's spirit."[61]

Although Chŏng Nae-hyŏk was not a member of the original core group of the coup, he was hand-picked by Park as the MCI minister for his reputation in the armed forces as being incorruptible and extremely capable. Park entrusted Chŏng with the crucial task of comprehensively reforming South Korea's electric power industry, which the U.S. Task Force on Korea had listed in its report of June 5, 1961, as one of the major economic problems that had faced the Chang Myŏn government. The task force recommended that the U.S. government urge South Korean authorities to take "essential steps to correct the present financial insolvency of Korean power companies . . . including a further rate increase, merger of the power companies to effect savings, and establishment of an independent rate commission."[62] Thus the United States advised the military junta that U.S. aid, especially for fiscal year 1962—which the task force estimated as reaching $282.5 million for economic assistance, $120 million for supporting assistance, and $86 million for a Food for Peace Program— would be provided on the condition that the South Korean power companies were overhauled.[63] The urgency of reform made Chŏng restructure the power industry in the fashion of a military combat operation. The MCI minister replaced the heads of the three electric companies and their eight affiliated companies with military officers on active duty.[64] By June 8, 1961, the electric companies had cut a total of 1,654 personnel after dismantling labor unions in each of the companies. Against this inefficient over-crowded industry, Chŏng acted as a surgeon, operating with the belief that "everything was possible under the revolutionary military junta."[65] On June 23, 1961, the SCNR legislated the establishment of the Korea Electric Company, which merged two distributors—Kyŏngsŏng and Namsŏn Electric companies—with Chosŏn Electric Company. Major General Pak Yong-jun, commander of the army's Ninth Division, was appointed the chairman of the new company. It had taken just one month for Minister Chŏng to complete the restructuring, a task that civilian governments since 1951 had not been able to accomplish.[66]

Park's Leap toward the Presidency

The KCIA's withdrawal from economic policymaking after mid-1962 did not mean that Kim Chong-p'il's radius of activities dramatically shrank. Although Kim became a political burden for Park after the failed currency conversion reform,[67] Park needed Kim's talents more than ever to pursue his own political ambitions, because the date for the transfer of power to civilians was rapidly approaching. No one in the mainstream faction could match Kim Chong-p'il in strategic thinking, vision, and organizational skill. The Park–Kim Chong-p'il axis was becoming a politically risky alliance, but it still remained a highly effective mechanism for consolidating Park's leadership position. Consequently, from the summer of 1962 onward Kim Chong-p'il was given the task of clandestinely (and illegally) organizing a new ruling Democratic Republican Party (DRP), under the pretext of establishing an Association of Comrades for National Reconstruction. In the context of the junta's outlawing of all political activities, the organization of the DRP meant that Park got a head start on preparations for the upcoming electoral contest.

Once the financial crisis triggered by the currency conversion reform was under control, Park shifted his attention to the transfer of power to an elected civilian government, which he officially announced on December 27, 1962, the day after the announcement of a newly revised national constitution. By then, the military junta thought that it had achieved its initial objective of rebuilding the state bureaucracy into a military-style organization, as well as laying the organizational basis of the DRP. Park believed he was ready to pursue his ultimate goal of becoming the president through competitive elections with the help of both state and party apparatus. Just as Park declared his intention to join the election, other coup leaders, especially the young colonels, made public their ambition to become the pillars of any future "civilian" government.

The announcement of Park's candidacy and the revelation of the organization of the DRP provoked an intense power struggle within the SCNR between the young "radical" colonels of the Kim Chong-p'il–led and KCIA-backed mainstream faction, on the one hand, and the "moderate" senior generals of the nonmainstream faction, on the other. Ironically, the final stage of power consolidation begun with the launching of the DRP was imploding the military junta from within by causing the nonmainstream faction to fear its exclusion from what they thought was destined to become the center of power in the soon-to-be-launched Third Republic.

In the face of opposition on multiple political fronts, Kim Chong-p'il was a sitting duck. The exposure of his political sins provided his opponents with many opportunities to strike back. First, there was the issue of illegally organizing the DRP through the KCIA-initiated "Operation Victory." At stake was the control of power after the transition to electoral politics, prompting the diverse factions of Kim Tong-ha, Kim Chae-ch'un, and others of the nonmainstream to fight back vigorously to snatch away the DRP from young colonels of Kim Chong-p'il's group. Second, Kim Chong-p'il was also condemned for his controversial negotiations with Japanese foreign minister Ohira Masayoshi on the issue of normalization of relations,[68] which generals of the nonmainstream used to criticize Kim Chong-p'il as a corrupt, power-hungry politician, ready to pursue a "humiliating diplomacy" and even sell out his country to realize his ambitions for power. Third, the KCIA-initiated a political fund-raising campaign for the DRP that snowballed into the "Four Scandals," damaging the credibility of Kim Chong-p'il even more. He was accused of rigging the Seoul stock exchange; of permitting duty-free imports of Japanese Datsun automobiles for resale in the South Korean market at double the import price under the name "Saenara" (New Country); of authorizing the duty-free importation of 880 pinball machines from Japan; and of illicitly authorizing the construction of a Walker Hill holiday resort aimed at attracting

U.S. GIs stationed in South Korea—all with the goal of acquiring operational funds for the DRP.[69]

Tensions exploded in January 1963, when Major General Kim Tong-ha of the marine corps reserves—also the chairman of the SCNR's Foreign Affairs and National Defense Subcommittee—joined several other moderate SCNR members in openly refusing to become members of the newly proposed DRP.[70] Kim Tong-ha was supported by military officers of the marine corps and the natives of Hamkyŏng provinces. As part of the nonmainstream faction, they looked at the DRP as nothing but "Kim Chong-p'il's private party."

Former prime minister Song Yo-ch'an also publicly demanded Park's resignation on January 7, 1963, declaring that "the core members of the military revolution should not participate in the future civilian-led government. If they do, there will be permanent [military] rule."[71] On January 16, even Yu Wŏn-sik, now dissatisfied with his marginalization from the center of power after the failed currency conversion reform, publicly declared that the DRP was "a political party that belonged to the Kim Chong-p'il faction and thus does not hold majority support."[72] The opposition within the SCNR reached a critical point when Commander Kim Chae-ch'un of the army's powerful Counter Intelligence Corps, Yu Yang-su, chairman of the SCNR's Finance and Economy Subcommittee, and defense minister Pak Pyŏng-gwŏn joined the chiefs of staff of the four military services in demanding Park's withdrawal of his candidacy in the forthcoming presidential election. They also demanded the removal of Kim Chong-p'il from the DRP. To paralyze the mainstream faction, they also urged Park to send Kim abroad at once and keep him in "exile" until the elections were held.

Although Park denied any knowledge of Kim Chong-p'il's clandestine preparations to establish the DRP, everyone thought that Park knew of Kim's activities from the very beginning and was wholly supportive of the DRP project.[73] In the face of mounting opposition, Park pursued a two-track response. First, he skillfully distanced himself from taking any blame for the currency conversion reform, the Four Scandals, and the Kim-Ohira memorandum on South Korean–Japanese normalization of relations by making Kim Chong-p'il take responsibility for the fiascos, as well as moving to cut Kim loose, albeit in a highly measured manner.[74] On February 25, 1963, Kim was forced to take his first exile abroad after initially refusing Park's advice. In less than a month, Kim had slid from his position as second-in-charge of the military junta to a man in exile and from Park's most trusted and astute lieutenant to scapegoat for all the illicit activities of the junta. Moreover, Kim's exile did not hurt Park's power position, because by then Park had laid the groundwork for his presidential candidacy. On the contrary, Kim's disgrace helped Park's consolidation of power, because Kim had by then grown into a politician of national stature.

Second, just as Park had chosen the strategy of purge to deal with the obstacle of Chang To-yŏng and his supporters from the P'yŏngan region in July 1961, Park again opted for a crackdown. From January to March 1963, the Park–Kim Chong-p'il axis carried out a total of eleven purges. The climax came in March, when Kim Tong-ha, Colonel Pak Im-hang, a moderate member of the SCNR, and Provost Officer Yi Kyu-gwang were arrested on the charge of plotting a counterrevolution. This incident, known as the "Alaska Operation" because of the geographical remoteness of Kim Tong-ha's native Hamgyŏng region, came to be the final blow for what remained of the Northern faction that had dominated the leadership of the South Korean armed forces since its establishment in the 1945–1948 period. The northwestern part of the faction had been purged with the arrest of Chang To-yŏng in July 1961. The remaining northeastern part was dismantled with the purge of Kim Tong-ha in March 1963.[75] A well-seasoned survivor with an exceptional ability to think strategically and move swiftly, Park had transformed the crisis into an opportunity for power consolidation.

Personal ambitions matter. The military coup of May 16, 1961, was Park's third or fourth attempt to seize power by force.[76] Park himself said that he wanted revolution or death, nothing in between.[77] He was driven by his desire for power, but he also sought power not only for its own sake but also for his vision of national reconstruction.

Ironically, however, for such a visionary man, Park lacked a concrete plan of action on the issue of national reconstruction when he launched the military coup. The junta's multiple reforms for state building, as a step toward national revolution, were without clear objectives, strategies, or defined plans. Lacking any grand strategies, the junta necessarily zigzagged from the day of the military coup, imprisoning the *chaebol* owners, only to release them to seek their cooperation in the first Five-Year Economic Development Plan; frequently replacing economic ministers and then making a U-turn to favor the rise of civilian technocrats; and imposing the currency conversion reform, only to rescind it within a few weeks. The revisions of the first FYEDP's gross domestic product target goals after a year and a half also illustrate the absence of any master plan. Many of the reform programs were drawn up by Kim Chong-p'il and his KCIA without internal consistency. They even undermined the reform programs initiated by the SCNR. As a whole, the junta's reform programs had no central coordination, not only because there were multiple centers of power competing for political hegemony, but also because the junta seized power without an agreed-upon programmatic plan.

Nevertheless, what is important is that Park zigzagged in strategy, but not in overall policy priorities. And it is in this sense that the personal ambitions of Park mattered for the fate of Park, the junta, and the country. The central issue for Park was economic development, and he linked this issue with the issue of state building through administrative reform. This was itself a great leap forward for the country. First, because the goal was economic development, Park zigzagged but also moved forward incrementally, learning through the policy failures of the 1961–1963 period what the goal of economic modernization entailed and how that goal could be achieved. Through a process of trial and error, he learned what not to do. Second, through the zigzags of economic policy, there emerged a set of institutions that were to make positive contributions to national reconstruction and economic modernization, once Park consolidated power and readjusted his goals and strategies from a position of political strength after 1963.

The swift changes in policy that lay ahead in 1964 were to show that Park was a quick learner regarding the management of both political power and economic issues. The junta years were a bridge to Park's new leadership style. During the military junta, Park was prepared to do whatever was necessary, including the purge of his own co-revolutionaries and risking economic destabilization, if his power was on the line. Sheer ruthlessness was enough for Park to "remake" himself to maintain his control over politics, and he demanded the same degree of commitment from his subordinates and his countrymen. A sea change had begun in South Korean society, with the people barely realizing that the road to a genuine revolution had commenced, with Park at the forefront.

PART II

POLITICS

CHAPTER FOUR

Modernization Strategy:
Ideas and Influences

Chung-in Moon and Byung-joon Jun

CERTAINLY, Park Chung Hee was a man of action. However, unlike the image portrayed by many historians, he was also a man of ideas and what he believed mattered greatly for South Korea. He mixed the Japanese ethos of top-down mobilization and the U.S. ideas of technocracy with Korean nationalism in most un-Japanese and un-American ways to clear the way for economic growth. As a leader, Park shared the spirit of the Japanese Meiji revolutionaries, Young Turks, and Bismarckian Germans, in which the state commanded the market to expedite the process of development,[1] as opposed to the Anglo-American version of modernization framed around market forces and evolutionary processes, but the way Park combined the ideas of statism, mercantilism, corporatism, and U.S. liberalism were distinctly his own. The new strategies and policies were not imposed from the outside; they were the product of ideologies, images, and information embedded in the inner world of Park Chung Hee. It is through these ideational dimensions that Park conceived, guided, and drove all of South Korea's modernization in the 1960s and 1970s.

On the economic front, Park adopted a strategy of economic nationalism that combined import protection, industrial policy, and export promotion to transform infant industries into internationally competitive engines of growth. To clear away societal obstacles and mobilize scarce resources for this dirigiste path to economic development, his political strategy centered on a guided democracy and state corporatism in which both civil society and political society were reorganized, controlled, and orchestrated by the state for the sake of efficiency, stability, and regime security. His social modernization strategy supplemented his economic and political strategies by making the South Korean people the targets of spiritual reform and resource mobilization by the state. Civil society was reorganized and mobilized for national harmony and economic prosperity along the military ideals of order, discipline, and collectivism. These three strategies of economic nationalism, guided democracy, and corporatist social mobilization made Park's modernization a classic and yet distinctive example of "revolution from above," tapping what Alexander Gerschenkron once termed the "advantages of historical backwardness" to beat the developed countries in the international marketplace and catch up on modernization.

To be sure, Park's threefold modernization strategies were reactive actions to cope with South Korea's state of underdevelopment. His choice of goals and strategies was also constrained by dominant societal interests, underlying coalitional dynamics and state-society power structures. On the one hand, Park, like Syngman Rhee and Chang Myŏn before him, faced a situation in which his country desperately needed a leader to preserve national security in the face of North Korean threats, ensure economic prosperity and welfare, and create a viable political system.[2] But such mandates did not in themselves decide the content of Park's approach to modernization. Nor were societal groups and their coalitional dynamics accountable for his choice of strategy. They shaped the range of strategic options, but not his choices within that range of options. Through his extreme concentration of power in the South Korean imperial presidency, Park was the one who defined policy agendas, shaped the social and political terrain, and altered South Korea's mode of interaction with global markets though the formation of a new coalition that consisted of the state, big business, academic technocrats, and small farmers at the expense of labor.

Throughout his eighteen years of rule, Park was the man on the commanding heights. External and internal constraints on his political maneuvering were severe, but Park looked at these as obstacles to be overcome, managed, and eventually incorporated as parameters influencing policy. They rarely stopped him from pursuing his goal. They did reshape his actions, policies, and strategies, but not his end-point of *pukuk kangbyŏng* ("rich nation, strong army"). It is natural that within the context of an imperial presidency, Park's own personal preferences, ideas, and leadership style came to be reflected in the nature and direction of his modernization strategy. Without taking account of his willingness to take risks and his goal of transforming South Korea into a second Japan in his lifetime, for example, it is difficult to explain the lightning speed with which South Korea concentrated scarce resources in a few high-risk heavy and chemical industrialization (HCI) projects. What really mattered in bringing about a sudden economic takeoff in war-devastated South Korea were the ideational dimensions that shaped Park's cognitive beliefs. As many analysts have argued, ideas embedded in ideologies, information, and images not only guide leaders' choice of policy measures to deal with pending problems but also provide them with the capacity to indoctrinate and mobilize their domestic populace.[3] Indeed, leaders are predisposed to see what they want to see. Their thoughts, policy preferences, and strategic choices are bounded by their own ontological locus. This ideational complex is not a mere summation of the individual's personality traits. It has rather a complex gestalt with its own structure and organization that must essentially be seen as a system.[4]

Park's ideational structure was complex, having a triple layer of ideas and images that were sometimes complementary and at other times contradictory. Although his association with Japan had shaped the foundations of his modernization strategy, Korean nationalism served as his primary driving force. The American factor also became a constant source of opportunities and constraints, critically conditioning the dynamics of his modernization strategy.

A Japanese Identity

Park Chung Hee, who became the "Japanese" Takagi Masao during the colonial period, was deeply influenced by Japanese colonial and military legacies.[5] Ambassador Okazaki Hisahiko lamented Park's death in 1979 as "the death of the last soldier of Imperial Japan."[6] This was not an exaggeration. Born under Japanese colonial rule, he received a Japanese education throughout his youth, absorbing imperial educational doctrines that glorified the Japanese emperor and indoctrinated the Koreans of his generation to be loyal imperial subjects.[7] Teaching only briefly, he changed careers and spent two years at the Manchurian Xinjing Officers School, which trained officers for the Manchukuo army, largely Chinese in both its officer corps and its ranks. As one of the top students in his class, he spent the last two of his four academy years at the prestigious Japanese Military Academy (JMA) in Zama, as part of a Manchukuo *ryugakuseo* class (the eleventh) that graduated with the fifty-seventh class of the JMA in 1944.[8] Park was proud of being a graduate of the academy and championed its spirit of discipline, leadership, and loyalty.[9] His Japanese education shaped his personality and his Weltanschauung. He emphasized attention to detail, precision, and decisiveness, and preached the value of self-sacrifice for the nation. Park was thoroughly militaristic in mentality, in the fashion of Japan of the 1930s and early 1940s.[10]

Park's Japanese identity influenced his modernization strategy in three critical ways. First is his admiration of the Meiji Restoration (1867/68–1912) and his incorporation into his modernization program of that era's nationalist ideological tenets, including *fukoku kyohei* ("rich nation, strong army") and *shokusan kogyo* ("production promotion").[11] The rise of a modernizing elite, the dissolution of old power bases, and bringing military force and industrial production under the guidance of the state, all of which were the central traits of the Meiji Restoration, became the references for Park's political and economic governance. The slogans of Park's modernization project echoed those of the Meiji Restoration. The South Korean state called for "production promotion, exports, and construction," urged "construction on the one hand and national defense on the other," and preached the virtue of "frugality, hard work, and saving."[12] When Park visited Japan in 1961, he told leaders Kishi Nobusuke, Ishii Mitsujirō, and Kosaka Zentaro of the impact of the Meiji Restoration on his thinking. "I am pushing for the modernization of my country as the modernizing elite of the Meiji Restoration did," Park said, and noted that he was "studying the history of the Meiji Restoration in that context . . . I am a graduate of the Japanese Imperial Military Academy, and I still believe that Japanese education is the best way to cultivate a strong army."[13]

Park's obsession with "rich nation" and "strong army" is evident in his selection of heavy and chemical industries as the strategic sectors that would pull South Korea out of economic backwardness and military vulnerability. He once told Kim Chŏng-ryŏm, then minister of commerce and industry, that "the power that enabled Japan to declare the Pacific War came from steel mills. Japan could produce tanks, cannons, and naval vessels because it had steel mills."[14] Believing in the power of steel, Park hurriedly designated the construction of an integrated steel mill as a priority project as early as 1962, in the formulation of the first Five-Year Economic Development Plan (FYEDP), despite U.S. reservations about the financial feasibility and economic viability of such a goal.[15] In July 1967, again in the face of criticism by the United States and the World Bank, Park repeated his identification of the steel industry as a strategic sector in the second FYEDP.[16]

The integrated steel mill project was a precursor to and an essential part of the 1970s' HCI drive, the mainstay of Park's economic modernization plans. His desire to pursue HCI thus began in the early 1960s, but was postponed until the promulgation of the authoritarian *yushin* constitution in 1972 because of the lack of foreign capital and technology and the limited state capacity for forced saving. The idea of HCI was strongly influenced by Park's Japanese ethos as well as by economic theories of unbalanced growth that were then prevalent. U.S. officials, civilian academics, and initially even the South Korean economic bureaucracy opposed HCI as a premature, risky, and abrupt shift of economic strategy, but Park, aware of the Japanese precedent, pursued the "big push" for HCI in the belief that it would enhance national security through its forward and backward linkages with the defense industry. The perceived security benefits outweighed the costs of weakening the comparative advantage of South Korea's labor-intensive export sectors.[17] Moreover, in his view, the heavy and chemical industries constituted the most effective long-term measure to ensure national wealth and military strength simultaneously. The costs were short term and the benefits long term, making Park perceive his role as asking his people to make the necessary sacrifices for the future of South Korea.

When President Richard M. Nixon declared his Guam Doctrine in 1969 to initiate U.S. military disengagement from Asia, Park's fear of the Americans' departure pushed him to initiate an aggressive HCI drive to develop a defense industry by 1973. For Park, it was a moment of realizing his lifetime goal of military self-help and strong defense. When Park received Fujino Chujiro, then president of the Mitsubishi General Trading Company, in February 1965, he recollected his experience under Japanese colonial rule: "While I was attending the Japanese Military Academy, I had a chance to visit Mitsubishi Heavy Machinery. I was deeply impressed by the production of naval vessels and submarines."[18] Park knew of the Japanese war economy of the 1940s and emulated its system of total mobilization.[19] The strong bureaucracy, primacy of production, strategic state intervention in markets, bureaucratic control over the financial sector, and *zaibatsu* corporate governance structures of Japan's wartime economic system resurfaced during Park's reign, albeit with innovations to fit the South Korean context.

Second, Japanese militarism left a lasting impact on the formation of Park's political modernization. His military coup d'état of May 1961 could itself be seen as emulating a series of military coups that shocked Japan during the Showa period of the 1930s. Although Park exalted the Meiji Restoration, the Japan he knew and emulated was that of the Showa period,[20] driven by the nationalist right-wing elements of the Japanese armed forces who sought to reestablish the authority of the imperial system and replace allegedly incompetent civilian party politics with military leadership. He particularly praised the patriotism, nationalism, and militarism of the officers who staged the February 26 Incident, an attempted coup led by ultranationalists in the Japanese imperial army in 1936.[21] As Gregory Henderson has argued, Park and his followers defined their military coup, like the ones in Japan, as an effort to save the nation from corrupt and incompetent civilian political factions and to create a new nation of wealth and strength through state power.[22]

The New Community Movement, part of Park's agricultural modernization, was also a product of learning from Japan of the 1930s. During the militarist era, the Japanese colonial government implemented a Village Promotion Policy based on the dense network of mass organizations (*yokusankai*) that it had created for the purposes of political control and mobilization. Much of this colonial experience was revived in Park's New Community Movement to make people in the countryside join his larger modernization drive.[23]

Third, Park and his staff also continued to learn from the trajectory of Japan's economic development in the postwar period. Yi Tong-wŏn, who served Park as chief of staff (1962–1964) and foreign minister (1964–1966), reports in his memoir of Park's appreciation of the Japanese model:

> *Yi:* Your Excellency, please don't worry! There will be a way out of this. Look at Great Britain! Like us, its geographic size is small, and its resource endowment is poor. Yet they conquered the world . . .
> *Park:* Why should we learn from a far away country like Great Britain? We have lots to learn from Japan, which is near to us.[24]

Yi Tong-wŏn describes Park as a man "busy studying Japan. He frequently took clippings from Japanese newspapers and read *The History of the Japanese Economy* until midnight. A great portion of Park's modernization policy emerged from the emulation of Japan. He compared South Korea's economic situation to that of Japan all the time, even through the 1970s."[25] The identification of Japan as a valuable source to learn from and imitate also meant that it was the target to catch up with and even surpass. The respect for Japan's accomplishments coexisted with Park's distrust of and enmity toward Japan. The two were not contradictory. They were different sides of the same coin.

South Korea's heavy and chemical industrialization plan exemplifies postwar Japan's influence on Park's thinking. The plan traced the origins of Japan's transformation into an economic superpower to its HCI-centered Long-Term Economic Plan promulgated in 1957. The strategy was judged as having enabled Japan to raise exports to the level of $10 billion within ten years by creating new frontiers of industrial growth.[26] The

Japanese experience was South Korea's road map for HCI in the 1970s, but even in the previous decade South Korea had experimented with its neighbor's ideas. The Machinery Industry Promotion Act, drawn up by South Korea's Ministry of Commerce and Industry (MCI) and legislated by the National Assembly in 1967, was in large part a replica of Japan's Temporary Measures to Promote the Machinery Industry introduced in 1956. Differences between the two laws were minor. South Korea's Electronics Industry Promotion Act (1969) shows an even greater similarity to Japan's Temporary Measure to Promote the Electronics Industry (1957).

The Park regime also introduced the concept of a general trading company *(shogo shosha)* borrowed from Japan. In 1972, Prime Minister Kim Chong-p'il invited Sejima Ryuzo, then vice president of Ito Chu Company and former staff officer of the Japanese army in Manchuria, to propose the establishment of a general trading company (GTC). The idea of establishing GTCs to coordinate the export drive and realize economies of scale in trade was circulated within the Ministry of Commerce and Industry (MCI) and other ministries for deliberation until MCI minister Yi Nak-sŏn, a member of the 1961 coup coalition and a confidant of Park during the junta years, reported to Park in January 1975 that the MCI was ready to propose the enactment of a law to establish GTCs. The idea was to promote export growth by selecting a few *chaebol* as the center for the country's exports and concentrating resources behind their conglomeration into export giants. Park's endorsement quickly followed, making the GTC operational that same year.

Compared with the Japanese GTC system, the South Korean model placed a greater emphasis on export growth and focused more on the exploitation of linkages between manufacturing and trading, but the idea of developing a few national champions to exploit economies of scale in global marketing; bringing small- and medium-sized exporters and importers under the umbrella of giant trading houses to facilitate the logistics of information sharing, quality control, and production coordination; and concentrating the channels of dialogue and cooperation within the state bureaucracy was Japanese.[27] At the same time, South Korea did not stop at imitation, but innovated, creating a GTC system that was more dependent on state support for survival, more hierarchical in organization, and more selective in the choice of strategic merchandise under the less favorable economic conditions that South Korea faced.

The anatomy of Park's modernization strategy demonstrates the depth of Japan's influence on him. The Japanese ethos, policy models, and institutions were instrumental in crafting the ideational foundations of Park's economic, political, and social modernization policies and goals. Moreover, learning occurred throughout his lifetime. The postwar Japanese ideas of industrial policy, administrative guidance, and GTCs shaped his decisions regarding modernization strategy and its institutional vehicles after his seizure of power in 1961. The scope of learning widened and its speed accelerated with the diplomatic normalization of relations with Japan in 1965 and the launching of heavy and chemical industrialization in 1973, but the most fundamental elements of his cognitive map—beliefs, norms, and values—were closely related to Japan of the 1930s, rather than to the pacifist and democratic postwar Japan. Nationalism, statism, and military values constituted his ethos.

Whereas imperial Japan constructed his personality, postwar Japan provided Park with instrumental ideas on how to ensure industrial and managerial efficiency, maximize the effect of state intervention on growth, and mobilize society for modernization. Undergirding this process of learning was the thick network of Japanese advisors that Park built up through his lifetime.

Industrializing Nationalism

Park was a self-proclaimed nationalist.[28] In spite of, or because of, this self-identification, his nationalist identity became a subject of intense political debate.[29] The conservatives of the post-Park period came to admire him as a true nationalist who had succeeded in establishing a new national pride and identity out of the shackles of defeatism, war, and poverty, whereas the liberal and radical intelligentsia branded him a betrayer of the ideals of democracy, national unification, and sovereignty that made up the progressive version of Korean nationalism.[30] Still others have emphasized his transformation over time from a soldier-revolutionary on the nationalist path to modernization during the early part of military rule to a proponent of "dependent development."[31] Sociologist Ko Yŏng-bok writes:

> Was [Park] a nationalist? The fact that he was a son of a poor farmer and that he experienced national discrimination under Japanese colonialism may well suffice to have made him a nationalist. Ill-treatment of Park by the American military authorities during his military career and the American government's overt pressures during the military coup could have bred nationalist sentiments in him. In light of all this, it seems quite natural for him to adopt nationalist democracy as his revolutionary ideology. But having realized the formidable barriers to the nationalist path to industrialization, his nationalism receded, and he eventually pursued a dependent capitalist path to industrialization.[32]

Implicit in Ko Yŏng-bok's appraisal is that Park was a pragmatist who adapted his nationalist ideals of modernization to the realities of South Korea.[33] The substance of Park's nationalism was not a constant, but a variable changing over time. For him, nationalism was an ideological construct with which to expedite economic modernization, to consolidate his fragile political power, and to mobilize civil society to fulfill his vision of transforming South Korea into an industrial powerhouse. It is this instrumental ideology of industrializing nationalism that persisted from the military coup in 1961 to his unexpected death in 1979.

Park ascribed what he saw as the mediocrity of five thousand years of Korean history to the lack of internal cohesion that continually invited foreign invasion, the loss of national identity, and the rise of flunkeyism as well as the lack of innovation in economic life and the resulting vicious circle of poverty and underdevelopment. Park's total negation of Korean history was as much a calculated political move as an outburst of nationalist ideological beliefs. The legitimization of his 1961 coup depended on his ability to put South Korea's past in the most unfavorable light possible and to project the future as one of "rich nation, strong army." The more effective Park was in projecting the image of a leader who had brought about this radical break in Korean history, the greater his mandate to rule the country.[34]

However, by 1966, if not earlier, Park began to realign his view. In his 1966 state of the union speech, Park argued that "in order to establish a firm national identity and to overcome social apathy, [South Korea] should reaffirm the superior legacies of [its] culture and tradition and foster the creation of a new culture on the basis of these legacies."[35] In his 1971 book *The Potential Power of Our Nation*, Park claimed that South Korea was different from other newly independent countries because it possessed rich historical and cultural legacies. "I am proud that for two thousand years prior to the late nineteenth century," Park wrote, "our history was the history of endless resistance to foreign invasion and the history of originality and creativity."[36]

With his rediscovery of Korea's national identity, Park began large public works programs to preserve and restore cultural relics and historical sites, and also sought to revive and re-create national myths, symbols, and ritual through the glorification of national heroes, including Admiral Yi Sun-sin (1545–1598) and King Sejong (1397–1450).[37] In 1968 Park issued the National Educational Charter, which defined "national revival" as the historical mission of his time. "Fostering national spirit" became the goal of modernization. The earlier defeatism disappeared. In its place was now the conservative version of an assertive nationalism that aimed to mobilize society to put forth the necessary effort to build up heavy and chemical industries. Park's plans derived not only from confidence built up during his country's recent high economic growth but also from a sense of crisis precipitated by the U.S. desire for military disengagement from East Asia and the erosion of alliance ties with the United States amid disputes over human rights in South Korea and its KCIA-orchestrated illegal lobbying in Washington. Park's political ambition to prepare for and then consolidate his authoritarian *yushin* regime also factored into his decision to invoke nationalism.

In the mid-1970s Park's ideological position underwent another metamorphosis. Throughout the 1960s, he had persistently condemned the Confucian tradition as the root cause of factionalism, formalism, flunkeyism, and impractical discourse, all of which he believed "deformed" political development, caused social stagnation, and retarded progress in science and technology.[38] In 1969, to weed out the Confucian tradition, he had even promulgated new family ritual codes that severely restricted South Koreans' practice of Confucian rituals. Reversing himself in 1977, Park asserted that the "tradition of loyalty and filial piety [was] rooted in love of, and dedication to, the community to which one belongs. The state [was] a larger community and, the family [was] a smaller community of people's life. Love toward [the] two communities was identical in substance."[39] To put the tradition on a legitimate footing, moreover, he negated the then prevalent dichotomous view of tradition and modernity as opposites and argued that "traditional thoughts and attitudes, mistakenly viewed as barriers to modernization, not only [serve] as the catalyst of modernization, but also [are] the source of national power that [propel] the process of modernization in the direction we desire."[40]

Park thus became a born-again Confucian, instructing the Ministry of Education to incorporate the traditions of loyalty and filial piety into the school curricula in 1977. The Academy of Korean Studies, modeled after the Academia Sinica of Taiwan, was established in 1978 to serve as the intellectual infrastructure for research in Korean studies and the dissemination of traditional values and historical ideas throughout society. The turn to Confucian values contradicted Park's past actions in 1961, but that past was now distant in the public's memory. To people of the late 1970s, Park was not a rebel with a vision of change, but the leader of mainstream society, his power successfully consolidated and secure in his role as the conservative guard of the *yushin* regime. To the dissident intelligentsia, he was the author of a repressive regime, to be overthrown by sporadic but intense popular protests. To radical religious activists and union organizers, he was in addition responsible for breaking up South Korea's homogeneity through the reproduction of class tensions and contradictions in the process of dependent development. Park wished to tame this unruly political and social terrain by invoking the traditional values of loyalty and filial piety as the Japanese military had in the 1930s.

Park's nationalist template therefore varied over time, changing as the domestic and external environments altered. Nevertheless, nationalism remained a consistent ideological theme that wove his different periods of rule into one integrated whole of top-down modernization. The nationalist ethos was what drove his modernization drive and shaped the nature and scope of his strategy. Given the concentration of power in the imperial presidency and the lack of countervailing power in society, Park's personality, value system, and leadership style had a visible impact in the political arena. For Park, U.S.-style liberal democracy encouraged social fragmentation and political strife. He sought a political system where unity, harmony, and sacrifice would prevail. The *yushin* system, established in defiance of democratic procedures, emulated the ideal of an institutionalized organic state corporatism and embodied Park's conservative nationalist political vision of single-mindedly pursuing economic growth. The vision of corporatist governance became one of the major themes in Park's speeches and writings in the late 1970s: "We are different from the West that pits the individual against the state. For us, the individual and the country [as a whole] are integral parts of a harmonious order . . . Our history is littered with good examples of national heroes who sacrificed personal interests for national interests . . . This is the potential power of our nation that has led our history."[41]

It is this conception of the "individual" and the "nation" that inspired the construction of Park's corporatist political template. The nation was greater than the mere sum of the individuals that constituted it. The individual's existence derived its raison d'être from its relationship to others and to the nation. To borrow an Aristotelian analogy, Park saw the nation as the "matter," and the state as the "form." "The nation is forever," Park declared, "[but] the life of the nation can be developed and grown only through the state. The ultimate goal of the [state], as the nurturer of our nation, is national unification and national renaissance."[42] With these words, Park embraced the Hegelian-like ethos that championed the virtues of the absolute state. It was this statist orientation with which Park organized, co-opted, and controlled civil society. In the name of the state and the nation, the *yushin* regime created tight corporatist networks of capital, labor, and farmers for a top-down mobilization led by the state that excluded and penalized any social forces that resisted. The dissident intelligentsia, coupled with religious activists, labor organizers, and opposition politicians, were the targets of exclusion, while Park formed a developmentalist coalition by co-opting and rewarding state bureaucrats, big business, small farmers, and mainstream intelligentsia in the 1970s.[43]

Nationalist ideology was also pronounced in the economic domain. Park conceived modernization mainly in terms of economic development, to be achieved on the basis of self-reliance and self-help.[44] With economic self-help, South Korea could reduce its dependence on the United States, catch up with North Korea and eventually even Japan, and enhance national power. Park intended to achieve this prerequisite of national survival, prosperity, and prestige by engineering the mercantilist strategy of export promotion and the economic nationalist path to heavy and chemical industrialization. As Alice H. Amsden and Robert Wade have correctly observed, even South Korea's transition to an outward-looking export strategy on the basis of economic stabilization and market liberalization between 1963 and 1966[45] was driven by Park's mercantile ethos, goals, and practices.[46] In 1967, South Korea took critical measures to liberalize its trade regime by changing its trade protectionist system from the "positive list system" to the "negative list system." Nonetheless, its protectionist barriers remained high, so that its import-liberalization ratio stood at 61.3 percent in 1978, far below that of Japan, which rose from 40 percent in 1960 to 90 percent in 1969, and even lower than the import-liberalization ratio of Taiwan, which hit 90 percent by the mid-1970s.[47]

The persistence of protectionism in spite of stabilization, liberalization, and export promotion was attributed in part to the continuing practice of import-substitution industrialization (ISI). Contrary to orthodox economic theory, the turn to export promotion did not end ISI in South Korea. On the contrary, Park saw the two as complementary, because given the lack of domestic demand and the underdevelopment of forwardly- and backwardly-linked industries, any ISI project had to be pursued as a project of export promotion and vice versa from the very start. The *yushin* regime allocated credit first to the heavy and chemical industries as targets of both export promotion and import substitution. While the average rate of real protection stood at 2.3 percent for all industries in 1978, the heavy and chemical industries enjoyed a protection ratio of 16.4 percent. For the six industries designated as strategic sectors—steel, nonferrous metals, machinery, chemical, shipbuilding, and electronics—the real market protection ratio reached 35 percent.[48]

Park's pursuit of ISI was visible even in the heyday of liberalization. As the Ministry of Commerce and Industry prepared to move to the negative list system to get South Korea into the General Agreement on Tariffs and Trade, the Economic Planning Board seized the South Korean–Japanese talks on normalization as an opportunity to construct an integrated steel mill. Resisting Japan's insistence that South Korea use reparation funds for the importation of Japanese consumer goods, the EPB succeeded in allocating the funds to the construction of the Pohang Iron & Steel Company.[49] When the opportunity to pursue heavy and chemical industrialization outside the market arose, as it did in the case of the normalization talks, Park did not hesitate to seize it, regardless of the risks and costs. Economic nationalism and mercantilism were alive and well even as an export-led development strategy was launched in the mid-1960s.

Park's export-led growth strategy was driven by economic nationalism. What looked like a liberal turn to the global market was in essence illiberal in nature, conceptualized as South Korea's only way to ensure national survival and wealth, implemented from the top down by the state, and mixing protectionist and liberalization measures to trigger an economic takeoff. The export sectors were the primary beneficiaries of a wide range of policy incentives, including preferential allocation of subsidized credits; exemption of tariffs on raw materials, intermediate goods, and capital goods; and a variety of tax incentives, license privileges, technological aid, and infrastructural benefits such as the provision of information and industrial complexes.[50] In other words, except for the labor-intensive light manufacturing industries, the export competitiveness of many South Korean goods was an artificial construct of the dirigiste state, not a product of comparative advantage. The letter and spirit of reciprocity, one of the major underlying norms and principles of the liberal global trading regime of the postwar era, were more often violated than upheld in South Korea's pursuit of national wealth and strength, even in the case of export industries.

The success of state-led export growth depended critically on the availability of foreign capital. Even before the Foreign Capital Inducement Act was introduced in 1966, Park saw access to foreign capital and technology as the key to fostering economic development in a resource-poor country like South Korea. On the issue of foreign capital, Park was a pragmatist: "I don't care [what] the national origin of capital [is]. I welcome capital from the United States, West Germany, Italy, and other European countries. Even if it is Japanese capital, I don't care as long as it is used for the economic development of our country."[51] Nonetheless, welcoming foreign capital did not mean lifting regulatory measures. On the contrary, Park put in place a diverse array of restrictions and regulations, particularly on foreign direct investment, in order to nurture the *chaebol* into national champions and harness foreign capital for Park's goals of economic independence. A great chunk of industries was off limits to foreign direct investment under the positive list system until the early 1980s, and the local operation of foreign business was closely restricted. In addition to the restrictive laws, protectionist institutions, bureaucratic red tape, and the *chaebol* conglomerates' opposition to foreign competition, public hostility to foreign investment prevented foreign investors from even owning land.

Several factors accounted for the heavy regulation. First, Park personally preferred foreign loans to foreign direct investment, because of his emphasis on greater autonomy and independence in the management of the national economy.[52] He thought he could strategically allocate foreign loans to target sectors for the realization of his developmental objectives if the state underwrote foreign loans. At the same time, it was difficult to secure foreign manufacturers who were willing to invest directly in joint ventures that could someday become their competitors. Second, even if Park were receptive to the hosting of foreign direct investment, the inflow of foreign direct investment would have remained small, because of South Korea's poor resource endowment, limited domestic market, unstable domestic politics, and security vulnerability. Consequently much of the foreign direct investment South Korea had was confined to the relatively competitive light industries located in special free export zones. The enclave nature of foreign direct investment saved South Korea from overhauling its legal system and institutional infrastructure to accommodate the needs of outside investors, which would have obstructed the state from developing national champions. Finally, Park's pursuit of heavy and chemical industrialization through ISI created myriad infant industries that had an interest in preventing the economic bureaucracy from undertaking more assertive liberalization measures regarding foreign direct investment.

The political and social domains were deeply affected by Park's nationalism as well. To establish a system of mobilization that could back his economic strategy, Park constantly invoked nationalist ideology and organized mass organizations from the National Construction Corps to the Movement for National Reconstruction and the New Community Movement to the home reserve forces in a classic top-down fashion with the help of the powerful state bureaucracy. For Park, nationalism was both a consummate ideal, valued for itself, and an instrumental means of legitimization.[53] To separate the two and identify Park as either a true believer or a manipulator of nationalism fails to capture the spirit of his regime. Park was both, resulting in the deep penetration of the nationalist ethos into every aspect of his modernization strategy. Park's nationalist ideology proved to be very effective in expediting the process of industrialization. If the Japanese ethos helped him shape the contours of modernization, nationalism provided Park with the locomotive of socioeconomic mobilization and depoliticization for his authoritarian ways of modernization and industrialization.

Administrative Democracy

Park also identified the goal of modernization as "the reconstruction of sound democracy." By this, he meant building a system of political rule that fit in with South Korea's historical conditions:

> The history of the importation of [Western] democracy has been a failure. The failure was an unavoidable result of the 'direct import' of exogenous democracy without filtering [it] through reflections on our history and the context of our life. The 'closed morality' of the kinship-based family community has bred political factionalism centered on local, familial, and religious ties, leading to the failure of democratic politics. We can import a form of democracy, but not its contents . . . [It] is fortunate that we have come to realize the relevance of the 'Koreanization' of democracy. Democracy is predicated not on irresponsible liberty, but on self-regulating and disciplined liberty, and, therefore, it is necessary to include leadership and guidance in our concept of democracy.[54]

Identifying more with populism or corporatism than with pluralist, procedural democracy, Park thought any idea of democracy had to embrace three political concepts. The first of the three prerequisites was "administrative democracy," which set the ideal of political order and efficiency over democratic procedures and the rule of law.[55] Instead of going through due legislative processes, administrative democracy relied heavily on the state bureaucracy to steer the process of modernization. The bureaucratic state was the coordinator that disciplined, mobilized, and directed civil society to implement the goals and visions of the executive leadership. This guidance depended not only on bureaucratic competence and institutional inertia but also on bureaucratic loyalty to the national leadership.

Consequently, in order to ensure the uninterrupted and effective guidance of social forces, Park sought to insulate state bureaucrats from contending political and social legislative pressures and to provide them with wide discretionary powers. He believed it was acceptable to transcend, circumvent, and even break legal procedures—if necessary—to achieve collective goals. The readiness to compromise the law was most evident when he dealt with corruption and organized crime. While having lunch with his staff on June 8, 1972, Park quipped: "If you rely on the rule of law too much, you cannot get things done. Wiping out gangsters is a case in point. If you have important tasks to implement, don't be constrained by the law!" The *yushin* regime was the epitome of administrative democracy, eliminating the time-honored but also time-consuming, conflict-ridden, and legally cumbersome processes of liberal democracy in favor of quick administrative "fixes."[56]

Park intended to make the executive branch strong and the legislative and judiciary branches weak. He viewed elections as wasteful and conflictive and wanted to restrain interest groups from damaging collective interests.[57] He was not an apologist for his turn to authoritarian rule. On the contrary, in his eyes, only a strong, tough state could carry out the mandates of national security and economic development. When his vision of the political system provoked resistance in some quarters of society, he refused to compromise and instead tried to forge national consensus and unity through coercion, intimidation, and repression, if necessary. His belief in the state-corporatist path to modernization led him to fight political battles on multiple fronts with a diverse array of political forces and social groups until they eventually cost him his life and his *yushin* regime.

Second, for democracy to be authentic, it had to be "nationalist democracy" *(minjokchŏk minjujuŭi)*. During his presidential election campaign in 1967, Park stressed that nationalist democracy rested on the rejection of the foreign-dominated modern history of South Korea. "We still live under the legacies of the five-hundred-year-old flunkeyism of the Chosŏn dynasty and Japanese colonialism. Vestiges of premodern feudal elements are not yet wiped out. We should overcome these legacies by becoming an independent and self-reliant people. My nationalism is to adapt foreign ideas, thoughts, and political institutions to befit our own reality and tradition."[58] For Park, Korean tradition consisted of two parts, one that was to be rejected, particularly the legacies of feudalism and flunkeyism *(sadaejuŭi)*, and another, involving national unity and cohesion, patriotism, and resistance against foreign interference and domination, that needed to be nurtured and embraced.

Third, Park emphasized that democracy had to be "Korean" *(han'gukchŏk)* in character in order to ensure political modernization. He summed up the essence of "Korean democracy" in 1978: "It is natural that insomuch as people cherish and love democracy, they unite and fight against the enemy when they face apparent threats to democracy by reducing the waste of national power and inefficiency associated with internal conflict and discord. *They overcome the national crisis by favoring content and substance, not forms and procedures, as well as valuing efficiency, not competition and compromise.* It is they who have grown democracy . . . The October Yushin has offered a decisive momentum for democracy which dovetails with our historical situation and reality" (emphasis added).[59]

Park saw executive dominance as central to his vision of Korean democracy. He stated, "It is a common trend among contemporary democracies in which the executive branch takes leadership in coping with complex policy problems. After having gone through a series of social crises, democratic states have realized that checks and balances among the three branches of government are not absolute. On the contrary, such arrangements of power have become rather obsolete in resolving complex problems of modern governance. As a result, organic integration of state power has become intensified."[60] For Park, efficiency, executive dominance, and guided democracy were the core traits of good polity, a belief that profoundly shaped the nature of the political terrain while he was in control. Power was concentrated in his imperial presidency and there was a lack of countervailing powers in society. His concept of "Korean democracy," based on state bureaucratic power and driven by beliefs in national corporate unity, was thus fundamentally authoritarian in character. Administration replaced politics to forge national consensus and unity, and performance pushed ideology to the sidelines as the mode of legitimization. Park built up his political constituency by getting things done, and he fought off the opposition through a complex mix of coercion, intimidation, and cooptation.

Park's Korean democracy was intended to let the state bring about social modernization in a top-down fashion. Social modernization, Park believed, required two cardinal strategies, one aimed at the creation of a new citizenry through spiritual reform and rebirth, and the other focused on social mobilization. Park wanted his great legacy to be the transformation of the psyche of South Koreans from the "traditional" type, embodying self-defeatism, nihilism, and fatalism, to the "modern" type, made self-reliant and entrepreneurial through extensive education, training, and indoctrination.[61] Having lived through a century of imperial conquest, internal war, economic stagnation, and political instability, much of South Korean society shared Park's negative image of the initial state of the country when he took power. To a people who had known only defeat, Park preached a "can do" *(hamyŏn toenda)* spirit, creating a new social energy and readiness for upward mobility and new opportunities with the delivery of economic growth.[62]

The military played a pivotal role in bringing about the transformation of the South Korean male population. Compulsory conscription produced a reservoir of literate, well-trained, and disciplined manpower with experience in large-scale collective organizational activities, and this resource proved to be instrumental in the country's economic takeoff. In particular, organizational experience in the military helped enable South Koreans to create modern forms of state, business, and group organization and to coordinate large collective projects efficiently. Park's use of mobilizational techniques constituted a striking application of military expertise to social tasks. From the 1961 National Reconstruction Movement to the New Community Movement initiated in 1970, the state bureaucracy penetrated, reorganized, and mobilized civil society for the goals of spiritual rebirth, societal transformation, and economic development.[63]

U.S. Influence

Compared with the influences of the Japanese ethos and Korean nationalism, the U.S. factor was less salient in shaping Park's ideas and strategies regarding modernization. This was in part due to his personality and upbringing. He was fluent in Japanese, but not in English.[64] Reticent and shy, Park found it difficult to reach out to the American community in South Korea and nurture enduring ties with its members.[65] More important, he suffered a "Red complex" of his own, because his name came up in connection with investigations into communist cells within the South Korean army after World War II. U.S. military intelligence put him on its watch list throughout his military career. When Park was agitating for the purge of military officers suspected of corruption and political collaboration with the overthrown Syngman Rhee in 1960 and 1961, U.S. military authorities at various points suggested that the newly elected Chang Myŏn government discharge Park from active service for fear of his leftist ideology.[66] On May 18, 1961, two days after the coup d'état, Park attempted to clear his alleged affiliation with communists in person by meeting with James H. Hausman, who was in charge of U.S. military intelligence in South Korea.[67]

Moreover, like many generals of his generation, Park visited the United States for six months of military training, but his experience at the U.S. Artillery School at Fort Sill, Oklahoma, hardly made him comfortable with the United States. The language barrier, his age difference compared with that of his American colleagues, and his educational background in the elite Japanese Imperial Military Academy made his life at Fort Sill difficult.[68]

Encountering U.S. culture and people for the first time when he was in his early thirties, Park kept his distance from the United States and distrusted its intentions. His complex image of the United States is summarized in *The State, the Revolution, and I*:

> First, the United States should realize that Western-style democracy is not fit for the [South] Korean reality . . . Expecting [South] Korea to develop Western-style democracy is like a foolish father who expects his children to grow up as adults overnight. Second, I admire America's democratic ideals and ambition and appreciate its economic aid very highly. But it should not expect an Americanization of [South] Korean society through the leverage of economic aid . . . Third, U.S. military and economic assistance should be tailored to our needs. We trust American policy advice, but U.S. assistance should be used for rebuilding our economy, not for consumption. The United States should not only increase its aid, but also change its aid policy drastically.[69]

The passage shows Park's mixed image of the United States and its intentions. Park was aware of the importance of U.S. aid for South Korea's prosperity and security,[70] but he was critical of U.S. attempts to interfere in South Korean economics and politics on the basis of that aid. He wanted to go his own way and saw the United States as wanting to balance, realign, and constrain his own ideational fixation with the dirigiste state, HCI projects, and mobilization strategies that grew out of his deep identification with the Japanese ethos and Korean nationalism. The dynamics of Park's modernization were shaped by the dialectical interplay of these two competing Japanese–South Korean and American worldviews.

The impact of this interplay was visible from the moment Park seized power in 1961.[71] Were it not for subsequent diplomatic and economic U.S. pressure to transfer power to civilians by 1963, the military junta could have stayed in power longer by unilaterally delaying the timing of presidential elections. Park's later declaration of the *yushin* constitution in order to govern South Korea with an iron fist for the rest of his life provoked the United States to seek to counterbalance his abuse of power through persistent diplomatic pressure for political liberalization, protection of human rights, and the rule of law. Park defied the pressure, only to see the United States increase opposition within the limitations set by the principles of sovereignty and noninterference in domestic affairs. However limited, these U.S. efforts constrained Park's political behavior significantly, periodically forcing him to soften, if not lift, repressive measures. U.S. intervention made America the primary source of democratic ideals and support for political opposition groups in South Korea, encouraging the formation of a transnational alliance between Americans and South Korean opposition groups against Park's authoritarian rule.[72]

The economic arena also saw serious conflict. Emulating Japan, Park tried to build a "rich nation, strong army" through the establishment of a dirigiste state. His penchant for top-down control was especially clear when he initiated the first Five-Year Economic Development Plan in 1962. He was then a novice in the art of governance, with an untamed ambition to catch up with Japan in his lifetime. Although in order to win U.S. support Park and his staff, in drawing up the plan, did refer to the U.S.-influenced Nathan Report, Tasca Report, the Three-Year Reconstruction Plan, and the first Five-Year Development Plan of the Chang Myŏn government, they formulated their plan without any serious consultation with the United States.[73]

Not surprisingly, when the military junta announced its first FYEDP, it provoked strong U.S. criticism. U.S. ambassador Samuel D. Berger and United States Operations Mission (USOM) director James Killen publicly questioned the junta's ability to raise $2.4 billion in foreign capital and obtain $1.4 billion in foreign—mostly U.S.—aid during the 1962–1966 period.[74] The United States viewed the first FYEDP as a shopping list full of wishful thinking rather than as a development plan with feasible target goals.[75] To discourage the implementation of the plan even further, the United States threatened to reduce or delay the delivery of its economic aid when political conflict arose with the junta in June 1962 over the currency conversion program and in January 1963 over the issue of extending military rule. The U.S. refusal to underwrite the first FYEDP, coupled with a series of economic policy failures and poor harvests, eventually made Park revise the plan and formulate the second Five-Year Economic Development Plan (1966–1971), which was more along the lines of the Fei-Ranis Report commissioned by the USOM.[76]

The issue of financial stabilization split the two allies even more. Upon seizing power in 1961, Park, like his civilian predecessors, tried to pursue expansionary fiscal and monetary policy in order to win public support through the provision of material incentives. In the early days of military rule, he even canceled farm debts as part of his war on usury. By contrast, since the days of Syngman Rhee's political rule the United States, as a donor of economic aid, had pressed hard for macroeconomic stabilization to arrest inflation and to maximize the impact of grants-in-aid. Like his civilian predecessors, Park resisted the U.S. pressures for interest hikes and currency devaluation in order to earn rents from selling U.S. dollars and aid goods in local markets at above the official exchange rates. The USOM succeeded in persuading Park to adopt an economic stabilization policy only after his domestic political situation stabilized with the electoral victory in October 1963. Even then, it was Killen's strategy of linking the release of U.S. economic and food aid to Park's implementation of fiscal and financial stabilization that pushed Park toward fiscal and monetary discipline in 1964 and 1965.[77]

Joel Bernstein replaced Killen as the director of the U.S. Agency for International Development (formerly USOM) in 1964 and influenced Park's choice of economic policy much more effectively, convincing Park and his staff of the importance of fiscal and monetary discipline, tax reform, export drive, and trade liberalization. Bernstein came to be known as Park's most trusted economic tutor, and strengthened his position within myriad bilateral forums of policy coordination between U.S. and South Korean officials.[78] Having learned the dangers of shock therapies through repeated policy failures during the military junta period, Park agreed to implement stabilization measures in 1964, paving the way to economic liberalization through the rationalization of South Korea's interest rates and foreign exchange regime. These began the transition to an export-led growth strategy.

At the center of financial stabilization was the interest-rate rationalization measure, begun in 1964 on the recommendation of a USAID-commissioned study by John Gurley, Edward Shaw, and Hugh Patrick.[79] Even at the height of U.S. influence, Park was his own master, integrating U.S. policy recommendations in the structure of his own priorities and strategies. To meet the need for capital to supply to the strategic firms and sectors at a preferential rate while accommodating the U.S. demand for interest-rate liberalization, Park increased deposit rates more than loan rates, producing a "reverse interest-rate system" in which deposit rates were higher than loan rates.

Unfortunately, the reversal of deposit and loan rates resulted in a rapid growth of the private curb market outside the state banking system to the level of 56 to 63 percent of total domestic credit by the end of 1964. At the same time, national savings was discouraged, prompting the United States to advise a doubling of the legal ceiling on interest rates.[80] In September 1965, Park undertook another interest-rate reform by doubling the ceiling on interest rates not only to remove the negative effects of low deposit rates on national saving but also to reduce the curb market and expand the state-owned commercial banks' share of savings. To link this effort at interest-rate liberalization with export growth, Park tapped both Japanese and U.S. expertise to lay the institutional foundations of an export-led growth strategy and to construct an outwardly looking incentive system.[81] In 1964, Amicus Most, an American businessman hired as an advisor to USAID, was instrumental in developing an extensive program for export expansion for MCI.[82]

In other words, although the United States was not able to socialize Park in its liberal mold, it exercised considerable influence in counterbalancing Park's Japanese ideas of economic modernization and his Korean nationalism during the mid-1960s. The security umbrella and military and economic assistance provided by the United States proved to be critical assets in the effort to restrain the most extreme dirigiste part of Park's Japanese ethos, but to collaborate positively on common goals, the United States needed something more. The threat of sanctions could not by itself induce Park's policy shift toward stabilization, liberalization, and export promotion. To explain the transformation of the U.S. role from a negative one of preemption and sanction to a positive one of collaboration, it is necessary to analyze the emergence of a new epistemic community between U.S. aid officers and South Korean economic technocrats during the mid-1960s. Ch'oe Kak-kyu, former deputy prime minister and EPB minister (1991–1993), recollected:

> We did not understand basic economic concepts like "present value" at the time. Even college professors did not understand the concept. Foreign exchange rates and prices constantly changed, and it was virtually impossible to plan for future repayment without calculating the present value of the foreign loans disbursed [by the EPB] in the local currency. We learned all this from USOM officials. The same can be said of the foreign exchange rate system. Were it not for their assistance, [we could not have thought up] the floating exchange rate system. We, economic technocrats, were adaptive and competent, but policy changes were possible because we had good tutors like the USOM officials.[83]

Most of the mid-level South Korean economic technocrats of the 1960s looked upon Killen and Bernstein as tutors, participating in a dense EPB-USOM policy network to import advanced U.S. economic and managerial expertise. The United States influenced Park's economic ideas by educating and co-opting his economic technocrats into the U.S.-led bilateral epistemic community. Moreover, the United States invited mid-level South Korean economic technocrats to its educational and research institutions for training. Programs had begun at the University of Minnesota, Vanderbilt University, and Williams College in the 1950s as part of U.S. assistance. Korean participants, upon their return home, spread the principles of a market economy and ways to streamline the country's inefficient administrative system.[84] It was this clustering of U.S.-trained and USOM-influenced economic technocrats in South Korea's elite economic ministries—the EPB, the Ministry of Finance, and the Ministry of Commerce and Industry—that became a new source of internal pressure for policy change during the mid-1960s. To assist the emerging bureaucratic enclaves of policy innovation from outside the state, moreover, the U.S. government helped Park establish the Korea Development Institute in 1971, which was to have a profound impact on the trajectory of economic development with its research activities.[85]

However, it is important to emphasize that Park determined how these institutional legacies of U.S. assistance actually affected economic development. Once U.S.-trained technocrats and U.S.-aided research institutions formed an enclave of innovation, they became the vehicle for Park's heavy and chemical industrialization, which was based on illiberal nationalist principles of control and mobilization. After some initial hesitation, the U.S.-trained technocrats turned into the advocates and agents of the state-led HCI drive in the 1970s, under Park's leadership. It was only after Park's death in 1979 that a new breed of U.S.-trained technocrats, armed with neoliberal economic ideas, joined Major General Chun Doo-Hwan in the search for a new formula for economic growth and political legitimization. Park maintained a complex love-hate relationship with the United States. He resented U.S. pressures for democratization, stabilization, and liberalization after he took power. After a brief interlude of collaboration post-1963, his relationship with the United States rapidly deteriorated with his declaration of the *yushin* constitution in 1972. Park opposed U.S. interference in domestic affairs in the name of human rights and democracy throughout the 1970s. Nevertheless, he recognized the importance of harnessing America's modern technology and organizational know-how for his illiberal goals. Additional considerations for Park were U.S. economic assistance, security guarantees, and policy ideas that were vital to South Korea's economic reconstruction. This dependence on the United States set limits on Park's dirigiste pathway to modernization. Park resented U.S. intervention, but it was precisely because the United States wielded stick and carrot to prevent the worst of Park's inclinations that Park was able to—albeit unintentionally—fine-tune his rough navigation of economic growth.

THE HISTORY of economic policy during Park's political rule demonstrates that ideas matter. Although structure, behavior, and leadership choice are critical in explaining the dynamics of Park's modernization, they cannot by themselves account for the mix of policy measures Park chose in order to accelerate South Korea's modernization. To explain why he combined instrumental U.S. policy ideas with his Japanese-like ethos of control and mobilization despite the high risk of policy failure, it is necessary to explore the inner structure of Park's ideational world. The ideological beliefs, images, and information that Park acquired through the process of political socialization offer valuable clues to the elucidation of his strategic choices, political maneuvers, and behavioral orientation. Equally critical, Park's ideational world was not monolithic, but composed of multiple ideas and influences, some complementary and some conflicting. Whereas the illiberal Japanese ethos of control and mobilization nurtured the foundations of his modernization strategy and framed it around the concepts of a commanding state, revolution from above, and "rich nation, strong army," Park's nationalist zeal shaped the direction of his political action, driving him to seize power through a military coup, construct an organic state corporatism, pursue mercantilistic economic policy, and mobilize civil society through indoctrination and top-down organization. The Japanese ethos and the nationalist zeal were complementary and mutually reinforcing in pushing Park to pursue the high-risk but high-yield modernization strategy of heavy and chemical industrialization. By contrast, the ideas of technocracy gained from the United States encouraged the risk taking by providing instrumental ideas. At the same time, the United States as an actor constantly counterbalanced the statist, mercantilist, and corporatist drive emerging from Park's Japanese ethos and Korean nationalism, altering his policy ideas during the critical transition period of the mid-1960s.

In this sense, Park's modernization strategy was an outcome of the dialectical interplay of his four ideas of statism, mercantilism, corporatism, and U.S. liberalism. It is misleading to give a monocausal explanation of the ideational background of Park's modernization strategy. The Japanese ethos, Korean nationalism, and U.S. ideas jointly shaped his thinking. Their dynamic interactions varied over time and across issues, making South Korean economic policy a hybrid mixture of ideas that defied the easy dichotomous classifications of state versus market, pluralism versus corporatism, and mercantilism versus laissez-faire. The longitudinal and cross-sectional variations of the way these ideas were mixed during Park's political rule suggest that political leaders' ideas and images are not fixed, sometimes complementing and other times contradicting each other as internal and external conditions alter. A recognition of the fluid and multidimensional nature of Park's ideas leads to an appreciation of both the continuity and the discontinuity in the history of South Korean modernization processes. The memory, experience, and learning of the Meiji Restoration, the Showa period, militarism, and the Village Promotion Policy during the colonial era all contributed to Park's modernization strategy. Even more important, he learned the ideas of industrial policy, export promotion, and administrative guidance from the postwar Japanese scene. The influence of the United States on Park was also powerful.

Finally, it should be noted that Park's ideational structure was by and large a reflection of the South Korean people. He represented not only the mind-set of older South Koreans who experienced Japanese colonial teachings during the 1930s, but also that of young military officers who yearned for greater autonomy and independence during the postwar era. Park's modernization can be seen as the crystallization of the aspirations of the South Korean populace, who struggled to overcome backwardness, poverty, and military vulnerability. However, as the widespread political opposition to Park's *yushin* regime in the 1970s demonstrates, a new generation of more affluent, urban, and educated youth was also rapidly emerging on the political scene to challenge Park's ideas and actions in that decade.

CHAPTER FIVE

The Labyrinth of Solitude:
Park and the Exercise of
Presidential Power

Byung-Kook Kim

THE POLITICAL LEADERSHIP of Park Chung Hee is key to understanding his success in prolonging his rule and bringing economic
growth. Yet most of the literature on South Korean politics and economics
during his rule simply takes his leadership as a given. Or worse, looking at
his leadership as based on his performance, observers assume that the historical achievement of growth necessarily conferred political leadership
upon him. There are three problems with such an argument. First, the
question is what kind of leadership Park had that enabled him to maximize the South Korean government's policy performance and legitimize his
rule. The issue is not that his legitimacy was defined in terms of his ability
to deliver economic growth and military security, but how Park was able
to bring about high performance in the first place.

Second, at the level of performance, the Park era was characterized by
economic crises as much as by modernization miracles. In 1962, the currency conversion reform paralyzed financial markets precisely when Park
was holding the line against rival military factions as well as Washington.
In 1972, his grip on power again seemed to be slipping away under the
pressures of corporate and financial distress, on the one hand, and the escalation of his lieutenants' and protégés' struggle over succession within
the Democratic Republican Party (DRP), on the other. And in 1979, the
bubble created by heavy and chemical industrialization (HCI) burst, inten-
sifying the political opposition's challenge to Park's power. Even during

normal times, when the economy was not on the brink of collapse, the *yushin* regime brought double-digit growth but at the cost of severely escalated social conflict: inflation rose; income and wealth became more concentrated.

Third, explaining Park's success in holding on to political power in terms of *long-term* and *macro* performance misses his struggle to make politically and economically important strategic choices and to craft the instruments through which he exercised power during severe dilemmas like those of 1962, 1972, and 1979. The spectacular achievements at the long-term macro level were a product of a series of politically difficult short-term policy choices on a range of issue-areas, which are lost so long as analysis remains focused on long-term macro trends. The power Park wielded was not a mere by-product of industrial growth; he worked hard to protect it even in boom years and to grow it through a series of policy choices.

To focus on how Park nurtured, organized, and expanded his power, we must set aside the myth that he was "above" politics. To be sure, he encouraged society to believe in this myth, but he did so because that was the way he wanted others to see him. The image helped him defend his power from political rivals, foes, and protégés. The real Park had a natural instinct for power, creating new opportunities by making strategic moves a step or two ahead of others and casting them as heroes or villains in his carefully scripted political drama. Park's manipulations were possible because he knew others' strengths and weaknesses, and because he engaged actively but silently in everyday politics and reached far down into political parties and state ministries for vital information. Park looked like a captive and his praetorians sometimes seemed to be his prison guard, but in reality it was he who ruled. Park revealed his inner thoughts only through the drama that he had set up in which he would use others to achieve his goals.

Nor was Park plagued by a sense of illegitimacy, another myth that many observers—in particular, his critics—have perpetuated. Chapter 5 will argue that after his 1963 electoral victory, it was not his weaknesses but his strengths that explain his political moves, at least until the last months of his life. In his 1967 election campaign, he beat Yun Po-sŏn by 10.5 percentage points. The gap narrowed in 1971 against Kim Dae-jung, but only to 7.6 points. The Democratic Republican Party's control of the National Assembly was slightly more erratic, but even in its worst election, it retained its majority status. The party's share in the National Assembly reached 62.8 percent in 1963, hit 73.7 in 1967, and fell to 55.4 in 1971. Even after 1972, when Park did away with direct presidential elections and filled a third of the National Assembly seats with hand-picked "Yujŏnghoe" members, his party picked up 38.7 percent of votes in 1973—down 10.1 percentage points from 1971, but still 6.2 points higher than the New Democratic Party's share. Only in 1978 did the DRP win fewer votes than the NDP in a National Assembly election; Park's party lost by 0.5 percent. The alleged illegitimacy problem haunted Park before 1963 and after 1972, but it was in the period between these two years that he made his most risky political choices: normalization of diplomatic relations with Japan, military intervention in Vietnam, the constitutional amendment for a third presidential term, the Emergency Decree on Economic Stability and Growth, and heavy and chemical industrialization. His decisions were hardly those of a weak and illegitimate leader. His risk taking bordered on recklessness, but he believed he could control situations. The problem with Park was overconfidence in his ability, not lack of confidence.[1]

What was Park's political leadership made of? Park was an institution builder who nurtured his power by ruling through a two-pronged structure, with the Korea Central Intelligence Agency protecting him in the political realm and the Economic Planning Board working with the Blue House Secretariat to lead state ministries in a concerted program of resource mobilization. To steer the two-pronged state in a direction that augmented his power, Park built an intricate system of checks and balances, selective co-optation and repression, and division of labor within each of the two spheres, while at the same time empowering the KCIA and EPB to plan, execute, and monitor what was needed to control the state politically and mobilize resources to modernize the country. Park chose to work through the KCIA and the EPB, but he was also careful not to become a captive of his guards, although his ability to do so declined precipitously as he unintentionally undermined his system of checks and balances in an effort to concentrate power in the Blue House to an extreme degree during the last months of the *yushin*. His political rule had distinctive strengths, but also weaknesses: he depended too much on the praetorian guards and the military rather than on the political parties, which were to bring him down in 1979.

Agents, Guards, and Staff

"Never have I thought of myself as a politician," Park once remarked.[2] These words hide as much as reveal his complex personality. Park never hid his distaste for elections and his contempt for legislators. They were divisive and costly, a luxury for South Korea.[3] In a deeper sense, however, he was political: he knew how to acquire and use power. When he set up a military junta in May 1961, Park was already a seasoned politico from Syngman Rhee's politicized military. He had seen how Rhee kept power not only by playing off Hamgyŏng and P'yŏngan natives against each other but also by establishing a tightly knit military security and intelligence complex to serve as a watchdog on all factions.

Park was a victim, excluded from key army posts because of his Kyŏngsang origins and at one time sentenced to life imprisonment for his leftist ideology. Park was Yi Yŏng-mun's deputy director at army headquarters' Intelligence Bureau and one of the brains behind Yi's aborted 1952 coup attempt.[4] As a witness, victim, and conspirator, his experience taught him three rules that served him well after he seized power in 1961: control the flow of information, divide and conquer, and use regionalist sentiments.

When Park chose artillery as his new field in 1952, he learned another rule: plan, execute, and monitor. "Unlike the infantry," writes Park biographer Cho Kap-che, "an artilleryman aims for a target lying beyond his sight. To improve his hit ratio, he has to check on his shell's location and correct his calculation of distance and direction. Working behind [the front lines], he is also trained to operate with a broad objective view. The artillery is multidimensional, systematic, and mathematical."[5] This discipline distinguished Park from Rhee. The two tried to put allies as well as foes under a tight watch by monopolizing intelligence services, breeding jealousy and distrust among factional leaders, and stirring up regionalist prejudices. But Park was more systematic and organized in pursuit of his goals and hence more successful. The centerpiece of Park's power apparatus was the Korea Central Intelligence Agency, established by law only twenty-four days after the May 16 coup of 1961.

The KCIA

Establishing the KCIA represented Park's first decision on what to do with his newly won power and how to guard it from allies and foes alike. Prepared by Lieutenant Colonel Kim Chong-p'il, whose life had been tightly intertwined with Park's by marriage as well as by career since 1949, Law no. 619 had only nine articles. Article 1 made the KCIA more like a Soviet KGB than an American CIA by placing domestic as well as foreign intelligence within its legal jurisdiction; by adding a criminal investigatory power to its arsenal; and by empowering it to "coordinate and supervise state ministries'—including the armed forces'—intelligence and investigation activities on issues related to national security." Through Article 3, the agency could "set up local branches when necessary." Article 7 stipulated that its agents could "receive support and assistance from all state institutions when necessary for [their] work."[6] In one law with nine articles, Kim Chong-p'il had set up the KCIA as a planner, an executor, and a monitor for his boss.

Park did amend Law no. 619 when he restored electoral politics in 1963, but only to block democratization from obstructing the KCIA's mandate. The amended law's Article 9 empowered the KCIA director to employ soldiers and bureaucrats for any given period on the agency's payroll. By a new Article 11, the KCIA director could also refuse requests for reports for or testimony to and questioning by National Assembly members or by a newly formed Board of Audit and Inspection on matters pertaining to "national secrets." With all rival coup leaders purged by 1963, Park also made it his presidential prerogative to appoint the KCIA director.[7]

From its inception, the KCIA was Park's favorite instrument of power. Unlike state ministries, it could ensure secrecy in both the formulation and the implementation of policy. By bringing people from line ministries and the armed forces into a working group, the KCIA could also rise above ministerial turf wars and devise policy solely from Park's perspective. Law no. 619 permitted the KCIA to hide its budget in the expenditures of other state ministries for reasons of national security, which enabled the agency to act outside the supervision of the National Assembly. Nevertheless, though the KCIA provided Park many advantages, it also entailed grave political risks. The KCIA's political intrigues, backed by terror and espionage, alienated party politicians and *chaeya* dissidents and stirred up antigovernment protests.[8] Worse, the KCIA might someday turn against Park and seize power itself.

To dodge popular fury, but also to keep the KCIA in line, Park always used it as a scapegoat and dismissed its director when public discontent increased and protests reached a dangerous level. For a surprisingly long time, his strategy worked. The ruling party, as well as the opposition, blamed three KCIA directors—a "showy" Kim Chong-p'il (1961–1963), an "illiterate" Kim Hyŏng-uk (1963–1969), and a "cunning" Yi Hu-rak (1970–1973)—for political excesses before turning against Park. Against such loyal praetorians, the ever suspicious Park built alternative information channels and put in place rival surveillance agents. The Presidential Security Service looked for any "irregular" activities. The Army Security Command joined in to keep the KCIA in check.[9]

Closely watched by its rivals, the KCIA seldom strayed from serving Park's interests, developing multiple roles and missions. As a political weapon for Park, the agency, under Kim Chong-p'il's leadership, set up the Democratic Republican Party as a new ruling party, with funds generated from wrongful operations in 1962, as we saw in Chapter 3.[10] Park used Kim as a scapegoat when he left the KCIA to join the DRP as its chairman in 1963, and forced Kim to go abroad in brief exile for the agency's illicit activities, while Park campaigned as the DRP's presidential candidate. When Park plotted to prolong his rule by amending the constitution to allow him to run for a third term in 1969 and then to stay in power for life through the declaration of the *yushin* constitution in 1972, the KCIA again became his main political instrument. To break Kim Chong-p'il's desire to succeed Park by fighting to retain the constitutional limit of two presidential terms, Park had the KCIA, now led by Kim Hyŏng-uk, bully Kim Chong-p'il's "crown prince" faction with threats of a purge, while DRP finance chairman Kim Sŏng-gon coaxed Kim Chong-p'il's followers to back down with soft talk in 1969.[11] The two-track strategy of repression and co-optation worked, persuading Kim Chong-p'il to support the constitutional revision.

Three years later, with Kim Chong-p'il tamed and Kim Sŏng-gon immersed in wishful thinking about instituting a parliamentary system after Park's third term ended in 1974, the KCIA on Park's orders struck against Kim Sŏng-gon and forced his retirement after abusive interrogations.[12] With such ruthless crackdowns on Park's one-time allies and followers in 1962, 1969, and 1972, the KCIA helped clear the way to Park's first election, third term, and the *yushin* regime. Even when Park was not plotting a political intrigue, the agency worked diligently in Park's shadow to build up and guard his power, intimidating legislators, feeding on jealousy and mistrust among opposition leaders, and harassing journalists.[13] During election season, moreover, the KCIA became a campaign strategist, a political fund-raiser, and a "pollster" for Park, given the institutional shallowness of the DRP.

The KCIA was also a critical player in foreign policy. When normalization talks with Japan became deadlocked over the issue of reparations, Park had Kim Chong-p'il, then the agency's director, fly to Tokyo in 1962 to broker a deal clandestinely and "shamelessly"—to quote protestors during South Korea's 1965 treaty crisis.[14] In 1972, when U.S. president Richard Nixon's trip to China rekindled South Korea's deeply ingrained mistrust of U.S. security commitments, Park again turned to the KCIA for covert operations. KCIA director Yi Hu-rak obliged, visiting the North Korean capital, P'yŏngyang, as Park's envoy in May after bilateral Red Cross talks on family reunions, and greeting the North's second deputy prime minister Pak Sŏng-ch'ŏl when he made a corresponding visit to Seoul a month later. The high-level exchange produced the July Fourth Joint Declaration for peaceful reunification and more. Soon after his return from the North, Yi Hu-rak urged Park to suspend direct presidential elections and amend the constitution to centralize his power, with the goal of defeating P'yŏngyang's totalitarian regime in a new era of détente. Park concurred. Having seen his national emergency declaration in December 1971 severely criticized and ridiculed for its blatant unconstitutionality and his belatedly legislated Law on Special Measures for National Security neutralized by opposition parties in early 1972, Park decided to draw up a new constitution and dissolve the National Assembly. This task, too, became Yi Hu-rak's. The KCIA director joined Park's presidential staff in weekly meetings to review plans for regime change prepared by his agents under the code name "Good Harvest" until August. Their document was then handed over to Minister of Justice Sin Chik-su and KCIA deputy director Kim Ch'i-yŏl for detailed legal work.[15] The KCIA's role as an instrument of foreign policy overlapped with, spilled over into, and was reinforced by its domestic role as the watchdog of Park's political interests, power, and mission.

Yet the KCIA's domestic and foreign agenda had profoundly negative consequences for Park's relationship with Tokyo and Washington after 1973. To slow down, if not reverse, the United States' staged military disengagement from South Korea, the KCIA brought in Pak Tong-sŏn, a lobbyist with an exclusive right to import U.S. rice into South Korea, and Kim Han-jo, a South Korean expatriate entrepreneur, into what the KCIA hoped would become a strong Washington lobby modeled after Taiwan and Israel's efforts to influence U.S. foreign policy. In August 1973, Yi Hu-rak had KCIA agents abduct South Korean opposition leader Kim Dae-jung from Tokyo, where he had been seeking political asylum in the wake of the *yushin* declaration, in order to stop him from building overseas anti-Park forces. These KCIA operations backfired, quickly developing into the Koreagate scandal with its resultant "Park bashing" in the U.S. Congress and a serious rift in relations with Japan.[16]

The strains on South Korea's relations with its two most important allies strengthened the domestic opposition, especially after South Korea recovered from the shock of Saigon's fall in 1975. The rise of opposition forces within society predictably dragged the KCIA further into political intrigues and foreign policy problems. To preempt the NDP's mobilization of societal opposition forces in 1979, Park expelled its leader, Kim Young-sam, from the National Assembly, only to see the opposition lawmakers resign en masse and the United States recall Ambassador William Gleysteen. The brutal repression of workers on strike at a small bankrupt

garment factory backfired as well, politicizing oppressive labor conditions. The residents of economically depressed Pusan and Masan in Kim
Young-sam's native South Kyŏngsang Province also broke out into a massive protest against Park's gross political blunders. At the center of each of
these missteps were KCIA director Kim Chae-gyu and Presidential Security
Service chief Ch'a Chi-ch'ŏl. They drew up "moderate" and "radical"
countermeasures that had more to do with internal power struggles than
with problem-solving.

Given the KCIA's multiple political roles, sweeping power, and cohesive
organization, its director served as a de facto senior presidential secretary
on domestic as well as foreign and security policy in Park's Blue House.
The president began his work every morning with reports from the KCIA
director. To guard his innermost thoughts on priority issues, Park met the
KCIA director alone, without even his chief of staff. The KCIA director
could also knock on his door anytime day or night, if necessary. There
were only two other people who enjoyed similar privileges: the head of the
army's Security Command and the Presidential Security Service chief. The
talk among these three praetorians could run for hours when Park faced
major issues.[17]

The Blue House

Park also knew that the KCIA was ill-equipped to handle economic issues.
When he entrusted it with handling economic policy in 1962, his move almost ruined South Korea's already feeble economy, as we saw in Chapter
3. From his 1962 policy disasters, Park learned what not to do: to use the
KCIA for economic policymaking rather than for political goals.[18] Nonetheless, it took time for him to learn what *to* do: where to put his trust
within the state bureaucracy and how to organize his presidential team in
the economic realm. In July 1961 Park had established the Economic
Planning Board as his pilot agency, but left it out in the cold during the
early military junta years because of his reliance on Kim Chong-p'il's
KCIA. The task lying before him after 1962 was to find ways to make the
EPB his lead economic agency in both name and reality and yet place it under his personal control. The issue of balancing institutional development
and patrimonial control was crucial for Park, because as with the KCIA,
the EPB was too powerful to be left alone. With its power to draw up the
nation's budget as well as to authorize foreign loans and investments,
which at the time were South Korea's main source of capital in the context
of low domestic savings, the EPB could independently raise money for industrial projects it deemed necessary to achieve the targeted rate of eco-

nomic growth without bringing in the Ministry of Finance for any close consultation. As with the KCIA, the EPB was kept under Park's tight rein with the help of his Blue House presidential Secretariat.

Set up to balance the goals of institutional development and patrimonial control, the Blue House resembled a mini-cabinet. At its apex sat the chief of staff with a rank equivalent to that of minister. Immediately below were the vice ministerial-level senior secretaries, whose number increased from one to six after a series of organizational overhauls in 1968 and 1969. Thereafter, until Park's death a decade later, the number of senior secretaries ranged from five to eight, each presiding over secretaries with a rank equivalent to that of general bureau director or assistant vice minister in the state bureaucracy. Each secretary, in turn, had exclusive jurisdiction over one or two state ministries with which to transform Park's vision into a detailed, workable policy package.[19] The organization of the Blue House thus more or less paralleled that of South Korea's state ministries. Because Park relied on his three praetorians—the KCIA, the Army Security Command, and the Presidential Security Service—to guard his power and deal with political issues, the "political" part of the presidential Secretariat always remained weak. Before 1968, Park did project an image of privileging politics within the organization of the Blue House by appointing a senior secretary with a "political" portfolio. This formal title, however, was misleading. The aide functioned more as a deputy chief of staff than as a senior staff member with an exclusive jurisdiction over political issues.[20] His role was to facilitate coordination between the chief of staff and nine lower secretarial units, only one of which dealt with the National Assembly and party politics. The 1969 reorganization seemingly set up a more secure place for politics within Park's Blue House by creating a separate political unit at a newly inserted vice ministerial layer of senior secretaries, but this new unit too defined its mission bureaucratically, as one of watching over seven "political" state ministries as diverse as Culture and Information, Education, Government Affairs, Justice, Foreign Affairs, Defense, and Home Affairs. For Park, the real counterpart to party politicians and legislators was his KCIA.

To be sure, Yi Hu-rak played a central political role during his tenure as chief of staff between 1963 and 1969, but he was more the exception than the norm. During these six years, Yi allied himself with KCIA director Kim Hyŏng-uk and DRP finance chairman Kim Sŏng-gon to squeeze Kim Chong-p'il out of power and prepare for Park's third presidential term in 1969. The three allied not only because they lacked personal charisma and popularity to compete with Kim Chong-p'il for the position of crown prince, but also because Park himself had no thought of retiring from politics. When Yi Hu-rak left, Park appointed Kim Chŏng-ryŏm—a hybrid technocrat with prior vice ministerial and ministerial experience in the strategic Finance as well as Commerce and Industry ministries—as the chief of staff. Kim Chŏng-ryŏm stayed on for nine long years until the DRP lost a National Assembly election in 1978. The successor was Park's reluctant old friend from his army years, retired general Kim Kye-wŏn, whom Park persuaded to become the chief of staff as a "companion" in his old age.[21]

The nature of the Blue House staff was primarily technocratic and bureaucratic. There were senior secretaries for political affairs, but their primary task was to check on and polish up political plans prepared by the KCIA. The real senior aide on politics, in short, was the KCIA, which explains why Park's Blue House political team remained organizationally weak both before and after 1968.

The Blue House staff as an organization was "80 percent economics," to quote a senior aide.[22] Moreover, unlike the KCIA and its rival security agencies, which Park staffed with his lifelong confidants from his military years in accordance with his military view of politics as a game of control, mobilization, and divide-and-conquer policies, the "80 percent economics" Blue House recruited its personnel from South Korea's state bureaucracy, the source of expertise in a thoroughly bureaucratized political society. Park knew the importance of the state bureaucracy and organized his daily schedule to win loyalty from state bureaucrats by personally visiting construction sites and closely monitoring governmental projects.

The strategic role of the Blue House does not mean that it was a large organization. Even after dramatic expansions in July 1967 and April 1968, Park's Blue House Secretariat had only 227 staff members, with 99 enjoying the civil service rank of Grade 3B (fifth-highest grade among 10) or higher. Park imposed an upper ceiling on his Secretariat's organizational growth because he desired his Blue House aides to remain as aides and to exercise power by working with and through—not around—state ministries.[23] In fact, the state bureaucracy constituted his single largest source of Blue House aides, supplying 37.9 percent of senior secretaries. The armed forces followed with a 27.6 percent share. Park also maintained a division of labor, recruiting his senior economic aides primarily from the elite EPB and Ministry of Finance and his Blue House spokespersons from among journalists, while retired military personnel took up posts in political and civil affairs. Park knew where power and expertise lay and acted accordingly, showering South Korea's bureaucratic elite with privileges. The crucial point, of course, was who controlled whom. The "guards" could build a "human curtain" *(in-ŭi changmak)* around Park and make him a captive of the state bureaucracy or of the guards themselves, distorting information, setting the national agenda, and formulating policy options to advance respective agencies' powers and privileges rather than Park's. To keep the Blue House Secretariat in line, Park could instill fear among his aides, but only to a limited extent, lest fear destroy any incentive they had for actively engaging in interministerial coordination to implement the policy goals that Park wanted them to work toward. The ideal aide for Park was Kim Chŏng-ryŏm. Brought in from South Korea's central bank to work on the KCIA's clandestine currency reform in May 1962, Kim Chŏng-ryŏm then saw his role as a "neutral" bureaucratic facilitator and as someone to "limit the damage of the KCIA-led currency conversion by drawing up a workable reform plan" based on his experience participating in a similar currency reform as a technocrat at the Bank of Korea in 1952.[24] The 1962 currency reform failed dismally, but Park took in Kim Chŏng-ryŏm as a top economic aide, making him finance vice minister in 1962 and trade and industry vice minister two years later. Subsequently, he became minister of finance as well as of trade and industry before heading Park's Blue House as the chief of staff from 1969 until December 1978.

Kim Chŏng-ryŏm's career exemplifies Park's systematic way of cultivating loyalty among his Blue House staff through predictable political patronage. Among the 29 senior secretaries of Park's presidential years (1963–1979), 44.8 percent rose to a cabinet post and 24.1 percent became legislators. Moreover, Park looked after his former presidential staff members even after they left the Blue House. Excluding the seven who were serving as senior secretary at the time of Park's death in October 1979, senior aides typically faced a 50 percent chance of moving on to another assignment during Park's political rule. Once Park made a technocrat part of his presidential staff, he promised lifelong political patronage. For an additional assurance of loyalty, Park also preferred to recruit rising young stars and Kyŏngsang natives, especially for strategic political and economic policy work. To build up personal ties as well as to develop an institutional memory of the Blue House, he had senior political and economic aides stay on in their posts for a little over two and a half years, on average. The tenure of other senior aides averaged longer, reaching a little over five years in the case of senior secretaries in protocol offices. Equally important, 48.3 percent of the senior secretaries had served as a mid-level secretary in the Blue House, resulting in a considerably higher total average years of service in the presidential Secretariat. The Blue House's protocol and civil affairs sections even appeared frozen, with their senior aides staying on in various capacities for an average of 5.3 and 8.0 years, respectively. The Blue House was an integral part of the state bureaucracy, recruiting its elite as secretaries and senior secretaries and sending them back to the ministries as high-level policymakers—with a reinforced sense of mission and loyalty inculcated by Park during their Blue House service.

Despite the systematic nurturing of bureaucratic support groups, however, Park knew that in the end it was only he himself who could truly look after his political interests. Consequently, he took a hands-on approach to crucial policy decisions and especially to monitoring policy and ministerial performance. Every month he held an Export Promotion Meeting with cabinet members and *chaebol* executives, and summoned bureaucrats for a "Report on Economic Trends."[25] In other policy areas, Park convened an Inspection and Analysis Meeting every quarter. After Nixon announced U.S. plans for a military disengagement from continental Asia, Park added a Quarterly Meeting on Defense Industry Promotion to the list of interministerial coordination meetings he chaired.[26] There was also the annual tour of inspection *(yŏndo sunsi)*, which occurred in January. Park toured all state ministries that month, with his entire cabinet and Blue House senior secretaries plus National Assembly leaders, including the Speaker, in tow. The tour was organized to review the annual work plans of the state ministries, as well as to "check on and boost up state bureaucrats' morale and capability."[27] Typically Park sat alone, motionless, in front of his delegation in a packed room, overwhelming all with his silence, while bureau directors of the state ministry under inspection each went through a thick briefing chart. Park spoke only occasionally to raise substantively very focused and strategic policy questions. To check on ministerial performance as well as to set clear goals, moreover, he preferred quantifying his questions and comments.[28] During his inspection tours, Park also tested the capabilities of each state ministry's rising stars and, when a person proved capable, he did not hesitate to call on the bureau directors directly and even on lower Grade 3A civil servants to answer his questions.[29] Many of the most talented bureaucrats were picked by Park to work as Blue House aides.

The Two Faces of Park

In the process of setting up the cohesive institutional mechanism of the KCIA, EPB, and Blue House Secretariat to help him plan, execute, and monitor both political and economic policies, and also enjoying newly won electoral legitimacy in 1963, Park was South Korea's unrivaled strong man by the mid-1960s. What occupied him thereafter was how to use the KCIA, EPB, and Blue House aides to guard and expand his power. To this end he drew up two strategies. For politics, Park adopted a negative strategy, seeking to prevent DRP faction leaders as well as opposition NDP politicians from becoming his political equals.[30] In the economic realm, by contrast, he developed a mobilization strategy with the positive goal of value creation, constructing a "market" driven by politically formulated goals operated from the top down by the dirigiste state and casting state and societal actors in the complementary roles he thought were necessary to make the dirigiste economy deliver his desired results. Surprisingly, Park got away with the two-track strategy for a long time, partly because he held overwhelming power through his control of the KCIA and the EPB.

In addition to this structure of dominance, Park's strategic mind mattered a great deal. Had he not always thought ahead of others and adjusted his moves in anticipation of how others would interpret and react to them, KCIA, EPB, and Blue House aides could not have served successfully to facilitate political preemption and economic mobilization. The three institutions realized their potential to wield power only because their boss, Park, acted with a strategic mind.

A Race against Time

Park's intention not to let anyone challenge him was nowhere more clearly revealed than when he named Chŏng Il-gwŏn, a retired general from the Hamgyŏng region, as prime minister in May 1965. "Do not socialize with generals who command key military units, nor with *chaebol* leaders," Park warned Chŏng. "Delegate the task of political fund-raising to EPB deputy prime minister Chang Ki-yŏng." Then Park added, "Be wary when people of the northern regions approach you, lest others perceive you as building a personal political power base."[31] Nor did Park hide his political calculations from Kim Chong-p'il. When Kim Chong-p'il returned in December 1964 from his second *oeyu*, or sojourn abroad, forced upon him by political rivals six months earlier for his shady role in negotiating diplomatic normalization with Japan, Park said the words Kim wanted to hear: "You will be my successor." Then he said: "Stay on guard. People let you alone now because I am here. When I am no longer here, everyone will try to go after you and slander you. That is why you should not get your hands dirty. Stay away from money. Do not appoint your people to any posts."[32] Park was warning Chŏng Il-gwŏn and Kim Chong-p'il to stay away from the three critical sources of political power in South Korea: guns, money, and regionalist organization.

The gentle Chŏng Il-gwŏn obliged and served an essentially ceremonial function, for which he was handsomely rewarded; he stayed on as prime minister until December 1970 and even functioned as foreign minister during early 1967. The young, charismatic, and ambitious Kim Chong-p'il obliged, too, when Park—after years of evasion—revealed his intention not to step down by changing the constitution through a referendum in 1969 to allow himself a third term. Kim Chong-p'il could not do otherwise, because having built a factional following through money-based politics, he could be charged with corruption and purged if he rebelled against Park. Besides, the KCIA was by then led by Kim Hyŏng-uk, who was waiting to topple Kim Chong-p'il from the position of first among equals in the political leadership of the DRP political coalition. To hang on to what power he had, Kim Chong-p'il had to shelve his presidential aspirations and campaign for Park's constitutional revision in 1969. He had reason to fear Park. Only a year earlier, Park had expelled National Assembly member Kim Yong-t'ae from the DRP on the charge of damaging party interests by clandestinely engaging in factional activities to back Kim Chong-p'il's presidential candidacy in 1971. Then, in April 1969, only three months before the DRP publicly endorsed Park's proposal for the constitutional amendment, Park expelled five more legislators when they led some forty DRP assembly members to vote with opposition NDP politicians to dismiss his education minister as part of a vote of no confidence against Park's plan for a constitutional change.[33] Behind these acts was the KCIA. "Director Kim Hyŏng-uk resorted to all possible means," former DRP president Chŏng Ku-yŏng recalled. "Kim Hyŏng-uk even dug up legislators' private lives for irregular or unethical activities to threaten them. Sometimes he pleaded. Other times he coerced. He won over legislators with money, too. Kim Hyŏng-uk approached different people in different ways."[34]

After taming Kim Chong-p'il in 1969, Park took on Kim Sŏng-gon as his next target. This power struggle ended even more swiftly and brutally because Kim Sŏng-gon, as the DRP's central political fundraiser, had become extremely vulnerable to charges of corruption. The purge came after Kim Sŏng-gon helped Park isolate Kim Chong-p'il. The opportunity to strike was ironically provided by Kim Sŏng-gon when he mobilized his faction within the DRP to dismiss the minister of home affairs, O Ch'i-sŏng, as a show of force against Park and even as a prelude to a transition to a parliamentary form of government after Park's third presidential term. With Kim Chong-p'il's faction disintegrating and the end of Park's third term expected in 1975, Kim Sŏng-gon thought he had the legislative support to enact a parliamentary governance structure. Suffering from a shady political image as a deal maker behind closed doors, but in command of political funding, Kim Sŏng-gon believed the establishment of a parliamentary government would be in his interest. To his surprise, Park struck hard, ordering the KCIA to bring him in for interrogation, along with twenty-two other DRP legislators, and forced his retirement from politics. Kim Sŏng-gon could only accept Park's verdict, lest he lose even more, including his business empire—the SSangyong Group.[35] Then, in December 1973, even Yi Hu-rak—who had led Park's campaign against both Kim Chong-p'il and Kim Sŏng-gon while serving as Blue House chief of staff and subsequently as KCIA director—had to retire from politics as well, once Park began to regard him as a political liability.[36] The fate of Kim Hyŏng-uk was far more tragic. Fearing revenge at the hands of those he terrorized while serving as KCIA director and also alarmed by a possible KCIA investigation into his illicitly amassed wealth, Kim Hyŏng-uk went into exile in New Jersey in 1973 and appeared in U.S. congressional hearings to testify against Park's regime in 1977, only to be kidnapped by unknown people in Paris in 1979 and never heard from again.[37]

The *silse*, or real power wielders, under Park were thus caught in a no-win situation if they harbored any ambition larger than serving Park's political interests. To build a factional power base, a *silse* had to raise money and attract supporters. But in doing so, he also put his political life in Park's hands. The *silse* had to surrender to Park's will, lest Park hand over the KCIA's secret file on the *silse*'s illicit activities to public prosecutors for criminal investigation. Understandably, no one dared to oppose Park when he clamped down. Having served as KCIA directors, Kim Chong-p'il, Kim Hyŏng-uk, and Yi Hu-rak all knew what was at stake.[38] The political game as structured by Park had no place for successors. Even before Park began preparing for his second presidential election in 1967, the first DRP president Chŏng Ku-yŏng—seeing no challenger emerging from within the DRP or from the fragmented NDP—became concerned about the political uncertainty that might ensue after Park's completion of his projected second term in 1971. Chŏng Kyu-yŏng urged Park not to lift the two-term restriction on presidential tenure "in spite of Park's ability to do so, because Park would only be disgraced if he revised the constitution."[39] Park understood Chŏng Ku-yŏng's concern, but evaded the question of constitutional revision. However, Park's intentions became clear through his political actions, letting Kim Hyŏng-uk crush Kim Chong-p'il in 1969 and Yi Hu-rak terrorize Kim Sŏng-gon in 1971. Park made these moves not because Kim Chong-p'il and Kim Sŏng-gon challenged his leadership, but because South Korea's constitution stood in his way to lifetime presidency. He was racing against the limits set by constitutional restrictions on consecutive presidential terms.

Park, however, could not have held on to power for so long had he only been ruthless. He was ruthless solely when power was at stake. Even for fallen *silse,* Park could be a caring father figure if the *silse* repented and vowed their loyalty to Park. Once Kim Chong-p'il was disgraced before his faction in 1969 as a weak leader unfit to challenge Park, Park made him prime minister, a post in which he served from June 1971 to December 1975. When Yi Hu-rak ended his seclusion in December 1978 to run for a National Assembly seat in the district of Ulsan and Ulju as an independent, Park had the DRP nominate an obscure figure as its candidate for the district and gave Yi party membership when he won a huge victory. Nonetheless, it was to those who did not harbor independent political ambitions that Park was the most benign. To win their loyalty and reward them for support, Park consistently built up the image of a boss who did not betray loyal followers. Among the 162 men who served as vice ministers or higher between 1963 and 1972, 37 held such posts twice and 35 more than three times. During the *yushin* era, consecutive post holdings increased even more. Among 91 vice ministers and higher-ranking officials of the *yushin* regime, 22 served in such posts twice and 24 more than three times. Moreover, once appointed, Park's power elite typically stayed. Before 1972, 50.4 percent had a tenure of two or more years; under the *yushin* regime, the share increased to 60.9 percent. Park tried to link the destiny of the political elite with his own personal political fate as consciously and as systematically as possible. For his political elite, joining Park was a lifetime commitment. They rose and fell together.

As Park tried to prolong his regime against the timetable set by the constitution, first in 1969 against the two-term limit and then in 1972 against the three-term, politics turned repressive, with NDP opposition politicians as well as DRP factional leaders selectively harassed, bribed, and blackmailed at each critical juncture. Behind every major political plot stood the KCIA. In his memoir, Kim Hyŏng-uk wrote:

> When Park made up his mind to push for a constitutional amendment to allow a third presidential term, I put all my energy behind it. The money required to buy support came from DRP's fund-raiser, Kim Sŏng-gon, under Park's orders . . . I chose not to suppress but to tame journalists with money . . . Only *Dong-A Ilbo*'s Ch'ŏn Kwan-u remained faithful to his principles.
> Converting opposition politicians into supporters for constitutional change was easier. I won over NDP National Assembly member Cho Hŭng-man and Sŏng Nak-hyŏn . . . I also had intermediaries to persuade Yŏn Chu-hŭm, Im Kap-su, and Han Tong-sŏk. I had to give not a little sum of money to do so.[40]

Against the opposition party's drive to mobilize popular support to defend the two-term limit, Kim Hyŏng-uk lined up veterans' associations, religious organizations, labor and business federations, and anticommunist leagues to come out in support of constitutional change.[41] Meanwhile thirty-eight universities were closed down on September 10, 1969, in order to stop the spread of student protests. Kim Hyŏng-uk was chagrined when all the members of the opposition NDP members except for Sŏng Nak-hyŏn, Cho Hŭng-man, and Yŏn Chu-hŭm agreed to withdraw their party membership and regroup into a parliamentary negotiation bloc, thus causing the dissolution of the party at an extraordinary party convention. This crafty procedure ensured that the three betrayers' National Assembly membership would be revoked under the law that canceled assembly membership in the case of party dissolution. To Kim Hyŏng-uk's relief, however, two other opposition legislators he had recruited to Park's side, Im Kap-su and Han Tong-sŏk, survived and joined the newly regrouped Sinminhoe (New Democratic Society) to vote on the bill for the constitutional amendment, because the opposition was unaware of their deal with Kim Hyŏng-uk. With their support, the DRP could meet the constitutional requirement of a two-thirds' majority in the National Assembly to initiate the process of constitutional revision. Even then, the DRP had to gather its 118 legislators plus previously expelled Kim Yong-t'ae and the two opposition legislators at 2:27 A.M. in an annex building to pass its bill, because the opposition occupied the National Assembly's plenary session hall. The vote took six minutes.[42] The constitutional amendment was put to a national referendum in October 1969, in which 77.1 percent of the electorate participated and 65.1 percent of the voters approved.

The KCIA's central political mission in more "normal" times, when neither electoral contests nor constitutional issues united opposition politicians, centered on breeding factional divisions inside the opposition bloc and, if possible, aiding those it chose to win party leadership. In the period before 1971 when Kim Sŏng-gon, who had once been a Liberal Party legislator with an extensive political network transcending party lines, controlled the DRP's political funds, he too joined in as a second channel of clandestine deal making, parallel to the KCIA's more repressive operations. Ironically, however, Park had at best mixed results in controlling opposition politicians. Kim Sŏng-gon and Kim Hyŏng-uk had secured the support of Yu Chin-san, a leading opposition figure, for the legislation of a repressive Press Ethics Committee Law back in 1964. In doing so, however, the DRP hurt Yu Chin-san's integrity and "inadvertently strengthened the hand of hard-liners within [the fragmented and contentious] opposition."[43] Once Yu Chin-san's moderate Democratic Justice Party was weakened, Yun Po-sŏn, a hard-liner, dominated talks on party merger among opposition politicians and eventually became the presidential candidate of the newly merged NDP three months before South Korea's 1967 election.[44]

In this way Kim Sŏng-gon and Kim Hyŏng-uk's deal making, designed to breed divisions among opposition politicians, tilted the balance of power within the opposition to the hard-liners, not the moderates—albeit after three years of confusing mergers and splits within opposition parties. Similarly, when the NDP readied for an extraordinary party convention to elect a new president after Yu Chin-san's death in 1974, the KCIA detained Kim Young-sam for a few days while Park tried to recruit Ko Hŭng-mun and Kim Ŭi-t'aek as proxies to block Kim Young-sam's election as the next NDP president.[45] The attempt failed, resulting in Kim Young-sam's campaign to amend the *yushin* constitution. Then in 1976, amid a Red scare caused by Saigon's fall, Park had an opportunity to tame the NDP—but, as in the past, only for a brief period. The centrist Yi Ch'ŏl-sŭng took over the NDP in 1976, only to be branded a collaborator, clearing the way for Kim Young-sam to get reelected as NDP president in 1979 despite PSS chief Ch'a Chi-ch'ŏl's support for the moderate Sin To-hwan and KCIA director Kim Chae-gyu's threats against the rebellious Kim Young-sam and his anti-mainstream faction.[46]

Modernizer

Whereas politics under Park was almost entirely driven by his will to power, economic policy showed another side of his personality: a leader with a vision. An incessant thirst for power was undoubtedly shared by most of his foes, rivals, and allies. Among Park's contemporaries, however, he was singular in articulating a vision that all South Koreans—even his foes—could share: to transform South Korea into a "second Japan," a militarily strong and economically prosperous state. Had Park sought power only for himself, he could not have held on to it for eighteen years. The economic vision distinguished him from all other political leaders and helped him to win absolute loyalty from his followers; it was his ultimate source of power. Park was well aware of this, and he jealously guarded his prerogatives over economic policy and carefully nurtured his image as a modernizer. By supporting EPB deputy prime minister Chang Ki-yŏng's refusal to join the DRP in 1964 and by protecting him from attempts within the DRP to challenge Chang with votes of no confidence in 1964 and 1965,[47] Park insulated the economic bureaucracy from unruly South Korean party politics. This did not mean that politics did not intervene in economic policymaking. On the contrary, Park warned DRP chairman Chŏng Ku-yŏng not to investigate the distribution of preferential loans and the terms of government guarantees on foreign loans when Chŏng voiced his concerns on corruption and inefficiency.[48]

Contrary to many theories regarding developmental states, Park could not or would not let economic policy be dictated only by technocratic rationality. To build a political coalition, he needed to secure a stable inflow of political funds through the nurturing of business allies and sponsors. The task was how to balance market requirements with political needs rather than choosing one over the other. He had to formulate a strategy that ensured not only high growth but also a material basis for regime stability. As part of this strategy, Park banished the DRP from economic policymaking processes and put state ministries under his exclusive political control. It was he who decided how the balancing act was to be pursued. To bring about a concert of state ministries to achieve his understanding of balancing acts, Park applied the principle of placing planning, executing, and monitoring powers all in one basket by consistently backing the EPB in interministerial policy struggles.[49]

Yet working through the state bureaucracy did not imply the delegation of power. Park saw himself as South Korea's agenda setter and intervened regularly in economic policymaking—with a clear sense of priorities—from early in his presidency. Even before Park expanded his Blue House in 1969 to prepare for heavy and chemical industrialization, he declared, "Professors should show me how to achieve my goal rather than teach me what I should strive for."[50] He treated *chaebol* owners similarly. The Hyundai Group's Chŏng Chu-yŏng was his type of entrepreneur, willing to tackle new business ventures against all odds once Park had made up his mind, with an unwavering belief in Park's pledge to rescue him if his business got into trouble. Against words of caution, Park asked what South Korea's alternative was. "The experts only try to discourage me by identifying risks and obstacles. Had I listened to their advice, I would have ended up doing nothing." When his aides called for scaling back his industrial projects to make them more viable, he answered: "We should even be prepared to replace our original investor with a new one if the original investor fails."[51]

Presidential activism and dominance were a constant during Park's political rule, but his style of leadership underwent a subtle change starting in 1969. Before 1969 Park proceeded project by project, with one or another aide acting as his *punsin*—literally, his "incarnation"—to monitor the process of policy formulation and implementation. This structure was necessary because with scarce capital and technology, Park could at best pursue a limited number of relatively simple industrial projects. Given their limited number and nature, Park could devote his full attention to economic policymaking and was confident of his ability to monitor projects with the help of his *punsin*. For example, Park entrusted the EPB with building an

integrated steel mill in 1961, only to see it get bogged down by a lack of interest among foreign investors. He jump-started the project in the mid-
1960s, but again the results were disappointing. This time, however, Park
made the EPB deputy prime minister accountable for the project, and
ended up dismissing his deputy prime ministers in 1967 and in 1969 when
talks with foreign bankers for commercial loans collapsed.

The pet project went forward only when Park decided to seek politically
motivated aid rather than commercial loans for the construction of the
steel mill. In 1969, senior secretary Kim Hak-ryŏl of the Blue House was
brought in as the EPB deputy prime minister to draw up a new plan to construct the mill with noncommercial foreign funds. A year earlier, Pak T'ae-
jun had been appointed president of the newly established Pohang Iron &
Steel Company and assigned the task of lobbying Japan to allocate $73.7
million of its reparation funds to the iron and steel company's purchase of
the necessary technology and production facilities.[52] These two confidants
of Park drove the integrated steel mill project with Park's full support. Kim
Hak-ryŏl had been Park's most trusted economic advisor since the early
days of the military junta, when he tutored Park on economic matters.[53]
Likewise, Pak T'ae-jun had been a loyal aide since he studied under Park
as a cadet at the Korea Military Academy in 1948. After joining the junta
as the chief of staff for Park in 1961 and participating in its Committee on
Industry and Commerce for three years, Pak T'ae-jun served as Park's secret envoy *(milsa)* in 1964 to break the deadlock in talks with Japan over
the issue of normalization of diplomatic relations.[54] Made for their role as
Park's *punsin*, Kim Hak-ryŏl and Pak T'ae-jun knocked on the doors of
Park's Blue House whenever political obstacles rose and state ministries
resisted.

To build up South Korea's technological capacity, Park recruited Ch'oe
Hyŏng-sŏp as his *punsin* in the area of science and technology. With Park's
support, Ch'oe drew up the charter for the Korea Institute of Science and
Technology in 1966 and headed it until he was made the science and technology minister in 1971. To guarantee budgetary stability and research
continuity, Ch'oe had the EPB channel money in the form of donations. To
ensure his scientists' autonomy in research activity, moreover, he secured
Park's support in legally banning state ministries from intervening in individual research projects and in exempting his institute from the National
Assembly's frequently politicized audits and inspections.[55] Similarly, when
Park found that Kim Hyŏn-ok—a loyal military comrade since Park's Logistics Headquarters Command years—was not only a workaholic but a
"bulldozer"-style leader, Park had him serve as the mayor of Seoul with
the mission to reconstruct the capital into a grayish yet modern city as rap-

idly as possible between 1966 and 1970.[56] In building a new state bureaucracy modeled after South Korea's half-American and half-Japanese military organization, Park chose Yi Sŏk-je as his minister of government in 1963. Yi had crossed the Han River with Park on May 16, 1961, and chaired the military junta's Legislation and Judiciary Committee, responsible for redrawing laws and purging "corrupt" bureaucrats as well as ordering a sweeping arrest of "leftists" in the early days of the coup. Yi Sŏk-je remained minister of government until 1969 in order to institutionalize a professional state bureaucracy, with its elite recruited from competitive civil service examinations and promoted on the basis of performance.[57]

In addition to the practice of working through confidant-led state agencies to realize his goals, Park resorted to the establishment of an interministerial task force within the Blue House when he thought he needed to take charge personally in the interests of coordination. The Kyŏngbu (Seoul-Pusan) Highway project was exemplary in this regard; Park was its planner, implementer, and monitor. Two and a half years after a state visit to West Germany, where he learned of the Autobahn, Park made public his plan to link Seoul with four major cities by constructing a highway system. The groundbreaking ceremony for the highway was held in the middle of his 1967 presidential campaign. After his landslide victory in both the presidential and the National Assembly elections in May and June of that year, he organized a Blue House task force with three military engineers and one construction bureaucrat to review six budget plans independently submitted by state ministries, Seoul City, the army's Engineering Corps, and Hyundai Construction Company. With the cost estimates varying widely between eighteen and sixty-five billion won, Park chose thirty billion won as the size of the government budget for Kyŏngbu Highway because it was an "approximately mid-figure," and ordered An Kyŏng-mo—a former construction minister with an engineering background—to organize a Planning and Research Corps for Constructing National Highways with relevant state ministries and *chaebol* construction companies. "The Corps," Kim Chŏng-ryŏm recalled, "was given a broad budget limit within which it was to build Kyŏngbu Highway rather than calculating costs based on its task." To skeptics and critics, who warned against a poorly built highway, Park simply said he would "repair after completing its construction."[58]

To purchase land before information on the highway leaked out and speculation broke loose, Park personally chose the path for the highway, using his ability to read maps as a former artilleryman. He then called in two top state bank executives under pledges of utter secrecy to order a land survey and directed provincial governors and the Seoul mayor to get landowners' consent to sell within one week by "mobilizing county magistrates, town heads, and other civil servants" under the Ministry of Home Affairs' control. All this was completed in less than three months for the project's most expensive portion, the section linking Seoul and Taejŏn. By the time of the groundbreaking ceremonies, thirteen construction companies—chosen by Park without public bidding—were already purchasing heavy construction equipment with state-guaranteed foreign commercial loans, as most had only outworn equipment unfit for building tunnels and bridges. Park also had to recruit thirty-four military engineers on active duty as supervisors at construction sites and fifty university graduates as inspectors while setting up a new civil engineering examination system.[59]

Park did not set his goals on the basis of the resources at his disposal. Rather, he defined his objectives first and let them identify what resources he needed to complete them. Encouraged by results, Park even moved up his target completion date for the highway by a year and daily checked work progress from a "situation room" set up in his Blue House. The 260-mile-long Kyŏngbu Highway was completed on July 7, 1970, a week after his revised target date and less than two and a half years since its groundbreaking ceremony. The total cost was forty-three billion won, thirteen billion won more than the original target goal.

After 1969, Park became more willing to let his Blue House economic teams act as more than facilitators for state ministries' work. This change in style had as much to do with Park himself as with the changing nature of state tasks and resource capabilities. He intervened extensively and deeply in ministerial operations before as well as after 1969, but the way he intervened changed after 1969. Before that time, Park chose indirect intervention through confidant-led state ministries and public enterprises (with the exception of the Kyŏngbu Highway project). He believed that relying too much on Blue House secretaries would demoralize the line ministries and make his coordination efforts harder, not easier.

After 1969, by contrast, he strengthened the policymaking role and capacity of his Blue House Secretariat and intervened more directly in policy formulation and implementation. The new approach began with a change in Blue House personnel. Park named Chang Tŏk-chin—a thirty-five-year-old Ministry of Finance bureaucrat—to the newly established post of Third Senior Secretary on Economic Affairs in April 1969 and O Wŏn-ch'ŏl—a forty-three-year-old assistant vice minister at the Ministry of Trade and Industry—to the newly created position of Second Senior Secretary on Economic Affairs in November 1971. The Third Senior Secretary position was created when many *chaebol*, laden with state-guaranteed foreign loans, showed signs of a severe liquidity squeeze during the global recession of early 1969. Their financial difficulties threatened the solvency of state-owned commercial banks. Because Park's high-risk, high-payoff modernization strategy of loan-financed industrialization rested on his ability to convince potential investors that the state would rescue them in difficult times, he faced the exceedingly arduous political task of forcing *chaebol* to make painful adjustments without actually threatening to bankrupt them. With the option of bringing in market forces as a disciplinary whip excluded from the outset, Park had to rely on the state's bureaucratic power to distribute adjustment costs among the stakeholders. This could be done only if Park personally took charge, working through a technically competent task force set up inside his Blue House Secretariat. The task of distributing adjustment costs through bureaucratic intermediation rather than through market forces provoked political resistance too powerful for any of the state ministries; it also was too complex a job for any single individual, including Park, to pursue in a sporadic manner.

Chang Tŏk-chin drew up a threefold strategy: rescue the MOF-controlled state commercial banks that had underwritten the *chaebol*'s foreign loans; funnel more resources into the faltering corporations in order not to waste their production facilities; but penalize the owners for mismanagement by liquidating their personal assets. Chang Tŏk-chin's team restructured 30 insolvent companies with foreign loans in May 1969 and another 56 firms under bank management by August 1969. Once the broad policy guidelines were established on financial and corporate restructuring, Park dismantled Chang Tŏk-chin's team and set up an interministerial Corporate Rationalization Committee headed by the EPB deputy prime minister in December 1970. After a heated debate over what constituted "insolvent companies," the EPB finally came up with a formula whereby 26 of the 121 companies with foreign debt were classified as "insolvent" and thus requiring state support. When the EPB measure proved to be inadequate in turning around the surviving *chaebol* conglomerates, keeping the state banks afloat, and reversing the pressures of the foreign exchange crisis, Park, on the recommendation of Chairman Kim Yong-wan of the Korea Federation of Industries, ordered the Blue House Secretariat secretly to draw up an Emergency Decree for Economic Stability and Growth in August 1972 to rescue the *chaebol* groups by freezing their private curb-market loans.[60] The corporate sector was too weak to be left to state ministries. Park had to take charge again and adopt what was a de facto breach of private property rights to keep the *chaebol* groups afloat and to prevent South Korea from defaulting on foreign commercial loans. And he could trust only his Blue House Secretariat to devise such a radical policy.

The establishment of the post of second senior secretary, by contrast, was a product of Park's own political decisions as well as South Korea's increased state capabilities. As Park's dogged attempts to build an integrated steel mill during the 1960s show, Park was infatuated with HCI long before he formally announced it in 1973 as South Korea's paramount policy goal. Park's decision to bring in O Wŏn-ch'ŏl as the second senior secretary in 1971 on the recommendation of the chief of staff, Kim Chŏng-ryŏm, was part of this lifelong ambition to emulate Meiji Japan's modernizers. With South Korea's gross national product increasing by 9.1 percent annually in real terms and its domestic savings rate cumulatively adding up to a 15.7 percentage point increase since 1962, Park thought that the time had come for him to pursue HCI in a more systematic manner even if foreign companies and banks only slowly came up with the required capital and technology. O Wŏn-ch'ŏl also fueled Park's "can do" *(hamyŏn toenda)* spirit by articulating what he called an "engineering approach" to minimize risks and costs.[61] With O Wŏn-ch'ŏl's expertise in industrial policy, Park believed he could draw up an HCI plan attractive even to skeptical foreigners. Whereas the HCI drive of the 1960s consisted of just a few projects, the HCI program Park envisioned after 1971 was on the scale of national restructuring, with the state subsidizing the *chaebol's* simultaneous entries into multiple unrelated industries. The program was economically too risky, technically too complex, and politically too controversial to be left to frequently bickering and generically conservative state bureaucracies. Park had to intervene more directly, regularly, and systematically from the Blue House than in the 1960s.

Even so, it is important not to exaggerate Park's shift in leadership style after 1969. The second senior secretary had only three MCI bureaucrats to assist him until he retired in December 1979 upon the death of Park Chung Hee. By tightly limiting O Wŏn-ch'ŏl's staff, Park made sure that O would be only a messenger of presidential orders, a monitor of policy implementation, and a facilitator of interministerial coordination. The bulk of the planning was done by the HCI Planning Corps, headed by either an EPB or an MoF bureaucrat during 1974. Thereafter the implementation of the 1974 plan was monitored through a weekly Working-Level Assistant Vice Ministerial Meeting. O Wŏn-ch'ŏl was in charge of both the planning and the working-level implementation meetings.

The relative limits to change in Park's leadership style were more visible in other policy areas. Pak T'ae-jun remained the Pohang Iron & Steel

Company's CEO even after Park's death in 1979, while Ch'oe Hyŏng-sŏp served as the science and technology minister for seven and a half years after leaving the Korea Institute for Science and Technology in 1971, during which time he created fourteen research institutes. Likewise, once Yi Sŏk-che showed his ability to control and reform state ministries, Park in 1971 made him head of the Board of Audit and Inspection, from which he lashed out against state bureaucrats' illegal activities in order to counter an increasingly serious moral hazard problem built into Park's bureaucratically driven economy. Park continued to rely on ministers as decision makers and presidential secretaries as personal staff in most policy areas even after launching HCI in 1973, because he knew that much of his power came from the politically loyal, but also technically competent and highly motivated, state bureaucracy. Park limited the number of staff in the Blue House Secretariat even when he entrusted them with his pet projects—Kyŏngbu Highway in 1967 and HCI after 1973—in order not to demoralize the state ministries.[62]

PARK HAD the necessary ingredients to become a powerful leader and leave a lasting mark on South Korean history. Following the lessons he learned during his military years, he concentrated planning, executing, and monitoring powers in two institutions—the KCIA for partisan political issues and the EPB for nation-building economic policy—with the Blue House Secretariat serving as his messenger, monitor, and coordinator among state ministries except when he had a goal he thought could be pursued more rapidly under his Secretariat's direct intervention. Park had a keen—even brutal—strategic mind, and he skillfully used the institutions of power to his advantage. He never shied away from sacrificing what he believed were secondary considerations once he made up his mind on policy priorities, and he had the KCIA and the EPB systematically mobilize multiple resources to achieve his overriding policy goals. Moreover, when he planned to extend his rule through a constitutional amendment or a palace coup, he could plead, cajole, threaten, repress, and even lie, depending on who his audience was. Against Park, by contrast, stood South Korea's organizationally fractured, ideologically shallow, and much less strategically minded political parties.

Yet despite his personal leadership strengths and powerful political machine, Park met with a sudden demise in October 1979. The causes were many. After his wife's assassination in 1975 with a bullet meant for him, his confidants said, Park lost his acumen, vigilance, and discipline, became frequently fatigued with work, and withdrew ever more into his deeply introverted personality. The success he had in purging rivals and repressing political opposition ironically also contributed to his fall. After Kim Chong-p'il's political eclipse, Kim Hyŏng-uk's exile, Kim Sŏng-gon's disgrace, Capital Garrison commander Yun P'il-yong's imprisonment, and Yi Hu-rak's retirement from public life—all occurring between 1969 and 1973—it took even more courage for his ministers and aides to speak out on politically sensitive issues, lest they too lose Park's personal favor. Moreover, the fall of second-tier leaders meant that the system of checks and balances was also seriously undermined, allowing "brute" PSS chief Ch'a Chi-ch'ŏl to monopolize Park's ear all the more in the late 1970s. The journalists sensed that Park's Blue House was showing signs of what might be called arteriosclerosis. The communications system within Park's political regime was breaking down.

Meanwhile, the opposition became increasingly radicalized as Yu Chin-san's "moderate line" and Yi Ch'ŏl-sŭng's "centrist platform" were successively branded as political sellouts by the hard-liners. Ironically, Park helped to undermine the moderate wing of the NDP—his natural ally—by harshly repressing its radical faction and abusing the stance of the moderates, who were more willing to negotiate. Park betrayed the NDP moderates' hopes, holding a summit with their leader only to buy time until old factional jealousies reemerged within the NDP to weaken its leadership, or until a new security crisis swept away the voice of political discontent. The NDP leader who brought Park down in 1979—Kim Young-sam—had been, in fact, a moderate only four years earlier, but became an uncompromising advocate of regime change after being, in his words, "duped" by Park with "tears in his eyes" at a summit meeting in 1975. At the meeting, Park promised "democratization," but urged Kim Young-sam to "keep [Park's] pledge secret in order to avoid many troubles." Kim Young-sam kept his end of bargain, but Park did not live up to his promise—enabling the NDP factional bosses to attack Kim Young-sam as a collaborator.[63] The summit cost him his NDP presidency. When Kim Young-sam was reelected as the NDP president in May 1979, he was not about to repeat his mistake. He publicly set forth his demands, mobilized society, and rejected compromise outright.

The personal crisis, malfunctioning *yushin* regime, and radicalized NDP would not have been fatal for Park had there not been a fourth factor: South Korea's societal transformation. With the nation's GNP growing at 9.5 percent per annum in real terms since the launch of the first FYEDP in 1962, the share of South Korea's primary sector in GNP and employment shrank precipitously, by 14.2 percentage points to 19.2 percent and by 27.2 percentage points to 35.8 percent, respectively, during Park's eighteen years of rule. The HCI share in South Korea's total industrial value-added correspondingly hit 54.7 percent in 1979, 28.9 points higher than its 1962 level. The economic growth and attendant social transformation provided the kindling for labor and other protest movements. South Korean society became differentiated in class structure as well as in degree of urbanization and education, with 57.3 percent of its population dwelling in cities and 19 percent possessing a high school diploma or higher according to South Korea's 1980 census. Those enrolled in college—a hotbed for political activism—totaled 556,484. Moreover, South Korea became a highly mobile society, where traditional mechanisms of social control were rapidly disintegrating. According to the 1980 census, 8.1 percent had changed their residence more than once during the previous year and 22.8 percent within the previous five years.[64] But because Park curbed party politics and suppressed interest groups in order to rule bureaucratically, political integration lagged behind social mobilization, making South Korea what William Kornhauser once called an atomized but volatile "mass society," with neither traditional primary networks nor modern group ties and associational institutions to ease political alienation and societal tension through interest intermediation.[65] Park did his best to contain and control the political effects of the massive social transformation that he had unleashed, issuing nine emergency decrees after 1972, but each decree only hardened the opposition's resolve to fight back and bring down Park's political rule.

Park's problem was that he was using the repressive political strategy of control, depoliticization, and co-optation, which, within the context of South Korea's vastly altered socioeconomic conditions, no longer worked as effectively as it had in the 1960s. The way Park employed the strategy of repression became more clumsy as time progressed and as he lost the vigilance, discipline, and system of checks and balances that had served him so well during the 1960s. When female workers of the bankrupt wig producer YH staged a sit-in at the NDP headquarters to demand payment of unpaid wages in August 1979, Park sided with hard-liner PSS chief Ch'a Chi-ch'ŏl and sent in the police. In the ensuing melee one of the workers was killed, confirming dissident forces' charge that the *yushin* regime was brutal.[66] When the opposition NDP struck back by organizing its own sit-in, Park escalated the conflict rather than seeking compromise, getting three NDP district leaders who were secretly on his payroll to apply for a court order to suspend NDP president Kim Young-sam's legal rights and duties as the NDP leader, because he was "elected by a party convention where many delegates were legally ineligible to vote." The court duly complied, appointing NDP party convention chairman Chŏng Un-gap of the anti-mainstream faction as the NDP acting president in September 1979. With Chŏng Un-gap accepting his new role and Yi Ch'ŏl-sŭng's centrist anti-mainstream camp supporting him on the ground that "even unjust laws [were] laws demanding compliance," Kim Young-sam fought back all the harder, publicly calling for Park's resignation and demanding U.S. intervention against the *yushin* regime.[67] Park refused to put the brakes on the escalating conflict and played into the opposition's hand, assembling the DRP and Yujŏnghoe legislators on October 4, 1979, to expel Kim Young-sam from the National Assembly. This act provoked Kim Young-sam's supporters in Pusan and Masan to revolt twelve days later.

South Korea was no longer the socially demobilized and politically passive traditional rural society it had been eighteen years earlier. There stood a new breed of opposition party leaders—Kim Young-sam and Kim Dae-jung—personifying the frustrations and hopes of the mass society and rejecting outright any political compromise, because, to quote Kim Young-sam when threatened by KCIA director Kim Chae-gyu, "losing a National Assembly seat or being jailed [makes us] look dead only temporarily. The reality is [we] will live eternally."[68] South Korea had outgrown Park because he had succeeded brilliantly in modernizing its economy while brutally repressing its political society. The old political strategy of control, depoliticization, and mobilization that worked so well for Park in 1965, 1967, and 1972 did not work in 1979. In fact, it only backfired and hardened his opponents' resolve to bring an end to his *yushin* regime.[69]

CHAPTER SIX

The Armed Forces

Joo-Hong Kim

THE SOUTH KOREAN armed forces became directly involved in politics with Park Chung Hee's military coup d'état in May 1961. The transition to "civilian rule" in October 1963 dismantled the military junta, but did not make the armed forces less of an actor in the country's politics. Park was to rule South Korea as a soldier-turned-civilian-politician and the armed forces served him both as the ultimate guarantor of political order in times of crisis and as a stable supplier of loyalists and supporters to man the key institutions of his political regime. The South Korean military belonged to what Samuel P. Huntington once called a "praetorian guard,"[1] putting Park's political interests before all others in the belief that his interests were its institutional interests as well as South Korea's national interests.

From Park's perspective, the armed forces were too important *not* to politicize. First, to perpetuate his reign, Park had to call on the armed forces, his most reliable power base, to check, control, and repress the opposition to his authoritarian rule and to preempt society from developing an independent base of power. Over the course of eighteen years, Park proclaimed martial law five times and invoked garrison decrees three times to quell mounting challenges from *chaeya* dissidents, opposition politicians, and new emerging social forces. To get the military to line up against the opposition in times of crisis, Park had to politicize it, making it his personal vehicle. Second, once a victim but ultimately the beneficiary of factionalism within the South Korean armed forces, Park knew that he had to use military factional rivalries to his personal advantage if he was to keep a tight rein on them. By doing so, he politicized the South Korean armed forces even more. He was a master of factional struggles and palace intrigues.

However, it is important to emphasize that the politicization of the armed forces did not necessarily hurt national modernization. In fact, long before Park's military coup, the outbreak of the Korean War (1950–1953) had transformed the once rag-tag army, consisting of former colonial officers and independence fighters of all ideological stripes split into innumerable factions, into a professionalized military with the potential to lead the country into modernity. As postwar South Korea became the front line of defense against communist aggression in East Asia, the United States poured in massive amounts of military aid to continue upgrading its ally's fighting capabilities. Included in the aid was training of the South Korean officer corps that would prove instrumental in the expansion of the military's role to nonmilitary nation-building activities in the 1960s. By the time Park launched his coup, the armed forces had become the most cohesive and modernized institution in South Korea. Indeed, members of the coup coalition succeeded in consolidating their power mainly because they were able to control, master, and harness the military institutions in all their complexity for the goal of nation building. At the same time, they were capable of using the organizational advantages stemming from the powers of military institutions to weaken civilian social forces and orchestrate modernization.

It cannot be assumed that the politicization of the armed forces and its expansion of the military's role into nonmilitary arenas obstructed its professionalization. On the contrary, during Park's long tenure, the military became an even more professionalized and formidable modern combat force. External security factors pushed Park to strengthen its esprit de corps. First, even after the devastation of North Korea's economy and society during the Korean War, its leader, Kim Il Sung, held on to his ambition to "liberate" the South from U.S. imperialism, allocating up to 25 percent of North Korea's gross national product to build up massive artillery batteries along the demilitarized zone (DMZ) and to forward-deploy much of its armed forces. To deter Kim Il Sung from launching a second Korean War, Park had to invest heavily in the professional training of his officer corps, the upgrading of weapons systems, and the building of a national defense industry. Second, in 1965 Park dispatched combat troops to South Vietnam as part of an effort to forge a robust alliance relationship with his seemingly fickle ally, the United States, which was increasingly eager to extricate itself from Asian security commitments. In the process, the Vietnam

War also became an opportunity to test and upgrade South Korea's military capabilities. After the combat troops were sent to Vietnam, the war itself became a rationale to keep up the pace of professionalization.

The question is, then, how such diverging images of the South Korean armed forces as a politicized and professional military could co-exist. Chapter 6 argues that the two images both constituted the South Korean reality, but were not as contradictory as they appeared because Park, aware of their potential contradictory institutional impacts, drew on a two-tiered strategy of dominance that balanced the requirements of securing a politically loyal but also institutionally professional military.[2] The first set of principles of dominance was insulation and monopolization. Both as a measure to preempt others from mobilizing military factional struggles to their personal advantage and as a way to build a professional combat force capable of meeting external security challenges, Park insulated the South Korean military from all political and social forces except himself. For Park, the insulation was a step toward his monopolization of the armed forces' loyalty as well as his protection of its esprit de corps and institutional capabilities. Under his strict control, the military was to be used only as an instrument of his rule in domestic political struggles and as a tool for military deterrence in inter-Korea relations. This dual strategy of insulation and monopolization was considerably facilitated by his victory in the 1961–1963 struggles among members of the junta to control the military. Uncovering some eleven or so "counterrevolutionary plots" allegedly prepared by rival generals in the junta, Park had purged from the armed forces all potential challengers to his leadership by the time he won the presidential election in 1963.[3] Thereafter, his task was to maintain this hard-won control despite political democratization and despite his own aging, which triggered competition for succession among the second tier of political leaders.

Second, Park adopted a dual-track promotion system, whereby the praetorian guards commanded strategic military intelligence units and the professional soldiers rose through the field army. The two tracks rarely crossed, deterring professionalization from obstructing Park's use of the armed forces as his personal praetorian guard in times of crisis and also preventing politicization from undermining the continued transformation of the South Korean armed forces into a professional institution. Once a graduate of the Korea Military Army entered the path of either a field command or a countersubversive security post, he usually remained within the track of his initial choice and enjoyed the privileges accruing to that career path. Those in the countersubversive security path were trusted by Park to participate in the innermost circles of decision making on vital political issues. They wielded immense power vis-à-vis field commanders, but they rarely got promoted to the rank of four-star general.[4] In a sense, the officers of the security forces traded in honor and prestige for power. By contrast, the officers in the field commander path ascended to the highest and most prestigious posts within the armed forces, including that of four-star army chief of staff. It was the field army's responsibility to maintain military deterrence against P'yŏngyang.

Moreover, Park adopted the strategy of divide and conquer toward security officers in order to preempt the formation of any rival to his leadership within the military. The Army Security Command (ASC) was closely watched over by the Capital Garrison Command (CGC), and the two were also kept in line by the Korea Central Intelligence Agency (KCIA) and the Presidential Security Service (PSS), the other core agencies of Park's security apparatus. Even so, Park knew that he had to decide personally on the promotions of high-ranking military officers in order to keep his most trusted lieutenants on their toes.[5]

Security Challenges and Professionalization

Military as an Instrument of Foreign Policy, 1963–1967

Park Chung Hee saw economic development and national security as inseparably linked; building a strong military required a strong industrial economy and vice versa. To focus on economic growth with the belief that this process would trickle over into a military build-up in the long run could not be his chosen strategy of modernization, because throughout his rule the North Korean military threat was real and imminent. Concentrating on economic growth was possible only if South Korea possessed strong defense capabilities to deter Kim Il Sung from waging war. The North had already surpassed its southern rival in terms of per capita GNP by 1958. To raise anxiety even more, the North-South gap continued to widen throughout the 1960s with Kim Il Sung's successful completion of the Three-Year Recovery Plan (1954–1956) and the first Five-Year Plan (1957–1961).[6] This rising economic gap also translated into a military gap, as it enabled P'yŏngyang to rebuild its armed forces. With as much as 25 to 30 percent of its GNP spent on defense, the North was able to maintain a standing army of more than 400,000 soldiers, with a population half the size of South Korea's.

Catching up with and eventually surpassing the North in both economic and military capabilities were extremely challenging tasks. The South Korean economy was too small, too poor, and too vulnerable to security threats to attract foreign capital. Consequently Park turned to state power and political bargaining to secure what the market could not make. Not only to strengthen the alliance with the United States—South Korea's last pillar of military deterrence and security—but also to secure capital, technology, and an export market through foreign policy, Park in the mid-1960s ventured into two controversial foreign policies in which the military played a critical role. One was to acquire reparation funds through the normalization of the diplomatic relationship with the country's former colonial power, Japan, which threw society into turmoil that could be controlled only by the military. The other was the dispatching of combat troops to South Vietnam as an ally of the United States for the purpose of military modernization, economic development, and alliance enhancement. Sending combat troops earned Park a steady inflow of U.S. aid (see Chapters 14 and 15).

In the case of normalizing relations with Japan, the military's role was that of a loyal guard defending Park and his regime from the massive demonstrations that broke out in June 1964. With the university campuses in revolt, Park had to suspend negotiations with Japan, but at the same time proclaimed martial law to clamp down on the opposition to clear the way for a resumption of the talks. Thus began the "June 3 Incident," when for the first time since the transition to civilian rule, Park had to mobilize four infantry divisions to defend his presidency.[7] The military having reestablished order, Park directed the police to take student leaders into custody and request arrest warrants from the court. When the court refused, twelve armed members of the airborne unit under the Capital Garrison Command broke into the court and forced the judges to issue the warrants.[8] Paratroopers also broke into the *Dong-A Ilbo* newsroom to threaten reporters and editors for their critical reports on the crackdown. The Counter Intelligence Command (CIC), the predecessor of the Army Security Command, also resorted to physical violence, terrorizing journalists at *Dong-A Ilbo* and the Dong-A Broadcasting System.[9]

In the end, it was the military—especially the CGC and the CIC—that protected Park's reign from the student activists and opposition politicians during the worst days of the June 3 Incident. The two security forces and other military leaders and their troops removed political obstacles to the South Korea–Japan normalization of relations that Park believed was a precondition for not only economic development but also the strengthening of South Korea's alliance with the United States. Moreover, by allowing the military to voice its concerns regarding Kim Chong-p'il's efforts to consolidate his front-runner position in the race for presidential succession, Park was able not only to find a scapegoat to protect himself from the angry public but also to eliminate a potential challenger to his power. Kim had been Park's right-hand man and also a secret negotiator of the normalization agreement. The 1964 treaty crisis showed the armed forces as the defender of Park's political rule, in cracking down on the political opposition, building a growth-friendly security environment, and weeding out potential challengers by playing into Park's game of divide and conquer.

By contrast, the dispatch of combat troops to South Vietnam caused far less domestic controversy. For most South Koreans who had experienced the horrors of the Korean War, anticommunism was a way of life and pro-Americanism an instrument for survival. No major political force could seriously challenge Park's call to help the U.S. war effort in South Vietnam as a way to repay the debts South Korea owed the United States for coming to its defense in June 1950. At the same time, the troop dispatch was defined as an opportunity to secure capital and export markets for economic modernization projects. Military interests proved critical as well, with the Vietnam War judged to provide the South Korean armed forces with an opportunity to gain invaluable combat experience and also to modernize its forces with cutting-edge U.S. weapons systems. Moreover, South Korean military intervention convinced the United States not to relocate some of its troops stationed in South Korea to the battlegrounds in South Vietnam. Accordingly, after President Lyndon B. Johnson formally requested in May 1964 that South Korea support U.S. efforts in South Vietnam, Park had by September sent 1,954 military officers, a number of Mobile Army Surgery Hospital (MASH) units, and ten Taekwondo martial arts instructors, all for noncombat purposes.[10]

The dispatch of combat troops was more challenging, but antiwar sentiment still proved to be too weak to prevent it. To prepare for this effort, Park sent Ch'ae Myŏng-sin, chief of army operations, on a fact-finding mission to assess the military situation in South Vietnam, only to hear Ch'ae advise against military intervention.[11] The ruling Democratic Republican Party (DRP) had its own internal fissure in 1964, with Acting Chairman Chŏng Ku-yŏng openly opposing the dispatch of combat troops for fear of tarnishing the image of the South Korean armed forces, whom some were already branding as mercenaries. Even National Assembly member Ch'a Chi-ch'ŏl—one of Park's most trusted lieutenants since his days as Park's bodyguard in the 1961 coup—joined some twenty DRP legislators in preparing a resolution to rescind the decision to dispatch combat troops. The opposition National Democratic Party (NDP), university students, and progressive intellectuals also opposed sending troops, but certainly not on the scale of the opposition they showed against Park's drive to normalize relations with Japan. The voice of the opposition was weak and dispersed. In January 1965, eight months after Johnson's formal request for military intervention and four months after the dispatch of noncombat troops, two thousand South Korean combat troops sailed to South Vietnam.

Given the political risks and dangers of sending combat troops to South Vietnam in the midst of social unrest caused by the South Korean–Japanese normalization of relations, Park was intent on winning as many economic and security concessions from the United States as possible. Before sending additional combat troops to make South Korea's military intervention full-scale in October 1965, Park asked for a U.S. pledge to increase bilateral economic assistance, to aid the strengthening of combat readiness of the South Korean armed forces, and to maintain the current level of U.S. military presence in South Korea despite the rapid escalation of U.S. troop requirements in South Vietnam. The negotiations were formalized in the Brown Memorandum of March 4, 1966, whereby the United States agreed to finance the cost of South Korea's troop dispatches to South Vietnam and to support the modernization of its armed forces with an eye to closing the military capability gap vis-à-vis the North.[12] It is estimated that through this agreement a billion dollars' worth of economic and military aid were transferred to South Korea during the 1965–1970 period, which amounted to as much as 19 percent of its total foreign exchange earnings.[13]

North Korean Threats, 1968–1971

The year 1968 ushered in a period of security transition. On January 21, thirty-one North Korean guerrillas successfully infiltrated the western front of the demilitarized zone, which was under the command of the U.S. Army Second Infantry Division, and marched to within one kilometer, or 0.6 miles, of the Blue House to mount a surprise attack on Park himself. A fierce gunfight broke out in the heart of Seoul, killing Ch'oe Kyu-sik of the Chongno Police Station and some of the passengers on a commuter bus that was blown up by the guerrillas. The "January 21 Incident" shook the South Korean military, showing the vulnerability of Seoul to guerrilla infiltration and exposing the South's unpreparedness for nonconventional military conflict despite its combat experience in South Vietnam and the modernization of its weapons systems. The tactical capability and the ideological resolve of the guerrillas to wage a suicidal mission were shocking as well. Among the thirty-one guerrillas, only one was captured alive. The rest fought to the last man, demonstrating the fighting spirit of North Korean special forces units. The news that it took only a single day for the guerrillas to move some 25 miles (40 kilometers) along the ridge of the western front to reach Seoul heightened the sense of vulnerability.

On January 23, two days after the failed North Korean commando attack, came the news of the North Korean capture of the USS *Pueblo,* an American intelligence vessel reportedly operating in the high seas east of Wŏnsan, North Korea. While in captivity, the U.S. crew members were forced to apologize publicly for entering North Korean territorial waters for the purpose of espionage. The question of how to counter the North Korean provocations created a rift in the South Korean–American alliance. Whereas Park demanded that the United States first deal with the North Korean guerrilla attack on the Blue House, Johnson focused on the release of the *Pueblo* crew. Moreover, in contrast to Park's readiness for military retaliation, Johnson chose to seek a negotiated settlement; he could not afford to risk war in another part of Asia when the situation in South Vietnam was continuing to worsen. Park felt abandoned by the United States when Johnson separately negotiated the release of the *Pueblo* crew without taking action to prevent the recurrence of North Korean guerrilla attacks against the South. The sense of betrayal was especially acute because Park thought he had risked his presidency to stand by Johnson in the Vietnam War. But he was also pragmatic enough not to escalate conflict with the United States.

On the contrary, Park transformed the rift into another opportunity to strengthen South Korean defense capabilities. To appease Park, U.S. presidential envoy Cyrus Vance visited Seoul to issue a joint communiqué in which the United States pledged to increase military assistance. In addition, Vance agreed to equip the newly established reserve forces, whose mission was to protect the rear from nonconventional threats; to hold a regular bilateral defense ministers' meeting to upgrade the alliance; and to reaffirm the policy of using the United States Forces in Korea (USFK) troops as a human "trip-wire" against invading North Korean military forces by maintaining their forward deployment near the DMZ.[14] The forward deployment ensured an automatic military engagement of the United States in the event of war on the Korean Peninsula, because the invading North Korean troops could reach Seoul only after running over the USFK troops stationed between the DMZ and Seoul on the flat western front.

The show of U.S. commitment to the defense of South Korea notwithstanding, military provocation by the North continued throughout the late 1960s. On October 30, 1968, over a hundred guerrillas landed at the east coast villages of Uljin and Samch'ŏk to harass the South Korean military from the rear. On April 15, 1969, North Korea shot down an EC-121 U.S. reconnaissance plane to test the allies' intentions and capabilities. On December 11 of the same year, the North hijacked a Korean Air domestic flight.[15] Presumably, Kim Il Sung engaged in military provocations in the belief that the South Korean masses would revolt to overthrow Park at the slightest sign of his weakness. The success of the North Vietnamese with guerrilla warfare encouraged Kim to experiment with nonconventional military actions as well.[16] To his disappointment, the South Koreans rallied behind Park's efforts to strengthen military capabilities. The new reserve forces joined the regular troops in antiguerrilla operations in Uljin and Samch'ŏk. Park also established the Third Military Academy to train junior army officers on a scale much larger than that of the Korea Military Academy (KMA);[17] established various special forces units for counterinsurgency and counterespionage operations; created new command posts to strengthen defense capabilities in the rear; adopted new weapons systems; and lengthened the service period of enlisted soldiers from two to three years.[18]

The security situation, however, continued to worsen. With the Guam Doctrine, announced in July 1969, newly elected U.S. president Richard M. Nixon began preparing for an "honorable" exit from the Vietnam War. Although the doctrine pledged continued U.S. support for the allies in Asia within the framework of existing defense agreements, it was interpreted by Park as a sign of weakening U.S. commitment to South Korea and to the East Asian region. With per capita GNP and gross military expenditures still lagging behind those of the North, South Korea became deeply unsettled by the Guam Doctrine. To raise its anxiety even more, the U.S. search for an exit from the Vietnam War culminated in national security adviser Henry A. Kissinger's secret visit to Beijing in July 1971 to prepare for a Sino-American summit meeting and China's entry into the United Nations as a permanent Security Council member. The coming of détente at the level of great power relations was, however, joined by an opposite trend of rising tensions on the Korean Peninsula. P'yŏngyang had announced its Four Military Principles to increase military pressure on Seoul in 1962.[19] And in January 1969, it embraced the simultaneous pursuit of conventional and nonconventional warfare should it launch a surprise attack on the South.[20]

With the change of U.S. military goals in the Vietnam War, Park lost his major source of leverage over U.S. policy. During the 1960s, Park had used Johnson's need of South Korean support for the war effort not only to secure U.S. assistance in the modernization of the armed forces and the development of his country's economy but also to win U.S. acquiescence in his increasingly heavy-handed treatment of his domestic political opposition. As the Guam Doctrine weakened Park's position, he frenziedly tried to control the damage. The goal was to get the United States to retract or scale down its rapidly emerging plan for troop reduction or withdrawal from South Korea. If that goal could not be achieved, the next was to get increased U.S. military assistance as a compensation for any removal of U.S. troops. At the same time, Park knew he was working against forces of change that were ultimately beyond his control, and began preparing for the worst by embarking on an ambitious plan to make South Korea self-sufficient in military defense through heavy and chemical industrialization.

The reduction and relocation of USFK military troops began in earnest in the early 1970s. Twenty-four thousand soldiers of the U.S. Seventh Infantry Division and three combat air force battalions left South Korea by March 1971, while the U.S. Second Infantry Division, with 20,000 soldiers, pulled back to Tongduch'ŏn, south of its original front-line military bases, making the First Infantry Division of the South Korean Army formally take over the defense of the western front from the U.S. Eighth Army. There were still a total of 46,000 USFK soldiers stationed on the Korean Peninsula, enough to maintain deterrence against the North. Nonetheless, the Guam Doctrine made Park realize that South Korea had to take charge of a substantial part of its own defense, and that meant more modernization for its military.

In the 1971–1975 period the Ministry of National Defense (MoND) pushed forward an aggressive military modernization project, with a U.S. military assistance program worth $1.5 billion secured by foreign minister Ch'oe Kyu-ha in his negotiations with U.S. ambassador William J. Porter finalized in February 1971, in return for accepting the U.S. withdrawal of one of its two ground divisions.[21] The Ministry of Commerce and Industry backed the MoND by starting the construction of a giant industrial complex in Ch'angwŏn in April 1974 in order to put in place an industrial infrastructure for the manufacture of military weapons. The Ministry of Science and Technology joined in the effort, creating the Agency of Defense Development[22] to take exclusive charge of the production of new weapons systems as well as taking over war matériel transferred from U.S. military troops leaving South Korea as part of a bilateral agreement signed in September 1973.[23] In this way Park began to implement his ambitious plan to develop the heavy and chemical industries as a self-sustaining basis for modernizing South Korean military capabilities to a level sufficient to deter a North Korean attack. While South Korea had agreed with the United States in February 1971 to establish a bilateral Security Consultative Meeting of their defense and foreign ministers as an effort at alliance building, Park focused on self-reliance, given the uncertainty of U.S. goals, intentions, and strategies.

Military Catch-Up, 1972–1979

To back the development of a national defense industry institutionally, Park appointed O Wŏn-ch'ŏl as second senior secretary for economic affairs in 1971 and entrusted him with the coordination of heavy and chemical industrialization (HCI). On the recommendation of O Wŏn-ch'ŏl, Park established a Defense Industry Bureau inside the Ministry of National Defense and organized a Logistics Council, chaired by the prime minister, to orchestrate interministerial coordination on defense industry policy in March 1973. Three weeks before, Park had enacted a Special Logistics Act for Procurement to support the *chaebol* conglomerates' entry into strategic HCI projects with the goal of transforming them into defense-related firms.[24] The MoND enthusiastically responded to Park's initiative, eventually creating the post of Assistant Vice Minister for the Defense Industry in September 1977 and spinning off its Defense Industry Bureau into three separate bureaus in December of the same year.[25] Park even developed, or tried to give the appearance of developing, a nuclear weapons program with the goal of either reversing President Jimmy Carter's campaign pledge of military withdrawal or securing South Korea's own instrument of deterrence (see Chapter 17).[26]

The inter-Korea balance of power began to shift visibly in favor of the South in the mid-1970s. The South Korean economy continued to grow at breakneck speed, outstripping the North in terms of per capita GNP in 1974 and enlarging the gap by over 50 percent of North Korea's per capita GNP in 1977. In the area of defense expenditures, the change was also dramatic. Whereas South Korea managed to provide only 50 percent of its total defense requirements through domestic resources in 1969, its ratio of self-sufficiency in defense expenditures surpassed 90 percent by 1975. Indirect U.S. military assistance ended in 1974, and direct U.S. military assistance terminated by 1978, but this did not threaten South Korean capabilities. After winning the $1.5 billion military assistance program from the United States in 1971, Park made an extra effort to extract domestic resources to maintain the armed forces at the level of 600,000 to 650,000 troops. In July 1975, he introduced a defense tax to support an increase in the defense budget from 4 percent to 5 percent of the country's GNP starting in 1976.

The weapons improvement program also made great headway during the *yushin* era (see Chapter 8). The 1971–1976 period saw the South Korean defense industry complex establish a solid base for research and development as well as for mass production of ammunition and light weapons such as M-16 rifles, mortars, and hand grenades through an intricate system of local content programs and technology licensing arrangements. In 1974, Park put in place the Yulgok Program, which ran until 1981, with the goal of rapidly moving into the next stage of improving defense capabilities. The mass production of basic light weapons and ammunitions was instituted during the first phase of Yulgok.[27] In September 1978, the South Korean armed forces celebrated the successful launching of a test missile named Paekkom (White Bear), a remodeled Nike-Hercules with a range of 112 miles (180 kilometers), in the presence of Park Chung Hee.[28] Not all defense industry programs contributed to South Korea's national interests as well as Park's political objectives in a positive way, however. The clandestine nuclear program brought more costs than benefits as it heightened U.S. fears of regional nuclear proliferation and damaged Park's relationship with Jimmy Carter beyond repair.[29] To preempt Park from going into the next stage of nuclear weapons development, the United States offered to deploy long-range missiles in South Korea.[30]

In spite of South Korea's successful catch-up militarily, North Korean threats continued into the 1970s. During the 1974–1978 period, the South Korean military discovered underground infiltration tunnels dug by the North to send its troops to the rear of the forward-deployed South Korean military troops. The first underground tunnel was found in Korangp'o on the western front bordering the DMZ in November 1974; the second in Ch'ŏlwŏn, lying on the central front in March 1975; and the third near P'anmunjŏm in October 1978. The second and third tunnels were large enough to accommodate five-ton trucks and 155mm howitzers. The South Korean armed forces estimated that as many as four columns of infantry soldiers could march down each of the two tunnels to attack South Korean military troops from the rear.[31] On August 18, 1976, two U.S. officers were brutally murdered by axe-wielding North Korean soldiers in the Joint Security Area at P'anmunjŏm. These North Korean provocations only worsened the South Koreans' sense of vulnerability. The North was putting military pressure on the South precisely when Carter's presidential campaign was making the future U.S. military role on the Korean Peninsula uncertain. The tunnels and the axe-murders only strengthened Park's resolve to counter the North with internal political unity and to build up South Korea's military capabilities.

At the tenth South Korean–American Security Consultative Meeting held in Seoul in July 1977, the representatives of the two allies' armed forces agreed to integrate operational command of the South Korean military troops with that of USFK troops and to establish a Combined Forces Command (CFC) by 1978, in order for the allies to fight effectively as a joint force and for South Korea to take a greater role in operational command and bear a larger share of the costs of deterrence. The two sides followed up with another Security Consultative Meeting in July 1978 to establish a joint Military Committee, the mission of which was to decide collectively on strategic issues.[32] With the Military Committee issuance of its Strategic Directive no. 1, the construction of the CFC began in July 1978 and was completed in three-and-a-half months.

In the newly organized CFC, the South Korean military took the posts of deputy commander and deputy chief of staff and filled the positions within personnel, intelligence, logistics, communications, and electronic engineering, whereas the United States held the posts of commander and chief of staff and was responsible for staffing operations and planning.[33] In a sense, the internal organization of the CFC reflected the transitional nature of the U.S.–South Korean security alliance, giving the South Korean military a greater voice in operational control, but not going so far as to give it an upper hand in wartime command. The latter rested solely with the USFK commander, who also served as the CFC commander. Even during peacetime, the most critical part of operational control—strategic planning—was controlled by the U.S.-dominated CFC staff of operations and planning. The USFK commander's role as head of the CFC as well as of the United Nations Command (UNC), responsible for overseeing the armistice agreement signed with North Korea in July 1953, ensured that the United States would continue to have a decisive influence on the South Korean military's strategic doctrine and options.[34]

Regime Security and Praetorian Guards

Taming Kim Chong-p'il, 1961–1969

In parallel with the efforts toward professionalization, Park worked relentlessly to monopolize the loyalty of the South Korean armed forces in order to preempt others from using the military against him and to defend his political rule. The central mechanism Park built up to turn the armed forces into his instrument of political control, repression, and preemption was a multilayered system of checks and balances he established among the military intelligence units. During the 1960s, the main target of political isolation was ironically Kim Chong-p'il, his right-hand man. Only a handful of Park's political confidants and lieutenants dared to harbor ambitions to succeed him on the basis of their extensive organized support within the DRP and the military. Kim Chong-p'il was one such person; he survived as the front-runner in competition for succession until the late 1960s. The core members of Kim Chong-p'il's mainstream faction held key posts in the DRP Secretariat, the KCIA, and the National Assembly until the constitutional revision of 1969 allowed Park's third presidential term. Being the front-runner in the race for succession as early as the mid-1960s meant that Kim Chong-p'il could readily win over new supporters who jumped on the bandwagon, but he was also the target of checks and balances by other aspirants for power, if not by the presidency itself. Ironically, it was Park who was most interested in keeping Kim Chong-p'il in line. Until power struggles surrounding the constitutional revision of 1969 seriously damaged Kim Chong-p'il's claim to the status of crown prince, Park's strategy of divide and conquer focused on building an anti-mainstream faction that would break Kim Chong-p'il's aspirations. As of the mid-1960s, Kim Chong-p'il commanded an impressive political arsenal. During the military junta period, he had been entrusted with the task of directing the KCIA (1961–1963), as well as clandestinely organizing the DRP Secretariat in preparation for the elections of 1963. Both tasks enabled him to build his own faction through political patronage. Once he seized control of the DRP Secretariat, Kim Chong-p'il also dominated the process of nominating DRP candidates for the 1963 National Assembly election.

It was not hard for Park to roll back Kim Chong-p'il's growing power, because the same sources of that power could be turned into political liabilities. Beginning in December 1962, Kim's rivals damaged his integrity by digging up his illicit activities, including raising funds for the birth of the DRP by illegal means. Moreover, Park, with his power consolidated after his election as president in 1963, then had less need of Kim Chong-p'il. The first layer of balancers Park found among military officers on active duty and in the reserves to check Kim Chong-p'il were those of the eighth KMA class and the senior generation that had participated in the 1961 coup and survived subsequent purges. Included in this first layer were Kim Hyŏng-uk, Pak Chong-gyu, and Yi Hu-rak, who became KCIA director (1963–1969), chief of the Presidential Security Service (1963–1974), and presidential chief of staff (1963–1968), respectively. These men were judged to be without any hope, ambition, or capacity to vie for presidential succession, given their lack of charisma, independent factional base, and public support. Their fate depended entirely upon Park, which made Park's interest become their interest. The three praetorian guards cooperated with the DRP's anti-mainstream faction led by Kim Sŏng-gon, a civilian politician of the dismantled Liberal Party, and his Gang of Four to isolate Kim Chong-p'il and eventually break his will to power.

The first opportunity to keep Kim Chong-p'il in line came in February 1963, when the rapidly emerging anti-mainstream faction forced Kim Chong-p'il to "retire" from public service on the charge of illegal fundraising and political corruption during the junta period. As we have seen in earlier chapters, when the normalization of diplomatic relations with Japan caused a political uproar in 1965, the same anti–Kim Chong-p'il faction in the Blue House, KCIA, Presidential Security Service, and DRP allied themselves for the second time—but this time, also with generals such as Kim Chae-gyu (Sixth Infantry Division), Kim Chin-wi (Capital Garrison Command), Chŏng Pong-uk (Twentieth Infantry Division), and Yi Pyŏng-yŏp (Thirty-Third Infantry Division), in command of the military troops to implement martial law in Seoul—in order to force Kim Chong-p'il's second "retirement" from politics. Long frustrated by the rise of Kim Chong-p'il and his eighth Korea Military Academy (KMA) class, these commanders joined KCIA director Kim Hyŏng-uk (a self-appointed leader of the anti-mainstream faction) in suggesting to Park that he remove Kim Chong-p'il from his DRP chairmanship.[35] The anti–Kim Chong-p'il faction in the DRP also saw the June 3 Incident as an opportunity to topple Kim Chong-p'il from his position as the de facto successor to Park. The drive to squeeze Kim out was led by the civilian politicians recruited by Park from the now dismantled Liberal Party.[36] Criticized by demonstrators as a betrayer of Korean nationalism and attacked by his rivals in both the military and the DRP, Kim Chong-p'il resigned on June 4 and went into "exile" abroad. Having made Kim Chong-p'il the scapegoat, Park signed a treaty normalizing relations with Japan.

At the same time, when Park, rather than Kim Chong-p'il, became the target of military discontent, Park lost no time in cracking down on protestors. Such was the case when more than twenty officers, including Wŏn Ch'ung-yŏn, a colonel in the reserves and Park's spokesperson during the junta years, were arrested by the CIC on the charge of plotting a military coup in May 1965. It is not clear what the officers were plotting, if they were indeed plotting at all. But a report that they had clandestinely met to exchange critical views of Park's way of political rule, including the dispatch of combat troops to South Vietnam, was enough for Park to act.[37] The intentions of Wŏn Ch'ung-yŏn and his group were less important to Park than the opportunity the incident afforded him to establish discipline over the armed forces before going further with the politically risky troop dispatch. The political situation was already tense, with society polarized over the parliamentary ratification of the bill to normalize relations with Japan. Park used Wŏn Ch'ung-yŏn's supposed attempt at counterrevolution as a pretext to tighten political control. On August 26, 1965, Park invoked a garrison decree and called on the Sixth Infantry Division to maintain order in Seoul for the second time in fourteen months. The troops were evacuated on September 2 and the garrison decree ended on September 25, as political protest over the normalization of relations with Japan subsided.

The 1963 and 1965 episodes of forced exile certainly damaged, but did not destroy, Kim Chong-p'il's political career. On the contrary, the crown prince returned to South Korea within a few months after the public uproar subsided. It was only when Park and the anti–Kim Chong-p'il coalition of praetorian guards, civilian DRP legislators, and next-generation military leaders successfully cajoled and threatened Kim Chong-p'il into accepting the constitutional amendment to clear the way for Park's third presidential term in 1969 that Kim Chong-p'il began losing his political clout as a primary contender for succession. The possibility that Park would remain in power indefinitely damaged the power base of the crown prince. Kim Chong-p'il's faction rapidly disintegrated; some members were disappointed by his inability to stand up to Park and others began to rethink what Kim's capacity for political patronage might now be.

To Kim Chong-p'il's discomfort, moreover, there also emerged by the early 1970s a second layer of balancers against him among the eleventh KMA graduating class under Park's patronage. The eleventh KMA class constituted the next generation of leaders in the South Korean armed forces. As such, they did not compete with Kim Chong-p'il for presidential power. Nor did they challenge the anti-mainstream faction of senior military leaders, civilian politicians, and presidential guards. They were Park's loyalists at the mid-level of South Korea's military leadership, then in control of major combat forces. As the first of KMA graduating classes to receive a full four-year program of military training and education, the members of the eleventh class prided themselves on being the first generation of South Korea's "professional" military officers and "genuine" KMA graduates. Moreover, too young to receive Japanese, Chinese, or Soviet military training during the era of Japanese colonialism and the Korean struggle for national liberation (1910–1945), the eleventh graduating class not only personified the spirit of national independence but also stood above the factionalism formed on the basis of pre-liberation political and educational affiliations. Park, too, thought that the eleventh graduating class could and should provide leadership for a new professionalized South Korean armed forces.[38]

Chun Doo-hwan was one of the eleventh KMA graduates who played a key role in creating a bridge between the young officers and Park. Chun Doo-hwan first met Park in May 1961. They then held the ranks of captain and major general, respectively. The young Chun Doo-hwan demonstrated his political value by organizing a public parade of eight hundred or so KMA cadets in support of the military coup. The parade helped turn the tide of public opinion in favor of Park, who was then struggling to put down Yi Han-lim's dissenting voice and win U.S. support. In July 1963, Chun Doo-hwan—by now a major—succeeded in deepening Park's trust by plotting with his KMA classmates, including Roh Tae-woo, to come to the aid of the anti-mainstream faction's campaign to oust Kim Chong-p'il and forty DRP politicians of the mainstream faction with the goal of consolidating Park's power base before the upcoming presidential election of October 1963. It was in this context that seven leaders of the eleventh KMA graduating class formed Ch'ilsŏnghoe (Society of Seven Stars), later renamed the Hanahoe (Society of One), as a secret society with the approval of Park Chung Hee.[39] Park was their invisible patron, entrusting the army chief of staff Sŏ Chong-ch'ŏl, CGC commander Yun P'il-yong, and PSS chief Pak Chong-gyu with the task of putting the members of the Hanahoe on the fast track to promotion. The secret society soon expanded to include members of the twelfth to twentieth KMA graduating classes.

The Hanahoe developed into a cohesive faction, recruiting only those military officers thoroughly screened and unanimously voted in by its members, and building strict internal rules and regulations on conduct.[40] To make its organization even more exclusive and cohesive, the Hanahoe recruited mostly KMA graduates from the Kyŏngsang region, the home of both Park Chung Hee and Chun Doo-hwan. Ultimately, however, it was the Hanahoe members' special relationship with Park and the privileges that relationship conferred on them that held them together. The army headquarters assigned Hanahoe members to the "political" units located inside or near Seoul—the CGC, ASC, PSC, KCIA, and Airborne Command, which lay outside the U.S.-dominated CFC command structure and hence were available for Park's mobilization without consultation with the United States.[41] When Hanahoe members were up for field duties on the front lines, the army headquarters typically assigned them to the First or Ninth Infantry Division stationed at the western front access route to Seoul.

In addition to the most coveted posts, Hanahoe members also enjoyed rapid promotion. The four key founding members—Chun Doo-hwan, Son Yŏng-gil, Kim Pok-tong, and Ch'oe Sŏng-t'aek—were promoted to brigadier general in 1973, the first among the eleventh graduating class to achieve that rank. The four were all from the Kyŏngsang region.[42] To consolidate their privileges, Hanahoe members—with the backing of their patrons, including Yun P'il-yong and Pak Chong-gyu—quickly developed a tradition of handing over key military posts among themselves. In particular, the Presidential Security Guard Unit 30 of the CGC, responsible for guarding the Blue House and hence located nearest to Park, saw its command post transferred from Son Yŏng-gil to Chun Doo-hwan (1967) to Pak Kap-nyong (1969). All three were Hanahoe members of the eleventh KMA graduating class. The next four commanders of the 1970s were similarly Hanahoe soldiers of the fourteenth to seventeenth KMA graduating classes. They were to prevent Kim Chong-p'il from dominating the next-generation leadership of the South Korean armed forces.

Regime Change, 1971–1972

By the time Park was elected president for a third time in 1971, there was in place an intricate multilayered system of checks and balances within the South Korean armed forces that seemingly ensured stability and order. Military politics was, however, anything but stable and orderly in the early 1970s. Not only a spread of sociopolitical tensions and economic problems, but also Park's transformation of those challenges into an opportunity to bring about his lifelong rule, dragged the praetorian part of the South Korean military deeper into political struggles and, in the process, unintentionally came to undermine the system of checks and balances.

The year 1971 was particularly filled with sociopolitical tensions and economic challenges. On August 10 of that year, some fifty thousand residents in Kwangju, Kyŏnggi Province, broke out in violent protests, burning down a police station and patrol cars and staging sit-ins at government buildings. They claimed that the government had not kept its promise to provide economic assistance for the resettlement of squatters forcefully removed from the slums in Seoul. To aid the police, the military had to be called in to suppress the riots.[43] The turmoil exposed for the first time the tensions that had been building up since Park embarked on his hyper-growth strategy in the mid-1960s. Then, on August 23, twenty-four commandos in a South Korean air force camp who were training to infiltrate North Korea in retaliation for the January 21 Incident of 1968 killed twelve guards to escape isolated Silmi Island and hijacked a bus to enter Seoul to voice their grievances concerning maltreatment. In the ensuing gunfight with the military forces, all the commandos committed suicide, but the breakout was enough to intensify societal concerns.

Regime opponents seeking democratization came forward as well. On

August 18, 1971, progressive professors at Seoul National University publicly criticized the police surveillance of student activists. University students followed with their own protest. The agenda quickly grew to include
the abolition of military drills on university campuses and the ousting of
"pro-Park" professors from the universities. On October 4, Korea University students began a sit-in to demand the punishment of corrupt politicians. Included in the list of politicians the students wanted purged were
DRP finance chairman Kim Chin-man, KCIA director Yi Hu-rak, and
CGC commander Yun P'il-yong. After the CGC's repeated intervention in
politics to weed out *chaeya* activists and terrorize opposition politicians,
its commander had become the symbol of the politicization of the South
Korea military.

Challenged by the mounting calls for democratization, but also sensing
an opportunity for counterattack amid the public's sense of crisis, Park
chose to move swiftly and decisively against the student protestors at Korea University, ordering Yun P'il-yong to send the CGC military police
onto the campus at dawn on October 5 to break up the sit-in, arrest student leaders, and close down classes. The defense minister threatened to
conscript any university students who refused to participate in campus
military drills, only to see demonstrations spread from Korea University to
other campuses. Clergy from many Christian denominations joined in
the rallies to denounce social injustice and political corruption. Park was
not intimidated by the coalescing of opposition forces. On the contrary,
he escalated the conflict, putting Seoul and its surrounding areas under a
garrison decree on October 15 and sending soldiers onto ten university
campuses to arrest the leaders of the student movements. In the end, more
than four thousand students were arrested and forcefully drafted into the
military.

As Park was challenged by society and as he sought to use this challenge
as an opportunity for instituting lifelong rule, then, the political role of the
South Korean military increased dramatically. Consequently, for the parliamentary election held on May 25, 1971, Park nominated forty-one retired generals as DRP candidates, giving the military the single largest
share, 46.6 percent, of the total number of nominees.[44] Although Park had
regularly appointed military officers on active duty and in the reserves to
important posts in the ruling political party, state bureaucracy, and state-
owned companies, the number of former military officers he recruited into
politics in 1971 was extraordinary.[45] Distrusting the incumbent DRP legislators, who split into rival factions to vie for power in anticipation of
Park's expected retirement after his third term (1971–1975), Park's loyal
military officers, once elected, were entrusted with checking Kim Chong-

p'il, whose supporters had opposed the extension of presidential terms to three in 1969, and Kim Sŏng-gon and his Gang of Four, whose loyalty could not be taken for granted in the event of the weakening of Kim Chong-p'il's mainstream faction.[46] The issue for Park in 1971 was not whether, but when and how, he would mobilize his praetorian guards to neutralize both Kim Chong-p'il and Kim Sŏng-gon in his bid for the extension of his rule. On December 6, 1971, Park declared a state of national emergency. The decree identified national security as the highest priority of the state and "disallowed" any social unrest threatening security. To overcome military security threats, South Koreans were called upon to restrain from "any irresponsible discussion" of security issues, to build up a "new belief system," and to endure temporary restrictions on civil rights.[47] The cabinet followed on December 7 with the preparation of a Military Establishment Protection Act, a Military Secret Protection Act, and an Amendment to the Requisition Act. These three bills laid the foundation for legally mobilizing the military for political purposes. A day earlier, Park had publicly presented his view of South Korea's changing security situation and its limited means to counter the external threat. "As it is impossible to defend against the [North Korean] invader's swords with the slogans of freedom and peace," Park declared, "[South Korea] should go forward with a firm determination to restrain a part of its freedom [for national security]."[48]

To strengthen his position further, Park called on the Speaker of the National Assembly on December 23 to speed up the enactment of a Special Law for National Security.[49] Passed on December 27, it enabled Park effectively to preempt any challenge to his rule, after the special law made clear that it was the president's duty to defend the state and that the office of the president wielded the powers to regulate the economy and order national mobilization for the purpose of defending state interests. Moreover, the special law stipulated that in the name of national security, the president could restrict the freedom of political association and demonstration, freedom of speech and the press, and workers' rights to collective action.[50]

To come up with a convincing security rationale for a regime change, however, Park thought he had to go beyond the traditional cold war rationale of containment, given the dramatically altered international security context of Sino-U.S. détente. Rather than justifying his turn to authoritarian rule only as a measure to prepare for confrontation with the North, Park combined the cold war rhetoric of military competition with the promise of reconciliation befitting the new era of détente. Park argued that by launching the *yushin* regime, the South strengthened not only its military deterrence but also its negotiating position vis-à-vis the North for co-existence. From the position of strength arising from internal political unity, Park argued, South Korea would negotiate favorable terms for unification. This newly added rationale of unification made it more difficult for not only the opposition NDP but also *chaeya* dissidents to oppose the promulgation of the *yushin* constitution in 1972. To undermine the opposition even more, Park appeared to be backing his words with concrete actions, sending KCIA director Yi Hu-rak to P'yŏngyang on a secret mission on May 2, 1972, to negotiate a mini-détente on the Korean Peninsula. After Yi's return, Park ordered him to draw up a "P'ungnyŏn saŏp" (Good Harvest Project), the blueprint for launching the *yushin* regime.[51]

Thereafter events moved rapidly. The two Koreas issued a Joint North-South Communiqué of July 4, 1972, to begin a dialogue for reconciliation based on the three principles of independence, peace, and national unity. At the same time, the Ministry of National Defense issued a statement cautioning against any euphoria and called for a strengthening of military deterrence. On National Armed Forces Day, October 1, Park himself came out to stress the importance of national security in the coming era of détente. On October 17, he declared martial law and deployed military troops in and around Seoul. The Army Security Command was ordered to investigate and arrest NDP legislators suspected of illegally raising political funds for Kim Dae-jung during his unsuccessful 1971 presidential bid. The ASC also searched for the opposition leader's sympathizers within the military and began cracking down on Kim Young-sam and his newly emerging faction within the NDP. The ASC, with its mission of counterintelligence and countersubversion within the military, now began to conduct regular investigations of civilian politicians.[52] The transition to authoritarian rule was completed when the State Council voted to submit the *yushin* constitution to a national referendum, which was duly held on November 22, 1972. Article 53 of the new constitution gave Park the power to take "emergency measures" for the maintenance of "national security" and "public peace and order."

Breakdown of Checks and Balances, 1973

While moving toward authoritarian rule on the basis of the armed forces' unswerving support in 1971–1972, Park also shook up the ruling coalition in order to clear away obstacles and nurture his bases of support. The objective was to adjust the control mechanism to the radical alteration in the parameters of power brought by the *yushin*. In the short run, the shake-up aided the launching of the *yushin* regime, but in the long run it damaged his regime's internal mechanism to correct extreme abuses of power and rectify the worst forms of policy distortions by seriously undermining the multilayered system of checks and balances Park had established within the 1961 coup generation and between the senior and Hanahoe officers. Ironically, it was the fall of Kim Chong-p'il from the position of crown prince that jeopardized the internal mechanism of checks and balances, because his fall reduced his rivals and foes' utility as instruments of checks and balances. Between 1971 and 1973, the ruling DRP saw Park lash out against Kim Sŏng-gon and his colleagues (Gang of Four), once they took over the mainstream role and used their newly found power to join the opposition NDP in a vote of no confidence against minister of home affairs O Ch'i-sŏng despite Park's explicit instruction not to weaken the cabinet. The military similarly saw CGC commander Yun P'il-yong stand trial under the charge of subversion on April 28, 1973. Park also dismissed Yi Hu-rak from his new post of KCIA director on December 3 of that year.

The purge of Yun P'il-yong shocked society, given his close ties to Park. The president had lavished him with patronage in spite of his failure to join his classmates of the eighth KMA graduating class in the 1961 coup.[53] Yun P'il-yong had risen from the rank of major in 1961 to that of major general by 1970. In those nine years of rapid promotion, he commanded the most powerful military units, from the Counter Intelligence Corps (1963–1968) to the Capital Garrison Command (1970–1973). In return for Park's political patronage, Yun P'il-yong diligently waged a "dirty war" on Park's behalf, suppressing political protests and cracking down on opposition politicians. By the early 1970s, Yun was singled out among military officers in uniform as a villain on the scale of Kim Hyŏng-uk and Yi Hu-rak in South Korean politics by political activists and dissidents. Yet Park came down hard on Yun P'il-yong, jailing him under the charge of subversion.

Yun had forgotten that he was only a caretaker of the Hanahoe, not its leader. His downfall began when PSS chief Pak Chong-gyu reported to Park on a discussion Yun had had with KCIA director Yi Hu-rak on the issue of succession. Park had reason to interpret Pak Chong-gyu's report with a grain of salt. As a political rival of Yi Hu-rak, Pak Chong-gyu had every reason to cast aspersions against Yun P'il-yong, who increasingly sided with Yi Hu-rak in palace politics. Yi Hu-rak was then at the zenith of his career, having orchestrated Park's victory in the 1971 presidential election against Kim Dae-jung. Yi Hu-rak had also triumphantly prepared the July 4 Joint Communiqué with Kim Il Sung, which opened the way for Park's promulgation of the *yushin* constitution in 1972. Alarmed by Yi Hu-rak's stunning political successes, Pak Chong-gyu was looking for a way to undercut his rival's political standing. When Sin Pŏm-sik, the president of a state-run newspaper, informed Pak Chong-gyu of Yun P'il-yong's talk with Yi Hu-rak on the subject of succession while playing golf in October 1972, the PSS chief promptly informed Park of their "disloyalty."[54]

Park was furious. He saw Yun P'il-yong as more threatening than Yi Hu-rak, because in his role as a caretaker of the Hanahoe on behalf of Park, Yun had managed to become its de facto leader. The Hanahoe was becoming a faction, with its top echelon ready for promotion to the rank of brigadier general and its rank-and-file members poised to monopolize mid-level positions in the military security forces. Park lost no time in ordering ASC commander Kang Ch'ang-sŏng to investigate Yun P'il-yong. Park's choice of Kang as the investigator on March 6, 1973, sealed Yun's fate. The two had been recognized by their superiors and classmates as having the makings of a future army chief of staff early in their military careers.[55] This was not the first time that they had confronted each other. In December 1967 Yun P'il-yong, then commander of the CIC, investigated Kang Ch'ang-sŏng for corruption. Kang Ch'ang-sŏng was the planning and management director at the KCIA and was rescued only by the last-minute intervention of Yi Chong-ch'an, Kim Kwang-uk, and Yi Tong-nam of northern and central regional origins. Kang Ch'ang-sŏng himself was a native of Kyŏnggi Province in the central region. It was during this time that Kang Ch'ang-sŏng came to learn about the Hanahoe. When Park appointed him as the ASC commander in August 1972, he set his mind on rooting out the Hanahoe and recruited non-Hanahoe officers into the ASC to investigate Hanahoe activities even before Park ordered him to crack down on Yun P'il-yong.

After forty days of investigation, Kang Ch'ang-sŏng's ASC charged Yun P'il-yong and his followers with plotting a military coup d'état. At the same time, the ASC accused them of having been involved in serious corruption that had endangered the morale of the armed forces.[56] On April 28, 1973, eleven officers, including Major General Yun P'il-yong, brigadier generals Son Yŏng-gil (chief of staff of the CGC) and Kim Sŏng-bae (director of promotion and personnel at army headquarters), and colonels Kwŏn Ik-hyŏn (Seventy-Sixth Regiment commander of the Twenty-Sixth Infantry Division), Chi Sŏng-han (chief of the Army Criminal Investigation Department), and Sin Chae-gi (chief of promotion and personnel, army headquarters), were sentenced to from two to fifteen years of imprisonment for crimes of embezzlement, bribery, abuse of authority, and desertion. Another thirty-one military officers were given dishonorable discharges.[57] Among the eleven "accomplices" sentenced to imprisonment, all but Kim Sŏng-bae and Chi Sŏng-han were Hanahoe members. These nine officers, moreover, all came from the Kyŏngsang region, the home of both Park Chung Hee and Yun P'il-yong. Worse for the Hanahoe, among the imprisoned were Son Yŏng-gil and Kwŏn Ik-hyŏn of the eleventh KMA graduating class, who had founded and led the group with Chun Doo-hwan. Chun escaped the purge because he was the one who reported Yun P'il-yong's conversation with Yi Hu-rak to PSS chief Pak Chong-gyu. Having escaped the purge, Chun tried to limit the damage by lobbying for clemency on behalf of other Hanahoe members. Park heeded his advice because he, too, could not afford to weed out the Hanahoe officers of the Kyŏngsang region altogether.

The exit of Yun P'il-yong ushered in a new era of military factionalism. Gone were the days of the "big game," where the prize was becoming Park's heir. Also gone were big players with big ambitions striving to develop an independent power base of their own, first in military security institutions and then in the DRP. The three core military praetorian guards in charge of the KCIA at one time or another during the 1961–1973 period all fell from grace by the first year of the *yushin* regime. Kim Chong-p'il became the prime minister on June 4, 1971, but he was no longer the embodiment of young South Korea he had once been. The three political defeats he suffered in 1963, 1965, and 1969 broke his spirit and dismantled his faction. The two other KCIA directors of the 1961–1973 period had much harder falls from Park's political grace. Fearing revenge by those whom he had harassed, abused, and terrorized, Kim Hyŏng-uk chose to go into exile in the United States on April 15, 1973. Yi Hu-rak retired to the countryside after his dismissal for having been implicated in the Yun P'il-yong incident and the kidnapping of Kim Dae-jung in Tokyo, until he won a seat in the National Assembly as an independent in the 1978 elections and was brought back into the DRP in 1979.

Even Pak Chong-gyu, whose rough style won him few friends, ended his twelve-year service as the PSS chief on August 21, 1974, when First Lady Yuk Yŏng-su died in an assassination attempt directed at Park. Like Kim Chong-p'il's rivals whose careers ended with the dismantlement of Kim Chong-p'il's mainstream faction, ASC commander Kang Ch'ang-sŏng too was forced to retire from active duty in January 1976 after serving as the Third District commander (1973–1975). He played a major role in cracking down on the Hanahoe officers of Kyŏngsang regional origin. But as things turned out, the purge of his rival, Yun P'il-yong, had damaged Kang Ch'ang-sŏng's political utility to Park, who stuck to his divide-and-conquer approach to power. Kang's experience was a reminder that a thing is cherished only if it is useful. And with the demise of these praetorian guards, the intricate system of checks and balances also was dismantled.

Guardian of the Yushin, *1972–1979*

Once the *yushin* was promulgated, the military was bound to increase its political role. The military's intervention in politics became an on-going affair after April 3, 1974, when, for the first time since the promulgation of the *yushin* constitution, students of Seoul National University, Sungkyunkwan University, and Ewha Womans University coordinated large-scale demonstrations against it, culminating in the organization of the National Democratic Young Students' Union and its Declaration of the People, the Nation, and Democracy. The *yushin* regime countered with the time-tested strategy of political repression, issuing Emergency Decree no. 4 to order the KCIA, ASC, and CGC's military police to launch wholesale arrests of student activists. Four student leaders, including Yi Ch'ŏl, were put on the wanted list and twenty-two others accused of participating in the People's Revolutionary Party were tried by an emergency court-martial. Included among the accused were Yun Po-sŏn, the former president of the Second Republic (1960–1961); Kim Tong-gil, a history professor at Yonsei University; and Kim Chi-ha, a renowned dissident poet. The court-martial found them guilty of violating Emergency Decree no. 1. Dissidents numbering about 180 were also imprisoned for violating Emergency Decree no. 4. Eight who were accused of being core members of the People's Revolutionary Party were sentenced to death and hurriedly executed on April 9, 1975.

Radical student protests briefly subsided in the aftermath of the death of First Lady Yuk Yŏng-su at the hand of Mun Se-gwang, a Korean-Japanese, on August 15, 1974. But with a massive demonstration staged by Korea University students on the first anniversary of the Declaration of the People, the Nation, and Democracy, Park was forced to declare Emergency Decree no. 7 on April 8, 1975. The new decree empowered the defense minister to restore order on the campuses by temporarily shutting down universities with the support of the armed forces. At the same time, a fully armed company of the CGC's military police occupied Korea University. On May 13, with South Vietnam and Cambodia on the brink of collapse and South Korea under a Red scare, Park issued Emergency Decree no. 9 to "guard national security and public order."

As the political opposition grew and the security crisis worsened, Park pursued even more systematically and extensively his practice of placing praetorian guards and professional officers on two mutually exclusive tracks of promotion. The big game was gone, but this did not end "politics." On the contrary, given the weakening of checks and balances, Park had to reach deep down personally into the military hierarchy for control more than ever. Nowhere was the heightened use of the two-track career policy more visible than in Park's recruitment of his generals for political roles. After proclaiming the *yushin* constitution, Park aggressively recruited generals in the reserves into public service, not only to cultivate his image as a patron of the armed forces' institutional interests but also to build up his network of loyal supporters in the strategic sectors of society. Among 588 retired generals in 1975, 53 held posts in the executive branch, 13 served as diplomats, 32 sat in the National Assembly, and 43 managed state-owned enterprises. There were 174 others in private business firms as owners, managers, and advisors. Universities also employed 24 retired generals. Still, there were 135 generals in the reserves (23 percent) without any employment.[58] The pool of the unemployed was large enough to make clear to all military officers the importance of cultivating Park's personal trust and patronage while serving in uniform.

As the opposition gained force in the 1970s, Park began to give junior officers their share of the political spoils. Under the Special Junior Officer Recruitment system introduced in 1977, the Ministry of National Defense opened up the jobs of Grade-3A—the lowest grade of the higher civil service—to KMA graduates who wanted to be discharged from military service after completing the legally obligatory service of five years and reaching the rank of captain or major. For those seeking careers in the higher levels of the civil service, the MoND only required that they finish a one-year education program at the KMA Administration Training Institute. The program was open to KMA graduates, but not to Third Military Academy graduates. The discrimination on the basis of schooling aimed to make the graduates of the four-year KMA identify with Park's political rule. Including the graduates of the second-tier, two-year Third Military Academy in the program would not only have reduced the number of civil service posts available to the KMA graduates, but also threatened the morale of higher-level civil servants by increasing the competition for promotion. There were simply too many Third Military Academy graduates to include in the program without hurting the balance Park wanted to achieve between professionalization and politicization and between economic growth and regime stability.

The officers-turned-bureaucrats took on the role of a royal guard for the *yushin* regime within the state bureaucracy. Not coincidentally, many of the junior officers took up posts in the more political state institutions responsible for control, such as the Ministry of Home Affairs, the

Board of Audit and Inspection, and the National Tax Administration.[59] The ministries responsible for economic coordination, including the Economic Planning Board (EPB) and the Ministry of Finance (MoF), were more insulated from the military.

On the other hand, Park did not construct multiple layers of checks and balances as he had done in the 1961–1973 period. Rather, Park let Ch'a Chi-ch'ŏl—a non-KMA retired army lieutenant colonel[60] and Park bodyguard in the days of the coup—dominate military and political affairs from his newly appointed post of PSS chief (1974–1979). In December 1974, Park made Kim Chae-gyu, a retired four-star general and a KMA graduate, his new KCIA director, but Kim Chae-gyu failed to keep Ch'a Chi-ch'ŏl in line. On the contrary, once in a position of influence, Ch'a Chi-ch'ŏl showed his ambition to become a de facto "vice president," to quote his critics. To strengthen his institutional base and secure military legitimacy, Ch'a Chi-ch'ŏl strengthened the Presidential Security Service, newly establishing the offices of the vice chief, the deputy for operations, and the deputy for administration and filled these posts with elite KMA graduates. The expanded PSS enabled him to cultivate close ties with the rising Hanahoe officers. Brigadier generals Chun Doo-hwan, Roh Tae-woo, and Kim Pok-tong from the eleventh KMA graduating class and leaders of the Hanahoe faction took turns as the deputy for operations during the 1976–1978 period. Ch'a Chi-ch'ŏl also expanded the Presidential Security Guard Units 30 and 33 from the status of a battalion to a regiment. In addition, he had a presidential decree enacted to give the PSS chief the command of the CGC in the event of a national emergency.[61] He even began to distribute informal "bonuses" and "grants" in the name of Park for the purpose of winning the support of the military.[62] More critically, Ch'a Chi-ch'ŏl intervened in the personnel policy of army headquarters and used his influence to promote loyal military officers to key command posts.[63]

The military establishment grew increasingly unhappy with Ch'a Chi-ch'ŏl's abuse of Park's trust. To most KMA graduates, it was outrageous that a retired officer with only an Officer Candidate School background exercised such influence over military matters. In particular, they were angered by the fact that the PSS chief, formally outside the chain of military command, would command the CGC during a national emergency.[64] Nevertheless, they kept their discontent to themselves, because they thought Ch'a Chi-ch'ŏl had Park's confidence. To be sure, Park's trust in Ch'a Chi-ch'ŏl was based not only on the PSS chief's unswerving loyalty but also on his ability to deliver a steady stream of high-quality intelligence reports on domestic political situations. The private intelligence team Ch'a Chi-ch'ŏl organized with Yi Kyu-gwang, uncle-in-law of Brigadier General Chun Doo-hwan, in charge of the Hanahoe after the purge of potential rivals in the Yun P'il-yong incident of 1973, proved to be very effective in gathering sensitive information on the daily activities of key military generals, DRP legislators, and opposition leaders. Ch'a Chi-ch'ŏl also owed his rise to Park's loss of confidence in the KCIA in the wake of the defection of some KCIA agents to the United States during the Koreagate scandal that rocked the U.S.–South Korean relationship. Equally critical, Ch'a Chi-ch'ŏl was able to increase his influence over the Army Security Command after the 1973 court martial of ASC commander Yun P'il-yong. After the transitional years of ASC commander Kim Chong-hwan (1973–1977), the post of ASC commander passed on to Major General Chin Chong-ch'ae (1977–1979) to bring better coordination of security intelligence policy among the different branches of the military in tandem with the launching of a Five-Year Plan for the Modernization of the Korean Armed Forces. The goal was to build an integrated security apparatus fit for the self-reliant armed forces Park envisioned for South Korea in the era of détente and U.S. military disengagement. As part of this effort, Chin Chong-ch'ae reorganized the ASC into the Defense Security Command (DSC) on September 26, 1977, in conformity with Presidential Decree no. 8704.[65] That tilted the balance of power even further away from KCIA director Kim Chae-gyu toward PSS chief Ch'a Chi-ch'ŏl.

Kim Chae-gyu tried to reverse the tide, and his attempt had partial success. When the DSC incorrectly reported the defection of a high-ranking South Korean military officer in October 1977, Kim Chae-gyu put pressure on the DSC to dissolve its Department of Intelligence and succeeded in prohibiting the DSC from sending its agents to government agencies and societal organizations for surveillance.[66] Such surveillance was to be the exclusive domain of his KCIA. Beyond this, however, Kim Chae-gyu had difficulty in keeping Ch'a Chi-ch'ŏl in check. On the contrary, he found himself on the defensive when Ch'a Chi-ch'ŏl outmaneuvered him in persuading Park to appoint Major General Chun Doo-hwan to head the DSC in March 1979. Whereas Ch'a Chi-ch'ŏl had cultivated close ties with the next-generation leader of the supposedly dismantled Hanahoe by appointing Chun Doo-hwan to the PSS post of deputy for operations before he moved to command the First Infantry Division in January 1978, Kim Chae-gyu's relationship with Chun Doo-hwan had been strained ever since Kim had sided against Yun P'il-yong when Yun had been appointed as the ASC commander (1967–1971). Moreover, in spite of his own South

Kyŏngsang origins, Kim Chae-gyu never hid his antipathy toward the eleventh KMA graduating class of Chun Doo-hwan, which he found to be too politicized and too arrogant.

Kim Chae-gyu appears to have recognized the danger of his fall sometime in mid-1979. With the opposition NDP garnering more votes than the DRP for the first time in the National Assembly election of December 1978, the ruling elite tried desperately to win back public support. Unable or unwilling to embark on political reform at the risk of disturbing regime stability, Park blamed the defeat on the failure of his economic team to prevent the coming of stagflation. To overcome the widespread legitimacy crisis of the *yushin* regime, Park turned to the proven strategy of winning public support through an improvement in his country's socioeconomic performance. In the ensuing reshuffling of the cabinet, presidential chief of staff Kim Chŏng-ryŏm (1969–1978) left the Blue House to become the ambassador to Japan, thus paving the way for the removal of the economic ministers who worked under him. The departure of Kim Chŏng-ryŏm also had an unexpected impact on the power dynamics of the Blue House. Kim, mild tempered but intelligent with a firm grasp of political and economic issues, had been a gentle and steadying influence on Park, as well as the last check on PSS chief Ch'a Chi-ch'ŏl within the presidential Secretariat. The new chief of staff, Kim Kye-wŏn, had once served as the army chief of staff, but despite a distinguished military career, he was brought in mainly as an old friend of Park who would keep him company in the "lonely" Blue House in his old age.[67]

With Paek Tu-jin—a non-elected Yujŏnghoe member handpicked by Park to become a National Assembly member—leading the National Assembly, Ch'a Chi-ch'ŏl joined the hard-liners of the DRP on October 15, 1979, to censure NDP president Kim Young-sam from the National Assembly for his interview with the *New York Times* critical of Park and for his support of the YH workers' strike (see Chapter 13). In the face of this unprecedented abuse of power, the people of Pusan and Masan in South Kyŏngsang Province—the home region of Kim Young-sam—rose up in massive anti-government protests. Martial law was proclaimed in Pusan on October 18 and a garrison decree invoked in Masan on October 20. In the midst of this political crisis, Kim Chae-gyu, Ch'a Chi-ch'ŏl, and Kim Kye-wŏn met with Park at one of the "safe houses" *(an'ga)* operated by the Blue House to hold private banquets. Discussion became heated, with crude but obsequious Ch'a Chi-ch'ŏl berating reticent and even shy Kim Chae-gyu in front of Park for his inability or unwillingness to suppress the Pusan-Masan demonstrations and for his failure to instigate a revolt against Kim Young-sam within the opposition NDP. Kim Chae-gyu advocated a "political solution" without explaining what that was and how it could be brought about amid mass revolt and political deadlock, while Ch'a Chi-ch'ŏl unambiguously took the hard-line position, seeking a military crackdown.[68] It is difficult to know exactly what Kim Chae-gyu thought at the dinner, because he was mostly silent, taking the tongue-lashing without protest. Then he suddenly shot Park and Ch'a Chi-ch'ŏl, killing them both. The Park era came to an abrupt end on October 26, 1979.

No one, including Kim Chae-gyu, was prepared for the post-Park era. The KCIA director desperately tried to persuade the martial law commander, General Chŏng Sŭng-hwa, to join him in what he would later call a "Revolution," only to be arrested for subversion not long after the shootings. The power vacuum was quickly filled by December, but in an unexpected direction. Although the NDP and DRP leaders prepared for a return to electoral politics, the real contest was taking place within the armed forces. Two groups of military officers emerged between October 26 and December 12. The "Old Military," consisting of generals with diverse school backgrounds from the KMA to the Officer Candidate School, coalesced around the martial law commander. The "New Military," by contrast, was more homogeneous but also lower in military rank, with its core recruited from the Hanahoe members with a four-year KMA educational background. Chun Doo-hwan's eleventh KMA graduating class sat at the top of the New Military, while those of the seventeenth KMA class supported the faction at its mid-level.

The New Military was destined to emerge triumphant for several reasons. First, since March 1979 its factional leader Chun Doo-hwan had led the Defense Security Command, with the power to coordinate the security intelligence agencies of all three branches of the armed forces. The only other security intelligence agency with coordinating powers was the KCIA, but it was delegitimized by its director's aborted "Revolution." In addition, Chun Doo-hwan was careful to neutralize the KCIA and purge its manpower immediately after the arrest of Kim Chae-gyu. In fact, the DSC literally took over the agency, purging all bureau directors just after arresting Kim Chae-gyu and placing its own people in their place. Chun Doo-hwan became acting KCIA director on April 14, 1980, thus formalizing what had been instituted since the arrest of Kim Chae-gyu. Even when Chun Doo-hwan became the acting KCIA director, he stayed on as the DSC commander, the seat of power.[69]

Second, at the time of Park's assassination, no military group could match the Hanahoe's sense of camaraderie. Moreover, not only the top echelon but also the mid-level members of the Hanahoe were at the prime of their military careers, in command of key military units around Seoul. The top echelon held the rank of major general and were in command of security intelligence agencies and infantry divisions, whereas the mid-level Hanahoe members were colonels in charge of regiments. They directly commanded combat troops, whereas the Old Military, headed by the four-star martial law commander, was much more disadvantaged in troop mobilization. It was this combination of a strong sense of camaraderie and a direct control over key military units that enabled the Hanahoe members' speedy and flexible collective action during the extremely uncertain period of regime transition. On December 12, 1979, DSC commander Chun Doo-hwan moved to arrest martial law commander Chŏng Sŭng-hwa for alleged involvement in the assassination of Park, while Chun's KMA classmate and Hanahoe comrade, Major General Roh Tae-woo, occupied Seoul with the heavily armed troops of the Ninth Infantry Division, formerly stationed on the front lines, even at the risk of weakening the military deterrence against North Korea.

Park thought that the military was too important to be left alone, and politicized the armed forces in order to make them the guardians of his regime. Yet he also believed he had to professionalize the South Korean armed forces, turning them into a modern institution capable of defending the country against another military attack from the North. Caught between these two competing requirements, Park compartmentalized the military into two tracks, one for soldiers raised to lead the "professional" field command posts and the other for those trained to become the "political" praetorian guard of the regime.

For most of Park's eighteen years of political rule, the two-track strategy worked. The South Korean military grew by leaps and bounds under his tutelage, becoming one of the largest standing armies in the world with the fighting skills and the weapons to match. Just as the South Korean economy transformed itself from one of the world's poorest to one of the most dynamic engines of growth, the South Korean military grew in terms of both quantity and quality. Continued aid and training provided by the United States proved crucial in this institutional transformation. The ambitious military modernization program orchestrated by Park, coupled with combat experience in the Vietnam War and military operations against North Korean guerrilla incursions, too, played a critical role in turning the South Korean military into a formidable fighting force by the time of Park's death.

Park's strategy to control the military and mobilize its security intelligence sector to defend his regime also worked remarkably well for most of his political rule. Park used KCIA director Kim Chong-p'il and his eighth KMA graduating class to drive out the rival generals of the Hamgyŏng and Pyŏngan regions during the 1961–1963 military junta years, only to weaken Kim Chong-p'il repeatedly during the 1963–1972 period of "democracy." For the progressive marginalization of Kim Chong-p'il, Park mobilized a heterogeneous group of military leaders and DRP legislators, whose common goal was to defeat Kim Chong-p'il's ambition to succeed Park. When these anti-mainstream leaders succeeded in destroying Kim's fighting spirit by 1969, Park got rid of them as he had done with Kim Chong-p'il. Park played the game of divide and conquer exceptionally well without hurting either the modernization of the South Korean armed forces or the life of his regime—but only until December 1978.

In 1979, Park was no longer in control of the situation. Rather than playing with the minds of his military praetorian guards, he let his follower—Ch'a Chi-ch'ŏl—play with his mind. Instead of maintaining a balance of power, he inadvertently destroyed it by demoralizing one of its two poles—Kim Chae-gyu. Most critically, rather than taking precautionary actions against Kim Chae-gyu as he did with so many of his military praetorian guards, he let that troubled man stay on in his too-important post for too long, trusting too much the friendship and loyalty forged over a lifetime of comradeship. The balancing act did not work in 1979, but that is not the real surprise. What is more impressive is that Park controlled the necessary checks and balances so successfully for so long.

CHAPTER SEVEN

The Leviathan:
Economic Bureaucracy under Park

Byung-Kook Kim

UNDER PARK CHUNG HEE, South Korea approximated the ideal-type "developmental state." The concept is Chalmers Johnson's, used with respect to Japan, and was from the 1980s on applied to South Korea by a diverse array of political economists and sociologists, including Peter Evans.[1] The ideal-type developmental state, Evans posits, possesses "corporate coherence" that endows its apparatuses with "a certain kind of autonomy" with which to transcend the interests of social forces in the formulation of goals and strategies and is "embedded in a concrete set of social ties" that link the state apparatuses to society. The state, having developed extensive institutional channels connecting it to the private sector, is posited as being able to reach down into the economy to assist and encourage economic growth in myriad ways. In other words, rather than replacing the private firm as a producer of goods and services, the developmental state continually negotiates and renegotiates goals and policies with the *chaebol* and others and backs the expansion of private entrepreneurial ventures with the goal of industrial growth. The ideal-type developmental state retains its autonomy, despite the complex interweavings of its connections with society.

Chapter 7 shares Evans's view that corporate coherence and embeddedness are key to the making of a developmental state, but unlike Evans, Chapter 7 emphasizes the primacy of politics in the South Korean context. Only with a political perspective zeroing in on Park's political calculations and roles can one explain many of the historical and theoretical puzzles surrounding the sudden rise of a developmental state during Park's rule and its complex character, from the patrimonial but rationalized state bureaucracy to the hierarchical but segmented power structures to the hybridization of predatory and developmental state roles. The corporate coherence of the South Korean developmental state was more a product of the "visible hand" of Park, who was imbued with a politically electrifying vision of transforming South Korea into a "second Japan" in his lifetime and equipped with a keen strategic mind to dexterously balance the political requirements of coalition building and the forces of the market, than a product of an institutional artifact developed autonomously, incrementally, and technocratically from within the state bureaucracy. Likewise, the South Korean developmental state was institutionally bound to society, but its embeddedness was more asymmetric and political, with Park making deals with *chaebol* groups in the corridors of the Blue House. Those deals framed the overall direction of bureaucratic action.

The primacy of politics is shown by the extremely ambitious goals for which the state was mobilized during Park's political rule. Certainly, he sought policy feedback from the *chaebol* and the state bureaucracy through multiple channels of communication, but only as advice on how to achieve what were his goals, and not others'. Park, setting his sights on goals that far exceeded what most at the time thought the country's small economy was capable of achieving, insistently held to his conception of Korea's becoming a "second Japan" in one generation. His vision included big business manufacturing a full line of industrial goods and exporting quality products under national brand names through their own trading houses. In a sense, Park faced a chronic capital shortage more because of his overly ambitious goals than because of South Korea's grim economic reality. His were anything but technocratically formulated goals. On the contrary, these dreams, as many saw them, drove Park into pursuing industrial projects that were too big for the domestic economy, but too small by international standards. When the *chaebol* resisted, the state bureaucracy wavered, and MNCs ignored, Park typically countered with even more ambitious investment proposals rather than scale down his original plan. Always aiming for the global market, Park frequently revised the production target upward until potential investors were tempted by the possibilities of growth that he offered. Even then, it was not foreigners but South Korean manufacturers who seized the risky but irresistible opportunity to transform themselves into industrial groups with their own international brand, technological capacity, domestic supply network, and overseas distribution facility, more or less on a par with Japanese multinationals. To his bureaucrats, grappling with formidable tasks, Park reiterated his emphasis on a "can do" spirit. However unreachable the goal looked, he argued passionately, it was achievable if one set one's mind to it. Park even suggested that rather than agonizing over what the goal and its instruments should be, state bureaucrats should plunge into the work and adjust policy as problems arose.

Reflecting his ambitions for his country, the strategy of development Park chose had to be one of high risk, high payoff, and high cost. To lure the *chaebol* to take part in his risky plans, Park explicitly or implicitly promised to rescue them if they faltered, and struggled mightily to make this pledge credible. The type of exchange Park engaged in with the *chaebol* was, then, political in nature, pledging his regime's support for the *chaebol* in return for their risk taking. Unable to specify a priori what level and what kind of political support would "match" an investor's risk taking, Park ended up giving a de facto blank check to the *chaebol* in his assurance that he would support their industrial projects with additional state resources if the investment foundered. As such, the politics of rent-seeking constituted an essential part of his development strategy. It was only through bank subsidies, state guarantees on loan payments, tax privileges, monopoly licenses, and tariff protections that Park could make his industrial projects attractive to the *chaebol*. Thus in the modernization of South Korea, development and rent-seeking were different sides of the same coin. The market was viewed only as an instrument of his political goals, a device of the dirigiste state to speed up modernization through telescoping the stages of economic development.

The problem with that strategy was that there would never be enough resources to achieve Park's goal. The most aggressive risk takers among the *chaebol*, by rushing into strategic sectors, did grow into global players with their own brands and technology, but they also became burdened with huge loans, which meant that their liquidity was severely squeezed during recessions. The state banks suffered, too, as business distress exponentially increased the number of nonperforming loans. Consequently, the developmental strategy came to acquire the character of stop-and-go policies. Once the emergency relief measures for the ailing companies had been implemented, Park immediately engineered another expansionary business cycle through inflationary financing and foreign loans, as if he had not learned any lesson from the painful adjustment. But he was not ignorant of the risks and dangers; rather, he thought that the goal of becoming a second Japan in his lifetime did not permit the luxury of market-led industrialization. The outcome was an economic system addicted to hypergrowth. The state banks, taxed with massive nonperforming loans, and the *chaebol,* suffering from a high debt-equity ratio, required double-digit macroeconomic growth to avoid a sharp deterioration on the balance sheet. The situation was sustainable only when markets continued to grow rapidly, thus driving the South Korean economy into a cycle of boom and bust and Park into stop-and-go policies.

The high risk, high payoff, and high-cost strategy of cyclically moving between hypergrowth and emergency adjustment measures required Park to secure concerted actions from the state. To lure big business into risky industrial projects during a growth phase and to assist their restructuring during the subsequent adjustment phase, Park had the Economic Planning Board (EPB) secure the budget and underwrite foreign commercial loans; the Ministry of Finance (MoF) follow suit with tax cuts, tariff protection, and bank subsidies; the Ministry of Commerce and Industry (MCI) provide investors with a monopoly of production during the infant-industry stage; and the Ministry of Construction (MoC) lower land costs, maximize spill-over effects, and facilitate the logistics of interfirm collaboration by locating related industries in a cluster in directly or indirectly subsidized special industrial zones. Even the Ministry of Labor (MoL) joined in to give an unambiguous signal on where Park's policy priorities lay, legally barring workers from organizing labor unions in newly designated strategic industries, while cooperating closely with the Ministry of Home Affairs (MHA) and the police to put workplaces under tight surveillance and weed out dissident *chaeya* activists from company unions.

To succeed in bringing about the state's concerted action, but without damaging his interest in building a cohesive ruling political coalition, Park adopted four principles vis-à-vis the state bureaucracy. First, Park *insulated* the economic bureaucracy from partisan politics, including factional rivalries within his ruling Democratic Republican Party (DRP), as well as from labor movements so that the economic bureaucracy could mobilize resources and balance the conflicting claims on industrial policy as he saw fit. Second, in order to develop the economic bureaucracy into a source of "neutral competence,"[2] Park *professionalized* the civil service by endowing it with a set of meritocratic rules on recruitment, promotion, and job security. Third, he also made the economic bureaucracy a *patrimonial* organization loyal only to him and constantly bending to his wishes. To accomplish this he chose the EPB and the MoF as coordinators and entrusted the two to serve as the hands of his "alter ego" *(punsin)* to control and mobilize the economic bureaucracy.[3] Fourth, however, Park tried to secure room for political coalition building at the same time and *segmented* economic ministries into the core, the strategic sectoral, and the auxiliary groups with varying institutional privileges and vulnerabilities. With these principles, the economic bureaucracy came to aggressively pursue goals handed down by Park rather than following its own internally generated rules and principles of investment policy. The South Korean economic bureaucracy came to possess what Max Weber called "purposive" rather than "procedural" rationality, wielding extensive discretionary powers to fine-tune the conflicting requirements of encouraging risk taking and minimizing moral hazards, but this purposive rationality was more a product of Park's political intervention than an outcome of bureaucratically generated neutral competence.

A Professionalized but Patrimonial State

Ironically, it was Park's electoral victory in 1963 that permitted the transition to a professional but patrimonial state. Far from creating tight political constraints on state ministries, the 1963 elections made the South Korean bureaucratic apparatus externally more insulated and internally more centralized, flexible, and coherent, because with the elections, many of the junta leaders moved from the seats of power—the Korea Central Intelligence Agency (KCIA), the Supreme Council of National Reconstruction, and the cabinet—to the DRP, which was too organizationally shallow and ideologically weak to dominate the processes of agenda formation and policy formulation. Nominated as DRP candidates for the National Assembly elections, they had authority but not power.[4] The resulting power vacuum was filled by civilian bureaucrats who depended solely on Park's patronage for promotion. The political parties and societal forces rarely took on an oversight role. The monitoring of bureaucratic performance was carried out by Park's presidential Secretariat and his lead economic agency, not the National Assembly. With a social structure too underdeveloped to construct a cohesive mass party system, and Park too dexterous in playing off rivals against one another, electoral democracy became an administrative or guided democracy long before Park declared the authoritarian *yushin* constitution in 1972 (see Chapter 8).[5]

To make the politically insulated state bureaucracy also a professionalized institution, Park began recruiting large number of Grade 3B—the grade at which the higher civil service began—bureaucrats through a highly competitive examination system (*haengjŏnggosi,* or *haengsi*). These *haengsi* bureaucrats symbolized the ideal of meritocracy and embodied "neutral competence," passing an extremely tough exam with an average entry barrier of 1:52 during the 1963–1979 period. Given South Korea's hierarchically structured educational system with a few elite universities hoarding the country's best minds, the civil service examination ensured Park a cohesive bureaucratic corps, with its members sharing close school and generational ties. This overlap in age and education helped foster a group identity among *haengsi* bureaucrats, which imbued the state bureaucracy with an esprit de corps.

Moreover, with an eye to nurturing professionalism, Park provided secure tenure once a college graduate entered the civil service. By Park's last years of rule, almost all Grade 2 and 3A vacancies went to internally promoted bureaucrats in sharp contrast to the period of Syngman Rhee (1948–1960) and Chang Myŏn's (1960–1961) rule, when over half of Grade 2 bureau directors were *tŭkch'ae,* or "specially appointed" non-career personnel.[6] Grade 3B showed a similar change, with Park reducing its *tŭkch'ae* share by two thirds and increasing its *haengsi* share fivefold. The strengthening of job security made a career bureaucrat view the ministry where he began his bureaucratic career as his "native home" *(ch'injŏng),* an object of loyalty and affection. Typically, he would stay in his home ministry most of his public life, ending up identifying its institutional goals and missions as his own, internalizing its distinctive culture, absorbing its specialized policy knowledge and experience, and rising and falling with its political fortunes and misfortunes. By nurturing common values and sharing a common fate, the bureaus and divisions of any given ministry came to acquire organizational unity.

Park's relationship with state bureaucrats, however, was not based on his blind faith in their loyalty. Park was aware of the danger that an externally insulated professional bureaucracy could become its own master, putting its institutional interests ahead of national goals. The danger of policy drift and deadlock could also be high as state ministries jealously guarded their turf against any attempt at coordination. Consequently, Park checked daily on bureaucratic implementation of his orders and directives through on-site inspections, keeping state ministries on a short leash. In a similar spirit, Park also strove to quantify target goals and guidelines as much as possible. Having quantified his goals, he could at the same time delegate power and keep a close eye on the bureaucrats' exercise of that power. When issues of paramount importance arose, or when interministerial conflicts resulted in a prolonged deadlock in spite of his lead agency's attempt at coordination, Park established an interministerial task force inside his Secretariat in the presidential palace, with a personal aide—usually a career bureaucrat transferred from one or another ministry—in charge of coordination as its secretary general.[7]

Fortunately for South Korea, however, Park also knew that there was an inherent limit to how much he could control through personal intervention. He could not simply lash out against the state bureaucracy's protection of its interests at the expense of the public interest, because he could not implement his plans if the line ministries were hostile to the plans' goal and spirit. Moreover, Park knew that he had the power to fight bureaucratic resistance with a long "stick," but he also understood that a too frequent use of sticks was likely to defeat his purposes by demoralizing the line ministries and seriously weakening their organizational capacity. If a state bureaucracy was driven into apathy, Park would be left without the instruments he needed to penetrate society and reshape its preferences. Thus he needed a strong state bureaucracy to be a strong president.

What he had to wield was two carrots and one stick to become not only a feared but also a beloved patron. Park organized the economic bureaucracy hierarchically into a pyramidal shape, with the goal of systematically pursuing the two-carrots-and-one-stick strategy of management. At the top of the pyramid stood the EPB as a superministry, with the MoF, whose policy preferences were intrinsically contractionary, and the MCI, whose policy preferences were intrinsically expansionary, assisting the EPB as its lieutenants. The elite EPB and MoF made up the bureaucratic core, with the mission to set agendas and policies of the other lesser but still strategic sectoral ministries, including the MCI, along the overall hierarchy of national priorities the EPB and MoF established under Park's leadership. Because it was these lesser sectoral ministries that were in direct contact with organized societal groups and therefore at risk of being captured by them, Park's treatment of the lesser sectoral ministries as second-class ministries explicitly or implicitly assumed the preemption of a spontaneous development of autonomous interest groups that could challenge the established priorities. By contrast, for the two core ministries, Park offered diverse privileges, including organizational growth, greater job security, and promotion opportunities in order to inculcate both with a sense of mission, an organizational interest in industrial transformation, and an unswerving loyalty to himself. In particular, the two core ministries frequently penetrated lesser sectoral ministries by controlling the staffing of their ministerial and even their bureau director posts in order to line up these lower ministries behind Park's goals. The capture of lesser sectoral ministries by the EPB and the MoF was possible because Park willed it, which in turn was possible because political parties and interest groups were too weak to resist Park.

Of the two core ministries, it was the EPB that Park chose as the overall coordinator. In his eyes, the board offered multiple organizational advantages as a lead agency. Unlike the MoF and MCI, whose sectoral organizational missions made each interface closely with the state banks and with *chaebol* as both a client and a patron of bureaucratic power, the EPB was a planner without a sector-specific mission. The agency identified the entire economy as its exclusive territory, setting the national agenda by budget planning and allocation, and influencing both real and financial sectors through fiscal expenditure as well as through license and approval powers over foreign loans and investments.[8] Established in 1961 by merging the Ministry of Reconstruction (MoR) with the MoF's budget bureau, the EPB was also manned by the "internationalists" of the South Korean state bureaucracy. The MoR and the MoF budget bureau had been reformist enclaves since 1957, importing from abroad modern planning and budgetary expertise under the close guidance of U.S. aid officials, and recruiting young talent from the less politicized central bank and research institutes for managerial positions.[9] These human resources became a source of the EPB's strength with Park's state reorganization in July 1961.

Discovering the EPB's potential as a lead agency in 1963, Park made its minister the country's deputy prime minister as well, with the legal prerogative to "orchestrate and coordinate" state policies.[10] Parallel to this effort to make the EPB minister first among equals in the economic cabinet, Park showered the EPB with diverse privileges that made it as much a "patrimonial" as a "professional" organization. With Park's blessing, the EPB enjoyed autonomy, recruiting 92.3 percent of Grade 1 bureaucrats from its own careerists. In its dealings with other economic ministries, however, the EPB was predatory, penetrating deep into their hierarchy for direct policy control. Between 1961 and 1980, the EPB sent 61.5 percent of its Grade 1 bureaucrats to the others as vice ministers and 38.5 percent of those even became ministers. Meanwhile, over a quarter of Grade 2 EPB bureaucrats entered other economic ministries as temporary transferees to head their respective planning and management offices (PMOs). Only nominally controlled by the prime minister, PMOs monitored and evaluated ministerial policies from inside the host ministries. By manning this strategic network of policy feedback and information flow with its own officials, the EPB could detect and correct cross-cutting ministerial actions early on, as well as hold the leaders of line ministries individually accountable to the president and his EPB confidants.

However, aware of the dangers of demoralization in host ministries triggered by the transfer of EPB and MoF bureaucrats to the lesser ministries' leadership posts, Park also carefully varied the degree of penetration across issue areas, with the effect of lining up the economic ministries into a hierarchical but segmented rank order. Entrusted with macroeconomic coordination, the EPB and MoF constituted a mini-state within Park's larger patrimonial state, protected from penetration by other economic ministries. At the same time, Park was interested in transforming the two core ministries into a cohesive presidential team, which resulted in the habitual circulation of their promising bureaucrats between each other and to the presidential Secretariat in the Blue House. The strategic post of vice minister was filled predominantly by careerists in both the EPB (76.9 percent) and the MoF (55.6 percent), but when an outsider was brought in, Park typically chose an EPB careerist for the post of MoF vice minister (22.2 percent) and an MoF bureaucrat for the post of EPB vice minister (23.1 percent). These two coordinating ministries were thus not only insulated from outside forces but also shared a common outlook on goals and strategies as a result of the staffing Park brokered at the top level of vice minister. Meanwhile, the transfer of EPB and MoF bureaucrats to the Blue House was also an opportunity to imbue them with Park's ideas on industrialization.

On the other hand, the two core ministries served as a major source of ministers and vice ministers for those that were responsible for developing strategic sectors with the potential for growth or charged with oversight of societal constituencies capable of affecting policy outcomes or electoral campaigns (Energy and Resources, or MER; Agriculture, Fishery, and Forestry, or MAFF; and Commerce and Industry). These strategic sectoral ministries sat at the mid-layer of the pyramidal economic bureaucracy, performing technically complex tasks that required a sector- and even product-specific expertise. The existence of powerful constituencies and the complexity of the expertise needed placed this mid-layer group of ministries in a gray area where neither a retired army general (without expertise) nor a career sectoral bureaucrat promoted internally from within the sectoral ministry (without a broad macroeconomic perspective) was thought to be able to offer effective leadership. Recruiting a former military general for ministership in these areas aided Park's efforts to win political loyalty among the armed forces, but at the cost of expertise. Internally promoting a careerist who had had lifelong contact with big business or agricultural cooperatives from inside the ministry, on the other hand, could make the MCI, MER, or MAFF a captive of its societal clients. Desiring neither, Park relied primarily on his hybrid EPB and MoF bureaucrats to steer this mid-layer group of economic ministries.

The flow of personnel—and hence power—was unidirectional, with the MCI and other strategic ministries recruiting as much as 60 percent of their ministers and vice ministers from the EPB and the MoF, without enjoying a similar privilege vis-à-vis the two coordinating agencies. Apparently, the type of bureaucrat Park preferred for a cabinet appointment in strategic issue-areas was a hybrid, who began his career in either the EPB or the MoF, but who had also served in line ministries as a vice minister or as a presidential aide on economic affairs at the Blue House after reaching the Grade 1 layer of the EPB or the MoF. Such a career trajectory helped create a coordinator with a broad macroeconomic perspective, expertise in micro sectoral issues, and an insider's understanding of line ministries, which were the object of control and coordination. This practice of penetration helped build a pool of generalists who understood micro industry issues and the role such issues played in establishing a coherent macroeconomic policy.

There were auxiliary agencies like the Ministry of Construction and the Ministry of Transportation (MoT), which sat at the bottom of the bureaucratic ranking created by Park and were locked in a very different pattern of interministerial power relations. The armed forces and the Ministry of Home Affairs together provided 67.7 percent of MoC and MoT ministers and 38.9 percent of MoC and MoT vice ministers, whereas the EPB and the MoF supplied only 16.1 percent and 27.8 percent, respectively. Park apparently regarded the MoC and the MoT as "auxiliary" economic ministries to be mobilized from the top down for the goals enumerated by Park in consultation with the EPB and the MoF, and he distributed the MoC and MoT leadership posts as spoils to the political arm of his ruling coalition, the armed forces and the MHA. Park could sacrifice the organizational interests of the MoC and the MoT without fearing too much loss of competence, because the two agencies performed technically simple tasks, such as clearing the land for highways and industrial complexes, laying down telephone lines, and building post offices. Not facing tight technical constraints, Park freely chose the MoC and MoT leadership from former military generals, to reward them for their role in enforcing martial law in politically difficult times, and from MHA bureaucrats, for ensuring electoral victories for the ruling DRP through the mobilization of its thick network of local intermediaries and grass-roots bureaucratic institutions. The former generals and MHA bureaucrats promoted to the top positions in the MoC and the MoT displayed unswerving loyalty to Park. They saw their ministerial roles as extensions of their previous careers as soldiers, police officers, or local magistrates, and they aggressively implemented decisions made by Park and his EPB-MoF advisors.

The internally hierarchical but segmented organization of the state profoundly simplified economic policymaking. The bureaucrats transferred from the EPB and the MoF to the top positions of the mid-layer sectoral ministries and the bottom-layer auxiliary ministries "edited" their respective host ministries' policy agendas, goals, and strategies from the macroeconomic perspectives of their home ministries and the Blue House, reinterpreting—if not outright suppressing—the host ministries' interests, which they saw as directly colliding with their home agency or presidential interests. The editing process effectively preempted any open resistance by the MCI and others to a macroeconomic policy that threatened their internal organization and societal clients. The hierarchical but segmented state organization did not, however, in itself ensure high economic growth. The pyramidal power structure Park built through a selective distribution of political patronage could become a catalyst for rapid growth only if its core group of EPB, MoF, and Blue House presidential staff members, in close collaboration with the MCI, set the agenda, formulated strategy, and monitored implementation on the basis of clear and viable goals. Without well-articulated and agreed-upon goals and strategies, along with effective monitoring, the same structure of hierarchical but segmented interministerial power relations could bring about disaster, because it would be mobilizing resources for the wrong reasons. The search for a viable strategy occurred through two stages.

Search for a Strategy, 1961–1967

The first Five-Year Economic Development Plan (FYEDP), begun in June 1962, had performed dismally, with South Korea's gross national product growing by 38 percent below the target level and local savings reaching only 21.6 percent of the original goal. The promised takeoff of investment never materialized, falling below its target by 38.3 percent in spite of—or because of—Park's overly aggressive efforts to force savings on society through inflation and even expropriation of the "illicit" private wealth of some *chaebol* groups. Moreover, the first FYEDP was fundamentally flawed, identifying capital- and technology-intensive heavy and chemical industrialization (HCI) as an engine of growth when South Korea's per capita GNP remained a meager eighty dollars. To implement the unrealistic first FYEDP, Park bypassed the EPB and MoF and used the KCIA as his think tank to mobilize resources through a politically as well as economically destabilizing program of forced savings.[11] The only sign of progress that emerged from the two years of military junta rule was the unforeseen export increase in the light industry sector, which Park had brushed aside as inconsequential for South Korea's modernization and therefore inappropriate for state assistance.[12] In November 1962, aware of the light industries–led export boom, Park ordered the EPB to initiate a comprehensive revision of the first FYEDP and to search for ways to make better use of market forces.[13]

The growth strategy South Korea came to adopt by the mid-1960s was a thoroughly politics-based policy package. Utterly failing to secure support from MNCs for his overly ambitious industrialization programs, Park turned to diplomacy to acquire the seed money to jump-start growth. Park normalized diplomatic relations with Japan in 1965 in spite of domestic opposition with the goal of securing reparation funds. The Japanese money was to finance the launching of a newly organized Pohang Iron & Steel Company after 1967. Then there was the dispatch of military troops to South Vietnam in 1965 that was rewarded by a boost in U.S. economic and military aid. In other words, Park was able to secure foreign capital only when he brought politics into a foreigner's—in this case, the Japanese and the American governments'—calculation of costs and benefits and replaced market rationales with political-security imperatives as the reason for financial support. Both efforts bore fruit—albeit after throwing Park into a severe political crisis at home. As reparations for its colonial rule, Japan pledged $600 million in grants and loans. The military intervention in the Vietnam War brought $920 million in U.S. military and economic assistance. With this money, Park and his patrimonial but rationalized state were able to experiment with their economic ideas of state-led development and to develop strategic sectors, including the steel industry.[14]

The new growth formula, consisting of the partly contradictory promotion of light industry exports and a drive toward HCI, was drawn up by the EPB incrementally over eight years. The first breakthrough came on deputy prime minister Chang Ki-yŏng's watch.[15] He constructed the expansionary part of Park's growth strategy and left a dynamic albeit financially fragile big business sector as his legacy.[16] The process began with a reform proposal whose main thrust was anything but expansionary. Since 1957, the United States Agency for International Development (USAID) had tried to ensure a more efficient use of its aid by South Korea to prepare the country for an eventual "graduation" from U.S. economic tutelage and patronage. The United States' goal was to force its client state to institute a financial stabilization program (FSP). As an integral part of this effort, USAID officials established a bilateral Economic Cooperation Committee (ECC) with the South Korean state ministries. In 1965, through the mechanism of the ECC, the two sides began to impose an upper ceiling on the South Korean money supply and set a lower ceiling on its foreign exchange reserves, with the understanding that they would be reappraised and redefined every three months. At the same time, the joint committee formulated a detailed schedule to reform interest rates and institute a single flexible exchange rate regime as proposed by USAID officials and advisors.[17]

However, Chang Ki-yŏng only partially accepted the USAID's advice for rationalization and stabilization, moving from a multiple to a single exchange rate regime, but consciously undervaluing the won in order to prevent a loss of international competitiveness. The interest rate reform saw a similar move; Chang Ki-yŏng followed the United States' advice to match the highly competitive private "curb markets" with a sharp increase in bank interest rates, but he set loan rates below deposit rates to subsidize industrial expansion.[18] This "reverse margin system" transferred income from state banks to the recipients of loans—mostly the *chaebol* in charge of Park's strategic industrial projects—squeezing out small- and medium-sized enterprises (SMEs) from financial markets by creating an excess demand for bank loans and unleashing powerful inflationary forces that disfavored wage earners and the middle class.

U.S. aid officials did not fight Chang Ki-yŏng's unorthodox growth strategy. On the contrary, they followed his "reform" with generous rewards, backing the MoF in the 1965 negotiations with the International Monetary Fund (IMF) on the issue of provisional arrangements, and facilitating commercial loans for South Korean business firms.[19] The United States also recognized the importance of Chang Ki-yŏng's leadership in the daily operations of the ECC and his contribution to the institutionalization of the financial stabilization program.[20] The U.S. accommodation of Chang Ki-yŏng's reform owed much to the rapidly emerging "honeymoon" *(milwŏl)* between Park and Lyndon B. Johnson. By 1965 Park resolutely sided with Johnson's regional security strategy, normalizing diplomatic relations with Tokyo and sending military troops to defend South Vietnam. Politically, Johnson needed Park as much as Park needed Johnson, which made the USAID tolerant of, if not receptive to, Chang Ki-yŏng's unorthodox ideas. Once the deputy prime minister secured his American partner's endorsement, he used the bilateral ECC to line up the other South Korean state ministries behind his growth policy. With Chang Ki-yŏng himself chairing the South Korean delegation to the ECC, and the international cooperation director of the EPB backing Chang Ki-yŏng from below within the bilateral committee as the secretary general of the South Korean representatives, the ECC de facto became an interministerial network through which U.S. pressures and influence were used by the EPB to neutralize MoF resistance to the reverse margin system of bank interest rates. The ECC became an instrument of Chang Ki-yŏng's economic policy that contradicted its original raison d'être of financial stabilization.

The risky expansionary strategy drew different reactions from different ministries. The MCI applauded, because it meant easy loans for its main clients, light industrial exporters and HCI investors. The MoF protested vigorously, because the EPB-formulated interest rate and foreign exchange reform reduced the MoF to the status of a mere resource mobilizer for industrial projects decided on by the EPB and the MCI. The strategy also entailed the danger of burdening the MoF's state banks with nonperforming loans. Against the MoF's opposition, Chang Ki-yŏng used Park's disciplinary whip. When finance minister Hong Sŭng-hŏn publicly rebelled against the reverse margin system in 1965, Park abruptly dismissed him. During Chang Ki-yŏng's three years as the deputy prime minister, the MoF saw its minister fired five times and its vice minister four times. The Ministry of Finance thought it had no choice but to rebel, because what Chang Ki-yŏng proposed meant a de facto divestiture of its coordinating authority on the basis of interest rate and foreign exchange policy. The MoF's ability to set the money supply autonomously through monetary policy instruments progressively declined as the EPB Budget Bureau set aside an increasingly large quantity of state resources for long-term investment projects, and as the EPB International Cooperation Bureau independently approved foreign loans and distributed international aid.[21]

The EPB prepared policy by working backward from Park's directives. Once the targets were set by Park, the EPB worked to calculate the resources required for implementation and meet any expected shortfall in capital, first by internal adjustment of budget policy and foreign capital licenses and second by influencing the MoF to change fiscal and monetary policy. A period of intense monitoring of industrial projects and regular feedback from the MCI, sectoral ministries, and auxiliary agencies would follow. The feedback allowed the EPB to prepare the necessary revisions of the original targets and measures of resource extraction and mobilization. In this way the superministry constantly revised its industrial targets to hit the right mix of goals and instruments that would get them nearer to fulfilling Park's directives. Targets were not sacred. On the contrary, frequent revision was believed necessary if Park's goals were to be realized.

It is important to emphasize that the significance of economic planning lay less in offering a technical master plan of industrial growth, with intricate modeling of targets and instruments, than in establishing institutional channels of communication and cooperation and institutional procedures for systematic agenda formation, resource mobilization, and policy feedback among the EPB, the MoF, the sectoral ministries, and the auxiliary ministries on an ongoing basis. Through these channels and procedures, the EPB effectively evaluated performance and adjusted policy strategies in a timely manner, as well as rapidly diffused new policy ideas and techniques throughout the state bureaucracy. In fact, as technical blueprints forecasting South Korea's future economic path, the EPB-formulated FYEDPs were more failures than successes. The first FYEDP (1962–1966) had to be revised downward after a year of implementation, only to see its new targets surpassed by actual policy results in 1963. In the case of the second FYEDP (1967–1972), the original targets were revised by the EPB upward only a year after its launch, in order to catch up with unforeseen hypergrowth. The real significance of economic planning was not technical but political, authorizing the EPB to intervene in other ministries' affairs and inculcate society with Park's brassy "can do" spirit and his daring "grow-at-all-costs" strategy. The EPB itself was well aware of the instrumental political role of economic planning and drew up its second FYEDP with a sense of political purpose and loyalty to Park.

Once the EPB extracted resources from society through its checks and balances against the MoF, it next needed a strategy for resource allocation. Again Park set the overall framework for ministerial decisions. Having learned during the junta years that coercion was counterproductive, only raising anxiety and distrust among *chaebol* groups, the USAID, and state ministries, the Park of the mid-1960s came to emphasize more carrots than sticks in his dealings with the *chaebol*. At the same time, however, Park kept three other parts of his earlier formula for state-business relations developed during the junta years. Those rules that survived were: (1) select a "national champion" from among the *chaebol* for each of the strategic industrial sectors and provide an integrated package of state assistance for its development; (2) rescue the national champion when it became trapped in a liquidity squeeze as a result of following Park's ambitious industrial policy, in order to make economic policy credible; (3) but also encourage one or another *chaebol* group to challenge the front-runner with an entry into the strategic industrial sector at an appropriate time, lest too much monopoly profit accrue to the front-runner, or lest the front-runner become too satisfied with monopoly profits and lose the incentive to expand, causing its performance to fall below the target level.

This mix of rules was a product not only of economic necessity but also of political choice. The concentration of resources in a few *chaebol* groups was unavoidable, as long as Park doggedly insisted on developing a full line of modern industries on an internationally competitive scale. Capital was too scarce, entry barriers too high, and investment too risky for big business to invest in industrial projects unless it was granted monopoly profits. At the same time, however, Park undermined this rule of monopoly by endorsing the principle of eventually establishing a system of oligopolistic competition among *chaebol* groups. This internal tension in Park's rules of resource allocation was to cost him much in the 1970s.

The *chaebol* responded enthusiastically. To secure a piece of the pie before the front-runners carved out their sectors of monopoly and shut down the entry points to strategic sectors, each of the *chaebol* aggressively lobbied for state licenses that would create the means to grow in a big way. With a stable supply of subsidized loans secured through the reverse margin system, and with the noncommercial grants and reparation funds provided through the tripartite regional security alliance that Park forged with Washington and Tokyo, Park had the credibility to promise the *chaebol* the growth opportunity of a lifetime. There developed an investment boom beginning in 1966. The ratio between target and actual investment stood at 124.7 percent in 1966 after annually averaging 161.3 percent for four years. Then, for the next five years, the same ratio averaged 73.4 percent.

Hitting the right balance between concentration and competition, however, was a difficult economic and political issue. Frequently Park ended up causing excess competition for state licenses and subsidies among the *chaebol,* making surplus capacity virtually a systemic trait of the South Korean political economy as early as 1969. This led to a severe liquidity crisis whenever export sales slackened and interest rates rose. But reducing surplus capacity with an exit policy for insolvent companies was not an easy option from Park's perspective. Allowing any of the state-backed *chaebol* to go under would not only create a systemwide panic by saddling state banks with huge nonperforming loans and disrupting production in vendor firms and affiliate companies vertically and horizontally integrated to the faltering *chaebol* but also bring Park's political credibility into question. Closing down a *chaebol* would be seen as a breach of his promises to other *chaebol* and to foreign and local lenders, which could cause a run on state banks, thus throwing the country's entire manufacturing sector into a liquidity squeeze.

Park constantly warned the *chaebol* of cuts in state assistance if they failed to meet their end of the political bargain to develop an internationally competitive business, but in reality he did not have an effective exit policy. Once the EPB guaranteed the foreign debts of an industrial producer and the MoF backed the EPB by continually rolling over loans provided by state banks despite a business's losses, the state banks lost the incentive of prudent regulation. Rather than making loans on the basis of their estimate of the future stream of the borrower's income, the state banks focused on securing the collateral to cover potential losses. The lack of prudential regulation encouraged the debtor to expand into uncompetitive industries with the expectation that it would be rescued with state subsidies if its business venture faltered. Consequently, Park faced the formidable task of weeding out moral hazards from the very start of economic growth processes. His choice of policy instruments was once again bureaucratic rather than market forces.

To induce big business to take risks in the direction of his goals, but at the same time to ensure the *chaebol*'s efficient allocation of productive resources, Park built a system of bureaucratic supervision and surveillance in the hope that it would serve as a functional substitute for the market's disciplinary mechanism of bankruptcy. This need to build a bureaucratic mechanism to minimize the problem of moral hazards constituted another prime driver in transforming the South Korean state bureaucracy into a Leviathan that had the capacity to reach deep down for control in virtually all aspects of business activities. The MCI began checking the status of export sales by commodity, company, and destination on a daily basis in 1962, in order to hold the *chaebol* to their export pledges. The EPB progressively strengthened the price stability law in 1961, 1962, 1973, and 1975, with the twin goals of countering inflation by establishing the "market price" in oligopolistic sectors and of taxing the "excess profits" accruing from international supply shocks. To bring down the level of state subsidies by encouraging major *chaebol* to go public, the Ministry of Finance provided tax breaks for business firms listed on the stock exchange beginning in 1968; established legal sanctions and financial penalties for the firms that rebuffed the MoF directive to go public in 1972; and set a detailed time schedule for the public listing of the subsidiaries and holding companies of each of the major *chaebol* after 1975. More important, the EPB made unfair and competition-limiting business practices the object of regulation by drawing up a Price Stability and Fair Trade Law in December 1975.

The effort to replace market discipline with bureaucratic supervision failed. The number of companies listed in the South Korean stock market reached 251 by October 1976, a tenfold increase since 1968, but because state banks were always ready to provide the *chaebol* with subsidized loans, the *chaebol* did not feel the need to raise funds through the stock market, which could threaten the majority shareholder's control over ownership and management. Moreover, in spite of bureaucratic threats, compliance with listing on the stock market was low, especially among the largest *chaebol*, because no matter how frequently the EPB threatened them with sanctions, they knew that the EPB would eventually back down and resume its role as an underwriter for their ventures.

Like the policy of encouraging firms to go public, the regulatory regime that the EPB constructed over prices was bound to lose its originally reformist purpose. Because Park built a profoundly expansionary export machine, the EPB had no choice but to use its regulatory power to control price hikes rather than to tax excess profits in oligopolistic industrial sectors. Moreover, big business always found legal loopholes to evade the EPB's directives on pricing policy and to neutralize its regulations. When the EPB did regulate prices at the expense of *chaebol* interests, the EPB's sister coordinating agency, the MoF, found itself granting more subsidies to the *chaebol* to compensate for the losses they accrued from complying with EPB requirements. The MCI, too, frequently joined in to compensate *chaebol* for their losses with the adjustment of its policy on production quotas and regulations. The *chaebol* were simply too weak financially for the EPB to use its regulatory power for the purpose of fair trade. On the contrary, rather than confronting the *chaebol*, the EPB and the MCI chose to work with them and harness the *chaebol*'s monopoly power to establish a "rationalization cartel." It was hoped that the cartel established among *chaebol* through the EPB's mediation would dampen the South Korean economy's dangerously expansionary bias and save it from a vicious circle of boom and bust.

Similarly, in an effort to replace market signals with administrative guidance, Park zeroed in on export targets to bring about economically functional firm behavior. To a certain extent, export targets did play that role. As Alice Amsden has argued, export targets were relatively objective and transparent criteria that helped economic policymakers in countering the South Korean economy's proclivity for rent-seeking, surplus capacity, and cyclical liquidity crisis.[22] In a similar way, Anne Krueger has distinguished the South Korean export machine from the Latin American import substitution model as an economic system with its own mechanism to correct policy biases and reestablish the market equilibrium. Fierce competition in export markets, Krueger argues, forced state ministries to readjust and restructure their expansionary policy periodically before it became too late to avoid the boom's becoming a dangerous bubble.[23]

At the same time, it is important to emphasize the limitation of export targets as a policy instrument to measure business performance and market efficiency. The firm's achievement of export targets did not necessarily mean that the firm's international competitiveness was on the rise, because with license privileges, bank subsidies, and tax deductions directly tied to the level of export sales, any increase of exports could mean rent-seeking as much as productivity-enhancing business activity. The factor and product markets were so systematically distorted to favor exports that an increase in exports did not necessarily imply a strengthening of international competitiveness. Nor did it mean Park's export machine had an internal corrective mechanism that corrected its own mistakes to avoid a dangerous bubble economy. On the contrary, with all policy instruments geared to concentrate resources in a few strategic industrial sectors and back their export sales, prices no longer accurately mirrored the South Korean resource endowment. Similarly, the rise of exports could have resulted from the firms' efforts to protect their licenses, subsidies, and tax privileges at home rather than from their competitiveness abroad. With the failure of the state's administrative efforts to weed out moral hazards, a number of strategic industries became financially insolvent, creating huge non-performing loans that threatened macroeconomic stability.

Adjustment Strategy, 1967–1972

In 1967, only three years after Chang Ki-yŏng's "rationalization reform," a number of *chaebol* with government-guaranteed foreign loans became lost causes, incapable of even paying back the interest they owed. Park sent a clear signal for policy change by dismissing Chang Ki-yŏng. Pak Ch'ung-hun, a former army general of soft temper, who had headed the Ministry of Commerce and Industry since 1964, became the deputy prime minister. Unfortunately, Pak Ch'ung-hun diagnosed South Korea's economic woes only in administrative terms. He saw the crisis as having been brought about by the lack of a bureaucratic mechanism for prudent supervision rather than by the intrinsic limitations of the state's expansionary modernization strategy.

In an attempt to ensure more effective supervision over foreign loans, Pak Ch'ung-hun established a foreign capital management bureau within the EPB. In 1968, he announced a rationalization program to merge or sell insolvent industrial companies to third parties with the goal of putting the companies on a financially sound basis as well as minimizing bank losses. But the liquidity crisis did not abate, because the corporate and financial distress South Korea was experiencing was on a scale that required extraordinary measures. To roll over foreign loans, it was not adequate just to merge insolvent companies into what was likely to be another business entity of financially questionable character. The industrial rationalization program faltered because no third party came up with the money to shore up the failing firms and the dangerously exposed state banks. The World Bank expressed serious concern over the state of the South Korean economy in 1969. More drastic measures were needed if Park was to prevent a market panic over the faltering *chaebol* and state banks.

Forced by events, Park replaced Pak Ch'ung-hun with Kim Hak-ryŏl as the deputy prime minister in 1969. Kim Hak-ryŏl was an elite MoF bureaucrat who had been dismissed from his finance ministership in 1966 for criticizing Chang Ki-yŏng's hyperexpansionary policy. A personal confidant of Park's since 1961, when he served as a private tutor on economic issues for the then SCNR chairman, Kim Hak-ryŏl was an advocate of economic contraction. Reflecting the unusual nature of his times, however, the "monetary conservatism" Kim Hak-ryŏl put forth was of an unorthodox kind. Rather than championing disciplined monetary policy to guard the interests of state banks, Kim Hak-ryŏl pulled the emergency brake on South Korea's overheated economy with the goal of saving industrial producers through the socialization of business losses. The emergency relief measure made the MoF intervene even more—not less—extensively into everyday business affairs with the effect of undermining the MoF's own banking constituency.

To deter the MoF from assembling a more orthodox adjustment policy package of interest hikes, which would have driven insolvent industrial producers into bankruptcy, Kim Hak-ryŏl set up a Blue House Task Force for Handling Insolvent Firms in 1969. Run jointly by the EPB and the MoF, the task force rescued ailing *chaebol* through bank subsidies and tax relief. The MoF reduced deposit interest rates cumulatively by over 60 percent and loan interest rates by almost 40 percent between 1969 and 1972, even when inflationary pressures were visibly deteriorating.[24] On the other hand, the rescue operation required the MoF to tighten its control over credit allocation to the SME sector, if it was to avoid colliding head-on with Park's other goal of macroeconomic stabilization. To cool down inflationary pressures in the midst of running a rescue operation for the *chaebol,* the MoF had to exclude small- and medium-sized firms as well as individual households from its extensive rationing of credit, and channel even more resources to the *chaebol.* In a similar spirit of emergency, the MoL forced the workers to shoulder an inordinate share of adjustment costs through wage restraints and even layoffs.[25]

Despite Kim Hak-ryŏl's adjustment strategy, the *chaebol* were on the brink of collapse and the South Korean economy was near default on foreign loans by 1972. In the face of these threats, Park drew up an Emergency Decree for Economic Stability and Growth (EDESG) on the recommendation of Chairman Kim Yong-wan of the Federation of Korean Industries. To rescue big businesses, the decree transformed informal curb-market loans into bank loans, repayable over five years with a grace period of three; forced state banks to cut interest rates by issuing special stabilization bonds; drastically raised depreciation ratios on fixed investment; and introduced tax exemptions on income for strategic industries.[26] This integrated effort to transfer income away from both informal curb-markets and formal state banks to ailing industrial producers effectively alleviated the liquidity crisis. The manufacturing sector's average financial cost stood at 5.7 percent of its total sales in 1973, still too high to make the *chaebol* financially stable, but 3.5 percentage points lower than during the height of the liquidity crisis in 1971.

Rescuing the *chaebol* through this politically orchestrated income transfer was intensely criticized by the opposition political party and the dissident *chaeya*. The twin strategy of business rescue and monetary contraction was, however, a logical outcome of Park's industrialization strategy. The financially vulnerable growth machine of the *chaebol* had been kept afloat since its inception only because Park had the EPB and the MoF underwrite its financial liabilities and socialize adjustment costs through the coercive mechanism of forced saving and even politically engineered income transfers to the *chaebol*. Herein lay the EPB's organizational distinctiveness. The superministry made mistakes—sometimes grave blunders, as in the case of Chang Ki-yŏng's reverse margin system that trapped South Korea in a liquidity crisis by 1972. Yet the EPB always emerged triumphant in the interministerial race to solve the issues at hand, because it could flexibly adjust its policy stand over time from expansion to contraction and vice versa on the basis of its organizational mission of macroeconomic planning. As a planning agency, the EPB had the entire economy as its turf and was not a captive of any sectoral interest, which enabled it to switch sides from expansion to contraction as South Korea went through a business cycle. Moreover, as planners, EPB staff always searched for stabilization measures that did not threaten the growth potential of the South Korean economy.

By contrast, the MoF—with its mission to maintain financial stability and its constituency residing in the weak state banks—was disadvantaged in assuming the role of macroeconomic coordinator when Park geared for high growth in 1964. Ironically, the same organizational characteristics also prevented the MoF from winning Park's trust when the opposite situation of contraction developed in the 1969–1972 period. Park then feared that the MoF would irreversibly damage the real sector in its pursuit of financial goals. To run to the other end of the policy spectrum and empower the MCI was equally inadvisable in 1969, because the adjustment policy required to deal with corporate distress directly collided with the expansionary ethos of the MCI. Whereas the MoF-centric coordination was likely to threaten corporate interests, the MCI was by definition excluded from Park's choice of institutional leadership because of its intrinsically expansionary organizational character.

The EDESG of 1972, however, brought only a brief respite. The *chaebol* escaped from their worst liquidity squeeze, but the recovery was soon swept away by the global oil crisis of that era. The timing of supply shock could not have been worse, hitting South Korea precisely when its unregulated informal curb markets—South Korea's more efficient financial sector, which had provided up to 40 percent of loans to *chaebol*—were paralyzed by the EDESG. The oil crisis again forced the MoF to dampen the effects of interest hikes on the *chaebol* by tightening its bureaucratic control of credit allocation. The double shock of the 1972 decree and the 1973 credit control put SMEs in a harsh credit crunch. From this pressing structural condition, Park drew up a strategy that directly contradicted orthodox economic thinking: if a company's low sales volume was the cause of high costs and low earnings, expand its production capacity further with policy loans and realize economies of scale through an aggressive export drive. Accordingly, Park geared himself up for what Yung Chul Park and Dong Won Kim have called the "gambler's approach" to growth: a strategy to "literally grow out" of a liquidity trap by engineering a new round of state-subsidized *chaebol* growth.[27] The new hypergrowth drive, launched only four months after the 1972 EDESG and continued in spite of the 1973 oil shock, however, was inseparable from and driven by the domestic political and economic turmoil that had been engulfing South Korea since 1969. The catalyst for the turmoil came from abroad.

HCI, 1973–1979

As Richard M. Nixon sought an exit from the Vietnam War, he set forth plans for a U.S. military disengagement from Asia in his 1969 Guam Doctrine. As part of this larger regional adjustment, Nixon unilaterally withdrew a third of the American armed forces stationed in South Korea by 1971, causing a deep sense of security crisis within Park's inner policy circle.[28] The same year, moreover, saw South Korea's long anticipated graduation from U.S. economic aid. The ending of aid programs was fully in line with Washington's foreign aid policy, but its timing was inauspicious. The termination of the aid strengthened Park's lifelong distrust of U.S. intentions. Ever since Secretary Dean Acheson publicly placed South Korea outside the U.S. defense line in the western Pacific in January 1950, thus inadvertently inviting the North Korean military invasion of the South five months later, South Korea looked at the United States as an ally who would abandon it when put under political pressure.

The South Korean domestic political situation was also becoming unstable. The opposition New Democratic Party (NDP) rallied around its presidential candidate, Kim Dae-jung, successfully mobilizing the urban electorate and Chŏlla regional voters into a formidable electoral coalition in

1971. The victory went to Park, but after 1971, the future defeat of the ruling Democratic Republican Party in a presidential election looked like a very real possibility. Most important, Park was scheduled to step down from the presidency in 1975 given the South Korean constitution's limitation of three terms for the president.

It was in this uncertain domestic and international context that Park declared the *yushin* constitution in October 1972, giving himself what was for all intents and purposes dictatorial power for life. The president viewed his "palace coup" primarily in terms of military security. The double crisis of military security and domestic instability, Park argued, called for a further concentration of power in the presidency. Once a new regime was put in place, moreover, there should follow a major reappraisal of South Korea's modernization strategy. The new regime, with its dramatically enhanced capabilities, deserved more challenging goals and strategies: heavy and chemical industrialization, or HCI. In Park's eyes, regime change and policy change were two sides of the same coin. In the "revolutionary" situation of 1972 and 1973, the experts' advice on budgetary balance and monetary discipline was brushed aside as a luxury before what Park judged to be a crisis threatening South Korea's very survival as a sovereign nation. This rationale of regime change and policy change made Park even more unresponsive—if not outright hostile—to market norms. The loss of monetary policy discipline was a cost he was willing to bear if it won him regime stability and military security.

The man he chose to orchestrate economic policy change on the basis of dramatically strengthened regime capabilities was O Wŏn-ch'ŏl. An MCI bureaucrat since 1962, and an engineer by training, O Wŏn-ch'ŏl possessed a thorough insider's knowledge of MCI's mechanisms of industrial policy, administrative guidance, and export promotion that was bound to assume a central role in Park's HCI drive. Personal ties between the two men went back to 1961, when O Wŏn-ch'ŏl served Park's military junta as a researcher. In 1971 he was brought in as the senior secretary on industrial affairs at the Blue House to prepare for developing a strategy to expand the heavy and chemical industries as the infrastructure for military security. Once the worst effects of the oil shock were met by 1974, Park appointed O Wŏn-ch'ŏl to oversee the newly established interministerial Heavy and Chemical Industrialization Planning Corps (HCI Planning Corps, or HCIPC). Holding these two posts until Park's death in 1979, O Wŏn-ch'ŏl left a lasting mark on South Korea's industrial policy.

O Wŏn-ch'ŏl was well prepared to act as Park's alter ego on behalf of the industrialization drive. In 1970, on the basis of a decade of service at MCI as an expert on industrial policy, O Wŏn-ch'ŏl, then assistant vice minister, had drawn up an overall blueprint for shifting the focus of development from the light to heavy and chemical industries in keeping with the Japanese model.[29] Much of the blueprint was to be formally incorporated into the strategic thinking of the HCI Planning Corps.[30] In contrast to orthodox economists' advice to wait until domestic demand reached the level of supporting mass production in the heavy and chemical industries, O Wŏn-ch'ŏl believed that supply was a greater bottleneck than demand, and that demand could be created abroad if production capacity was expanded to allow economies of scale. In his view, downscaling HCI projects to fit the South Korean domestic demand level would make the projects a losing proposition and deprive South Korea of its opportunity to join the club of industrial societies. The only option, as he saw it, was to expand HCI projects to internationally competitive scales for export promotion, with state-guaranteed foreign loans and state-subsidized bank loans.

The idea of export-led HCI instantly caught Park's attention. A soldier more than a politician and a dreamer with the eyes of a realist, much like the Japanese Meiji oligarchs, Park had seen iron and steel as symbols of national strength ever since he had seized power in 1961. After the *yushin* regime was imposed, HCI became more than a personal preference; it provided Park with an opportunity to solve the twin crises of military security and regime legitimacy, as well as to rescue the *chaebol* from their slide into a deep recession in the middle of the oil crisis.[31] In January 1973, Park publicly announced the spectacular goal of achieving more than a sixfold increase in exports and more than a threefold growth in GNP by 1981. Initially, the EPB and the MoF reacted with incredulity to O Wŏn-ch'ŏl's idea of investing over $9 billion in six strategic heavy and chemical industries by 1981 to deliver Park's promise of hypergrowth. Because South Korea was in the midst of the oil crisis, which shook its economy to the core, the EPB and the MoF were then putting into place a sharp monetary contraction to adjust to post-oil-shock realities.[32] O Wŏn-ch'ŏl's plan seemed to counter all that they were trying to do.

Park let the EPB and the MoF stabilize the badly shaken South Korean economy by issuing the Presidential Emergency Measure for Stabilizing People's Livelihood in January 1974. Even before the economy was stabilized, however, Park began laying the institutional groundwork for an aggressive pursuit of HCI. Aware of the EPB's skepticism regarding his HCI drive, Park dramatically strengthened the power of his presidential Secretariat by relying on chief of staff Kim Chŏng-ryŏm (1969–1978) as a de facto macroeconomic coordinator and O Wŏn-ch'ŏl as the engine for HCI. O Wŏn-ch'ŏl's post of senior secretary on industrial affairs had been newly created to balance the post of senior secretary on economic affairs that typically went to an EPB or MoF career bureaucrat. Parallel to the strengthening of Blue House capabilities, Park also transformed both the EPB and the MCI into colossal organizations, with newly created sectoral bureaus in charge of heavy and chemical industries, in order to back the Blue House-initiated HCI drive bureaucratically. Their organizational growth gave the EPB and MCI an institutional stake in HCI too.

At the same time, Park knew that given the huge scale of resource mobilization required for HCI, no one ministry could propel the drive. To prevent projects from getting lost in bureaucratic bickering, Park established the interministerial Council for Promoting Heavy and Chemical Industries (CPHCI). Personally chaired by Park himself and with cabinet ministers recruited as regular council members, the CPHCI was given the mission of setting the agenda, designing a concerted effort of resource mobilization and allocation, and laying out a division of labor among the economic ministries in that push toward HCI. The real driver of HCI was, however, not the council but O Wŏn-ch'ŏl's HCI Planning Corps, which Park organized as the secretariat of CPHCI. Moreover, to win bureaucratic support for HCI, draw on the expertise and resources of each of the line ministries in the direction of HCI, and achieve even greater control over the policy agendas, Park had O Wŏn-ch'ŏl's Planning Corps work directly with Grade 1 and 2A bureaucrats (assistant vice ministers and bureau directors) from the relevant line ministries in weekly working-level meetings, thus enabling the Planning Corps to go over the heads of cabinet ministers to influence sectoral policy directly.

The organizational change brought clear winners and losers. The biggest winners were the two members of the presidential staff, Kim Chŏng-ryŏm and O Wŏn-ch'ŏl, who exercised discretionary power over macroeconomic and industrial policy, respectively, to move the state bureaucracy toward heavy and chemical industrialization. The EPB and especially the MCI also benefited a great deal, each adding four or more new sectoral bureaus and doubling their Grade 2A slots in January 1973.[33] Park had to strengthen the presidential Secretariat and the EPB because the institutional vehicle of industrial policy, the MCI, was a relatively weak agency, frequently captured by its *chaebol* clientele, "robbed" of the best of newly appointed *haengsi* bureaucrats by the elite EPB and MoF, and tilted decisively toward expansion without an eye to macroeconomic issues. More critically, the MCI possessed an arsenal of license powers with which to design industrial policy, but those powers could not be actualized unless the EPB backed its license decisions with budget and foreign loans and the MoF with tax relief and bank subsidies. The MCI could fight off MoF resistance only if the EPB, now transformed into a planning agency with sectoral expertise, put its weight behind the MCI.

This is not to belittle the role of the EPB and the MoF. On the contrary, the success of increasing industrialization depended on Park's winning their institutional loyalty to HCI. It was they who controlled strategic policy networks, commanded indispensable economic resources, and, most important, possessed South Korea's best bureaucrats. Simply silencing the EPB's voice of caution and ordering the MoF to obey Park's HCI directives unswervingly could not ensure the mobilization of the bureaucracy in the direction of HCI. Fully aware of the importance of winning bureaucratic support, Park continued his old habit of showering the MoF and especially the EPB with organizational privileges. The 1973 presidential order issued to construct an institutional infrastructure for HCI expanded the organization of the EPB even more than that of the MCI. The HCI Planning Corps, moreover, sought active support from the EPB by bringing in its economic planning director, Sŏ Sŏk-chun, as the deputy chief of the Planning Corps in May 1974.[34] With his loyalty to HCI proven, Sŏ Sŏk-chun saw his EPB career flourish, becoming the assistant vice minister for planning in December 1974 (when he was only thirty-six years old) and the vice minister by December 1977. Sŏ Sŏk-chun was a symbol of success, becoming the first among EPB careerists to reach the EPB vice ministership. Moreover, his promotions, after he briefly served in the HCI Planning Corps, were all made within the internal hierarchy of the EPB, which was also unprecedented. This extraordinary career trajectory, possible only with Park's backing, sent out a clear message to EPB bureaucrats: work for HCI and be rewarded with power and honor.

With the center of power tilted toward the presidential Secretariat and away from the economic bureaucracy, and toward the EPB and the MCI within the economic bureaucracy, Park could embark upon HCI as soon as the immediate goal of stabilization to absorb the effects of the oil shock was achieved in 1974. The Council for Promoting HCI was personally presided over by Park himself once every month and by Prime Minister Kim Chong-p'il once every two weeks in between, approving the HCIPC-prepared overall timetable of investment and the HCIPC-formulated interministerial division of labor by April 1973. A flurry of rule making, sectoral planning, and institution building ensued throughout 1973. In May, the MCI announced a set of policy rules and guidelines on the debt-equity ratio, production capacity, joint ventures, foreign loan, export targets, and technology licensing arrangements for firms entering the heavy and chemical industries. To bring about a timely execution of the MCI investment programs, the MoC drafted a Law for Promoting the Industrial Complex by July, with its discretionary power to expropriate land considerably strengthened. To maximize the benefits of industrial clustering, the MoC also established an Industrial Complex Development Company to oversee the simultaneous construction of three massive HCI complexes in the southern provinces. More critically, after a long consultation with the EPB, the MoF drafted a controversial National Investment Fund (NIF) Law in July, which the DRP-controlled National Assembly duly enacted in August.[35] The NIF was an outright forced savings program, legally requiring nonbank financial institutions with a "public character"—welfare pension funds, insurance, and trusts, among others—to purchase NIF bonds. The law also envisioned state agencies' purchase of NIF bonds with budgetary funds, interest and dividend incomes, and capital gains. The money raised was subsequently channeled to the *chaebol* entrants in the heavy and chemical industries in the form of concessionary policy loans via state banks. To bring more funds under the NIF's direct control, Park had the DRP legislate the MoF-drafted Law on National Welfare Pensions a month after the establishment of the NIF. Henceforth, 8 percent of wage income was to be levied as pension funds, with employers and employees each contributing half. Much of that money was to be used to back HCI. The MoF also doubled the nominal capital of the Korea Development Bank and quintupled that of the Korea Export-Import Bank in December 1973 with an eye to increasing policy loans.[36]

Having completed most of its four groundbreaking tasks—rule making, sectoral planning, institution building, and forced saving—the cabinet-level CPHCI went into a de facto adjournment with its eighteenth meeting in February 1974. The much more challenging stage of implementation began. With O Wŏn-ch'ŏl enjoying Park's complete trust, the rules and plans of the Council for Promoting HCI—in actuality, of O Wŏn-ch'ŏl—became institutionalized. The economic ministries were unsure who was really giving the orders, Park or his confidant O Wŏn-ch'ŏl, when the HCI Planning Corps chief "relayed" a presidential policy directive. The weekly Working-Level Interministerial Meeting of Assistant Vice Ministers, organized in place of the Council for Promoting HCI, never digressed from its mission of establishing at the working level an ongoing mechanism to coordinate the actions of the economic ministries in the interests of implementing the HCIPC-formulated set of HCI goals and strategies. Convening over eighty times between 1974 and 1979, the working-level meeting never became an agenda setter. Passively formulating an interministerial program of coordination to solve micro policy issues identified by O Wŏn-ch'ŏl's Planning Corps, the working-level meeting was a club of assistant vice ministers only in name. Before long, the member ministries began sending bureau directors and even division chiefs in place of assistant vice ministers.

As the Planning Corps became increasingly sure of its control over economic ministries and their loyalty to Park's HCI drive, it too reorganized into a small staff organization. The Planning Corps had been staffed by over sixty bureaucrats from the EPB, MCI, MoC, and Ministry of Science and Technology (MST) while the cabinet-level Council for Promoting HCI was in operation to draw up basic goals, rules, and strategies. Once the project entered the implementation stage in 1974, the number of HCIPC personnel fell to below forty. Now mainly a surveillance mechanism checking on its member ministries' timely execution of policy rather than Park's personal vehicle to draw up and inculcate the state bureaucracy with basic goals, rules, and strategies, the HCI Planning Corps no longer needed to be large. On the contrary, by returning most of the transferees back to their home ministries in the implementation stage, the Planning Corps could even strengthen its supervisory power over state ministries. The returnees could serve as the eyes and ears of the Planning Corps in their respective home ministry, checking on ministry policy as well as transmitting the HCI vision of the Planning Corps to the economic bureaucracy.

To be sure, in the effort to grow out of economic woes by means of HCI, Park was helped by an unexpected turn of events abroad. The oil-rich Middle Eastern countries aggressively embarked on modernization with their vast amounts of oil money. To win a share of this booming market before other nations rushed in, Park had the EPB vice minister head an interministerial task force of bureau directors to "exclusively" coordinate state support for *chaebol*-initiated Middle East construction projects. The prime minister also played a role in this effort to penetrate the Middle East markets, lining up state ministries behind the EPB-coordinated policy package in a newly formed Commission for Enhancing Cooperation with Middle Eastern Economies.[37] As with O Wŏn-ch'ŏl's Planning Corps for HCI projects, it was the working-level interministerial team, led by the vice minister—not the commission of economic ministries chaired by the prime minister—that crafted the basic framework of state support for Middle East business ventures. The working-level team had the MoF prepare tax deductions for both construction companies and workers employed in Middle East economies; the MoC discourage "excessive competition" among South Korean construction companies by encouraging their formation of cartels under a newly drafted Law to Promote Overseas Construction; and the EPB manage the construction workers' remittance of overseas earnings by issuing a Principle for Administering Overseas Construction Earnings in 1976.

Partly as a result of this integrated program, South Korea enjoyed a "Middle East boom" for a decade. By 1985 its construction companies were to earn over $80 billion from the Middle East, much of which was transferred to their affiliate companies in the South Korean manufacturing sector for investment. In 1979 alone, over eleven thousand South Korean workers were sent to work in the Middle East. For an economy that saw its "Vietnam boom" disappear after 1971, the Middle East boom was a godsend. By taking early advantage of opportunities in the Middle East, South Korea was able to break out of one of its structural afflictions, foreign exchange constraints, which was obstructing its heavy and chemical industrialization.

The HCI drive was an unambiguous success in terms of its own goals. The fourth FYEDP (1977–1981) had more or less achieved the target goal of HCI investment by 1979, two years ahead of schedule. By contrast, light industries visibly suffered, with actual investment standing at only 46.2 percent of the target goal in 1981. The spectacular overachievement in HCI was possible only because Park channeled 79 percent of available funds into these industries in 1977 and 1978 at the expense of light industries. The annual growth rate of investment in production facilities shot up even higher, reaching 26.6 percent in 1977 and 40.5 percent in 1978.

The HCI investment boom also translated into other successes. The heavy and chemical industries furnished over half of the South Korean GNP by 1978, three years earlier than Park's original plan of 1973. With an annual GNP growth rate of 11.2 percent after 1973, per capita GNP topped $1,000 in 1978—again, three years earlier than the original plan. Growth in exports was equally dramatic, growing sixfold between 1972 and 1977 and even producing a small but unprecedented current account surplus in 1977. The sense of triumph, however, lasted only briefly. The current account showed a deficit of a billion dollars in 1978 and over four billion dollars by 1979, although exports grew annually by 21.1 percent. The investment boom had become a dangerous "bubble."[38] Most of the HCI projects showed very low returns—if not outright losses.[39] Park achieved his 1973 goals, but at high economic costs, including the cycle of boom and bust, the spiral of price increases, and financial vulnerabilities.

The strategy to grow out of illiquidity could not continue indefinitely. The consumer price index rose by 10.2 percent in 1977, despite extensive price controls and the selective rationing system put in place by the EPB. Black markets thrived and speculation spread. But because Park was solidly behind the HCI effort, the EPB had to continue along the expansionary path for one and a half year more. The planners devised only stopgap measures, tackling inflation mainly as a problem of supply bottlenecks and imbalances rather than as a result of systemic economic contradictions. Likewise, the MCI worked to halt inflation on the assumption that economic priorities remained unchanged. Trying to dampen price increases with an expansion of the supply of goods, the MCI included 151 new items in its list of those automatically approved for import in 1978.[40] In a similar spirit, the EPB used the recently legislated Law on Price Stability and Fair Trade to correct price distortions through an even tighter regulation on monopolistic goods and their distribution system.[41] These efforts on the supply side of issues notwithstanding, inflation reached 14.4 percent in 1978. Only then did Park realize the futility of his efforts at price control. He had offered a meek supply-side reform for what was essentially a crisis triggered by easy credit and excess demand. With Ayatollah Khomeni's Iran suspending oil exports and other members of the Organization of Petroleum Exporting Countries (OPEC) declaring a price hike of 14.5 percent in December 1978, adjustment became even more urgent for South Korea.

Looking for a way out of stagflationary pressures, Park brought in Sin Hyŏn-hwak, who had a distinguished record of service at the Ministry of Reconstruction (the EPB's predecessor) in 1959–1960, as the deputy prime minister in December 1978. Given the profound financial vulnerability of *chaebol* firms, however, three months passed without meaningful change in policy. In March 1979, Park called Sin Hyŏn-hwak to the presidential palace and ordered him to assemble an adjustment package. As Sin Hyŏn-hwak later recollected, Park was by then South Korea's "leading expert" on economic issues, "fully aware of what was required of him to put the economy back onto the path of growth without anyone telling him so. The initiative for adjustment came from Park."[42] Once Park ordered economic adjustment, the EPB assembled the Comprehensive Measure for Economic Stabilization (CMES) within a mere twenty days.[43] This speed was possible because a number of EPB bureaucrats had already become advocates of change and reform, even drafting a Fiscal and Monetary Policy for Currency Stabilization for in-house review a year before Sin Hyŏn-hwak came to head the EPB. Brushed aside by top EPB officials as politically untenable, the draft proposal acquired a new life when Park independently came to the same conclusion and ordered Sin Hyŏn-hwak to draw up an adjustment policy.

The CMES proceeded on five different policy fronts. To reduce budget expenditures, it had the EPB slow down—if not halt—HCI investment programs and also end the price support for rice. To relieve inflationary pressures, the MoF was to ram through an interest hike.[44] For those firms suffering a liquidity squeeze as a result of this sudden shift in monetary policy, the EPB was to offer an "industrial rationalization program," with the MoF providing loans and tax cuts for companies under bankruptcy protection.[45] Equally critical, the EPB publicly pledged price decontrol to correct the distorted incentive structures. To continue the earlier effort to correct the supply bottlenecks that were causing inflationary pressures, the EPB advocated trade liberalization as well.[46]

The changes, however, came too late. The economy was trapped in a deep stagflationary crisis, precisely when Park's ruling coalition was simultaneously challenged on the political front. Under Kim Young-sam's leadership, the opposition National Democratic Party garnered more votes than Park's Democratic Republican Party in the hotly contested 1978 National Assembly election, encouraging the NDP to take an increasingly intransigent stance against the regime, calling for direct presidential elections and even joining the workers' struggle for economic justice. The repression of the NDP that ensued only made Park's political position more untenable. When Park had Kim Young-sam censured and expelled from the National Assembly in 1979, Kim Young-sam's regional stronghold of South Kyŏngsang Province became thoroughly alienated from Park, leading to a wave of political protests and labor strikes that paralyzed Pusan City and crippled the Masan Industrial Complex. In the face of this regime crisis, Park's confidants and protégés fought each other over political options, until, as we saw in Chapters 5 and 6, KCIA director Kim Chae-gyu—a "soft-liner" who advocated dialogue with the NDP—assassinated Park on October 26, 1979, in a moment of despair and misguided heroism.

IN RETROSPECT, the state Park built with the engineering mind of an artillery officer exhibited a strong predatory quality, but the predatory character it showed was qualitatively different from Africa's and Latin America's "classic" predatory states. The South Korean state generated rents for its business allies, but unlike the African and Latin American counterparts, it explicitly tied the provision of rents to the risky FYEDP investment projects and the development of export markets that these clients had to undertake. This game of exchanging political support for business performance acquired complexity and subtlety when Park returned to making HCI his top priority after 1973, but the game of political exchange was already in place in 1961 when Park put the leading *chaebol* owners under house arrest to negotiate their terms of participation in the ambitious first FYEDP projects. Tying rents to investment in FYEDP projects, however, did not make Park's politics of modernization any less disruptive than the African and Latin American predatory states' game of rent-seeking. Once state subsidies poured into one or another front-runner, other *chaebol* groups who had hitherto been passive, if not outright skeptical, toward state plans showed an intense interest in entering the industry despite the risk of heavy losses. To stay out of FYEDP projects was to pass up one's opportunity to become a global market player.

The profoundly expansionary bias built into Park's export machine inevitably threw South Korea into a political and economic cycle of boom and bust. Trapped in the increasingly illiquid corporate structure he himself created after 1964, however, Park was not able to put in place an orthodox adjustment policy. Because of the need to guard his image as a credible and trustworthy patron of risk-taking firms, Park frequently ended up delaying adjustment and overlooking disequilibrium until business difficulties developed into a systemwide crisis, threatening South Korea's entire financial and industrial system in the 1969–1972 and 1979–1982 periods. Even then Park shied away from closing down failing *chaebol*. Rather, despite increasing the risk of moral hazards, he came to the rescue of ailing industries. In 1972 Park relieved financial pressures on the *chaebol* by a freeze on interest payments on informal curb-market loans as well as by an injection of relief loans. Then in 1979 he began an "industrial rationalization program," which subsidized a program of "business swap" between failing *chaebol* groups in the hope of reducing surplus capacity.

Looking back on the cycles of boom and bust, some speak of good fortune. "The policymakers were lucky," write Young Chul Park and Dong Won Kim. "In each case of [restructuring], an upturn in the world economy rescued [South] Korea."[47] To a certain degree, this was true. Without a turnaround in export markets, the *chaebol* would have suffocated under massive debts. Yet when adjustment success becomes a pattern repeated in crisis after crisis, as happened in the case of South Korea under Park, simply identifying the friendly helping hand of Fortune will not do. Fortune helped only because South Korea helped itself by socializing investment risks and business losses through the patrimonial but rationalized developmental state apparatus. Fortune provided a helping hand only for those prepared to seize it, and South Korea was one of the few who were armed with the requisite political organization and societal structure.

Facing an amorphous society with neither an organizationally unified labor movement nor a strong political party system firmly rooted in social cleavages, and also wielding a massive arsenal of coercive and repressive power developed by state institutions during South Korea's colonial and cold war eras, Park could force society to bear a disproportionate share of adjustment costs through wage cuts and job losses. He could also inject massive relief loans for ailing *chaebol* without precipitating a serious banking crisis, because South Korea was then financially a closed economy, with the EPB and the MoF tightly controlling transnational flows of capital. Relief loans, moreover, were not wasted, because of the existence of an economic bureaucracy capable of socializing business risks and implementing productive investment. By coordinating industrial rationalization programs and maintaining business confidence in Park's rules of political exchange, the EPB-led hierarchical but segmented economic bureaucracy kept the financially vulnerable *chaebol* on the growth track for almost two decades. The risky strategy to grow out of financial illiquidity paid off handsomely for both political and business leaders, albeit at high economic costs, because South Korea was under tight authoritarian rule, strict capital regulation, effective bureaucratic leadership, and, most important, Park's patrimonial but also organized way of intervening in the market.

CHAPTER EIGHT

The Origins of the *Yushin* Regime: Machiavelli Unveiled

Hyug Baeg Im

> When we look into [the new princes'] actions and their lives, we
> will find that fortune provided nothing for them but an opportu-
> nity; that gave them material, on which they could impose what-
> ever form they chose. Without the opportunity their strength
> [*virtù*] of mind would have been vain, and without that strength
> [*virtù*] the opportunity would have been lost.
>
> —NICCOLÒ MACHIAVELLI, *THE PRINCE*

ON OCTOBER 17, 1972, Park Chung Hee turned back the clock on
South Korea's constitutional progress by replacing the existing constitution with a new one under the pretext of the need for "revitalizing reform" *(yushin)*. The decision, Park argued, was made to permit South Korea to adjust more flexibly to the rapidly changing international security
order from the cold war to the emerging environment of détente; to ameliorate the rising military tensions on the Peninsula brought about by
North Korean military provocations in the late 1960s; if possible, to prepare the ground for the peaceful reunification of the two Koreas; to tackle
the task of increased industrialization with an eye to continuing hypergrowth; and, ironically, to establish a more efficient "Korean-style democracy"[1] that could enable the country to carry out the goals of military security, inter-Korea reconciliation, and economic modernization. Yet despite
his promise to "nurture and develop liberal democracy more steadfastly,
substantively, and efficiently," the *yushin* regime imposed an unvarnished
dictatorship.[2] The new constitution bestowed on Park the power to rule
without constraints in the absence of legislative and judicial checks-and-
balances. Also, under the new regime, Park was de facto granted a lifelong presidency. His electoral victories were now guaranteed by a rubber
stamp vote in the hand-picked National Congress for Unification (NCU or
yuchŏnghoe). The contentious National Assembly was also undermined
from within, as NCU members now took up a third of the National As-

sembly seats. To facilitate his imperial rule, Park relied on his time-tested centers of coercive power, which included the Korea Central Intelligence Agency (KCIA), Army Security Command (ASC), and Presidential Security Service (PSS). No longer willing to take any chances on retaining his power, Park was determined to turn South Korea into a garrison state.

At the same time, however, the *yushin* regime retained the Third Republic's (1963–1972) features of technocracy. The revitalizing reform was not "sultanic." Rather, it was a modern form of authoritarian rule.[3] Even during the Third Republic, much of "politics" had been replaced by administration, with former military officers and bureaucratic technocrats taking over many of the roles and functions of interest group representation and intermediation previously held by legislators of the pre-1961 period, but this trend toward the bureaucratization of politics strengthened during the *yushin*. For these technocrats with the self-proclaimed mission of pursuing state-directed industrialization and military build-up, the paramount concerns were effectiveness and performance. The *yushin* regime stunted what potential the Third Republic had for democratization, but it was at the same time one of the factors that contributed to South Korea's transformation into a model East Asian developmental state.

That the *yushin* was a garrison state is clear. The continuity it had with the formally democratic but technocratic and frequently authoritarian Third Republic, however, has made it a historical as well as a theoretical controversy. At the center of the issue is whether the *yushin* represented a change of regime, or merely a change within a regime. Depending on how the *yushin* and its relationship with the past are viewed, the Third Republic also assumes a different status in South Korean political history, either as a brief democratic interlude abruptly terminated by Park or as a period of soft authoritarianism that was a cousin to both the pre-1960 dictatorial rule of Syngman Rhee and the post-1972 *yushin* regime. Complexly intermingled with this question of historical continuity is the issue of motives. The die-hard loyalists of Park take seriously his discourse of revitalization, portraying him as a "Meiji revolutionary" who launched the *yushin* to catch up economically with the West, modernize the armed forces in deterrence against the North, and ensure national survival in the hazardous era of détente. The Park they imagine is a Nietzschian superhero tackling the impossible task of transforming South Korea into a second Japan in his lifetime, albeit through an authoritarian route.

In contrast to his supporters who follow a voluntarist line of thought, positing Park to have chosen the path of *yushin* out of his own will to power and his ambition to leave a permanent mark on South Korean political history as a modernizer, the critics of Park usually take a structuralist perspective.[4] The advocates of structural determinism fall into two groups. Privileging economic forces as the prime driver of political change, some have argued that Park was structurally bound to impose the *yushin* regime in order to overcome the economic challenges inherent in the stage of heavy and chemical industrialization (HCI). Faced with a profound lack of capital and technology needed to enter the next developmental stage of HCI, Park is portrayed as launching the *yushin* to mobilize and concentrate resources through the centralized and concentrated power of the state. As such, the *yushin* is presented as a political institution that achieved what the market was unable to achieve.

Others have identified the structural prime driver as more sociopolitical than economic, arguing that Park chose the *yushin* in order to silence social tensions inherent in his trickle-down hypergrowth strategy and to repress political discontent emanating from his strategy of rule based on Kyŏngsang regionalism, money politics, and selective coercion. Whether the economic or sociopolitical variant, the structuralists are alike in that they look at Park's justification of the *yushin* in terms of the need to ward off external security challenges and telescope stages of industrialization in a single generation's time only as a pretext to prolong his political rule in the face of economic and sociopolitical crises.

Consequently, beneath the debates surrounding the questions of regime continuity or change, political motives, and structural forces stands the issue of agent and structure. The voluntarist privileges the role of Park the person, zeroing in on his vision, strategy, and leadership to explain why he chose the politically and economically challenging path of *yushin* in 1972, whereas the structuralist conceptualizes Park as a captive of structures, driven into the launching of *yushin* by the political, economic, and social contradictions of his earlier modernization strategy of hypergrowth cum authoritarian rule. Despite the vastly diverging ways the voluntarist and structuralist portray the relationships between the agent and structures, political institutions and economic development, and intentions and strategies, they agree that the *yushin* constituted a clear instance of historical discontinuity separating the post-1972 period from the pre-1972 period in terms of political regime, developmental stage, and economic strategy.

Chapter 8 takes a third view. First, it will argue that the journey toward the *yushin* regime needs to be conceptualized in terms of evolution, not discontinuity. The seeds of Park's shift toward authoritarian rule and HCI—the two essential traits of the *yushin*—were sowed when Park pushed for a constitutional revision to allow a third presidential term in 1969 and brought in O Wŏn-ch'ŏl of the Ministry of Commerce and Industry (MCI) to the Blue House as a newly established senior secretary on industrial affairs in 1971 to develop the heavy and chemical industries as the infrastructure of military security. Once this seed was sowed, Park helped the forces of authoritarian rule and HCI to sprout by clearing away both political and economic obstacles, including next-generation second-tier party and military bosses of the ruling coalition and financial vulnerabilities of the *chaebol*, through purges and emergency measures in 1971 and 1972. In other words, Park moved incrementally toward the *yushin* over a period of three years. The inauguration of the *yushin* in October 1972, followed by the announcement of HCI in January 1973, was more the outcome of his three-year-long preparation for lifelong rule than the beginning of his scheme to put in place a garrison state with the mission to aggressively pursue HCI.

Second, Chapter 8 recognizes that the launching of *yushin* brought a qualitatively different type of politics by making presidential elections a de facto rubber-stamp process of perpetuating Park Chung Hee's political rule, but at the same time it echoes the findings of Chapters 5, 6, and 7 that the 1972 enactment of indirect presidential elections masks the continuity of the extreme centralization of power in the presidency throughout the Park era. Strong control mechanisms were already in place during the Third Republic, making its "democracy" a bureaucratically driven "administrative democracy," to quote Park. Many of the political and economic policies required to put South Korea onto the track of hypergrowth during the 1960s, from the risky normalization of relations with Japan, to the potentially contentious dispatch of military troops to South Vietnam, to the launching of an extremely regressive "reverse margin system" of interest rates, were chosen without any effective legislative checks-and-balances. The imperial presidential system was not the outcome of the *yushin*. On the contrary, it was already in place during the Third Republic and became progressively strengthened through the politics of purges and rule-by-emergency power during the 1969–1972 period. At best, the Third Republic was soft authoritarianism with the potential to turn into liberal democracy through competitive presidential elections. The significance of the *yushin* lay in weeding out this potential rather than in destroying democracy.

Third, in analyzing Park's gradual dual-track preparation for the *yushin* through political purges and economic emergency measures, Chapter 8 hopes to put the agent and structures on an ontologically equal footing. The Third Republic found itself under severe pressures on financial, military-security, and social fronts beginning in the late 1960s, partly as a result of the tensions and contradictions built into its trickle-down grow-at-all-cost strategy of modernization and partly as an unexpected outcome of global recession and regional détente. However, in contrast to the structuralist portrayal of these triple pressures as crises that constrained Park's room for maneuver and maybe even determined his choice of options, Chapter 8 argues that the political meaning of those pressures was openended, decisively shaped by what Park could make out of them. That is, structural constraints certainly tightened and deepened beginning in the late 1960s, but they were challenges rather than crises, turning into an opportunity once the Machiavelli in Park enabled him to see those pressures as a lever to further his vision of nation building and, with it, his will to power. In fact, if the structural pressures engendered a crisis, it turned out to be a crisis of anti-Park rather than pro-Park forces, democracy rather than soft authoritarianism, market mechanisms rather than the dirigiste developmental state, after Park harnessed the triple structural pressures to advance his vision of *puguk kangbyŏng* (rich nation, strong army).

Fourth, by putting Park the agent on an equal footing with structural pressures, Chapter 8 complements Chapters 5, 6, and 7 in identifying his leadership as the missing link in the explanation of South Korea's politics of modernization, but it strives to do so through focusing on the Machiavellian *virtù* of Park at play in the transition years of 1969–1972. Park started early in 1969 to prepare for the *yushin* and moved incrementally through a carefully synchronized and sequenced series of political purges, institutional changes, economic emergency measures, and inter-Korea dialogue with a strategic mind. Each of the steps Park took looked like a marginal change, but their cumulative consequences were profound—in effect, clearing the way to the promulgation of *yushin* in October 1972. In explaining how Park was able to move from one critical juncture to another in his journey to the *yushin* without much sustained political resistance during the 1969–1972 period, it will be argued that it was Park's strategic choice to perpetuate himself in power more than any structural necessities that moved him to the launching of the *yushin* regime. Although elected for a third term only a year earlier, Park felt limited by the existing constitution in extending his rule. The *yushin* was then a political act through which he removed the structural obstacles that constrained his will to power and that obstructed the realization of his vision for modernization. He could have retired after serving his third presidential term in 1975 and become a hero, but he did not.

As his promulgation of *yushin* demonstrated, Park was never a faithful believer in democracy. After three years of military rule, he returned to electoral democracy in 1963 under pressure from both the United States and his domestic political opposition. What Park truly desired was to emulate Meiji Japan's spirit of top-down modernization. Even during the Third

Republic, Park did not shy away from compromising democratic principles and norms when he thought it necessary to bring about economic
modernization.[5] Park even named his new bureaucratic-authoritarian regime after the Meiji *ishin* (*"yushin"* in Korean). Meiji Japan was governed
by a system of political rule emphasizing absolute loyalty to the state, with
the emperor at the top, but managed by former samurai bureaucrats in alliance with conservative party politicians and big business. They were
united by the common vision of rapid industrialization. Park saw in Meiji
ishin a model for good governance and built his own *yushin* regime after
the century-old Japanese idea of state-led modernization.

Purging and Taming the Praetorian Guards

Park won the presidential election of 1967 by a landslide. He could have
celebrated his victory, but he did not. Rather, Park immediately focused on
the upcoming National Assembly elections to make preparations for lifelong rule. To do so, he had to revise the constitution to allow for a third
presidential term. That required the Democratic Republican Party's control of two thirds of the National Assembly seats. Only after the passage of
a constitutional amendment in the legislature could he put the amendment
to a public referendum for approval. In the National Assembly elections
held one month after the presidential election, Park was accused by the
press of resorting to money politics *(kŭmgwŏn chŏngch'i)* and bureaucratically driven politics *(kwan'gwŏn chŏngch'i)* even when it was certain that
the DRP would win a majority. The press reports of vote buying alienated
some urban voters, but did not bring about a change in campaign strategy.
Soon the critics began charging that Park had a hidden agenda in winning
two thirds of the National Assembly seats: to remove the constitutional restriction that permitted only two consecutive presidential terms. The anxiety of the opposition was only aggravated when some of the DRP leaders
began openly appealing to the electorate to give the DRP a two-thirds majority in order to enable Park to run for a third term in 1971.[6] The Kim
Chong-p'il–led mainstream faction within the DRP was on guard too, lest
the constitutional revision irreparably damage the crown-prince status of
its boss, but they could not politicize the issue of constitutional revision on
the basis of the isolated instances of talks on it.

The National Assembly election of 1967 gave the DRP two thirds of the
seats. However, the struggle for constitutional revision had to wait until
the first half of Park's second term passed. In this struggle to introduce a
third term for the president, Park had an unquestionable upper hand. In

control of a powerful security apparatus, a colossal economic bureaucracy, and two thirds of the National Assembly seats, Park could co-opt, silence, and even destroy potential foes. Moreover, having delivered his election promise of economic growth, military security, and political stability since 1963, Park could also claim that he had the public with him in introducing a third presidential term. The extremely favorable economic conditions of 1969 also strengthened his political hand. At the time of the constitutional revision in 1969, the GNP grew in double digits (15 percent), the harvest was good (7,737,000 rice bags), rural income climbed by 21 percent, the unemployment rate decreased to 4.8 percent, and the inflation rate fell from 11 percent in 1968 to 9 percent. This was the first time price levels had dropped since 1962, stabilizing voters' economic life.[7]

In fact, the most serious challenge to the constitutional revision came from within the ruling DRP, not from the opposition. Kim Chong-p'il's mainstream faction preferred to maintain the constitutional limitation of two presidential terms, with an eye to the presidential succession and a possible generational change of leadership in 1971. Against such a political challenge, Park was to use intra-DRP factional struggles to steer the issue of constitutional revision in the direction he preferred. His strategy was the time-tested policy of divide and rule. For this he found a willing instrument in the anti-mainstream faction. Without a leader who could match Kim Chong-p'il in charisma, mass support, and organizational prowess, the anti-mainstream faction looked at the constitutional revision as an opportunity to not only consolidate the power of Park—their patron in intra-DRP factional struggles against Kim Chong-p'il—but also defer the question of presidential succession to a more favorable time. The first political leader to bring up the issue of constitutional revision publicly was acting DRP chairman Yun Ch'i-yŏng of the anti-mainstream faction. On January 7, 1969, Yun called for a constitutional revision to clear the way for a third term for Park, "the greatest leader since the founding of the Korean nation by Tan'gun 5,000 years ago."[8] As usual, Park maintained a low profile on the issue of constitutional revision until he thought his proxies had succeeded in establishing the subject's legitimacy.

The mainstream faction's initial reaction was negative, believing that with Park prohibited from entering the 1971 race, power would go to its boss, Kim Chong-p'il. To show its discontent over the talk within the DRP regarding constitutional revision, the mainstream faction went against the party line in joining the opposition's no-confidence vote against minister of education Kwŏn O-pyŏng in April 1969, thus demonstrating the faction's voting power when aligned with that of the opposition. Concerned about the escalation of factional struggles and determined to reestablish party discipline, Park took the matter into his own hands, purging Yang Sun-jik, Ye Ch'un-ho, Chŏng T'ae-sŏng, and Kim Tal-su of the mainstream faction from the DRP. That Park was willing to give up the hard-won DRP control of two thirds of the National Assembly seats to crack down on the opponents of constitutional revision revealed how much he wanted to extend his political rule and how much he distrusted Kim Chong-p'il. The purge brought a further shift in the balance of power within the DRP toward the anti-mainstream faction—to the effect of raising the status of the "Gang of Four"(Kim Sŏng-gon, Paek Nam-ŏk, Kil Chae-ho, and Kim Chin-man) to the new mainstream. By contrast, Kim Chong-p'il began losing credibility even among his faction members because of his failure to stand up to Park on the issue of presidential succession. In their eyes, Kim Chong-p'il was letting his men be crushed by Park for looking after Kim Chong-p'il's interests. The reality, however, was more complex. Having been forced to "retire from public service" and "go into exile" twice in 1963 and 1965 for his role in political fund-raising and normalization of relations with Japan, Kim Chong-p'il knew his political vulnerabilities. With the anti-mainstream in control of the key institutions of power, from the Korean Central Intelligence Agency (KCIA) to the Army Security Command (ASC) to the Blue House presidential Secretariat, Kim Chong-p'il did not dare to oppose Park on the issue of constitutional revision. Besides, Park hinted to Kim Chong-p'il that he would be the heir in 1975.

Once Park secured Kim Chong-p'il's reluctant support for the constitutional revision, the Gang of Four swiftly led the passage of the bill for the revision in the National Assembly, where the DRP made up for its losses of seats with defectors from the opposition to obtain the votes required for putting into motion the constitutional revision. Then followed the national referendum, which Park claimed was a vote of confidence for his government. The strategy was to mobilize public support by heightening people's fear of the disorder that could result from Park's defeat in the referendum.[9] As expected, the referendum was approved by a huge margin.

The alliance of Park and the Gang of Four, however, masked their irreconcilable interests. For Park, the 1969 constitutional revision was only one of the many hurdles he had to overcome in order to realize his ultimate goal of lifelong rule and "revitalizing reform."[10] The Gang of Four also thought that the 1969 revision was not the end but the beginning of regime change, but the change it envisioned was vastly different. Like Kim Chong-p'il, the Gang of Four assumed that Park would retire after his third term and it planned to take power at that point. Lacking the charisma and mass support base of Kim Chong-p'il, the Gang of Four hoped to institute a parliamentary or semi-presidential system at the end of Park's third term, with presidential power drastically weakened and most of the rights, duties, and functions of governance entrusted to the cabinet, led by the prime minister.[11] Such a power scheme had no place in Park's plans for South Korea. Park was determined to stay on even after 1975 and worked to centralize his power, whereas the Gang of Four preferred to share power through the strengthening of legislative powers.

Park moved swiftly to keep the Gang of Four in check after the 1969 constitutional revision. His two most powerful praetorian guards—chief of staff Yi Hu-rak and KCIA director Kim Hyŏng-uk—were forced to step down as Park's gesture of accommodating the public's demand to weed out corruption and abuses of power. At the same time, though, Park must have also welcomed the effects of their dismissal on the balance of power within the DRP. Because Yi Hu-rak and Kim Hyŏng-uk were allies of the Gang of Four, their dismissal helped put the brakes on the rise of the Gang of Four. In a twist of political irony, Park appointed the much weakened Kim Chong-p'il as prime minister. Kim was no longer the charismatic leader he had been before 1969, with his will to power broken and his faction in disarray, but even with his political decline, he was the closest thing to a crown prince that Park had ever had. Now his role was to give what remained of his mass popularity to strengthen Park's cabinet and check the Gang of Four. What remained of Kim Chong-p'il's faction spearheaded a counterattack against the new mainstream in 1971. Minister of home affairs O Ch'i-sŏng embarked on a campaign to break up the power base of the Gang of Four in the central and provincial governments. The Gang retaliated by joining the opposition political parties' vote of no confidence against O Ch'i-sŏng in October 1971, against Park's explicit order to vote the motion down. In particular, Kim Sŏng-gon wanted to show his newly enhanced power not only to his mainstream faction but also to Park. The vote of no confidence turned out to be a disaster for the Gang of Four. Tortured and humiliated by KCIA agents, Kim Sŏng-gon and his men stepped down in disgrace. Kim Sŏng-gon had forgotten that revolt was never an option, given his personal vulnerabilities. Once the owner-manager of the Ssangyong Group and the main fund-raiser for the DRP during the 1960s, Kim Sŏng-gon had too many weaknesses to survive any public assault on his integrity. He had joined the no-confidence vote on the assumption that Park had to step down in 1975 as he had pledged in the 1971 presidential campaign. Had he known of Park's true intentions to stay on even after 1975 with the help of the military, which was to be unveiled only a year later, Kim Sŏng-gon would not have dared to challenge Park in October 1971.

The 1969 constitutional revision was, then, the first and the most critical of the steps to Park's road to the *yushin*. It paved the way for him to run for a third presidential term, which in turn provided a setting that led to the weakening of all potential power contenders within the DRP, including Kim Chong-p'il and the Gang of Four. The ruling DRP was transformed from a coalition of loyalist party bosses to a system of one-man rule without independent bosses by October 1971. Moreover, once the second-tier next-generation DRP bosses were either disgraced, co-opted, or purged, Park did not return to the pre-1971 practice of raising a group of party bosses with an eye to divide-and-rule. After the purge of the Gang of Four, Park made sure that no one stood between himself and the National Assembly. He took charge of party affairs directly from the Blue House. In undermining the power bases of all major DRP leaders, Park cleared the road toward his lifelong presidency. Or, to put it another way, the extreme personalization of power in the coming *yushin* political order was already visible in its early preparatory stages of 1969–1972.

To be sure, the power vacuum was promptly filled by the KCIA, PSS, and ASC, but the rise of military praetorian guards did not threaten Park because it did not mean the rise of potential alternative centers of mass-based or faction-driven power. On the contrary, influencing party politics mainly through political coercion, bribery, and surveillance, the heads of the KCIA, PSS, and ASC came to depend more on Park for their political survival the more they succeeded in their role as praetorian guards, because they became the targets of public discontent and distrust.

It was in this context of the dismantlement of alternative centers of political power that Park ordered a clandestine preparation for the *yushin*. According to the testimony of chief-of-staff Kim Chŏng-ryŏm, Park began secretly preparing for the *yushin* constitution from April 1971, when he ran for his third presidential term.[12] Park's support came from three forces: (1) Yi Hu-rak and the KCIA's agents; (2) Kim Chŏng-ryŏm and the Blue House presidential Secretariat; and (3) Sin Chik-su and bureaucrats from the Ministry of Justice. These three lieutenants of Park shared the common vision of establishing one-party rule after the model of Kuomintang-ruled Taiwan. In particular, Taiwan's National Congress became their benchmark when designing the National Congress for Unification, whose members, hand-picked by Park, were to occupy one third of the seats in the National Assembly. The *yushin* planners also looked to the emergency powers that the French Fifth Republic had conferred on its president as a model.

In May 1972, the support group assembled in one of Park's security-cleared houses *(an'ga)* in Kungjŏngdong to plot regime change in earnest. In August 1972, they organized a team to work on the specifics of constitutional revision under the name P'ungnyŏn saŏp (Good Harvest Project). As the team worked on constitutional revision, Yi Hu-rak visited P'yŏng-yang to discuss inter-Korea reconciliation in May 1972 to create a political environment favorable to the regime change. The key members in the constitutional revision group included KCIA deputy director Kim Ch'i-yŏl, minister of justice Sin Chik-su, and senior secretary for political affairs Hong Sŏng-ch'ŏl. Legal scholars were also brought in to give advice, but their role was minor. Two professors, Han T'ae-yŏn and Kal Pong-gŭn, only modified phrases of the *yushin* constitution drafted by the justice ministry. Kal Pong-gŭn was also dispatched to France on a fact-finding mission, but this came after, not before, the promulgation of the new constitution. Park kept a very low profile throughout the Good Harvest Project, but the *yushin* constitution was essentially his work, with Sin Chik-su serving as an expert on the legal issues of constitutional revision. Ironically, when Park geared up to launch the *yushin* in October 1972, all that remained in the way of his permanent rule was the 1969 constitutional revision that he had pushed to allow him a third term. To remove this constraint was to break his 1971 election pledge not to seek another re-election. Park knew that to go back to the public with another proposal for a one-term extension was bound to be received with cynicism, if not intense political resistance. Park needed a political vision on a broader scale to justify a second constitutional revision, and 1972 was marked by his search for this grand vision. Eventually he landed on the idea of *yushin*, but before he implemented it, he had to tame the opposition.

Confronting the Opposition

In the late 1960s, the NDP remained thoroughly demoralized by its 1967 electoral defeat. But this did not imply that Park faced no opposition forces outside of his own ruling party. The opposition political party was in disarray, but there emerged a loose but contentious coalition of student activists, dissident *chaeya* intellectuals, and religious leaders that joined NDP politicians in raising a serious moral critique of Park's way of doing politics and economics. It took the constitutional revision of 1969 to unite the opposition movements from their internal disunity and anomie.[13] The constitutional revision rekindled the dissident intelligentsia's distrust of Park and revived their criticism of his abuse of democratic procedures. The economy helped the opposition, too. Under the impact of a global recession and the pressures of the bubble that had developed in the domestic economy through the 1960s, the South Korean economy began to slow down after 1969, which quickly spread fears of a stagflation and strengthened the latent popular discontent over Park's trickle-down policy of "growth first and distribution later." Labor issues were also thrust onto central stage as student activists, dissident intellectuals, and religious leaders began to focus on labor rights and urban poverty as much as on Park's violations of liberal political ideas in an attempt to fundamentally reorient the intelligentsia-centered *chaeya* into a broader mass-based dissident movement, with or without the support of conservative NDP politicians. Student activists tried to organize the workers on the basis of their "right to survival." Christian groups began to demand social justice, speaking on behalf of workers and the urban poor.[14] Their social activism worked, because Park's decade-long strategy of export-led industrialization had transformed what once was a homogeneous society, living in a condition of "equality-in-poverty," into a heterogeneous class society, with a rising income gap between capital and labor, urban and countryside areas, and Chŏlla and Kyŏngsang provinces.

The spread of social protests soon began affecting the NDP. Conservative in its broad ideological stance since its inception, but also in competition with the DRP for votes in elections, the NDP began to take on labor issues as part of its strategy to make an electoral comeback from its 1967 defeat. Increasingly, its leadership pledged to support the struggle of the poor in alliance with middle-class intellectuals, setting up investigatory teams to monitor working conditions and initiating legislative programs to deal with distributive issues. The NDP called for an increase in the government's purchasing price for agricultural products, a ban on foreign rice imports, the establishment of a minimum wage system, and the improvement of labor conditions.[15] In April 1971, student activists, religious leaders, and NDP politicians jointly established the People's Council for the Preservation of Democracy as an umbrella organization to coordinate all antigovernment struggles on political, economic, and social issues.

In the midst of the NDP's gradual redefinition of party identity and its incremental expansion of its legislative agendas and electoral strategies, Park confronted the challenger of his lifetime—Kim Dae-jung of South Chŏlla Province, who became the NDP's presidential candidate in 1971 on a progressive platform. The candidacy of Kim Dae-jung opposed Park in a comprehensive manner. The young opposition leader sided with the cause of human rights against Park's "dictatorship," cultivated the image of a labor rights activist in direct opposition to Park's "crony capitalism" with the *chaebol,* and formulated the doctrine of "mass (participatory) economics" in contrast to Park's "unjust" and "unworkable" growth-first strategy. Kim Dae-jung's formula for sustainable and just growth consisted of better welfare for the people, fairer distribution of wealth, heavier taxes on the rich, joint management by employers and workers, and an "agricultural revolution" to increase rural income.

In a brave break with anti-communist cold war political orthodoxy, Kim Dae-jung even advocated a three-stage peaceful unification with the North in direct opposition to Park's *myŏlgong t'ongil* (destroy communism, unify the nation). In the early 1970s, when the tragic memory of the Korean War was still alive and strong, and when the emerging global security order of détente was causing an intense sense of insecurity and vulnerability, these were revolutionary policy proposals—and in the eyes of the conservative mainstream of society, heresy. To the discomfort of Park, during the 1971 presidential campaign, a year before the launching of *yushin,* Kim Dae-jung also claimed that "there [was] proof of Park's attempt to rule for life as a Generalissimo," forcing Park to pledge that "1971 [would] be the last time [he would] be asking [the public] to vote for [him]."[16]

Unfortunately for Park, Kim Dae-jung's mix of new policy ideas delivered votes in 1971.[17] Park played on the public fear of military insecurity by accusing Kim Dae-jung of being a communist sympathizer and isolated his Chŏlla constituency by strengthening the Kyŏngsang-Ch'ungch'ŏng regionalist alliance forged since the 1961 military coup. The regionalist electoral strategy exploited the retirement of Yun Po-sŏn, the previous favorite son of Ch'ungch'ŏng provinces, from the leadership of NDP after his second defeat at the polls in 1967. In the absence of Yun Po-sŏn, Kim Chong-p'il—now resigned to the position of an anti-mainstream leader—seemed to be mobilizing Ch'ungch'ŏng voters on behalf of Park. Although Kim Dae-jung was defeated by 946,928 votes, many saw him as the real winner because he campaigned under very unfavorable conditions: a McCarthyist Red scare, regionalist mobilization, bureaucratic dominance, and money politics. And under these conditions, Kim Dae-jung came to symbolize anti-Park political forces.

A greater setback for Park came in the National Assembly elections that followed a month after the presidential contest of 1971. Despite the NDP's internal split into "radical" Kim Dae-jung–led Chŏlla and "moderate" Kim Young-sam–led South Kyŏngsang natives, the opposition did extremely well in the urban sector. In large cities, the NDP took 33 seats and the DRP, 7 seats. In medium- and small-sized cities, the National Assembly seats were distributed by a ratio of 44:19, again in favor of the NDP. The DRP was able to maintain a majority over the NDP by a ratio of 113:89 in the National Assembly only because of its victories in the overrepresented rural sector. The countryside chose the DRP over the NDP by a ratio of 67:19.

Consequently, the DRP felt the results of the 1971 National Assembly elections as a major blow. The elections showed a clear urban-rural cleavage, with the cities supporting the NDP and the countryside siding with the DRP. This was not good news for the ruling coalition. As industrialization accelerated the migration of the rural population to the urban sector, the electoral future for Park and the DRP looked increasingly uncertain in the long run. Moreover, the opposition party's share of National Assembly seats hit 43.6 percent in 1971, which was the best it had done in the history of South Korean politics. To Park's alarm, the NDP had 20 more seats than the minimum (69) required to stop another attempt at constitutional revision,[18] so he could not again seek to prolong his rule through constitutional procedures. Under the circumstances, Park could only resort to extra-constitutional measures to stay in power after his third term expired in 1975.

The electoral success of 1971 emboldened the NDP and its social allies, and they raised their voices throughout the early 1970s. University students protested against the Student Corps for National Defense (SCND), which Park introduced with the goal of operating military training programs on campuses. When the residents of urban slum areas were driven out of their homes to clear the way for city remodeling, they broke out in violent protests to resist Park's forced migration policy. Some of the workers at Hanjin Company set its headquarters on fire in protest against a delay in the payment of wages, signaling the emergence of a more contentious labor force. The middle class, especially its intellectual component, also joined the opposition movement in greater numbers. Professors at Seoul National University announced their "declaration of independence" from the powerful. The Korean Journalist Committee declared it would defend the freedom of the press, while young judges called for judicial independence.

At the same time, it is important to note that, as of late 1971, the opposition movements had not gained enough force to change Park's course of political action. Having weeded out the next-generation aspirants for power from the DRP, still marshaling a legislative majority in the National Assembly, and commanding the loyalty of the KCIA, ASC, PSS, and the Ministry of Home Affairs (MHA) in control of the police, Park had the means to suppress any serious challenge to his rule. Contrary to the intentions of the opposition movements, in fact, the opposition's persistence in protests even after the 1971 elections more strengthened his distrust of the dissident intelligentsia as an irresponsible, if not dangerous, force of the Left and confirmed his belief in the need to bring about a revitalizing reform to restore order, maintain prosperity, and enhance military security, than weakened his sense of historical mission, his will to power, and his confidence in his abilities to steer the course of South Korean politics and economics. Rather than retreating to accommodate societal pressures, Park moved forward—this time, seeking a change of regime rather than a change within the regime.

First, Park lost no time in repressing protests. The Army Security Command cracked down on students protesting against the SCND. In October 1971, Commander Yun P'il-yong ordered his Capital Garrison Command soldiers to quash student protestors at Korea University. Ten days later, Seoul was placed under a garrison decree. Second, in December 1971, Park crossed the bridge of no return with the declaration of a state of emergency and the enactment of the Special Law for National Security.[19] The state of emergency formalized the establishment of a "national security state," with its six articles defining national security as the first of state priorities, forbidding any social unrest threatening national security, disallowing the press from "discussing national security issues in a careless way," calling upon the public to carry out their duties to defend national security, and justifying restrictions on freedoms and civil rights in the event of a national security crisis. By contrast, the Special Law for National Security provided the president with a wide range of emergency powers, including the power to declare a national emergency, to order economic emergency measures by presidential decree, to prohibit outdoor demonstrations, to restrict the freedoms of speech and the press, and to limit the collective action of workers.

With this special law, South Korea no longer had even a semblance of democracy. The change was to be most visible in the shifting role of the military. To be sure, Park had repeatedly used the armed forces to defend his rule during political crises in the 1960s (see Chapter 6), but from December 1971 on, military intervention in politics was to become part of everyday life. And with the military's political backing, Park gambled on the *yushin*. Because the NDP controlled 43.6 percent of the assembly seats, more than enough to block another constitutional revision, Park chose to bring a regime change through a "palace coup" when he was in a position of strength—that is, in October 1972, only a year since his third presidential election and still three years before the end of his third term. In October 1972, a majority of the South Korean electorate still endorsed Park as their leader for the modernization he had brought to society, and their belief in him was alive and strong. However, before making that final move, Park first had to resolve the country's financial crisis.

Resolving the Financial Crisis

The 1969–1972 period saw a severe financial crisis developing parallel to the transformation of the opposition into a more ideologically charged and socially broad-based political force. Like the radicalization of the opposition, however, the financial crisis did not persuade Park to retreat and critically reappraise his vision, goals, and strategies. Rather, it became a stepping stone for Park's regime change. The economy's entrapment in a vicious circle of inflation, current account deficit, and economic recession had multiple causes.[20] The "golden age" of global economic growth and stability ushered in by the Bretton Woods system, which the Allied nations adopted in 1944 to rebuild the global economic system, was coming to an end in the early 1970s. Faced with an increasing deficit in its balance of payments, the United States suspended the convertibility of the dollar into gold, imposed wage and price controls at home, and introduced a tax on imports in August 1971, thus triggering the other developed countries' rush to adopt a floating exchange rate system and take protectionist measures in the midst of a growing worldwide recession.

Because exports to the United States constituted 40 percent of total South Korean exports, Nixon's economic policy seriously hurt South Korea, especially its light industries. Moreover, with Japan's decision to follow the U.S. initiative with the adoption of a floating exchange rate system, which brought a revaluation of the yen, the cost of Japanese parts and components, intermediary products, and capital goods, upon which South Korea depended for economic growth since its manufacturers' integration into the Japanese regional production networks through licensing agreements and joint ventures in the 1960s, South Korea saw its export competitiveness decline. The imports from Japan accounted for 40 percent of South Korea's total imports. To trigger an even greater sense of economic vulnerability, many of the Japanese producers, including Toyota (see Chapter 10) accepted Zhou Enlai's "Four Principles," whereby foreign companies entering the Chinese market had to terminate their business with South Korea and Taiwan.[21] And Nixon's decision to gradually disengage the U.S. military presence in South Korea made multinational corporations even less willing to invest there for fear of military risks and dangers. These economic and security troubles caused foreign investors and creditors to panic, leading to an upsurge in the outflow of capital. For a country still dependent on foreign loans to finance about 25 percent of its total imports, and burdened with massive foreign loans to be refinanced, the rising instability in financial markets constituted a grave threat to the sustainability of the entire economy.[22]

Under the pressure of capital flight, foreign exchange rates climbed up, making banks pressure their industrial clients to speed up payments on the principal and interest on dollar-denominated foreign loans. The banks' reluctance to roll over loans, in turn, drove a number of the foreign-loan-financed manufacturers to the brink of business failure.[23] By 1969, eighty-six major companies found it difficult to pay the interest on their state-guaranteed foreign loans, instantly transforming corporate distress into bank crisis and domestic financial instability into foreign debt crisis. With a steep increase in deficit in the current balance of payments, whether South Korea could recycle foreign debt became the hot issue of the day.[24] Fearing South Korea's default on foreign loans, the United States pushed Park to accept an International Monetary Fund (IMF) rescue operation. The IMF partnered with the World Bank and other international agencies to provide relief loans on the condition that South Korea devalue its currency, deflate its expansionary monetary policy, and work for a greater fiscal balance.[25] South Korea signed a stand-by loan agreement of $25 million with the IMF in 1968, which it renewed again in 1969.

On the surface, most of the macroeconomic indicators, from growth rates to the consumer price index, to investment and consumption, moved outside the danger zone; some even seemed to be signaling the usual adjustment after a period of high growth. However, in possession of micro financial information at the firm level, Park knew that the South Korean economy was on the verge of collapse under the pressure of massive non-performing loans (NPLs). Behind the spectacular growth of the 1960s lay the absence of independent institutions to put in place modern-day prudential regulations over the state's underwriting of foreign loans. To correct the financial imbalance resulting from the absence of prudential regulations and to induce corporate restructuring as an integral part of the debt rescheduling and write-offs required to create greater financial balance, South Korea agreed with the IMF on a stand-by loan agreement to put in place a ceiling on myriad financial indicators, including the growth rate of foreign credit, the size of the central bank's credit to government entities, new foreign loans, and the financial institutions' possession of foreign currency. Moreover, in the negotiations for additional financial assistance in June 1971, the IMF demanded that South Korea restrict the inflow of short-term foreign capital, pursue a deflationary fiscal policy, devalue the currency from 329 to 450 won per dollar, tighten monetary policy, reduce bank loans, cut government spending, and abolish export subsidies. The

South Korean negotiators accepted all except the abolition of export subsidies. On the issue of the exchange rate, they partially accommodated the IMF, settling on 371.6 won per dollar.

To the disappointment of Park, the IMF's shock therapies proved to be insufficient to arrest the tides of financial and corporate distress. The rate of inflation rose sharply due to the devaluation. The easy monetary policy Park pursued to help him win the 1971 elections also became a factor in driving up prices.[26] For the first time since Park embarked on export-led industrialization in 1963, the South Korean economy experienced a recession, taxing the manufacturers with even greater NPLs.[27] The steep increase of bad loans by the manufacturers discouraged many of the state banks from rolling over loans to help the firms pay back the principal and interest, lest their own financial solvency came to be further tied to the financially vulnerable manufacturers. As a consequence, many large companies of the *chaebol* went bankrupt, prompting Federation of Korean Industries president Kim Yong-wan to appeal to Park for state rescue. Given the colossal size of the NPLs, the FKI president asked Park to convert the private curb-market loans held by business firms into low-interest bank loans, to reduce corporate taxes by a half, and to relax the tight monetary policy.[28] Receptive to the demands of big business, Park resorted to the emergency powers recently vested in him by the 1971 Special Law for National Security. In August 1972, he issued an Emergency Decree on Economic Stability and Growth (EDESG).

The financially most critical and politically most controversial of the policy measures adopted by the emergency decree was the measure to temporarily freeze the business companies' payment of the principal and interest on allegedly "usurious" private curb-market loans. The measure sought to relieve the pressures of financial and corporate distress and, with it, prevent default on foreign loans by transferring much of the costs of adjustment from the *chaebol* and state banks to the private lenders in the curb market. There was also an injection of massive policy loans, which again reaffirmed the time-honored principle of socializing corporate restructuring costs to continuously generate hypergrowth rather than weed out moral hazards to stop the vicious circle of financial distress. Given the scale of the financial crisis brewing in 1972, the emergency decree distinguished itself from previous rescue operations in the size of preferential policy loans.[29] The emergency decree converted the high-interest short-term bank loans held by business firms into low-interest long-term loans through the issuing of special bonds worth 200 billion won and by the establishment of a public fund to finance industrial rationalization programs. (See Chapter 9.)[30] Apparently Park thought that his regime could suffer irreparable political damage if he failed to contain and remedy the financial and corporate distress. Believing the situation to be in urgent need of repair, Park brushed aside the criticisms of the EDESG's infringement of private property rights and its further concentration of income in the *chaebol*. The emergency decree worked. The *chaebol* were relieved of the pressures of the liquidity squeeze and the South Korean economy rebounded remarkably, increasing investment by 40 percent and export by nearly 100 percent in 1973. The growth rate in the first quarter of 1973 hit 19.3 percent, three times that of the same period in 1972.[31]

Having put the *chaebol* on a more solid financial footing through the EDESG, Park was now in a position to take an economic gamble to justify his long-prepared political gamble of regime change. With the *chaebol* out of the liquidity squeeze and the danger of default on foreign loans overcome, Park could launch heavy and chemical industrialization in earnest as a showcase of the soon-to-be-unveiled *yushin* regime's capabilities. As shown below, that program of regime legitimation also had the benefit of constructing an industrial base for national security and an engine of hypergrowth. Most important, by adjusting the overheated economy through the socialization of corporate restructuring costs, Park's EDESG further consolidated his symbiotic partnership with the *chaebol*. The manufacturers were in debt to Park for their survival in 1972, and they were ready to repay him with an aggressive pursuit of his new economic goal of HCI. More generally, by overcoming the seemingly intractable financial crisis, Park once again strengthened his popular image as the leader who delivered. Having stabilized the financial markets, strengthened the *chaebol*'s trust and loyalty, and proved his capacity for problem-solving through his EDESG, Park was a half step away from the goal of regime change. To take that remaining other half step, Park had to come up with a forward-looking grand vision capable of justifying the imposition of an authoritarian regime. The search for such an idea ended with the launching of inter-Korea dialogue in the security realm and the pursuit of heavy and chemical industrialization in the economic realm.

Transforming Security Crisis into a Political Opportunity

Park was in a position of strength in 1972, but even then he needed to develop a rationale for regime change if he was to not only justify his planned actions but also defend his very position of strength. The rationale was provided by South Korea's rapidly changing security environment. In many ways, the *yushin* regime emerged as Park's reinvigoration of South Korean cold war ideas and their adjustment to the new global and regional security environment of détente. The impetus for the change came with the retrenchment of U.S. military engagement in East Asia under President Richard M. Nixon's Guam Doctrine of 1969. The United States was then trying to end the Vietnam War through diplomacy, launching a détente with the Soviet Union and eventually with China to bring North Vietnam to the negotiating table. The timing of the adjustment in U.S. global and regional security policy could not have been worse for Park, because North Korean military threats were on the rise on the Peninsula, following Kim Il Sung's announcement of the aggressive "Four Military Principles." Tensions remained high on the Korean Peninsula into 1968 and 1969, with North Korea shooting down a U.S. reconnaissance plane and sending armed guerrillas into Seoul and, then, into the Uljin and Samch'ŏk areas (see Chapter 6). In 1970, a South Korean marine broadcasting ship was seized by North Korea on the Yellow Sea, and in the Tongjakdong National Cemetery a bomb exploded that had been planted by North Korean agents. Armed guerrillas from the North continually infiltrated the South via the Kyŏngnyŏlbi archipelago, Kunja Gulf, and East Sea.

The contradictory trends of global-regional détente and the rise of military tensions on the Korean Peninsula brought domestic political fissures. Park held the orthodox view, diagnosing the continuing military threats from the North in the new era of global-regional détente to pose a security challenge of unprecedented scale, forcing South Korea to face threats from the North with much weakened U.S. support and possibly even under diplomatic isolation. The South was then tailing far behind the North in winning support from "non-aligned" countries of the Third World. By contrast, Kim Dae-jung saw the situation as requiring a paradigmatic shift in security policy. As already noted, during the 1971 election, Kim Dae-jung had announced his own proposal for a mini-détente on the Korean Peninsula that called for the establishment of peace and ultimately a negotiated unification of the two Koreas through diplomatic dialogue with the United States, the Soviet Union, Japan, and China. Kim Dae-jung also criticized Park's cold war strategy of military confrontation as a conspiracy to bring about Park's permanent rule by exaggerating North Korean security threats.[32] Against such charges, Park argued that the United States' military disengagement from East Asia might have brought détente to the great powers at the global level but not necessarily to the Korean Peninsula, because of the existence of the two separate states on the peninsula with mutually incompatible national identities, regimes, and military alliances with the rival great powers. Contrary to Kim Dae-jung's assertion that the global-regional détente opened a window of opportunity to bring about inter-Korea reconciliation, Park argued that South Korea became *more* vulnerable militarily as a result of the unilateral U.S. actions. In his eyes, the U.S. reduction of its military presence in East Asia was premature, occurring at a time when the South was still struggling to catch up with the North in military capabilities. The result of the U.S. decision would be a break in the inter-Korean military balance in favor of the North, which could lead to the repeat of an all-out North Korean invasion.[33] Presenting the Six-Day War in the Middle East as an example of modern warfare, Park warned that South Korea should not lower its guard, lest the North launch a blitzkrieg to capture Seoul and then to present the action as a fait accompli to the United States in the hope of negotiating a new armistice. In return, critics accused Park of deliberately resisting the coming of détente to the Korean Peninsula for the sake of his own political interest in remaining in power under the pretext of combating the continuing North Korean military threat. In the event of détente on the Korean Peninsula, critics predicted that peace and coexistence would finally reign.

The mounting criticisms and dissent against cold war orthodoxy did not change Park. To prevent South Korea from becoming "another South Vietnam," which had aligned with the United States only to be abandoned by it in the midst of military conflict, Park called for "recharging the security state." Describing South Korea as in a state of war because the armistice of 1953 had not been replaced by a peace treaty among the warring parties of the Korean War, Park established new reserve forces 2.5-million-men strong to defend the rear area. The president also set up the Student Corps for National Defense with the goal of operating military training programs on campuses, and the defense industries were promoted as never before. Then, in December 1971, Park declared a state of emergency and enacted the Special Law for National Security.

As soon as Park made his regime a garrison state in December 1971, two problems arose. First, in order to put the garrison state on a solid basis, Park needed to come up with a more positive, forward-looking programmatic vision in addition to the existing negative doctrine of security threats. Second, during the 1971–1972 period, the number of North Korean military provocations decreased dramatically. The great powers' détente at the global level was finally affecting the North Korean regime. To continue on the path of Kim Il Sung's "Four Military Principles" entailed too many risks for North Korea, as it could no longer assume that the Soviet Union and China would support it in an escalation of military conflict. For the North as much as for the South, the détente meant an adjustment in its strategic doctrine. Consequently North Korea began to look to the option of dialogue with the South as a strategy of national survival.[34]

With the North searching for a new strategy of national survival, and himself in need of a forward-looking vision on the Korean Peninsula for domestic political reasons, Park seized upon the first signs of North Korea's receptivity to the idea of inter-Korea dialogue to develop a two-track strategy of military build-up and national reconciliation with an eye to strengthening the garrison state created by the Special Law for National Security. The second track of dialogue had been in the making since August 15, 1970, when Park delivered an Independence Day celebration speech that announced his intention to bring about inter-Korea dialogue under the principle of "fair competition based on good will." A year later, Park followed up with the proposal to bring about a reunion of the families separated from each other by the national division through the offices of the Red Cross in the two Koreas. The initiative was supported by the United States, which was then concerned about the danger of military instability following the staged reduction of U.S. troops in South Korea.[35]

Under rising security dilemmas of its own, North Korea promptly agreed to Park's proposal of North-South Red Cross talks. Inter-Korea dialogue could provide the North with an opportunity to secure foreign investment and find relief from the pressure to build up its military capability at an economically dysfunctional rate. The subsequent dialogues resulted in the Joint Declaration of July 4, 1972, which ameliorated many of the security dilemmas confronting Park Chung Hee and Kim Il Sung. First, the joint declaration reduced military tensions by getting the North to tone down the "Four Military Principles." By recognizing each other as de facto, if not de jure, sovereign states, the two Koreas progressed, however cautiously, toward a state of peaceful coexistence. Second, by conferring on Park and Kim the legitimacy of working together in the interest of establishing a new peace regime on the Korean Peninsula, the joint declaration enabled the two leaders to reorganize their respective systems of political rule to better fit in with the requirements of the emerging world order of détente. Park was to launch the *yushin* within four months, whereas Kim had completed the ongoing consolidation of his *yuil* regime whereby the Workers' Party, the military, and the state were under the sole *(yuil)* command of and with the *suryŏng* (Leader) in body and spirit. Third, the joint declaration created an opportunity for Park Chung Hee and Kim Il Sung to muster popular support by playing to the mass desire for national reunification.

It was from this joint declaration that Park found the positive, forward-looking vision he needed to supplement the negatively defined cold war doctrine of anticommunism to simultaneously muster popular support and military deterrence. Arguing that the establishment of a "Koreanized administrative democracy" (see Chapter 4) or an authoritarian regime would be far more effective in negotiating the issues of peace, coexistence, and unification with North Korea's monolithic Stalinist regime, Park proposed to launch the *yushin*. Interestingly, a similar idea was being parlayed by Kim Il Sung in the North. Ten days after Park promulgated the *yushin* constitution on December 17, 1972, Kim Il Sung revised his constitution, which completed North Korea's long process of centralization of power in Kim Il Sung and the construction of a uniquely North Korean–style socialist system based on the Juch'e ideology. By declaring P'yŏngyang rather than Seoul to be the capital of his Democratic Peoples' Republic of Korea, Kim Il Sung also appeared to recognize national division as a permanent, not temporary, state of politics.[36]

For Park, however, inter-Korea dialogue was a double-edged sword, rallying popular support for the *yushin* regime for its alleged effectiveness in bringing about a peaceful reunification, on the one hand, but potentially weakening the South Korean people's perception of the North as a military threat, on the other. Once the public perception of North Korean threats subsided, it would be inevitable that Park's rationale for legitimizing the *yushin* on the basis of fear of the North would also weaken. Having an enemy state only forty miles north of Seoul helped Park's political rule by providing a rationale for social and political repression. Park knew he had to engage in the strategy of inter-Korea dialogue without undermining his other strategy of legitimating the *yushin* regime on the basis of perpetual ideological rivalry and confrontation with those across the border. Presumably, a similar political dilemma haunted Kim Il Sung too, dampening the two leaders' enthusiasm to engage in a negotiation for unification once they completed the consolidation of their own power. By the mid-1970s, the two Koreas were to return to the old pattern of military tension and conflict. In contrast to the relatively brief inter-Korea dialogue, the developmental strategy of heavy and chemical industrialization, which Park launched to demonstrate the *yushin* regime's superior capabilities in problem-solving, continued to the end of his rule.

To be sure, the early 1970s were not the first time Park had spoken of HCI. On the contrary, he was obsessed with it from the very moment of taking power in 1961. In spite of such continuity in his personal infatuation with HCI, however, the HCI drive of the *yushin* period differed from his earlier HCI attempts in two fundamental ways. First, whereas Park of the 1960s concentrated on HCI projects as separate investment projects to be planned and implemented individually on a case-by-case basis without systematic links between the projects, Park of the post-1973 period took HCI as a macroeconomic strategy, simultaneously pursuing a wide range of investment projects on multiple fronts, with an integrated view of their forward and backward linkages to each other and to other sectors in the economy. The HCI drive of the *yushin* era differed from the HCI projects in priority, scope, scale, and style.

Second, in the post-1973 period, Park was prepared to pay the extremely high costs of the HCI drive, including the cost of political alienation and discontent that arose from the authoritarian ways the HCI drive was pursued. Given South Korea's low per capita income, small economy, and lack of industrial linkages, Park had to resort to forced savings, fiscal and financial subsidies, and labor repression to mobilize resources to the scale required for his ambitious HCI goals. Consequently, the top-down HCI drive proceeded in tandem with society's deepening sense of alienation. Nevertheless, Park stuck to his goal of HCI rather than downscaling his economic program to fit with the only slowly changing national capabilities. By contrast, in the 1960s, with the exception of building an integrated steel mill (see Chapter 11), Park was ready to back down in the face of market pressures.

The question is why Park adopted the HCI drive as the macroeconomic strategy in 1973. Most critics argue that he chose the HCI drive because the politically illegitimate *yushin* needed a justification. The HCI drive is looked upon as a defensive measure adopted against the powerful rise of societal resistance against authoritarian rule. Essentially, the critics view the Park of 1972 as having been in an acute political crisis where his legitimacy was denied by societal forces, and identify the *yushin* as the only option left for him to survive and the HCI drive as the instrument to justify the promulgation of authoritarianism. Upon a closer inspection, however, the reality looks much more complex.

First, it is not clear whether the turn to HCI—and, for that matter, the promulgation of the *yushin* regime itself—actually helped to strengthen Park's political rule.[37] On the contrary, even before the launch of HCI in 1973, Park was firmly in control of domestic politics and in possession of the power to enact what he thought was required for modernization, as the adoption of the Emergency Decree for Economic Stability and Growth in August 1972 demonstrates. Moreover, Park was capable of ruling over South Korean society through his emergency powers even before the launching of the *yushin* and the HCI drive, as the declaration of a state of emergency and the enactment of the Special Law for National Security in December 1971 show. In other words, apart from removing all constitutional constraints on his reelection, it is not clear what added value the *yushin* and the HCI drive had for his political power. More specifically, in sharp contrast to the critics' argument that Park promulgated the *yushin* to strengthen his regime's capacity to suppress the resistance of workers, students, and dissident intellectuals against authoritarian rule, Park of the pre-1972 period already possessed a powerful security state with such capabilities. To undermine the critics' argument even more, Park could also suppress societal resistance *legally* with the enactment of security laws in 1971. If Park was solely concerned with the need to suppress societal resistance, he did not need the *yushin*. Nor did he have to pursue the HCI drive. The EDESG of 1972 had already resolved the financial crisis.

Second, the focus on HCI was nothing new.[38] On the contrary, among the six heavy and chemical industries identified by Park in January 1973 as the strategic sectors for export-led development, the nonferrous metal and petrochemical industries had been the target of import-substituting industrialization through the end of the 1960s. Also, the other four industries had been designated as future export industries because of their labor- and capital-intensive character. Although some analysts have argued that Park instituted the *yushin* regime in order to preempt workers from demanding wage increases and labor rights in the strategic heavy and chemical industries,[39] Park already had a powerful labor control mechanism in place before he launched the *yushin* regime.

This is not to argue that economics and politics had nothing to do with the promulgation of the *yushin* and its HCI drive. On the contrary, they both originated as a distinctive political and economic strategy, but the political and economic prime drivers were not Park's crisis of legitimacy and capabilities. Economics and politics of a different sort were at play. It was the removal of constitutional restrictions on the number of presidential terms more than any threats of societal resistance, domestic political instability, industrial conflict, and economic crisis that appears to have motivated Park's move to the *yushin* regime in October 1972. That is, it was more Park's political strengths than his weaknesses that explain the timing and character of regime change. In fact, the political and economic crises many analysts speak of occurred first in 1971–1972, which Park put to rest through the EDESG, and then in 1978–1979 as a result of the repressive politics of the *yushin* and the too premature, too expansionary HCI drive. That is, economic and political crisis was more the outcome than the cause of the *yushin* and the HCI drive. The HCI drive was extremely ambitious. In January 1973, three months after the declaration of *yushin*, Park announced a plan to raise exports to the level of $10 billion and per capita GNP to $1,000 by 1981 on the assumption that his HCI drive would successfully upgrade the South Korean industrial structure. Rather than the HCI drive requiring the regime change to the *yushin*, it is more likely that the *yushin* regime, instituted as a remedy to the political problem of constitutional restraints on presidential terms, needed the HCI drive to justify itself.[40]

Ironically, the security crisis precipitated by Nixon's Guam Doctrine and the ensuing U.S. military disengagement itself removed what could have been the most challenging obstacle to the launching of the *yushin*—potential U.S. opposition. Because South Korea remained a client state of the United States despite this U.S. doctrine, it was important that Park not weaken South Korea's military alliance with the United States in his pursuit of the *yushin*. Having learned the advantages of presenting his political choice as a fait accompli to the United States when that choice affected his vital political interest of staying in power during the junta years (see Chapters 1 and 2), Park was careful not to reveal his plan for regime change until the very last minute of regime transition. At the same time, Park understood that the U.S. interest in maintaining South Korea's political stability to keep up military deterrence against the North would prevent the United States from outright opposing the launching of the *yushin*. Besides, the Guam Doctrine had set into motion U.S. military disengagement from the Korean Peninsula, which Park thought undermined what political leverage the United States had over him. Consequently, Park secretly prepared for the regime change without consulting the United States. When he notified the United States of the regime change at the last minute, the State Department's immediate response was to cautiously distance itself from the newly promulgated authoritarian government, lest the United States become hopelessly caught between the ideologically polarized pro- and anti-*yushin* forces.[41]

At the same time, the timing of Park's move worked in his favor. The United States was then preoccupied with the task of implementing the Guam Doctrine, and as part of its effort to pull back from its overseas military commitments, it withdrew 20,000 troops from South Korea in the early 1970s. In the context of military withdrawal, the United States was not in a position to proactively engage in South Korea's domestic political developments, certainly not to the extent that it did during the 1961–1963 period of military rule.[42] Moreover, as noted earlier, Park was qualitatively different from the man he had been in the junta years. Having won his third presidential bid less than a year earlier, the Park of October 1972 commanded sizable popular support. Moreover, unlike the unstable military junta, whose incessant internal power struggles prevented Park from dominating the political scene and opened an opportunity for the United

States to penetrate and influence the core coup leadership, in 1972 no politicians could claim to be Park's rival. The DRP was under his direct control, with the second-tier next-generation bosses either tamed, purged, or publicly discredited (see Chapter 5), the state bureaucracy had been transformed into a patrimonial but rationalized instrument of economic modernization (Chapter 7), the opposition was struggling to unify the rival forces of Kim Dae-jung and Kim Young-sam, and the dissident *chaeya* was still in the making (Chapter 13). Without credible forces of opposition within both the DRP and the NDP to ally with, and recognizing Park's strong hold over South Korean political society, the United States adopted the strategy of wait-and-see when Park rammed through the *yushin* constitution in 1972.

U.S. domestic politics also helped Park's cause. Unlike John F. Kennedy, who scarcely hid his contempt for authoritarian rule during the junta years, Nixon was willing to tolerate Park's turn to repressive politics. Moreover, Nixon's national security adviser, Henry A. Kissinger, was a realist, taking the shifting balance of power as the main driver of foreign policymaking. Kissinger focused on the task of bringing about Sino-American rapprochement to end the Vietnam War and build a new global order of détente. The issue of South Korea's democratization was judged in terms of its relationship with this overriding issue of military security. Besides, Kissinger was a conservative, valuing Park for his ability to rule with effectiveness. As defined by Nixon and Kissinger, the first priority of the United States was to promote détente, stability, and deterrence on the Korean Peninsula rather than to push for the development of South Korea as a showcase of democracy in East Asia. The United States tried not to destabilize what was an already volatile political situation by intervening in South Korean domestic affairs against Park. To discourage Nixon and Kissinger from confronting Park on the issue of democracy even more, the United States needed Park's cooperation in bringing about its "honorable" exit from the Vietnam War. At the United States' request, Park agreed to postpone South Korea's second stage of military withdrawal from South Vietnam from the end of 1972 to June 1973, making South Korean troops the largest force among the foreign military forces aiding South Vietnam at the time of the promulgation of the *yushin*. For the United States, which was then negotiating a peace treaty with North Vietnam in Paris, Park's postponement of military withdrawal by a half year was crucial in maintaining the pressure on North Vietnam to speed up the negotiation process. To make the military and political value of South Korea's ground troops even more important in Nixon's strategic calculations, the United States itself had withdrawn its ground troops. The promulgation of the *yushin* constitution came in October 1972, in the middle of Kissinger's negotiations with North Vietnam, which most likely prevented Nixon from opposing Park in a clear way in the critical early days of regime change, even if Nixon had been interested in doing so.

Park Chung Hee's Virtù and Fortuna

In many respects, Park would have made Niccolò Machiavelli very proud. For Machiavelli, the "new" prince, destined to uplift society to glory, was a person with the ruler's *virtù*. The new prince envisioned by Machiavelli "continuously [made] subjects passive but content, rule[d] over them with [a] lion's strength but with the slyness of [a] fox, receive[d] respect from his supporters but [was] a figure of fear, brutal but generous, and . . . able to avoid flatterers." Above all, the new "prudent prince [did] not keep his word when to do so would [have gone] against his interest, or when the reasons that made him to pledge it [were] no longer valid . . . [The new] prince never lack[ed] for legitimate excuses to explain away his breaches of faith."[43] The foremost *virtù* of the ruler was, in other words, the quest for power and the ability to grow it continuously.

In the transition to the *yushin* regime, Park amply demonstrated his Machiavellian virtues. The president had the ability to turn political, economic, and international challenges into an opportunity for power aggrandizement, to successively eliminate the alternative options to his leadership within the DRP, to make people accept his terms of governance, to provide the right structure of incentives to the guardians of power to get them to work on behalf of his political interests, and to be feared enough to exact the acquiescence of many of the opposition. Park was "sly as a fox" in using the public fear of security threats, social discord, and political instability to build the institutional infrastructure of a security state. He was also a "lion," forcing the opposition to think twice before challenging his vision of what regime change should entail.

In addition to his political leadership, Park was aided by many fortuitous events or circumstances. These events, however, could have become either a crisis or an opportunity, and it was Park who turned those events into opportunities. At first glance, it appears that *fortuna* lent its hand to Park, but upon a closer examination, it was Park who transformed the events into *fortuna* to clear the way for the promulgation of the *yushin* regime. First, the coming of détente and the accompanying U.S. retrenchment of its forward-deployed military posture in East Asia provided Park with greater room to maneuver in domestic politics by triggering a Red scare in society and by reducing the United States' capacity to intervene against Park in South Korean domestic politics on the basis of its military and economic patronage. By timing the transition to the *yushin* regime in October 1972, when the United States was busy negotiating the terms of peace with North Vietnam, Park was able to prevent the United States from voicing its dissent during the crucial days of regime change. Second, like the security crisis triggered by Nixon's Guam Doctrine, Park made South Korea's financial and corporate distress work in favor of his political interests and goals by using it to justify the establishment of presidential power to declare emergency economic measures. With the newly acquired power to shape the market through presidential decrees, Park effectively resolved the country's mounting corporate and financial distress in August 1972. The EDESG contributed to his power consolidation not only by clearing the financial obstacles to HCI, with which he planned to legitimize the turn to the *yushin* regime, but also by strengthening his alliance with the *chaebol* on the basis of asymmetric political exchange. Third, even the repeated military provocations of North Korea during the 1968–1971 period and Kim Il Sung's peace overtures in 1972 became instruments for Park in persuading the public why the *yushin* regime had to be established. He packaged the *yushin* as the answer to both South Korea's fear of military invasion and its hope for peaceful coexistence with the North. Fourth, the eruption of social dissension after the 1971 presidential election had the effect of justifying the move to the authoritarian *yushin* regime by raising the specter of political instability.

In the last analysis, it was Park's vision to become the Meiji of South Korea that got him to use his *virtù* to transform the multiple political, economic, and security challenges into *fortuna*. In the first instance, Park launched the *yushin* to prolong his political rule. But the prolongation of his rule was also deemed essential for building a wealthy and powerful nation. The *yushin* was an instrument to transform South Korea into a second Japan. Unfortunately for Park, the same instrument also planted the seeds of ideological illegitimacy that would lead to his downfall in 1979.

ECONOMY AND SOCIETY

CHAPTER NINE

The *Chaebol*

Eun Mee Kim and Gil-Sung Park

Faced with south korea's unique transformation into a modern industrial economy in a mere generation's time, many observers fall back on simple images to explain the state-business relationship that enabled the nation's hypergrowth. Some analysts project an image of "Korea, Inc.," where the state and the *chaebol* deeply penetrated each other's organizations by personnel exchanges at the top of their hierarchies, seeking to influence decisions and to learn from the other's organizational features and functions.[1] The *chaebol* is portrayed as an organization created and managed by the state for national interests, with Park sitting on top as the CEO. There are others who agree with the proponents of Korea, Inc., that the state-*chaebol* relationship was extremely close during Park's political rule, but give it the opposite characterization of "crony capitalism." In this view, the *chaebol* captured the state to pillage banks and sabotage market forces in pursuit of rents. Rather than the *chaebol* serving national interests as defined by the state, it was the state that came to the aid of rent-seeking *chaebol* conglomerates in the literature of crony capitalism.

The two views both have the historical facts wrong. Indeed, the state-*chaebol* relationship was extremely close, but the nature of that closeness cannot be adequately captured by static, unidimensional concepts like those of Korea, Inc., or crony capitalism. The *chaebol* were neither captives of the state nor its masters. They were organizations based not only on traditional family ties but also on modern rational business enterprises that made their own decisions, albeit within the confines of state policies.[2] As Stephan Haggard argues, it is more useful to view the state-*chaebol* relationship as an ongoing negotiation, continually reinterpreted and remade under the pressures of socioeconomic and political change.[3] Even during Park's rule, when the *chaebol* were reborn into industrial conglomerates under massive political patronage, their relationship with the state was more complex than those images of unidirectional power flow that the proponents of Korea, Inc., and crony capitalism portray.

The transfer of elite bureaucrats to the *chaebol* did not occur with great frequency during Park's rule.[4] In fact, because the locus of decision making and coalition building resided at the top of the state organization, Park's Blue House, there was less need for the *chaebol* to invite retired career bureaucrats to act as go-betweens in the way the Japanese *keiretsu* did through *amakudari*.[5] Big deals were made directly between Park and the owner-managers of his choice, so that the *chaebol* were less interested in securing *amakudari*-like channels of coordination with state ministries. Moreover, deal making in the Blue House took place in ways that made the concept of leader-follower less relevant. To be sure, Park had the power to make or break any one *chaebol* group, but Park could not weaken the *chaebol* as a class if he was to transform South Korea into an industrial economy in his lifetime. On the contrary, after committing a series of economic policy blunders in 1961–1962 that almost cost him his military junta (see Chapters 2 and 3), Park came to recognize that the *chaebol* were more experienced in running a business entity, just as he was more knowledgeable about running the state. As long as the *chaebol* accepted the broad direction of economic policy and refrained from getting entangled in partisan politics, Park let the *chaebol* be the CEOs of South Korean economic development, implementing politically formulated and bureaucratically elaborated goals with great autonomy and discretion. In fact, the *chaebol* came to be the source of major innovative policy ideas, from the construction of special export zones and industrial complexes to the launching of Japanese-style general trading companies, to the entry into the Middle East construction boom in the mid-1970s.

Just as it is wrong to view Park and the *chaebol* in terms of leader and follower, it is not constructive to ask who was more indispensable and who was less powerful. Rather, Chapter 9 proposes to look at the state-*chaebol* relationship as a partnership, asking how each party complemented the other. And this was a partnership between visionaries. Park strove to become the Meiji of South Korea, whereas the leading *chaebol* groups hoped to grow into conglomerates on a par with the Japanese *keiretsu*. Sharing the *han*, or anguish, of being born into one of the world's poorest countries, only recently liberated from Japanese colonial rule and scarred by three years of a violent cold war conflict–turned–civil war, Park and the *chaebol* were united by the vision of pulling South Korea and its people out of their absolute poverty, and drawn together by their fearless "can do" spirit and ethic of hard work. For Park the *chaebol* were indispensable for his political project of "rich nation, strong army" *(puguk kangbyŏng),* and for the *chaebol* Park was indispensable for their growth into a corporate empire. As Yi Chun-lim once recollected, "it was not really that one led the other into something that he did not want to do. Park and [big business] formed a full-fledged partnership on the basis of broad trust, common vision, and hard work."[6] In the eyes of David Kang, this partnership was one of "mutual hostages," with the state and the *chaebol* each preventing the other from taking measures that threatened vital interests. By contrast, Chapter 9 presents the partnership to be that of "mutual guarantors," each enabling the other to achieve its vital interests.

Because the partnership was based on asymmetric political exchange, where Park defended *chaebol* allies from the threats of business failure in return for their plunging into his risky industrial projects, it imbued both the state and the *chaebol* with contradictory traits. The state was both predatory and developmental (see Chapter 7), generating rents to lure the *chaebol* into the risky frontiers of growth, but at the same time bureaucratically regulating and politically disciplining rent-seekers to keep rent-seeking below a systemically dangerous level. Likewise, the *chaebol* were both cronies and entrepreneurs, cultivating Park's support to secure licenses, subsidies, and loans, but also harnessing the rents for investment in his industrial programs as part of their original pledge to line up behind his vision of nation building. Consequently, during the Park era, the state-*chaebol* relationship was characterized by a constant effort to balance between the predatory and the developmental tendencies of the state, the cronyism and the entrepreneurial energy of the *chaebol,* and the generation of rents and the regulation of the ensuing moral hazards.

Park knew that the balancing act required for the state-*chaebol* partnership he envisioned would be an extremely challenging political task. To generate rents for the *chaebol* willing to invest in risky projects, but without worsening the moral hazards to the level of triggering a systemic crisis, Park developed a set of rules and norms for the state-*chaebol* partnership. First, in order to ensure that his business "cronies" were also individuals with a conquering entrepreneurial spirit, Park chose partners from the *chaebol* with a proven track record of risk taking, managerial capability, and high performance. To be sure, Park preferred allying with the *chaebol* from his Kyŏngsang region in order to insure against the danger of non-Kyŏngsang business groups coalescing around one or another alternative regional center of political power, but he did not shy away from partnering with non-Kyŏngsang entrepreneurs like Chŏng Chu-yŏng of Hyundai (Kangwŏn Province), Kim U-jung of Daewoo (Kyŏnggi), and Cho Chung-hun of Hanjin (Seoul) when they shared his visionary mind, "can do" spirit, and entrepreneurial capabilities. Even then, however, Park was aware of the need to keep his *chaebol* partners in line and check their abuse of his trust. The best way to do so was to take advantage of their rivalry. Consequently, as a second rule of thumb, he built a structure of oligopolistic competition in the strategic industries over time, searching for challengers among second- or third-tier medium-sized *chaebol* groups to compete with the front-runners.

Third, as the proponents of Korea, Inc., and crony capitalism argue, Park backed his *chaebol* allies with massive subsidized resources, but contrary to the portrayal of guaranteed business success, he was prepared to let failing *chaebol* groups go under, once he thought he had exhausted relief measures. This was an extremely costly way to balance between the requirements of socializing business risks and disciplining the moral hazards, but it was nonetheless effective in moving state-*chaebol* relations toward hypergrowth. On the one hand, by supporting hard-pressed business partners until he exhausted all possible policy options during a period of macroeconomic adjustment, Park crafted the image of a reliable patron who backed words of support with concrete actions when his business partners were in trouble. This image made his words of commitment credible, thus making his task of mobilizing the *chaebol* behind risky industrial projects that much easier. When Park had to pull the plug from the weakest of the *chaebol* to save the stronger of the South Korean big businesses and to stabilize the economy during a period of adjustment, on the other hand, most of the *chaebol* looked at his action not as a breach of his earlier promise of unswerving support but as an unavoidable adjustment forced upon him by the financially fragile South Korean economy, because he resorted to restructuring the weakest of the *chaebol* only after he had exhausted all options of keeping those *chaebol* groups afloat through state support.

That the weakest of the *chaebol* would be allowed to fall—albeit after the failure of a concerted rescue operation by the state—was a rule that prevented the moral hazards from rising to the level of a systemically destabilizing scale. The rule was economically inefficient, wasting too many resources in keeping alive too weak business ventures for too long, but it was a politically effective strategy to retain the trust and loyalty of big business while at the same time preventing the worst forms of moral hazards. As a result of this economically costly but politically effective balancing act, the Park era came to be characterized by both spectacular business successes and spectacular business failures. The likes of Chŏng Chu-yŏng, Kim U-jung, and Cho Chung-hun grew into industrial tycoons during Park's eighteen years of rule, but there were also many more would-be *chaebol* leaders who fell while attempting to seize what they thought was the opportunity of their lifetime to build a corporate empire. In sharp contrast to the arguments of Korea, Inc., and crony capitalism that the *chaebol* had an easy way to the top, the Park era was Janus-faced, where an opportunity for hyper corporate growth could turn into a dangerous moment of adjustment and maybe even business failure. The opportunity and the risk that came with it resulted in a continuous reordering of the Big Ten. It was only in the late 1970s that the structure of the South Korean business community stabilized.

Fourth, aware of the danger that the *chaebol* could use their rents to become alternative centers of political power either on their own or as a junior ally of party politicians, Park made it very clear to big business that his support for their industrial ventures came on the condition that they did not seek political power themselves. To be sure, there were *chaebol*-turned-politicians like Kim Sŏng-gon of Ssangyong, who raised political funds for the ruling Democratic Republican Party (DRP) by leveraging his business background, but they were more the exception than the rule. Park preferred the *chaebol* to remain entrepreneurs. When he relied on the likes of Kim Sŏng-gon to raise political funds, Park made it clear that they worked solely for him under his trust. When they strayed from their role of caretakers to seek their own power, as Park thought Kim Sŏng-gon did in 1972, Park swiftly cracked down on the real or imagined challengers in order to send a clear message to all that DRP fundraisers were only caretakers, that the ultimate power rested solely in the hands of Park, and that the *chaebol* should not seek political power for themselves. The rule that the *chaebol* should not themselves become political powers was essential for Park's ability to choose his partners largely on the basis of performance, to keep the *chaebol* in line through oligopolistic rivalry, and to discipline the worst forms of moral hazards by letting the weakest of the *chaebol* go under during a period of adjustment. The transformation of the *chaebol* into an alternative center of political power either on their own or as a junior ally of party politicians would have obstructed the already very challenging task of balancing between predatory and developmental tendencies of the state, between cronyism and entrepreneurial energy of the *chaebol*, and between the generation of rents and regulation of the ensuing moral hazards.

This is not to argue that Park had in place these four rules and norms governing state-*chaebol* relations from the very start of his rule. On the contrary, these rules and norms emerged out of political conflicts, policy mistakes, and learning throughout the eighteen years he was in power. They were continually made and remade as Park zigzagged to find an appropriate formula for the state-*chaebol* partnership that would enable him to use the rents for economically productive purposes. Chapter 9 analyzes this making of rules and norms governing state-*chaebol* partnership during the Park era.

Partnering with the *Chaebol,* 1961–1963

When Park seized power in 1961, his first priority was winning public support for his military coup. Having overthrown the democratically elected government of Chang Myŏn by brute force under the pretext of cleaning up corruption, establishing political order, and building state competence, Park necessarily came to justify his coup by stressing his ability to generate economic growth. The technocratic rationale made Park search for ways to win over the business community, because only with its support could he make economic growth happen. Consequently the first months of military rule saw Park busy with the task of selecting entrepreneurs that he could trust and work with to devise a new set of rules and norms governing the state-*chaebol* relationship in the direction of launching an economic takeoff. The objective was to get the *chaebol* to collaborate in state-formulated industrial projects through an asymmetric exchange of political support and risk taking between the state and the *chaebol*.

Despite his statist ideology, Park knew that he would be able to achieve his economic goals only with the private sector's cooperation. Consequently, he sought to strengthen state leverage, but he did so not to expand the state's direct productive capacities at the expense of the *chaebol*, but to secure the private sector's compliance with state-formulated policy objectives. And to induce the *chaebol* to venture into more risky kinds of production and marketing activities, Park was ready to assist his strategically chosen *chaebol* partners in strengthening their corporate capabilities. To strengthen state leverage with which to persuade the *chaebol* into collaborating with the military junta, Park centralized power in the Economic Planning Board (EPB) and used it to encourage the *chaebol* into taking risks in return for his political support. He also nationalized all commercial banks with an eye to controlling the sources of capital. At the command of the Ministry of Finance (MoF), banks no longer acted as the agents of commercial financial transactions. Rather, they became an instrument through which the state could secure business compliance with the goals of industrial policy and macroeconomic planning. By implicitly threatening to revoke preferential bank loans if the borrower failed to meet state-set targets, the MoF used commercial banks as both carrot and stick in its efforts to reshape the preferences, interests, and strategies of business companies in the direction of the first Five-Year Economic Development Plan (FYEDP).

Once Park lined up his powerful arsenal of centralized economic bureaucracy and state-owned commercial banks by July 1961, he began looking for his business partners. His choice was the *chaebol,* whose owner-managers he had initially put under house arrest on the charge of illicit wealth accumulation immediately after the military coup. Although the public remained critical of these large companies' activities of rent-seeking during Syngman Rhee's rule (1948–1960), Park soon came to value their leaders' proven record of business success. And in any case, the economics of scale necessary to fulfill Park's vision of building a modern industrial economy in his lifetime could not be achieved by relying on small- and medium-sized enterprises (SMEs). The large enterprises with access to capital and technology were the only actors capable of participating in large-scale infrastructure projects and mass-producing manufactured goods for export.

On the other hand, Park excluded multinational corporations (MNCs) from his potential business partners out of both choice and necessity. Still fresh in the minds of South Koreans were memories of Japanese colonial exploitation, which made the option of generating economic growth through foreign direct investment (FDI) unpopular. An admirer of the Japanese Meiji Restoration that modernized through the nurturing of "national champions," Park also personally preferred to maintain national ownership of productive assets and chose foreign commercial loans over FDI to build infant industries. To keep Park on the nationalist path to modernization, moreover, South Korea was not a hospitable investment site for MNCs, suffering as it did from chronic political instability, limited domestic markets, and poor resource endowment. The economy was then still struggling with post–Korean War reconstruction as well.

By contrast, the option of replacing private producers with state-owned enterprises (SOEs) as an engine of growth was briefly experimented with in mid-1962, when Park came to be frustrated by the lack of progress in the *chaebol* groups' pledged investment in the first FYEDP projects. Endorsing the radical ideas of forced savings drawn up by the Kim Chong-p'il–led Korea Central Intelligence Agency (KCIA), Park identified a newly strengthened state-controlled Korea Industry Development Company (KIDC) as a conduit to channel the money in frozen bank accounts to FYEDP projects during the currency reform of June 1962. This brief play with radical statism ended as a political fiasco, with the United States lashing back with an interruption of aid because it charged that the military junta was trying to move toward a socialist economy.[7] Securing over 90 percent of the national budget from U.S. aid-generated counterpart funds as late as 1961, Park could not but backtrack from both the currency reform and the KIDC-channeled project financing. The junta found itself returning to the original task of negotiating a state-*chaebol* relationship that would transform the *chaebol* into a willing partner of the state in economic development.

For South Korea, the exclusion of statist options in the early stage of economic development was to clear the way to hypergrowth. The SOEs of South Korea did not have the capital, technology, or managerial expertise required for developing the modern manufacturing sector. They had also been the hotbed of corruption and inefficiency during Syngman Rhee's political rule, supporting his Liberal Party as a source of electoral funds. The military junta's rhetoric of anticorruption notwithstanding, it was unlikely that the politically fragile coup makers—externally lacking ideological legitimacy and internally trapped in intense factional power struggles—could remain disciplined in their exercise of power and resist the temptation of corruption. The expansion of SOEs would only have provided the rival factions of the junta an added incentive to use the state apparatus for rent-seeking.

Certainly by mid-1962, if not from the very day of the military coup in May 1961, then, teaming up with large domestic enterprises constituted the less politically risky and more economically viable option for Park. Consequently, he personally chose some of his life-long business partners from among the *chaebol* on the basis of two potentially contradictory criteria. On the one hand, Park searched for *chaebol* owners with a solid business track record to tap the best of South Korea's entrepreneurial resources. In particular, he looked for businessmen with a zeal for growth and an appetite for risk taking. Park was looking for business leaders who resembled himself: visionaries. Chŏng Chu-yŏng of Hyundai captured this spirit more than any other among the *chaebol*. At the same time, however, Park patronized Kyŏngsang-born *chaebol* owner-managers when possible, in order to give his regionalist ruling coalition a solid financial base. The strategy of choosing *chaebol* partners on the basis of entrepreneurial performance and regional background with an eye to balance the requirements of economic growth and political coalition building originated during the junta years when Park was challenged by coup makers from the

P'yŏngan and Hamgyŏng region (see Chapters 1 and 2), but it came to be continually strengthened even after his presidential election in October 1963. However, it is important to emphasize that the partnership required two willing partners. Park's choice also had to be the choice of the entrepreneurs if it was to result in actual investment. From their perspective, the junta's vision of a big push into industrialization presented not only new opportunities but also new challenges. Depending on the outcome of their risk taking, the old-timer entrepreneurs might either construct an empire of affiliate firms across unrelated industries, or see their companies shaken from their foundations under financial pressures. To stay out of the race to grow entailed costs as well, because the second-tier firms were likely to take the risk to push aside the front-runners with the goal of winning Park's political support. Once overtaken by the rising stars, the front-runners would find themselves without the privileged access to bank loans that they had earlier enjoyed.

Ironically, the business leaders' efforts to establish channels of communication and cooperation with the new rulers of South Korea began in the worst possible situation for them, when the coup makers, with an eye to winning popular support, initiated an investigation into their wealth gained in the 1950s. The day after the coup, Park arrested twenty-one business leaders on charges of illicit wealth accumulation. Some younger officers in the junta even called for the execution of some of the *chaebol* leaders in order to clean up corruption once and for all. By the end of May 1961, the Supreme Council for National Reconstruction (SCNR) had formally established an investigatory committee and put the issue at the top of its agenda. The swiftness with which the military junta went after the large entrepreneurs and the seriousness of the charges indicate that its mainstream faction, led by Park and Kim Chong-p'il, had formulated a fairly detailed plan to prosecute these individuals prior to launching the coup. The entrepreneurs were accused of illegally acquiring state-invested properties, unjustly purchasing state-owned foreign exchange at preferential rates, profiting from unfair bidding, illicitly benefiting from state-distributed foreign loans, evading taxes, and illegally transferring property to foreign countries in return for providing Liberal Party politicians with political funds.[8]

Since the *modus operandi* of business firms during the Liberal Party regime had been rent-seeking, which made corruption part of everyday business practices, most *chaebol* owner-managers of the day were vulnerable to the military junta's charges. Those running businesses in the lucrative "three white industries" (sugar refineries, flour mills, and textile mills), in particular, became a target of investigation because their prosperity owed much to the state's preferential distribution of U.S. aid goods, import licenses, production permits, and preferential bank loans. The oligopolistic market that ensured high profits for the three white industries was a state-sanctioned and -maintained structure. Under investigation were two of the most successful business tycoons: Yi Pyŏng-ch'ŏl, of Samsung, whose illicit wealth was officially estimated at 800 million won (19 percent of the total illicit wealth), and Hong Chae-sŏn, of Kŭmsŏng Textiles, which later became Ssangyong.[9]

As dramatically as the junta demonstrated its power to shake up and challenge big business in May 1961 with its investigation into Liberal Party–brokered business deals, its gesture to put the past behind it and move forward to construct a growth machine with the same *chaebol* owner-managers as its junior partners came abruptly. On June 27, Yi Pyŏng-ch'ol returned from Japan to face charges. What awaited him, however, was not imprisonment but a historic meeting with Park Chung Hee. There Yi Pyŏng-ch'ol convinced Park that the prosecution would inadvertently prevent Park from pursuing economic growth by irreparably damaging business confidence. The Samsung *chaebol* leader added that Park would benefit more by having the business leaders work for South Korea's rapid industrialization than by putting them in jail, which only wasted their talents. Park knew better than anyone that he had to work with big business if he were to put the country on the track to growth. Much of the managerial expertise, organizational capabilities, capital, and technology required for modernization were in the hands of the *chaebol*, not the armed forces. Moreover, even compared to the state bureaucracy, the *chaebol*, with their entrepreneurial spirit, looked like the ideal vehicle for penetrating export markets.

Equally critical for Park, relying on the *chaebol* as an instrument of modernization did not threaten his political interests, because the *chaebol* were not the "conquering bourgeoisie," sure of their historical mission and ideological legitimacy. Rather, the leading business groups were seen as rent-seekers, living off state licenses and loans and accused of illicit wealth accumulation. They were not in a position to claim political legitimacy, which made Park less hesitant in making a U-turn to partner with them and support their diversification and conglomeration. Thus began in June a series of arm-twisting and behind-the-scenes negotiations between the state and the *chaebol*, out of which new terms of political exchange were drawn up to clear the way for business investment in FYEDP projects.

In August, with Park's blessing, the business leaders launched a National Association of Company Presidents, which was to become the Federation of Korean Industries (FKI) in 1968. Established as a summit organization of large industrial conglomerates, the FKI not only served as a channel to voice and defend the collective interests of big business but also enabled the state to control, shape, and influence those interests. The sense of camaraderie developed by the FKI was to help the state and the *chaebol* to jointly tackle the challenging task of negotiating the market shares required for the establishment of "industrial rationalization cartels" aimed at preventing "excessive competition" among rival conglomerates.[10] At the same time, Park organized the FKI to monopolize the political loyalty of its members and preempt not only the opposition but also his potential rivals within the ruling coalition from securing an independent source of political funds. Once he had herded all of big business into the FKI, Park preferred to make business deals with the *chaebol* on an individual basis, often behind closed doors and in one-on-one conversations directly with their owner-managers, rather than in the open through the official channels of the FKI.

Ironically, it was the issue of illicit wealth accumulation that Park leveraged to construct a system of state-*chaebol* coordination on his terms. He could destroy any uncooperative *chaebol* owner-manager by levying exorbitant fines, or protect cooperative ones by acquitting them of shady business deals. It was through the adjustment of fines that Park thought he could set the *chaebol* groups' terms of participation in FYEDP projects and their place in partisan politics. The negotiation for the acquittal of the business owners from the charges against them was a well-orchestrated play, with Park as its producer interested in getting maximum compliance from his future partners. The *chaebol* owner-managers, including Yi Pyŏng-ch'ol, who were under house arrest, well understood Park's intentions. They knew that the politics of rapid industrialization—not elections—was the only game in town and that they had to help Park achieve his economic vision and ambitions if they were to survive. They also understood that the most critical issue was not the threat of imprisonment, which was not going to happen, once Park met with Yi Pyŏng-ch'ol on June 27 to start talks on state-*chaebol* cooperation, but Park's decision on the two closely coordinated issues of how much to levy in fines and how to distribute FYEDP projects among the *chaebol*. Depending on the nature of the projects allotted and the level of fines imposed, the owner-managers had an opportunity to grow into an industrial conglomerate in both name and reality, or could go insolvent under the pressure of market forces and legal fines.

For the two parties to come to a final deal, however, several attempts at negotiation were necessary. In August 1961, the junta enacted a Special

Law on the Disposition of Illegally Accumulated Capital, which allowed the business leaders convicted of illegal wealth accumulation to "donate" to the state the factories they were to construct under state guidance in lieu of a fine. This was the *chaebol* owner-managers' idea. By persuading Park to enact the special law rather than to expropriate the illicitly accumulated wealth immediately, the business leaders bought time to gain Park's trust through their participation in various FYEDP projects and to use that trust to renegotiate the fines later.[11] With the strategy of renegotiating the terms of the fines and maybe even winning their revocation from a position of political strength, eighteen of the original twenty-one illicit wealth accumulators began building the factories Park had designated for them.

As the owner-managers hoped, Park soon discarded his plan to nationalize the factories to be built by the illicit wealth accumulators. Rather than nationalization, Park went back to the option of levying fines. But by January 1962, he had reduced the fines twice, by 90 percent in the first round and again by a half in the second round. In the end, the *chaebol* owner-managers got away with a mere slap on the wrist. Apparently Park never intended to punish the *chaebol* for their past shady business deals. On the contrary, from the beginning the top priority was getting the *chaebol* to acquiesce in his vision of modernization and accommodate the state's administrative guidance on investment. The issue of illicit wealth accumulation was a mere instrument in this game of arm-twisting to "persuade" the *chaebol* to collaborate with Park.

Once Park ventured into negotiating new terms of state-*chaebol* cooperation, moreover, big business inevitably came to increase its leverage on Park. First, once resources were concentrated in the *chaebol* groups' investment projects, Park was bound to look at the business failure of *chaebol* conglomerates as the political failure of the developmental state he was building up as the partner to the *chaebol*. Consequently, the balance of power shifted toward the *chaebol,* because the state thought their bankruptcy threatened the financial viability of the state itself. Second, the political weakness of the *chaebol* became a source of influence on economic policy, because it allowed Park to support big business without fear of inadvertently fostering an alternative center of political power. Confident of the business groups' political weakness, but also fearing the negative political fallout of economic recession, Park made subsidies available for the *chaebol* to enter new frontiers of growth.

Third, the dynamics of political exchange itself strengthened the hands of the *chaebol*. Because the owner-managers made their entry decision on the basis of Park's pledge of support, the withholding of state subsidies during business difficulty would be perceived as a breach of the political understanding between Park and the *chaebol,* which could irreparably damage Park's credibility and, hence, his ability to persuade future investors to take risks. In a sense, the moment that Park and the *chaebol* agreed to pursue FYEDP projects jointly as part of their efforts to put the issue of illicit wealth accumulation behind them, they both lost much of their political maneuverability. The state could not withdraw support as it liked. Nor were the *chaebol* free to exit from their lines of business simply because of financial losses. The alliance between Park and the *chaebol* meant that they were each other's guarantor and that they had to weather corporate and financial distress together.

Even during the formative era of military rule, it was not unusual to see the *chaebol* helping Park formulate goals and the state bureaucracy implementing *chaebol* ideas. It was Yi Pyŏng-ch'ol who persuaded Park to make concessions on the issue of illicit wealth accumulation in return for *chaebol* participation in FYEDP projects in June 1961. Thereafter, Park periodically consulted Yi Pyŏng-ch'ol for advice, and even backed Yi's effort to organize big business as the first president of the newly established FKI. In that role, Yi Pyŏng-ch'ol led a delegation of business leaders to the United States and Western Europe as part of efforts to attract foreign capital. At stake was nothing less than the survival of their businesses, as the owner-managers worked to construct the factories they were required to build in return for Park's agreement to defer and reduce their fines. Shortly after the trip, on January 11, 1962, the FKI submitted a proposal for the construction of the Ulsan Industrial Complex. Three weeks later, Park held a groundbreaking ceremony. The Ulsan project was to popularize the idea of building a cluster of backwardly- and forwardly-linked industries in a geographically compact area with an eye to facilitating well-coordinated collective actions between the state and the business community, suppliers and assemblers, and industrial and service sectors. A myriad of industrial complexes and export zones eventually emerged throughout South Korea during the 1963–1979 period.

Kim Ip-sam, the FKI executive vice chairman during the entire Park era, once recollected that "Park himself confessed on several occasions that he knew nothing about the economy in meetings with business leaders immediately after the 1961 military coup."[12] Many of the innovative ideas that later became his trademark were of *chaebol* origin. "The strategy of export promotion was first suggested by Chŏn T'aek-bo of Ch'ŏnusa, a producer of leather goods and toys. The idea of attracting foreign capital and commercial loans through the construction of industrial complexes was likewise put forth to Park by business leaders during the early days of military rule." To be sure, Kim Ip-sam acknowledged that these ideas bore fruit only because "Park was an extraordinary person, open to new ideas and capable of transforming them into a detailed workable action program," and "a quick learner . . . intensely interested in the economy. He studied hard to learn about economic issues and to discover ways to bring about economic development. Nevertheless, the point is that it was the *chaebol* who had the ideas and the means to attain economic development." Even during the "easy" stage of developing light industry in the 1960s, Park needed the *chaebol* as much as the *chaebol* needed him for the generation of industrial growth. The mutual dependence of the two was to become even more apparent in the 1970s, when Park embarked on the riskier program of heavy and chemical industrialization (HCI).

Rebirth of the *Chaebol*, 1964–1967

In the initial years of the first FYEDP, the economy performed dismally despite a comprehensive reorganization of the state and a visible shift of political priorities toward economic growth. Unfavorable external economic conditions were initially blamed, but Park soon realized that the problem had deeper roots. After the radical measures of forced saving, including the currency reform and the KIDC debacle of June 1962, paralyzed the economy, Park ordered the EPB to revise the first FYEDP in December of the same year. The revised plan, announced in February 1964, called for concentrating resources in a few strategic industries and promoting exports in order to withstand the whims of the world market. The principles of resource concentration and export promotion signaled that Park was now emulating Meiji Japan in his strategy of modernization, in which the state worked exclusively with the economic powerhouses of the *zaibatsu* to grow through export markets. But unlike the pre–World War II Japanese *zaibatsu*, which possessed both industrial firms and financial institutions within their group organization, the *chaebol* of the mid-1960s were strictly manufacturing entities. The nationalization of commercial banks by the junta in 1961 helped the Ministry of Finance to control the *chaebol*.

Once Park secured *chaebol* participation in FYEDP projects, a handful of top-ranking *chaebol* groups came to enjoy privileged access to the state bureaucracy, including the Blue House. Some of the *chaebol* were showered with preferential bank loans, state-guaranteed foreign loans, and oligopolistic entry licenses in return for not only taking the risk to develop state-designated industries, but also supplying political funds to Park's ruling Democratic Republican Party. Although Park discouraged big business from itself becoming a player in party politics, he did let a handful of the *chaebol* owner-managers' extended family members become second-tier leaders in the ruling coalition by taking on crucial DRP posts. Kim Sŏng-gon of Ssangyong rose to the position of DRP finance chair, serving Park's interests in holding Kim Chong-p'il's DRP mainstream faction in check. Both as an old-time civilian politician with a Liberal Party background and as a former entrepreneur with an extensive personal network throughout the South Korean business community, Kim Sŏng-gon was made for the task of building an anti-mainstream faction in the interest of maintaining a balance of power within the DRP.

The state-*chaebol* partnership Park constructed was Janus-faced. The partnership was fed by the rents generated through subsidized bank loans, state-guaranteed foreign loans, and selectively distributed licenses, but the politics of rent-seeking did not degenerate into the classic predatory type of plundering, because, in the last analysis, the *chaebol* as exporters lived in a competitive world of global market forces, and because they remained accountable to Park as the state-designated vehicles for building a "rich nation, a strong army." Park tied the state provision of rents to the *chaebol* partners' ability to achieve FYEDP target goals, withdrawing the sources of rents when he thought the recipients had failed to deliver their part of the bargain without justifiable cause.

Park's strategy worked because the state's capacity for generating rents was dramatically strengthened through a series of policy decisions during the mid-1960s. The signing of a normalization treaty with Japan in 1965 not only resulted in a lump-sum transfer of Japanese money in the form of reparation funds, but also cleared the way for the entry of Japanese capital on a commercial basis. To facilitate foreign loans and FDI institutionally, the National Assembly enacted the Foreign Capital Inducement Law, drafted by the Ministry of Finance, in 1966. Park's 1964 decision to dispatch combat troops to South Vietnam in support of U.S. war efforts also provided the *chaebol* with the opportunity to earn foreign exchange. The war produced two Cinderellas, Hanjin as a transportation magnate in control of a shipping company, an airline, and a bus and truck company, and Hyundai as a construction conglomerate.

It soon became clear that the key to business growth was access to state-guaranteed foreign loans. The manufacturing sector took 52.1 percent of South Korea's total foreign loans in 1966 and 69.1 percent in 1968, a huge jump from 10.3 percent in 1962.[13] Moreover, in order to encourage the *chaebol* to take risks and foreign commercial banks to lend money to the risk-taking *chaebol*, the state guaranteed repayment of 90 percent of the foreign commercial loans, either directly (40 percent) or indirectly through state-owned banks (50 percent). Such a socialization of the financial risk and costs by the state ended up in driving the *chaebol* to finance their business expansion and diversification aggressively through the available loans.

The benefits accruing to a *chaebol* from being designated as a recipient of state-guaranteed foreign loans exceeded the simple sum of foreign loans and included a wide range of privileges from low interest rates on domestic loans, to easy access to scarce foreign exchange, and even to legal prohibition of labor organizations. The benefit of low interest domestic loans became particularly great when Park introduced a "reverse interest rate system" in 1965, which put the domestic bankers' deposit rates above lending rates.[14] To make loan-financed business growth even more irresistible, the average rate of inflation was then roughly 21 percent per year—3 to 5 percentage points below the state-owned banks' lending rates. Equally critical, whereas the South Korean domestic banks' interest rates ranged between 24 and 26 percent during the 1965–1970 period, the rates on export-policy loans, many of which were provided to the foreign loan–financed *chaebol,* stood in the range of 6.0–6.5 percent. The press even charged that some *chaebol* were re-lending their bank loans in the private curb market, where interest rates hit 50–60 percent, rather than investing in risky manufacturing projects.[15] It was in a certain sense profitable for companies to acquire as many domestic bank loans as possible.

At the same time, Park allowed the *chaebol* to organize their corporate governance structures, inter-firm relations, and internal hierarchy in the direction that would enable them to raise capital with a minimum threat to their corporate control. The *chaebol* established multiple businesses with a minimum amount of equity capital through a system of cross-shareholding and cross-loan guarantees, while legally protected from threats of hostile takeovers. The *chaebol* also had their subsidiaries support each other through insider trading and subsidies, while centralizing internal decision-making processes through the establishment of a planning and management office with an eye to orchestrate a concerted action of mutual assistance among their affiliate firms. What we know as the *chaebol* of today emerged from these organizational experiments of the mid-1960s: a group of business firms that seem to be independent but are actually run by one owner-manager family through an opaque corporate governance structure, including cross-shareholding, cross-loan guarantees, inter-firm insider trading and subsidies, and centralized planning and management offices. This structure enabled a *chaebol* to participate as a monolithic actor in diversified unrelated markets, with systematic control over affiliated firms with regard to financial, personnel, and management issues. As such, the *chaebol* constituted the South Korean business firms' way of mobilizing scarce resources and managing business risks that included market uncertainty and international disadvantage.

Consequently, despite inter-firm and inter-sectoral variations in organization, the *chaebol* exhibited several common characteristics. First, all firms in the group were controlled by a central company, which was typically operated by an owner-manager family. Second, most of the member firms were of a significant size, and they worked under the coordinated initiative of the centralized management at the top. Third, they tended to be involved in multiple sectors, with the managers transferred from one sector to another, thus ensuring unity of strategy and cross-fertilization of experience.

The mid-1960s saw a furious competition among entrepreneurs to enter the club of *chaebol*. Chungang and Ssangyong competed for the license to construct a cement factory, Han'guk and Yŏnhap Steel for a cool strip iron mill, and Taehan Electric Wires and Gold Star for production of electrical products. The winners of licenses were provided with state guaranteed foreign loans, which were the ticket to corporate expansion. The foreign-loan financed projects of the mid-1960s went to Kŭmsŏng Chemicals, Ssangyoung Cement, Sinjin Motors, Samyang, Taehan Industries, Inchŏn Heavy Industries, Yŏnhap Steel, and Hyundai Engineering and Construction, many of which formed close alliances with Park.[16] The Lucky-Gold Star Group also consolidated its political edge when it beat its rival, Taehan Electronic Wire Company, in securing foreign and domestic loans at preferential rates. In particular, Park formed a special partnership with Chŏng Chu-yŏng of Hyundai, based on their shared vision of rapid industrialization and their similar orientation toward risk taking, "can do" spirit, and sheer drive. In spite of its second-tier status within South Korean big business at the time of the 1961 coup, Hyundai was chosen over other more established business groups as a partner in national reconstruction because of its owner-manager's credibility as a risk taker.

The 1960s' competition for loans and licenses dramatically restructured big business. Faced with a politically driven high-risk and high-payoff marketplace, four of the ten largest *chaebol* in 1960 dropped from the top ten list by 1965. The second- and third-largest *chaebol* of 1960—Samho and Kaep'ung—joined the list of declining *chaebol* and dropped from the top ten list by the early 1970s. In their place was a new group of bold risk takers: Hanjin, Sinjin Motors, Ssangyong, Hyundai, Hanhwa, and Taenong. These new *chaebol* invested more in the heavy and chemical industries, Park's strategic sector, whereas the old *chaebol* were largely involved in light manufacturing and in commerce. By the end of 1969, foreign loans were concentrated in the hands of the largest *chaebol,* including

Ssangyong, with a total of $150 million, and Lucky-Gold Star, with $123 million.[17]

The rise of Hyundai during the late 1960s was particularly spectacular. Established in 1947, Hyundai Construction remained a solo operation without affiliate companies and subsidiaries until 1955, although it made its name as a construction magnate during the Korean War (1950–1953) by signing numerous exclusive construction contracts with the U.S. military to build barracks and other army facilities along the rapidly changing front lines.[18] With many of the lucrative businesses, including the three white industries, under the control of the older *chaebol* groups, Hyundai could find new markets only through a major expansion of the economy.[19] The military coup created opportunities for corporate growth for the latecomers by shaking up the state-business nexus that had been previously mediated and constructed by the Liberal Party and through opening up the heavy and chemical industries as a new frontier of growth without any established front-runners. The 1960s saw Hyundai transformed into an industrial conglomerate with six affiliate companies by entering these new frontiers of growth: Hyundai Construction (1947), Hyundai Marine and Fire Insurance (1955), Hyundai Securities (1962), Inchŏn Iron and Steel (1964), Hyundai Oil Refinery (1964), and Hyundai Motors (1967).[20]

By contrast, Samsung's case was more turbulent. After close collaboration during the junta, its relationship with Park soured when one of its affiliate firms was charged with the smuggling of saccharin in 1967. Yi Pyŏng-ch'ol was forced to "donate" to the state its foreign loan–financed Han'guk Fertilizer Company as part of an effort to win back Park's trust. The damage was already done, however. In spite of the nationalization of the fertilizer company, the public remained furious, accusing Samsung of illegally profiting from state-guaranteed foreign loans and charging the Park regime with corruption. To appease the populace, Yi Pyŏng-ch'ol's son, Ch'ang-hŭi, was arrested, while Yi Pyŏng-ch'ol stepped down from his position as Samsung's group chair.[21] After this incident, Yi Pyŏng-ch'ol kept a healthy distance from politics and sought ways to secure less politically vulnerable sources of capital, including joint ventures with foreign capital. He was also more guarded regarding the use of state-controlled and, hence, politically vulnerable bank loans than Hyundai's Chŏng Chu-yŏng and Daewoo's Kim U-jung because of his less adventurous management style. Moreover, because Samsung was already in control of many of the commanding heights in the South Korean economy as its largest *chaebol*, Yi Pyŏng-ch'ol could afford the luxury of letting other *chaebol* groups enter state-designated strategic industries and test the waters before he decided on his business options.

In spite of the differences in management styles, however, the powerful and charismatic owner-managers of both old and new *chaebol* groups, from Yi Pyŏng-ch'ol of Samsung to Chŏng Chu-yŏng of Hyundai and Ku Cha-gyŏng of Lucky-Gold Star, were all self-made visionaries with distinct management styles. The founders typically tapped the resources of their entire extended families, recruiting brothers and in-laws into the management and pooling together the family wealth.[22] Later they became powerful CEOs, making up what the press called the "royal family of the founder," enjoying unparalleled access to top managerial posts and making strategic and operational managerial decisions unilaterally, without the watchful eyes of auditors and minor stockholders. The "imperial" corporate governance structure relied on the leadership of owner-managers for firm growth, making the *chaebol* organizationally flexible in adjusting to changes in market signals, but at the cost of hasty decision making.

Financial Crisis and Corporate Restructuring, 1968–1972

Backed by Park's expansionary drive, manufacturing firms increased in number at a rate of roughly a thousand per year during the 1960s. Although most of the newly established manufacturers were small- and medium-sized enterprises in light industry, the decade also witnessed the launching of 509 large-sized enterprises. The takeoff period of 1963–1969 was particularly productive, with 409 large firms newly established. Industrial concentration increased as well, as the *chaebol* diversified into unrelated industries. Industrial concentration had been high even before Park's big push, with 12.5 percent of business firms accounting for 39.8 percent of South Korea's total value-added and 36.6 percent of its total production in 1960. By 1968, however, large firms, accounting for 12.4 percent of South Korea's total number of business enterprises, were responsible for 65.2 percent of the total value-added and 64.8 percent of the total volume of production.

However, it was at the height of hypergrowth that the South Korean economy began showing signs of trouble. The root cause lay in Park's failure to fine-tune the conflicting requirements of competition and concentration. On the one hand, South Korea had to concentrate resources in a few strategic projects if it was to exploit the economies of scale within its given conditions of limited markets and scarce resources. On the other hand, for firms to have an incentive to cut costs and open up new markets, there had to be competitors. The challenge was to establish the "right" number of firms, neither too many nor too few, that would ensure market competition without getting caught in a downward spiral of surplus capacity, low profits, and financial distress. By the end of the 1960s, it became clear that Park had failed in getting that right number of firms. The intrinsic difficulty in forecasting future market conditions was part of the problem, but Park also faced intense business lobbying for entry licenses. Consequently the heavy concentration of wealth in the leading *chaebol* took place with too much duplication of investment projects, which began to pose a serious threat to the sustainability of not only those *chaebol* but the entire national economy. A large number of foreign loan–financed *chaebol* started to show signs of insolvency by 1967, but Park could only defer adjustment because of great political pressure to increase the money supply to ensure a DRP victory in both the National Assembly and the presidential elections of 1967.

Park faced the grim reality of the financial crisis only in 1968. The crisis was attributed to three factors.[23] First, the *chaebol* had become heavily indebted after five years of hypergrowth, with a large portion of capital financed by short-term private loans on the curb market and foreign commercial loans. The high debt-equity ratios meant that the economic recession then triggered by a global downturn immediately turned into a corporate crisis, as many of the firms could not even pay the interest they owed out of their declining profits. Of the total corporate funds available in 1968, debt totaled a hefty 72.5 percent, of which 24.5 percent were foreign loans and 15 percent were informal curb-market loans.[24] To ease pressures on the current account, the state tightened regulations on foreign capital and raised interest rates, only to see the financial burden on small- and medium-sized enterprises increase. Real interest rates were near two-digit figures in contrast to the negative rates the *chaebol* enjoyed.[25] The interest rates for private curb-market loans ranged from 40 to 70 percent,[26] further aggravating not only the SMEs' but also increasingly the *chaebol*'s financial positions.

To make the situation worse, the United States, South Korea's leading export market, was under rising protectionist pressures, preventing the South Korean textile industry from leading economic growth through exports. The economy was in a slump throughout 1970. The decade of export-driven hypergrowth based on labor-intensive industries, moreover, had brought about a decrease in surplus labor and a rise in real wages, resulting in the loss of comparative advantage. As the global economy hit a deep recession with a downturn in the economies of industrialized nations, South Korean began feeling the crunch.[27] More than 200 firms went bankrupt in 1971, although the state tried to come to the rescue by taking over 30 of them.[28]

The FKI stepped in to voice the collective needs of *chaebol* conglomerates, calling on the state to take the steps necessary to tackle the liquidity crisis. To underline the gravity of corporate financial distress, which macro indicators like the annual GNP growth rate concealed, the FKI even proposed cutting the government budget and tax revenue by half. Realizing the gravity of the situation, Park announced an Emergency Decree for Economic Stability and Growth (EDESG) on August 3, 1972, on the recommendation of FKI chairman Kim Yong-wan, as we saw in Chapter 7. The EDESG had been in preparation since September 1971, with Kim Yong-hwan of the Ministry of Finance in charge of the working-level task force established within the Blue House. The announcement of the measure was originally planned for January 1972, but was put off until political conflict over the legislation of a special law on national security subsided. To prevent any leaks of the emergency measure, Kim Yong-hwan, as the secretary for foreign capital, received the signatures of the prime minister, the EPB deputy prime minister, and the MoF minister, among other relevant cabinet members, without explaining the contents of the decree.[29] Despite this secrecy, the press later charged that information on the EDESG had been leaked to a few *chaebol* conglomerates so that their owner-managers could secretly prepare for the shock of the emergency measure.[30]

To rescue the financially weak business community, the EDESG allowed corporate debtors to repay their private curb-market liabilities over five years with a three-year grace period at a monthly interest rate of 1.35 percent (or an annual rate of 16 percent), when the monthly interest rates in the curb market stood at 3.84 percent on average. The emergency measure also allowed debt-equity swaps at the request of lenders. It was estimated that the EDESG reduced corporate borrowers' financial burden by two-thirds on average.[31]

The emergency decree was successful in relieving the pressures of the liquidity squeeze, but at the cost of paralyzing the private curb market that had served as a source of capital for hard-pressed firms, when regular bank financing was unavailable or when a quick loan without extensive paperwork was needed to cover unforeseen operational costs.[32] Although the EDESG was originally designed to help firms of all sizes, the greatest beneficiaries were the *chaebol,* because they accounted for 64 percent of the private curb-market loans. Parallel to the freeze on curb-market loans, the state banks lowered interest rates by 3.5 percent from 19 to 15.5 percent, again benefiting the *chaebol* the most, as the largest debtors.[33] Moreover, the *chaebol* conglomerates with heavy investment in strategic industries and export sectors were given the additional benefit of financial subsidies in the form of "industry rationalization funds."[34] In return for their participation in the state's risky program of heavy and chemical industrialization during the uncertain 1970s, they received generous state support, including low interest rates on bank loans, tax cuts, state guarantees on foreign loans, and preferential licenses. Saved by the emergency decree, big business came back strong, leading the economy to grow by a phenomenal 16.5 percent in 1973.

In the end, the EDESG had the effect of consolidating the *chaebol*'s place in the South Korean economy by not only putting the *chaebol* on a more financially sound base but also enabling them to exploit new opportunities in HCI-led corporate growth from that position of financial strength. The EDESG, followed by heavy and chemical industrialization, sealed a rock-solid partnership between the state and the *chaebol*.[35] Once the front-runners among the *chaebol* entered strategic heavy and chemical industries after the mid-1970s, the entry opportunities were rapidly closed down, with the effect of protecting the front-runners' market share and political privileges. The HCI *chaebol* grew exponentially during the 1970s. Daewoo, established only in 1967, became the Cinderella of the following decade, growing over 54 percent annually. Hyundai also grew at 38 percent to become the largest *chaebol*, surpassing Samsung. The business community's internal hierarchy, once it had been reordered by the EDESG and HCI drive during the 1970s, was to survive for decades to come.

First, the top-ranking *chaebol* groups' conglomeration and diversification into unrelated business sectors intensified with the HCI drive. Whereas Lucky-Gold Star concentrated on producing electrical appliances and electronic goods, Hyundai embodied the image of heavy and chemical industry *chaebol* by expanding its presence in the automobile sector and entering the shipbuilding and steel industries. The synergy effects accruing from myriad backward and forward linkages were seen as justifying their respective specialization into electronics and HCI. Nonetheless, the sectoral specialization of these *chaebol* conglomerates should not be exaggerated. Hyundai went on to enter the electronics industry in 1983 and the oil refinery business in 1993. Moreover, its corporate origins traced to Hyundai Engineering and Construction, yet by 1971 it was also operating department stores and hotels. Lucky-Gold Star similarly operated large businesses outside the electrical appliance and electronics industry, running an oil refinery from 1963 on, setting up as a metal maker in 1971, and diversifying into the financial sector in the late 1980s.

Second, the *chaebol*'s pattern of investment since the late 1960s closely maps onto and followed the Park regime's economic planning and was concentrated in the state-designated strategic industries, demonstrating that state subsidies and support played an important role in investment decisions made by the *chaebol*. Apparently, by coming to the rescue of faltering firms between 1968 and 1972, Park succeeded in making his pledge of support politically credible to the *chaebol*, which helped his mobilization of business support behind the post-1972 HCI drive.

Third, by the mid-1970s, many *chaebol* conglomerates began to enter the construction industry to exploit the growing domestic real estate market and the Middle East construction boom. Non-bank financial institutions (NBFIs) also attracted major investment when the Ministry of Finance chose to develop NBFIs under the private sector's leadership with the goal of developing new sources of capital and reducing demands on state bank loans. The financial and corporate distress of the early 1970s had persuaded the MoF to develop the stock market as a supplement to the existing bank-centered financial system.

Finally, by the early 1970s, the two older and largest *chaebol* groups— Samsung and Lucky-Gold Star—diversified into not only the light and heavy manufacturing sectors, but also the services sector, including nonbank financial institutions, hotels, and department stores. Unlike Hyundai and Daewoo, the aggressive front-runners among the new *chaebol*, which were known to be favored by Park for their risk taking, Samsung and Lucky-Gold Star did not seek extensive loan packages as aggressively as Hyundai and Daewoo. Consequently, they were slower in growth and in diversification. When they entered the state-targeted heavy and chemical industries, they did so much later and on a smaller scale, after the frontrunners had tested the waters. The late entry into HCI was owed in part to their top management's conservative business strategy of following the proven path of specializing in the production of consumer goods. However, in Samsung's case, politics also factored in to delay its entry into HCI. Since 1966, when Samsung's fertilizer firm had been caught smuggling 60 tons of OTSA (used for the manufacture of saccharin) with the help of state-guaranteed foreign loans, Samsung's relationship with Park had remained uneasy, preventing it from forging close-knit ties to his industrial projects and goals.[36]

Of the Big Three, Hyundai was the most dynamic. By 1972, Chŏng Chu-Yŏng laid the foundation to become the heavy and chemical industry magnate of South Korea, with six of his eight major firms each building an empire in the construction, iron and steel, oil refinery, and automobile industries. As Yi Chun-lim once recalled, the Hyundai Group's diversification was driven by its desire to control the markets:

[Chŏng Chu-yŏng] established an iron and steel plant to secure a reliable source of steel for Hyundai Construction. The public then complained about shoddy buildings, but at the time, there could be only shoddy buildings. We could secure steel supplies from a U.S. supplier only at the end of the year, when there were only a few months left to meet the construction deadline . . . [W]e ended up constructing gray concrete buildings with steel beams in the middle of the winter cold, when the cement kept getting frozen. That was why Chŏng Chu-yŏng decided to build his own iron and steel plant.

Besides, Hyundai was the largest construction company, capable of building the iron and steel plant with a steady demand for its products . . . All in all, this was a good deal. Chŏng Chu-yŏng's ideas in establishing Hyundai Motors and Hyundai Oil Refinery were similar: Hyundai was its own largest supplier and customer. Why should Hyundai pay another company for what Hyundai could produce?[37]

As each of the *chaebol* conglomerates expanded its empire through diversification and conglomeration, it came to need a new corporate governance structure to help the owner-manager *ch'ongsu* (commander in chief) maintain his tight rein over subsidiaries and affiliate firms. The structure of family ownership-management had to be modernized if the *chaebol* were to remain an effective business organization in spite of rapid conglomeration and diversification. The pioneer in organizational innovation was Samsung, who as South Korea's largest *chaebol* had already faced the dilemma of family ownership-management and entrepreneurial effectiveness in the late 1950s *chaebol*. The establishment in 1959 of a secretariat, with full-time staff members to help the *ch'ongsu* systematically manage the growing Samsung Group, was a precursor to the modernized corporate governance structure that emerged out of the 1964–1972 corporate expansion. Yi Pyŏng-ch'ol once argued that the secretariat "must become one with the group chairman, putting into practice his management philosophy."[38] To enable the chairman to control and direct the burgeoning business group as if it were a single business entity, the secretariat enjoyed the prerogative of making policy and investment decisions for each of the member firms from the collective perspective of the entire business group. The Samsung chairman's secretariat consisted of some twenty staff members, neither too many to threaten the autonomy of affiliate firms by hoarding power, nor too few to be unable to make strategic business decisions. Yi Pyŏng-ch'ŏl saw the secretariat as his eyes and ears to monitor performance and advise on strategic issues from a macro perspective.

Needless to say, the ultimate source of the power wielded by Yi Pyŏng-ch'ŏl and his secretariat lay in the myriad cross-shareholding and circular shareholding that glued the member firms together. Through this mechanism, Yi Pyŏng-ch'ŏl and his family were able to launch new business entities with a minimum input of family wealth. Once Yi controlled parent companies with a large personal stake, he used the parent companies to establish new firms and the subsidiaries to launch still another layer of business firms. Then, from his secretariat, Yi Pyŏng-ch'ŏl effectively controlled the entire business group without any checks and balances by professional managers or, more important, by minor stockholders. Even after some of the member companies went public under Park's pressure to ameliorate societal discontent over the concentration of wealth in the mid-1970s, the opaque corporate governance structure of cross-shareholding and centralized managerial power enabled Yi Pyŏng-ch'ŏl to make strategic business decisions for the firms listed on the stock exchange as if they were still family businesses.

Completion of the *Chaebol* Structure, 1973–1979

The HCI drive announced by Park on January 13, 1973, allowed the *chaebol* to complete their structure. Aware of the need to concentrate resources in order to realize economies of scale in the capital-intensive heavy and chemical industries, but also wary of the risks and dangers of stagnant monopolies, Park chose the strategy of getting the *chaebol* to construct an oligopolistic structure of competition in five industries: nonferrous metal, petrochemical, machinery, shipbuilding, and electronics. The sixth industry selected for massive state support—steel—was reserved for state ownership and management. Selected on the basis of Park's trust in their owner-managers' commitment, ten *chaebol* groups became the dominant players in the other five heavy and chemical industries.[39] As the HCI drive progressed, business concentration accelerated. Some 70 percent of investment funds were channeled into a few large *chaebol* in support of Park's HCI drive, and most of the top ten *chaebol* conglomerates, except Samsung and Lucky-Gold Star, came to be Park's creation, pulled out of the second tier of the South Korean business community by him and diversified into unrelated industries under his patronage. These *chaebol* were chosen by Park as national champions on the basis of their performance, their loyalty, and their willingness to take risks. The risk taking was rewarded handsomely with oligopoly rights in strategic industries.

This is not to argue that the *chaebol* itself was Park's creation. On the contrary, as was already visible in Samsung's choice to supplement the strategy of funding industrial projects with state-brokered loans with joint ventures after the political fiasco of saccharin smuggling in 1967, the two largest business groups in South Korea—Samsung and Lucky-Gold Star—

chose the option of teaming up with MNCs to secure scarce resources and minimize risk when they entered the electrical and electronics industry in the 1970s.[40] Samsung gained contracts for technology transfers for Samsung Electronic Devices from Nippon Electric and Joowoo (Japan) and for Samsung Electronic Parts from Sanyo, among others.[41] Similarly Lucky-Gold Star collaborated with firms such as AT&T (United States), Mitsubishi Corporation (Japan), and Siemens Aktien Gessellschaft (West Germany).[42] Lucky-Gold Star opted for joint ventures outside the electrical and electronics industry, too. Among its affiliate companies, the Honam Oil Refinery signed a 50:50 joint venture with Caltex, Gold Star Company secured direct investment from the International Finances Corporation, and Lucky partnered with the National Plastic Company of Japan.[43]

Despite the variation in the *chaebol* groups' readiness to grow through risky state-brokered bank loans, or with MNCs as their partners in joint ventures, the HCI-driven 1970s were for all conglomerates—whether the old or new, the cautious or adventurous, or the political cronies or entrepreneurs—a lifetime opportunity for hypergrowth. To be sure, Samsung and Lucky-Gold Star fell behind, but still grew fast enough to remain within the Big Four. The two older *chaebol* groups annually grew by 17.2 percent in terms of total assets. The HCI drive of the 1970s, then, promised hypergrowth for all conglomerates. Equally critical, the continued corporate growth of Samsung and Lucky-Gold Star demonstrated that although state support and guidance were important, they were not the whole story. They showed that there were alternative ways to prosper, even in the most dirigiste period of the Park era.

Once Park decided to pursue HCI, export promotion became an added reason to strengthen business concentration. In the absence of sufficient domestic demand, Park designated the heavy and chemical industries as export sectors when they were only infant industries. He set the goal of increasing HCI exports to a level of 60 percent of total exports by 1981. Incredibly, the target goal was achieved.[44] The success was partly owed to the establishment of general trading companies (GTCs) in the mid-1970s. Shaken by the 1973 oil crisis and challenged by the rising tide of trade protectionism in the markets of advanced industrialized nations, Park pushed through the legislation of a law on GTCs in 1975 on the recommendation of the *chaebol*. Modeled after the Japanese *sogo shosa,* organized to deal with exports and imports of diversified products in multiple markets, the GTCs, it was hoped, would put limited resources to their best use.

From the standpoint of the state, the establishment of the GTCs was crucial to its goal of export growth. In the eyes of the *chaebol,* the GTCs became another instrument of conglomeration and diversification. The acquiring of a GTC instantly provided the *chaebol* with additional privileged access to preferential policy loans. The trading house also helped the *chaebol* in bringing small- and medium-sized producers into their network of vertical and horizontal *kyeyŏlhwa* (affiliation). There were also the benefits of building up high-quality manpower, gathering quality information on overseas markets, and acquiring managerial expertise inside the *chaebol* organization, which could assist their pursuit of new business opportunities. Moreover, because the *chaebol* were forbidden to own commercial banks, GTC export credits could help finance their sprawling industrial empires. The organization of *chaebol* came to look like a concentric circle of firms, with the GTC at the core, assisting affiliate firms with export credits, market information, and managerial expertise and coordinating their collective actions. By 1979, half of South Korean exports were handled by *chaebol*-owned GTCs.[45]

The Park regime was shrewd in utilizing export credits as both carrot and stick to discipline the *chaebol* in the direction of government goals. Every year, the Ministry of Commerce and Industry (MCI) announced the minimum amount of paid-in capital and total export volume, as well as the minimum number of export items, export destinations, and overseas branches, that a GTC had to meet to retain its GTC status. For those that met the requirements, the state banks provided loans up to the dollar amount on their letters of credit at preferential foreign exchange and interest rates. GTCs with exceptional export records were even exempt from showing their letters of credit in order to receive credit from domestic banks and could borrow up to 1.5 months' worth of their past export record.[46] Conversely, in the case of a GTC that failed to meet the target goals, the MCI immediately revoked its GTC license. During the 1974–1978 period, it was those *chaebol* with HCI affiliate firms and GTCs that grew into a formidable power bloc in the South Korean economy.

As in the case of launching GTCs in 1975, it was the *chaebol* that initiated the idea of exploiting the Middle East boom of the mid-1970s to earn badly needed foreign exchange to stabilize the South Korean economy and fund HCI-led economic growth. This period looked extremely gloomy for the resource-poor, export-dependent South Korea, with the 1973 oil crisis shaking it from its foundations by pushing up the price of crude oil from $1.75 per barrel to over $10 in less than two years. Whereas the Japanese automakers developed fuel-efficient cars on the basis of their technological capabilities to break out of the dual challenges of rising oil import bills and stagnating export sales, Chŏng Chu-yŏng looked to the Hyundai Construction Company rather than to Hyundai Motors for an exit strategy. He had no choice; Hyundai Motors, only established in 1967, was struggling to raise the local content of its products, let alone innovate with foreign technology. By contrast, Hyundai Construction had more than ten years of experience building infrastructure in Thailand and South Vietnam.

Hyundai went to the Middle East in the fall of 1975, with the same spirit of learning-by-doing that had proved fruitful in Southeast Asia in the 1960s. A breakthrough came when Chŏng Chu-yŏng successfully bid for the Jubail Industrial Harbor project in Saudi Arabia, the crown jewel of Middle East construction projects worth $931 million,[47] which was nearly half of South Korea's annual national budget. The state became aware of the vast opportunities to earn foreign exchange in the global recycling of oil money and swiftly changed gears in a way typical of Park. The MoF channeled massive policy loans, while the Ministry of Construction (MoC) relaxed regulation on overseas construction and restrained "excess competition" among South Korean construction companies bidding for construction projects in the Middle East through the formation of cartels. Taking these measures as the state's signal to emulate Hyundai, second-tier *chaebol* companies rushed into the Middle East construction market. Until the bubble burst in the mid-1980s, the boom was to provide South Korea with massive foreign exchange earnings with which to weather the 1973 and 1979 oil shocks. It is estimated that the earnings in the Middle East construction markets contributed about 10 percent to South Korea's GNP growth from the late 1970s to the early 1980s.[48]

In the areas of state guidelines and regulations too, the *chaebol* proved crucial in prodding the state to look into new ways to achieve its policy goals. The EPB came to learn about the new possibilities for raising funds in international markets when Daewoo became interested in pioneering this frontier. Daewoo's mid-level managers worked closely with mid-level MoF career bureaucrats, who defined their role as facilitating the business activities of private firms, to devise new regulatory rules on international financing.[49] Similarly, when the Ministry of Transportation (MoT) announced broad long-term guidelines to modernize the South Korean transportation system, Hyundai Motors quickly responded with its own plan in August 1973 to help the MoT realize its goal.[50]

As each of the *chaebol* dramatically expanded its empire during the 1970s to seize the business opportunities of HCI, it felt the pressures of further centralizing its corporate governance structures. As in the 1960s, the innovator was Samsung. The Samsung chairman's secretariat enhanced its responsibilities for strategic decision making and business monitoring and grew in personnel. The secretariat became the "brain" of the Samsung Group, establishing mid- and long-term goals for the entire conglomerate, coordinating personnel policy among the member firms, making strategic investment decisions, analyzing the impact of state policy and the trends of overseas markets, and providing support to member firms in the areas of public relations, overseas market expansion, and computerization, among others.[51] The secretariat grew to seven teams with 40 elite staff in 1972, and to twelve teams with 71 staff by 1978. By 1980, it was to have ten teams with 139 staff.[52] The other *chaebol* conglomerates soon came to look at the Samsung chairman's secretariat as a model. Ssangyong established a Central Office for Coordination in 1969, Sŏn'gyŏng (Sunkyong, which later became the SK group) an Office of Planning and Coordination in 1974, and Hyundai a Central Office for Planning in 1979.[53]

In 1978, Samsung pioneered another managerial innovation to strengthen its coordination capabilities by dividing up highly heterogeneous member firms into six smaller subgroups along the sectoral lines of trading, heavy and chemical industries, light manufacturing, electronics, construction, and services. The reorganization allowed the Samsung Group to balance the business requirements and goals of specialization and conglomeration, managerial professionalism and family control, and group control and firm autonomy. Through the reorganization, member firms came to work more effectively within a unified small subgroup structure while Samsung retained its family-management style.

From the standpoint of the *chaebol,* the Park era presented a tremendous opportunity for corporate growth as well as for corporate crisis. For those *chaebol* willing to work with Park under the rules of high risk and high payoff and capable of achieving the goals set by the regime, the state promised and delivered privileged access to resources. Whereas Hyundai was given lucrative government contracts, Daewoo was offered opportunities to take over and turn around insolvent business firms with generous loan packages. On the other hand, what Park perceived as a breach of the political exchange he had contracted for with the *chaebol* met with harsh punishment, as in the case of Samsung with the Han'guk Fertilizer incident. At the same time, however, Park's ability to wield the stick was a variable, not a constant, being formidable during the early years of his political rule, when strong preexisting ties between the state and the *chaebol* were lacking. As the ties between the two deepened and widened with the launching of FYEDP projects, and as Park committed political support in return for the *chaebol*'s entrepreneurial leadership, the state saw its stick getting shorter and thinner.

The Park era was one of reorganizing big business in South Korea. Of the ten largest *chaebol* groups of the early 1960s, only three remained in the same exclusive club of the Big Ten by the early 1970s. The number was to fall to two by 1980. Thus the 1960s were a turbulent time for the old *chaebol,* but a tremendously profitable time for the new *chaebol.* By the early 1970s, there existed a group of highly motivated *chaebol* owner-managers who were poised to take advantage of state subsidies to build the heavy and chemical industries. The Park regime rewarded their risk taking by limiting other firms' entry into HCI development, which conferred on the entrants oligopolistic profits with which to weather the difficulties of HCI projects. This strategic choice resulted in the segmentation of big business, with the Big Four undergoing the process of remarkable conglomeration and diversification within the heavy and chemical industries. The structure of big business created by Park's HCI drive remained the same until the Asian financial crisis shook the *chaebol* from top to bottom in 1997–1998.

The *chaebol* groups' business success sustained South Korean economic development in spite of the oil shocks and rising trade protectionism, and economic development in turn allowed the Park regime to acquire instrumental legitimacy and sustain itself. The *chaebol* were dynamic players, sometimes following Park, other times leading the state, and still other times partnering with multinationals rather than with the state in their search for corporate growth.

CHAPTER TEN

The Automobile Industry

Nae-Young Lee

SOME SAY THAT the rise of South Korean automakers was a miracle. Others portray it as a necessary outcome of the work of a technocratically driven developmental state, visionary entrepreneurs with a "can do" spirit, or their partnership based on asymmetric political exchanges. Still others argue that it was neither a miracle nor a product of a superior state or *chaebol* institutional capabilities. They brush automaker success aside as growth generated through a massive injection of resources rather than as a continuous improvement of productivity. For some, the automakers had an easy way to growth, with the state subsidizing their entry into new lines of production, taking over the costs of adjustment during crisis, and awarding rents with which to make up business losses. Chapter 10 takes the South Korean auto industry as a case study to critically review all three schools of thought. By tracing the industry's volatile history of hypergrowth, structural crisis, and top-down restructuring, and through identifying the formidable challenges of forging a national champion, it will argue that, in contrast to developmental state theories, the South Korean state pursued a strategy technocratically full of limitations, but successful in achieving an auto industry take-off because it not only backed the automakers with massive support but also let failing ones go under.

The problem with the miracle thesis is that by focusing on the outcome of hypergrowth, it ignores the politically and economically challenging processes of coalition building, risk taking, innovation, and restructuring which brought about that outcome. Indeed, the outcome was beyond all imagination. The South Korean auto industry was born only in 1962 with the assembly of a Nissan passenger car model, but by 2001 it had become the fifth-largest automobile producer and the sixth-largest exporter in the world. The outcome, however, looks like less of a miracle when the processes of the industry's development are analyzed. In a word, getting the industry to take off and grow into a major player in global markets was an extremely challenging task, and South Korea ended up paying massive political and economic costs in the process. What looked like a miracle was, then, a product of bold risk-taking, hard work, and great sacrifice over four decades.

The trajectories of the South Korean automakers show the challenging processes of developing a dynamic auto industry under national ownership. Saenara Motors, launched in 1962 as an assembler of Nissan passenger car models, fell only a year later in the midst of political and economic crisis. Sinjin Motors, allied with Toyota, took over Saenara in 1965, only to forge a joint venture with General Motors in 1972 amid the withdrawal of Toyota under the pressures of Zhou Enlai's "Four Principles" and Park's turn to the manufacturing stage of auto production. General Motors-Korea (GMK) underwent an equally rocky development, with its South Korean shares transferred from failing Sinjin to a state development bank (1976) to Daewoo (1978), while General Motors withdrew entirely from GMK (1981) in a dispute over management control and M&As (mergers and acquisitions). The MNC was to return to take over faltering Daewoo Motors in 2002.

The fate of other automakers was also tumultuous. Asia Motors produced cars with Fiat technologies for eight years (1968–1976) until Kia Motors—a latecomer with its own modern integrated assembly lines established in 1970—took it over to roll over Hyundai's expansion of market shares. As part of the state's effort to rescue the auto industry through competition-limiting industrial rationalization measures in 1980, Kia Motors was given a monopoly over production of commercial vehicles while Hyundai and Daewoo held a duopoly over the passenger car market. The market segmentation was lifted by the state in 1986 after the auto industry recovered from the worst of corporate distress. However, Kia Motors survived only twelve more years; it collapsed in mid-1997, dragging the entire economy into a severe liquidity squeeze. A year later Kia Motors was taken over by Hyundai.

The miracle, if there was any, was not that of the auto industry, but of Hyundai Motors, which introduced its own independent passenger car model in 1976 and began exporting to U.S. markets in 1986. By 2000

Hyundai Motors enjoyed a 70 percent share of the South Korean domestic market, boasted an annual production volume of 1.5 million cars, and annually exported more than 800,000 cars to over 180 countries. Even for Hyundai Motors, however, its "miracle" came only after it weathered severe crises in 1972, 1979–1980, and 2000. With its greatest patron—Park Chung Hee—assassinated in 1979, in particular, Hyundai Motors had to resist the pressures of economic stabilizers within the state to merge with GMK (now renamed Saehan) under unfavorable terms. Had it merged with GMK on the basis of 50:50 equity shares, as GMK demanded in spite of its limited market share and smaller asset size, Hyundai as a producer with the ambition to become a multinational with its own brand name rather than functioning as a subsidiary of an established MNC would have disappeared. That would also have removed much of the drive for export-led growth built into the *chaebol*-owned auto industry.

The history of South Korea's auto industry also raises doubts regarding those who explain its hypergrowth in terms of state or *chaebol* capabilities. The South Korean auto industry was a graveyard of would-be *chaebol*. If there was any message in its history of crisis-ridden hypergrowth, it is that the forging of a national champion was an extremely challenging task, even with the state backing the automakers with subsidized loans, license privileges, and trade barriers. Ironically, Park and his state bureaucracy were one of the root causes of their ordeal. His state apparatus did put its technocratic rationality to work, drawing up industrial policy and engaging in administrative guidance fashioned after the Japanese model of economic growth, but this did not protect the automakers from getting trapped in a destructive cycle of boom and bust, because the goal for which technocratic rationality was mobilized was anything but a technocratically rational one. Park intended to grow the infant automakers into a global player on a par with Japanese automakers in his lifetime, producing autos with their own national brand name under an economically sustainable cycle of model changes, and in collaboration with a dense network of nationally owned but foreign technology–licensed suppliers as well as an extensive global distributive system of sales and services. The goal contradicted South Korea's national capabilities. The initial conditions of a small domestic market, technological deficiency, capital shortage, limited human resources, and underdeveloped related industries made it the least likely place for developing internationally competitive automakers. Moreover, it was unlikely that MNCs would support a strategy that aimed to weaken their control over global markets through the forging of independent national champions.

Given Park's strong grip on the state, technocrats did not have the option of toning down, if not entirely rejecting, his goal. Rather, they ended up reversing the order of policy thinking, identifying the determinants of a *chaebol* assembler's successful take-off, from its supplier networks to backwardly- and forwardly-linked industries, to market size, as the target to be restructured and reshaped by the state-brokered take-off of the *chaebol* assembler. The transformation of a *chaebol* assembler into a national champion was not only a goal but also a means to create the industrial structures and market conditions that helped the assembler achieve that goal. That is, the *chaebol* assembler was to pull its suppliers and related industries out of underdevelopment with its hypergrowth. Such circular reasoning put the state on a highly risky policy track. To ensure that the growth of the auto industry triggered the development of related industries and vice versa, Park housed Hyundai Motors in Ulsan, which he had designated as a special industrialization zone in 1966, in part because it was on the coast, with a deep harbor that could accommodate large container ships, and in part because it was located in his native Kyŏngsang region. Moreover, Ulsan's geographical proximity to P'ohang, the site of an integrated steel mill then under construction, and to Pusan, South Korea's largest port, serving as the gateway to the Japanese market, worked in its favor. The strategy was to get the automakers and related industries to promote each other's growth as consumers and suppliers, respectively.

Similarly, Park, rather than being discouraged by the absence of globally competitive vendor firms, looked at it as a reason to develop *chaebol* assemblers. Again, they were to sow the seed for a dense web of robust vendor firms rather than wait until their suppliers' maturation to acquire international competitiveness. The political drive to build a thick network of vendor firms and subsidiaries began in 1973, when Park chose the automobile industry as one of the strategic sectors in the drive for heavy and chemical industrialization (HCI). To exploit the synergy effects of industrial clustering, many of the parts-and-components producers located their factories in Ulsan and other industrial zones near their assemblers. The state also emulated Japan in encouraging vendor firms to affiliate *(kyeyŏlhwa)* vertically and horizontally around a *chaebol* assembler, while at the same time supplying as many standardized parts and components as possible to multiple assemblers, with an eye to strengthening their ability to engage in coordinated actions, pool resources, and exploit greater economies of scale. The *kyeyŏlhwa* was South Korea's way to counter the obstacles of small markets, limited resources, and weak supplier networks through a state-brokered and -subsidized restructuring of inter-company relations and product standardization.

Likewise, the state's policy on corporate ownership structures was drawn more ideologically than technocratically. Park was aware of the dangers of MNC domination. Because multinationals chose sites and scales of production, automobile models, and their cycle of change from the perspective of their headquarters' interest in maximizing profits at the global level and operating a worldwide division of labor among its subsidiaries,[1] their market domination usually ended up stagnating the auto industries of developing economies. In a few large third world economies like Brazil, some of the multinationals were ready to transform their subsidiaries into a producer of major parts and components in the 1970s as part of their strategy to produce a "World Car," but none would have welcomed any of its subsidiaries' hypergrowth on the scale that Park envisioned for South Korean automakers. The market was too small, with annual domestic sales totaling less than 150,000. There was also a grave security risk.

The dangers of MNC domination, however, do not mean that the opposite strategy of maintaining local ownership by automobile producers with the goal of export promotion, rather than focusing solely on the domestic market, and of seeking maximum linkage effects, despite initial difficulties, was technocratically rational. But this was exactly what Park pursued. He assumed that locally owned automakers by definition had an organizational interest in producing cars under their own national brand name and developing into a national champion. The assumption would turn out to be correct only in the case of Chŏng Chu-yŏng (Hyundai) among his numerous *chaebol* partners. With this assumption, Park forged a dual alliance between the dirigiste state and local capital as the driving force to upgrade the auto industry. Although South Korean automakers imported key technologies and auto parts from MNCs, Park and his *chaebol* partners, especially Chŏng Chu-yŏng, resisted foreign domination by holding on to the principles of local ownership and national management. As Chŏng Chu-yŏng argued and Park agreed, no multinational was ready to join Park's vision of HCI, which, if successful, would compete with the MNC for a larger share in global markets on the basis of national brand name and product models. The strategy entailed high risk and high costs, given the formidable entry barriers of the capital- and technology-intensive auto industry.

To sum up, the "technocratic" strategies of maximizing linkage effects with related industries, consolidating vendor firms into a closely-knit web of *kyeyŏlhwa*, and maintaining the national ownership of the auto industry emerged out of Park's Napoleonic ambitions, his distinctive understanding of Japan's path to the modernity, and his nationalist beliefs and prejudices. To call such strategies "technocratic" hides as much as it reveals about South Korea's political and economic mechanisms of industrial hypergrowth. Certainly, the state behaved technocratically, searching for a strategy that most effectively achieved a given set of politically formulated goals within the constraints of resource scarcity. However, because those goals were set by a man who aspired to become a "Meiji," the state's technocratic strategy turned out to be a carefully calculated but still dangerous gamble, if not wishful thinking. The strategies' technocratic limitations were visible in policy outcomes. The South Korean automakers remained too small, too backward, and too poor to construct worldwide supply and marketing networks through the end of the Park era. The state's designation of the auto industry as a strategic HCI sector guaranteed massive financial incentives to those who pursued the state's goals, but the massive injection of resources aggravated surplus capacity and corporate distress. Through the Park era, the backward and forward linkage effects with related industries and vendor firms, as well as the ownership policy, proved to be more an obstacle than an opportunity for growth, as they undermined the fledgling auto industry's competitiveness.

Alongside the state's calculated but risky gamble to pursue Park's goal of forging a national champion, the local automakers' entrepreneurial spirit and managerial know-how shaped the auto industry's trajectory of development. The state created a business environment for risk taking, but it was the local automakers, especially Hyundai Motors, who actually took the risk of entering the manufacturing stage in a big way. They individually advised Park on broad policy guidelines and were ultimately responsible for implementing state policies. For the state to have its way, it needed business cooperation and business talent. Moreover, once the investment was made, the balance of power between the state and big business changed from one of state dominance to one of state-*chaebol* symbiosis, because the state defined the survival of the automakers, heavily financed by state loans, as in its own political interest. At the same time, the state apparatus became internally more fragmented and burdened with increasing interagency rivalry and conflict as it grew in the process of orchestrating the HCI drive. The expansion of the state's role, power, and resources ironically undermined state autonomy by provoking societal interests, especially the *chaebol*, to influence the state's exercise of power in the direction of their interests.

The importance of *chaebol* capabilities, however, should not be overemphasized. Different local automakers ended up pursuing different business strategies with varying levels of success, showing not only that state policy alone did not determine industrial performance, but also that the *chaebol* automakers varied strikingly in their corporate capabilities. Whereas Hyundai Motors pursued the high-risk, high-payoff strategy of developing into a locally owned exporter of independently designed passenger car models in the way Park wanted, Sinjin opted to form a 50:50 joint venture with General Motors in the hope that this move would minimize business risk and serve as a political safety net. Kia, as a distant third-ranked automaker, emulated Hyundai—but in very un-Hyundai ways, manufacturing an outdated Mazda model for its mini-export drive. The winner was Hyundai, which bet on the risky "Pony project" in the mid-1970s. That triumph came not in Park's lifetime, however, but in the mid-1980s with a steep rise in exports to U.S. markets. Then there were Saenara, Sinjin, and Asia Motors, which all fell while trying to become *chaebol*.

The main objective of Chapter 10 is to show that forging a national champion was a political game much more challenging for Park to play than it has been portrayed in developmental state theories and the *chaebol* literature. The problem was that the ambition to build a dynamic auto industry capable of challenging MNCs in Park's lifetime could not be technocratically achieved. Rather this ambition dragged the developmental state into calculated but dangerous policy gambles and taxed his financially overburdened *chaebol* partners with surplus capacity. Whatever technocratic and entrepreneurial capabilities South Korea's state apparatus and big business possessed—and they did have capabilities—those capabilities could not guide South Korea out of its destructive cycle of crises because of the overly ambitious goals that drove policy in the first place. Yet Park held on to his ambition. More incredibly, despite its vulnerabilities, the South Korean auto industry continued on its track of crisis-ridden hypergrowth, while Hyundai Motors laid the ground for its eventual transformation into a national champion. What made this possible was the combination of two seemingly contradictory measures. On the one hand, for the automakers that made Park's ambition their passion, he provided massive subsidized resources during good times while taking over a major share of their adjustment costs during bad times. At the same time, however, Park was not afraid to let failing automakers go under. On the contrary, he seized the opportunity for the state to thoroughly restructure failing automakers before or as part of their takeover by a third party. With bank debts rescheduled, excess workers laid off, and production lines streamlined under state support, Park thought the South Korean auto industry could start anew its task of forging a national champion.

Assembly Stage, 1962–1969

The development of South Korea's auto industry began in earnest in 1962, when local entrepreneurs were encouraged by the military junta to enter the auto market as assemblers of licensed foreign models.[2] Park and his staff sought to develop the industry not only for its own sake but also as an engine for growth for the myriad of related industries that fed into and out of the process of car making. Included in the sectors that Park hoped the auto assemblers would trigger growth were not only the parts-and-components sector of the auto industry but also the steel, machinery, electronic, and chemical industries. To promote the auto industry, the military junta adopted the Five-Year Plan for the Promotion of the Automobile Industry and the Law for the Protection of the Automobile Industry in 1962, which prohibited the import of finished vehicles, barred the import of parts and components except for the assembly of finished vehicles, and reduced taxes and tariffs on parts and components imported for the assembly of finished vehicles.[3]

The choice of the local producers who were to implement the 1962 policies was heavily influenced by political calculations, given intense factional struggles within the military junta. The mainstream, consisting of Kim Chong-p'il and his colonels at the Korea Central Intelligence Agency (KCIA), was then clandestinely organizing the Democratic Republican Party (DRP) to aid Park's 1963 bid for presidential power. They turned to the auto industry to raise some of the required political funds. Having become the junta's bridge to Japanese political and business leaders in his capacity as a key negotiator of diplomatic normalization of relations between the two countries, Kim Chong-p'il helped Pak No-jŏng, a Korean expatriate businessman living in Japan, win a license to assemble Nissan cars. Thus was born Saenara Motors, which began importing semi-knock-down (SKD) kits of Nissan's Bluebird model in 1962 duty-free to be put together in South Korea. The imported price of one SKD kit stood at 130,000 won, whereas the assembled vehicle fetched a price of 250,000 won in the marketplace. With this huge profit margin, Saenara was able to contribute political funds to Kim Chong-p'il. Saenara, for its role as both a pioneer in the automobile industry and a source of political funds, was granted tax exemptions for five years.

Despite its profitability, Saenara Motors collapsed in July 1963 when the junta could not let the company import SKD kits in the face of the shortage of foreign currency in the aftermath of the disastrous currency reform of June 1962. Moreover, not only the civilian opposition but also the rivals of Kim Chong-p'il within the junta began accusing him of working with Pak No-jŏng to earn monopoly profits. In a complaint to the National Assembly, Pak No-jŏng disclosed the amount of political contributions he had made.[4] Along with three other political scandals,[5] the Saenara incident provoked calls for the removal of Kim Chong-p'il from his positions of power in the KCIA and the forthcoming DRP. Kim survived the attack, but Saenara ended up under the joint management of the Ministry of Commerce and Industry (MCI) and Hanil Bank.

The second opportunity to establish an automobile assembler came with Park's electoral victory in 1963. With the transition to electoral democracy, most of the coup makers took seats in the National Assembly, contending for the position of a crown prince at the expense of losing opportunities to shape state policy. Moreover, the center of gravity in economic policymaking moved from the KCIA to state ministries because Park—more sure of his political legitimacy and public support after the 1963 elections—felt less need to fall back on the KCIA's clandestinely prepared economic shock therapies. The change came with the MCI's announcement of a Promotion Plan for the Automobile Industry in August 1964. Through the plan, the MCI intended to construct a parts-and-components sector around a single assembler, which would purchase the bankrupt Saenara. Fierce competition broke out among major industrial firms to take over Saenara with the expectation of monopolizing the automobile market. The bidding initially drew five companies, who were then joined by two firms, Sammisa and Sinjin, both of which had strong political ties to the ruling political coalition.

The bidding contest was seen as a proxy battle between two second-tier political leaders. Sammisa was backed by Kim Chong-p'il, the leader of the declining "mainstream" faction in the National Assembly, whereas Sinjin secured the political support of Yi Hu-rak, the chief of staff for the president and a central figure in the rising "anti-mainstream faction." Using his position as chief of staff, Yi tried to build his own political faction, which prompted him to think about fund-raising. To challenge Kim Chong-p'il's position as the heir to Park within the ruling elite, Yi needed allies in both the South Korean and the Japanese business communities, who would help him raise political funds just as Kim Chong-p'il's business associates had done for him during the junta years. The Sammisa-Sinjin rivalry also echoed the competition between Nissan and Toyota over the establishment of a foothold in the South Korean market with the normalization of relations in 1965.[6] Nissan drew on the ties it had established with Kim Chong-p'il from the days of Saenara Motors, whereas Toyota aligned with Yi Hu-rak.

The licensing committee members were MCI bureaucrats and Hanil Bank representatives. Their initial choice was Sammisa, which DRP politicians saw as attesting to the resilience of Kim Chong-p'il's mainstream faction. Then, two months later, the MCI and Hanil Bank reversed their decision and chose Sinjin as the new owner of Saenara, under the pretext of Sinjin's "superior quality," to quote MCI minister Pak Ch'ung-hun.[7] It was rumored at the time that Park himself ordered the MCI to overturn the initial decision because he was worried about Kim Chong-p'il's growing power.[8] One source of Park's own power stemmed from the uncertainty over whether there would be a presidential succession and who would be the heir in case Park opted for a power transfer. The resilience of Kim Chong-p'il's mainstream faction threatened to make him a de facto heir. Park chose to weaken Kim's source of political funds, Sammisa, in favor of Yi Hu-rak, who lacked personal charisma and thus posed less of a threat. Consequently, Sinjin took over the Saenara plant in November 1965 and began assembling a Toyota model, Corona, with a local content of 21 percent in May 1966 under a licensing arrangement.[9] With the production of the Toyota Corona, Sinjin saw its total assets increase more than tenfold over the next three years, from 300 million won in 1965 to 3.2 billion won in 1968. The domestic market for passenger cars and commercial vehicles increased rapidly, although the number of assembled vehicles still stood at the meager level of 30,096 units in 1968.

Ironically, the profitability of Sinjin became a source of its political difficulties. The auto industry drew the interest of South Korea's second-tier business groups, who were searching for ways to diversify. Tempted by the profitability of Sinjin, but also sensing the growth potential of South Korea's auto markets, newly established Hyundai Motors and Asia Motors petitioned the state for licenses to enter the industry. They argued that Sinjin was too dependent on Toyota's capital and technology, which prevented it from contributing to the development of a local parts and components sector. The criticism drew its power from Sinjin Motor's resistance to the state's pressures to raise the local content on the ground that the domestic market was too small. Sinjin simply wanted to maintain its assembly operations by continually importing Toyota SKD kits rather than replacing some of the imported parts with locally manufactured ones. This position, however, was politically untenable, because the press had already zeroed in on Sinjin's monopoly profits. The price of a Toyota Corona hit 870,000 won, whereas the same model was sold in Japan at less than half that price. Although the price differential was inevitable because the small number of cars Sinjin produced forced it to forgo economies of scale, it provoked public outcry, thus enabling Hyundai and Asia Motors to challenge Sinjin's monopoly status only four years after the passage of the 1964 Promotion Plan for the Automobile Industry.

Park and the MCI bureaucrats were themselves dissatisfied with the slow growth of the local parts and components industry and Sinjin's risk-averse strategy of remaining a mere assembler of imported Toyota SKD kits. Park had chosen the auto industry as a strategic sector for its massive linkage effects, but Sinjin Motors negated that rationale by choosing to live off monopoly profits. O Wŏn-ch'ŏl, then the assistant vice minister for mining and manufacturing at the MCI, evaluated Sinjin as too oriented toward short-term profit maximization and disinterested in contributing to the long-term development of the industry through a timely increase of local content.[10] Thus Park authorized the entrance of Hyundai Motors in 1967, followed a year later by Asia Motors. Hyundai produced vehicles with imported SKD kits and technology from Ford; Asia Motors produced passenger cars and buses under a technology license arrangement with Fiat. By 1968 the South Korean automobile industry had three assemblers—Sinjin, Hyundai, and Asia—with licensing arrangements with Japanese, American, and European multinationals, respectively. The entries soon backfired. With a wide variety of models produced inefficiently with relatively low domestic content ratios, the three assemblers were on the verge of becoming mere MNC-controlled inefficient automakers, much like those of Latin America.

Search for a Strategy, 1969–1973

Ironically, Park searched for ways to move the auto industry into the manufacturing stage precisely when the industry had become too crowded with the entries of Hyundai and Asia Motors. Moving from the labor-intensive assembly stage to the capital- and technology-intensive manufacturing phase would surely make the industry even more inefficient and the loan-financed automakers even more vulnerable to the danger of being unable to meet their payment obligations should a recession develop. Park knew of the danger, but would not let it stand in the way of his efforts to build a national champion. On the contrary, confident of the state capacity to relieve corporate distress and make industrial adjustments in hard times, and captivated by his own vision of HCI, Park ordered MCI minister Kim Chŏng-ryŏm in October 1968 to raise the local content of locally assembled vehicles. The question he struggled with was not whether, but how to move into the manufacturing stage. The technocrats were to answer that question.

In December 1969, with Kim Chŏng-ryŏm in control of the Blue House as the chief of staff, new MCI minister Yi Nak-sŏn made public a Basic Promotion Plan for the Automobile Industry. To develop the parts and components industry, schedules to increase local content were set up by the MCI for each passenger car model. The ministry also listed the auto parts chosen for domestic production. Presumably, the automakers' license to assemble cars depended on their timely implementation of the local content program. In parallel to these bureaucrats' stick, the Ministry of Finance (MoF) offered carrots, pledging to provide preferential access to foreign and domestic loans to the automakers that met the MCI-formulated local content schedules.[11] Then, in February 1970, Yi Nak-sŏn designated the construction of an engine plant as a concrete way to achieve the goals of the Basic Promotion Plan. To prevent the problem of surplus capacity from increasing to a threatening level, only one assembler was to be chosen among Asia, Hyundai, and Sinjin as the producer of engines for the entire passenger car industry, on the basis of three criteria: that it establish a joint venture with a multinational in the production of engines, that it export surplus engines in excess of domestic consumption, and that it involve as many domestic vendor firms as possible in the development of locally produced engines. The assembler chosen was expected to become a dominant producer, because the other two assemblers would use its engines for their products. By expressing its preference for a joint-venture operation, the MCI also prompted the assemblers to strengthen their foreign business alliances to secure the necessary technology. The parts and components industry welcomed these policies, because the higher local content requirement meant that they would be protected from imports in developing key auto parts.

The dominant assembler, Sinjin, was the first to respond positively to the new state initiative. In March 1970, Sinjin and its licensor, Toyota, submitted a plan to the MCI to establish a joint venture for the production of Sinjin automobiles, not just engines. It looked like Sinjin had formulated the winning strategy until the next month, when China's premier Zhou Enlai announced that as part of the "Four Principles," the Chinese would prohibit Japanese companies with business operations in South Korea or Taiwan from entering the China market. Five days later, Toyota decided to withdraw from South Korea in order to enter the China market, judging it to be potentially more promising than the South Korean one. Desperate to secure an alternative foreign partner, Sinjin contacted various MNCs until it hit upon General Motors.

Park enthusiastically endorsed Sinjin's partnership with GM for not only economic but also security reasons. The United States' 1969 Guam Doctrine that sought U.S. military disengagement from East Asia had instilled in South Korea a fear of abandonment. The entry of a major U.S. company like General Motors was judged as verifying continued U.S. commitment to the defense of the southern half of the peninsula. Taking advantage of these security concerns, General Motors was able to win major concessions in its negotiations with Sinjin. GM was to control the financing, receive a 3 percent royalty based on total sales, and charge a management fee of $750,000 per year. The result was the birth of General Motors–Korea in June 1972, a 50–50 joint venture with General Motors and Sinjin each investing $24 million.

Hyundai Motors also welcomed Yi Nak-sŏn's Basic Promotion Plan, but for a different reason. As a newcomer to the auto industry, Hyundai looked at the plan as an opportunity to surpass Sinjin in market share and technological leadership in one stroke. Characteristically, Hyundai aggressively approached Ford regarding the establishment of a joint venture, but it soon decided to go it alone, concluding that the two had unbridgeable differences on strategic issues ranging from the scope of the business to the size of exports to the control of management. As a multinational that needed to maintain the division of labor among its subsidiaries worldwide and interested in maximizing profits at the level of its entire global operations rather than with any particular business entity in that chain of production, Ford was insistent on limiting the joint venture to the engine plant. Ford was less interested in establishing a new manufacturing hub in South Korea than in transforming it into one of the sources of engines in Ford's global production network. By contrast, Hyundai wanted to develop the joint venture into an integrated automobile manufacturer rather than a mere engine producer. Linked with the issue of production was the issue of sales. Whereas Hyundai hoped to utilize the worldwide sales network of Ford to export the fully assembled vehicles of the joint venture, Ford was interested only in exporting the joint venture–manufactured engines to its other subsidiaries as goods internally traded within Ford's production chain.

As Hyundai geared up to proceed on its own, Park and his MCI bureaucrats reconsidered their options. South Korea was then in the middle of regime change, with Park imposing the *yushin* constitution top-down in October 1972 and plunging into the HCI drive in January 1973 to demonstrate the superior regime qualities of the *yushin*. Moreover, as detailed in Chapter 7, Park put in place an institutional mechanism of forced savings to back the *chaebol* groups' massive entries into the heavy and chemical industries with subsidized loans by establishing a National Investment Fund in July 1973. To back the HCI drive with industrial policy, the MCI also created three new posts of assistant vice minister as part of its effort to reorganize its functions, powers, and staff along the sectoral lines of HCI. One new division was to focus on the automobile industry. In other words, not only the Park regime's political interest in putting the auto industry on a new footing, but also its institutional capabilities to do so increased dramatically in 1972 and 1973 due to the launching of *yushin*. Consequently, Park approved of his MCI technocrats' critical reassessment of their previous attempt to develop auto assemblers through a high degree of linkage with the local parts and components industry. The outcome was the extremely ambitious Long-Term Plan for the Promotion of the Automobile Industry, which the MCI announced in April 1973 and the cabinet adopted in July of the same year.

Although the Long-Term Plan was much more carefully prepared than Yi Nak-sŏn's Basic Promotion Plan of 1969, it looked nationalistic to the point of being unrealistic. The emphasis on raising the ratio of local content remained as high as in the Basic Promotion Plan, but this time, the MCI required the additional development of "original" South Korean models. The idea was that of Kim Chae-gwan, who was brought in from the Korea Institute of Science and Technology (KIST) to take the job of the assistant vice minister of heavy and chemical industries. He saw that the development of original South Korean models was the key to breaking out of the auto industry's stagnation.[12] Up to that time, the South Korean industry had assembled their MNC licensors' passenger cars, whose models altered frequently not only to satisfy changing consumer tastes, but also to raise entry barriers to a prohibitively high level. Consequently the South Korean auto assemblers faced a severe problem of market size in two senses of the term. First, given the country's low per capita income, the domestic market for passenger cars was inherently limited. Second, the frequent change of models, in addition to the assemblers' desire to carry a full range of models with the goal of realizing economies of scope, resulted in the assembly of too many foreign models for too short periods, thus preventing the realization of economies of scale even more.[13] The inefficient assemblers, in turn, failed to serve as the engine of growth for the parts and components industry.

To break out of the vicious circle of too many models, too frequent model changes, too small a market, and too few linkage effects, the Long-Term Plan proposed to manufacture an indigenous South Korean model with an engine size smaller than 1.5 liters as a "citizen car" and to produce it on a much longer cycle than that used by MNCs. The plan also envisioned suppressing the demand for larger cars by levying a luxury tax while increasing the local content of citizen cars to over 95 percent by 1975. In addition, it pledged to promote the parts and components industry by designing a special industrial zone for vendor firms as well as by supplying loans in keeping with the new policy.[14] It was thought that more than 80 percent of the total domestic demand for passenger cars would be met by these indigenous models through diverse tax incentives. To protect the producers of the citizen car, the plan also allowed the assembling of foreign models of medium- or large-size passenger cars at a much lower local content ratio. The measure enabled the automakers to recover some of the losses incurred in the production of citizen cars through the sale of more profitable medium- or large-size cars.

Initially not only the Long-Term Plan but also the larger HCI drive met with skepticism from South Korea's two economic coordinators, the Economic Planning Board (EPB) and the MoF, who saw both as premature and too ambitious. The total number of vehicles produced in South Korea remained just 26,334 in 1973. But Park was determined to pursue his vision, believing that what economic disadvantages South Korea possessed could be readily overcome by its political advantages. Under the newly promulgated *yushin* regime, which concentrated political power in the Blue House, Park thought he could make a credible commitment to the development of heavy and chemical industries so that the *chaebol* would take the risk of entering the targeted sectors, including the auto industry. With an eye to strengthening the state's ability to mobilize resources, Park established a cabinet-level interministerial Committee to Promote Heavy and Chemical Industrialization and organized its planning corps under the office of the second senior secretary on economic affairs, O Wŏn-ch'ŏl, at the Blue House. With Park's unwavering support, O Wŏn-ch'ŏl was able to orchestrate HCI projects by getting the entire state bureaucracy to assist in their implementation. The specific task of upgrading the automobile industry fell to the MCI, which meant that Kim Chae-gwan not only was the architect of the Long-Term Plan, but also became its implementer. The question was which of the South Korean automakers would take the bait.

Hyundai's Pony Project, 1973–1979

The 1973 Long-Term Plan placed the auto industry at a cross-roads. By tying state subsidies to the production of indigenously designed citizen cars, the plan closely coincided with the interests of Hyundai, which wanted to produce its own models under a national brand for the export market after the breakdown of its joint venture negotiation with Ford. Indeed, demonstrating the close alliance that had developed between the MCI and Hyundai on the basis of their common interests in challenging the multinationals' global auto industry, the Long-Term Plan was prepared by Kim Chae-gwan in close consultation with Hyundai's management.

By contrast, GMK found it difficult to follow Hyundai Motor's example, even with the state's pledge that it would back up those who took risks. In 1973 GMK enjoyed the largest market share, 40 percent, and had no intention of export promotion, which could undermine General Motors' hold over the world market. Moreover, the Long-Term Plan weakened many of the advantages GMK enjoyed as an auto producer. With the introduction of tight regulations on the number of models and the cycle of model changes an assembler could produce and adopt, respectively, GMK was obstructed from exploiting its greatest source of comparative advantage, product differentiation. In addition, the high local content requirement reduced GMK's cost advantage by forcing it to rely on South Korean parts and components as much as its rival Hyundai did. Most detrimental of all to GMK interests was the plan's goal of developing an original model rather than pursuing the GMK strategy of assembling any of the many models it produced through its worldwide production networks. As part of an MNC with an interest in profit maximization at the global level, GMK believed it was economically irrational to develop a new model just for the small South Korean market. GM's South Korean partner, Sinjin, was also reluctant to pursue an independent strategy, because it profited from assembling foreign models that beat any Hyundai cars. The interests of both General Motors and Sinjin lay in maintaining the status quo.

Unlike in Latin America, where multinationals typically defeated their host governments' efforts at independent development, in South Korea the state prevailed for several reasons. First, because General Motors entered the South Korean automobile market only in 1971, its joint venture had not had time to construct a strong political base. Its cars' low local content made its business profitable, but also weakened GMK's political clout by depriving it of the opportunity to surround itself with parts and components producers with an interest in manufacturing GM models.

Second, as Peter Evans has noted, the role of the local partner of a multinational lies in the development of political safety nets for the joint venture, but unfortunately for GMK, Sinjin's political influence was on the wane. The political patron of Sinjin, Yi Hu-rak, was not in a position to intervene on the side of GMK. Before 1973, as chief of staff to the president (1963–1969) and the director of the Korea Central Intelligence Agency (1970–1973), Yi Hu-rak had the political clout to protect Sinjin. But he was ousted from power in 1973 after becoming implicated in army security commander Yun P'il-yong's "aborted counter-revolution attempt" of 1972 (see Chapter 6). The kidnapping of opposition leader Kim Dae-jung from Japan by KCIA agents in an attempt to destroy anti-Park movements abroad also made Yi Hu-rak a political liability rather than an asset for Park, because the scandal entangled Yi in diplomatic conflict between South Korea and Japan. Once he resigned from his post as KCIA director in 1973, Yi Hu-rak was never again part of Park's inner circle. Hyundai

Motors, by contrast, maintained a close working-level alliance with MCI bureaucrats and enjoyed Park's trust. The Hyundai Group's risk-taking business strategy fit well with Park's ambitious HCI drive, and consequently Hyundai's support for the Long-Term Plan strengthened Park's trust of MCI bureaucrats.

Third, despite a decade of hypergrowth, the state still enjoyed an upper hand over the private sector. With tight control over capital markets and the imposition of high nontariff trade barriers, the state had ample policy instruments with which to influence the private sector. In particular, state control over foreign loans enabled Park to reshape the private sector's investment patterns as well as to increase the autonomy of the state vis-à-vis both the *chaebol* and the MNCs.[15] Moreover, with second-tier *chaebol* like Hyundai and later Daewoo willing to take risks in order to catch up with the front-runners, Park had ample political space in which to play off the *chaebol* conglomerates against one another to achieve his goals. In addition, given the loan-financed nature of corporate growth, the expansion of *chaebol* groups did not mean that they were growing more independent; on the contrary, the rising debt-equity ratio made them even *more* dependent on the state.

Finally, it was Park's strong commitment to the nationalist automobile policy that worked most decisively against GMK. After the 1972 promulgation of the *yushin*, Park exercised absolute authority over South Korea's policy choices. In September 1973, Park issued a Directive for the Promotion of the Automobile Industry, by which he pledged to transform the willing assemblers into national champions with massive policy loans.[16] With Park's support of the 1973 Long-Term Plan, there emerged a powerful nationalist coalition of mercantilistic MCI bureaucrats, backed by O Wŏn-ch'ŏl's Blue House team of coordinators, on the one hand, and the independence-oriented Hyundai Motors, on the other. Together they competed with the internationalist coalition of General Motors and Sinjin for market share.

Once the 1973 Long-Term Plan put in place the new rules of the game and made massive state resources available for the would-be producers of citizen cars, it was the task of the automobile producers to transform the plan into a workable business strategy. In this sense, it was the *chaebol* more than the state that ultimately decided the success or failure of the plan in the marketplace. The local content increased and the parts and components industry grew as a result of the 1973 policy shift, but the production of indigenous models was a different story. Not only GMK but also Kia, newly in control of Asia Motors, was reluctant to develop genuinely original models in fear of a steep increase in business risks. The two chose to bring out the models previously produced by their licensors for European markets with only minor modifications under the new brand names of Camina and Brisa, respectively. Thus GMK and Kia accommodated the state only partly, manufacturing independent, but not original, models. Only Hyundai Motors developed an original model, Pony, against all odds.

As Park had to win over reluctant EPB and MoF bureaucrats with his charisma and power, Hyundai founder and owner-manager Chǒng Chu-yǒng had to overrule the skepticism of many of his men at Hyundai, who thought the financial and technological barriers too great. The Pony Project was pushed by Chǒng Chu-yǒng and his younger brother and the president of Hyundai Motors, Chǒng Se-yǒng. Chǒng Chu-yǒng was the man Park valued as his business partner—an ambitious, audacious personality willing to take on anything with a "can do" spirit. With his family's controlling shares of the Hyundai Group and under the opaque corporate governance structure of *chaebol,* Chǒng Chu-yǒng was able to introduce the Pony in the local market after three years of development in 1976. The citizen car became an instant hit, enabling Hyundai Motors to increase its market share from 19 percent to 39 percent in a mere year. By 1979, it was to command a market share of 51 percent. The introduction of citizen cars, coupled with a continued hypergrowth of per capita GNP, meanwhile helped expand South Korea's total number of auto production over seven times to 204,447 between 1973 and 1979. The success was owed to several factors.

First, the Pony Project succeeded because it was an integral part of the larger HCI drive, which provided Hyundai Motors with a supply of internationally competitive inputs. In particular, as shown in Chapter 7, the Pohang Steel & Iron Company, a state enterprise promoted as a national champion with Japanese reparation funds since 1967, had by the mid-1970s begun supplying steel products at a lower cost than the Japanese steel mills.[17] The rapid expansion of automobile production, based in part on the steel industry's timely provision of internationally competitive steel products, in turn contributed to the productivity and profitability of the steel industry.

Second, fortunately for Hyundai Motors, its development of the Pony coincided with an increasing liquidity in the international financial markets because of a massive infusion of petrodollars. After the 1973 oil crisis, global financial institutions began recycling the great sums of oil money by expanding their loans to oil importers at relatively low interest rates. Taking advantage of the large supply of petrodollars, some late developers, including South Korea, embarked on "indebted industrialization."[18]

Hyundai was a beneficiary of the ample liquidity, financing more than 70 percent of its required capital through foreign loans, which totaled $61.2 million by 1976. The automaker borrowed money from Suez Bank (France), Barclays (England), and Mitsubishi Bank (Japan), and the foreign loans were guaranteed by the state.

Third, the Pony Project yielded positive results because it effectively exploited the opportunities of collaboration provided by the highly competitive world automobile industry. In order to overcome the technological gap, Hyundai Motors had actively sought technological licensing arrangements since it had been established in 1967 with support from Ford. Once it launched the Pony Project, Hyundai Motors began diversifying its sources of technology. Ironically aided by its image of technological backwardness, which made MNCs underestimate Hyundai's potential as a competitor, Hyundai Motors was able to obtain technology from several sources in the development of its Pony model. The car design came from Italy, its internal combustion engine from England; and the engine block design, transmission, and axles from Japan.

Among foreign sources, it was Mitsubishi Motors that Hyundai came to rely on the most. In May 1973, Chŏng Chu-yŏng and Chŏng Se-yŏng visited Mitsubishi to request technological and managerial assistance in the development of the Pony, although its primary licensor since 1967 had been Ford. The transnational coalition building had begun the year before, when the Hyundai Group entered the shipbuilding industry with the assistance of Mitsubishi. Hyundai's Ulsan shipyard was a replica of the Mitsubishi shipyard, and Chŏng Chu-yŏng hoped to replicate the Hyundai-Mitsubishi alliance in the automobile industry. During the development of the Pony, the engineers of Mitsubishi Motors resided in Hyundai Motors' Ulsan plant to design the layout of the assembly lines and to supervise their construction. Hyundai engineers were also sent to the Mitsubishi plant to be trained by its engineers. Parallel to the training, Hyundai Motors began importing key parts and components of internal combustion engines, transmissions, and axles from Mitsubishi Motors. At the same time, Mitsubishi Trading Corporation supplied loans to finance the construction of the Pony assembly lines in the Ulsan plant. The Hyundai-Mitsubishi alliance in the automobile industry was part of the larger trend of South Korean–Japanese collaboration emerging across industries. In addition to the two countries' cultural similarity and geographical proximity, the organizational similarity of group-based investment coordination between the South Korean *chaebol* and the Japanese *keiretsu,* and the dense web of personal ties developing between the top managers of the two countries over years of collaboration contributed to the development of close ties between various industries of the two countries.

Fourth, massive state support was also crucial to the development of the Pony model. The Ministry of Finance had state banks provide policy loans at preferential interest rates based on the newly established National Investment Fund. It also exempted the automakers from paying corporate taxes for the first three years of a new plant's operations and returned up to 10 percent of the capital invested to the automobile producers as "investment tax credits."[19] Moreover, from the outset, Park made himself available to Chŏng Chu-yŏng to gather information on the automaker's needs.

Fifth, Hyundai Motors succeeded because its competitors blundered. In particular, the front-runner, GMK, made the strategic mistake of choosing the outmoded Chevrolet 1700 as its citizen car and selling it under the local brand name of Camina. The model was too heavy, too large, and too fuel-inefficient for the South Korean market, where the price of gasoline was one of the highest in the world. The 1973 oil crisis dealt a blow to the sales of the Camina, forcing GMK's market share down from 23 percent in 1975 to 16 percent by 1977. With the decline, the South Korean major shareholder of GMK, Sinjin, suffered financial difficulties and ended up selling its stake to the state-owned Korea Development Bank in 1976. When Daewoo purchased the original Sinjin shares in 1978, the joint venture changed its name to Saehan Motors and then to Daewoo Motors with the departure of General Motors in 1981.

Liquidity Squeeze and Adjustment, 1980–1981

For a moment, Hyundai Motors thought its victory was near. The automaker had defeated GMK, the joint venture of the world's largest MNC, in the South Korean market with its own indigenous model. Just as the Pony was introduced in the domestic market, moreover, Hyundai turned to the export market, shipping its citizen cars to Central American markets. The euphoria, however, soon turned into a sense of crisis as the exports failed to get picked up in developing economies. Entry into developed economies was unthinkable, given the low quality of the Pony, the prohibitively high marketing barriers, and the lack of advanced managerial know-how. To make the situation worse, the 1979 oil crisis buried the domestic market in a severe stagflation, throwing the entire automobile industry into a new vicious circle of rising interest rates, declining domestic sales, slow exports, and large excess production capacities. Moreover, politics took an unexpected turn with the death of Park Chung Hee in October 1979. Chŏng Chu-yŏng's greatest patron had suddenly disappeared. After a brief period of political opening, Chun Doo-hwan seized power via a military rebellion in December 1979 and a national subversion in May 1980, with the effect of aggravating the already difficult economic situation.

The year 1980 was the worst for the South Korean economy since Park's seizure of power in 1961, spreading rumors of its imminent collapse under the pressures of rising corporate distress. To deal with the issue of economic stabilization, as well as to clear the way for the launching of an authoritarian Fifth Republic (1980–1988), Chun Doo-hwan organized the Special Committee for National Security Measures (SCNSM). The SCNSM's Economic Committee became primarily responsible for restructuring the heavy and chemical industries, including the automobile sector. Within Chun Doo-hwan's inner policy circle, however, developing a consensus on how to deal with the problem of surplus capacity in the automobile industry was difficult. The familiar conflict between proponents of stabilizers and mercantilists resumed—but in the economically fragile and politically uncertain context of 1980 and 1981.

The proponents of financial stabilization consisted of the EPB, MoF, Bank of Korea, and Korea Development Institute (KDI), which all shared pessimistic views regarding the growth potential of the auto industry. In keeping with classical comparative advantage theories, they argued that South Korea's lack of technology and capital prevented the country from developing a competitive automobile industry on its own. Officials from the World Bank and the International Monetary Fund agreed, advising South Korea to concentrate on the development of its parts and components industry, not the assembling of indigenous models.

The mercantilist proponents of growth through the socialization of adjustment costs were made up of the MCI and its research wing, the Korea Institute of Economics and Technology. They believed that the South Korean automobile industry faced only temporary difficulties, which could be overcome by export promotion. Drawing on the insights of product lifecycle theory and the infant industry argument, the mercantilists argued that with the standardization of auto production technology around the world and the rising costs of labor in developed economies, competitiveness was rapidly shifting from advanced to developing countries. Therefore any drastic restructuring of the South Korean automobile industry would prevent South Korea from exploiting the window of opportunity to develop a locally owned automobile industry. In their eyes timing was crucial. The year 1980 should be not a moment of downsizing but a time of perseverance, with the state continuing its protectionist policies and promotional measures for the automobile industry with an eye to getting it ready for another round of hypergrowth when the global recession ended.

In the end, the SCNSM's Economic Committee settled on state-brokered mergers of failing automakers as a way to relieve the problem of large surplus capacity. The industrial rationalization measure proposed to merge Hyundai and Saehan into one passenger car producer and make Kia the sole producer of commercial vehicles. The measure represented the victory of EPB-led stabilizers, who hoped to reduce the number of automakers in the passenger car and the commercial vehicle sectors with the goal of realizing greater economies of scale and tapping the superior resources of General Motors. The idea profoundly aggravated market uncertainty. In a mere eight years since the launching of the 1973 Long-Term Plan, General Motors had changed its joint venture partner from Sinjin to the Korea Development Bank to Daewoo. Now it was under state pressure to team up with Hyundai Motors. Kia had likewise taken over Asia Motors, only to give up passenger car assembly lines in return for the monopoly on production of commercial vehicles. The 1980 merger policy was paradoxical in character. The stabilizers justified it as a measure to reduce the role of the state in economic management, which they blamed for causing severe surplus capacity, but ironically the merger policy ended up being extremely interventionist. It was the state, not the *chaebol,* which tried to orchestrate the state withdrawal from the market.

To reshuffle the automobile industry along the lines of the 1980 merger policy, the EPB-led stabilizers needed to overcome two hurdles. First, Daewoo and Hyundai had to agree on who would be the sole South Korean partner with General Motors in the newly proposed joint venture in the passenger car industry. Then there had to be another agreement between the South Korean partner and General Motors on the ownership structure of the new joint venture. Of the two issues, it was the first, concerning domestic ownership, that was easier to resolve. The breakthrough here came with the state's strategy of bringing about an intersectoral business exchange between Daewoo and Hyundai. In 1980, the two *chaebol* conglomerates were suffering from surplus capacity in the electricity generator sector along with the auto industry. Zeroing in on the pair's overlapping businesses, the stabilizers proposed that Hyundai and Daewoo each choose one sector and give up the other. The stabilizers expected Hyundai to choose the electricity generator sector, because they believed that the passenger car industry could develop only with help from General Motors, Daewoo's joint venture partner.

To the EPB's surprise, Hyundai opposed any idea of an intersectoral business exchange on the grounds that it was more competitive than Daewoo in both sectors, although it too suffered from surplus capacity. The persistent pressure from SCNSM eventually forced Hyundai to accept its merger plan, but when given the right to choose its sector for specialization, Hyundai chose the passenger car industry against the advice of the SCNSM's Economic Committee. After Hyundai's decision, Kǔm Chin-ho, chairman of the Industry Subcommittee of the SCNSM's Economic Committee, announced in August 1980 that Daewoo's share in Saehan Motors would be acquired by Hyundai Motors in exchange for Daewoo's takeover of Hyundai's electricity generator business and that Kia would be given the exclusive right to produce commercial vehicles in return for its exit from the passenger car industry. As their end of the bargain, both Daewoo and Hyundai would withdraw from the commercial vehicle sector.

Next the stabilizers turned to the issue of ownership shares between Hyundai and General Motors in the new joint venture. Six meetings were held in August and September of 1980 between the representatives of the two companies, only to become deadlocked over the issues of equity ratio and export. Hyundai argued that the equity share of General Motors in the new joint venture needed to be calculated on the basis of not only GM's share of Saehan Motors (50 percent), but also the total assets of Saehan and Hyundai Motors. Because General Motors owned a 50 percent share of the smaller of the two automakers, Chŏng Chu-yŏng argued that the equity share of General Motors in the new joint venture should be only 20 percent and that the management rights ought to be exercised by Hyundai. By contrast, General Motors insisted on having 50 percent of the equity, or at minimum 33 percent of the shares to enjoy veto power.

The conflict over equity shares and management rights reflected the irreconcilable differences in the two sides' marketing strategy. General Motors insisted that the new joint venture would be a subsidiary in GM's international production network, producing only models based on the multinational's design and technology. To be sure, GM proposed building a large parts and components production network in South Korea and selling that plant's products to the world market through the GM distribution network as part of its larger ongoing effort to redesign the division of labor among its subsidiaries with the goal of manufacturing "world cars." However, it was also keen on preventing its subsidiaries from disrupting its grand vision of specialization and integration within and through its internal organization by pursuing their own independent marketing strategy. To balance these two requirements, General Motors took the position that the new joint venture with Hyundai should export vehicles only through the existing sales networks of General Motors and that it should not export cars to any market already dominated by GM subsidiaries. Hyundai, by contrast, wanted to remain independent in management, freely selecting models for both the domestic and the export market without any restrictions.[20]

Given the differences in the two parties' definition of the mission, role, and organization of the joint venture, negotiations stalled until the military junta turned power over to the Fifth Republic with its leader, Chun Doo-hwan, ascending to the presidency in 1980. Upon the return to "normalcy," the MCI regained control of industrial policy and decided to nullify the August 1980 merger agreement between Hyundai and Saehan in the face of the deadlock in the Hyundai–General Motors negotiations. The U-turn was made in 1982 also because forcing a merger on unwilling private companies was criticized as an unconstitutional infringement on private property rights by both the *chaebol* and the media.

The political struggle over the August 1980 merger policy revealed the rapidly changing nature of the South Korean state and its relationship with big business. First, with the death of Park the state's policy orientation changed fundamentally in the early 1980s, with the EPB-led proponents of economic stabilization and liberalization replacing the nationalistic-mercantilist bureaucrats like O Wŏn-ch'ŏl in key decision-making positions. The August 1980 merger policy for the automobile industry was part of this larger political and economic change. The days of growth at all costs and extreme risk taking were over. The massive policy arsenal developed by the state, along with the authoritarian political mechanisms of control, was now harnessed for stabilization and liberalization. Second, the nullification of the merger policy also showed that after two decades of hypergrowth, the *chaebol* came to acquire the power to resist the state. The death of Park also helped strengthen *chaebol* power, because Chun Doo-hwan lacked the charisma, experience, and expertise that Park developed over the eighteen years of his rule. The strong state could no longer have its way when the private sector's interests and preferences diverged substantially from state priorities. The state needed the *chaebol*'s cooperation more than ever before.

With the breakdown of negotiations between Hyundai and General Motors, the automobile industry came to have a dual structure, with Hyundai and Saehan (its name now changed to Daewoo Motors) dominating the passenger car sector and Kia Motors producing commercial vehicles as a monopoly assembler. The nullification of the Saehan-Hyundai merger proved to be beneficial to South Korean national interests. The stagflationary crisis soon ended, and the auto industry entered another period of dynamic growth by the mid-1980s. The remarkable turnaround was brought by a boom in both domestic and export markets. In particular, Hyundai's successful entry into the North American market in 1984 constituted a turning point, enabling South Korea to possess an independent automobile industry that competed with MNCs under its own national brands. The success in exports had several causes.

First, the South Korean producers overcame some of their production and marketing deficiencies by strengthening their strategic alliance with MNCs. After 1982 Daewoo returned to its joint venture with General Motors and Kia developed an alliance with Ford and Mazda with the goal of obtaining advanced technologies and key parts and components, as well as securing access to the multinationals' marketing networks to enter the global marketplace. It was, however, the Hyundai-Mitsubishi axis that posed the greatest challenge to the MNC-centric order of the world automobile industry. In return for its support for Hyundai's export strategy, Mitsubishi took a 10 percent ownership of Hyundai in 1981 and raised its share to 14.7 percent by 1985. The Japanese automaker benefited from Hyundai's export growth through its role as a licensor of key technologies and a supplier of major parts and components. In 1987 Mitsubishi upgraded its alliance with Hyundai by selling Hyundai's Excel under the name of Precis through its marketing network in the U.S. market. Whereas Hyundai's close collaboration with Mitsubishi proved crucial to its export success in the small-size passenger car sector, the alliance offered Mitsubishi Motors an opportunity to catch up with Toyota and Honda in the U.S. market.

Second, U.S. trade policy toward Japanese automobile exports helped Hyundai's penetration of the North American market. The United States began pressuring Japan to impose voluntary export restraints in 1982. Faced with these rising protectionist challenges, but also under the pressure of a shift in comparative advantage away from low-end toward high-end automobiles, the Japanese automakers began shifting the focus of their production from small-size cars to medium-size and even luxury cars. This situation enabled Hyundai to enter the U.S. market for small-size cars in the mid-1980s.

Third, once the overseas markets for small-size cars opened up, it was the South Korean automakers, not other developing country producers, that rapidly filled the vacuum, because they possessed a relatively cheap but productive labor force. Until the "Great Workers' Strike" broke out in the aftermath of a democratic breakthrough in June 1987, moreover, the workers in the automobile industry, as in other heavy and chemical industries, were legally prohibited from organizing labor unions. The quiescent labor sector, depoliticized through military-like labor practices, was another contributor to the competitiveness of the South Korean automobile industry.[21] Labor productivity was much higher in South Korea than in Mexico and Brazil, although their wages were higher.[22]

Fourth, the auto industry's export success owed much to Park's original decision to develop a locally owned automaker within the structure of *chaebol* conglomerates. By encouraging local ownership, Park hoped to create an automaker that saw its interest to lie in challenging MNCs. By choosing his partner from *chaebol* groups, Park sought to build an automaker that tapped the resources of its affiliate companies in unrelated industries to overcome managerial, technological, and financial barriers. As he intended, Hyundai Motors, lacking resources, developed on the basis of pooling resources and sharing risks at the level of the entire Hyundai Group. The organizational strength of the group offset the weakness of the automobile company. Even Daewoo, the South Korean partner to General Motors in the joint venture, which presumably faced fewer organizational limitations than Hyundai Motors because it could draw on the resources of the world's largest multinational, was one of the newly emerging *chaebol* conglomerates in the 1970s. The organizational features of the *chaebol*, including cross-shareholding and cross-loan guarantees that put affiliate companies under the tight control of a single owner-manager, made it possible to mobilize resources for the targeted automobile sector in spite of, or because of, high business risks.[23]

Fifth, with the ambition to grow into a MNC-like producer of indigenous models, South Korean automakers strove to develop autonomous technological capabilities through extensive research and development programs and technological licensing. Total R&D expenses increased six times, from 36.6 billion won in 1984 to 228.3 billion won in 1990.[24] To be sure, the technological gap still remained huge into the mid-1990s, preventing Hyundai Motors from competing against global firms on an equal footing. Similarly, the construction of a stable long-term relationship between the assemblers and vendor firms in the spirit of *kyeyŏlhwa* improved the quality of parts and components and lowered their prices, but until the mid-1990s, this was not enough to make Hyundai stand on a par with the best of the global players. Nonetheless, the institutional infrastructure of Hyundai Motors' spectacular export success after the mid-1990s was being constructed during the 1980s and early 1990s by its investment in R&D, technological licensing, and integration of parts and components producers into its network of *kyeyŏlhwa*.

THE HISTORY OF the South Korean automobile industry represents the general pattern of industrial development under Park Chung Hee. Like the macro economy that successfully upgraded its industrial structure through state intervention and export promotion, the auto industry developed from the assembly to the manufacturing stage and progressed in the local manufacture of capital- and technology-intensive parts and components. Both the macro- and the micro-industrial stories tell of a developing country that changed its comparative advantage with a mix of private entrepreneurship and public initiatives. The costs of dirigiste hypergrowth were as high as its benefits. The economy ran into severe stagflationary crises in 1969–1972 and 1979–1982, and the automobile industry suffered from chronic surplus capacity. As the change of General Motors' partner in its joint venture from Sinjin to the Korea Development Bank to Daewoo in the 1970s, as well as the bankruptcy of Saenara in the 1960s, demonstrated, the South Korean automobile industry was not only the incubator but also the burial ground of would-be *chaebol*. The rise of Hyundai Motors and the demise of Sinjin were the different sides of the same high-risk, high-cost, high-payoff HCI drive.

The cases of Hyundai and Sinjin give a clue to South Korea's eventual success in forging national champions. Certainly, state subsidies, industrial policy, local ownership, *chaebol* governance structures, transnational alliances, "can do" spirit, and disciplined workforces put its infant automakers on a path to hypergrowth. But hypergrowth also inevitably ended in a bust, dragging many of its automakers to the brink of bankruptcy. To explain how South Korea's auto sector was able to get back on the track of hypergrowth rather than remain paralyzed, we need to look at Park's dealing with *chaebol* failures, not just *chaebol* successes. When faced with an automaker under severe distress, Park tried to jump-start it with state support as part of his end of his political bargain. However, Park was willing to let an automaker go under when he thought he had exhausted his options. Then he rammed through an extensive restructuring program, replacing its owner-managers with state-designated caretakers, rescheduling its debts, streamlining its lines of production, and laying off workers with an eye to recreate it into a business asset attractive enough for a takeover by a third party. Obviously such a restructuring entailed a huge cost. Nonetheless, it was an effective way to adjust without throwing away the failed automaker's production facilities, technologies, and skilled workers. Those assets were now in possession of its acquirer, to be used for the next window of opportunity for hypergrowth. In short, the hypergrowth was possible because Park was politically capable of and prepared to pay for the adjustment costs of hypergrowth.

CHAPTER ELEVEN

Pohang Iron & Steel Company

Sang-young Rhyu and Seok-jin Lew

IN EXPLAINING SOUTH KOREA'S macroeconomic takeoff, Park Chung Hee's leadership was one of many factors. By contrast, in the development of POSCO (the Pohang Iron & Steel Company), his leadership was the pivotal variable, dwarfing all others in determining the scale and speed of the effort. To recount the story of POSCO is to retell the story of Park as the soldier and the modernizer. When his people yearned to escape from the hunger they endured during the lean months of spring, Park envisioned the building of an industrialized nation, with the steel industry as the engine of growth for the rest of the heavy and chemical industries, from machinery to automobiles to shipbuilding to the defense industries.[1] "Steel is national power," said Park at the celebration of POSCO's tenth anniversary. Park put the steel industry at the top of his list of strategic industries as early as 1961, when he promulgated the first of his Five-Year Economic Development Plans (FYEDPs).

Beyond Park's own identity as a modernizer of South Korea in the style of Meiji Japan leaders, there were also domestic political factors that drove Park to the construction of a modern integrated steel mill. Lacking the credentials of a liberal democrat, Park portrayed his Democratic Republican Party (DRP) regime as a political force that promised to lift South Korea out of its poverty and military insecurity. Constructing an integrated steel mill on the scale of POSCO fit in perfectly with Park's strategy of legitimization based on performance. Steel was a measure of military prowess, economic modernization, and technological progress. By extension, it was also a living proof of Park's political leadership.

This is not to claim that Park's construction of an integrated steel mill constituted a mere instrument of political legitimization. On the contrary, it legitimized his rule only because it served real needs. Seoul lagged far behind P'yŏngyang in military capabilities when Park seized power through a military coup in May 1961. Military deterrence was secured only with support from his U.S. ally, but his relationship with that patron was anything but secure. Washington cracked down on his junta for toying with "socialist" economic ideas in June 1962 and even withheld aid to dissuade Park from extending military rule in March 1963. Moreover, as the Vietnam War escalated, there spread rumors of the United States relocating some of its troops stationed on the Korean Peninsula to South Vietnam. Anxious to tie his ally's hands, Park dispatched military troops to Saigon in 1965, thus forging a "honeymoon" *(milwŏl)* with Washington—but only for three years. South Korea's security dilemma worsened on all fronts. The North Korean guerrillas staged their mini "war of liberation," even coming close to attacking the Blue House in January 1968. The same year P'yŏngyang captured a U.S. reconnaissance naval vessel, the *Pueblo*, in the waters of the East Sea and again dispatched its highly trained guerrillas into Kangwŏn Province to test South Korea's military preparedness. In the face of the heightened North Korean military threat, the United States surprised Park by calling upon its Asian allies and client states to shoulder the burden of defending Asia from communist threats and swiftly moved toward an exit from the Vietnam War, one consequence of which was the withdrawal of the U.S. Seventh Infantry Division from South Korea by 1971.

South Korea was militarily vulnerable throughout the eighteen years of Park's rule. The value of steel as a defense industry traced its origin to both real and perceived security threats. To cope with the country's security challenges, Park argued, the South had to make building its own defense industry a national priority. Steel was the center of this political effort.

The powerful image of industrial linkage effects also gave added force to the plan for an integrated steel mill. As early as 1961, Park embraced the strategy of heavy and chemical industrialization (HCI) to surmount the obstacles of increasing trade deficits, dwindling foreign exchange reserves, and falling growth rates. Among the myriad heavy and chemical industries, it was the steel industry that Park had to develop first, because without a stable supply of quality steel, South Korea could not vertically diversify into other heavy industries upstream. Moreover, as a decade of hypergrowth dramatically raised the South Korean domestic demand for steel, much of which had been met by imports, producing quality steel products domestically would also alleviate balance-of-payments difficulties. By 1970, iron and steel were the country's second largest imports, next to crude oil. These rationales of industrial linkage effects and import substitution made the military security strategy of steel industry development a good economic strategy as well.

Not only driven by his own ambition to become a "Meiji," but also in need of justifying his rule with developmental showcase projects in addition to resolving military threats and clearing a way to HCI-led hypergrowth, Park never wavered from his goal of building an integrated steel mill after his seizure of power in May 1961. The issue was not whether, but how, to build it. Given the lack of capital, technology, and market, it was not surprising that Park's search for a viable strategy ended in repeated failure, until the dynamics of economic modernization and regional military security converged to support his lifetime fascination with the steel industry in 1969. Implementation proved to be far more challenging than the formulation of the goal of constructing an integrated steel mill.

Yet within thirty years of its establishment, the Pohang Iron & Steel Company (or POSCO, as it came to be popularly known in the 1990s) completely changed the global map of steel production. The World Bank, which had turned down POSCO's 1968 loan request on the grounds that South Korea had no comparative advantage in the production of steel, by 1981 called it "the world's most efficient producer of steel."[2] The bank's original assessment, however, was not without reason. During the 1960s just ten developing countries had integrated steel mills, half of which had an annual production capacity of more than half a million tons. South Korea trailed far behind, in possession of only small steel mills with electric furnaces. Depending on imported scrap iron, these mills all suffered from high production costs. Even by the standards of the third world, South Korea was a late-late developer, fit only for the production of light industry goods like textiles, shoes, and wigs. But it nevertheless plunged into the development of an integrated steel mill only a few years after horizontally expanding into light industry.

The transformation of the South Korean steel industry is the story of one single company, POSCO. Formally founded in April 1968, the construction of its integrated steel mill began in April 1970 and was completed in July 1973 with an annual production capacity of 1.03 million tons. This Phase I alone cost $123.7 million. The expansion of production capacity continued rapidly, culminating in the completion of Phase IV by May 1983, which endowed POSCO with an annual production capacity of 9.1 million tons. With the death of Park Chung Hee in October 1979, the task of turning POSCO into a world leader in the production of steel fell on the shoulders of Pak T'ae-jun (often transliterated as Park Tae-joon), whom Park handpicked in 1968 to construct and manage POSCO. The company completed the building of its second mill, Kwangyang Integrated Steel, in 1992 to boost its total annual production capacity to 21.1 million tons. By 2000 POSCO was the second-largest steel producer in the world, surpassed only by Nippon Steel, with an annual production capacity of 28 million tons. To achieve this rank, POSCO had increased its production capacity by 28 times in twenty-seven years. More incredibly, from the very first year of its operation, POSCO was profitable. By 2000 its operating profit rate ran 18 percent. Only the China Steel Corporation of Taiwan performed better.[3]

How was this "miracle" possible? Or was it a miracle? The existing literature on South Korea's industrial upgrading is firmly entrenched in either developmental state theories or neoclassical economics, but we argue that neither approach adequately explains the history of POSCO.[4] Although works on South Korea's developmental state bring out the centrality of the state's mission, ideology, organization, strategy, and "embeddedness" in shaping its pathway from the periphery to modernity, they lack an analysis of the political process by which the South Korean state made strategic choices and implemented its chosen route of development. Moreover, they zero in on the study of POSCO development after 1973, when most of the politically challenging decisions on its scale of production, funding, ownership structure, transnational coalition, and marketing had already been made. Focusing on the process and including the pre-1973 period of strategic decisions brings out three stories that have been hitherto inadequately dealt with in developmental state theories and neoclassical economics.

First, there was nothing "technocratic" about South Korea's choice of developing a modern integrated—let alone, export-driven—steel industry. As the World Bank diagnosed in 1968, South Korea was without markets and resources to tackle the task. Yet, as early as March 1962, under pressure from the military junta, four *chaebol* groups joined forces to establish Korea Integrated Steel, Ltd., only to see it collapse owing to a lack of investment funds. However, rather than discouraging South Korea, the failure only led to its renewed attempts to construct an integrated steel mill in 1964 and 1967. That it was Japan's 1969 provision of reparation funds rather than commercial loans that eventually enabled South Korea to launch its steel project attested to the centrality of Park and his ambition, not his state's technocratic prowess. The goal of building an integrated steel mill cannot be explained by global market conditions or national capabilities. It was Park who decided to build POSCO against all odds. To explain his preferences and interest, Chapter 11 looks into not only the interplay of military security, domestic politics, and economic imperatives as understood by Park, but also his lifelong ideological vision of "rich nation, strong army" *(puguk kangbyŏng)* modeled after Meiji Japan.

Second, the analysis of South Korea's efforts to overcome its lack of technology, capital, and human resources in developing POSCO into a player in the world market reveals that the key to its success lay as much with Park's manipulation of great power relations as with its state's "Weberian" internal organizational resources. It took seven years for Park to hit on a foreign policy strategy that got international geopolitics to provide South Korea's strong, autonomous state with an opportunity to develop a transnational coalition of the technology, capital, and human resources required for the construction of an integrated steel mill. Until 1969 many of Park's initiatives were defeated by the American refusal to assemble an investor group of international financial organizations, bankers, and multinational corporations (MNCs) behind Park's vision of statist development. That left only the option of using the Japanese reparation funds for the construction of POSCO, which profoundly influenced not only its technology and marketing strategy but also its organizational ethos. The funding also put POSCO on a financially strong basis from its very inception, as Japan provided reparation funds on a noncommercial basis, either as grants-in-aid or as low-interest loans, to compensate for colonial wrongdoings. Chapter 11 makes the building of a transnational coalition the key story of POSCO and foreign policy the central part of economic policymaking.

Third, unlike developmental state theories, the story of POSCO puts the issue of moral hazard and rent seeking at the center of analysis. On the one hand, POSCO combined features that bred moral hazard. The company was funded by the politically driven Japanese reparation funds, whose noncommercial character presumably gave stakeholders greater leeway in rent seeking. Moreover, it was a state-owned enterprise (SOE) with a governance structure allegedly incapable of keeping under control the forces of rent seeking and moral hazard. Lastly, whereas Park opted to construct an oligopolistic industrial structure in each of the heavy and chemical industries reserved for the *chaebol* in order to balance the conflicting requirements of competition and concentration, he made POSCO a monopoly. Consequently, the risks of rent seeking and moral hazard, which were built into the macroeconomic growth machine built by Park (see Chapter 7), were that much greater. Yet POSCO was profitable and dynamic, growing into a world player within a mere decade. This spectacular performance requires a multi-level analysis encompassing a wide set of variables, from POSCO's unique political relationship with Park and the state bureaucracy, to its extensive transnational networks with the bureaucrats, bankers, big business, and Liberal Democratic Party (LDP) bosses of "Japan, Inc.," to the internal organizational workings of POSCO, including corporate strategy, managerial practices, and company unionism. At the center stood Pak T'ae-jun, POSCO's founding president. Enjoying an unparalleled degree of trust from Park and an extensive delegation of power, Pak T'ae-jun maintained the internal cohesion of POSCO's state-business alliance and transnational coalition at all levels of corporate life by serving as political entrepreneur, mediator of interests, facilitator of dialogue, and business strategist all at the same time. Only forty-one years old when appointed in 1968, Pak T'ae-jun stayed on as POSCO's top leader until he joined the National Assembly as a Democratic Liberal Party (DLP) member in 1992.

The Wrong Start, 1961–1969

Military Junta Years

The frustrating search for a viable formula of development for the steel industry began with the military junta. South Korea was then not a fertile ground to build a modern integrated steel mill. The gross national product stood at only $1.9 billion, and per capita income roughly $80. Moreover, the country's first electric furnace-based steel company began operation only in 1963, producing a meager twelve tons of crude steel. In lieu of the capital, technology, and markets required to construct a modern steel industry, the junta was determined to sow its seed through the mobilization of political power. The junta was then in the middle of prosecuting the *chaebol* for the wealth they had allegedly hoarded through illicit means during Syngman Rhee's First Republic (1948–1960). Although the junta initially wavered between the radical position of imposing heavy penalties in the interest of satisfying the public demand for justice and the moderate stance of light fines to protect economic stability, it quickly came to link the issue of illicit wealth accumulation with its industrial policy with an eye to transform the *chaebol* into a partner for growth. The idea was to lure the *chaebol* into the junta's pet industrial programs, including its steel mill project, by linking the reduction of fines directly to their entries into strategic industries. As part of this effort at arm-twisting, the junta invited the top *chaebol* groups to bid for an entry license for the steel industry in October 1961.

Running for political cover, the Federation of Korean Industries (FKI), the umbrella business association established by the *chaebol* at the prodding of Park, welcomed the junta's initiative. After reviewing the many investment plans announced by the junta, the FKI chose Samhwa as its candidate for pursuing the integrated steel mill project. But the attempt failed to bear any fruit. The project was revived in January 1962 as the FKI renewed its effort to reach a political *modus vivendi* with Park through its participation in FYEDP projects. Four *chaebol* groups jointly launched a Private Investment Council with the explicitly stated goal of developing the South Korean steel industry.[5] With public and private funds, they established Korea Integrated Steel, Ltd., in March 1962, and signed an agreement with a West German steel producer for a feasibility study in April. The venture fell apart when it failed to secure investment funds both domestically and internationally.

The problem was that despite an endorsement by the Van Fleet Commission, a private American advisory group, the request of Korea Integrated Steel for funds got nowhere with the United States Agency for International Development (USAID) or with the United States Export-Import Bank. One reason for their refusal was the danger of sending the wrong signals regarding U.S. policy on the issues of military rule and fiscal stabilization. The Kennedy administration was then twisting the arm of Park and his mainstream faction to set a date for the restoration of civilian rule as well as to keep inflation under control through budget cuts and tax increases. To approve Korea Integrated Steel's request for loans when Park was strenuously resisting U.S. efforts at democratization and stabilization was judged to jeopardize United States interests. Besides, the USAID argued that the top priority of the junta should be not the steel industry but the energy, transportation, machinery, and communication sectors. The U.S. denial of the requests made the Van Fleet Commission instantly deem the integrated steel mill project not feasible, because it was only with the U.S. provision of low-interest loans and grants-in-aid that the international financial community would join in support of the project.[6] The commission soon dissolved itself.

In July 1962 came a third attempt at the steel mill project—this time, from the Economic Planning Board (EPB). With an eye to securing Park's trust, the superministry proposed the creation of an international financial consortium around the World Bank and the United States Operations Mission (USOM) in charge of administering aid in South Korea. Unfortunately for the EPB, USOM was then using its aid as an instrument both to streamline Park's ambitious first FYEDP through the readjustment of investment priorities and strategies and to force Park to deliver on his earlier promise to democratize.[7] USOM's pressure on Park to change his target goals on the money supply, budget, foreign exchange reserve, and price stability to more realistic levels increased throughout 1963, culminating in Park's abandonment of his inwardly-focused unbalanced growth strategy based on heavy and chemical industrialization. Park could not pursue HCI without U.S. support, because without a dynamic domestic capital market, it was only through close collaboration with USOM that South Korea had any chance of getting the seed money to finance HCI projects. The EPB's attempt at jump-starting the integrated steel mill project was defeated by this larger political and economic conflict with USOM over the issues of macroeconomic growth strategy and democratization.

The signs of a U-turn in economic policy, however temporary, surfaced as early as December 1962, even before the United States confronted Park head-on with the question of the restoration of civilian rule and used aid to pressure Park to retreat in March 1963. The previous December, the EPB had successfully persuaded Park to scale down his HCI ambitions until the economy was ready to tackle the task. Park heeded the EPB's advice because he had no choice. Since, under U.S. pressure, Park had given up on the KCIA-initiated idea of financing HCI with the money "frozen" through the currency reform of June 1962, he thought he could only rely on the private sector to implement FYEDP projects. The dependence on the private sector, in turn, meant that Park had to give a green light to the revision of the first FYEDP because no *chaebol* was capable of pursuing HCI projects without U.S. endorsement and loans. Unlike the original drafting of the first FYEDP in 1961, in which the EPB competed with the military junta, *chaebol* owner-managers, professional economists, and U.S. aid officials for influence, the plan's revision was thoroughly dominated by the EPB, resulting in a shift of policy emphasis from import-substitution strategy with the steel industry at its core toward a strategy of export promotion focusing on light industry. The advocates of HCI-led unbalanced growth had to wait for another opportunity for vertical integration.

On the other hand, for Park, the change of policy direction toward export-promotion in 1964 was tactical, not strategic. He chose to slow down rather than to scrap his HCI drive. Rather than plunging into a "big push" with a wide array of heavy and chemical industry projects launched simultaneously across multiple industries, Park became more selective in his choice of HCI projects. Among those selected for continued efforts at development was the steel industry. In light of the alterations in South Korea's overall strategy of modernization that came with Park's approval of the revised first FYEDP, the Ministry of Commerce and Industry (MCI) engaged in an extensive discussion of the industry's fundamental importance, focusing on:

1. Whether to include the steel industry in the category of "strategic sectors" deserving a concerted program of state assistance;

2. How to secure the capital and technology required for its development, and what budgetary programs to cut in order to channel resources into the steel industry;

3. Whether to nurture the steel industry as an export sector from the
very outset of import substitution, thus raising the target scale of
production to an internationally competitive level; and

4. Whether to entrust the task of developing the steel industry to the
hands of the private or the public sector.

As expected, the result of these internal debates was the MCI's reaffirmation of the goal of constructing an integrated steel mill on an internationally competitive scale, which was widely known to be Park's preference and also in the organizational interest of MCI. Nonetheless, the
painful experiences of the 1961–1963 period made the MCI and EPB
come up with a new strategy to deal with the structural obstacles Park and
his FKI partners had tried to grapple with since 1961. Reflecting Park's
"can do" spirit and his obsession with steel, the MCI and EPB unequivo-
cally reconfirmed the steel industry as a strategic sector, but also proposed
to make it an export sector, thus putting into motion Park's fourth attempt
at constructing an integrated steel mill. The South Korean economy was
then engulfed by the vision of an export drive after the model of Japan.
The decision to pursue an export-led steel industry had the effect of dramatically raising the size of funds needed, because export competitiveness
rested on economies of scale. Partly because of this upward adjustment of
target goals and partly because of the *chaebol* groups' failure to assemble a
transnational coalition of investors in 1961 and 1962, the MCI and EPB
also opted for public ownership of the integrated steel mill. Building an internationally competitive integrated steel mill was too big a project for any
one *chaebol* group. Entrusting the monopoly production of steel to a single *chaebol* would also entail the additional cost of politically alienating
the rest of the South Korean business community and causing a public uproar over distributive implications. The only remaining unanswered question was how to secure the money and technology required for the development of a state-owned and export-oriented integrated steel mill.

The Wrong Partner

The failure to bring in the United States as a partner or a patron in the development of an integrated steel mill in 1961 and 1962 did not lead Park
to look elsewhere for potential investors in his fourth bid to construct an
integrated steel mill. Even when Park backed the *chaebol* groups' recruit-

ment of a West German steel producer for a feasibility study in 1962, he looked to the United States for financial support. In his state visit to the United States in 1965, Park even went out of his way to inspect an integrated steel mill in Pittsburgh and discuss the possibility of developing an indigenous steel industry with Koppers. The hope to partner with the United States continued into 1967, because he thought that the trust and support of the superpower he had won through the dispatch of combat troops to South Vietnam would result in his hoped-for donor's change of heart. Although huge Japanese reparation funds were ready to flow into South Korea as the result of Park's normalization of relations with Japan in 1965, he hoped to construct an integrated steel mill on the basis of U.S.-brokered commercial loans and/or international aid. Yet the United States still could not or would not take on the role of a partner or a patron. In the eyes of U.S. policymakers imbued with the neoclassical conception of economic rationality and a static view of comparative advantage, Park's steel mill project was based on wishful thinking or, even worse, on recklessness.

In addition, USOM had been urging South Korea to become less dependent on U.S. aid by diversifying its sources of capital to Japan. This encouragement was consistent not only with the United States' long-standing policy of reducing grants-in-aid since it had begun to register a trade deficit in 1958, but also with its long-standing military security strategy to integrate East Asia's "free countries" into a loose regional alliance system, with Japan increasingly sharing the burden of regional and peninsula security as a junior partner of the United States. For this, the United States had been pressuring Japan to supply more development funds for the East Asian region, as well as normalization of its diplomatic relations with South Korea.[8] To make the USAID and United States Export-Import Bank even more reluctant to finance the development of the South Korean steel industry, U.S. steel producers were also worried about losing the South Korean market to newly established local producers at a time when Japanese and European steel producers were threatening the U.S. home market and saturating the world market.[9] Nonetheless, Park still looked to the United States for leadership when he announced the integrated steel mill project with the promulgation of the second FYEDP in 1967 in the middle of his presidential campaign. Based on the MCI-EPB policy review since 1964, the second FYEDP designated the steel industry, along with the petrochemical and machinery industries, as South Korea's "core" sector. The drive to build an integrated steel mill reached a new height when Park dismissed deputy prime minister and EPB minister Chang Ki-yŏng in October 1967 for his failure to make any progress on fund-raising. Pak Ch'unghun was then made EPB minister with explicit instructions to launch

POSCO. To raise money, the EPB jump-started its negotiations with the Korea International Steel Associates (KISA), which it had established with Koppers, Blaw-Knox, and Westinghouse Electric International from the United States, Demag and Siemens from West Germany, Wellman Engineering from the United Kingdom, Ensid from France, and Impianti from Italy in December 1966 with the goal of constructing an integrated steel mill. Japan did not join KISA because its steel producers could not reach a consensus on the goal and method of participation. In October 1967, KISA reached an agreement with Pak Ch'ung-hun to build an integrated steel mill with an annual production capacity of 600,000 tons.

KISA soon collapsed, however. In November 1968, after a feasibility study, the World Bank recommended that South Korea give priority to its machinery industry rather than to its steel industry.[10] According to the bank's "Evaluation Report of the [South] Korean Economy in 1968" submitted to the Third General Assembly of the International Economic Consultative Organization for Korea, plans to develop an integrated steel mill were premature because of the lack of capital, technology, and market.[11] South Korea's comparative advantage was thought to lie in the labor-intensive machinery industry.[12] After the World Bank's negative appraisal, KISA's British and West German members declined to finance the project. In April 1969, USAID urged the EPB to support the country's existing small-scale electric-furnace steel mills rather than seeking to construct a new integrated steel mill. Questioning South Korea's ability to repay any KISA-incurred foreign debt, the World Bank refused to provide a loan. The United States Export-Import Bank, too, announced that it would not provide loans.[13] Without support from its member countries and international lending agencies, KISA soon dissolved. Like Chang Ki-yŏng, Pak Ch'ung-hun was also dismissed—but in June 1969, after several more unsuccessful attempts at mobilizing international support for the steel project.

The Japan Card, 1969–1973

Another "Japan, Inc."

As KISA was collapsing in May 1969, the indefatigable Park began toying with the idea of engaging in political, rather than commercial, negotiation to secure Japanese consent to the use of reparation funds for the steel mill and adopted a two-track strategy. Park entrusted the EPB with negotiations at the intragovernmental level while employing newly established POSCO's Pak T'ae-jun to do the groundwork for negotiations with Japan through his talks with the Japanese private sector. The change in Park's strategy was signaled by the appointment of Kim Hak-ryŏl, one of his most trusted aides, to the post of deputy prime minister and EPB minister in June 1969. The EPB negotiators formally proposed that some of the Japanese reparation funds be allocated to the POSCO project.[14] They expected Japanese steel producers to assist POSCO if much of the funding was to come from reparation funds, permitting the Japanese to construct POSCO with Japanese plants and technology.

The bilateral talks were begun informally even before the dismissal of Pak Ch'ung-hun in June 1969. POSCO president Pak T'ae-jun, in his role as a facilitator, pursued the strategy of first contacting Japanese big business for support and then approaching Japanese LDP bosses and bureaucrats on the basis of the response from Japan's business circles. The goal was to get Japanese big business to lobby for POSCO from within Japan on behalf of South Korea.[15] In February 1969, three months before the United States Export-Import Bank formally turned down POSCO's request for a loan, Park dispatched Pak T'ae-jun to meet with the leaders of the Japanese steel industry.[16] Although Japanese steel producers and plant manufacturers feared that support for POSCO might boomerang and create a rival able to compete on the world market, they, as expected by EPB, kept their misgivings to themselves and came out in support of the POSCO project as a means of getting a share of the new markets created by reparation monies.[17] In response to Pak T'ae-jun's overtures, Fuji Steel, Yawata Steel, and NKK submitted a positive appraisal to EPB in August 1969 on the basis of their joint feasibility study.[18] The report became a basis for bilateral discussion at the Third Annual Korea-Japan Ministerial Meeting and was instrumental in persuading the Japanese state to support the POSCO project.[19]

Aside from delivering a positive report to the political authorities, leaders of the Japanese steel industry also lobbied for POSCO in the corridors of the Japanese bureaucracy. Initially, the idea of tapping the reparation funds drew support from Japanese steel producers, plant manufacturers, and LDP politicians, but not bureaucrats, except the Ministry of Foreign Affairs. Because the 1965 Normalization Treaty stipulated that any diversion of the reparation funds for projects not enumerated in the original agreement required prior consultation with and consent of the Japanese government, the Japanese business and political elite's endorsement of the EPB's proposal caused interministerial conflict in Japan. The Japanese finance ministry, concerned that the reallocation could cause a budget shortage, opposed the plan. Japan's Ministry of International Trade and Industry was also in opposition, wanting to guard Japanese export interests from potential South Korean competition. But with the support of

LDP politicians and business leaders, the foreign ministry was able to override these two ministries. Nagano Shigeo of Fuji Steel and Inayama Kazuhiro of Yawata Steel led the drive, arguing that the economic development of South Korea was the key to the prosperity and security of Japan.[20] "The future fate of the Japanese industries," Nagano Shigeo stated in a newspaper interview, "totally rests on the five hundred million people of Indochina, the natural resources of Indonesia and the prosperity of [South] Korea fighting communism [on] the front-lines in Asia."[21]

In bilateral negotiations, South Korea followed the likes of Nagano Shigeo and Inayama Kazuhiro in appealing to regional security interests. As Park's messenger, Kim Hak-ryŏl justified the use of reparation funds as part of Japan's responsibility to share South Korea's burden of fighting the cold war as a front-line state for the entire "Free World," including Japan: "[South] Korea is building its economy while fighting North Korean military aggression. In order to ensure peace and prosperity in the Asia-Pacific region, Japan with its strong economy needs to cooperate with [South] Korea, [who disproportionately bears the costs of military deterrence for the entire region] with its army of six hundred thousand. The POSCO project is a perfect opportunity for [building security] cooperation between the two countries."[22] Park thus asked Japan to pay some of the costs incurred by South Korea to secure a favorable regional security environment.

By contrast, Japan's calculation was more complex. Economically, its business community saw the launching of POSCO as an opportunity to make a deep inroad into the South Korean economy, which not only increased Japanese plant exports but also established a new division of labor within the steel industry between Japan and South Korea. The establishment of a Japanese presence in a strategic South Korean sector as critical as the steel industry was also judged to put the Japanese *keidanren* groups in a position of strength to penetrate related heavy and chemical industries. Moreover, through the use of reparation funds, Japanese producers could collaborate without incurring any financial risk. Political stability and peace on the Korean Peninsula were also critical to Japanese national interests, which Japanese politicians and bureaucrats thought the POSCO project served well. Japanese conservatives believed that Park's strong political leadership, coupled with the developmental state supporting modernization, would enable South Korea to overcome the political, economic, and security challenges of the 1970s. Coming to the aid of the integrated steel mill project also provided Japan's ruling LDP with an opportunity to show its U.S. ally its commitment to sharing the cost of regional military security.

Equally critical, unlike the United States and the World Bank with their neoclassical stance, Japan evaluated the POSCO project through its own time-tested dynamic theories of comparative advantage and recognized South Korea's ability to learn quickly with Japanese assistance. Japan had no ideological inhibitions holding it back from promoting the development of an infant steel industry, because it had grown out of poverty through the same belief in state activism. The two countries talked in a political language they both readily understood. Interestingly, after Japan's decision to support the integrated steel mill project in September 1969, the World Bank reappraised it as viable, so long as South Korea provided necessary infrastructural support, including the construction of ports, roads, and water service. The Japanese pledge to provide reparation funds in the form of grants-in-aid and low-interest loans instantly cleared away the World Bank's fear of a financially vulnerable POSCO.

The deal was finally sealed at the Third Annual Korea-Japan Ministerial Meeting in August 1969. Under political pressure and aware of the prohibitively high barriers against the construction of an integrated steel mill on a commercial basis, Kim Hak-ryŏl adopted brinkmanship tactics, bluntly stating that there would be "no joint communiqué unless Japan agreed to the construction of POSCO" using Japanese reparation funds and technology. The Japanese agreed, thus setting in motion the construction of the steel mill. In September of the same year, Japan set up the Akazawa Commission to coordinate Japanese actions. The former head of Fuji Steel's foreign operations, Ariga Toshikiko, oversaw the transfer of funds and technology in his capacity as the director of the Japan Group, a consortium of Japanese companies involved in the POSCO project. The Japan Group handled all procurement of machinery and equipment, worth $107 million, from Japanese sources. The export of a steel plant amounted to another several million dollars, which the Japanese steel industry welcomed as a way to overcome market difficulties created by the United States' imposition of voluntary export restraints (VERs).

That business, political, and bureaucratic leaders agreed to back POSCO within a mere nine months of negotiations was remarkable, given Japan's slow policymaking processes driven by the principle of consensus building. The singularly decisive force moving Japanese policymaking processes forward arose from the fact that the project, as proposed, required only the diversion of part of the already committed preferential loans earmarked as reparation payments. To be sure, there was a limit to which the EPB could build a transnational alliance using a reparations-based strategy. With the funds soon exhausted, the bilateral economic relationship between South Korea and Japan soon reverted back to commercial relations driven primarily by profit motives, prompting POSCO to put its steel mill on a profitable basis as quickly as possible. POSCO was born out of political negotiation, but its survival required competitiveness in the world marketplace. Park was its mother and the EBP its midwife, but its husbandry needed a capable CEO, in addition to the continued support of its mother and midwife. That CEO was Pak T'ae-jun.

Developmental State

As chief of staff Kim Chŏng-ryŏm recalled, Park remained the "driving force" behind the POSCO project after 1969, too.[23] Wielding even greater power and authority than in the 1960s, Park made sure that interministerial bickering would not slow down the construction of POSCO and obstruct its profitable operation. During the 1970–1973 period alone, Park made thirteen visits to the construction site to demonstrate to the state bureaucracy his unequivocal interest in the project. Equally critical, he had Pak T'ae-jun report directly to him on the recruitment of top managers.[24] Moreover, upon Pak's plea, Park exempted POSCO from making contributions to his political party's coffers. He was not to let POSCO falter under political pressures after all the troubles he had gone through since 1961.

Interestingly, Japan joined in this effort to put POSCO on the right track. As part of the deal, the Japanese steel producers asked Park to strengthen state capabilities to establish a solid institutional foundation for POSCO. Echoing their request, Akazawa Shouichi, head of the Japanese Economic Planning Agency's coordination bureau, gave South Korean deputy prime minister Kim Hak-ryŏl three prerequisites for Japanese cooperation in the steel industry in his capacity as the chief of the Japanese delegation:

1. The South Korean state should continue playing an active role in the mobilization of domestic capital in order to minimize the financial risks and costs entailed in the construction and operation of POSCO;
2. As in Japan, South Korea should enact a special industry law in support of POSCO in order to ensure POSCO a stable supply of electricity and industrial water at discount prices; and
3. The South Korean state should assume responsibility for constructing the infrastructure for POSCO, including the building of a breakwater and rock wall.[25]

Park agreed, ordering the EPB in June 1969 to design a comprehensive plan to promote the development of the project. In collaboration with the

Ministry of Commerce and Industry, the EPB drafted a Steel Industry Pro-motion Act (SIPA) in January 1970. Following Akazawa's advice, the SIPA stipulated that only a steel producer with an integrated steel mill with an annual production capacity of more than 100,000 tons would be eligible for state support, from long-term, low-interest, and state-guaranteed for-eign loans, to financial subsidies for raw material procurement, to state construction of ports, railroads, paved roads, and other infrastructure. Be-cause of the stipulation on production capacity, POSCO was the only steel producer legally eligible for such support in South Korea.

The EPB could have made the promotion act exclusively for POSCO, but it chose not to do so by drawing up an industry law. Apparently, the EPB feared that a special law tailored only to the needs of POSCO would run the risk of making POSCO a perpetual infant company, constantly looking to the state for subsidies and frequently captured by external rent-seekers, including bureaucrats, politicians, and business forces. By con-trast, adopting an industry law would keep POSCO on its toes and pres-sure it into raising productivity because under an industry law, entry was, in principle, not closed to outsiders. Provided that a would-be steel pro-ducer met the scale requirement, that company could become eligible for the same state support as POSCO. The possibility of industry entry by an-other business firm was very low at that time, given the prohibitive entry barriers. Yet the possibility was left open, which the EPB hoped would force POSCO into productive activities. The same entry principle, more-over, would leave the excluded private business groups less frustrated. The existing electric furnace-based steel producers could endure with the hope that they too would be able to meet the scale requirement and enjoy state support through growth.

POSCO's Pak T'ae-jun opposed the adoption of a special company law even more aggressively than the EPB. Pak argued that the state could inter-vene in support of POSCO as extensively under a general industry law as under a special company law, and that the risk of POSCO's becoming a captive of rent-seekers was much higher in the case of the latter. To mini-mize inefficiency, Pak also argued that the general industry law should be time-bound, to be terminated after the completion of POSCO's expansion stage. Presumably, the prospect of the termination of the law's benefits would give POSCO an incentive to build up its comparative edge through innovation in the short run. In the long run, this stipulation would under-cut the *chaebol* groups' entry into the steel industry. The would-be *chaebol* steel producer would be unable to enjoy state support at the level of POSCO because, by then, the time-bound industry law would have been terminated. Moreover, by enabling Pak to argue that he had a specific deadline to meet in making POSCO a self-sustaining profitable business venture, the specification would have provided him and POSCO with an unprecedented level of freedom from the state bureaucracy. However, Pak T'ae-jun was frustrated by EPB bureaucrats, who prepared the Steel Industry Promotion Act as a general industry law without any time limit. The bill was duly enacted by the National Assembly in January 1970.

By the time POSCO completed the construction of its integrated steel mill in 1973, it boasted powerful patrons and effective intermediaries working on its behalf within the country's innermost policy circles. The central figure was its CEO, Pak T'ae-jun himself. Having served as the chief of staff to then-junta chairman Park Chung Hee in the first year of military rule, Pak T'ae-jun enjoyed the unswerving trust of the president.[26] Park was always ready to uphold Pak's stand on both strategic and technical business issues, with an eye to strengthening Pak's political credibility within the state bureaucracy, the Democratic Republican Party, and POSCO itself, because Park knew the importance of the protection of CEO prerogatives if he was to achieve his political goal of modernization. Pak T'ae-jun remained "Mr. POSCO" with easy access to Park through the very end of the *yushin* regime in 1979, deciding with Park virtually every strategic business issue pertaining to POSCO.

Working in close cooperation with Pak T'ae-jun inside the state bureaucracy was the EPB. The two had the combined resources required to put POSCO on the right track. Whereas Pak had Park Chung Hee's personal trust as a professional manager with absolute loyalty to Park, the EPB boasted of Park's institutional confidence after its successful orchestration of an economic takeoff in 1964. They had made a great team in 1969, with the EPB negotiating the terms and conditions of Japanese support at the ministerial level and Pak backing that negotiation with his private talks with Japanese steel producers and LDP bosses. Later, interests of the two diverged over the Steel Industry Promotion Act, but after this brief conflict, the EPB and Pak T'ae-jun collaborated closely to achieve their common goal of making POSCO an efficient state enterprise.

The relationship between Pak and the EPB was not zero-sum. On the contrary, with the division of labor constructed by Park, Pak T'ae-jun and the EPB were both tsars in their respective spheres of influence. Whereas Pak T'ae-jun enjoyed a high level of managerial autonomy regarding POSCO's internal issues, the EBP was the implementer within the state bureaucracy of Park's ambition to transform South Korea into a major steel producer. The superministry transmitted Park's policy decisions and Pak T'ae-jun's business ideas to the wider state bureaucracy, monitored bureaucratic execution of presidential orders, and drew up a division of labor among relevant ministries to provide POSCO with a concerted program of state support. That South Korea developed POSCO in a coherent, effective, and coordinated manner owed much to the availability of the EPB as the executor of Park's presidential vision. Equipped with powers to allocate the budget and approve foreign loans, the EPB was taken seriously by all state actors. The others cooperated with the EPB in the hope of winning EPB support both in the budget and in foreign loans, without which no programmatic action was possible, given their centrality as the source of financing. The support of such a superministry became part of Pak T'ae-jun's leverage in securing assistance from line ministries.

In fact, EPB was as much an "owner" of the POSCO project as Pak T'ae-jun was. With Park's delegation of power, the EPB thoroughly dominated other state ministries in the formulation of POSCO policy. The MCI was legally in charge of the steel industry,[27] but it was viewed as at best a junior partner in the launching of POSCO or, at worst, a sectoral ministry captured by the small-size, electric furnace–based steel producers, to be kept in close check if the EPB was to carry out Park's vision of catching up with the Japanese steel industry—ironically, with Japanese money and technology. Even the elite Ministry of Foreign Affairs (MFA) had to move aside to give the EPB the spotlight in negotiations with Japan over reparation funds and technology licensing. Under the special Presidential Order of June 7, 1969, it was the EPB, not the MFA, that headed an interministerial task force for the construction of POSCO to coordinate the MFA's negotiations with Japan on the use of reparation funds, the MCI's preliminary preparation of the Steel Industry Promotion Act, Pak T'ae-jun's business strategy, and the development of the infrastructure of POSCO, led by the Ministry of Construction (MoC).

POSCO's Search for Autonomy, 1973–1981

Building a Second Integrated Steel Mill

Even before completing the construction of POSCO in July 1973, Park planned to expand its production capacity radically. The HCI drive was already in full swing by early 1973, with the state announcing myriad development plans, policy guidelines, and political manifestos for a wide range of heavy and chemical industries, many of which the MCI and other line ministries had been preparing since the late 1960s. What had been isolated instances of line ministries drawing up a wishful list of projects became merged into a concerted, integrated program of HCI and, in the process, was transformed into an even more ambitious plan to upgrade the South

Korean industrial structure. The deteriorating condition of military security put the HCI drive on a qualitatively different plane as well. With President Nixon's visit to China in 1972, the U.S. Seventh Infantry Division's withdrawal from South Korea in 1971, and the U.S. military disengagement from South Vietnam in 1972, Park's urgency in developing the steel industry as part of South Korea's modern defense industries rose dramatically. Politically, too, the HCI drive made sense for Park, who was in need of a showcase project to justify the launching of his authoritarian *yushin* constitution in October 1972. He also faced the triple woes of falling growth rates, worsening balance of payments, and declining foreign exchange reserves, all of which he hoped to reverse with the half-import-substitution, half-export-promotion of heavy and chemical industries.

The launching of HCI profoundly strengthened the status of the steel industry within the hierarchy of the national agendas. Park looked at the steel industry as the engine of deepening industrial development. This change of perception within the inner policy circles led to the announcement in July 1973 of plans to construct a second integrated steel mill upon the completion of POSCO. To support the simultaneous development of the shipbuilding, electronics, machinery, and nonmetal materials industries, Park called for increasing the South Korean steel production capacity from one million tons in 1973 to ten million by 1980. That required not only POSCO to undergo expansion, but also the construction of a second integrated steel mill.

The 1973 HCI drive also brought a shift in the balance of power within the state bureaucracy. As HCI began, the EPB, as the lead agency in charge of macroeconomic growth and stability, argued for a more moderate shift toward HCI, whereas the MCI, as the agent of industrial transformation, advocated a massive entry into the heavy and chemical industries. Park favored an even more radical change, prodding MCI to raise the scale of its plans to the level of the best of Japan's industries. Park's intervention resulted in the declining influence of the EPB. Eventually Park had the newly established cabinet-level Heavy and Chemical Industrialization Promotion Committee (HCIPC) make strategic decisions, with EPB-MCI bureaucrats then translating those decisions into feasible policies. To ensure bureaucratic loyalty and control, Park had his second senior economic secretary, O Wŏn-ch'ŏl, a former MCI assistant vice minister already transferred to the Blue House in 1971, steer the HCIPC as head of the HCI Planning Corps (see Chapter 7). Nominally under the prime minister–chaired HCIPC, the Planning Corps prepared plans, guidelines, and strategies for the members of the HCIPC to review and approve. In its role as a secretariat, the Planning Corps came to influence the agenda of the HCIPC and structure the options of Park in decisive ways. Under O Wŏn-ch'ŏl's patronage, the Bureau of Steel at the MCI came to dominate the expansion of POSCO as well as the construction of a second integrated steel mill.

Such an upgrading of the steel industry in the hierarchy of national priorities posed not only an opportunity for POSCO, but also a serious challenge to its status of national champion. In November 1973, Park established Second Integrated Steel, Ltd., with its equity capital provided entirely by the state. Renamed Korea Integrated Steel, Ltd., in September 1974, the company signed a joint venture agreement with U.S. Steel to construct an integrated steel mill with an annual production capacity of seven million tons. The foreign partner was to provide 20 percent of the required investment. The challenge was thwarted only because the U.S. company demanded that it be guaranteed a 20 percent profit margin. Moreover, the South Korean negotiators could not accept U.S. Steel's demand that the South Korean state block POSCO from entering the market for steel plate. In April 1975, POSCO absorbed Korea Integrated Steel, Ltd., as part of its internal expansion program. Ironically, it was the foreign steel producer's effort to keep POSCO from diversification that tipped the state toward the protection of its monopoly status in 1974. Until 1978 there would be no talk of launching a second integrated steel mill to break that monopoly.

The real test of POSCO's ability to guard its interests came when its third expansion phase neared its end in 1978. With the scheduled completion of Phase III, the issue of whether South Korea should build a second integrated steel mill resurfaced. This time, second senior economic secretary O Wŏn-ch'ŏl called for the Hyundai Group's entry into the steel industry with the goal of creating a private competitor for POSCO. The MCI and the Ministry of Construction (MoC), by contrast, supported POSCO. A deadlock ensued until Pak T'ae-jun met with Park on October 26, 1979, a few hours before his assassination. The aging president sided with POSCO. Although objections were raised at the ministerial level, Park's decision was honored by Chun Doo-hwan's Fifth Republic (1980–1988). With it, POSCO came to consolidate its dominant market position.

Going It Alone

The slogan at POSCO was "Catch Up with Nippon Steel." To do that, the company had to strengthen international competitiveness, which was possible only when POSCO increased its own capacity for technological innovation and expanded production to meet world standards. In 1981,

POSCO announced its plan to construct the Kwangyang Steel Mill in South Chŏlla Province and approached Japanese steel producers for support. This time, however, the earlier transnational alliance was not to repeat. The world steel industry was suffering from severe surplus capacity, and the global market was in a deep recession. Moreover, to the Japanese steel producers' surprise, POSCO had proved to be a formidable challenger to the Japanese steel industry, undergoing four phases of expansion without hurting its profit level. The month of August 1981 even saw South Korean steel exports to Japan surpass South Korean steel imports from Japan, causing an outcry among Japanese steel producers, who believed that they had inadvertently undermined their market position by assisting POSCO. Accordingly, Nippon Steel turned down POSCO's 1981 overture and even tried to give the Kwangyang project a bad name in global markets through its influence at the International Iron and Steel Institute. Only Chairman Yoshihiro Inayama of Keidanren supported the Kwangyang project, but even then only at the "personal level" in the words of Pak T'ae-jun.[28]

POSCO transformed the challenge into an opportunity to diversify its sources of loans, technology, and production facilities. Austria and West Germany were particularly responsive, providing production facilities at low prices in order to reverse their falling export receipts. Alarmed by their willingness to cooperate with POSCO, but also fearful of losing the South Korean market for production facilities, estimated at $2.3 billion, some of the Japanese changed their stance and promised technological cooperation, which enabled POSCO to construct the Kwangyang Steel Mill.[29] Having strengthened POSCO's ability to independently raise funds abroad, engage in technological innovation, and capture new export markets through the realization of economies of scale, Pak T'ae-jun was able to assemble a coalition of foreign technology licensers, plant suppliers, and bank lenders for the Kwangyang investment project on a strictly commercial basis.

The leadership of Pak T'ae-jun proved to be an even greater asset for POSCO after the death of Park in 1979. Before the demise of the *yushin* regime, Pak T'ae-jun served as the link between POSCO and the ultimate center of power, Park Chung Hee. From warding off political party pressures for financial contributions to the struggle against foreign lobbyists' pressures for concessions[30] to the defense of POSCO's organizational interests in interministerial turf wars, it was Park who swung the balance of power in a direction favorable to POSCO. The president was a safety net, protecting POSCO from rent-seekers and bureaucratic intruders during its formative years and giving it the time it needed to build up its corporate identity, institutional autonomy, and technological capabilities to grow out of the infant stage. When Park died, Pak T'ae-jun faced a true test of his leadership, which he passed masterfully. He was a model "network organizer," to borrow Ken-ichi Imai's concept describing the Japanese style of political organization.[31] Consolidating the powerful support group he had built up for POSCO within the South Korean state bureaucracy and the ruling political party as well as among foreign steel producers, Pak T'ae-jun himself became the safety net for POSCO after October 1979.

With Pak T'ae-jun's network warding off would-be rent-seekers, POSCO was able to decide its investment, procurement, and outsourcing policy autonomously according to the requirements of global markets, even during the Fifth Republic. That was unusual among South Korea's state enterprises, which were notorious for being heavily influenced by outsiders in personnel and investment policy. In addition to its insulation from external political forces, POSCO also had a diverse array of support from the developmental state that ensured large profits. With these state supports, POSCO was able to finance the four phases of expansion, the results of which were a greater exploitation of the economies of scale, an enhancement of international competitiveness, and a reasonable level of profits. The virtuous cycle of profitability and expansion also strengthened POSCO's political autonomy. Since the mid-1990s, POSCO has been able to raise funds directly in capital markets, freeing it from dependence on the state for subsidies and loans and, conversely, from vulnerability to external political intervention in internal business operations.[32]

THE CONCEPT OF "strong state" is inadequate in explaining the successful development of POSCO into a national champion. Much more critical was the establishment of a developmental coalition with all crucial actors with the necessary resources on board. The coalition building was an extremely challenging task for Park, even with the massive carrots he could and did offer to potential coalition partners. The outcome was a spectacular success, but the process by which South Korea got there was nothing spectacular. Even with the strong state's guarantee of a stable supply of subsidized policy loans, trade protection, license privileges, and industrial peace through repressive company unionism, it took a decade to build an integrated steel mill on the scale Park envisioned.

POSCO's success was the product of leadership and risk taking. Without Park's unswerving commitment to the development of the South Korean steel industry and Pak T'ae-jun's ability to gain the support of political leaders, bureaucrats, and business elites both at home and abroad, POSCO could not have become what it is today. These two great political entrepreneurs secured funds for POSCO only after repeated failures, and they protected its institutional integrity from powerful external rent-seekers during its formative years. It was the enormous dedication and leadership of Pak T'ae-jun and Park Chung Hee that guarded and nurtured POSCO into a world-class steel producer.

The political leadership that proved crucial for POSCO's success involved either risk taking or recklessness, depending on the ideological baggage of who is doing the evaluating. A series of foreign lenders from USAID and the United States Export-Import Bank to the World Bank to eight KISA member-states turned down Park's request for funds because his vision of making South Korea a "steel power" *(ch'ŏlgang kangguk)* contradicted the wisdom of neoclassical economics. South Korea's ability to secure Japanese support in 1969 did not imply that the Japanese thought differently. Despite Japan's talk of dynamic comparative advantage, its LDP bosses, *keidanren* leaders, and bureaucrats decided to support the POSCO project only because it was to be funded by the reparation funds, because it was judged as serving Japan's geopolitical need to bring South Korea firmly into a U.S.-centered regional security alliance, and because it was expected to remain an inefficient infant industry. Among the three rationales, the first two were not economic, but political. The story of POSCO has a happy ending; it succeeded. But the process of developing POSCO was often mired in setbacks, making its success anything but inevitable, necessary, or natural. It was politics, not economics, that made possible the development of POSCO into a world-class steel producer.

CHAPTER TWELVE

The Countryside

Young Jo Lee

SINCE THE MOSTLY left-leaning peasant organizations were eradicated in the course of the revolutionary challenge and counterrevolutionary reaction during the 1945–1953 period, there have been no autonomous peasant movements to speak of in South Korea. This absence, however, does not mean that the peasantry have been unimportant in politics. The dominant view of their role is that of *yŏch'onyado* (the countryside for the government, the city for the opposition).[1] Its advocates make four propositions. First, after the land reform of the early 1950s, the country-side turned into a strong support base for the ruling coalition even when it pursued an economic strategy hostile to rural interests. Second, farmers did so because immersed in traditional culture, raised in political conform-ism, and looking to clan leaders, village elders, and local officials for guid-ance,[2] they lacked a sense of individual autonomy and "civic capacity"[3] and became available for top-down mobilization in support of the ruling coalition.[4] Third, those in power commanded an extensive state and party organization with which to hand down "carrots" to reward their rural supporters and to wield "sticks" to punish their rural adversaries selec-tively with the goal of top-down mobilization. Fourth, sure of the country-side's political backing, the ruling coalition was able to turn terms of trade against the farmers toward urban-based manufacturers with an eye to gen-erating export-led industrial hypergrowth.

Essentially, the four propositions of *yŏch'onyado* add up to the image of the South Korean farmers as a sort of safety net for Park Chung Hee (1961–1979). In the eyes of *yŏch'onyado* advocates, the steady flow of electoral support from the countryside, even when Park financially squeezed it to secure the necessary resources for industrial development, allowed him to "afford" electoral competition during the 1960s and to contain the politically contentious city with top-down rural electoral mobilization during the 1970s, despite his personal distaste for elections and his modernization strategy's "selective affinity" with authoritarianism rather than with democracy.[5] Equally critical, from the perspective of *yŏch'onyado* advocates, support in the countryside helped cushion Park's political dilemmas with regard to modernization. Park knew that the primary beneficiary of his modernization effort—the "modern" and "dynamic" urban sector, uprooted from traditional ways of life—would oppose him on mainly ideological grounds. However, Park stuck to his goal of modernization because he knew also that the rural sector would come to his rescue by overwhelming the votes of growing but still minority pro-opposition city dwellers.

That there was solid rural support for Park during his political rule is beyond dispute. What is at issue is rather the farmers' political motivation and capabilities and Park's political strategy to reshape them. Were the farmers mere captives of cultural conformism? Did Park's local electoral machines unilaterally control and mobilize the rural population without any direct or indirect feedback from the farmers? Was Park only exploiting the countryside to generate macroeconomic hypergrowth? By going beyond the national or regional aggregation of votes to decipher variations in rural support for Park over time and across regions, Chapter 12 brings out the complexity of South Korean rural politics that advocates of the *yŏch'onyado* thesis overlook. First, it will be argued that Park's rural strategy was a variable, tilting toward the farmers' interest during his junta years (1961–1963), only to swing to the opposite strategy of agricultural squeeze (1964–1968), then to a politically timely but economically unsustainable Bismarckian alliance of "rye and steel" on the basis of simultaneously supporting the farmers' price for rice and the *chaebol* groups' entry into heavy and chemical industries (1968–1979). As his zigzags in rural politics showed, Park saw farmers as rational actors, evaluating the benefits and costs of his agricultural policy and acting on those evaluations in elections with their votes. Rural votes were not consistently pro-Park; they had to be nurtured with incentives. Consequently, Park had to be a rational mobilizer as well, changing his rural strategy as his political fortunes waxed and waned and his primary political goals altered.

Second, however, rationality had a competitor—not from traditional culture and political conformism, as suggested in the *yŏch'onyado* thesis, but from volatile regionalist sentiments that continually redefined their object of loyalty and their target of opposition through electoral struggles. This power of regionalism was also variable, surfacing in a most decisive way in a region with its favorite son bidding for presidential power and authority. Kyŏngsang voters, whether rural or urban dwellers, sided with Park across presidential elections. In a similar spirit, South Ch'ungch'ŏng rallied behind Yun Po-sŏn of the opposition in 1963 and 1967, and Chŏlla around Kim Dae-jung in 1971. The rural areas without a presidential candidate from their region, like those in Chŏlla in 1967 and Ch'ungch'ŏng in 1971, were ready to give greater weight to economic interests in their electoral calculations. By contrast, in National Assembly elections, clientelism became the primary mode of political mediation as rural voters responded most immediately to economic incentives. To mete out individual rewards and sanctions, the state developed into a political machine, with the power to affect almost all facets of everyday life in the countryside.

The "Green Uprising," 1961–1963

Having toppled Chang Myŏn's democratically elected government (1960–1961), Park knew that his best chance of political survival rested in his ability to take advantage of public discontent over Chang Myŏn's ineptitude. To differentiate himself from Chang Myŏn, he zeroed in on delivering economic growth and national security.[6] During the junta years Park believed that an improved rural standard of living was a prerequisite of economic development, with the raised purchasing power of the farmers inducing expanded industrial production. The export-led industrialization (ELI) strategy, often regarded as a hallmark of Park's economic development scheme, was not yet in his "toolbox."

In addition to his belief in the rural sector's potential to back up, if not lead, hypergrowth, Park also sought a political cushion in the countryside. Economically vulnerable, socially deprived, and politically unorganized, South Korean farmers constituted a natural target for political mobilization. With a few carrots, they could be won over as a pillar of political order. Most South Korean farmers were small but independent "owner-farmers,"[7] living at or below subsistence level.[8] The state had also, since 1950, plundered farmers' livelihoods, forcing them to sell grain at below-market prices with an eye to stabilizing the price of grain sold in the urban sector.[9] The state even ended up purchasing grain at below the farmers' production cost.[10] Abetting this policy was massive agricultural aid provided by the United States under Public Law 480. The easy availability of

U.S. grain aid undoubtedly provided a disincentive for the state to increase domestic production through higher grain prices. In lieu of price incentives for farmers, the state had to secure its stock of grain by relying on local administrative channels, including the agricultural cooperatives. The purchase was made mainly as part of a rice–fertilizer barter or as an in-kind farmland tax.[11]

To make the farmers an even more attractive target for political mobilization, they made up 58.3 percent of South Korea's total population in 1961. Moreover, unlike the urban political scene, dominated by opposition politicians and activists who thought their Student Revolution of April 19, 1960, had been thwarted by Park's military coup, the countryside not only lacked their own horizontal organization, but also was in the tight control of the state bureaucracy, especially the Ministry of Home Affairs (MHA). Once the leftist forces were rooted out by the end of the Korean War in 1953, the state ceased to place much political value on even the rightist Korean Farmers' Association (KFA), which largely fell into oblivion after 1955. In the absence of autonomous rural forces, Park could cultivate rural support through bureaucratically driven political mobilization that amounted to what Samuel P. Huntington once called the "Green Uprising," in which "one segment of the urban elite develop[s] an appeal to or [makes] an alliance with the crucial rural voters and mobilize[s] them into politics so as to overwhelm at the polls the more narrowly urban-based parties."[12] But in contrast to Huntington's party-led Green Uprising, the top-down mobilization of farmers during Park's junta years began as a bureaucratic enterprise propelled by the military and state ministries.

The State as a Political Machine

The tools for mobilizing the rural population were extensive. The most critical was the MHA, with its organization of control, regulation, and mobilization reaching all the way down to the village level.[13] During the 1960s, its Bureau of Local Administration presided over 14,000 sub-county offices of the *myŏn*, the lowest and smallest administrative unit in South Korea, with the authority to administer some 36,000 villagers. The *myŏn* office placed village heads on its payroll, having appointed them to their posts itself.[14] Each of the *myŏn* also had a *chisŏ*, or police substation, directly under the MHA's other, more coercive, bureau, the Bureau of Public Safety. The MHA therefore had the power to affect almost all facets of everyday life in the countryside, from issuing birth certificates and death reports to the administration of curfew rules to criminal investigations.

The National Agricultural Cooperative Federation (NACF) constituted another powerful instrument in Park's efforts to shape the farmers' political preferences and behaviors. Over 90 percent of South Korean farmers belonged to local branches of the NACF. More a centrally controlled and directed bureaucracy than a voluntary association of farmers, the NACF was an arm of the state with the mission of implementing national economic policy at the local level. "The only thing cooperative about the organization," S. H. Ban and his colleagues write, "is the fact that farmers must buy one or more shares in their primary cooperatives" in order to be cooperative members.[15] The real location of power was the Ministry of Finance (MoF) and the Ministry of Agriculture and Forestry (MAF), whose representatives intervened at all levels of NACF activities with the power accrued from their control over the supply of low-interest credit, the marketing channels for grain, and critical agricultural inputs like fertilizer. Because the NACF was the only source of credit, marketing, and fertilizer for most farmers, the MoF and MAF bureaucrats could readily influence the farmers' economic decisions. Needless to say, these powers of the MoF and MAF secured through the NACF became a source of leverage for MHA bureaucrats in mobilizing votes for Park and Democratic Republican Party (DRP) candidates in the upcoming elections of 1963.

Park constructed a dense machinery for political propaganda in the countryside as well. During the junta years he launched the People's Movement for National Reconstruction (PMNR), with the goal of instilling in farmers the spirit of hard work, frugality, perseverance, and self-help. Park envisioned that the PMNR would take charge of the old and new organizations of political socialization and propaganda at the village level to remold the farmers into model citizens. These organizations ranged from Youth for National Reconstruction to Women for National Reconstruction to 4-H clubs. The military junta also began constructing a wired broadcasting system to facilitate propaganda work. Even villagers in the remotest area were provided with loudspeakers that were connected to an amplifier-equipped "wired broadcast station," which was run privately but under the tight control of the *myŏn* office. It is estimated that some 400,000 loudspeakers were distributed and installed in rural villages during the junta years. Even sparsely populated mountainous Kangwŏn Province reportedly supplied 3,000 loudspeakers to each of its counties.[16] Through these broadcasting networks, local MHA officials played propaganda songs, announced state policy guidelines, and disseminated Park's public speeches every day to the villagers. The villagers had no choice in the selection of stations.

The Ministry of Education (MoE) also put the schools to work in the project of political socialization. Every morning the loudspeakers at the schools blared out propaganda songs like "This Is a Year for Work." Schoolmasters joined in this concerted program of "reeducation," delivering scarcely disguised propaganda regarding the junta's policies and achievements at weekly all-school meetings.

As an additional means of cultivating rural support, Park publicly portrayed himself as a "son of the soil." During the seasons of rice planting and harvesting, newspapers carried photographs of Park working in the rice paddies and drinking rice wine *(makkŏlli)* with the farmers in order to project the image of a commoner, or *sŏmin*. To a significant degree, he saw himself as a commoner. This enduring image had a potentially powerful effect in the mobilization of rural support for Park. Many ousted Democratic Party leaders, including President Yun Po-sŏn, had been from the traditional elite, who saw their power as stemming in part from their gentry lineage and schooling abroad. By contrast, Park came from a modest social background, and he was proud of it.

Economic Carrots

Park Chung Hee's strategy of rural mobilization would have been far less effective had he only constructed a dense web of control mechanisms and propped up his image with modern propaganda techniques. The sticks were more effective if they were mixed with the lure of carrots. The image of "a son of the soil" Park tried to create for himself could acquire public credibility only if it was backed by incentives. The junta leader knew of the importance of carrots, and he liberally dispensed them when he seized power. Park did not need much political imagination to know where to focus to win the farmers' trust and support. In most peasant homes, expenditures were larger than incomes, resulting in debt accumulation in 92 percent of rural households by September 1960. The average size of the debt per rural household stood at 66,932 hwan, almost twice its liquid assets. Most of the loans carried usuriously high interest rates of 5 to 10 percent a month. Since rural households typically did not earn enough income to pay back the principal and interest, rural debt accumulated at an alarming annual rate of 19.3 percent between 1958 and 1960.[17]

After servicing their debts once the harvest was over, about one third of rural households ran out of food by the spring and were forced to borrow money or grain again from loan sharks, relatives, or neighbors. Another 10 percent, deprived of even this option, survived by subsisting on grass roots and tree bark *(ch'ogŭnmokp'i)*. To make the situation worse, the spring of 1961 was extremely lean due to a bad harvest in the previous fall. According to the conservative estimate of Chang Myŏn's government,

342,147 rural households, making up 14 percent of the total population, harvested only half the annual average.[18] According to field reports, in some areas as many as two thirds of the households ran out of food.[19]

On May 25, 1961, nine days after he ousted Chang Myŏn, Park pledged to free the farmers of any legal obligations to pay back high-interest debts. By the end of October, out of the total rural debt of 79.4 billion hwan, 48 billion hwan was reported to the MAF for review, 26.7 billion hwan of which was found to be usurious.[20] In contrast, the military junta threatened to crack down on the *chaebol* with fines on their "illicit wealth accumulation" during the rule of Syngman Rhee and Chang Myŏn, and also to strengthen regulatory efforts to weed out tax delinquency and noncompliance by the rich. The crackdown on usurious rural loans, coupled with an agricultural price support law enacted in June 1961, reflected Park's populism. Not yet tamed by the harsh realities of the South Korean economic situation, Park at that time viewed agricultural development as a prerequisite of industrialization. Moreover, industrialization was to be led by small- and medium-sized enterprises (SMEs), focusing on import substitution and drawing funds from domestic savings, rather than by foreign loans. The fruits of industrialization should be evenly shared, not left to the market's trickle-down mechanism alone. In this 1961 scheme of economic change, agricultural development mattered, because it would raise the purchasing power of the rural population, thus providing an expanded market for manufactured goods. Without a thriving agricultural sector, Park repeatedly declared, any talk of national development was bound to be an "empty promise."[21]

In August 1961, the military junta merged the Agricultural Bank with the Farm Cooperatives Association into the newly formed NACF, with the effect of instantly transforming 17,000 local cooperative units into de facto bank branches.[22] In addition to the revitalization of the dormant rural cooperatives by enabling them to provide farmers with a full range of services, including credit provision, common purchases, common sales, and debt extension, the merger sought to further tighten the junta's grip on the countryside. Two days later, the Financial and Monetary Committee raised the money allocated for the state to make advance payments for the rice it was purchasing in the third quarter. The bill totaled 11.1 billion hwan, 1.7 billion hwan more than the original plan.[23] In December 1961, Park ordered the provincial governors to devise measures to eradicate the problem of grain shortage in the countryside during the lean months of the spring.[24] The next month, he provided in-kind loans of half a million *sŏk* (1 *sŏk* = 180 liters) of grain to some 310,000 grain-depleted rural households.[25] The MHA vigorously carried out Park's instructions, even dismissing the head of the Puyŏ county office in South Ch'ungch'ŏng Province for his failure to "earnestly" investigate the conditions of the grain shortage in February 1962.[26]

The junta also implemented agricultural restructuring and farmland development policies, enacting a Farmland Improvement Law in 1961 and a Land Clearing Promotion Law a year later. Then followed the establishment of a Council on the Improvement of Agricultural Structure. Although this project ultimately ended in failure, the junta later experimented with a collective farm project in 1963.[27] To back the restructuring program with a concrete incentive structure, Park raised the state's purchase price of rice by 46 percent over the previous year amid a strong show of approval by the mass media and the farmers.[28] The very next year, however, under the pressures of price instability, the powerful Economic Planning Board (EPB) allied with the MoF to keep the purchase price of rice under the rate of inflation. The EPB-MoF reversal of the price support program for grains in 1962 was a harbinger of things to come. In 1964, Park was to make a fundamental change of direction in his macroeconomic policy that put agricultural development at the lower end of national priorities. Until then, Park zigzagged between the junta-initiated "populist" programs of agricultural development and the EPB- and MoF-recommended budget cuts. Fortunately for Park, the zigzags did not alter the public perception of his economic strategy as fundamentally "favoring agriculture," or *chungnong,* to quote the catchphrase of his junta years. The images that formed during the early period of Park's leadership were powerful. Once the anti-elite, pro-commoner image of Park took root in the public mind during 1961 and 1962, the image came to acquire a life of its own, surviving future policy zigzags.

Park thus devised a strategy of bringing about a Green Uprising with two carrots of rural debt relief and grain price support, one stick of the threat of repression, and the modern-day politics of image making. The instrument for channeling the carrots, wielding the stick, and creating the image of a "son of the soil" was South Korea's powerful state bureaucracy, not its ideologically shallow and organizationally thin political party system. What clientelistic networks the political parties possessed were thoroughly captured by ousted LP and DP politicians at that time. Making Park rely on the state bureaucracy even more, the Young Turks, led by Kim Chong-p'il, were not able to complete their clandestine organization of the DRP until December 1962.[29] Before then, Park had to choose a bureaucratic, rather than a political, path to his Green Uprising out of not only his distaste for politics but also his lack of a party. The question was whether, why, and how the farmers of South Korea would respond to Park's political overtures.

Elections, 1963

The presidential election that the military junta promised in 1961 as a way to "return power to the civilians" was finally held on October 15, 1963. Although seven candidates entered the race, the real contest was between the DRP's Park Chung Hee and the hurriedly assembled Civil Rule Party's Yun Po-sŏn, who had served as president in Chang Myŏn's government. Park won the election by the slimmest of margins, winning 42.6 percent of the votes against Yun Po-sŏn's 41.2 percent.

Park enjoyed a clear advantage over the opposition in terms of organization and campaign funds. He used the state bureaucracy, including the police, extensively to mobilize votes. The myriad parastatal organizations like the NACF and the PMNR also actively joined his election campaign, enabling the DRP to reach deep down into the villages for support. Although it was called "the freest and fairest election in [South] Korean history,"[30] the 1963 presidential election was marred by irregularities. By ruling that the MHA-appointed head of a rural village or an urban bloc was not a civil servant, and thus was free to join political parties and conduct campaign activities,[31] the Central Election Management Committee opened a way for the state bureaucracy to marshal its power behind Park in the election without breaking the law that barred civil servants from getting involved in political activities. The heads of rural villages and urban blocs were on the public payroll, but freely canvassed households to solicit support for Park.

The September and October issues of *Chosun Ilbo* carried reports of irregularities every day. Some village heads forced farmers to apply for DRP membership under the threat of abruptly ending their grain rations.[32] County officials and policemen were transferred to their hometowns before the election to persuade relatives and friends, apparently in accordance with an MHA directive.[33] The Seoul City police department was found to be asking its officers to submit a list of relatives and local notables with the power to influence the vote in their hometowns.[34] The MHA itself was accused of setting up coordination committees at every level of public administration to facilitate cooperation among and between state ministries and parastatal organizations on behalf of Park's candidacy.[35] The mayors of Pusan and other cities threw feasts in honor of the elderly to campaign for Park.[36] In the special classes the schools organized for parents and students to learn civic duties,[37] various pro-Park nongovernmental organizations came to give lectures on "current affairs," and to hold exhibitions on past corruption.[38] The regional chapters of the PMNR also ran educational programs on election procedures for schoolteachers, families of public officials, and local notables.[39]

The Comrades of May, an organization of retired army officers, joined in this flurry of propaganda, organizing a series of "nonpolitical" lecture tours across the country.[40] Forty-four military officers on active duty were also put on a nationwide tour to give "educational" lectures at 1,115 high schools and colleges.[41] Through these and many other efforts, Park managed to register a total of 1,568,006 men and women as DRP members. The DRP additionally held 629 rallies with an alleged participation of some 2.64 million people by the time of the election.[42] Considering the organizational advantage Park enjoyed through his control over the state bureaucracy and parastatal agencies, many critics claimed that the 4.7 million votes cast for Park were "much too few" to claim electoral victory.

In the end, it was the countryside that came to Park's rescue. The DRP candidate carried 50.8 percent of the rural vote, whereas Yun Po-sŏn garnered 57.1 percent of the urban vote. Put differently, the rural votes accounted for 74.2 percent of the total votes cast for Park and only 59.2 percent of Yun Po-sŏn's.[43] The strategy of bringing about a Green Uprising with two carrots, one stick, and the modern-day politics of image making apparently worked in 1963, except in the two predominantly rural Kangwŏn and Ch'ungch'ŏng provinces. The voters in Kangwŏn, known for political conservatism stemming from their province's role as a frontline military post, were judged to have opposed Park for his earlier leftist political activities. The electorate in Ch'ungch'ŏng, by contrast, cast a regional vote, siding with Yun Po-sŏn, a native of Asan, a village in South Ch'ungch'ŏng Province.

Park's successful Green Uprising strategy, however, does not necessarily validate the *yŏch'onyado* thesis that portrays the farmers as voting for Park out of their political conformism on the basis of traditional culture. First, of the rural electorate, 50.8 percent sided with him, but an almost equally large bloc of 49.2 percent of the rural electorate did not. Second, those who backed Park might have chosen to do so after a rational calculation of benefits arising from his Green Uprising strategy, or simply because they were hopelessly trapped in South Korea's allegedly conformist culture that made them follow the wishes of local elders and state bureaucrats. Lacking extensive public survey data, we need to defer judgment until we analyze the electoral consequences of Park's switch to the policy of agricultural squeeze in 1964.

The interviews I conducted in February 2001 reveal not only the potential but also the limitations of Park's Green Uprising strategy, as well as the complexity of South Korean farmers' political psyche. "The state told us to report our debts," a farmer in North Kyŏngsang Province recollected. "They told us they would write off usurious debts. They thought they were doing us a favor, but wasn't it their responsibility? I reported, but for nothing. I still had usurious debts. Worse, it became even more difficult for me to borrow money," because there were no longer lenders willing to lend even at usurious interest rates.[44] The issuance of a new currency in June 1962 with the goal of unearthing the supposed underground economy's illicit wealth also failed to secure wide support from farmers. A peasant from South Ch'ungch'ŏng Province complained in a newspaper interview that replacing the hwan with the won at the ratio of 10:1 "was bad. Now it is even harder to make a living because the money is reduced while expenses remain the same."[45] The image of the farmer emerging from these interviews is of a rather sophisticated economic actor aware of the unintended adverse consequences of Park's 1961 *chungnong* strategy of debt relief as well as his 1962 radical currency reform. How that awareness of the boomerang effects of Park's policy was translated into farmers' electoral decisions is far from obvious.

Equally interesting, many of the farmers interviewed did not identify themselves with Park despite his carefully cultivated image of a "son of the soil." Some mistrusted his intentions. "Park might have been a peasant's son," a farmer said. "Still, he was different from us wretches. He attended the Normal School and the Japanese Military Academy in Manchuria. At the time we did not believe him that much. The state always says it is working for us. It was so under Japanese rule. So was Syngman Rhee. Just wait and see. That was what we thought about Park, until much later."[46] Whether Park was able to overcome such sentiments during the three years of junta rule is unclear. The existence of political mistrust, however, cautions against the portrayal of South Korean farmers as political conformers, readily available for top-down mobilization regardless of the distributive character of state policy. On the contrary, the interviews show that even a genuinely *chungnong* state elite would have had difficulty in being accepted as an ally of the farmers in the countryside. To achieve such an alliance, the state elite would need to side consistently with the farmers in economic policy.

The National Assembly elections held on November 26, 1963, soon after the presidential election, also showed both the potential and the limitations of Park's Green Uprising strategy. For the DRP, the stakes were as high as in the presidential election. To ratify the highly contested treaty normalizing relations with Japan, the DRP needed a comfortable legislative majority, and it campaigned vigorously. Throughout the campaign, the press reported many irregularities. The National Assembly election looked even more like a politics of vote buying and bureaucratic mobilization than had the presidential election. The DRP's post-election report did not shy away from what had occurred, and cited a "timely emission of campaign funds" that "reached to the farthest end through efficient transmission channels" as one of the factors that brought its victory at the polls.[47] This time, Ch'ungch'ŏng and Kangwŏn provinces switched sides to give more votes to DRP candidates. Apparently, the strategy of Green Uprising, backed with carrots, surpassed the power of Ch'ungch'ŏng regionalism and Kangwŏn security ideology in shaping the farmers' voting behavior in what was a more clientelistic National Assembly election.

The most critical cause of the DRP's landslide victory in the 1963 National Assembly election, however, stemmed from South Korea's new electoral system that privileged the political party with the largest vote and severely punished the remaining fragmented political bloc. In 1963, it was the DRP who received the largest vote, and the opposition bloc that fragmented. The votes the DRP won amounted to only 32.4 percent of the total, far less than Park's 42.6 percent in the presidential race a month earlier, but the DRP nonetheless won 88 seats, which represented two thirds of the directly contested single-member plurality National Assembly seats, due to the splintering of the opposition into eleven political parties. The DRP on average faced five opposition candidates per electoral district. And because the electoral system allotted 50 percent of the 44 "listed" seats to the political party with the largest number of National Assembly seats, Park came to enjoy the luxury of winning 22 additional listed seats.[48] The total of district and listed seats added up to 110, giving the DRP a stable majority in the 175-member National Assembly.

Agricultural Squeeze, 1964–1968

Even before civilian rule was restored in 1963, Park and his bureaucrats were busy redrawing their strategy of economic development. The turn away from the policy of *chungnong* began silently but unmistakably when Park ordered the EPB to review economic policy in December 1962, and the changes became explicit by May 1964. The policy reorientation had much to do with the mounting economic problems Park faced in implementing his "catch-all" first Five-Year Economic Development Plan (FYEDP). The most serious issue was the shortage of investment capital, which Park had to cover with budget deficits, which in turn aggravated inflation and, through it, social instability. In the course of preparing for the historic presidential and National Assembly elections of 1963 and also laying the groundwork for economic takeoff, the military junta had formulated overambitious and even contradictory goals for its first FYEDP (see Chapters 3 and 7).

Not surprisingly, the first FYEDP failed to produce the expected results. The investment targets were more or less met, but only at the expense of a ballooning fiscal deficit. Rampant inflation broke out in late 1962, triggered by a poor harvest. Between December 1962 and May 1964, the consumer price index rose by 58 percent and the wholesale price index by 66 percent,[49] reducing the real income of the majority of households. There was no easy way out of the inflation. Government revenues proved to be extremely inelastic to the rise in prices and nominal income. U.S. aid and public enterprise profits were declining in real terms as well. The private savings rate also fell, because individuals shifted from the accumulation of liquid assets and productive investment to the acquisition of a broad range of real goods and commodities in order to protect themselves from inflation. Eating up the real interest rate, high inflation frustrated Park's hope of accumulating investment capital through higher domestic savings. The economy suffered from a decline in the level of productive investment during the latter days of military rule in real terms.

Facing a budget deficit, Park gave the green light to the EPB's search for a new strategy of modernization. From the policy failures of 1961 and 1962, Park learned an elementary economic principle: raise revenue, reduce consumption, and increase investment. In May 1963, the EPB began preparing for a move toward a balanced budget. Reflecting Park's obsession with growth, the pilot agency intended to bring about a balanced budget not by any slackening in the effort to keep up a high level of investment, but by a new political drive to raise the tax burden and reduce "secondary" expenditures, including budget support for agricultural products. After the 1963 elections consolidated Park's power, Park began to put in place the EPB's newly formulated economic policy. And with it began the politics of agricultural squeeze.

A Double Squeeze

The search for investment capital for South Korea's burgeoning export manufacturers pitted the EPB against the MAF over the 1964 budget. Whereas the MAF proposed that the state increase its purchasing price of grain by 35 percent,[50] the EPB, which held the budgetary powers, insisted on placing as tight a ceiling on such budget increases as possible. Twelve days before the 1963 National Assembly elections, the MAF announced a 27 percent raise, a moderate increase given South Korea's two-digit inflation rate.[51] After the election, economic logic began to get the better of political moves, and the policymakers' mantra changed from "balanced" to "unbalanced" growth,[52] with resources transferred from the rural to the urban sector for the benefit of export industries. At the center of this policy U-turn was the state's low purchasing price for grain. By maintaining the MAF's grain purchases at below-market prices, the EPB weeded out one source of inflationary pressure and increased its chances of balancing the budget. The policy also ensured a steady supply of workers for light industries, then the mainstay of South Korea's exports, by encouraging the hard-pressed farmers to flee the stagnant countryside for jobs in the urban sector. The MAF's purchasing price for grain from the farmers was to remain lower than market prices throughout the 1961–1975 period except in 1972. To keep grain prices artificially low, the MAF set quotas for grain delivery for the farmers.[53] The farmers were indirectly taxed by the state in the input market, too. In the early 1960s, Park pushed to develop a fertilizer industry not only for domestic consumption but also for export promotion. To this end, nine companies were created. Three were joint ventures with U.S. fertilizer firms producing compound fertilizer. To persuade the foreign companies to enter into the joint ventures, the EPB guaranteed each of the three an annual minimum return of 20 percent by promising to purchase a set quantity of fertilizer. The rigid guarantee on profits, coupled with South Korea's comparative disadvantage in the production of ammonia from naphtha, made the locally produced fertilizers much more expensive than foreign ones, effectively closing off export as an option for the industry. The producers, in effect, came to live off the domestic fertilizer market, which became saturated by 1970.[54] To pass the high costs of production on to the farmers, the MAF erected stiff trade barriers against cheaper foreign products and handled all domestic demand for fertilizers through its parastatal organization, the NACF.[55] The state monopoly over the supply of fertilizers kept the price up, forcing the farmers to de facto subsidize South Korea's uncompetitive fertilizer industry.

The increasingly high price of fertilizer greatly contributed to the worsening terms of trade for the rural households. The price of fertilizers jumped 80 percent in 1964 alone, followed by another 44.4 percent increase in 1965.[56] A small farmer reportedly spent 55 percent of farming costs on fertilizer in 1966.[57] Nor did high prices mean timely delivery; farmers complained of a constant delay. The companies also forced the farmers to buy unpopular potash fertilizer along with more popular ones.

The press reported that the farmers were getting rid of the potash fertilizer at the fire-sale price of 200 won per bag or less, far below the NACF's price of 500 won.[58]

Elections, 1967

The 1967 presidential and National Assembly elections were held at the height of the agricultural squeeze. As in 1963, Park fully mobilized not only the DRP but also the MHA and other support institutions in the countryside to win votes. The presidential election was held on May 11, again between Park and Yun Po-sŏn. Yun Po-sŏn ran as the candidate of a newly established New Democratic Party (NDP), which had united the opposition only three months earlier through a merger of two parties. Despite the merger, Park managed to win a decisive victory, garnering 51.4 percent of the total vote, up 8.8 percent from 1963. By contrast, Yun Po-sŏn saw his level of popular support remain virtually the same at 41 percent. Minor candidates took 7.6 percent of the votes.

Major changes in voting patterns were apparent. Whereas Park won the southern provinces and lost the northern ones in 1963, he won the east coast region and lost the west coast four years later. The east coast included not only the predominantly rural Kangwŏn and North Ch'ungch'ŏng provinces he had lost in 1963, but also Pusan City, South Korea's second largest city after Seoul. The split, however, was far from being urban versus rural. Along the west coast, where Park performed dismally, lay South Korea's "rice bowl," North and South Chŏlla provinces, which had voted for him in 1963. Whereas Park had won all of the 34 counties in the Chŏlla provinces while losing 6 of their 7 cities in 1963, he lost 23 of the 34 counties and 6 of the 7 cities in 1967.

The swing of Chŏlla voters constitutes a better barometer of rural sentiment, because their vote was less influenced by regionalist sentiments. In contrast to South Ch'ungch'ŏng Province that had its favorite son (Yun Po-sŏn) running as the NDP presidential candidate and North and South Kyŏngsang provinces theirs (Park Chung Hee) as the DRP presidential candidate, North and South Chŏlla provinces had neither of their favorite sons (Yi Ch'ŏl-sŭng and Kim Dae-jung) vying for national leadership. The South Ch'ungch'ŏng and Kyŏngsang voters whose favorite son was bidding for presidential power followed their regionalist instinct, whether they were from the rural or the urban sector. By contrast, without a regionalist option, the Chŏlla voters could be presumably more faithful to their agricultural interests than to any identity-based sentiments, beliefs, or images. The dramatic decrease in the farmers' support for Park in North and

South Chŏlla provinces showed that he could hardly take rural support for granted. The farmers' support for him was neither automatic nor unchanging outside his home provinces. The image of a "son of the soil" that he had carefully cultivated during the military junta years could still positively influence farmers' voting decisions when Park zigzagged between budgetary support and cuts as in 1962 and 1963, but not when he unambiguously turned to a policy of agricultural squeeze after 1964.

Equally critical, the presidential election of 1967 warned the NDP not to assume that the urban sector would automatically support the opposition candidate. Park carried 50.4 percent of the total urban vote, as opposed to only 37.7 percent in 1963. To be sure, he lost Seoul City, South Korea's breeding ground of urban opposition. Even here, however, his performance improved markedly from 1963, trailing behind Yun Po-sŏn's 49 percent by only three percentage points. The distribution of Seoul votes in 1963 had been 30:65 in favor of Yun Po-sŏn. Park's enhanced ability to get urban votes was attributable to South Korea's economic hypergrowth since 1964, the first fruits of which were enjoyed by the city dwellers. Park had succeeded in transforming "economic development [into] the ideology of the day,"[59] which helped legitimize his presidency and won him an unprecedented level of urban votes. As a 1966 survey of 1,515 professionals and journalists revealed, even South Korea's highly contentious and moralistic intelligentsia came to place economic development as the highest priority of the country. Many even thought individual freedom could be sacrificed for economic development,[60] thus forgiving much of Park's authoritarian excesses committed in the 1963–1967 period in the name of economic growth and military security.

As a matter of course, Park played up his leadership in economic development for electoral purposes. The EPB published its second FYEDP in the summer of 1966, providing Park with a year of propaganda before the 1967 elections. Under the slogan of "Uninterrupted Progress," the DRP portrayed Park as the architect of the "Miracle of Han River," orchestrating a concerted program of modernization through tapping the innovative spirit of the military, state bureaucracy, business community, and people. The ruling party sold his reelection as necessary to the successful implementation of the second FYEDP, which formalized the policy U-turn that had been taking place since 1964. The DRP spoke of the *chungnong,* but as revealed in the second FYEDP, it had replaced the strategy of Green Uprising with that of industrial revolution to appeal to the electorate in 1967. And it worked.

The next month, on June 8, 1967, South Korea held National Assembly elections. Although eleven political parties put up candidates, the race was between the two major parties, the DRP and the NDP. They campaigned fiercely, fully recognizing what was at stake. The DRP aimed to win two thirds of the National Assembly seats, which would enable it to push through a constitutional revision to allow a third term for Park in 1971. The NDP fought an uphill battle to prevent the constitutional revision. Unfortunately for the NDP, the outcome was an even more decisive triumph for the DRP than in the presidential election of May 11. The ruling DRP won 129 legislative seats; the NDP, 45; and a newly formed splinter force (Mass Party), 1. Unlike in the presidential election, the DRP swept both rural areas and small cities. Even in North and South Chŏlla provinces, 20 of the 22 rural districts and 6 of the 8 urban districts sided with DRP candidates. The election saw the residents of small cities ally with the rural electorate against South Korea's NDP-led largest urban centers. The NDP successes were concentrated in major cities, including Seoul and Pusan. The opposition party carried only 3 electoral districts outside of the major cities.

The dramatic change in rural political sentiments, especially those of the two Chŏlla provinces, in just a month cautions against facile generalizations, including that of *yŏch'onyado*. To be sure, widespread irregularities contributed to the DRP's landslide victory in the 1967 National Assembly election. As the opposition party reported, vote buying, intimidation, and ballot stuffing were common in many of the districts.[61] The court even ordered one DRP member to turn over his National Assembly seat to the NDP opponent after the election in a rare moment of judicial independence. In order to ameliorate public discontent, the DRP also had to expel six members after the election for engaging in electoral irregularities. Nonetheless, the large margin by which the DRP won the National Assembly election showed that there was more to its victory than simply the effect of the irregularities.

The fundamental cause of the DRP's ability to turn the tide of Chŏlla's rural opposition and South Ch'ungch'ŏng's regionalist resistance in a mere month after the presidential elections was specific to the nature of National Assembly elections. Unlike the presidential contests, where national agendas dominated electoral contests and society polarized around the leadership of Park, the National Assembly elections were predominantly "local," with the rural electorate voting on criteria that were different from the ones they used during the presidential elections. Too far from the center in both the psychological and the physical senses of the term, and too weak to have a meaningful influence on the outcome, farmers were likely to see the presidential elections more as a plebiscite to express discontent regarding the national political leadership than as an opportunity to make a choice about their future. By contrast, in the National Assembly elections, the farmers sided with the candidate who could deliver particular economic and social benefits, that is, the candidate who could build a bridge, develop schools, empower the NACF and other collective village organizations with bigger budgets, and, more generally, open the door to the local centers of power including the MHA, the MAF, and the police. What farmers looked for in their national assemblyman was the ability to link the village with the state bureaucracy located in distant Seoul. That ability of intermediation was best secured by voting for the DRP, not the NDP, which was mostly excluded from the national and local centers of power. DRP candidates knew how to twist the arms of EPB and MoF bureaucrats to get money for village projects.

Accordingly, it is possible to explain the DRP's retake of Chŏlla and other rural provinces in the 1967 National Assembly election without assuming the conformist culture of South Korean farmers. Given the extreme centralization of power in the state bureaucracy and the insulation of state ministries from all outside forces except the Blue House, the DRP, and the *chaebol,* voting for the DRP in clientelistic National Assembly elections was what could be expected of a "rational peasant" constantly calculating benefits and costs of his political choices and weighing the pros and cons of backing an opposition candidate.

The Second Green Uprising, 1968–1979

Important as it was for Park's ability to fund export-led industrialization, the agricultural squeeze was creating serious political problems by the late 1960s. During the 1962–1971 period, the primary sector, which included agriculture and the relatively small fishery and forestry concerns, grew annually by 4 percent on average, 14.2 percentage points below the growth of the manufacturing sector.[62] On a per household basis, rural income stood at 55.8 percent of the urban sector's income level in 1967, a drop of 47.5 percentage points since 1963 when the ELI strategy was beginning to take shape.[63] And this worsening of the urban-rural income gap occurred when the poorest of rural households continually migrated to the burgeoning cities. According to MAF data, the share of the poorest rural households with less than 0.5 hectares of farmland declined from 42.9 percent in 1960 to 35.9 percent in 1965 and to 31.6 percent in 1970 due to migration.[64] A total of 1.5 million people, or 10 percent of the total farming population, left the countryside between 1968 and 1970.[65]

By the late 1960s, migration came to be seen as a source of concern rather than a blessing in disguise to be welcomed by the state for its role in keeping low the reproductive costs of industrial labor. First, the size of the rural population began to decrease even in absolute terms after 1967, shrinking the *p'yobat,* or "field of votes," for the DRP in clientelistic National Assembly elections. Second, the increase of unemployed squatters in the urban sector became in itself a cause of social unrest, as a 1971 riot on the outskirts of Seoul demonstrated.[66] Migration threatened the political stability of the city by flooding it with an army of urban poor without a stable source of employment. Third, the low-grain-price policy unexpectedly but inevitably discouraged grain production and encouraged food consumption precisely when the United States began to end its PL480 assistance. As a result, South Korea had to draw on its scarce foreign exchange to import grain. Available statistics show that from 1969 through 1972, grain imports alone accounted for more than 10 percent of total imports, taking resources away from the strategic manufacturing sector.[67] Both politically and economically, agricultural policy was in need of adjustment. Park's second U-turn came in 1968.

A Two-Tier Price System, *New Seeds, and* Saemaŭl Undong

The year 1968 saw Park's initiation of a two-tier price system for barley.[68] Under the scheme, the MAF purchased barley at above-market prices and sold it to urban dwellers at below-market prices through NACF-monopolized distribution networks. The goal was to encourage the consumption of barley over rice, which the MAF thought would raise rural income, help the urban poor to reduce their dependence on costly imported rice, and reduce the trade deficit. The catalyst for introducing the new system was the scheduled termination of PL480 aid from the United States, but the new policy was also politically motivated. The MAF announced it as part of Park's program to drum up rural support for a national referendum on the constitutional revision to permit a third presidential term. Between Park's victory in the 1969 national referendum and the 1971 presidential elections, the MAF expanded the two-tier price system to include rice. The move signaled a fundamental reorientation of Park's political strategy and economic policy. The inclusion of rice was bound to cost the government much more money, thus necessitating a change in resource allocation.

Fertilizer policy was altered, as well. Mindful that the state guarantee of high profits for the three largest joint venture producers hurt the farmers by raising fertilizer prices, the MAF collaborated with the MoF in establishing a public fund to supply fertilizer to farmers at prices below what the state had paid. The deficits arising from the Grain Management Fund for price support and the Fertilizer Fund for fertilizer support were to be financed in an inflationary manner with credits from the Bank of Korea. At the same time, Park embarked on an overly ambitious program of heavy and chemical industrialization (HCI). Park was designing his own Bismarckian alliance of "rye and steel" to withstand the opposition he expected from his turn to authoritarian rule in October 1972. Park aggressively courted big business with large investment projects in the heavy and chemical industries, while luring the farmers with the state's support of grain and fertilizer prices. Yet the Park-style rye-steel alliance suffered from internal dissension from the start. The business community was unhappy with the tight monetary policy that aimed to dampen the inflationary pressures caused by the simultaneous pursuit of HCI and the second Green Uprising. For the *chaebol,* South Korea's small-size farmers exploiting their families' manpower just to survive could not be the "Junkers" of Bismarckian Germany deserving a status of junior partnership in Park's *yushin* coalition. Rather than working with the farmers to back Park's conservative path to modernity, the *chaebol* frequently tried to pass the burden of adjustment to the countryside by lobbying to scale down Park's policy of high grain and low fertilizer prices.[69]

The conflict between big business and the rural sector surfaced in the form of interministerial disputes. In 1972, the EPB proposed to raise the purchase price for rice by only 5 percent over the previous year in order to hold down inflation at 3 percent. The MAF balked and eventually succeeded in increasing the purchase price by 8 percent. Then, twelve days prior to the national referendum on the newly promulgated authoritarian *yushin* constitution, Park abrogated the EPB-MAF compromise and ordered a 13 percent raise. In addition, Park ordered the MAF to pay the same price for the less popular high-yield rice (HYR) as for more popular types and to purchase as much as the farmers were willing to sell.[70] Politics got the better of economics. At the same time, Park knew that relying on subsidies alone was not tenable in the long run, and he had the MAF undertake research and development to help the farmers' competitiveness and lessen the pressure on the state budget. In 1971, the MAF proudly introduced a new HYR under the name *t'ongilbyŏ,* or Unification Rice. The new seed helped to boost rural income, given the MAF's policy of purchasing *t'ongilbyŏ* at high prices and in large amounts despite its unpopularity due to its poor taste.

Parallel to these efforts at price support, Park launched the *Saemaŭl Undong,* or New Village Movement, in 1970, which was to symbolize the turnaround in his rural political and economic strategy. In spite of its modest and almost chance beginnings, the *Saemaŭl Undong* would soon develop into a full-fledged integrated rural development program. The origins of the New Village Movement are found in the NACF's distribution of 335 bags of unmarketable surplus cement to the countryside, to be used "for village projects [that met] the villagers' common needs" and to be chosen on the basis of "general consensus."[71] Initially, the *Saemaŭl Undong* failed to produce much in the way of positive results because, in the words of Park's advisor on agricultural affairs, it was conceived as a "spiritual revolution" based on the principles of "self-reliance, self-help, and cooperation."[72] In other words, Park initially did not plan to commit much money to the *Saemaŭl Undong*. At most he was thinking about financing public projects that "beautified" the villages. Thus in its early stages, the farmers looked at it cynically as another pretext for the state to meddle in village affairs and tighten the grip of administrative control in return for cosmetic changes to their material life.[73]

Despite its inauspicious start, however, it is wrong to brush aside Park's pledge of rural development as only rhetoric. Many of the ideas Park set forth in his speeches on the *Saemaŭl Undong* traced their origin to the ideas of balanced growth that Park espoused in his earlier writings of the junta years and that he reluctantly renounced in favor of export-led industrialization under the pressures of inflation in 1964. "Our industry," he solemnly declared, "can develop only when our farmers become well-to-do and the rural communities develop rapidly. Well-to-do farmers generate a great deal of purchasing power, providing one of the basic conditions for industrial development. When industries develop rapidly, the resources thus generated are made available . . . for reinvestment in the agricultural sector. Viewed in this way, agriculture and industry are inseparable."[74] These words began acquiring political credibility when Park rejected pressures to scale down, if not scrap altogether, the two-tier price system for barley and rice in 1973 and 1974 when a profound stagflationary crisis was sweeping over South Korea in the aftermath of the oil shock stemming from the Middle East. As soon as South Korea got out of the recession in 1975 with the help of a construction boom in cash-rich Middle Eastern countries (see Chapter 9), Park earnestly launched the *Saemaŭl Undong* by securing budgetary support for the MAF's Grain Management Fund, Fertilizer Fund, and HYR development programs, in addition to rural public construction works. The net flow of resources into the countryside climbed dramatically in 1975 and stayed high through the end of the *yushin* regime.

Elections

As Park prepared for the simultaneous pursuit of HCI and agricultural development in the late 1960s, the opposition readied for an electoral rematch. Lacking power to shape economic policy, the New Democratic Party focused instead on putting its house in order. The opposition forces were determined not to repeat the 1963 and 1967 mistake of agreeing on their unified candidate too late in the presidential race. In September 1970, the NDP held its national convention and nominated a young politician, Kim Dae-jung, as its presidential candidate. A native of South Chŏlla Province and a political entrepreneur with progressive ideas, Kim Dae-jung proved to be an unflagging election campaigner. By the middle of the 1971 presidential campaign, Park's team felt the pressure. Even in Taegu, North Kyŏngsang Province, the native home of Park Chung Hee, Kim Dae-jung drew a crowd of 300,000. There he warned that Park would become South Korea's "Generalissimo Chiang Kai-shek" if elected for a third term in 1971. In response, Park tearfully announced in unequivocal terms that this would be his final electoral bid for presidential power.

In the end, Park won with 53.2 percent of the total votes against Kim Dae-jung's 45.3 percent. Charges of electoral irregularities were again brought up. At the aggregate level, the rural-urban cleavage line reemerged too—this time, in favor of Park for attempting a second Green Uprising since 1968. Park carried 58 percent of the rural votes, an increase of 5.8 percentage points over the 1967 presidential contest.

However, it is also important to note that with the favorite sons of Kyŏngsang and Chŏlla provinces respectively heading the DRP and the NDP, rural votes there served as regional imprimaturs rather than as a plebiscite on Park's agricultural policy. The Kyŏngsang provinces backed Park with 74.7 percent of their total votes, whereas the Chŏlla provinces lined up behind Kim Dae-jung with 62.3 percent of their votes. The urban areas of the two regions, which included Pusan City, in South Kyŏngsang Province, also split along regionalist lines rather than rural-urban cleavages. Unlike in 1967, when the Chŏlla voters took the role of "rational voters," punishing Park for his 1964–1968 policy of agricultural squeeze, they sided against Park in spite of his second attempt at a Green Uprising since 1968. The 1971 presidential election was a thoroughly regionalist contest where the outcome was largely shaped by Kyŏngsang and Chŏlla provinces. Unfortunately for Kim Dae-jung, not only were there more voters in the Kyŏngsang provinces, but also the turnout was higher. In the Kyŏngsang provinces and Pusan City, Park won 1,586,006 more votes than Kim Dae-jung, whereas Kim Dae-jung garnered 621,906 more votes than Park in the Chŏlla provinces. The difference was 964,100 votes, roughly equal to the national differential of 946,928 votes.

It is ironic that Park attempted his second Green Uprising precisely when the two largest regions were overtaken by regionalist rivalries, thus making his strategy of two carrots, one stick, and the modern-day politics of image making to mobilize the farmers top-down that much less effective. Not only the countryside but the entire nation became increasingly affected by the contagious politics of regionalism, in sharp contrast to the 1963 and 1967 presidential elections, when only South Ch'ungch'ŏng and Kyŏngsang voters showed such inclinations. Park had embarked on buying rural votes with a generous economic program when a large chunk of South Korea's rural sector, the Chŏlla provinces, increasingly refused to be bought off because of their favorite son's political ascendance.

In retrospect, the Chŏlla provinces show how volatile rural sentiments could be and why Park could not take rural support for granted. The journey of the Chŏlla region in South Korea's presidential elections was as remarkable as Park's constant switch of agricultural policy. The Chŏlla region's rural electorate endorsed Park for his efforts at rural reform in 1963, only to change sides to support the NDP's Yun Po-sŏn at the height of the agricultural squeeze in 1967. Then, in a show of regionalist preference provoked by Kim Dae-jung's NDP candidacy in 1971, the Chŏlla voters sided against Park in spite of his efforts to promote a second Green Uprising after 1968. The South Korean farmers were far from being what the advocates of *yŏch'onyado* thought they were. Their votes were influenced more by economic calculation and regionalist identity than by cultural conformism. They even voted against Park in ever larger numbers as he increased his ability to reward with two carrots, punish with one stick, and engage in the politics of image-making through the continuous strengthening of the organizational capabilities of the MHA, MAF, NCAF, and *Saemaŭl Undong*. The state's institutional ability to force the farmers' acquiescence rose in tandem with the Chŏlla farmers' increasing resistance against that state in presidential elections.

The National Assembly elections, coming only a month after the presidential election, were driven by a different dynamic. Whereas the presidential election often served as a plebiscite on Park's leadership, the National Assembly contests again involved the particularistic economic game of clientelism. Under the system that elected "district" *(chiyŏkku)* legislators on a simple plurality rule and that allotted 50–66 percent of listed "national" *(chŏnkukku)* seats to the political party with the largest number of votes, the DRP captured 86 district seats and 27 listed seats, while the NDP won 65 and 27, respectively. The ruling party won a comfortable majority, which ensured legislative support for Park's economic policy, but it was 23 seats short of acquiring two thirds of National Assembly seats. Consequently, the DRP was prevented from passing another constitutional revision to extend Park's presidential rule. Introducing another change in the constitutional restriction on presidential terms would require an extra-constitutional measure, leading to Park's decision to rely on the national referendum in 1972 (see Chapter 8). Until then, the press called the 1971 election an NDP victory because the NDP almost doubled its seats from the 1967 National Assembly elections. In reality, the 1971 National Assembly elections were a victory for the DRP as well. The ruling party was able to hold on to its majority status because the rural voters in the Chŏlla provinces opted for the DRP candidates, after having voted for NDP's Kim Dae-jung in the presidential election. The DRP won 14 of South Chŏlla Province's 17 rural districts and 6 of North Chŏlla Province's 9 rural districts. Regionalist loyalty did not stand in the way of the Chŏlla voters, who wanted to vote for the DRP because they looked at the National Assembly elections as an opportunity to choose an intermediary between the village and the state bureaucracy. That goal was best served by electing DRP candidates.

The *Yŏch'onyado* Thesis Revisited

The relationship between rural voters and the Park regime was much more complex than the prevailing views of *yŏch'onyado* would suggest. As shown by a regression analysis of Jae-On Kim and B. C. Koh on the voting patterns of the South Korean electorate, the "explanatory power" of urbanization fluctuated greatly throughout Park's political rule, from as high as 66 percent in the 1971 election to as low as 2 percent in the 1967 election.[75] The rural electorate voted quite differently from one election to another, as the choices of the Chŏlla voters show. They endorsed Park for rural reform in 1963, only to dump him in favor of the NDP's Yun Po-sŏn at the height of the agricultural squeeze in 1967. Then, enthusiastically reacting to their favorite son's NDP candidacy in 1971, the Chŏlla voters voted against Park despite his U-turn on agricultural policy. In contrast to the image of pliable and malleable farmers portrayed by the advocates of the *yŏch'onyado* thesis, South Korea's rural population expressed its discontent when it was discontented.

Even regionalism included some characteristics of economic voting, in addition to being wedded to the politics of identity. The farmers in the Kyŏngsang provinces consistently backed Park not only out of regionalist loyalty but also because of what Albert O. Hirschman termed the "tunnel effect."[76] The tunnel effect occurs when those who have fallen behind choose not to rebel but to persevere, in the belief that they too will share the fruits of economic growth like those who have already made advances.

The sight of frontrunners in the race to modernity does not create alienation, but rather the hope for a better future for those left behind. Kyŏngsang farmers were in no better condition than Chŏlla farmers, but unlike Chŏlla farmers, they had relatives and friends in nearby Kumi and Ulsan, which were then rapidly becoming major industrial centers. Those in Kyŏngsang believed their prosperity would one day trickle down to them as well. "We did not expect much change for us," a farmer of North Kyŏngsang Province recollected. "Was there any period when farmers were fairly treated? No. Still, since Park was from the Kyŏngsang provinces, we thought there would be something for us. Isn't there a saying, 'We better choose red skirts if the price is same'? We thought that a Kyŏngsang president would be somehow better for us than a Seoulite or Chŏlla president."[77]

Rural votes in National Assembly elections that had a different tone and rhythm from those of presidential elections must also be considered. The *yŏch'onyadŏ* occurred much more consistently in National Assembly elections than during presidential elections, but contrary to the prevalent image of the "conformist farmer," the rural electorates' votes for the DRP appear to be based on a rational calculation of benefits and costs, not the conformist act of following the village elders and local bureaucrats' wishes. Take the example of the Chŏlla voters once more. In 1967 and 1971, they voted overwhelmingly against Park in the presidential elections, but backed DRP candidates by a large margin in the National Assembly elections held only a month later. Apparently they viewed the presidential election as a plebiscite to express their grievances, and the following month's elections as a selection of the intermediary who would lobby most aggressively for the village in interministerial struggles over budget allocations. Because the assembly elections immediately followed the presidential election during the 1961–1972 period, which consistently resulted in the victory of Park, that meant backing the DRP in the National Assembly elections.

In the case of the rural voters in the Kyŏngsang provinces, both regionalist loyalty and economic calculation worked in the same direction. "We voted for the DRP candidate for the National Assembly," an interviewee recollected, "thinking that he would get one more road or one more bridge for the village. What could a national assemblyman with membership in the NDP do for us? Obviously, voting for the DRP candidate does not guarantee that he will actually deliver on his election pledges. If he does not accomplish much, we can throw him out of office one way or another. It is no accident that there has been no national assemblyman who served three or more terms in our districts. After two terms, they all fell because they became very unpopular."[78] Another farmer was equally cynical and mistrustful of all party politicians: "Those rascals were the same. They all were after their own selfish interests. Whoever won, what difference would it make? We voted for the one who treated us better, with the gift of a pair of rubber shoes or even a bowl of *makkŏlli*." It was the DRP candidates, with the state bureaucracy's resources, who could lure the voters with economic incentives. The same farmer reported of the NDP candidate who once pleaded with the farmers that they "drink the *makkŏlli* the DRP offered, but vote for NDP." "But men are not like that," the interviewee admitted. "In the end we voted for whoever gave or promised us economic goods, even if that meant only a bowl of *makkŏlli*."[79]

Apparently, many of the rural population voted in accordance with their needs, expected or current. Some voted for the DRP candidate in expectation of a greater supply of local public goods, like the construction of bridges and roads. Others voted for whichever candidate provided the most immediate individual utility, like the bowl of *makkŏlli*. They did so not only because Park's formidable political machine, driven by the MHA, MAF, NACF, and other bureaucratic organs, bid vigorously for electoral support with the mix of two carrots and one stick, but also because the expected difference between DRP and NDP candidates was in many ways seen as minimal from the farmers' perspective. The NDP did not differ from the DRP ideologically except on the issue of liberal democracy. More critically, the NDP remained a party of notables, without the organizational ability to develop a concrete program of policy action. Besides, the NDP saw itself as the heir to the ideals of the urban-based Student Revolution of April 19, 1960, which Park thwarted with his coup d'état the next year. Because "those rascals were the same," it was neither unethical nor irrational for the farmers to "sell" their vote to the highest bidder. More often than not, the highest bidder was the better-financed DRP candidate.

This is not to deny that top-down mobilization occurred in the countryside for the electoral victory of Park and the DRP. Park had at his disposal a vast array of means for mobilization and used them to get votes. That power fundamentally arose from his modernization of the state apparatus, but it was also South Korea's close-knit traditional rural society that facilitated the use of bureaucratic power on behalf of electoral mobilization. Because of the self-contained nature of South Korea's rural villages, DRP organizers and state bureaucrats could easily distinguish NDP and DRP supporters from each other. Anonymity barely existed, if at all. A villager could not meet NDP campaigners without his neighbors' knowledge of it. Word would soon spread of his political preference, making him vulnerable to the DRP's revenge. The following excerpt from an interview is revealing.

I think it was 1963. My wife campaigned for an opposition candidate who was a distant relative of hers. Since she was meeting various people, everybody in the village came to know of her political work. After the election, an NACF representative abruptly told me to pay back the loans I had borrowed from the NACF. I had borrowed the money to send the kids to school in Taegu. The NACF representative knew of this all along, but suddenly asked me to pay back because I was using the loans not for farming, but for family purposes. I begged for his understanding, but one day he came over with his people and attached red tags to everything I had in the house. We could not use any of those household goods [because the red tag-attached goods were to be confiscated to pay for the loans]. I had to borrow "quick money" from private lenders at exorbitantly high interest rates to pay back the farming loans. Eventually, I ended up losing two *majigi* [patches] of rice paddies.[80]

The farmer's recollection is consistent with the MAF's change in agricultural policy in 1964. To counter the rampant inflation that started in late 1963, the NACF under MAF guidance began calling in many outstanding farming loans. With his wife out of favor with the local political authorities, our interviewee had little chance of being exempt from this crunch.

However, it is also true that the same tight-knit traditional rural society provided a protective shield for some NDP supporters. Another farmer recalled: "It was not difficult to guess who voted for the NDP candidate. Everyone in the village knew each other's business. But what could one do if his relative or neighbor voted for the opposition? Living in the same neighborhood with the same people throughout life and knowing everyone in the village so well, how could he dare to report NDP supporters to the local authorities? That would have made them lifelong enemies. It was out of the question for most of us to take action against NDP supporters simply because the village head asked us to do so."[81]

The interviews reveal rural voters to be very different from those envisioned under the prevailing interpretation of *yŏch'onyado*. Some South Korean farmers, like those of South Ch'ungch'ŏng Province in 1963 and 1967 and the Chŏlla provinces in 1967 and 1971, expressed their grievances by voting for the opposition. But more often they let themselves be mobilized less because of cultural conformism than because of the payoff structure. They not only calculated the pros and cons of not supporting Park, but also took into account the expected utility to them of the DRP versus the NDP before making their rational choice in the National Assembly elections. This strategy of survival was one the farmers had learned from living in a subsistence economy, where the difference between survival and starvation was very thin. Because of the fragility of rural life, most farmers tended to keep quiet about their problems until they became unbearable. Essentially embodying the "rational peasant" of James C. Scott, the South Korean farmers preferred to minimize losses rather than maximize gains because the penalties for failure were severe.[82] By contrast, in the presidential elections, not only the Kyŏngsang (1963, 1967, and 1971) and Ch'ungch'ŏng (1963 and 1967), but also the Chŏlla (1971) voters followed their regionalist instinct rather than their narrowly defined economic interests, when their regionalist favorite sons ran as presidential candidates. Otherwise, they treated the presidential election as a plebiscite on Park's agricultural policy.

In keeping with the rational peasants' behavior in the National Assembly elections, Park was a rational mobilizer. Knowing that the South Korean farmers tried to minimize losses rather than to maximize gains, Park equipped his rural political machine with two carrots and one stick. Park knew he could mobilize the farmers without giving them much, and he followed this instinct. When he found it difficult to pursue "balanced growth," it was the countryside that was to bear the brunt of budget reductions, as in the 1964–1968 period of agricultural squeeze. Park tried to get the most out of the little he did for South Korean farmers. He held the National Assembly elections soon after the presidential race in order to make the villages view his DRP candidates as an attractive choice to link villagers to the state bureaucracy. When Park resorted to the policy of agricultural squeeze to propel his export-led industrialization drive, he was careful not to make the agricultural squeeze too obvious by resorting to indirect methods of forced savings, such as inflationary financing. During the election year, he also tried to prop up, however temporarily, his image as a "son of the soil" by reducing the direct outflow of resources from the countryside, while increasing direct subsidies to the rural sector. And understanding villagers' low expectations of any marked difference between DRP and NDP candidates in the National Assembly elections, Park had his DRP candidates focus on promising locally prized construction projects, or simply give away a pair of rubber shoes, a bowl of *makkŏlli*, a towel, or even outright cash to secure a legislative majority.

CHAPTER THIRTEEN

The *Chaeya*

Myung-Lim Park

S OUTH KOREA IS KNOWN globally for its success as a state—and for
good reason. Energized by Park Chung Hee's vision and power (1961–
1979), and empowered with technocratic rationality, discretionary power,
and esprit de corps, the South Korean state achieved economic hypergrowth from the top down in one generation. In the literature on developmental states, it is a rare case, having largely beaten the market in the syn-
chronization of its *chaebol* partners' massive entries into new frontiers of
growth under their own brand names, product cycles, and distributive networks. Behind this widely celebrated story, however, lies another, much
less known tale of the *chaeya*. These dissident intelligentsia seemed to face
a losing battle, trying to reshape politics not from the inside but from outside South Korea's *chedogwŏn,* or official institutions of political rule, in
the belief that moral integrity, partisan neutrality, and intellectual independence constituted their source of power and would ultimately carry the
day.[1] To go inside the *chedogwŏn* to have an impact on politics and gain leverage over policy was interpreted as threatening this source of power, because it would transform the *chaeya* into merely another political force
with vested interests in the status quo and would weaken its members' will
to resist. The *chaeya* gave up opportunities to develop a political party for
fear of getting compromised by "dirty politics." Yet the *chaeya* still had a
crucial impact on South Korean politics, shaping national agendas, empowering social forces, and even laying the ground for regime change in

1979 by forcing Park and his developmental state into a risky strategy of repression and confrontation.

The paradoxical coexistence of a strong state and a contentious civil society during Park's political rule constitutes two sides of the same coin. South Korea's strong state was also a hard state that, for the sake of hypergrowth, refused to develop a dense web of institutional linkages to social forces, which Park thought cost state autonomy, damaged technocratic rationality, and required budget support. However, by refusing to institutionalize the politics of give-and-take, the state also left itself vulnerable to challenges from below. The question is why those challengers turned out to be the *chaeya* rather than the farmers and the workers. By analyzing the dissidents' changing ideological visions, diffuse yet cohesive *inmaek* (human networks), social support bases, and complementary but also competing relationships with social forces as well as opposition politicians, Chapter 13 traces the roots of the *chaeya*'s ability to engage the state in continual political contests despite its members' organizational weakness.

That the *chaeya* made up a nonparty, non-interest-group, extra-parliamentary opposition movement formed outside the *chedogwŏn* is clear. That this form of opposition was consciously chosen by its members, who envisioned the *chaeya* foremost as a group of activist intellectuals standing above politics to speak for moral principles and to guard national interests, is also obvious. However, such a broadly agreed-upon combination of identity, mission, and role did not mean that the *chaeya* developed in predictable ways. On the contrary, the moral principles and national interests for which they were to speak were anything but obvious. The political strategy, coalition partners, and ideational innovation required for the *chaeya* to transform into a guardian of those moral principles and national interests were even less clear. Consequently, there was no one static *chaeya* to speak of during Park's rule. Rather, it was a constantly evolving group of intellectual activists, maintaining their raison d'être as a moralistically packaged political force of nonparty and non-interest-group activists, but undergoing a qualitative change in ideology, organization, societal base, and relationship with opposition party politicians in 1964–1965, 1969, 1970, and 1972–1979.

First, ideologically the myth is that the *chaeya* were a collection of born radicals, if not leftists. The reality was the opposite. Many of the founders of South Korea's modern *chaeya* were Christian refugees from the North and took a staunch anticommunist stand. Yet these same activists steadily radicalized as Park evolved from a military coup leader with a reformist agenda (1961–1963) to a popularly elected "soft-authoritarian" modernizer (1963–1972) to a security czar with a *"yushin"* dictatorship (1972–1979). The *chaeya* evolved in tandem with Park, from anticommunist to pro-democracy activists, from pro-American to nationalist agitators, and from conservative reformers to radical supporters of distributive justice. Three historical events, in particular, profoundly reshaped the *chaeya* movement. By opposing the normalization of relations with Japan in 1964, the *chaeya* became a force of Korean nationalism very early in their history. The 1969 struggle against the constitutional revision to clear the way for Park's third presidential term added the image of freedom fighters. The profound soul-searching precipitated within the *chaeya* by the public suicide of Chŏn T'ae-il in 1970 ushered in another popular image—this time, as social reformers on the side of the oppressed *minjung* (people).

Because it was historical events rather than some preconceived theoretical or ideological worldview through which the *chaeya* added new political identities on top of their founding generation's anticommunist conservatism, the *chaeya* movements' ideology at the end of the journey in their struggle against Park was an amalgam of diverse—even contradictory—norms, values, and ideas. At the close of the *yushin* era, the *chaeya* were anticommunist, nationalist, Christian, liberal democratic, and social reformist.[2] But this did not prevent the *chaeya* from becoming a major force in South Korea. On the contrary, by being a number of things at the same time, they were able to appeal to a diverse array of societal forces. The *chaeya* activists' critique of authoritarian rule stoked the sense of injustice, anger, and hostility within society and persuaded a sizable number of students, workers, and members of the urban poor to join the intelligentsia-led moral crusade against Park. To be sure, their strength in attracting multiclass support also became a source of political weakness by obstructing them from building a consistent ideological platform. Nevertheless, they were still able to challenge Park and his regime because sharing a common enemy provided them with a group identity despite their diverse ideological origins.

Second, organizationally the *chaeya* formed a horizontal network. However, as the activists' identity expanded from nationalists to freedom fighters to social reformers, and as Park tightened his capacity for political control and repression, the *chaeya*, emerging from a geographically dispersed and ideologically heterogeneous rank and file, increasingly needed to supplement this horizontal network with a national umbrella organization to orchestrate a synchronized attack on the regime. The experiment began with the *chaeya*'s attempts at opposing the normalization of relations with Japan in 1964 and blocking Park from revising the constitution in 1969. With the slide into authoritarian rule, the *chaeya* furthered their organizational experiment, establishing the National Council for the Safe-guard of Democracy in 1971, the People's Congress for the Restoration of Democracy in 1974, the National Coalition for Democracy in 1978, and the National Coalition for Democracy and Unification in 1979. Rather than forming a tightly knit hierarchical organization on a permanent basis, the *chaeya* preferred to coalesce and disband as event-driven opportunities arose and disappeared. The hit-and-run strategy of guerrilla warfare not only provided the *chaeya* with political flexibility but also ensured the autonomy of its members. Besides, that strategy was the only way to fight the garrison state and escape its tight surveillance.

In addition to these efforts to establish a single umbrella organization at the national level to coordinate opposition efforts, the *chaeya* engaged in institutional innovations at the local and sectoral levels. A diverse array of church groups coalesced into the National Catholic Priests for the Realization of Justice and the Korean National Council of Churches. There were also the Korean Urban Industrial Christian Missionaries and the Young Catholic Workers, organized to empower the workers. Still others organized into myriad human rights watch groups. From these organizations was to emerge the second generation of religious *chaeya* leaders: Protestant ministers Kim Sang-gŭn, Yi Hae-dong, Cho Sŭng-hyŏk, O Ch'ung-il, and In Myŏng-jin; Catholic priests Kim Sŭng-hun, Ham Se-ung, and Mun Chŏng-hyŏn; and Buddhist monk Chin Kwan. On the other hand, it was from the student movements, singularly notable for their intensity and persistence, that the third generation of *chaeya* leaders emerged: Yi Pu-yŏng, Chang Ki-pyo, Kim Kŭn-t'ae, Kim Chi-ha, Cho Yŏng-rae, Yi Sin-bŏm, Yi Ch'ang-bok, Yi Ch'ŏl, Yu In-t'ae, Sim Chae-gwŏn, Cho Sŏng-u, Yi U-je, Na Pyŏng-sik, Pak Kye-dong, and Han Kyŏng-nam.

Third, throughout the history of *chaeya* development, religious groups constituted its most critical ally. The churches and temples provided a sanctuary for *chaeya* activists to hide from the police, as well as to organize political protests beyond the reach of the authorities. The church also tapped its extensive organizational network to raise funds for the *chaeya* on a regular basis. With the press under severe censorship, the church functioned as a "counter-media" as well, alongside underground study groups on the university campuses, disseminating contentious political ideas to a wide circle of people through many forms of publication. Consequently, wherever the *chaeya* did not have a well-developed activist-led local organization, it came to be the church that served as the focal point of the opposition. Through church networks, religious sermons, and church pamphlets, the *chaeya* coordinated the strategy of opposition among its rank-and-file members dispersed across diverse regions. The knowledge that other regions were waging struggles similar to theirs built up the local *chaeya* activists' confidence that they would eventually be victorious.

Equally important, the religious community helped the *chaeya* expand their agendas of political resistance and develop their identity as a force of liberation by providing a set of new values, norms, and ideas. The transformative impact of religion on the *chaeya* was most visible in the areas of human rights and labor issues. Equipped with the Christian notion of "natural rights," the church lashed out against the *yushin* regime's human rights violations. The church–state confrontation dramatically escalated when radical sectors of the religious community began importing liberation theology and embraced the right to a minimum standard of living as an integral part of human rights after the tragic death of Chŏn T'ae-il, a garment factory worker in one of the Ch'ŏngyech'ŏn sweat shops, in 1970. The clergy-intelligentsia coalition led the Korean Urban Industrial Christian Missionaries, Christian Academy, and Young Catholic Workers in organizing militant trade unions, especially in small- and medium-sized enterprises, where the working conditions were dismal. Fourth, the development of the *chaeya* as a political force was tied to the changing nature of political parties and electoral politics, especially the opposition strategy of the New Democratic Party (NDP), in complex ways. Ironically, it was the profound weakness of the National Assembly and the political parties that gave birth to the *chaeya* and fueled its continuous growth. Lacking the channels of representation and deprived of effective spokesmen for their economic interests and political values, South Korean societal forces turned to the intelligentsia-led *chaeya* for an alternative leadership. South Koreans may not have agreed on the specifics of the *chaeya*'s political agenda and especially its reconciliatory views toward North Korea, but they valued its role in placing what checks and balances it could on the Park regime, a role that the National Assembly failed to play and that the NDP only partially fulfilled. The lack of autonomous interest groups capable of organizing the workers and farmers made the intelligentsia-led *chaeya* even more the voice of societal interests.

The *chaeya*–NDP relationship was driven by forces of both collaboration and competition. When political interests converged, as in their common struggle to oppose the 1964 normalization of relations with Japan, the 1969 constitutional revision, and the 1972 promulgation of the *yushin* regime, the two collaborated closely by taking complementary roles, with the *chaeya* supporting the NDP through its moral authority and its army of student activists and the NDP providing the *chaeya* with an opportunity to shape national politics. The height of their collaboration came when the NDP, emboldened by its victory in the 1978 National Assembly elections and prodded by *chaeya* activists, elected "unyielding" Kim Young-sam over "compromising" Yi Ch'ŏl-sŭng as its party leader the next year. The subsequent explosion of *chaeya* protests and NDP struggles drove a fatal split between "soft-liner" Kim Chae-gyu's Korea Central Intelligence Agency (KCIA) and "hard-liner" Ch'a Chi-ch'ŏl's Presidential Security Service (PSS) over how to deal with the *chaeya*–NDP challenge, which sowed the seeds for Park's downfall in October 1979.

The complementarity of NDP–*chaeya* political roles, however, should not be overdrawn. The two joined forces to bring down the *yushin* in 1979, but during Yi Ch'ŏl-sŭng's NDP leadership (1976–1979), their relationship showed signs of strain. Whereas the *chaeya* adopted a strategy of intransigent opposition during most of Park's political rule, exposing his regime's moral faults, articulating social agendas, organizing popular forces, and escalating political confrontation with an eye to triggering a radical change of political regime and, after 1970, also of socioeconomic institutions, NDP party bosses typically stopped short of embracing regime change as their top priority except during Kim Young-sam's 1979 assault on Park and his *yushin* regime. Fighting for votes in a society whose memories of Pyŏngyang's military invasion in 1950 were still vivid, South Korea's opposition party could not let itself become a mere replica of radical *chaeya* activists, lest it acquire the vote-losing image of a leftist party. Even in 1979 with "unyielding" Kim Young-sam in charge, NDP bosses had their eyes focused on restoring liberal democratic principles rather than on bringing about a deeper socioeconomic transformation. Consequently, *chaeya* activists were always ahead of NDP bosses in expanding their agendas of political resistance, making the *chaeya* and the NDP not only players of complementary roles in political struggles against Park but also competitors occupying different ends of the opposition ideological spectrum. They looked like a united political force, but they were not. The endpoints of their political struggles against Park were different.

Early *Chaeya* Activists

Treaty Crisis and Nationalist Ethos, 1964–1965

When Park took power in May 1961, he met almost no resistance from university students or civic activists. On the contrary, many leaders of the protest movements that had brought down Syngman Rhee (1948–1960) and carried Chang Myŏn's Democratic Party into power in 1960 had publicly endorsed Park in the belief that he espoused the political ideals of those earlier student-led uprisings. Some of the activists even looked to the military, dominated by Kim Chong-p'il's young eighth graduating class of the Korea Military Academy, as the heirs to their 1960 student revolution to bring about a national rejuvenation.[3] Park actively encouraged such a perception. "Whereas the April Nineteenth Student Revolution succeeded only in toppling Syngman Rhee [without bringing a change of system through reform]," Park declared, "the May Sixteenth Military Revolution will lash out against the system [that survived the demise of Syngman Rhee]. The military will attack its democratic disguise and overthrow it from inside."[4]

The early support for the military coup was nowhere more visible than in *Sasanggye,* a magazine that served as a public forum for leading intellectuals. The June 1961 issue declared that "the Military Revolution of May 16, 1961, constitute[s] the last effort to save the nation from the dire predicament it faced. [Park has led] a nationalistic military revolution aiming to wipe out corruption and disorder, to preempt communist subversions, and to guide the future of the nation onto the right path. The military ha[s] embarked on an inevitable course of action in light of the exigency confronting South Korea."[5] The positive appraisal of *Sasanggye,* whose leaders were to become the founding generation of South Korea's modern *chaeya* movements after 1964, was due to its radical conservatism. Most of the founding generation of the *chaeya*—including Ham Sŏk-hŏn,[6] Kye Hun-je,[7] Mun Ik-hwan,[8] Chang Chun-ha,[9] Paek Ki-wan,[10] An Pyŏng-mu,[11] and Yi Yŏng-hŭi[12]—were refugees from North Korea, deeply immersed in Christianity and staunchly anticommunist due to their experience with communist rule during the post-liberation years of left–right conflict.[13]

The early enthusiasm of *Sasanggye* waned as the military junta turned to political repression and approached Japan for normalization of diplomatic relations. These two issues were to trigger political turmoil in 1964, pitting university students and intellectuals against Park and his Democratic Republican Party (DRP) in open conflict. The *Sasanggye* was at the center of this transformation of the progressive wing of South Korea's intelligentsia. First, the conflict involved a clash of two opposing worldviews—pragmatism and moralism, realism and idealism—over how to interpret Korean nationalism, what to make of its political mission, goals, and functions, and who "owned" it as a spokesperson for the national ethos. Whereas Park took the stand of a pragmatic leader ready to ask society to hold back its national pride and restrain anti-Japanese sentiments in order to gain Japanese reparation funds with which to build "a rich nation and a strong army" *(puguk kangbyŏng),* the *chaeya* took a moralistic posture. Unforgiving where Japan's colonial exploitation was concerned, the *chaeya* opposed the normalization of relations unless Japan unambiguously apologized for its past wrongdoings.

Second, it was a clash of two ideologically diverging paradigms of modernization. Against Park's economic strategy of "growth first, distribution later," which he justified not only in terms of what was required in a resource-poor country that needed to modernize but also in his belief that the benefits of growth would "trickle down" through the market, the *chaeya* spoke for distributive justice. In the area of political rights, too, a sharp division emerged. Whereas Park rejected Western democracy in favor of what he called "administrative" or "guided" Korean democracy, the *chaeya* was propelled by a vision of Western liberal values. The defining feature of its top leadership's ideology was procedural democracy, not populism, let alone Marxism-Leninism, which Park claimed was its hidden agenda.

The gap was unbridgeable. Park pushed for the normalization of relations with Japan to secure a new source of funding for economic development and to lay the groundwork for a trilateral security collaboration between Seoul, Tokyo, and Washington through a tightening of America's system of cold war bilateral military alliances, whereas university students, opposition party politicians, and dissident intellectuals demanded Japan's unambiguous apology for its colonial wrongdoings as a prerequisite for progress in bilateral relations. On March 9, 1964, in lieu of any such apology and wary of the danger that Japanese money might be channeled to DRP fund-raisers, the opposition political parties joined with some two hundred leaders of civil society to establish the National Committee for Opposition to Humiliating Diplomacy toward Japan and began staging protests nationwide. Initially, the opposition defined its protest movements as a struggle against Park's betrayal of Korean nationalism. Eventually, participants zeroed in on the political system Park personified as the target of resistance. Severely criticizing Park's notion of "nationalistic democracy" as authoritarian, student activists held a "funeral for nationalistic democracy" on May 20. They also denied Park's claim that he was the successor to the ideals of the April Nineteenth Student Revolution. On the contrary, in their eyes, Park was a reactionary coup-maker—not a revolutionary—who had reversed the historical tides of anticolonialism and antifeudalism embodied in their earlier protests.[14]

Thus were born the modern *chaeya*. The *chaeya* in their own eyes were a force of conscience in a struggle against the unjust and malign Park Chung Hee. *Chaeya* activists were the "practical" scholars, not the *ŏyŏng* (government-patronized unprincipled scholars). Driven by a sense of moral superiority, the *chaeya* helped NDP politicians in launching a frontal attack on state authority on June 3, 1964. Approximately ten thousand students took to the streets of Seoul and other major cities to force Park's resignation. The police reported that the protestors burned down a police station. Angry students even marched toward the Blue House, making political authorities nervously recollect the public outcry that had toppled Syngman Rhee only four years earlier. Park responded immediately. He declared martial law to prohibit political assemblies and demonstrations in Seoul. He also imposed censorship on the press, closed down all schools, permitted the arrest of protest leaders and organizers without warrants, and established a military court to judge violations of martial law. The swift crackdown broke the momentum of the student protests and drove the opposition political parties into silence—only for a while, but long enough to let the DRP-majority National Assembly enact the treaty bills in 1965.

The turmoil over the treaty irreversibly transformed the *Sasanggyo* and the progressive parts of South Korea's vocal intelligentsia into members of the anti-Park forces. "Having come to resemble the last days of Syngman Rhee's Liberal Party rule," the *Sasanggye* declared, "the three years of military rule have put the [South] Korean people in the worst chaos and hardship since the days of the Tan'gun [founding father of ancient Korea]."[15] Labeling the gap between its ideal of independence and Park's "subservience" toward foreign powers unbridgeable, the *Sasanggye* saw the emergence of a polarized political landscape pitting the *minjung* (people) against the "ruling clique" over the issues of national pride and democratic values.[16] Thus began the political competition between the *chaeya* and Park to control, command, and represent or personify the forces of Korean nationalism, democratic ideals, and egalitarian ethos. The *chaeya* capitalized on anti-Japanese Korean nationalism to build an independent base of power from which to challenge Park and the DRP. Moreover, because it was the United States who aggressively pushed for the normalization treaty in the hope of constructing trilateral regional ties between the United States, South Korea, and Japan to repel and contain the expansion of communism, the *chaeya*'s opposition to the treaty had the potential to develop into an anti-American movement. But that was only a potential, left for future *chaeya* leaders to bring to life.

Constitutional Revision and Democracy, 1969

A second transformation occurred in 1969, when the DRP, with the help of the KCIA, prepared for a constitutional revision to enable Park's bid for a third presidential term. The initiative moved the issue of democracy to the core of the *chaeya* agenda. By prompting the hitherto fragmented and isolated *chaeya* forces to join the opposition political party in one unified but still loose national organization, Park's 1969 campaign for constitutional revision also marked a turning point for the *chaeya* as an organization. In July 1969, the New Democratic Party partnered with *chaeya* leaders of diverse backgrounds to establish the National Committee to Oppose the Constitutional Revision (NCOCR) under the leadership of Reverend Kim Chae-jun.

The NCOCR issued what amounted to be a declaration of just war. "The Park regime," its manifesto stated, "[is using] the threat of North Korean military invasion for the purpose of political propaganda. However, the real threat that [could] encourage the North to invade the South [is] the destruction of national consensus and the spread of social unrest triggered by Park's dogged effort to bring about a constitutional revision." With these words the NCOCR used Park's doctrine of national security to delegitimize Park himself. The committee went on to warn that Park might institute lifelong dictatorship if he were permitted to prolong his political rule for four more years. The *chaeya* leaders also harshly criticized his proudest accomplishment, economic development, by accusing him of leading South Korea into "bankruptcy" and "obstructing efforts to democratize the economy."[17] The inability of many of the *chaebol* producers to pay back the interest on state-guaranteed foreign loans in the late 1960s made this accusation credible. The NCOCR, furthermore, distinguishing between the "regime" and the "state," warned Park not to confuse his fate with that of the state. "Adolph Hitler and his Nazi Party thought of themselves as the state," Reverend Kim Chae-jun asserted. To guard South Korean democracy, "it [is] necessary to remember that the fascists justified their existence in terms of the need to stem communism."[18]

However, while trying to obstruct Park from using South Korea's cold war ideologies to crack down on opposition forces, the *chaeya* also kept their distance from the "far left," not only because of their staunchly anticommunist stand, but also because of the need not to give Park an excuse for cracking down. When the underground Unification Revolution Party (URP) formed in 1969 with North Korean communist ideology as its guiding principle, no *chaeya* activists sought membership. Not only was the URP ideologically pro–North Korea; it also had organizational links with Pyŏngyang.[19] Although the founding generation of *chaeya* leaders were anti-Park, pro-unification, and egalitarian, North Korean attempts to generate a support base among *chaeya* activists failed dismally.

To the disappointment of NCOCR leaders, their plea to the literati, art-ists, professors, and religious leaders not to be bought off by the DRP and the KCIA did not win broad support within society. The *chaeya* turned to its proven strategy of mobilizing students by organizing a series of lectures, but this too failed to trigger a mass protest against the constitutional revision. Student activists issued public statements of opposition, took to the streets for demonstrations, and staged a hunger strike, but none of these provoked anything that resembled the anti-treaty protest of June 3, 1964. When the constitutional revision was approved by 65.1 percent in a national plebiscite with 77.1 percent voter participation in October 1969, student protests declined rapidly, forcing the *chaeya* to wait until the 1971 presidential election to reenter politics with some force.

Despite the defeat in 1969, however, the *chaeya* grew as a political entity in both organizational capabilities and ideological identity. Particularly crucial was the entry of South Korea's Christian community into politics in support of antisystem protests. Christian minister and NCOCR president Kim Chae-jun personified religion driven reform efforts, calling on the Christian community to "fulfill the holy duty, show the resolve [to fight injustice], and organize popular movements of resistance."[20] To be sure, the Christian community was not a unitary actor united against Park and his regime. On the contrary, the religious activists' entry into politics split South Korean Christians into "progressives" and "conservatives," a division that was to have a lasting impact. The vocal progressive minority was destined to serve as a sanctuary for dissident *chaeya* activists, while the conservative majority became unswervingly loyal supporters of Park's staunchly anticommunist stand during the 1970s.

As Park's victories in 1964 and 1969 demonstrate, it is important not to exaggerate the *chaeya*'s power during the pre-*yushin* era (1961–1972). The dissident intelligentsia's ability to produce a persuasive discourse of radical political resistance had noticeably weakened since Park's reestablishment of competitive elections in 1963. In spite of the selective use of political repression to preempt the rise of political rivals and to stabilize his regime, Park regularly held competitive elections and won by sizable margins. The DRP even won two thirds of the seats in the National Assembly in 1967, enabling it to set into motion the 1969 revision to the constitution without violating constitutional procedures. Moreover, despite the rising income gap between classes and regions, it was undeniable that Park had lifted even the most underprivileged sectors of South Korean society out of absolute poverty. The people's national pride had been damaged by Park's "humiliating diplomacy" in 1964 and their democratic aspirations scarred by his extension of his rule in 1969, but they also knew that the country was on the path to modernization.

Against the reality of economic growth, military modernization, and regular elections, the *chaeya*'s rhetoric of economic bankruptcy and fascist threat backfired, making the *chaeya* look too radical for the public to place the nation in its hands. Mainstream journalists, academics, and writers remained strikingly indifferent to the *chaeya*'s political agenda. Disenchanted, student activists accused the press of having lost the spirit of resistance it once possessed as a force of national independence during Japanese colonial rule and as an advocate of democracy against Syngman Rhee a decade earlier. Some student leaders even claimed that the press was propping up Park's political rule.[21] The mainstream academic community was targeted for criticism as well, depicted as betraying the ideals of the student revolution it had led in April 1960.[22]

Moreover, the *chaeya* of 1969, despite their split from the conservative mainstream of South Korea's intelligentsia, were primarily an intelligentsia-based opposition movement centered around a few spiritual leaders of national stature. The National Committee to Oppose the Constitutional Revision, then applauded as a turning point in *chaeya* organization, was led by a small group of notables with an agenda focused mainly on the ideological issues of nationalism and democracy. The unity it boasted of was one of ideological outlook rather than of organizational cohesion. When the *chaeya* ventured into economic areas, its critiques were more on moral than on policy grounds. Activists deplored social alienation and economic injustice, but their discourse was devoid of class ideologies. Consequently the *chaeya* of 1969 did not qualitatively differ from the opposition NDP in political orientation. Its members were largely conservative.

The Expansion of *Chaeya* Agendas

Minjung *Issues, 1970*

The year 1970 brought change of another order of magnitude for the *chaeya*. On November 13, Chŏn T'ae-il—a twenty-two-year-old tailor and union organizer employed in one of the clothing sweatshops in downtown Seoul—poured gasoline over his body and died by suicide. The news of his death shocked society, because while engaging in the usual *chaeya* discourse of reform and distributive justice, he also demanded that the political authorities abide by the existing labor laws. The suicide exposed the grim reality of labor exploitation hidden beneath South Korea's modern-looking legal system. As seen by Chŏn T'ae-il, the problem was not the lack of legal provisions for the protection of workers' rights. On the contrary, South Korean labor laws looked very "modern," having been literally copied from the labor laws of industrial democracies. The state, however, chose not to implement key provisions, in effect depriving workers of their legally guaranteed rights.

The death of Chŏn T'ae-il became a watershed in the history of *chaeya* activism, labor movements, and party politics.[23] Seoul National University students immediately organized a Student Committee for Preparing the Safeguard of Civil Rights. Other universities held memorial services in honor of Chŏn T'ae-il. Still others formed a fact-finding commission with the goal of bringing about "the improvement of working conditions and the guarantee of the workers' rights to form labor unions." The Christian community was also shaken, and prayers were said for Chŏn T'ae-il nationwide. Young activists like Chang Ki-p'yo—a dissident later identified by Reverend Mun Ik-hwan as "the sharpest of all knives that cut through the turbulence of the 1970s and 1980s"[24]—chose to join the *chaeya* and become professional revolutionaries out of their anger and frustration over the death of Chŏn T'ae-il. The transformed life of Chang Ki-p'yo signaled the emergence of a new breed of *chaeya* activists, who were more sensitive to the issues of the people *(minjung)* and more aware of the need to build a broad social alliance to bring about fundamental changes in the system. From their organizational experiments would emerge the *nohak yŏndae,* or the worker-student alliance that served as the bastion of radical opposition against what the *chaeya* then called Chun Doo-hwan's "new colonial state monopoly capitalism" (1980–1988).[25]

Korea University's Institute of Labor, established in 1965, also began reaching out to scholar-activists to teach trade union leaders, labor administrators, clergymen, and student leaders on the issues of labor-management relations, labor laws, and labor movements. At the same time, the Institute of Labor periodically conducted surveys of working conditions to raise public awareness of labor issues, as well as holding a series of lectures for rank-and-file members of the unions to transform their political consciousness.[26] Among the scholar-activists at the Institute of Labor were Cho Ki-jun, Cho Tong-p'il, Kim Yun-hwan, Kim Nak-jung, Yi Mun-yŏng, Kim Kŭn-su, and Kwŏn Tu-yŏng.

The impact on the Christian community was equally transformative. Since the late 1960s, its progressive sector had been trying to replace the dominant conservative theology with liberal doctrines, including liberation theology. It was the death of Chŏn T'ae-il that enabled these Christians to take an unequivocal stance on the issue of social justice and not only side with but also go beyond the NDP politicians in their struggle against Park. Their political activism led to the spread of the liberal Urban

Industrial Christian Missionaries throughout the 1970s. The missionaries constructed a web of religion-labor linkages that sought to redress labor and poverty issues from a progressive theological stand.[27] Their spokesman was Reverend Kim Chae-jun, who had led *chaeya* struggles against the 1969 constitutional revision in the belief that "the Christians and the Church [had to seek salvation] by waging the struggle for justice."[28] The progressives believed their movement was a *"Missio Dei,"* or Mission of God.[29]

The radicalization of the *chaeya* was nowhere more visible than in the concept of the *minjung* that permeated all the writings of dissident intellectuals. As defined by *chaeya* activists, the *minjung* were agents with the will to act, whereas the *taejung* (masses) were not. Possessing independent minds that they could use to resolve issues on their own terms, the *minjung* could become a force of change if the intelligentsia made them realize their revolutionary potential and organized them. Once the passive *taejung* were transformed into self-conscious and self-willing *minjung,* the *chaeya* argued, they would take hold of their own lives and fight to bring down the structures of injustice. Reflecting the revolutionary spirit that swept university campuses during the early 1970s is this excerpt from an activist study group at Seoul National University: "The *minjung* have finally overcome the sense of hopelessness and frustration and begun to create a new history. They have come to reject the unjust social order hitherto imposed upon them and demand a humane order . . . The *minjung* will seize history only when their struggle is guided [by student activists] along the right path."[30]

The *chaeya* radicalized even more when the Park regime forcibly relocated three thousand squatters from Seoul to the "Kwangju relocation complex" (present-day Sŏngnam) as part of its effort to "clean up" the capital city. Uprooted from their base of life overnight, the angry squatters raided public buildings and set a police station on fire on August 10, 1971, demanding the establishment of poverty-assistance measures. The violent explosion of mass discontent, the first of its kind under Park's rule, exposed South Korea's lack of a welfare safety net and the accompanying danger of political instability in many of its rapidly growing cities.[31] Together with Chŏn T'ae-il's suicide, the squatters' revolt visibly demonstrated that Park's strategy of export-led industrialization had failed to answer the needs of many of the urban poor despite the hypergrowth it had generated for a decade. With the exception of the issues of anti-Americanism, national unification, and socialism that dominated the *chaeya* movements of the 1980s, then, all major political, economic, and social agendas of today's South Korea made their emergence during the early 1970s.

It is important to note that student activists still remained the core of the resistance after 1970 although, unlike in the 1960s, they were complemented by and fused with protest movements based in other societal groups. While reaching out to labor and the urban poor for support, the *chaeya* also kept up their activities aimed at strictly student-related political issues, because it was from the university campuses that the *chaeya* recruited their future leaders as well as their rank-and-file members. In 1971 alone, over two thousand university students demonstrated every day against the military education program newly instituted by Park; they believed that the program had been established to incapacitate their resistance movements by creating a Red scare on the campuses.

Presidential Election, 1971

The 1971 presidential election was an important opportunity for the *chaeya* to test their dramatically strengthened organizational capabilities. They plunged into electoral contests to support NDP candidates because, even with Park's tightening of authoritarian political rule, elections mattered. Given Park and his DRP-KCIA power elite's superior capabilities to mobilize society from the top, elections were unlikely to bring about a change in South Korea's top political leadership. Nor did they adequately express the hopes and fears of societal groups, because South Korean political parties, including the NDP, lacked organizational linkages to society and because interest groups were preempted by the Park regime from developing their own distinctive agendas, strategies, and organizations of collective political action. Elections were more a plebiscite vote on his leadership than an occasion to articulate and organize the country's top policy agendas. Ironically, however, because elections were plebiscites, they did matter. They indicated the public mood and, in doing so, influenced more than the dynamics of political confrontation between the Park regime and the NDP-*chaeya* opposition. To use the NDP's electoral performance as leverage over Park, the *chaeya* sought to strengthen solidarity with the NDP in 1971.

Strengthening the *chaeya*'s incentives for solidarity with the NDP even more, conservative Yi Ch'ŏl-sŭng backed progressive Kim Dae-jung over moderate-conservative Kim Young-sam in the opposition political party's election of its 1971 presidential candidate on regionalist grounds. Kim Dae-jung represented a new breed in NDP factional politics. Whereas Yi

Ch'ŏl-sŭng boasted of his anticommunist political credentials built during his student-activist days of post-liberation Left–Right ideological struggles, and Kim Young-sam of his spirit of moderation and his centrist role in legislative politics since 1954, Kim Dae-jung had entered South Korean politics as a leftist in 1945. Until 1946 he had participated in the Committee for the Preparation of Korean Independence and the leftist People's Committee, and worked in the New People's Party, because, he said, he "did not have a clear understanding of either communism or nationalism." Disillusioned by the pro-Soviet orientation of Korean communists, Kim Dae-jung quickly severed his ties with them and embraced the nationalist principle of "Independence First."[32] This early involvement in communist activities came to haunt Kim Dae-jung, once he acquired national political stature in 1971. Ironically, it was Park with his own brief period of participating in the leftist organization, who played on the public distrust of Kim Dae-jung's ideology to short-circuit his political career.

By contrast, what the Right thought was Kim Dae-jung's political fault was an ideological plus in the eyes of many *chaeya* activists. Whereas Park converted to South Korea's political conservatism, Kim Dae-jung evolved into a progressive thinker, fitting in well with the *chaeya* that, for the most part, were a "liberal reformist movement."[33] Its members objected to Park because he placed national security and economic growth before democracy in the hierarchy of national priorities. The *chaeya* embraced democracy as its top priority because "democracy was a catalyst [or a precondition] for economic development, not its obstacle," to quote the words of Kim Dae-jung. The two were in a virtuous circle, democratization facilitating economic development and vice versa, as in Western Europe.[34] Park took the opposite stand, asserting that "for developing countries, economic modernization [is] an absolute precondition for the growth of democracy . . . Democracy blossoms only on the fertile soil of economic development."[35]

On April 19, 1971, Kim Chae-jun (a minister), Ch'ŏn Kwan-u (a journalist), and Yi Pyŏng-rin (a lawyer) became co-chairs of the National Council for the Safeguard of Democracy (NCSD). The council was the representative of the progressive wing of South Korea's religious forces, press, intellectuals, and legal community, thus bringing the hitherto dispersed factions of the *chaeya* into a nationwide organization of solidarity against Park. Students, for their part, formed the National Student Alliance for the Safeguard of Democracy (NSASD), as civil society's watchdog over the presidential election. Under the leadership of the NCSD, a total of 6,139 students, youth leaders, literati, and religious activists jointly set up local election-monitoring commissions throughout the country.[36] Despite

Park's electoral victory, the *chaeya*—unlike in 1967 and 1969—managed not to collapse and instead drew on their strengthened organizational capabilities. From March to November 1971, a total of 269 student demonstrations broke out, with 62,264 students participating.[37] As their protests refused to subside, Park was forced to issue a decree on October 25 authorizing a military presence on university campuses. Armed military troops marched onto the campus of every major university in Seoul, resulting in the arrest of as many as 1,889 student activists.

The repression backfired, triggering a proliferation of underground campus newspapers, which soon became the *chaeya*'s primary mechanism of disseminating radical ideas to bring about what *chaeya* activists called the *ŭisikhwa,* or the raising of the students' consciousness to the reality of social injustice and political repression. The underground publications that came to acquire influence over the student body included Seoul National University's *Chayu-ŭi Chong* (The Bell of Liberty), *Ŭidan* (The Righteous Platform), *Hwalhwasan* (The Active Volcano), *Hwaetpul* (The Torch), and *Chŏnya* (The Eve); Korea University's *Hanmaek* (The Pulse of the Han [Korean]), *Sanjisŏng* (The Living Intellectual Spirit), and *Sannara* (The Nation Alive); Ewha Womans University's *Saeŏl* (The New Soul) and *Saetpyŏl* (The Morning Star); Yonsei University's *Naenara* (My Country); the Korean Student Christian Federation's *Kwangya-ŭi Sori* (The Voice of the Field); Chŏnnam University's *Noktu* (Mung Beans, a popular alias of Chŏn Pong-jun, a leader of the 1894–1895 peasant uprising against Japanese imperialism and the Chosŏn dynasty's exploitative feudalism); and Pusan University's *Hanŏl* (The Soul of the Han [Korean]).[38] As the titles suggest, the student activists of the early 1970s not only focused on political democratization but also zeroed in on *minjung* issues from the rights of workers to the structure of urban poverty. Highly critical of the mainstream press for having compromised its role as the watchdog of the state, the underground newspapers, weeklies, and monthlies vigorously called on students to rise up against social injustice and political repression.

The increasing criticism of these mainstream press had an awakening effect on journalists. On April 15, 1971, *Dong-A Ilbo* announced a "Declaration on Freedom of the Press" and pledged to fight censorship. *Hankook Ilbo, Chosun Ilbo, JoongAng Ilbo,* Munhwa Broadcasting Company, and *Haptong T'ongsin* (Hapdong News Agency) soon joined the cause with their own manifestos.[39] On July 28, a total of 153 judges confronted the Public Prosecutor's office with their demand for the independence of the judicial branch, the first judicial defiance of its kind since the establishment of the Republic in 1948. On August 23, a group of university professors denounced the military troops' occupation of the campus, and declared their support for the academic community's freedom and autonomy. The *chaeya* thought Park was under attack on all fronts, with the press, judiciary, and academia, in addition to urban squatters and union organizers, starting to challenge him for their political and civil rights.

Against the rising tide of opposition, Park chose to raise—not reduce— the level of political repression. He issued a "garrison decree" in October 1971, only to follow it with an even more drastic measure of regime change a year later. The launching of the *yushin* regime in October 1972 silenced the NDP and reduced *chaeya* activities—but only very briefly. Contrary to Park's calculations, the *yushin* measures not only strengthened but also radicalized the dissidents. The turn to a blatantly authoritarian form of political rule ironically gave the *chaeya* a clear set of radical goals and strategies. The elimination of competitive elections also provided the *chaeya* with an opportunity to penetrate deeply into society and shape public opinion from a position of moral and ideological strength.

Radical Political Mobilization

Confronting the Yushin, 1972–1974

Reflecting the changes that had occurred in the *chaeya*'s composition, ideology, and organization during the 1969–1972 period, it was the Christian activists, in collaboration with student radicals, who launched the first waves of political resistance against the *yushin* constitution by holding an anti-*yushin* Namsan Easter service on April 22, 1973. The Christian-led resistance signaled serious trouble for Park, because of South Korean Christians' intimate ties with religious forces abroad. Repression became a highly costly political option. Any arrest of Christian activists instantly triggered diplomatic protests and especially eroded support for Park in America.

The news of the Namsan Easter service soon reached the university campuses to ignite new waves of political protest. Korea University students launched anti-Park protests in May and June 1973, only to see their leaders arrested by the police. After several months of silence, Seoul National University students held a street demonstration on October 2, calling for "the termination of fascist rule by the security forces, the re-establishment of liberal democracy with basic rights of the people re-instituted, the eradication of subservience to Japan, and the construction of a nationalist economy based on the principles of national autarky and people's right to the minimum standard of living."[40] Because of press censorship, the student protestors could not reach out to the public for support. Nonetheless, the news of their resistance spread to other sectors of the *chaeya*, to be interpreted as a call to rise up against Park.

Reverend Kim Chŏng-jun, a leading thinker on *minjung* theology and a dean of Hansin University, shaved his head in protest against the crackdown on student activists. *Chaeya* leaders like Chang Chun-ha, the editor of *Sasanggye*, and Paek Ki-wan began a nationwide effort to collect a million signatures for the revision of the *yushin* constitution on December 24, 1973. The signature drive immediately found support among the literati community, religious leaders, students, and NDP politicians, becoming a catalyst for a wide range of moderate societal leaders to merge forces with the hitherto radical-dominated *chaeya* movement. The infusion of moderates, from Cardinal Kim Su-hwan and Buddhist monk Pŏpjŏng, to intellectuals like Yi Hŭi-sŭng, Paek Nak-chun, Pak Tu-jin, Yi Sang-ŭn, and Kim Yun-su, to Reverend Kim Kwan-sŏk and politicians Kim Hong-il and Yi In dramatically strengthened the *chaeya*'s standing in the eyes of the general public.[41] In only eleven days, the signature drive succeeded in getting 30,000 people to sign in support of the revision of the *yushin* constitution. Park reacted by issuing Emergency Decree no. 1, which prohibited any denunciation of the *yushin* constitution. That prompted Christian leaders to issue another declaration of opposition—this time, not only against the *yushin* but also against Emergency Decree no. 1.

On April 3, 1974, the police, in cooperation with the KCIA, arrested 2,000 student activists under the charge that they had clandestinely organized a subversive National Democratic Youth Students Alliance (NDYSA) at North Korea's instigation. The same day, Park authorized Emergency Decree no. 4 in order to quell student protests. The decree prohibited student rallies and demonstrations, empowered the state to close down schools that were found to violate the decree, permitted the mobilization of the armed forces whenever necessary for the purposes of public security, and dramatically increased the legal punishment for the instigators of demonstrations to include the death sentence.[42] The promulgation of Emergency Decree no. 4 occasioned the arrest of 2,000 people, 203 of whom were sentenced to imprisonment by the military court. The court verdicts added up to a total of 1,800 years, and included eight death sentences.[43]

The NDYSA was a fabrication. The student activists had been planning to instigate a nationwide anti-*yushin* demonstration as part of their effort to forge a broad alliance of resistance among diverse student forces, but they had not organized the NDYSA. The *yushin* regime's invention of NDYSA activities had the effect of strengthening the *chaeya*'s sense of solidarity and the expansion of its forces in society. The arrest of former president Yun Po-sŏn, Bishop Chi Hak-sun, Reverend Pak Hyŏng-gyu, poet Kim Chi-ha,[44] and professors Kim Tong-gil and Kim Ch'an-guk on charges of aiding the students' organization of NDYSA from behind the scenes made the *yushin* regime's legal case seem all the more untenable in the eyes of the general public. The Christian opposition, in particular, strengthened after the April 1974 crackdown. Park's attempt to weed out all sources of opposition on university campuses in one single stroke only provoked stronger resistance from below. With the public questioning the *yushin* regime's intentions, repression became increasingly ineffective in silencing the *chaeya*.

On the other hand, the "Declaration for the *Minjung,* Nation, and Democracy," which the student activists announced before their arrest on April 3, 1974, showed the student movements' radicalization since the promulgation of the *yushin* constitution. These activists claimed to lead a "nationalist democratic movement representing the will of the *minjung* and pursuing genuine freedom and equality." Their agenda was a precursor to the 1980s' radical *samminjuŭi* (Peoples' Three Principles) of *minjungjuŭi,* nationalism, and democracy. Unlike the more liberal-bourgeois color of the pre-*yushin* student movements, the student activists of April 1974 had a clearly defined social and political agenda that included confiscating the "illicit wealth" accumulated by *chaebol* owner-managers and politicians, reducing taxes on the popular sector, guaranteeing minimum subsistence earnings for the masses, recognizing workers' right to collective action through an overhaul of the labor laws, releasing all *chaeya* activists from prison, replacing the *yushin* regime with a genuinely democratic political order, dismantling the KCIA-led coercive security apparatuses, and building an "autonomous" national economic system through a decisive shift away from the exploitative export-led industrialization drive. The 1974 declaration also appealed for the participation of workers in company management and industrial policymaking. To show the *yushin* regime the power of the *chaeya* opposition, the declaration's authors also called on students to gather in front of the Seoul city hall and move along to the Ch'ŏnggyech'ŏn to show solidarity with the workers in the clothing sweatshops where Chŏn T'ae-il had once worked.

Three months after the crackdown, the *yushin* regime reversed itself and lifted Emergency Decree no. 4, realizing that the measure had unexpectedly strengthened the *chaeya*'s resolve to resist. The overture toward dialogue did not work. On the contrary, political protests broke out every day through the end of 1974. Some university students staged hunger strikes. Many more went to the streets to confront the police. In Kwangju, the authorities had to cancel classes at seven high schools in order to prevent demonstrations. By October 30, 1974, the Ministry of Education (MoE) had to close down a total of 44 universities and issue an administrative order to 13 others among South Korea's 77 four-year universities to stop the spread of protests. Finally, on December 25, leaders from all corners of society—opposition politicians, Catholic activists, Protestant leaders, Buddhists, journalists, professors, writers, judges, and feminist leaders—created the People's Congress for the Restoration of Democracy (PCRD), with the goal of bringing down the *yushin* regime. The PCRD leadership consisted of many of South Korea's most renowned public figures: Catholic priests Yun Hyŏng-jung and Ham Se-ung; lawyers Yi Pyŏng-rin, Hong Sŏng-u, and Han Sŭng-hŏn; feminist leaders Yi T'ae-yŏng and Kim Chŏng-rye; opposition politicians Kim Young-sam, Kim Dae-jung, Yang Il-dong, and Kim Ch'ŏl; writer Kim Chŏng-han; journalist Ch'ŏn Kwan-u; Reverend Kang Wŏn-ryong; professors Paek Nak-ch'ŏng and Kim Pyŏng-gŏl; and philosopher Ham Sŏk-hŏn.

Adopting self-determination, peace, and righteous conscience as its "principles guiding action" and the restoration of democracy as its goal, the PCRD defined its campaign of resistance as a "people's movement." For the first time in the *chaeya*'s history, the PCRD strove to organize political struggle in a systematic way, establishing a six-member operations committee and a secretariat at the center and "chapters" in the provincial areas. By March 1975, the PCRD had managed to establish seven chapters at the city and province level and twenty at the county level, with leadership coming mostly from the local clergy and opposition party branch. A month earlier, the People's Congress had proclaimed the Democratic People's Charter—as opposed to the *yushin* regime's National Education Charter—in which the PCRD declared that "in an act of conscience . . . we hope to devote ourselves to a nationwide people's movement for the establishment of democracy." In a separate statement addressed to the *minjung*, the PCRD called for a "movement to encircle [and isolate] the dictatorial regime" in the "spirit of intransigence and disobedience." PCRD leaders seemed to be considering launching a civil disobedience movement.

The "People's Coalition," 1975–1979

By March 1975, discontent had become so pervasive that each protest drew students by the thousands. For the first time since the promulgation of the *yushin* constitution, demonstrations were drawing in nonactivist students in large numbers. To preempt a further escalation of political conflict, the *yushin* regime reverted back to the strategy of political repression and issued Emergency Decree no. 7 on April 8, 1975. With it, the military sent troops to occupy the campus of Korea University. In the month of April alone, a total of twenty-five universities were forced to cancel lectures. A Seoul National University student, Kim Sang-jin, committed suicide by disembowelment during a demonstration rally after reading a "Declaration of Conscience" and an "Open Letter to the President," in which he cried out: "How can we tolerate dictatorial rule anymore? . . . Democracy grows on the blood. Comrades! Do you have the courage to give your lives so that the leaves of democracy can flourish eternally on this land?"[45]

Tensions built up until the fall of Saigon in April 1975, which gave the *yushin* regime some breathing space. Taking advantage of the severe sense of security crisis precipitated by the communist takeover of Indochina, Park pursued a two-track strategy of engineering anticommunist rallies to appeal to the conservatives for ideological backing for his rule, on the one hand, and increasing the level of repression to isolate the opposition from nonactivist students, on the other. The second part of the strategy culminated in the promulgation of Emergency Decree no. 9 for the Preservation of National Security and Public Order on May 13, 1975. The decree prohibited anyone from engaging in activities to "deny, oppose, distort, slander, revise or abrogate the *yushin* constitution," as well as from "initiating a petition for constitutional revision."[46] The National Assembly, dominated by Park's DRP and the additional hand-picked *Yujŏnghoe* members his majority entitled him to appoint, followed up with its own resolution to "repel the North Korean puppet regime and to safeguard [South Korea's] liberal democracy." The Ministry of National Defense (MND) reinstituted the Student Defense Corps (SDC) in face of vigorous student opposition, with the goal of triggering another Red scare on the campuses to isolate student activists from the general student body.

The promulgation of Emergency Decree no. 9 took the level of repression to new heights and gave the South Koreans only two options: acquiesce in the *yushin* regime or engage in a total struggle for the restoration of democracy.[47] The *chaeya* took the second option, brushing aside the decree as illegitimate and issuing a Declaration of National Democratic Salvation at Myŏngdong Cathedral on March 1, 1976, in support of restoration of democracy, reform of the economic system, and peaceful unification, in addition to the resignation of Park.[48] For the first time, the *chaeya* came out publicly to support the removal of Park from power. Previously, their demands had included only the dismantlement of the *yushin* regime. And by including peaceful unification in their agenda along with democracy and economic reform, the authors of the Declaration of National Democratic Salvation recognized the close link between the issues of national division and domestic politics. As Park's periodic Red scares demonstrated, the division of the Korean Peninsula into two hostile regimes had discouraged the development of South Korean democracy by enabling Park to crack down on protest movements in the pretext of national security. *Chaeya* activists victimized by cold war ideas and ideologies came to believe that South Korean democracy could grow only if national unification proceeded simultaneously with—if not preceded by—democratization.[49] The declaration of March 1, 1976, was primarily the work of Mun Ik-hwan, a once-moderate Protestant minister who had become a radical out of rage over the allegedly accidental death of Chang Chun-ha, a leader of the *Sasanggye* intellectuals.

The declaration led to the establishment of a closer alliance between the conservative NDP and the radical *chaeya*. The two realized that they could not effectively counter Emergency Decree no. 9 without pooling their scarce political resources. The seeds for the alliance had been sown when the *yushin* regime began cracking down on the *chaeya* even more aggressively after the "Myŏngdong Declaration." The opposition political party then unambiguously came out in support of the *chaeya*, demanding the release of its leaders from prison. Political resistance was led by the progressive sector of the Christian community, who organized a Committee for Justice and Peace and stated that Park no longer commanded any moral authority over the nation. The *yushin* regime, however, did not back down. On the contrary, it rounded up and imprisoned the leadership of the *chaeya*.[50] The *chaeya* leaders, too, refused to compromise. During his trial, Yi T'ae-yŏng foresaw the coming of a "war between the people and the [Park] regime, and a showdown between the judiciary branch and the citizens."[51] When the state prosecutors taunted the *chaeya* dissidents for risking "the collapse of the entire country in their struggle for freedom and democracy, much like in [the fallen] South Vietnam," the *chaeya* defendants argued that it was the *yushin* regime, not the *chaeya*, that endangered national security by precipitating political instability and disharmony through its divisive authoritarian rule. To allay public fears of North Korea–instigated political instability, moreover, the *chaeya* leaders declared that they were staunchly anticommunist.[52]

The radicalization of society continued at a rapid pace under the impact of Emergency Decree no. 9. In a massive assault on the intelligentsia, many of the country's leading progressive thinkers were driven off their campuses, including Yi Yŏng-hŭi[53] and Chŏng Ch'ang-ryŏl at Hanyang University; Han Wan-sang[54] and Paek Nak-ch'ŏng at Seoul National University; Kim Tong-gil, Sŏng Rae-un, and Sŏ Nam-dong at Yonsei University; Kim Yong-jun and Yi Mun-yŏng at Korea University; An Pyŏng-mu at

Hanshin University; and Yi U-jŏng from Seoul Women's University. To counter Park, the dissenters organized the Council of Unjustly Dismissed Professors to continue their struggle. Contrary to the *yushin* regime's intention to sever these scholars' ties with the wider intelligentsia and the general student body, their dismissal had the opposite effect of transforming them into the martyrs of human rights on the university campuses and strengthening their moral power over the public. Their expulsion from the campus, in fact, facilitated the professors' active participation in *chaeya* activities, giving them the time, moral legitimacy, and political networks required to organize resistance movements. In the process, they instilled a *"minjung* consciousness" in student activists from South Korea's elite universities.

Christian church groups raised their level of resistance too, establishing the Council of Human Rights Movements in December 1977, the first of many alliances of nongovernmental organizations that were to emerge in defense of human rights during the 1970s.[55] The National Catholic Priests for the Realization of Justice similarly had been demanding Park's repeal of the emergency decrees, which the group saw as "in violation of natural law and human conscience," since the imprisonment of Bishop Chi Hak-sun in July 1974. The rising *chaeya* pressures on the *yushin* regime persuaded even Yi Ch'ŏl-sŭng, the leader of what was then the mainstream faction of the moderates within the NDP, to make a public demand for the repeal of Emergency Decree no. 9, the release of political prisoners, and the establishment of an independent constitutional commission to review the *yushin* regime. Yi Ch'ŏl-sŭng had been an advocate of "Reform through Participation" because he feared the domino effects of the fall of Saigon. With the weakening of Yi Ch'ŏl-sŭng's hold over the NDP and the *chaeya*'s deep penetration into society, the *yushin* regime encountered great difficulty in selling the 1976 court ruling on the Declaration of National Democratic Salvation that "while the constitution guarantee[s] the right of disobedience as a natural right, [this right of civil disobedience cannot] supersede the state's emergency measures."[56]

On March 4 of the same year, twelve *chaeya* organizations came together under the umbrella of a newly established National Coalition for Democracy and National Unification (NCDNU). Its composition showed how far the *chaeya* had come in institutional development. Whereas the *chaeya* of the early 1970s possessed only one symbolic figure of resistance in the person of Chŏn T'ae-il, the *chaeya* of the late 1970s was spearheaded by a group of widely respected public figures, who had gained moral clout in withstanding harsh state repression: Kim Chi-ha (literary community), Yi Yŏng-hŭi (academia), Kim Dae-jung (politics), Chi Hak-sun (Catholic Church), Mun Ik-hwan and Pak Hyŏng-gyu (Protestant church), and Song Kŏn-ho (journalism). Whereas Chŏn T'ae-il came from the lower stratum of the population, the *chaeya* leaders of the late 1970s were part of South Korea's burgeoning middle class.

It was not the *chaeya,* however, that brought down the *yushin* regime. The political turmoil in the Pusan-Masan area that ultimately triggered the regime collapse in 1979 was spontaneous, with its immediate cause lying in the Pusan-Masan residents' outrage at Park's order to his lieutenants in the DRP, KCIA, and PSS to expel their regional favorite son, NDP leader Kim Young-sam, from the National Assembly for his intervention on the side of the workers in an isolated labor dispute and for his interview with the *New York Times* that urged the United States to force democratization on Park.[57] This was the first time the National Assembly had expelled one of its members in the history of South Korean politics. In protest, the United States summoned Ambassador William H. Gleysteen, Jr., back to Washington. The confrontation between the *yushin* and the loose coalition of the NDP and *chaeya* activists unexpectedly ended when KCIA director Kim Chae-gyu assassinated Park on October 26, 1979, during a meeting with Park and PSS chief Ch'a Chi-ch'ŏl over how to handle a mass revolt in Pusan and Masan in support of Kim Young-sam.[58] The protagonists in the political showdown of October 1979, in other words, were Park's security forces and opposition NDP parliamentary forces—not the *chaeya.* Moreover, the issue that galvanized the Pusan-Masan people was not the *chaeya*'s "new" radical agendas of national unification and distributive justice, but the political parties' traditional regionalist rivalries (see Chapters 5 and 6).

The importance of the NDP opposition and partisan conflict in making the *chaeya*-instigated ideological polarization a moment of regime change underlines the centrality of political parties even during authoritarian rule. In contrast to the *chaeya,* which came out to challenge Park from the very outset of his decision to launch the *yushin,* the NDP zigzagged from "moderate" Kim Young-sam's two-track strategy of dialogue and resistance (1974–1976), to Yi Ch'ŏl-sŭng's "compromising" strategy of reform-through-participation (1976–1979), to "unyielding" Kim Young-sam's confrontational strategy of regime change and democratic revival (1979). The NDP eventually decided to challenge Park in 1979 because, with the abolition of direct presidential elections, the transformation of the National Assembly into a rubber stamp through Park's appointment of a third of the parliamentary members with the hand-picked *Yujŏnghoe,* and the successive promulgation of emergency decrees, it had become constitutionally barred from taking power. The NDP ended up defining its political objective as nothing less than the overthrow of the *yushin* regime. With the paralysis of the legislative branch, the NDP went to the streets to appeal directly to the public and fight the state in an all-out confrontation. This partisan conflict ultimately led to the collapse of the *yushin* regime.

MODERN South Korean politics have been marked by a persistent clash of two protagonists: the hard state and the contentious society. During much of its postwar era, South Korea experienced "moments of madness" (to borrow Aristide Zolberg's phrase referring to French history) that periodically swept over society to alter the political landscape in unexpected directions.[59] The country swung between the extremes of stable authoritarian rule and outbursts of political protest. Modern South Korean politics constituted a battlefield, where the hard state, insulated from society, clashed against the organizationally weak, but spiritually resilient and contentious, *chaeya* in what looked like an endless cycle of repression and resistance.

The *chaeya* of 1964–1979 was a popular movement that found its raison d'être in raising a moral critique against authoritarian rule. What gave birth to it and accelerated its growth into a major force by the late 1970s was ironically Park himself. Every impetus for the *chaeya*'s growth came from Park's political choices: the signing of the normalization treaty with Japan in 1964, the constitutional revision to introduce a third presidential term in 1969, the promulgation of the *yushin* constitution in 1972, and the declaration of nine emergency decrees between 1973 and 1975. The *chaeya* demonstrated during the 1960s, but its efforts did not yield as spectacular results as in the *yushin* era, because in the earlier decade the institution of competitive elections provided an outlet for political discontent. Conversely, when Park promulgated the *yushin* constitution in 1972, he closed down all open and competitive avenues of political dialogue, negotiation, and compromise, thus making not only the public turn to the *chaeya* for an articulation of society's suppressed ideas and interests, but also the NDP join forces with the *chaeya* for the sake of its political survival.

Politics became a zero-sum game after 1972, because South Korea's two power blocs held opposing worldviews, eliminating any possibility of reaching a modus vivendi. The opposition bloc of *chaeya* activists and NDP politicians championed political liberty, social justice, and human rights, whereas the ruling DRP coalition placed national security and economic growth before democratic ideals. Once the two were put on a collision course with Kim Young-sam's takeover of the NDP leadership in 1979, it was difficult for either side to back down, because of the disastrous consequences this would bring to the internal cohesion of their respective power blocs. A dynamic of escalation was also built into the politics of confrontation that was difficult to stop. The *yushin* regime's repression made the *chaeya* even more contentious. The *chaeya*'s resistance, in turn, made the *yushin* resort to even more repression. The vicious circle of repression and resistance feeding on each other continued until the ruling coalition was left with the unattractive options of either violently repressing mass protestors or surrendering to the opposition by October 1979. The *yushin* regime was paralyzed over the choice of its next political move until KCIA director Kim Chae-gyu cracked under pressure and assassinated his lifetime mentor, Park, "not because [he] did not love Caesar, but because [he] loved Rome more," as Kim said with reference to Marcus Junius Brutus during his trial of December 18, 1979.

Compared with Syngman Rhee's political rule, at least three factors worked in favor of the *chaeya*. First, Park was far more repressive than Syngman Rhee, making the *chaeya*—not the National Assembly or the political parties—that much more important as an actor of democratic resistance. Second, Park's modernization drive brought not only economic growth but also an aggravated sense of relative deprivation in society. The accompanying economic differentiation created a huge industrial working class with the potential to turn against the political authorities in distributive struggles. Third, slowly coming out of the shock of the Korean War and rapidly acquiring the contentious ideas of liberal democracy under the tutelage of the United States, the Christian community and the intelligentsia began to engage in political activism. However, many aspects of these three factors did not play out to their full antisystem potential during Park's political rule, despite the *chaeya* activists' continuous radicalization, because the workers still remained under tight state control. The *chaeya* of the 1964–1979 period reached out to labor for support, but still the workers' participation was not extensive, making the *chaeya* still an intelligentsia-based protest movement without dense and wide ties to popular forces even during the October 1979 mass revolt.

It was only after Park's death on October 26, 1979, that the *chaeya* transformed into groups with well-developed linkages to the student protest movements, religious communities, and industrial workers. The abrupt demise of the *yushin* regime before the full-scale mobilization of popular forces by the coalition of *chaeya* activists and NDP politicians, however, made the 1980s a painful transition to democratic rule. On the one hand, the *yushin* constitution was repealed, but its apparatus of political and social control survived the death of Park. The institutional legacy of Park made it possible for Chun Doo-hwan's military faction to seize political power by launching a coup d'état on December 12, 1979, and expand martial law to the entire country on May 17, 1980. On the other hand, the *chaeya* was too weak to stop Chun Doo-hwan's march to power, but it was also too strong to be silenced by the coup-makers. The distribution of power between the military and the *chaeya* ushered in the continuation of the "Park regime without Park" for eight more years, while the state-*chaeya* confrontation continued.

PART IV

INTERNATIONAL
RELATIONS

CHAPTER FOURTEEN

The Vietnam War:
South Korea's Search for
National Security

Min Yong Lee

A U.S. SENATOR ONCE called South Korea's military troops fighting in South Vietnam "mercenaries."[1] By contrast, many of Park Chung Hee's domestic critics believed that South Korea dispatched its combat troops because of U.S. political pressure. Either way, Park was portrayed as a man of moral shortcomings, a willing mercenary on a military mission abroad either for money or a reluctant instrument of U.S. imperial ambitions. The reality, however, was much more complex. Presumably Park could have accommodated U.S. demands by going only part way, limiting the dispatch of military troops to noncombat forces. Or he could have sent a smaller force of combat troops. But Park picked one of the best units in South Korea's army, the Tiger Division, responsible for the defense of Seoul, to be the first combat force to be sent in 1965.[2] The White Horse Division that followed in 1966, too, had an impeccable reputation. Moreover, it was not U.S. policymakers but Park who proposed sending the South Korean combat troops in 1961. At the height of the allied military intervention, some 50,000 South Korean soldiers fought side by side with 550,000 U.S. troops in South Vietnam.

The Vietnam War became important to South Korea because Park made it important. Even if the threat of a "domino effect" was real, there was always the politically easy option of a free ride, letting the United States provide regional stability and containment by itself. Moreover, South Korea was neither an ally of South Vietnam nor a member of the Southeast Asia

Treaty Organization (SEATO). On top of that, the South Korean military situation at home was itself precarious, depriving Park of the luxury of worrying about other countries' security problems. Given the North Korean military threat, South Korea was not a likely candidate to provide the most significant support out of all other nations for the U.S. military campaign in South Vietnam. Yet it participated in the Vietnam War with the second-largest number of military troops after the United States.

Chapter 14 argues that despite the huge economic benefits, Park's most compelling reason to intervene militarily in the Vietnam War was political: to prevent the United States from redeploying its troops from South Korea to South Vietnam; to acquire a modern armed forces with combat experience; and to make himself an indispensable strategic ally of the United States in its cold war campaigns, with an eye to discouraging U.S. political forces from joining South Korean opposition politicians and *chaeya* activists in an anti-Park transnational coalition. Park hoped to make South Korea an anchor in his ally's Asia policy by helping the United States where it most needed help. The U.S. good will Park secured by coming to the rescue of Lyndon B. Johnson in the Vietnam War and, by extension, by helping to counter some of the U.S. domestic political turmoil over war efforts in South Vietnam (by showing that the United States was not alone in its stance there), was intended to influence U.S. policy in the direction of strengthening South Korean national security and ensuring regime stability. Economic motives were secondary for Park.

The primacy of politics in Park's decision to dispatch combat troops to South Vietnam owed to South Korea's deeply ingrained fear of abandonment. Ever since secretary of state Dean Acheson had placed South Korea outside the U.S. defense perimeter in January 1950,[3] thus inadvertently luring Kim Il Sung into a miscalculated military invasion of the South the following June, the South Korean ruling political elite always remained fearful that the United States would abandon the South if put under political pressure. To be sure, Harry S. Truman brushed aside his secretary of state's "Acheson Line" to militarily intervene in the defense of the South in the Korean War, thus ensuring that U.S. credibility would become entangled in and U.S. interests coincide with the survival of South Korea as a sovereign state. In spite of Truman's policy reversal, however, South Korea was never able to overcome the shock of the Acheson Line. When added to the lack of a sense of common values, shared destiny, and similar history in the way that the United States had with Western Europe, the seeming ambiguity of South Korea's geopolitical value, which its political elite thought caused the United States' policy zigzags in 1950, made Park and his people worry that the United States might revert back to Acheson's position if the regional security situation or domestic U.S. public opinion altered dramatically.

South Korea's fear of abandonment was kept alive, moreover, by the fact that the Mutual Defense Treaty promulgated in October 1953 did not have a provision for "automatic response" that would have obliged the United States to immediately intervene militarily in the event of armed attack by a third party. South Korea thought the lack of such a provision deprived it of protection against the volatile opinion of U.S. public, which typically looked at South Korea as an ally of limited strategic value, not worthy of a strong security commitment. A precipitous decline in U.S. military aid, from an annual average of $232 million during the 1956–1961 period to $154 million for the 1962–1965 period,[4] was also seen as signaling a decline in U.S. military commitment, although the reduction was actually made by the United States as part of an effort to cope with its rising balance-of-payments problems.

Undergirding South Korea's fear of U.S. abandonment was its fear of North Korea. At that time, it looked as if the North had beaten the politically unstable, economically stagnant, and internationally isolated South in the competition to become the sole legitimate state on the Korean Peninsula. The P'yŏngyang leadership had created a monolithic party-state that had mobilized popular forces into a stable pillar of political order, pursued heavy and chemical industrialization as an engine of economic growth, built up a powerful military force out of the ashes of the Korean War, and developed the indigeneous ideology of Chuch'e to strengthen its nationalist credentials. While Park struggled just to survive in 1961, Kim Il Sung wrapped up his consolidation of political power, visiting Moscow and Beijing in July of 1961 to establish formal alliance relations. The following year, Kim Il Sung adopted the "Four Military Principles" *(sadae kunsa rosŏn)*[5] with the goal of transforming North Korea into a thoroughly militarized garrison state. To test Park's resolve and demoralize his people, Kim Il Sung increased the North's aggression against the South, violating the Armistice Agreement on 736 occasions in 1961 alone. Military provocations had averaged less than 200 instances annually before 1960.

It was against this backdrop of military insecurity that Park decided to dispatch combat troops to South Vietnam in support of President Lyndon B. Johnson's war efforts. For Park, the military intervention looked like a rare opportunity to redress—however temporarily—the imbalance in the existing bilateral alliance relations that put South Korea's destiny in U.S. hands. For the first time in the volatile and fragile alliance relationship, South Korea was to have leverage over U.S. security policy by joining the United States' war in a distant place. In return for helping Johnson where he was most vulnerable in U.S. domestic politics, Park expected to secure his cold war partner's firm assurance that the United States was committed to the defense of South Korea. Believing that the U.S.–South Korean alliance lacked the kind of geopolitical, ideological, and historical interests required for a strong partnership, Park chose to create such an interest by committing combat troops to South Vietnam. The military campaign, pursued in tandem with a political overture toward Japan, would also appeal to American planners' regional strategy of forging a trilateral cold war network of deterrence among Seoul, Tokyo, and Washington against the trilateral alliance network among Beijing, Moscow, and P'yŏngyang.

The primacy of politics in Park's decision to join U.S. war efforts in South Vietnam owed much to his domestic political interests as well. By becoming an indispensable partner of the United States in its military campaign, Park hoped to deter the patron-state from meddling in South Korean domestic politics on the side of the opposition. As we saw in Chapters 1 and 2, Park struggled to win U.S. recognition of his coup as a fait accompli during the junta years (1961–1963), eventually conceding to reinstate a system of competitive elections. Once he won a presidential election in 1963, Park knew he had to secure new policy instruments that could transform the guarded, conditional support of the United States into the more proactive political backing required for the launching of his modernization project. Those instruments were his two-track strategy of cold war alliance building: military intervention in the Vietnam War and normalization of relations with Japan. By accommodating the United States' vital security interests, Park thought he could secure U.S. endorsement of his rule and prevent domestic political critics and opponents from building a broad anti-Park coalition with U.S. support. As the model of democratic rule upheld by the opposition political parties and even the *chaeya* dissidents (Chapter 13), the United States profoundly reshaped the parameters of South Korea's opposition political movements.

Politically delinking the domestic opposition from the United States was critical for Park because his modernization project challenged U.S. values in basic ways. Park dreamed of building a "security state" that championed national security over democracy, "planned rationalism" over laissez-faire market principles, and state control over civil society empowerment. To build such a state, Park thought he needed U.S. acquiescence to his authoritarian rule. And he succeeded in acquiring it so as long as he maintained a sizable troop presence in South Vietnam. When university students rushed into the streets to demonstrate against his policy of diplomatic normalization with Japan in June 1964, the U.S. ambassador Samuel D. Berger and the United States Forces in Korea (USFK) commander

Hamilton H. Howze visited Park to recommend the declaration of martial law. When Park sought a third presidential term through a constitutional revision in 1969, the United States stayed out of the domestic political turbulence, thus tacitly supporting Park's political move. More fundamentally, the United States helped Park to become the paramount political leader when it withdrew its traditional policy recommendation of financial stabilization and fiscal balance and instead joined in the process of debt-financed economic hypergrowth on Park's terms in 1964 and 1965 (see Chapter 7)—the two years that saw the signing of a treaty to normalize relations with Japan as well as the dispatch of military troops to South Vietnam. For Park, the decision to intervene in the Vietnam War also aimed to bury any lingering doubts the United States and the South Korean conservatives had about his ideological beliefs on the basis of his 1945–1948 leftist activities. From the outset of his political rule in May 1961, Park consciously built up an image of a cold war warrior against the North, lest the opposition accuse him of being a communist sympathizer. As the leader of the military junta, Park warned, "the international communist conspiracy" was an imminent threat to the "free world." The dispatch of combat troops to South Vietnam was an integral part of his effort to demonstrate his ideological conversion. In his eyes, the Vietnam conflict occurred as part of global communist expansionism. When the Soviet Union resumed the testing of nuclear weapons on August 30, 1961, he warned that "[t]he more the Western world seeks peace, the deeper the Communists' penetration into the Free World will be. The Communists are immoral in their exploration of nuclear weapons . . . They will continue to seek countries to infiltrate."

Emphasizing the primacy of politics does not mean that economic motives mattered little. Once Park chose to enter the Vietnam War in a massive way because of military-security and domestic-political interests, he concentrated on extracting as much economic aid from the United States as possible. At the time of Park's ascent to power in 1961, U.S. aid constituted a lifeline for South Korea, supplying over 73 percent of its annual imports and sharing about 12 percent of its gross national product. Unfortunately for Park, his rule coincided with a sharp decline in annual U.S. economic aid from $230 million during the 1959–1963 period to $110 million in the 1964–1968 period. The drop compelled Park to pursue a quick settlement with Japan on the terms of diplomatic normalization, including on the size and conditions of reparation funds (see Chapter 15). The decision to intervene in the Vietnam War followed a similar logic. To slow down the trend of aid reduction by winning the hearts of U.S. policymakers with the dispatch of South Korean troops, as well as to secure an export market for South Korean goods and services with U.S. support in South Vietnam, Park plunged into his Vietnam venture. The Vietnam War turned out to be an economic godsend, especially with the special procurement arrangements Park negotiated with the United States.

Buildup to Involvement

Interestingly, talk of South Korea's participation in the Vietnam War began well before the advent of Park in 1961. In February and May 1954, then-president Syngman Rhee proposed to the United States that South Korea was ready to send its troops to South Vietnam for the containment of communist expansion.[6] In return for dispatching troops, Rhee demanded that the United States provide assistance for the establishment of five new South Korean combat divisions. President Dwight D. Eisenhower turned down Rhee's offer on the grounds that "U.S. public opinion would not support the maintenance of U.S. Forces in Korea if [South] Korean forces were withdrawn from [the Korean Peninsula] for actions elsewhere."[7]

Rhee had made his proposal to offset the possible weakening of the United States' security commitment to South Korea. After the armistice was signed in July 1953 to end the Korean War, the U.S. Department of Defense began drawing up a plan to reduce the level of its USFK troops. The plan, completed in January 1954 and put into effect two months later, aimed to reduce the U.S. military presence in South Korea from eight divisions to two. For Rhee, getting involved in the Vietnam War was a way to slow down the U.S. plan for troop reduction and to ensure continued security guarantees from the United States after the withdrawal of six divisions.

To tie down the United States and limit its options, Rhee even threatened to "march north at the earliest possible time to save [the] North Korean brethren from the sure death they [are] facing."[8] The specter of another war on the Korean Peninsula—this time, through South Korea's initiative—was thought to pressure the United States into a position more supportive of South Korean security concerns. Like Park a decade later, Rhee also believed that he needed to appeal to the United States' cold war project of building a strong anticommunist front in Asia. In June 1954, he took the initiative to establish an Asian People's Anti-Communist League, a regionwide network of rightist parastatal organizations, with South Vietnam as a member-state. In 1957 and 1958, Rhee held a summit meeting with Ngo Dinh Diem of South Vietnam to forge common ground in their fight against communism.

When Park seized power in 1961, he too tried to use the Vietnam War to win U.S. support for his fragile military junta. In his state visit to Washington in November 1961, Park told President John F. Kennedy that South Korea was ready to dispatch troops to South Vietnam "if requested." He argued that South Vietnam could survive only with outside help.[9] Kennedy's reply must have disappointed him. The president simply said that he would keep Park informed of future developments, hoping that the situation in South Vietnam would not deteriorate to the point that South Korean assistance would be needed. Contrary to later critics of Park, the South Korean decision to participate in the Vietnam War was made voluntarily, not under U.S. pressure. Kennedy had not yet decided the extent to which the United States would get militarily involved in South Vietnam.

The beginning of the U.S. change in posture—and with it, the leverage South Korea gained over its large ally—came in February 1962, when Kennedy set up a Military Assistance Command in Vietnam (MACV) within the South Vietnamese command structure, which led to the deployment of 12,000 U.S. troops within a year. In April 1962, Park received an official request from Ngo Dinh Diem for South Korean military assistance. In the next month, Park sent a military mission led by Major General Sim Hŭng-sŏn to South Vietnam to examine ways to assist it militarily. After two months of fact-finding efforts, the mission reported that it would be advisable to assist in the areas of infrastructure building and medical care, rather than providing direct military assistance in the form of combat troops.[10]

Park drew a vastly different conclusion. In August 1963, only two months before his presidential election, Park shared his inner thoughts with close confidants, including his minister of internal affairs Pak Kyŏng-wŏn and minister of national defense Kim Sŏng-ŭn, along with the chiefs-of-staff of the army (Min Ki-sik), navy (Yi Myŏng-gi), and air force (Chang Sŏng-hwan), and the commander of the marine corps (Kim Tu-ch'an). "In case the United States requests the dispatch of troops to South Vietnam," Park declared, he was "obliged [to accommodate it] out of both economic and security considerations."[11] Here, too, Park was thinking of the possibility of being involved in the Vietnam War well in advance of an official request from the United States.

The United States made a formal request for South Korean troops on May 1, 1964, when President Johnson prepared for a massive escalation in his country's military engagement. Park promptly ordered his cabinet to plan for the dispatch of troops. The intervention began with a dispatch of 140 noncombat troops, including a Mobile Army Surgical Hospital (MASH) and 10 martial arts instructors, which was unanimously approved by the National Assembly. The opposition parties, which held 37 percent of the National Assembly seats, did not object because the scale of troop dispatch was small and limited to noncombat missions. On September 22, these noncombat troops arrived in South Vietnam, the first of what eventually became a major deployment.

In December of the same year, South Korea received the second American request for help. Park responded by sending some 2,000 noncombat medics and military engineers. This time, getting the legislature's approval proved to be more difficult, as conflicting opinions began to surface. Although supporters of the second dispatch emphasized the moral obligation of South Korea as an ally of the United States to intervene in the Vietnam War, opponents criticized it as fighting a proxy war on behalf of a superpower patron.[12] The critics included a number of opposition party politicians as well as a few junior DRP assemblymen, including Ch'a Chi-ch'ŏl, one of Park's most trusted confidants, who had served Park as a bodyguard during the uncertain days of the 1961 coup.[13] Others called upon the United States to increase economic and military assistance to South Korea in return for the second troop dispatch. The voices of opposition, however, were mostly scattered, weak, and ill-articulated.

For its part, the United States also did not hesitate from using its USFK troops as direct leverage to get Park involved militarily, once Johnson decided to enter the Vietnam War in a massive way. In 1964, U.S. ambassador Winthrop Brown hinted that some of the USFK troops might have to be withdrawn if Park decided not to dispatch troops to South Vietnam.[14] Three years later, amid a presidential election campaign, Park recollected: "Had we decided not to dispatch our troops to South Vietnam, I assume that two combat divisions of the United States forces stationed in South Korea would have been transferred to South Vietnam . . . If we had turned down the request, we would have risked a power vacuum in the demilitarized zone (DMZ), giving another chance for the North to attack."[15]

In the end the National Assembly approved the bill for the second dispatch by a vote of 106 to 11. Eight assemblymen abstained, while fifty legislators opted to waive their right to vote. The four opposition political parties were unable to mend their factional differences to come up with one collective voice. In fact, for the opposition, the more critical of the two political issues was the impending normalization of relations with Japan, which galvanized the opposition parties, *chaeya* dissidents, and student activists. By contrast, the ruling Democratic Republican Party (DRP) showed strong unity on the issue of troop dispatch, once Park showed his resolve to build a robust alliance with the United States through the expansion of South Korean military intervention in the Vietnam War.

On the other hand, the command structure of the allied military forces was a contentious issue from the very start of South Korea's military intervention. The U.S.–South Korean talks in early 1964 failed to establish a combined command structure, because South Korea held on to the right to command its own military troops in direct opposition to South Vietnam's proposal to put the South Korean armed forces under South Vietnamese operational control. The United States accommodated South Korea, scrapping the idea of a combined command structure.

First Dispatch of Combat Troops

As Park was eagerly waiting for the United States' request for troops in early 1964, the United States was busy with the construction of a multinational military coalition to fight in South Vietnam. Initially, Johnson worked to send U.S. ground forces with support from some twenty-five allied countries, including South Korea. The goal was to widen international support for the U.S. war effort so as to mute domestic opposition to the war at home. But unable to convince most of its allies, especially the Western Europeans, the United States had to settle for a small contingent of supporting nations.[16]

Ironically, the United States discounted the value of South Korean support in the initial stage of international coalition building. Not only was South Korea not a member of the United Nations or SEATO, thus lacking the international status that would lend legitimacy to U.S. war efforts, but its armed forces were under the USFK commander's operational control, which made its troops look more like a proxy of the United States than like an independent force. To discourage the United States further, South Korea had a security problem of its own as a divided nation under threat from the superior North Korean armed forces, which the United States thought would prevent its active military intervention elsewhere. The South Vietnamese, for their part, were reluctant to see South Korean forces operating on their soil.[17] But with most other countries declining the United States' request for troops, Johnson turned to South Korea for major support. In early 1965 the U.S. secretary of defense, Robert S. McNamara, recommended that the total number of foreign combat troops in South Vietnam be increased to 175,000 from 75,000 soldiers. To meet this new target, Johnson needed Park.[18]

Throughout 1964, the two allies had engaged in informal discussions on the issue of combat troops. During this period Park encouraged U.S. officials to send a larger number of U.S. combat troops along with South Korea's in order to bring about a swift resolution of the Vietnam War. In October 1964, he told the State Department's assistant secretary for East Asian and Pacific affairs, William P. Bundy, that the United States seemed to lack the resolve to win the conflict. Park went on to say that he was "ready to support the United States if President Johnson requests our military cooperation."[19]

To be sure, from the very outset of the bilateral talks Park defined the issue of intervention primarily in terms of military security, but at the same time, it was also true that he showed much interest in the potential economic benefits of troop dispatch. In late 1964, foreign minister Yi Tong-wŏn recommended that Park focus primarily on economic side-payments if the dispatch of combat troops was inevitable. By contrast, defense minister Kim Sŏng-ŭn advised Park to consider the troop dispatch more from the perspective of improving South Korean military capabilities than of resolving the Vietnam conflict. Park agreed on both counts, but added that "it would be selfish to stress benefits too much when the United States is facing a critical situation on the battlefield."[20]

In April 1965 the bilateral negotiations for troop dispatch became public. Henry C. Lodge, a special envoy of Johnson, visited Park to discuss the conditions for South Korea's expansion of its military intervention. Park followed with a summit meeting with Johnson in May. Although the two leaders' joint statement did not mention the issue of troop dispatch, it was agreed at the summit that South Korea would send one combat division. In return, the United States stipulated in the joint statement that it would continue to maintain its forward-deployed force posture in South Korea, that it would amend the Military Assistance Transfer Program to equip South Korean troops with cutting-edge military equipment, and that it would provide a loan of $150 million through the United States Agency for International Development (USAID).[21]

Then, on June 23, 1965, defense minister Kim Sŏng-ŭn met with USFK commander Howze to present the following ten conditions for the first dispatch of combat troops:

- Maintain the current level of United States and South Korean military troops in South Korea;
- Make three South Korean reserve divisions combat-ready by fully arming their troops, as well as modernizing South Korea's seventeen regular army divisions and one marine division in firepower, maneuver, and signal capabilities in order to avoid any weakening of the South Korean defense posture by the troop dispatch to South Vietnam;
- Maintain the same level of aid through the Military Assistance Pro-

gram (MAP) as before the deployment of South Korean troops in
South Vietnam;

- Confirm as early as possible the mission, bivouac area, and command
  channels of KFV troops in South Korea, and provide a U.S. plan for
  logistical support for South Korean combat in South Vietnam;
- Establish a small planning group to determine the organization of the
  South Korean army division destined for service in South Vietnam;
- Provide communication equipment for the Korean Forces in Vietnam's (KFV's) exclusive use, with the goal of facilitating communication between the South Korean military establishment and its troops'
  headquarters in South Vietnam;
- Provide transportation for the dispatch of South Korean military
  troops and for their subsequent rotation and replacement, as well as
  assisting with the transport of military supplies;
- Provide the South Korean soldiers in Vietnam with combat-duty pay
  at the same rate as paid to U.S. military personnel, pay gratuities and
  compensation for line-of-duty deaths or disability, and cover for the
  salaries of South Vietnamese workers hired by the KFV military units;
- Provide the South Korean air force with four C-123 aircraft for the
  purpose of medical evacuation and liaison between South Korea and
  South Vietnam;
- Provide a field broadcasting installation with the goal of enabling the
  South Korean military troops to conduct anticommunist broadcasts,
  psychological warfare, and jamming operations, as well as bringing
  South Korea's home news, war news, and entertainment programs to
  its soldiers in South Vietnam.[22]

The United States' acceptance of these ten conditions helped Park in preventing the public's anger over the speedy passage of his 1965 bill to dispatch combat troops. To ensure the prompt deployment of these troops,
the United States also had to agree with South Korea on July 13, 1965,
that there would be no reduction of USFK military troops without prior
consultation; that the MAP for 1966 would include an additional $7 mil-
lion to finance the provision of combat equipment for three South Korean reserve divisions; that the South Korean armed forces would be modernized in firepower, communications, and mobility; and that the United
States would share the financial burden of transporting South Korean military troops to South Vietnam.[23]

There was, however, a clear limitation on what the United States was
prepared to give in return for the South Korean dispatch of combat troops.
As Park readied for the dispatch of troops to South Vietnam in early 1965,

his foreign minister, Yi Tong-wŏn, had requested that U.S. ambassador Brown begin negotiations to include a new clause in the Mutual Defense Treaty that would require each of the allies to dispatch military troops automatically when the other party faced armed aggression.[24] The United States did not respond favorably to the idea of such a revision, although it was willing to reaffirm its commitment to the defense of South Korea verbally. On July 16, three days after the agreement on South Korea's dispatch of combat troops, the United States tried to satisfy Park by having Ambassador Brown and USFK commander Howze write a letter that reconfirmed the U.S. commitment.[25] Park was disappointed, but not discouraged from dispatching combat troops to South Vietnam.

Having secured political, military, and economic rewards, Park presented the National Assembly with bills on the dispatch of combat troops to South Vietnam and the normalization of relations with Japan on July 14, 1965. The action triggered a heated debate in the National Assembly. Dissenting views emerged even within the ruling DRP. The DRP chairman, Chŏng Ku-yŏng, warned of heavy casualties. Park's response, however, was resolute. Obviously displeased, Park remarked: "A powerless ruling party that fears challenges should be dismantled."[26] With public hostility against the proposed treaty of diplomatic normalization growing and with university students demonstrating fiercely in the streets in ever larger numbers, the opposition political parties chose to boycott the vote on the two bills. The ruling party, enjoying a majority in the National Assembly, rammed through the treaty bill on August 11 without the presence of opposition members. Ignited by this cavalier action, most of the opposition party legislators submitted their resignations. Park was not persuaded to negotiate. Two days later, the DRP-dominated National Assembly approved the bill on the dispatch of combat troops to South Vietnam by a vote of 101 in favor, 1 against, and 2 abstentions—again with the opposition legislators boycotting the session.

With the first dispatch of combat troops in 1965, the issue of combined command resurfaced. This time, it was the United States that requested South Korea to turn over its operational control in order to bring about greater effectiveness in the allies' war efforts. South Korea rejected the request, because it believed that placing its combat troops under a de facto U.S.-centric combined command structure made it look like a "mercenary." Moreover, defense minister Kim Sŏng-ŭn argued that "if we give our operational command to the United States, our forces might end up being deployed in extremely dangerous areas, resulting in a higher number of casualties. To avoid unnecessary military casualties and to protect the South Korean civilians dispatched to rehabilitate damaged areas, our forces should remain autonomous and be deployed in relatively safe rear-areas."[27]

Reflecting the concerns of the Ministry of National Defense, KFV commander Ch'ae Myŏng-sin maintained that "the Vietnam War [was] fought mainly at the political rather than at the military front. [The task] was preventing South Vietnam from being overthrown by the North Vietnamese." By extension, South Korea's rehabilitation activities in damaged areas were as vital as U.S. combat activities on the front for the survival of South Vietnam as a sovereign state. Consequently, it was critical that public support for its military troops both at home and within South Vietnamese society did not get damaged by the allies' dispute over the issue of operational control. General William C. Westmoreland, the commander of the United States Forces in Vietnam, and Major General Stanley R. Larsen eventually agreed with Ch'ae Myŏng-sin to recognize South Korea's right to command its own troops independently.[28] The two allies established a Free World Military Assistance Policy Council to give each a fair share of decision-making power in military operations. Even then, they agreed to recognize each other's right to command their respective military units.

The South Korean military forces conducted both combat and peace-keeping operations, but they did not play a leading role in the war. The Korean Forces in Vietnam had as their primary responsibility restoring order and rehabilitating damaged areas,[29] and were deployed mainly in the coastal areas adjacent to three of the five major harbors in South Vietnam: Qui Nhon, Nha Trang, and Cam Rahn. These three harbors were logistically important for war efforts, but also relatively safe, away from the front lines. Despite U.S. complaints about South Korea's restriction of its military operations to the defense of the harbors and adjacent areas,[30] Ch'ae Myŏng-sin stuck to the strategy of deploying KFV troops mainly in the coastal areas. He was extremely successful, maintaining peace in an area of 7,438 square kilometers (2,872 square miles) where some 5 percent of the South Vietnamese lived. Among the military operations the KFV troops conducted, 1,171 were large-scale and over 576,000 were small, company-based actions.[31]

Second Dispatch of Combat Troops

Despite the escalation of foreign military presence, the Vietnam War did not go well for the United States. With the North Vietnamese forces infiltrating South Vietnam to support guerrilla warfare, Westmoreland recommended in December 1965 that the total number of combat troops be increased to 443,000 soldiers from 275,000. The recommendation led Johnson to request an additional dispatch of South Korean combat troops. In addition to the rising tide of antiwar sentiment at home, the economics of troop deployment encouraged the United States to turn to South Korea for additional troops. In terms of U.S.-paid monthly allowances, the South Korean captains received $190, far below the sums earmarked for the Americans ($570), Filipinos ($475), and Thais ($407) in the same military rank. Only the Vietnamese captains received less ($123) than the South Korean captains.[32] The Pentagon estimated that it cost $5,000 to support one South Korean soldier's year-long deployment in South Vietnam, less than half of what it cost to support an American soldier ($13,000).[33]

The idea of sending one more combat division raised heated debate in the National Assembly. The advocates argued for committing the additional combat troops on the grounds that the fate of South Vietnam was directly tied to South Korean security, that the military intervention had thus far benefited South Korea by ensuring a strong U.S. guarantee of South Korean security, that the dispatch of a second combat division was necessary to support the military operations of the South Korean troops already deployed in South Vietnam, and that the South Korean armed forces would gain precious combat experience by fighting in the Vietnam War. The advocates were various DRP leaders and state bureaucrats, including Chairman Min P'yŏng-gwŏn of the National Assembly's Defense Committee and minister of defense Kim Sŏng-ŭn. On the opposite side was once again Ch'a Chi-ch'ŏl, claiming to represent the DRP's junior National Assembly members. Prime Minister Chŏng Il-gwŏn was also known to caution against the additional dispatch of combat troops in his typically gentle way.[34]

But it was from the opposition political parties that the most explicit objection was voiced. Led by Pak Sun-ch'ŏn and Yun Po-sŏn, the opposition argued that South Korean security would be better enhanced by adding to the Mutual Defense Treaty a provision for "automatic" U.S. intervention in the event of armed attack, rather than by dispatching combat troops to South Vietnam. In their eyes, moreover, it was not right to intervene in another country's civil war without a UN resolution. Doing so, in fact, was likely to isolate South Korea in the international community for fighting in a "wrong" war. The opposition also warned that the second dispatch of combat troops would not be the end of U.S. requests for South Korean troops, because the war situation was continuing to deteriorate. The critics additionally charged that the economic benefits accruing from any additional troop dispatches would be less than what Park's political propaganda claimed. Emphasizing the dangers of underestimating political and military risks, they noted that U.S. policy toward Southeast Asia was anything but stable and that the people of South Vietnam seemed to lack resolve in fighting communism.[35]

By contrast, Park welcomed the U.S. request for a second dispatch of troops as an opportunity to zero in on the issue of revising the Mutual Defense Treaty as well as on the expansion of U.S. military and economic assistance to South Korea. On January 15, 1966, defense minister Kim Sŏng-ŭn reported that South Korea was investigating the possibility of increasing its combat troops in response to South Vietnam's request for additional forces. KFV commander Ch'ae Myŏng-sin had also supported the idea of a second troop dispatch when Park visited Saigon on January 14, 1966, for a summit meeting.[36] The negotiations for the second dispatch were held not with South Vietnam, but with the United States. After tough and lengthy negotiations involving fifty bilateral consultations, Kim Sŏng-ŭn and Yi Tong-wŏn delivered a memorandum to their American counterparts with six major requests.

The memorandum called for the United States to finance the "complete" equipping of three South Korean army divisions; to give an unequivocal security assurance that the United States would automatically intervene in case of an armed attack from the North, without prior consent of the U.S. Congress; to assist in the improvement of KFV capabilities; to suspend the implementation of the MAP transfer program, which had envisioned the reduction of U.S. military aid through South Korea's sharing a greater burden in the procurement of military supplies; to help South Korea's expansion of exports to South Vietnam; to encourage economic cooperation among South Korea, the United States, and South Vietnam; and to provide a $50 million package of USAID loans and other financial assistance.[37] Moreover, Yi Tong-wŏn asked the United States to agree to each of these requests in writing. The United States' initial response, delivered by Ambassador Brown, was lukewarm at best, positively responding only on the issues of modernizing the South Korean armed forces. Park and his staff were furious.

To break the deadlock over the issue of revising the Mutual Defense Treaty, Vice President Hubert H. Humphrey visited Seoul to meet with Park on February 23, 1966. During his stay, Humphrey reassured Park that the United States would immediately intervene in case of an armed attack from the North. The vice president also promised to make further economic concessions, including an increase in the overseas allowances for KFV troops in South Vietnam paid for by the United States and an increase in the United States' role in facilitating the expansion of South Korean exports to South Vietnam.[38] South Korea had been demanding that the United States drastically increase the overseas allowances for the South Korean soldiers to the level of Southeast Asian troops fighting in South Vietnam. But Yi Tong-wŏn was not persuaded, demanding that Humphrey examine the possibility of revising the Mutual Defense Treaty. When Humphrey turned down the request on the grounds that the issue was under the jurisdiction of the U.S. Congress, beyond the influence of the executive branch, the South Korean leaders protested even more, because they were aware of the growing antiwar and isolationist forces within the United States, which they thought would make U.S. intervention in a future military conflict on the Korean Peninsula that much more difficult.[39]

On March 4, the United States came back with a proposal to provide additional military and economic assistance in the form of a written memorandum by Ambassador Brown. Initially, the memorandum involved sixteen items in all, ten on military assistance and six on economic assistance. After minor revisions to make room for expanded assistance, the "Brown Memorandum" was formally exchanged between the two allies on March 7. The memorandum called for the United States to:

- Provide over the next few years substantial military equipment for the modernization of the South Korean armed forces;
- Equip as necessary and finance all additional costs of the additional South Korean military troops deployed in South Vietnam;
- Provide training programs for KFV troops in South Vietnam and finance the replacement of its personnel;
- Contribute to the improvement of South Korea's anti-infiltration capabilities to deter North Korea from waging guerrilla war and destabilizing South Korea;
- Provide equipment and facilities to expand South Korea's ordnance map with the goal of increasing ammunition production within South Korea;
- Provide communications facilities exclusively for KFV use in South Vietnam, in order to enable direct communication between the South Korean government and its KFV troops in South Vietnam;
- Provide four C-54 aircraft to the South Korean air force with the goal of strengthening its support for KFV troops in South Vietnam;
- Improve military facilities for troop welfare from proceeds of the excess sales of MAP;
- Assume the costs of overseas allowances paid to KFV forces at the rate agreed on March 4, 1966;
- Provide death and disability gratuities resulting from casualties in

South Vietnam at double the rates recently agreed to by the Joint
United States–South Korea Military Committee.

There were also six agreements on economic assistance, whereby the
United States pledged:

- To provide South Korea with a budgetary fund equal to the net additional costs of deploying additional military troops in South Vietnam
  and of mobilizing and maintaining in South Korea one combat-ready
  reserve division, one brigade, and their support units;
- To suspend the MAP transfer program as long as there were two
  South Korean army divisions deployed in South Vietnam;
- To procure as much as possible from South Korea the military supplies, services, and equipment used by South Korean troops in South
  Vietnam, and to procure as much as South Korea can provide in a
  timely manner, at a reasonable price, and under the principle of fair
  competition any goods purchased by USAID for use in its projects for
  rural construction, pacification, relief, and supply in South Vietnam;
- To increase technical assistance to South Korea in the general area of
  export promotion;
- To provide new USAID loans to support South Korea's economic development, in addition to its already pledged loan of $150 million;
- To provide $150 million in program loans in 1966, for the purpose of
  supporting South Korean exports and development projects in South
  Vietnam.[40]

By contrast, on the issue of revising the Mutual Defense Treaty, the
United States maintained its stance that any revision could only be initiated by Congress. To ameliorate South Korea's frustration, Ambassador
Brown wrote his second letter on the issue on March 8, 1966, with the
hope that the reaffirmation of U.S. security commitment would minimize
the political damage arising from the absence of a treaty revision.[41] In contrast to the United States' readiness to make military and economic concessions as an inducement for Park's second dispatch of combat troops to
South Vietnam, it never thought of making concessions on an issue as fundamental and strategic as its range of strategic-military choices in the event
of an armed attack against South Korea. For their part, Park and his
confidants tried to use their commitment of troops to South Vietnam as leverage to tie down the United States' military options on the Korean Peninsula for good. Park's failure to do so, despite what the press called the
"honeymoon" *(milwŏl)* between Seoul and Washington since 1964, con-

firmed his earlier fears of U.S. ambivalence toward its security commitment to South Korea.

In the end, with his eye on the military and economic concessions enumerated in the Brown Memorandum, Park put the bill for a second dispatch of combat troops to a vote in the National Assembly in March 1966. Park was sure of his legislative victory. With the DRP controlling 110 of the total 175 legislative seats and the major opposition political parties still staging their boycott of the National Assembly since the passage of the treaty bill to normalize relations with Japan in August 1965, the bill passed with 95 in favor, 27 against, and 3 abstentions. Although defeated, the opponents of the war were gaining in number. Only one DRP legislator had opposed the first dispatch of combat troops in 1965; now a total of 27 DRP legislators voted against the second dispatch in 1966. But even combined with the opposition New Democratic Party (NDP), the opponents of the war still remained a minority. The two rounds of troop dispatch were to increase annual U.S. military aid to South Korea from $163 million during the 1961–1965 period to $336 million in the next five years.

Military Disengagement

South Korea's second dispatch of combat troops ended with the deployment of the White Horse Division in 1966, but U.S. requests for more South Korean troops continued through 1967. Then came two political-military shocks that brought a freeze to South Korea's military presence in South Vietnam, followed by its phased pullout of combat forces from Saigon. The shocks were triggered by North Korea's escalation of provocations toward the South in January 1968 and newly elected president Richard M. Nixon's "Guam Doctrine" of July 1969. The shocks developed into a security crisis with profound domestic political repercussions for South Korea (see Chapters 6 and 8), when the United States unilaterally countered North Korean provocations with a mixture of benign neglect and negotiation against South Korea's hard-line posture and, again unilaterally, an expansion of its policy of military disengagement from South Vietnam to include its USFK troops stationed in South Korea against vigorous South Korean protests. It was the United States' unilateralist style of response that transformed the security shocks into a crisis of alliance—and a crisis in South Korean domestic politics.

The first of the two shocks began on January 21, 1968, when thirty-one North Korean commandos tried to raid the Blue House to assassinate Park. Two days later, military tensions worsened even more with North

Korea's seizure of the *Pueblo,* a U.S. intelligence ship, which was operating in the East Sea. The United States and South Korea responded very differently to the two North Korean provocations. Whereas Park reacted in a rage, calling for immediate military retaliation, U.S. ambassador William J. Porter and USFK commander Charles H. Bonesteel called for restraint from any military response.[42] The United States opted instead for dialogue with the North Koreans for the return of the *Pueblo* crew and adopted a policy of hands-off vis-à-vis the issue of North Korea's failed commando attack.

Within South Korea, some of the hard-liners urged military sanctions not only to deter further North Korean provocations, but also to curb the United States' unilateral negotiations for the return of the *Pueblo*'s sailors. A few even called for the withdrawal of military troops from South Vietnam to protest the United States' separate negotiations with the North over the *Pueblo* crew in the middle of South Korea's security crisis.[43] The United States quickly came down on Park, with Cyrus R. Vance, a special envoy, warning that U.S. troops would be pulled out of South Korea if South Korea acted similarly in South Vietnam.[44] Park was furious, feeling betrayed after having taken risks in joining the United States' Vietnam venture. Park even toyed with the idea of launching a unilateral retaliation against the North Korean military bases responsible for the preparation of the commandos' raid against the Blue House.

The United States' attempt at a separate deal with the North was Park's wake-up call regarding South Korean security vulnerabilities. The sense of betrayal and insecurity spreading throughout his inner policy circles had an instant negative impact on the United States' request for the dispatch of a third combat division to South Vietnam. Before North Korea's provocations in January 1968, Park had toyed with the idea of sending civilian personnel to the rear areas in place of a third combat division.[45] Now, in dispute with the United States, Park shelved plans for further military or civilian deployment on the grounds that South Korea faced a growing security threat from North Korea—possibly, all alone. As the United States' negotiations with the North Koreans over the *Pueblo* proceeded, Park began to stress the importance of enhancing self-defense capabilities. In April 1968, he established a 2,500,000 men-strong reserve force. He also moved to build production facilities for weapons, starting with M-16 rifles and ammunition.[46]

Meanwhile, the military situation in South Vietnam deteriorated from bad to worse throughout 1968, forcing Johnson to search for ways to "Vietnamize" the Vietnam War. His successor, Richard M. Nixon, followed with the Guam Doctrine, which led to the policy of reducing the number of U.S. troops in South Vietnam from 550,000 soldiers in 1968 to 430,000 by 1970. By December 1972, the United States completed the withdrawal of its combat troops, leaving only 24,000 behind for non-combat purposes. That instantly prompted its allies to pull out their troops as well. Park announced South Korea's military disengagement from South Vietnam in his 1971 New Year's Address.[47] The first stage of troop with-drawal began in December of the same year.

Initially, the United States tried to limit its military disengagement to South Vietnam. In August 1969, a month after publicly declaring the Guam Doctrine, Nixon held a summit meeting with Park in San Francisco to pledge not to reduce the number of USFK military troops stationed in South Korea.[48] Then, in March 1970, contrary to his earlier assur-ance, Nixon had Ambassador William J. Porter inform Park of the United States' decision to reduce USFK troops. The news confirmed the doubts Park had developed about U.S. intentions since the United States' 1966 re-fusal to revise the Mutual Defense Treaty and its 1968 separate negotia-tions for the return of the *Pueblo*'s sailors. The USFK presence in South Korea was gradually reduced from 64,000 soldiers in 1969 to 40,000 in 1972. Aware that South Korea could trust only its own military capabili-ties to protect vital national interests, Park followed the United States in bringing KFV troops home to shore up military deterrence against rising North Korean threats.

At the same time, Park intended to get whatever leverage he could by linking the speed, scale, and timing of KFV troop withdrawal with the United States' concessions on South Korean security issues. Although U.S. policy regarding East Asia had fundamentally changed toward military disengagement, the idea of leveraging based on the Vietnam War had worked so well for Park in the mid-1960s that he clung to this negotiating strategy of issue linkage through much of the 1969–1973 period. The strategy worked—but only partly—because the United States also sought a similar deal. When Porter informed Park of the United States' decision to withdraw its troops from South Korea in March 1970, he also suggested that this move could be postponed to correspond with South Korea's time table for its own troop withdrawal from South Vietnam. Park strongly ob-jected, but at the same time, he recognized the utility of linking the timing of the two military withdrawals to his advantage, once he became sure of the irreversibility of the United States' plans.[49]

Moreover, Park adopted the strategy of extracting as much military and economic aid as possible from the United States as the price of his acquies-cence. At the Third Annual Bilateral Defense Ministerial Meeting held in July 1970, South Korea demanded that the United States support its military modernization program before reducing the USFK presence. Unable to bridge their differences, the allies had no provision for U.S. military reduction in their joint statement. A month later, Vice President Spiro T. Agnew visited Seoul to persuade Park. Negotiations continued under the leadership of the chairman of the Joint Chiefs of Staff, Sim Hŭng-sŏn, and USFK commander John H. Michaelis. Before the two countries succeeded in exchanging a memorandum in November 1970 after ten rounds of negotiation, they had to overcome several hurdles. Hindering their easy agreement, the allies had different conceptions of South Korea's strategic role, potential capabilities, and preferences. Fearful of being abandoned by the United States to face the North and its Soviet and Chinese allies alone, the South Korean side began negotiations with an extensive shopping list of cutting-edge military equipment, estimated to be worth $4 billion, whereas the United States offered a military sales list ranging between $1 billion and $1.5 billion. Moreover, with an eye to establish self-sufficient defense capabilities on the basis of rapid and extensive military modernization, South Korea wanted to bring its KFV troops home with all of their U.S.-financed military equipment used in the Vietnam War. The United States, by contrast, allowed only two of the six KFV regiments to leave South Vietnam with their equipment.[50] In the end, the two sides ended up issuing a joint statement on February 6, 1971, whereby the patron state agreed to assist South Korea's Five-Year Military Modernization Plan (1971–1975) with an appropriation of $1.5 billion.[51] The assistance was conceived as helping South Korea fill in any power vacuum that could result from the reduction of USFK troops by 20,000 soldiers.[52]

The agreement did not stick, however. The United States soon revealed its plan to further reduce its USFK troop levels in 1973. As expected, Park resisted. To cut off the U.S. troop reduction at the level of 20,000, he once again fell back on the the Vietnam card, proposing to keep his troops in South Vietnam beyond 1972, in return for a U.S. pledge not to push its policy of military withdrawal from South Korea any further in April 1971. Initially, the talks got nowhere. The United States rejected linking the time table of KFV troop withdrawal with its level of USFK troop reductions by telling the South Koreans that it was inappropriate for the United States to intervene in what it saw as a bilateral issue between South Korea and South Vietnam.[53] With its military disengagement from South Vietnam proceeding rapidly, the United States was intent on not playing into Park's hands. Rather, the United States only promised to maintain its troop presence in South Korea through 1974, without any definitive word on its long-term policy for the Korean Peninsula. U.S. policymakers were not being disingenuous. In the middle of constructing a new regional order of détente, they had yet to formulate a new long-term vision for the United States–South Korean alliance that fit in with the still-evolving broader policy of détente. In spite of, or perhaps because of this lack of new U.S. strategic doctrine, Park continued to delay the withdrawal of KFV troops from South Vietnam in hopes of influencing U.S. policy toward the Korean Peninsula.

The problem with Park's strategy of issue linkage was that his instrument of leverage on the United States' regional and peninsular security policy—the speed, scale, and timing of his withdrawal of KFV troops from South Vietnam—worked only while there were KFV troops deployed in South Vietnam to assist the United States' orderly military pullout. Park refrained from carrying out his threat of early military disengagement because that would have depleted the ability of his only source of leverage, KFV troops, to attempt to slow down, if not reverse, the United States' policy of USFK troop withdrawal. Consequently, he initially planned to pull out 17,000 KFV soldiers before February 1972, but ended up bringing home only 10,000 by February. Formally, it was South Vietnam's request for a slowdown in KFV troop withdrawal that put in motion his change in the speed, scale, and timing of the first of South Korea's three stages of military withdrawal. However, given Park's agenda of shaping the United States' emerging security strategy, he must have welcomed South Vietnam's request as an opportunity to protect his source of leverage over U.S. policy from getting depleted prematurely. By then the United States had more or less completed the withdrawal of its combat troops from South Vietnam, making South Korea's remaining troops that much more critical for the U.S. effort to pressure North Vietnam into peace negotiations, as well as to keep South Vietnam alive with an eye to the United States' claim that it had exited "honorably" and "responsibly" from the Vietnam War.

As Park waited for an opportunity to employ leverage through South Korea's second and third stages of troop withdrawal in April 1972, Nixon requested that South Korea maintain its combat troops in South Vietnam to back up his pressure on North Vietnam in the coming peace talks. With most of the U.S. ground troops withdrawn by then, the KFV troops were one of the few instruments Nixon had to force North Vietnam into serious peace talks. In return for Park's delay in troop withdrawal, Nixon promised to support military and financial assistance for the operations of KFV troops in South Vietnam.[54] Park responded positively, delaying his troop withdrawal until the United States signed a peace agreement with North Vietnam. When the two adversaries signed the Paris peace agreement in January 1973, Park moved to complete the second and third stages of the South Korean withdrawal of ground troops within two months. Again,

South Vietnam asked for a delay, but this time Park went ahead with his plan once he confirmed that the United States did not intend to provide any further assistance for KFV troops in South Vietnam. The time table for late withdrawal turned out to be a fruitful bargaining chip in negotiations with the United States, but only in the short run. The issue of USFK troop reduction was to return when Jimmy Carter was elected U.S. president in 1976 (see Chapter 16). However, buying time for even a short period was crucial for Park because it was long enough for him to lay the ground for his plans for *puguk kangbyŏng* (rich nation, strong army).

Legacies

The Vietnam War proved to be a profitable political venture for Park. First, the South Korean military intervention set the stage for Park to play a more active role in international politics. In 1966, he called for a Manila Summit Conference for anticommunist countries in the region to collectively reconfirm their commitment to military victory in South Vietnam.[55] The conference was held regularly through 1972. Park also joined in efforts to launch an Asian and Pacific Council (ASPAC). Proposed initially in 1964, ASPAC held its first meeting in Seoul in 1966 to discuss noncommunist Asian countries' common political and security interests. The organization included ten countries: South Korea, Japan, Thailand, Malaysia, the Philippines, Taiwan, South Vietnam, Australia, New Zealand, and Laos. The United States, though not a direct participant, fully endorsed the launching of ASPAC. For a country as profoundly isolated in international arenas as South Korea had been since its independence in 1948, any role in international organizations—however minor—was perceived by society as a victory for the South Korean government in its competition with North Korea to be recognized as the sole legitimate government on the Korean Peninsula.

Second, the Vietnam War had a windfall effect on the South Korean economy by providing scarce capital with which to spur its ambitious five-year development plans. According to one estimate, the United States expended $927 million during the 1965–1970 period as financial support for South Korea in return for its troop dispatch to South Vietnam.[56] Another source has estimated the total South Korean earnings from the Vietnam War to be over a billion dollars between 1965 and 1972.[57] Coinciding with the normalization of relations with Japan in 1965, which brought $800 million in grants and preferential loans as reparations for Japanese colonial wrongdoings, Park's intervention in the Vietnam War enabled South

Korea to support financially the risky policy transition to export-led industrialization in 1964. The reparation funds and the Vietnam windfall served as seed money to start strategic industrial projects and to ameliorate the foreign exchange bottleneck, which typically worsens during the stage of economic takeoff. Apart from these grants and loans, the troop dispatch helped South Korea's transition to export-led industrialization by increasing exports to South Vietnam by tenfold between 1964 and 1973. South Korea also reaped an indirect benefit in gaining U.S. assistance in securing foreign loans, which reached $2.7 billion by 1971.[58]

Third, the military intervention in South Vietnam proved to be a turning point for South Korean military capabilities. Although the Korean War had transformed the South Korean armed forces into a large modern organization of 600,000 men, it remained weak in morale and backward in equipment well into the early 1960s. U.S. military assistance, providing around 60 percent of South Korea's total military expenditure in the 1950s, had been mostly spent on the maintenance of the armed forces rather than on their modernization. The intervention in the Vietnam War helped not only to reverse Kennedy's plan to reduce United States military aid to South Korea, but also to increase it in three stages, the first of which came with the deployment of KFV troops in South Vietnam; the second, with the heightened North Korean military provocation and the United States' policy of benign neglect and separate dealmaking toward those provocations during the late 1960s; and the last, as part of the efforts to win Park's acceptance of the United States' troop reduction from South Korea in 1971. Consequently, during the 1965–1971 period, South Korean military capabilities rose significantly, adding 170 aircraft, 190 missiles, 25 naval ships, and 630 combat vehicles with the help of the United States.[59] The Vietnam War also proved to be a major morale booster for the South Korean military. The war not only became an occasion for providing over 300,000 soldiers with combat experience, but also enabled the South Korean armed forces to improve the living standards of its officers by providing proper services with proper allowances.

At the same time, the Vietnam War was not all about profits and benefits. South Korea faced a huge downside of approximately 16,000 casualties, 4,960 of whom were killed, 10,962 wounded, and 6 missing in action. By 1992, a total of 36,926 Vietnam veterans were found to be struggling with the effects of their exposure to Agent Orange in South Vietnam, prompting successive South Korean governments to draw up plans for compensation and medical treatment.[60]

During the years of South Korea's intervention in the Vietnam War, antiwar sentiments[61] grew over time, but not to the level of triggering the intense partisan conflict and political instability found in the United States. The South Korean opposition political parties made some damaging moral criticisms on the floor of the National Assembly, but they were seldom able to spread their partisan conflict to the world outside. The general public remained more or less silent on the issue, not only because the state made systematic efforts to control the mass media[62] but also because most South Koreans of the 1964–1973 period harbored complex, if not ambiguous or contradictory, perspectives on the war and South Korea's intervention, views that fell somewhere between national pride and shame, pragmatic endorsement and normative rejection, and internationalist inclinations and isolationist urges.

In contrast to the mid-1960s, when sending combat troops was judged to have enhanced South Korea's standing in global politics, the same military intervention increasingly became a diplomatic liability for South Korea during the early 1970s by isolating it among "nonaligned" third world nations. South Korean efforts to participate in the conferences of Afro-Asian nations were turned down by the nonaligned countries on the grounds that South Korea had sent troops to South Vietnam as a proxy of the United States. The Third Summit Conference of Nonaligned Nations in 1970 dealt a particularly damaging blow to South Korea's international standing when the conference sided with North Korea by passing a resolution for the withdrawal of USFK military troops and the dissolution of the UN Command in South Korea. Five years later, North Korea and North Vietnam were admitted as new members to the club of nonaligned nations, whereas South Korea and the Philippines—the two participants in the U.S.-led war efforts in South Vietnam—were barred from entering the Summit Conference of Nonaligned Nations.

Another negative legacy was Park's increasing mistrust of the United States, which seriously damaged the two countries' relations after 1972. As dramatic as the strengthening of alliance ties brought by the South Korean dispatch of troops in 1964 was the increase of Park's suspicions of the United States after Nixon's unilateral declaration of military disengagement from continental Asia in 1969. The disappointment was great because Park's expectations had been great since 1964. In Park's eyes, South Korea had supported U.S. war efforts in South Vietnam unswervingly despite potentially grave political and military risks to his leadership, regime, and country, but the United States repaid his loyalty with a betrayal, seemingly ready to abandon Park when larger East Asian regional power configurations and American domestic politics required it to do so.

The Vietnam War put Park and the United States on a roller-coaster ride, ending their "honeymoon" in only six years and replacing it with a relationship of deep distrust. To be sure, the end of the Vietnam War was bound to increase the divergence of the two countries' national interests by eliminating the regional security rationale for a stronger United States–South Korean alliance, but it was also true that the divergence of national interests looked bigger to Park than it actually was because he judged it from the perspective of a man who had been betrayed by what he thought to be a loyal ally. The South Korean military involvement in the Vietnam War was thus in many ways damaging as well as helpful to the cohesion of the United States–South Korean security alliance, the effect of which was to be fully played out after 1976 (see Chapter 16).

In fact, Park's domestic political fortunes correlated directly with the degree of South Korea's involvement in the Vietnam War. The deeper the South intervened, the more stable Park's basis of power became, owing to strong U.S. support for his regime. The United States was then an unquestioned hegemon, enjoying strong South Korean public support for its role as the underwriter of security, the patron of economic growth, and the tutor of liberal democracy. Its strong endorsement of Park conferred on him an aura of legitimacy. Conversely, the withdrawal of military troops from South Vietnam in 1972 as part of the U.S. military disengagement removed any restraint the patron-state might have had in intervening in South Korean domestic politics against Park's authoritarian rule. Especially after 1976, when Jimmy Carter pledged a full military withdrawal from South Korea and launched his human rights diplomacy against Park, the United States became a destabilizer of Park's regime.

The Vietnam War reveals the complexity of the bargaining strategy a mid-sized power like South Korea can adopt vis-à-vis a great power in the context of a patron-client relationship. As the weaker side in the alliance, South Korea was not in a position to reject any U.S. request for combat troops outright. Aware of the geopolitical constraints arising from the asymmetrical power relations between the United States and South Korea, but also in need of U.S. support for his own domestic reasons, Park was predisposed to take the initiative on the issue of troop dispatch to South Vietnam. This initiative seemed to be risky politically, but it turned out to be an effective way for Park to avoid U.S. pressure and to gain bargaining leverage in negotiations with the United States on political, security, and economic issues. South Korea was a client state, but it managed to find not insignificant room for political maneuvering in its dealings with its patron. The client state guarded its national interests and Park his regime interests by taking the initiative to court the United States rather than waiting to respond to the superpower's pressures. The episode illustrates that a mid-sized power can make up for its disadvantages in power capabilities with the advantages gained when its political leadership is willing to take risks, to formulate policy with speed, to withstand domestic challenges for the advantage of foreign policy, and to organize a concerted program of actions across state ministries in building its bargaining position vis-à-vis the United States.

On the other hand, the impact of the Vietnam War on alliance relations was a variable, not a constant. When the United States had the intention to intervene massively in the Vietnam War, as it did in much of the 1960s, Park's proactive posture toward the Vietnam War won him the reputation of a credible partner in the United States, and his strategy of leveraging the Vietnam War secured for Park a long list of political, economic, and military concessions from his stronger ally. However, when U.S. intentions dramatically altered to that of rapid military disengagement from South Vietnam and continental Asia after 1968, the same uncompromising anticommunist position came to be viewed as a liability obstructing the United States' construction of a new order in the spirit of détente. The 1960s' strategy of leveraging the KFV troops to win concessions similarly came to offend the U.S. Senate and, more critically, encouraged Nixon to tilt even more toward unilateralism on the issue of USFK troop reduction, thus revealing that the alliance remained fragile even a decade after jointly waging war in South Vietnam. After the Vietnam War, the alliance entered its most conflictive phase since its inception in 1954. The level of alliance cooperation was contingent on the nature of great power relations in the larger regional and global arenas, as well as on the situation of the battlefields of South Vietnam.

The Vietnam War also provided a turning point for Park's domestic political leadership. With his troops fighting in South Vietnam, Park could persuade Johnson to increase aid and loans for South Korea's economic development projects, to back Park's expansionary economic policy in the mid-1960s, and to take a low profile in South Korea's domestic politics, which de facto helped Park's efforts to revise the constitution to allow a third presidential term in 1969. As long as the United States fought in South Vietnam, it tried not to get in the way of Park in South Korean domestic politics. All this would change when Nixon decided to seek an "honorable exit" from the Vietnam War. With U.S. troops withdrawn from South Vietnam, U.S. political leaders could more openly and aggressively take on Park in the area of South Korean domestic politics during much of the 1970s.

CHAPTER FIFTEEN

Normalization of Relations with Japan: Toward a New Partnership

Jung-Hoon Lee

ANYONE EVEN REMOTELY familiar with East Asian history will attest to the unique and complex nature of South Korean–Japanese relations. The paradox of the relationship is that while the two sides remain vulnerable to recurrences of disputes over unresolved colonial legacies, they have enjoyed since the mid-1960s a symbiotic relationship. Despite sporadic anti-Japan outbursts in South Korea, Japan has for nearly four decades been South Korea's top trading partner, second only to the United States. The 1990s and the new millennium saw expanded security cooperation between the two, yet anti-Japan protests still flared when it came to the issue of sovereignty over the two islets and assorted rocks that make up Tokdo (or Takeshima in Japanese), or to the issue of Japanese apology for colonial wrongdoings. Although the legal treatment of the 680,000 Korean residents in Japan has improved, the Japanese government's inability to deal with the "comfort women" issue from the colonial era has raised doubts about Japan's sincerity in dealing with its militarist past. Many of the issues that cast a shadow over the South Korean–Japanese relationship now, from history questions and identity conflicts to political apologies to fishery and territorial rights, were as salient at the time of diplomatic normalization with Japan in 1965 as they are today. The "political" side of the South Korea–Japan relationship looks frozen while its "economic" side has continuously improved into a close partnership.

In many ways this duality of fragile political relations and robust economic cooperation between South Korea and Japan has affected the way in which Park Chung Hee is viewed for his efforts to normalize diplomatic relations with Japan in 1965. Rather than securing a "genuine" Japanese apology and repentance for colonial wrongdoings and forcing Tokyo to unambiguously recognize South Korea's sovereignty over Tokdo, as demanded by the *chaeya* and opposition parties, Park chose the pragmatic approach in order to achieve economic gains as well as political stability. Should Park be extolled for bringing about modernization by, among other things, steering South Korean–Japanese relations onto a new, cooperative path, or should he be denounced for brushing aside the public call for settling for good the history issue in favor of a quick economic gain? Just as there is much controversy in evaluating Park's eighteen-year rule, his role in establishing a new South Korean–Japanese relationship is also full of contrasting assessments. There is little doubt that Park broke the shackles of the past and put the bilateral relationship on a more positive and mutually beneficial course for the first time in the twentieth century. But it is also evident that genuine reconciliation did not keep pace with the surge in broader bilateral relations.

On the question of whether Park sacrificed an opportunity for a genuine reconciliation, it is extremely difficult to answer due to the lack of hard evidence. Now, not as often asked, but perhaps the more pertinent question might be to ask whether political reconciliation was possible at all, had Park's dealings with Japan taken a different course. Could Park have brought about a genuine reconciliation between South Korea and Japan, had he taken a more uncompromising position in dealing with the issues of the past? What would have been required of Japan to satisfy South Korea's demand for historical rectification, and was Japan prepared to meet its requirements? Given the state of South Korean–Japanese relations during Syngman Rhee's rule (1948–1960), it is difficult to imagine that Park could have in any way made a difference by adopting a more anti-Japanese attitude. It is more likely that historical reconciliation remained elusive for the two countries in the mid-1960s, as it is today. Apparently, Park thought history could never be rectified. At best, South Korea had to live in the shadow of its tragic past while trying to put itself on a new track of historical development through Park's strategy of *puguk kangbyŏng* (rich nation, strong army).

With regard to Japan, the significance of Park's rise to power was that, in him, South Korea finally had someone who was not just eager, but actually had the political strength to normalize relations with the country's former foe and colonial overseer, despite vociferous domestic opposition.

Park's predecessor, Chang Myŏn (1960–1961), had been just as eager to improve relations with Japan, but was unable to deliver because of his weak domestic political standing. But Park, who as we have seen had come to power in an undemocratic fashion, needed to find as many ways as he could to make up for his obvious lack of electoral legitimacy so that he could consolidate his power, govern the contentious society of South Korea, and lay the ground for industrialization. This is where the Japanese settlement came in. Uninhibited commercial ties with Japan were considered paramount not only because they would help to strengthen the financial basis of Park's ruling political coalition, but also because they would help fuel Park's development plans and, through them, enhance his political legitimacy on the basis of economic performance. Moreover, by accommodating the United States' long-standing policy to strengthen the trilateral security ties between South Korea, Japan, and the United States for common regional security interests, the treaty initiative also aimed to strengthen military deterrence against North Korea, as well as prevent the United States from intervening in South Korean domestic politics on the side of the opposition. Like Park's decision to dispatch combat troops to South Vietnam in 1965 (see Chapter 14), the treaty initiative was another instance where Park used foreign policy as an instrument of economic modernization, power consolidation, and military deterrence.

From Park's point of view, normalizing relations with Japan without its unambiguous apology did not make him any less a nationalist. Under the Park regime, to be *panil* (anti-Japan) was set aside to make way for a more pragmatic but still nationalistic *kŭkil* (beat Japan) approach. The normalization of relations with Japan was conceived as an instrument to secure the capital, technology, and markets required for South Korea to catch up with and eventually beat Japan in Japan's own game of statist modernization. To be sure, many South Koreans accused Park of having pro-Japanese *(ch'inil)* tendencies, a view that some still hold today. These opponents ignored the fact that the reconciliation issue—via a proper Japanese apology and demonstrated repentance—was really beyond anyone's power to resolve at the time. For the anti-Japanese nationalists, determined to force Japan to make amends for Korea's humiliating colonial experience, Park was a convenient target to vent their deep sense of frustration over what had happened in the past and how little could be done about it. The volatility of South Korean–Japanese relations is, if anything, indicative of Park's conscious, as opposed to indiscriminate, attempts to deal with the conflicting claims of geopolitics, geoeconomics, domestic politics, and historical legacies despite charges otherwise by the anti-Park, anti-Japanese elements in South Korea over the years.

Converging Interests and Diverging Identities

The normalization treaty brought out the sharp contrast between Park and Syngman Rhee in their approach to Japan. Personifying anti-Japanese Korean nationalism, Rhee demanded an unambiguous apology from Japan for all its colonial wrongdoing. When Japan failed to come forward, Rhee deliberately fostered anti-Japanese sentiments not only to satisfy his genuine hatred of Japan but also to mobilize the public behind his Liberal Party (LP) for the goal of political stability. Having fought all his life for independence from Japan, his instinct after liberation was to continue to oppose Japan. The more the Japanese resisted repentance, the more intensified his anti-Japanese political campaigns became.

Consequently, for six years after South Korea's liberation from Japan in 1945, the two countries lived in isolation from each other, almost completely lacking formal channels of contact. It was only with the intensification of the cold war in East Asia and the subsequent negotiations for the San Francisco Peace Treaty that the stage was set for dialogue on the issue of diplomatic normalization. Even then, the gap remained too wide for the intermittent bilateral talks to yield any concrete results. Rhee saw no urgent need to cooperate with Japan, especially in the context of the continued U.S. military commitment to South Korea. Japan, too, was in no hurry to normalize relations. Certainly, it wanted to resolve the conflict over territorial waters and fishery rights with South Korea but not at the political cost of making a public apology for its colonial rule. The result was lackluster negotiations for diplomatic normalization throughout the 1950s.

With the inauguration of Chang Myŏn's Democratic Party (DP) government in 1960, there developed a greater interest in improving South Korean–Japanese relations. In contrast to Syngman Rhee, whose main concern was the strengthening of the U.S.–South Korean alliance to deter the North, Chang made economic growth his highest priority because he saw it as the only way to give his fragile DP government political legitimacy. The recognition of the importance of economic growth in generating legitimacy naturally encouraged Chang to develop closer ties with Japan, whose economy was becoming increasingly stronger. He looked to Japan as a source of much-needed economic assistance rather than as a perpetual enemy that had to be brought to its knees. To encourage bilateral cooperation, Chang invited Japanese politicians and business leaders to South Korea, liberalized sales of Japanese products, and refrained from making inflammatory remarks about Japan. But as he sought to advance normalization talks, he was overwhelmed by opposing forces, including the student-led dissident movements that took advantage of his lack of leadership within the faction-ridden DP. In the end, Chang could not act on his desire to bring about a political, economic, and historical settlement with Japan. Japanese prime minister Ikeda Hayato did not help, either, adopting a wait-and-see posture in dealing with Chang Myŏn's political overtures to extract maximum South Korean concessions. Time was obviously a crucial factor for the weak Chang Myŏn government, under siege by mass demonstrations. Unfortunately, time ran out. Just as Chang boldly tried to break the deadlock, he was forced out of the office by Park's 1961 military coup.

Park Chung Hee had a reputation as a Japan-hand with an earlier career in the Japanese Imperial Army. Enraging his critics, Park made clear his admiration for the Meiji modernizers of nineteenth-century Japan and eagerly pursued a normalization treaty with Japan once he assumed power. But contrary to the image of a colonial collaborator that his political opponents and *chaeya* activists drew of Park, he did not think that his emulation of the Meiji modernizers made him any less a nationalist. On the contrary, his talk of Meiji Japan was heavily marked by nationalist ideas and spirit. Park admired Japan's modernizers because he too wanted to make South Korea economically prosperous and militarily strong like Meiji Japan. Park was more than a military strongman. He was a deeply committed leader, with a self-defined mission to deliver South Korea from deep poverty. For Park, Meiji Japan constituted a model to emulate for Korean nationalists; it showed the way to the "rich nation, strong army."

Even if Park were a Japan sympathizer, his personal predilection was only a secondary factor in his decision to turn to Japan for economic and technological assistance. The needs of his time compelled Park to lean on Japan, inextricably tying South Korea's economic future with that of its neighbor. At the time of Park's ascent to power, the per capita annual GNP stood at $80, only $9 more than its level at the end of the Korean War in 1953. The annual growth rate remained 1.1 percent, the trade deficit hit $310 million, the unemployment rate reached 11.7 percent, and inflation ran at 10.5 percent. Moreover, the United States was decreasing aid to South Korea as part of its global foreign policy to replace grants-in-aid with loans. Having hovered at over $200 million until 1963, U.S. aid would drop to $149.3 million in 1964 and to $131.4 million in 1965. As his chief of staff Yi Tong-wŏn suggested and Park agreed, given South Korea's inability to contract foreign loans and technology licensing on a commercial basis, it needed to turn to diplomacy to achieve what South Korea could not achieve through market forces.

In fact, had his country found alternative sources of foreign capital and technology, Park would have thought twice before risking the kind of political crisis that he brought on himself during the 1963–1965 period by rushing into the normalization of relations with Japan. In the short run, the rapprochement hurt rather than helped Park's efforts to consolidate his domestic base of power as he was drawn into the emotionally charged politics of national identity. That he risked his political rule in ramming through the normalization of relations with Japan showed his lack of alternative market-based ways to secure capital and technology. To his vehement domestic opposition, Park defiantly said, "Spit on my grave," believing that economic growth would in the end justify his decision to settle with Japan. Fortunately for Park, the first Five-Year Economic Development Plan (FYEDP) was successful beyond all expectations by 1964, making Park confident of South Korea's growth potential and consequently even more focused on the normalization treaty.[1]

Then there were security reasons to normalize relations with Japan, too. The United States argued and Park agreed that the containment of communist threats in East Asia could not be effective so long as the United States' alliances with South Korea and Japan were left uncoordinated. Cold war tension had heightened worldwide in the early 1960s. With the U-2 spy plane incident and crisis situations brewing in Cuba, Congo, Laos, and South Vietnam, the predominant view in the United States was that the Soviets were winning the cold war. Having been himself one of the chief proponents of this view, John F. Kennedy won the 1960 presidential election on the strength of, among other things, his firm commitment to anticommunism. The young military officers who overthrew Prime Minister Chang Myŏn in May 1961 also cited South Korea's domestic weakness in the face of a growing communist threat from the North as the most important reason for the coup.

The year 1961, then, looked promising for a breakthrough in South Korean–Japanese relations. The military coup freed South Korea from Syngman Rhee's stubbornly anti-Japanese posture as well as from Chang Myŏn's political drift and administrative ineffectiveness. Park appeared to have the strength to take on the challenges of anti-Japanese public sentiment as well as the bureaucratic imbroglio. The military junta looked like it possessed the political strength as well as the will not only to bring the normalization treaty to a successful conclusion but also to steer the nation on the path of export-led growth on the basis of that treaty. The question was how to get diplomacy to do the work the market would not do for South Korea.

Yi Tong-wŏn advocated the strategy of securing Japanese capital and technology on the basis of a political understanding on a range of issues that were of interest to Japan:

> What is lacking in natural resources and financial instruments can be made up through strategically timed diplomatic manoeuvres. Foreign policy can either make or break a nation. If [the military junta] can concentrate on the strengthening of economic ties with the United States as much as the security ties, and on the normalization of relations with Japan, South Korea can secure large amounts of economic assistance in a timely manner. With the resources secured through diplomacy, I believe [the military junta] will have a chance at creating an economic miracle.[2]

Even before Yi Tong-wŏn advanced the idea of diplomacy-led economic modernization, Park had politically committed himself to the policy of reaching a quick settlement with Japan on the bilateral issues of the day in order to clear the way for economic cooperation. As early as May 22, 1961, only six days after the military coup, Park had foreign minister Kim Hong-il, a lieutenant general in the reserves, hold a press conference to announce that the junta was interested in resuming talks with Japan on the issue of normalization of relations at the earliest possible date.[3] On July 15, Yi Tong-hwan, a graduate of Tokyo University and then the vice chairman of the Korean Trade Association, was appointed the minister plenipotentiary to the South Korean representative office in Japan, with the goal of making full use of the private sector's ties to Japanese political and business leaders to make the Japanese audience receptive to the idea of early diplomatic normalization.[4] The driving force behind the South Korean initiative was Kim Chong-p'il, Park's right-hand man and the director of the newly established Korea Central Intelligence Agency (KCIA).

For the United States, once the early jitters over the military coup in May 1961 were overcome, Park's rise to power was seen as an opportunity to consolidate the Seoul-Tokyo link in the U.S. system of bilateral security alliances. The Kennedy administration was particularly hostile to communism,[5] and saw the staunchly anticommunist Park as a welcome addition to its list of junior security partners in the third world.[6] Although the United States highly regarded Chang Myŏn's democratic credentials, it was also true that an increasing number of U.S. officials had become skeptical of Chang's ability to check the growing leftist forces in South Korea. Now, with a pragmatic and powerful military leader at the helm, the United States hoped to contain leftist forces in South Korea, as well as forge a triangular East Asian security alignment between the United States, Japan, and South Korea, as the emerging superpower had advocated since the days of secretary of state John Foster Dulles. Shortly after the coup, the U.S. House Committee on International Relations recommended that the National Security Council take measures to improve South Korea–Japan relations: "Discuss with the Japanese Prime Minister during his forthcoming visit, the U.S. planning for [South] Korea and the ways in which economic and political differences between [South] Korea and Japan can be bridged . . . It should be understood that while the United States will not participate actively in negotiations, it should be prepared to act as a catalyst in seeking a settlement. The Prime Minister should be encouraged to continue efforts recently begun to develop Japanese trade with [South] Korea, and to provide economic assistance for [South] Korean development coordinated with American programmes."[7] Presumably, it was for this prospect of building a trilateral security network that Kennedy received Park in Washington on November 14, 1961, to extend the United States' continued support for South Korea, a move that was received as an endorsement of Park's political leadership.[8]

Just as the news of the military coup in South Korea caught the United States by surprise, Japan was caught off guard when Park seized power in 1961. Understanding the full meaning of Park's rise to power took time. Only a week before the military coup of May 1961, a Japanese parliamentary delegation on a visit to Seoul had given a rosy picture of the political situation. Iseki Yujirō, as a Foreign Ministry member of the delegation, assured Ikeda that the Chang Myŏn government was "extremely stable."[9] Noda Uichi, the head of the delegation, echoed the optimism, praising the successes of Chang Myŏn and encouraging the Japanese Diet to have confidence in his ability to see through the normalization talks.[10] Naturally, the news of the coup was not taken well by these South Korea watchers, who were busy convincing their government to work with Chang Myŏn to bring about wider economic cooperation with South Korea. Also, like Kennedy, Ikeda Hayato was not happy to see a democratically elected civilian government forcibly displaced by a military coup. Reports of Park's earlier involvement in communist-inspired political activities did not help, either. Concerned about the future course of South Korea and the possible negative fallout for Japanese security, Ikeda anxiously gathered what information there was on Park, then a relatively unknown leader.

Soon the new South Korean leader's diplomatic overtures shifted the mood in Japan in Park's favor. For many Japanese politicians and bureaucrats, the military coup came to be seen as a window of opportunity to pursue the normalization talks on the basis of pragmatism. Whereas Chang Myŏn had proved to be politically too weak to shake off the constraints of South Korean public opinion, Park seemed capable of overcoming the sociopolitical hurdles in the normalization of relations between the two countries in order to achieve success for his ambitious economic development programs. Such views were given much credence when Park used force to clamp down on the press, political parties, intelligentsia, and interest groups to implement his vision of modernization. Former prime minister Kishi Nobusuke once observed: "Fortunately, South Korea is under a military regime where Park Chung Hee and a handful of leaders can decide things on their own . . . We [need to] persuade Park. [We] can expect him to deliver, [especially since] there is no National Assembly to [constrain him]. If the newspapers oppose, Park can be expected to seal [*fuzuru*] them off."[11]

Kishi had been at the forefront of the Japanese conservatives' initiative to cultivate a close relationship with South Korea. This time, spurred on by the emergence of a pragmatic military junta, he argued strongly for a speedy settlement of the property claims in order not to jeopardize Japan's future security interests. In his eyes, the collapse of Park's military junta might give way to the rise of anti-Japanese political forces in South Korea. In an unambiguous way, Kishi explained his rationale for working closely with the junta:

> Imagine what it would be like for Japan if communists were able to stretch their influence all the way down to Pusan . . . The reason that our forefathers, at least from the Meiji period onward, went through so much trouble over the Korean Peninsula—[including the waging of] the Sino-Japanese War [1894–1895] and the Russo-Japanese War [1904–1905]—was not because of their imperialistic ambitions, but because of their concern for Japan's security that has always faced the dreaded possibility of hostile forces emerging in [the Korean Peninsula] . . . This is why Japan must normalize diplomatic relations with South Korea, provide substantial economic aid along with the United States, and thereby help build South Korea's economic foundation . . . If we do not do anything and allow Park to fail, most grave consequences will follow. Now is not the time to sit idly by.[12]

The specter of a "red flag fluttering over Pusan" *(pusan chŏkkiron)* had been frequently raised by Japanese conservatives to justify their call for diplomatic normalization with South Korea. This time, with the sense of uncertainty, opportunity, and urgency ushered in by the military coup, Kishi worked to mobilize LDP support for the normalization of relations. By identifying his security worries with the geopolitical concerns of Japan tracing back to the Meiji period, Kishi defined his South Korea policy to be in line with Japan's traditional policy toward the Asian continent.

Concurring with him was Kōnō Ichirō, the agricultural minister and a major LDP faction leader. Not a usual South Korea hand, but an expert on the Soviet Union and, to a lesser extent, China, Kōnō became interested in the normalization talks primarily as part of Japan's regional policy to counter the Soviet and Chinese threats. In his talks with Ikeda, Kōnō advised: "We have before us the best *chance* since the end of the war to resolve the Japanese–South Korean problem. Undergoing a serious economic crisis, South Korea is in most urgent need of money. Now is the time to negotiate."[13] Kōnō also urged that Sugi Michisuke, a business magnate from the Kansai area and the chairman of the Japan External Trade Organization (JETRO), head the Japanese delegation to the sixth round of normalization talks scheduled to begin in October 1961.[14]

For Prime Minister Ikeda Hayato, however, cooperating with Park was not as easy as it was made out to be by Kōnō and Kishi. First, Ikeda was not yet convinced of the military junta's ability to put its house in order and overcome its political challenges. Second, he was unsure of his own ability to align Japanese public opinion behind the negotiation of the claims issue. The situation was also not helped by Park's authoritarian style of rule, which had the effect of bringing together the Japanese opposition parties, press, and intelligentsia, as well as the more liberal elements within the LDP, to oppose any political deals with what they regarded as a repressive military regime. There were in addition Japanese leftists who had organized a Liaison Council in January 1961 to coordinate their campaign against the normalization of relations with South Korea on the grounds that it would entail the danger of getting dragged into a U.S.-centric military network in East Asia and maybe even an unwanted military conflict.[15] The council consisted of representatives from the Japanese Communist Party, the Japanese Socialist Party, the General Council of Trade Unions *(Sohyo),* and the Japan–North Korea Association, among other political and social organizations. In such a context of domestic political polarization, it was the United States that had to step in to push Ikeda to the negotiating table.

Early Overtures

In October 1961, under the direction of Park, Kim Chong-p'il made a secret trip to meet with Ikeda Hayato to arrange Park's state visit to Japan on his way to Washington the following month. Kim used the trip to widen South Korea's points of contact in Japan, meeting unofficially with Kishi Nobusuke, Ishii Mitsujirō, Satō Eisaku, Kōnō Ichirō, and Ōno Bamboku. This was the first of many informal meetings Kim was to have with the leaders of the Japanese Liberal Democratic Party (LDP) through the course of the normalization talks. Park had high hopes for a speedy settlement. By sending the most diverse and certainly the largest ever delegation to the negotiations, Park showed his readiness to cover all areas of contention.

The junta leader had U.S. secretary of state Dean Rusk as a friendly mediator. With North Korea concluding mutual defense treaties with the Soviet Union and China, respectively, in July 1961,[16] Rusk took on the role of mediator between Seoul and Tokyo, visiting Japan in November 1961 to meet with Ikeda to persuade him of the importance of seeking an early settlement with South Korea. Rusk urged Japan to share with the United States the burden of financing South Korea's economic development programs by seeing to the resolution of the property claims.[17] By contrast, Ikeda explained to Rusk the difficulties of cooperating with South Korea:

> The [Japanese] opposition parties, including the Democratic Socialist Party, are strongly against spending vast sums of money to settle the claims issue. Whereas in South Korea the military regime can put into effect its decisions instantly, in Japan things have to be put through the Diet proceedings. It is simply not possible for us to do things in the way they do them . . . We run the risk of going through a security treaty crisis all over again [like the one in 1960 provoked by the United States–Japan Mutual Security Treaty].[18]

Before the meeting was over, however, Ikeda came to agree with Rusk that he would try his best to help South Korea's economic development and to settle many of the outstanding differences between the two countries. The Japanese prime minister sensed that the United States looked at his South Korea policy as a testing ground for Japan's commitment to the U.S.-Japanese security alliance and to the principle of burden sharing in regional geopolitics. Aware of what was at stake, Ikeda replied that he would begin serious negotiations with the new military regime in South Korea.[19] Ikeda backed the resumption of normalization talks started in October 1961 and consented to hold a meeting with Park. For the junta chairman, who needed to demonstrate to his people that the military coup had the backing of the international community, Ikeda's show of interest was a positive development that could help consolidate his power base.

On November 11, less than three weeks after Kim Chong-p'il's secret trip to Japan, Park made the first official trip to Japan by a South Korean head of state in the postwar period.[20] Before his departure, Park simply expressed his hope to have "frank talks" with the Japanese.[21] Once in Japan, he did not shy away from giving his positive views on Japan at the risk of alienating South Korean domestic political forces. At the state banquet hosted by Ikeda Hayato on the day of his arrival, Park pleasantly surprised the Japanese by arguing that "it would be neither wise nor beneficial to dwell on the [colonial] past and . . . both nations should try their utmost to promote cooperation for common goals and ideals."[22] The next day, speaking to Kishi Nobusuke, Ishii Mitsujirō, and other senior LDP leaders, Park did not hide his admiration for the Meiji modernizers, and reaffirmed his commitment to the construction of a "rich nation, strong army" in the same way that the Meiji leaders had done.[23] Deeply moved by Park's respect for Japanese ethos and history, one of the attending LDP leaders likened Park to the *ishin no shishi* (Meiji patriots).

Park was committed to concluding an agreement should there arise an opportunity to make a deal on the spot. However, despite Ikeda's public commitment to an early settlement, Park found the Japanese prime minister to be extremely cautious in the face of increasing domestic pressure to call off the normalization talks with Park. The Japanese public became agitated over Park's use of force to silence the South Korean opposition. Even within the LDP, an anti-treaty camp emerged to make it difficult for Ikeda to forge a forward-looking South Korea policy, especially since the opponents included major LDP leaders like the minister of international trade and industry, Satō Eisaku, and the finance minister, Mizuta Mikio. Satō Eisaku was particularly vehement in his opposition to the settlement of the property claims issue, apparently trying to prevent his political rival, Ikeda, from accomplishing a major diplomatic feat. The opposition of Mizuta Mikio was another headache for Park, because he headed the Finance Ministry in charge of dispensing state money and regulating banks and nonbank financial institutions. Mizuta could slow down, if not block, the normalization talks.

The visit of November 1961 did not result in substantive breakthroughs on the issues of normalization. The Japanese press remained mostly uninterested in Park's visit, giving only scant coverage to the Park-Ikeda meeting, while repeating the existing Japanese demand that the two countries should deal with the issues of property claims and reparations from an "economic" rather than from a "political" perspective. By emphasizing the economics rather than the politics of the issues of property claims, the Japanese were arguing that the size of reparations would be much smaller than Park hoped. With the Japanese press and public outlook unchanged,[24] Ikeda's space to maneuver in Japanese domestic politics was severely constrained.

Park had some trouble understanding the domestic political difficulties his Japanese counterpart faced. On the basis of his political experience in South Korea, where power was concentrated in the chairman of the military junta, Park assumed that the establishment of mutual trust, friendship, or simply political give-and-take at the level of the top authorities between the two countries would ensure a speedy resolution of the territorial, fishery, history, and reparation issues. His lack of experience in diplomatic affairs and his oversimplified image of the Japanese decision-making process were the causes of his eventual disappointment over the results of his trip, especially since he initially thought the trip was a diplomatic triumph.[25]

Nonetheless, Park's Tokyo visit of 1961 was important in three respects. First, it assured the Japanese that Park was not going to politicize the territorial, fishery, history, and ideological issues inherited from the colonial past, certainly not to the extent Syngman Rhee had done in the 1950s. The Japanese understood that Park had opened a window of opportunity for cooperation, with or without a genuine reconciliation at the level of the two peoples. Second, the Tokyo visit indicated that Park would step back from Syngman Rhee's unilaterally declared "Peace Line" to bring about a settlement on the issues of territorial waters and fishery rights if Japan was prepared to deal favorably with the issues of property claims and reparations.[26] Third, it also signaled to the United States that South Korea was moving toward the U.S. policy of strengthening the trilateral relationship between South Korea, Japan, and the United States for common regional security interests. These three were major accomplishments for a bilateral relationship marked by mistrust and animosity. But they were not enough to bring about a breakthrough in the negotiations.

The main obstacle was the issue of property claims. Contrary to Park's hope for Japanese flexibility, the Ikeda cabinet reiterated the Japanese position that the issue had to be settled in a way that the Japanese public could understand and endorse. Specifically, the Japanese negotiators insisted that the issue of property claims was not an issue of overall damages inflicted on South Korea during the colonial period. If there was to be compensation for colonial damages, Iseki Yujirō, the Asian Affairs Bureau director in the Japanese Foreign Ministry, argued, it had to be limited strictly to the unpaid salaries, pensions, bonds, and debentures of South Korean workers and investors, among others. Moreover, the claimants had to back their demand with solid legal proof. There were reports in the Japanese press that the Foreign Ministry and the Finance Ministry were considering a settlement amount in the range of $20-$80 million. By contrast, Park was aiming for a figure between $600 million and $900 million.[27]

With renewed confrontations over the territorial issue of Tokdo, the Peace Line, and the property claims, and facing the Japanese delegation's criticism of the South Korean refusal to permit the establishment of a Japanese representative office in Seoul, Park had to cancel his plans for an overnight stay in Japan on his way home from the United States. The situation was not helped by the upcoming Upper House elections in Japan, which prevented the pro–South Korea members of the Diet from turning the tide on the politically sensitive issue of property claims. As an effort at damage control, Ikeda reached out to both Japanese and American advocates of a quick settlement in January 1962 with an official statement that political stability in South Korea served Japanese security interests and that his government was prepared to pursue negotiations for diplomatic normalization in earnest.[28] To break the deadlock, South Korean foreign minister Ch'oe Tŏk-sin met with his Japanese counterpart, Kosaka Zentarō, on March 15, 1962. Six days later, KCIA director Kim Chong-p'il made his second visit to Japan to reinforce the foreign ministers' meeting. Neither effort proved to be successful, despite Kim Chong-p'il's show of enthusiasm and determination. If anything, his visit to Japan only increased South Korean opposition to the normalization of relations. The timing of his visit did not help either, as it coincided with President Yun Po-sŏn's resignation in March 1962 in protest against Park's authoritarian rule, which strengthened the anti-treaty forces in Japan. The outbreak of student demonstrations in South Korea forced Kim Chong-p'il to cut his visit short. Subsequently, the normalization talks were suspended for five months.[29]

It was in this context of drift, if not deadlock, in the South Korean–Japanese talks that the U.S. government intervened to convince the Japanese leaders of the importance of reaching a quick settlement with South Korea. Kennedy urged former prime minister Yoshida Shigeru in May 1962 to help facilitate the talks. Other U.S. officials followed suit with a similar message in talks with Japanese political leaders.[30] In the end, however, the United States could not force Ikeda to unambiguously commit his political career to the normalization of relations with South Korea. The Japanese prime minister was reluctant to push the normalization talks forward, lest, as he explained to Rusk, they trigger another political crisis like the one generated over the 1960 signing of the United States–Japanese mutual security treaty. Extremely cautious, Ikeda even tried to mollify the Left with the idea of pursuing a separate overture toward North Korea in August 1962. Ikeda suggested that Japan could "someday" negotiate a separate deal with Pyŏngyang on the issues of property claims, implying that Seoul could not claim jurisdiction over the entire Korean Peninsula.[31] The idea of a separate deal with the North added another reason, in addition to anti-Japanese nationalist sentiments, for the South Korean public to oppose Park's diplomatic initiative.

Fortunately for Park, Ikeda Hayato's resounding reelection as the LDP president on July 14, 1962, appeared to encourage him to take a more forward-looking policy regarding South Korea.[32] With the launching of a new cabinet, Ohira Masayoshi, the newly appointed foreign minister and Ikeda Hayato's close lieutenant, began tackling the normalization talks. Ohira was given the task of settling the outstanding issues as quickly as possible. In the most detailed effort yet, Ohira proposed a four-point guideline for settling the claims issue. First, he proposed that Japan would make only private settlements, the total of which would not exceed $70 million. Second, a grant in the amount of $100 million would be provided in the form of economic assistance. Third, he set forth the idea of supplying South Korea with long-term low-interest loans to aid the launching of its first FYEDP. Fourth, the settlement would be made with the understanding that it dealt only with the claims issues made by the people living to the south of the armistice line.[33] The willingness to make only private settlements meant that Japan was unwilling to apologize for its colonial past. Ohira and others believed that an apology could damage Japan's national identity and global reputation. The restriction of the claims settlement to residents in the South, by contrast, was conceived to ameliorate the leftist opponents in Japan. However, given that this was the first time the specifics of property claims were proposed, Park welcomed Ohira's initiative, especially with regard to the structural formula of categorizing the claims into private claims, grants, and loans.

When the talks resumed on August 21, 1962, Sugi Michisuke and Pae Ŭi-hwan immediately set up a series of working-level meetings to work out the details. But with no progress on the actual amount of property claims, Kim Chong-p'il had to make his third trip to Japan. On his way to Washington at the State Department's invitation, Kim Chong-p'il made a three-day layover in Tokyo in October 1962 to negotiate the amount with Ohira. Under instructions from Park, Kim set his target at between $600 million and $900 million.[34] From here on, Park kept a close watch on the negotiation process, making specific orders to Kim Chong-p'il on some of the details of settlement issues, including the total amount of property claims to be received from Japan.[35]

The stopover meeting was exploratory at best. It was not until Kim Chong-p'il and Ohira held their second meeting upon Kim's return from the United States that the negotiations began in earnest. The Japanese foreign minister expected Kim to ask for $800 million on the basis of his earlier talks with South Korean deputy prime minister Kim Yu-t'aek in September 1961. In a sharp contrast to the Japanese offer of $50 million, the South Koreans thought Kim Yu-t'aek's figure was a concession by the South Korean side, being much lower than Rhee Syngman's demand for $2 billion and Chang Myŏn's figure of $1.2 billion.[36] Ohira was more gener-

ous—but not much from the South Korean perspective. Ohira had originally proposed $170 million in private settlements and grants, plus an
undefined amount of long-term low-interest loans. Incidentally, the Japanese foreign affairs and finance ministries had suggested that the entire
package should remain below $100 million.[37]

Ohira once recollected the following from his talk with Kim Chong-p'il:

> I can well understand the feelings of your people toward Japan. However, I
> [do not] think there is any benefit for your country in saying only resentful
> things about Japan . . . Our two countries are perpetual neighbours, so
> [should we not] make up our minds to discard, like ash in an ashtray, every-
> thing that is past and have some vision for the future? If there is such a senti-
> ment on your side, Japan, too, will be sensible enough to behave accordingly.
> Now that you have become independent and are faced with the difficult task
> of building up your nation, Japan, as your country's perpetual neighbour, will
> be willing to assist your future progress with substantial economic coopera-
> tion [38]

After intense haggling, the two sides finally agreed on the figures of
$300 million in grants, $200 million in ODA (Official Development Assistance) loans, and over $100 million dollars in commercial loans.[39] In-
cluded in the $300 million in grants was the write-off of a $45.7 million
debt that South Korea owed to Japan. To make the deal more acceptable
to Japanese legislators and bureaucrats, and also taking into account Japan's lack of foreign exchange reserves, Ohira proposed making the payments over an extended period of time. Kim Chong-p'il agreed to receive
both the grants and the ODA loans over ten years. By contrast, the commercial loans were to be provided even before the conclusion of diplomatic normalization on a case-by-case basis.[40] Finally, aware of each
other's domestic political vulnerabilities, the two agreed to different inter-
pretations of the deal. Whereas Kim Chong-p'il saw the deal to be a settlement of property claims and reparations for Japan's colonial wrongdoings,
Ohira Masayoshi claimed that it was Japan's economic assistance to South
Korea. With their terms of agreement written down on a piece of paper at
the end of the meeting, the controversial "Kim-Ohira Memorandum" was
brought into existence.[41]

The Kim-Ohira Memorandum settled what was considered to be the
key issue for a comprehensive settlement. Park had already indicated that
he was ready to resolve the issues of fishery rights and the Peace Line dispute if the Japanese showed good faith on the property claims issue. But
aware of the danger of nationalist backlash in South Korea against the
Kim-Ohira Memorandum, the two negotiators agreed to keep the agreement secret.[42] It was not until January 29, 1963, that the actual contents of

the memorandum were revealed by the Japanese Foreign Ministry. As fore-seen by Park and Kim Chong-p'il, the revelation of the terms of the agree-ment greatly angered the South Korean opposition, which was already re-sentful of Kim Chong-p'il's resort to "one-man diplomacy" *(ilin oegyo)*.[43] Moreover, the secretive nature of the negotiations worsened public fears of a sell-out. Nationwide demonstrations quickly followed, forcing Park—hitherto believed, especially by the pro-treaty group in Japan, to have been impervious to public opinion—to stall the talks for a good part of the 1963–1964 period.

Treaty Crisis

As in the jump-start of negotiations in October-November 1961, it was once again the United States that brought South Korea and Japan to the negotiating table in the mid-1960s. The United States was never directly involved in the negotiations. Rather, it actively mediated behind the scenes, steadily applying pressure on Seoul and Tokyo to work out a treaty on mutually agreeable terms. Even in the spring of 1963, when the United States was at odds with Park over his attempt to renege on his earlier promise to turn over the government to civilians (see Chapter 2), the United States continued its effort to bring together its two East Asian al-lies.[44] Through the good offices of Rusk, ambassador to South Korea Sam-uel D. Berger, ambassador to Japan Edwin O. Reischauer, under secretary of state for political affairs W. Averell Harriman, and assistant secretary of state for East Asian and Pacific affairs William P. Bundy, the United States played the intermediary role throughout the critical 1964–1965 period.

The United States' role of mediation heightened in 1964 because of the intensification of military conflict in Indochina. The events in South Viet-nam unfolded rapidly. The overthrow and death of President Ngo Dinh Diem in 1963 led the National Front for the Liberation of South Vietnam (NLF) to hope that South Vietnam would become a neutral state under a coalition government. But President Lyndon B. Johnson moved in the opposite direction, adamantly pressing for an early military victory. For Johnson, neutrality was tantamount to a communist takeover of South Vietnam.[45] Johnson's resounding victory in the U.S. presidential election in November 1964 led to an escalation of bombing expeditions against North Vietnam under Operation Rolling Thunder. Arguing that he had to provide security for Americans, Johnson also called for the dispatch of ground troops in large numbers. By the end of 1965, United States military forces in South Vietnam numbered 184,314. The undeclared war in Indo-china was fully under way.

Against this background, the United States eagerly awaited the normalization of relations between South Korea and Japan. In order to effectively carry out its military campaign in South Vietnam, the United States counted on Japan's logistical support and South Korea's supply of combat forces. As part of his political campaign to project the image of unity in the free world behind U.S. war efforts in South Vietnam, Johnson also sought solidarity among his anticommunist allies in East Asia and, in particular, a strong regional support network tying together South Korea and Japan. During his meeting with Park on October 2, 1964, U.S. national security adviser McGeorge Bundy acknowledged that South Korea had valid reasons to demand Japan's apology for its wrongdoings committed during the colonial era. He also encouraged Japanese foreign minister Shiina Etsusaburō to visit Seoul.[46] When Park showed his willingness to back the United States in the Vietnam War, Bundy pledged to offer his personal commitment to persuade Japan to make concessions to South Korea.[47] The United States' deepening entrapment in South Vietnam was rapidly changing South Korea's political and economic fortunes.

This tilt toward South Korea was a reversal—however brief and limited—in the United States' foreign policy in East Asia, which had traditionally been defined from the vantage point of Japan. Even as late as in the fall of 1964, cold war expert George F. Kennan reiterated what had always been the United States' position on the relationship between South Korea and Japan:

> Those in [South] Korea who oppose the establishment of acceptable relations with the overwhelmingly peace-loving Japan of the present day show scant appreciation for the advantages of American protection and little inclination to be helpful to the United States in the exercise of the responsibilities it has assumed in that area . . . If the regime in South Korea, whose domestic failures are serious in any case, is forced to remain a dead weight on American policy towards Japan, it will eventually compel a reconsideration of American policy towards [South] Korea generally; for [South] Korea is important, but Japan is more important still.[48]

To be certain, Japan remained the United States' most important ally in East Asia despite the much enhanced U.S.–South Korean relationship amid the Vietnam War. Nonetheless, the war had far-reaching consequences on the politico-strategic landscape of the East Asian region, forcing significant changes in the way the United States conducted its East Asia policy. With the prospect of South Korean combat troops fighting alongside U.S. troops in South Vietnam, the United States became more understanding of the problems South Korea had encountered with Japan in the normalization talks. Kennan was right to suggest that South Korea was less strategically important to the United States than Japan. But having failed to take fully into account Johnson's slide into the Vietnamese quagmire, Kennan was unable to assess accurately the political implications of South Korean troop engagement in the Vietnam War. Park, thanks to the war, was able to influence the direction of U.S. policy toward the normalization talks more than Kennan might have imagined. Rather than being a "dead weight," South Korea was on its way to becoming a central part of U.S. policy in East Asia.

The final push for the conclusion of the normalization talks would not begin until late 1964, when, by fortuitous coincidence, the two sides appointed new foreign ministers who were both strong pro-treaty advocates: Yi Tong-wŏn in South Korea and Shiina Etsusaburō in Japan. Formerly Park's chief of staff, Yi Tong-wŏn was selected with a mission to conclude the normalization talks regardless of the level of domestic political backlash. Right away, the new South Korean foreign minister proposed to alternate the venue between Seoul and Tokyo. Until then, the talks had been held only in Tokyo. Yi also proceeded to conduct "open diplomacy" in order to reduce public distrust. Having fought against the Japanese colonial rule in his youth and also against the U.S. military occupation in the post-independence period, Yi Tong-wŏn felt confident that he could appeal to the public.

In Japan, Sato Eisaku became the new prime minister on November 9, 1964, upon Ikeda Hayato's retirement from public life due to illness. A younger brother of former prime minister Kishi Nobusuke, Sato Eisaku shared Kishi's support for a quick settlement with South Korea. In his first Diet address as prime minister on November 20, Sato expressed his intention to "resolve the outstanding problems quickly and justly as desired by the majority of people in both Japan and South Korea."[49] In his first press interview, he optimistically remarked that the talks were near completion, requiring only minor adjustments before a treaty could be signed.[50]

For Park and Yi Tong-wŏn, these words of enthusiasm coming from a man known for his cautious approach prompted great hope for a quick settlement. Still, Sato was by nature more of a consensus builder than a charismatic politician willing to take risks.[51] When the time came for tough decision-making, it was Foreign Minister Shiina who stepped forward to meet the challenge. Following the prime minister's address to the Diet, Shiina remarked:

As soon as the negotiation agenda is agreed, we would like to resume the talks on the outstanding issues, with special reference to the fishery dispute. Moreover, if my visit to South Korea is required to enhance in any way the understanding between the two countries, I am willing to take the earliest possible opportunity to work out such an arrangement.[52]

Shiina Etsusaburō was neither a pro–South Korea politician nor a noted expert on international relations when he was appointed the foreign minister in 1964. Having led the Ministry of International Trade and Industry (MITI) and served as the chief cabinet secretary and state minister under Prime Minister Kishi Nobusuke, Shiina was known more for his economic than for his foreign policy expertise.[53] As to his views on South Korea, little was known except that he was hardly a South Korea sympathizer.[54] The surprise was that much greater when Shiina put his political career on the line by making independent decisions on some of the key settlement issues. If there ever was a turning point in the normalization talks, it was when Shiina stood on the arrival platform at the Kimpo airport to publicly "apologize" for the pain Japan inflicted on the Korean people during the colonial era. With the Japanese national flag *hinomaru* flying high on the Korean Peninsula for the first time since the end of colonial rule in 1945, the foreign minister made his elusively worded, but still significant arrival statement on history issues:

As neighbors, [South] Korea and Japan have long enjoyed cultural, economic, and other meaningful and friendly exchanges throughout [their] history. It is in this respect that I find it most regrettable that we had to go through this most unfortunate [colonial] period in our history. I feel deeply reflective [*fukaku hansei suru*] about this ... I will do my utmost best to realize our mutual hope to establish a new starting point in our history to guarantee friendship for many years to come.[55]

The reception accorded to Shiina by the South Korean government was first class, quite a contrast from the one accorded to his predecessor, Kosaka Zentarō, in 1960. More important, Shiina quickly earned the South Korean leadership's confidence with his earnest and humble manner.[56] The two sides quickly set up meetings to hammer out three key issues: (1) whether South Korea's jurisdiction covered the entire peninsula or only its southern part below the armistice line; (2) how the normalization of relations would affect the status of their old treaties, including the 1910 annexation document; and (3) which of the two countries had sovereignty over Tokdo. It was not until the night before Shiina was scheduled to return to Japan that the two sides agreed on a carefully worded set of principles. With regard to the status of the old "unequal treaties" forced on the

Chosŏn Dynasty (that is, Korea) on or before the annexation in August 1910, the two sides avoided the issue of the legality of Japan's annexation of Chosŏn by simply declaring the treaties to be "*already* null and void" (Article II). As for the issue of the geographic reach of South Korea's jurisdiction in the Korean Peninsula and, hence, the legitimacy of North Korea's claim to being a sovereign state, Yi Tong-wŏn and Shiina Etsusaburo agreed that the government in the South to be "the *only* lawful Government in Korea as specified in the Resolution 195 (III) of the United Nations General Assembly" (Article III).[57] On the other hand, they could not find a mutually agreeable formula on the question of Tokdo. Faced with an unbridgeable difference, Yi Tong-wŏn and Shiina Etsusaburo decided to put the issue of territorial dispute on hold in order to proceed with the Basic Relations Treaty.

To capitalize on the momentum generated from Shiina Etsusaburo's Seoul visit, working-level negotiations quickly resumed in Tokyo on the remaining issues in March 1965. In a month, the two sides settled on all issues. On the issue of fishery rights, the two countries established a joint control zone in addition to exclusive territorial waters. Some restrictions were made on the number and size of fishing boats, and also on the volume (165,000 tons) of the total catch in the joint control zones. Violators of these restrictions were to be "handled with domestic measures including appropriate penalties." As for the rights of ethnic Koreans living in Japan, those who had resided in Japan before its surrender to the Allied forces on August 15, 1945, and their direct descendants were to be granted permanent resident status by the Japanese government. For the yet-to-be-born "third generation" and beyond of ethnic Korean residents in Japan, South Korea and Japan agreed to "consult" on their legal status anytime within twenty-five years after the 1965 agreement went into effect. The Japanese also agreed to return or "transfer" a number of old Korean books and treasured art objects taken away during the colonial era. The only major dispute that would not be included in the treaty was the territorial issue over Tokdo. The closest the Japanese could get was to include a passage in the treaty that would say that all bilateral disputes would be settled through diplomatic means. These stipulations in their draft form came to be known as the April Third Agreement. With only the final text left to be produced, the fourteen years of intermittent and emotion-laden negotiations were brought to a close.

The news of the settlement quickly galvanized opposition forces in both South Korea and Japan. The political resistance became particularly serious in South Korea, where the dissident intelligentsia organized the Committee for the Struggle against Humiliating Diplomacy with Japan to spearhead nationwide protests on April 9, 1965. On April 14, over 5,000 students took to the streets in Seoul, resulting in the death of a Dongguk University student in one of the confrontations with the police.[58] The incident led to even more vigorous demonstrations, forcing the government to issue a garrison decree to maintain political order.

What triggered the spread of opposition demonstrations was the public perception that the South Korean negotiators had yielded too much. The demonstrators demanded Japan's apology for the forced annexation in 1910. They also took issue with the inability of the Park government to call the Japanese money "reparations." Contrary to South Korea's constitution, the treaty documents' failure to state explicitly South Korea's claim that its territorial jurisdiction extended over the entire Korean Peninsula was another criticism the Park government had to cope with. Finally, the abolition of the Peace Line, to the dismay of South Korean fishermen, was repeatedly criticized by opponents. The opposition vehemently protested that this all added up to a national sell-out.

To effectively resist Park's initiative on the normalization issues, the two largest opposition parties—the Democratic Justice Party (DJP) and the Democratic Party (DP)—merged on May 30, 1965, to establish the Popular Party *(Minjungdang)*. The seriousness of the situation prompted the United States to intervene by sending deputy assistant secretary of state for East Asian and Pacific affairs Marshall Green on April 29 and, in his capacity as chairman of the Policy Planning Council at the State Department, Walt Rostow on May 2 to give moral support to the hard-pressed Park. Park was not about to reconsider the signing of the treaty on account of the opposition; nevertheless, he did have to postpone it until the domestic situation cooled down.

The treaty documents were signed at the Japanese prime minister's official residence, and the treaty bills were ratified by the South Korean National Assembly and the Japanese lower house on August 14 and November 12, 1965, respectively. The Japanese upper house followed with its ratification on December 11. Throughout 1965, Park resolutely put down anti-treaty demonstrations. Some universities were closed down to contain the spread of demonstrations. In Japan, contrary to the LDP leadership's fear that the treaty would trigger a security crisis, there were only some qualms about the way the bills were handled in the Diet. With the ratification process completed, the treaty documents were officially exchanged on December 18, 1965, at the central government building in Seoul.

The treaty was not about which side got the better of the other. Rather, it was about what the two sides could agree on within the tight constraints of their respective domestic political and economic situations in 1965. As much as the normalization treaty failed to reconcile the two countries' historically constituted self-identities, this failure of political reconciliation was counterbalanced by the firm interest-based groundwork laid for a much better future relationship. Economically, Japan's assistance in the form of private property claims, grants-in-aid, and commercial loans, as well as technology transfers, helped to build the foundation for South Korea's economic growth. Militarily, the normalization treaty reinforced the security of both South Korea and Japan by consolidating—albeit with some limitations—U.S.-South Korea-Japan triangular security cooperation against the threat of communist aggression and expansion in East Asia. Politically, the normalization treaty sowed the seeds for the development of a closer relationship between the two countries on the basis of shared values and interests. The opposition attacked the treaty as a sell-out, but its rather exaggerated claim that the treaty was a replica of the Ŭlsa Treaty of 1910 backfired. The parallels drawn by the opposition between the 1910 and 1965 treaties made the opposition look more radical, alienating many of the moderate opponents of the treaty.

Beyond the Settlement

The timing for the settlement was right. Economically, South Korea was in dire need of foreign capital to move ahead with its ambitious economic development plans. For its part, Japan had fully recovered from World War II and was searching for a new role in global and regional arenas. Putting its militarist past behind it, Japan was keen on building a new reputation for itself as a pacifist liberal democracy. The settlement with South Korea was in a sense a litmus test for Japan's genuine conversion into a liberal democratic player. The timing of the intensification of the Vietnam War in the mid-1960s also contributed to the settlement. Considered central to U.S. efforts to consolidate an anticommunist military front in East Asia was a good working relationship between South Korea and Japan. The coinciding of the anticommunist Park and Sato governments also helped to bring the erstwhile enemies together. The two leaders shared pragmatic goals of military deterrence and economic cooperation. Without the convergence of these economic and security interests in the conclusive stage of the normalization talks, it would have been difficult to motivate the two countries' leadership to reach a comprehensive settlement in the mid-1960s.

Moreover, in the mid-1960s, state-centric, export-led industrialization faced little resistance from great powers and the world economy, in contrast to the 1970s and 1980s when the forces of protectionism in developed countries would certainly have narrowed the window of opportunity for late developers relying on state-subsidized programs of export promotion. In the 1990s and thereafter, the forces of financial globalization would have made it even more difficult for a state to use subsidized "policy loans" for developmental goals. In other words, South Korea may have faced much more difficulty in relying on the same growth strategy had it pursued it at a later stage. The normalization treaty with Japan was instrumental in jump-starting the whole process of development at the most opportune time.

On the other hand, for the South Korean–Japanese bilateral relationship, the ratification of the treaty in 1965 was followed by remarkable cooperation through the end of Sato Eisaku's premiership in 1972. Within a year after their normalization of relations, Japan surpassed the United States as South Korea's single largest trading partner. Japanese exports to South Korea surged from an annual average of $180 million in 1965 to $586 million in 1970. From 1971 to 1973, the figure tripled to $1.8 billion. South Korean exports to Japan also increased substantially, but not enough to prevent South Korea's trade deficit from rising equally high. The expansion of commercial activities between the two countries constituted one of the engines driving South Korea's hyper economic growth. At the same time, Japan's economic assistance and compensation became Park's seed money to finance some of his strategic FYEDP projects and laid the basis for heavy and chemical industrialization in the 1970s. Besides the booming bilateral trade and the timely implementation of economic assistance programs, the two countries raised their level of cooperation in the military realm under the watchful eye of the United States. In the Nixon-Sato joint communiqué issued on November 21, 1969, a "Korean clause" was introduced whereby South Korea's security was to be considered essential to that of Japan.[59]

But at the same time, it is important to underline the limits of the two countries' rapprochement. The eclipse of Sato Eisaku's leadership, which coincided with a series of dramatic changes in East Asian security relations—Nixon's declaration of the Guam Doctrine (1969), China's entry into the United Nations (1971), and Nixon's visit to China (1972)—ushered in a difficult period for Park. First, Japan followed the American lead in improving bilateral relations with communist China. What is more, Prime Minister Tanaka Kakuei reviewed his nation's relations with the two Koreas. Arguing that the newly initiated Red Cross meetings between the two Koreas at P'anmunjŏm in September 1971 had the effect of reducing military tension on the Korean Peninsula, Tanaka departed from the "one Korea policy" espoused by his predecessors. Tanaka resorted to a more pragmatic and flexible approach in dealing with the two Koreas, not un-like the days of Hatoyama Ichiro (1954–1956). Tanaka argued that the détente on the Korean Peninsula rendered the 1969 "Korean Clause" no longer pertinent.

Other events also erupted to test the strength of South Korean–Japanese relations following the normalization. One of the most damaging was the kidnapping of Kim Dae-jung, the South Korean opposition leader then living in Japan, by KCIA agents in August 1973. The candidate of the New Democratic Party (NDP) in the 1971 presidential election, Kim Dae-jung was then trying to mobilize international opinion in denouncing Park's promulgation of the *yushin* constitution in November 1972 that was to perpetuate his political rule. Park accused Kim Dae-jung of plotting to set up a provisional government in Japan. He also accused Kim of links with pro-Pyongyang *chosoren* in Japan. When Kim Dae-jung was kidnapped from his hotel in Tokyo on August 8, 1973, by KCIA agents, Park's image became seriously tarnished. Angered by the event that took place on Japanese soil, many Japanese opinion leaders became openly critical of Park's dictatorial rule. Damage might have been contained at the governmental level, but Park became angry at what he considered Japanese intervention in South Korean domestic politics. In February 1974 he banned the circulation of *Asahi Shimbun,* a Japanese progressive daily newspaper.

When, in August 1974, an ethnic Korean residing in Japan, under a false Japanese identity, shot and killed South Korea's first lady in an assassination attempt on Park, emotions flared to new heights. South Koreans held the Japanese government responsible for the incident. When the Japanese government refused to apologize for what had taken place, as demanded by the Park government, widespread demonstrations were touched off, even leading to a raid on the Japanese embassy in Seoul. Shiina Etsusaburō's timely mediation helped to calm the raw nerves, but the damage was already done. The bilateral relationship was at its lowest possible point since the 1965 normalization of relations. But even then, the South Korean–Japanese relationship survived. As in the two countries' signing of a normalization treaty in 1965, it was regional power politics that halted the deterioration of relations during the 1970s. The United States' military withdrawal from South Vietnam in 1973 and the subsequent communist takeover of Saigon in 1975 alarmed Japan and moved it to combine its new engagement strategy of détente with its earlier cold war position of military containment. Given the continued military threats from China and North Korea, Japan could not maintain Tanaka Kakuei's alleged policy of "equidistance" between the two Koreas. Instead, Tanaka's successors came to reaffirm the "Korean Clause" in the

1969 Nixon-Sato joint communiqué that had held South Korea to be the sole legitimate state on the Korean Peninsula. Prime Minister Miki Takeo, who replaced the scandal-plagued Tanaka Kakuei in December 1974, decided to part with the equidistance policy, convinced that a communist takeover of the Korean Peninsula would pose a serious problem for Japan's own security interests. This meant patching up the differences Japan had with South Korea over the kidnapping of Kim Dae-jung.

Alarmed by the specter of a domino effect triggered by the fall of South Vietnam, Park also left behind the issue of his wife's death. The rapprochement continued under both Fukuda Takeo and Ōhira Masayoshi, the last two Japanese prime ministers Park faced before his own assassination in October 1979. In fact, just a few months prior to his death, Park was able to take the bilateral relations to new heights, going beyond economic cooperation to lay the foundation for cooperation in the security realm. Beginning with historic visits to South Korea by both Nagano Shigeo, chief of staff of Japan's Land Self-Defense Forces (SDF), and Yamashita Ganri, head of the Japanese Defense Agency, lawmakers from both sides established a formal parliamentarian council to discuss security issues.[60] The South Korean–Japanese relations had indeed come a full circle. The outstanding territorial, history, and political issues notwithstanding, the two nations managed to go back to the cultivation of a mutually beneficial, comprehensive relationship that they began with the normalization of relations in 1965 on the basis of common security interests.

At the same time, it is also important to note that the dynamics of market integration unleashed by Park's decision to normalize relations with Japan in 1965 became a new safety valve, in addition to the old security rationales of cold war containment, protecting South Korean–Japanese relations from political setbacks and conflicts. As their bilateral economic cooperation continuously deepened and widened, South Korea and Japan thought they could not afford to let political conflicts disrupt their relationship. It was in this creation of new economic rationales for nurturing a robust South Korean–Japanese relationship that Park's greatest legacy lay.

Just as Syngman Rhee's political rule marked the coming of a distinctive era in South Korean–Japanese relations, Park's rise to power ushered in a new era in the two countries' relationship. Having set the normalization of relations with Japan as a national foreign policy goal, Park, by the time of his death, achieved what he set out to do. Despite bad patches in the first half of the 1970s, South Korea and Japan came to enjoy flourishing commercial ties, all the while consolidating their anticommunist security link. Respect from Japan may not have come at a national level for South Korea, but it certainly came at the individual level as many Japanese leaders in the government and big business came to appreciate Park's developmental vision, leadership style, and commitment to strengthening bilateral ties. Japanophile that he may or may not have been, Park's pragmatic and forward-looking vision helped to reshape South Korean–Japanese relations. Founded in the spirit of the normalization treaty of 1965, the new, carefully cultivated South Korean–Japanese relationship has in many ways contributed to South Korea's growth as an economically vibrant, modern nation as we now know it. This is what Park wanted all along.

CHAPTER SIXTEEN

The Security, Political, and Human Rights Conundrum, 1974–1979

Yong-Jick Kim

R ELATIONS BETWEEN South Korea and the United States took a sharp downward turn in the mid-1970s with the inauguration of President Jimmy Carter, who introduced a new South Korea policy that diverged from the United States' traditional cold war stance in three crucial respects. First, Carter put the issue of human rights abuses by President Park Chung Hee's *yushin* regime (1972–1979) at or near the top of the U.S. foreign policy agenda. Second, Carter campaigned for the complete withdrawal of U.S. ground troops from the Korean Peninsula as part of America's military disengagement from East Asia that had begun with Richard M. Nixon's 1969 Guam Doctrine. The disputes over human rights and military withdrawal almost crippled the alliance as they spilled over and magnified political tensions that culminated in the third conflict, which became known as "Koreagate" and involved the *yushin* regime's alleged effort to buy support in the U.S. Congress with illegal funds.

The crisis in the alliance developed over time. The human rights dispute began with U.S. congressional hearings in 1974 and 1975, when Park turned to emergency decrees to crack down on the rising opposition. The ensuing repression prompted many U.S. legislators to argue for cuts in military aid in order to compel Park to be more responsive to U.S. concerns on human rights. Then came the plan for U.S. ground troop withdrawal in 1977 on the basis of Carter's presidential election pledge in 1976. The Koreagate scandal also began developing in the mid-1970s, with media reports of illegal South Korean lobbying on Capitol Hill, which aggravated the situation even further. With anti-Park sentiment growing in the United States, the Carter administration persisted in a punitive South Korea policy that, had it been successful, could have seriously damaged the U.S.–South Korean security alliance.

In an interview with the *Washington Post* on January 16, 1976, then–presidential candidate Carter declared his intention to withdraw ground troops and nuclear weapons from the Korean Peninsula. The Trilateral Commission, a new multinational private group organized by David Rockefeller, convened in May 1976 in Kyoto and gave Carter's new policy credibility with its endorsement of troop withdrawal. In March 1977, Carter officially declared his plan to withdraw U.S. ground troops from South Korea completely within four to five years. Over Park's strong protests, Carter was implementing his election pledge at a pace alarming to South Koreans. The following two and a half years bore witness to what were undoubtedly the two countries' worst bilateral relations since the end of the Korean War in 1953.

To oppose Carter's new policy, Park adopted the strategy of categorically denying the existence of any human rights problems in South Korea. Claiming that Carter had failed to understand South Korea's unique circumstance of national division and military confrontation with the "rogue state" of North Korea, Park's advisors criticized Carter's policy of military withdrawal not only as an act of betrayal but also as an ill-informed policy that would hurt the U. S. interest in maintaining the status quo on the Korean Peninsula. The Carter administration, by contrast, stressed that human rights abuses were neither necessary nor justifiable even in South Korea's difficult military situation. On the contrary, such practices were a direct result of Park's attempt to maintain authoritarian rule in the face of rising domestic political opposition. On the whole, the two governments never questioned the strategic importance of the U.S.–South Korean alliance; nor were they really disputing the existence of human rights abuses. Park could not escape charges of oppression and torture by both U.S. officials and domestic political opponents. The real question was the legitimacy of U.S. intervention in South Korean domestic politics. Given the extensive U.S. role in South Korea, from a supplier of economic aid to a provider of military deterrence to a patron of democracy, the United States was de facto intervening in South Korean domestic politics, whether it did or did not act on its missionary instincts to spread democratic values. As Park's opponents in South Korea and the United States argued, inaction strengthened Park's hold over domestic politics as much as action weakened it by depriving him of economic, military, and ideological resources.

The United States' hegemonic presence in South Korea made any action or inaction by the United States automatically an act of intervention.

Ironically, the three disputes that profoundly destabilized South Korea and threatened its military deterrence were of Park's own doing. To defend his *yushin* regime, Park relied on emergency powers to repress *chaeya* dissidents and opposition party politicians, which only strengthened his opponents' will to resist. To slow down, if not reverse, the United States' military disengagement as enunciated in its Guam Doctrine, Park had Pak Tong-sŏn lobby for U.S. congressional support, which boomeranged into not only U.S. investigations but also domestic criticisms.

The three disputes, however, came to an anticlimactic ending. The bilateral disputes over U.S. ground troop withdrawal, Koreagate, and human rights violations did not end with Carter's victory, not because Park resisted, but because U.S. domestic politics turned against Carter and U.S. policymakers redefined American strategic interests after the euphoria of détente receded with a crisis in the Middle East. When Carter linked the issue of human rights abuses with his campaign pledge of troop withdrawal, the U.S. Department of Defense (DoD) and Congress—not South Korea— put the brakes on Carter's foreign policy experiment. Despite the earlier threats of intervention, the sanctions the United States actually imposed proved to be very mild due to not only regional geopolitical constraints but also the internal divisions within the Carter administration and its uneasy relationship with Congress. With regard to Koreagate, the Ethics Committee of the House of Representatives ended up reprimanding only three of the congressmen accused of accepting money from Pak Tong-sŏn after two years of intense investigation. On the issue of troop withdrawal, Carter made a U-turn after his decision to pull back 2,400 ground troops, including 800 combat soldiers, prompted U.S. advocates for a continued military presence in South Korea within the DoD, the U.S. armed forces, and Congress to join together in restraining him. Fortunately for the alliance between the two countries, the damage was limited.

The Origins of Park's Troubles, 1972–1974

The Yushin *Regime*

The dispute between South Korea and the United States over human rights issues originated from the launching of the *yushin* regime in October 1972. In Park's eyes, the *yushin* constitution was a legitimate response to the perceived weakening of the U.S. military commitment to South Korea that came with the ending of the Vietnam War. Ten thousand U.S. troops were withdrawn from South Korea by 1970 and the Seventh Infantry Division departed in 1971, although the military threat from North Korea remained unchanged. Park countered the security vacuum with the announcement of a national emergency in 1971 and the declaration of the *yushin* constitution in 1972.[1] With it, Park thought he could put the South on the path to his twin objectives of "self-reliant defense" and heavy and chemical industrialization.[2]

The United States was caught off guard. Park had kept his plans secret until the final moment, and the United States saw the declaration as unwarranted, since political-military tensions on the peninsula were becoming more relaxed through the North-South dialogue that Park launched immediately before establishing his *yushin* regime.[3] The effect on the opposition forces in South Korea was far worse. In August 1973, Kim Dae-jung, who had been the presidential candidate of the New Democratic Party (NDP) in 1971, was abducted from Japan, where he had been granted political asylum since the promulgation of the *yushin,* by Korea Central Intelligence Agency (KCIA) operatives. Earlier in the year, Kim Dae-jung had organized the Alliance for Democracy and Unification in Korea *(Hanmint'ong)* to lead anti-*yushin* movements in the United States and Japan. His abduction in broad daylight in downtown Tokyo seriously damaged Park's image in the eyes of South Korea's two most important foreign patrons. Kim Dae-jung reappeared five days later in the vicinity of his Seoul residence, to the relief of opposition politicians, *chaeya* dissidents, and Japanese and U.S. policymakers.[4] The damage was done, however, as high-level leaders at the KCIA were deeply implicated in the abduction. The *yushin* regime flatly denied Park's involvement in the incident, but it knew it had to accommodate public opinion. KCIA director Yi Hu-rak was dismissed several months later.[5]

The frequent use of repressive measures to silence criticism and to put down *chaeya*-led student protests became the hallmark of the *yushin* regime. On January 8, 1974, Presidential Emergency Decrees nos. 1 and 2 were promulgated, which enabled the military court to try anyone who "den[ied], oppose[d], misrepresent[ed] or defame[d] the constitution." As justified by Park, these decrees were necessary "to safeguard the right to national existence and to lay a strong foundation for prosperity and national unification."[6] The political consequences of political rule by emergency decrees were dire, forcing Park to issue two more emergency decrees by April 1974. Presidential Emergency Decree no. 4 continued for five months, and resulted in the round-up of more than 1,000 dissidents for police interrogation and the trial of 253 by an emergency court martial.[7] In the midst of widespread sympathy for Park over the death of the nation's first lady at the hand of an ethnic Korean resident of Japan who was aiming to assassinate him, Park removed the decree as a gesture of political reconciliation on August 23, 1974, only to see a greater challenge from the opposition. The escalation of political conflict led Park to issue Emergency Decree no. 7 in April 1975 and no. 9 in May 1975. The *yushin* became rule by emergency decrees.

Human Rights Movement

As Park tightened his grip on political society, the anti-*yushin* movement grew both in numbers and in intensity. The movement was initially led by church leaders and student activists, but quickly expanded to include opposition NDP politicians. In October 1974, the NDP came under the leadership of hard-liner Kim Young-sam with the platform of "clear opposition" *(sŏnmyŏng yadang)*. The opposition party soon joined forces with *Dong A Ilbo* and Dong-A Radio to agitate for the Movement for the Amendment of the *Yushin* Constitution. The journalists of the newspaper and radio station protested against censorship, issuing a "Declaration for the Practice of Freedom of Speech" on October 24, 1974, which by mid-December had resulted in the business community's cancellation of their advertising under pressure from the political authorities. Christian leaders had been vocal in their opposition, organizing a Human Rights Committee on May 17, 1974, to support the "prisoners of conscience" *(yangsimbŏm)* and their families, in addition to the promotion of human rights.[8] Toward the end of 1974, these different groups of the anti-*yushin* movement launched the People's Congress for the Restoration of Democracy as an umbrella organization to challenge Park.

The driving force of the anti-*yushin* movement in South Korea consisted of the Alliance for Democracy and Unification in Korea *(Mint'ongryŏn)*, the Coalition for the Restoration of Democracy in the Motherland *(Chominryŏn)*, and the Alliance of Korean Youth *(Hanch'ŏng)*.[9] Combining forces with other nongovernmental organizations (NGOs) to coordinate a political challenge to Park, these dissident groups received support from abroad, including from Reverend Pharis J. Harvey's North American Coalition for Human Rights in Korea, Asia Watch, Amnesty International, and the International Human Rights Law group. The NGO-led human rights campaign paid off when prominent Americans began criticizing Park for his political repression. Former U.S. ambassador to Japan Edwin O. Reischauer wrote an article in the *New York Times* to call for a reexamination of current U.S. policy toward South Korea. Arguing that the U.S. commitment to democracy in South Korea was seriously threatened by

Park's *yushin* regime, and asserting that Park's resort to political repression to stay in power would only increase domestic political conflict that could drive the Korean Peninsula into a Vietnam type of quagmire, Reischauer proposed to put human rights at the top of the U.S. agenda. Until Carter's ascent to the presidency in 1977, however, this was a minority position—albeit with an increasing number of supporters in the United States.[10]

The United States Divided, 1974–1976

U.S. Congressional Hearings on Human Rights Abuses

During the Gerald R. Ford administration (1974–1977), the human rights dispute between South Korea and the United States centered on congressional hearings. Donald M. Fraser, chairing the U.S. House Subcommittee on International Organizations and Movements, on July 30, 1974, held joint hearings with Robert N. C. Nix of the House Subcommittee on Asia and Pacific Affairs on human rights in South Korea. Representative Fraser was to become a key investigator of the illegal South Korean lobbying campaign allegedly to buy support in the U.S. Congress. Much of his work was supported by American human rights lawyers and church leaders, as well as by dissident South Korean intellectuals working on anti-*yushin* campaigns.[11]

The House hearings succeeded in identifying human rights abuses in South Korea and the Philippines as a genuine challenge for U.S. foreign policy. At the hearings, New York attorney William H. Butler, in his capacity as a member of the Amnesty International mission to South Korea, criticized the *yushin* regime for its "mass arrests, prolonged detention without trial," "other denials of due legal process," and "constant surveillance by the KCIA."[12] Jerome A. Cohen of Harvard Law School testified that the choice facing the United States was not one of choosing security at the expense of human rights, or human rights at the expense of security interests. Rather, Cohen saw military security and human rights interests to be mutually complementary. He asserted that continuing U.S. support for Park despite his resort to authoritarian rule and political repression would severely damage South Korea's internal cohesion, which would render the society vulnerable to communist infiltration and subversion.[13]

Representative Fraser expressed frustration over the *yushin* regime's negative response to the rising tides of criticism within Congress regarding South Korea's human rights abuses. When Fraser visited South Korea in March 1975, the *yushin* regime refused to allow him to meet with victims of state torture. U.S. human rights activists, including Cohen, echoed Fraser's warning that Park's oppressive rule risked not only weakening South Korean democracy but, more seriously, bringing on another war on the Korean Peninsula by breeding domestic political instability in the South. Thus arose the liberal strand of intellectuals, human rights activists, and the left wing of the Democratic Party that directly linked the issue of human rights to military aid.[14] The Republicans were more cautious, putting security interests above human rights interests in the bilateral relationship. The Park sympathizers saw South Korea's history of national division, civil war, and military confrontation as compelling Park to choose the path of authoritarian modernization. At the hearings, Franz Michael of George Washington University explained the *yushin* regime as a response to answer the security dilemmas brought by the weakening of U.S. commitment to the defense of South Korea. Chong-Sik Lee of the University of Pennsylvania saw the "threatening international environment" as the basis for Park's fear and his resort to authoritarian rule in 1972. Lee recommended that the United States pursue a policy of mutual dialogue and persuasion rather than the path to sanctions.[15]

In December 1974, Fraser proposed reducing military aid to South Korea from the original request of $165 million to $145 million. Fraser also called for inserting a human rights clause in the bill that made an additional supply of military assistance worth $55 million contingent on Park's effort to make substantial progress in the human rights conditions in South Korea. The direct linkages Fraser made between military aid and human rights constituted a "major psychological blow" to the *yushin* regime.[16] On April 2, 1976, with the support of 118 congressmen from both parties, Fraser petitioned the U.S. government to reconsider the program of military support for South Korea on the basis of an "intensification of the longstanding crisis of democracy in South Korea."

Deepening Security Crisis in the Korean Peninsula

While some members of the U.S. Congress began toying with the idea of making military aid an instrument of human rights diplomacy, the presidents of the two countries doggedly held on to the traditional policy of putting security interests ahead of other goals and values. In fact, the security dilemmas brought by the deepening crisis in Indochina had only strengthened their view that the core value of the bilateral relationship was military security. In August 1974, when Park narrowly escaped the assassination attempt that took the life of his wife, it was alleged that the assailant, an ethnic Korean resident of Japan, had been trained by a sympathizer of North Korea. In November 1974, the South Korean armed forces discovered a North Korean–built underground tunnel four feet high and three feet wide south of the demilitarized zone.

The Ford administration recognized Park's security concerns as legitimate, although it was careful not to make them a rationale for political repression. As early as February 1974, secretary of defense James R. Schlesinger testified before the House Armed Service Committee that a continued U.S. military presence in South Korea was vital for the security of Northeast Asia. On March 20, national security adviser Henry A. Kissinger confirmed to minister of foreign affairs Kim Tong-jo that there would be no more withdrawals of United States military troops from the South. Peter Hayes has argued that it was Kissinger who reversed Schlesinger's plan for continuing with the phased withdrawal operation previously drawn up by his predecessor as secretary of defense, Melvin R. Laird.[17]

Amid the strengthening of the communist challenge in Cambodia and South Vietnam, Ford made sure not to inadvertently encourage North Korea into military ventures by hurting the credibility of the U.S. military commitment to South Korea. Despite the spread of opposition to his traditionalist South Korea policy among many of the Christian human rights organizations in the United States, Ford paid an official visit to South Korea in November 1974 with the goal of demonstrating the strength of the alliance. In a joint declaration, Ford reaffirmed the United States' commitment to deliver "prompt and effective assistance" to South Korea in the event of an armed attack "in accordance with the Mutual Defense Treaty." As for the U.S. troops stationed in South Korea, he assured Park that there was "no plan to reduce from the present level."[18] In response, Park reiterated his commitment to continue dialogue with the North with the goal of easing tensions and building peace on the Korean Peninsula. But despite Ford's show of political support at the summit meeting, Congress sought to prevent Park from feeling wholly confident of its support; the legislators reduced military assistance to South Korea by $20 million until Ford submitted a report on the improvement of Park's human rights record.[19]

Then came the news of the evacuation of what remained of U.S. military forces from South Vietnam in April 1975, followed by the report of South Vietnam's unconditional surrender to the North Vietnamese. At the same time, to Park's alarm, Kim Il Sung, the leader of North Korea, visited Beijing on April 18 to discuss the possibility of waging a military offensive on the Korean Peninsula. Although Zhou Enlai rejected the idea a day before the communist takeover of Saigon,[20] Park issued a "Special Statement on National Security." The news that Kim Il Sung was sounding out Zhou

Enlai on the idea of military engagement in the midst of the collapse of South Vietnam triggered a Red scare in the South. In his speech, Park appealed for public unity and warned of the danger of an imminent war on the Korean Peninsula. Two weeks later, Park declared Emergency Decree no. 9 to strengthen the power of the *yushin* regime. Saying national security was at stake, the decree tried to silence the voice of human rights activism. Moreover, Park began to consider developing nuclear weapons capabilities in fear of the possible removal of the U.S. nuclear umbrella. In an interview with the *Washington Post* in June 1975, Park asserted that South Korea had the capability to develop nuclear weapons and hinted that it might go nuclear if the United States removed its nuclear weapons from South Korea. The nuclear option was aborted under strong pressure from the United States, who warned that pursuing the idea would threaten the break-up of the bilateral security alliance (see Chapter 17).[21]

Despite the unfavorable House hearings on human rights abuses and the confrontation over nuclear development, official U.S. policy emphasized stability on the Korean Peninsula and close cooperation with South Korea until 1975. The continuity of its security-first orientation was reconfirmed on May 11 of that year with the rejection of Representative Fraser's revised foreign aid bill that proposed to reduce military aid to South Korea for fiscal year 1976–1977.

The "Carter Shock," 1976–1977

Carter's Campaign Pledge of Troop Withdrawal

In spite of their defeat in 1975, Representative Fraser and progressive Democrats in Congress increased pressure on Park to improve human rights conditions in South Korea. Playing into their hand was the escalation of political conflict there, which led to Park's decision to use force. In March 1976, eleven dissidents, all Christian activists, were arrested under the charge of plotting to overthrow the government. The crackdown was triggered by their declaration of resistance at Myŏngdong Cathedral. The arrests immediately provoked a response from United Methodist churches in the United States, which had had a large missionary presence in South Korea for over a century and were in close contact with South Korean dissidents in the 1970s to call for reconsideration of U.S. support to the *yushin* regime.[22] In June 1976, the general assembly of the United Presbyterian Church in the United States sent letters to both Park and Ford to request a fair trial for the detained dissidents. Two months earlier, Fraser had also sent a letter to Ford along with the signatures of 118 congressmen, urging reconsideration of military support to the *yushin* regime due to the "intensification of the longstanding crisis of democracy in South Korea."[23] When the dissidents were found guilty of subversion, a total of 154 congressmen co-signed a letter to Park, warning that disrespect for human rights seriously undermined U.S–South Korean relations.

The progressive Democrats' challenge to the traditional U.S. policy toward South Korea reached a new level when one of the Democratic Party's presidential candidates, Jimmy Carter, promised in a campaign speech in Chicago on June 23, 1976, that if elected, he would withdraw U.S. ground troops from South Korea. Carter had revealed his idea of a complete military withdrawal in a meeting held by the Trilateral Commission in Kyoto in May 1975.[24] Since then, he had developed a powerful rationale that directly linked Park's record of human rights abuses to the issue of troop withdrawal, asserting that the *yushin* regime's "internal repression [was not only] repugnant [but also] undermine[d] the [public] support for commitment of continued U.S. military presence."[25] Carter also criticized Ford's record on human rights issues during a televised debate in October 1975, especially condemning his inaction on the issue of the Soviet Union's violations of the Helsinki agreement.[26]

By the time of the U.S. presidential election campaign in 1976, human rights activists had succeeded in persuading many U.S. politicians that blind support for Park could trap the United States in another unwanted war in Asia. Park's opponents argued that because his rule-by-decree had destabilized South Korea, he had provided the North with an opportunity for armed attack. Once the North invaded, the United States would have to intervene because of the "human trip-wire" role that its Second Army Division, stationed near the demilitarized zone (and on the likely route that invading North Korean troops would take), played. Reverend James Sinnott of the Maryknoll Order, who had served as a missionary in South Korea, advised linking the troop withdrawal with the human rights issue and making future aid conditional upon improvement in that situation.[27]

By championing the liberal-idealist side of U.S. foreign policy, Carter declared that human rights constituted "a standard within the community of nations" and that the United States' endorsement of human rights as a moral principle signified the "exertion of American power and influence."[28] In his inaugural address, Carter declared that "because we are free we can never be indifferent to the fate of freedom elsewhere . . . [O]ur commitment to human rights must be absolute."[29] In his memoir, Carter recollected that "[as] President, I hoped and believed that the expansion of human rights might be the wave of the future throughout the world, and I wanted the United States to be on the crest of this movement."[30] In the eyes of national security adviser Zbigniew Brzezinski, Carter's human rights policy aimed at bringing the conduct of foreign affairs in line with American political values. However, Brzezinski also viewed human rights policy as a pragmatic instrument of U.S. hegemony that could meet the "Soviet ideological challenge" and "shape a world more congenial to American values and more compatible with American national interests."[31]

Carter's Strategic Reviews

Initially Carter's South Korea policy harnessed the issues of troop withdrawal and human rights to move Park in a direction that was compatible with both U.S. values and U.S. interests. Heading a country that endorsed democratic values and survived on U.S. military support, Park saw the two-track pressure as highly damaging to his political rule. Of the two components of Carter's South Korea policy, it was the human rights component that took Carter more time to develop, whereas his decision to withdraw U.S. military forces from the South virtually came with the inauguration. On February 1, 1977, Vice President Walter F. Mondale stated in a Tokyo news conference that the United States was phasing out ground military troops in South Korea in "close consultation and cooperation" with both Japan and South Korea. Next, in a press interview on March 9, shortly before his meeting with South Korean foreign minister Pak Tong-jin, Carter unilaterally announced his intention to withdraw all U.S. ground troops from the South in four to five years. In his meeting with Pak, Carter focused more on his concern for human rights violations than on the issue of military withdrawal. For Carter, the policy of military withdrawal was a fait accompli that the South had to accommodate. All that minister Pak could demand was South Korea's right to prior consultation before any decision on the specifics of troop withdrawal was made.[32]

Carter's plan for troop withdrawal was based on the Presidential Review Memorandum 13 (PRM-13), which Brzezinski had signed on January 26, 1977. PRM-13 was still in the early stages of its formal drafting by the National Security Council (NSC), but the core concept of the policy change was already decided. Reaffirming his campaign promise, Carter made it clear that the principle of troop withdrawal was not to be questioned and that the task of the Policy Review Committee (PRC) was limited to designing the specifics of the implementation of his election pledge.[33] Moreover, the PRC was instructed not to "examine the consequences of partial or complete troop withdrawal."[34] On February 18, Carter directed Brzezinski to "examine the alternative national objectives and strategies" outlined in another memorandum, PRM-10. Drawn up to guide and ensure the strategic flexibility of the United States, PRM-10 examined, among other key issues, the withdrawal of military troops from South Korea.[35] The PRM-10 Force Posture Study presented a cautious but generally optimistic view of the reduction of U.S. military forces deployed in South Korea, encouraging Carter to continue on the track of withdrawal.

Carter's policy of troop withdrawal was conceived of as an integral part of his larger regional strategy of military disengagement from the East Asian continent. Optimistically viewing the regional security situation in East Asia, PRM-10 defined the primary objective of the United States in the region as maintaining the status quo among the great powers rather than the containment of communist threats.[36] In its eyes, the U.S. defense posture was moving toward "an offshore military posture which avoid[ed] automatic involvement" on the Asian continent.[37] To foreshadow intense bilateral conflict, PRM-10 de facto assumed a dramatically altered role for South Korea in U.S. military policy, emphasizing the United States' strategic need to secure "flexibility" in the Korean Peninsula. Moreover, in contrast to the traditional policy of waging a massive counterattack on the North after the first stage of repelling the North in the event of war, PRM-10 mainly concentrated on necessary measures to offset North Korea's initial armed attack.

The U.S. Security Community's Opposition

Opposition to Carter's policy of troop withdrawal, however, was already visible in the early stage of reviewing the new policies within the U.S. security community. Fortunately for Park, the support for Carter's policy of troop withdrawal was not strong within the United States. Basing his decision on PRM-10 and PRM-13, without consulting the Joint Chiefs of Staff, Carter saw many in his own administration oppose his South Korea policy. These included not only the Department of Defense and the three armed services but also many personnel on the Policy Review Committee.

William H. Gleysteen, destined to serve as the U.S. ambassador to South Korea during 1978–1981, was one such official caught by surprise by Carter's troop withdrawal policy. A core member of the interagency group that had prepared PRM-13, Gleysteen later recalled that at the initial stage of planning, most of the officials in the group opposed Carter's plan.[38] Troop withdrawal was unpopular in the State Department and especially in the Defense Department, but Carter's adamant position on the issue rendered any substantive debate nearly impossible at this early stage.[39]

On May 19, 1977, Major General John K. Singlaub, the chief of staff of the U.S. Forces in Korea (USFK), openly criticized Carter's withdrawal policy in an interview with the *Washington Post,* warning that the policy, if carried out, would lead to another war on the Korean Peninsula. Although his action was interpreted as open insubordination, Singlaub felt justified in opposing Carter given the USFK's recent reassessment of North Korea's enhanced military capabilities. In effect, Singlaub claimed that Carter's decision was based on outdated intelligence reports. The president recalled Singlaub immediately, but Carter's action galvanized the opposition even more, especially in Congress and among the military. The House Armed Services Committee responded by holding hearings on the Singlaub incident six days later, on May 25.

Carter was not deterred. He issued Presidential Directive 12 on May 27 to withdraw one brigade (6,000 soldiers) by 1978 and another brigade no later than June 1980. The final stage of ground troop withdrawal was to be decided later in consultation with Congress and allies in East Asia.[40] Twenty days earlier, the Joint Chiefs of Staff (JCS) had recommended a phased, partial reduction of 7,000 troops through 1982. Carter rejected this recommendation in favor of his more sweeping withdrawal plan when he issued Presidential Directive 12.[41] The directive was drawn up unilaterally without prior consultation with South Korea. The United States later explained Carter's decision as based on the reassessment of "military balance, [South Korean] capabilities, and the international situation," but this did not alleviate Park's sense of betrayal.[42]

Park's Response

To prevent Park from protesting Presidential Directive 12, which would strengthen the hand of Carter's opponents in Congress, Philip C. Habib, under secretary of state for political affairs, and General George S. Brown, chairman of the JCS, were dispatched to South Korea in May 1977. Habib and Brown conveyed Carter's plan to complete the withdrawal of USFK ground troops within the next five years. Because Park had already expressed his concern over the declining credibility of the U.S. commitment to the defense of South Korea in his letter to Carter on February 26, Park chose not to question the wisdom of the directive, but the timing of Carter's decision to implement his 1976 election pledge was disturbing. The mood within Park's inner policy circle at the Blue House was far worse than what Park conveyed in his meeting with Habib and Brown. In private, Park's key national security advisers strongly opposed Carter's troop withdrawal policy, warning that it would put the U.S.–South Korean security alliance in a precarious state. Aware of Carter's commitment to the new policy, Park focused on limiting the damage rather than reversing the decision. To Habib and Brown, after explaining the crucial role the USFK played as a deterrent against the Soviet Union and North Korea, Park requested that the United States reaffirm its commitment to the 1953 Mutual Defense Treaty and sought an increase in military assistance programs to fill the vacuum created by the staged withdrawal of USFK ground troops. In addition, Park urged that the United States maintain the headquarters of the Second Infantry Division in South Korea despite the withdrawal of its brigades, with the goal of demonstrating the United States' support for the defense of South Korea. Park also hoped for the continued deployment of tactical nuclear weapons in South Korea.[43]

At the Tenth Annual Bilateral Security Consultative Meeting (SCM) held on July 26, 1977, the two allies agreed on compensatory measures. Secretary of defense Harold Brown had to modify the timetable for troop withdrawal in the face of opposition by South Korean defense minister Sŏ Chong-ch'ŏl, delaying the withdrawal of the Second Infantry Division's two combat brigades from 1978 to 1981. The South Koreans argued that the withdrawal of these brigades would severely damage deterrence unless the South Korean military was given time to catch up with the North and take on the role of trip-wire previously handled by the American troops in the western front. As a measure to counterbalance the effect of U.S. troop withdrawal, Sŏ Chong-ch'ŏl demanded the sale of cutting-edge fighter planes as well as the establishment of a Combined Forces Command (CFC) prior to the withdrawal of USFK ground troops.[44] The United States agreed to launch the CFC as the war-fighting headquarters because CFC not only satisfied South Korea's desire to secure a U.S. commitment to the defense of South Korea in the uncertain era of troop withdrawal, but also enabled the USFK to continue maintaining operational control over the 600,000-men-strong South Korean armed forces.

To secure Park's consent, the United States agreed to a $1.9 billion program of compensatory military assistance, which included the transfer of USFK-owned military weapons systems ($500 million), support for the South Korean armed forces' modernization plan ($300 million), and commercial sales of military weapons ($1.1 billion).[45] Park thus used the U.S. troop withdrawal as an opportunity for upgrading South Korean military capabilities. There was also an agreement to hold annual joint military exercises in order to ready the two allies' military troops for coordinated military action in the event of war. As a result of his negotiations, Park not only earned time to prepare the South for the troop withdrawal, but also built the institution (CFC) and the means (military weapons systems) to enhance his country's alliance with the United States.

For Carter, the primary objective was to phase out the Second Infantry Division's human trip-wire role, thus reducing the danger of getting trapped in an unwanted war on the Asian continent.[46] As recommended by Brzezinski, Carter was emphasizing political and economic coordination among the advanced democracies in Western Europe and Japan, at the expense of late developers like Taiwan, South Korea, and the Philippines.

Dissension over Human Rights Issues

The other half of Carter's South Korea policy, human rights activism, was more directly inherited from the congressional activities of the mid-1970s. As secretary of state Cyrus R. Vance once recognized, Carter's human rights policy was "framed in collaboration and consultation with Congress."[47] Positing human rights as the basic tenet of his foreign policy, Carter dramatically moved away from the traditional security-first stand to a position of human rights activism. The shift was made possible by the rapidly altering status of South Korea in U.S. strategic calculations. With troop withdrawal, Carter could deal with human rights issues more strictly as human rights issues without fearing adverse geopolitical implications. Ironically, however, the troop withdrawal strengthened Park's leverage as well. Given Carter's determination to fulfill his campaign pledge to withdraw ground troops, Park had less incentive to heed the United States' concern over human rights abuses. On the contrary, Park bluntly accused Carter of unjustly intervening in South Korea's domestic politics.

The Carter administration created a "human rights bureau" in the State Department and placed it under the leadership of assistant secretary of state for human rights and humanitarian affairs Patricia Derian. The new bureau adopted an activist posture, arguing that "human rights conditions had to be met before security aid could be given."[48] Particularly during Carter's first year in office, his activist human rights policy came into conflict with regional bureaus in the State Department as well as with the Department of Defense, failing to make much progress. The Interagency Group on Human Rights and Foreign Assistance was established to resolve bureaucratic struggles on April 1, 1977, but to no avail. The interagency group came to be known as the Christopher Group, after its chair, deputy secretary of state Warren M. Christopher, and became an "arena of debate." However, it was unsuccessful, unable to carry out its mission of resolving interagency conflicts over the proper place of human rights in U.S. foreign policy.[49]

Linking human rights directly with military security policy constituted a key element in the liberal critique of American foreign policy in congressional debates. Again Fraser led the liberal camp, arguing that military assistance to South Korea should be decided by the *yushin* regime's human rights practices. In this sense, Fraser was a critic of Carter, who initially pushed for troop withdrawal without framing it as a sanction on Park's human rights abuses. Carter's PRM-13 did call for investigation of human rights issues, but the thrust of its policy recommendations dealt with troop withdrawal as a narrowly conceived security issue.[50] In Fraser's eyes, this perspective was precisely the problem with Carter's South Korea policy. Fraser urged Carter to make the troop withdrawal conditional, to be reversed if the human rights situation improved. For Fraser, removing ground troops was the last option to take after all others were exhausted. But contrary to Fraser's position, Carter had decided to withdraw USFK ground troops even before formulating his human rights policy.

The military pullout was implemented in a unilateral way, precluding any attempt to "use [it] as leverage to gain concessions" on human rights issues.[51] To Carter's political opponents in Congress, the policy of military withdrawal only revealed his obstinate desire to deliver on his election pledge, because there appeared to be no urgent strategic imperatives to pull out the ground troops in such a hurry. Nor did the economics of military retrenchment make any sense, since the United States had to pay for South Korea's military modernization in return for its Asian ally's acquiescence. The lack of coordination between human rights and security policy, moreover, meant that the United States lost an opportunity to improve the South Korean human rights situation.[52] When the Carter administration justified its withdrawal policy as a change brought on by the economic growth of South Korea and the coming of détente with the Soviet Union and China, many security experts in Congress pointed to the continued military rivalry among the great powers and cautioned against any abrupt changes in American foreign policy.[53] Although Congress, often led by Democrats critical of Park, urged Carter to use the issue of troop withdrawal to gain Park's concessions on human rights, Vance expressed caution in applying the principle of human rights in the conduct of foreign policy, urging Congress "to be flexible and pragmatic in dealing with specific cases that might affect [American] national security." He championed "flexibility rather than rigidity in implementing foreign policy."[54]

Park did not budge. Not only did he denounce Carter's human rights policy as interference in South Korea's domestic affairs,[55] but his aides criticized the policy as hypocritical and insensitive, turning a blind eye to the deplorable human rights conditions in the totalitarian communist countries while "crucifying" America's friendly South Korean ally that suffered under a serious security threat. At a Blue House reception, Park asserted that "the protection and the survival of the thirty-six million [South] Korean people [constitutes] the highest [possible] form of [protecting] freedom, human rights, and democracy."[56] Still, Park conceded to some U.S. demands. Contrary to his earlier denial of the existence of political prisoners, Park grudgingly released fourteen leading dissidents from prison on July 17, 1977. He also set free ten more people, arrested for their public call to abolish the *yushin* constitution, on March 1, 1978, only to see them rejoin the dissident *chaeya*.[57]

Carter's human rights policy was thus a policy that satisfied neither the human rights activists nor the security advocates. By emphasizing "positive incentives" rather than negative sanctions like aid withdrawal to punish "governments guilty of serious violations of human rights,"[58] Carter's key advisors still viewed human rights as secondary to "military, economic, and strategic considerations."[59] Vance later recalled that "given the importance of South Korea for the security of Japan and for [the United States'] political and military position in East Asia, [it was] recommended that [the United States] continue to press hard on [the] issue [of human rights], but not to tie it to [American] economic or military assistance."[60] Vance argued that the decision to withdraw ground troops from South Korea was a strategic one that needed to be made on the basis of military security calculations.

Another Quagmire: Koreagate, 1976–1978

The Koreagate Investigation

On October 24, 1976, the *Washington Post* reported the illegal lobbying of congressmen by South Korean lobbyists, thus opening up what the press was to call "Koreagate," hearkening back to the Watergate scandal that had led to President Richard Nixon's resignation. Identified by the *Washington Post* as the "most sweeping allegations of congressional corruption ever investigated by the federal government," Koreagate centered around Pak Tong-sŏn, a South Korean businessman and unregistered lobbyist. The newspaper cited FBI sources reporting that a number of U.S. government officials and congressmen had been on Pak Tong-sŏn's payroll for their pro–South Korea positions. The *New York Times* followed with an estimate that as many as 115 members of Congress might be implicated in Koreagate. Senator Howard H. Baker gave another estimate, suggesting that about 50 congressmen had been the target of Pak Tong-sŏn's bribery. The charges were serious, prompting U.S. media to work on tracking down those who had been bribed for nearly two years. Needless to say, bilateral relations between the two countries suffered in consequence.[61]

Over the next twenty-four months, Koreagate developed into a major political scandal. Not only the Justice Department but also the House and Senate ethics committees as well as the House Committee on International Organizations and Movements investigated South Korea's systematic efforts to bribe congressmen through Pak Tong-sŏn. Soon the investigators zeroed in on other South Koreans for illegal lobbying, including the former ambassador to the United States, Kim Tong-jo; a Baltimore-based businessman, Hancho C. Kim; Suzi Park Thomson, former secretary to retired House Speaker Carl B. Albert; and Pak Bo-hŭi, Mun Sŏn-myŏng's aide in the Unification Church.

The investigations by Fraser's Subcommittee on International Organizations eventually led to a comprehensive review of U.S.–South Korean relations. Citing U.S. intelligence sources, the Fraser report found that Park began organizing his Washington lobby in 1970, when Nixon announced the withdrawal of the U.S. Seventh Army Division from South Korea. The goal was to build a lobby in Washington that would work to prevent the United States from going further down the road of troop reduction and to secure U.S. assistance in the modernization of the South Korean armed forces. When Koreagate erupted, the *yushin* regime adopted the strategy of denying all allegations.[62] When former ambassador William J. Porter acknowledged the U.S. Central Intelligence Agency's past practice of eavesdropping on the Blue House to back the United States' claim that it had the evidence to trace the ties between the Washington lobbying and Park Chung Hee, the *yushin* regime accused the United States of violating the universal norm of respect for national sovereignty. *Yushin* backers also called Carter's moralistic foreign policy hypocritical, given U.S. interference in South Korea's internal affairs.[63]

The Fraser report concluded that Pak Tong-sŏn's lobbying efforts had proved effective, getting Congress to approve a $1.5 billion military aid program to South Korea for fiscal years 1971–1975.[64] In addition, the report revealed that since 1972, Park's Washington lobby increasingly came to rely on the KCIA to run the illegal lobbying. Moreover, the Fraser committee found that the KCIA had been threatening and intimidating anti-*yushin* Korean Americans prior to the outbreak of Koreagate.

In this context of extensive congressional investigations into the *yushin* regime's human rights violations and illegal Washington lobbying, the news that former KCIA director Kim Hyŏng-uk would testify at the hearings of the Fraser committee seemed to indicate that the very foundations of the *yushin* regime were being threatened. Kim had been a key member of Park's inner circle, serving as the KCIA director for six years (1963–1969), a period when Park made fundamental decisions that shaped the character of his political rule, including the dispatch of combat troops to South Vietnam (1965), normalization of relations with Japan (1965), and the constitutional revision to allow a third presidential term (1969). Since 1973, Kim had been in what he termed "exile." Despite the *yushin* regime's attempts to stop Kim Hyŏng-uk from testifying, sometimes with threats and other times with the offer of ambassadorial positions in Mexico or Brazil,[65] the former KCIA director stood before the Fraser committee and said that he himself had helped Pak Tong-sŏn get the highly lucrative license for importing American rice to South Korea in return for Pak Tong-sŏn's efforts to lobby for South Korea in Washington. Kim Hyŏng-uk also revealed that he had transferred $3 million to U.S.-based banks for Pak Tong-sŏn as "loans" for his operating the George Town Club.[66]

Kim Hyŏng-uk blamed Park Chung Hee for the lobbying scandal. But despite Kim's testimony, the Fraser committee could not come up with definitive evidence of Park's direct link to the illegal lobbying activities.[67] Summoning Pak Tong-sŏn to the hearings thus became imperative. Carter wrote a letter urging his return to the United States.

Escalation of Conflict

Congress also delayed approving the Carter administration's military aid bill. The *yushin* regime reacted as expected, rejecting outright Congress's request for the testimony of Pak Tong-sŏn and Kim Tong-jo. To the surprise of Park's political opponents in South Korea, the U.S. congressional hearings and investigations triggered nationalistic reactions, making South Korean society rally around the head of the *yushin* regime. Some student activists and political dissidents demanded that Park completely disclose the details of the Koreagate scandal, but the public mood was hardly "anti-Park." In the midst of the Koreagate scandal, the South Korean National Assembly adopted a bipartisan resolution in June 1978 to oppose the U.S. troop withdrawal policy.[68] Park's problem had less to do with his mass base of support than with the rising fragmentation within the ruling elite. The mounting criticism in the United States could not be taken lightly by the political elite because South Korea depended on U.S. military, economic, and political support for national survival. The rift in the alliance was to fracture the *yushin* regime's internal cohesion, with dire consequences in October 1979 (see Chapters 5, 6, and 13).

In 1977 Leon Jaworski succeeded Philip A. Lacovara as special counsel for the House Committee on Standards of Official Conduct. Backed by Speaker Thomas P. O'Neill and Chairman John J. Flynt of the House Ethics Committee, Jaworski kept up the pressure on Park by arranging an ethics hearing. On October 31, 1977, the House passed a resolution demanding South Korea's cooperation in the investigation into Koreagate.[69] In the end, the two disputing allies compromised in December 1977 by having Pak Tong-sŏn questioned by Jaworski's men in Seoul. The United States also agreed to give Pak Tong-sŏn immunity from prosecution during his subsequent visit to the United States for further interrogation. In January 1978, the U.S. prosecutors went to Seoul to question Pak Tong-sŏn. In February, South Korea acceded to the terms of Pak Tong-sŏn's testimony before the House and Senate ethics committees. The actual testimony was an anticlimax, with Pak Tong-sŏn simply denying that he was an agent of the South Korean government and that he conspired with Representative Otto E. Passman to buy influence for South Korea.[70]

Kim Tong-jo was another person Jaworski wanted to summon.[71] But South Korea rejected his request on the grounds that the former ambassador to the United States enjoyed diplomatic immunity. Congress cut economic aid by $56 million to pressure the South to hand over Kim Tong-jo to U.S. investigators, only to find South Korea even more adamant. Ambassador Gleysteen actively mediated between Seoul and Washington and arranged a compromise solution whereby the United States would interrogate Kim Tong-jo through a written questionnaire. As expected, in September 1978 Kim Tong-jo denied all allegations of bribery in his written response.

The congressional investigations and hearings continued after the testimony of Pak Tong-sŏn and Kim Tong-jo, but with much reduced media scrutiny and public attention. The issue soon became buried. Despite the anticlimactic end of the scandal, Koreagate damaged the integrity of Congress, particularly its Democratic members. Park and his *yushin* regime suffered much more. Throughout the two-year-long Koreagate dispute, the U.S. media zeroed in on the seamy side of Park's political rule, making it more difficult for the advocates of the U.S.–South Korean alliance to stop the tides of U.S. military withdrawal and human rights activism.

The Anticlimax: Revision of Carter's Troop Withdrawal Plan, 1977–1979

The U.S. Congress Steps In

While Koreagate was in full swing and the human rights dispute had deteriorated into a contest of wills, many senators on the Committee on Foreign Relations began to advise caution regarding Carter's troop withdrawal plan. In June 1977, the Senate passed Democratic Majority Leader

Robert C. Byrd's amendment that required the president to consult with Congress on the issue of troop withdrawal from South Korea. The Byrd amendment was brought about by Carter's earlier failure to consult with Congress.[72] On January 9, 1978, Senators John H. Glenn and Hubert H. Humphrey warned in their report to the Committee on Foreign Relations that Carter's decision to remove U.S. ground troops "reduce[d] the deterrent effect" on the North, which enjoyed military superiority over the South by deploying its military troops in an offensive posture. In the senators' eyes, the reduction of U.S. military assistance, coinciding with the precipitous fall in South Korean confidence in the United States' commitment to the defense of South Korea, also came at the wrong time. The Glenn-Humphrey report warned that "each phase of U.S. troop withdrawal should be approached most cautiously" and demanded the submission of "a detailed Presidential report prior to each withdrawal phase."[73]

After holding its own hearings, the House Armed Services Committee issued a report highly critical of Carter's troop withdrawal policy in April 1978, describing it as "lacking advice, assistance, recommendations, or estimates" of the JCS. Closely supervised by Chairman Samuel S. Stratton, an outspoken critic of Carter's troop withdrawal policy, the report argued that troop withdrawal should proceed with a transfer of military equipment worth $800 million. Deeming the North to be superior in military capabilities, it also warned of the destabilizing effects that Carter's policy of troop withdrawal would have on the Korean Peninsula and in East Asia generally.[74] By this time, the opposition against troop withdrawal had become bipartisan as key Democrats like Glenn, Sam Nunn, Henry M. Jackson, and Gary W. Hart joined the Republican critics.[75]

When Carter held a summit meeting with Fukuda Takeo in 1977, the Japanese prime minister reluctantly agreed to Carter's plan of troop withdrawal. However, encouraged by the changing tides of opinion in the Congress, Fukuda urged Carter to reconsider his decision, especially in the absence of adequate compensatory measures to prevent a power vacuum from developing on the Korean Peninsula. Fukuda's growing anxiety over the destabilizing impact of Carter's withdrawal policy was widely shared in Japan. Only two years earlier, its Defense White Paper had classified the Korean Peninsula as "one of the highest threat areas in the world," because it was thought that North Korea might miscalculate and believe that it would go unpunished in the event of war with the South.[76]

Becoming increasingly isolated, Carter announced on April 21, 1978, that troop reduction would be limited to only one battalion in 1978 and that the withdrawal of the other two battalions would be postponed until a year later. Carter justified the adjustment of his original plan as forced on him by the delay in Congress's passage of a military equipment transfer bill he had submitted to counter the possible danger of military imbalance on the Korean Peninsula.[77] Despite his placing the blame on Congress for its inaction, the adjustment was clearly a victory for the opponents of troop withdrawal. Congress eventually unanimously passed Carter's bill to transfer military equipment worth $800 million.

The Armstrong Report

In reversing the political climate in Washington, it was the U.S. intelligence community that played a pivotal role. In December 1975, John Armstrong, a young intelligence analyst in the Defense Intelligence Agency, reported a dramatic surge in North Korean military capabilities since 1972. In January 1978, General John W. Vessey, commander of the USFK, urged the Defense Department to reassess the military capabilities of North Korea upon hearing Armstrong's startling intelligence analysis.[78] The news of the ensuing Defense Department review was leaked to the *Army Times* in January 1979, making the Armstrong report itself a political issue. Moreover, from mid-1978 on, the result of more extensive studies of North Korean military capabilities became available as classified intelligence reports, putting Carter even more on the defensive. The Armstrong report and others suggested that the North Korean armed forces were two times larger in size than the South Korean military.[79] When some of the findings were made public, Congress gained the upper hand over Carter on the issue of troop withdrawal.

The National Security Council (NSC), too, began preparing Presidential Review Memorandum 45 (PRM-45) on the basis of new estimates regarding the North Korean military in January 1979. PRM-45, which called for a "comprehensive review of U.S. objectives and policies toward [South] Korea," was a product of combined efforts by the National Security Council and the State Department. Vance had assistant secretary of state Richard C. Holbrooke orchestrate a concerted effort to reverse Carter's troop withdrawal plan by preparing PRM-45, reappraising the military balance on the Korean Peninsula and planning Carter's tour of East Asia.[80] PRM-45 had the effect of transforming the "isolationist" Carter administration into a supporter of containing threats from the Soviet Union and its allies, including North Korea.[81] Gleysteen recalled that the presence of Vance at the NSC meeting on PRM-45 in May 1979 was a precursor to the reversal of Carter's troop withdrawal policy.[82]

As noted above, Brzezinski had once taken the position that human rights activism could be a valuable instrument for promoting U.S. values and interests in the third world as well as in other democratic nations. However, he soon realized that human rights activism could severely damage U.S. interests by exacerbating the superpower rivalry with the Soviet Union and by alienating authoritarian regimes in geopolitically crucial third world countries. In 1978, facing the reality of power politics, the Carter administration was active in the selling of newly developed aircraft to South Korea, delivering eighteen F-4E Phantom jets out of a total of thirty-seven contracted for sale by 1979 and planning for a sale of sixty F-16 fighters worth $1.2 billion in the 1980s. Aiming to maintain deterrence against the North, the United States reconfirmed its provision of a nuclear umbrella for South Korea, in addition to holding regular massive joint military exercises.[83] Ironically, the more Carter pushed for an active human rights policy toward South Korea, the more he was pressured by Congress and the Defense Department to support traditional containment policy and to increase military aid to South Korea with the goal of minimizing the damage to deterrence.

The Park-Carter Summit

By the late 1970s, maintaining the military balance on the Korean Peninsula came to be widely recognized within the U.S. foreign policymaking community as a key precondition for the continuance of Carter's troop withdrawal policy. Drawing on new intelligence reports, the U.S. army and the CIA came out with a strong recommendation to suspend Carter's troop withdrawal plan. In June 1979, the JCS also officially put its weight behind the suspension of troop withdrawal. Carter signed PRM-45, and he publicly made the U-turn in July 1979 when he visited South Korea to hold a summit meeting with Park.

Having been consulted on the drafting of PRM-45, Ambassador Gleysteen had been preparing for the Park-Carter summit meeting since late 1978 to improve strained U.S.–South Korean relations. To clear the way for Carter's U-turn on the issue of troop withdrawal, Holbrooke stated before the Senate Foreign Relations Committee in April 1979 that "further withdrawals [were] in abeyance until [the United States] complete[d] [its] reassessment of North Korean military capabilities."[84] In May 1979, however, Carter toyed with the idea of holding a trilateral meeting between Seoul, Pyŏngyang, and Washington either during or after his summit meeting with Park rather than making any public statement on troop withdrawal policy. The idea of holding a trilateral peace talk had been suggested earlier by Yugoslav president Josef Tito, upon Kim Il Sung's proposal for a U.S.–North Korean summit meeting to ease tensions on the

Korean Peninsula. Gleysteen succeeded in thwarting Carter's proposal by arguing that it would only raise a sense of anxiety, anger, and betrayal in South Korea. With the memory of the United States' unilateral pullout from South Vietnam and the consequent demise of Nguyen Van Thieu's government, Park could interpret Carter's initiative as the beginning of the application of the "Vietnamese solution" to the inter-Korea situation.[85]

The historic meeting between Carter and Park took place on June 30, 1979, a day after Carter spent the first night of his visit in Camp Casey with American soldiers. The summit was the first held since U.S. military aid in the form of grants ended in 1976. Park began the summit meeting with a lengthy lecture on the North Korean military threat, which ended with a strong rebuke of Carter's troop withdrawal policy. As recollected by a South Korean official, Carter was in a fury. Rather than pledging a freeze in the troop withdrawal plan, Carter demanded an increase in South Korea's defense expenditures and a significant improvement in its human rights conditions in return for retracting his idea of holding the trilateral peace talks. Park's reply was terse, pledging to accommodate Carter's human rights request by lifting Emergencey Decree no. 9, but in the eyes of all the participants, the summit was a disaster. There was a heated discussion among the Americans about the issue of troop withdrawal in Carter's limousine ride to the U.S. ambassador's residence, with Gleysteen, Vance, and secretary of defense Harold Brown all siding against any further troop withdrawal.[86] Carter yielded, enabling Gleysteen to hold a meeting with Park's chief of staff Kim Kye-wŏn, at which the South Koreans pledged to increase military expenditure to up to 6 percent of gross domestic product and to make a significant move on human rights,[87] in return for Carter's promise to accommodate Park's demand for the continued stationing of the U.S. Second Infantry Division and the maintenance of the CFC.[88] Park released a total of 180 political prisoners after Carter's departure. In Washington, Brzezinski announced a de facto freeze on any troop withdrawals until 1981.

HUMAN rights disputes in the 1970s seriously strained U.S.–South Korean relations. The dispute, however, could have been restrained, had there not developed simultaneously the United States' congressional investigations of Koreagate and Carter's policy of troop withdrawal. As Brzezinski once recalled, the problem for Carter was that it was exceptionally difficult to apply the general principle of human rights to the particular case of South Korea, where security interests were at stake.[89] The United States could not put pressure on Park for human rights progress to the point of endangering bilateral relations, because it had vital strategic interests in South Korea.

More important, however, the security alliance survived without serious damage in the long run. The turnaround in relations came in the late 1970s as abruptly as the crisis had arrived in the mid-1970s. The way both changes occurred demonstrates that the simultaneous development of the human rights, Koreagate, and troop withdrawal disputes was brought about as much by domestic political changes in the two allies as by the transition to détente in regional power politics and Nixon's Guam Doctrine. The domestic political consequences of the Vietnam debacle constituted a core intermediating variable in bringing the two unequal allies into a direct political collision. The way their domestic politics (mal)adjusted to the fluid international environment aggravated the disputes. Park's sense of military insecurity led him to launch the *yushin* regime, which in turn sowed the seeds for a human rights dispute, and even Koreagate, by making Park believe that he had power not only to silence the opposition but also clandestinely to buy influence in the U.S. Congress. In a similar way, the Carter administration reacted to the Vietnam debacle with a military disengagement from Asia, which translated into the withdrawal of ground forces from South Korea. The legacy of Watergate, which helped "outsider" Carter win the 1976 presidential election with a highly moralistic political agenda on human rights and public ethics, was also part of the picture. These forces of moralism found their target in Park's *yushin* regime.

Carter's South Korea policy was initially driven by his personal conviction. What tamed it was not Park's political protests, but the U.S. Congress's intervention. Even more crucial than this process of interbranch checks and balances in torpedoing Carter's troop withdrawal policy was the resistance from the Department of Defense, the Joint Chiefs of Staff, and senior officials of the State Department. The opposition to troop withdrawal built up early within the Carter administration, providing advocates of a strong U.S.–South Korean alliance in the U.S. Congress with an opportunity to freeze Carter's troop withdrawal policy and bring about the anticlimactic eclipse of both the human rights and the Koreagate disputes. Making a concerted effort to reevaluate North Korean security threats with new intelligence, the defense community proved to be effective in overturning Carter's South Korea policy by 1979.

In the end, the primacy of security interests prevailed and the commitment to the existing alliance was renewed. The change in Carter's position was nowhere more evident than in the 1979 Carter Doctrine, which called for a new cold war to contain communist threats after the Soviet Union's invasion of Afghanistan.[90] Carter's freeze on troop withdrawal from South Korea in 1979 was an integral part of his strategic rethinking at the global level. Just as the Vietnam debacle triggered the policy of troop withdrawal in the early and mid-1970s, it was the Afghan war that encouraged an about-face in U.S. policy toward South Korea on issues previously deemed of highest importance. In his last year as president, Carter abandoned his zeal for human rights issues. Instead, he focused on the strategic value of the U.S.–South Korean alliance.

However, it is important to emphasize that despite the eventual defeat of Carter's South Korea policy, the four years of Carter's presidency irreparably damaged the *yushin* regime. The prolonged dispute on human rights, military withdrawal, and Koreagate not only discredited Park in South Korean domestic politics, thus energizing the opposition political parties and *chaeya* movements (see Chapter 13), but, more important, fractured Park's inner circle into hard-liners and soft-liners on the issues of whether the *yushin* regime could survive domestic political turmoil and how it should deal with the United States. It was this divide within the political elite that eventually led to the assassination of Park by KCIA director Kim Chae-gyu on a chilly night in October 1979.

CHAPTER SEVENTEEN

The Search for Deterrence: Park's Nuclear Option

Sung Gul Hong

WHEN IT COMES TO issues involving nuclear weapons on the Korean Peninsula, North Korea, not the South, comes to most people's minds. But in the early 1970s, it was the South that became embroiled in conflict with the United States over the issue of nuclear sovereignty. In November 1971, a year before promulgating his *yushin* regime, Park Chung Hee asked O Wŏn-ch'ŏl, then a newly appointed member of the Blue House senior staff and in charge of developing defense-related heavy and chemical industries: "Our national security is vulnerable because of the uncertainty surrounding continued U.S. military presence on the Korean Peninsula. To become secure and independent, we need to free ourselves from dependence on U.S. military protection . . . Can we develop nuclear weapons?"[1] This was not a question. Park was instructing O Wŏn-ch'ŏl to draw up concrete plans.

Park sought or pretended to seek the "super weapon" to maximize South Korean security. Frustrated by the unilateral U.S. policy of military disengagement after the adoption of Richard M. Nixon's 1969 Guam Doctrine, Park had his Agency for Defense Development (ADD) begin research and development on nuclear weapons design, delivery systems, and explosion technologies. To assist the ADD, the Korea Atomic Energy Research Institute (KAERI) also made efforts to import nuclear reprocessing and fuel fabrication technologies and facilities from France and Belgium. Because reprocessing the spent fuel could produce weapons-grade plutonium, KAERI's attempt to purchase French technology was viewed by the United States as driven primarily by military goals, although KAERI justified its efforts as a search for alternative forms of energy. To alarm the United States even more, South Korea also imported a Canadian heavy-water reactor, CANDU, departing sharply from its past practice of purchasing U.S.-made light-water reactors. Although Park never publicly admitted his commitment to developing nuclear weapons, it was becoming increasingly clear that he was interested in acquiring a nuclear bomb similar to the one dropped on Nagasaki in 1945. Yet eventually, under strong U.S. pressure, both multilaterally and bilaterally, Park's efforts didn't materialize.

Few countries seriously consider the option of going nuclear even when hard pressed by external security threats. But even fewer countries give up nuclear programs once they have committed themselves to the project. Why did Park launch his nuclear initiative in the first place, and why did he retreat when the United States put pressure on him? How did the conflict with the United States over nuclear issues influence what was already becoming a troubled alliance? What was at stake for Park and his American counterparts in the nuclear conflict?

Four general points can be made on the nature of U.S.–South Korean relations. First, the nuclear conflict shows not only the weakness but also the strength of the bilateral relationship. Park toyed with the nuclear option in the early 1970s, when the alliance entered one of its most rocky periods since the end of the Korean War. Fear bred mistrust and vice versa, trapping the allies in a spiral of conflict across a variety of issues. Clashes were contagious, making each of the allies pressure the other by mobilizing resources in unrelated areas, only to produce new frontiers of conflict. The original seed for the alliance crisis was Nixon's unilateral decision to withdraw the Seventh Infantry Division in 1971 to win the support of U.S. voters. Fearful of the United States' abandonment of South Korea, Park pursued the nuclear option, which only made the United States hostile. In addition, Park hired Pak Tong-sŏn to try to fight U.S. unilateralism by purchasing support in Congress through illegal lobbying. He also clamped down on his domestic opposition under the pretext of a national security crisis. These countermeasures, however, boomeranged into the Koreagate scandal and conflict over human rights in South Korea, controversies that greatly weakened U.S. support for Park and his regime. At the same time, given their geopolitical interest in avoiding a total collapse of the alliance, both South Korea and the United States tried to stop, if not reverse, the deterioration of their relationship. Conflict spread and worsened, but there existed a safety net that kept the alliance from collapsing.

Second, among the bilateral conflicts of the 1970s, the nuclear conflict was unique in the sense that the outcome was a clear U.S. "victory." Even in extremely asymmetric relationships such as the one between the United States and South Korea, the weaker party usually has some leverage, because the stronger member to some extent depends on the weaker one to realize its goals. It was through these U.S. interests that South Korea protected itself from the worst of U.S. unilateralism. The United States refrained from escalating conflict with South Korea, lest its client state became threatened with instability. Consequently, Koreagate ended as an anticlimax, with Pak Tong-sŏn free from U.S. prosecution. The human rights disputes heated up, but they did not lead to any sustained U.S. intervention. Even Carter's plan to withdraw all U.S. ground troops from the Korean Peninsula by 1981 was rescinded in 1978. In each of these bilateral confrontations, South Korea succeeded in holding its ground until the United States reversed its policy, not because South Korea had the power to stop the United States, but because the strategic importance of the Korean Peninsula to the superpower made it reluctant to fully flex its muscles (see Chapter 16). But where the nuclear issue was concerned, the United States resorted to every possible means to stop Park. Compromise was unthinkable, because what was at stake was the stability of the postwar U.S.-led regional and global regime of nuclear nonproliferation. Park did try to bargain throughout the 1970s, arguing that he was seeking nuclear technology strictly for economic purposes. When the United States came back harder against him, he zigzagged, clandestinely pursuing nuclear programs, only to engage in risky diplomatic dialogues with U.S. officials under intense pressure. In the end, he realized that there could be no negotiation on the nuclear issue.

Third, the nuclear conflict demonstrates that it was military issues that decisively shaped Park's political relationship with the United States. Both good times and bad times in the alliance relations were primarily the result of military issues. When the United States increased its military presence in East Asia to fight the Vietnam War during the mid-1960s, Park's relationship with the U.S. political leadership improved significantly because of the value South Korea had as an ally that was willing to send combat troops to South Vietnam with the goal of assisting U.S. war efforts and sharing the burden of "collective security." When the United States began military disengagement from South Vietnam in the early 1970s, Park lost the leverage he had had on U.S. policy toward South Korea. On the contrary, he found himself desperately pleading with the United States not to include South Korea among the countries targeted for military disengagement. When the pleading failed to reverse the U.S. decision, Park resorted to a wide range of countermeasures. The speed and scope with which the bilateral political relationship either improved or deteriorated with a change in U.S. security policy were remarkable. Moreover, once the United States decided on a new course of policy on the basis of its altered regional and global security calculations, South Korea could only negotiate the terms of the change, not the direction of the change. It is difficult to find any other bilateral relationship in which both conventional and nonconventional nuclear military issues dominated general political relations to the extent that they did in U.S.–South Korean relations.

Fourth, despite the unique character of nuclear issues, the conflict over Park's nuclear development program once again demonstrates that commercial interests were always closely intertwined with military and security issues in the two countries' relations. Initially, Park thought he could outmaneuver the United States by contracting with French and Canadian suppliers for nuclear technology and equipment. To a certain extent, his strategy worked, luring these suppliers to act as a protective shield for his plans. At the same time, once the alternative suppliers showed an interest in the sale of nuclear reactors and propellant facilities, commercial interests became another reason for the United States to press hard on South Korea and France to cancel their commercial deals. The sale of French nuclear technology could mean that the growing South Korean market for nuclear energy would become dominated by French suppliers.

With these general features of United States–South Korean security relations outlined, we turn to a more in-depth analysis of Park's motives in toying with the nuclear option, the channels and processes of U.S. intervention against Park's nuclear initiative, and the factors that enabled the United States to successfully stop the program.

From Research to Weapons Development

South Korea began its nuclear research in 1956, three years after it signed a mutual defense treaty with the United States. The program was strictly one of research aimed at the peaceful use of atomic energy.[2] As part of an effort to secure the blessing of the United States, South Korea joined the International Atomic Energy Agency (IAEA), which put South Korea's infant research program under international surveillance in 1957. In 1964, South Korea ratified the Partial Test Ban Treaty. In 1968 it signed the Nuclear Non-Proliferation Treaty (NPT), although the actual ratification was postponed because of North Korea's delay in becoming an NPT member-state. The United States did not press South Korea to ratify the NPT immediately, because it thought that IAEA inspection and regulations were sufficient to restrict South Korean nuclear activities to peaceful research. Besides, the South Korean nuclear program was then assisted by the United States, giving its officials ample opportunity to control what the South Koreans were doing.

Parallel to these efforts to launch a research program was the need to construct an institutional base. In March 1956, Rhee established a nuclear energy section within the Ministry of Education to conduct basic research on nuclear energy. The Atomic Energy Law was promulgated in 1958, and the Office of Atomic Energy (OAE) was established directly under the president to coordinate the research, development, and use of peaceful atomic energy. The Korea Atomic Energy Research Institute was launched in 1959 as an affiliate of the OAE, resulting in the assemblage of the General Dynamics–designed Triga Mark-II (250kw) research reactor three years later with U.S. assistance.

What started out as an energy research and development program, however, came to acquire a military dimension when the security environment swiftly deteriorated in the late 1960s. Park began to question the seriousness of the U.S. security commitment to South Korea when Nixon followed up on his 1969 Guam Doctrine with the removal of some 20,000 U.S. ground troops from South Korea, the pursuit of détente with China, and an exit from the Vietnam War. Park was shocked to think that the United States was abandoning its East Asian allies because of domestic political pressure. The shock was especially great because Park thought he had taken a significant domestic political risk for his U.S. ally in the 1960s when he dispatched combat troops to South Vietnam. When the two allies began to negotiate the terms of U.S. military disengagement, Park reportedly asked the journalists gathered at the Blue House: "The pressing question for South Korea is how long can we trust the United States."[3] He began to emphasize the principle of "self-defense" *(chawi)* and then "self-determination" *(chaju),* with an eye to reducing dependence on what he thought was an unreliable superpower ally.[4]

Before seeking to acquire nuclear military capability, however, Park did try to strengthen South Korea's security environment through both diplomacy and conventional military measures. It was their failure that made Park turn to the nuclear option. When the United States withdrew its Seventh Infantry Division from South Korea in 1971, Park tried to counterbalance the U.S. military retrenchment by establishing a 2.5-million-strong army reserve. The Agency for Defense Development (ADD), established in August 1970, was intended to pursue modernization programs for South Korea's armed forces. With declining military aid from the United States,

Park also introduced in 1974 a national defense income tax surcharge of
10 percent to finance the Forces Improvement Plan (1974–1981), with the
goal of surpassing North Korea on defense expenditures by 1976.[5] To do
so, South Korea raised defense expenditures from 5 percent of its gross national product to nearly 7.5 percent.[6] The gap began to narrow considerably when South Korea increased its defense expenditures from $719 million in 1975 to $1.5 billion in 1976, and again to $1.8 billion dollars in
1977. During the same period, North Korean defense expenditure grew at
a much lower rate, rising from $770 million in 1975 to $1 billion in 1977.[7]

In spite of these impressive efforts to catch up militarily, the South still
lagged behind the North in armed forces, air force, and naval military capabilities by a considerable margin in the late 1970s. It was only the U.S.
military troops stationed in the South that kept the North deterred from
waging war, but it was precisely this U.S. role in deterrence that was questioned after the end of the Vietnam conflict. Given the continued military superiority of North Korea and the uncertainty of U.S. intentions,
Park seems to have concluded that a conventional military buildup was
not enough to deter North Korean military attacks. *JoongAng Ilbo* sets
the date of Park's decision to develop nuclear programs as March 1971.[8]
Pak Kŭn-hye, his daughter, also recollects that Park launched a nuclear
(weapons) development program when the United States unilaterally implemented its decision to pull out the Seventh Infantry Division in July
1971 despite his repeated pleas to the White House to reconsider the decision.[9]

Upon Park's request to draw up a plan to develop strategic weapons in
November 1971, O Wŏn-ch'ŏl met with science and technology minister
Ch'oe Hyŏng-sŏp and KAERI director Yun Yong-gu to pursue nuclear
weapons in a clandestine program.[10] Given the adverse impact the news of
nuclear weapons development would have had on already difficult U.S.–
South Korean relations, as well as the U.S. ability to track down any military program of this scale through its massive intelligence network in
South Korea, Park pursued it with utmost secrecy.[11] He could do so because with power centralized around him since the 1969 constitutional
amendment to clear the way for his third bid for presidential power in
1971, Park did not need the endorsement of others on what he thought
was of paramount importance. Nor was he the kind of man who would
put such an important issue to open debate.[12]

What made Park's intentions ambiguous even to his Blue House confidants and ADD researchers was the difficulty in separating military from
economic intentions in any nuclear development program. Much of what
was needed for the development of nuclear weapons was also required for

the peaceful use of nuclear energy. And South Korea had ample need to develop nuclear energy in order to reduce its dependence on oil. A twelve-year plan (1969–1981) for nuclear research, prepared by KAERI in 1968 and approved by the cabinet as a blueprint for national energy autonomy in 1969, envisaged the construction of the means for nuclear fuel fabrication, a uranium refinement factory, and a reprocessing facility by 1981. To implement the plan, KAERI began negotiating with foreign nuclear suppliers for joint research programs on nuclear fuel fabrication and reprocessing as early as 1972. The same year Yŏngnam Chemical Co. began to negotiate with Nuclear Fuel Services, Skelly Oil Co., and Mitsubishi Petroleum in order to import a facility with the capacity of reprocessing one ton of spent fuel per day. The construction site for the reprocessing facility was to be in Onsan, South Kyŏngsang Province. Yŏngnam Chemical Co. partnered with KAERI for the project, but due to the Nuclear Fuel Service's failure to secure the U.S. government's approval of the sale, the project was dropped prematurely.

The central person in jump-starting the nuclear project was Yun Yong-gu, appointed to the post of KAERI director in August 1971 with the mandate to develop nuclear fuel fabrication and reprocessing technology as one of the top priorities of the institute.[13] KAERI contacted Algon Nuclear Lab, a U.S. research institute, for the provision of manpower training and the supply of necessary technology for reprocessing, only to be turned down. It appears that at that point South Korea was trying to acquire reprocessing technology for peaceful purposes, because KAERI targeted a U.S. institute as its partner. Any effort to develop nuclear weapons would have been easily detected by the United States. Upon the failure of talks with Algon, KAERI turned elsewhere for the technology transfer it needed. To Yun's delight, France, Belgium, and Canada showed interest. Consequently, the South Korean project for developing nuclear energy for peaceful purposes was already under way when Park decided to develop nuclear weapons sometime in 1971. Reflecting Park's interest in the nuclear program as a potentially military project, KAERI efforts to license nuclear technology were dramatically accelerated after 1971.

In May 1972, a South Korean delegation of scientists and bureaucrats led by Ch'oe Hyŏng-sŏp made an official visit to France and Great Britain. Then followed an agreement with France on the sale of nuclear reprocessing and fuel fabrication technology. For France, in addition to its traditional ambition to carve out its own place in the area of global security independent from the United States, commercial interests drove it into becoming a willing supplier of nuclear technologies and facilities. Ch'oe's initiative constituted a welcome opportunity to penetrate an American-dominated burgeoning commercial nuclear market. In October 1972, KAERI actively began negotiating the transfer of reprocessing technology with the French Atomic Energy Commission. A separate negotiation to import test facilities for mixed nuclear fuel fabrication was also under way with Belgonucléaire, a Belgian company.

Reprocessing Technologies

In March 1973, Ch'oe Hyŏng-sŏp recruited Chu Chae-yang as the first vice director of KAERI. Chu became the recruiter of overseas South Korean scientists and engineers for nuclear development. By July of that year, fifteen overseas scholars with expertise in nuclear engineering, chemical engineering, and chemistry joined KAERI. Enjoying relatively high salaries and provided with accommodations, these overseas scientists joined some twenty-five local researchers in a "special project team." As recollected by one of the returnees, KAERI recruited the overseas scientists and engineers without informing them of its plan to acquire reprocessing technology. Even within KAERI, information was tightly controlled, with the scientists outside the "special project team" kept in the dark about the team's activities.[14] This secrecy was to raise U.S. suspicions that KAERI was pursuing its nuclear research projects not only for the peaceful use of atomic energy but also for the development of nuclear weapons. The special project team, consisting of some forty members, took charge of research and development as well as commercial negotiations with research institutes, business firms, and state agencies in France, Belgium, Great Britain, and Canada for the licensing of nuclear technologies.

The scale and complexity of the research projects, however, required the organization of an institutional support network outside KAERI. In the Blue House, O Wŏn-ch'ŏl and Secretary Kim Kwang-mo spearheaded the drive to develop nuclear programs. At the Ministry of Science and Technology, Ch'oe Hyŏng-sŏp mobilized ministerial resources to assist KAERI's research activities. The Ministry of National Defense was excluded from the entire project not only because of its lack of expertise but also because of its wholesale institutional integration with the U.S. military establishment, which made the clandestine development of nuclear weapons impossible. Principally, it was KAERI's special project team headed by Chu Chae-yang that was in charge of acquiring technological capabilities for nuclear fuel fabrication and reprocessing. By contrast, research and development on weapons design, a delivery system, and explosion technology were conducted separately by the ADD. There thus emerged a division of labor, with KAERI focused on obtaining weapons-grade fissile materials and the ADD on manufacturing weapons and the delivery system. Because KAERI and the ADD could pursue their respective technological missions independent of each other, the division of labor helped Park's effort to hide the nuclear weapons program from the United States as long as possible.

In late 1973, the ADD submitted a secret plan to develop nuclear weapons for Park's review. Proposing to develop a plutonium bomb of 20 kilotons, which was similar in size to the bomb dropped on Nagasaki, the ADD plan estimated a total budget of $1.5 to $2 billion, to be disbursed over six to ten years. Initially, the ADD chose the bomber as its delivery vehicle, but it later opted for missiles when South Korea successfully tested the launching of a medium range surface-to-surface missile (Paekkom) in 1978.[15] KAERI and its scientists were excluded from the ADD-led planning process, although it was they who worked to acquire reprocessing capabilities. The exclusion of KAERI scientists from the development of nuclear weapons, delivery systems, and explosion technology was intentional; it minimized the danger of information leakage. The KAERI scientists certainly knew that the technological capabilities they developed for peaceful uses of nuclear energy could also be used for the development of nuclear weapons, but whatever they conjectured remained mere conjecture because they were never at any point told about the planned military nature of their work. The key hurdle in developing nuclear weapons was the acquisition of weapons-grade plutonium.

The negotiation with France for technology transfer initially went smoothly, resulting in two interim contracts between KAERI and French companies by April 1975, one with CERCA for nuclear fuel fabrication and another with Saint-Gobain Technique Nouvelle for spent-fuel reprocessing.[16] KAERI had also been negotiating a separate deal with Canada since April 1973 for the construction of a heavy-water reactor called CANDU, in order to acquire spent fuel required for the production of plutonium. Although South Korea's first large-scale nuclear reactor, Kori 1, was under construction with U.S. assistance, KAERI calculated that it would be difficult, if not impossible, for South Korea to reprocess the spent-fuel rods from Kori 1 because of the United States' participation. Moreover, with the target date for the completion of construction set for 1978, KAERI thought it needed another source of spent fuel if it was to back up the ongoing research programs on nuclear fuel fabrication and reprocessing technology.[17] It was in this context that Saul Eisenberg, an Israeli-Austrian lobbyist representing the Canadian Atomic Energy Commission, approached South Korea with the idea that if South Korea purchased a CANDU reactor, Canada was willing to provide an NRX reactor.

Because the Canadian NRX was a heavy-water reactor using natural uranium, its purchase would enable South Korea to secure natural uranium with relative ease. Moreover, because it was possible to remove high-quality spent fuel without having to shut down the NRX research reactor, Eisenberg's proposal had an added advantage of maintaining the secrecy of KAERI's research and development programs. Canada, for its part, was actively looking for overseas markets where it could sell its heavy-water reactors, making the deal even more likely. By mid-1975, negotiations with Canada had progressed considerably, getting South Korea to choose the Canadian CANDU for its Wŏlsŏng 1 nuclear power plant. As a package deal, Canada agreed to provide a 30,000-kilowatt NRX reactor—but on the condition that South Korea accept the U.S. demand that it ratify the NPT. Canada was under strong U.S. pressure to get South Korea to ratify the NPT prior to the package sale of the CANDU reactor and the NRX research reactor.[18] The United States by then understood Park's seriousness in developing a nuclear option.[19]

South Korea concurred, quickly ratifying the NPT to show its peaceful intentions. At the same time, both the United States and South Korea knew that the South was coming close to the acquisition of capabilities to develop nuclear weapons with the purchase of the NRX research reactor, which produced spent fuel. With sufficient weapons-grade fissile material, South Korea was expected to construct its own nuclear weapon within four to six years.[20]

The South Korean access to the French and Canadian nuclear suppliers had important political implications for U.S.–South Korea relations. First, encouraged by the initial success in the import of nuclear technology and facilities, Park thought he had finally escaped from total dependence on the United States for nuclear research and development. This sense of confidence combined with the specter of security crisis encouraged Park to emphasize the doctrine of self-reliance in national defense that he had developed since the early 1970s. Second, by having sources other than the United States for nuclear development, Park was able to pursue his nuclear program with a degree of strategic ambiguity. Because nuclear technology could be put to both economic and military purposes, there was always uncertainty regarding Park's intentions in developing nuclear programs. This ambiguity yielded Park some leverage over U.S. policy toward South Korea. At the same time, however, it was also true that his attempt to secure leverage out of the strategic ambiguity of his nuclear programs could backfire if it was overplayed, which could cause the United States to conclude that Park was intent on violating IAEA and NPT regulations. Such a conclusion could trigger U.S. sanctions.

The South Korean purchase of French and Canadian nuclear technology had important economic implications as well. The South Korean nuclear market was no longer a monopoly of U.S. nuclear companies, which prompted the U.S. nuclear industry to seek countermeasures to repel the challenges from nuclear suppliers elsewhere. Ironically, the U.S. industry's defensive measures could go both ways in strengthening or weakening South Korea's hand vis-à-vis the United States in the game of securing access to nuclear technology and maintaining the nuclear card as an option. The U.S. companies could take defensive measures and put pressure on U.S. policymakers to crack down on Park's pretensions of nuclear self-reliance, or they could aid South Korea by making more concessions in bidding for its purchase of their technology.

In spite of the advances made in the diversification of its nuclear technology suppliers, South Korea of the mid-1970s was far from becoming a nuclear power. It still needed to develop a workable weapons design, obtain weapons-grade fissile material, and build or purchase a delivery system. Furthermore, South Korea needed to acquire technologies in chemical engineering and machinery to deal safely with hazardous plutonium. As a researcher in charge of weapons design at the ADD once testified, the development of a workable weapons design was relatively easy and nearly complete in 1975.[21] The acquisition of weapons-grade fissile material was also a relatively easy task, because of the availability of the NRX reactor from which spent fuel was obtained to be reprocessed. Likewise, the acquisition of a delivery system did not pose a major challenge, because the U.S.-manufactured F-4D/E fighter planes, initially supplied to South Korea as a concession for its military intervention in the Vietnam War and later purchased by the South as part of its military modernization program to make up for the loss of firepower brought on by U.S. military disengagement, could deliver nuclear weapons weighing up to 4,000 pounds. South Korea had also been developing its own surface-to-surface ballistic missiles since the early 1970s, which could serve as a delivery system.[22] The acquisition of technologies to assemble nuclear weapons needed time, but given the vibrancy of South Korea's heavy and chemical industries in the 1970s, this too did not constitute an insurmountable problem. Building a reprocessing plant was expected to cost some $51 million over four years, which was not particularly burdensome for an economy of South Korea's size.[23]

For the United States, the stakes were high. First, the NPT regime could be weakened. Second, South Korea's acquisition of nuclear weapons at the time of U.S. military disengagement could mean an erosion of U.S. influence in one of the most volatile regions of the world. The regional nuclear arms race that could break out as a result of South Korea's acquisition of nuclear capabilities was judged to endanger U.S. security interests. By contrast, as Park saw it, he was going to be a winner whether his nuclear weapons program proceeded without U.S. interruption or not. If the program escaped U.S. surveillance, Park would acquire an independent source of nuclear deterrence against North Korea in what seemed to be an irreversible era of U.S. military disengagement. On the other hand, if the program was revealed, he thought he could use the dismantlement of the nuclear weapons program as a bargaining chip with which to extract U.S. concessions on security issues.

Missile Development

Integral to the nuclear weapons program was the development of missiles as a delivery system. O Wŏn-ch'ŏl was at the center of Park's missile initiative. In December 1971, after Park conveyed to O his decision to acquire strategic missile capabilities, O summoned to the Blue House Ku Sang-hoe, later to be known as the father of South Korean missile development. There he was personally ordered by Park to spearhead the development of ballistic missiles. Park personally wrote down a list of specific characteristics he wanted to see in the missile program, and handed the memo to O Wŏn-ch'ŏl.[24] Most critically, Park directed O to develop an independent missile development system, with the goal of producing surface-to-surface ballistic missiles with a range of 200 kilometers (roughly 125 miles) at the first stage, and then progressively expanding the range in later stages. Park also identified the ADD as the coordinator for research and development.[25] By September 1972, a group of scientists and engineers from the ADD, the Korea Institute of Science and Technology (KIST), the Korea Advanced Institute of Science and Technology (KAIST), and the Korea Central Intelligence Agency (KCIA) was able to assemble a missile development plan, with the title "The Promotional Plan for the Aerospace Industry." The actual plan, however, focused on developing ballistic missiles, calling for the successful testing of mid-range surface-to-surface missiles by the end of 1976 and long-range missiles by the end of 1979.

In February 1973, Park approved the "Basic Plan for Developing Ballistic Missiles" and ordered its implementation as part of the Yulgok project to modernize the South Korean armed forces. Its inclusion in the Yulgok project virtually guaranteed state financial support. The actual implementation began in 1975, with an infusion of 6.2 billion won from the state. In 1976, the bill stood at 5.7 billion won.[26] By December 1976, the construction of the Taejŏn Machine Tool Center was completed to serve as a technical base for the development of ballistic missiles. The ADD actively sought to purchase the necessary propellant and guiding technologies, parts, and components on the international market, as well as to recruit several South Korean scientists and engineers from the United States.

To develop a missile design, the ADD chose McDonnell Douglas (MD) as its preferred licensor, because MD manufactured the Nike-Hercules (NH) missiles used by U.S. ground troops in South Korea. Moreover, MD was suffering financial difficulties in the mid-1970s, which the ADD thought would make it eager to sell missile design technologies. To the disappointment of MD, however, the ADD was asked to get permission from the State Department. When the State Department would not approve the sale of missile design technologies, the ADD proposed a joint research project to increase the range of NH missiles from 180 kilometers (112 miles) to 240 kilometers (150 miles). MD concurred, but at a price of $30 million, which forced the ADD to divide the research project into three stages and to conclude a contract for the first stage of joint research in the amount of $1.8 million. As part of this first stage, which was essentially a feasibility study, ten ADD researchers were sent to MD for six months. Upon the completion of the six-month-long feasibility study, the ADD acquired basic design technologies for ballistic missiles and canceled the remaining two stages of joint research.[27]

Acquiring the propellant technology was also a difficult process. Because U.S. companies were legally required to secure the State Department's prior approval in the sale of propellant technologies, the ADD initially chose to contact a French company, SNPE, for the purchase of technology, equipment, and parts and components. Then, in the middle of negotiations with SNPE, the ADD, hearing of Lockheed's plan to close down its propellant plant in California due to financial distress, swiftly contacted Lockheed for the purchase of some of the equipment at the plant. Lockheed counterproposed that the ADD buy all of the equipment in the California plant, with the pledge that it would get the necessary permission from the State Department. In the end, the ADD invited both Lockheed and SNPE to bid for the project, and eventually chose the option of buying Lockheed's California factory at the price of $2.6 million— but without the manufacturing technology. The manufacturing technology was excluded from the deal because of strong opposition from the State Department. Consequently, the ADD had to conclude a separate deal with SNPE to acquire the manufacturing technology at a cost of $3 million.[28] The deal with Lockheed came through only because the United States was internally divided, with the U.S. embassy in Seoul joining the Defense Department in supporting the Lockheed plan and the State Department remaining strongly opposed on the following grounds:

> [Deputy Secretary of Defense] William P. Clements' memorandum of January 23 contends that the Lockheed plant would enable [South Korea] to achieve substantial savings in reloading motors for the US-made rockets it now possesses. The memorandum further states that it is desirable for the ADD to undertake research and test programs for anti-tank and other rocket ordnance . . . The Department of State believes that [remained classified] President Park, through the ADD, is embarked upon an ambitious program to develop advanced weapons systems which will be "strategic" in the context of the Korean Peninsula. In addition to advanced missiles the ADD has been directed to supervise production of a prototype nuclear weapon . . . Linkage of nuclear weapons development to an advanced missile capability would have the most serious strategic implications given [South Korea's] geographic location.[29]

After the construction of the Taejŏn Machine Tool Center and the relocation of the Lockheed propellant factory to South Korea, the missile development program quickly gained momentum. At the same time, with the heightened activities of the ADD and KAERI in overseas nuclear and missile markets, U.S. surveillance of South Korea was also increasing. The chief of staff at the Blue House, Kim Chŏng-ryŏm, once recalled that the greatest obstacle in the missile development program was the United States' objection. Ambassador Richard L. Sneider repeatedly expressed strong objections to the South Korean missile program in a monthly luncheon meeting he held with Kim Chŏng-ryŏm.[30] To secure U.S. guiding technology and equipment, which were required to complete the development of ballistic missiles, the ADD had to agree with the United States to limit the range of the South Korean missiles to 180 kilometers (112 miles) and the warhead weight to 1,000 pounds.

The Trial of Park's Nuclear Ambitions

Park's nuclear weapons program proceeded uninterrupted until mid-1974. The United States paid relatively little attention to the issue of nuclear proliferation in developing countries until then, giving Park a window of opportunity to construct an institutional basis for research and development and contract with foreign companies for the sale of technology and/or facilities for the development of nuclear and missile capabilities. With India's successful nuclear test in May 1974, the U.S. attitude changed dramatically, leading the State Department to investigate other potential challengers of the NPT regime. It was against this background that the United

States became aware of South Korea's negotiations to purchase reprocessing technologies and facilities from France and Canada in late 1974 and ordered the U.S. embassy in Seoul to appraise South Korean intentions in acquiring nuclear reprocessing facilities. A telegram from the embassy to the State Department on October 28, 1974, demonstrates U.S. concern: "Embassy is currently preparing analysis of [the] potential in [South] Korea for developing nuclear weapons and we plan to address related questions of surface-to-surface missile development . . . in the context of our nuclear weapons analysis."[31]

A few months later, the State Department informed a branch of U.S. intelligence—most likely the Central Intelligence Agency—of the need to investigate South Korea's nuclear development program.[32] In early 1975, the United States conducted a survey of potential nuclear proliferation in the third world and put South Korea in the group of developing countries with the capability to develop nuclear weapons within a decade. The State Department was then of the opinion that the South Korean acquisition of nuclear weapons would break down regional stability by compelling China and the Soviet Union to provide the North with strategic nuclear weapons in the event of military belligerency on the Korean Peninsula.[33]

Anxious about the dangers of nuclear proliferation, the United States proposed that the member states of the Nuclear Suppliers Group (the United States, the United Kingdom, Canada, France, West Germany, Japan, and the Soviet Union) convene a meeting to develop common guidelines on export policy, including the export of nuclear technology, parts and components, and facilities, with the goal of restraining sales of sensitive nuclear materials. To the U.S. query on the French sale of a reprocessing plant to South Korea, the French answered that it would seek to have IAEA safeguards on the completion of the deal. In addition to such efforts to mobilize multilateral support for restricting the South Korean nuclear program to peaceful uses, the State Department also resorted to bilateral pressure to stop the program from developing into a military one by pushing for South Korea's ratification of the NPT. At the same time, the United States tightened its surveillance over South Korean nuclear facilities and strengthened intelligence on research activities.

The U.S. embassy in Seoul took the most alarmist view. In its eyes, given the South Korean people's "diligent nature" and Park's commitment, South Korea could develop its own nuclear weapon by the early 1980s. The embassy also argued that the United States should not underestimate South Korea's ability to obtain nuclear technology and equipment from a third country through commercial deals. The embassy believed that South Korea would push ahead with its nuclear weapon development program despite the high political and economic costs involved and that its successful acquisition of nuclear weapons would mean a precipitous decline in U.S. influence on South Korea. The embassy recommended that the United States take explicit action to prevent South Korea from continuing with its nuclear weapons program.[34] Groping for ways to stop South Korean efforts, Ambassador Sneider met with Park on May 1, 1975, to discuss South Korea's missile development program. Predictably, Park reiterated his firm commitment to building his country's defense capabilities, including its missile stock, as a preparatory measure for the planned U.S. military reduction of forces, if not withdrawal. By contrast, Sneider pointed out that the missile development program entailed too great a financial cost for the objective of self-reliance and that South Korea needed to take into account U.S. concerns before proceeding further. Incidentally, Park emphasized that he had no plans to develop nuclear weapons.[35]

On July 2, Robert S. Ingersoll, then deputy secretary of state, drew up a memorandum for the White House to lay out the options for defeating South Korean efforts to acquire nuclear weapons.[36] Recollecting how he secured cooperation from France and Canada in preventing the earlier deals that might have evolved into a nuclear weapons program,[37] Ingersoll stressed that South Korea's nuclear weapons program directly threatened U.S. security interests in the East Asian region. On the other hand, in Ingersoll's view, there was a significant role to be played by the United States as a licensor and donor if South Korea's attempt to acquire the reprocessing technology was strictly motivated by the economic need to secure an alternative form of energy in the era of high oil prices and South Korea's fragile access to Middle Eastern sources of oil and gas. Considering the stakes at hand, Ingersoll urged the United States to act right away. To dissuade Park from toying with the risky nuclear weapons strategy, Ingersoll recommended that the United States clearly state its deep concern over South Korea's nuclear reprocessing program and warn that future U.S. nuclear assistance, including the pending U.S. Export-Import (EX-IM) Bank loan for Kori 2, would be terminated in the event of Park's use of the technology for military purposes.[38] Moreover, Ingersoll urged the United States to pressure South Korea not to proceed with its planned construction of a pilot reprocessing plant. In return for South Korea's acquiescence, he thought the United States could invite South Korea to participate in a regional reprocessing plant.[39]

By October, the U.S. embassy had asked at least twice that Park stop his nuclear reprocessing program, only to see him reject the demand. Instead, Park offered the "concession" of allowing U.S. inspection of the planned reprocessing facilities as a gesture of his goodwill toward the United

States. In the same vein, South Korea had ratified the NPT in April 1975, after seven years of postponement, when the United States succeeded in persuading France and Canada to join it in pressing for South Korea's ratification of the NPT as a precondition for the French and Canadian sale of nuclear technology. Faced with the united front of its suppliers, South Korea quickly agreed, and the ratification took less than two minutes in the National Assembly. However, given the long record of South Korea's attempts at going around the United States to develop nuclear capabilities, the damage to the two countries' relationship could not be healed by the ratification of the NPT alone. On the contrary, the skeptics within the U.S. government argued that the ratification was only an opportunistic move aimed at silencing U.S. objections to the French sale. Moreover, the South Korean ratification came only after a U.S. congressional resolution calling for the U.S. EX-IM Bank to defer its approval of loans for the construction of the Kori-2 reactor.[40] In view of the situation, Sneider thought the United States had four options:

(1) We can now let [the] question lie fallow without further reply, letting ROKG [the Republic of Korea Government] discover for themselves [the] difficulty of proceeding without our support in [the] nuclear field; (2) We can acquiesce in [the] reprocessing sale, accepting ROK offers of bilateral U.S. as well as international inspection; (3) We can raise this issue once again directly with President Park [to seek] compromise of a moratorium on reprocessing contract, which we have heard may be feasible; or (4) we can confront Park personally with uncompromising line.[41]

The first two options prevented an escalation of nuclear conflict that was certain to damage the already fragile alliance, weakened by human rights disputes, the Koreagate scandal, and the U.S. military withdrawal (see Chapter 16). However, either option would come with the cost of letting South Korea take the initiative in defining the security situation on the Korean Peninsula as well as in the East Asian region. Depending on South Korea's understanding or misunderstanding of U.S. security interests, an arms race in Northeast Asia could break out. The first two options, in other words, counted on South Korea's ability to realize, without hostile U.S. pressure, that its decision to push ahead with the nuclear weapons program would hurt its own interests by prompting the United States not only to refuse the pending Kori-2 loan but also to cut U.S. military assistance. In light of the risks and limitations of the first two options, the third option urged the United States to confront Park directly and seek a compromise. In this scenario, the United States would look for a two- to three-year moratorium on the South Korean purchase of a reprocessing plant.

Like the first two options, however, the third option did not foreclose Park's development of nuclear weapons in the future. Sneider explained:

> We should stress that this [third] approach [of agreeing on a moratorium] would permit an expanding flow of technological and economic benefits from [the United States], including offer of some training of ROK technicians in [the] reprocessing field. We should deal directly with Park's longer-term concerns, stating that in our view ROKG is in [a] strong security position and we see no need for concern; but if they are indeed worried about [the] withdrawal [of the U.S.] nuclear [umbrella], which we do not anticipate, we would be glad to discuss this contingency. We must, at [the] same time, make clear that [the] spectrum of our relations and our ability to support ROK not only in nuclear power development but across the board will be impaired without Park's cooperation.[42]

The fourth option was much more confrontational, asking Park to back down without any corresponding concessions from the United States. What exactly the United States decided to do to force Park's surrender of his nuclear ambitions remains classified, but the actions must have had potentially serious political fallout. Of the four options, Sneider recommended the third but with a cautionary note that the United States should engage in a "truly serious and strict application of our multilateral approach to nuclear reprocessing. To be tough with [the South] Koreans while giving the appearance of lenience toward other countries . . . in [the] same [situation] would cause [the South] Koreans to conclude that [the United States] has serious doubts about relationship of trust, which underpins the alliance, and will probably cause permanent damage to [the] spirit of cooperation needed for assuring [South] Korean security."[43]

Thereafter, the United States began pressing Park to give up the nuclear reprocessing deal with France. In addition to Sneider, Philip Habib, a former U.S. ambassador to Seoul and then the assistant secretary of state, played a central role. On December 10, 1975, Sneider asked the State Department to communicate with the South Korean ambassador to the United States, Ham Pyŏng-ch'un, regarding the profoundly negative consequences South Korea would encounter if it continued the nuclear reprocessing effort.[44] Ham Pyŏng-ch'un was scheduled to meet with Park in a week to convey the message to Park and his staff at the Blue House. In a telegram to the secretary of the state, Sneider reported:

> Conversation with Prime Minister [Kim Chong-p'il] indicates that to be effective, our approach must emphasize adverse impact on our broader relationship with ROKG . . . if it persists in completing [the] French reprocessing deal. This point is reinforced by [the] initial negative reaction to [the] approach to [Prime Minister Kim Chong-p'il] which I received from Deputy [Prime Minis-

ter] Nam [Tŏk-u] this morning. Thus, in [our] approach to [Ham Pyŏng-ch'un], I believe we must make it indelibly clear that *far more than our nuclear support is at stake here, that if ROKG proceeds as it has indicated to date, [the] whole range of security and political relationships between [the United States] and ROK will be affected,* including potential for adverse congressional action on security assistance for [South] Korea. (Emphasis added)

When Sneider realized that his effort to persuade Park during the months of October and December 1975 had failed, he recommended that the State Department issue an ultimatum that included the possible reconsideration of South Korea's overall bilateral security and political relations. What Sneider meant to say when he warned that the "whole range of security and political relationships between the United States and South Korea will be affected" is unclear, but it is safe to infer that he thought the very alliance itself could be irreparably damaged in the event of Park's continuing pursuit of nuclear weapons development. The United States was in possession of a vast arsenal to directly reshape Park's preferences. The superpower could reduce or cancel its military aid program for the South Korean forces' modernization program, withdraw the remaining U.S. ground troops stationed in South Korea, or even rescind its pledge of providing a nuclear umbrella for the South Korean people.

On December 16, 1975, Vice Minister Yi Ch'ang-sŏk of the Ministry of Science and Technology and Director Yun Yong-gu of KAERI visited Ambassador Sneider under instructions from Prime Minister Kim Chong-p'il. The two South Korean officials asked Sneider what concessions the United States was willing to make in return for the cancellation of the nuclear reprocessing deal with France. A U.S. embassy telegram to the State Department reported that Vice Minister Yi Ch'ang-sŏk raised a series of questions:

(A) Would USG [the United States Government] be willing to provide technology and capital assistance to [South Korea's] commercial fuel fabrication project?; (B) [w]hen and where would [the U.S.-proposed] Asian regional nuclear fuel reprocessing center be established, what would it do, who would participate, what would be [the] ROK role, and would [the United States] train [South] Korean technicians in advance?; (C) [w]ould USG give support and training for [South Korea's] long-range nuclear power development program in design and manufacturing capability, reactor safety, [and] waste management technology, and would USG allow employment by South Korea of American experts required for these projects?; (D) [w]ill USG guarantee enrichment services to meet all future [South] Korean requirements and reprocessing services before commercial operation of [the U.S.-proposed] multinational regional reprocessing center?; and (E) [w]ill USG assist ROK with loans for purchase of U.S. natural uranium and nuclear power reactors?[45]

Pointing out that the issues raised by Yi Ch'ang-sŏk were not only technical but also political, Sneider responded that the real question was whether South Korea was prepared to jeopardize its vital partnership with the United States not only in nuclear and scientific areas but also in broader political and security areas.[46] Sneider could not be certain of the South Korean intentions at the meeting with Yi Ch'ang-sŏk and Yun Yong-gu. Only when he met with chief of staff Kim Chŏng-ryŏm to hear the same South Korean concerns was he assured of the South Korean intention not to take any further action on the purchase of the French reprocessing plant until the United States formally replied to the South Korean questions.

On January 5, 1976, Sneider sent a telegram to secretary of state Henry A. Kissinger for his immediate attention. Without spelling out what the State Department had previously instructed him, Sneider requested that it reconsider and modify its instructions because the "potential gains [were] not commensurate with risks involved and potential disruption to [the United States'] basic relationship [with South Korea]. Nor [were the] tactics [proposed previously] consistent with [the United States'] longer-term interests in [South] Korea." Sneider wrote that he was "convinced [that the U.S.] objective of discouraging nuclear proliferation by blocking [the construction of a] reprocessing facility in [South] Korea [could] be achieved without forcing confrontation and humiliating . . . loss of face and prestige for President Park."[47] Because a substantial part of this document remains classified, the exact nature of the telegram exchanges between the U.S. embassy in Seoul and the State Department from December 1975 to January 1976 cannot be determined. However, given Sneider's telegram of December 10, 1975, which called for an explicit warning to Park on the danger of conflict across the whole range of security and political relationships between the two countries and his other telegram of January 5, 1976, which urged the reconsideration of the "disruptive" U.S. policy toward South Korea, it is likely that the United States was driving Park into a corner in the months of December 1975 and January 1976.

At the end, Park agreed to hold off the nuclear deal with France, but at the same time, he continued to press for U.S. compensation in return for the upcoming cancellation of negotiation talks. By the time Sneider met Nam Tŏk-u on January 14, 1976, it was clear that a group of U.S. officials would fly in from Washington to hammer out the details of South Korea's cancellation of the French deal.[48] Although the United States had already secured French and Canadian assurance to abide by the IAEA safeguards and NPT regulations in their provision of reprocessing technologies to South Korea, it strove to cancel the French deal in order to weed out any possibility of South Korea's clandestine development of nuclear weapons and the risk of triggering a nuclear arms race in the region. At the same time, the superpower must have considered the need to protect commercial interests for the U.S. nuclear industry from the threat of French penetration into the South Korean market. Under mounting pressure from the United States, Park broke off the deal with France. Whether he had folded his nuclear ambitions as well was not certain. For the time being the United States had succeeded in putting the brakes on Park's nuclear program by getting him to stop the French reprocessing deal.[49]

Park's Nuclear Calculus

The cancellation of the French deal makes Park's intentions even more perplexing. At first glance, Park looked like he lacked a sound security motive in developing nuclear weapons. The United States, after all, had deployed tactical nuclear weapons, including Honest John nuclear missiles, as early as January 1958 in order to back up its security commitment to South Korea.[50] To be sure, Park perceived this security commitment as wavering because of the Guam Doctrine, despite the continued presence of tactical nuclear weapons in South Korea. Like many others there, Park feared that the United States could remove its nuclear umbrella as unilaterally and abruptly as it had decided to withdraw the Seventh Infantry Division in 1971. Similarly, there was no guarantee that the United States would not withdraw the remaining U.S. ground troops from South Korea. To intensify Park's fears even more, the change in U.S. military policy coincided with an alarming rise in North Korea's conventional military threat in the early 1970s.

However, these tides of change only explain that South Korea faced a security crisis, not that its options were restricted to nuclear development. Park could have concentrated his efforts on increasing South Korea's conventional military capabilities if his objective was simply to counterbalance North Korean conventional military capabilities. Moreover, Park had been actively engaging in a conventional military buildup under the Forces Improvement Plan (1974–1981), according to which South Korea was to outspend the North in defense expenditures by 1976.

To explain Park's strong commitment to the nuclear option, it is necessary to go beyond the macro analysis of aggregate military data and look at the geopolitical nature of South Korean defense in depth. As a retired army general, Park was aware of South Korea's strategic vulnerabilities that could not be reduced by simply adding to conventional military capabilities. Given the extraordinary proximity of Seoul, the capital city with a

third of the nation's population and economic concerns, to the demilitarized zone (about 30 miles), South Korea was extremely vulnerable to a
surprise attack. The North knew of this geopolitical weakness, locating its
heavy artillery forces along the demilitarized zone in order to put the
northern part of Seoul within range of artillery attack. Because any North
Korean surprise attack could devastate heavily populated Seoul within
hours, the South thought war would be disastrous even if it won the war.
Moreover, Park feared that given the geopolitical realities, the North
might choose to launch an attack to occupy only Seoul and then to negotiate an armistice with the United States, knowing that the superpower
would be extremely reluctant to engage in another war on the Asian continent after its Vietnam debacle. For Park, the key issue was political rather
than military. Distrusting U.S. intentions, Park thought that he had to opt
for nuclearization in order to make the North give up any thought of waging a total or a limited war. Certainly, as a geographically small country,
South Korea could not contemplate having a second-strike nuclear capability, which would argue against the nuclear option. However, within the
context of wavering U.S. security commitments, Park could easily have
thought that the possession of a primitive nuclear weapon or even the
mere ability to produce a nuclear weapon could deter the North from a
surprise attack in the fear of "an armed conflict escalating into a nuclear
war."[51] Park wanted to instill in North Korea the fear of nuclear annihila-
tion.[52]

What Park thought about the consequences of the nuclear proliferation
that his strategy was likely to trigger remains unknown. It is easy to imagine that South Korea's development of nuclear weapons would provoke
the North to do the same. This would be consistent with North Korea's
massive conventional military buildup, especially in its offensive capabilities, that was initiated in 1976.[53] The prospect that Japan would jump on
the nuclear bandwagon was also a possibility, throwing the entire Northeast Asian region into a nuclear arms race. The actions of South Korea, in
other words, would trigger the others' counteractions, which were likely
to worsen rather than ameliorate South Korea's security dilemmas. In contrast to the lack of information regarding Park's thinking about the threat
of nuclear proliferation and its impact on long-term South Korean security
interests, there is no ambiguity regarding U.S. preferences. The superpower looked at Park's nuclear program as directly threatening U.S. interests in East Asia. Whereas Park could have entertained the thought that a
totally nuclearized East Asia could be stable by instilling in the new nuclear states the fear of mutual destruction, which would make them more
cautious before venturing into a belligerent act,[54] the United States could

only conclude that nuclear proliferation damaged its security interests irreparably by reducing its influence over both allies and foes.

Domestic politics also mattered in South Korea's choice of nuclearization. The way it mattered, however, was different from the other theoretically more well known cases, where the nuclear option was decided jointly by the nuclear energy establishment of state-run laboratories and civilian institutions, military, and politicians frequently driven by their narrow parochial interests without consideration of the wider geopolitical consequences of the acquisition of nuclear weapons.[55] By contrast, in the case of South Korea, the decision to pursue nuclearization was made decisively by Park before as well as after the promulgation of the *yushin* constitution in 1972. Although the U.S. embassy in Seoul once entertained the idea that bureaucratic politics might be encouraging Park to pursue the construction of a nuclear reprocessing plant,[56] the available evidence shows that bureaucratic rivalries and politics did not figure in as a factor in South Korea's decision to make nuclear bombs. This lack of bureaucratic drivers, however, does not relegate domestic politics to a marginal place. On the contrary, the extreme level of concentration of power in Park constituted the enabling factor that allowed him to dominate the agenda setting, choose the high-risk nuclearization strategy, orchestrate the clandestine pursuit of nuclear weapon and missile development, and swiftly change gears toward negotiation, once the United States came down hard on the purchase of reprocessing technology.

At the same time, the vision of self-defense should not be underestimated in the explanation of Park's nuclear decision. Park's senior aides recollect that he was a man thoroughly humiliated by his unsuccessful pleas to the United States for the delay, if not the reversal, of partial U.S. ground troop withdrawal in the early 1970s. This humiliation came after Park's domestically risky decision to commit combat troops to fight the Vietnam War alongside the hard-pressed U.S. military forces, the combination of which made Park bitter toward his unreliable and, worse, "unfaithful" ally. He was also troubled by the U.S. refusal to militarily punish North Korea for its commando attack on the Blue House in January 1968 and its guerrilla infiltration into the Uljin-Samch'ŏk area in November of that year. By contrast, the eagerness of the United States to negotiate with the North over the release of the USS *Pueblo* crew confirmed Park's perception that the United States cared only for American lives and interests (see Chapter 14). This long list of what Park saw as U.S. betrayals shows that his talk of self-defense was not only rhetoric for domestic political consumption. On the contrary, Park wanted greater independence from the United States. As he saw it, having nuclear weapons constituted the quickest way to achieve independence as well as to ensure South Korea's national security in the absence of a firm U.S. commitment.

The regional danger of nuclear proliferation appears to have been considered in Park's nuclear calculus, but not in the way the United States calculated. Whereas the ally saw Park as the villain who could trigger a nuclear arms race in Northeast Asia, Park saw his move as a defensive action against Japan, which already had its own reprocessing plant in Tokai Mura. Although Park never openly expressed his thoughts on Japan's nuclear program, it was a source of both fear and envy for him.[57] When combined with Japan's missile capabilities, which gave it the possibility of developing its own independent formula for deterrence in another time,[58] South Korea could well have aimed at becoming another Japan, a nonnuclear power that could become a nuclear power in a rapid fashion if South Korean security was threatened even more.

However, alternatively, it is possible that Park never intended to develop nuclear weapons, and instead pursued his program only to gain bargaining leverage against the United States. If this was his intention, he badly miscalculated. The nuclear issue was too critical for the United States to accept the principle of nonproliferation as an object of negotiation. Moreover, given its hegemonic presence in South Korea's economic, political, and military institutions, the United States could subdue Park's nuclear ambition by threats of sanctions and force. In addition to the option of canceling the EX-IM Bank loan for South Korea's nuclear program, the United States had a massive power advantage stemming from South Korea's structural dependence on the United States for both prosperity and security. Park could not have lost sight of the fact that the United States imported over half of South Korea's exports, as well as underwriting its military security. Sneider's diplomatic efforts during the months of December 1975 and January 1976 aimed to make clear to Park that any further move on nuclearization could only jeopardize South Korea's future.

Sneider's decisive and unambiguous intervention brought about a moment of truth. Until then, no one in South Korea, including even Park, had talked about the nuclear program in anything other than the context of the peaceful uses of atomic energy, with the intention to hide the nuclear weapons program from the United States. Once the United States confirmed Park's nuclear intentions and began pressing hard for the abandonment of his plans, Park swiftly changed his strategy from one of silently acquiring fissile materials to that of negotiating for U.S. concessions. Park revealed his views on nuclear armament openly in his interview with Robert D. Novak of the *Washington Post* on June 12, 1975, in which he argued that South Korea had to go nuclear if the U.S. nuclear umbrella were to be removed. In an interview with the *Korea Herald* on June 26, 1975, science and technology minister Ch'oe Hyŏng-sŏp openly supported Park's statement by saying that South Korea had already acquired the capacity for developing nuclear weapons.

In many of the telegrams exchanged between the State Department and the U.S. embassy in Seoul during the critical mid-1970s, it was the telegram of December 11, 1974, that reported South Korea's possible intention to develop nuclear weapons for the first time. After that, in the telegram dated February 26, 1975, Sneider reported on his meeting with foreign minister Kim Tong-jo, where he demanded South Korea's early ratification of the NPT. In this he was joined by the Canadians, in the middle of negotiations with South Korea on the sale of CANDU technology.[59] By March 4, 1975, the State Department agreed with the U.S. embassy in Seoul that South Korea was proceeding with initial phases of nuclear weapons development.[60] In July of that same year, the United States implicitly revealed its knowledge of the South Korean nuclear weapons program by having Sneider meet with Ch'oe Hyŏng-sŏp, Kim Tong-jo, and Kim Chŏng-ryŏm in succession to argue against South Korea's construction of a reprocessing plant, but without directly mentioning the nuclear weapons program in order to avoid direct confrontation with Park.[61]

In August 1975, after Park's interview with Novak, U.S. defense secretary James R. Schlesinger, with Sneider, met with Park to warn of the negative impact of South Korea's nuclear weapons program on U.S.–South Korean relations. In the meeting, Park denied any intention to develop nuclear weapons and assured Schlesinger of his commitment to the NPT. Then Park went on to explain his interview with Novak as a hypothetical statement, explaining what South Korea would do in the event of the removal of U.S. nuclear deterrence. The corollary was that there would be no South Korean nuclear weapons if the United States continued its provision of a nuclear umbrella. If he had not announced the nuclear option in the event of the removal of U.S. nuclear deterrence, Park argued, it was certain that the morale of the South Korean people would suffer a blow in the uncertain post–Vietnam War era of U.S. military retrenchment.[62] Park's pursuit of the acquisition of reprocessing technology continued unabated till December 1975, when Sneider and Habib threatened Park with a dramatic change of the entire political, economic, and security relationship if South Korea did not stop its reprocessing program. This threat worked, and Park gave up his reprocessing program.

At the same time, Park thought he did gain a U.S. concession. Although the United States did not plan to remove its nuclear umbrella, Park thought this was a real possibility. Consequently, as Mitchell Reiss has explained,

South Korea was "sending the simple message to Washington that the price of South Korea's nuclear abstention was the retention of the American military presence in the country."[63] The distrust of U.S. military commitment continued, but through the nuclear conflict, Park came to be assured of at least the continued provision of the U.S. nuclear shield.

Park's Nuclear and Missile Programs after 1976

A group of U.S. officials visited Seoul on January 22, 1976, to discuss the cancellation of the French reprocessing deal. In return, the United States pledged its continued assistance to South Korea's nuclear development for the peaceful use of atomic energy. However, this was to be only a temporary halt in South Korea's nuclear weapons program. As Pak Kŭn-hye recalled, Park put the nuclear weapons program on hold when President Gerald R. Ford reconfirmed the U.S. security commitment to South Korea.[64] When Ford's successor, Jimmy Carter, aggressively pushed for the withdrawal of all U.S. ground troops from South Korea, Park renewed the nuclear weapons program.

The situation, however, had greatly changed since Park had initiated the nuclear program in early 1972. The situation in 1976 did not permit nuclear weapons development, because the IAEA safeguards had been strengthened and the NPT ratified during the 1974–1976 nuclear dispute. Moreover, U.S. surveillance of South Korean nuclear activities had become much tougher and tighter through the U.S. provision of nuclear training, technology, and facilities for the peaceful use of atomic energy during the mid-1970s. Under these circumstances, it was not possible for South Korea to reprocess the spent fuel from light-water reactors as well as heavy-water reactors. The only way to continue the nuclear weapons program was to accumulate nuclear technologies indirectly to become a potential nuclear developer after the model of Japan.[65] Instead of directly owning nuclear weapons, O Wŏn-ch'ŏl argued, South Korea needed to have the technology and the capability to develop the nuclear bomb whenever necessary, like Japan and Western European countries.[66]

KAERI's nuclear reprocessing program was renamed the Chemical Fuel Replacement Project. When Carter was elected president in 1976, Park ordered O Wŏn-ch'ŏl to pursue a full-scale development of the South Korean nuclear industry as quietly as possible.[67] In December 1976, the Korea Nuclear Fuel Development Institute (KNFDI) was established in Taedŏk to head the Chemical Fuel Replacement Project. The KNFDI's mission was to develop South Korean capabilities for nuclear fuel fabrication. At the same time, the KNFDI strove to acquire plutonium by reprocessing the spent fuel. In Park's eyes, his 1976 agreement with the United States concerned only the cancellation of the French reprocessing deal, not a South Korean renunciation of its right to develop reprocessing technology through its own efforts. Because the technology learned and acquired through non-military nuclear programs could turn into military technology, Park thought he could leave open the option of going nuclear, although he had agreed to live up to the NPT and cancelled the reprocessing deal with France.

Upon the establishment of the KNFDI in 1976, most members of the original special project team, including Vice Director Chu Chae-yang, were transferred from KAERI to KNFDI. Chu Chae-yang led the KNFDI as its president, making KNFDI more or less an expanded version of the KAERI special project team. By establishing KNFDI, South Korea wanted to acquire reprocessing technology indirectly through learning civilian nuclear technologies and acquiring nonmilitary nuclear equipment and facilities. No longer able to rely on either French or Canadian support, South Korea decided to develop its own indigenous research reactor to acquire the spent fuel for the production of weapons-grade plutonium. Despite many technological difficulties, the KNFDI scientists and engineers were able to complete the construction of a nuclear fuel fabrication facility by October 1978. Another research team, led by Kim Tong-hun at KAERI, succeeded in producing a detailed design of a research reactor in 1979. The United States kept a close watch on all of this. Robert Steller, a science attaché in the U.S. embassy in Seoul, better known locally as a CIA agent with special expertise in nuclear weapons, frequently visited KNFDI without giving prior notification of his visit.[68] However, because KNFDI's research project closely paralleled the development of South Korea's civilian nuclear energy industry, the United States could not come up with convincing evidence of military intentions in order to stop KNDFI's research activities.

It is wrong to dismiss Park's nuclear ambition as a personal fixation. Only a week after his presidential inauguration, Carter ordered the Defense Department to prepare a secret plan to remove all nuclear weapons from South Korea.[69] Upon strong opposition from the U.S. military establishment, Carter was unable to remove all strategic nuclear weapons. Such an action would have triggered the threat of nuclear proliferation. The episode demonstrates not only that Park's fear of abandonment was grounded on an objective situation of wavering U.S. security commitment, but also that Park's previous play of the nuclear card succeeded in restraining the isolationist tendencies of U.S. foreign policy in the post–Vietnam War era. While KNFDI kept busy learning nonmilitary nuclear technologies, the ADD continued to develop missiles—albeit under close U.S. surveillance. In September 1978, South Korea successfully tested the surface-to-surface missile named Paekkom (White Bear) on the west coast of the Korean Peninsula. However, because South Korea had accepted the U.S. demand to limit the missile range to 180 kilometers (112 miles) as a pre-condition of purchasing U.S. missile technology, the success came at the cost of tight military restrictions. Whereas the international Missile Technology Control Regime (MCTR) allowed the development of missiles with a range of 300 kilometers (187 miles) for military purposes, and up to 500 kilometers (311 miles) for research objectives, the bilateral U.S.–South Korean agreement allowed only for the development of missiles with the shorter range of 180 kilometers.

After Park's death in 1979, the entire missile program was downsized. With an eye to winning support for the new military regime inaugurated in 1980, Chun Doo-hwan put the ADD through a major organizational over-haul, dismissing over 800 ADD employees by 1982. As later argued by O Wŏn-ch'ŏl, Chun Doo-hwan's organizational restructuring profoundly damaged South Korea's capabilities for developing long-range missiles, while the North was to acquire the Taep'odong, with a striking range of over 6,000 kilometers (3,728 miles).[70]

THE 1970s constituted the most trying period for U.S.–South Korean re-lations since the Korean War ended in 1953. A wide range of political is-sues, from U.S. troop withdrawal to the Koreagate scandal, seriously ham-pered the bilateral relationship. To compound the already fragile situation, Park challenged the United States where it was most sensitive: nuclear weapons development.[71] For Park, however, the nuclear card ultimately entailed more costs than benefits. First, South Korea could not pursue the clandestine development of weapons indefinitely, given U.S. intelligence capabilities and South Korea's military integration into the U.S. armed forces. Second, because of the hegemonic presence of the United States in South Korea's economic, political, and military realms, Park had to ac-commodate U.S. pressure, once his nuclear weapons program was re-vealed. Third, the United States was not interested in exchanging Park's nuclear card with a U.S. concession on troop withdrawal, which Park wanted to prevent. At best, he secured U.S. financial and technological as-sistance, the acceptance of which entailed further restrictions on the South Korean nuclear program. Fourth, the accommodation of U.S. demands did not transform his political image in the United States to that of a reliable ally. On the contrary, that he had toyed with the nuclear card was enough to make him an unpredictable and even dangerous client who needed to be restrained in the eyes of U.S. policymakers.

PART V

COMPARATIVE PERSPECTIVE

Nation Rebuilders: Mustafa Kemal Atatürk, Lee Kuan Yew, Deng Xiaoping, and Park Chung Hee

Ezra F. Vogel

O F THE MANY outstanding national leaders in the twentieth century, only four who inherited countries in great turmoil modernized their nations by building new systems and initiating very rapid growth, causing transformations that continued after them: Atatürk in Turkey, Lee Kuan Yew in Singapore, Deng Xiaoping in mainland China, and Park Chung Hee in South Korea. Japan, Taiwan, and Hong Kong underwent great system changes and grew very swiftly, but in these societies the leverage to guide fundamental change came from powerful outsiders who controlled local developments: in Japan, from the Allied Occupation; in Hong Kong, from Great Britain's colonial government; and in Taiwan, from the newly arrived Kuomintang army. No country where fundamental changes were introduced from within and that achieved sustained rapid growth did so without having a strong authoritarian leader who guided those changes. Comparing these four leaders can highlight the common features of such transformative leadership in the twentieth century and clarify what features were unique to Park Chung Hee.[1]

After World War I, Atatürk took an ancient empire that was being dismembered, firmed up some of the remaining borders, and built new institutions to remake Turkey into a modern, Western-style and Western-oriented nation. He formed a provisional parliament in 1920 when he was thirty-nine, declared his nation independent in 1923, and continued to rule until his death in 1938.

Lee Kuan Yew helped hasten the British withdrawal from Singapore and then became prime minister of self-governing Singapore in 1959 at the age of thirty-five. When Malaysia cast Singapore out and forced it to be independent in 1965, Prime Minister Lee struggled to establish a new nation, guarantee its security, and transform it into a clean, orderly, attractive, and prosperous city with a broad social security net for its citizens. Lee continued as prime minister until 1990, when he passed the torch to Goh Chok Tong.

Deng took the world's most populous nation, devastated by the Great Leap Forward and the Cultural Revolution, with a system that was not working, and held it together while reorienting its basic direction through his policy of reform and opening. Under Deng's leadership, China began its transition from a poor backward country to one of the world's leading nations. He became the preeminent leader in 1978 at age seventy-three and even when he passed the chairmanship of the Chinese Communist Party to Jiang Zemin in 1989, Jiang continued to report to him through 1992.

Park Chung Hee took a poorly functioning chaotic democracy in a divided country, under acute threat from the North, and held it together. With military-style discipline and determination, he set South Korea on a path to become one of the world's leading middle-sized powers. Park was forty-three when he led the coup in 1961 and remained president until he was assassinated in 1979.

Background and Leadership Style

Atatürk, Lee, Deng, and Park all came from countries that had fallen far behind the industrialized West. The four men shared a deep patriotism, a passion to end the domination of Western powers they believed to be inimical to the interests of their people and to strengthen their country.

Turkey after World War I was a dispirited, defeated country in danger of being broken up by the Allied powers. Lee headed a tiny nation struggling to defend itself from communist insurgency without help from the outside. Deng became top leader in China after it was torn apart by the ten years of the Cultural Revolution. Park became head of a divided country, still not recovered from its civil war, under threat from an aggressive North Korea. These four leaders were convinced that given the conditions they faced, democratic structures and practices of advanced industrial Western societies could not hold their countries together, to say nothing of enabling their states to become powerful and prosperous.

All four men had been hardened by struggle and were comfortable with the hierarchy and discipline they knew in the conflicts they experienced before taking power. Atatürk and Park were professional soldiers, and Deng had spent twelve years in the army fighting first the Japanese and then the Kuomintang. Lee was not a soldier, but he had led his fellow Singaporeans in dangerous political struggles, first against the British and then against the communists fighting to take over his country. After these four leaders rose to power they did not hesitate to use the authoritarian systems they had known earlier to respond to the continuing threats they faced after taking power.

As much as they were repelled by the domination of their countries by the industrial powers, in their youth all four men had acquired a deep understanding of Western (in Park's case, Japanese) imperialists and were ready to take advantage of what they had learned from them in order to modernize. They could separate the fight against imperial powers from the imperial powers' knowledge and structures, which they were prepared to use in full measure.

The four had a sense of history, a keen understanding of the great powers and how those powers had affected weaker nations' security and development. Western countries had built up their institutions and modernized over a longer period of time, but these late industrializers, by government-led borrowing of technology and institutions, could modernize at a far faster pace than the earlier industrializing nations. None of the four leaders was an economist or a businessman, but each was ready to seek advice from and work with people, including foreigners, who knew how to make the economy function and grow.

They were all skilled in maintaining power. Their long tenure in office meant that they could consolidate the building of new institutions and witness the economic takeoff that they had launched. Two of the four, Atatürk and Park, died in office, but their legacy and the institutions they had built survived their period of rule. The success of all four in bringing order and then economic progress gained them enough support that the public could tolerate and in some cases even welcome their authoritarian leadership.

The four faced the same fundamental questions: How could they gain and keep power against possible rivals? How could they overcome the opposition of those with traditional thinking and those who felt their interests were not served by rapid modernization? How could they work with their core supporters and their staff to provide coherent effective programs? How could they provide for their nation's security and get the foreign cooperation they needed to help guarantee that security and gain assistance in achieving economic growth?

Because the details of Park's background and rule are developed in earlier chapters, here I concentrate primarily on the other three leaders to highlight how Park's background and approach differed.

Early Education: Local Roots
and Foreign Learning

Atatürk, born in 1881, grew up in Salonica, a city with a strong Islamic tradition that also had a large Jewish population. The port and, after 1888, the railway linked Salonica with Istanbul and European cities. Atatürk's family was well versed in the Koran and his mother saw that he had good training in the Islamic tradition, but his father, who died when Atatürk was eight, was a civil servant who wanted his son trained in modern affairs. New elite educational institutions had been introduced in the 1880s, and military institutions were given government support to import modern weapons and training needed to fight the advanced European countries. Germans helped provide the Turks with training, arms, and equipment. Atatürk attended a civil service preparatory school and then switched to a military preparatory school, followed by a military high school, where he was second in his class. He went on to the War College in Istanbul, where he graduated eighth in a class of seven hundred, and then to Staff College for its three-year course, completing his studies in 1902. Though familiar with traditional Islamic culture, he, like many of his classmates, became convinced that this culture impeded Turkey's adaptation to the modern world. He sought modern learning from Europe.

Atatürk's thirteen years of military training, including the highest training Turkey had to offer, gave him an excellent grounding in math, in which he especially excelled, and in science and technology. He also studied literature and political history. He took the initiative to get enough extra training in French to become fluent, and then through French, to acquire a broader knowledge of Western civilization. He was attracted to Western ideas of positivism and rationality. He socialized with secular patriotic fellow students and had acquired a passion for politics by the age of sixteen, when, during the Turkish-Greek War of 1897, he joined in demonstrations against the Greeks.

Lee Kuan Yew, born in 1923, grew up in Singapore, a more British and Chinese city than the rest of Malaya. The majority of youths of Chinese ancestry in Singapore went to Chinese-dialect schools, but Lee was in the significant minority, generally from wealthier families, who went to English-language schools. Lee went briefly to Chinese schools, but, having spoken English at home, spent six years in an English-language primary school. When he and fellow students in their last year of primary school took the examination for future study, he passed with the highest scores. Along with some 150 other top students in Singapore, Lee was accepted into Raffles Institution, the outstanding secondary school in Singapore. Raffles was modeled on English public schools and many teachers were English. Many graduates went off to the leading universities of England. Like other students in the British colonies, Lee studied English literature, the history of the British Empire, mathematics, and geography, but he decided he wanted to become a lawyer. In the Senior Cambridge University entrance examinations held in Singapore, Lee scored the best in all Malaya. In 1940, because of the war in Europe, Lee chose to remain in Singapore and attend Raffles College.

Immediately after the war, Lee went to England for further study. At Cambridge he concentrated in law but also acquired a strong background in history and comparative politics. Like many students in Britain from the colonies, he was influenced by Harold Laski and his socialist agenda, in which governments accepted responsibility for helping to provide housing, employment, social security, and medical care. While still in England, however, Lee came to realize that governments that accepted social responsibility without a secure competitive economic base were in trouble.

Cambridge provided excellent training in writing, public speaking, and reasoning. Lee took a special interest in Great Britain's empire. At the time, colonialism in South and Southeast Asia was already under siege. Lee, like many students from the colonies, took an active role in debates about independence struggles.

In China, leftists then classified their country as "semi-colonial," but Deng, born in 1904, grew up in a village in the southwest, remote from the coastal areas where colonialists were concentrated. At age five, he began attending a private school to study the Confucian classics, and two years later, he entered the public lower primary school in a nearby market town. The Qing dynasty had fallen shortly before he started, and the school was experimenting with new educational materials that included math, science, and business as well as history and literature. After four years there, he passed exams to enter a school equivalent to a junior high school, from which he graduated at fourteen. Along with about one percent of his age group, he passed the examination to the Guang'an County Middle School, the only such school in his county of some 200,000 people.[2] After scarcely a year there, Deng's father sent him to a school in Chongqing preparing students for a work-study program in France. In July 1920, after a year of study, Deng was the youngest of those who passed the written and oral examinations given by the French consulate. A month after graduation, at age sixteen, Deng and eighty-two other students from Sichuan left by boat for France.[3]

On the way, the boat stopped in Shanghai, Hong Kong, Vietnam, Singapore, and Sri Lanka, where Deng had a chance to observe the cruel, condescending way in which whites mistreated locals and rich local businessmen mistreated their workers. Later, when he learned what Marxists said about imperialism and capitalism, their words resonated with what he had seen.

Deng's funds to study in France proved inadequate, so that except for a few months studying French language and customs,[4] he received no training and had to settle for factory jobs with low pay and poor working and living conditions. His education in France came primarily from analyzing what he saw or experienced in Paris, Lyons, and other cities, and what he saw was rich capitalists exploiting the labor of poorly paid workers. Unlike Atatürk, Deng did not master French.

Park Chung Hee, unlike Deng who grew up in a landlord family and Lee and Atatürk who grew up in middle-class families, grew up in a poor tenant farm family and suffered as a child from malnutrition. Like the other three, however, Park had roots in traditional society yet also excelled in schools that provided modern Western training. He grew up in rural North Kyŏngsang Province, near the rail line between Pusan and Seoul that had recently been built by the Japanese. He was a top student at the Manchurian Military Academy in the Japanese puppet state of Manchukuo and while still a student was recognized as a person destined to rise to high positions.

In Atatürk's youth, foreign powers invaded Turkey, but his education was still directed by Turks. In Deng Xiaoping's youth, imperial powers had nibbled at the periphery of China, but until he went to France all his teachers were Chinese. Lee Kuan Yew grew up in schools controlled by Great Britain, but in his youth, the occupation by Britain was far less pervasive and far less humiliating than the massive Japanese presence in Korea, during which Koreans spoke only Japanese in schools, took Japanese names, and knew that any signs of Korean loyalty would be brutally punished.

Though thoroughly indoctrinated with the occupier's worldview in Japanese-run schools, Park felt a sense of national shame that he could not hold his head up as a Korean in his own country. He was sufficiently imbued with the Confucian respect for authority he learned as a child that throughout his life, he aimed to build a modern Confucian state whose authority would also be respected. He greatly admired the industrial modernization Japan had achieved through the Meiji Restoration. During his service in the Japanese-led Manchurian military, he had to keep his national identity as a Korean under control until, when he was twenty-eight,

Japan was defeated and he left the Japanese military. Because of his deep involvement with Japan's forces, Park, like many Koreans of his generation, had more difficulty defining his national identity than Atatürk, Lee, or Deng. Even though he later received great help from the United States militarily and economically, Park remained less comfortable with Westerners than with Japanese. He began working with the American military after 1945, and had more direct contact with Americans than Atatürk, Lee, or Deng. But because his elder brother, shot by rightists during the Taegu uprising of 1946, took part in leftist activities, Park was suspected of communist leanings and was alienated from the U.S. military.[5]

Young Adulthood: Anticolonialism and Breaking with the Colonial Powers

During the childhood of the four leaders, colonialism around the world was strong, but they came to power after its strength had peaked. The growing attacks on colonial powers with the rise of nationalism and the thirst of countries for independence gave them hope that the trend of history was on their side. China had never been fully colonized, but foreigners had enclaves along the coast. Turkey was colonized only in the years immediately after World War I, but foreign businesspeople had dominated the economy before that. Although Atatürk and Deng did not live in colonies, they came to share Lee and Park's passion against outside domination. All four fervently wanted to establish governments that served the interests of their people, not those of the outside powers. They all had confidence that they understood and served the needs of their country better than the outside powers and, given those needs, could rule more effectively than outsiders. They did not believe that the American vision of Western-style democracy was appropriate for their country, at least in their time.

In their youth their personal relations with individual colonialists were complex. All had been selected for advancement by representatives of imperial powers, who gave them opportunities because their talent had been recognized through examinations. They were all befriended by individual imperialists. And yet their observations of the injustice and suffering that their fellow countrymen endured at the hands of colonialists turned them into ardent nationalists. Their lives became totally consumed in the effort to build a strong independent nation.

Ironically, Atatürk, who fought European imperialism, was himself from a former empire, the Ottoman, which in the sixteenth century was one of the great powers in the world. But the Ottoman empire had begun to fall apart far earlier than the European empires which, with industrialization, were able to extend the life and the reach of imperialism. From the late nineteenth century until World War I, the Ottoman empire was under continuous strain as local areas within the empire demanded more autonomy and European powers expanded their influence into the remains of the empire.

Turkey, the remaining core of the old Ottoman empire, successfully defended itself against the Greeks in the thirty-day war of 1897, but just before World War I it lost most of its territory in the Balkans and North Africa. Turkey's effort to defend itself against the more powerful European powers by modernizing its army without a strong industrial base strained its financial resources, forcing it to go into debt to Europeans, mostly Germans, who lent it money. The Turkish investment in its military was not enough to stem the tide of the advancing European powers, and Turkey became known as the "sick man of Europe."

Atatürk, in his early twenties, had become aware that Turkey would never regain control over the Balkans or its North African territories, and he believed that Turkey should defend its core territorial base, where it would build a strong modern nation. In 1907 he cast his lot with other "Young Turks" in the CUP (Committee for Union and Progress Party). In 1908 the Young Turks seized power from Sultan Abdul Hamid II and took over the leadership of Turkey. But Atatürk, who was not given a high position by the Young Turk leaders, came to realize that the new power holders were merely replacing one group of leaders with another without making the institutional changes needed to strengthen the country. Atatürk was shocked and dismayed when he learned that Young Turk leaders, desperate to be on the good side of the winners in World War I, had allied with Germany. When the gamble failed, Turkey was confronted by the predatory Allied powers of Europe, which sent in occupation troops.

Lee Kuan Yew, before going to England to study, had enjoyed the benefits given to talented youth in Singapore, and was not a passionate anti-colonialist. His grandfather was an Anglophile and Lee attended English schools while some 90 percent of the children of Singapore's ethnic Chinese community attended Chinese schools. Lee later wrote that he first questioned whether the British had the ability to rule Singapore for the good of the local people when the Japanese captured Singapore in 1942. The Japanese conquest of Western colonies in Southeast Asia destroyed the myth that Western powers were invulnerable. Lee's doubts about colonialism grew stronger while he was in England, because he could see that the British elite he met were more concerned with advancing their own financial interests in the colonies than with benefiting the local population. He observed British who did not rent to non-Caucasians or welcome them on sports teams.[6]

Lee's anti-colonialism intensified after he returned to Singapore from England in 1950. He became increasingly upset at the concentration of power in the hands of British officials. He legally dropped "Harry" from his given name, "Harry Kuan Yew Lee," and thereafter used the name "Lee Kuan Yew." As a lawyer he took on clients disadvantaged under British rule. His experience defending postal workers and other union members and students reinforced his conviction that the government leaders were not dealing fairly with the local populace, that the government was vulnerable to well-organized legal protests, and that by giving legal advice, issuing carefully worded public statements, and taking part in political groups, he could contribute to independence for Singapore.[7] In November 1954, he and others formed the Political Action Party to show the rottenness of colonial rule and gather public support for ending it.[8]

Deng Xiaoping and his fellow Chinese who went to France had the confidence that came from being selected as a promising young elite, but in France they were poverty-stricken workers and identified with the downtrodden. They started study groups, in which fellow students reported on the Russian Revolution that had occurred three years before Deng arrived in France and on Marx's and Lenin's writings.

One year before Deng went to France, he had taken part as a fifteen-year-old in the explosive May 4, 1919, patriotic demonstrations in China. To Deng and his comrades in France, the rich exploitative capitalists and warlords in China were not capable of bringing order to their nation or looking out for the benefit of the common people. Like Atatürk, Deng came from an ancient civilization that was being dismembered and whose leadership was not up to the task of defending the country. A revolution along the lines of the Russian one seemed to Deng and others to be the only way to build a strong China that could improve the lives of ordinary people. In June 1922, only a year after the Communist Party was founded in China, Zhou Enlai and others in France helped to found a communist organization of youth in Europe. Deng Xiaoping joined the communist-led Youth League that year, and in June 1923 he went to Paris to become a professional worker in the league. He worked part time in factories to earn money for survival. In July 1924, one month before his twentieth birthday, Deng joined the Communist Party.[9]

In early 1925, after Deng joined other Chinese students in demonstrating against the French government's cooperation with the Chinese government, French police began searching for him. Deng escaped to Moscow and studied for a year at the newly established Sun Yat-Sen University there to train workers for the Communist International. Deng studied Soviet views on economics, history, the contemporary world, the theory and practice of the Russian Revolution, nationality and colonialism, and social development in China. He also took part in military training.

Although his experiences in France and Moscow radicalized Deng, he still felt China could learn a great deal from Western countries. Deng and others who became communists in France later became among the more cosmopolitan leaders of the Chinese Communist Party leadership. After returning to China some died in the revolutionary struggle, but many others, including Zhou Enlai, Li Fuchun, Nie Rongzhen, Li Weihan, Chen Yi, and Deng became revolutionary leaders and, after 1949, important officials.[10]

Park Chung Hee was one of the small number of talented Koreans admitted to the Manchurian Military Academy and later spent two years at the Japanese Military Academy in Zama. Like other Korean youth in the Manchurian (Manchukuo) army, Park served throughout World War II. As an officer under the Japanese military, Park had to assist in keeping control over Koreans, but he and his fellow Koreans in the Manchurian army were acutely aware that they lacked the full privileges and opportunities that Japanese of comparable ability were given. Nonetheless, the model of dedicated Japanese patriots in the Japanese army serving their emperor stayed with Park when he later sought to build a strong Korea.

In 1946 Park became a student in the second class of the Korea Military Academy. In the immediate period after World War II, before the sharp lines of the cold war were drawn, he cooperated with people who were communists. For this he was condemned to death, saved only by former superiors who knew him well. Before the Korean War began, however, he had cast his lot with the anticommunists. During the war, he served as an official in military intelligence and was considered an outstanding young officer. But like other soldiers of his age who had served in the Manchukuo army, Park lacked the unblemished patriotic credentials of the other three leaders considered in this chapter who fought for independence in their countries and of Koreans young enough to have escaped service under the Japanese. Many Koreans who suffered under Japanese colonialism found it difficult to give Park and his generation who cooperated with the Japanese the undivided respect accorded to those with a purer patriotic history.

Rise to Power

Long before they rose to power, all four leaders began considering how to rebuild their countries. They had sufficient confidence in their own ability that they were prepared at the appropriate time to break with superiors who held different views. Toughened through conflict, they did not shy away from confrontation, but they were shrewd enough not to take on battles without purpose or prospects for success. They were ambitious, with no hesitation about taking leadership roles, but power was to be used for a cause, to strengthen their country, firm up its borders, and enrich their people.

Atatürk rose to prominence through his heroism and success as a military leader. In 1915 he distinguished himself as one of the most outstanding front-line commanders in the defense of the Gallipoli peninsula, where he played a major role in stopping the French and British troops from storming the peninsula and marching on to Istanbul. At the peak of the fighting, with a fever, he heroically led his troops for four days with virtually no sleep to stop the advance. In 1917–1918 on the Caucasus front, Atatürk again distinguished himself in leading troops into battle, becoming a national hero. Through careful study of enemy strategy he was unusually successful in anticipating what the other side might do. In a crunch, if his superiors asked him to move in ways not in keeping with his analysis, he would disobey orders so he could defeat the enemy. His intensity and determination helped inspire his troops, who were willing to engage in pitched battles even when facing almost certain death, sometimes without adequate ammunition or supplies.

After the loss in World War I, the senior leaders of the CUP were discredited both for having allied with Germany and for being ready to sign a humiliating treaty that would have divided Turkey among the victors. Atatürk did not rank high enough in the CUP to take part in the decision to ally with Germany, and he was convinced from the beginning that it was a mistake. After the Germans lost, he was distraught that the CUP leaders and the sultan wanted to accept the terms dictated by the victorious Allies.

Long interested in political issues, Atatürk in 1919, as a highly regarded military hero, split with the capitulationist sultan and emerged as the leader of high-level military officers determined to maintain an independent Turkey. Before taking the bold step of splitting with the sultan, Atatürk secretly recruited key military commanders to his cause without first announcing that he intended to get rid of the sultan. Taking advantage of people's fury over the Allied occupation, over incidents like the Greek military's killing of several hundred Turks in Smyrna, and over the Allied powers' plans to dominate Istanbul, he gained popular support for his aim of driving out the foreigners. In 1919 after issuing a Declaration of Independence, he formed his own Nationalist Congress, and in April 1920 called a provisional parliament, the Grand National Assembly, to reject the victors' demands and fight for national independence. Military commanders, troops, and ordinary citizens rallied to his cause.

As massive Greek forces, supported by British, Italian, and French troops, marched into Turkey, Atatürk led his forces in resisting them. With Atatürk as commander in chief, the Turkish side fought heroically, driving out the Greeks and attacking the invading armies of Italy, Britain, and France until they decided it was not worth it to continue their occupation. Troops under Atatürk also forcefully pushed the Armenians back from territories that had once belonged to Turkey and reestablished an earlier border. Atatürk's independent government became the government of Turkey.

With widespread popular support for maintaining Turkey's independence, Atatürk in 1922 abolished the sultanate. He calculated that trying to abolish the caliphate at the same time would stir up too much opposition, so he used religious supporters in his struggle against the sultan and waited several years before taking on the caliph and religious officials.

On November 20, 1922, Turkey and the Allied powers began to negotiate a peace treaty in Lausanne. Atatürk sent his former chief of staff, Ismet Pasha, who turned out to be a brilliant and stubborn negotiator. Unlike in China, where the leaders were determined to claim the territory the country had possessed at its peak, including Tibet, Taiwan, and islands along the coast, Atatürk accepted the reality that Turkey no longer had the ability to maintain all the territory of the former Ottoman empire such as the Balkans and the north African territories. But Atatürk insisted that Turkey should include Istanbul, Thrace, and other areas the Allies had intended to occupy immediately after their victory in World War I. Through persistence in the Lausanne discussions, Turkey was able to get a favorable treaty, signed on July 24, 1923, and in early October the Allied troops left Constantinople. This success enabled Turkey to become the first of the vanquished Central powers to sign a treaty with the Allied powers and emerge as an independent nation. A few months later, on October 29, 1923, Atatürk, with widespread popular support, proclaimed the Turkish Republic with himself as president.

Lee Kuan Yew rose to power in a series of political campaigns and elections that began with the formation of the Political Action Party (PAP) in 1954. In 1959, when he was first elected prime minister, Singapore was part of a British colony, separated from the rest of Malaya by a causeway. In 1963 when Malaysia achieved independence from Britain, Singapore became part of independent Malaysia. When Malaysia included Singapore, the population was fairly evenly divided between Malays and ethnic Chinese. But in 1965 Malay leaders, fearing that the ethnic Chinese who constituted 75 percent of the Singapore population might collaborate with the ethnic Chinese minority elsewhere in Malaysia to overwhelm the Malays, expelled Singapore, giving the Malays a clear majority. Lee and his allies, bitterly disappointed by the expulsion, began to build Singapore as an independent country.

Lee, observing the momentum of history against imperialism, was optimistic that Britain would recognize that it could not perpetuate its rule in Singapore and that he could negotiate the terms of the turnover of power with wise and civil British officials who accepted the inevitable. His assessment proved correct.

In Singapore, unlike the other three countries, Lee and his allies could deal with the British through discussions and gain power through legal means, including voting. When the leaders formed the PAP in 1954, they knew they did not yet have the votes to win an election. Instead Lewe and his team took a long-term perspective, aiming to show the rottenness of the current system while building up popular support to prepare for a later election that was eventually set for 1959. PAP leaders realized that to win an election they had to appeal to the 75 percent of the population who were ethnic Chinese, many of whom had communist leanings. Since the Communist Party was strong and effectively organized, PAP leaders determined that they would need communist support if they were to win elections. In 1959, while Singapore was still under British rule, Lee Kuan Yew sought and received some communist help in his first election as prime minister of Singapore. By the September 1963 general election, however, Lee, after building up a stronger degree of support, split with the communists and his PAP still won a decisive victory.

In December 1978 when top Chinese Communist Party leaders chose Deng, then seventy-three, to be their preeminent leader, it is hard to imagine how he could have been better prepared for the position. He had been a military leader for twelve years, including being front secretary for some 500,000 troops in the critical campaign of the civil war, at Huai Hai. He had been the top official in Southwest China, serving as first party secretary from 1949 to 1952, with overall responsibility for establishing order in a region of some 100 million people. He had been finance minister in 1953–1954, had played a key role in the quarrel with the Soviet Union in the early 1960s, and had represented China in the first appearance of a high-level Chinese leader at the UN. For years he had joined Mao or Zhou Enlai in seeing foreign leaders and after Zhou became ill in 1973 was the key leader who met foreign visitors. He was general secretary of the Communist Party from 1956 to 1966, in charge of the front line of Party activities, covering all major areas of political and economic activity throughout the country. He had been a favorite of Mao's from 1931, but after 1949 his experience was not in making revolution but in building the Party and the country. He had proved himself as a strategist, as a communicator of Party policy, and as a leader who could command respect and get people to work together.

In his last year of life, Mao became convinced that Deng's thinking differed from his own and chose Hua Guofeng to be his successor. But in the April 5, 1976, demonstrations in Tiananmen Square, the public made it clear not only that they were mourning Zhou Enlai's death but that they supported Deng, who had provided such outstanding leadership while he was de facto premier in 1975. The decision to elevate Deng to the top position in December 1978 was made by a small group of high Party officials, and their decision in turn was based on their familiarity with Deng's ability and experience, their conviction that he understood China's problems, and their confidence that he would exert forceful leadership to bring about fundamental policy change. Hua Guofeng had been only a provincial Party secretary, with little experience in policy circles in Beijing and no experience in foreign affairs. He was beholden entirely to Mao and had announced his determination to be faithful to all of Mao's directives. The top Party leaders, dismayed at the errors of Mao in the Great Leap Forward and the Cultural Revolution and convinced that continuing to follow Mao's directives would be disastrous when the country needed fundamental change, passed the baton to Deng. Not being Mao's chosen successor, Deng had the leeway to distance himself from Mao's policies.

Park, unlike the other three leaders, had not built up a large public following before he took over the top office. Unlike the other three, he lacked experience in communicating with various groups and the general public to gain their support. He rose to power by building support among a small group of military officers, forging a secret plot and staging a coup. A few weeks after the coup, when Park emerged as the supreme leader, he was not well known to the public. He was not sociable by nature, and he took office without developing the skills to persuade the public to support him and his cause.

Atatürk had legitimacy to rule because of his military heroism and proven dedication to the country. Lee had legitimacy because of his election. Deng had legitimacy because of his long and dedicated service in high positions and his selection by a small group of Party elders. Park had no legitimacy aside from raw power. Whatever resistance the public may have had to authoritarian rule and to some decisions the leaders made, their ability to unify their country, provide security against the outside, and maintain stability helped provide an acceptance of their rule that would later be further strengthened by the benefits of economic growth.

Approach to Rule: Politics and Security

All four men mastered what it took to gain and retain power. They understood power instinctively and were sensitive to threats to their power. But to them, power was pursued not for its own sake, but as a means to accomplish something bigger. They shared similar goals: protecting the independence of their native land from attacks, enriching their people, strengthening their nation, and gaining the respect of other countries. They were single-minded and unwavering in the pursuit of these goals. "Greatness," Atatürk once said, "consists in deciding only what is necessary for the welfare of the country and making straight for the goal."[11] The other three would not have disagreed.

No issue was more basic than defending their nations' borders from outside threats and for all four this was crucial. Atatürk was concerned about the invasions of the British, the French, the Greeks, and the Russians. Lee was concerned about the communists in Singapore and nearby areas and about his aggressive neighbors, Indonesia and Malaysia. When Deng came to power in 1978, he was aware that Vietnam and the Soviets, who had just signed a new treaty, had designs on controlling Southeast Asia and encircling China. It was only nine years after the Sino-Soviet clash on their border, and the Soviets still had an estimated one million troops stationed nearby. Vietnam, confident following its defeat of the United States three years earlier, was ready to cooperate with the Soviets against the Chinese.

Park was aware when he came to power that the American commitment to South Korea could not be taken for granted. To retain U.S. support he sent large numbers of his best troops to fight in Vietnam. When U.S. officials took strong stands on issues such as human rights, he could not ignore those views. At the same time, especially after Jimmy Carter became president, Park also had to make contingency plans for what to do if U.S. troops withdrew.

From his observations in Manchuria, where the Japanese had worked to build an industrial base to serve their military needs, and from his analysis of how the United States defeated Japan, Park was convinced that a nation's industrial base was crucial in determining the outcome of a war. He knew that in the 1960s and early 1970s North Korea had a stronger industrial base than South Korea because of the Japanese concentration of industry in the North during the Japanese occupation and because of further industrial assistance from the Soviet Union and China.

He was also aware of how deeply committed the North was to uniting the peninsula on its terms, how daring the North was prepared to be, and how willing the North was to use any means to achieve victory over the South. Park's fears were genuine, but he also used fear of the North as a rationale for tightening authoritarian controls in the South. Park worked closely with a small group of staff members and went all out to build a strong military and to hasten the establishment of industry.

Although these four leaders did not have detailed plans when they came to power, they did have a sense of direction for what they wanted to achieve. They were not ideologues and were pragmatic and smart enough to keep learning in an effort to get results. The nature of their rule evolved, but by the time Atatürk, Lee, Deng, and Park had been in power for nineteen, thirty-one, fourteen, and eighteen years respectively, a new approach to rule had taken root and continued as the basis for the governments that followed.

Atatürk's overall goals were presented as the "Six Arrows": republicanism, secularism, nationalism, populism, statism, and reformism. Atatürk wanted to establish a homogeneous Turkish nation-state with modern Western-style political institutions, including a parliament, elections, and parties. Religion, the spiritual force that had underpinned political rule for so long, was eliminated from political activity. Education was secular. Although he felt he needed support from some religious groups when he was abolishing the sultanate in November 1922, by early 1924, after he had proclaimed the Turkish Republic with himself as president, he felt confident enough to abolish the religious side of traditional rule, the caliphate.

Atatürk introduced a totally secular modern culture. Religious ministries were abolished, separate religious schools closed, education secularized, and religious courts eliminated. He adopted a new judicial system, with codes for commercial, maritime, and criminal law based on the Swiss civil code and Italian penal code. In 1928 Atatürk removed Islam as a formal religion from the constitution. He introduced the Gregorian calendar, Western numerals, international weights and measures, the use of surnames, and made the weekly holiday the Western Sunday rather than the Islamic Friday. In 1928 he introduced the Latin alphabet to replace the Arabic-Persian writing script. Women were given the right to vote and enter public service. He toured the country to persuade people to make the changes.

Atatürk's style in dealing with big controversial issues was the blitzkrieg, suddenly taking bold action and presenting others with a fait accompli so they had little choice but to accept the results. To establish the republic, he plunged the nation into a ministerial crisis and then he rammed through the constitution. To minimize opposition, he took up one issue at a time, concentrated on getting it through and cooperating with one group without revealing that he intended to attack that group at a later date.

Lee Kuan Yew, later reflecting on his perspective when he became prime minister in 1959, said, "I had begun to realize the weight of the problems that we were to face—unemployment; high expectations of rapid results; communist unrest; more subversion in the unions, schools and associations; more strikes, fewer investments; more unemployment; more trouble."[12] When Singapore was part of Malaysia, it was under no serious security threat, but when separated in 1965, Singaporean leaders worried about their vulnerability to attacks by Malaysia and Indonesia as well as by communists. When Malaysia cast Singapore aside, Lee and many of his associates in the PAP were dismayed, frightened, and depressed.

To cope with Singapore's security problems, Lee built up a small modern military force and strong internal security forces. He instituted compulsory military service and required veterans to remain in the reserves for several years after their discharge from active duty, thus giving Singapore the capacity to mobilize large numbers in an emergency. Singapore also acquired airplanes, tanks, and other military equipment. Lee benefited from cooperation with another small country that had learned how to defend itself from the threats of neighbors, Israel. At the time of independence, 80 percent of Singapore's military forces were Malay. Lee feared that if there were race riots between Malays and Chinese, it was questionable whether the troops would defend ethnic Chinese. He therefore increased the proportion of forces that were ethnically Chinese or Indian.

Lee realized that Singapore, once it was on its own, was too small to defend itself against a major threat from the outside. Lee was able to persuade the British to postpone their navy's plans to pull out of Singapore. He realized that with threats from communists and from Islamic Malaysia or Indonesia, both hostile to Singapore, only the United States could help. In anticipation of the departure of the British navy, Lee concentrated on building closer relations with the United States. To deepen his ties, he spent several months in the United States, where he consulted with academics, business leaders, and political leaders to better understand their thinking and increase his support base.

Lee's approach was first to think through issues logically, next to get other leaders on board, and then to sell his plan to the public with tightly reasoned and highly articulate personal presentations. Lee considered it important to maintain his authority and was ready, when challenged in public debate, to push his opponents to the wall, embarrassing them by the weight of forceful arguments.

Deng's slogan for his new era was "reform and opening." Deng was acutely aware that China had fallen decades behind and that the country needed to import technology, machinery, investment, and management skills from Japan and the West. In his visits to Japan in October 1978 and to the United States in January 1979, he proved very popular, paving the way for substantial help from the two countries most able to assist China's development. He recognized that opening the doors to foreign investment would pose problems for Chinese companies that could not compete and that foreign ideas about freedom would create demands that he did not believe China could grant and still stay together, but he never wavered in his commitment to remain open and face those risks.

Deng was convinced that the Soviet Union was in deep trouble because it was exhausting itself spending on national defense. He was determined that China work to create a peaceful environment so that it could attract foreign investment, promote trade, and keep military expenses low.

Deng realized that many "leftists" in China were uncomfortable with the changes needed to achieve a dynamic economy. He used the goal of "four modernizations" (industry, agriculture, science-technology, and national defense) to drive reforms. China was big enough that it could try experiments in various localities. If they didn't work, drop them. If they worked, apply them on a large scale. But Deng, unlike Soviet Union leaders, did not want to open markets suddenly with a "big bang." China had such massive underemployment that it needed to hold on to its state industry sector to provide jobs. New growth was initially to come from outside the state system.

Deng concentrated on big strategic decisions. He was known for distinguishing important issues that demanded his attention from less important issues that he could leave to underlings. He avoided personally going out on a limb to support controversial policies, but gave leeway to those beneath him who were prepared to do so. Once enough positive feedback had been gathered for a given experiment, he declared his personal support.

Deng spent mornings by himself reading reports and thinking through issues. He commonly met with other officials in the afternoon or evening. Once he had determined key strategies, he presented them to the public in a clear, simple, and straightforward way. Deng, who like other Party leaders sought to understand what had gone wrong in the Cultural Revolution, concluded that the problem was not just Mao but the system, which had concentrated too much power in one individual. To provide predictability and ensure that policies would be at least vetted by key officials, Deng, unlike Mao, held regular meetings of the central committee and Party congress. While Lee, in his small city-state, could manage things by personal conversations and speeches, Deng had to present his views to a massive country that when he took power had virtually no television system. Deng's style in public was aloof and formal, but in private conversations, he could be disarmingly direct and humorous, while occasionally inserting colorful popular aphorisms.

Park Chung Hee, unlike Atatürk and Deng, was not constrained by a strong traditional society, because South Korean society had been torn apart by the Japanese occupation and the Korean War. His instinct was to use a hierarchical disciplined system, and he placed former military officers who accepted this style in key positions. He was constrained by the democratic system, including a National Assembly and an electoral system, introduced since the foundation of the Republic in 1948 but still not yet firmly rooted by his immediate predecessor, Chang Myŏn. Park had to revive and keep the National Assembly for fear of losing the support of the United States, but since the National Assembly was weak, he could manipulate it. In the 1970s when he decided to remain in office beyond term limits and squeezed the society for all possible funds for investment in the development of heavy and chemical industries, he rammed through the *yushin* constitution that enabled him to run roughshod over the National Assembly.

Park pushed others as he pushed himself, to the limits of human endurance. Lacking communication skills to persuade or at least mollify the opposition, he relied on more repressive means, especially the Korea Central Intelligence Agency. He dealt harshly with opponents. When opposition grew after the launching of *yushin* in 1972, he responded in the way he knew, by tightening controls. Deng suppressed opposition when he judged that public demonstrations threatened stability, but Park suppressed opposition almost continuously.

Approach to Rule: Economic Growth

All four leaders linked their countries to international markets. The stability and openness that all four achieved enabled them, with proper incentives, to attract foreign investment. They all made good use of their initial comparative advantage, low cost labor, to produce goods for export to earn foreign exchange to buy more technology from abroad and to enrich their people. Only Deng inherited a socialist economy and, like the others, soon accepted a market economy.

Atatürk aimed first to make political and social changes and then, de-

spite his lack of interest in economic issues, to modernize the economy. After stabilizing the country, he pursued a relatively open liberal market
economy and attracted foreign investment. With investment in industry
and infrastructure, the country began to grow rapidly until the growth
spurt was slowed down by the global depression in 1929–1931. From the
time the depression broke out, the government made greater efforts to promote the economy by planning and financing industries, promoting sectors
like textiles, iron and steel, glass, and ceramics. Between 1933 and 1939
the GNP growth rate was 9.1 percent, one of the highest in the world. By
1939 Turkey was able to produce not only most of its consumer goods but
most of the basic capital goods that it needed.

Lee Kuan Yew, to build up industry, relied on multinational industrial
companies. With a tiny population, then less than three million, Singapore
could not build up its industry through sales to the local market, so it
made no sense to protect the home market as Japan and Korea did. Local
merchants, overwhelmingly of Chinese ethnic background, were shrewd
bargainers and traders but they had little experience in manufacturing.
Even if they could manufacture goods, they lacked the global networks to
provide outlets for their production. Singaporean leaders sought large, stable multinational companies that would be committed to Singapore for a
long period of time, and in order to attract such companies they gave very
favorable conditions. Singapore built an industrial zone in Jurong to provide appropriate facilities. It succeeded in attracting well-known international corporations. Singapore has continued this strategy, training local
people and upgrading its industries as they moved into electronics and bio-
technology.

Although all four of the countries encouraged their students to learn foreign languages, only Singapore went so far as to make English the standard language for public schools. This made it easier for Singaporeans to
benefit from international educational institutions and to take part in international commercial and political discussions.

Lee Kuan Yew and his team had a socialist vision of providing welfare
benefits. They also wanted to give Singaporeans a stake in the system, and
they concluded that nothing would do more to achieve this than home
ownership. In February 1960, only a few months after taking office, Lee
established the Housing and Development Board, initially designed to provide low-income housing for workers. Under the British colonial government, to provide modest pensions, a Central Provident Fund had been established, with matched contributions from the worker and his employer.
Lee and his team expanded the percentage going into the fund so it would
be enough to allow an employee to use the accrued fund to make a down
payment on an apartment. The government built the apartment buildings

and sold the apartments to the workers. In new buildings, apartment size and quality were gradually upgraded and people could sell their older apartments and purchase new ones. In 1996, of the 725,000 flats under the Housing Board, over 90 percent were owned by the occupants.[13] In addition there was a private housing market, primarily for people who were not citizens.

The Singapore government used housing to reduce ethnic separatism, mixing ethnic groups in a given apartment building, and for family policy, giving discounts to younger couples who bought an apartment near where their parents' apartment was located. Later Singapore began allowing families to use money accumulated in the Provident Fund to pay for medical care as well as for housing and retirement benefits. After Deng Xiaoping became the preeminent leader of China in December 1978, he first allowed Chen Yun, the most respected official in managing the economy, to undertake retrenchment to ensure that there was enough grain, that the economy was not overheated, that there was enough foreign currency to repay foreign loans and purchases, and that the budget imbalance did not get out of hand. Deng was impatient to speed up growth, but having experienced the Great Leap Forward when haste made waste, he initially yielded to Chen Yun.

In Deng's efforts to get enough grain, he allowed experiments in "contracting responsibility down to the household," whereby the community owned the land but let the individual farm family be responsible for tilling it. The experiment, which began first in poor mountainous villages to ease the opposition of leftists who feared the socialist system was being replaced by capitalism, was an immediate success and grain production shot up. In addition the population, earlier required to stay in a given locality, was given greater flexibility in moving to towns and later to cities.

Deng not only allowed but welcomed foreign investment. Foreign companies built factories and brought in technology, machinery, and management skills. China initially encouraged a "processing industry," in which foreign companies supplied the materials, machinery, and product design while Chinese supplied the labor and passed the products on to outsiders.

Deng allowed the formation of small household enterprises, but initially, to avoid becoming capitalist, they could not employ more than seven workers. Gradually they were allowed to expand. Rural towns and villages, were allowed to form "collective enterprises" that had far more flexibility than state enterprises that were constrained by planning, but once the collective enterprises grew and could provide employment opportunities, pressure was placed on state enterprises to become more efficient and competitive or else go out of business. Planning increasingly gave way to markets. Deng, trying to keep down leftist opposition, allowed the new overall economic system to be called "The Early Stage of Socialism with Chinese Characteristics."

Park drew heavily on Japanese practices. He imported technology, management systems, and organizational structure from Japan. Once a local industry was capable of producing certain goods, he protected that industry from foreign imports. Once low-wage, labor-intensive industries were established, Park began to introduce higher technology and heavy industry. But compared with Japan, where ministries played a major role in shaping plans, Park centralized decisions more in his own hands.

Compared with the other three leaders, Park personally played a more proactive role in promoting industry. Worried about possible Japanese domination of Korea's industry, Park kept tighter control over foreign investment. He identified able business executives like Chŏng Chu-yŏng (Hyundai) and Yi Pyŏng-ch'ol (Samsung), who had management abilities, the same all-out dedication Park did, and Japanese connections to get technology. He helped provide the capital needed so that after they proved themselves in one sector, they could expand into another. Where possible, he supported competing companies in a given sector to heighten their performance.

Park suppressed wages and used police to subdue the labor movement so that Korean goods would remain competitive. The number of hours that laborers worked was the highest in the world. Especially in the 1970s, the whole country was straining to make its economic breakthrough, which came with enormous speed.

Park, worried about U.S. troop withdrawal and competition from the North, pushed the development of heavy and chemical industries far harder and faster than Japan or any other country pushed industrialization at a comparable stage of development. This effort constrained the availability of finance and resources, leading to debt, inflation, and political turmoil. Amid this turmoil, Park was assassinated by his childhood friend and intelligence chief Kim Chae-gyu, who said at his trial that he feared more massive crackdowns like those Park had carried out in Pusan and Masan. Despite the enormous social costs, the plans met their targets and after Park's successors made needed corrections to the country's macroeconomic policy, heavy industry development continued to take off.

The Inner Circle, Bureaucrats, and Intellectuals

In all four cases the strong leader required a small group of dedicated fellow leaders who were absolutely committed to the same goals and could be counted on to make an extra effort to overcome difficulties they confronted as they engineered fundamental changes in society. Although some in the inner circles split off on certain occasions, a core of trusted allies remained. Before coming to power, each of the four leaders had a deeply committed inner circle that had bonded and developed common goals so they could move quickly and firmly as they confronted myriad issues after they came to power. They also needed to link to a broader group of knowledgeable specialists to deal with complex issues related to the economy, science and technology, and foreign relations.

Atatürk's core team consisted of military officers who had been together for many years, but they were a highly select elite who had received not only modern military training but a broad background in European culture and history. They had bonded through life-and-death struggles in which many of their comrades had fallen. When Allied powers invaded, Atatürk assembled a small core of military officers he could count on, ostensibly to round up weapons to pass on to the victorious Allies, but in fact secretly committed to working with Atatürk to establish their own government. He took this small group with him to Anatolia, where they worked together to build a base before declaring their independence. Atatürk used his time in Anatolia to forge a clearer understanding of not only a common core of ideas but how to respond to the issues he and his officers would face once in power.

Lee Kuan Yew, through Raffles Institution and Raffles College, through meetings with Singaporeans studying in England and through his work as a lawyer defending labor union leaders and other leftists, came to know many of the talented people of his age in Singapore whose views were similar to his. Lee valued academic excellence. The inner core backing him had performed well on their school and university exams. The PAP brought together like-minded people who fought together in the struggle for independence and then in the struggle against the communists. A high proportion of this group was ethnic Chinese. The inner circle also contained a small group of Indian ethnics and Caucasians, but virtually no Malay ethnics. In the small city of Singapore their members had a broad base of common experience and personal connections. Theirs was the most cosmopolitan of the four circles of leaders, and Singapore was small enough to ensure they could meet and reach common understandings.

In China the leaders who worked closely with Deng were all longtime members of the Communist Party, but since China was so huge they came from different regions and social class backgrounds and therefore had very different perspectives. Even those in Deng's top circles who had known each other for decades represented widely different kinds of units, each with their own subcultures. Although the politburo and the Party secretariat were small and could make decisions, it was difficult for them to form a small, intimate, closed group. The Party had over the years developed strong methods for preventing factionalism, making it risky for any small group, even one that included Deng, to have full and frank discussions apart from others. Although discussions had implications for personal relations, issues were discussed in a formal way in terms of common principles so that if discussions were reported to a wider group, they could be defended.

But Party discipline ensured that those below Deng could be counted on to follow agreements made at higher Party levels. Deng was concerned with achieving overall goals and was not constrained by personal loyalties. When he considered it necessary for the sake of Party goals, Deng removed in turn the three people he worked with most closely in the reform period: Hu Yaobang, Zhao Ziyang, and Yang Shangkun. There were no permanent friendships, only various levels of cooperation between comrades serving the same Party.

Like Atatürk, Park had a core group of former soldiers he was close to, but the bond came not from fighting together but from the intense loyalties of certain classmates at the Korea Military Academy that was established after World War II. Park relied particularly on those in his class and several who were in the eighth and eleventh classes. The South Korea Military Academy did not provide the broad cultural training that Turkish military academies had, but since it drew on the American military's modern equipment, academy students learned how to manage modern technology that had not yet spread to other parts of Korean society. Older academy students had received Japanese education in school and younger ones learned about the world through the U.S. army. Academy students were powerfully nationalistic and moved by the commitment they had observed earlier among young Japanese officers.

Park's core group was the least cosmopolitan of the four, and Park himself lacked experience negotiating with politicians and making appeals to the broader public. After taking power in 1961, Park assigned graduates from the military academy to serve in other sectors, including foreign policy, the bureaucracy, construction, and economic affairs. Since the academy had recruited some of the brightest people in the society, many of them, though lacking in expertise, proved to be very able and learned quickly on the job.

Park, lacking intimate relations with many other groups in the society from whom he might get accurate information, relied heavily on the KCIA to carry on secretive work and report to him. Despite the agency's activities, many people believed that Park was bringing needed order to society, and he was popular enough to be elected president in 1963. Although the counting of votes in his later election in which he ran against Kim Dae-jung is deeply suspect and his ultimate abolition of direct presidential elections shows he feared the results, he still had acceptance among some of the electorate. They believed he imposed much needed order, provided security against the North, and brought economic growth.

Once the core team in each country took over responsibility for ruling, they were confronted with complex issues such as foreign relations, economics, and technology for which they had at best limited experience. Deng had far more experience than the other leaders, but he too lacked the detailed understanding needed to deal with the new age. Deng did have experience dealing with a range of bureaucrats and had specialists he could call upon. Nor were the other three leaders, bright and self-assured, afraid to select the best and the brightest; indeed, they sought them out. For political assignments, however, the four still used people in their inner circles.

In Singapore, since the number of bureaucrats was small enough, talented young people were rotated to many different departments, enabling them to understand how their own work fit in with the overall needs of the community. In China, with such a huge government, even Party members who became specialists and worked in different organizations tended to develop their own culture and to pursue their own narrow sectional or regional interests. Members of the inner core were needed to provide coordination between units and to ensure that overall interests were represented.

Though Park Chung Hee had by the late 1960s over two hundred people on his personal staff at the Blue House, when needed he brought in specialists from the bureaucracy or elsewhere to join him there. He chose to bring in a small number of people, such as O Wŏn-ch'ŏl, who led the heavy and chemical industry initiative, and to give them broad responsibilities.

The four leaders felt a sense of urgency in reshaping their countries and had little interest in or patience for academic discussions that were not directly related to the practical issues they faced. They all realized that they needed talented officials and supported high-quality schools, universities, and research institutes, but they were far more interested in issues relating to technology, economics, and management than in philosophy, religion, literature, and other fields in the humanities and social sciences. They were all secular and believed in science and the Enlightenment. Atatürk was especially critical of traditional religious practices that provided such resistance to his efforts at modernizing thinking. Although the others were less openly critical of religion, they tended to view it in the same light.

All of the four bristled when anyone criticized them personally. All worried that any unanswered critique might affect their authority, prestige, and ability to rule. All were ready to counterattack or even to silence outspoken critics. Compared with Atatürk, who was revered as a military hero, Lee who was elected to office, and Deng who was selected by a Party Plenum, Park, coming to power by a coup, had far less legitimacy. Because of this, because he had so few acquaintances in the intellectual community, and because he felt vulnerable to both domestic and U.S. criticism, he relied less on persuasion and more on fear, intimidation, and crackdowns on those who dared to criticize him publicly.

Park Compared with Other Rebuilders: Coping with Domestic and Foreign Opposition

Park's efforts to resolve the generic problems he faced had many similarities to the other leaders' efforts. Like the others he assembled a very able group of committed generalists and developed long-range goals for the nation with a pragmatic approach to finding ways to achieve them. Like the others he transformed the early struggles against colonialism into struggles to defend the country, keep order, build a modern nation, bring modern industry, and enrich the people. But Park's rise to power and his ensuing approach had significant differences from those of the other transforming leaders.

1. Park came to power by a coup, with a lower level of legitimacy than any other leader.

2. Because South Korea had had a more democratic system before he came to power than any of the other countries, his repressive regime, especially his forceful imposition of the *yushin* constitution in 1972, was seen at home and abroad as reversing the trend toward democracy.

3. It was more difficult for Park and many of his supporters to be seen as genuine patriots because they were compromised by having worked with the country that had been seen as Korea's main enemy, Japan. The issue was especially difficult for Park, for not only had he served in the Japanese army during the colonial period but in 1965, to get the external technical, managerial, and financial help he needed to launch industrialization, he normalized relations with Japan and worked closely with the Japanese.

4. Park's total mobilization for economic progress and his tight control over available capital and resources, especially during the heavy and chemical industrialization drive, went beyond that of the other three leaders. It was such a strain to get the needed resources that Park tried to get control over funds everywhere. Because of the political resistance to these efforts, he chose to force through the *yushin* constitution to give him tighter political control.

5. Park did not have the broad contacts outside the military that the other three leaders had, nor the extent of experience in persuading the public outside his narrow circles, nor the natural ability to manage public relations. Because he had significant domestic opposition, he relied heavily on the KCIA, military intelligence, and the police to clamp down still further on his opponents.

6. Despite his authoritarianism, Park could not fully ignore two significant groups that objected to his autocratic behavior, the U.S. government and Christians. He was more dependent than the other three leaders on U.S. government support for security, since the presence of U.S. troops on South Korean soil was so essential to protecting South Korea from large-scale attacks by the North. He therefore was in a weak position to resist U.S. pressure for greater democracy and respect for human rights. Because of the strong Protestant and Catholic churches in Korea, with membership that was above 15 percent of the population, and strong international Christian support, those who opposed Park's authoritarianism could rally their churches, as in the days of Japanese colonialism. Because of this foreign support, Park's ability to crack down on Korean Christians was severely constrained; they formed a base of resistance that was beyond his power to fully control.

None of the other three did more than Park in raising the people's standard of living, and in strengthening the country. All four leaders had intense single-minded devotion to their nation, but none more so than Park. None did more to launch heavy industry. But because of the issues of legitimacy, the lack of "thoroughgoing" patriotism in his relations with Japan, his difficulty in managing public relations, and the limitations on his ability to silence domestic critics and their foreign supporters, expressions of opposition to Park were stronger than for Atatürk, Lee, or Deng. With more determined opponents, Park used more sustained forceful methods to keep them under control than the other leaders did.

Public Memory of the Rebuilders

In Turkey, Atatürk has remained a hero in the public's eyes not only for his military victories, patriotism, and economic progress but for his determination to leave their feudal past behind and link Turkey to the modern West. Except for religious extremists who resent his secularism, people in Turkey revere him as the great man who set Turkey on a new path and brought enlightenment to his people.

Lee Kuan Yew, the only rebuilder who lived on to greet the twenty-first century, has been a hero in Singapore since his early days as prime minister. Singaporeans are proud that their leader became a major world leader and that their nation has earned a reputation as clean and green. Singapore is small enough that Lee's presence and influence has been felt everywhere, long after his retirement, like a patriarch in an extended family. Singaporeans are grateful for his brilliant and courageous leadership that brought Singapore through a dangerous period that no other leader could have achieved. Some Singaporeans believe that Lee Kuan Yew remained stricter than necessary as a taskmaster, too ready to look down on people of lesser ability, too harsh toward potential rivals, and that the well-ordered society he created is a little dull. But the dominant view is one of huge respect for a man of extraordinary intellect, wisdom, and dedication who played the decisive role in making Singapore an unusually well ordered, prosperous, secure, and attractive place to live.

The Chinese Communist Party made an official evaluation of Mao but not of Deng. The official evaluation of Mao in 1981 declared that 70 percent of his actions were contributions and 30 percent were errors, and that the 30 percent were largely in his later days. Until his death, Mao was treated as a god, and a minority remains nostalgic for what is remembered as a simpler but less corrupt and more equal society. Most people, however, believe Mao was leading China down the wrong path. They are enormously grateful that Deng turned China around and opened it up in many ways that have benefited the people and the country.

Many people, especially intellectuals and liberal Party leaders, are critical of Deng for his failure to do more to stop corruption and allow greater freedom, for his 1987 sacking of Hu Yaobang, who stood for a more humane and democratic rule, and above all for the 1989 crackdown around Tiananmen Square, when hundreds of citizens were shot on the streets of Beijing. Now that a generation is growing up on the coast with a comfortable standard of living, many say that in launching his reforms and opening, Deng did not do enough to combat the evil side-effects of his policies, particularly corruption, inequality, and the unrestrained selfishness that comes from the passion to get rich.

The picture of Deng that has been presented in the public media, especially in 2005, the year of the hundredth anniversary of his birth, is an official picture of a hero who always made correct decisions and lacked personal foibles. The public has little sense of what he was like as a person except that he was a family man as well as a dedicated official.

The public overwhelmingly believes that Deng is the leader who set China on the correct path of reform and opening that has improved the lives of the people, decreased the fear in their daily lives, ended the century of failures and humiliation, and created a strong China that they can be proud of. Even among intellectuals who criticize Deng for not doing more to promote democracy, there is almost universal appreciation for his successes in launching reform and opening, and a conviction that no other leader could have accomplished what he did. Many Chinese believe his contributions not only exceed Mao's but that he did more for China than any leader in recent centuries.

Of the four leaders, Park Chung Hee remains the most controversial in his own country. He was hated and feared for his illegal seizure of power by a coup, the repression of opposition, the military clampdowns, the climate of fear, the harshness of the *yushin* constitution, and his disregard for democratic procedures and the rule of law.

Since Chun Doo Hwan, who seized power in 1980, and Roh Tae-woo were Park's underlings before they became his successors, the South Korean public also links Park to the repression during their rule and especially the horror of the slaughter of civilians by Chun Doo Hwan's troops in Kwangju. Since the South Korean media has become freer, media opinion has been dominated by intellectuals who were suppressed during earlier eras and who in the new, freer environment have poured out their grievances against Park. Many Koreans consider the authoritarian governments of Park and his immediate successors unworthy of a nation that boasts such a rich history, such high standards of education, and such high levels of science and technology.

Because Park normalized relations with Japan in 1965, Koreans' view of Park cannot be separated from the widespread hatred of Japanese colonial occupation. Park's service in the Japanese army, his use of the prewar Japanese model, and his readiness to work closely with Japan all contributed to the controversy surrounding him.

Yet South Koreans know that Park held their nation together at a critical moment and made it possible to create the modern prosperous nation that people today enjoy. The pain and suffering during the era of Park and his successors has made it difficult for people to deal with his rule in an objective way. Both the horrors and the successes were beyond the range of ordinary human experience. Park aroused such passions that it has taken several decades after his death for the Korean public to begin to look at him with some detachment, engage in an objective analysis of him and his rule, and seek an understanding of how and why the troubled past caused such pain and yet laid the grounds for the prosperity and eventually the freedom they enjoy now.

CHAPTER NINETEEN

Reflections on a Reverse Image: South Korea under Park Chung Hee and the Philippines under Ferdinand Marcos

Paul D. Hutchcroft

P ARK CHUNG HEE and Ferdinand Marcos were both born in 1917, came of age while their respective countries were under colonial rule, emerged as national leaders in the 1960s, and proclaimed martial law at virtually the same time in late 1972. The countries they ruled each had deep historical and economic ties with the United States and Japan, and in the postwar years both South Korea and the Philippines hosted major U.S. military bases and were strongly aligned with the West. In declaring martial law, the incumbent presidents claimed that harsh measures were necessary to defend against a range of challenges and promote democratic foundations appropriate to national circumstances. Although both men enjoyed a strong base of power, they at the same time feared popular electoral rivals, made constitutional changes ensuring their continuance in office, and carried out horrific repression against movements of political opposition. The two authoritarian regimes were based on a high concentration of personal authority and power, with a relatively weak role for the ruling political party in each country.

Despite these striking similarities, the regimes of these two leaders produced huge contrasts in political-economic outcomes: rapid industrialization in Korea and disastrous economic predation in the Philippines. "More than any other single political figure," leading historians conclude, "Park . . . shaped the modern South Korean political economy, and his legacy was both admirable and appalling." The assessment of Marcos by his former chief ideologue tells an entirely different story: "He believed he could have a vision for society . . . and still loot it." According to Transparency International, Marcos ranks as the second-most successful kleptocrat in history, stealing roughly $5–$10 billion during his two decades in the presidential palace.[1]

How are these highly contrasting outcomes to be explained? The analysis below demonstrates the importance of both structure and agency. On the one hand, Park had the advantage of certain structural preconditions much better suited to positive developmental outcomes. His dictatorship both inherited and nurtured a far more institutionalized civilian and military bureaucracy than did the dictatorship of Marcos. One can observe within the Park regime an often paradoxical mix of institutionalization and personalization; Marcos, on the other hand, both inherited and nurtured a thoroughly patrimonial bureaucracy. In addition, state-society relations in Korea and the Philippines can be viewed—at various points in both the colonial and the postcolonial eras—as the reverse image of each other. In general, the Korean state historically faced weak countervailing forces in society. The dominant political-economic elite in the Philippines, by contrast, historically demonstrates a remarkable capacity both to plunder the state and to fend off challenges from below.[2]

Differences in the nature of state institutions and state-society relations are an essential but by no means complete part of the story. One must also examine important individual differences in the two leaders, beginning with the very notable contrast in their personal backgrounds: Park went from humble peasant origins to colonial and postcolonial military service to his 1961 seizure of political power, while Marcos came forth from a minor provincial elite family and used a range of ingenious political tactics to ascend to the highest post in the land in 1965. Once in office, both presidents were interested in maximizing power and authority, but their broader goals were the reverse image of each other: Park was obsessed with national economic development and seems to have accumulated little personal wealth while Marcos's developmentalist rhetoric masked an underlying commitment to promoting the economic success of his family and his cronies. Although one can say that both regimes were personalistic, the Marcos regime was thoroughly familial in character as well.

This chapter examines the combination of structural and agency-based factors that explain the starkly varying political-economic outcomes of the two authoritarian regimes. Given the rich and textured detail provided in earlier chapters of this volume, less attention will be given to Park and Korea as compared to Marcos and the Philippines. To enhance my analysis of the combined importance of structure versus agency, I conclude with counterfactual speculation that imagines Park at the helm in the Philippines and Marcos in charge of South Korea. As I shall argue, both dictators began their rule with structural factors highly conducive to their respective personal goals: rapid development in one case and systematic plunder in the other.

State-Society Relations in Korea and the Philippines: The Looking Glass of the Recent Past

The historical character of state-society relations in Korea and the Philippines have been the mirror image of each other in many ways. Scholars of modern Korean history and politics commonly describe a highly centralized and overbearing state able to exercise a considerable degree of control over a weak and poorly organized yet often "contentious" society. Within the society, explains Carter Eckert, the bourgeoisie has been "a decidedly unhegemonic class, estranged from the very society in which it continues to grow."[3] In the Philippines, by contrast, a strikingly decentralized and porous state has been continually raided by a hegemonic oligarchy that maintains strong clientelist linkages with a range of other societal groups. While the country has a long history of popular resistance and revolutionary activity, the national oligarchy that emerged in the early twentieth century still dominates both state and society—even though its composition and economic base have evolved significantly over time, and its dominance has occasionally come under challenge. In each country, the dynamics of state-society relations have been dramatically shaped both by colonialism and by postcolonial ties to foreign powers.

In the late Chosŏn dynasty in Korea and the late Spanish colonial era in the Philippines, both central states faced major restraints in the exercise of authority. The character of these restraints, however, varied considerably. The Korean monarchy faced a powerful *yangban* aristocratic class that enjoyed not only effective control over the bureaucratic structure but also hereditary rights over land. The *yangban* in many ways undermined the power of the central state, but their status was at the same time ultimately derived from their position within the state. Each *yangban* family owed its origin to an ancestor who had passed the difficult state examination. As Hagen Koo explains, "The yangban class had no interest in weakening state power; rather it sought to use state power only for its own interests."[4]

The late Spanish colonial state in the Philippines faced an even greater range of challenges, and—quite unlike the Chosŏn state—never achieved a substantial degree of centralization. First, the government based in Manila was so understaffed that it had to rely heavily upon ecclesiastical personnel in order to extend its reach throughout the archipelago.[5] Second, the Muslim population in the southern portion of the archipelago was effectively independent until nearly the closing years of Spanish colonial rule.[6] Third, and of greatest relevance here, the particular character of the colony's agricultural commercialization throughout the nineteenth century "gave rise to a new class of . . . landowners who were quite separate from the bureaucracy." This provincially based elite had an economic base firmly outside the central state.[7]

As a "new imperialism" swept the globe, both the Chosŏn dynasty and the Spanish colonial regime were forcibly removed by two rising industrial powers, Japan and the United States. In each case, the new colonials built upon the foundations of well-established polities, successfully co-opted many elites into colonial structures, and in the process brought enormous transformation to subject states and to state-society relations. There was tremendous divergence, however, in the character of the colonial states that each established.

As Japan colonized Korea through a large, coercive, and Japanese-dominated bureaucratic apparatus, the power of the *yangban* class was severely diminished in the political realm but substantially retained in the agricultural economy. The Japanese gradually promoted economic change that in comparative perspective might be considered oxymoronic: colonial industrialization. In this top-down process, encouraged by new and sophisticated colonial financial institutions, Japanese capital (that of both state and *zaibatsu*) was overwhelmingly dominant and Korean entrepreneurs decidedly marginal.[8] To the extent that Korean elites enjoyed any substantial degree of economic power, therefore, it was primarily as landlords; those branded "Japanese collaborators" became "the object of an intense national hatred."[9]

American colonial rule in the Philippines was put in place after rapid defeat of the Spanish and in the midst of a fierce, protracted war with nationalist forces throughout the archipelago.[10] Intent on ending a conflict that was tying down 72,000 American troops and facing increasing opposition at home, Governor-General William Howard Taft initiated a "policy of attraction" that promised Philippine elites a major role in governance—and sought to make the "modern lawyer-politician" the dominant figure in Philippine society.[11] Elections for municipal and provincial posts were instituted in 1901 and 1902; in 1907, a significant amount of authority was given over to a national representative assembly; and in 1916, the creation of a Senate was accompanied by the explicit promise of future independence. As elections were held and legislatures convened, relatively little attention was given to the creation of a modern administrative apparatus. The representative institutions enabled local caciques, or local political bosses, to consolidate their hold on the national state, and fostered the creation of what Benedict Anderson calls "a solid, visible 'national oligarchy.'" This oligarchy—both Manila-based politicos and provincial lords—took advantage of their independent base of power, and came to exercise powerful, particularistic control over all levels of the governmental apparatus through a spoils system that had become well entrenched at the national level early in the century.[12]

American colonial rule is essential to understanding both the origins of the modern Philippine state and the many basic elements of modern-day Philippine society and democracy. The outcome was, in many ways, the reverse of the colonial-era transformation found in Korea: while the Japanese turned the *political-economic* elite of the Chosŏn dynasty into a tightly controlled *economic* elite harnessed to their colonial goals, the Americans transformed the *economic* elite that had emerged in the late Spanish era into a broadly influential *political-economic* elite that soon proved capable of frustrating major U.S. goals of colonial "tutelage." In stark contrast to the powerful and highly centralized Japanese colonial state in Korea, the American colonial state in the Philippines was remarkably weak and decentralized.

Through their control of the political apparatus, Philippine oligarchs continually created more economic opportunities for themselves (for example, land-grabbing through control of the land titling process). Collaboration with the Americans created many opportunities for gaining greater degrees of legislative authority and local autonomy, and with the creation of the Philippine Commonwealth in 1935 all branches of government were effectively turned over to the oligarchy that the Americans had created.[13] Commonwealth president Manuel L. Quezon was a consummate Philippine "lawyer-politician": he emerged from provincial roots with the backing of influential American colonials, and proved masterful in using the rhetoric of American democracy and subtle understandings of American institutions simultaneously to consolidate his provincial base of power and build a nationwide network among other provincial powerholders. In many ways, Quezon was the antecedent of Marcos: both men skillfully manipulated diverse components of the political system to accumulate personal power, and spawned regimes "characterized by corruption and cronyism."[14]

Change and Continuity in State-Society Relations:
From Independence to the Early 1960s

The end of World War II brought independence both to Korea and to the Philippines, and the inauguration of the two new governments was presided over by the same U.S. military official: General Douglas MacArthur. Although the experiences of colonization and processes of decolonization were extremely distinct in nature, one can nonetheless observe a surprising degree of convergence in the character of the states and elites that initially emerged in the Republic of the Philippines and the Republic of Korea.

In Korea, independence came suddenly and resulted in a partitioning of the nation that remains in place more than six decades later. The landlord class was challenged everywhere by a nationalist and "contentious" civil society born in the colonial era.[15] In the North, under Soviet occupation, this class was quite thoroughly stripped of their landholdings. In the South, on the other hand, American occupation provided a necessary degree of protection to Korean landlords, and permitted them to regain a measure of political influence. For the post of the presidency, the Americans needed a figure who could combine fierce anticommunism with anti-Japanese nationalist credentials. Syngman Rhee fit the bill, and after taking the helm he worked out a marriage of convenience with the opposition Korean Democratic Party, "the organ of landed wealth and local power."[16] Through its association with Rhee, the landlord class sought to defend its economic positions and regain the political clout it had lost during the Japanese colonial era, and thus consolidate itself as a *political-economic elite*.

In the Philippines, entirely unlike Korea, the impact of the Pacific War was to cement closer ties than ever to the former colonial power. MacArthur's promised return conquest of the Philippines and the fulfillment of prewar promises of independence seem to have brought unprecedented legitimacy for deep American involvement in postwar politics. When granted on July 4, 1946, independence was accompanied by provisions clearly advantageous to the landed oligarchy that controlled the state. In exchange for military bases coveted by Washington and economic concessions desired by some elements of American business, the United States provided the Philippines with both continuing access to its market as well as postwar rehabilitation assistance. In part because the grantor of independence was a rising superpower, it was especially difficult for the Philippines to emerge as a truly sovereign nation. Even in the postcolonial era the oligarchs have remained highly dependent upon U.S. aid, investment, and counterinsurgency support. Although the country as a whole has faced no serious external threat, oligarchs have needed external support to sustain an unjust, inefficient, and graft-ridden political and economic structure. Washington, in turn, received unrestricted cold war access to two of its most important overseas military installations.

As in Korea, the Philippine elite faced major challenges from below in the late 1940s. The Hukbalahap (People's Anti-Japanese Army), formed in 1942, battled against both the Japanese and their landlord collaborators. Despite their frequent willingness to cooperate with U.S. forces, the Huks soon found themselves enemies of the state being reestablished by MacArthur and his many oligarchic friends (some of whom had collaborated with the Japanese during the war). By late 1946, after efforts at parliamentary struggle were obstructed and repression of the peasantry worsened in the countryside, the Huk units were once again in full-scale rebellion.[17] The Philippine government had major difficulties in meeting this challenge; as in Korea in the late 1940s, one finds a weak and corrupt state highly dependent upon the United States for its basic survival.[18]

The Huk Rebellion peaked between 1949 and 1951, after which counterinsurgency efforts began to achieve considerable success. Especially important was the role of U.S. advisors in cultivating Ramon Magsaysay, "America's boy."[19] The major reason for the Huk's decline, explains Benedict Kerkvliet, was that "peasants in Central Luzon liked Magsaysay, first as secretary of defense (1950–1953) and then as president (1954–1957), because he had personal contact with villagers and because the military became less abusive under his leadership."[20] The eventual defeat of the Huks was achieved far more by symbolic actions than by substantial concessions, and in its wake came no major change in the character of either the state or state-society relations. Agrarian discontent was temporarily ameliorated through resettlement in the southern island of Mindanao, and U.S. proposals for land redistribution were blocked.[21] With the root causes of insurgency unaddressed, the Left would soon rise again.

In contrast to the Huk Rebellion, the impact of the Korean War on the South Korean state and state-society relations was nothing short of cataclysmic. "No single event in modern Korean history," Hagen Koo writes, "has influenced state formation more than the Korean War."[22] Of particular importance, especially as we compare state-society relations with those of the Philippines, is the issue of land reform. Prior to the war, reformist measures pushed by the Americans had been obstructed by the landed class; during the North Korean occupation, however, revolutionary land reform greatly weakened this class; after the war, American pressure forced Rhee to carry through earlier reform measures. With the landlord class thus wiped out, the Rhee regime no longer faced the threat of a nascent political-economic elite challenging it from within. Bruce Cumings writes of the war as a "great equalizer," not only undermining the landed elite but also spawning a new group of entrepreneurs thriving on opportunities brought forth by massive social dislocation.[23]

While the South Korean state of the late 1940s was "extremely unstable and fragile"—not unlike its Philippine contemporary—the war brought considerable consolidation of state authority under the Rhee regime.[24] This is reflected in the emergence of a modern and efficient army, the enshrinement of the unchallenged ideology of an "anti-leftist state," and efforts to control popular sectors.[25] Massive quantities of U.S. aid provided the Rhee regime with myriad opportunities for allocating particularistic benefits and strengthening its base of political support. Rhee actively resisted American attempts to reintegrate Korea into colonial-era trading patterns, using his leverage in the geopolitical realm simultaneously to promote an alternative national development strategy and to strengthen his own regime. He nurtured a much stronger domestic capitalist class, largely dependent upon the state for its success, and ensured that the allocation of benefits would generate large contributions for the ruling party.[26] In the late 1940s Rhee's regime needed to accommodate the demands of an economic elite; by the late 1950s, it quite effectively manipulated a qualitatively different sort of economic elite now rooted much more in industry and commerce. At least in the political realm, Rhee was quite successful in achieving his goals: "By the late 1950s," conclude Eckert and his colleagues, "Rhee had made the political system largely his own."[27]

In the Philippines, as well, the political economy of the 1950s was characterized by corrupt rent-seeking and import-substitution industrialization (ISI). While at first glance this might seem to reveal major similarities with Rhee's Korea, closer analysis reveals substantial differences. Broadly speaking, one can observe that if rent-seeking in Korea promoted the consolidation of political power in the ruling regime, rent-seeking in the Philippines benefited a political-economic elite that was not only diffuse but expanding in size. Reacting to a major balance-of-payments crisis in 1949, the newly created Central Bank of the Philippines instituted import and exchange controls with the strong backing of the United States and U.S. investors. The allocation of import and exchange licenses was rife with corruption, and several scandals erupted in the course of the decade over particularly favorable allotments provided to those with the best political connections. One (perhaps apocryphal) incident symbolizes the plunderous manner in which licenses were sometimes obtained: in the late 1950s, it is said, opposition congressman Ferdinand Marcos "burst into [the] office" of a Central Bank official who had refused to license the imports of "a well-heeled Chinese businessman" and pointed a revolver at the head of the official until "the documents were signed and turned over to him."[28]

As in the case of Korea under Rhee, economists find little rationality in the process by which Filipino individuals and industries were selected.[29] Unlike in Rhee's Korea, however, it is more difficult to discern any regime-based political logic behind the madness of this period's rampant rent-seeking. Industrialization was a major goal of national development planning, but Filipino leaders generally did not share Rhee's nationalist aversion to the liberal prescriptions of American economic planners. (Indeed, rather than resisting dependence on the former colonial power, a major economic priority was continued access to U.S. markets.) Reflecting the highly decentralized character of political and economic power in the Philippines (especially under democratic institutions), the central allocation of economic benefits did little to promote the centralization of political power. Rather, the period of controls provided one more source of booty for an oligarchy whose strategies of capital accumulation had long depended on favorable access to the state apparatus. As a rule, what the oligarchs grabbed from the state was theirs to keep; the beneficiaries of the system had little if any obligation to contribute to (1) larger developmental objectives (in some cases, "industrialists" requested a foreign exchange license to support manufacturing ventures and then diverted the proceeds to import finished goods); (2) the coffers of the state (there were minimal taxes on the sale of foreign exchange); or (3) political parties (payoffs tended to go not to parties but rather to politicians). Finally, one can observe that—unlike in Korea—the Philippines saw no major transformation of the character of the elite from the late 1940s to the late 1950s: while the elite expanded in size and acquired more diverse economic interests, it remained a powerful political-economic elite.

In both Korea and the Philippines, changes in U.S. policy encouraged important shifts in development strategy. In Korea, the reduction of U.S. aid in the late 1950s eventually brought down the Rhee-era political economy, and contributed to the end of the Rhee regime.[30] Also in the late 1950s, the United States reassessed its support for the system of controls in the Philippines. A process of decontrol followed in 1960, and in 1962 the peso was devalued by roughly 50 percent.

By the end of the 1950s, after many years in which civil society had been quiescent, student activists began to challenge the autocratic basis of Syngman Rhee's rule. The students' April 1960 "revolution" brought the opposition Democratic Party to power, but a mere thirteen months later it was toppled in a military coup led by Park Chung Hee. In the wake of the coup, the new military government arrested the richest men in the country and condemned them as "illicit profiteers."[31] Subsequent compromises notwithstanding, this event highlights not only the clear separation between state and society that existed at the outset of the Park era, but also the highly asymmetric relationship between the country's political and economic elites.[32]

Such a bold attack by the state on the business community would be absolutely unimaginable in the Philippine context, where the institutions of the state were commonly overwhelmed by the particularistic demands of a single dominant elite enjoying power in both the political and the economic realms. Instead of being dispossessed of their land, as in Korea, landlords came to possess much more diversified economic interests across a range of sectors. Politics was above all a fight for spoils, and continuing corruption scandals provided a steady supply of political ammunition as the two elite parties attacked each other, exchanged members, and rotated in power.[33] When the Marcos era began in 1965, unaddressed grievances in the countryside and widespread disenchantment with corruption, electoral abuse, and economic travails helped to activate students, remobilize popular sectors, and reinvigorate leftist movements that had been temporarily vanquished in the 1950s.

Park and Marcos before 1972: Rising to Power and Consolidating Presidential Authority

At the outset of Park's rule in South Korea and Marcos's in the Philippines, many elements of divergence between the social, institutional, political, political-economic, and geopolitical contexts stand out, most notably what can be broadly characterized as (1) the historical legacies of state centralization versus decentralization; (2) long-standing experiences with authoritarian rule versus democratic institutions; (3) the "equalizing" impact of thorough postwar land reform versus mere land resettlement schemes and enduring inequalities; (4) a clear versus a thoroughly blurred distinction between political and economic elites; (5) economic elites dependent on and manipulated by the state versus political-economic elites able to pillage and manipulate the state; (6) a concerted postwar process of political centralization versus enduring patterns of decentralization; (7) nationalist assertion versus the endurance of colonial-era economic patterns; (8) a solidly anti-leftist state versus (what we know in hindsight was) a much more tentative defeat of a leftist challenge from below; and (9) external threat versus absence of threat. In this section, I will build on this analysis and trace the two leaders' respective paths to power, their goals once in power, and their subsequent decisions to discard democratic institutions and declare martial law.

Personal Backgrounds

In the mid-1960s, as American troops were dispatched to Vietnam in ever greater numbers, two of the United States' major allies in Asia were President Ferdinand Marcos and President Park Chung Hee. The two new leaders met each other at conferences of U.S.-backed regional organizations, proclaimed "free world" solidarity in treks to Lyndon Johnson's Washington, and—in exchange for American assistance—supported U.S. counterinsurgency efforts in Vietnam: Korea with nearly 50,000 combat troops and the Philippines with a much smaller engineering battalion of 2,000 soldiers.[34] Within this larger geopolitical context, we find both important similarities and important differences between the two presidents and their rise to power.

Park and Marcos were both men of provincial origins, born and raised under colonial rule. But while Park grew up in a peasant family, Marcos's forebears enjoyed substantial landholdings in the hardscrabble Ilocos region of northwest Luzon and held such posts as judge, mayor, and village head. Ferdinand's family moved to Manila when he was young, and his father, after finishing law school, was elected to Congress in 1924. Ferdinand was preparing to follow in his father's footsteps, but in the late 1930s was among those accused in the 1935 killing of an Ilocano politician who had defeated his father in a congressional race that year. In a nationally celebrated 1940 case, law student Ferdinand Marcos pled his innocence before the Philippine Supreme Court and had his earlier conviction for the murder overturned. In the same period in which Park found social mobility through a career in the Japanese colonial military establishment, therefore, Marcos became yet another of the "modern lawyer-politicians" bred under American colonial rule.

After his first election to Congress in 1949, Marcos displayed no strong political convictions but did show considerable political acumen. His electoral success was advanced at least in part by the mythology of his heroic role as a guerrilla fighter during the Japanese occupation; while falsely claiming to be the recipient of some thirty medals for battling the Japanese, Marcos may in fact have spent part of the war years collaborating with the Japanese. Also of considerable political value, particularly as he moved from a local congressional constituency to a national senatorial constituency in 1959, was his 1954 marriage to Imelda Romualdez, a former beauty queen from the Visayas (a vote-rich region in the center of the archipelago).[35] In 1963, Marcos was elected president of the Philippine Senate. After switching from the Liberal to the Nacionalista Party prior to the elections, Marcos defeated the incumbent (Liberal Party) president, Diosdado Macapagal, and took office at the end of 1965.

Prior to assuming the presidency, both Park and Marcos overcame major early adversities that nearly cut their careers short: Park's conviction for involvement in the leftist Yŏsu-Sunch'ŏn rebellion, and Marcos's trial for murder. But the terrain of their journeys was entirely distinct. Park was a military man who came to power via a coup d'état, and his transition to electoral politics in 1963 was in large part due to U.S. pressure. A diminutive, introverted man, Park had an almost total lack of political charisma and "never hid his distaste for elections and contempt for legislators."[36] Marcos, in contrast, was in fact the grand master of the Philippine game of politics. His ascension to the presidency came not via a coup, but through many years of electoral ambition. A man of athletic prowess and extraordinary charisma, Marcos wooed large crowds not only through impassioned speeches but also with love songs he sang in duet with Imelda. International correspondents frequently compared the First Couple's glamour to that of the Kennedys, and upon his inauguration in 1965 *Time* magazine put Marcos on its cover and hailed his "dynamic, selfless leadership."[37]

Goals

Even though both Park and Marcos were products of the social and political milieu from which they emerged, their personal preferences and leadership styles are of course essential to understanding the character of their respective presidencies. While the two men certainly shared the desire to concentrate and retain power to the fullest possible extent, their use of power was distinct. Park Chung Hee followed previous presidents of much higher social status and combined "a peasant['s] suspicion of the wealthy" with Japanese-style mercantilist goals of promoting "a rich nation and a strong army."[38] Scholars of Korean political economy rarely give any hint that Park used his position to build up a substantial personal fortune.[39] Marcos, by contrast, was the classic provincial parvenu determined not only to emulate but to overtake the country's most wealthy families. The objective of national economic development was decidedly secondary to the promotion of a rich family and a strong retinue.

Marcos spoke frequently of promoting the goal of national economic development, and beginning with his first term as president sponsored major infrastructural projects throughout the archipelago. But these expenditures, supplemented with smaller "community development" grants at the barrio level, were "parceled out for maximum political advantage."[40] Amid the rhetoric of "nation building," rumors of the First Couple's overseas real estate investments, Swiss bank accounts, and crony privilege were already prominent in the Manila press in the late 1960s.[41] Whereas Park manipulated external relations with the overarching goals of national security and national autonomy, Marcos's considerable skills of diplomacy were oriented primarily toward personal gain. In exchange for sending an engineering battalion to Vietnam, Marcos received large, off-the-books payments from the United States; U.S. officials with knowledge of the arrangements, reports Raymond Bonner, "have no doubt that many of the millions . . . went into [Marcos's] pockets or, more accurately, into his overseas bank accounts."[42] The reelection campaign of 1969 offers perhaps the greatest evidence of personal political goals trampling national welfare: after the treasury was raided and opponents were cowed by the administration's extensive mobilization of official and private forces of coercion, the defeated candidate grumbled that he had been "out-gooned, out-gunned, and out-gold[ed]." In the wake of the election came the country's worst balance-of-payments crisis since 1949.[43] The personal aggrandizement for which Marcos became famous can thus be traced to the earliest years of his presidency.

Institutional Context

As both men skillfully consolidated the political base of their regimes, they built on very distinct institutional foundations and very distinct visions for institutional reform. Unlike in the Philippines, Park worked in a "thoroughly bureaucratic" environment: he "knew where power and expertise lay and acted accordingly, showering Korea's bureaucratic elite with privileges."[44] Benefitting from the earlier centralization of the political system under Rhee, Park proceeded to establish the Korea Central Intelligence Agency (given the extremely broad writ of guarding power and managing elections) and the Economic Planning Board (tasked with overseeing rapid industrialization).[45] Within a system he dubbed "administrative democracy," Park worked carefully and steadily to create a more meritocratic bureaucracy.[46] Despite his own background in the military, and his own obsession with the tasks of economic coordination, Park generally insulated military officers from key agencies of the economic bureaucracy (including the Economic Planning Board and the Ministry of Finance).[47] As the president nurtured the growth of strong and clearly delineated bureaucratic institutions, he simultaneously made sure to retain his own personal control over them. Building on the country's long tradition of meritocratic rule, Park centralized authority over the bureaucracy in the Blue House and achieved military-like discipline from his top bureaucrats.

Marcos inherited a bureaucracy that had long been poorly institutionalized and manipulated for particularistic purposes by a wide range of politicians and oligarchic families. Rather than seeking to strengthen bureaucratic institutions and insulate them from patronage networks, Marcos instead sought to centralize patronage networks under his own control. There was no major new initiative of bureaucratic reform under his constitutional presidency; if anything, he further subverted the bureaucracy's already minimal degree of institutional integrity. In addition to "harnessing" the military to patronage projects beneficial to the regime, he blatantly used the regulatory authority of the Central Bank to bail out his friends and punish his enemies.[48] Unlike Park, who was building up the Korean bureaucracy in order to promote his own developmental goals, Marcos was undermining the Philippine bureaucracy to bolster a far more thoroughly personalistic regime.

Government-Business Relations

Through a combination of clearer economic goals and stronger institutional instruments, the pre-1972 Park regime accomplished a far greater political-economic transformation than did its counterpart in the Philippines. Taking advantage of its superior power over the fledgling business class, the government forced the nationalization of all commercial banks. By controlling access to funds, the state encouraged a nascent and dependent business class to move into increasingly sophisticated industrial production organized around huge diversified family conglomerates. Businesspersons were no longer denounced as "illicit profiteers," but for many years they continued to be marshaled to the rhythms and beats emanating from the major economic policymaking agencies. Even so, the Korean state's power was by no means absolute; rather, its symbiotic relationship to business in these years has been described as "asymmetric political exchange."[49]

One can similarly observe a huge power disparity in the Philippines in the early 1960s, but the balance of power was tilted in precisely the opposite direction. If money is indeed power, analysis of the financial sector is once again instructive. While businesspersons in Seoul were being arrested and subsequently lost control over their banks, nearly all major families in the Philippines were taking advantage of new incentives to establish private banks. In essence, government resources were made available to the banks and their owners could freely proceed to milk the loan portfolios for the benefit of diversified family conglomerates. If in Korea the government used the banks to execute "national macroeconomic goals, not profit-mongering through lucrative money lending," the outcome in the Philippines was exactly the reverse. Nationalization of the private banks would have been unthinkable; quite the contrary, families were given new opportunities for private plunder at the public trough.[50]

Development Strategies

The 1960s were a time of transition for both the Korean and the Philippine political economies. In Korea, a reduction in U.S. aid encouraged greater attention to export promotion. American advisors argued against excessive investment in heavy and chemical industries, but Park and his advisors developed their own game plan as they pushed for goals that the Americans considered wildly ambitious. Reparations of $800 million from Japan, as well as roughly $1 billion in payment from the United States for Korean involvement in Vietnam, provided resources both for regime consolidation and for huge industrial projects. American markets provided an outlet for Korean exports. As the Japanese economy moved to higher-wage and higher-technology industries, South Korea began to take over lower-wage, labor-intensive production from Japan. The race to catch up with Japan and overcome competition with North Korea produced a national obsession with rapid economic growth. Through control of the financial sector that was in many ways reminiscent of the colonial-era industrialization of Korea under Japanese rule, Park employed a set of Gerschenkronian "institutional instruments" that enabled Korea to develop its economy and heighten its national power at the same time. In the 1970s, Park moved to heavy industry; in his own formulation, "Steel = National Power." "Essentially taking on a political task which transcended Korea's national capacity," writes Byung-Kook Kim, Park pursued "a strategy of unbalanced growth, with a few *chaebol* chosen as 'national champions,' enjoying a diverse array of politically provided economic privileges and benefits." His regime pursued what Woo calls "impossible debt-equity ratios," thus ensuring that the country was always on the precipice of crisis.[51]

In the Philippines, the United States also played a major role in trying to engineer a new economic strategy in the 1960s. Unlike in South Korea, however, American advice was not so much *countered* via alternative policy ideas as it was *undermined* by policy drift (unlike their Korean counterparts, Filipino policymakers had little familiarity with Japanese-style state-led development). The process of decontrol in the early 1960s brought strikingly little sense of direction to the country's economic policy. From the standpoint of a diversified Philippine family conglomerate, things probably didn't look so grim—especially if favorable access to the political machinery provided opportunities for a range of particularistic privileges: loans from state banks, special government favors for their own banks, logging and mining concessions, preferential tax exemptions, advantageous treatment on tax assessment and payments, special tariff walls or exemptions, favorable arrangements from the Bureau of Customs, and so on. Precisely because the overall policy regime was so lacking in direction, families could move in many directions in pursuit of greater wealth.[52] In Korea private talents were quite effectively marshaled to public goals; in the Philippines public resources were widely looted for the benefit of a powerful oligarchy. As Park threw caution to the winds in pursuit of his goal of rapid industrialization, Marcos moved the country toward crisis in order to ensure his reelection in 1969.

Overcoming Opposition and Centralizing Power

Despite major contrasts in personal background, goals, institutional context, government-business relations, and development strategies, Park and Marcos shared a genius for centralizing political power in the office of the presidency and perpetuating their power despite numerous obstacles. In the face of opposition, both proved to be ruthless leaders ready to use any means—including the destruction of democratic institutions—in order to keep themselves in power.

In the 1971 elections, Park for the first time faced a political opponent articulating issues of substance; he managed to defeat Kim Dae-jung by a narrow margin, but in the process his Democratic Republican Party lost the two-thirds majority needed to amend the constitution. It became clear that Park's political support base had weakened, especially in the urban areas but also in the rural areas, where the government's presence was highly intrusive. Kim Dae-jung, meanwhile, tapped a huge reservoir of anti-government resentment in the Chŏlla region. With no further constitutional options for extending his rule, Park resorted to more extreme measures. He declared a national emergency at the end of 1971, and then martial law in October 1972. As David I. Steinberg explains, the timing "was not unrelated to the fact that three weeks earlier, without public U.S. objection, President Marcos in the Philippines had also declared martial law. It is said that President Park had his staff monitor the U.S. reaction to that move, and when Washington did not object, Park felt free to follow his own inclinations."[53]

Marcos's declaration of martial law followed years of economic problems and growing political turbulence. Throughout the 1960s, Philippine students became increasingly politicized and radicalized, provoked by campus issues, the presence of U.S. bases, the U.S. war in Vietnam and the deployment of Philippine troops there, inequitable social structures and the need for agrarian reform, and electoral fraud and demands for constitutional reform. The new Communist Party of the Philippines was officially launched in late 1968, proclaiming the virtues of guerrilla struggle in the countryside but finding its greatest success in the urban areas, especially among students. The reelection of Marcos was controversial, not least because all candidates (led by Marcos) reportedly spent the equivalent of nearly one-fourth of the national budget. Coming at a point in which the country's exports remained sluggish, this huge binge of election spending brought on a balance-of-payments crisis, followed by a devaluation that fueled inflation. This situation, in turn, heightened mass demands for change. In early 1970, student protests in the now-legendary First Quarter Storm reached the gates of Malacañang Palace.[54]

Just as Park had amended the constitution in 1969 in order to circumvent a two-term limit that would remove him from office in 1971, Marcos sought constitutional revision of the two-term limit that would have removed him from office in 1973 (riding on strong reformist sentiment that already existed in favor of cleaning up Philippine politics, culminating in the opening of a Constitutional Convention in June 1971).[55] Unlike Park in 1969, however, Marcos faced a much more developed system of elite contention within long-standing democratic institutions, as well as much stronger societal opposition; as a result, he encountered far greater difficulty in engineering a smooth and predictable process of constitutional change. Marcos took a beating in the congressional elections of 1971, with major opposition gains and even higher levels of "turncoatism" from the ruling party than had been experienced by previous presidents in midterm polls. As Thompson explains, Marcos was guilty of "two political sins": family and friends were strongly favored over partymates in the allocation of state patronage, and the president had touted the idea of having the First Lady succeed him as the Nacionalista presidential candidate in 1973. The elections themselves achieved new heights of violence, epitomized by the bombing of the opposition party's senatorial rally in August 1971.[56]

Faced with this combination of a stagnating economy, student unrest, growing political opposition, and problems forcing his self-serving version of charter change through the Constitutional Convention, Marcos came to see martial law as the best option for perpetuating his rule. Such a radical step required careful preparation, particularly since Marcos lacked what was so important to Park: an external threat "that was omnipresent but also convenient for stifling domestic or foreign opposition to any action that the government cared to make."[57] Marcos substituted his genius at political manipulation, constructing a plot intended to strike fear in the populace and thereby justify martial law as the only way for the country to preserve itself from multiple threats of disorder. In August 1972, Manila was rocked by a series of bombings that were blamed on the Communist Party but nonetheless suspected at the time (and later confirmed) to have been orchestrated by the Palace itself.[58] The denouement came on September 21, 1972, when President Marcos declared martial law and thereby brought an end to over thirty-five years of postwar democratic institutions.

Dictatorships Compared: Regime, State, Economy, and Society from 1972 to 1979

At virtually the same time, therefore, two major Asian leaders resorted to martial law in order to ensure their perpetuation in office—Park when he was unable to obtain a fourth term through constitutional means, and Marcos as he faced major obstacles to gaining a third term. The authoritarian transitions in the two countries, however, varied enormously. In Korea, one finds a comparatively smooth and uncontested shift from semi-authoritarian to authoritarian rule. Along with draconian new security measures, Park proclaimed a new ideology based both on a Korean *yushin,* or restoration, inspired by Japan's Meiji Restoration, and on a "Korean democracy" that exalted the virtues of executive dominance (built on the fiction of purportedly democratic institutions that were severely weakened but not dismantled). Rights were severely restricted, the National Assembly was emasculated, and presidential elections became meaningless exercises dominated by a body of presidential appointees. Legitimacy was to come, most importantly, from the regime's relentless pursuit of heavy and chemical industrialization (HCI).[59]

Societal opposition was far more vocal and active in the Philippines than in Korea, and Marcos feared widespread popular resistance to his declaration of martial law. Whereas Park had seemingly felt secure in his ability to impose martial law, and did not need to arrest opposition forces, Marcos knew he could take no chances. He took his opponents by surprise, with nighttime arrests of "some 8,000 individuals—senators, civil libertarians, journalists, student and labor leaders, and even scions of a few of the country's elite families." Opposition newspapers, meanwhile, were closed down. As in Korea, this U.S.-supported dictator declared the unsuitability of American-style democracy, and proclaimed the advent of a Philippine-style "democracy" more suited to the needs of the "new society" that he would be building. In addition, he claimed to be leading a "revolution from the center," able to deal with the dual threats facing the country from left and right.[60]

The sudden nature of this authoritarian onslaught served Marcos's purposes, and through arrests and repression and torture he quite easily stifled those most likely to register fierce opposition to martial law. At the same time, many elements of society were genuinely convinced that extreme measures were necessary to deal with the country's problems, and were ready to give him the benefit of the doubt as he centralized power in the Palace, disarmed the private armies of local bosses, and proclaimed ambitious goals for land reform. The Communist Party had yet to emerge as a major threat to the government, but was active enough to provide easy rationalization for repressive measures. Nonetheless, even Marcos seems to have been somewhat surprised at the relative quiescence of the traditional (that is, nonleftist) opposition, given his earlier fears of their potential to put up resistance.

Five key factors explain this outcome. First, "the Marcos regime left most members of the Philippine elite alone." Only two major politicians were held in prison longer than a few weeks, and relatively few families experienced confiscation of their properties. Second, the centralization of state patronage in the hands of one leader meant that "government largesse was available only to those in his good graces." Given the dominance of patronage over policy in Philippine politics, "it is understandable that most formerly anti-Marcos politicians did not denounce the regime but instead tried to ingratiate themselves with it."[61] Third, Marcos obtained critical support from the United States. As a man whose primary loyalty was to personal interests rather than to any state or national interests—however defined—Marcos saw that American strategic needs presented ample opportunity for private gain. Especially at a time when the military bases were offering such important support to U.S. forces in Vietnam, Marcos could approach Washington aid-givers from a strong position. Indeed, the United States rewarded martial law with large increases in grants and loans.[62] Fourth, this American seal of approval gave the regime ready access to billions of dollars of multilateral assistance and commercial loans. The abundance of external resources, soon to include cheap petrodollar loans at negative real rates of interest, gave many the impression that the country was on the road to rapid development. Fifth, Marcos also began martial law with the good fortune of high international commodity prices, which, Rigoberto Tiglao explains, "generated windfall profits for the Philippine economic elite, dispelling whatever doubts it still had about the Marcos dictatorship."[63]

With the opposition effectively tamed and U.S. support firmly in place, Marcos consolidated his dictatorship without any strong challenge. A combination of carrots and sticks pushed the delegates of the Constitutional Convention to rapid and overwhelming passage of a charter drawn up by the Palace, and in early 1973 the new constitution was given sham approval through the convening of "citizen's assemblies" throughout the country. The judiciary was forced into submission, and Congress voted to dissolve itself in exchange for appointment to an Interim National Assembly (the promised basis of the new parliamentary-style government for which elections were not actually held until 1978).[64] Whereas Park was confident enough to accommodate a National Assembly within his authoritarian structures, Marcos dismantled the Congress altogether and offered only the prospect of a new assembly in its stead.

In summary, both Park and Marcos wrote constitutions ensuring executive dominance and worked assiduously to achieve a maximum personal concentration of power. Yet there remained enormous differences in the character of the two regimes, as demonstrated in the following examination of institutions, government-business relations and development strategies, and societal opposition.

Institutions: Ruling Parties, Bureaucracies, and Military

Ruling Parties. The ruling Democratic Republican Party in South Korea had become of marginal importance to the Park regime by the late 1960s, as those (notably Kim Chong-p'il) who favored a strongly institutionalized party were pushed to the sidelines. After the inauguration of the *yushin* regime, explains Hoon Jaung, the DRP was "nothing more than a puppet of the president who maintained a highly centralized personal leadership within the regime."[65]

Marcos had no allegiance to the Nacionalista Party on whose ticket he won the presidency in 1965, especially after the defection and dissidence of many party members in the 1971 elections. It was not until 1978, in preparation for elections to the long-promised Interim National Assembly, that the Marcos regime launched its own ruling party, the Kilusang Bagong Lipunan (New Society Movement [KBL]). The rhetoric of a "new society" and the emergence of new faces notwithstanding, the old, informal patronage politics of the pre–martial law years remained the fundamental basis of the KBL. Throughout much of the country, politicians flocked to the KBL for the benefits that it could dispense. Three major cronies of Marcos became regional party chairmen, tasked with ensuring a KBL victory and at the same time given the opportunity to achieve political dominance over other local powerholders.[66] The patronage dispensed by this political machine was an important bulwark for the regime, complementing its elaboration of hollow democratic structures and extensive use of coercion. The home regions of the First Couple (Ilocos in northern Luzon and Leyte in the Visayas) were perceived to have been particularly favored, and are the areas in which the regime was widely thought to have enjoyed its greatest degree of popular support.

In two major ways, however, the emergence of the KBL represented a major break from pre–martial law patterns. To a far greater extent than any Philippine president since Manuel Quezon and his Nacionalista Party in the 1930s, Marcos and his KBL achieved a remarkable centralization of patronage resources. This is not to say that Marcos had the capability to launch a full-scale assault on local power, for the clans were far too entrenched for him to attempt such a thing; he could, however, restructure local power by favoring his allies at the expense of his enemies.[67] Second, to a degree unprecedented in Philippine history, the ruling family lorded over all formal political institutions, the ruling party included. One would never use the term "conjugal dictatorship" to describe the Park regime,[68] but it is in fact a very apt description of the regime of Ferdinand and Imelda. The First Couple attempted to promote themselves as "Father and Mother of the Nation" in barrio-level youth organizations, and in the Palace hung an oil portrait of the couple, drawing on pre-Hispanic imagery, that portrayed the President as *Malakas* (strong) and the First Lady as *Maganda* (beautiful). In addition to her many official positions, the First Lady headed up Manila's KBL ticket in the 1978 elections, using every possible means of electoral fraud to trounce imprisoned opposition leader Benigno Aquino, Jr., at the polls.[69]

In sum, the ruling parties of Park and Marcos were both weakly institutionalized (especially as compared with the authoritarian ruling parties found in nearby Taiwan and Indonesia). Park provided little scope to his ruling party, while Marcos delayed the formation of a new ruling party for many years. When he did form the KBL in 1978, his model was a more centralized version of the patronage-oriented parties of the pre–martial law years. Tellingly, neither the DRP nor the KBL survived the demise of its authoritarian leader.

Bureaucracies. After the declaration of martial law in Korea, Park maintained his earlier goal of building bureaucratic capacity, with a particular focus on the economic policymaking agencies central to his ambitious goals for HCI; as before, he exercised a highly personal mode of rule over the institutions that he nurtured. In the Philippines, by contrast, the post–martial law period was one in which the task of bureaucratic reform was given new attention after relative neglect. Marcos promoted "a sweeping rationalization of the Philippine administrative structure" and created both the National Economic Development Authority and the Development Academy of the Philippines in 1973. NEDA was established as a means of centralizing economic planning functions in one agency, and the talented technocrats at its helm oversaw development efforts in thirteen newly established regions throughout the archipelago. DAP had as a major goal the training of more effective bureaucrats and the improvement of bureaucratic systems.[70]

Simultaneous to this "rationalization," however, was a wildly patrimonial system in which there was no effective separation between the official and private spheres. Although resolution of national problems and defense of the state provided the official rationale for declaring martial law, it became increasingly clear over the course of the decade that personal and regime interests continually outflanked all other motivations for martial law. "From one point of view," Benedict Anderson colorfully explains, "Don Ferdinand can be seen as the Master Cacique or Master Warlord, in that he pushed the destructive logic of the old order to its natural conclusion. In place of dozens of privatized 'security guards,' a single privatized National Constabulary; in place of personal armies, a personal Army; instead of pliable local judges, a client Supreme Court; instead of myriad pocket and rotten boroughs, a pocket or rotten country, managed by cronies, hitmen, and flunkies."[71]

While only a few cronies were able to combine access to officially granted privileges with the formal assumption of official positions, First Lady Imelda Marcos was able to have her cake and eat it, too.[72] She assumed the posts of governor of Metro Manila, minister of human settlements, chair of the Southern Philippine Development Authority, founder of the Cultural Center of the Philippines, and "presidential envoy plenipotentiary" (often on quite sensitive missions) throughout the martial law years. Funds "saved" from the regular budgets of government ministries were commonly redeployed into special projects of the First Lady, who combined her official roles with enormous informal influence throughout the government. As Marcos faced increasing health problems in the later years of his rule, "she became in many ways the country's *de facto* president."[73]

How is one to understand this mixture of administrative rationalization and patrimonial goals? As a former Palace insider explains, Marcos would utilize the skills of competent officials, but at the same time try to limit their "political clout" and keep them "segmented . . . in their fields."[74] The technocrats, in particular, played the essential role of formulating lofty development plans essential to securing loans from multilateral institutions and foreign banks. Once the funds were obtained, "the political leadership then allowed the unconstrained introduction of exceptions that made complete mockery of the spirit and letter of the plans." In the same way that Weber allows for a "bureaucratic rationalization of patrimonial leadership" that does not undermine the essential nature of that leadership,[75] one can say that Marcos's bureaucratic reform and use of technocratic skills only streamlined his plunder of the state.[76] An important consideration in the relative portions of the mix, it seems, is a regime's security of tenure; if there is a feeling that the regime will endure into the long term, there is no necessity to maximize gains in the short term. After the declaration of martial law, Marcos likely felt secure enough in his position to know that he, personally, would be able to reap the benefits of a better-run state apparatus.

Militaries. Park inherited a much stronger military apparatus in the 1960s than did Marcos, and the continual presence of an external threat as well as fear of U.S. force withdrawals under Nixon's Guam Doctrine led not only to the rapid modernization of the armed forces but also to the emergence of a robust defense industry to support it. Park viewed the United States as an ultimately unreliable ally, and built up a highly disciplined, efficient, and modern military "under the banner of self-reliant defense." Although the defense budget grew sixfold between 1972 and 1978, the military as an institution was not given strong roles in either domestic politics or economic policy. Opportunities for rent-seeking by military officers, moreover, were kept in check.

The military that Marcos inherited in 1965 had little concern for issues of external security; ironically, the only potential external threat faced by the Philippines was that which arose from the possibility that U.S. military bases might draw the country directly into cold war conflict. In the late 1960s Marcos had already deployed the military in "development-oriented" patronage projects. With the declaration of martial law came a major expansion in the size of the Philippine military, from 57,000 in 1971 to 113,000 in 1976 and 158,000 in 1985. Unlike Park, who responded to the Guam Doctrine with a rush toward self-reliance, Marcos continued and even deepened the country's reliance on American military aid. Indeed, as explained above, the myriad forms of external assistance that came from hosting U.S. bases were critical to regime sustenance. And while Park put concerns over external defense at the forefront of state policy, Marcos's primary goal was not to protect the country from external threat but to reward military supporters and ensure their ability to defend the regime against internal challenges. The military came to enjoy new stature: as one officer explained in 1975, "we in the military were mud before martial law. . . . Now the people come to the military tribunal seeking justice."[77]

As the largely imaginary internal threats used to justify martial law in 1972 evolved into a powerful Muslim secessionist challenge in the South and growing insurgency by the New People's Army throughout the archipelago, Marcos's coercive resources were stretched to the limit. In Korea, Park deployed a colossal number of KCIA agents against an opposition that faced major obstacles of organization and a complete lack of arms; in the Philippines, Marcos had about one-third of that number in the combined forces of his army, navy, air force, and constabulary to confront a Muslim insurgency that had at least 15,000 fighters by the mid-1970s and a communist insurgency that by the early 1980s numbered 5,000 to 7,000 guerrillas.[78] Another way of highlighting the contrast in the two countries' security apparatuses is to examine the number of civilians per soldier in 1975: 55 in Korea and 628 in the Philippines.[79]

What Marcos lacked in sheer numbers, however, he more than made up for in the brutal and public nature of his response to insurgency: under his dictatorship, 3,257 were killed, 35,000 tortured, and 70,000 imprisoned. "Even at its peak," explains Alfred W. McCoy, the Marcos regime "lacked the communication and information systems for a blanket repression . . . [Despite growth in the size of the military,] it was still poorly financed and lacked efficient communications . . . Instead of a machinery that crushed all resistance, the Marcos regime used the spectacle of violence for civil control, becoming a theater state of terror. In the first three years, the military incarcerated some fifty thousand people. But faced with rising insurgency, the regime soon abandoned this costly enterprise. . . . Arrests declined, but 'salvagings' [extrajudicial executions] climbed." The roughly 2,500 "salvagings" committed by Marcos's security forces had a purposefully public character: victims' corpses—mutilated from torture—were commonly displayed as an example for others not to follow. Conversely, the far fewer number of political prisoners and far fewer deaths from domestic political conflict in Korea as compared with the Philippines, notes Byeongil Rho, are associated with the "more institutionalized repressive capacity of the Korean state."[80]

Ironically, despite its smaller size, the Philippine military seems to have had far greater influence on the political dynamics of the Marcos regime than did the Korean military on the political dynamics of the Park regime. Two major factors may account for this difference: the greater ability of the Philippine military to assume posts outside strictly defense functions (e.g., as diplomats, heads of government agencies, and regional development officers), and far greater opportunities to use their official positions for private enrichment. As Rigoberto Tiglao explains, "Military officers became managers and directors of government-owned corporations as well as private economic establishments" that had been seized from selected "oligarch" opponents of the regime. In addition to the enormous rents that could be extracted in these fields of endeavor, generals and their subordinates often engaged in "illegal activities such as gunrunning, protection rackets, narcotics trafficking, smuggling, carnapping, and illegal gambling. The biggest carnapping ring, it was widely known, had been managed all along by a leading general . . . The remunerative possibilities were endless so long as one's loyalty to the Marcoses was not in question."[81]

Government-Business Relations and Development Strategies

As Park patterned *yushin*-era "revitalization" after the experience of late-nineteenth-century Japan, Chung-in Moon and Byung-joon Jun explain, he "envisioned himself as a modernizing Meiji samurai." In the Philippines, meanwhile, some viewed Marcos's development strategy as an attempt "to assign the country's own version of *zaibatsu* leaders to the strategic economic sectors." But Marcos proved not to be a modern-day samurai modernizer, as he and his so-called *zaibatsu* had strategies that did more to undermine than to promote the national economy. While in Korea the lasting achievement of the 1970s was rapid industrialization in the heavy and chemical industrial sectors, the same decade in the Philippines is remembered as a period of mere "debt-driven growth," lacking in any clear development strategy.[82]

For Park, HCI not only furthered a long-term obsession but more immediately resolved what Byung-Kook Kim has called the "double crisis of military security and domestic instability."[83] In declaring martial law, Marcos pledged economic reforms that would usher in equality of opportunity and save the country from "an oligarchy that appropriated for itself all power and bounty."[84] But while Marcos did, indeed, tame selected oligarchs most threatening to his regime, a "new oligarchy" (of Marcos and his relatives and cronies) achieved dominance within many economic sectors. In exchange for the dismantling of democratic institutions, the Filipino people enjoyed only fleeting economic gain. While foreign loans sustained growth in the 1970s, crony abuses brought economic disaster in the early 1980s. Most fundamentally, martial law perpetuated important shortcomings of Philippine capitalism, because Marcos was merely expanding earlier patterns of patrimonial plunder. Particularistic demands continued to prevail, with the difference that one ruler was now appropriating a much larger proportion of the state apparatus toward the service of his own private ends. The cronyism of the Marcos regime in this period is more obvious than that of the pre-1972 period, since the regime had more centralized control over the state apparatus and enjoyed a much longer tenure in office. But amid important changes in the political economy was a remarkable continuity in the nature of business-government relations; as Emmanuel de Dios explains, "the crony phenomenon was no more than a logical extension and culmination of the premartial law process of using the political machinery to accumulate wealth."[85]

In addition, Marcos brought no fundamental shift in development policy—there was continued promotion of exports, but at the same time continued protection of ISI firms. Manufactured exports did, indeed, post major gains in the late 1970s and the 1980s, but its major supporters, the technocrats and the multilateral agencies, were unable to do much more than create one more avenue of diversification for the major family conglomerates to pursue. As long as external funds were readily available, it was most expedient simply to let debt drive growth. Throughout the Marcos years, de Dios concludes, "the issue of the development strategy could be essentially avoided."[86]

Unlike his counterpart in Korea, Marcos quite clearly had no "obsession" to promote the rapid industrialization of the economy. The increased prominence of talented technocrats and strong ties with the United States ensured a flood of loans from the multilateral agencies and foreign banks, and improved ties with Japan simultaneously yielded a harvest of increased aid, loans, and investment. Yet while Park used Japanese assistance to build his own steel plant in the early 1970s, Marcos allowed the Kawasaki Steel Corporation to move the most pollution-intensive phase of steel production from Japan to Mindanao in the mid-1970s. The sintering plant, wholly owned by Kawasaki and the biggest single Japanese investment in the Philippines at the time, was built on land that had been acquired (through the eviction of small farmers and fisherfolk) by the Marcos-controlled Philippine Veterans Investment and Development Corporation and then leased to Kawasaki. And while Park promoted "policy loans" to promote HCI, one finds in Marcos's Philippines a host of "behest loans"—that is, loans from the two major government-owned banks made at the behest of the Palace—to promote crony enrichment. Recipients commonly squandered their loot: when rehabilitation of the failed state banks was undertaken in 1986, the vast bulk of their loans were declared non-performing. In all sectors of the economy, there are countless tales of the First Couple and their relatives and friends gaining access to officially granted privileges and producing little or no positive benefit for larger developmental objectives. It is not surprising that the term "crony capitalism"—now used worldwide—was first coined to describe the political economic system of Ferdinand Marcos. If analysts of Park's Korea note "private agency with a public purpose," the common pattern under Marcos was public agency with a private purpose.[87]

Mounting Societal Opposition: Civil and Political

Contrary to the objectives of the Park regime, the strategy of HCI and rapid economic growth did not resolve the problem of legitimacy. Rather, it "broadened the structural base of the opposition through the rapid expansion of the working and middle class population, and . . . eroded the legitimacy of . . . authoritarian rule."[88] In 1979, after the harsh repression of workers in the YH incident and the emergence of more assertive leadership within the opposition New Democratic Party, the forces of civil society developed closer ties with political society.[89] The new coalition between the NDP and the "triple solidarity" (of students, workers, and the churches) made possible a determined, vigorous, and broad-based movement to topple the *yushin* regime. Because the political system was so thoroughly "anti-leftist," there was no strong radical component within the opposition. The absence of radicals no doubt facilitated the emergence of a broad-based coalition, the demands of which centered on the quite moderate demand of "restoration of democracy." Faced with such a conservative opposition, it was difficult for the dictatorship to legitimize its brutal repression.[90] Disagreement within the regime on how to respond to this democratic discontent led to the shocking assassination of Park by his KCIA chief in October 1979, after which the democratic movement itself was temporarily subdued by murderous rampages unleashed against it.

In the Philippines, one can observe far greater ideological variance among the opponents of the regime. As explained above, elites generally accepted martial rule in the early years. The Liberals, the major pre–martial law opposition party, "virtually disintegrated" after 1972. The party's leading figure, Senator Benigno Aquino, Jr., was imprisoned, and the rest of the party was deprived of the usual sustenance of electoral mobilization and the subsequent spoils for those who emerged victorious at the polls.

During early martial law, the only serious resistance to the regime was the rebellion of the Moro National Liberation Front in Mindanao and the Sulu archipelago. Although the uprising tied down a large proportion of Marcos's troops, the threat was limited to a region of the country far from Manila.[91]

Pressures for both domestic and international legitimation encouraged Marcos to call elections in 1978 for the long-promised Interim National Assembly of his "New Society" faux-parliamentary democracy. With electoral rules wildly skewed in favor of the regime, many opposition politicians urged a boycott; Aquino, however, declared that the prospect of "half a parliament" was better than none, and campaigned for a seat from jail. He worked out a temporary alliance with the Manila branch of the Communist Party of the Philippines to overcome his major logistical disadvantages, and relied on his wife, Corazon, and youngest daughter, Kris, to woo the crowds. A massive "noise barrage" the night before the elections demonstrated the depth of opposition to the regime, but the next day Marcos's newly formed KBL won an overwhelming victory—albeit marred by massive electoral fraud. Even unknown candidates of the ruling party outpolled Aquino in Manila.

The gap between the moderate traditional opposition and the radical armed opposition was far more pronounced than the gap that existed at the same time between political and civil society in Korea. "While the radicals [in the Philippines] had long ago given up the idea of a peaceful transition," explains de Dios, "the moderates and conservatives had participated in the elections, half-hoping that Marcos would voluntarily share meaningful power." The moderates reacted with great frustration to the fraud of the 1978 elections, and some within their ranks desperately turned to violent tactics themselves as a means of "bargaining . . . for electoral opportunities."[92] The rest of the martial law period saw major tension in relations between the "traditional politicians" and the Left: the politicians were sometimes willing to work out short-term accommodation with the Left in order to bring down the regime, but at the same time had a strong motivation to bring down the regime as quickly as possible in order to defeat the long-term threat of the Left—and ensure the restoration of the institutions of pre–martial law democracy under which they had functioned so well before 1972.

Korea-style "triple solidarity" was not appropriate to Philippine conditions. The role of the Catholic and Protestant churches was broadly similar, as opposition groups in both countries received critical sanctuary and valuable support from activist clergy and laity and church organizations. Examination of the roles of students and workers, however, reveals many more differences than similarities. Whereas activist students in Korea massed in the streets, many of their counterparts in the Philippines headed to the hills instead, devoting their lives to the revolutionary movement. Organizing efforts in the Philippines focused far more attention on the countryside than on the cities, and it was among peasants rather than workers that the Left achieved its greatest strength.[93] Enduring inequalities made the Philippine countryside far more conducive to organizing than the Korean countryside, and the strength of the Philippine working class could not rival that of its counterpart in a substantially more industrialized Korea.

By the end of the decade, the Communist Party was fast becoming the threat that Marcos had falsely claimed it to be in 1972. As the country's sole ideologically driven party, the CPP was eventually able to adjust and even thrive in the new environment of political repression. As the New People's Army built up strong bases of support throughout diverse regions of the archipelago, it came to be the hope of many Filipinos—across different social strata—who desperately sought the demise of the Marcos dictatorship. The traditional politicians, by comparison, looked liked impotent has-beens.[94] The CPP steadily built support for itself and a range of affiliated organizations, not only in the countryside where its base was strongest but also in urban areas among workers and destitute squatters.[95] In Korea, the establishment of a highly repressive "anti-leftist" political system had been accompanied by a sweeping process of land reform that served to ease radical demands for change. In the Philippines, communism had never been as thoroughly marginalized, and a combination of repression, military abuses, and unresolved social injustices brought forth a new leftist movement far stronger in both territorial scope and cross-class support than that which had been defeated in the 1950s.

For many years, the Philippine regime skillfully played on the deep divisions within opposition forces, using measures of liberalization to lure moderates back into its tightly circumscribed arena of political activity and punishing those who remained "outside the fold of the law." In 1983, however, the assassination of Benigno Aquino brought forth a torrent of anger from throughout Philippine society and engendered countless new alliances among moderate and radical groups determined to bring down the dictatorship. An economic crisis and increasing outrage over crony abuses further undermined the legitimacy of the regime. Marcos responded with a limited degree of liberalization, but—as is the pattern with personalistic dictatorships—there were clear limits to the degree to which the regime was willing to share power.

Given this basic characteristic of the Marcos dictatorship, many expected that only the radical opposition could succeed in toppling the regime. Marcos did indeed have to be "brought down because he would never step down,"[96] in a massive 1986 "People Power" uprising that served as an inspiration to democrats the world over—including many in Korea. But the regime that replaced him was dominated not by leftists but by forces of the traditional elite. Upon taking power, President Corazon Aquino and her major allies concentrated first on restoring the pre–martial law structures of Philippine democracy. The prevailing attitude within the Palace, a top aide explains, was "anything that the dictator built let us destroy."[97]

Structure, Agency, and Divergent Outcomes

In truth, the Marcos dictatorship really didn't do much building. His successor inherited a bureaucracy that remained weak and overwhelmed by patronage pressures, a highly factionalized military inclined to frequent coup attempts, and an economy that was in a shambles. The contrast between Korea and the Philippines is striking. Park survived eighteen years in power, but his regime endured in many ways long after his death. Marcos, in contrast, survived a bit more than twenty years in power, but his regime effectively collapsed immediately upon his downfall.

Along with reverse images in both the state-society relations of Korea and the Philippines as well as the personal goals of Park and Marcos, this analysis has further demonstrated a corresponding reverse image in political-economic outcomes: rapid economic development versus crony-capitalist economic decay. In explaining these highly divergent outcomes, what is the relative importance of structural versus agency-based variables? While such a question is probably impossible to answer with any degree of certainty, it is useful to speculate (by way of counterfactual fantasy) as to what would have been the outcome if a person of Park's vision and goals had emerged as leader of the Philippines in 1965, and a person of Marcos's vision and goals had emerged as leader of South Korea in 1961.[98] It is my sense that *a Filipino Park* would have been continually frustrated by the failure of state institutions to respond to his commands, and would have faced major obstacles in nurturing stronger institutions and moving toward rapid industrialization. Like President Getúlio Vargas of Brazil in the 1930s, perhaps, much could have been accomplished but major compromises would have been necessary along the way. *Marcos as leader of South Korea*, on the other hand, could have enjoyed many opportunities to raid institutions for his own benefit and to build on the centralized power base bequeathed by Rhee. A stronger bureaucracy and military might present obstacles to a thoroughly plunderous agenda (particularly to the extent that it would threaten the country's territorial integrity and national security), but at the same time a Korean Marcos would not have any need to accommodate himself to local power (conveniently smashed a decade earlier). Because institutions are easier to break down than to build up, one might speculate further that the frustrations of a Filipino Park would be much greater than those of a Korean Marcos.

To return to historical reality, both structure *and* agency are essential to understanding President Park's developmental achievements in Korea and Marcos's predatory debacle in the Philippines.[99] I would propose that the patterns of state-society relations and the institutions inherited by President Park of South Korea were necessary but not sufficient elements of his accomplishments. He relied on the structures that preceded him and then brought forth—through his own efforts and vision—the extraordinary transformation of the Korean political economy. Conversely, the personal goals that he pursued with such relentless fervor can also be viewed as necessary but not sufficient elements of his success. Without the inheritance of structures so conducive to his goals, it is difficult to imagine Park achieving such high levels of economic achievement.

While Park is recalled for things both "admirable and appalling," Marcos's name tends to bring forth almost entirely unambiguous memories of brutality, looting, and decay. Paraphrasing Marx very loosely, one can say that while Marcos could not choose the circumstances under which he made history, he inherited extremely favorable circumstances as he systematically plundered his country and subverted its institutions for his own self-aggrandizing goals.

CHAPTER TWENTY

The Perfect Dictatorship?
South Korea versus Argentina,
Brazil, Chile, and Mexico

Jorge I. Domínguez

AUTHORITARIAN RULE ESTABLISHED through an act of force, such as a military coup, poses several distinct challenges for the authoritarian ruler. The first is how to install the regime; that is, how to survive past the initial moments of the overthrow of the old regime in order to establish a pattern of rule that will last. This requires reducing the need for initial repression, unifying the coup leadership, and arranging for succession rules to stabilize and broaden the support coalition for the new dictator. A second challenge is the choice of institutional means. Will the new dictator delegate significant executive decision-making powers to competent civilians in specialized areas in which civilians excel? Will the new regime employ consultative procedures, legislative assemblies, and partisan organizations to shape the new rules for governing, obtain political information, and reduce the resort to repression? And what will be the relative role of the police and the military in enforcing compliance? A third challenge is the choice of a strategy to govern the society. Will regime leaders claim to rule seeking the consent of the governed through explicit ideological appeals? Will the regime tolerate, and make use of, societal pluralism? Will it activate or deactivate citizen engagement?[1]

A politically effective military dictatorship—the "perfect dictatorship"—is likely to display the traits listed below to be able to endure while at the same time incurring low costs of repression. Such dictatorships may or may not generate high rates of economic growth and may or may not adapt to unfolding societal trends. The criteria for the "perfect dictatorship" are political.

1. The "perfect dictatorship" provokes little societal resistance at its installation in order to cut its costs.
2. Its leaders at the time of installation act jointly and cooperatively to consolidate the regime.
3. Its leaders at the time of installation broaden the support coalition by agreeing upon succession rules to rotate the presidency through elite agreement within the authoritarian regime to prolong its duration.
4. Regime designers delegate policymaking and executive authority to civilians in areas of their competence, including economic policy.
5. Regime designers choose institutional means that emphasize consultation and employ restricted-scope legislatures and political parties within the authoritarian context to diversify the tool kit for ruling and policymaking, expand the coalition in support of the regime, and gather political information.
6. Regime executives prefer political means to brute repression as ways to cope with opposition and protest in order to reduce the costs of rulership and sustain a broad base of support for the regime.
7. The regime eschews ideological appeals, depriving civil society and the opposition of independent standards to hold the dictator accountable.
8. Regime designers compel political, economic, and social actors into regime-licensed organizations to maximize state control over the society, harness economic and social forces toward the government's goals, while employing a minimum of military force.
9. Regime executives employ political strategies to deactivate the population politically and constrain independent voices in civil society.

   In this chapter, I argue that the regimes that faced the most difficult installation had the strongest incentives to develop a wide array of consultative and information-gathering mechanisms. They were more likely to retain elections and parliaments, albeit in authoritarian contexts, and to find means to deal with organized labor that did not just rely on crude repression. Regimes of difficult installation were less likely to experience a single towering personalist leader and more likely to require a wider elite coalition; the authoritarian regime became consolidated through the institutionalization of rules for presidential succession. In contrast, authoritarian regimes that faced easier installations did not discover in time the incentives to widen their political base and sharpen their political tools. Thus they were more likely to be short-lived, or less politically effective and more reliant on repression over time. Not surprisingly, nonpersonalist authoritarian regimes were likely to endure longer than those in which a single ruler towered over others; more importantly, nonpersonalist authoritarian regimes governed by civilians were more likely to endure than nonpersonalist authoritarian regimes in which only military officers served as president.

The Countries

The response of the Park Chung Hee regime in South Korea to the three challenges noted at the outset of this chapter can be usefully compared with the similar responses in four Latin American countries also under authoritarian regimes at the same historical moment: Argentina, Brazil, Chile, and Mexico. I will argue that both initial conditions and ongoing economic circumstances suggest that Park's authoritarian regime was the most likely to succeed politically, that is, rely less on crude repressive measures and last longest. I focus mainly on analytical time, that is, the unfolding of decisions regardless of the starting date of each regime. My examination looks only at regimes established mainly by national military leaders in countries where ethnic, racial, or religious divisions did not play an overt role in the organization of national politics before or after the establishment of the authoritarian regime.

Park Chung Hee's rule began with the military coup of May 16, 1961. Dictatorships began in Argentina in 1966 and again in 1976 (after a three-year interlude of civilian rule), in Brazil in 1964, and in Chile in 1973. The Mexican authoritarian regime, a distant heir to the Mexican revolution of the second decade of the twentieth century, was actually founded in 1929, when General Plutarco Elías Calles convened the victorious generals from two decades of civil war to create a single political party that would rule for the next seven decades. This party allocated opportunities and rewards and administered penalties. Thus the Mexican authoritarian regime, too, began as the rule of military leaders accustomed to using force in domestic politics. All five political regimes emerged from the political actions of top-ranking soldiers, and all but Mexico's were founded between 1961 and 1973. The four Latin American authoritarian regimes out-lived that of Park, who was assassinated on October 26, 1979.

South Korean society is much more ethnically and linguistically homogeneous than that of any Latin American country, including the four considered here. Nonetheless, in no Latin American country before 1980 were there nationally organized political parties or social movements based on race, ethnicity, or language. The troubling social differences within the respective societies along these lines had yet to be mobilized politically, and none of these differences was politically significant for the founding or evolution of the various authoritarian regimes.

Park's South Korea had reason to fear for its international military security and was rightly concerned about a possible invasion from North Korea. As a result, South Korea's military was much more professional, ready for modern warfare, than its Latin American counterparts. South Korean military leaders experienced the Korean War personally. No Latin American authoritarian regime objectively faced a comparable situation. And yet in the 1970s Argentina, Brazil, and Chile each prepared for war with a neighbor. Argentina and Chile came to the brink of war.[2] The Brazilian military leaders who seized power in 1964 had fought on the Italian front during World War II in the Brazilian battalion deployed for war. In the 1970s, the South American dictatorships shared with the Park regime an obsessive fear of domestic subversion associated with international communism, in particular from Cuba.[3]

In the 1960s, Park's South Korea adopted a political economy that differed from Latin America's in significant respects. It emphasized high growth through export promotion with little reliance on foreign direct investment. Historically, Latin America had relied more on import substitution and foreign direct investment. Yet by the end of the 1960s Brazil's authoritarian regime also adopted a high-growth manufactured export-promoting economy that resembled and succeeded like South Korea's through the 1970s. In the early 1970s, Chile abandoned import substitution to emphasize exports.

Park inherited a bureaucracy that was already more professional than those in Latin America, though he would make it much more professional, and he also was heir to a weak labor movement. Chile had Latin America's best bureaucracy. Argentina and Chile had powerful nationally mobilized labor movements while the Brazilian and Mexican labor movements were about as weak as South Korea's.

The South Korean, Brazilian, and Argentine regimes installed in the 1960s, Mexico's after its revolution, and the Chilean in 1973 were all quite novel. In Mexico, the ancien régime had truly collapsed and a new one had to be built from scratch. In the other four countries, the bureaucratic-military-authoritarian regimes had no parallel in each country's respective national history. There had been military dictators in South America, but none approximated the experiences of the 1960s and 1970s in the harshness of their rule and the ambitiousness of their efforts to remake society.

On balance, these regime dissimilarities and the range of variation suggest that the task of building a "perfect dictatorship" should have been easiest in South Korea. Park could mobilize public support around a genuine, credible threat of North Korean attack. The South Korean military was professional. The Park regime's low reliance on foreign direct investment also buttressed nationalist pride and support. South Korea's high economic growth could rally additional backing for the regime. South Korean rulers had the least reason to worry about ethno-linguistic heterogeneity or organized labor union strength. They could also rely on the best bureaucracy.

South Korea and these four Latin American countries also shared sufficient social, economic, and political traits to permit comparison, as evident in Table 20.1. The time frame is the 1960s, when General Park rose to power and military coups overthrew constitutional governments in Argentina and Brazil. Authoritarian rule prevailed in Mexico. The seeds were also being sown for the Chilean military coup that took place in 1973. South Korea ranks at or near the median in this comparison, although its specific ranking varies across indicators. South Korea seems closer to Mexico and Brazil than to Argentina and Chile; the latter are consistently more socially and economically developed. South Korea never ranks first; Argentina characteristically outranks it.[4]

The authoritarian regimes established in South Korea and these four Latin American countries arose from the actions of high-ranking military leaders in societies that were not politically activated along the lines of race, ethnicity, or language and that shared certain characteristics of low to middle levels of social and economic development by world standards. None was among the world's least educated countries, nor was any of them among the most developed countries. The international circumstances were also remarkably similar. The anticommunist authoritarian regimes of the 1960s and early 1970s were close U.S. allies during the cold war. Anticommunism was a specific motivating element in military intervention in politics in Brazil, Chile, and South Korea. South Korea fits comfortably in a comparison surrounded by Latin American cases, notwithstanding the differences noted above that make South Korea the "most likely to succeed" at becoming a "perfect dictatorship."[5]

Table 20.1 Comparative rank order of social, economic, and political indicators in the 1960s

Population in 1965	Gross national product per capita in 1965	Percentage living in cities of 100,000+ in 1960	Percentage literate age 15+ in 1960	Deaths from domestic political violence 1948–1967
Brazil	Argentina	Argentina	Argentina	Argentina
Mexico	Chile	Chile	Chile	South Korea
South Korea	Mexico	Brazil	South Korea	Mexico
Argentina	Brazil	South Korea	Mexico	Brazil
Chile	South Korea	Mexico	Brazil	Chile

Source: Charles Lewis Taylor and Michael C. Hudson, *World Handbook of Political and Social Indicators* (New Haven: Yale University Press, 1972), tables 3.4, 4.1, 4.5, 5.1, and 5.5.

The Installation of the Authoritarian Regime

What happens the morning after a successful military coup? New authoritarian regimes face two immediate and one medium-term installation problems. First, they must seek sufficient consent from the governed. At a minimum, this consent is passive: acquiescence or tolerance of the new rulers, no or low levels of violent political resistance, and no or low levels of strikes or other forms of nonviolent resistance against the founding coup. More actively, new dictatorships seek some claim to legitimacy, asserting that the immediate past was unacceptable and had to be overcome to secure a brighter future. Dictatorships seek historical and prospective bases of legitimacy because they lack procedural legitimacy, that is, they have gained power by violating the constitution in the absence of free and fair elections.

The second installation problem faced by new authoritarian regimes is to sort out who is in charge. Sometimes there is one undisputed leader; at other times there is a military junta. This also raises the third or medium-term installation problem: is the dictatorship to be personalist or institutionalized? The most successful authoritarian regimes, historical bureaucratic empires, had means of succession from one monarch to the next and featured bureaucratic organizations for the sharing and exercise of power.[6]

Military regimes, born from a coup, have had to face this question repeatedly. Samuel Huntington long ago recognized the conflict that, in the aftermath of a coup, soldiers face between "their own subjective preferences and values and the objective institutional needs of society." New political institutions are needed, he argued, not just to "reflect the existing distribution of power" but also "to attract and to assimilate new social forces as they emerge and thus to establish an existence independent of those forces which initially gave them birth." These political institutions should also be capable of regulating succession and providing for the transfer of power from one leader or group of leaders to another without recourse to direct action in the form of coups, revolts, or other bloodshed.[7] Well-installed authoritarian regimes, therefore, settle upon succession procedures early on to enable the regime to broaden the support coalition and last beyond the lifetime of its founder. One measure of a well-installed dictatorship, therefore, is how many peaceful successions it manages within the framework of the authoritarian regime.

The South Korean military coup of May 16, 1961, held promise for the installation of an effective authoritarian regime. No military coup is free from some violence, arrests, and other means of conflict and repression. By these standards, this coup entailed rather low levels of violence or other forms of resistance. The new government repressed the organized labor movement and provided few inducements for organized labor support for the regime but, at its birth, it also faced relatively little resistance from organized labor. Moreover, the rebellious officers had a legitimating claim: to overcome a recent past of corrupt practices in government, to accelerate the prospects for economic growth, and thus to build a stronger South Korea to face its communist enemy to the north. There was also little difficulty in establishing who was in charge. General Park Chung Hee was the coup's principal leader and the head of the military junta.[8]

Park's political role from the start was so great that he reduced the likelihood of collegial rule. He soon marginalized his most important comrade in coup plotting, Kim Chong-p'il. He ordered the court martial of General Yun P'il-yong in 1973 on the basis of slender information that General Yun had begun to think about Park's succession.[9] Park took no credible steps to provide for his own succession, never transferred power peacefully, and was assassinated while still serving as president.

The Park regime's political installation record looks somewhat worse than Argentina's, roughly comparable to Brazil's. At first, the June 1966 coup in Argentina held even more promise of installing an effective authoritarian regime. "There was almost no opposition to the coup within the armed forces, and there was practically no civilian attempt to prevent it," writes Guillermo O'Donnell. He adds that "the coup had the approval of most of the population and of nearly all social organizations . . . [including] a considerable part of the popular sector, and was endorsed by a majority of political and union leaders."[10] The claim to legitimacy was the search for Argentina's modernization and faster economic growth as well as the eradication of corruption, for all of which "order" was the key.

South Korea and Argentina in 1966 were similar on two other dimensions. There was also no doubt in Argentina in 1966 about who was in charge: the army's commander in chief Lt. General Juan Carlos Onganía, whose ascendancy had been undisputed since armed clashes in 1962–1963. Onganía's towering role made it difficult to create institutionalized procedures within the dictatorship to respond to crises with flexibility. In South Korea, Park's comparable dominance during the 1960s gradually reduced his regime's capacity for flexible response as well.

The Argentine authoritarian regime unraveled more quickly than South Korea's, however. In April and May 1969, there were massive uprisings in Argentina's major urban centers, particularly among blue-collar workers, events known as the "Cordobazo." The government had suppressed channels of popular representation so well that it lacked information about discontent. On June 8, 1970, the commanders of the army, navy, and air force deposed Onganía. His successor, Roberto Levingston, a junior general, was overthrown in 1971 by General Alejandro Lanusse, who ended the military regime in 1973.

At its installation moment, the subsequent Argentine dictatorship, which began with a coup on March 24, 1976, improved somewhat on the 1966 pattern and, hence, also on what had taken place in South Korea. Between 1973 and 1976, Argentina was governed by three Peronista presidents: provisionally by Héctor Cámpora, and then by Juan Domingo Perón (who died in office) and was succeeded by the vice president, his wife, María Estela Martínez (Isabel) de Perón. By the time of her overthrow, Argentina had sunk into chaos. In the first quarter of 1976, the annualized inflation rate was 3,000 percent; labor unions were vigorously militant. Extensive civil violence broke out, including terrorist and paramilitary assassinations and kidnappings. "To no one's great surprise, and to the undisguised relief of many ordinary Argentines (including Peronists), the armed forces . . . deposed the now thoroughly discredited Peronist regime. There was no resistance."[11] The legitimating claim was similar, only more urgent. Argentina had to stabilize its economy and end civil violence. The armed forces chose to employ very high levels of repression, however, even though there had been little resistance to the coup.[12]

The Argentine military had also learned from its previous dictatorship and, as we shall see, from the Brazilian experience. Upon taking power in 1976, the military issued a "Statute of the Revolution" that stipulated a single, five-year mandate for any presidential incumbent. In 1976, General Jorge Videla, chief of the army, became president while agreeing on the termination date for his time in office. From the start, a presidential succession was scheduled for, and took place in, March 1981. At that moment, however, Argentina was in the midst of a financial crisis. The new president, General Roberto Viola, was overthrown in December 1981; his successor, General Leopoldo Galtieri, ousted in July 1982, was held responsible for Argentina's defeat at war with the United Kingdom over islands in the South Atlantic Ocean.

Thus Argentina's starting circumstances were slightly more auspicious for the installation of dictatorship at both times (but especially in 1976) than in South Korea, because in Argentina there was little opposition and extensive support for both coups. Onganía's and Videla's predominance was comparable to Park's, and neither had a good strategy for institutionalized succession. But the Argentine military in 1976 had a better plan to institutionalize authoritarian rule than Park or Onganía did.

The Brazilian armed forces overthrew President João Goulart in a revolt between March 30 and April 2, 1964. The general confederation of workers called for a general strike, but the workers did not respond. Loyalist troops failed to fight the military rebellion. Calls for a popular uprising went unheeded. Brazil, too, had suffered from intense and widespread social conflict and from high inflation in the months preceding the coup (though at rates much lower than in Argentina and Chile at the time of the 1976 and 1973 coups, respectively). The Goulart government had been politically weak and presided over economic stagnation. Goulart had been elected vice president in October 1960 and acceded to the presidency in August 1961 only because President Jânio Quadros resigned. In circumstances similar to South Korea's at the time of the 1961 coup, the Brazilian armed forces claimed legitimacy to overcome these ills.

Initial conditions were less favorable in Brazil than in South Korea, however, because the organization of power in the new regime took some time to construct. The war minister, General Dantas Ribeiro, was immobilized in the hospital. The chief of the Army General Staff, General Humberto Castello Branco, took the lead in the military conspiracy but political complexity deferred his becoming president until April 11. Castello Branco was elected to the remainder of the presidential term—that is, the Brazilian constitution was not set aside but would be amended tortuously and painfully in subsequent years. The Congress was purged; political parties were dissolved, and presidential elections and gubernatorial elections were made indirect. But the notion that no single person had seized power remained entrenched.

The military reached consensus on General Arthur Costa e Silva, chosen as president in October 1966. The Brazilian authoritarian regime thus completed its installation featuring institutionalized succession within the authoritarian regime. There would be a total of four peaceful transitions of presidential power during the authoritarian regime (and thus five military presidents) before its end in 1985. The difficulty in making the coup and consolidating the regime at the start led the Brazilian military to install more collegial and eventually more effective procedures of rule than in South Korea, Argentina of 1966, or Chile, and more successful than in Argentina of 1976–1983.[13]

In short, at the start the installation of dictatorship in Brazil was less propitious than in South Korea in terms of leadership unity and about the same in terms of resistance to the installation. But the Brazilian dictatorship was more effective at establishing workable succession rules.

The Park regime's installation looks better than the opening moments of General Augusto Pinochet's dictatorship in Chile. There was more resistance to the overthrow of constitutionally elected president Salvador

Allende in Chile in 1973 than in South Korea's comparable moment in 1961. The brutality of immediate military repression of that resistance in Chile in 1973 exceeded repression levels in South Korea in 1961. During the last twelve months of Allende's presidency, the annualized inflation rate was 286 percent; social conflict was widespread and intense. Chileans were more divided than South Koreans and Argentines at the moment of the founding coup, but many Chileans welcomed the dictatorship and most acquiesced to it in order to "rescue" Chile from chaos and confrontation—the new military regime's claim to legitimacy.

In contrast to Argentina, Brazil, and South Korea, military authority in Chile at the time of the coup was in flux. Before the coup, the Chilean military's chain of command snapped several times and a military mutiny occurred in June 1973. Pinochet was sworn in as commander in chief of the army only nineteen days before the coup that overthrew Allende. In the air force, General Gustavo Leigh was appointed commander in chief only twenty-nine days before the coup. In the navy, Vice Admiral José Toribio Merino was appointed chief only four days before the coup. All three had conspired not just against Allende but also against the officers whom they replaced. These three coup plotters were joined by the chief of police to create a four-man ruling junta. Moreover, Generals Sergio Arellano and Oscar Bonilla, "both more dashing and respected than Pinochet, emerged as heroes of the coup with new sources of power." Bonilla became interior minister; Arellano, commander of the garrison for the capital city. Within six months, both generals met mysterious deaths. Pinochet's predecessor as army commander in chief, General Carlos Prats, remained popular in the army and in Chile; he was assassinated in September 1974. The military junta made Pinochet the chief executive only in June 1974. In July 1978, Pinochet ousted General Leigh from the junta (not unlike the case of General Yun in South Korea in 1973) for deigning to discuss transition scenarios. In part because Pinochet had such difficulty in establishing his primacy, he took no steps to organize his succession within the authoritarian regime. Until the day of his defeat in a plebiscite in 1988, he never believed that he would stop serving as Chile's president until his death.[14] The Chilean installation was thus more troubled at the outset than South Korea's— greater initial resistance, lower leadership unity—and equally poor in the shared failure to institutionalize succession within the regime.

The Mexican authoritarian installation was initially the most troubled. Resistance to new rulers was high and leadership unity was low. The Mexican revolution began in October 1910, swiftly overthrew President General Porfirio Díaz, but continued for much of that decade as various factions fought each other. In 1920, the most powerful revolutionary commander, General Venustiano Carranza, who had become president of Mexico, attempted to impose his chosen successor for the presidency. Carranza's gambit failed. He was killed in May 1920. The second great survivor of the revolution, General Francisco (Pancho) Villa, signed a peace agreement in July 1920. There was, however, no one winner but a triumvirate. General Adolfo de la Huerta became provisional president until General Alvaro Obregón was elected president later that year. General Plutarco Elías Calles followed, being elected in 1924 after the government beat back General de la Huerta's rebellion. Obregón was reelected in 1928 but was assassinated by a religious fanatic before his presidential inauguration. Religious civil war flared in various regions of Mexico between 1926 and 1929. The elections of the 1920s were uncompetitive and fraudulent.

Faced with civil war, the assassination of Mexico's president-elect, and prospects for further instability, in 1929 President Calles acted as if he had read Thomas Hobbes's *Leviathan*. Because men live in a perpetual state of war without a leviathan, "the life of man [is] solitary, poor, nasty, brutish, and short." Therefore, men agree on a covenant: "I authorize and give up my right of governing myself, to this [single party], on this condition, that thou give up thy right to [it], and authorize all [its] actions in like manner."[15] On the occasion of his last message to Congress, Calles called for the formation of a single party. The National Revolutionary Party, founded in March 1929, included all the powerful military leaders and civilian bosses. Until 1934, Calles ruled indirectly through puppet presidents: Emilio Portes Gil, Pascual Ortiz Rubio, and Abelardo Rodríguez. Calles also tried to control Lázaro Cárdenas, elected in 1934, but Cárdenas broke Calles's power and, in April 1936, exiled him.[16]

Anchored in a single party, eventually known as the Institutional Revolutionary Party (PRI), the Mexican authoritarian regime lasted until the 1990s. The first president of Mexico ever elected from the opposition, Vicente Fox, took office only in December 2000. A key to the regime's success was its no-reelection rule, which applied to presidents, governors, mayors, members of Congress, and subnational legislators. You obey me today, the regime's key rule implied, in the certainty that I will step down on schedule and you will then have your chance to rule. Starting at the end of Cárdenas's six-year term in 1940, there were ten peaceful presidential successions within the same single-party regime. In addition to its hold on the presidency until 2000, the ruling party controlled every governorship until 1989 and both chambers of Congress until 1997; it typically claimed three-quarters to nine-tenths of the valid votes cast in every presidential election until 1988.

In Mexico, more than in Brazil in 1964 but unlike in South Korea, Argentina, and Chile, the contestation at the start of the authoritarian regime forced a collegial outcome. This contributed to a longer-lasting and more stable authoritarian regime. The early emergence and consolidation of rule by Park, Pinochet, and Onganía worked to the detriment of the installation of a long-term institutionalized authoritarian regime.

The Choice of Institutional Means

Every authoritarian regime studied here chose the same institutional means for executive decision making. The new ruler delegated significant powers to civilians in specialized areas of the regime. These regimes differed, however, in their choice of institutional means for rule making and information gathering. The Chilean and Argentine militaries abolished parliament, while the Brazilian and Mexican militaries retained parliaments. South Korea retained a parliament during 1961–1972 but gutted it during the so-called *yushin* period, 1972–1979. The "parliamentary dictatorships" employed consultative procedures, legislative assemblies, and party organizations to shape the new rules for governing; in general, the greater the resort to these procedures, the lower was its resort to police or military repression.

President Park relied on highly talented and admirably trained civilian economic policy officials, privileging the role of the Economic Planning Bureau.[17] South Korea's economic growth during the Park era was stunning. President Onganía chose a comparably talented civilian minister of the economy and labor (who also controlled the finance ministry), Adalberto Krieger Vasena, who served from 1967 through 1969. Inflation fell, average annual industrial wages in real terms did not decline, and the growth rate of per capita gross domestic product reached 7 percent in 1969, Krieger's last year.[18] President Videla's economic policies were less successful, though he also relied on a bright civilian minster of the economy, José Martínez de Hoz. Unable to cut the budget deficit because of military and other pressures, Martínez de Hoz manipulated the exchange rate to bring down inflation but ultimately failed.[19]

The Brazilian military likewise hired talented and hardheaded civilian finance ministers. Key reforms were enacted under Roberto Campos and Octávio Gouvéia de Bulhões, with Campos in the lead as planning minister. The military government's economic growth policy, however, can be traced to the appointment of Antonio Delfim Neto in March 1967. The rate of economic growth doubled from 4.8 percent in 1967 to 9.3 percent in 1968; it stayed above that rate for four consecutive years, with growth rates in the 1970s averaging 8 percent through 1976. This period was known as the Brazilian economic "miracle." The military government's economic policies were less successful thereafter, but civilian officials continued to design and implement economic policy.[20]

President Pinochet made famous his "Chicago Boys"—civilian economic policy officials trained at the University of Chicago. However, Chilean economic policy in the 1970s and early 1980s was unevenly successful at best, plunging Chile into a financial panic in 1983.[21] A different set of civilian ministers engineered Chile's economic recovery for the balance of the 1980s.

The last general to serve as president of Mexico, Manuel Ávila Camacho, stepped down in 1946. Civilian economic policy officials prevailed throughout Mexican twentieth-century history, and certainly during the years of the Mexican "miracle," 1940–1960, when the average annual growth rate exceeded 6 percent. Mexican economic malperformance occurred only later.[22]

The South Korean and Brazilian regimes, Mexico's from the 1940s through the 1960s, Argentina's in 1966–1973, and again in 1981–1982 also worked closely with industrialists. They all privileged the development of manufacturing, including heavy industry, concentrated in large business conglomerates, creating oligopolies in the hopes that the firms would become "national champions." Mexico remained strongly supportive of manufacturing even through the 1970s and early 1980s, but political disputes arose frequently between entrepreneurs and leading government officials during those years over issues other than the shared support for the growth of manufacturing. The Chilean regime and the Argentine dictatorship in 1976–1981, on the contrary, followed policies that weakened manufacturing capacities and industrial interests.[23]

In sum, there is no variation among these regimes in their willingness to delegate economic and other policies to talented civilian ministers. As a set, they differed from other authoritarian regimes of the 1970s, such as Peru under military rule, which appointed only military officers to cabinet posts. There are some differences, however, in the willingness to work closely with leading industrialists. The authoritarian regimes in Chile and Argentina 1976 were markedly less supportive of the development of manufacturing. And conflicts over some issues emerged in the 1970s and 1980s in Mexico between business and the state.

The authoritarian regimes under study differed in their willingness to retain a parliament and lawful political parties. The Argentine and Chilean dictatorships disbanded Congress and proscribed political parties for nearly all of their duration, necessarily relying on secret police and brute repression to cope with the opposition and obtain pertinent political information. They were sophisticated dictatorships in some economic policies but rather primitive in their politics.

The Mexican single-party regime, in contrast, never dispensed with its Congress during its decades in power and, by definition, it featured a ruling party. The party was organized into worker, peasant, and "popular" (catch-all) sectors; labor and peasant union leaders and many middle-class groups were thus linked directly to the ruling party. Nominations of candidates for the presidency remained the informal but effective prerogative of the incumbent president until the 2000 election. Nominations for other ruling party posts were negotiated within narrow ruling circles to ensure control from the top and party discipline. The main long-term opposition party, the National Action Party (PAN), was founded in 1939 and was never banned. It was cheated from many subnational electoral victories during its history; it won the presidency for the first time only in 2000. The regime tolerated other small parties but these, unlike the PAN, were often co-opted. The ruling party won elections by using legal and illegal means, including fraud. Outgoing President Cárdenas set the example in the 1940 presidential election, ensuring the election of his chosen successor over a strong opposition candidate.

Posts in Mexico's Congress rewarded politicians from various regions and from the party's various sectors to sustain the broad ruling coalition; membership in the Congress "nationalized" regional and sectoral politicians. The no-immediate-reelection rule enabled many politicians to rotate as members of Congress. The Congress also gave the opposition voice without power. In the early 1960s, the constitution was amended to ensure some opposition party representation in the Chamber of Deputies elected from party lists. In 1977, the constitution was amended again to ensure that there would be no fewer than 100 opposition deputies in the 400-member chamber. A decade later, as part of the start of the political transition, the opposition was guaranteed 200 seats in a 500-member chamber. Until the 1988 elections, Congress posed no serious challenge to the president's powers; between 1988 and 1997, the president needed support from the PAN when he wished to amend the constitution. In short, the choice of consultative, partisan, and legislative institutional strategies gave the Mexican authoritarian regime "safe" instruments with which to reward supporters, discipline members, and allow the opposition to vent its grievances without resorting to violence or harming policies. It was a brilliant political strategy for authoritarian rule.

The Brazilian military government stumbled onto a similar scheme. Its approach proved to be less successful than in Mexico but rather more so than in Argentina and Chile. As already noted, after the 1964 coup the Brazilian military purged the Congress, weakened it institutionally, and in 1965 disbanded the preexisting political parties. But the toothless Congress continued, and new political parties were founded. Politicians were herded into an official party, the National Renewal Alliance (ARENA), or the tolerated opposition, the Brazilian Democratic Movement (MDB). In the late 1960s and early 1970s, the opposition held about one-third of the seats in the Chamber of Deputies, a much higher proportion than in Mexico before the start of its democratic transition.[24] The Congress and the tolerated opposition party voiced discontent without impairing executive policies. The government employed cooptation strategies and patronage to woo selected opposition members and keep ARENA party members of Congress and subnational politicians in line.

This strategy served the government well even in the 1982 legislative elections, the last held under dictatorship. ARENA won 49 percent of the seats in the Chamber of Deputies; by that point, the government had authorized the creation of other parties so ARENA remained the largest party. And ARENA held two-thirds of the Senate seats.[25] ARENA was never as central to the Brazilian military regime, however, as the PRI was in Mexico. The Brazilian executive was beholden to the top military officer corps and independent from ARENA, whereas in Mexico the president was a successful PRI politician.

The South Korean experience was superior to Mexico's and Brazil's in the 1960s but inferior in the 1970s. Mexican and Brazilian authoritarians relied increasingly upon political strategies for governing. The South Korean sequence was the opposite, that is, there was decreasing use of political strategies from the 1960s to the 1970s. South Korea moved away from subtle authoritarian rule (Brazil, Mexico) toward the more primitive exercise of power (Argentina, Chile).

The Park regime began with the construction of the Democratic Republican Party (DRP) and the toleration of a significant opposition. In 1963, Park won the presidency with 42.6 percent of the vote, just 1.5 percentage points ahead of opposition candidate Yun Po-Sŏn. In 1967, Park widened his margin of victory to 10 percentage points over Yun. In 1971, Park also won comfortably, although his margin of victory narrowed slightly. During these years, the National Assembly included substantial opposition representation and, especially between 1963 and 1967, noteworthy opportunities for individual Assembly members to propose bills. The Assembly also typically modified about half of all executive bills. Yet as the years passed, the political space shrank for Assembly member initiatives or for

DRP-led amendments of executive bills. In contrast to ARENA in Brazil and the PRI in Mexico, the DRP steadily atrophied as time wore on.[26]

Some blame for the weakness of the South Korean opposition rests with the opposition itself and some with government efforts to weaken it. In the 1963 legislative elections the combined opposition parties won half the votes while the government won only one-third (this did not happen at all during the first half of the Brazilian authoritarian regime, and it happened only as part of the end of the Mexican authoritarian regime), but the single-member plurality district electoral law, and the division of the opposition into four major parties, left the government with 63 percent of the seats. In 1963, the South Korean opposition would have benefited from being forced into a single party like Brazil's MDB. By the 1967 election, excellent economic growth performance and resort to election rigging gave the DRP a majority of the votes and nearly three-quarters of the seats. In the 1971 legislative election, the distribution of seats resembled the distribution of votes more closely because government and opposition parties had become regionally concentrated and thus able to win single-member district seats relatively proportionate to their national share of the votes (the DRP, nonetheless, still won more seats than its share of the national vote). With nearly 45 percent of the seats, the opposition could block constitutional amendments.[27]

Compare the Park regime's response to the 1971 parliamentary elections with the Brazilian dictatorship's response to the 1974 parliamentary elections. In Brazil, the opposition MDB won sixteen out of twenty-two senators and nearly doubled its share of the popular vote in the Chamber of Deputies, reaching almost 38 percent of the votes. In anticipation of the next elections, Brazil's military government amended the constitution, arrogating to itself the power to appoint one-third of the Senate and gerrymandering the Chamber of Deputies to increase the representation of the rural areas, where it was stronger. Soon thereafter, however, the government also relaxed its political party law, permitting various parties to organize, and it adopted a much more tolerant attitude toward labor union strikes.[28] The government began to loosen the historical state-corporatist control over labor unions, enabling independent labor unions to organize. The government preferred that labor protest focus on business firms, not on the state. To cope with the more complex political situation, the government increased its reliance on the official ARENA party. ARENA incorporated most of the appointed senators. The net result retained sufficient space for the opposition and sufficient power for the government. The government preferred to rely on political instruments instead of brute repression. A sharper, more destabilizing political crisis was avoided. Higher levels of repression were unnecessary and the cost of coercion was reduced. Bolívar Lamounier summarized the regime's strategy well in comparative perspective: "Between the impossibility of a lasting Mexicanization, and more dictatorial immobilism, General Geisel [the fourth consecutive military president in Brazil] opted for a third road, which was gradual and secure decompression."[29]

The Park regime's response to the April and May 1971 election challenges was less effective in maintaining an authoritarian regime that relied on the consent of the governed or at least their toleration, with low resort to repression. Park could not Mexicanize and would not even attempt to Brazilianize South Korea's political system. Along with other factors, the 1971 elections led Park to install the *yushin* regime the next year. Under the *yushin* constitution, Park could control the appointment of one-third of the National Assembly members. Because South Korea's parliament was unicameral, this was a much greater proportionate power of appointment than the Brazilian authoritarians would obtain a few years later. In contrast to the rising role of ARENA in Brazil, Park chose to rely less on the DRP because he was assured of support from his appointees. The electoral law and the government's manipulation of the political process greatly weakened the opposition parties as well. The *yushin* regime also imposed tougher controls over Korean labor unions. Park relied increasingly on the Korea Central Intelligence Agency and other repressive forces to provide him with information to put down the opposition.[30]

The installation of the *yushin* regime, as Hyug Baeg Im indicates in Chapter 8, was directly related to the regime's founding flaw—a flaw that authoritarians had avoided in Brazil and Mexico. Park insisted on remaining in power, forcing an amendment of the constitution to enable him to run for a third reelection in 1971 against the opposition of members of his own coalition, and employing this succession crisis as a tool to enable the subsequent construction of the *yushin* regime. The authoritarian regimes in Brazil and Mexico were spared these succession troubles because they had arranged for the rotation of presidential power within the authoritarian regime.

In conclusion, Mexican authoritarians institutionalized means for consultation and thus fashioned policies that gathered support. Their choice of means also made it easy to obtain political information about opponents. The ruling PRI managed the choice of incumbents at election time with relative ease. The Brazilian dictatorship was less capable, but it also employed various consultative mechanisms, retained a parliament, permitted a strong lawful opposition and, for most of its duration, preferred to co-opt rather than to repress. These two authoritarian regimes were prepared to repress, of course, and at times did so. One should not confuse an "intelligent dictator" with a democrat.

The means for stable and politically successful authoritarian rule, with low levels of repression, created in Mexico and to some extent in Brazil, were for the most part absent in Argentina (especially in the late 1970s) and in Chile. The remarkable South Korean feat is that its ruler exchanged the more politically effective means of the 1960s for the less politically effective means of the 1970s.[31]

The previous choices about means for rule making, information gathering, and representation had consequences for the enforcement of compliance. The fewer the channels for peaceful expression of dissent are, the greater the likelihood of protest and repression is. The authoritarian regimes in Argentina (especially 1976), Chile, and South Korea under *yushin* were highly repressive. Torture became an administrative practice, large numbers of political prisoners were held, and labor union protest was dealt with harshly. In contrast, levels of political imprisonment were much lower in authoritarian Brazil. Both torture and political imprisonment were lower still in authoritarian Mexico.[32]

The Labor Question

Mexican authoritarians relied on two sets of instruments to control organized labor. One set included state controls on worker participation, selective repression of labor opposition movements, and cooptation of labor leaders; this set made the regime authoritarian. But the long-term stability of authoritarian rule in Mexico also rested on the alliance forged between the 1920s and the 1940s that linked national political elites to key elements of organized labor. Despite at times contradictory policies, the national political elite valued this alliance at least until the mid-1990s and supported its labor union allies in return for their backing the regime.[33] Few strikes got "out of control" during the long decades of PRI rule; repression was limited even at those times. This fact does not excuse the regime's authoritarian practices, but it makes clear their political effectiveness.

The Brazilian military government installed in 1964 inherited the labor code first elaborated in 1943, which intended unions to collaborate with the government to promote social peace. It gave the Labor Ministry broad powers over the unions, including the capacity to intervene in union elections and replace union leaders. Strikes were extremely rare. General nationwide labor confederations were prohibited. This scheme for labor control came to be known as state corporatism.[34] In 1964, the government used this labor code to the hilt to get rid of union leaders it disliked and to crush union power.

Brazil's economic "miracle" transformed the social and economic basis for labor unions. From 1960 to 1980, the number of people employed in secondary economic activities nearly quadrupled. They were geographically concentrated. In the 1970s, about half of all secondary-sector employment was located in the state of São Paulo, making it easier for labor activists to organize unions. Led by metalworkers, in 1978 a wave of union strikes swept over the manufacturing sector, especially in São Paulo. This labor upsurge led to the foundation of the Workers' Party (PT) in 1979, made possible by the regime's changes in the electoral law, permitting the creation of new parties, and in labor laws to permit wage increases and the emergence of interunion organizations.[35] There was no "Cordobazo" in Brazil in 1978, because the dictatorship—led by President General Ernesto Geisel—knew how to adjust. There was also less need for brute repression.

The political ineptitude of the Argentine regimes stands out in contrast. Mention has been made of the "Cordobazo" labor union and other protests in May 1969 that led eventually to the unraveling of the Argentine authoritarian regime founded in 1966. The Onganía regime had sought to subordinate, not to destroy, organized labor; the latter thus remained strong enough to provide eventually the major impetus for the regime's termination. Nevertheless, this military regime generally preferred to co-opt than to repress the labor unions. In 1976, the Videla dictatorship believed it had to avoid that "mistake." In addition to the thousands of people murdered by the security forces, the Videla government attacked the General Confederation of Workers (CGT) to abolish "political unionism," destroying the CGT's capacity to coordinate hundreds of labor unions and drastically curtailing their economic power. Labor unions suffered much more from this second authoritarian regime, but in the 1980s they reemerged nearly as strong as ever to reclaim their power after this dictatorship collapsed in 1983. Argentine organized labor's political and economic militancy remained vibrant during the 1980s.[36]

The Chilean authoritarian regime was extremely hostile to the labor movement. Its economic and social policies led to a drop in real wages, increased unemployment, heightened repression, and severe limitations on the capacity of unions to represent their members. The immediate post-coup repression of labor was at least as severe as in Argentina. Yet in Chile, government authorities innovated a more successful labor policy; labor minister José Piñera was its architect. His "Labor Plan" greatly curtailed the ability of organized labor political networks to affect elections of any kind, but it created a space for labor unions at the plant level. The Labor Plan markedly weakened the areas eligible for collective bargaining, yet at the same time such bargaining remained a tool available for unions. Although it became very difficult to call a strike legally, strikes were not banned. The outcome permitted a limited role for labor unions. In the 1980s, while the unions were key actors in the political opposition to the dictatorship, they were never powerful enough to overthrow it or to prevent the accomplishment of its economic objectives.[37] The Chilean labor movement had been one of Latin America's most powerful before the 1973 coup, certainly far more so than South Korea's in either 1961 or 1972. The Chilean dictatorship, unlike Argentina's, dealt with its labor unions harshly but not stupidly.

The effectiveness of the South Korean authoritarian response to the same set of problems declined from the 1960s to the 1970s. In the 1960s, the Park regime attempted to Brazilianize the labor movement, employing the tools of state corporatism to enhance state control over the unions. It deposed and arrested the union leaders it disliked; it banned some nationwide union federations. It created procedures to interfere regularly with the selection of union leaders and prohibited union political activities. It mandated the creation of joint labor-management committees as the site for collective bargaining. But it also permitted the persistence of industrial-level unions. The South Korean economic "miracle" in the 1960s was closest in some respects to Brazil's in the late 1960s and early 1970s. Both countries grew at comparably very fast rates during a short time. Yet, in time, they would differ. The Brazilian dictatorship responded to the increased economic significance of labor and activity through a managed opening. President Park installed the repressive *yushin* regime.

The *yushin* system eliminated the influence of industrial-level unions and removed the legal basis for collective action. It ruled via emergency decrees, viewing any form of labor protest as a challenge to the regime itself. The system drove labor union leaders and workers, lacking lawful peaceful means to express their normal grievances, to the opposition.[38] The *yushin* regime faced intensified labor protests in 1978 and 1979 at exactly the same historical moment as the Brazilian dictatorship did. The *yushin* system collapsed and Park was assassinated (though for reasons unrelated to the labor protest); the South Korean military employed even higher levels of brute repression. The Brazilian military regime's accommodationist tactics, in comparison, were more effective politically and less costly; the regime endured another half-dozen years.

Compared with President Geisel, President Park was less successful in managing labor politics. Compared with both Geisel and Park, the Mexican PRI incarnated genius in managing labor politics. In general, South Korea under *yushin* and Argentina after 1976 were the least politically effective authoritarian regimes in their handling of the labor question, while Mexico's and to a lesser extent Brazil's authoritarian regimes were the most effective.

Governing the Society

An authoritarian regime faces three important choices to govern society. Will it fashion an ideology to persuade citizens to consent to its rule? Will it tolerate and make use of societal pluralism to permit the articulation of civil society interests? And will it activate or deactivate citizen engagement to advance its ends?

The Mexican authoritarian regime was founded in response to the Mexican revolution but, except during the presidency of Lázaro Cárdenas, it was not particularly revolutionary. It deemphasized both ideological appeals, except in the most general way, and regime-sponsored political activation of citizens. It valued nationalism and the defense of the state's international sovereignty. Government-sponsored school textbooks exalted the accomplishments and good intentions of Mexican governments over the twentieth century and supported the president's legitimacy. Government officials spoke the language of social justice, at times genuinely, at times to justify the extensive state involvement in the economy and society. The state promised economic growth and delivered it from the 1930s to the end of the 1960s. But none of this was part of a well-articulated ideology. There were no "sacred" ideological texts. The government and the PRI avoided creating a standard by which they could be judged. Election turnouts were low. Independent popular political movements were few and fragmented, and most were based only in specific regions. Through the 1950s Mexicans had low interest and low involvement in politics.[39]

The most important and enduring political legacy of the Lázaro Cárdenas presidency was the corporatist organization of politics. The government fostered the organization of social and economic groups subordinated to the state and the ruling party. The PRI, as noted, was organized into sectors for workers, peasants, and middle-class associations. But the state also required nearly all business firms to join state-chartered business organizations to "represent" and control business interests. The Roman Catholic church, Mexico's largest, had been militarily and politically defeated by President Calles during the "Cristero" war (1926–1929); it operated politically with great caution. This system of corporatist controls functioned relatively effectively, with few changes, from the 1930s to the 1980s. Its breakdown was coterminous with the regime transition toward democracy.[40] The corporatist system, though frayed, even helped Mexico overcome its economic depression of the 1980s.[41]

The Brazilian, Chilean, and both Argentine authoritarian regimes justified their rule in the name of the nation, patriotism, modernization, public order, morality, anticommunism, measures against corruption, economic reorganization and growth, and a deep distrust of "politics."[42] These pronouncements were vague, albeit frequently repeated, providing little guidance for political action and little or no risk of being held as a standard for assessment. These notions—as those of Mexican authoritarians—were what Juan Linz calls "mentalities" rather than ideologies. "It is more difficult to conceive of mentalities as binding," Linz wrote, "requiring a commitment of the rulers and the subjects irrespective of costs and of the need of coercion to implement them. Mentalities are more difficult to diffuse among the masses, less susceptible to be[ing] used in education."[43] Nor can mentalities be readily used to hold rulers accountable.

The Chilean and Argentine (especially post-1976) dictatorships had a similar approach toward citizen participation: don't! They banned political parties, smashed many labor unions and social movements, and mostly failed to develop channels to engage popular participation. Military regimes in both countries cultivated friendly labor union leaders, but these efforts had little impact on the broader labor movement. The Pinochet government also employed a national network of Women's Centers. Although these had charitable purposes, they were also means to obtain support among conservative women.[44] But because the government distrusted civil society and especially mass politics, these endeavors failed to activate participation: they emphasized compliance.

In Argentina and Chile, these policies had broader consequences for societal pluralism and the articulation of interests. Organizations to represent workers, peasants, or the poor more generally were repressed. Business organizations, albeit under constraints, continued to function. The constraints on business were greater in Argentina between 1976 and 1980 because government authorities disdained the competence of business executives and intervened in the management of business federations. But the asymmetry in organization and potential for representation between upper-class and lower-class organizations prevented the sort of social pact that was the bread and butter of elite politics in Mexico, where they cushioned the impact of business-government disagreements between 1970 and 1982 and the economic crisis that followed in Mexico in the early 1980s. In Argentina and Chile under dictatorship, for several years the state and business federations had no partners with whom to negotiate. This regime failure to permit and make use of societal pluralism proved fatal for Argentine dictatorships. In Chile, it required a much larger dose of repression to keep the dictatorship in power at the time of economic crisis in the early to mid-1980s. The Mexican authoritarian regime, however, endured the economic depression of the 1980s, ending only in the 1990s.[45]

The Brazilian authoritarian regime, though similar to the others in its reliance on mentality rather than on ideology, differed from the Chilean and Argentine dictatorships in its approach to societal pluralism, which it addressed through state corporatism. The Brazilian dictatorship did not activate citizen participation but held elections, tolerated an opposition, and was less likely to repress than in Argentina or Chile. Employing the 1943 Labor Code, in its first decade the Brazilian dictatorship increased the level of labor repression well above the standards prevailing before the 1964 coup; after 1979, however, its policies toward labor and labor unions became more tolerant. The Brazilian regime for the most part tolerated business organizations; it permitted these organizations to become sources of opposition to government policies in economic and political spheres. Brazilian business leaders understood sooner than their Chilean counterparts that political authoritarianism had costs and that they would wield greater influence under democratic politics. They favored the "softer" themes of the authoritarian regime and in the end would help foster the transition to democracy.[46] The Brazilian regime's approach to societal pluralism came closer to Mexico's than to Argentina's or Chile's.

President Park's ideas about economic modernization, nationalism, and rejection of democratic politics echo well the themes from Latin American authoritarians. But Park's ideational formulations went beyond these mentalities. He sought to reshape the school curriculum and affect how Korean families related to the nation. There was an attempt to indoctrinate civil society, not just to repress it. Park displayed anti-elitist and populist values, including egalitarianism, to cope with elements of opposition in cities and especially in universities. He cultivated support in the rural areas, with some success, in part through the New Community Movement. This movement was more effective in the 1960s than in the 1970s because, with the success of Korean industrialization policies, the size of the rural sector shrank.[47]

In these ways, the Park regime in the 1960s created ideational standards against which it could subsequently be judged: was the egalitarian populist promise fulfilled and were communities empowered? Although the extent of effective participation in the New Community Movement was limited, it was more extensive than anything promoted by ruling South American dictatorships and was exceeded only in Mexico, whose ruling party developed similar forms of limited rural engagement over a longer span of time.

From the 1960s to the 1970s, the Park regime's approach to societal pluralism veered away from the Mexican comparison and resembled Argentina of 1976 and Chile more closely. As noted earlier, Park emulated Brazilian state corporatism toward labor unions in the 1960s but turned toward sharper repression of urban labor in the 1970s, departing from both the Brazilian and the Mexican patterns. Park's economic strategy chose certain business firms as "national champions," nurturing their development as *chaebol*, subordinating their strategies to governmental objectives managed through highly competent bureaucracies (echoes of the Argentine military's disdain for business acumen in the late 1970s), and sacrificing the development of a broader-based medium- and small-sized set of business firms that might have served as a proxy for civil society. The lack of strong labor federations and the lack of business federations that might have represented civil society indirectly deprived the South Korean regime of the Mexican-style social pact that might have smoothed political and economic crises. The South Korean government also entered into conflict with Christian churches to an extent unrivaled in Latin America (the only distant parallels were the critical postures of the Chilean and Brazilian Roman Catholic Bishops' Conference toward dictatorship years after each coup).[48]

By the late 1970s, the South Korean authoritarian regime was as unable as the Argentine and Chilean authoritarian regimes to address societal pluralism to advance its objectives, harness national efforts toward regime goals, and reduce the costs of repression. The *yushin* regime gave up on state corporatism, practiced briefly in South Korea during the 1960s, relying more on overt repression of labor and greater guidance of big business. But by having earlier emphasized the values of egalitarianism and limited forms of participation in the New Community Movement, the South Korean regime made itself somewhat vulnerable to the criticism that, through the establishment of *yushin*, it broke its own promises to the Korean nation. It sowed the least effective combination of variables to foster its own political objectives: it created ideological standards, gave up on state corporatism, and increased repression.

The Perfect Dictatorship?

Authoritarian regimes are often politically ineffective because many military officers who create and lead them do not care for or understand politics well. Authoritarian regimes often depend on just one leader, seek to ban politics, and resort to repression as their means of coping with disagreement. The politics of such regimes is at times so primitive that, by the second half of the twentieth century, they were less likely to survive for long in increasingly complex modern societies. Nonetheless, there is variation in the political performance of authoritarian regimes.

The authoritarian regimes under consideration also varied regarding economic outcomes. South Korea and Brazil had generally excellent economic growth results. Chile and the second Argentine dictatorship had poor economic growth results. Chile under General Pinochet has an international reputation for having engineered an economic miracle. Yet the best the Pinochet regime could muster during its second decade in power (1981–1990), after it had presumably purged the Chilean economy of all its viruses, was an annual average growth rate of gross domestic product per capita of 1.4 percent.[49] Mexico and the first Argentine dictatorship had periods of excellent economic growth results (in Mexico, this first-rate performance lasted from the late 1930s to the late 1960s) followed by economic downturns. The relationship between dictatorship and economic growth is therefore indeterminate.

The analysis of the political effectiveness of dictatorships in South Korea, Argentina, Brazil, Chile, and Mexico is summarized in Tables 20.2 20.3, and 20.4.

Argentina in both 1966 and 1976 and, to a lesser extent, South Korea had propitious circumstances at the start of the installation of the Onganía, Videla, and Park regimes. There was low resistance to the respective coups and substantial leadership unity. Where the installation was more difficult because the resistance was greater and there was no leadership unity, as in Brazil and Mexico, the likelihood that regime installers

Table 20.2 Comparative rank order for authoritarian political effectiveness: Performance during the installation of the regime

Rank	Low Resistance	Leadership Unity	Succession Rules
1 Best	Argentina 1966*	South Korea*	Mexico
2	Argentina 1976*	Argentina 1966*	Brazil
3	South Korea**	Argentina 1976*	Argentina 1976
4	Brazil**	Chile	Argentina 1966*
5	Chile	Brazil	Chile*
6 Worst	Mexico	Mexico	South Korea*

* Indicates ties.
** Indicates a second-level of ties in the "low resistance" column.

Table 20.3 Comparative rank order for authoritarian political effectiveness: Choice of institutional means

Rank	Delegate to civilian elites	Use legislature and political parties	Co-opt > Repress labor unions
1 Best	S. Korea *Yushin**	S. Korea 1961–72	Mexico
2	S. Korea 1961–72*	Mexico	Brazil
3	Brazil*	Brazil	S. Korea 1961–72
4	Argentina 1966*	S. Korea *Yushin*	Argentina 1966
5	Mexico	Argentina 1966*	Chile
6	Argentina 1976	Argentina 1976*	S. Korea *Yushin*
7 Worst	Chile	Chile*	Argentina 1976

* Indicates ties.

Table 20.4 Comparative rank order for authoritarian political effectiveness: Governing the society

Rank	Eschew Ideology	State Corporatism	Deactivate Participation
1 Best	All alike, except:	Mexico	Mexico
2		Brazil	Brazil
3		S. Korea 1961–72	S. Korea 1961–72
4		Argentina 1966	Argentina 1966
5		Argentina 1976	S. Korea *Yushin**
6		S. Korea *Yushin*	Argentina 1976*
7 Worst	South Korea	Chile	Chile*

* Indicates ties.

would agree on succession rules within the authoritarian regime was much greater. Those authoritarians who had to work harder at stabilizing their coalition at the moment of installation discovered the utility of succession rules early and to good effect. (Chile was an exception; installation was difficult, and yet General Pinochet succeeded in imposing his will over his coup allies and over societal opposition.)

The regimes that experienced difficult installation (Brazil and Mexico) were also more keenly aware of the need to expand and sustain the coalition to support the authoritarian regime and to gather political information useful for governing. They were, therefore, more likely to employ some legislative institutions and one or more political parties to advance their goals. These legislatures and parties were deeply constrained in their powers and their capacities; they differed from legislatures or parties in democratic political systems even though they carried out some of the same roles. Regimes with installation difficulties also learned earlier about the costs of repression. They preferred cooptation to repression to cut the cost of rulership and sustain a broad base of support. In this regard, the South Korean regime in the early 1960s scores high: its willingness to create a National Assembly and accept political parties is greater than might have been expected from its circumstances at installation.

The regimes with installation difficulties (Brazil and Mexico) and South Korea 1961–1972 followed similar strategies to govern society. They deactivated political participation and, for the most part, employed low levels of repression to accomplish this purpose, reducing the incentive for opponents to rise in protest. They employed state-corporatist instruments to control the society and harness it toward regime ends. Brazil and Mexico—but not South Korea 1961–1971—eschewed ideological appeals in order to deprive their critics of a standard by which to hold them accountable.

Argentina and Chile had primitive and politically ineffective authoritarian regimes. In order to govern, they bashed heads. They banned legislatures and parties, found it difficult and distasteful to co-opt critics, repressed brutally, and eschewed state-corporatist strategies. They deactivated political participation by force, thereby giving their opponents strong incentives to organize to defeat them. Argentina's second dictatorship was generally a worse performer than its first dictatorship; alas, even though the second dictatorship at its start learned the utility of succession rules, its leaders broke those rules soon after the first scheduled succession.

The Park regime's political effectiveness systematically deteriorated from the 1960s to the 1970s. By comparative political standards, it was an above-median performer in the 1960s (most often resembling Brazil) but a below-median performer in the 1970s. The Park regime in the 1960s employed the legislature, sponsored an official political party, preferred to co-opt rather than to repress, attempted to frame organized labor within a state-corporatist scheme, and promoted political deactivation in urban areas but with low levels of repression. (The Park regime was the only one to create a fairly formal official ideology.) The founding of the *yushin* regime in 1972 led to worse performance on all of these dimensions. The longer Park ruled, the more politically underdeveloped his regime became. This pattern of political decay continued under his immediate successors.

Analytically, this chapter has proceeded in three steps across time. The first step shows broad, sufficient similarities between the cases to permit comparison. This step of the analysis also indicates that South Korea had the apparently most propitious hypothesized conditions prior to regime installation to meet the criteria for a "perfect dictatorship" sketched at the outset. Nevertheless, Park's South Korea would become less politically effective than authoritarian regimes in Mexico and Brazil. Why did this happen?

The second step answers one part of this puzzle. It turns out that the hypothesized "propitious conditions" prior to installation proved counterproductive for longer-term authoritarian regime political efficacy. Instead, difficult installation circumstances are more likely to provide incentives for the authoritarian coalition to be politically innovative and to approximate the criteria of the "perfect dictatorship." Five years after regime installation, this foundational variable correctly ranks four (see Table 20.5) of the five countries in terms of the cumulative political efficacy of their respective dictatorships: Mexico, Brazil, South Korea, and Argentina. However, Chile had an authoritarian installation but the behavior of its rulers resembled Argentina 1976 and eventually South Korea's *yushin* rather than Mexico and Brazil. Moreover, regime trajectories changed not just in response to the initial installation but at some later time in Argentina 1976, Chile, and South Korea. Why did this happen?

The third step takes note that Generals Galtieri in Argentina, Pinochet in Chile, and Park in South Korea cared more for their personal power than for the construction of a broader-based authoritarian regime. Pinochet's response to a difficult installation was not to shift away from repression but to impose his personal rule and repress more. Galtieri and especially Park, in turn, undid the more effective political means adopted earlier in their respective authoritarian regimes, concentrated power, and repressed more in the regime's later years. Not every founding dictator behaved this way, and not every founding dictator who attempted to lengthen his rule succeeded, as the greater political success of authoritarian rule in Mexico and Brazil shows. Twenty years after installation, only the authoritarian regimes founded in Mexico and Brazil survived.

Table 20.5 Comparative rank order for authoritarian political effectiveness: Time dimension

Rank	At installation[a]	Installation + 5 years	Installation + 20 years[b]
1 Best	Argentina 1966	Brazil	Mexico
2	S. Korea	Mexico	Brazil
3	Argentina 1976	S. Korea	
4	Brazil	Argentina 1976	
5	Chile	Chile	
6 Worst	Mexico	Argentina 1966	

a. This column combines the two first columns in Table 20.2 prior to establishing succession rules.

b. The other authoritarian regimes no longer existed.

Politically effective dictators seek political stability and economic growth. They hope that both goals will reinforce each other, but they value political stability more. Politically effective dictators prefer cooptation and preemption to repression and *ex post* responses to crises—they are proactive, not merely reactive. These are qualities, to be sure, that resemble those of effective democratic rulers.

"The perfect dictatorship is not communism, nor is it the Soviet Union, nor is it Fidel Castro: it is Mexico."[50] So alleged Peruvian novelist and essayist Mario Vargas Llosa in August 1990 during a series of round tables convoked in Mexico City by the dean of Mexican letters, the late Octavio Paz. Vargas Llosa noted that the long-term permanence of a single party in power, the manipulation of elections, and the suppression of domestic criticism marked this dictatorship. He also emphasized the political effectiveness and complexity of the Mexican regime's procedures and institutions.

Park Chung Hee was an economic-growth visionary. The initial conditions that he faced at the start of his authoritarian regime and Korea's high economic growth performance made the Park dictatorship the "most likely to succeed" politically. It should have relied less on crude repression and it should have lasted the longest. Yet Park's authoritarian regime was less politically successful from its first to its second decade and generally less successful than those installed in Brazil and Mexico. Park's choice of politically inept strategies leading up to and under the *yushin* system was a mistake. Park's political errors probably contributed to his assassination and certainly to the death of the *yushin* system.

CHAPTER TWENTY-ONE

Industrial Policy in Key Developmental Sectors: South Korea versus Japan and Taiwan

Gregory W. Noble

A REMARKABLE SURGE in the production and export of commodity manufactures dramatically lifted the standard of living in South Korea, and became one of the most enduring legacies of the Park era. By the end of Park's rule, labor-intensive manufactures such as textiles were increasingly joined by capital-intensive heavy industrial goods.

Explaining South Korea's industrial accomplishment and placing it in comparative perspective is no easy task. Some authors have compared Korea, particularly under the second half of Park's reign, to the bureaucratic authoritarian regimes of Latin America in the same period.[1] This perspective highlights the dilemmas of growth and the wary but interdependent relationship between generals and economic bureaucrats, but ultimately proves limiting, if not misleading. The immediate stimuli for South Korea's *yushin* constitution were security concerns and politics (Park's attempts to justify a third presidential term, and then the ruling party's loss of the two-thirds legislative majority necessary to revise the constitution) rather than a crisis of accumulation. Latin America's pattern of industrialization, with its mobilized labor unions, abundant natural resources, and high levels of direct foreign investment also was dramatically different from that of Korea.

An alternative approach focuses on the similarities linking South Korea and its East Asian neighbors, Japan and Taiwan.[2] The three Northeast Asian economies not only shared important geographic and demographic legacies such as dense populations and a paucity of natural resources, but also were deeply influenced by Chinese culture, by the developmental state first created in Meiji Japan, and by the postwar American attempt to contain Asian communism through economic development. War, inflation, and land reform distributed wealth and income far more widely than in Latin America or other developing areas. Rapid growth in postwar Japan provided South Korea and Taiwan both a model for development and a tangible stimulus in the form of trade and investment.

By the late 1960s, economic development in all three countries was characterized by strikingly high levels of educational attainment, savings, investment and growth, and impressive improvements in public health indicators such as infant mortality and life expectancy.[3] In all three, political parties supported by organized labor remained weak, while the government intruded heavily in economic activity, protecting domestic markets, promoting favored industries, and exercising decisive influence over the allocation of capital.

Nevertheless, without completely denying the manifest similarities, many regional experts highlight the differences across the three countries and caution against generalizations about any one "East Asian model of development."[4] Japan enjoyed a larger population base, a longer history of development, a more independent business class, and an earlier development of democratic institutions than did its two former colonies, leading to a more stable and balanced pattern of economic development. During the rapid growth period, the Japanese government generally held inflation in check and balanced its budgets. Japan's capacious domestic market meant that even behind protectionist barriers a large number of domestic firms competed at efficient scale in most industries, although competition was more often oligopolistic and restrained than perfectly free. Large companies and business groups coexisted with a much larger mass of independent small firms. Exports, though important to pay for raw materials and other necessary inputs, remained modest compared with domestic production. Taking advantage of skilled engineers and workers, Japanese companies combined the mass production of commodities with more specialized and flexible production of consumer durables and capital equipment.[5]

Taiwan had but one-sixth the population of Japan and a later start in development. However, its entrenched and stable ruling party, developed in competition with the Chinese Communist Party and re-formed in Taiwan after the loss of the mainland, and its powerful state structure, enriched by the legacy of the Japanese colonial period and rationalized with help from the Americans, allowed Taiwan to maintain extraordinary macroeconomic stability and intervene only selectively in the workings of the private sector. The bitter experience of wartime hyperinflation also inclined Taiwan's government toward conservative macroeconomic management. Taiwan grew on the back of exports of labor-intensive goods, most produced by small local enterprises, with a secondary role for state-owned enterprises (SOEs) supplying upstream commodity inputs such as metals, machinery, and petrochemicals, and a tertiary role for foreign investors, particularly in electronics. Private business groups, mostly owned by ethnic "Taiwanese" rather than by the émigrés from mainland China who dominated the government, were smaller, less tightly integrated, and less diversified than in Japan or South Korea (though perhaps more significant than many analysts have realized).[6]

Lacking the support of the cohesive and deeply rooted political parties that governed Japan and Taiwan, Park and other Korean presidents relied directly upon the military-bureaucratic machinery of the state, largely neglecting hard to organize areas such as the small business and rural sectors. Severely damaged by fighting in World War II and the Korean War, and unable to match the balance and stability of Japan and Taiwan, South Korea under Park adopted an aggressive macroeconomic policy to try to catch up with North Korea, which had inherited most of the peninsula's industrial base and grew rapidly in the 1950s and 1960s. Park accepted high rates of inflation and foreign debt, refusing to slow down even after the oil shock of the early 1970s.

In the dash to development, Park and his successors aggressively channeled capital to favored large private firms, particularly the diversified, family-controlled *chaebol* business groups, as well as to major public firms such as the Pohang Iron & Steel Company (POSCO) and Korea Telecom.[7] The *chaebol* produced most of Korea's exports, often from plants proudly hailed as the largest in the world. Problems of monopoly and moral hazard, however, were much more severe in Korea's limited domestic market than in Japan. The use of export performance measures as a proxy for efficiency only partly ameliorated the task of implementing effective administrative guidance, and did little to encourage firms to maintain sound financial structures. Some observers have lauded the South Korean *chaebol* for their speed, power, and aggressive investments in new plants and research and development.[8] Others (particularly after the Asian financial crisis of the late 1990s) assailed their lack of financial discipline and transparency and their tendency to focus on mass production of low-margin commodities.[9] Virtually all analysts agree, however, on the centrality of the *chaebol* to the industrial structure crafted by Park. And if Park was able to control the business octopuses he fostered, after his death many observers concluded that the *chaebol* had grown powerful enough to check or override the state.[10]

The differences across the political economies of the East Asian countries were not, however, as stark as implied by this static picture of giant Korean *chaebol,* tiny Taiwanese enterprises, and loose Japanese business networks. Over a longer time span, and in a number of key industries, the three countries shared important commonalities. In the first half of the Park era South Korea did not look so different from Taiwan (and earlier Japan). Only with the massive heavy industrial push under the *yushin* constitution of the 1970s did Korea diverge dramatically from Japan, whose earlier heavy industrialization occurred within a much larger and more balanced economy, and Taiwan, whose "ten major construction projects" of the late 1970s were but a weak echo of Park's drive for heavy and chemical industrialization (HCI).

Once in place, the Korean *chaebol* were able to strengthen their position, but even before Park's death important policy changes began to reduce Korea's distinctiveness. In mid-1979, Park and his advisors hammered out a financial stabilization policy. After his death, the new Chun administration (1980–1988) imposed fiscal restraint. Over the 1980s, inflation rates declined, largely converging with those of Taiwan. In the 1990s, the South Korean government largely stopped providing policy loans. Initially the *chaebol* were still in an advantageous position to gain credit on normal commercial grounds, and also aggressively entered the nonbank financial sector, but many collapsed or disintegrated during and shortly after the Asian financial crisis. In contrast, from the late 1980s, large firms and groups in Taiwan assumed a greater prominence in the economy, somewhat shrinking the gap with Korea.

In specific important industrial sectors, moreover, similarities across the three countries were often more important than differences. These similarities resulted from the economic requirements of the sector more than from the peculiarities of the country. Thus in textiles, all three countries nurtured a core group of large, upstream suppliers of fibers, which in turn supported a much larger group of mid-sized fabric producers and a mass of garment firms downstream. In the 1960s and 1970s, both South Korea and Taiwan led the world as shoe producers, though Korea's were mostly athletic shoes, while firms from Taiwan were more active in women's fashion shoes. In electronics, all three specialized in mass-produced consumer items, including radios, television receivers, and, from the mid-1970s, videocassette recorders, computers, and monitors. All came to produce the semiconductors used in consumer electronics. All, with limited exceptions in Japan, remained stronger in consumer electronics than in industrial electronics and software. It is true that Japanese and later large Korean firms were more likely to develop their own brands, while Taiwanese firms tended to remain smaller, more specialized, and more reliant upon original equipment manufacture (OEM), following the specifications and carrying the brands of multinational corporations. Yet even Japanese and Korean firms engaged in significant amounts of OEM production during their periods of rapid growth—South Korea became the world's leading producer of microwave ovens, for example, by supplying General Electric and other foreign brands.

Moreover, strategies often converged over time. In semiconductors, large Korean firms began aggressive mass production of memory chips in the late 1970s under Park's heavy industry drive. The Taiwanese remained much more cautious until 1987, when Taiwan Semiconductor Manufacturing (TSM) pioneered the concept of the "pure-play" fabrication facility that did not design its own semiconductors but produced only the designs of customers. Together with its compatriot United Microelectronics (UMC), Taiwan Semiconductor came to control 80 percent of the large and rapidly growing fab market. Korean firms like Hyundai and Samsung soon vowed to join them. Thus differences across countries were often less significant than differences across industries, and despite some differences in timing and emphasis, South Korea and Taiwan were often in the same broad industrial categories at roughly the same level of sophistication, usually a decade or so behind Japan.

Broad similarities of approach were particularly visible in key industrial sectors such as electric power, steel, and two of the major consumers of steel: shipbuilding and automobiles. Four themes reappear in the development of steel and autos in Northeast Asia: (1) underlying similarities across the leading East Asian capitalist economies in crucial developmental sectors; (2) the influence of sectoral requirements in determining policy approaches and patterns of industrial organization in all three countries; (3) repeated but incomplete attempts in Korea to reverse the hard-charging, high investment policies just before and after Park's death; and (4) the lasting effects of South Korea's aggressive use of subsidized credit in both private and public sectors.

In autos and steel, a surprising degree of commonality in ownership, firm size, and relations with the government joined the three countries. South Korea, like Taiwan, found little alternative to creating a state-owned enterprise to promote its integrated steel industry. In autos, Korea relied on private firms, but so did Taiwan. At several critical junctures, industrial requirements clearly curbed divergent political tendencies. Both countries encouraged private firms to participate in the founding of integrated steel mills, but the capital requirements were too daunting for the private sector in either economy. In the late 1970s and early 1980s, Taiwan attempted to use a state-owned enterprise, China Steel, to energize a stagnant auto industry, but eventually recognized that the requirements of the two industries were too different. The large scale required for modern steel plants made it difficult for small economies like South Korea and Taiwan to have more than one integrated steel company. The Japanese economy was large enough by the late 1950s that it could allow several companies to develop large modern steel plants. High Japanese officials were convinced of the dynamism of private companies competing with each other and permitted several private companies to make steel, always in close interaction with the government, which helped ensure adequate financing.

Creating and Promoting Big Steel

Integrated steel mills process iron ore and coal into iron and steel. They are highly capital intensive, with a few firms operating at massive economies of scale. The crucial technology largely has come embedded in capital equipment imported from Europe (and later occasionally Japan). As a result, the key to economic success is not innovation or cheap labor costs, for with the new technology few workers are required. Rather, the key is effective construction and management of production capacity, combined with stable and sustained growth in demand.[11] In Northeast Asia, increasing demand, partly a function of economic growth in rapidly developing countries and partly a function of government protection and promotion, sustained a virtuous cycle of profitability, continued investment, and increasing economies of scale and productivity. This led to declining costs and even more robust profits and investments.

In all three of the industrialized economies of Northeast Asia, integrated steel production was founded, protected, and promoted by the government. The Asian steel mills bore little resemblance to the politicized and inefficient state-owned enterprises often seen in other developing countries and even in less crucial sectors in Northeast Asia. In the 1950s and 1960s the Japanese steel industry was somewhat more diverse and competitive, but state-sanctioned cartels among the oligopoly of six major producers were pervasive, and after Fuji and Yawata recombined to form Nippon Steel in 1970, market shares in the industry settled into an extraordinarily stable balance, thanks in good measure to close cooperation and support from the Ministry of International Trade and Industry (MITI, after 2001 renamed METI). To provide the economies of scale, Korea and Taiwan created state-owned enterprises and blocked competing investments by private firms, but they accorded the national champions quasi-private status to ensure that they would remain competitive in global markets.

Japan

Local and central governments were central to the modern Japanese iron and steel industry from its origins in the 1850s.[12] The government founded Yawata Steel, the first large-scale integrated mill, at the time of the Sino-Japanese War (1894–95) with the explicit goal of creating an autonomous munitions capability. Private niche producers appeared as well, often linked to user industries such as shipbuilding or machinery, many of which were also dominated by the military. One of these producers, Nippon Kōkan, became the second major integrated mill, but remained far smaller than Yawata. In 1934 Yawata absorbed several smaller mills and changed its name to Nippon Steel. After the war, the Allied Occupation broke up Nippon Steel into Yawata and Fuji Steel, resulting in three integrated steel mills. Nippon Steel had largely complemented and supported the private firms, but the new, privatized offspring competed directly with them. In response, Kawasaki Steel, a small, maverick company, mobilized support from Liberal Democratic Party (LDP) politicians to overcome opposition from the Bank of Japan, the existing integrated makers, and parts of MITI, to create a large integrated mill on the waterfront in Chiba Prefecture, across the bay from Tokyo.[13] Kobe Steel and Sumitomo Metals soon followed with giant seaside plants. Over the course of the 1960s the Japanese steel industry expanded from 30 million tons of capacity to over 100 million tons, making it the most productive and sophisticated and second largest (after the Soviet Union) in the world.

Most of the capital to build these impressive steel plants came from the abundant savings of Japan's large domestic economy, channeled through private Japanese banks, but the Japan Development Bank and the World Bank provided vital assistance to Kawasaki, Kobe, and Sumitomo in their efforts to break into integrated production.[14] Most of the crucial technology came in the form of equipment and licenses from Europe for such breakthroughs as basic oxygen furnaces and continuous casting. Unlike their American rivals, Japanese steel companies were unburdened by excess capacity and outdated plants, and avidly sought out advanced European technologies.[15] Over time, Japan became a net exporter of steel technology and equipment, but most technology remained embedded in capital equipment and the most important technologies generally came from Europe.

The economic viability of the Japanese industry thus depended less on innovation or product differentiation, the opportunities for which were limited in steel, and more on efficient siting and organization of giant coastal steel plants and maintenance of high levels of capacity utilization. As the industry embarked on gigantic and risky investments in the 1950s and 1960s, the government and leading firms tried to enforce controls and cartels on prices, production, and new investment. Rapid growth in demand created many opportunities to cheat on the cartels, however, especially for aggressive, newer companies such as Sumitomo. MITI and the firms (including Sumitomo) concluded that the industry needed stability. After the merger of Fuji and Yawata, Nippon Steel emerged as a clear price leader with the resources and will to modulate production to maintain order. The Japanese steel industry settled into a remarkably stable oligopoly, adjusting exports—often determined cooperatively—as necessary to maintain order in domestic markets, and threatening would-be importers of cheap foreign steel with loss of access to high-end products.

Although the top five steel firms relished their independence and initiative, the Japanese government was intimately involved in all aspects of the steel business: siting, capacity forecasts, public works procurement, technology imports, and trade and investment relations with the outside world, including financing construction of Korea's Pohang Iron & Steel Company and the Baoshan plant in Shanghai. For Japanese officials and steel executives, steel was the rice of industry. After the great expansion of the 1960s subsided, steel mills remained prized customers of the Japanese banking system, though they no longer received preferential capital from the government.

Taiwan

At first glance, the creation of the integrated steel industry in Taiwan looks like a virtually paradigmatic case of the Taiwan government's insistence on using state-owned enterprises to provide inputs to small private processors downstream. China Steel Corporation was founded from a conviction that Taiwan needed to deepen its industrial structure and strengthen its defense capacity. China Steel became highly successful, producing steel of respectable quality at internationally competitive prices. It initially focused primarily on the domestic market while exporting as necessary to maintain high levels of capacity utilization and economies of scale. As in Japan and

South Korea, the growth of steel production was closely linked with ship-building, which absorbed a high proportion of steel production. China Steel expanded less aggressively and remained focused on serving its domestic customers. Unlike POSCO at the end of the Park era, it did not erect a second plant, so that by the beginning of the twenty-first century it produced less than one-third as much steel as POSCO in an economy over half as large as South Korea's. If China Steel's development was less spectacular (and less well publicized), for many years it was far more profitable than POSCO, which poured resources into expansion.

Before becoming an archetype of domestically oriented state-owned enterprise, however, China Steel traveled a more complicated and revealing developmental path. Far from insisting on state ownership, the government of Taiwan pushed for well over a decade to create a private integrated steel mill.[16] During the 1950s the government aggressively supported the expansion of Tangrong, a private, Taiwanese-owned minimill firm (minimills use electric arc furnaces to melt steel scrap, rather than making steel from iron ore as integrated plants do). In 1956 the government floated a plan to build a 200,000-ton integrated plant using raw materials from the Philippines, but ran into a veto from American aid officials. In 1968 the government established a preparatory office for an integrated steel mill, and in 1970 it signed a tentative agreement with Australia. In December 1971 China Steel was founded with more than 50 percent private capital. When international financial turmoil scotched the deal with Australia, China Steel turned to an Austro-German consortium, but in July 1973 that deal, too, fell through. As in Japan and South Korea, the domestic steel industry was considered so crucial for building downstream industries that the government persevered. Mired in the stagnation following the oil shock, private investors proved unable to make up for the loss of European capital, so when the government increased its investment to fund plant construction, China Steel automatically turned into a state-owned enterprise. With help from the engineering arm of United States Steel, the first stage officially reached completion in December 1977 with a rated production capacity of 1.5 million tons per year.

Organizationally, the company retained its private form. The founding general manager of the company, William Chao (Zhao Yaodong), accepted the job from President Chiang Kai-shek only on the condition that the company not be treated as an SOE: "I'm willing to do my best. But any company, whether national or private, that is run according to the current national enterprises law will fail. So I have one request: let me run it on my own, and I will accept full responsibility."[17] Pushing the necessary provisions through the Legislative Yuan to secure independence in personnel and procurement was not easy, but Chao brought impressive credentials and connections to the job. His father was closely associated with the CC (Central Club) clique, the most powerful faction in the Kuomintang, and served from 1942 to 1951 as general manager of the Chiao Tung Bank (Jiaotong Yinhang), China's main development bank, while Chao himself earned a master's degree in engineering from MIT before successfully constructing a clutch of textile factories in Taiwan and Southeast Asia. Even so, Chao relied upon the political support of China Steel's chairman, the admiral-turned-politico Ma Jizhuang, to shepherd the special provisions for China Steel through the sometimes-recalcitrant legislature.[18]

With forceful and effective leadership from Chao and a little lucky timing, China Steel operated smoothly and profitably almost from the beginning. Three expansions brought capacity to eight million tons and used up the available space along Kaohsiung's harbor. China Steel drew up plans to build a new plant in Southeast Asia, but the legislature blocked the plan on the grounds that it would "hollow out" Taiwan's industrial base. China Steel retained a domestic monopoly on integrated production, but its grip on the market loosened in the late 1980s as the company lost the right to vet steel imports. In 1989 the government began to privatize China Steel. In 1995 it officially became a private company when the government's equity share fell below 50 percent.[19]

South Korea

As in Taiwan, the decision to erect a giant integrated iron and steel plant reflected the South Korean government's deep concerns about industrial upgrading and national security. During World War II, President Park Chung Hee had observed firsthand how the creation of the Manchurian industrial base sustained the Japanese war effort. A more puzzling question is why the government did not rely on the *chaebol,* as it had in so many other sectors.[20] In fact, as in Taiwan, the Korean government initially tried to persuade private firms to participate in the construction of an integrated plant.[21] The first plans to build an integrated plant gained the support of the ruling Liberal Party as early as 1958, but difficulties in acquiring international financial support and increasingly severe economic and political problems at home doomed the idea.[22]

Park Chung Hee pushed for a public effort right after the military coup. In response, a business consortium proposed a private-sector alternative. By March 1962, a public-private joint venture appeared. After providing some initial encouragement, the Van Fleet Commission (1962–1963) concluded that the plan would fail without support from USAID and the Ex-Im Bank. The U.S. mission's commitment to economic stabilization meant that such support would not be forthcoming. As in Japan and Taiwan, the high barriers to entry in the steel industry made it crucial to obtain cheap capital. At least some of the financing would have to come from abroad, necessitating solid credit ratings.

Despite these setbacks, the South Korean government remained committed to economic planning and self-sufficiency. The partition of the Korean Peninsula had left the North with most of the existing iron and steel plants, and through the 1960s the North outpaced the South in industrial development. Moreover, the South Korean government felt a new security threat after 1965, as the acceleration of the war in Vietnam, the outbreak of the Cultural Revolution in China, and the *Pueblo* incident heightened the all-too-recent memories of communist invasion. The perception of a growing security threat decreased political resistance to an essentially military regime.

Rapid growth in demand for steel also made an integrated plant seem more feasible, and the South Korean government had some success in negotiations with the United States and Europe. During a visit to Pittsburgh in May 1965, President Park met with the head of Koppers, a leader in steel engineering, to explore plans for creating an international consortium to build an integrated plant in Korea. A year later, the World Bank issued a positive technical report on the feasibility of a 500,000-ton mill.[23] Park incorporated plans for a steel mill in the second five-year development plan. In April 1967, an American-European consortium reached agreement on a 600,000-ton mill for South Korea. In rapid succession, the government selected Pohang as the site (June 1967), formed an integrated steel mill committee to develop detailed plans (November 1967), and established Pohang Iron & Steel Company (April 1, 1968).

Heading the new company was General Pak T'ae-jun, Park's chief of staff in the first year of the military junta's Supreme Council for National Reconstruction. He enjoyed the complete trust of President Park.[24] Even more than China Steel's "Ironhead" Chao in Taiwan, Pak T'ae-jun combined formidable technical and organizational skills with personal charisma. Stories of Pak's extraordinary determination, energy, powers of observation, and obsession with cleanliness and order became legendary in Korea. Pak also brought to POSCO deep connections with Japan, where his family had moved shortly before the war. After graduating from high school in Japan, Pak received a degree in engineering from Tokyo's prestigious Waseda University. He served as an emissary from President Park to Japan in preparation for the normalization of diplomatic relations in 1965, and developed personal relationships with the heads of the Fuji, Yawata, and Kawasaki steel companies.[25]

Pak T'ae-jun's management style closely resembled that of large Japanese companies during Japan's rapid growth period, but he also promoted military-like discipline and radiated passionate allegiance to "steel patriotism." Military regimentation reflected not only Pak's own background as a general but also the martial character of Park Chung Hee's whole regime, which was reflected in the organization even of light industrial sectors such as textiles.[26] As in Japan, Pak implemented a stiff examination system, offered permanent employment to white- and blue-collar workers alike, and based pay largely on seniority. Like China Steel's Chao, Pak insisted on managerial independence as a precondition for accepting the daunting task of building an integrated steel mill. President Park gave Pak T'ae-jun complete control over procurement and personnel, and assented to his demand that POSCO remain free to refuse requests for political donations. Like China Steel, POSCO was incorporated as a joint-stock corporation, largely free from the constraints binding other state-owned enterprises.[27]

Creation of an integrated mill was incomplete without a foreign partner. The Americans, the World Bank, and the Europeans soon cooled to the idea of building an integrated steel plant in a country as poor as Korea still was in the mid-1960s, partly because integrated mills in other developing countries were proving to be major disappointments. Desperate to get the company under way, Park used his personal connections to convince Japan to redirect reparations and foreign loans originally slated for agriculture and fisheries into the construction of a steel mill.[28] Leaders of the Japanese steel industry believed that peaceful relations in Asia required the development of healthy economies, and that steel, like electric power, was an important building block for their economies. Park was able to enlist the support of Japanese steel executives in a plan to build a one-million-ton plant. With their help, he succeeded in overcoming concerns about feasibility, timing, and precedents, converting to his cause first Japan's economic ministries, then the ruling LDP and Prime Minister Sato. Once the Japanese government was on board, it pushed the World Bank to issue a somewhat more supportive report so as to improve POSCO's image in the international financial community.

In the first stage of construction, engineering and equipment came almost entirely from Japan, but with unusually high rates of participation by the South Korean side. Construction of POSCO shattered industry records for speed and cost containment.[29] In later phases, the company steadily decreased its reliance on Japan, taking on increasing portions of the planning and engineering work itself, ordering directly from plant engineering firms rather than from other steelmakers, and diversifying sources of supply.[30] As the company matured, it became increasingly independent of the government and capable of financing most of its new construction from retained earnings. It remained a public enterprise throughout the Park period, however, and the government continued to provide myriad direct and indirect subsidies and accepted very low rates of return.[31]

Shortly before his assassination, President Park personally approved POSCO's plans to construct a brand-new steel mill in Kwangyang, along the coast southwest of Pohang. As early as 1972, a private group led by Hyundai had sought to build a second mill, but President Park backed Pak T'ae-jun, who had made POSCO such a success. After President Park's death, Chun Doo-hwan confirmed POSCO's plans to build a second plant at Kwangyang. Domestic sources provided two-thirds of the funding for the new mill, three-quarters of which came from POSCO itself. For the first time, POSCO looked beyond Japan for procurement of the single largest and most costly piece of equipment in an integrated mill, choosing Britain's Davy McKee to supply the first blast furnace. Despite political instability, domestic economic crisis, world recession, and the covert opposition of Japanese and Western steelmakers, POSCO succeeded in building a whole new greenfield site ahead of time and under budget. As soon as the blast furnace was blown in, POSCO began further expansion at Kwangyang.

The steel produced at Pohang and Kwangyang went to many of the same markets as did China Steel's: construction, appliances, autos, and shipbuilding, though the latter two industries were more successful in South Korea than in Taiwan. South Korean steel exports, mostly to Japan and the United States, fluctuated more than at China Steel and hit higher peaks—over 40 percent soon after the completion of the Pohang and Kwangyang plants.[32] On balance, though, the two companies followed similar paths to similar destinations.

Contrary to legend, the World Bank and the advanced countries, including Japan, were not uniformly hostile to POSCO (or China Steel or, earlier, the Japanese steelmakers). Rather, their stances varied depending upon the economic and political circumstances and apparent local capacities. They gladly sold expertise and equipment when the projects seemed feasible and unthreatening, but they opposed construction or expansion of capacity when Korea (and Taiwan) seemed either too weak, and thus likely to flounder, or too aggressive, thus posing a strategic threat to a capital-intensive industry chronically threatened with overcapacity, riddled with subsidies, and constrained by strong unions. By the time of the construction of the Kwangyang mill in the early 1980s, Western suppliers simply went along with a company that had clearly established itself.

With the construction of the Kwangyang works, POSCO solidified its position as South Korea's national champion in steel, and long maintained a monopoly on integrated production. Privatization, first mooted in 1975, finally began in 1988, but the government's share of equity holdings declined only gradually, and little changed in the operation of the company.[33]

For many years, POSCO and the government blocked the Hyundai group from building a competing integrated plant to supply its auto operations.[34] When Hyundai constructed a plant to produce cold-rolled steel coils in the late 1990s, contributing to local overcapacity, POSCO refused to supply Hyundai with hot-rolled steel inputs, even at prices higher than it could obtain by exporting. Hyundai assailed POSCO for attempting to maintain a monopoly by blocking new entrants; POSCO replied that Hyundai's actions were typical of the mindless, octopus-style diversification of the *chaebol*, since no other auto assembler in the world made its own steel. In 2006, the Hyundai-Kia automotive group finally broke POSCO's monopoly on integrated steel production. Hyundai procured governmental permission to build two new blast furnaces at a plant acquired from Hanbo Iron & Steel, which had collapsed in the Asian financial crisis, at the southwestern port of Tangjin. Once the only auto company relying on a single supplier—POSCO—of cold-rolled steel for car bodies, Hyundai-Kia became the only automotive group in the world to produce the full range of steel products needed to produce cars.[35]

Similar patterns can be observed in one of the steel industry's key customers: the shipbuilding industry. Japan's postwar rise to dominance in ships took advantage of cheap steel and inexpensive wages—crucial in a labor-intensive industry—as well as an important prewar and wartime legacy of maritime skills and links to the machinery industry. South Korea's *chaebol* combined their experience in another closely related industry, construction, with a massive allocation of government-directed capital to come from nowhere and catch up with Japanese shipbuilders in the late 1970s. Despite technological weaknesses and recurrent crises, South Korea eventually surpassed Japan in total orders. Even more concerned about the defense implications of shipbuilding than Korea, Taiwan created a state-owned enterprise next door to China Steel in Kaoshiung in the late 1970s. However, with less experience in construction, less domestic competition, and less aggressive government support, China Shipbuilding remained a laggard.

Autos

In contrast to steel, the auto industry in East Asia was only moderately capital intensive and was based on a mixture of imported technology, local adaptations, and incremental innovations. The industry's structure combined large assembly firms with a host of smaller suppliers of parts and components. The organizational problem was less the creation of an efficient hierarchy and more one of balancing cooperation and competition in a market-based business network. Despite the huge scale and engineering complexity of steelmaking, a modern, up-to-date integrated steel plant could be purchased, installed, and working within a couple of years. The auto industry involved much more complex relations with suppliers. Cars required continuous adaptations and it took much longer to catch up to the mature auto industries of Europe and North America.

In all three of the industrialized powerhouses of Northeast Asia, two private firms led the auto industry with considerable support from the government. Policy toward the auto industry was less dirigiste than in the case of steel. Government procurement constituted only a small share of demand, and competition among producers was more important. Competitive success in autos depended not on the efficient creation and utilization of capacity to produce relatively standardized products for industrial users, but on the development of high quality products and the marketing and servicing of appealing new models for individual households. During the rapid growth period, lower economies of scale and capital requirements led to a less stable industrial structure as new firms entered despite government preferences for consolidation. Nonetheless, the influence of the government remained pervasive in all three auto industries. Today Japan and South Korea rank among the world's greatest success stories in automobiles, while Taiwan is at best an also-ran. But through the end of the Park period—and after years of extraordinarily subsidized exports by Hyundai—the Korean auto industry produced little more than that of Taiwan, with only half the population of South Korea. Only a drastic reorganization shortly after the death of President Park turned things around.

Japan

Analysts have often held up automobiles as a crucial example of a Japanese industry that defied government edicts and disproved statism.[36] Particularly after the prolonged recession of the 1990s, autos and electronics came to be hailed as the outward-oriented, market-led exceptions to the general pattern of statism and politicization dogging Japan. Analysts point in particular to two crucial episodes. In the 1950s, a plan by MITI to foster economies of scale by consolidating the auto industry into two giant groups foundered on opposition by the smaller automakers. Then in the early 1960s MITI failed to prevent the entry of Honda, which eventually became the third-largest auto producer in Japan. Governmental efforts notwithstanding, the rapid expansion of demand in a large economy, plus later opportunities to export, left Japan with far more auto producers than in the United States—nine or ten by some counts (though only five were independent producers of cars).

This story of market triumphalism builds on some important facts, but it is incomplete and deeply misleading. It glosses over the Japanese auto industry's virtually complete protection against imports and foreign direct investment during the rapid growth period (nor were the multinationals simply uninterested in Japan—before World War II, General Motors and Ford developed significant operations in Japan, just as they invested heavily in Europe, but they were pushed out as Japan mobilized for war). Market triumphalism also misses the significant government support given the auto industry in the 1950s and even the 1960s. Toyota and particularly Nissan developed on a wartime base and were treated as crucial national companies. They received preferential funding both from public banks and from long-term trust banks heavily influenced by MITI and the Ministry of Finance.[37] The Japanese auto industry was not competitive internationally until the early 1970s, more than a decade after Toyota and Nissan first began exporting compact cars, and the Japanese market remained essentially closed to imports until the early 1980s. The government supported the efforts of the largest companies to develop economies of scale by discouraging new entrants.

In the domestic market for regular-sized passenger cars, Toyota and Nissan were completely dominant, and they developed and nurtured the parts infrastructure that supplied the others, including Honda and producers of the minicar segment created by the Japanese tax system; indeed, several of the other assemblers, such as Hino and Daihatsu, were subordinates of the two leaders. While nearly all of the assemblers cultivated suppliers' associations, most suppliers to Toyota provided parts to all of the assemblers except Nissan and vice versa.[38]

Honda was genuinely entrepreneurial, to be sure, but when it ventured into auto assembly it was already one of the world's largest manufacturers of motorcycles. It depended upon the protected domestic supplier base, but never managed to challenge Toyota and Nissan in the domestic market, instead relying primarily on exports. More important, no other firms tried to enter the industry after Honda in 1964. After Honda's entry, MITI had some minor success in encouraging consolidation and rearrangement of the assembly industry, notably the merger of Prince into Nissan. The government also supported the grouping of several different companies into the Toyota and Nissan families. Even more significant was public financing that encouraged the consolidation and rationalization of the parts industry in the 1960s, a move that even critics of MITI concede had considerable impact.[39] Parts firms were also beneficiaries of both LDP largesse aimed at small companies and technical assistance from both MITI and local governments.[40]

Thus, through the mid-1980s, when Japanese auto firms began to make major investments in North American and European assembly operations, the auto industry was a highly protected Japanese oligopoly, albeit considerably more complex and varied than steel. The government provided some financial support to assemblers in the 1950s and to parts firms in the 1960s, and enjoyed some success in encouraging consolidation.[41]

Taiwan

The pioneer of Taiwan's auto industry was not a state agency but an off-shoot of a Shanghainese textile group called Yulon (Yulong, formerly spelled Yue-loong), whose founder had studied mechanical engineering at Shanghai's Tongji University and received an engineering degree in Germany.[42] Yulon began assembling Jeeps in 1958 and soon shifted to Nissan passenger cars. Yulon was lucrative, but not surprisingly, given Taiwan's tiny market and limited industrial capacities, it made little progress in improving quality or expanding local content. Starting in 1967, the government opened the industry to new assemblers, most of them native Taiwanese, who then aligned with Japanese automakers (as well as Ford, but even Ford relied primarily on its Japanese affiliate Mazda to supply the Taiwanese market). The government consistently subordinated auto policy to finance and diplomacy. It sought to build up domestic capabilities without threatening the interests of foreign investors or trade partners, leading to repeated reversals of policy. Protection against imports, in particular, was less extreme and less consistent than in South Korea or even Japan. Not surprisingly, despite Taiwan's increasing levels of income and industrial sophistication, its auto industry fell into the same rut that afflicted most other developing countries. Production fell far below minimum efficient scale. Local content was low and dependence on outsiders high. The numerous assemblers relied on product differentiation strategies rather than cost reduction based on mass production, making it even more difficult to attain economies of scale. Given the tiny volume of orders, suppliers did not form pyramidal *keiretsu* structures as in Japan, but sold to all assemblers equally; assemblers, in turn, lacked the volume, resources, or incentive to support the technological upgrading of suppliers. Taiwan's parts firms were unusually successful at exporting, but only of noncritical replacement parts such as wheels and bumpers.[43]

In the late 1970s and early 1980s the government, stimulated by the manifest failure of existing policies and the growth of South Korean exports, proposed to break through the impasse with a joint venture between China Steel and a major international assembler to produce compact cars for both domestic and foreign sales. The government announced the ambitious plan without even consulting the existing assemblers, most or all of whom would have been wiped out. In the end, this "typically Taiwanese" approach of bypassing local private business groups in favor of state-owned enterprises and foreign investors fell through. Although Toyota agreed to the broad outlines of Taiwan's plan, it refused to provide a written guarantee of export performance. Taiwan's economic policy leadership split over the promotion of auto assembly versus the export of auto parts: those supportive of parts insisted that Toyota abide by the export requirement. With the failure of the international joint venture, the government adopted a slow and cautious policy of tariff reduction and liberalization.[44] The number of assemblers increased to over a dozen, including five major firms.

Yet the policy gradually took effect. Local content increased, quality improved, and over the 1990s domestic production gradually displaced many of the imports. Local firms began to invest in significant design capacities, modifying Japanese models for the local market and even developing (in conjunction with the quasi-governmental Industrial Technology Research Institute and foreign advisors) an independent engine for compact cars and small commercial vehicles. Yulon bought the Philippine operations of then-ailing Nissan. Both Yulon and its sister firm China Motors, an affiliate of Mitsubishi Motors, made serious investments in mainland China, eventually producing far more units in China than on Taiwan.[45] Exports of auto components, including a minority of more sophisticated parts, continued to increase rapidly.[46]

South Korea

The great success of South Korean firms at exporting automobiles attracted far more international attention than Taiwan's experience.[47] Early

Korean policy toward the auto industry, however, looked depressingly like that in Taiwan and other developing countries: attempts to promote a consolidated and internationally competitive local assembly industry were ineffective and often politicized. Soon after the coup, the government passed special legislation to promote import-substituting industrialization for the auto industry.[48] The pioneer was Kim Chong-p'il, nephew of President Park, founder of the KCIA, organizational force behind the ruling Democratic Republican Party, and brother of the managing director of Hanil Bank. Kim supported the establishment of Saenara ("new nation") Auto Company, reportedly to raise funds for the ruling party.[49] The government allowed the company to assemble Nissan Bluebirds without paying any duty or tax. Unfortunately for Kim, disputes over monopoly profits and political contributions drove the highly lucrative business into bankruptcy. In November 1965, factional struggles culminated in the takeover of the company by Sinjin, which had links to Nissan's archrival Toyota. Again (and as in Taiwan), the company was initially lucrative but subject to criticism for its high prices.

In 1967 the government allowed two new firms to enter, purchasing market competition at the cost of a predictable proliferation of models and inability to attain economies of scale. To counter these problems, in 1969–1970 the government developed plans to encourage the creation of a single engine plant. Such a plant would have conflicted with the division of labor set up by the international assemblers, for whom the Korean market was still far too small to merit special attention. The plan also ran afoul of Zhou Enlai's proclamation of the "four principles" guiding Sino-Japanese interrelations before the normalization of diplomatic relations, under which China would not deal with Japanese firms investing in Taiwan and Korea.

In June 1973, just before the oil shock began to shake the global economy, the South Korean government embarked on a much more aggressive policy to encourage local firms to design independent models.[50] The new policy, formalized in 1974, required assemblers to increase drastically their use of local components, design independent models, and limit the engines of mainstream models (80 percent of production) to no more than 1.5 liters. Only Hyundai developed a car that could be considered even reasonably independent. The *chaebol*, with government support, were able to draw on organizational skills developed in one sector and apply them to new sectors. Hyundai hired an Italian firm to design the body of its new Pony model, and manufactured the engine, gearbox, and rear axle under license from Mitsubishi. George Turnbull, a former executive with British Leyland, managed the project.[51] Foreign loans guaranteed by the Korean government supplied more than 70 percent of the capital, while policy loans and generous tax provisions also helped.[52] Domestic demand grew rapidly from an extremely low base.

Most accounts of the Korean auto industry give great credit to the Long-Term Development Plan of 1974, but it is important to recognize the severe limitations of the industry through the end of the Park regime. Even at its peak of 113,564 passenger cars and 78,576 trucks in 1979, the volume of production was still far from achieving economies of scale, and not much higher than in Taiwan.[53] Hyundai began exporting in 1976, but volumes were tiny—the first export order comprised six cars for Ecuador.[54] Quality was terrible. Most telling, the cars were dumped overseas at astonishingly low prices—less than half the price charged in the domestic market.[55] Such tactics not only grossly violated norms of international trade, they were also economically unsustainable. In the words of a Hyundai executive, "Between 1972 and 1978 Hyundai Motors was essentially a bankrupt company supported by other Hyundai companies."[56] And Hyundai was the strongest of the Korean automakers.

To make matters worse, the South Korean economy crashed in 1980. As Park's heavy industry drive reached a climax in the late 1970s, inflation, debt, and low capacity utilization plagued the economy. In the December 1978 National Assembly elections, the leading opposition party gained a plurality of votes, though the electoral rules under the *yushin* constitution kept the ruling party in power. The Park administration began to retrench, but the second oil shock only exacerbated the problems. Then in October 1979, Park was assassinated. By 1980, Korea's auto industry was in desperate straits. Production dropped by half, and barely improved in 1981 to about 69,000 passenger cars and 52,000 trucks. Trivial levels of exports provided little relief. Despite Korea's strong overall industrial base and experiment in exports, production languished behind even that of Taiwan, which produced about 137,000 light vehicles in 1981. South Korean production capacity was woefully underutilized and quality continued to lag. The Park administration had stumbled on a contradiction: overcoming the forbidding barriers to genuine localization of production in automobiles required a longer period of stability than Park's hard-charging, crisis-prone style of economic management could provide.

Faced with disaster, the Chun administration pushed a series of macroeconomic stabilization measures that succeeded in taming inflation, while its industrial policy focused on cutting and rationalizing excess capacity. Many analysts assert that the government's effort to merge the leading auto assemblers failed. Alice Amsden, for example, dismisses the merger campaign as "short-lived and abortive."[57] Instead, she and other analysts stress the political power and increasing size of the *chaebol*, particularly Hyundai. It is true that the initial merger efforts foundered, but compelling firms to merge against their wishes is always difficult (as it was in Japan), and it should come as no surprise that a policy that amounted to asking affiliates of GM (Saehan, soon to become Daewoo) and Ford (Hyundai) to merge their operations was doomed to failure.[58]

And yet, in the end the Chun government *did* succeed in imposing reorganization, largely by imposing limitations on the smaller players. Mergers continued, including the absorption of Jeep producer Kŏhwa by Tonga (later Ssangyong).[59] More important, from early 1981 through the end of 1986, the government strictly limited the number of producers. It pushed Kia out of passenger cars, leaving only leaders Hyundai and Daewoo. A similarly strict division of labor governed trucks, where Kia received a monopoly in light trucks in return for exiting passenger cars. At the same time, the government changed tack on the introduction of foreign capital, encouraging each of the companies to strengthen its links with major global assemblers. From 1982 to 1986, Daewoo established a new joint venture with GM, Kia took capital injections from Mazda and its American parent Ford, and Hyundai accepted both technology and a 10 percent capital share from the Mitsubishi group.[60] However, in line with the Korean government's exacting policies on direct foreign investment, Hyundai retained management control and the right to import parts and technology from Mitsubishi's competitors and to compete in third markets.[61] The government also provided support to parts makers. Hyundai and Daewoo, the only passenger car producers, first established supplier associations during this crucial period.[62]

In standardizing engine sizes at 1.5 liters and reducing producers to just two firms, Korea distinguished itself from virtually all other developing countries, and finally made it possible to gain economies of scale in auto assembly.[63] In 1983 production of light vehicles barely eclipsed the level reached in 1979, and even then it was only about 25 percent higher than that of Taiwan. From 1984, exports, led by Hyundai's redesigned Pony, began to play a significant role. In 1986, the last year under the enforced division of labor, passenger car production exceeded 450,000—four times the peak of 1979 and almost eight times the level of 1980, the last year before the enforced rationalization. In 1987 production almost doubled again to 789,819 units. During the same period, production in Taiwan, which failed to implement rationalization policies, barely doubled. Aggressive investments by large business groups were not sufficient: only government-enforced rationalization enabled South Korea to attain the economies of scale vital to competing in automobile manufacturing. And even that rationalization was temporary and unexpected, coming in response to the economic and political crisis surrounding Park's death. Fortunately for the Korean auto industry, that extraordinary period lasted long enough to allow Korean companies to make a critical breakthrough in production efficiency.

The South Korean firms differed from the Japanese in some critical areas, especially in relations with suppliers. Assemblers such as Hyundai tended to deal directly with, and often supported financially, their full range of vendors, rather than developing a tiered pyramid of cooperating suppliers. The main contractors delivered most of their output to one assembler, and few exported, a sharp contrast with Japan and even Taiwan.[64]

Organizationally, the Korean auto firms largely followed the Japanese approach. Only Hyundai developed significant independent skills in body, chassis, and engine design, and even then only slowly; most of the Korean firms continued to rely on Japan.[65] After an abortive initial campaign to storm the North American market, they concentrated on exports to less developed countries, before returning to North America. Even more than the Japanese in the rapid growth period, they were heavily indebted and, with the occasional exception of Hyundai, at best marginally profitable.[66]

As the Chun administration's rationalization measures wore off, the typical tendency of *chaebol* to use preferential credit to expand aggressively reasserted itself. Kia's return to passenger car production in 1987 caused few immediate problems; indeed, Kia soon passed Daewoo to become the second-largest producer. However, Ssangyong also moved into passenger cars and in late 1994 the government yielded to heavy political pressure to allow the Samsung group to enter auto production. The specter of excess capacity was only partly banished by renewed success in exports. Even before the collapse of the Thai baht sparked the Asian financial crisis of 1997, several *chaebol*, including Kia, fell into insolvency. Although Kia had been relatively specialized and well run as an auto company, it overinvested in autos, the truck maker Asia Motors, and specialty steels. By late 1998 Kia fell under the control of Hyundai in a merger of the largest and second-largest auto producers that gave Hyundai around three-quarters of the domestic market.

Ssangyong failed in 1997 and was acquired by Daewoo in early 1998. Within a couple of years Daewoo, which had passed Kia to rank number two, then collapsed, leaving billions in debts and leading to numerous indictments. Samsung, the late entrant, fell into the hands of Nissan, its technology supplier, and thus into the Renault camp. Even Hyundai, the strongest and most independent Korean firm, sold a 10 percent share to Daimler-Chrysler. With the partial exception of a couple of firms in the

Hyundai-Kia group, Korean suppliers remained very weak compared with their competitors in Europe and Japan.

Nonetheless, Korea strengthened its position as one of a handful of leading automobile production sites, and Hyundai began to challenge Toyota for leadership of the global assembly industry. President Park's dream of a proudly independent Korean industry may have faded a bit in the face of global consolidation that affected even the United States and Japan, but without question Korea's success in automobile design, production, and assembly surpassed anyone's expectations.

DESPITE the many important differences separating South Korea from the other major industrial powers in East Asia, when it came to key developmental projects such as promoting the steel and automobile industries, Japan, Taiwan, and South Korea adopted and implemented policies that were more similar than regional specialists have usually appreciated. Often the differences were greater across industry than across country. Korea's giant steelmaker the Pohang Iron & Steel Company not only looked rather like Japan's Nippon Steel, one of the major forces behind POSCO's initial design and construction, but also followed a path of development remarkably similar to that of China Steel in Taiwan, though with the construction of the Kwangyang mill, POSCO traveled further down that path. In autos, Korea closely followed the Japanese pattern. The Korean auto industry became far more successful than its counterpart in Taiwan, but as this chapter has emphasized, South Korea did not pull decisively ahead until the Chun administration reorganized the industry in the turmoil surrounding the death of President Park. Industries matter: for integrated steel makers, installing and managing capacity will always be crucial, while automakers in all countries focus more on new model design and relations with subcontractors and dealers. Governments often exercise determinative influence over steel companies, but they typically have more complex relations with auto firms.

Of course, to say that the governments of Northeast Asia all adopted dirigiste approaches to development, but promoted autos quite differently from steel, does not mean that their approaches to development were identical. Indeed, I have argued elsewhere that variations in the political systems of the three countries carried important implications for industrial policy.[67] Significant differences show up even in the two strategic industries discussed here. Japan, for example, had by far the largest and most advanced economy in Northeast Asia; government intervention, even in steel and autos, tended to be more indirect (especially after about 1970) and more often explicitly politicized.

The defining difference between South Korea and the others was the aggressive use of preferential credit and governmental loan guarantees. Those loans and guarantees, it should be noted, went not just to the *chaebol* but to public enterprises as well. The biggest difference between POSCO and China Steel, which generally followed remarkably similar developmental trajectories, was the aggressive support the South Korean government gave to growth even at the expense of low rates of profitability. Taiwan, always more cautious than Korea, grew even more so over time. In the case of semiconductors, for example, Taiwan's government played a crucial pioneering role, but quickly privatized production facilities. It continued to support the industry with tax breaks and research funding, but it left financing largely to the companies themselves, which increasingly tapped the equity markets rather than depending on banks owned or directed by the government.

Similarly, the provision of financing to successful exporters in Korea profoundly affected small- and medium-sized enterprises. Contrary to the virtually universal impression, the share of employment and output coming from small firms was nearly as large in Korea as in Taiwan,[68] but as we noted in the case of the auto industry, small firms in Korea were more dependent on large assemblers for help in finance and exporting. On the other hand, while large *chaebol* business groups played a more important role in Korea than in Taiwan, the materials reviewed here do not suggest that they became genuinely independent of government support and control either during the Park regime or after its demise.

Thus, notwithstanding some important differences, particularly regarding the greater use of subsidized credit in Korea, the review of the auto and steel industries given above suggests that policy toward crucial industries during the rapid growth period was surprisingly similar—and statist—across the three countries. Differences were more likely to stem from variation across industries rather than from fundamental differences in government policy.

How should we account for the remaining differences, the particular style of statism, especially the South Korean government's greater decisiveness and willingness to allocate capital and assume risk? Formal institutional factors no doubt explain some of the differences. During the periods of most rapid growth only Japan had a fully democratic political system, so naturally the Japanese government was more sensitive to political concerns. In that period, Japan and Taiwan conducted local elections and used a multi-member electoral system infamous for its tendency to promote factionalism, while South Korea had a strong president but no local elections. The Korean government under Park and his successors was less compelled to factor local reactions or factional implications into its policymaking. The lack of local elections helps explain why the Korean government focused on assemblers such as Hyundai to the near exclusion of part suppliers, while Japan and even Taiwan provided significant support to parts companies.

In Taiwan, local business had grown up under Japanese occupation and was familiar with Japanese ways of doing business. But the government and the ruling party, the Kuomintang, had experience in governing on the mainland, relatively independent from Japanese influence. Because Park and his officials had grown up under the Japanese, the approach and institutional structure they introduced made much deeper use of the Japanese structures.

At least as important as institutional structures were differences in the goals and capabilities of the ruling parties in the three countries.[69] The KMT lost the mainland when it failed to control inflation, corruption, and instability. After the outbreak of the Korean War in 1950 caused the American navy to begin patrolling the Taiwan Strait, the main threat to Taiwan came in the form of subversion and capital flight rather than invasion. As a result, while the KMT prized industrial development, it never accorded it priority over economic stability or diplomatic support. The party could afford to focus on broad economic and political goals partly because the KMT brought to Taiwan a formidable political organization rendered even more capable by the reforms of 1950–1951. The KMT did not require campaign contributions from big business, nor did it contest the limited election campaigns held on Taiwan primarily on the basis of the party's contributions to economic development.

In contrast, the historical lesson impinging on Park and other South Korean leaders was the need to repel external invasion and influence, first from Japan, then from North Korea. Moreover, while Korean presidents exercised a degree of direct administrative control unprecedented in Japan or even in Taiwan, they could not rely on strong, well-organized parties to maintain social support. Reliance on the *chaebol* reflected not only a recipe for rapid industrial growth but also a search for allies and contributors.

Thus, as regional specialists emphasize, differences in the political regime and ruling parties of the Northeast Asian countries have led to important differences in industrial policy, with equally important consequences for industrial structure and patterns of economic specialization. In the key periods of industrial development during and immediately after the Park era, and particularly in core sectors such as steel, autos, and electricity, however, outsiders are right to detect a broadly similar, and highly statist, approach to development. President Park Chung Hee may have pushed that development more resolutely and in some ways more successfully than any other leader, but he was building on precedents set in Japan and he was often matched by the KMT in Taiwan.

After Park's death, the system he created fell into crisis twice. Immediately after Park's assassination, President Chun implemented a vigorous, but still largely statist, stabilization and reorganization of the economy. The government privatized banks, but retained virtually complete control over them. In part, the failure of the reforms to persist reflected quite specific factors, such as North Korea's assassination of Kim Chae-ik and other liberalizing advisors in the Rangoon bombing of 1983. At a more fundamental level, though, in the 1980s the system created by Park was still capable of sustaining rapid investment and growth.[70] In contrast, the transition to lower rates of investment and growth in Taiwan occurred "naturally" at the same time as Chun's reorganization, and genuinely private Taiwanese banks appeared at the beginning of the 1990s, though the market share of government banks declined only slowly.[71]

By the early 1990s, however, there were ominous signs that Park's system was running out of gas. The *chaebol* were no longer capable of wringing adequate returns out of their huge investments.[72] Banks and *chaebol* teetered on the edge of insolvency, and finally fell over. Once again, a new president was left to deal with the excesses bequeathed by his predecessor. Kim Dae-jung tackled the task of financial reform with more vigor than had Chun, but it was hard to fix the banks and trust companies without undertaking fundamental changes to the industrial system inherited from Park Chung Hee. Fifteen years after Park's death, the positive elements of his legacy were greatly reduced. The task of revitalizing and reorganizing the South Korean economy and the *chaebol*-oriented financial system fell to Kim Dae-jung, his successors, and the Korean people.

Conclusion:

The Post-Park Era

Byung-Kook Kim

P ARK CHUNG HEE DIED on October 26, 1979. So ended his developmental era. Or did it? Given his great successes and dismal failures, and his profoundly effective but costly authoritarian way of rulership, it was inevitable that even after his death Park lived on as either a hero or a villain in South Korea's politics. In the three decades after Park's death, the memory of his powerful and controversial rule still towered over the country. In what can be called the "post-Park era," allies and enemies still defined themselves and each other by their attitudes toward Park and his political, economic, and coercive systems. Not only did the structures that he created continue after his death but the forces that supported and opposed him both remained vigorous. By making Park a hero or a villain and deeming his leadership indispensible or dispensable for South Korea's progress, the conservative and progressive forces of the post-Park era hoped to legitimate their past, win the present, and shape the future. Virtually all discussion of Park has been contaminated by the power of Park's image, whether positive or negative. The deep involvement of all parts of society in the "pro-Park" and "anti-Park" battle has made it impossible to achieve the detachment necessary for an objective discussion of who he was, what he did, and whether his vision still has relevance today.

The effort to achieve a more balanced understanding of Park and his place in South Korean political history requires an acknowledgment of both his successes and his failures. It requires abandoning the sharp distinction widely used by South Korean intellectuals between Park's "modernizing era" and post-Park "globalization" and "democratization" to permit a more nuanced understanding of how the institutions of the Park era survived and were adapted to fit the emerging democracy and the globalized political economy. To understand how the Park legacy was adapted and changed by his supporters and his opponents as they confronted the challenge of democratization and globalization in the three decades after his death, it is useful to distinguish the post-Park politics of reform along three institutional dimensions.

First, this chapter will focus on Park Chung Hee's legacies for South Korea's economic system and his successors' two decades of reform aimed at taming its extremely destabilized character through a diverse array of restructuring programs. All successors—whether military or civilian, conservative or progressive, Kyŏngsang- or Chŏlla-born—projected one or another kind of reformist image, reshaping South Korea's developmental state and *chaebol* industrialists in a more market-friendly and less dirigiste direction. Their risky efforts at partial reform continued until an Asian regional crisis took down South Korea in 1997. Only then did its political authorities adopt a strategy of systemic change. Ironically, however, it took South Korea's "Weberian" state bureaucracy inherited from Park's developmental era to weed out Park's other legacy of structural pressures for boom and bust from South Korea's hypergrowth economy. Even then, its powerful state only shed its developmentalist ethos. Transforming into a regulatory state, it regained the commanding heights in South Korea's much changed neoliberal economy. Likewise, *chaebol* industrialists purged their overly expansionist "gene," but kept much of their "imperial" corporate governance structures.

Second, South Korea's post-Park political system also lived in the shadow of Park. Given their weaker political standing in South Korean politics, in fact, many of his successors ended up copying Park's triple strategy of electoral mobilization: regionalist agitation, ideological mobilization, and money politics. The politics of regionalist agitation, already contagious during Park's last years of rule, only became more aggravated, with smaller regions developing their own "mini" regionalism to split away from larger voter blocs. The Ch'ungch'ŏng broke its ties with Kyŏngsang voters and became a swing variable in elections after its regionalist leader, Kim Chong-p'il, lost all hope of presidential succession. The political opposition also fractured into Kim Dae-jung's Chŏlla and Kim Young-sam's South Kyŏngsang factions, which evolved into rival parties as democratization proceeded. The politics of ideological mobilization likewise escalated during the post-Park era too, but with a major twist. The "left-right" struggle Park waged in an attempt to delegitimize his opponents as an ideologically heretical leftist force transformed into a "progressive-conservative" electoral contest for power. The progressive forces, continually evolving and splitting into *undong'gwŏn* (*chaeya* activists), NGO leaders, and party politicians in tandem with democratization, but maintaining their raison d'être as a moralistically organized transformative political force, packaged their "progressivism" in terms of "anti-Park" beliefs. The conservatives responded in a mirror image, personifying their modernization ideals in a continually re-created, reinterpreted, and relived image of Park. The third instrument of electoral mobilization, money politics, also worsened until two former presidents were prosecuted under charges of military mutiny, national subversion, and corruption in 1995.

By contrast, Park Chung Hee's third system of political coercion, which included the Korea Central Intelligence Agency (KCIA), the Presidential Security Service (PSS), and the Army Security Command (ASC), began collapsing after the 1987 democratic breakthrough. The security agency still plans, executes, and monitors key elements of South Korea's policy toward P'yŏngyang, and even intervenes in domestic politics as a strategist, but it has more or less stopped dirtying its hands with the politics of selective coercion, especially since Roh Moo-hyun's presidency (2003–2008). Likewise, the military has become a "modern" institution of national defense, as Park hoped, but has given up its other role as a watchdog for regime stability in the midst of Kim Young-sam's crackdown on the *Hanahoe* (Society of One) in 1993.

The Economic System

Successes and failures coexisted side by side nowhere more clearly than in the economic arena. Park built the South Korean banking system, corporate community, and labor market with an eye focused on the maximization of economic growth. It was the socialization of the risks and dangers in corporate expansion that enabled Park Chung Hee to achieve his goal of grow-at-all-costs. To his aides who warned of the serious socioeconomic dislocations that would result from his expansionary industrial policy, he answered: "Push society to its limits when you can."[1] When political protests spread and social unrest worsened, he defiantly declared: "Spit on my grave!"[2] He was not ignorant of the dangers of "modernization Park-style." A good listener rather than an overbearing speaker, Park always let his advisors air their doubts and worries, and yet he chose to take the risky strategy of grow-at-all-costs.

The economic system performed as Park Chung Hee intended, growing at a double-digit rate during much of his rule, but, as his advisors warned, it also periodically became paralyzed under the pressures of financial and corporate distress, at high social costs. The periodic implosion of financial and corporate distress, in particular, came to constrain his policy options and even threaten the sustainability of his economic system itself. Financing corporate growth primarily through state-guaranteed foreign loans and state-channeled bank loans, the *chaebol* became extremely vulnerable to financial distress during recessions. Their vulnerability became Park's vulnerability as well, forcing him to come up with ever larger industrial projects and ever more policy loans[3] in order to keep the failing *chaebol* afloat during economic downturns. When Park died in 1979 amid a liquidity crisis, which had become a generic trait of his economic system since the late 1960s, he left behind a manufacturing sector with a staggeringly high debt-equity ratio of 488 percent.[4]

From Park's seemingly reckless policy gambles, however, also arose a group of industrial combines unique among third world big business. Whereas most third world industrialists grew as subsidiaries and joint ventures of multinational corporations (MNCs), each of the *chaebol* came to possess its own international brand, domestic supply network, technological capacity, and overseas distribution facility, with which it strove to acquire independent capabilities to generate corporate growth across unrelated business sectors. The *chaebol* wanted to become MNCs in their own right.[5] In the process of their corporate expansion, the country annually increased its GDP more than 8 percent in real terms. The downside was the very sharp business cycle of boom and bust that profoundly destabilized and polarized South Korean civil society.

The *chaebol*, in fact, embodied both the strengths and the weaknesses of the economic system constructed during the Park era. The most critical problem with Park's export machine lay in its propensity to head toward a liquidity crisis by utterly failing to devise a viable "exit policy" for shaky *chaebol* groups. By forcing state banks to underwrite investments and assume business risks through subsidized policy loans, Park encouraged *chaebol* groups to become reckless and diversify into unrelated industries without adequate risk management. Once investments were made with bank loans, the *chaebol* became burdened with an extremely vulnerable debt-equity structure that prevented their owner-managers from corporate restructuring for fear of losing ownership and management control. On the contrary, the financially weak *chaebol* sought ever more bank loans for business growth, lest any stagnation in their business sales trigger a liquidity trap within the context of their extremely high debt-equity ratio.

However, by taking on more loans, they sowed the seeds for even bigger financial crises and dragged society into a cycle of boom and bust.

To be sure, Park could have chosen to deal with the root cause of South Korea's vicious circle of boom and bust by making the *chaebol* more cost-conscious and less sloppy in their risk calculation. He could have established a banking system that made loans on the basis of borrowers' objective cash flow rather than on the basis of state bureaucrats' administrative guidance, but he did not, because the restructuring of banks would have threatened his entire export growth machine. The regimen for banks would have worked only if Park had moved to strengthen the market threats of bankruptcy and downsize *chaebol* combines, which in turn would have required massive debt-restructuring and layoffs. The system of company unions would have been at stake too, because the workers had implicitly agreed to forgo their rights to collective action because of Park's pledge to deliver job security and steady wage increases by continually generating economic hypergrowth. Layoffs threatened this implicit class bargain and would have taken away any restraint the workers might have felt in demanding political rights and strengthening their industrial and national labor federations.

Coupled with these structural barriers against systemic reform, there was also Park's vision of transforming South Korea into a second Japan with an army of national champions in his lifetime. This goal constantly encouraged Park to take chances when a new frontier of economic growth arose.

There was also the problem of capital scarcity, which had originally made Park base his growth strategy on bank subsidies, *chaebol* organization, and company (as opposed to industrywide) unionism. Because domestic resources were limited, Park would have had to turn to foreign direct investment sooner or later if he had decided to restructure the *chaebol* in any meaningful way. Lifting entry barriers, however, would have posed multiple political dangers for Park. The foreign investors would have recapitalized insolvent corporations and banks only if excess employees could be dismissed quickly and redundant production lines closed down. Such investors would also call for a thorough reform of South Korea's corporate governance structure, because only when account books were clean and transparent, majority shareholders legally accountable, and opaque cross-shareholding among subsidiaries discontinued could banks establish prudent supervision over corporate borrowers. Even with just a few commercial banks under foreign control, Park would have seen his discretionary power over credit allocation and industrial policy rapidly slip away and his personal ties to *chaebol* weakened. Park instead tried to tame the excesses of the developmental state's expansionary nature by imposing more regulations each time he faced a severe banking crisis.[6]

In lieu of structural reform, Park had to fall back on the strategy of "industrial rationalization" to cool down the overheated economy with shock therapies such as foreign exchange devaluation, interest hikes, debt restructuring, and wage controls,[7] but at the same time put in place safeguards to prevent these measures from disintegrating the *chaebol*, South Korea's microfoundation of economic hypergrowth. To stave off disintegration, he got the state to broker, coordinate, and subsidize business swaps between rival *chaebol* as well as state banks to subsidize the restructuring of corporate debts. The state-brokered and -subsidized business swaps were thought of as a substitute for market-led M&As (mergers and acquisitions), reducing surplus capacity, holding executives accountable for mismanagement, and resolving financial distress, but without a spread of corporate bankruptcy. Unfortunately, however, industrial rationalization could never serve as such a substitute for market-led M&As, because its mechanism of state-brokered business swaps and corporate takeovers was designed more as a rescue operation than as a disciplinary measure. Consequently, it helped the *chaebol* weather two or three years of hard times, but did not make them financially any stronger. On the contrary, the strategy of industrial rationalization Park-style trapped the *chaebol* in deeper moral hazards, as they diversified and conglomerated in the belief that state rescue could be relied on in the event of external supply or demand shock. Consequently, the task of interrupting the cycle of boom and bust at the macro level and of disciplining the *chaebol* conglomerates' moral hazards at the micro level without paralyzing the sources of growth was passed on to Park's successors.

Unfortunately, however, until the Asian financial crisis struck South Korea in 1997, Park's successors—whether authoritarian or democratic—were all alike in waiving the option of disciplining the *chaebol* with a credible exit policy on the basis of the market threat of bankruptcy, lest the U-turn in corporate finance and industrial policy trigger massive corporate and bank failures. Like Park, they resorted to secondary measures to tame the *chaebol* conglomerates' excessive appetite for loans, and like Park, they failed, albeit to varying degrees. Having seen the stagflationary crisis of 1979 bring down Park, Chun Doo-hwan (1980–1988) severed the cycle of boom and bust at the macro level by ending the practice of easy government loans and other monetary policies, but he failed in the other task of weeding out the moral hazards of the *chaebol* at the micro level because he resorted to his predecessor's strategy of industrial rationalization out of fear of systemic instability. In 1981, emulating Park in industrial policy,

Chun Doo-hwan oversaw a limited business swap among South Korea's top *chaebol* groups to reduce surplus capacity and encourage specialization, only to see another liquidity crisis descending upon smaller *chaebol* and construction groups in 1985, which he met with massive rescue money.[8] In other words, the old ways of doing business continued, albeit with a subtle but critical shift in policy priorities. Chun provided privileges and benefits for the *chaebol*, but he also made sure that these subsidies were made within an overall framework of conservative monetary policy and, in doing so, purged from his predecessor's growth model one of the causes of systemic instability. The policy innovation he pushed through was a change within Park's growth model, not a fundamental "neoliberal" overhaul of South Korea's financial as well as corporate governance structures.

Nor did the democratic breakthrough of June 1987 bring about the needed U-turn. In fact, Roh Tae-woo (1988–1993) remained within Park's paradigm of developmental statism and Chun's notion of stabilizing growth. The series of industrial policies Roh proposed were a replica of Chun's program to tame rather than to discipline the *chaebol*. The loose ceiling Roh placed on bank loans and cross shareholding to restrain *chaebol* groups from risky empire building was originally introduced in 1984.[9] The idea of transforming the *chaebol* into "specialized" industrial conglomerates with four or five "core areas" of production through swapping secondary "unrelated" businesses with other *chaebol* groups similarly traced its origin to Chun's 1985 policy that required the *chaebol* to sell their unrelated businesses before entering a new product market.[10] The May 1990 measure that prohibited the *chaebol* from purchasing large land parcels as well as entering "unproductive" industrial sectors[11] also echoed Chun's September 1980 measure.[12] Roh briefly toyed with the radical "public concept" of land in 1991 to place a ceiling on land ownership by big business, to levy special taxes on "unearned incomes" from real estate speculation, and to order the sale of idle land with a threat of credit reduction, tax investigation, and expropriation, but even this did not imply a paradigmatic shift in policy for the *chaebol*. The public concept of land was brought into policy to hold down land prices and channel capital into more productive business fields.[13] As such, it only represented a strengthening of the traditional industrial policy to force the *chaebol* to focus on main businesses, not a search for alternative forms of business organization.

The idea of substituting the threat of exit for state-brokered, -coordinated, and -subsidized business swaps reappeared during Kim Young-sam's presidency (1993–1998) under the 1993 policy of "sectoral specialization." Under the policy, each of the top *chaebol* groups chose six or seven of its affiliate firms operating in two or three "core sectors" as its "lead companies," on the understanding that the state would lift restrictive regulations on bank loans for these companies in return for their restraint on issuing new loan guarantees to other affiliate firms. The outcome was anything but specialization. As in the case of Roh's main firm policy of 1991,[14] the lead company policy of Kim Young-sam worsened moral hazards and fueled corporate expansion. Lured by the promise of financial privileges, the top thirty *chaebol* registered a total of 112 affiliate firms as their lead companies in January 1994. Moreover, because the South Korean economy was reclassified from having 73 to having 15 industrial sectors under the lead company policy, the *chaebol* faced no real constraints on their options for corporate expansion, as their horizontal diversification and vertical integration within the chosen sectors were by definition acts of corporate specialization.[15] Even this loose policy of specialization collapsed when the Samsung Group successfully lobbied in December 1994 to establish an integrated passenger car plant in Pusan—a regional support base of the then-ruling Democratic Liberal Party. The president approved Samsung's entry into the automobile industry with his eye on winning the 1996 National Assembly election, although the decision brought down the minimal restriction his lead company policy had set on entry into noncore sectors.

It was only the Asian financial crisis, coupled with the presidential election of "progressive" Kim Dae-jung (1998–2003), that forced South Korea to give up Park's idea of state-brokered, -coordinated, and -subsidized business swaps and to tackle the root cause of the *chaebol* groups' entrapment in moral hazards by packaging financial, corporate, and labor reforms as integrated measures of system restructuring. The state now wore the hat of regulator rather than that of modernizer and oversaw asset revaluation, debt prioritization and rescheduling, injection of new working capital, and management and ownership change in both financial and corporate sectors in a typically dirigiste South Korean way,[16] setting a 200 percent upper limit on debt-equity ratios for the *chaebol* in February 1998 through administrative guidance. By July 1999, nineteen of its original thirty merchant banks were shut down, twenty-six commercial banks consolidated into twelve through M&As and liquidations, and eighteen investment trust companies streamlined into four, while a flurry of legislative activism developed market exit mechanisms, including a public asset management company, bankruptcy laws, M&A markets, prudential regulations, and the lifting of legal upper ceilings on foreign ownership in equity, bond, and money markets.[17] The prolonged systemic crisis also ended up dissolving Daewoo and splitting the Hyundai Group by 2000, thereby burying South Korea's myth of *taema pulsa* (the big never die),[18] as well as its state elite's hope for bureaucratically engineered and politically safer schemes of corporate rationalization. The failure of South Korea's two largest *chaebol* persuaded the survivors to become more cost-conscious and slimmer agents of economic growth.

In other words, Kim Dae-jung's politics of system restructuring did not dismantle the *chaebol*. On the contrary, the survivors of debt restructuring were reformed *chaebol* with new patterns of behavior. The sight of their weaker brethren collapsing under massive nonperforming loans unambiguously signaled that South Korea was entering a brave new era, where the *chaebol* could not fall back on a state rescue operation in times of corporate distress. Consequently, the survivors adopted new patterns of behavior while retaining much of their *chaebol* organizational characteristics of family ownership, cross-shareholding, and an imperial structure of decision making. The new *chaebol* was more obsessed with cash flow than with sales growth, less prepared for bold risk taking, and more wary of the threats of hostile takeover, becoming slimmer in structure, conservative in finance, cautious in market entry, but still organizationally centered around the owner family. The change of behavior was nowhere more visible than in its massive piling up of retained earnings,[19] once it succeeded in reducing bad loans and liquidating losing businesses. The banks changed too, but not in the direction of policy objectives. Whereas the state hoped for a rebirth of the South Korean banks as genuine financiers that made loans on the basis of an objective assessment of a borrower's future streams of cash flow as well as its capabilities of risk management, the banks that emerged out of the shock of debt restructuring were risk averse rather than carefully risk calculating banks. They recovered financial solvency after a massive injection of public money, but lacking expertise and experience in risk management, they focused on South Korea's relatively safe household markets, with real estate taken as collateral.[20] And with these transformations of the *chaebol* and banks, South Korea shed the worst forms of moral hazard but also graduated from hypergrowth.

The Political System

For almost three decades after Park's death there were struggles between a political elite aiming to maintain the political system Park created and those determined to create a more democratic and open country. When the opposition's hope for an early victory over dictatorship vanished in May 1980, the year after Park's death, with Chun Doo-hwan's military

coup d'état, those opposed to Chun—and by extension, Park—nevertheless sought to build their base of support and take advantage of opportunities. Park's rule had been at the center of political contention ever since
Park overthrew the democratically elected Chang Myŏn in May 1961. The
debate became even more heated after Park's death.

When Park was assassinated, the coalition that supported Park's authoritarian developmental coalition first rallied behind Kim Chong-p'il and after May 1980 behind Chun Doo-hwan. They dominated the political scene
until June 1987, when the democratic breakthrough irreversibly terminated their monopoly of political power. The survival of the protagonists
of the Park era did not mean that the system of political rule and the patterns of economic growth after 1979 were unchanged by the powerful
forces of democratization and globalization. The three decades after Park's
demise witnessed the spirit of reform spread incrementally to all corners of
South Korean society, and the cumulative effect was nothing less than a
systemic transformation. The protagonists of the Park era survived because they adapted to the forces of democratization and globalization by
adopting new ideas, opening up new linkages to society, and experimenting with new forms of organization. Various factions of the Park coalition
for development played a game of party mergers, splits, and cooperation
with opposition politicians and *chaeya* dissidents in order to maximize
their power.

In the course of political transformation, elections became the "only
game in town." Even Park had had to face elections and to accomplish this
he put together a strategy of regionalist agitation, ideological mobilization, and money politics as a basis for building a broad ruling coalition.
Initially, the strategy worked extremely well. Syngman Rhee's fall in 1960
had meant the demise of his staunchly anticommunist northern natives. In
their place, Park forged a cohesive power elite[21] as well as a loyal mass following early in his political rule by favoring his fellow Kyŏngsang natives.
Against his regionalist bloc stood the Chŏlla natives, whose stake in top
executive posts fell below their population share by 8.7 percentage points
during Park's rule. To tighten his grip on power, Park filled strategically
critical political posts through his control over elections, legal procedures,
intelligence, and military power, mainly with the natives of his Kyŏngsang
region. The regional composition of the South Korean business community also changed visibly under Park, as he discriminated against northern
chaebol during his military junta years and against Chŏlla *chaebol* after
the restoration of electoral politics in 1963. With foreign capital entering
en masse after 1963 and loan rates falling below deposit rates in 1965,
Park had the powerful instrument he needed to reorganize the business

community around Kyŏngsang *chaebol*. The Ssangyong and P'anbon *chaebol*, each launched by a Kyŏngsang native, newly entered the ranks of South Korea's top ten *chaebol* only four years after Park's coup d'état, making Kyŏngsang natives a majority in that elite group.[22] By 1979, the northern *chaebol* had all dropped off the list. Equally critical, only once, in 1965, did a Chŏlla entrepreneur find his name listed among South Korea's ten largest industrialists.[23]

In addition, Park added a mass component to his regionalist coalition strategy early in his rule. To build up a stable electoral constituency as well as to exploit backward and forward linkage effects, he opted to house factories and plants of related industries in a few geographically compact industrial complexes. In 1962, Park chose Ulsan-Mip'o of North Kyŏngsang Province as a center for his strategic heavy and chemical industries. By the time he died, Park had constructed seven more national industrial complexes, four of which were located in his Kyŏngsang region, whereas the rival Chŏlla region hosted only one, in its Yŏch'ŏn–Kwangyang area.[24] Among the four largest industrial complexes, as measured by employment, three resided in the Kyŏngsang region.[25] By locating industries linked to each other at different points in the chain of production together on South Korea's southeastern Kyŏngsang shores, near Japanese suppliers, consumers, technology licensors, and investors, Park secured the synergy effects of transnational ties and linkages as well. There emerged a dense cross-border network of production,[26] with Japanese "lead" companies outsourcing some of their business activities to South Korean subcontractors, suppliers, distributors, or service providers much along the "flying geese" model of regional division of labor and thus helping South Korea's search for export markets. However, by backing the Kyŏngsang region in intra-elite as well as mass struggles over political and economic resources, Park alienated rural Chŏlla voters so that they joined urban Seoul dwellers in opposing his political rule, beginning with the 1967 presidential and National Assembly elections. This Chŏlla-Seoul axis was to find its vehicle in 1971 when Kim Dae-jung of the Chŏlla region ran a presidential race against Park. Chŏlla voters remained even more united behind Kim Dae-jung after his abduction from Tokyo by KCIA agents in 1974, taking his experience as their own.

To put Park on the defensive even more, the Kyŏngsang region also showed signs of an internal split under the forces of "mini" regionalism. Ironically, much of the split was Park's own doing. Certainly, Kim Young-sam, born in Kŏje, an island near Pusan in South Kyŏngsang Province, became the opposition New Democratic Party (NDP) leader on his own credentials when Yu Chin-san died in April 1974; he boasted of the ability

to get the votes in Pusan, South Korea's second-largest city and traditionally the rival to Taegu, a northern Kyŏngsang city near Park's home. However, it was Park's political crackdown in 1979 that awakened Pusan and
other parts of South Kyŏngsang Province to their own mini regionalism,
with Kim Young-sam as the symbol and the instrument of their ambition.
When YH workers staged a protest at the NDP headquarters in August
1979, Kim Young-sam as the party's president sided with the workers in
unambiguous ways, thus developing the image of a defender of labor
rights. Park hit back by instigating a court order to suspend Kim Young-
sam's duties as the NDP president in September, only to see Kim Young-
sam heighten his struggle with a call for "peaceful regime change"[27] and
pressure on the United States to oppose the *yushin* regime.[28] The Democratic Republican Party (DRP) legislators expelled Kim Young-sam from
the National Assembly in early October on Park's order,[29] but the crackdown only triggered mass protests in Kim Young-sam's home province and
Park's declaration of martial law over Pusan and a garrison decree over
Masan, followed by the dispatch of marine and airborne military units.[30]
Like Kim Dae-jung's 1971 presidential election and 1974 abduction from
Tokyo, the events of 1979 made South Kyŏngsang Province identify with
Kim Young-sam.

The system of regionalist elections, then, eventually worked as much
against as for Park by driving each of South Korea's major regions or sub-
regions to coalesce around one or another native political leader to vie for
power at the national level. In spite of the spread of regionalism, however,
it is important to note that regionalism's grip on South Korean party politics was not as strong as it would come to be after the demise of the *yushin*
regime, and that it was the political choices of Park's successors that made
regionalism the primary cleavage of party politics and the central organizing principle of the South Korean political parties. As late as 1978, on the
basis of deep anti-party sentiments pervading South Korean society, independent candidates won 28.1 percent of the vote, up 9.5 percentage points
from the 1973 National Assembly election.

In Kim Dae-jung's native South Chŏlla Province and Kim Young-sam's
home South Kyŏngsang Province, the outcome of the 1978 National Assembly elections contradicted the myth that South Korean party politics
was under the unbreakable influence of regionalism even more by the
end of Park's political rule. The DRP took 8 of the 10 first places in
South Chŏlla Province, and the NDP none of the 9 first places in South
Kyŏngsang Province.[31] That Yi Ch'ŏl-sŭng from Chŏnju, North Chŏlla,
tried to lead the NDP into accepting Park's *yushin* and pursuing "reform
through participation" as a "centrist integrationist" between September
1976 and May 1979, in opposition to Kim Dae-jung's "radical" *chaeya*

position of democratic struggle, moreover, should caution us against interpreting North Chŏlla Province's award of 4 of the 12 National Assembly seats to the NDP in 1978 as a vote for Kim Dae-jung. They might have been as much a vote for Yi Ch'ŏl-sŭng as for Kim Dae-jung. In other words, Kim Dae-jung and Kim Young-sam came to enjoy unswerving loyalty from their respective regions only after Park died in 1979, or, more accurately, only after Chun Doo-hwan's repression of the Kwangju Democratic Uprising in 1980 irreversibly split the Chŏlla from the Kyŏngsang region and threw the northern and southern parts of the Kyŏngsang region into a family feud.

It was the leaders of the post-Park era who groomed regionalism into the principal basis for political organization in South Korea. The most critical and tragic turn of events that made regionalism the main recipe of political struggle occurred in 1980, when Chun Doo-hwan led a bloody repression of political protests in Kwangju. Before the Kwangju Democratic Uprising, Chŏlla voters had been a house divided, some backing the centrist Yi Ch'ŏl-sŭng, others the dissident Kim Dae-jung, and still others the modernizer Park. After the military massacred the "citizen army" making its last stand in the capitol building of South Chŏlla Province on May 27, the voters of both northern and southern parts of the Chŏlla region lined up uniformly behind Kim Dae-jung as the personification of Kwangju's hopes and anguish, as well as progressive ideological ideals. This deep hostility against Chun Doo-hwan's military coalition of Kyŏngsang origin also metastasized into a culture of mutual distrust between Kim Dae-jung and Kim Young-sam, when "progressive" Kim Dae-jung broke away from "moderate conservative" Kim Young-sam's New Korea Democratic Party to launch a separate presidential campaign in 1987, the outcome of which was the victory of Roh Tae-woo, Chun Doo-hwan's handpicked successor, in a four-way presidential race. Then, in 1990, under the banner of conservative unity, Kim Young-sam merged his forces with the heirs of the authoritarian *yushin* and the Fifth Republic (1980–1988) and the regional leaders of the Ch'ungch'ŏng region and North Kyŏngsang Province—Kim Chong-p'il and Roh Tae-woo, respectively—in order to isolate progressive Kim Dae-jung of the Chŏlla in a bid for presidential power in 1992. The break and merger of 1987 and 1990, criticized as acts of betrayal by Kim Young-sam and Kim Dae-jung respectively, transformed their provincial homes into mutually unforgiving rivals.

After the 1987 democratic breakthrough, it was the combination of regionalism and progressive-conservative ideological conflict that gave South Korean party politics its basic contours and parameters. The Chŏlla gave Kim Dae-jung between 83.5 and 97.3 percent of its votes in the post-

1987 direct presidential elections.[32] Alarmed by the Chŏlla voters' rallying around Kim Dae-jung, the electorate of Pusan and South Kyŏngsang Province sided with Kim Young-sam by 53.7 percent in 1987 and 72.8 percent in 1992. Until Roh Moo-hyun of the postwar generation was elected president in 2002, South Korean party politics came to be thoroughly dominated by the politicians, whose leadership was built up either by opposing Park as a leader of democratic struggles in the case of Kim Young-sam and Kim Dae-jung, or by crafting the image of a trusted lieutenant of a modernizer Park in the case of Kim Chong-p'il.

The tenacity of regionalist party politics turned into the enduring legacy of money politics as well. Because South Korea's regionalism lacked any programmatic vision, both the Park and the post-Park era were prevented from building a strong political party system on the basis of balancing what Angelo Panebianco once argued are two necessary ingredients for strong party organization: "selective incentives" such as power, prestige, or money that lure the elite into becoming party careerists; and "collective" or ideological incentives that gain mass support for the political party from the rank and file as well as from the electoral constituency.[33] As these collective incentives were in short supply with the constitutional revision to clear the way for a third presidential term in 1969 and for lifelong rule in 1972, and his anticommunist cold war ideologies failed to develop a proactive programmatic vision for the public, Park Chung Hee came to rely not only on regionalist agitation and McCarthyist Red scares but also on money politics to build a political machine. Without any real rank and file willing to pay annual dues for a commonly held political value, the DRP had to raise campaign funds from *chaebol* groups by promising subsidies and license privileges and using those funds to hire local brokers as campaign workers. To keep able local brokers on its side between elections, the DRP also had to maintain large district party chapters nationwide with some of the local brokers on its payroll. Thus formed a "chain of prey" *(mŏki sasŭl),* with party leaders, *chaebol* groups, and local power brokers feeding on each other to buy influence. The use of "selective incentives" had negative consequences on South Korea's moral fabric as well as on its economy,[34] diverting scarce resources from productive activities precisely when the overexpansionary export machine ran into a liquidity problem.

In contrast to regionalist party politics that only worsened and ideological mobilization that evolved into progressive-conservative rivalries after the democratic breakthrough of 1987, money politics came to be incrementally but irreversibly foiled after 1995. Even during the presidency of Roh Tae-woo, the reformist National Assembly had tried to wage a moral crusade against money politics by holding assembly hearings on the human rights abuses and corruption committed during Chun Doo-hwan's rule, but the hearings produced at best a mixed outcome. Wary of political paralysis and its impact on economic stagnation, but also satisfied with the political damage inflicted on Roh Tae-woo with the revelation of the human rights abuses and corruption committed by Chun Doo-hwan, Roh Tae-woo's mentor, the opposition let Chun Doo-hwan go free—but on the condition that he turns over all remaining political funds and go into "exile" in a secluded Buddhist temple in Sŏlak for two years. The two issues of human rights abuses and corruption, however, refused to go away, even after Kim Young-sam, in his capacity as the newly elected president, purged 11 National Assembly members with shady records of illicit wealth accumulation and abuse of human rights; arrested, retired, or dismissed 23 military generals on active service or in the reserves for questionable roles in Chun Doo-hwan's 1979 military mutiny and 1980 coup d'état, bribery, or human rights abuses; indicted 7 business executives for shady deals; and brought a criminal charge against a public prosecutor who had hunted down dissidents since the time of the *yushin*. The turning point came in 1995, when the slush funds stashed away by Roh Tae-woo were discovered, forcing Kim Young-sam to order another round of investigation. This time, the procurator general arrested Roh Tae-woo after interrogating some forty *chaebol* owners as "references" and "accomplices" and also moved against Chun Doo-hwan for the 1980 military coup as well as for illicit wealth accumulation.

Despite the prosecution of Chun Doo-hwan and Roh Tae-woo, however, progress came slowly because the political parties of the post-1987 democratic era still based their organization on regionalist agitation and the ill-articulated rhetoric of progressive and conservative ideologies, failing to develop beyond the stage of "cadre" parties. Possessing neither a coherent ideological vision nor a densely organized network of linkages to social forces, the post-1987 political parties turned to the old game of money politics, albeit in much more discreet ways, in order to maintain the dense network of local power brokers and to run the costly nonprogrammatic election campaigns. Consequently, in spite of the sporadic crackdowns on money politics, parties were shunned by the public as the culprits of money politics that eroded South Korea's fragile moral fabric, weakened its once dynamic export machine, and obstructed the policymakers' focus on policy by breeding regionalist prejudices and populist sentiments. However, because they *were* political parties that by definition assumed the role of articulating public sentiments into goals, agendas, and strategies of reform and developing the basic political language or discourse with which to aggregate conflicting demands of society, the post-1987 political parties were constantly called on to break away from the politics of regionalist agitation, ideological rhetoric, and money politics that they themselves practiced and, in the process, became the targets of their own prosecutorial politics. Essentially, the post-1987 political parties lived in a transitional era, where careers were made through the old ways of regionalist agitation, ideological prejudices, and money politics, but were judged by the unsystematically imagined but electrifying new vision of transparent and responsive democracy. Until this gap between the reality and the ideal was bridged, many of the post-1987 party politicians were destined to fall, much like their pre-1987 predecessors, during the post-1987 democratic era.

The Coercive System

The system of selective coercion was the most dysfunctional of the three systems. In fact, it is uncertain whether the coercive system actually helped even Park, because with every act of coercion, he created one more enemy and weakened his own legitimacy. But what was important was that Park thought the KCIA to be *the* indispensable pillar of his political rule, and he acted on this belief. During the military junta years, Park had the KCIA orchestrate the purge of rival northern military factions, silence *chaeya* dissidents and opposition politicians with a show of force, and clandestinely organize the DRP in preparation for electoral politics. The KCIA's role as a watchdog continued into the Third Republic (1963–1972). When Park prepared for his third term via a constitutional change in 1969, the KCIA bribed both ruling and opposition party legislators to do what Park wanted.[35] The intelligence agency also did not shy away from terrorizing party leaders when it thought it necessary, as it did when some of Kim Chong-p'il's mainstream faction stood in the way of Park's desire for a third term in 1969, when DRP finance chairman Kim Sŏng-gon sided with opposition legislators in a vote of no confidence against cabinet ministers in 1971,[36] or when Kim Dae-jung frontally challenged the legitimacy of the *yushin* regime from exile in 1973.[37]

However, it was the restraint rather than the actual use of force that showed the power of the KCIA. The intelligence agency kept extensive files on the everyday lives of South Korean party, military, business, and *chaeya* leaders, including their wealth, sexual habits, tax reports, and social circles, to keep opponents in line. Even Kim Chong-p'il had his house searched three times by KCIA agents, to be reminded of his vulnerability.[38]

The impact of silent surveillance on the South Korean elite was powerful. Aware of the watchdogs' shadow over their lives, members of the elite thought twice before challenging Park and usually moderated their critique of his authoritarian rule on the assumption that he would correspondingly refrain from threatening their vital interests. It was only in 1976, three and a half years after the launching of the *yushin* regime, that the radical *chaeya* led by Kim Dae-jung publicly called for an end to Park's authoritarian rule. The NDP, led by the centrist Yi Ch'ŏl-sŭng and later the reformist Kim Young-sam, unambiguously sided with the *chaeya* position of dismantling the *yushin* only when Park threatened in 1979 to take away even the limited political pluralism he had granted since 1972. The implicit understanding of the "formally ill-defined . . . but actually quite predictable"[39] limits on the exercise of power reached between Park and his rivals before 1978 had enabled Park to isolate the more intransigent *chaeya* from the moderate NDP opponents so that he could repress the *chaeya* in unforgiving ways. The breakdown of that implicit understanding, as demonstrated in the DRP's 1979 expulsion of Kim Young-sam from the National Assembly, united NDP politicians with the *chaeya* in demanding the end of the *yushin* regime.

The KCIA was more brutal when the target of repression lay outside the political elite. In 1969, it rounded up over a hundred *chaeya* intellectuals on the charge of operating a P'yŏngyang-funded underground communist cell with its headquarters in East Berlin,[40] and tried their leaders under the draconian national security laws. The McCarthyist witch hunt broke out again in 1974, with over a thousand dissidents interrogated for their alleged organizing of a "People's Revolutionary Party" to instigate student protests to overthrow the *yushin* regime. The 1974 crackdown ended in a particularly tragic way. The prosecutors demanded that the newly established Emergency Military Court issue 14 death penalties, 15 life imprisonments, and 18 twenty-year imprisonments in July 1974.[41] The same day Park announced Presidential Emergency Decree no. 7 to close down a rebellious Korea University. On April 8, 1975, the Supreme Court confirmed 8 of the proposed 14 death penalties, which the state swiftly carried out within a day.[42] By 1979, Park had had his security and legal apparatus imprison a total of 1,184 people for opposition activities.[43] After the death of Chŏn T'ae-il in 1970, the *chaeya* labor activists were also tracked down and repressed by the police forces. The church joined the list of victims when some of its progressive activists joined the elders of the opposition to call for the dismantlement of the *yushin* and the guarantee of labor rights in 1976.

The use of the KCIA as an instrument in power struggles hurt Park profoundly in the long run. Apart from getting Park stuck in an ideological war with both "progressive" Kim Dae-jung and "moderate conservative" Kim Young-sam, who by 1979 had transformed into intransigent anti-*yushin* "radicals" with a regional power base from which to launch a sustained siege against Park, the use of the KCIA also entailed the danger of inadvertently breaking up the system of checks and balances that Park had nurtured within his inner circle of praetorian guards, technocratic aides, and party bosses during much of the Third Republic. The problem was that the watchdog could become the master itself by hoarding power while tightening the ropes of repression. Park was aware of this danger and tried to maintain the checks-and-balances system. Before the constitutional revision of 1969 that opened the way to Park's third term, KCIA director Kim Hyŏng-uk was only one among equals in the president's inner circle, typically flexing his muscle as the "operational man" in charge of doing the dirty work, for which he would later be "slandered" and "remain sleepless at night," to quote his words.[44] The idea man was the "clever" Yi Hu-rak who presided over the imperial Presidential Secretariat,[45] whereas the soft talker Kim Sŏng-gon was a deal-maker in the National Assembly, co-opting one or another opposition legislator by tapping the dense political network he had developed as a Liberal Party politician and a business tycoon before 1961, or by generously disbursing money from the DRP political funds.[46] There was also the "elder," Chŏng Ku-yŏng, who raised a critique of state policy or even urged power sharing with Kim Chong-p'il in front of Park, in his unique capacity as the president's personal counsel *(sangŭiyŏk)* between 1965 and 1974.[47] In other words, before 1972 Park had channels to make deals with opposition party bosses, at the same time that he loosed KCIA agents to suppress more hostile forces.

Unfortunately for Park, not only the mechanism of limited political pluralism but also the system of checks and balances within the inner circle collapsed as he tried to counter the opposition's assault on the *yushin* in 1979. By then, Kim Sŏng-gon had been purged, Yi Hu-rak had retired into oblivion, and Chŏng Ku-yŏng had died of old age, leaving only KCIA director Kim Chae-gyu and Presidential Security Service chief Ch'a Chi-ch'ŏl as the top aides. The inner circle no longer had a strategist, a deal-maker, or a critic. Moreover, the two praetorian guards were deadlocked over how to deal with Kim Young-sam's call for democratization, with a "quixotic" Kim Chae-gyu advocating dialogue with the opposition and a "rugged" Ch'a Chi-ch'ŏl calling for a war against the opposition party and *chaeya* leaders. The collapse of the checks and balances was Park's own doing. Despite the repeated failures of both soft-line Kim Chae-gyu and hard-line Ch'a Chi-ch'ŏl to prevent Kim Young-sam's assault on the *yu-*

shin regime, Park kept on calling on the two security heads to stop the opposition.[48] When socioeconomic adversity, regionalist animosity, and ideological discontent converged to ignite mass protest in Pusan and Masan, Kim Chae-gyu snapped and became a most unlikely "revolutionary," killing Park in October 1979 to "restore liberal democracy . . . with as little sacrifice as possible," to quote Kim Chae-gyu's testimony in his trial by a military court.[49]

Like the political system of regionalist elections based on money politics and supplemented by cold war ideology and the economic system of debt-financed growth, the coercive system did not die with the demise of Park. On the contrary, it heavily influenced the political path of the post-Park era by providing the military heir to the *yushin* regime with an opportunity to strike back at the opposition and snatch power from the three Kims in May 1980. Certainly, the garrison state was shaken by Park's death, but it also quickly recovered from its paralysis once Chun Doo-hwan's Army Security Command, emerging out of the feud between the KCIA and the PSS triggered by the regime crisis without any organizational damage of its own, took over the then-demoralized KCIA. The takeover enabled the ASC to supplement its brute force with the KCIA's powerful arsenal of surveillance, which it used to lash out against the three Kims. And with it, Chun Doo-hwan resolved the problem of the politically dysfunctional KCIA-PSS power rivalry. Thereafter, power was centralized in the ASC. The ASC led the way to the launching of the Fifth Republic by arresting army chief-of-staff Chŏng Sŭng-hwa and his moderate faction of senior military officers on the charge of conspiring with Kim Chae-gyu in December 1979 and by brutally repressing the Kwangju Democratic Uprising in May 1980. The "Spring of Seoul" abruptly ended, bringing the military back into power with Chun Doo-hwan as the heir to Park.

In spite of the direct lineage the Fifth Republic traced to the *yushin* regime, and the personal ties Chun Doo-hwan had with Park since his organization of a military parade by the Korea Military Academy cadets in support of Park in the early days of the 1961 coup d'état, Chun Doo-hwan knew that he could consolidate his rule only when he succeeded in differentiating himself from his patron. Consequently, Chun Doo-hwan attempted a U-turn across issue areas upon the inauguration of the Fifth Republic. He adopted a single seven-year term for the president, pledged to put the issues of social justice at the core of the national agenda, and embarked on a program of economic liberalization. Except for the promise of serving only one presidential term, however, he failed to break away from the Park era. On the contrary, the Fifth Republic ended up being an extension of authoritarian developmentalism, perfecting rather than dismantling Park's model of economic growth by purging the financial excesses built into it through a tight control over the money supply. The rhetoric of social justice and financial liberalization dissipated too, because Chun Doo-hwan never was what he thought he was, a "neoliberal" with the mission to "dissolve" the developmental state even at the risk of confrontation with the *chaebol*.[50] Likewise, the garrison state remained intact, but this time with the balance of power tilted toward the ASC, as the university campuses turned into breeding grounds of radical ideas and *chaeya* organizations in the aftermath of the bloody repression of the 1980 Kwangju Democratic Uprising. Ironically, with an eye to giving the Fifth Republic a democratic face, Chun Doo-hwan restored the rights of some of the former NDP politicians to run for election in 1984, but this gesture of political opening resulted in a strong resurgence of the opposition in the 1985 National Assembly elections and only prompted Chun Doo-hwan to rely even more on the security apparatus to oppose his adversaries.

The coercive system was shaken up from the bottom only when middle-class groups openly, unambiguously, and decisively sided with the *chaeya* and the opposition political party to force direct presidential elections on Chun Doo-hwan and his successor, Roh Tae-woo, in June 1987. Protests spread to the industrial complexes in July and August. The intelligentsia of the "386 Generation"[51] also increasingly radicalized, initially toying with dependency theory and liberation theology, then embracing Marxist ideas and Leninist organizations, and later landing in North Korea's home-grown Chuch'e (or Juche) ideology. These intellectuals were searching for an ideology that negated not only Park and Chun but also the South Korean national identity of liberal democracy, market capitalism, and alliance with the United States.[52] Certainly, most of the 386ers eventually grew out of their fixation with Marxist-Leninist ideas and Chuch'e beliefs after the collapse of the Soviet Union and its East European satellite states in 1991 and the paralysis of the North Korean economy in the mid-1990s. However, the 386ers' spirit of resistance and their doubts about the South Korean national identity survived, getting the political parties to pressure for the withdrawal of the security apparatus from domestic political affairs. The 1988 National Assembly hearings on human rights violations, followed by the 1993 purge of Chun Doo-hwan's *Hanahoe* faction from the military and the 1995 trial of Chun Doo-hwan and Roh Tae-woo on the charges of military mutiny, national subversion, and corruption, made the security agencies lose their appetite for any role in political repression. The days of terrorizing the political parties and the *chaeya* with threats of torture were over for good with the progress of democratization.

However, this did not mean that the heirs to Park's security agencies completely withdrew from domestic politics. The politics of terror ended, but given the ideologically shallow and organizationally weak regionalist parties' entrapment in a destructive cycle of party splits and mergers, the leaders of democratic South Korea were repeatedly tempted to use the security apparatus as their praetorian guard in covert political operations. As late as the 1997 presidential election, the National Security Planning Agency—the successor to the KCIA—wiretapped *chaebol* executives, party politicians, and newspaper owners, among others, to trace the flow of election campaign funds, and also tried to get North Korea to stage a military incident in the hopes of triggering a war scare that could tilt the undecided toward the ruling political party. Reorganized into the National Intelligence Service during Kim Dae-jung's presidency, the security agency spearheaded peace talk with P'yŏngyang in 2000 and 2007, eventually clearing the way to a summit meeting with Kim Jung-il of the North. It was revealed in 2005 that illegal wiretapping continued under Kim Dae-jung; according to the Public Prosecutor's Office, some 1,800 people were wiretapped by the National Intelligence Service to gather a diverse array of information concerning such issues as the presidential primaries and intra-party factional struggles, labor strikes and medical reforms, and inter-Korea economic programs. Apparently, the organizational capabilities of the security apparatus to plan, execute, and monitor made the leaders of democratic South Korea repeatedly turn to this system to engineer a political coup at the country's critical moments of domestic political development.

TOWARD THE END of the third decade after Park's death, new perspectives and new issues were becoming more central to South Koreans. The fear of communism and North Korea that underpinned authoritarian rule in South Korea had dissipated. North Korea had fallen so far behind that it had become an object less of fear than of pity. The United States that had been so powerful and so essential to the security of South Korea had lost some of its power and lustre, allowing South Korea to become more independent in foreign policy and to strengthen its ties to China, other countries, and international organizations. The financial crisis of 1997–1998 forced South Korea to become more dependent on the international economic system, thus weakening its power to remain a developmental state. The *chaebol* also transformed in tandem with South Korea's thoroughly restructured banks and nonbank financial institutions, becoming slimmer in structure, conservative in finance, and cautious in risk management.

The presidents, more influenced by democratic standards, were continuing to weaken the country's coercive institutions. The influence of Park Chung Hee and the institutions he established were not dead, even three decades after his death. However, the post-Park era, during which he and his institutions continued to dominate the South Korean economy, politics, and coercive institutions, was over.

Notes

Introduction

1. The kind of policy and institutional change occurring under Park Chung Hee's rule was too discontinuous to make Morton H. Halperin's bureaucratic politics analysis analytically relevant. Morton H. Halperin, *Bureaucratic Politics and Foreign Policy* (Washington, D.C.: Brookings Institution, 1974).

2. Alice Amsden, *Asia's Next Giant: South Korea and Late Industrialization* (New York: Oxford University Press, 1989); and Jung-en Woo, *Race to the Swift: State and Finance in Korean Industrialization* (New York: Columbia University Press, 1991).

3. Robert Wade, *Governing the Market: Economic Theory and the Role of Government in East Asian Industrialism* (Princeton: Princeton University Press, 1990).

4. Juan J. Linz, "An Authoritarian Regime: The Case of Spain," in *Cleavages, Ideologies, and Party Systems,* ed. Erik Allardt and Yrjö Littunen (Helsinki: Academic Bookstore, 1964), 297.

5. Denny Roy, "Singapore, China, and the 'Soft Authoritarian' Challenge," *Asian Survey* 34, no. 3 (March 1994): 231–242.

6. David Kang, *Crony Capitalism: Corruption and Development in South Korea and the Philippines* (Cambridge: Cambridge University Press, 2002).

7. Peter B. Evans, *Embedded Autonomy: States and Industrial Transformation* (Princeton: Princeton University Press, 1995).

8. Peter H. Smith, *Labyrinths of Power: Political Recruitment in Twentieth-Century Mexico* (Princeton: Princeton University Press, 1979).

9. Byung-Kook Kim and Hyun-Chin Lim, "Labor against Itself: Structural Di-

lemmas of State Monism," in *Consolidating Democracy in South Korea,* ed. Larry Diamond and Byung-Kook Kim (Boulder: Lynne Rienner Publishers, 2000), 111–137.

10. Joel D. Aberbach, Robert D. Putnam, and Bert A. Rockman, *Bureaucrats and Politicians in Western Democracies* (Cambridge, Mass.: Harvard University Press, 1981).

11. Roderic Ai Camp, *Political Recruitment across Two Centuries: Mexico, 1884–1991* (Austin: University of Texas Press, 1995), 243–258.

12. U.S. House of Representatives, *Investigation of Korean-American Relations* (Hearing before the Subcommittee on International Organization of the Committee on International Relations, House of Representatives), Part I (June 22, 1977), 11.

13. Consult Robert A. Packenham, *The Dependency Movement: Scholarship and Politics in Development Studies* (Cambridge, Mass.: Harvard University Press, 1998), for a critical review of dependency theories.

14. Peter B. Evans, *The Dependent Development: The Alliance of Multinational, State, and Local Capital in Brazil* (Princeton: Princeton University Press, 1979).

15. Consult Park Chung Hee, "Kwangbokchŏl kyŏngch'uksa, August 15, 1972" [Speech in Commemoration of Liberation Day], in Park Chung Hee, *Park Chung Hee taet'ongryŏng yŏnsŏlmunjip chekujip* [Speeches of Park Chung Hee], vol. 9 (Seoul: Secretary Office of the President, 1973), 265–268; and Park Chung Hee, "Kinkŭp choch'i saho sŏnp'oe chŭ'ŭmhan t'ŭkpyŏl tamhwa" [Special Speech on the Occasion of the Declaration of Emergency Decree no. 4, April 3, 1974], in Park Chung Hee, *Park Chung Hee taet'ongryŏng yŏnsŏlmunjip chesip'iljip* [Speeches of Park Chung Hee], vol. 11 (Seoul: Secretary Office of the President, 1975), 127–128.

16. Mark Hiley, "Industrial Restructuring in ASEAN and the Role of Japanese Foreign Direct Investment," *European Business Review* 99, no. 2 (1999): 80–90; and Chungsoo Kim, "Economic Cooperation in Northeast Asia," *Korean Journal of International Studies* 22, no. 1 (1991): 55–74.

17. Han'guk kidokkyo kyohoe hyŏpŭihoe [Korean Council of Christian Churches], *1970nyŏndae minjuhwa undong: kidokkyo undongŭl chungsimŭro I-V* [Democratization Movements of the 1970s: A Focus on Christian Movements], vols. 1–5 (Seoul: Korean Council of Christian Churches, 1987).

18. Consult Park Chung Hee, *Kukkawa hyŏkmyŏnggwa na* [The Nation, the Revolution, and I] (Seoul: Hyangmunsa, 1963).

19. Hyung-A Kim, *Korea's Development under Park Chung-Hee: Rapid Industrialization, 1961–1979* (London: RoutledgeCurzon, 2004), 110–111.

20. Temporary Special Law on Mediation of Labor Unions and Labor Disputes in Foreign-Invested Companies (legislated in December 1969), and Special Law on National Security (adopted in December 1971).

21. Cho Kap-che, *Nae mudŏm-e ch'im-ŭl paet'ŏra* [Spit on my grave], vols. 1–5 (Seoul: Chosun Ilbosa, 1999), and vols. 6–8 (Seoul: Chosun Ilbosa, 2001), based on Cho Kap-che's newspaper series of 564 articles published between October 29, 1997, and December 30, 1999.

1. The May Sixteenth Military Coup

1. Cho Kap-che, *Nae mudŏm-e ch'im-ŭl paet'ŏra 2: chŏnjaeng-gwa sarang* [Spit on My Grave, vol. 2: War and Love] (Seoul: Chosun Ilbosa, 1998), 216–238.

2. Don Oberdorfer, *The Two Koreas: A Contemporary History* (Reading, Mass.: Addison-Wesley, 1997), 32.

3. Chŏng Chae-gyŏng, *Park Chung Hee Silgi* [Park Chung Hee's Real History] (Seoul: Chimmundang, 1994).

4. Cho Kap-che, *Nae mudŏm-e ch'im-ŭl paet'ŏra 3: hyŏngmyŏng chŏnya* [Spit on My Grave, vol. 3: On the Eve of Revolution] (Seoul: Chosun Ilbosa, 1998), 196–197.

5. The Korea Military Academy was founded in May 1946 as Chosŏn Guard Military Academy *(Chosŏn kyŏngbi sagwan hakkyo),* changing its official name to the Korea Military Academy in September 1948. Beginning with a two-year program, it instituted a four-year curriculum from 1951 on, and produced its first class of cadets who had gone through the four-year program in 1955. The 1955 class included Chun Doo-hwan and Roh Tae-woo, who were to stage another successful coup in December 1979. The relationship between Park and the KMA was a special one. Park had pinned much hope on the academy's first graduating class, which was the first to contain "purely" Korean officers, not graduates of Japanese military schools like himself and others who dominated the military in the early years of the Republic. Indeed, Chun and Roh regarded Park as their mentor, and his vision of eventually handing over the control of the South Korean army to graduates of the KMA greatly influenced their decision to stage a coup in 1979, wresting power from the likes of Chŏng Sŭng-hwa, who had become the de facto leader of the South Korean military in the immediate aftermath of Park's assassination in October 1979.

6. After the coup, the Manchurian group started to decline because of Park's fear that members of the faction might challenge his power. Park did not appoint any members of the Manchurian faction to important government posts, even after consolidating his rule. Chŏng Il-gwŏn rose to the second-highest post of prime minister in 1965, but this was mainly a ceremonial position without power. After the coup Park arrested Kim Tong-ha, Pak Im-hang, and Pak Ch'ang-am—members of the Manchurian faction who participated in the coup—for their resistance to Park's political plan and their ambition for supremacy. General Yi Han-lim, another prominent general of the Manchurian faction, was exiled to the United States after unsuccessfully trying to stop the coup in its first three days.

7. According to Cho Kap-che, Park may have thought of the coup when he was under General Yi Yong-mun as early as 1952. The dream ended abruptly with General Yi's death in a traffic accident. See Cho Kap-che, *Nae mudŏm-e ch'im-ŭl paet'ŏra 3,* 32–51.

8. Ibid., 144–145. When Park Chung Hee was assigned to the post of commander of logistics in Pusan, he discussed the coup with his colleagues, includ-

ing a novelist, Yi Pyŏng-ju, after observing the government's illegal election campaign on March 15, 1960.

9. President Yun Po-sŏn and Prime Minister Chang Myŏn were in the same Democratic Party at the time of the Second Republic's birth (June 1960), but belonged to its Old and New Factions, respectively. This factionalism paralyzed the Chang Myŏn government before splitting the Democratic Party into two in 1962.

10. Kim Hak-jun, *Han'gukmunje-wa kukchejŏngch'i* [Korean Matters and International Politics], 4th ed. (Seoul: Pagyŏng-sa, 1999), 445.

11. The outbreak of the Korean War and the ensuing cold war made defense the top national priority, forcing South Korea to allocate 6–7 percent of its gross national product (GNP) and some 50 percent of its government budget to the defense sector every year throughout the 1950s. Kukpang kunsa yŏnguso [Research Institute for Defense and Military History], *Kukpang Chŏngch'aek Pyŏnch'ŏnsa 1945–1994* [History of Change in Defense Policy 1945–1994] (Seoul: Kukpang kunsa yŏnguso, 1995), 72.

12. Cho Kap-che, *Nae mudŏm-e ch'im-ŭl paet'ŏra* 3,138–139.

13. On the eve of the 1961 coup, a total of 7,049 officers had been trained and educated in the United States since the establishment of the Republic. In 1953 alone, 983 officers received training in the United States, as opposed to 613 civilians. Park Chung Hee was one of the beneficiaries, receiving training at Fort Sill in Oklahoma in 1953–1954. Cho Kap-che, *Nae mudŏm-e ch'im-ŭl paet'ŏra* 3,70–73.

14. Kang Ch'ang-sŏng, *Ilbon/Han'guk Kunbŏljŏngch'i* [Military Factional Politics in Japan and Korea] (Seoul: Haedong munhwasa, 1991), 351.

15. Ibid., 173–194. The SCNR describes all sorts of corruption in the military, for example, generals took military property by truck, officers took military property by jeep, whereas sergeants took out military property on their backs for personal use.

16. Ibid., 197.

17. Cho Kap-che, *Nae mudŏm-e ch'im-ŭl paet'ŏra,* 3: 128–235.

18. Kukkachaegŏn ch'oegohoeŭi Han'guk kunsahyŏngmyŏngsa p'yŏnch'an wiwŏnhoe [Compilation Committee on Korean Military Revolution History, Supreme Council of National Reconstruction], *Han'guk kunsahyŏngmyŏngsa, sang* [History of the Korean Military Revolution, vol. 1] (Seoul: Kukkachaegŏn ch'oegohoeŭi Han'guk kunsahyŏngmyŏngsa p'yŏnch'an wiwŏnhoe, 1963), 199.

19. Cho Kap-che, *Nae mudŏm-e ch'im-ŭl paet'ŏra,* 3: 328–331.

20. Cho Kap-che, *Nae mudŏm-e ch'im-ŭl paet'ŏra,* 4: *Kukka kaejo* [Spit on My Grave, vol.4: National Reconstruction] (Seoul: Chosun Ilbosa, 1999), 26.

21. See "Text of Korean Rebels' Communiqué," *New York Times,* May 17, 1961.

22. Cho Kap-che, *Nae mudŏm-e ch'im-ŭl paet'ŏra* 4: 29–30, 57–59.

23. Then an army captain, Chun Doo-hwan was a main actor responsible for organizing a parade in support of the military coup by KMA cadres. This

was the first and last of this kind of intervention by cadets in politics in the history of modern South Korea.

24. Kukkachaegŏn ch'oegohoeŭi Han'guk kunsahyŏngmyŏngsa p'yŏnch'an wiwŏnhoe, *Han'guk kunsahyŏngmyŏngsa*, 1: 329.

25. Ibid., 278.

2. Taming and Tamed by the United States

1. The counterpart fund consisted of South Korean won-denominated funds generated by the sale of foreign exchange provided by grants-in-aid and aid goods to domestic users that were then to be jointly managed by the South Korean and U.S. governments.

2. The U.S. National Security Council (NSC) document 5514 of 1955 defined U.S. objectives to be "[assisting] the Republic of Korea (ROK) in order to enable it to make a substantial contribution to free world strength in the Pacific area, to prevent more of the Korean Peninsular from coming under Communist domination either by subversion or aggression, and to develop ROK armed forces sufficient for internal security and capable of defending ROK territory short of attack by a major power." "Statement of Policy on U.S. Objectives and on Courses of Action in Korea," *Foreign Relations of the United States* [hereafter FRUS], 1955–1957, 23:44.

3. "Evaluation of Alternative Military Programs for Korea," January 14, 1957, NSC 5702, *FRUS*, 1955–1957, 23:374–384.

4. "Statement of U.S. Policy toward Korea," *FRUS*, 1955–1957, 23:491–498. As will be seen below, the reduction of ROK forces met strong resistance from the ROK government.

5. As such, it shared the spirit of the report of the Massachusetts Institute of Technology's Center for International Affairs submitted to the Senate Foreign Relations Committee. Donald S. Macdonald, *U.S.-Korean Relations from Liberation to Self-Reliance: The Twenty-Year Record* (Boulder: Westview Press, 1992), 26–27. It was presumed that Kennedy's transition team participated in the deliberations. Jung-en Woo, *Race to the Swift: State and Finance in Korean Industrialization* (New York: Columbia University Press, 1991), 75.

6. *FRUS*, 1958–1960, 28:700.

7. Report by Hugh D. Farley, *FRUS*, 1961–1963, 22:424–425.

8. Telegram from Embassy in Seoul to Department of State, March 11, 1961, John F. Kennedy Library, Boston [hereafter JFKL].

9. "Short-range Outlook in the Republic of Korea," Special National Intelligence Estimate [hereafter SNIE] 42–61, *FRUS*, 1961–1963, 22:430–435.

10. Memorandum from Robert W. Komer to Rostow, March 15, 1961, *FRUS*, 1961–1963, 22:426–427.

11. Memorandum from Rostow to Kennedy, March 15, 1961, *FRUS*, 1961–1963, 22:428.

12. Memorandum from Director of Central Intelligence Dulles to President Kennedy, May 16, 1961, *FRUS*, 1961–1963, 22:456–457.

13. Citing Kim Chong-p'il, Cho Kap-che writes that Kim Chong-p'il's Korean Central Intelligent Agency (KCIA) discovered the operation, and secretly expelled two officers. Cho Kap-che, *Nae mudŏm-e ch'im-ŭl paet'ŏra 5: Kim Chong-p'il-ŭi p'ungun* [Spit on My Grave, vol. 5: The Adventures of Kim Chong-p'il] (Seoul: Chosun Ilbo-sa, 1999), 393.
14. Telegram from the Department of State to the Embassy in Korea, May 16, 1961, *FRUS*, 1961–1963, 22:455.
15. *New York Times*, May 18, 1961.
16. *New York Times*, May 19, 1961.
17. It was at Green's discretion to withhold it, however. Memorandum for McGeorge Bundy on Proposed Message to Lieutenant General Chang To-yŏng by L. D. Battle, May 25, 1961, JFKL.
18. Telegram from the Embassy in Korea to the Department of State, June 13, 1961, *FRUS*, 1961–1963, 22:487.
19. Ibid., 488.
20. Macdonald, *U.S.-Korean Relations*, 216.
21. *FRUS*, 1961–1963, 22:482–486.
22. Telegram from the U.S. embassy in Korea to the Department of State, October 28, 1961, *FRUS*, 1961–1963, 22:522 and passim.
23. Letter from the Ambassador to Korea (Berger) to Secretary of State Rusk, *FRUS*, 1961–1963, 22:543.
24. During his farewell visit to SCNR chairman Park in Washington in November 1961, Secretary Rusk joked that Park "was very strongly represented in Washington, not only by [Korean] Ambassador Chŏng but by Ambassador Berger as well." *FRUS*, 1961–1963, 22:541.
25. Telegram from the Embassy in Korea to the Department of State, July 27, 1962, *FRUS*, 1961–1963, 22:590–591.
26. Telegram from the Department of State to the Embassy in Korea, August 5, 1962, *FRUS*, 1961–1963, 22:591–592.
27. He mobilized various sources, including not only Ambassador Chŏng but General Van Fleet, who wrote a personal letter to the president. *FRUS*, 1961–1963, 22:608, 615.
28. Cited in Macdonald, *U.S.-Korean Relations*, 219.
29. Cho Kap-che, *Nae mudŏm-e ch'im-ŭl paet'ŏra* [Spit on My Grave], 5:144–147.
30. Ibid., 217. Cho writes that it was on February 13, not 17, and cites an interview with Pak Pyŏng-gwŏn, where he denied that anything similar to an ultimatum had been made on that day.
31. *FRUS*, 1961–1963, 22:622, 626–627.
32. Telegram from the Department of State to the Embassy in Korea, March 16, 1963, *FRUS*, 1961–1963, 22:630–631.
33. Ibid., 639–641, but *FRUS* does not mention the content of the letter. Nor does *FRUS* list the letter.
34. *FRUS*, 1961–1963, 22:642–644.
35. Telegram from the Embassy in Korea to the Department of State, July 15, 1963, *FRUS*, 1961–1963, 22:652–656.

36. Telegram from the Embassy in Korea to the Department of State, September 2, 1963, *FRUS, 1961–1963*, 22:660.
37. Telegram from the Department of State to the Embassy in Korea, October 22, 1963, *FRUS, 1961–1963*, 22:667.
38. The Sixth National Assembly had a total of 175 seats, comprising 131 district and 44 party-list seats. Of the 110 seats won by the DRP, 22 of those seats were allocated from the party-list seats. The Democratic Justice Party, which had won the next largest number of seats, had a total of 41 seats, of which 14 were from the party-list seats.
39. In 1964, negotiations between South Korea and Japan for diplomatic normalization caused a severe political crisis and forced Kim Chong-p'il to go on his second exile. Berger's term was terminated in July 1964 and Kim returned to South Korea in January 1965. Kim remained behind the scenes until the normalization treaty was ratified. When he sought center stage again, however, his utility to Park was not the same as before. By that time, Park commanded greater public support and control of the state apparatus and political power.
40. *FRUS, 1961–1963*, 22:474 475.
41. Ibid., 475. Komer's memo reflected both his enthusiasm for applying the Rostovian model of economic development to the South Korean case and his frustration with bureaucratic intransigence to policy change. See the next section.
42. Comment by Bundy to Kennedy, cited in Woo, *Race to the Swift*, 76.
43. Telegram from the Embassy in Korea to the Department of State, October 28, 1961, *FRUS, 1961–1963*, 22:522.
44. Memorandum by Robert H. Johnson, June 6, 1961, *FRUS, 1961–1963*, 22:470.
45. Tadashi Kimiya, *Han'guk-ŭi naep'ojŏk kongŏphwa chŏllyak-ŭi chwajŏl: 5.16 kunsa chŏngbu-ŭi kukkajayulsŏng-ŭi kujojok han'gye* ["The Failure of the Inward-looking Deepening Strategy in South Korea: The Limits of the State's Structural Autonomy in the 5.16 Military Government"] (Ph.D. diss., Korea University, 1991), 33–57.
46. *Chaejŏng kŭmyung 30nyŏnsa* [Thirty Years of Fiscal and Financial Policy] (Seoul: Committee to Publish "Thirty Years of Fiscal and Financial Policy," 1978), 99–103.
47. Macdonald, *U.S.-Korean Relations*, 218. The quotation within the quote is from the source.
48. Telegram from the Embassy in Korea to the Department of State, July 23, 1962, *FRUS, 1961–1963*, 22:581–585.
49. Macdonald, *U.S.-Korean Relations*, 293. It is a matter of contention whether it was the lack of consultation or the seemingly socialist nature of the plan that made Washington particularly unhappy. While U.S. diplomatic documents generally refer to the former, there is evidence that the latter was no less important. Kim Chin-hyŏn, then an economic reporter for the *Dong-A Ilbo*, said that he personally heard from Berger that the United States took the issue— the "socialist" nature of the plan—so seriously that it was even contemplating the termination of diplomatic relations with South Korea. Stunned, Kim asked

Berger if he could write about it. Berger answered in the affirmative, but Kim did not write the story.

50. Telegram from the Embassy in Korea to the Department of State, July 15, 1963, *FRUS*, 1961–1963, 22:655. Yet it seemed that withholding the aid was largely motivated by political concern. In the same telegram, Berger reports that "timing of latest developments (appointing Kim Hyŏng-uk to KCIA director) worth mentioning. That they came after additional US food commitment and additional $15 million support assistance announced . . . is probably not just coincidence. [Park] knows US reaction to these moves will be adverse but, encouraged by Kim Chong-p'il, he believes that US is so committed in Korea that we will have to accept his actions." Ibid., 653.

51. Cited in Macdonald, *U.S.-Korean Relations*, 295–296.

52. Memorandum from Robert W. Komer to Rostow, March 15, 1961, *FRUS*, 1961–1963, 22:426.

53. Notes of the 485th Meeting of the National Security Council, June 13, 1961, *FRUS*, 1961–1963, 22:479–480.

54. Memorandum from Komer to Bundy, December 20, 1961, *FRUS*, 1961–1963, 22:548–549.

55. Memorandum from the JCS to Secretary of Defense, April 10, 1962, *FRUS*, 1961–1963, 22:554.

56. "The Outlook for South Korea," SNIE 42–62, April 4, 1962, *FRUS*, 1961–1963, 22:553.

57. "Korea: A Political-Military Study of South Korean Forces," as an attachment to letter from McNamara to Hamilton, April 27, 1962, *FRUS*, 1961–1963, 22:562.

58. Robert Komer's memo to Forrestal, July 31, 1962, JFKL.

59. Robert Komer, Memorandum for the Record, May 4, 1962, *FRUS*, 1961–1963, 22:562–564.

60. Yi Tong-wŏn's memoir, reported in the *JoongAng Ilbo*, August 7, 1999. Although the circumstances were more complicated, Yi was generally right.

61. Cho Kap-che, *Nae mudŏm-e ch'im-ŭl paet'ŏra* [Spit on My Grave], 5:190–191.

62. Telegram from Embassy in Seoul to Department of State, March 11, 1961.

63. Cho Kap-che, *Nae mudŏm-e ch'im-ŭl paet'ŏra* [Spit on My Grave], 5:57. The point was shared by Americans. Memorandum of Discussion, June 15, 1962, *FRUS*, 1961–1963, 22:575–576.

64. Telegram from the Department of State to the Embassy in Korea, August 5, 1962, *FRUS*, 1961–1963, 22:592.

65. The Korean Task Force Report of June 5, 1961, gave wide discretion to the newly appointed ambassador to meet the needs of the highly fluid situation in post-coup South Korea.

66. See note 27 above.

67. See above notes 23 and 33.

68. In this regard, the ending paragraph of the book by Donald Macdonald, then the Korean desk officer in the State Department, is apt. "While [Park Chung Hee and the military leadership] do deserve much of the credit [for sustained

rapid economic growth], it must be recognized . . . that it was the American effort of the previous fifteen or more years . . . that prepared the material and social ground for Korea's economic take-off. . . . Moreover, if it had not been for the guidance and restraining hand of the United States, its ambassadors [including Berger] and its aid chiefs [including Killen], and their staffs, the economic excesses of the military might well have jeopardized [South] Korea's economic future." Macdonald, *U.S.-Korean Relations,* 301.

3. State Building: The Military Junta's Path to Modernity through Administrative Reforms

1. See "Choguga! Tangsinŭn yŏngyŏng?" [Fatherland! Will you wilt forever?, in *Wŏlgan Chosun Palgul: Han'guk hyŏndaesa, pijaryo 125 kŏn* [The Monthly *Wŏlgan Chosun's* Discoveries: Korea's Modern History, 125 Secret Materials] (Seoul: Chosun Ilbosa, January 1996), 199–200. See also Yi Sŏk-jeche, *Kak'ha, Uri hyŏngmyŏng hapsida* [General, Let's Have a Revolution] (Seoul: Sŏjŏkp'o, 1995), 75–76.

2. Berger to the Secretary of State, October 28, 1961, National Security Files, Box 128, Country File: Korea, John F. Kennedy Library, Boston [hereafter NSF: Korea, JFKL], cited by Jung-en Woo, *Race to the Swift: State and Finance in Korean Industrialization* (New York: Columbia University Press, 1991), 79.

3. The name of the Ministry of Commerce and Industry was changed in the 1980s to the Ministry of Trade and Industry (MTI). This chapter, however, uses the earlier name, to reflect the period covered.

4. The other two leading groups consisted largely of: (1) a mixed group of generals from Park's Manchurian days; and (2) a colonels' group of the fifth class of the Korea Military Academy. See Chapter 1 above.

5. *Military Revolution in Korea* (Seoul: Secretariat of the Supreme Council for National Reconstruction, 1961), 25–26.

6. Yi Sŏk-chje, *Kak'ha* [General], 136.

7. Interview with Yi Sŏk-che. Details of Yi's account on this topic are also available; see ibid., 132–137.

8. Yi Kyŏng-nam, "Tak'ument'ari: Panhyŏngmyŏng" [A Documentary: Counterrevolution], *Sindonga,* November 1982, 183–201.

9. Hahn-Been Lee, *Korea: Time, Change, and Administration* (Honolulu: East-West Center Press, 1968), 167.

10. McConaughy to Task Force on Korea, "Revised Progress Report on Follow up Actions," 6–7.

11. Born in Puyŏ in South Ch'ungch'ŏng Province on January 7, 1926, Kim Chong-p'il was a junior at the Teachers College, Seoul National University, when the Republic was inaugurated in 1948. He immediately joined the army that year and was selected to enter the KMA a year later, graduating as a member of its eighth class. Kim began his military career as an intelligence officer and rose to head the North Korean Section of the army's Intelligence Bureau by 1952. In that capacity, he had access to the personnel files of many in the

South Korean officer corps, which he was to use later for the identification and recruitment of the members of both the coup coalition and the post-coup military junta. Park and Kim first met in 1949, after Park was dismissed from the army in 1948 (see Chapter 1) and was then allowed to work as a civilian at the Intelligence Bureau. Despite many differences in character, upbringing, and style of leadership, Park and Kim instantly became close. When Kim married Park's niece, Yŏng-ok, in late 1951 in Taegu, where both Park and Kim were stationed as intelligence officers, their loyalty to each other became even stronger. The relationship turned into a revolutionary partnership when, as we saw in Chapter 1, Park initiated a military reform campaign with Kim and his group of young colonels after President Rhee's resignation on April 26, 1960. See *Han'guk kunsa hyŏngmyŏngsa, I* [A History of the Korean Military Revolution], vol. 1 (Seoul: Kukka chaegŏn ch'oegohoeŭi Han'guk kunsa hyŏngmyŏngsa p'yŏnch'n wiwŏnhoe,1962), 915; and Kim Hyung A, *Korea's Development under Park Chung Hee: Rapid Industrialization, 1961–1979* (London: Routledge Curzon, 2004), 22–27.

12. Berger to Secretary of State, October 16, 1962, Box 127, NSF: Korea, JFKL.
13. Ibid.
14. The KCIA was founded on June 10, in accordance with the Supreme Council for National Reconstruction Law promulgated the same day.
15. *Han'guk kunsa hyŏngmyongsa, II* [A History of the Korean Military Revolution], vol. 2 (Seoul: Kukka chaegŏn ch'oegohoeui han'guk kunsa hyŏngmyŏngsa p'yŏnch'anwiwŏnhoe, 1962), 610.
16. Marshall Green [the U.S. deputy chief of mission in Seoul] to Secretary of State, June 3, 1961, Box 128, NSC: Korea, JFKL.
17. Ibid.
18. Kim Ch'ung-sik, *Namsan ŭi pujang-dŭl, 1* [The KCIA Directors, vol. 1] (Seoul: Dong-A Ilbosa, 1992), 50.
19. Cho Yong-jung, "Tak'yument'ari: kukka chaegŏn ch'oego hoeŭi" [A Documentary: The Supreme Council for National Reconstruction], *Sindonga,* May 1983.
20. Cho Kap-che, *Naemudŏm-e ch'imŭl paet'ŏra: Kukka kaejo* [Spit on My Grave], vol. 4:150.
21. The SCNR later announced that the Military Administration dismissed 35,684 persons out of a total bureaucracy of 241,877 during the period from June 20 to July 20. See Military Revolution in Korea, Secretariat of the Supreme Council for National Reconstruction, 1961, 31.
22. For details of the guidelines, see Cho Kap-che, *Nae mudŏm-e ch'im-ŭl paet'ŏra,* 4:. 138.
23. *Hankook Ilbo,* May 22, 1961.
24. Embtel 1667 (section one of two), May 25, 1961, Box 128A, NSF: Korea, JFKL.
25. As the youngest ever director-general of the MoF's elite Financial Management Bureau (1959–1960), Kim Chŏng-ryŏm was hand-picked as the MoF vice minister soon after the disastrous currency conversion reform of 1962.

He was to become vice minister of the Ministry of Commerce and Industry (MCI) in 1964, the MoF minister in 1966, the MCI minister in 1967, and the chief of staff to the president in 1968.

26. O Wŏn-ch'ŏl eventually moved to the MCI as bureau director and then assistant vice minister (1961–1971). He was to become one of the architects of heavy and chemical industrialization as second senior economic secretary to the president during the *yushin* regime (1972–1979).

27. Kim Hak-ryŏl was the holder of the highest scores in the civil service examination of 1950. He transferred from the MoF's Taxation Bureau to the newly established Economic Planning Board to head its Budget Bureau in July 1961. Reportedly a "tutor" to Park on economic issues, Kim Hak-ryŏl was promoted to EPB vice minister (1962–1966) to play a key role in revising the first FYEDP and preparing the second (1967–1971). In 1966 Park promoted Kim Hak-ryŏl to the post of finance minister before he was appointed senior economic secretary to the president, serving from 1966 to 1969. He rose to deputy prime minister and EPB minister (1969–1972).

28. This new mode of merit-based recruitment and promotion was later given further impetus by the introduction of the National Civil Service Law in 1963. Kim Kyŏng-nak, "Kunsa chŏngbu insa haengjŏng kaehyok p'yŏng'ga" [Assessment of the Personnel Administration Reform under the Military Government] (MA thesis, Seoul National University, 1968), 59–62.

29. During this period, Kim worked outside both the MoF and the MCI twice. In June 1963, he served for about nine months as a member of the South Korean delegation appointed to negotiate with the Japanese government on normalization. Kim was out of work for about eleven months, however, from September 1966 when he resigned from the MoF as its minister until October 1967 when he was appointed minister of commerce and industry.

30. Park Chung Hee, *Our Nation's Path* (Seoul: Hollym Corporation, 1970), 201. First published as *Uri minjok uinagial-gil* [Our Nation's Path] (Seoul: Dong A ch'ulp'absa, 1962).

31. The illicit profiteering by the *chaebol* was one of the major issues in the masses' call for an anticorruption campaign immediately after the April Student Revolution in 1960, and thus the interim government under Hŏ Chŏng passed a law in the National Assembly in May of the same year to punish those "illicit profiteers." See "Pujŏng ch'ukjaeja ch'ŏri chŏnmalsŏ" [The Final Report on the Prosecution of Illicit Profiteers], *Sindonga*, December 1964, 158–177.

32. Embtel 530, September 29, 1961, Box 128, NSF: Federation of Korean Industries Korea, JFKL; *Chŏnkyŏngryŏn 40-nyŏnsa, sanggwon* [A Forty-Year History of the Federation of Korean Industries], vol. 1 (Seoul: Chŏnkyŏngryŏn 40-nyŏnsa p'yŏnch'an wiwŏnhoe, 2001), 207.

33. Yi, in fact, was picked up by a KCIA agent from the airport. Yi Pyŏng-ch'ŏl, *Hoamjajŏn* [Yi Pyŏng-ch'ŏl's Autobiography] (Seoul: JoongAng Ilbosa, 1986), 110–112. "Hoam" is Yi's penname.

34. *Chŏnkyŏngryŏn 40-nyŏnsa* [A 40-Year History of the Federation of Korean

Industries], 1:207; O Wŏn-ch'ŏl, *Han'gukhyŏng kyŏngje kŏnsŏl: enjiniŏring ŏp'ŭroch'i* [Korean-Style Economic Development: An Engineering Approach], vol. 1 (Seoul: Kia kyŏngje yŏn'guso, 1996), 19.

35. Cited in Ambassador Berger's report to Secretary of State, September 29, 1961, Box 128, NSF: Korea, JFKL.

36. *Chŏnkyŏngryŏn 40-nyŏnsa* [A 40-Year History of the Federation of Korean Industries], 1:207; Cho Kap-che, *Nae mudŏm-e ch'im-ŭl paet'ŏra* [Spit on My Grave], vol. 4:192–193.

37. Embtel 530, September 29, 1961, Box 128, NSF: Korea, JFKL.

38. Ibid.

39. The immediate predecessor to the FKI was originally established under the Chang Myŏn administration on December 13, 1960.

40. For this new arrangement, the Special Measure for the Control of Illicit Profiteering was revised twice, on October 26 and November 20, 1961.

41. Kim Chin-hyŏn, "Pujŏng ch'ukjaeja ch'ŏri chŏnmalsŏ" [The Final Report on the Prosecution of Illicit Profiteers], 172–173.

42. In his determination to protect Yi Chu-il, Park had Yi accompany him on his official visit to Washington in November of that year.

43. Cho Kap-je, *Nae mudŏm-e ch'im-ŭl paet'ŏra: Kukka kaej* [Spit on My Grave], vol. 4:257.

44. Kim Chŏng-ryŏm, *Han'guk kyŏngje chŏngch'aek 30-nyŏnsa: Kim Chŏng-ryŏm hoegorok* [A 30-year history of Korea's economic policy] (Seoul: JoongAng Ilbo, 1990), 84; Kim Ch'ung-sik, *Namsan-ŭi pujangdŭl, 1* [The KCIA Directors], vol. 1 (Seoul: Dong-A Ilbosa, 1992), 64–65.

45. Author interview with Yi Sŏk-che, June 2005; see also Cho Yong-jung, "Tak'yument'ari: Kukka chaegŏn ch'oego hoeŭi" [Documentation: The Supreme Council for National Reconstruction], *Sindonga*, May 1983, 130–131.

46. Yi claims to have prepared about thirty-five programs. See Yi Sŏk-che, *Kak'ha* [General], 62–63, 83–84.

47. Ibid.,168–169.

48. Ch'a Kyun-hŭi, a career financial expert, was the first vice minister of the EPB (June 1962-June 1963).

49. Kim served as ambassador plenipotentiary in Japan (1957–1958) and Britain (1958–1960). Kim began his career as a bank officer in April 1938 and, in February 1949, he became director-general of the Financial Bureau, Bank of Korea.

50. JoongAng Ilbo, *Sillok Park Chung Hee* [A Historical Record: Park Chung Hee] (Seoul: JoongAng M&B, 1998), 124. See *Chŏnkyŏngryŏn 20-nyŏnsa* [A 20-Year History of the Federation of Korean Industries] (Chŏn'guk kyŏngjein yŏnhaphoe, 1983), 252.

51. All quotes in this paragraph from Park Chung Hee, *Our Nation's Path*, 217.

52. Yi Sŏk-che, *Kak'ha* [General], 200.

53. Embtel 293, August 12, 1961, Box 128, NSF: Korea, JFKL. Correction issued: August 14, 1961.

54. Author interview with Minister Chŏng, June 2005. Minister Chŏng later served as chairman of the National Assembly from 1981 to 1984, until he resigned from his official position as a consequence of an alleged corruption scandal. For details on the background for Chŏng's involvement in the currency reform, see his autobiography, *Kyŏkpyun-ui saengaer-ŭl tora bomyŏ* [Looking Back on the Rapid Changes in My Life] (Seoul: Han'guk sanŏp kaebal yŏn'guwŏn, 2001), 268–272.

55. See Donald S. Macdonald, *U.S.-Korean Relations from Liberation to Self-Reliance: The Twenty-Year Record* (Boulder: Westview Press, 1992), 218.

56. *Chŏnkyŏngryŏn 20-nyŏnsa* [A 20-Year History of the Federation of Korean Industries], 205. There were two key reasons for the revision: U.S. pressure to downsize and a critical shortage of government holdings of foreign currency.

57. Macdonald, *U.S.-Korean Relations from Liberation to Self-Reliance*, 219.

58. The minister of the MoF changed three times in the first year of military rule: Major-General Paek Sŏn-jin (May-June); Kim Yu-t'aek (June-July); and Ch'ŏn Pyŏng-gyu (July 1961–June1962).

59. In particular, Kim Chŏng-ryŏm's influence in assembling an economy-oriented technocracy, especially in the 1970s as the chief of staff who was also designated by Park as his "economic manager," cannot be stressed enough.

60. Both held Ph.D.s from the United States, the former in mechanical engineering and the latter in metallurgic engineering. Ham is known to have been Minister Chŏng's brain trust, who inspired him to promote MCI-led industrialization.

61. Chŏng Nae-hyŏk, *Kyŏkpyun-ŭi saengaer-ŭl tora bomyŏ* [Looking Back on the Rapid Changes in My Life], 252.

62. Presidential Task Force on Korea, "Report to the National Security Council," June 5, 1961, Box 127, NSF: Korea, JFKL, 21–22.

63. Ibid., appendix C.

64. Colonel Cho In-bok became president of Kyŏngsŏng Electric Company. Two other newly appointed presidents were Colonel Hwang In-sŏng at Chosŏn Electric Company and Colonel Kim Tŏk-jun at Namsŏn Electric Company.

65. Chŏng Nae-hyŏk, *Kyŏkpyunui saengaerŭl tora bomyŏ* [Looking Back on the Rapid Changes in My Life], 253–254, 275.

66. *Minju Han'guk Hyŏngmyŏng ch'ŏngsa* [A History of the Democratic Korean Revolution] (Seoul: Minju han'guk hyŏngmyŏng ch'ŏngsa p'yŏnch'an wiwŏnhoe, 1963), 161–164, 325, 352.

67. Macdonald, *U.S.-Korean Relations from Liberation to Self-Reliance*, 219.

68. For details of the secret agreement between Kim and Ohira, see Yi To-sŏng, ed., *Sillok, Park Chung Hee-wa Han-il hoedam: 5.16-esŏ choinkkaji* [A True Record, Park Chung Hee and Korea-Japan Normalization Talks: From May 16, 1961 to the Signing of the Agreement] (Seoul: Hansong, 1995).

69. Kim Ch'ung-sik, *Namsan-ŭi pujangdŭl: Chŏngch'i kongjak saryŏngbu KCIA* [The KCIA Directors: KCIA, Headquarters of Political Maneuvering], 1:72–77.

70. As early as October 1961, U.S. ambassador Berger warned in his telegram report to the secretary of state that Kim Chong-pil's dominance would be a factor in any factional fight in the SCNR. See Embtel 640 (section two of two), October 28, 1961, Box 128, NSF: Korea, JFKL.

71. Cho Yong-jung, "Tak'yument'ari: Kukka chaegŏn ch'oego hoeŭi" [Documentation: The Supreme Council for National Reconstruction], 160.

72. Ibid., 166.

73. Kim Ch'ung-sik, *Namsan-ŭi pujangdŭl* [The KCIA Directors], 1:66.

74. Kim's power within the KCIA was drastically reduced immediately after February 21, when Kim Chae-ch'un was appointed director of the KCIA. He dismissed thirty-one who were mostly from members of Kim Chong-pil's team, in the eighth class of the Korea Military Academy. Major General Kim Yong-sun, who had succeeded Kim as the second director of the KCIA, in 1963, served for only forty-five days, to be replaced by Kim Chae-ch'ua.

75. Cho Yong-jung, "Tak'yument'ari: Kukka chaegŏn ch'oego hoeŭi" [Documentation: The Supreme Council for National Reconstruction], 155–162.

76. According to Chŏng Chae-gyŏng, the three earlier attempts were (1) on May 8, 1960, known as "5.8 kyehoek [May 8th plan]" but abruptly canceled because of the student revolution on April 19; (2) on April 19, 1961, on the first anniversary of the April 19 revolution; and (3) on May 13, 1961. Chŏng Chae-gyŏng, *Wi'in Park Chung Hee* [The Great Man Park Chung Hee] (Seoul: Chimmundang, 1992), 152.

77. In the poem that Park reportedly delivered to his brother-in-law just before the coup, Park pledges "to commit *k'waedo halbok*," the traditional Japanese samurai-style suicide. See ibid.

4. Modernization Strategy: Ideas and Influences

1. Robert E. Ward and Dankwart A. Rustow, eds., *Political Modernization in Japan and Turkey* (Princeton: Princeton University Press, 1964).

2. Park Chung Hee, *Minjok chunghŭng-ŭi kil* [The Road to the Revival of Our Nation] (Seoul: Kwangmyŏng ch'ulp'ansa, 1978), 6.

3. Albert S. Yee, "The Causal Effects of Ideas on Policies," *International Organization* 50, no. 1 (Winter 1996): 69–108; Geoffry L. Taubman, "Combating the Phantom Menace: Foreign Ideas, Domestic Political Change and Responses to Globalization," paper presented at the annual meeting of the International Studies Association, Los Angeles, 14–18 March 2000, 7.

4. Gordon J. Direnzo, *Personality, Power and Politics: A Social Psychological Analysis of the Italian Deputy and His Parliamentary System* (Notre Dame: University of Notre Dame Press, 1967), 5.

5. Takagi Masao was Park Chung Hee's Japanese name. During the Japanese colonial period, all Koreans were forced to change their Korean names into Japanese as a way of homogenizing Japanese and Koreans into one *(naesŏn ilch'e)*.

6. Okazaki Hisahiko, *Kukka to joho: Nihonno gaikou senryakuwo motomete*

[The State and Intelligence: Searching for Japan's Foreign Policy] (Tokyo: Bungeishunju, 1984), 116.

7. Yi Ki-t'aek, "Park Chung Hee-wa Ilbon" [Park Chung Hee and Japan], in *Hyŏndaesa-rŭl ŏttŏk'e polgŏtin'ga* [How to View the Modern History of Korea], vol. 4, ed. Dong-A Ilbosa (Seoul: Dong-A Ilbosa, 1990), 190.

8. Han Yong-wŏn, *Ch'anggun* [Founding of the Military] (Seoul: Pakyŏngsa, 1984), 34–38. Cho Kap-che, *Nae mudŏm-e ch'im-ŭl paet'ŏra2: chŏnjaeng-gwa sarang* [Spit on My Grave, vol. 2: War and Love] (Seoul: Chosun Ilbosa, 1998), 2:127–131; Sin Yong-gu, *Park chung hee chŏngsin punsŏk: sinhwa-nŭn ŏpta* [The Psychoanalysis of Park Chung Hee: There Is No Myth] (Seoul: Ttŭindol, 2000),135–140.

9. A testimony by Kim Chong-sin in *The Observer,* March 1991, 188.

10. Cho Kap-che, *Nae mudŏm-e ch'imŭl paet'ŏra* [Spit on My Grave], 2:57; Kim Hyŏng-uk and Pak Sa-wŏl, *Kim Hyŏng-uk hoegorok 2: han'guk chungang chŏngbobu* [Kim Hyŏng-uk's Memoir: The Korea Central Intelligence Agency] (Seoul: Ach'im, 1985), 2:187.

11. Richard Samuels, *Rich Nation, Strong Army: National Security and Technological Transformation of Japan* (Ithaca: Cornell University Press, 1994), 35–38; Kim Chŏng-ryŏm, *A! Park Chung Hee: Kim Chŏng-ryŏm chŏngch'i hoegorok* [Ah! Park Chung Hee: Kim Chŏng-ryŏm's reflections on politics] (Seoul: JoongAng M&B, 1997), 116–117.

12. Kim Chŏng-ryŏm, *A! Park Chung Hee* [Ah! Park Chung Hee], 116–117; JoongAng Ilbo Sillok Park Chung Hee sidae t'ŭkbyŏl ch'wijaet'im, *Sillok Park Chung Hee* [A Historical Record: Park Chung Hee] (Seoul: JoongAng M&B, 1998), 117–119.

13. Yi Sang-u, *Park Chung Hee, p'amyŏl-ŭi chŏngch'igongjak* [The Ruined Political Maneuvering of Park Chung Hee] (Seoul: Dong-A Ilbosa, 1993), 23.

14. JoongAng Ilbo Sillok Park Chung Hee sidae t'ŭkbyŏl ch'wijaet'im, *Sillok Park Chung Hee* [A Historical Record: Park Chung Hee], 193.

15. Kimiya Tadashi, "Han'guk-ŭi naep'ojŏk kongŏphwa chŏnllyak-ŭi chwajŏl: 5.16 kunsa chŏngbu-ŭi kukkajayulsŏng-ŭi kujojŏk han'gye" [The Failure of the Inward-looking Deepening Strategy in South Korea: The Limits of the State's Structural Autonomy in the 5.16 Military Government] (Ph.D. diss., Korea University, 1991), 131–136.

16. Ryu Sang-yŏng, "Han'guk sanŏphwa-esŏŭi kukka-wa kiŏp-ŭi kwan'gye: P'ohang chech'ŏl-gwa kukka chabonju-ŭi" [Government-Business Relations in the Industrialization of South Korea: Pohang Iron & Steel Company and State Capitalism] (Ph.D. diss., Yonsei University, 1995), 90–105.

17. Kim Chŏng-ryŏm, *Han'guk kyŏngje chŏngch'aek 30nyŏnsa: Kim Chŏng-ryŏm hoegorok* [A 30-Year History of Korea's Economic Policy: The Recollections of Kim Chŏng-ryŏm] (Seoul: JoongAng Ilbosa, 1990), 322–324; O Wŏn-ch'ŏl, *Han'gukhyŏng kyŏngje kŏnsŏl 5: enjiniŏring ŏp'ŭroch'i* [Korean-Style Economic Development: An Engineering Approach] (Seoul: Kia kyŏngje yŏn'guso, 1996), 5:11–31.

18. Kim Yŏn-gŭk, "Park Chung Hee-wa hujino-ŭi widaehan ujŏng" [The Great

Friendship of Park Chung Hee and Hujino], *Wŏlgan Chosun*, January 1997, 330.

19. Noguchi Yukio, *Senkyuhyakunenyonjunen Taisei* [The 1940 System] (Tokyo: Tokyo Keizai Shimbunsa, 1995).

20. Yi Sang-u, *Park Chung Hee p'amyŏl-ŭi chŏngch'igongjak* [The Ruined Political Maneuvering of Park Chung Hee], 23; Ch'oe Yŏng, *Park Chung Hee-ŭi sasanggwa haengdong* [Park Chung Hee's Thoughts and Behavior] (Seoul: Hyŏnŭmsa, 1995), 19; JoongAng Ilbo, Sillok Park Chung Hee sidae t'ŭkbyŏl ch'wijaet'im, *Sillok Park Chung Hee* [A Historical Record: Park Chung Hee], 117–119.

21. Yi Pyŏng-ju (Park Chung Hee Sojang, Kŭ ch'ŏngryŏmhan yuadokchon; wŏllojakka Li Pyŏng-ju-ŭi) "Taet'ongnyŏngdŭlŭi ch'osang 2" [The Portrait of Presidents 2], *Wŏlgan Chosun*, July 1991, 480; Cho Kap-che, *Nae mudŏm-e ch'im-ŭl paet'ŏra* [Spit on My Grave], 2:125–126.

22. Gregory Henderson, *Korea: The Politics of the Vortex*, trans. Pak Haeng-ung and Yi Chong-sam, *Soyongdoli-ŭi Han'guk chŏngch'i* (Seoul: Hanul Academy, 2000 [1968]), 507n6.

23. Cho Kap-che, *Naemudŏm-e ch'im-ŭl paet'ŏra* [Spit on My Grave], 2:79–80.

24. JoongAng Ilbo, Sillok Park Chung Hee sidae t'ŭkbyŏl ch'wijaet'im, *Sillok Park Chung Hee* [A Historical Record: Park Chung Hee], 115.

25. Yi Tong-wŏn, *Taet'ongryŏng-ŭl kirimyŏ* [Missing the President] (Seoul: Koryewŏn, 1992), 64.

26. Planning Unit, Heavy-Chemical Industrial Policy Committee, *Chunghwahak kongŏphwa chŏngch'aek sŏnŏn-e ttarŭn kongŏp kujo kaep'yŏllon* [On Reorganization of Industrial Structures following the Declaration of Heavy-Chemical Industrial Policy], January 1, 1973, 9–14; quoted in Cho In-wŏn, *Kukka-wa sŏnt'aek* [The State and Choice], 183.

27. Cho Tong-sŏng, *Han'guk-ŭi chonghap sangsa* [The General Trading Company of South Korea], vol. 1 (Seoul: Pŏmmunsa, 1983), 14; idem, *Han'guk-ŭi chonghap sangsa* [The General Trading Company of South Korea], vol. 2 (Seoul: Pŏmmunsa, 1983), 165–170; Yi Chong-yun, *Muyŏk palchŏn-kwa chonghap sangsa* [The Development of Trade and the General Trade Company] (Seoul: Pakyŏngsa, 1987), 33–43.

28. The term *industrializing nationalism* was suggested by Ezra F. Vogel. We thank him for his suggestion. On Park's self-proclaimed nationalism, see Park Chung Hee, *Kukka-wa hyŏngmyŏng-gwa na* [The Nation, the Revolution, and I] (Seoul: Hyangmunsa, 1963).

29. Chŏn Chae-ho, *Pandongjŏk kŭndaejuŭija Park Chung Hee* [Park Chung Hee as a Reactionary Modernizer] (Seoul: Ch'aekseang, 2000), 23–34.

30. On conservative opinion, see Yi Chŏng-sik, *Yushin-ŭi chŏngch'i nolli* [The Political Logic of Yushin] (Seoul: Pakyŏngsa, 1977); Chŏng Chae-gyŏng, *Hanminjok-ŭi chunghŭng sasang: Park Chung Hee taet'ongryŏng-ŭi chŏngch'i ch'ŏlhak* [The Thought of Revival of Our Nation: The Political Philosophy of President Park Chung Hee] (Seoul: Sinhwa ch'ulp'ansa, 1979); Han Sŭng-jo, *Yushin kaepyŏk sasang-ŭi kwagŏ, hyŏnjae, mirae* [Past, Present, and Future of Yushin Reform Thought] (Seoul: Sŏhyanggak, 1977). On lib-

eral opinion, see Kang Man-gil, "Han'guk minjokchuŭiron-ŭi ihae" [Understanding Nationalism in Korea], in *Han'guk-ŭi minjokchuŭi undong-gwa minjung* [Nationalist Movements and the Minjung in Korea], ed. Yi Yŏng-hŭi and Kang Man-gil (Seoul: Ture, 1987); Pak Hyŏn-ch'ae, "Pundan sidae han'guk minjokchuŭi-ŭi kwaje" [The Task of Korean Nationalism in the Era of National Division], in *Han'gukminjokchuŭiron* [On Nationalism in Korea], vol. 2, ed. Song Kŏn-ho and Kang Man-gil (Seoul: Ch'angjakkwa pip'yŏngsa, 1983).

31. Son Ho-ch'ŏl, *Han'guk chŏngch'ihak-ŭi saegusang* [New Design for Korean Political Science] (Seoul: Pulbit, 1991); Chŏng Yun-hyŏng, "Park Chung Hee chŏnggwŏn-ŭi kyŏngje kaebal inyŏm" [The Idea of Economic Development in the Park Chung Hee Government], in *Han'guk chabonjuŭi sŏnggyŏk nonjaeng* [Debates on the Character of Capitalism in South Korea], ed. idem (Seoul: Taewangsa, 1988); Kimiya Tadashi, "Han'guk-ŭi naep'ojŏk kongŏphwa chŏllyak-ŭi chwajŏl: 5.16 kunsa chŏngbu-ŭi kukkajayulsŏng-ui kujojŏk han'gye" [The Failure of the Inward-looking Deepening Strategy in South Korea: The Limits of the State's Structural Autonomy in the 5.16 Military Government].

32. Ko Yŏng-bok, "Park Chung Hee-ŭi kŭndaehwa inyŏm" [Park Chung Hee's Ideology of Modernization], in *Hyŏndaesa-rŭl ŏttŏk'e polgŏtin'ga*, 4:271.

33. Yang Sŏng-ch'ŏl, *Park Chung Hee-wa Kim Il Sung* [Park Chung Hee and Kim Il Sung] (Seoul: Hanul, 1992), 84.

34. Ibid., 252–256.

35. Sim Yung-t'aek, *Charip-e-ŭi ŭiji: Park Chung Hee taet'ongryŏng ŏrok* [The Will of Self-Reliance: Quotations from President Park Chung Hee] (Seoul: Hallim ch'ulp'ansa, 1972), 229.

36. Park Chung Hee, *Minjok-ŭi chŏryŏk* [The Potential Power of Our Nation] (Seoul: Kwangmyŏng ch'ulpa'nsa, 1971), 16.

37. Chŏn Chae-ho, "Tongwŏndoen minjokchuŭi-wa chŏnt'ong munhwa chŏngch'aek" [Mobilized Nationalism and Policies for Traditional Culture], in *Park Chung Hee-rŭl nŏmŏsŏ: Park Chung Hee-wa kŭ sidae-e taehan pip'anjŏk yŏn'gu* [Beyond Park Chung Hee], ed. Han'guk Chŏngch'i Yŏnguhoe [Study Group on Korean Politics] (Seoul: P'urŭnsup, 1998), 244.

38. Park Chung Hee, *Kukka-wa hyŏngmyŏng-gwa na* [The State, the Revolution, and I], 254; idem, *Uri minjok-ŭi nagal-gil* [Our Nation's Path] (Seoul:Tonga ch'ulp'ansa, 1962), chap. 5.

39. Park Chung Hee, *Minjok chunghŭng-ŭi kil* [The Road to Revival of Our Nation], 22.

40. Ibid., 32.

41. Ibid., 73–74.

42. Yang Sŏng-ch'ŏl, *Park Chung Hee-wa Kim Il Sung* [Park Chung Hee and Kim Il Sung], 262.

43. Byung-kook Kim, *Pundan-gwa hyŏngmyŏng-ŭi tonghak: han'guk-kwa meksik'o-ŭi chŏngch'i kyŏngje* [The Dynamics of National Division and Revolution: The Political Economy of South Korea and Mexico] (Seoul: Munhakkwa chisŏngsa, 1994), 183–200, 350–365.

44. Sim Yung-t'aek, *Charipe-ŭi ŭiji* [The Will of Self-Reliance], 37. See also Park Chung Hee, *Kukka-wa hyŏngmyŏng-gwa na* [The State, the Revolution, and I], 45.

45. Stephan Haggard, Byung-kook Kim, and Chung-in Moon, "The Transition to Export-led Growth," *Journal of Asian Studies* 50, no. 4 (1991): 850–873; Yi Wan-bŏm, "Che ilch'a kyŏngje kaebal ogaenyŏn kyehoek-ŭi ipan'gwa miguk-ŭi yŏkhal" [Designing the First Five-Year Economic Development Plan and the Role of the United States], in *1960nyŏndae-ŭi chŏngch'i sahoe pyŏndong* [Political and Social Changes in the 1960s], ed. Academy of Korean Studies (Seoul: Paeksansŏdang, 1999), 126–133; Byung-Kook Kim, *Pundan-gwa hyŏngmyŏng-ŭi tonghak* [The Dynamics of National Division and Revolution], 365–381; Kim Chŏng-ryŏm, *Han'guk kyŏngje chŏngch'aek 30nyŏnsa* [A 30-Year History of Korea's Economic Policy], 106–117.

46. Amsden, *Asia's Next Giant;* Robert Wade, *Governing the Market: Economic Theory and the Role of Government in East Asian Industrialization* (Princeton: Princeton University Press, 1990).

47. Kim Sang-on et al., *Han'guk kyŏngje-ŭi kujobyŏnhwa* [The Structural Change of the Korean Economy] (Ulsan: Ulsan University Press, 1997), 64; Sŏng Pyŏng-t'ak, *Hanil yanggug-ŭi kyŏngje pigyo* [Comparison of Korean and Japanese Economy] (Seoul: Hyungsŏl Ch'ulp'ansa, 1994), 227, 246–247.

48. Kim Sang-on et al., *Han'guk kyŏnje-ŭi kujobyŏnhwa* [The Structural Change of the Korean Economy], 61–62.

49. Kim Chŏng-ryŏm, *Han'guk kyŏngje chŏngch'aek 30nyŏnsa* [A 30-Year History of Korea's Economic Policy], 135–140; Ryu Sang-yŏng, "Han'guk sanŏphwa-esŏŭi kukka-wa kiŏp-ŭi kwan'gye" [Government-Business Relations in Industrialization of South Korea], 109–117.

50. Economic Planning Board, *Kaebal yŏndae-ŭi kyŏngje chŏngch'aek: kyŏngje kihoegwŏn 20nyŏnsa* [Economic Policy during the Developmental Decades: Twenty Years of the Economic Planning Board] (Seoul: Miraesa, 1982), 40; Stephan Haggard and Chung-in Moon, "The South Korean State in International Economy: Liberal, Dependent, and Mercantile?" in *Antinomies of Interdependence,* ed. John Ruggie (New York: Columbia University Press, 1983), 47–60.

51. Sin Pŏm-sik, ed., *Park Chung Hee taet'ongryŏng sŏnjip* [Selected Works of President Park Chung Hee] (Seoul: Chimun'gak, 1969), 199.

52. Stephan Haggard and Tun-jen Cheng, "State and Foreign Capital in East Asian NICs," in *The Political Economy of the New Asian Industrialism,* ed. Frederic C. Deyo (Ithaca: Cornell University Press, 1987).

53. For debates on this issue, see Yang Sŏng-ch'ŏl, *Park Chung Hee-wa Kim Il Sung* [Park Chung Hee and Kim Il Sung], 84; Pak Myŏng-rim, *Han'guk chŏnjaeng-ŭi palbal-gwa kiwŏn* [The Korean War: The Outbreak and Its Origins], vol. 2 (Seoul: Nanam, 1996), 548.

54. Park Chung Hee, *Uri minjok-ŭi nagal-gil* [Our Nation's Path], 129, 130.

55. Ibid., 257–258.

56. Sŏn U-Yŏn, "Park Chung Hee yuksŏng chŭngŏn sang" [Verbal Testimony by Park Chung Hee 1], *Monthly Chosun,* March 1992, 158–159.

57. Chŏng Sang-ho, "Yusandoen minjuhwa, kyŏngjaeng-ŭi pujae-wa t'onghap-ŭi

pin'gon" [An Aborted Democratization, an Absence of Political Competition, and Poverty of Integration], in *Park Chung Hee-rŭl nŏmŏsŏ* [Beyond Park Chung Hee], ed. Study Group on Korean Politics, 109–132.

58. Park Chung Hee, *Choguk kŭndaehwa-ŭi chip'yo* [Index of Modernization of Our Fatherland] (Seoul: Koryŏ sŏchŏk, 1967), 48.

59. Park Chung Hee, *Minjok chunghŭng-ŭi kil* [The Road to the Revival of Our Nation], 47–50.

60. Ibid., 61–62.

61. Park Chung Hee, *Kukka-wa hyŏngmyŏng-gwa na* [The State, the Revolution, and I], 252–256.

62. See Chapter 14 below.

63. Park Chung Hee, *Kukka-wa hyŏngmyŏng-gwa Na* [The State, the Revolution, and I], 134–138; Yi Sŏk-che, *Kak'ha, Uri hyŏngmyŏng hapsida* [General, Let's Have a Revolution] (Seoul: Sŏjŏkp'o, 1995), 81; Yi Pyung-dong, "Park Chung Hee-wa saemaŭl undong" [Park Chung Hee and the New Community Movement] in *Hyŏndaesa-rŭl ŏttŏk'e polgŏtin'ga* 4 [How to View the Modern History of Korea], vol. 4, ed. Dong-A Ilbosa (Seoul: Dong-A Ilbo, 1990), 356–381; Chŏn Chae-ho, *Pandongjŏk kŭndaejuŭija Park Chung Hee* [Park Chung Hee as a Reactionary Modernizer], 79–84; Office of the President, *Saemaŭl undong: Park Chung Hee taet'ongryŏng yŏnsŏlmun sŏnjip* [New Community Movement: Selected Speeches of President Park Chung Hee] (Seoul: Office of the President, 1978).

64. Henderson, *Korea, The Politics of the Vortex,* trans. Pak Haeng-ung and Yi Chong-sam, *Soyongdoli-ŭi Han'guk chŏngch'i,* 506.

65. Kim Un-t'ae, ed., *Han'guk chŏngch'iron* [On Korean Politics] (Seoul: Pakyŏngsa, 1991), 438.

66. Yi Sang-u, *Park Chung Hee p'amyŏl-ŭi chŏngch'igongjak* [The Ruined Political Maneuvering of Park Chung Hee], 71; Yi Ki-hong, *Kyŏngje kŭndaehwa-ŭi sumŭn iyagi* [A Behind-the-Scenes Story of Economic Modernization] (Seoul: Voice, 1999), 41.

67. James H. Hausman and Chŏng Il-hwa, *Han'guk taet'ongryŏng-ŭl umjigin migun taewi: hausŭman chŭngŏn* [A U.S. Army Captain Who Maneuvered Presidents of South Korea: The Testimony of Hausman] (Seoul: Han'guk-munwŏn, 1995), 58–59.

68. Cho Kap-che, *Naemudŏm-e ch'im-ŭl paet'ŏra* [Spit on My Grave], 3:70. Cho offers a counterargument.

69. Park Chung Hee, *Kukka-wa hyŏngmyŏng-kwa na* [The State, the Revolution, and I], 231–232.

70. Pak Kŭn-hye's testimony in Cho Kap-che, "Park taet'ongryŏng-ŭi ch'ŏngwadae ilgi wŏnbon" [Original Version of President Park's Blue House Diary], *Wŏlgan Chosun,* April 1989, 321.

71. Yi Tong-wŏn, *Taet'ongryŏng-ŭl kirimyŏ* [Missing the President], 57–58; Kang Sŏng-jae, "Park Chung Hee-ege ŏnsŏng-ŭl nopin bŏgŏ taesa" [Ambassador Berger Who Raised His Voice to Park Chung Hee], *Sindonga,* January 1987, 332–337; W. D. Reeve, *Republic of Korea: A Political and Economic Study* (London: Oxford University Press, 1963), 177–178.

72. Man-wu Yi, "Double Patronage toward South Korea," in *Alliance under Ten-*

sion: The Evolution of South Korean–U.S. Relations, ed. Man-wu Yi, Ronald D. McLaurn, and Moon Chung-in (Boulder: Westview Press, 1988), 35–36.

73. Kim Chin-hyŏn and Chi Tong-uk, "Han'guk changgi kaebal kyehoek-ŭi naemak" [The Inside Story of Korea's Long-Term Economic Development Plan], *Sindong-A,* September 1966, 100–120; Anne O. Krueger, *The Developmental Role of the Foreign Sector and Aid* (Cambridge, MA: Council on East Asian Studies, Harvard University, 1979), 77–78; Yi Yong-wŏn, *Che-i konghwaguk-kwa Chang myŏn* [Chang Myŏn and the Second Republic] (Seoul: Pŏmusa, 1999), 48–49; Yi Ki-hong, *Kyŏngje kŭndaehwa-ŭi sumŭn iyagi* [A Behind-the-Scenes Story of Economic Modernization], 263–267; Yi Wan-bŏm, "Che ilch'a kyŏngje kaebal ogaenyŏn kyehoek-ŭi ipangwa mikug-ŭi yŏkhal" [Designing the First Five-Year Economic Development Plan and the Role of the United States], 93–94.

74. From Seoul to Secretary of State, Embtel 699 (Seoul), November 11, 1961, in *5.16 kwa Park Chung Hee chŏngpuŭi sŏngnip: chŏnmunch'ŏl* [The 5.16 Coup and the Inauguration of the Park Chung Hee Government: Collection of Telegrams], ed. Institute for the Modern History of Korea, Academy of Korean Studies (Sŏngnam: AKS, 1999).

75. Cho Kap-che, *Naemudŏm-e ch'im-ŭl paet'ŏra* [Spit on My Grave], 5:47.

76. John C. H. Fei and Gustav Ranis, "Han'guk kyŏngje-ŭi changgi kaebal pangan" [Long-term Economic Development Plan of the Korean Economy], trans. Sindong-A Editorial Borad, *Sindong-A,* March 1965, 190–216.

77. Haggard, Kim, and Moon, "The Transition to Export-led Growth," 862–868; Im Ch'ŏl-gyu, "Yusom" [USOM], *Sindong-A,* May 1965, 151–170.

78. Subcommittee on International Relations, U.S. House of Representatives, *Investigation of Korean-American Relations* (Washington, D.C.: U.S. GPO, 1978), trans. Research Group of Korean-American Relations, Seoul National University, *P'ŭreijŏ pogosŏ* [The Fraser Report] (Seoul: Silch'ŏnmunhaksa, 1986), 252.

79. David C. Cole and Yong Chol Pak, *Financial Development in Korea, 1945–1978* (Cambridge, Mass.: Council on East Asian Studies, Harvard University, 1983), 201, 298–303.

80. Ibid.,163–165; Haggard, Kim, and Moon, "The Transition to Export-led Growth."

81. Research Group of Korean-American Relations, Seoul National University, *P'ŭreigŏ pogosŏ* [The Fraser Report], 244–245. For an opposing view, see Yi Wan-bŏm, "Che ilch'a kyŏngje kaebal ogaenyŏn kyehoek-ŭi ipan-gwa miguk-ŭi yŏkhal" [Designing the First Five-Year Economic Development Plan and the Role of the United States], 133–134.

82. See Amicus Most, *Expanding Exports: A Case Study of the Korean Experience* (Washington, D.C.: USAID, 1969). See also Haggard, Kim, and Moon, "The Transition to Export-led Growth."

83. Kim Hŭng-gi, ed., *Yŏngyok-ŭi han'guk kyŏngje: pisa kyŏngjhe kihoekwŏn samsipsamnyŏnsa* [The Glory and Hardships of the Korean Economy: 33 Years' Untold History of the Economic Planning Board] (Seoul: Maeil Business Newspaper, 1999), 103.

84. Song In-sang, *Puhŭnggwa sŏngjang* [Reconstruction and Growth] (Seoul: 21segibuksŭ Saenal, 1994), 249.
85. Kim Hŭng-gi, ed., *Yŏngyok-ŭi han'guk kyŏngche* [The Glory and Hardships of the Korean Economy), 255; Ch'oe Hyŏng-sŏp, *Ch'oe hyŏng-sŏp hoegorok: Puli kkŏjiji annŭn yŏn'guso* (Institute Working 24 Hours: A Memoir of Hyŏng-sŏp Ch'oe) (Seoul: Chosun Ilbosa, 1995), 52–65.

5. The Labyrinth of Solitude: Park and the Exercise of Presidential Power

I would like to express my gratitude to Yi Su-hyŏn for assisting me with the collection and classification of the Blue House Secretariat's personnel information during Park Chung Hee's political rule. Without her assistance, this essay would not have been possible. The research was supported by a Korea University Grant.

1. National Election Commission, Republic of Korea, "Chungang Sŏngŏ Kwanri Wiwŏnhoe: Yŏkdae Sŏngŏ Chŏngbo Sisŭt'em [National Election Commission Republic of Korea: Information Database of Past Elections]," National Election Commission, Republic of Korea, http://www.nec.go.kr/sinfo/index.html.
2. Kim Ch'ung-nam, *Sŏnggonghan taet'ongryŏng, silpaehan taet'ongryŏng* [Successful Presidents and Failed Presidents] (Seoul: Chŏnwŏn, 1992), 286.
3. Consult Park Chung Hee, *Uri minjok-ŭi nagalgil* [Our Nation's Path] (Seoul: Tonga ch'ulp'ansa, 1962) and *Kukka-wa hyŏngmyŏng-gwa na* [The State, the Revolution, and I] (Seoul: Hyangmunsa, 1963) for Park's authoritarian political beliefs.
4. See Cho Kap-che, *Nae mudŏm-e ch'im-ŭl paet'ŏra 3: hyŏngmyŏng chŏnya* [Spit on My Grave, vol. 3: On the Eve of Revolution] (Seoul: Chosun Ilbosa, 1999), 28–51.
5. See ibid., 65.
6. Law on Korea Central Intelligence Agency, Law no. 619, promulgated on June 10, 1961.
7. See ibid., as amended by Law no. 1510 of December 14, 1963, as well as the Law on Korea Central Intelligence Agency Employees promulgated on May 31, 1963.
8. Consult New Democratic Party's floor leader Kim Young-sam's "Kukchŏng chŏnban-e kwanhan chilmun" [Questions on the National Political Situation] raised on June 13, 1969, at the second plenary meeting of the seventieth National Assembly session. The full text is quoted in Kim Young-sam, *Kim Young-sam hoegorok 1: minjujuŭi-rŭl wihan na-ŭi t'ujaeng* [The Recollections of Kim Yŏng-sam, vol. 1: My Struggle for Democracy] (Seoul: Paeksan sŏdang, 2000), 263–280.
9. See Kim Chin, *Ch'ŏngwadae pisŏsil 1: yuksŏng-ŭro tŭlŏbon Park Chung Hee sidae-ŭi chŏngch'i kwŏllyŏk pisa* [The Blue House Secretariat, vol. 1: The Untold Story of the Park Chung Hee Era Told by the Voices of Witnesses] (Seoul: JoongAng Ilbosa, 1994), 9–221, for Park's complex relationship with his security forces.

10. See Kim Hyŏng-uk and Pak Sa-wŏl, *Kim Hyŏng-uk hoegorok 1: 5.16 pisa* [The Recollections of Kim Hyŏng-uk, vol. 1: The Untold Story of the May Sixteenth Military Revolution] (Seoul: Ach'im, 1985), 193–220, 234–243, 253–279.

11. Consult Kim Hyŏng-uk and Pak Sa-wŏl, *Kim Hyŏng-uk hoegorok 2: han'guk chungang chŏngbobu* [The Recollections of Kim Hyŏng-uk, vol. 2: The Korea Central Intelligence Agency] (Seoul: Ach'im, 1985), 13–15, 119–128, 231–240, 273–314.

12. Consult Kim Hyŏng-uk and Pak Sa-wŏl, *Kim Hyŏng-uk hoegorok 3: Park Chung Hee wangjo-ŭi pihwa* [The Recollections of Kim Hyŏng-uk, vol. 3: The Secrets of Park Chung Hee's Dynasty] (Seoul: Ach'im, 1985), 100–107.

13. See Kang Sŏng-jae, *K'udet'a kwŏllyŏk-ŭi saengri* [The Physiology of Military Coup d'état Power] (Seoul: Dong-A Ilbosa, 1987), 142–176.

14. Cho Kap-che, *Nae mudŏm-e ch'im-ŭl paet'ŏra 5: Kim Chong-p'il-ŭi p'ungun* [Spit on My Grave, vol. 5: The Adventures of Kim Chong-p'il] (Seoul: Chosun Ilbosa, 1999), 180–187.

15. See Kim Ch'ung-sik, *Namsan-ŭi pujangdŭl 1* [The KCIA Directors, vol. 1] (Seoul: Dong-A Ilbosa, 1992), 342–423.

16. Consult ibid., 2:14–54, 246–278.

17. Consult Kim Chŏng-ryŏm's *A! Park Chung Hee: Kim Chŏng-ryŏm chŏngch'i hoegorok* [Ah! Park Chung Hee: Kim Chŏng-ryŏm's reflections on politics] (Seoul: JoongAng M&B, 1997), 74–75.

18. See Byung-kook Kim, *Pundan-gwa hyŏngmyŏng-ŭi tonghak: han'guk-kwa meksik'o-ŭi chŏngch'i kyŏngje* [The Dynamics of National Division and Revolution: The Political Economy of South Korea and Mexico] (Seoul: Munhak-kwa chisŏngsa, 1994), 346–365.

19. *Taet'ongryŏng pisŏsil p'yŏllam* [A Handbook on the Office of the President] (Seoul: Administrative Staff Office, Office of the President, 1997).

20. Interview with Sŏ Pong-gyun, who served as senior secretary for political affairs in 1966, with status equivalent to that of a vice minister.

21. JoongAng Ilbo Sillok Park Chung Hee sidae t'ŭkbyŏl ch'wijaet'im, *Sillok Park Chung Hee* [A Historical Record: Park Chung Hee] (Seoul: JoongAng M&B, 1998), 336.

22. Interview with Chŏng So-yŏng, who served as a secretary for macroeconomic policy with jurisdiction over the EPB and MoF between 1963 and 1969. Chŏng So-yŏng became MoF vice minister in 1968, returning to the Blue House to serve as senior secretary on economic affairs between 1969 and 1973.

23. Kim Chŏng-ryŏm, *A! Park Chung Hee: Kim Chŏng-ryŏm chŏngch'i hoegorok* [Ah! Park Chung Hee: Kim Chŏng-ryŏm's Reflections on Politics], 52–55.

24. Cho Kap-che, *Nae mudŏm-e ch'im-ŭl paet'ŏra* [Spit on My Grave], 5:104–105.

25. See Yung Whee Rhee, Bruce Ross-Larson, and Garry Pursell, *Korea's Competitive Edge: Managing the Entry into World Markets* (Baltimore: Johns Hopkins University Press for the World Bank, 1984), 9–38.

26. Consult Kim Chŏng-ryŏm, *Han'guk kyŏngje chŏngch'aek 30nyŏnsa: Kim*

Chŏng-ryŏm hoegorok [A Thirty-Year History of Korea's Economic Policy: The Recollections of Kim Chŏng-ryŏm] (Seoul: JoongAng Ilbo, 1990), 419.

27. See O Wŏn-ch'ŏl's *Han'gukhyŏng kyŏngje kŏnsŏl: enjiniŏring ŏp'ŭroch'i 1* [Korean-Style Economic Development: An Engineering Approach], vol.1 (Seoul: Kia kyŏngje yŏn'guso, 1995), 240. O Wŏn-ch'ŏl entered public service as a head of the research division in Park's military junta in 1961 and soon transferred to MTI to become Chemical Industry Division director (1961–1964), First Industry Bureau director (1964–1968), Planning and Management director (1968–1970), and assistant vice minister of mining and industry (1970–1971).

28. Ibid., 3:262–265.

29. Interview with Kim Chŏng-ryŏm and Yang Yun-se. Yang Yun-se met with Park on a weekly basis to advise on foreign loan and foreign investment policy as the director of the EPB Division on Foreign Capital Management (Grade 3A) during the 1962–1966 period.

30. Yi Sang-u, "Park Chung Hee-nŭn yongin-ŭi ch'ŏnjaeyŏnna?" [Was Park a Genius in Using People?], *Sindong-A,* September 1984, 268–289,

31. Chŏng Il-gwŏn, "Na-wa Park taet'ongnyŏng: 'kun'gwa chŏngch'i chagŭmen kwanyŏhaji masio'" [President Park and I: "Do not get involved with military and political fund-raising"], *Sindong-A,* February 1987, 251–267.

32. Cho Kap-che, *Nae mudŏm-e ch'im-ŭl paet'ŏra 7: sŏngjang sok-ŭi kŭnŭl* [Spit on My Grave, vol. 7: The Dark Shades of Growth] (Seoul: Chosun Ilbosa, 2001), 47.

33. Yi Yŏng-sŏk, *JP wa HR: Kim Chong-p'il-gwa Yi Hu-rak-ŭi chŏngch'i pihwa* [JP and HR: The Untold Political Story of Kim Chong-p'il and Yi Hu-rak] (Seoul: Wŏnŭm ch'ulp'ansa, 1983), 89–94, 119–126.

34. Chŏng Ku-yŏng, *Chŏng Ku-yŏng hoegorok: silp'aehan tojŏn* [The Recollections of Chŏng Ku-yŏng: The Failed Challenge] (Seoul: JoongAng Ilbosa, 1987), 264.

35. Kim Ch'ung-sik, *Namsan-ŭi pujangdŭl 1* [The KCIA Directors], 1:364–372.

36. Ibid., 2:14–81.

37. Consult Kim Hyŏng-uk and Pak Sa-wŏl, *Kim Hyŏng-uk hoegorok 3: Park Chung Hee wangjo-ŭi pihwa* [The Recollections of Kim Hyŏng-uk, vol. 3: The Secrets of Park Chung Hee's Dynasty], 263–351.

38. The files the KCIA kept on its former directors were used not by Park but by Chun Doo-hwan when he launched a military coup in 1980. The army security commander cleared his way to power in May 1980 by simultaneously arresting key DRP leaders—Kim Chong-p'il, Yi Hu-rak, Kim Chin-man, Pak Chong-gyu, and O Wŏn-ch'ŏl—on charges of "illicit wealth accumulation" while cracking down on major opposition politicians and dissident activists on charges of "instigating social instability and unrest in labor unions and on university campuses." See *Dong-A Ilbo,* May 19 and June 18, 1980.

39. Chŏng Ku-yŏng, *Chŏng Ku-yŏng hoegorok: silp'aehan tojŏn* [The Recollections of Chŏng Ku-yŏng: The Failed Challenge], 15, 139.

40. Kim Hyŏng-uk and Pak Sa-wŏl, *Kim Hyŏng-uk hoegorok 2: han'guk*

chungang chŏngbobu [The Recollections of Kim Hyŏng-uk, vol. 2: The Korea Central Intelligence Agency], 282–284.

41. Ibid., 285.

42. Ibid., 307–314.

43. Ibid., 136, 14.

44. Consult Ch'oe Han-su, *Han'guk chŏngdang chŏngch'i pyŏndong 1* [Change of Korean Party Politics], vol. 1 (Seoul: Semyŏng sŏgwan, 1999), 209–210, 217, 221, 231.

45. Kim Young-sam, *Kim Young-sam hoegorok 2: minjujuŭi-rŭl wihan na-ŭi t'ujaeng* (The Recollections of Kim Young-sam, vol. 2: My Struggle for Democracy) (Seoul: Paeksan sŏdang, 2000), 43–51.

46. Cho Kap-che, *Yugo! 1* [The Death of Park!], vol. 1 (Seoul: Han'gilsa, 1987), 77–80.

47. David C. Cole and Princeton N. Lyman, *Korean Development: The Interplay of Politics and Economics* (Cambridge, Mass.: Harvard University Press, 1971), 96. See also Chŏng Ku-yŏng, *Chŏng Ku-yŏng hoegorok: silp'aehan tojŏn* [The Recollections of Chŏng Ku-yŏng: The Failed Challenge], 124–130.

48. Chŏng Ku-yŏng, *Chŏng Ku-yŏng hoegorok: silp'aehan tojŏn* [The Recollections of Chŏng Ku-yŏng: The Failed Challenge], 121.

49. See Chapter 7 below.

50. Cho Kap-che, *Nae mudŏ-me ch'im-ŭl paet'ŏra 7* [Spit on My Grave], 7:297.

51. Ibid.

52. O Wŏn-ch'ŏl, *Han'gukhyŏng kyŏngje kŏnsŏl: enjiniŏring ŏp'ŭroch'i 2* [Korean-style Economic Development: An Engineering Approach], 2:227–241.

53. An Mun-sŏk, "Kim Hak-ryŏl-ron: kyŏngje kihoek p'ungt'o-ŭi chosŏngja" [Kim Hak-ryŏl's Leadership Style: The Groundbreaker of Economic Planning], in *Chŏnhwan sidae-ŭi haengjŏngga: Han'gukhyŏng chidojaron* [Public Entrepreneur in a Time of Turbulence: A Leadership Model in Korea], ed. Yi Chong-pŏm (Seoul: Nanam, 1994), 43, 53.

54. Cho Kap-che, *Nae mudŏm-e ch'im-ŭl paet'ŏra 3: hyŏngmyŏng chŏnya* [Spit on My Grave), 3:136, and *Nae mudŏm-e ch'im-ŭl paet'ŏra 6: maengho-nŭn kanda* [Spit on My Grave, vol. 6: The Tiger Corps Is Going to Vietnam] (Seoul: Chosun Ilbosa, 2001), 46.

55. Yŏm Chae-ho, "Kwahak kisul-ŭi chŏndosa: Ch'oe Hyŏng-sŏpron" [A Preacher of Science and Technology: Ch'oi Hyŏng-sŏp's Leadership Style], in *Chŏnhwan sidae-ŭi haengjŏngga* [Public Entrepreneur in a Time of Turbulence], ed. Yi Chong-pŏm, 104–132.

56. Ch'oe Sŏng-mo, "Seoul-ŭi sŭk'ai rain-ŭl pakkun chŏngnyŏl-ŭi haengjŏngga: Kim Hyŏn-okron" [The Passionate Administrator Who Changed the Skyline of Seoul: Kim Hyŏn-ok's Leadership Style], in *Chŏnhwan sidae-ŭi haengjŏngga* [Public Entrepreneur in a Time of Turbulence], ed. Yi Chong-pŏm, 60–101.

57. Cho Kap-che, *Nae mudŏm-e ch'im-ŭl paet'ŏra 4: Kukka kaejo* [Spit on My Grave, vol. 4: National Reconstruction] (Seoul: Chosun Ilbosa, 1999), 47, 107; and *Nae mudŏm-e ch'im-ŭl paet'*, 7:20–27.

58. Kim Chŏng-ryŏm, *Han'guk kyŏngje chŏngch'aek 30nyŏnsa: Kim Chŏng-*

ryŏm hoegorok [A Thirty-year History of Korea's Economic Policy: The Recollections of Kim Chŏng-ryŏm], 238, 252.

59. Ibid., 239–243.
60. Ibid., 256–257, 263–268, 273.
61. See O Wŏn-ch'ŏl, *Han'gukhyŏng kyŏngje kŏnsŏl: enjiniŏring ŏp'ŭroch'i 3* [Korean-style Economic Development: An Engineering Approach], 3:259–279, and Kim Chŏng-ryŏm, *Han'guk kyŏngje chŏngch'aek 30nyŏnsa: Kim Chŏng-nyŏm hoegorok* [A Thirty-year History of Korea's Economic Policy: The Recollections of Kim Chŏng-nyŏm], 322–323.
62. Interview with Kim Chŏng-ryŏm.
63. Kim Young-sam, *Kim Young-sam hoegorok 2: minjujuŭi-rŭl wihan na-ŭi t'ujaeng* [The Recollections of Kim Young-sam, vol. 2: My Struggle for Democracy], 82–88.
64. Korea National Statistical Office.
65. William Kornhauser, *The Politics of Mass Society* (New York: Free Press of Glen Co., 1961).
66. See Chapter 12 below.
67. Kim Young-sam, *Kim Young-sam hoegorok* [The Recollections of Kim Young-sam], 2:135–161.
68. Ibid., 159.
69. Yi Sang-u, *Kwollyŏk-ŭi mollak: yushingwŏllyŏk-e chŏhanghan panch'eje min gwŏn undongsa* [The Demise of the Powerful: The History of the Anti-system Human Rights Movements against the *Yushin*] (Seoul: Dong-A Ilbosa, 1987).

6. The Armed Forces

1. Samuel P. Huntington, *Political Order in Changing Societies* (New Haven: Yale University Press, 1968), 203–210, 225–233. Also see Amos Perlmutter, *The Military and Politics in Modern Times* (New Haven: Yale University Press, 1977), 13.
2. Concerning the relationship between professionalism and political intervention by the military, see Morris Janowitz, *The Professional Soldier: A Social and Political Portrait* (New York: Free Press, 1960).
3. For detailed description of factions and power struggles in the South Korean military, see Han Yong-wŏn, *Han'guk-ŭi kunbujŏngch'i* [Military Rule of Korea] (Seoul: Taewangsa, 1993), 222–255; Kang Ch'ang-sŏng, *Ilbon/Hanguk kunbŏl jŏngch'i* [Japan/Korea Politics of Military Factions] (Seoul: Haedong munhwasa, 1991), 331–356.
4. Kim Chae-hong, *Kun: chŏngch'ijanggyo-wa p'okt'anju* [Military 1: Politicized Military Officers and Boiler-makers] (Seoul: Dong-A Ilbosa, 1994), 226–227.
5. Even chiefs of staff did not attend the meeting where President Park deliberated on the promotion of generals. See Kim Sŏk-ya and Kodani Hidesiro, *(Sillok) Park Chung Hee-wa Kim Chong-p'il: : han'guk hyŏndaejŏngchi'isa*

(True Record) [Park Chung Hee and Kim Chong-p'il] (Seoul: P'ŭrojekt'ŭ 409, 1997), 70.

6. Chŏng Ch'ang-yŏng, *Pukhan kyŏngje ch'eje-ŭi kaebanghwa yoin: punsŏk-kwa chŏnmang* [Factors Inducing Open Economy for North Korea: Analysis and Prospects] (Seoul: ROK Unification Board, 1985).

7. Ch'oe Ch'ang-gyu, *Haebang 30nyŏnsa 4: Chesam gonghwaguk* [History of Thirty Years since Emancipation, vol. 4: The Third Republic] (Seoul: Sŏngmun'gak, 1976), 248–249.

8. These soldiers were eventually court-martialed and found guilty. Yi Sang-u, *Park chŏnggwŏn 18nyŏn: kŭ kwŏllyŏk-ŭi naemak* [Eighteen Years of Park's Regime: Secrets of its Power] (Seoul: Dong-A Ilbosa, 1986), 270–273.

9. Kim Ch'ung-sik, *Namsan-ŭi pujangdŭl* [The KCIA Directors], 3rd ed., vol. 1 (Seoul: Dong-A Ilbosa, 1992), 103–106.

10. *Kŏn'gun 50nyŏnsa* [Fifty Years of Armed Forces Building] (Seoul: Kukbang kunsa yŏn'guso, 1998), 204–205. Also see Han Yong-wŏn, *Han'guk-ŭi kunbujŏngch'i* [Military Rule of Korea], 294.

11. Kim Hyŏng-uk and Pak Sa-wŏl, *Kim Hyŏng-uk hoegorok 2: han'guk chungang chŏngbohu* [The Recollections of Kim Hyŏng-uk, vol. 2: The Korea Central Intelligence Agency] (Seoul: Ach'im, 1985), 153–154.

12. For the details of the Brown Memorandum, refer to U.S. Congress, Committee on International Relations, Subcommittee on International Organization, *Investigation on Korean-American Relations* (Washington, D.C.: U.S. GPO, 1978).

13. Bruce Cumings, *Korea's Place in the Sun: A Modern History* (New York: Norton & Company, 1997), 321.

14. Ch'oe Ch'ang-gyu, *Haebang 30nyŏnsa* [History of Thirty Years since Emancipation], 4:423. At their summit in Honolulu on April 17, 1968, Park and Johnson agreed to regular bilateral meetings between their defense ministers, the first of which was held on May 27–28, 1968. The meeting was enlarged to become the Security Consultative Council in 1971. See ROK Ministry of National Defense, *Kukbang paeksŏ* [Defense White Paper], *1991–1992* (Ministry of National Defense, 1992), 188–193.

15. See Public Relations Association of Korea, *A Quarter Century of North Korean Provocations* (Seoul: Public Relations Association of Korea, 1974), 64–70; ROK Ministry of National Defense, *Kukbang paeksŏ* [Defense White Paper], 429–436.

16. Ch'oe Ch'ang-gyu, *Haebang 30nyŏnsa* [History of Thirty Years since Emancipation], 4:419–420.

17. Third Military Academy of the ROK Army, *Yukkun chesamsagwanhakkyo samsimnyŏnsa* [Thirty-Year History of the Third Military Academy] (Yŏngch'ŏn: Third Military Academy, 1998), 24–27.

18. *Kŏn'gun 50nyŏnsa* [Fifty Years of Armed Forces Building], 241–243.

19. North Korea's "Four Military Principles" called for the arming of all North Koreans, the development of all soldiers into military leaders, the fortification of all the land of North Korea, and the modernization of weapons. See Yu Wan-sik, *Kim Il Sung chuch'e sasang-ŭi hyŏngsŏng kwajŏng yŏn'gu* [A Study

of the Formation Process of Kim Il Sung's *Chuch'e* Ideology] (Seoul: Unification Board, 1977).

20. Kŭktong munje yŏn'guso, ed., *Pukkoe kunsa chŏllyak charyojip* [The Puppet North Korea's Military Strategy: Documents] (Seoul: Kŭktongmunje yŏn'guso, 1974), 327–329; *Pukhanch'ongram* [Encyclopedia on North Korea] (Seoul: Pukhan yŏn'guso, 1983), 1468–1470.

21. In the joint communiqué on February 6, they agreed to U.S. military assistance to South Korea, South Korea's exclusive responsibility for defending the DMZ, allied defense of South Korea in case of unprovoked war, and the establishment of an annual security consultative meeting. See *Kŏn'gun 5onyŏnsa* [Fifty Years of Armed Forces Building], 248.

22. Originally launched as the Research Agency for Defense Science, the agency was officially changed to ADD in 1971. Ibid., 292.

23. Han Yong-wŏn, *Han'guk-ŭi kunbujŏngch'i* [Military Rule of Korea], 298.

24. *P'alsibnyŏndae pangwi sanub-ŭi kibon chŏngch'aek* [A Basic Policy for the Defense Industry in the 1980s] (Seoul: Kukbang kwanri yŏn'guso, 1981), 17.

25. *Kŏn'gun 5onyŏnsa* [Fifty Years of Armed Forces Building], 296.

26. According to former U.S. ambassador William Gleysteen, Park recognized that ROK-U.S. relations were endangered by his nuclear development program and tacitly agreed to renounce it. See William H. Gleysteen, Jr., *Massive Entanglement and Marginal Influence* (Washington, D.C.: Brookings Institution, 1999). Korean translation: *Allyŏjiji an-ŭn yŏksa,* trans. Hwang Chŏng-il (Seoul: JoongAng M&B, 1999), 41.

27. *Kŏn'gun 5onyŏnsa* [Fifty Years of Armed Forces Building], 293–296, 303–305.

28. The Nike-Hercules was originally a surface-to-air missile, but the Agency for Defense Development converted it into a surface-to-surface missile. The South Korean government had tried to improve its range and guidance system, but had been constrained by technological dependence on the United States. See Yi Sŏng-su, "Mugi ijŏn-ŭi kukchejŏngch'ihak: han'guk-ŭi kyŏng'u-rŭl chungsim-ŭro" [The International Politics of Arms Transfers: A Case of Korea] (MA dissertation, Seoul National University, 1986), 136.

29. Kim Chŏng-ryŏm, *A! Park Chung Hee: Kim Chŏng-ryŏm chŏngch'i hoegorok* [Ah! Park Chung Hee: Kim Chŏng-nyŏm's reflections on politics] (Seoul: JoongAng M&B, 1997), 305.

30. Kim Chae-hong, *Kun1: chŏngch'ijanggyo-wa p'okt'anju* [Military 1: Politicized Military Officers and Boiler-makers], 364.

31. *Kŏn'gun 5onyŏnsa* [Fifty Years of Armed Forces Building], 275–280.

32. See ROK Ministry of National Defense, *Kukbang paeksŏ* [Defense White Paper], *1991–1992,* 191–192.

33. Yu In-t'aek, *Hanbando kunsamunje-ŭi ihae* [Understanding Military Affairs on the Korean Peninsula] (Seoul: Pŏmmunsa, 1996), 40–45.

34. Peacetime operational control was returned to the ROK armed forces on December 1, 1994. Ministry of National Defense, *ROK-US Alliance and USFK* (Seoul: Ministry of National Defense, 2003), 53.

35. Kim Hyŏng-uk and Pak Sa-wŏl, *Kim Hyŏng-uk hoegorok* 2 [The Recollections of Kim Hyŏng-uk], 2: 116–123, and 123–128.

36. Kim Sŏk-ya and Kodani Hidesiro, *(Sillok) Park Chung Hee-wa Kim Chong-p'il: han'guk hyŏndaejŏngchi'isa* [(True Record) Park Chung Hee and Kim Chong-p'il] (Seoul: P'ŭrojekt'ŭ 409, 1997).

37. Kim Hyŏng-uk and Pak Sa-wŏl, *Kim Hyŏng-uk hoegorok* [The Recollections of Kim Hyŏng-uk], 2:157–158.

38. Kang Ch'ang-sŏng, *Ilbon/Han'guk kunbŏl'jŏngch'i* [Japan/Korea Politics of Military Factions], 360; Gregory Henderson, *Korea: The Politics of the Vortex* (Cambridge, Mass.: Harvard University Press, 1968). Korean translation: *Soyongdoli-ŭi Han'guk chŏngch'i*, translated by Pak Haeng-ung and Yi Chong-sam (Seoul: Hanul Academy, 2000), 502–503.

39. Kang Ch'ang-sŏng, *Ilbon/Hanguk kunbŏljŏngch'i* [Japan/Korea Politics of Military Factions], 358.

40. Kim Chae-hong, *Kun: chŏngch'ijanggyo-wa p'okt'anju* [Military 1: Politicized Military Officers and Boiler-makers], 281–285.

41. Kim Chin, *Ch'ŏngwadae pisŏsil* [Presidential Secretariat of the Blue House] (Seoul: JoongAng M&B, 1993), 417.

42. Kang Ch'ang-sŏng, *Ilbon/Hanguk kunbŏljŏngch'i* [Japan/Korea Politics of Military Factions], 364–365.

43. Ch'oe Ch'ang-gyu, *Haebang 30nyŏnsa* [History of Thirty Years since Emancipation], 4:500–502.

44. Kim Ch'ung-sik, *Namsan-ŭi pujangdŭl* [The KCIA Directors], 1:329.

45. See Korea Military Academy, *Armed Forces and National Development* (Seoul: KMA, 1981), 158, table 5–3. For a time-series comparison, see C. I. Eugene Kim, "The Value Congruity between ROK Civilian and Former Military Party Elites," *Asian Survey* 18 (1978): 840.

46. The Gang of Four included Kim Sŏng-gon (chairman, Central Committee of the DRP), Kil Chae-ho (DRP secretary-general), Paek Nam-ŏk (DRP chairman), and Kim Chin-man (chairman, Financial Committee of DRP).

47. For the full text of the Proclamation of the State of National Emergency, see *Chosun Ilbo* (December 7, 1971). Kim Sŏng-jin, presidential press assistant, said, "The emergency shall continue until the threat from North Korea disappears."

48. See Park Chung Hee's Kukka Pisang Satae Sŏnŏn [Special Statement on the Proclamation of the State of National Emergency], as reported in *Chosun Ilbo*, December 7, 1971.

49. For the full text of Park's official letter to the chairman of the National Assembly to urge for the passage of the Special Law for Defending the State, see *Chosun Ilbo*, December 24, 1971.

50. Kim Chae-hong, *Kunbu-wa kwŏllyŏk: 6 kong kunbu-ŭi inmaek* [The Military and Political Power] (Seoul: Nanam, 1992), 257–258.

51. No Ka-wŏn, *Ch'ŏngwadae kyŏnghosil* 2 [Presidential Security Service of the Blue House, vol. 2] (Seoul: Wŏlgan mal, 1994), 140–156.

52. Kim Hyŏng-uk and Pak Sa-wŏl, *Kim Hyŏng-uk hoegorok* 3: *Park Chung Hee*

wangjo-ŭi pihwa [The Recollections of Kim Hyŏng-uk, vol. 3: The Secrets of Park Chung Hee's Dynasty] (Seoul: Ach'im, 1985), 134–137.

53. See ibid., 3:165–167.
54. See No Ka-wŏn, *Ch'ŏngwadae kyŏnghosil 2* [Presidential Security Service of the Blue House], 2:207.
55. Kim Chin, *Ch'ŏngwadae pisŏsil* [Presidential Secretariat of the Blue House], 38–39.
56. Kang Ch'ang-sŏng, *Ilbon/Hanguk kunbŏljŏngch'i* [Japan/Korea Politics of Military Factions], 372–378.
57. Kim Chin, *Ch'ŏngwadae pisŏsil* [Presidential Secretariat of the Blue House], 12–13.
58. See KMA, *Armed Forces and National Development,* 154–161.
59. The *Yushin* Junior Officials numbered a total of 784 over eleven years. Among these officers, 85 were from the navy and the air force; 89.2 percent were from the Korea Military Academy (KMA). See KMA, *Yukkun sagwan hakkyo 50nyŏnsa* [Fifty Years of the KMA] (Seoul: KMA, 2000), 872–890.
60. While in the army as a student soldier during the Korean War, Ch'a applied to enter the eleventh class of the KMA but failed. He subsequently enlisted in the Officer Candidate School (OCS). See Kim Chin, *Ch'ŏngwadae pisŏsil* [Presidential Secretariat of the Blue House], 105.
61. Ch'a Chi-ch'ŏl's base of power was the Committee for Presidential Security, which he organized with the Capital Garrison commander, the commissioner general of the national police headquarters, the mayor of Seoul, and some cabinet ministers as members. See Kim Chae-hong, *Kun 2: haekkaebal kŭkpijakchŏn* [The Military, vol. 2: Secret Development of Nuclear Program] (Seoul: Dong-A Ilbosa, 1994), 45–46.
62. Kim Chin, *Ch'ŏngwadae pisŏsil* [Presidential Secretariat of the Blue House], 112–113.
63. Chŏng Sŭng-hwa, *1212 sakkŏn: Chŏng Sŭng-hwa-nŭn malhanda* [The December 12 Incident: Chŏng Sŭng-hwa Says] (Seoul: Kkach'i, 1987), 144.
64. According to General Chŏng Sŭng-hwa, he became aware of the presidential decree that allowed the security chief to command the Capital Garrison force just after he got into office as the army chief of staff on February 1, 1979. General Chŏng and Ch'a Chi-ch'ŏl were thenceforth in opposition. In March 1979, General Chŏng recommended to Park Chung Hee that he appoint General Chun Doo-hwan as the security commander. As his reason for the recommendation, he wrote: "To check Ch'a Chi-ch'ŏl's rampant abuse of power and to speak for the military's interests." See Chŏng Sŭng-hwa, *1212 sakkŏn: Chŏng Sŭng-hwa-nŭn malhanda* [The December 12 Incident: Chŏng Sŭng-hwa Says], 21–23.
65. Defense Security Command, *Taegong 30nyŏnsa* [Thirty Years of Counter-Communist Activities] (Seoul, 1978), 559.
66. Chosun Ilbo Wŏlgan chosunbu, *Pirok: han'guk-ŭi taet'ongnyŏng* [Confidential Records: Presidents of Korea] (Seoul: Chosun Ilbosa, 1993), 242–243.

67. Kim Chin, *Ch'ŏngwadae pisŏsil* [Presidential Secretariat of the Blue House], 105.
68. Kim Chae-hong, *Park Chung Hee-ŭi yusan* [The Legacy of Park Chung Hee] (Seoul: P'urŭnsup, 1998), 47.
69. Kang Ch'ang-sŏng, *Ilbon/Hanguk kunbŏljŏngch'i* [Japan/Korea Politics of Military Factions], 370–381.

7. The Leviathan: Economic Bureaucracy under Park

The research for this chapter has been supported by a Korea University Grant.

1. Chalmers Johnson, *MITI and the Japanese Miracle: The Growth of Industrial Policy, 1925–1975* (Stanford: Stanford University Press, 1982); Peter Evans, *Embedded Autonomy: State and Industrial Transformation* (Princeton; Princeton University Press, 1995), 12–14.
2. On neutral competence, see Hugh Heclo, "OMB and the Presidency: The Problem of 'Neutral Competence,'" *Public Interest* 38 (Winter 1975): 82.
3. On patrimonialism, consult Reinhard Bendix, *Max Weber: An Intellectual Portrait* (Berkeley: University of California Press, 1977), 344–347.
4. Yi Yŏng-sŏk, *JP wa HR: Kim Chong-p'il-gwa Yi Hu-rak-ŭi chŏngch'i pihwa* [JP and HR: The Untold Political Story of Kim Chong-p'il and Yi Hu-rak] (Seoul: Wŏnŭm ch'ulp'ansa, 1983).
5. Consult Park Chung Hee, *Uri minjok-ŭi nagal-gil* [Our Nation's Path] (Seoul: Dong-A ch'ulp'ansa, 1962), 39–40, 198–205.
6. For a general review of Rhee's personnel administration, see Pak Tong-sŏ, *Han'guk kwallyo chedo-ŭi yŏksajŏk chŏn'gae* [The Historical Development of the Korean Bureaucratic System] (Seoul: Han'guk yŏn'gu tosŏgwan, 1961).
7. O Wŏn-ch'ŏl, *Han'gukhyŏng kyŏngje kŏnsŏl: enjiniŏring ŏp'ŭroch'i* [Korean-style Economic Development: An Engineering Approach] (Seoul: Kia kyŏngje yŏn'guso, 1996), 3:209–257.
8. Russell Mardon, "The State and the Effective Control of Foreign Capital: The Case of South Korea," *World Politics* 43, no.1 (October 1990): 115–122, 126–137.
9. See Hahn Been Lee, *Korea: Time, Change and Administration* (Honolulu: East-West Center Press, 1968), and Pak Hok, *"Rŭppo kŭmyunggye-rŭl umjigin inmaek, hanŭn inmaek-ŭl chungsim-ŭro"* [Report, The Driving Force behind the Financial Community: A Focus on Former Bank of Korea Human Networks], *Dong-A Ilbosa*, November 1980, 188–196. Also the interview with EPB vice minister Ch'a Kyun-hŭi (1962–1963).
10. The Government Organization Law (originally no. 660) as amended by Law no.1506, December 14, 1963.
11. See Chapters 2 and 3 for economic policy during the junta years.
12. Youngil Lim, *Government Policy and Private Enterprise: Korean Experience in Industrialization*, Korea Research Monograph no. 6 (Berkeley: Institute of East Asian Studies, University of California, 1981), 16–17.

13. Interview with EPB Planning Bureau director Chŏng Chae-sŏk (1962–1963).

14. Kim Chŏng-ryŏm, *A! Park Chung Hee: Kim Chŏng-ryŏm chŏngch'ihoegorok* [Ah! Park Chung Hee: Kim Chŏng-ryŏm's reflections on politics] (Seoul: JoongAng M&B, 1997), 191.

15. Sin Song-sun, "Kyŏngje kihoegwŏn [Economic Planning Board]," in *Han'guk-ŭi kyŏngjegwallyo* [Economic Bureaucrats in Korea], ed. Yu Sŭng-sam (Seoul: Kyŏnghyang sinmun, 1979), 38–40, 56–57.

16. Stephan Haggard, Byung-Kook Kim, and Chung-in Moon, "The Transition to Export-led Growth in South Korea: 1954–1966," *Journal of Asian Studies* 50, no. 4 (November 1991): 850–873.

17. Economic Planning Board, "Kijunhwanyul insang-gwa oehwan chŭngsŏje ch'aet'aek" [An Increase of the Basic Exchange Rate and the Adoption of a System of Foreign Exchange Certificates, May 5, 1964], and "Kŭmni hyŏnsilhwa taech'aek" [Policy to Make Interest Rates Realistic, September 30, 1965].

18. Chang Ki-yŏng, "Wae kŭmni-rŭl hyŏnsilhwa haetnŭn'ga?: han chŏnch'ŏlsu-ŭi paegŭijonggundam" [Why Were Interest Rates Rationalized? The story of a former switchman], *Dong-A Ilbosa*, December 1965, 84–87.

19. Interview with Yang Yun-se, who simultaneously served as ECC secretary general and EPB International Cooperation Division chief between 1962 and 1966.

20. Economic Planning Board, *Kaebal yŏndae-ŭi kyŏngje chŏngch'aek: kyŏngje kihoegwŏn 20nyŏnsa* [Economic Policy during the Developmental Decades: Twenty Years of the Economic Planning Board] (Seoul: Miraesa, 1982), 58–59.

21. Consult David Cole and Yung Chul Park, *Financial Development in Korea, 1945–1979* (Cambridge, Mass.: Harvard University Press, 1983), and Anne O. Krueger, *The Developmental Role of the Foreign Sector and Aid* (Cambridge, Mass.: Harvard University Press, 1979), for the effects of industrial and foreign capital policies on MoF's room for maneuvering monetary policy.

22. Alice H. Amsden, *Asia's Next Giant: South Korea and Late Industrialization* (New York: Oxford University Press, 1989), 146–147.

23. Krueger, *The Developmental Role of the Foreign Sector and Aid*.

24. Robert Wade, "East Asian Financial Systems as a Challenge to Economics: Lessons from Taiwan," *California Management Review* 27, no. 4 (Summer 1985): 293.

25. Economic Planning Board, "Mulga anjŏng-ŭl wihan pisangdaech'aek" [An Emergency Measure to Stabilize Prices], November 3, 1969.

26. Eun Mee Kim, "From Dominance to Symbiosis: State and Chaebol in Korea," *Pacific Focus* 3, no. 2 (Fall 1988): 112–116.

27. Yung Chul Park and Dong Won Kim, "Korea: Development and Structural Change of the Banking System," in *The Financial Development of Japan, Korea, and Taiwan: Growth, Recession, and Liberalization*, ed. Hugh T. Patrick and Yung Chul Park (New York: Oxford University Press, 1994), 213–214.

28. Chae-Jin Lee and Hideo Sato, *U.S. Policy toward Japan and Korea: A Changing Relationship* (New York: Praeger, 1982).

29. O Wonch'ŏl, *Han'gukhyŏng kyŏngje kŏnsŏl* [Economic Development Korean-Style], 3:179–208.

30. On South Korean industrial policy, see Larry E. Westphal, "Industrial Policy in an Export-Propelled Economy: Lessons from South Korea's Experience," *Journal of Economic Perspectives* 4, no. 3 (Summer 1990): 44–54.

31. O, *Hangukhyŏng kyŏngje kŏnsŏl* [Economic Development Korean-Style], vol. 5.

32. Economic Planning Board, "Yuryu p'adong-e taech'ŏhagi wihan mulga anjŏng taech'aek" [A Price Stabilization Measure to Counter the Oil Crisis], December 4, 1973; "Kungmin saenghwal anjŏng-ŭl wihan taet'ongnyŏng kin'gŭpchoch'i" [A Presidential Emergency Measure to Stabilize the People's Livelihood], January 14, 1974; and "Chonghap mulga anjŏng taech'aek" [A Comprehensive Measure to Stabilize Prices], February 5, 1974.

33. Presidential Order no. 6454, January 16, 1973.

34. Chunghwahak kongŏp ch'ujin ch'agwanbogŭp silmu p'alch'a hoeŭi [Minutes of the Eighth Working-Level Vice Assistant Minister Meeting for Heavy and Chemical Industrialization Promotion], May 3, 1974.

35. Ministry of Finance, *Chaejŏng kŭmyung 30nyŏnsa* [Thirty Years of Finance and Monetary Policy] (Seoul: Ministry of Finance, 1978), 259–260.

36. Ibid., 260–261.

37. Economic Planning Board, "Chungdong chinch'ul ch'okchin pangan" [A Measure to Promote the Entry into Middle East Markets], December 5, 1975.

38. Stephan Haggard and Tun-jen Cheng, "State and Foreign Capital in the East Asian NICs," in *The Political Economy of the New Asian Industrialism*, ed. Frederic C. Deyo (Ithaca: Cornell University Press, 1987), 123–125.

39. Richard M. Auty, "Creating Competitive Advantage: South Korean Steel and Petrochemicals," *Tijdschrift voor Economische en Sociale Georgrafie* 82, no. 1 (1991): 19–28.

40. Economic Planning Board, "Suip chayuhwa sich'aek" [A Measure to Liberalize Imports], May 1, 1978; September 12, 1978; January 1, 1979.

41. Economic Planning Board, "Yut'ong kujo kaesŏn taech'aek" [A Measure to Improve the Distribution System], February 25, 1974.

42. Interview with Sin Hyŏn-hwak.

43. Stephan Haggard and Chung-in Moon, "Institutions and Economic Policy: Theory and a Korean Case Study," *World Politics* 42, no. 2 (January 1990): 216–220.

44. Economic Planning Board, "Haban'gi kyŏngje unyŏng-gwa taech'aek" [The Economic Management for the Second Half of 1979 and Policy Measures], July 13, 1979.

45. Economic Planning Board, "Chunghwahak t'uja chochŏng" [Coordination of Investment in Heavy and Chemical Industries], May 25, 1979.

46. Korea Development Institute, *Kyŏŋggi anjŏnghwa sich'aek charyojip: 79.4.17 kyŏngje anjŏnghwa chonghap sich'aek-ŭl chungsim-ŭro 1–2* [The Collected Documents of Economic Stabilization Measures: A Focus on the April Seventeenth 1979 Integrated Measures for Economic Stabilization], vols. 1–2 (Seoul: Korea Development Institute, 1981).

47. Park and Kim, "Korea," 214.

8. The Origins of the *Yushin* Regime: Machiavelli Unveiled

1. See Secretary Office of the President, *Park Chung Hee taet'ongryŏng yŏnsŏl munjib che gujip 9* [Collection of President Park Chung Hee's Speeches, vol. 9] (Seoul: Secretary Office of the President, 1973), 299.

2. Ibid.

3. Hyung-Baeg Im, "The Rise of Bureaucratic Authoritarianism in South Korea," *World Politics* 39, no. 2 (1987).

4. Han Pae-ho, *Han'guk chŏngch'i pyŏndongnon* [Political Changes in Korea] (Seoul: Pŏmmunsa, 1994), 2.

5. Park Chung Hee, *Kukkawa hyŏngmyŏnggwa na* [The Nation, the Revolution, and I] (Seoul: Hyangmunsa,1963), 167.

6. Yi Sang-u, *Park Chung Hee sidae* [The Era of Park Chung Hee], vols. 1–3 (Seoul: Chungwonmunhwa, 1986), 198; Kim Hyŏng-uk, *Hyŏngmyŏng-gwa usang: Kim Hyŏng-uk hoegorok* [Revolution and Idol: Kim Hyŏng-uk Memoirs] (Seoul: Chŏnyewŏn, 1991), 203–205; and Chŏng Ku-yŏng, *Chŏng Ku-yŏng hoegorok: silp'aehan tojŏn* [The Recollections of Chŏng Ku-yŏng: The Failed Challenge] (Seoul: JoongAng Ilbosa, 1987), 329–330.

7. Ryu Kŭn-il, *Kwŏnwijuŭich'ejeha-ŭi minjuhwa undong yŏn'gu: 1960–70nyŏndae chedo'oejŏk pandaeseryŏk-ŭi hyŏngsŏnggwajŏng* [A Study of the Democratization Movements under Authoritarian Regimes] (Seoul: Nanam, 1997), 68–69.

8. Yi Sang-u, *Park chŏnggwŏn 18nyŏn: kŭ kwŏllyŏk-ŭi naemak* [Eighteen years of Park Chung Hee Government] (Seoul: Dong-A Ilbosa, 1986), 198.

9. Ibid., 199.

10. Yi Kyŏng-jae, *Yushin k'udet'a* [*Yushin* Coup d'État] (Seoul: Ilwŏlsŏgak, 1986), 203.

11. Yi Sang-u, *Park chŏnggwŏn 18nyŏn: kŭ kwŏllyŏk-ŭi naemak* [Eighteen Years of Park's Regime: Secret of the Power] (Seoul: Dong-A Ilbosa, 1986), 203.

12. Ibid.

13. Ryu Kŭn-il, Kwŏnwijuŭich'ejeha-ŭi minjuhwa undong yŏn'gu: 1960~70nyŏndae chedo'oejŏk pandaeseryŏk-ŭi hyŏngsŏnggwajŏng [A Study of the Democratization Movements under Authoritarian Regimes: The Formation Process of Extra-Institutional Opposition Forces in the 1960s and 1970s] (Seoul: Nanam, 1997).

14. Kim Yŏng-sun, "Yushinch'eje suripwŏnin-e kwanhan yŏn'gu: chŏngch'ikyŏngjehakjŏk chŏpgŭn" [A Study of the Establishment of the *Yushin* Regime: Political Economy Approach], in *Onŭl-ŭi Han'guk chabonjuŭi-wa kukka* [Current Capitalism in Korea and the State], edited by Han'guk sanŏp sahoe yŏn'guhoe (Seoul: Han'gilsa, 1988), 62–63.

15. Ibid., 63.

16. Kim Chin, *Ch'ŏngwadae pisŏsil 1: yuksŏng-ŭro tŭlŏbon Park Chung Hee sidae-ŭi chŏngch'i kwŏllyŏk pisa* [The Blue House Secretariat, vol. 1: The Untold Story of the Park Chung Hee Era Told by the Voices of Witnesses] (Seoul: JoongAng Ilbosa, 1995), 196.

17. Kim Dae-jung, "Dae-jung kyŏngjeron 100mun 100tap" [A Theory of Mass Economics: A Hundred Questions, A Hundred Answers], Kim Dae-jung

chŏnjip p'yŏnch'anwiwŏnhoe, ed., in *Kim Dae-jung chŏnjip 2: Dae-jung kyŏngjeron* [A Complete Collection of Kim Dae-jung's Works, 2: Mass Economics] (Seoul: Han'gyŏnggwayŏn, 1989).

18. Kim Yŏng-sun, "Yusinch'eje suripwŏnin-e kwanhan yŏn'gu" [A Study of the Establishment of the Yushin Regime], 68.

19. Pae Kŭng-ch'an, "Niksŭn taktŭrin-gwa tongasia-ŭi kwŏnwijuŭi ch'eje-ŭi tŭngjang: Han'guk, P'ilip'in kŭrigo Indonesia-ŭi pigyo punsŏk" [The Nixon Doctrine and the Rise of Authoritarian Regimes in East Asia: A Comparative Analysis Among Korea, Philippines, and Indonesia], *Korean Political Science Review* 22, no. 2 (1988), 329; Kim Yŏng-myŏng, "Yushin ch'eje-ŭi surip-gwa chŏn'gae" [The Establishment of the Yushin Regime and Its Development], *Han'guk chŏngch'i oegyosa nonch'ong* 15 (1997), 208); and Son Hak-kyu, *Authoritarianism and Opposition in South Korea* (London: Routledge, 1989).

20. Chŏng Yun-hyŏng, "Yushin ch'eje-wa 8.3 choch'i-ŭi sŏnggyŏk" [The *Yushin* Regime and the Nature of the August 3 Measure] in *Han'guk kyŏngjeron* [A Theory of the Korean Economy] (Seoul: Kkach'i, 1987).

21. Yi Sŏng-hyŏng, "Kukka, kyegŭp mit chabon ch'ukchŏk" [The State, Class, and Capital Accumulation] in *Han'guk chabonjuŭi-wa kukka* [Capitalism and the State in Korea], ed. Ch'oe Chang-jip (Seoul: Hanul, 1985), 248.

22. Jung-en Woo, *Race to the Swift: State and Finance in Korean Industrialization* (New York: Columbia University Press, 1991), 124.

23. The rate of export increase slowed down steadily from 42 percent in 1968, to 34 percent in 1969, to 28 percent in 1970.

24. In 1968, the trade deficit amounted to $1 billion, by 1970, total foreign debts amounted to $2.5 billion and the repayment of principal and interest amounted to $160 million.

25. Yi Sŏng-hyŏng, "Kukka, kyegŭp mit chabon ch'ukjŏk" [The State, Class, and Capital Accumulation], 257.

26. The monthly inflation rate in April 1970 was 8.4 percent and the fiscal deficit from January to April 1970 amounted to 18.5 billion won.

27. The economic growth rate decreased from 13.8 percent in 1969, 7.6 percent in 1970, 8.8 percent in 1971, to 5.7 percent in 1972. Yi Sŏng-hyŏng, "Kukka, kyekŭp mit chabon ch'ukchŏk" [The State, Class, and Capital Accumulation].

28. Kim Chŏng-ryŏm, *Han'guk kyŏngje chŏngch'aek samsimnyŏnsa: Kim Chŏng-ryŏm hoegorok* [A 30-Year History of Korea's Economic Policy: The Recollections of Kim Chŏng-ryŏm] (Seoul: JoongAng Ilbosa, 1990), 263.

29. Given the fact that the interest rate for private loans was 3.84 percent per month at the time of the Emergency Decree, the readjusted interest rate of 1.35 percent reduced the burden of interest payments for the concerned firms by one third. Ibid., 269.

30. Ibid., 269–271.

31. Kim Chŏng-ryŏm, *A! Park Chung Hee: Kim Chŏng-ryŏm chŏngch'ihoegorok* [Ah! Park Chung Hee: Kim Chŏng-ryŏm's Reflections on Politics] (Seoul: JoongAng M&B, 1997), 280.

32. Kim Chae-hong, *Munminsidaeeŭi kunbuwa kwŏllyŏk* [The Military in the Age of Civilian Rule and Power] (Seoul: Nanam, 1992), 97.

33. Ibid., 97–102.

34. Young Whan Kihl, *Politics and Policies in Divided Korea* (Boulder: Westview Press, 1984), 57.

35. The testimony of the U.S. ambassador to South Korea, William Porter, before the Committee on Foreign Relations of the U.S. Senate, February 24, 1970, indicates that the United States advised South Korea to initiate talks with the North.

36. Yi Sang-u, *Park Chung Hee sidae* [The Era of Park Chung Hee], 239–241.

37. Yi Chŏng-bok, "Sanŏphwa-wa chŏngch'i ch'eje-ui pyŏnhwa" [Industrialization and Change in the Korean Political System], *Korean Political Science Review* 19 (1985): 67.

38. Tun-jen Cheng, "Political Regimes and Development Strategies: South Korea and Taiwan," in Gary Gereffi and Donald L.Wyman, eds., *Manufacturing Miracles: Paths of Industrialization in Latin America and East Asia* (Princeton: Princeton University Press, 1990).

39. Hyug Baeg Im, "The Rise of Bureaucratic Authoritarianism in South Korea," 254–257.

40. Park Chung Hee, *Kukka-wa hyŏngmyŏng-gwa na* [The Nation, the Revolution, and I]

41. "We were not consulted about the decision and quite obviously not associated with it." U.S. Senate Staff Report, "Korea and Philippines: November 1972," February 8, 1973.

42. Ibid.

43. Niccolò Machiavelli, *The Prince*, trans. and ed. Robert M. Adams (New York: W. W. Norton, 1977), 50.

9. The *Chaebol*

We gratefully acknowledge the research assistance provided by Hee Eun Kim, Bo Ram Kwon, and Kyung Mi Yoon of Ewha Womans University and Won Jun Jang and Sang Geun Lee of Korea University.

1. Consult Paul J. DiMaggio and Walter W. Powell, "The Iron Cage Revisited: Institutional Isomorphism and Collective Rationality in Organizational Fields," *American Sociological Review* 48 (1983): 147–160; Walter W. Powell and Paul J. DiMaggio, eds., *The New Institutionalism in Organizational Analysis* (Chicago: University of Chicago Press, 1991).

2. Eun Mee Kim, *Big Business, Strong State: Collusion and Conflict in South Korean Development, 1960–1990* (Albany: State University of New York Press, 1997).

3. Stephen Haggard, "Business, Politics and Policy in East and Southeast Asia," in *Behind East Asian Growth: The Political and Social Foundations of Prosperity*, ed. H. Rowen (New York: Routledge, 1998), 82–83.

4. Less than 8 percent of the ministers and vice ministers of the Park era went on to work for leading *chaebol* groups. Calculated from http://db.chosun.com.

5. *Amakudari*, or "descent from heaven," refers to the Japanese corporate practice of hiring retired state bureaucrats for high-ranking managerial positions.

6. Interview on February 5, 2001, with Yi Chun-lim, who rose to the rank of CEO of Hyundai Engineering and Construction, Hyundai Heavy Industries, and Hyundai General Trading Company.

7. Kim Byŏng-kuk, *Pundan-gwa hyŏngmyŏng-ŭi tonghak: han'guk-kwa meksik'o-ŭi chŏngch'i kyŏngje* [The Dynamics of National Division and Revolution: The Political Economy of Korea and Mexico] (Seoul: Munhak-kwa chisŏngsa, 1994).

8. *Han'guk yŏn'gam* [Korea Yearbook], (Seoul: Han'guk yŏn'gamsa, 1961, 1962).

9. Leroy P. Jones and Il Sakong, *Government Business and Entrepreneurship in Economic Development: The Korean Case* (Cambridge, Mass.: Harvard University Press, 1980), 353.

10. Mark L. Clifford, *Troubled Tiger: Businessmen, Bureaucrats and Generals in South Korea* (New York: M. E. Sharpe, 1998), 63.

11. Kim Chin-hyŏn, "Pujŏng ch'ukchae ch'ŏri chŏnmalsŏ" [The Final Report on the Prosecution of Illicit Profiteers], *Sindonga*, December 1964, 174.

12. Interview with Kim Ip-sam, former executive deputy chairman of the FKI (1960–1981) conducted on February 9, 2001.

13. Pak Tong-ch'ul, "1960nyŏndae kiŏpchiptan-ŭi hyŏngsŏng-gwa kujo" [The Formation and Structure of Business Groups in the 1960s], in *1960nyŏndae han'guk-ŭi kongŏphwa-wa kyŏngjegujo* [The Industrialization and Economic Structure of South Korea in the 1960s], ed. Han'guk chŏngsin munhwa yŏn'guwŏn [Academy of Korean Studies] (Seoul: Paeksansŏdang, 1999), 50.

14. Eun Mee Kim, *Big Business, Strong State*, 110.

15. Pak Tong-Ch'ul, "1960nyŏndae kiŏpchiptan-ŭi hyŏngsŏng-gwa kujo" [The Formation and Structure of Business Groups in the 1960s], 52.

16. Pak Tong-ch'ul, "1960nyŏndae kiŏpchiptan-ŭi hyŏngsŏng-gwa kujo" [The Formation and Structure of Business Groups in the 1960s], 19.

17. Kang Ch' ŏl-gyu, Ch'oe Chŏng-p'yo, and Chang Chi-sang, *Chaebol: sŏngjang-ŭi juyŏk-in'ga tamyok-ŭi hwasin-in'ga* [*Chaebol*: Are They the Main Contributor to Economic Development or the Devil of Greed] (Seoul: Pibong ch'ulp'ansa, 1991), 134.

18. Based on an interview with Yi Chun-lim on February 5, 2001, and also from Chŏng Chu-yŏng, *Yi ttang-e t'aeŏnasŏ: na-ŭi salaon iyagi* [Born in South Korea: My Life Story] (Seoul: Sol chulp'ansa, 1998).

19. Kim Sang-gwŏn, "Kiŏpchiptan-ŭi sŏngjang-gwa tagakhwa kwajŏng" [Growth and Diversification of Business Groups], in *Han'guk-ŭi kiŏp chiptan* [South Korea's Business Groups], ed. South Korea Economic Research Institute (Seoul: South Korea Economic Research Institute, 1995), 43.

20. Donald Kirk, *Korean Dynasty: Hyundai and Chŏng Chu-yŏng* (New York: M. E. Sharpe, 1994).

21. Eun Mee Kim, *Big Business, Strong State*, 132.

22. Chŏng Chu-yŏng, *Yi ttang-e t'aeŏnasŏ* [Born in South Korea].

23. David Cole and Y. C. Park, *Financial Development in South Korea, 1945–1978* (Cambridge, Mass.: Harvard University Press, 1979).

24. Bank of Korea, *Flow of Funds Account*.

25. Bank of Korea, *Economic Statistics Yearbook*.

26. Eun Mee Kim, *Big Business, Strong State*, 147.

27. Kim In-yŏng, *Han'guk-ŭi kyŏngje sŏngjang: kukka chudoron-gwa kiŏp chudoron* [South Korea's Economic Development: State-Led Arguments and Corporate-Led Arguments] (Seoul: Chayugiŏp Center), 105.

28. Ibid., 104.

29. Kim Yong-hwan, *Imja, chane-ga saryŏnggwan anin'ga: Kim Yong-hwan hoegorok: kyŏngjegaebalgyehoek-butŏ IMF oehwan wigi-kkaji kyŏktonggi-ŭi han'guk kyŏngjesa* [You are the Real Commander: Memoir of Kim Yong-hwan: A History of the Rapidly Changing Korean Economy from the Five Year Economic Development Plans (FYEDP) to the IMF Foreign Exchange Crisis] (Seoul: Maeilgyŏngje sinmunsa, 2002).

30. Eun Mee Kim, *Big Business, Strong State,* 149.

31. Bank of Korea, *8.3 Kin'gŭp kyŏngjejoch'i chonghap pogosŏ* [Full report on the president's Emergency Decree of August 3, 1972] (Seoul: Bank of South Korea, 1973); Kim Chŏng-ryŏm, *Han'guk kyŏngje chŏngch'aek 30nyŏnsa: Kim Chŏng-ryŏm hoegorok* [A 30-Year History of Korea's Economic Policy: The Recollections of Kim Chŏng-ryŏm] (Seoul: JoongAng Ilbosa, 1990), 269; Eun Mee Kim, *Big Business, Strong State.*

32. Eun Mee Kim, *Big Business, Strong State,* 147.

33. Sŏ Chae-jin, *Han'guk-ŭi chabon'ga kyegŭp* [Capitalist Class of South Korea] (Seoul: Nanam, 1991), 3.

34. Eun Mee Kim, *Big Business, Strong State.*

35. Ibid.

36. Ibid., 146, 157.

37. Interview with Yi Chun-lim.

38. South Korean Economic Research Institute, *Han'guk-ŭi kiŏp chiptan* [South Korea's Business Groups] (Seoul: South Korean Economic Research Institute, 1995).

39. See Kim Yun-t'ae, *Chaebol-gwa kwŏllyŏk* [Chaebol and Power] (Seoul: Saeroun saramdŭl, 2000), 125; and Seok Ki Kim, "Business Concentration and Government Policy: A Study of the Phenomenon of Business Groups in South Korea, 1945–1985," D.B.A. dissertation, Harvard University (1987).

40. Eun Mee Kim, *Big Business, Strong State.*

41. Ibid.

42. Ibid.,161–164.

43. Ibid.

44. Alice Amsden, *Asia's Next Giant: South Korea and Late Industrialization* (New York: Oxford University Press, 1989).

45. Myoung-Han Kang, *The Korean Business Conglomerate: Chaebol Then and Now,* Korea Research Monograph (Berkeley: Institute of East Asian Studies, University of California, Berkeley, 1960), 180.

46. Ibid.

47. Richard M. Steers, *Made in South Korea: Chung Ju Young and the Rise of Hyundai* (London: Routledge, 1999), 109–110.

48. Haeoe kŏnsŏl hyŏphoe [International Contractors Association of Korea], *Haeoe kŏnsŏl hyŏphoe 5nyŏnsa* [5 Years of the Foreign Construction Committee] (Seoul: International Contractors Association of Korea, 1982).

49. Interview with a former executive of Daewoo on December 22, 2000.

50. Seok-Jin Lew, "Bringing Capital Back in: A Case Study of the South Korean Automobile Industrialization," Ph.D. dissertation, Yale University (1992).

51. South Korean Economic Research Institute, *Han'gugŭi kiŏpchiptan* [South Korea's Business Groups].

52. Samsung's Secretarial Office, *Samsung 6onyŏnsa* [Sixty Years of Samsung] (Seoul: Samsung's Secretarial Office, 1998).

53. Samsung's Secretarial Office, *Samsung 6onyŏnsa* [Sixty Years of Samsung]; Hyundai Engineering and Construction, *Hyundai kŏnsŏl 5onyŏnsa* [Fifty-Year History of Hyundai Engineering and Construction] (Seoul: Hyundai Engineering and Construction, 1997); Ssangyong, *Ssangyong 5onyŏnsa* [Ssangyong's Fifty Years] (Seoul: Ssangyong, 1989); Sŏn'gyŏng's Public Relations Office, *Sŏn'gyŏng 4onyŏnsa* [Sŏn'gyŏng's Forty-Year History] (Seoul: Sŏn'gyŏng's Public Relations Office, 1993).

10. The Automobile Industry

1. Douglas Bennett and Kenneth Sharpe, *Transnational Corporations versus the State: The Political Economy of the Mexican Auto Industry* (Princeton: Princeton University Press, 1985); Rhys Jenkins, *Transnational Corporations and the Latin American Automobile Industry* (Pittsburgh: University of Pittsburgh Press, 1987).

2. Korean Automobile Industries Cooperative Association (KAICA), *Chadongch'a chohap 20 nyŏnsa* [The Twenty-Year History of the Korean Automobile Industries Cooperative] (Seoul: KAICA, 1983).

3. Chuk-Kyo Kim and Chul-Huei Lee, "Ancillary Firm Development in the Korean Automobile Industry," in *The Motor Vehicle Industry in Asia: A Study of Ancillary Firm Development,* ed. Konosuke Odaka (Singapore: Singapore National University, 1983).

4. Hyung-Wook Kim and Saul Park, *KCIA Chief's Testimony: Revolution and Idol,* vol. 1 (New York: Korean Independent Monitor, 1984), 195–197.

5. The three scandals included KCIA-orchestrated stock market speculation, the irregular construction of Walker Hill Hotel, and the illegal operation of slot machines. Like the Saenara debacle, they were caused by Kim Chong-p'il's efforts to finance Park's entry into the 1963 presidential election on the ticket of the yet-to-be organized DRP. Ibid., 1:193–198.

6. Dal-Joong Chang, *Economic Control and Political Authoritarianism: The Role of Japanese Corporations in Korean Politics, 1965–1979* (Seoul: Sogang University, 1985), 118–132.

7. *Dong-A Ilbo,* August 26, 1965.

8. *Sindonga,* (November 1984), 420–421; *Sindonga,* (March 1989), 309–314.

9. Dal-Joong Chang, *Economic Control and Political Authoritarianism,* 127.

10. O Wŏn-Ch'ŏl, *Han'gukhyŏng kyŏngje kŏnsŏl: enjiniŏring ŏp'ŭroch'i 4* [Korean-Style Economic Development: An Engineering Approach, vol. 4] (Seoul: Kia kyŏngje yŏn'guso, 1996), 118.

11. Ibid., 4:119–135.

12. Korea Institute of Science and Technology, *On the Foundation of the Heavy*

Industry Development: The Analysis of the Machinery and Material Industry (Seoul: KIST, 1970).

13. Seok-Jin Lew, "Bringing Capital Back In: A Case Study of the South Korean Automobile Industrialization" (Ph.D. diss., Yale University, 1992), chap. 4.

14. Ministry of Commerce and Industry, *Changgi chadongch'a kong'ŏp jinhŭng kyehoek: han'gukhyŏng sohyŏngsŭngyongch'a-ŭi yangsanhwa* [Long-term Plan for the Promotion of the Automobile Industry: Mass Production of Compact Korean Automobiles] (Seoul: Ministry of Commerce and Industry, 1974), 301; Byung-Kook Kim, "Bringing and Managing Socioeconomic Change: The State in Korea and Mexico" (Ph.D. diss., Harvard University, 1987), 221–229.

15. Jung-En Woo, *Race to the Swift: State and Finance in Korean Industrialization* (New York: Columbia University Press, 1991).

16. O Wŏn-ch'ŏl, *Han'gukhyŏng kyŏngje kŏnsŏl: enjiniŏring ŏp'ŭroch'i 4* [Korean-Style Economic Development: An Engineering Approach, vol.4], 164–165.

17. Alice Amsden, *Asia's Next Giant: South Korea and Late Industrialization* (New York: Oxford University Press, 1989), 291–318.

18. Jeff Frieden, "Third World Indebted Industrialization: International Finance and State Capitalism in Mexico, Brazil, Algeria, and South Korea," *International Organization* 35 (Summer 1981).

19. Kyu-Uck Lee, *Industrial Development Policies and Issues* (Seoul: Korea Development Institute, 1986).

20. Hyundai Motors, *Hyundai chadongch'a isimnyŏnsa* [Twenty Years of Hyundai Motors] (Seoul: Hyundai Motors, 1988), 382–384.

21. On the industrial relations of the South Korean automobile industry, see Korea Institute of Labor, *Chadongch'a kong'ŏp-ŭi nosa kwan'gye* [Labor Relations in the Auto Industry] (Seoul: Han'guk nodong yŏnguwŏn, 1989); and Kyu-Han Bae, *Automobile Workers in Korea* (Seoul: Seoul National University Press, 1987).

22. John Krafcik, "A First Look at Performance Levels at New Entrants Assembly Plants," research manuscript, International Motor Vehicle Project, MIT, 1991.

23. On the organizational features of the *chaebol,* see Richard Steers et al., *Chaebols: Korea's New Industrial Might* (New York: Harper & Row, 1989); and S. Yoo and S. M. Lee, "Management Style and Practice in Korean Chaebols," *California Management Review* 29 (1987).

24. Korea Institute for Economics and Technology (KIET), *Chadongch'a sanŏp changgi palchŏn kusang* [Long-Term Plan of the Auto Industry] (Seoul: Korea Institute for Economics and Technology, 1990), 68.

11. Pohang Iron & Steel Company

1. Park Chung Hee, *Kukka-wa hyŏngmyŏng-gwa na* [The Nation, the Revolution, and I] (Seoul: Hyangmunsa, 1963), 114.

2. Robert Wade, *Governing the Market: Economic Theory and the Role of*

Government in East Asian Industrialization (Princeton: Princeton University Press, 1990), 319; World Bank, *Korea: Managing the Industrial Transition,* 1 (Washington, D.C.: World Bank, 1987), 45.

3. *POSCO Weekly,* May 31, 2001.

4. For developmental state theories, see Alice H. Amsden, *Asia's Next Giant: South Korea and Late Industrialization* (New York: Oxford University Press, 1989); Chalmers Johnson, "Political Institutions and Economic Performance: The Government-Business Relationship in Japan, South Korea, and Taiwan," in *The Political Economy of the New Asian Industrialism,* ed. Frederic C. Deyo (Ithaca: Cornell University Press, 1987).

5. *Dong-A Ilbo,* January 31, 1961.

6. "Memorandum for Mr. McGeorge Bundy: Accomplishment of American Investment Group Headed by General Van Fleet in Korea (June 19, 1962)," National Security File, John F. Kennedy Library [hereafter JFKL].

7. "From Berger and Killen to Secretary of State" (July 30, 1962), National Security File, JFKL.

8. Department of State, "Japan: Department of State Guidelines for Policy and Operations (October 1961)," Thompson Papers, Box 17, JFKL.

9. Beginning in 1969, the United States put in place voluntary export restraint (VER) arrangements with Japan and Europe in the steel industry.

10. Pak T'ae-jun, "Pak T'ae-jun hoegorok: bulch'ŏrŏm salda" [Pak T'ae-jun Memoir: Living like Fire], *Sindonga,* June 1992, 465.

11. The IECOK was formed in 1966 to finance the South Korean Second Five-Year Economic Development Plan.

12. Pohang chonghapchech'ŏl chusikhoesa, *Pohang chech'ŏl 20nyŏnsa* [History of POSCO: 20 Years] (Pohang: Pohang chonghapchech'ŏl chusikhoesa, 1989), 136–137.

13. In 1956, Taiwan also made an attempt to push a heavy and chemical industrialization drive by constructing an iron mill, but gave up the project because the United States refused to support the construction, stating that it was an extravagance (Noble, *Collective Action in East Asia*) (Ithaca: Cornell University Press, 1998), 73.

14. Ho-sŏp Kim, "Policy-Making of Japanese Official Development Assistance to the Republic of Korea, 1965–1983" (Ph.D. diss., University of Michigan, 1987), 133–134.

15. Ibid.

16. While Pak T'ae-jun was approaching Japan for the use of reparation funds, the EPB was also trying to reverse the United States Export-Import Bank's decision between February and May 1969.

17. Interview with Ariga Toshihiko by Sang-young, Tokyo, January 29, 1993.

18. Fuji Steel and Yawata Steel combined in March 1970 to form Nippon Steel.

19. *Nihon Keizai Shimbun,* August 23, 1969.

20. *Mainichi Shimbun,* August 28, 1969.

21. *Nihon Keizai Shimbun,* September 6, 1969. To be sure, Chinese premier Zhou Enlai's 1970 declaration of the "Four Principles" was to have a chilling effect on South Korean–Japanese economic ties during the early 1970s by getting Japanese companies to readjust downward the importance of trading relations

with South Korea and Taiwan in order to increase economic transactions with China. The Four Principles even made Toyota Motors divest and withdraw from the South Korean market in 1972 (see Chapter 10). The Japanese steel industry, however, was largely unaffected by the Chinese Four Principles, and the POSCO project was able to proceed with the support of Japan's business and political leaders.

22. *Mainichi Shimbun,* August 28, 1969.

23. Kim Chŏng-ryŏm, *Han'guk kyŏngje chŏngch'aek 30nyŏnsa: Kim Chŏng-ryŏm hoegorok* [A 30-Year History of Korea's Economic Policy: the Recollections of Kim Chŏng-ryŏm] (Seoul: JoonAng Ilbosa, 1990), 36. In sharp contrast, Taiwan's Kuomintang regime refused to construct a large integrated steel mill for fear of upsetting the steel industry it then had, dominated by small- and medium-sized enterprises. The Taiwanese Kuomintang regime did not want to undermine its monopoly of political power by creating *chaebol*-like industrial conglomerates. See Gregory W. Noble, *Collective Action in East Asia: How Ruling Parties Shape Industrial Policy* (Ithaca: Cornell University Press, 1998), 72–92.

24. O Wŏn-ch'ŏl, "Sanŏp chŏllyak kŭndaesa 120" [History of Industrial Strategy], *Han'guk kyŏngje sinmun* [Korean Economic Daily], May 24, 1993.

25. POSCO, *POSCO I Visited: Its Secret of Success* (Pohang: POSCO, 1994), 94.

26. Their friendship went back to 1948, when then-cadet Pak T'ae-jun met then-instructor Park Chung Hee at the Korea Military Academy. On the eve of the military coup in May 1961, Park Chung Hee even entrusted the lives of his family to Pak. In addition to this unequivocal support from South Korea's highest political authority, Pak's experience gained from operating Korea Tungsten Corporation, a state enterprise, for four years before joining POSCO as its CEO in 1968 prepared Pak well for his managerial tasks at POSCO.

27. Kim Chŏng-ryŏm, *Han'guk kyŏngje chŏngch'aek 30nyŏnsa* [A 30-Year History of Korea's Economic Policy], 135.

28. Interview with Pak T'ae-jun by Sang-young Rhyn, Seoul, March 29, 2001.

29. *POSCO I Visited,* 1994, 414–418.

30. Procurement for the construction of POSCO was carried out without kickbacks. Pak T'ae-jun received a written mandate directly from the president that he used to block pressure from domestic and foreign lobbyists. POSCO, *Pohang chech'ŏl 20nyŏnsa* [History of POSCO 20 Years] (Seoul: POSCO, 1989), 168–170; interview with Pak T'ae-jun, Tokyo, January 27, 1993.

31. Ken-ichi Imai, "Japan's Corporate Networks," in *The Political Economy of Japan 3: Cultural and Social Dynamics,* ed. Shumpei Kumon and Henry Rosovsky (Stanford: Stanford University Press, 1992), 229.

32. Interview with Pak T'ae-jun by Sang-young Rhyn, Tokyo, January 27, 1993.

12. The Countryside

1. Jae-On Kim and B. C. Koh, "The Dynamics of Electoral Politics," in *Political Participation in Korea,* ed. Chong Lim Kim (Santa Barbara, Calif.: Clio Books 1980), 67–68.

2. Yun Ch'ŏn-ju, "Ŭpmin-ŭi t'up'yo haengt'ae: ŭp-ŭi kŏnsŏl-ŭn minjujŏngch'i hyangsang-ŭl ŭimihanda" [The Voting Behavior of Townspeople: Improving Democratic Politics through Developing Towns], *Aseayŏn'gu* [*Asian Studies*] 7 (June 1961).

3. Chong Lim Kim, Young Whan Kihl, and Seong-Tong Pai, "The Modes of Citizen Participation: An Analysis of Nation-Wide Survey Results," in *Political Participation in Korea,* ed. Chong Lim Kim (California: Clio Books, 1980).

4. Ibid.

5. See Park Chung Hee, *Uri minjok-ŭi nagal gil: sahoejaegŏn- ŭi inyŏm* [Our Nation's Path: The Ideology of Social Reconstruction] (Seoul: Tonga ch'ulp'ansa, 1962); and *Kukka-wa hyŏngmyŏng-gwa na* [The Nation, the Revolution, and I] (Seoul: Hyangmunsa, 1963). Also consult James Palais, "'Democracy' in South Korea, 1948–72," in *Without Parallel: The American-Korean Relationship since 1945,* ed. Frank Baldwin (New York: Pantheon Books, 1974), 332; and Joungwon Alexander Kim, *The Divided Korea: The Politics of Development, 1945–72* (Cambridge, Mass.: East Asian Research Center, Harvard University, 1975), 248.

6. Park Chung Hee, *Kukka-wa hyŏngmyŏng-gwa na* [The Nation, the Revolution, and I], 177.

7. Ministry of Agriculture and Forestry (MAF), as quoted in *Chosun Ilbo,* June 21,1961: 1. According to a field study of Ch'ungju and Chŏngwŏn, North Ch'ungch'ŏng Province, commissioned by the U.S. Operations Mission (USOM), 88 percent of the rural households were owner-farmers; 8 percent, part owner-part tenants; and the remaining 4 percent, pure tenants. Statistics: *Chosun Ilbo,* March 5, 1961, 4.

8. The rural household owned less than one hectare (that is, less than 2.47 acres) of farmland on average, which produced barely enough to sustain a family of six members. *Chosun Ilbo,* June 21, 1961, 1.

9. See S. H. Ban et al., *Rural Development: Studies in the Modernization of the Republic of Korea, 1945–1975* (Cambridge, Mass.: Council on East Asian Studies, Harvard University, 1980), 234–245.

10. For example, in 1960, the government purchase price of an 80 kg bag of rice was 1,059 wŏn, about 81 percent of the production cost. Ibid., 240.

11. Ibid., 237.

12. Samuel P. Huntington, *Political Order in Changing Societies* (New Haven: Yale University Press, 1968), 74–75.

13. For details of administrative control in the Park era, see Sŏ Chu-sŏk, "Park Chung Hee sidae-ŭi kungmint'ongje: haengjŏngch'echerŭl chungsimŭro" [Citizen Control in the Park Chung Hee Era: With Reference to Administrative System], paper presented at a special conference on the Park Chung Hee era, organized by the Korean Political Science Association, April 7, 2000.

14. The village heads *(ijang)* in the rural area and the block heads *(t'ongjang)* in the cities were not government officials in the formal sense. However, they were virtual extensions of and appendages to the local administration. As such, they were paid various "allowances" in return for their services.

15. Ban et al., *Rural Development,* 272.

16. *Chosun Ilbo*, September 6, 1963, 3.
17. *Chosun Ilbo*, May 14, 1961, 1, 2.
18. *Chosun Ilbo*, March 17, 1961, 3.
19. *Chosun Ilbo*, April 29, May 2–5, 1961; May 9, 1961, 1.
20. Ministry of Agriculture and Forestry (MAF), "Nongjŏng pansegi" [A Half Century of Agricultural Administration], 2000. Available at http://www.maf.go.kr/intro/.
21. Park Chung Hee, *Kukka-wa hyŏngmyŏng-gwa na* [The Nation, the Revolution, and I].
22. Gilbert T. Brown, *Korean Pricing Policies and Economic Development in the 1960s* (Baltimore: Johns Hopkins University Press, 1973), 49.
23. *Chosun Ilbo*, July 13, August 4, 1961.
24. *Chosun Ilbo*, December 24, 1961, 1.
25. *Chosun Ilbo*, January 31, 1962, 1.
26. *Chosun Ilbo*, February 20, 1962, 1.
27. MAF, "Nongjŏng panseki" [A Half Century of Agricultural Administration].
28. *Chosun Ilbo*, September 18, 1961, 1.
29. Yi Yŏng-jo, "Minjugonghwadang ch'angdang kwajŏng e kwanhan han yŏn'gu" [A Study of the Formation Process of the Democratic Republican Party] (M.A. thesis, Seoul National University, 1982).
30. *Time*, October 25, 1963.
31. *Chosun Ilbo*, August 30, 1963, 1.
32. *Chosun Ilbo*, August 31, 1963, 7; September 7, 1963, 2.
33. *Chosun Ilbo*, September 3, 1963, 7.
34. *Chosun Ilbo*, September 4, 1963, 7.
35. *Chosun Ilbo*, September 3, 1963, 7.
36. *Chosun Ilbo*, September 4, 1963, 7; September 10, 1963, 7.
37. *Chosun Ilbo*, September 11, 1963, 7; September 27, 1963, 7.
38. *Chosun Ilbo*, September 18, 1963, 1.
39. *Chosun Ilbo*, October 2, 1963, 7.
40. *Chosun Ilbo*, October 17, 1963, 3.
41. *Chosun Ilbo*, September 27, 1963, 1.
42. Democratic Republican Party (DRP), *Kyŏngnang-ŭl hech'igo: minjugonghwadang 2nyŏnsa* [Through the Raging Waves: A Two-Year History of the DRP] (Seoul: Minjugonghwadang chungang samuguk, 1964), 104, 120.
43. Calculated from the Central Election Management Committee's data.
44. Interview, February 23, 2001.
45. *Chosun Ilbo*, September 6, 1963, 3.
46. Interviews, February 21, 2001.
47. DRP, *Kyŏngnang-ŭl hech'igo* [Through the Raging Waves], 139.
48. The election law favored the leading party, by providing that it receive half of the listed "national" seats if it won less than 50 percent of votes; two-thirds of the seats if it won 50 or more percent of votes.
49. BOK (Bank of Korea), *Kyŏngje t'onggye yŏnbo, 1965* [Economic Statistics Yearbook, 1965], (Seoul: Bank of Korea, 1965).
50. *Chosun Ilbo*, October 22, October 24, 1963.

51. *Chosun Ilbo,* November 15, 1963, 2.

52. It was at this time of strategic change that Albert O. Hirschman's *The Strategy of Economic Development* (New Haven: Yale University Press, 1958) was published by the Korea Productivity Center, on which the government had strong influence. The book, advocating the unbalanced growth strategy, became a bible for technocrats and some intellectuals.

53. S. H. Ban et al., *Rural Development,* 240, table 105, and 247, table 109.

54. Avishay Braverman, Choong Yong Ahn, and Jeffrey S. Hammer, *Alternative Agricultural Pricing Policies in the Republic of Korea: Their Implications for Government Deficits, Income Distribution, and Balance of Payments,* World Bank Staff Working Papers no. 621 (Washington, D.C.: World Bank, 1983), 130, table 12.

55. Braverman, Ahn, and Hammer, *Alternative Agricultural Pricing Policies in the Republic of Korea: Their Implications for Government Deficits, Income Distribution, and Balance of Payments,* 5–6, 109–117.

56. *Chosun Ilbo,* January 24, 1967, 1; January 27, 1967, 1.

57. Yi Kwan-ch'ŏl, "Ŏnŭ nongmin-ŭi kagyebu: Ssalnongsa-nŭn chŏkja. Su'ip 7manwŏnjŭng, chich'ul 10manwŏnjŭng" [The Accounts of a Peasant Household: Growing Rice Is a Losing Business. Income at 70,000 Won and Expenditure at 100,000 Won], *Chosun Ilbo,* January 31, 1967, 1. See also *Chosun Ilbo,* April 14, 1967, 2.

58. Sŏng Sin-gŭn, "Han nongmin-ŭi ch'ehŏmgi: non'gap kyesok harak. Nonp'ara ija patnŭn'gŏsi nongsa poda natda" [Experiences of a Peasant: The Price of Farmlands Falls Continuously. It is Better to Sell Farmlands and Earn Interest than Growing Rice], *Chosun Ilbo,* February 1, 1967, 1.

59. J. A. Kim, *The Divided Korea,* 271.

60. Sung Chick Hong, *The Intellectual and Modernization: A Study of Korean Attitudes* (Seoul: Social Research Institute, Korea University, 1967).

61. New Democratic Party (NDP), *6.8 Pujŏngsŏn'gŏbaeksŏ* [White Paper on Election Rigging in the June 8th Election] (Seoul: NDP, 1967).

62. Edward S. Mason et al., *The Economic and Social Modernization of the Republic of Korea* (Cambridge, Mass.: Council on East Asian Studies, Harvard University, 1980), 98, table 12.

63. See ibid., 428, table 127.

64. Ministry of Agriculture and Forestry, "Nongjŏng panseki" [A Half Century of Agricultural Administration].

65. *Korea Annual,* 1972. See also Man-gap Lee, "Pushing or Pulling" in *Report of the International Conference on Urban Problems and Regional Development* (Seoul: Yonsei University, 1970); John E. Sloboda, "Off-Farm Migration," in *Rural Development,* ed. Ban et al.; Kazuo Kuramochi, "Rodoreki no kyokyu to roson no henyo" [Labor Supply and Changes of Rural Villages], in *Kankoku kogyoka-no kozo* [The Structure of Korean Industrialization], ed. Tamio Hattori (Tokyo: Ajiakeizai kenkyusho, 1987), 172–173.

66. Chae-Jin Lee, "South Korea: Political Competition and Government Adaptation," *Asian Survey* (January 1972), 42.

67. Economic Planning Board,, *Korean Economic Indicators* (Seoul, March 1982), 70.
68. Economists had long recommended the two-tier grain price system. See Chu Chong-hwan, "Kukka kyŏngje-e issŏsŏ nong' ŏp: chŏngch'aekchŏk koch'al" [Agriculture in the National Economy: A Policy Review], *Chosun Ilbo,* January 26, 1967, 1.
69. Kira N. Greene, "Agricultural Policies and Political Competition in Korea, 1962–1988" (Ph.D. diss., Stanford University, 1997), 129–131.
70. *Chosun Ilbo,* November 11, 1972, 2.
71. Mick Moore, "Mobilization and Disillusion in Rural Korea: The Saemaŭl Movement in Retrospect," *Pacific Affairs* 57, no. 4 (Winter 1984–85): 587.
72. Jin-Hwan Park, "Introduction," in *Saemaŭl: Korea's New Community Movement,* by Park Chung Hee (Seoul: Secretariat of the President, Republic of Korea, 1979), 1. These goals are almost the exact replica of those of the PMNR of the junta period: hard work, frugality, perseverance, and self-help.
73. It was in 1973, after the *yushin* era began, that the *Saemaŭl undong,* aided by increased government investment, began to show positive results in rural life. See Ban et al., *Rural Development,* 275–280.
74. Park Chung Hee, *Saemaŭl: Korea's New Community Movement,* 129.
75. Jae-On Kim and B. C. Koh, "Regionalism and Voter Alignment," in *Party Politics and Elections in Korea,* ed. C. I. Eugene Kim and Young Whan Kihl (Silver Spring, Md.: Research Institute on Korean Affairs, 1976).
76. Albert O. Hirschman, "The Changing Tolerance for Income Inequality in the Course of Economic Development," *Quarterly Journal of Economics* 87 (November 1983): 544–565.
77. Interview, February 21, 2001.
78. Interview, February 21, 2001.
79. Interview, February 21, 2001.
80. Interview, February 22, 2001.
81. Interview, February 23, 2001.
82. James C. Scott, *The Moral Economy of the Peasant* (New Haven: Yale University Press, 1976), chaps. 1 and 2.

13. The *Chaeya*

1. A survey of *chaeya* leaders of the 1970s showed their moralistically articulated self-identity. Only 14.9 percent saw themselves as engaging in "political activities," whereas 24 percent thought they were participating as "citizens." On the other hand, 64.9 percent said that they had joined the *chaeya* out of their sense of "moral imperatives," while 32.4 percent identified "reform as their prime motive." See Ryu Kŭn-il, *Kwŏnwijuŭich'ejeha-ŭi minjuhwa undong yŏn'gu: 1960–70nyŏndae chedo'oejŏk pandaeseryŏk-ŭi hyŏngsŏngggwajŏng* [A Study of the Democratization Movements under an Authoritarian Regime: The Formation Process of Extra-Institutional Opposition Forces in the 1960s and 1970s] (Seoul: Nanam, 1997), 112.

2. Given South Korea's anticommunist political culture, the *chaeya* dissidents' public declarations were devoid of any Marxist-Leninist anti-imperialist ideas. But these ideas had been present in *chaeya* circles from the bottom up for a long time. The *chaeya* leaders of the 1970s included writings by Mao Zedong (1), Marx (3), V. I. Lenin (6), and Ho Chi Minh (14) among their 15 most frequently used sources of political ideas. The Christian teachings of Ham Sŏk-hŏn (4), Pak Hyŏng-gyu (10), Dietrich Bonhoeffer (11), and Jesus (13) were also at the top. Among South Korea's founding generation of *chaeya* leaders, Yi Yŏng-hŭi (2), Chang Chun-ha (5), and Kim Chi-ha (15) also left a lasting legacy. Two modern Korean nationalist leaders, Sin Ch'ae-ho (7) and Kim Ku (8), were also revered. Ibid., 117–118.

3. Kukka chaegŏn ch'oegohoeŭi han'guk kunsa hyŏngmyŏngsa p'yŏnchan wiwŏnhoe [Compilation Committee on Korean Military Revolution History, Supreme Council for National Reconstruction], *Han'guk kunsa hyŏngmyŏngsa, sang* [A History of the Korean Military Revolution, vol. 1] (Seoul: Kukka chaegŏn ch'oegohoeŭi [Supreme Council of National Reconstruction],1962) 274; Cho Hŭi-yŏn, "50, 60, 70nyŏndae minjok minju undongŭi chun'gaegwajŏng-e kwanhan yŏn'gu" [Research on the Evolution of Nationalist Democracy Movements], in *Han'guk sahoe undongsa: han'gukpyŏnhyŏgundong- ŭi yŏksa-wa 8onyŏndae-ŭi chŏn'gaegwajŏng* [History of Korean Social Movements: A History of Korean Revolution and the Process in the 80s], ed. Cho Hŭi-yŏn (Seoul: Chuksan, 1990), 75.

4. Park Chung Hee, *Kukka-wa hyŏngmyŏng-gwa na* [The Nation, the Revolution, and I] (Seoul: Hyangmunsa, 1963), 74.

5. *Sasanggye* (June 1961): 34–35. However, it only took a month for the magazine to modify its evaluation of the coup. In its July 1961 issue, p. 35, Chang Chun-ha suggested that the significance of the May16 coup could not be found in its continuity with the April 1960 uprising. Ham Sŏk-hŏn derided the coup for the first time, saying that "soldiers should not engage in revolution." See *Sasanggye* (July 1961): 26–47.

6. Ham Sŏk-hŏn (1901–1989) hailed from Yongch'ŏn, North P'yŏngan Province, after being arrested for his participation in Cho Man-sik's rightist-nationalist political organization. Ham Sŏk-hŏn advocated democratization as the best way to prevail over the North in the struggle over regime legitimacy.

7. Kye Hun-je (1921–1999) was born in Sŏnch'ŏn, North P'yŏngan Province. During the 1945–1948 post-liberation era, Kye Hun-je joined the rightist-nationalist camp headed by Kim Ku and took part in a protest movement against the installment of the United Nations trusteeship over the Korean Peninsula.

8. Born into a family with strong Christian traditions, Mun Ik-hwan (1918–1994) migrated to the South after witnessing a brutal confrontation between the Christian church and communists in the Soviet-occupied North Korea. Mun Ik-hwan, *Kasŭm-ŭro mannan p'yŏngyang: Mun Ik-hwan, Yu Wŏn-ho byŏnhoindan sanggo iyusŏ* [Visiting P'yŏngyang with an Open Heart: A Statement of Reasons for an Appeal to the Supreme Court by the Defense Counsel of Mun Ik-hwan and Yu Wŏn-ho] (Seoul: Samminsa, 1990), 14–17.

9. During the post-liberation era, Chang Chun-ha (1918–1975), a fervent anti-

communist, worked for conservative Kim Ku as his secretary and served as dean of academic affairs at the Central Training School of the rightist youth group Korean National Youth (KNY), led by Yi Pŏm-sŏk. Chang Chun-ha was born in Ŭiju, North P'yŏngan Province, and studied theology during his youth. Chang Chun-ha sŏnsaeng ch'umomunjip kanhaeng wiwŏnhoe [Publishing Committee for Anthology in Memory of Chang Chun-ha], *Minjokhon, minjuhon, chayuhon: Chang Chun-ha-ŭi saengae-wa sasang* [National Spirit, Democratic Spirit, Free Spirit: The Life and Philosophy of Chang Chun-ha] (Seoul: Nanam, 1995); Sŏ Chung-sŏk, "Pundanch'eje t'ap'a-e momdŏnjin Chang Chun-ha" [Chang Chun-ha: His Fight to End the Divided Korean Peninsula," *Yŏksa pip'yŏng* [Critiques of History] 28 (Fall 1997): 62–85.

10. Paek Ki-wan (1933-) followed Kim Ku in becoming a pro-unification activist after starting out his political career as a radical anticommunist. Paek Ki-wan was also a northerner, born in Kim Ku's Hwanghae Province.

11. An Pyŏng-mu, the "father" of the uniquely Korean *minjung* theology, was born in South P'yŏngan Province. Like many refugees from the North, An Pyŏng-mu harbored strong anticommunist sentiments after witnessing the atrocities committed by the communists in the North, but also hoped to transcended left-right struggles. In 1951, he launched the publication of the monthly magazine *Yasŏng* (Being in the Opposition). By the late 1960s, he developed what he called *minjung* theology, which he hoped would free society from the powers of the conservative South Korean church and its orthodox theology. An Pyŏng-mu, *Minjungsinhak iyagi* [The Story of Minjung Theology] (Seoul: Han'guk sinhak yŏn'guso [Korea Institute of Theology], 1987), 17–20.

12. Born in Unsan, North P'yŏngan Province, the hypocrisy and deceit Yi Yŏng-hŭi saw during the Korean War led him to hold a "religious-like conviction of denying any loyalty to anything." Yi Yŏng-hŭi, *Yŏkchŏng: na-ŭi ch'ŏng-nyŏnsidae* [My Life Journey: My Youth] (Seoul: Ch'angjak-kwa pip'yŏngsa, 1988), 241.

13. Many of the founding generation also jointly or individually progressed toward an unwavering pro-unification stand during their later years, putting unification before all other political values. They did so not only because they longed for reunion with their native provincial homes, but also because they felt an urgent need to deny Park and his regime the pretext for repression in the name of national security.

14. Student Coalition for the Opposition of Shameful Korea-Japan Talks, "Minjokjŏk minjujuŭi-rŭl changryehanda" [A Funeral for Nationalistic Democracy]," in *Minjok, minju, minjung sŏnŏn* [Declaration of the Nation, Democracy, and Minjung], ed. Kim Sam-ung (Seoul: Ilwŏlsŏgak, 1984), 41–42; see also 6.3 Tongjihoe [Compilation Committee of the History of the June Third Student Movement], *6.3 Haksaeng undongsa* [History of the 6.3 Student Movement] (Seoul: 6.3 Tongjihoe, 1994), 90.

15. *Sasanggye* (July 1964): 26–27.

16. "Special Edition: The Debacle of Abnormal Diplomacy," *Sasanggye* (May 1964): 28–58.

17. "Declaration of the National Committee for Struggle against the Third-term Constitutional Revision," *Sasanggye* (August 1969): 132–133.
18. Kim Sam-ung, ed., *Minjok, minju, minjung sŏnŏn* [Declaration of the Nation, Democracy, and Minjung], 82–99.
19. Taedong p'yŏnjippu, ed., *T'onghyŏkdang: yŏksa, sŏnggyŏk, t'ujaeng, munhŏn* [The Unification Revolution Party: History, Character, Struggle, Documents] (Seoul: Taedong p'yŏnjippu, 1989); Narasarang p'yŏnjippu, ed., *T'ongil hyŏngmyŏngdang* [The Unification Revolution Party] (Seoul: Narasarang, 1988).
20. "Dear Faithfuls around the Nation!" *Sasanggye* (October 1969): 108–111.
21. Korea University Student Council, "Open Letter to the Press," *Sasanggye* (September 1969): 143.
22. Seoul National University Student Council, "Message to Professors Nationwide," *Sasanggye* (October 1969): 158.
23. Ch'oe Chang-jip, *Han'guk-ŭi nodong undong-gwa kukka* [The State and Labor Movements in Korea] (Seoul: Yŏlŭmsa, 1988); Ch'oe Chang-jip, *Han'guk hyŏndae chŏngch'i-ŭi kujo-wa pyŏnhwa* [The Structure and Transformation of Contemporary Korean Politics] (Seoul: Kkach'i, 1989).
24. Mun Ik-hwan, "Igŏn k'allal-ida" [This Is the Blade of a Knife], in *Haebang- ŭi nolli-wa chajusasang: kunkmin yŏrŏpun'kkye tŭrinŭn kŭl* [The Logic of Liberation and the Philosophy of Autonomy: To the People of South Korea], ed. Chang Ki-p'yo (Seoul: Ch'in'gu, 1988), 7.
25. The farmers did not join the *chaeya* until the 1980s. The experience of the "class war" precipitated by the spread of radical leftist labor-peasant movements and the ensuing political repression during the late 1940s made the South Korean peasants one of the last sectors within society to look at political activism as a viable option.
26. Kodae nodongmunje yŏn'guso [Korea University Institute of Labor], *Kodaenoyŏn 30nyŏnsa: 1965–1998* [30 Years' History of the Korea University Institute of Labor] (Seoul: Koryŏdaehak nodongmunje yŏn'guso) [Korea University Institute of Labor Issues], 1998).
27. Ch'oe Chang-jip, *Han'guk-ŭi nodong undong-gwa kukka* [The State and Labor Movements in Korea].
28. "Dear Faithfuls around the Nation!"
29. Han'guk kidokkyo sahoemunje yŏnguwŏn [Korean Christian Institute of Social Research], *1970nyŏndae minjuhwa undong-gwa kidokkyo* [Christianity and Democratization Movements in the 1970s] (Seoul: Han'guk kidokkyo sahoemunje yŏnguwŏn, 1983), 41–91, 110–126.
30. Sahoebŏb hakhoe, Seoul National University, "Kwangju taedanji pinmin silt'ae chosabogosŏ" [Survey on the Poverty Situation of the Kwangju Complex], (October 1971), 3, and Han'guk kidok'kyo sahoemunje yŏnguwŏn, *1970nyŏndae minjuhwa undong-gwa kidokkyo* [Christianity and Democratization Movements in the 1970s], 99.
31. Urban poverty was a serious social problem by the early 1970s. Between 1960 and 1966, a total of 1,409,000 people had migrated from the countryside to the city. The rate of rural-urban migration accelerated even more during the

1966–1970 period, resulting in the cumulative net migration of 2,271,000 people to the city. The population of Seoul, in particular, shot up from 2,445,000 in 1960 to 5,536,000 by 1970. *Tonga yŏn'gam 1970* [Tonga Year Book 1970 edition] (Seoul: Dong-A Ilbosa, 1970), 529.

32. Kim Dae-jung, *Haengdonghanŭn yangsim-ŭro* [With Conscience in Action] (Seoul: Kŭmmundang, 1985), 44–46.

33. Ch'oe Chang-jip, "Kunbu kwŏnwijuŭi cheje-ŭi naebu mosun-gwa pyŏnhwa-ŭi donghak" [The Internal Contradictions and the Dynamics of Change in the Military Authoritarian Regime], in *Hyŏndae han'guk chŏngch'i-ui kujo-wa pyŏnhwa* [The Structure and Transformation of Contemporary Korean Politics], by Ch'oe Chang-jip, 194.

34. Son Se-il, "Sindonga int'ŏbyu—chŏn sinmindang taet'ongryŏng hubo Kim Dae Jung-ssi" [A Sindonga Interview—Former New Democratic Party Presidential Candidate Kim Dae Jung], *Sindonga* (February 1975) no.126: 78.

35. Park Chung Hee, "1972 New Year Press Conference" (January 1, 1972), in the Secretarial Office of the President, *Park Chung Hee taet'ongryŏng yŏnsŏlmunjip che gujip* [Collection of President Park Chung Hee's Speeches, Vol. 9], (Seoul: Secretarial Office of the President, 1965–73), 25.

36. Han'guk kidokkyo sahoemunje yŏnguwŏn, *1970 nyŏndae minjuhwa undong-kwa kidokkyo* [Christianity and Democratization Movements in the 1970s], 103.

37. *Haptong yon'gam* [Haptong Year Book] (Seoul: Haptong t'ongsinsa, 1972), 102.

38. Kim Ŏn-ho, "Rŭppo, ŏnron chayu undong" [Free Press Movement], *Sindonga* (March 1975): 92; and Cho Sang-ho, *Han'guk ŏnron-gwa ch'ulpan chŏnŏllijŭm* [The Korean Press and Print Journalism] (Seoul: Nanam, 1999), 148.

39. Kim Ŏn-ho, "Rŭppo, ŏnron chayu undong" [Free Press Movement].

40. Han'guk kidokkyo sahoemunje yŏn'guwŏn, *1970nyŏndae minjuhwa undong-gwa kidokkyo* [Christianity and Democratization Movements in the 1970s], 258.

41. Kim Sam-ung, *Minjok, minju, minjung sŏnŏn* [Declaration of the Nation, Democracy, and Minjung], 174.

42. Park Chung Hee, "Kin'gŭp choch'i sa-ho sŏnp'o chŭŭmhan t'ŭkpyŏl tamhwa" [Special Address on the Occasion of the Promulgation of Emergency Decree no. 4], in the Secretarial Office of the President, *Park Chung Hee taet'ongryŏng yŏnsŏlmunjip che sipiljip* [Collection of President Park Chung Hee's Speeches, 11]: 128–129.

43. Han'guk kidokkyo sahoemunje yŏn'guwŏn, *1970nyŏndae minjuhwa undong-gwa kidokkyo* [Christianity and Democratization Movements in the 1970s], 139.

44. With his poem "O chŏk" [The Five Enemies], Kim Chi-ha came to symbolize the spirit of resistance among South Korean intellectuals.

45. Kim Sam-ung, *Minjok, minju, minjung sŏnŏn* [Declaration of the Nation, Democracy, and Minjung], 267–268.

46. Han'guk kidokkyo kyohoe hyŏpŭihoe [Korean Council of Christian

Churches], *1970nyŏndae minjuhwa undong: kidokkyo in'gwŏn undong-ŭl chungsim-ŭro* 2 [Democratization Movements in the 1970s: A Focus on Christian Human Rights Movements, vol. 2] (Seoul: Korean Council of Christian Churches, 1987): 664–665.

47. Yi Kwang-il, "Panch'eje undong-ŭi chŏn'gaegwajŏng-gwa sŏnggyŏk" [The Process and Nature of Anti-System Movements], in *Park Chung Hee-rŭl nŏmŏsŏ* [Beyond Park Chung Hee], ed. Korean Politics Research Society (Seoul: P'urŭnsup, 1998), 182.

48. Han'guk kidokkyo kyohoe hyŏpŭihoe, *1970nyŏndae minjuhwa undong* [Democratization Movements of the 1970s], 2:685–687 and Kim Sam-ung, *Minjok, minju, minjung sŏnŏn* [Declaration of the Nation, Democracy, and Minjung], 269–267. The original draft of this declaration was written by Mun Ik-hwan. The process of drafting is discussed in Han'guk kidokkyo kyohoe hyŏpŭihoe, *1970nyŏndae minjuhwa undong* [Democratization Movements of the 1970s], 2:688–689.

49. Han'guk kidokkyo kyohoe hyŏpŭihoe, *1970nyŏndae minjuhwa undong* [Democratization Movements of the 1970s,], 2: 687; Kim Sam-ung, *Minjok, minju, minjung sŏnŏn* [Declaration of the Nation, Democracy, and Minjung], 272–273.

50. Mun Ik-hwan, Ham Se-ung, Kim Dae-jung, Moon Tong-hwan, Yi Mun-yŏng, Sŏ Nam-dong, An Pyŏng-mu, Sin Hyŏn-bong, Yi Hae-dong, Yun Pan-ung, Mun Chŏng-hyŏn were arrested and convicted. Yun Po-sŏn, Ham Sŏk-hŏn, Chŏng Il-hyŏng, Yi T'ae-yŏng, Yi U-jŏng, Kim Sŭng-hun, Chang Tŏk-p'il, Kim T'aek-am, An Ch'ung-sŏk were indicted without physical detention and convicted. Han'guk kidokkyo kyohoe hyŏpŭihoe, *1970nyŏndae minjuhwa undong* [Democratization Movements of the 1970s], 2:690–694.

51. Han'guk kidokkyo kyohoe hyŏpŭihoe, *1970nyŏndae minjuhwa undong* [Democratization Movements of the 1970s], 2:700.

52. See Han'guk kidokkyo kyohoe hyŏpŭihoe, *1970 nyŏndae minjuhwa undong* [Democratization Movements of the 1970s,], 2:697–818, for the court deliberations.

53. The works of journalist-turned-professor Yi Yŏng-hŭi were particularly liberating for student activists. By espousing a critical worldview free from the fetters of the cold war and anticommunism, his works were interpreted as bringing a "Copernican" transformation of student perceptions by the progressives, and as heretical Marxist-Leninism by the conservatives. The radical student movements called him the "Master of Thought." In his book *Usanggwa Yisung* [Idol and Rationality], Yi Yŏng-hŭi lashed out against the *yushin* regime as the "idol" standing in the way of the rationality that the *chaeya* represented. See Kim Chae-myŏng, "An Intellectual in the Age of Transformation: Professor Yi Yŏng-hŭi" *Choson Monthly* (October 1988): 213–333; Cho Sang-ho, *Han'guk ŏnron-gwa ch'ulpan chŏnŏllijŭm* [The Korean Press and Print Journalism], 183–200.

54. In parallel to An Pyŏng-mu and Sŏ Nam-dong's development of an indigenous *minjung* theology, Han Wan-sang developed what he called "*minjung* sociol-

ogy" in the hope of liberating academia from the repressive influences of standard modernization theories.

55. For details on the South Korean church and the human rights movement, see Han'guk kidokkyo kyohoe hyŏpŭihoe, *1970nyŏndae minjuhwa undong* 5 [Democratization Movements of the 1970s, vol. 5].

56. Han Sŭng-hŏn et al., *Yushin ch'eje-wa minjuhwa undong* [The *Yushin* Regime and the Democratization Movement] (Seoul: Ch'unch'usa, 1984), 296–308.

57. Kim Young-sam warned in the interview with the *New York Times* that "the United States should not repeat in South Korea what it did in Iran." By that, he meant that an anti-American popular revolution could break out if the United States kept backing Park's authoritarian rule. Han Sŭng-hŏn et al., *Yushin ch'eje-wa minjuhwa undong* [The *Yushin* Regime and the Democratization Movement], 331.

58. William H. Gleysteen, Jr., *Massive Entanglement, Marginal Influence: Carter and Korea in Crisis* (Boulder: Westview Press, 1988), 37.

59. Aristide R. Zolberg, "Moments of Madness," *Politics and Society* 2, no. 2 (Winter 1972): 183–207; Pak Myŏng-rim, "Tŭkbyŏl kihoek: haebang 5onyŏn, han'guk hyŏndaejŏngch'i-ŭi pansŏng-gwa chŏnmang 'sudong hyŏng myŏng-gwa kwanggi-ŭi sun'gan" [Contemporary Korean Politics: Passive Revolution and Moments of Madness, 1945–1995], *Sahoebip'yŏng* [Critical Review on Society], vol. 13 (Seoul: Nanam, September 1995).

14. The Vietnam War: South Korea's Search for National Security

1. U.S. Senate, "United States Security Agreements and Commitments Abroad" (hereafter U.S. SACA), Hearing before the Committee on Foreign Relations, 91st Congress (Washington, D.C., 1970), 1566–1568.

2. Kukpang kunsa yŏn'guso [Research Institute for Defense and Military History], *Kŏn'gun 5onyŏnsa* [Fifty Years' History of the Korean Armed Forces] (Seoul: Kukpang kunsa yŏn'guso [Research Institute for Defense and Military History], 1998), 210.

3. Yong Sun Yim, ed., *Handbook on Korean-U.S. Relations* (Seoul: Asia Society, 1985), 6.

4. Sungjoo Han, "South Korea's Participation in the Vietnam Conflict: An Analysis of the U.S.-Korean Alliance," *Orbis* 21, no. 4 (Winter 1978): 902.

5. The guidelines called for instilling cadre potential in every soldier, modernizing the entire military, arming the entire population, and turning the whole nation into a fortress.

6. Yi Ki-jong, *Han'guk kukchegwan'gyesa* [History of South Korea's International Relations] (Seoul: Hyŏngsŏlch'ulp'ansa, 1992), 160–161; Dong-Ju Choi, "The Political Economy of Korea's Involvement in the Second Indo-China War" (Ph.D. diss., University of London, 1995), 90–92. See also Memo for NSC, March 2, 1954, NSC Series, Policy Papers Sub-series, Box 10, WHO File, DDE Library; Kukpang kunsa yŏn'guso [Research Institute for Defense and Military History], *Kukbangsa yŏnp'yo 1945–1990* [A Chronology of

National Defense History] (Seoul: Kukpang kunsa yŏn'guso [Research Institute for Defense and Military History], 1994), 154, 157.

7. George McT. Kahin, *Intervention: How America Became Involved in Vietnam* (Garden City, N.Y.: Anchor Press, 1987), 42.

8. Kyudok Hong, "Unequal Partners: ROK-US Relations during the Vietnam War" (Ph.D. diss., University of South Carolina, 1991), 89.

9. Department of State, "Memo for Conversation, Park and Kennedy," November 14 and 15, 1961, Box 128, John F. Kennedy Presidential Library; Hong Kyu-dŏk, "P'abyŏng oegyo-wa anbo sindŭrom: 6onyŏndae han'guk oegyo chŏngch'aek- ŭi p'yŏngga" [The Diplomacy of Dispatching Troops to Vietnam and Security Syndrome: An Evaluation of South Korea's Foreign Policy in the 1960s], *Kukche chŏngch'i nonch'ong* 22:2 [Korean Journal of International Relations 22, no. 2] (1992): 27; and Dong-Ju Choi, "The Political Economy of Korea's Involvement in the Second Indo-China War," 93–94.

10. Kukpang kunsa yŏn'guso [Research Institute for Defense and Military History], *Wŏlnam p'abyong-gwa kukkabaljŏn* [The Dispatch of Troops to Vietnam and National Development], (Seoul: Kukpang kunsa yŏn'guso [Research Institute for Defense and Military History], 1996), 163.

11. Kim Sŏng-ŭn, "Chŏnhwan'gi-ŭi naemak: wŏlnam p'abyŏng" [The Dispatch of Korean Troops to Vietnam: Unknown Story of a Transition Period], *Chosun Ilbo*, November 25, 1981.

12. *Dong-A Ilbo*, January 12, 1965.

13. Park ordered some of his DRP legislators to oppose the troop dispatch to obtain leverage vis-à-vis the United States. See Yi Tong-wŏn, *Taet'ongryŏng-ŭl kŭrimyŏ* [Missing the President] (Seoul: Koryŏwŏn, 1992), 118–126.

14. Kukpang kunsa yŏn'guso [Research Institute for Defense and Military History], *Wŏlnam p'abyŏng-gwa kukkabalchŏn* [The Dispatch of Troops to Vietnam and National Development], 175.

15. Secretarial Office of the President, ed., *Park Chung Hee taet'ongryong yŏnsŏlmunjip*, [Collection of President Park Chung Hee's Speeches, vol.1], (Seoul: The Secretarial Office of the President, 1973), 191–193.

16. Only five nations dispatched troops to South Vietnam: South Korea, 50,000; Thailand, 11,570; Australia, 7,600; the Philippines, 2,060; and New Zealand, 550. Sungjoo Han, "South Korea's Participation in the Vietnam Conflict," 893–896.

17. Ibid., 897.

18. Lyndon B. Johnson, *The Vantage Point: Perspective of the President, 1963–69* (New York: Holt, Rinehart and Winston, 1971), 142–146.

19. Yi Tong-wŏn, "Che samgong oegyo pihwa: kŭ yŏksa kŭ hyŏnjang" [The Third Republic: Its Hidden Diplomatic Stories: Their History and Their Sites], *Kukmin Ilbo*, October 31, 1989.

20. Yi Tong-wŏn, *Taet'ongryŏng-ŭl kŭrimyŏ* [Missing the President], 112–114.

21. War History Compilation Committee, the Ministry of National Defense, *Kukpang choyakjip* [The Treaties of National Defense] (Seoul: Ministry of National Defense, 1981), 708–710.

22. Stanley Larsen and James Lawton Collins, Jr., *Allied Participation in Vietnam* (Washington, D.C.: Department of the Army, 1975), 124–125.

23. Kukpang kunsa yŏn'guso [Research Institute for Defense and Military History], *Wŏlnam p'abyŏng-gwa kukkabaljŏn* [The Dispatch of Troops to Vietnam and National Development], 183.

24. Yi Tong-wŏn also demanded that the United States support the modernization of South Korean forces, provide financial support for South Korean troops in South Vietnam, procure military supplies for South Korean troops in South Vietnam, and support South Korea's access to the South Vietnamese market. Kukpang kunsa yŏn'guso [Research Institute for Defense and Military History], *Wŏlnam p'abyŏng-gwa kukkabaljŏn* [The Dispatch of Troops to Vietnam and National Development], 176–177.

25. Dong-Ju Choi, "The Political Economy of Korea's Involvement in the Second Indo-China War," 156.

26. Yi Sang-u, *Che samgonghwaguk oegyo pisa* [The Untold Diplomatic Story of the Third Republic] (Seoul: Chosun Ilbosa, 1985), 262.

27. Kim Sŏng-ŭn, "Wŏlnam p'abyŏng" [The Dispatch of Korean Troops to Vietnam], *Chosun Ilbo*, December 6, 1981.

28. Chŏng Su-yong, "Han'guk-ŭi petŭnamjŏn p'abyŏng-gwa hanmi tongmaeng-ch'eje-ŭi pyŏnhwa" [South Korea's Dispatch of Combat Troops to Vietnam and the Change in the South Korea–U.S. Alliance] (Ph.D. diss., Korea University, 2001), 235.

29. Ministry of National Defense, *Kukbangsa, 3* [The History of National Defense, vol.3] (Seoul: Ministry of National Defense, 1990), 351–352.

30. Kukpang kunsa yŏn'guso [Research Institute for Defense and Military History], *Wŏlnam p'abyŏng-gwa kukkabaljŏn* [The Dispatch of Troops to Vietnam and National Development], 201.

31. Kukpang kunsa yŏn'guso [Research Institute for Defense and Military History], *Kŏn'gun 5onyŏnsa* [Fifty Years' History of the Korean Armed Forces], 220.

32. Yi Sang-u, *Che 3konghwaguk oegyo pisa* [The Untold Diplomatic Story of the Third Republic], 283.

33. Frank Baldwin, "America's Rented Troops: South Koreans in Vietnam," *Bulletin of Concerned Asian Scholars* (October–December 1975), fn 36.

34. Interview with Chŏng Il-gwŏn, as reported by Yi Ki-jong, *Han'guk kukchegwan'gyesa* [History of Korea's International Relations], 239.

35. Kukpang kunsa yŏn'guso [Research Institute for Defense and Military History], *Wŏlnam p'abyŏng-gwa kukkabalchŏn* [The Dispatch of Troops to Vietnam and National Development], 200.

36. Hong Kyu-dŏk, "P'abyŏng oegyo-wa anbo sindŭrom" [The Diplomacy of Dispatching Troops to Vietnam and Security Syndrome], 169–170.

37. Kukpang kunsa yŏn'guso [Research Institute for Defense and Military History], *Wŏlnam p'abyŏng-gwa kukkabaljŏn* [The Dispatch of Troops to Vietnam and National Development], 193.

38. Ibid., 192.

39. Yi Tong-wŏn, *Taet'ongryŏng-ŭl kŭrimyŏ* [Missing the President], 133–134.

40. Kukpangbu, Kunsa p'yŏnch'an yŏn'guso [War History Compilation Committee, the Ministry of National Defense], *Kukpang choyakchip* [The Treaties of National Defense], (Seoul: Kukpangbu, Kunsa p'yŏnch'an yŏn'guso [War History Compilation Committee, the Ministry of National Defense], 1997–2006), 265–266.

41. U.S. SACA, 1531.

42. U.S. SACA, 1604–1607. Also see *Dong-A Ilbo*, February 8 and March 11, 1966.

43. Yang Sŏng-ch'ŏl and Mun Chŏng-in, "Hanmi anbo kwan'gye-ŭi chaejomyŏng: p'uebŭloho sagŏn-ŭi wigi mit tongmaeng kwanlli sarye-rŭl chungsim-ŭro" [Reconsideration of Security Relations between South Korea and the U.S.: Focusing on the Crisis and Alliance Management during the Pueblo Incident], in *Han'guk-kwa miguk: chongch'i anbo kwan'gye* [South Korea and the U.S.: Political and Security Relations], ed. An Pyŏng-jun (Masan: Far East Research Institute, Kyungnam University, 1988), 69.

44. See *Dong-A Ilbo*, January 30, 2001.

45. There existed a critical gap in the two countries' interpretation of Park's original position. The United States thought he agreed to the dispatch of a third combat division, but South Korea thought it was committed only to the dispatch of civil personnel. See Frank Baldwin, "America's Rented Troops: South Koreans in Vietnam," 35. Also consult *Dong-A Ilbo*, November 11, 1966.

46. Kukpang kunsa yŏn'guso [Research Institute for Defense and Military History], *Kukpang chŏngch'aek pyŏnch'ŏnsa: 1945–1994* [Changing Nature of Korean National Defense Policy: 1945–1994], (Seoul: Kukpang kunsa yŏn'guso [Research Institute for Defense and Military History], 1995), 166.

47. Kukpang kunsa yŏn'guso [Research Institute for Defense and Military History], *Kŏn'gun 5onyŏnsa* [Fifty Years' History of the Korean Armed Forces], 218.

48. Ministry of Foreign Affairs and Trade, "Hanmi chŏngsang'gan tandok hoedamrok mit yang'guk kakryo hoeŭirok" [The Documents of the Summit Meetings and Bilateral Ministerial Talks between Republic of Korea and the United States] (Seoul: Diplomacy Archives Division, 2005), Registration no. 3017, Film No. C-0033, 430–442.

49. Pak Sil, *Park chung hee taet'ongryŏng-gwa miguk taesagwan* [President Park and the U.S. Embassy] (Seoul: Paegyang ch'ulp'ansa, 1993), 175–176.

50. Kyudok Hong, "Unequal partners: ROK-US Relations during the Vietnam War," 227–228.

51. Sungjoo Han, "South Korea's Participation in the Vietnam Conflict," 907.

52. Kukpang kunsa yŏn'guso [Research Institute for Defense and Military History], *Kŏn'gun 5onyŏnsa* [Fifty Years' History of the Korean Armed Forces], 248.

53. U.S. Department of State, Briefing Memorandum to the Secretary, April 20, 1971. (Maryland National Archives V.)

54. Memorandum, April 26, 1972, "Meeting with Foreign Minister Kim Yong Sik of South Korea," RG59, State Department Documents, Subject Numeric Files, 1970–73 Political and Defense Box, 2423. (Maryland National Archives V.)

55. Ministry of Foreign Affairs, *Han'guk oegyo 30nyŏn: 1948–1978* [Thirty

Years' History of Korean Foreign Policy: 1948–1978], (Seoul: Ministry of Foreign Affairs, 1979), 30.

56. U.S. SACA, 1970, 1571.

57. Dong-Ju Choi, "The Political Economy of Korea's Involvement in the Second Indo-China War," 211.

58. Kyŏngje kihoegwŏn [Economic Planning Board], *Kaebal yŏndae-ŭi kyŏngje chŏngch'aek: kyŏngje kihoegwŏn 20nyŏnsa* [Economic Policy during the Developmental Decades: Twenty Years of the Economic Planning Board] (Kwach'ŏn: Kyŏngje kihoegwŏn [Economic Planning Board], 1982), 90.

59. Kukpang kunsa yŏn'guso [Research Institute for Defense and Military History], *Wŏlnam p'abyŏng-gwa kukkabaljŏn* [The Dispatch of Troops to Vietnam and National Development], 250–251.

60. Kukbang Kunsa Yŏn'gusa [Research Institute for Defense and Military History], *Wŏlnam p'apyŏng-gwa kukkabaljŏn* [The Dispatch of Troops to Vietnam and National Development], 266; Hŏ Chin, "Han'gukgun-ŭi wŏlnam ch'amjŏn-gwa ch'amjŏn kunin-ŭi hyŏnsil" [The Participation of the Korean Troops in Vietnam and Their Reality], *Han'guk Kunsa* [Korean Military Affairs], no. 9 (Seoul: Korea Institute for Military Affairs, 1997), 51.

61. Yi Yŏng-hŭi, *Petŭnam chŏnjaeng: 30nyŏn petŭnam chŏnjaeng-ŭi chŏn'gae-wa chonggyŏl* [The Vietnam War: The Evolution and Conclusion of the Thirty Years' Vietnam War] (Seoul: Ture, 1985).

62. Yi Yŏng-hŭi, a *chaeya* leader and also a journalist at the *Chosun Ilbo* during the Vietnam War, said that major daily newspapers were told not to report any negative news on the KFV troops in South Vietnam, although international news agencies reported atrocities committed by some South Korean troops during combat. "Yi Yŏng-hŭi sŏnsaeng'i hoegohan kwang'giŭi petŭnam chŏnjaeng" [Mr. Yi Yŏng-hŭi's Recollection on the Insane Vietnam War], *Hankyoreh 21*, vol. 57 (May 4, 1995), 43.

15. Normalization of Relations with Japan: Toward a New Partnership

1. During the first FYEDP years (1962–1966), the GNP grew at an average annual rate of 7.9 percent. By 1966, the GNP totaled $3.6 billion, $1.1 billion more than projected earlier by South Korea's economic planners. See Paul. W. Kuznets, "Korea's Five-Year Plans," in *Practical Approaches to Development Planning: Korea's Second Five-Year Plan*, ed. Irma Adelman (Baltimore: Johns Hopkins University Press, 1969), 66.

2. This is quoted in the third part of a series titled *Samgong oegyo pihwa: kŭ yŏksa kŭ Hyŏnjang* [The Third Republic: The Hidden Diplomatic Stories], written by Yi Tong-wŏn for *Kukmin Ilbo*. See *Kukmin Ilbo*, October 7, 1989.

3. *Dong-A Ilbo*, May 23, 1961.

4. Having attended the same college as Ikeda Hayato, Ohira Masayoshi, and Kosaka Zentaro, Yi Tong-hwan was counted on to facilitate South Korea's lobbying efforts in Japan on the strength of his school background. Kim Tong-jo, *Hoesang 30nyŏn: Hanil hoedam* [Recollecting Thirty Years: Korean-Japanese Talks] (Seoul: JoongAng Ilbosa, 1986), 212–213.

5. See John F. Kennedy's remarks in Chicago on April 28, 1961, *Public Papers of the Presidents of the United States, John F. Kennedy, 1961* (Washington, D.C.: U.S. GPO, 1962), 340–341.

6. Following his meeting with Park Chung Hee in Washington on November 14, 1961, Kennedy endorsed the "positive steps taken by [Park] in strengthening the nation against Communism and in eliminating corruption and other social evils." Kennedy went on to assure Park that "the U.S. government would continue to extend all possible economic aid and cooperation to [South Korea] in order to further long range economic development," which would in turn help to "maintain a strong anti-Communist posture in [South] Korea." See the Kennedy-Park Joint Statement, ibid., 720–721.

7. U.S. House Committee on International Relations, *Investigation of Korean-American Relations: Appendixes to the Report of the Subcommittee on International Organizations*, vol. 1 (Washington, D.C.: U.S. GPO, 1978), 46.

8. In return for U.S. support, Park reiterated his earlier pledge to return the government to civilian control in the summer of 1963. U.S. Department of State, *Bulletin*, vol. XLV, no. 1171 (December 4, 1961), 928–929.

9. Nikkan Kankei o Kenkyu Suru Kai, *Shiryo: Nikkan kankei, I* [Materials: Japanese-South Korean Relations vol. 1](Tokyo: Gendaishi Shuppankai, 1976), 36.

10. See Yi To-hyŏng, *Hŭkmak: Hanil kyosŏp pihwa* [Black Screen: The Secret Stories of the Korean-Japanese Talks] (Seoul: Chosun Ilbosa, 1987), 108–109.

11. See Ooka Eppei, "Jiyu Kankoku o mamoru: Nikkan kaidan no mondaiten o sagaru" [Defend Free Korea: Searching for the Problems of Japanese-South Korean Talks], *Chuo Koron* (January 1962): 284.

12. Ibid.

13. Ibid., 288.

14. Sugi was Kōno's leading financial backer from the Kansai area. For a discussion of Sugi's selection as the chief delegate, see ibid. For full details on the sixth round of talks, see the South Korean Foreign Ministry's "Che yukch'a hanil hoedam hoeŭirok 1,2,3,4" [Official Records on the Sixth Round of Talks 1,2,3 & 4], (ROK Foreign Ministry, 1962).

15. For an overview of the position the Japanese leftists took on the South Korean-Japanese talks, see Kawakami Jotaro (chairman of the JSP and a moderate), "Party Stand on Japan-ROK Normalization Talks," *Japan Socialist Review* (October 1, 1962), 7–18.

16. For details on the background of the mutual defense treaties concluded by North Korea, see Byung Chul Koh, *The Foreign Policy Systems of North and South Korea* (Berkeley: University of California Press, 1984), 205–206.

17. See Yamamoto Tsuyoshi, *Nikkan Kankei* [Japanese-Korean Relations] (Tokyo: Kyoikusha, 1978), 67–68.

18. *Ekonomisuto*, November 21, 1961.

19. *Asahi Shimbun*, July 20, 1961.

20. President Syngman Rhee visited Japan on several occasions, but none of them were in an official capacity.

21. *Dong-A Ilbo*, November 12, 1961.

22. Kim Tong-jo, *Hoesang 30nyŏn* [Recollecting Thirty Years], 225.

23. Ishii Mitsujiro, *Kaiso hachij_hachinen* [Recollecting Eighty-eight Years] (Tokyo: Karucha Shuppansha, 1976), 441–442.

24. *Asahi Shimbun*, November 14, 1961.

25. Interview with Pae Ŭi-hwan, chief delegate to the sixth round of talks (May 22, 1992).

26. The "Peace Line" refers to South Korean territorial waters unilaterally declared by Syngman Rhee. Some of these waters were claimed by Japan as well, causing much conflict and tension between the two countries.

27. See an article series called *Nikkan kosho hiwa* [The Secret Stories of Japan-ROK Negotiations], contributed by Shimamoto Kanero in *Yomiuri Shimbun*, January 21, 1992.

28. *Japan Times*, January 20, 1962.

29. "Hanil hoedam-ŭi kyŏngwi" [The Circumstances of Korean-Japanese Talks], in *Hanil hoedam paeksŏ* [The White Papers on the Korean-Japanese Talks] (Seoul: Government of the Republic of Korea, 1965), 156–157.

30. For Kennedy's meeting with Yoshida Shigeru, see *Asahi Shimbun*, May 12, 1962.

31. Ikeda's reply to Okada Haruo, a left-wing member of the JSP, at the lower house's Foreign Affairs Committee meeting on August 29, 1962, as reported by *Japan Times*, August 30, 1962.

32. In the LDP national convention held on July 14, 1962, Ikeda reemerged as the head of the party, receiving 391 votes out of 466 cast. *Asahi Shimbun*, July 15, 1962.

33. Yi To-Hyŏng, *Hŭkmak* [Black Screen], 138–139.

34. Taking into consideration Japan's limited foreign exchange reserves ($1.4 billion), Kim Chong-p'il is said to have advised against demanding high payments if Park was serious about bringing an end to the claims issue. Interview with Pae Ŭi-hwan (May 22, 1992).

35. See Yi Wŏn-dŏk, *Hanil kwagŏsa ch' ŏri- ui wŏnjŏm: Ilbon-ŭi chŏnhuch' ŏri oegyo-wa hanil hoedam* [The Starting Point for Korea and Japan's Settlement of the Past: Japanese Post war Diplomacy and Korea-Japan Normalization], 172. (Seoul: Seoul National University Press, 1996).

36. See Yi Sŏk-ryŏl and Cho Kyu-ha, "Hanil hoedam chŏnmalsŏ" [An Account of the Korean-Japanese Talks], *Shindong-A* (June 1965), 114.

37. The Japanese foreign affairs and finance ministries' proposal was released just prior to the bilateral foreign ministerial meeting in March 1962, prompting the South Korean side to dismiss it as "preposterous" and threaten to discontinue the talks. See *Mainichi Shimbun*, March 9, 1962; and *Dong-A Ilbo*, March 10, 1962.

38. Seizaburo Sato, Ken'ichi Koyama, and Shunpei Kumon, ed., *Postwar Politician: The Life of Former Prime Minister Masayoshi Ohira* (English translation by William R. Carter of the Japanese biography *Ohira Masayoshi: hito to shiso*) (Tokyo and New York: Kodansha International, 1990), 202.

39. Yi Sŏk-Ryŏl and Cho Kyu-ha, "Hanil hoedam chŏnmalsŏ" [An Account of the Korean-Japanese Talks], 118.

40. Ibid., 118.

41. In comparison, Japan's reparations payment to the Philippines (1956) amounted to $550 million in goods and services plus $250 million in commercial loans. The settled amount for Indonesia (1958) was $223 million in goods and services plus $400 million in commercial loans. For Burma, it was $200 million plus $50 million (1954). See Lawrence Olson, *Japan in Postwar Asia* (London: Pall Mall Press, 1970), 13–32.

42. ROK Foreign Ministry, *Hanil hoedam ryaksa* [Short History of the Korean-Japanese Talks] (Seoul: Asian Bureau, Foreign Ministry, Republic of Korea, 1984), 97.

43. For Ohira's public revelation of the secret agreement on property claims, see *Mainichi Shimbun*, January 30, 1963.

44. Kennedy opposed Park's proposed extension of military rule, but he was careful not to make this a public U.S. stand. In a news conference held in April 1963, Kennedy stated that the leadership situation in South Korea was ultimately a judgment that the people and the responsible officials of South Korea had to make. See *Public Papers of the Presidents of the United States, John F. Kennedy, 1963, 305*. The State Department, however, did warn that "the military junta's effort to continue military rule for four more years could constitute a threat to stable and effective government." U.S. Department of State, *Bulletin*, vol. XLVI, no. 1198 (June 11, 1962), 573.

45. Quoted in George McTurnan Kahin and John W. Lewis, *The United States in Vietnam*, rev. ed. (New York: Dell, 1969), 152.

46. Series no. 46, *Kukmin Ilbo*, October 25, 1989.

47. Ibid.

48. George F. Kennan, "Japanese Security and American Policy," *Foreign Affairs* 43, no. 1 (October 1964): 19–20.

49. South Korea's Foreign Ministry, *Hanil hoedam ryaksa* [Short History of the Korean-Japanese Talks].

50. *Asahi Shimbun*, November 11, 1964.

51. For an analytic comparison of Kishi Nobusuke and Sato Eisaku, see Pak Kyŏng-sŏk, *Ilbon chamindang: kyŏlsŏng-gwa chidojadŭl* [Japan's Liberal Democratic Party: Its Formation and Its Leaders] (Seoul: Hyŏndae Chisiksa, 1990), 79–84.

52. Shiina Etsusaburo Tsuitoroku Kankokai, *Kiroku Shiina Etsusaburo* [A Record: Etsusaburo Shiina] (Tokyo: Record Issuance Committee of Etsusaburo Shiina, 1982) ,35–36.

53. Interview with Shiina Motoo (October 26, 1992).

54. If anything, Shiina was more an ultranationalist who was proud of Japan's colonial past. During a no-confidence motion against Shiina in the Diet on February 15, 1965, a JSP member accused Shiina of being a former imperialist and therefore unfit to preside over the South Korea–Japan negotiations. In one of his earlier writings, *Toka to Seiji*, Shiina wrote: "If Japan's annexation of Korea constituted in any way an act of imperialism, then it was a 'glorious imperialism.'" See South Korea's Foreign Ministry, *Hanil hoedam ryaksa* [A Brief History of the Korea-Japan Talks], 105.

55. Quoted in Shiina Etsusaburo Tsuitoroku Kankokai, *Kiroku Shiina Etsusaburo* [A Record: Etsusaburo Shiina], 49.

56. After the official luncheon on the day of his arrival, Park told Yi Tong-wŏn that "Shiina appears sincere enough for us to trust and work with." Quoted in Series no. 53, *Kukmin Ilbo,* November 2, 1989.

57. The inevitable discrepancy in the two countries' interpretation of Articles II and III was to become a source of political friction in the future.

58. *Dong-A Ilbo,* April 15, 1965.

59. Jung-Hoon Lee, "Korean-Japanese Relations: The Past, Present and Future," *Korea Observer* 21, no. 2 (Summer 1990), 171.

60. Chong-sik Lee, *Japan and Korea: The Political Dimension* (Stanford: Hoover Institution Press, 1985), 100–101.

16. The Security, Political, and Human Rights Conundrum, 1974–1979

1. See the testimony of Yi Hu-rak, then the director of the Korea Central Intelligence Agency, in *Kim Dae-jung napch'i sagŏn chinsang* [The True Story behind the Kidnapping of Kim Dae-jung], ed. Kim Dae-jung napch'i sagŏn-ui chinsang kyumyŏng-ŭl wihan simin-ŭi moim [A Citizen Meeting to Find Truth about the Kidnapping of Kim Dae-jung] (Seoul: P'urŭn namu, 1995), 143, and Kim Chŏng-ryŏm, *A! Park Chung Hee: Kim Chŏng-ryŏm chŏngch'i hoegorok* [Ah! Park Chung Hee: Kim Chŏng-ryŏm's reflections on politics] (Seoul: JoongAng M&B, 1997), 168.

2. See Cho In-wŏn, *Kukka-wa sŏnt'aek* [The State and Choice] (Seoul: Nanam, 1998) and Chapters 5, 7, and 8 above.

3. U.S. House of Representatives, *Investigation of Korean-American Relations* (October 31, 1978), 39. Hereafter *Investigation of Korean-American Relations.*

4. See *Kim Dae-jung napch'i sagŏn-ui chinsang kyumyŏng-ŭl wihan simin-ŭi moim* [A Citizen Meeting to Find Truth about the Kidnapping of Kim Dae-jung].

5. See *Investigation of Korean-American Relations,* 149.

6. Hak-Kyu Sohn, "Political Opposition and the *Yushin* Regime: Radicalisation in South Korea, 1972–79" (Ph.D. diss., Oxford University, 1988), 121.

7. Yi Sang-u, *Pirok Park Chung Hee sidae* [Hidden Record of the Park Chung Hee Era], vol. 3 (Seoul: Chungwŏnmunhwa, 1985), 61; Sohn, "Political Opposition and the *Yushin* Regime," 24.

8. Sohn, "Political Opposition and the *Yushin* Regime," 127.

9. See Chung-in Moon et al., *Alliance under Tension: The Evolution of South Korean-U.S. Relations* (Boulder: Westview Press, 1988), chap. 5, 118–119.

10. Chae-Jin Lee and H. Sato, *U.S. Policy toward Japan and Korea: A Changing Influence Relationship* (New York: Praeger, 1982), 90.

11. Robert Boettcher, *Gifts of Deceit: Sun Myung Moon, Tong-sun Park and the Korean Scandal* (New York: Holt, Rinehart and Winston, 1980), 232.

12. Ibid.

13. *Human Rights in South Korea and Philippines: Implications for U.S. Policy,* hearings by the Committee on Foreign Affairs, May-June 1975, 11–12. Hereafter *Human Rights Hearings,* 1975.

14. Mun Ch'ang-gŭk, *Hanmi kaldŭng-ui haebu* [Anatomy of Korea-U.S. Conflicts] (Seoul: Nanam, 1994), 276.

15. *Human Rights Hearings,* 1975, 75 and 234–235.

16. Lee and Sato, *U.S. Policy toward Japan and Korea,* 92. See Boettcher, *Gifts of Deceit,* 142, 34.

17. Peter Hayes, *Pacific Powderkeg: American Nuclear Dilemmas in Korea,* Korean translation (Seoul: Hanul, 1993), 112–113.

18. War History Compilation Committee, *Kukpang choyakchip* [The Treaties of National Defense] (Joint Communiqué of Ford-Park Summit Meeting) (Seoul: Ministry of National Defense, 1981), 755.

19. Lee and Sato, *U.S. Policy toward Japan and Korea,* 92.

20. Don Oberdorfer, *The Two Koreas: A Contemporary History* (Indianapolis: Basic Books, 1997), 63.

21. Ibid., 71–72; Hayes, *Pacific Powderkeg,* 285–286.

22. A letter from Bishop Paul Washburn and T. Jones to President Ford, March 25, 1976. Gerald R. Ford Presidential Library (hereafter Ford Library).

23. A letter from Donald Fraser and another 118 congressmen to President Ford, April 2, 1976. Ford Library.

24. Oberdorfer, *The Two Koreas,* 85–86.

25. Lee and Sato, *U.S. Policy toward Japan and Korea,* 92.

26. The Helsinki agreement's basket three clause dealt with freedom of travel, marriage between citizens of different states, and reunion of families. Kenneth Thompson, *Morality and Foreign Policy* (Baton Rouge: Louisiana State University, 1980), 73.

27. *Human Rights Hearings,* 1975, 94–95.

28. Jimmy Carter, *Keeping Faith: Memoirs of a President* (New York: Bantam Books, 1982), 143.

29. Zbigniew Brzezinski, *Power and Principle: Memoir of the National Security Adviser, 1977–1981* (New York: Farrar, Straus and Giroux, 1983), 125.

30. Carter, *Keeping Faith,* 144.

31. Brzezinski, *Power and Principle,* 123.

32. Pak Tong-jin, *Kil-ŭn mŏlŏdo ttŭt-ŭn hana* 9 [A Long Road but One Wish, a Memoir] (Seoul: Dong-A Ch'ulp'ansa, 1992), 106.

33. Lee and Sato, *U.S. Policy toward Japan and Korea,* 108.

34. William Gleysteen, *Massive Entanglement, Marginal Influence: Carter and Korea in Crisis* (Washington, D.C.: Brookings, 1999), 23.

35. See Presidential Review Memorandum [PRM]/NSC-10, February 18, 1977, and Harold Brown's memorandum as well as the Final Report of Military Strategy and Force Posture Review at the Jimmy Carter Presidential Library. Hereafter Carter Library.

36. PRM/NSC-10, February 18, 1977, 29.

37. PRM/NSC-10, 32 and IV-23.

38. Gleysteen, *Massive Entanglement, Marginal Influence,* 23.

39. Cyrus Vance, *Hard Choices: Critical Years in American Foreign Policy* (New York: Simon and Schuster, 1983), 129.

40. "Transfer of Defense Articles to the Republic of Korea: Message from the President," *Department of State Bulletin,* December 12, 1977, 853.

41. Lee and Sato, *U.S. Policy toward Japan and Korea,* 109; Senators H. Humphrey and J. Glenn, *U.S. Troop Withdrawal from the Republic of Korea, a Report to the Committee on Foreign Relations, U.S. Senate* (Washington, D.C., January 9, 1978), 19–20.

42. Philip C. Habib, "Withdrawal of U.S. Ground Forces from South Korea," *Department of State Bulletin,* July 11, 1977.

43. The initial PRM-13 included removal of most of the nuclear weapons of the Second Division of the USFK. See Hayes, *Pacific Powderkeg,* 132. Kim Chŏng-ryŏm, *Han'guk kyŏngje chŏngch'aek 30nyŏnsa: Kim Chŏng-ryŏm hoegorok* [A 30-Year History of Korea's Economic Policy: The Recollections of Kim Chŏng-ryŏm] (Seoul: JoongAng Ilbosa, 1995), 353–354; Lee and Sato, *U.S. Policy toward Japan and Korea,* 111–112.

44. War History Compilation Committee, *Kukpang choyakchip* [The Treaties of National Defense], 769.

45. Lee and Sato, *U.S. Policy toward Japan and Korea,* 114.

46. See Harold Brown, *Thinking about National Security* (Boulder: Westview Press, 1983), 125.

47. "Human Rights and Foreign Policy," address by Secretary Vance, *Department of State Bulletin,* May 23, 1977.

48. A. Glenn Mower, *Human Rights and American Foreign Policy: The Carter and Reagan Experience* (New York: Greenwood Press, 1987), 71.

49. Ibid., 73.

50. For Carter's attempt at linking the issues of troop withdrawals and human rights, see Kōji Murata, *Daitōryōno zasetsu* [Frustration of a President] (Tokyo: Yuhikaku, 1998), 127, and Victor Cha, *Alignment despite Antagonism: The US-Korea-Japan Security Triangle* (Stanford: Stanford University Press, 1999), 145.

51. Humphrey and Glenn, *U.S. Troop Withdrawal from the ROK,* 21.

52. See Cha, *Alignment despite Antagonism,* 144 and n15, and Oberdorfer, *The Two Koreas,* 85.

53. William Gleysteen, former ambassador to South Korea, recalls the situation: "Anti-Korean fireworks in Congress, magnified by Korea bashing in the media, must have encouraged Carter to think he would have support for or at least acquiescence to his position on the troop issue. In any event, he failed to consult Congress before making up his mind." Gleysteen, *Massive Entanglement, Marginal Influence,* 22.

54. Mower, *Human Rights and American Foreign Policy,* 28.

55. Kim Chŏng-ryŏm, *A! Park Chung Hee* [Ah! Park Chung Hee], 207.

56. *Korea Herald,* September 2, 1977.

57. Humphrey and Glenn, *U.S. Troop Withdrawal from the ROK,* 59–60; *Department of State Bulletin,* January 1978.

58. Brzezinski, *Power and Principle,* 126.

59. Mower, *Human Rights and American Foreign Policy* , 30.

60. Vance, *Hard Choices*, 32.

61. See Boettcher, *Gifts of Deceit*, 241–266.

62. See *Investigations of Korean-American Relations*, 124 n40; Kim Chŏng-ryŏm, *Han'guk kyŏngje chŏngch'aek 30nyŏnsa*, 440.

63. See editorials of *Korea Herald* and *Seoul Sinmun* on April 5, 1978.

64. U.S. Congress Committee on Ethics, "Korean Lobby Probe Ended Lamely," *Congressional Quarterly*, 1980, 44.

65. Kim Hyŏng-uk and Pak Sa-wŏl, *Kim Hyŏng-uk Hoegorok 3: Park Chung Hee wangjo-ŭi pihwa* [The Recollections of Kim Hyŏng-uk, vol. 3: The Secrets of Park Chung Hee's Dynasty, vol. 3] (Seoul: Munhwa Kwangjang, 1987), 253–254.

66. Boettcher, *Gifts of Deceit*, 258–259.

67. *Investigations of Korean-American Relations,* part 7, Hearing, House of Representatives, 95th Congress (Washington, D.C.: U.S. GPO, 1978), 8.

68. See Hak-Kyu Sohn, *Authoritarianism and Opposition in South Korea* (London: Routledge, 1989), 116–117, and the *Korea Herald*, June 2, 1978.

69. Boettcher, *Gifts of Deceit*, 280–281.

70. "Korean Lobby Probe Ended Lamely," *Congressional Quarterly*, 37.

71. In Fraser's early human rights hearings in 1974, Yi Chae-hyŏn testified that Ambassador Kim Tong-jo distributed money to U.S. congressmen.

72. Lee and Sato, *U.S. Policy toward Japan and Korea*, 116.

73. Humphrey and Glenn, *U.S. Troop Withdrawal from the ROK*, 1–5, 40.

74. Lee and Sato, *U.S. Policy toward Japan and Korea*, 118–119, and "Pullout Review in Order," an editorial of the *Korea Herald*, April 11, 1978.

75. Vance, *Hard Choices*, 129.

76. See Lee and Sato, *U.S. Policy toward Japan and Korea*, 119–120, and Cha, *Alignment despite Antagonism*, 153.

77. See abstract of Statement by President Carter, *Department of State Bulletin*, April 1978.

78. Oberdorfer, *The Two Koreas*, 101–102.

79. Brown stated that from 1970 to 1977, the number of North Korean ground troops increased by about 30 percent, and tank and artillery inventory almost doubled. See Brown, *Thinking about National Security*, 123.

80. See Hayes, *Pacific Powderkeg*, 140–141, and also refer to James V. Young, "70nyŏndae 3 dae sagŏn makhu pisa" [Hidden History of Three Key Incidents of the 1970s], *Wŏlgan Chosun* [Monthly Chosun], 1995.

81. Hayes, *Pacific Powderkeg*, 144.

82. Gleysteen, *Massive Entanglement, Marginal Influence*, 29.

83. Lee and Sato, *U.S. Policy toward Japan and Korea*, 121.

84. "East Asia: FY 1980 Assistance Proposals," *Department of State Bulletin*, April 1979.

85. Gleysteen, *Massive Entanglement, Marginal Influence*, 44; and Oberdorfer, *The Two Koreas*.

86. See Gleysteen, *Massive Entanglement, Marginal Influence*, 48, and Vance, *Hard Choices*, 130.

87. Gleysteen, *Massive Entanglement, Marginal Influence,* 47–48, and Oberdorfer, *The Two Koreas,* 106–107.
88. Gleysteen, *Massive Entanglement, Marginal Influence,* 48–49; War History Compilation Committee, *Kukpang choyakchip,* 779.
89. Brzezinski, *Power and Principle,* 127–128.
90. For Carter doctrine, see Brzezinski, *Power and Principle,* 426–469, and Robert Schulzinger, *U.S. Diplomacy since 1900,* 4th ed. (New York: Oxford University Press, 1998), 332.

17. The Search for Deterrence: Park's Nuclear Option

1. *JoongAng Ilbo,* November 3, 1997.
2. See the "Agreement for Cooperation between Governments of the Republic of Korea and the United States Concerning the Civil Uses of Atomic Energy," Ministry of Science and Technology (MoST), *Wŏnjaryŏk kwan'gye pŏmnyŏngjip* [A Collection of Laws and Regulations of Atomic Energy] (Seoul: MoST, 1977), 809–860. Quoted in Young-Sun Ha, *Nuclear Proliferation: World Order and Korea* (Seoul: Seoul National University Press, 1983), 82.
3. Don Oberdorfer, *The Two Koreas: A Contemporary History* (Reading, Mass.: Addison Wesley, 1997), 13.
4. See also Park's speech celebrating National Military Day on October 1, 1970, available online at http://www.516.co.kr/library/sp/f-speech.htm.
5. Taik-young Hamm, *Arming the Two Koreas: State, Capital and Military Power* (London: Routledge, 1999), 80.
6. See Mitchell Reiss, *Without the Bomb* (New York: Columbia University Press, 1988), 82.
7. Institute for Strategic Studies, *The Military Balance,* various issues.
8. *JoongAng Ilbo,* November 3, 1997.
9. See Kang Yong-wŏn, "Pak Kŭn-hye Chŭngŏn: Abŏjiŭi Chukŭmgwa Haekkabal" [Pak Kŭn-hye's Testimony: Father's Death and Nuclear Development"], *Monthly Chosun,* April 1994, 228–229.
10. Ch'oe Hyŏng-sŏp had served as the director of KAERI twice, in 1962–1963 and 1964–1966. When he was appointed the minister of science and technology in June 1971, Ch'oe initiated a fifteen-year Nuclear Power Development Plan. He was to serve in that position for seven and half years. Yun Yong-gu was appointed as the director of KAERI in August 1971, and served until March 1978.
11. Even to the ADD researchers, Park tried not to issue an explicit order for the development of nuclear weapons, lest the United States trace the program to the Blue House and accuse it of undermining the NPT regime. A former ADD researcher, in charge of nuclear weapons design between April 1971 and early 1975, reportedly said that when he met Park on the occasion of his appointment, Park emphasized, "we need to develop *superweapons,* and this has to be done secretly" (italics added). Although the ADD researcher recollected that the term "superweapons" generally referred to chemical weapons among

South Korean scientists, he thought Park meant to say the development of nuclear weapons. See *JoongAng Ilbo,* November 10, 1997.

12. There exist different accounts on Park's pursuit of nuclear development. On the basis of interview with a high-ranking South Korean official, a U.S. congressional report argues that it was the Weapons Exploitation Committee (WEC), established within the Blue House, that voted unanimously to proceed with the project. By contrast, Seung-young Kim relies on his interview with former South Korean army generals to argue that it was the South Korean armed forces that raised the possibility of nuclear armament as an option to counter North Korea's superior conventional military capabilities. See U.S. House of Representatives, *Investigations of Korean-American Relations,* Report of the Subcommittee on International Organizations of the Committee on International Relations (Washington, D.C.: U.S. GPO, 1978), 80, and Jacques E. C. Hymans, Seung-Young Kim, and Henning Riecke, "To Go or Not to Go: South and North Korea's Nuclear Decisions in Comparative Context," *Journal of East Asian Studies* 1, no. 1 (February 2001), note 15.

13. KAERI, *Han'guk wŏnjaryŏk yŏn'guso 40 nyŏnsa* [Forty-year History of KAERI] (Seoul: KAERI, 1990), 55.

14. Interview with a key nuclear engineer in the special project team, November 2000.

15. *JoongAng Ilbo,* November 13, 1997. Ku Sang-hoe, who was in charge of missile development, recounted the complete story of South Korean missile development in *Sindonga,* from February to April 1999.

16. Saint-Gobain Technique Nouvelle and CERCA agreed to provide KAERI with $46 million and $2.6 million in commercial loans, respectively. See *JoongAng Ilbo,* November 6, 1997.

17. The bilateral Agreement for Cooperation with the United States for the peaceful use of atomic energy explicitly prohibited any use of American-supplied material for military purposes. See Article X(2), *Agreement for Cooperation between the Government of the United States of America and the Government of the Republic of Korea Concerning Civil Uses of Atomic Energy.* Signed November 24, 1972; entered into force March 19, 1973. 24 UST 775; TIAS. 7583. Quoted in Reiss, *Without the Bomb,* 85, 293.

18. Cable from U.S. Ambassador Richard L. Sneider to Secretary of State Henry A. Kissinger, "Non-proliferation Treaty," February 26, 1975.

19. Telegram from the State Secretary to Embassy Seoul, "ROK Plans to Develop Nuclear Weapons and Missiles," March 4, 1975, MLF MR Case no. 94–146, Document no. 49.

20. See the U.S. Energy Research and Development Agency's report of April 1977 as cited in U.S. Senate, Committee on Governmental Affairs, *Nuclear Proliferation Factbook,* 96th Cong., 2nd Sess. (Washington, D.C.: U.S. GPO, 1980), 325.

21. *JoongAng Ilbo,* November 3, 1997.

22. See Ku Sang-hoe, "A Retrospective of Dr. Ku Sang-hoe, a Living Witness of Korean Missile Development," *Sindonga,* February, March, and April, 1999.

23. Reiss, *Without the Bomb,* 91.

24. Ku Sang-hoe, "A Retrospective."
25. O Wŏn-ch'ŏl, "Chun Doo-hwan and the U.S. Intervention in the Development of Ballistic Missiles," *Sindonga*, January 1996, 395–396.
26. Ibid., 397.
27. Ibid., 399–400.
28. Ibid., 401. Also see telegram from Embassy Seoul to the State Secretary, "Lockheed Proposals for ROK," October 28, 1974.
29. George S. Springteen, "Sale of Rocket Propulsion Technology to South Korea," a Memorandum for Lieutenant General Brent Scowcroft, the White House, February 4, 1975, 3.
30. *JoongAng Ilbo*, May 3, 1997.
31. Telegram from Embassy Seoul to the State Secretary, "Lockeed Proposals for ROK," October 28, 1974, MLF MR Case No. 94–146, Document no. 52.
32. Telegram from the State Secretary to Embassy Seoul, "ROK Plans to Develop Nuclear Weapons and Missiles," December 11, 1974, MLF MR Case no. 94–146, Document no. 47.
33. Telegram from the State Secretary to Embassy Seoul, "ROK Plans to Develop Nuclear Weapons and Missiles," March 4, 1975, MLF MR Case no. 94–146, Document no. 49.
34. Telegram from Embassy Seoul to the State Secretary, "ROK Plans to Develop Nuclear Weapons and Missiles," March 12, 1975, MLF MR Case no. 94–146, Document No. 28.
35. Telegram from Embassy Seoul to the State Secretary, "Meeting with President Park: Missile Strategy," May 1, 1975, MLF MR Case no. 94–146, Document no. 54.
36. Robert S. Ingersoll, Acting Secretary, "Approach to South Korea on Reprocessing," A Memorandum to the Assistant to the President for National Security Affairs, July 2, 1975, MLF MR Case no. 94–146, Document no. 14.
37. At first, France was reluctant to cooperate with the United States due to its economic interests in the nuclear deal with South Korea. However, France eventually renegotiated with South Korea to include a clause on the non-replication of equipment for a period of twenty years. South Korea accepted this condition and on September 22, 1975, the safeguards agreement among the IAEA, France, and South Korea entered into force. See Reiss, *Without the Bomb*, 92.
38. At that time, South Korea was seeking a U.S. Export-Import Bank loan of $132 million and an additional commercial loan of $117 million guaranteed by the U.S. government for the construction of the Kori-2 reactor.
39. The idea of building an East Asian regional reprocessing plant was first mentioned in this document without much detail. However, this idea never materialized.
40. Reiss, *Without the Bomb*, 92.
41. Telegram from Embassy Seoul to the State Secretary, "ROKG Nuclear Reprocessing," October 31, 1975, MLF MR Case no. 94–146, Document No. 31.
42. Ibid.
43. Ibid.

44. Telegram from Embassy Seoul to the State Secretary (immediate), "ROK Nuclear Reprocessing," December 10, 1975, MLF MR Case no. 94–146, Document no. 36.

45. Telegram from Embassy Seoul to the State Secretary (immediate), "ROK Nuclear Reprocessing," December 16, 1975, MLF MR Case no. 94–146, Document no. 40.

46. Ibid.

47. Telegram from Embassy Seoul to the State Secretary (immediate), "ROK Nuclear Reprocessing," January 5, 1976, MLF MR Case no. 94–146, Document no. 42.

48. Telegram from Embassy Seoul to the State Secretary (immediate), "ROK Nuclear Reprocessing," January 14, 1976, MLF MR Case no. 94–146, Document no. 43.

49. Telegram from State Department to Embassy Seoul, "ROK Nuclear Fuel Reprocessing Plans," June 30, 1975, MLF MR Case no. 94–146, Document no. 13.

50. Peter Hayes, *Pacific Powderkeg: American Nuclear Dilemmas in Korea* (Lexington: Macmillan, 1991), 35.

51. Victor Cha at Georgetown University provided me with this excellent comment.

52. According to O, Park never intended to use the would-be nuclear weapons against North Korea. Private conversation with O, November 18, 2009.

53. Hayes, *Pacific Powderkeg*, xxxix.

54. Such an argument of nuclear optimism is set forth by Kenneth N. Waltz in "Nuclear Myths and Political Realities," *American Political Science Review* 84, no. 3 (September 1990): 731–745. This line of nuclear optimism is contrasted to the nuclear pessimism addressed mainly by Scott C. Sagan and Peter D. Feaver. For the details of the debate, see David J. Karl, "Proliferation Pessimism and Emerging Nuclear Powers," *International Security* 21, no. 3 (Winter 1996/97): 87–119; and Scott D. Sagan and Kenneth N. Waltz, *The Spread of Nuclear Weapons: A Debate* (New York: W. W. Norton, 1995).

55. Consult Scott D. Sagan, "Why Do States Build Nuclear Weapons? Three Models in Search of a Bomb," *International Security* 21, no. 3 (Winter, 1996/97): 54–86, for such a view.

56. See Telegram from Embassy Seoul to the State Secretary, "ROKG Nuclear Reprocessing," October 31, 1975, NLF MR Case no. 94–146, Document no. 31.

57. Reiss, *Without the Bomb*, 91.

58. For this argument, the author owes special thanks to Victor Cha of Georgetown University.

59. Telegram from State Department to Embassy Seoul, "Non-proliferation Treaty," February 26, 1975, MLF MR Case no. 96–146, Document no. 53.

60. Telegram from the State Secretary to Embassy Seoul, "ROK Plans to Develop Nuclear Weapons and Missiles," March 4, 1975, MLF MR Case no. 94–146, Document no. 49.

61. Oberdorfer, *The Two Koreas*, 71.
62. Memorandum of Conversation, Participants: President Park Chung Hee, Senior Protocol Secretary Ch'oe Kwan-su, Secretary of Defense James R. Schlesinger, and Ambassador Richard L. Sneider, MR 94–143, no. 19.
63. Reiss, *Without the Bomb*, 104–105.
64. Kang Yong-wŏn, "Pak Kŭn-hye Chŭngŏn" [Pak Kŭn-hye's Testimony], 228–229.
65. Cho Ch'ol-ho, "Park Chung Hee Haekchongch'aek-kwa 1970nyŏndae huban hanmigwangye" [Park's Nuclear Policy and the U.S.-Korea Relations in the late 1970s], paper presented at the Winter Conference of the Korean Association of International Studies, 2002.
66. O Wŏn-ch'ŏl, "A Brutal Fight between Park and Carter," *Sindonga*, November 1974, 426.
67. Ibid., 430.
68. *JoongAng Ilbo*, November 10, 1997.
69. Memorandum of Conversation, Subject: Secure telephone conversation with Secretary Harold Brown on Wednesday, January 26, 1977.
70. O Wŏn-ch'ŏl, "Chun Doo-hwan and the U.S. Intervention in the Development of Ballistic Missiles."
71. Etel Solingen has a similar view. Too much was at stake for Park to continue his nuclear program after all. See Etel Solingen, *Nuclear Logics* (Princeton: Princeton University Press, 2007), 82–99.

18. Nation Rebuilders: Mustafa Kemal Atatürk, Lee Kuan Yew, Deng Xiaoping, and Park Chung Hee

1. For Atatürk and Turkey, see Andrew Mango, *Atatürk: The Biography of the Founder of Modern Turkey* (Overlook Press, 1999); Lord Kinross, *Atatürk: A Biography of Mustafa Kemal, Father of Modern Turkey* (Quill, 1964); Lord Kinross, *The Ottoman Centuries: The Rise and Fall of the Turkish Empire* (Quill, 1979); Ali Kazancigil and Ergun Ozbuden, eds., *Atatürk: Founder of a Modern State* (C. Hurst and Co., 1981).

   For Lee Kuan Yew and Singapore, see Lee Kuan Yew, *The Singapore Story: Memoirs of Lee Kuan Yew* (Prentice Hall, 1998); Lee Kuan Yew, *From Third World to First: The Singapore Story: 1965–2000* (Singapore: Singapore Press Holdings, 2000); Kernial Singh Sandhu and Paul Wheatley, eds., *Management of Success: The Moulding of Modern Singapore* (Institute of Southeast Asian Studies, 1989).

   For Deng Xiaoping and China see Deng Maomao [Deng Rong], *Deng Xiaoping: My Father* (New York: Basic Books, 1995); Deng Rong, *Deng Xiaoping and the Cultural Revolution: A Daughter Recalls the Critical Years* (Foreign Language Press, 2002); Richard Evans, *Deng Xiaoping and the Making of Modern China* (Penguin Books, 1993); Benjamin Yang, *Deng: A Political Biography* (M. E. Sharpe, 1998); and Richard Baum, *Burying Mao: Chinese Politics in the Era of Deng Xiaoping* (Princeton: Princeton University Press, 1994). I have also drawn on my own interviews on Deng and his era.

For Park Chung Hee and South Korea, see the chapters in this book and the references they cite.

I am indebted to the book contributors and especially to Ozkul Akin, Ed Baker, Vin Brandt, Byung-Kook Kim, Dick Samuels, and Nur Yalmon, who carefully read and commented on my manuscript.

2. Deng Maomao, *Deng Xiaoping: My Father*, 40–41.

3. Ibid., 42–51.

4. Ibid., 59–60, 99.

5. I am indebted to Hyung-A Kim and her manuscript "Who Was Park Chung Hee" for providing the background on which the above comments draw.

6. Lee Kuan Yew, *The Singapore Story*, 113–114.

7. Ibid., 146–176.

8. Ibid., 137–145, 177–193.

9. Ibid., 73, 104–109.

10. Deng Maomao, *Deng Xiaoping, My Father*, 75–103.

11. Lord Kinross, *Atatürk*, 54.

12. Lee Kuan Yew, *The Singapore Story*, 306.

13. Lee Kuan Yew, *From Third World*, 119.

19. Reflections on a Reverse Image: South Korea under Park Chung Hee and the Philippines under Ferdinand Marcos

Sincere thanks to Ezra Vogel for bringing me into this project, and to both him and Byung-Kook Kim for their very helpful support and suggestions as I have developed the comparative analysis in this chapter. I am also indebted to the participants in the August 2000 conference, where contributors to this volume first presented their papers. I enjoyed my often-lengthy discussions, both during and after the conference, with Seung-Mi Han, Hyug Baeg Im, Hoon Jaung, Joo-Hong Kim, Yong-Jick Kim, Min Yong Lee, Young Jo Lee, Chung-in Moon, Wookhee Shin, David I. Steinberg, and Meredith Woo-Cumings. Their many insights were enormously beneficial to a scholar who had no previous academic background in Korean history or politics, and I am grateful to them for assisting and tutoring me. Valuable comments on earlier drafts were provided by Patricio Abinales, Jorge Domínguez, Sung Chull Kim, Kevin McGahan, Aloysius M. O'Neill, Rigoberto Tiglao, and Meredith Woo-Cumings. Any errors, of course, are mine alone.

1. Carter J. Eckert, Ki-baik Lee, Young Ick Lew, Michael Robinson, and Edward W. Wagner, *Korea Old and New: A History* (Seoul: Iljogak, 1990, for the Harvard University Korea Institute), 372; interview, Adrian Cristobal, former special assistant (to President Marcos) for special studies, June 19, 1989; BBC, "Suharto tops corruption rankings," March 25, 2004, at http://news.bbc.co.uk/2/hi/3567745.stm.

2. The structural preconditions examined here are in the realms of administration and state-society relations. Beyond the scope of this analysis is an additional precondition in the economic realm that would generally be seen as highly *disadvantageous* to the country's developmental prospects, namely South Korea's relative lack of natural resources. All the more impressive, therefore, is Park's ability to shape a successful strategy of rapid economic development around the basic precondition of resource scarcity.

3. Hagen Koo, "Strong State and Contentious Society," in Koo, ed., *State and Society in Contemporary Korea* (Ithaca: Cornell University Press, 1993), 232; Carter J. Eckert, "The South Korean Bourgeoisie: A Class in Search of Hegemony," in Koo, *State and Society,* 96.

4. Koo, "Strong State and Contentious Society," in Koo, *State and Society,* 235.

5. Onofre D. Corpuz, *The Bureaucracy in the Philippines* (Manila: University of the Philippines Institute of Public Administration, 1957), 118–122; Peter W. Stanley, *A Nation in the Making: The Philippines and the United States, 1899–1921* (Cambridge, Mass.: Harvard University Press, 1974), 10–11, 38.

6. James Francis Warren, *The Sulu Zone, 1768–1898* (Quezon City: New Day Publishers, 1985), 121–123, 253–255. Late nineteenth-century Spanish attempts at enforcing the political unity of the Philippine archipelago came a full millennium after the political unification of the Korean Peninsula under Wang Kŏn. See Bruce Cumings, *Korea's Place in the Sun* (New York: W. W. Norton, 1997), 39–40. It is also worth noting that the Chosŏn dynasty (dating to 1392) was almost two centuries older than the Spanish colonial state in the Philippines.

7. Harold Crouch, *Economic Change, Social Structure, and the Political System in Southeast Asia: Philippine Development Compared with the Other ASEAN Countries* (Singapore: Institute of Southeast Asian Studies, 1985), 10.

8. Jung-en Woo, *Race to the Swift: State and Finance in Korean Industrialization* (New York: Columbia University Press, 1991), 19–42. This book provides an enormously rich analysis of the interplay of many factors, from colonial foundations to postwar geopolitics, and through it I received my first—and most enduring—introduction to Korean political economy.

9. Koo, "Strong State and Contentious Society," in Koo, *State and Society,* 234.

10. The following draws on Paul D. Hutchcroft, "Colonial Masters, National Politicos, Provincial Lords: Central Authority and Local Autonomy in the American Philippines, 1900–1913," *Journal of Asian Studies* 59, no. 2 (2000): 277–306.

11. Quoted in David Joel Steinberg, ed., *In Search of Southeast Asia: A Modern History* (Honolulu: University of Hawaii Press, 1987), 277.

12. Benedict Anderson, "Cacique Democracy and the Philippines: Origins and Dreams," *New Left Review,* no. 169 (1988): 11–12 (quote at 11).

13. See Hutchcroft, "Colonial Masters," 294–299. On land and land-grabbing, see Leonard F. Gesick, *History of American Economic Policy in the Philippines during the American Colonial Period, 1900–1935* (New York: Garland Publishing, 1987), 178–230.

14. Alfred W. McCoy, "Quezon's Commonwealth: The Emergence of Philippine Authoritarianism," in *Philippine Colonial Democracy,* ed. Ruby R. Paredes, Yale University Southeast Asia Studies Monograph no. 32 (New Haven: Yale University, 1989), 115–116; on Quezon's rise, see Michael Cullinane, *Ilustrado Politics: Filipino Elite Responses to American Rule, 1898–1908* (Quezon City: Ateneo de Manila University Press, 2003), 176–194.

15. Koo, "Strong State and Contentious Society," in Koo, *State and Society,* 237–238.

16. Eckert et al., *Korea Old and New*, 341–342; Cumings, *Korea's Place in the Sun*, 215–216, quote at 215.

17. Stephen Rosskamm Shalom, *The United States and the Philippines: A Study of Neocolonialism* (Quezon City: New Day Publishers, 1986), 1–69; Benedict J. Kerkvliet, *The Huk Rebellion: A Study of Peasant Revolt in the Philippines* (Berkeley and Los Angeles: University of California Press, 1977), 143–202.

18. Frank H. Golay, *The Philippines: Public Policy and National Economic Development* (Ithaca: Cornell University Press, 1961), 71–72, 80.

19. Shalom, *The United States and the Philippines*, 86–93.

20. Kerkvliet, *The Huk Rebellion*, 238.

21. Shalom, *The United States and the Philippines*, 84–85; David Joel Steinberg, *The Philippines: A Singular and a Plural Place*, 4th ed. (Boulder: Westview Press, 2000), 26.

22. Koo, "Strong State and Contentious Society," in Koo, *State and Society*, 240.

23. Cumings, *Korea's Place in the Sun*, 270, 302, quote at 270.

24. Jang Jip Choi, "Political Cleavages in South Korea," in Koo, *State and Society*, 22.

25. On the "establishment and institutionalization of the anti-leftist State," see Chang Hun Oh, "A Study of the Dynamics of an Authoritarian Regime: The Case of the *Yushin* System under Park Chung Hee, 1972–1979" (Ph.D. diss., Ohio State University, 1991), 61–62.

26. Woo, *Race to the Swift*, 43–69; see also Cumings, *Korea's Place in the Sun*, 306–307. In Woo's vivid terms, one finds at this point "a capitalism without the capitalist class. . . . [W]hat powerful group exists today in Korea, mostly the chaebŏl, had to be built *by* the state" (p. 14).

27. Eckert et al., *Korea Old and New*, 351; see also Cumings, *Korea's Place in the Sun*, 341. As Byung-Kook Kim explains, the *yangban* class was "destroyed by a triple shock of Japanese colonial rule, land reform, and civil war." See Byung-Kook Kim, "The Leviathan: Economic Bureaucracy under Park Chung Hee," a paper presented at the Conference on the Park Chung Hee Era, August 2000, Seoul, Korea.

28. This discussion draws on Hutchcroft, *Booty Capitalism: The Politics of Banking in the Philippines* (Ithaca: Cornell University Press, 1998), 71–77. The Marcos incident is reported in Sterling Seagrave, *The Marcos Dynasty* (New York: Harper and Row, 1988), 162; a similar story is found in Primitivo Mijares, *The Conjugal Dictatorship of Ferdinand and Imelda Marcos I* (San Francisco: Union Square Publications, 1986 [1976]), 262.

29. Golay, *The Philippines*, 141, 163–164, 239; Laurence Davis Stifel, *The Textile Industry: A Case Study of Industrial Development in the Philippines*, Southeast Asia Program, Cornell University, Data Paper no. 49 (Ithaca, N.Y., 1963), 70, 74, 80.

30. Woo, *Race to the Swift*, 71–72.

31. As Jung-en Woo explains, "it was a crime to have indulged in the political economy of the Rhee era." *Race to the Swift*, 83.

32. See Stephan Haggard, Byung-Kook Kim, and Chung-In Moon, "The Transi-

tion to Export-led Growth in South Korea, 1954–1966," *Journal of Asian Studies* 50, no. 4 (1991): 850–873, at 858–859.

33. On "The Rules of Pre-Martial Law Philippine Politics," see Mark R. Thompson, *The Anti-Marcos Struggle: Personalistic Rule and Democratic Transition in the Philippines* (New Haven: Yale University Press, 1995), 15–32.

34. Raymond Bonner, *Waltzing with a Dictator: The Marcoses and the Making of American Policy* (New York: Times Books, 1987), 50.

35. David Joel Steinberg, *The Philippines*, 115–117; Bonner, *Waltzing with a Dictator*, 11–17. On the Marcos medals, see Alfred W. McCoy, *Closer than Brothers: Manhood at the Philippine Military Academy* (New Haven: Yale University Press, 1999), 159–180.

36. See Chapter 5 above.

37. The First Lady loved to entertain foreign dignitaries, and at one 1966 gathering in Manila she sang and danced for a group of leaders that included Lyndon B. Johnson and Park Chung Hee. Her orchestra, meanwhile, played "Deep in the Heart of Texas" and "Arilang." Bonner, *Waltzing with a Dictator*, 51, 61.

38. Woo, *Race to the Swift*, 81.

39. As Kim Hyung-A concludes, "Park was found to have amassed very little personal wealth of any significance" in his eighteen years in power; since his death, moreover, "there is no new evidence that challenges Park's financial probity." Kim, *Korea's Development under Park Chung Hee: Rapid Industrialization, 1961–79* (London: RoutledgeCurzon, 2004), 192. The only reference I have found linking Park to corrupt behavior comes from David C. Kang, who notes in passing that "after Park's death, half a million dollars was found in his personal safe." See Kang, *Crony Capitalism: Corruption and Development in South Korea and the Philippines* (Cambridge: Cambridge University Press, 2002), 104. Given the highly liquid form of these assets, however, it is not clear whether this cash was part of a personal fortune or just a cache of money used to pay off regime stalwarts and opposition politicians. More damning would be revelations that Park demanded a share in the *chaebol* that he nurtured throughout his presidency, or stashed away huge sums (à la Marcos and Mobutu) in foreign bank accounts and real estate.

40. Thompson, *Anti-Marcos Struggle*, 34–35.

41. Petronilo Bn. Daroy, "On the Eve of Dictatorship and Revolution," in *Dictatorship and Revolution: Roots of People's Power*, ed. Aurora Javate-de Dios, Petronilo Bn. Daroy, and Lorna Kalaw-Tirol (Metro Manila: Conspectus, 1988), 15–16; Belinda A. Aquino, *Politics of Plunder: The Philippines under Marcos*, 2nd ed. (Quezon City: Kadena Press, 1999), 20–25.

42. Bonner, *Waltzing with a Dictator*, 75; McCoy, *Closer than Brothers*, 29.

43. Thompson, *Anti-Marcos Struggle*, 36–37; Bonner, *Waltzing with a Dictator*, 76–77; McCoy, *Closer than Brothers*, 29; Jose Veloso Abueva, "The Philippines: Tradition and Change," *Asian Survey* 10, no. 1 (1970): 56–64, at 62.

44. See Chapter 5 above.

45. John Kie-chiang Oh, *Korean Politics* (Ithaca: Cornell University Press, 1999), 52–53; Chapters 5 and 7, above.

46. See Chapters 4 and 7 above.

47. See Chapter 6 above.

48. Carolina G. Hernandez, "The Role of the Military in Contemporary Philippine Society," *Diliman Review* 32, no. 1 (1984): 1, 16–23, at 18–19; Hutchcroft, *Booty Capitalism*, 90–102.

49. See Woo, *Race to the Swift*, 84, 101–117. The term "asymmetric political exchange" is inspired by the analysis of Byung-Kook Kim. See Chapter 7 and Chapter 9.

50. Woo, *Race to the Swift*, 84; Hutchcroft, *Booty Capitalism*, 84–90.

51. Woo, *Race to the Swift*, 85–117, 130, quote at 109; Park quote is from Cumings, *Korea's Place in the Sun*, 299; Byung-Kook Kim, Chapter 7.

52. See Hutchcroft, *Booty Capitalism*, 82–84.

53. Sunhyuk Kim, *The Politics of Democratization in Korea: The Role of Civil Society* (Pittsburgh: University of Pittsburgh Press, 2000), 55–56; C. I. Eugene Kim, "The Meaning of the 1971 Korean Elections: A Pattern of Political Development," *Asian Survey* 12, no. 3 (1972): 216; Cumings, *Korea's Place in the Sun*, 361; David I. Steinberg, *The Republic of Korea: Economic Transformation and Social Change* (Boulder: Westview Press, 1988), 57.

54. Joel Rocamora, *Breaking Through: The Struggle within the Communist Party of the Philippines* (Metro Manila: Anvil Publishing, 1994), 11–13; David Wurfel, *Filipino Politics: Development and Decay* (Ithaca: Cornell University Press, 1998), 107; Hutchcroft, *Booty Capitalism*, 111–112.

55. Wurfel, *Filipino Politics*, 106–112.

56. Thompson, *Anti-Marcos Struggle*, 43–44; for evidence linking the Communist Party to the bombing, see Gregg Jones, *Red Revolution: Inside the Philippine Guerrilla Movement* (Boulder: Westview Press, 1989), 59–69.

57. Steinberg, *The Republic of Korea*, 57.

58. See Mijares, *Conjugal Dictatorship*, 160; McCoy, *Closer than Brothers*, 192.

59. Chang Hun Oh, "The *Yushin* System under Park Chung Hee," 21–28. See also Chapters 4, 7, and 8 as well as In-sub Mah, "Rule by Emergency Powers," a paper presented at the Conference on the Park Chung Hee Era, August 2000, Seoul, Korea.

60. Rigoberto Tiglao, "The Consolidation of the Dictatorship," in *Dictatorship and Revolution: Roots of People's Power*, ed. Aurora Javate-de Dios, Petronilo Bn. Daroy, and Lorna Kalaw-Tirol (Metro Manila: Conspectus Foundation Incorporated, 1988), 26; Abueva, "Ideology and Practice," 34.

61. Thompson, *Anti-Marcos Struggle*, 60.

62. Anderson, "Cacique Democracy and the Philippines," 21; Wurfel, *Filipino Politics*, 191. Raymond Bonner's *Waltzing with a Dictator* gives a very good sense of how the Marcoses were adept at maneuvering in Washington circles. Fortunately for Marcos, Richard Nixon and Henry Kissinger had proven to be frequent supporters of dictatorships worldwide, and exhibited no problems accepting Marcos's arguments in favor of emergency rule.

63. Tiglao, "The Consolidation of the Dictatorship," 38.

64. Thompson, *Anti-Marcos Struggle*, 60–61; Wurfel, *Filipino Politics*, 114–117.

65. Hoon Jaung, "The Abortive Modernization Experiment of Party Politics: The

Failure of Democratic Republican Party," a paper presented at the Conference on the Park Chung Hee Era, August 2000, Seoul, Korea, 40.

66. Thompson, *Anti-Marcos Struggle*, 44, 60, 61; Wurfel, *Filipino Politics*, 130–131, 237.

67. Alfred W. McCoy, ed., *An Anarchy of Families: State and Family in the Philippines* (Madison: University of Wisconsin-Madison Center for Southeast Asian Studies, 1993).

68. The term comes from the title of a book written by a former Marcos aide, Primitivo Mijares (*Conjugal Dictatorship*, cited above).

69. Aquino, *Politics of Plunder*, 88; Thompson, *Anti-Marcos Struggle*, 76–78.

70. Wurfel, *Filipino Politics*, 135; Abueva, "Ideology and Practice," 52; Robert B. Stauffer, "The Political Economy of Refeudalization," in *Marcos and Martial Law in the Philippines*, ed. David A. Rosenberg (Ithaca: Cornell University Press, 1979), 200; interview, Carmensita T. Abella, Vice President of DAP, August 28, 1986.

71. Anderson, "Cacique Democracy and the Philippines," 20.

72. Whatever the precise origins of her power, there is no question that at some point after 1972 she was able to establish a relatively autonomous power base within the regime. According to a former Marcos advisor, Imelda could threaten Marcos with an exposure, or a "big public divorce, and Marcos never wanted to call her bluff." Interview, Adrian Cristobal, June 19, 1989. Wurfel describes it as a relationship of "mutual blackmail" (*Filipino Politics*, 241).

73. Paul D. Hutchcroft, "Oligarchs and Cronies in the Philippine State: The Politics of Patrimonial Plunder," *World Politics* 43, no. 1 (April 1991): 414–450, at 436; biography of Madame Imelda Romualdez Marcos, Office of Media Affairs, 1984; Thompson, *Anti-Marcos Struggle*, quote at 52. The First Lady's prominent roles caused considerable dissension within the regime, as many technocrats, as well as many among the relatively more professionalized elements of the military, resented her ability to influence key policies and appointments.

74. Interview, Francisco S. Tatad, former Information Minister (under President Marcos), August 22, 1989. In Weber's words, "the ruler's personal discretion delimits the jurisdiction of his officials." Max Weber, *Economy and Society* (Berkeley: University of California Press, 1978), 1029.

75. Raul V. Fabella, "Trade and Industry Reforms in the Philippines: Process and Performance," in *Philippine Macroeconomic Perspective: Developments and Policies*, ed. Manuel F. Montes and Hideyoshi Sakai (Tokyo: Institute of Developing Economies, 1989), 197; Weber, *Economy and Society*, 1098 (see also p. 1028).

76. Marcos's modest land reform was similarly counteracted by the regime's rampant land grabbing, and modest bank reforms were counteracted by the bank grabbing of Marcos and his cronies. See Hutchcroft, *Booty Capitalism*, 140–142.

77. Davide Commission Report, 52; McCoy, *Closer than Brothers*, quote at 207.

78. Wurfel, *Filipino Politics*, 159, 266. Wurfel writes that unofficial estimates of the size of the Moro National Liberation Front reached as high as 60,000 fighters.

79. Byeongil Rho, "State Capability and Third World Politics: A Comparative Analysis of South Korean and Philippine Cases" (Ph.D. diss., State University of New York at Albany, 1992), 331. I am grateful to Rigoberto Tiglao for pointing me to this analysis.

80. McCoy, *Closer than Brothers*, 193, 205–206 (quote at 205). Rho reports that in 1976 there were roughly 120 political prisoners in Korea, while in 1977 there were some 4,700 political prisoners in the Philippines. Between 1972 and 1977, there were 10 deaths from domestic political conflict in Korea and 3,588 deaths in the Philippines. Rho, "State Capability and Third World Politics," 332–333, quote at 333.

81. Tiglao, "The Consolidation of the Dictatorship," 53.

82. See Chapters 4, 7, 9, 10, and 11, above; Tiglao, "The Consolidation of the Dictatorship," 49, citing economist Bernardo Villegas of the Center for Research and Communications. The term "debt-driven growth" comes from Manuel F. Montes, "Financing Development: The 'Democratic' versus the 'Corporatist' Approach in the Philippines," in *The Political Economy of Fiscal Policy*, ed. Miguel Urrutia, Shinichi Ichimura, and Setsuko Yukawa (Tokyo: United Nations University, 1990), 90.

83. See Chapter 7.

84. Ferdinand E. Marcos, *The Democratic Revolution in the Philippines* (Englewood Cliffs, N.J.: Prentice-Hall International, 1979 [1974]), 6.

85. De Dios, "Philippine Policy-Making," 114. "Crony" is used to describe those whose positions are particularly favored by the current regime, regardless of their origins. An "oligarch" may not be a current crony but in either case has already established his or her fortune in earlier dispensations. Under the Marcos regime, both "old oligarchs" and "new men" gained "crony" status, and they were referred to collectively as the "new oligarchy." According to the regime's chief ideologue, the impulse for crony capitalism was present from the start, but Marcos knew he had to take "measured steps" and wait for further opportunities to present themselves. Interview, Adrian Cristobal, June 19, 1989.

86. Manuel F. Montes, "Philippine Structural Adjustments, 1970–1987," in *Philippine Macroeconomic Perspective: Developments and Policies*, ed. Montes and Sakai, 45–90, at 71–73; World Bank, "Philippines Staff Appraisal Report on the Industrial Finance Project," Report no. 3331-PH (Washington, DC, 1981), 1; Emmanuel S. de Dios, "The Erosion of the Dictatorship," in Javate-de Dios et al., *Dictatorship and Revolution*, 119–120; and de Dios, "Philippine Policy-Making," quote at 116.

87. Hutchcroft, "Oligarchs and Cronies," 429–430; Wurfel, *Filipino Politics*, 200; Woo, *Race to the Swift*, 88, 133–170, quotes at 163, 169; Joel Rocamora, "Japanese Capital in the Philippines: Exploiting to Develop," *Southeast Asia Chronicle*, no. 88 (1983): 10–13, at 11–12; Mamoru Tsuda, *A Preliminary*

Study of Japanese-Filipino Joint Ventures (Quezon City: Foundation for Nationalist Studies, 1978), 34–35 (see also p. ii of Renato Constantino's foreword to the book); and Hutchcroft, *Booty Capitalism*, 188. On the origins of the term "crony capitalism," see Benjamin Trinidad Tolosa, Jr., "Calling to Account: Good Governance, Global Financial Regularization and the Symbolic Labor of Securities Research" (Ph.D. diss., University of Minnesota, 2001), 6.

88. In-Sub Mah, "Emergency Powers," 2.

89. Sunhyuk Kim, *The Politics of Democratization in Korea*, 51–55.

90. Sunhyuk Kim, *The Politics of Democratization in Korea*, 61–62; Chang Hun Oh, "Dynamics of an Authoritarian Regime," 78, 298, 302.

91. Thompson, *Anti-Marcos Struggle*, 61. Throughout this study, Thompson provides a fascinating account of the complex linkages among the various oppositions to martial law: traditional politicians, communists, and Muslims.

92. De Dios, "Erosion," 70–71, 74 (quotes at 71, 74); Thompson, *Anti-Marcos Struggle*, 74–80.

93. See Kathleen Weekley, *The Communist Party of the Philippines: 1968–1993: A Story of Its Theory and Practice* (Quezon City: University of the Philippines Press, 2001), 111–114.

94. On the adjustment of the CPP to new conditions, see Rocamora, *Breaking Through*, 15–18, and Tiglao, "The Consolidation of the Dictatorship," 63–66. On relations between the CPP and the "caciques," see Patricio N. Abinales, *Images of State Power: Essays on Philippine Politics from the Margins* (Quezon City: University of the Philippines Press, 1998), 137–165.

95. De Dios, "Erosion," 128–130; Rocamora, *Breaking Through*, 21–27; Tiglao, "The Consolidation of the Dictatorship," 58–66.

96. Mark R. Thompson, "Off the Endangered List: Philippine Democratization in Comparative Perspective," *Comparative Politics* 28, no. 2 (1996): 179–205 (quote at 180).

97. Interview, Aniceto Sobrapeña, Cabinet Secretary in the administration of Corazon Aquino, 1987–1992, July 24, 2000.

98. This counterfactual fantasy sets aside, for the sake of simplicity, questions about whether a fierce nationalist like Park would likely have emerged from a Philippine military that had little concern about external threats and competition, and little if any animosity toward the former colonial power, or whether someone like Marcos would rise to the top of the Korean political system. It is perhaps somewhat easier to imagine a self-aggrandizing politico like Marcos arising from the ranks of Korean congresspersons, but by the end the 1950s—after Rhee's success at centralizing the political system—it seems unlikely that such a politician could have had the same sort of independence and strong local base that Marcos enjoyed as he ascended to higher office.

99. The complementary nature of structure and agency in the two cases could at least in part be attributed to the way in which Park and Marcos were shaped by the contexts from which they emerged. It must quickly be emphasized, however, that a range of different individuals can arise from precisely the same

context. One can imagine highly divergent outcomes, for example, if Fidel Ramos rather than his second cousin Ferdinand Marcos wielded the powers of martial law in the Philippines after 1972.

20. The Perfect Dictatorship? South Korea versus Argentina, Brazil, Chile, and Mexico

This chapter is part of a project focused on the Park Chung Hee regime in South Korea led by Professors Byung-Kook Kim and Ezra Vogel. It draws on the works of South Korean authors for this project as the basic source of information about the Park regime. Thus I am greatly in debt to all colleagues in this project for their research, insights, and generosity. Earlier versions were presented at the Annual Meeting of the American Political Science Association, held in Boston, Mass., in 2001, and at the Harvard Government Department Comparative Politics Workshop on 5 October 2005. I am especially grateful to Hillel Soifer for his comments. All mistakes are mine alone.

1. The classic theoretical and comparative analysis is Juan J. Linz, "Totalitarian and Authoritarian Regimes," in *Handbook of Political Science: Macropolitical Theory* (Reading, Mass.: Addison-Wesley, 1975).
2. See David Mares, *Violent Peace: Militarized Interstate Bargaining in Latin America* (New York: Columbia University Press, 2001).
3. Jorge I. Domínguez, *To Make a World Safe for Revolution: Cuba's Foreign Policy* (Cambridge, Mass.: Harvard University Press, 1989), chap. 5.
4. See Meredith Woo-Cumings, ed., *The Developmental State* (Ithaca: Cornell University Press, 1999) and Stephan Haggard and Robert R. Kaufman, *The Political Economy of Democratic Transitions* (Princeton: Princeton University Press, 1995).
5. My task is to assess how authoritarian regimes can be politically effective. I do not endorse such regimes and hope none reappears.
6. S. N. Eisenstadt, *The Political Systems of Empires* (New York: Free Press, 1963).
7. Samuel P. Huntington, *Political Order in Changing Societies* (New Haven: Yale University Press, 1968), 244–245.
8. See Chapter 1 above. On the relatively low level of resistance, see also Chapter 13 above. On organized labor, see Ho Keun Song, "State and Labor under the Park Chung Hee Regime." This paper was prepared for the project that gave rise to this book.
9. See Chapter 6 above.
10. Guillermo O'Donnell, *Bureaucratic Authoritarianism: Argentina, 1966–1973, in Comparative Perspective* (Berkeley: University of California Press, 1988), 39–40.
11. William C. Smith, *Authoritarianism and the Crisis of the Argentine Political Economy* (Stanford: Stanford University Press, 1989), 230–231.
12. David Pion-Berlin, *The Ideology of State Terror: Economic Doctrine and Political Repression in Argentina and Peru* (Boulder: Lynne Rienner, 1989), and Smith, *Authoritarianism*, 231.

13. Thomas Skidmore, *Politics in Brazil, 1930–1964: An Experiment in Democracy* (London: Oxford University Press, 1967), 294–313.

14. Pamela Constable and Arturo Valenzuela, *Chile under Pinochet: A Nation of Enemies* (New York: Norton, 1991), chaps. 1–4, and pp. 297, 310–11; Arturo Valenzuela, *The Breakdown of Democratic Regimes: Chile* (Baltimore: Johns Hopkins University Press, 1978), 55 and *passim*.

15. Thomas Hobbes, *Leviathan,* ed. Michael Oakeshott (New York: Collier, 1962), 100, 132.

16. Robert E. Scott, *Mexican Government in Transition,* rev. ed. (Urbana: University of Illinois Press, 1964), 115–125; Enrique Krauze, *Mexico: Biography of Power,* trans. Hank Heifetz (New York: Harper Collins, 1997), 426–435.

17. See Chapter 7 above.

18. O'Donnell, *Bureaucratic Authoritarianism,* 104, 108, 113.

19. Guillermo A. Calvo, "Fractured Liberalism: Argentina under Martínez de Hoz," *Economic Development and Cultural Change* 34, no. 3 (April 1986): 511–529.

20. Edmar␣I.␣Bacha, "Issues and Evidence on Recent Brazilian Economic Growth," *World Development* 5, nos. 1–2 (1977): 47–64; Albert Fishlow, "Some Reflections on Post-1964 Brazilian Economic Policy," in *Authoritarian Brazil,* ed. Alfred Stepan (New Haven: Yale University Press, 1973).

21. Sebastian Edwards, "Stabilization with Liberalization: An Evaluation of Ten Years of Chile's Experiment with Free-Market Policies, 1973–1983," *Economic Development and Cultural Change* 33 (1985): 223–254.

22. Regarding the successful growth model, see Daniel Levy and Gabriel Székely, *Mexico: Paradoxes of Stability and Change,* 2nd ed. (Boulder: Westview, 1987), chap. 5.

23. For a comparison between the Argentina 1966 and Brazil cases with the Chile and Argentina 1976 cases, see Hector Schamis, "Reconceptualizing Latin American Authoritarianism in the 1970s: From Bureaucratic-Authoritarianism to Neoconservatism," *Comparative Politics* 23 (1991): 201–220. See also David Collier, ed., *The New Authoritarianism in Latin America* (Princeton: Princeton University Press, 1979) for discussion of Argentina, Brazil, and Chile. On Mexico, see Roderic Ai Camp, *Entrepreneurs and the State in Twentieth Century México* (New York: Oxford University Press, 1989) and Dale Story, *Industry, the State, and Public Policy in Mexico* (Austin: University of Texas Press, 1986). For state protection for national manufacturers in Brazil and Mexico to the end of the 1970s, with weaker instances in Argentina and Chile, see Jorge I. Domínguez, "Business Nationalism," in *Economic Issues and Political Conflict: U.S.–Latin American Relations* (London: Butterworth, 1982).

24. Frances Hagopian, *Traditional Politics and Regime Change in Brazil* (Cambridge: Cambridge University Press, 1996), 184–185.

25. Scott Mainwaring, *Rethinking Party Systems in the Third Wave of Democratization: The Case of Brazil* (Stanford: Stanford University Press, 1999), 94–98.

26. See Hoon Jaung, "The Abortive Experiment of Party Politics: The Failure of

the Democratic Republican Party." This paper was prepared for the project that gave rise to this book.

27. See Kim Soo Jin, "A Study of Opposition Parties in the Park Chung Hee Era." This paper was prepared for the project that gave rise to this book.

28. Luciano Martins, "The 'Liberalization' of Authoritarian Rule in Brazil," in *Transitions from Authoritarian Rule: Latin America,* ed. Guillermo O'Donnell, Philippe Schmitter, and Laurence Whitehead (Baltimore: Johns Hopkins University Press, 1986), 83–86.

29. Bolívar Lamounier, "Authoritarian Brazil Revisited: The Impact of Elections on the *Abertura,*" in *Democratizing Brazil,* ed. Alfred Stepan (Oxford: Oxford University Press, 1989), 70.

30. See Chapters 5, 6, 8, and 13 above.

31. Huntington's *Political Order,* published in 1968, scored Mexico and South Korea as comparably successful authoritarian regimes (see p. 261), which at the time they indeed were.

32. For comparative data on torture and political imprisonment, see Jorge I. Domínguez, Nigel Rodley, Bryce Wood, and Richard Falk, *Enhancing Global Human Rights* (New York: McGraw-Hill, 1979), 93–102.

33. Kevin J. Middlebrook, *The Paradox of Revolution: Labor, the State, and Authoritarianism in Mexico* (Baltimore: Johns Hopkins University Press, 1999), 29–30.

34. On Brazilian state corporatism, see Philippe Schmitter, *Interest Conflict and Political Change in Brazil* (Stanford: Stanford University Press, 1971).

35. Margaret Keck, "The New Unionism in the Brazilian Transition," in *Democratizing Brazil,* ed. Alfred Stepan (Oxford: Oxford University Press, 1989).

36. Smith, *Authoritarianism and the Crisis of the Argentine Political Economy,* 231, 263–265, and chap. 6.

37. Manuel Barrera and J. Samuel Valenzuela, "The Development of Labor Movement Opposition to the Military Regime," in *Military Rule in Chile: Dictatorship and Oppositions,* ed. J. Samuel Valenzuela and Arturo Valenzuela (Baltimore: Johns Hopkins University Press, 1986).

38. See Ho Keun Song, "State and Labor under the Park Chung Hee Regime." This paper was prepared for the project that gave rise to this book.

39. Wayne A. Cornelius, *Mexican Politics in Transition: The Breakdown of a One-Party-Dominant Regime,* Monograph Series no. 41 (La Jolla: Center for U.S.-Mexican Studies, University of California-San Diego, 1996), 89–98; Roderic Ai Camp, *Politics in Mexico: The Decline of Authoritarianism,* 3d ed. (New York: Oxford University Press, 1999), chaps. 3 and 8.

40. Camp, *Politics in Mexico,* chap. 6; Cornelius, *Mexican Politics in Transition,* 51–56.

41. Ian Roxborough, "Inflation and Social Pacts in Brazil and Mexico," *Journal of Latin American Studies* 24 (October 1992): 639–664.

42. O'Donnell, *Bureaucratic Authoritarianism,* 51–61; Pion-Berlin, *The Ideology of State Terror,* 97–101; Skidmore, *Politics in Brazil,* 304, 314; Constable and Valenzuela, *Chile under Pinochet,* 62–63.

43. Linz, "Totalitarian and Authoritarian Regimes," 267.

44. Constable and Valenzuela, *Chile under Pinochet,* 161–162.

45. Carlos Acuña, "Business Interests, Dictatorship, and Democracy in Argentina," and Blanca Heredia, "Mexican Business and the State," both in *Business and Democracy in Latin America,* ed. Ernest Bartell and Leigh Payne (Pittsburgh: University of Pittsburgh Press, 1995).

46. Leigh A. Payne, *Brazilian Industrialists and Democratic Change* (Baltimore: Johns Hopkins University Press, 1994).

47. See Chapters 4, 12, and 13 above. Also see Seung-mi Han, "The New Community Movement (Samaŭl Undong) and the Formation of State Populism: An Analysis of the Ethos of Development Project in Korea." This paper was prepared for the project that gave rise to this book.

48. See Chapters 7, 9, 10, and 11 above. See also Mah In-Sub, "Rule by Emergency Powers." This paper was prepared for the project that gave rise to this book.

49. Naciones Unidas, Comisión Económica para América Latina y el Caribe, *Balance preliminar de las economías de América Latina y el Caribe* (Santiago, Chile: Naciones Unidas, 2001), 86.

50. Quotation from Jorge Chabat, "Mexico's Foreign Policy in 1990: Electoral Sovereignty and Integration with the United States," *Journal of Interamerican Studies and World Affairs* 33, no. 4 (Winter 1991): 12.

21. Industrial Policy in Key Developmental Sectors: South Korea versus Japan and Taiwan

1. Hyug Baeg Im, "The Rise of Bureaucratic Authoritarianism in South Korea," *World Politics* 39, no. 2 (January 1987), 231–257; see also Chapter 8 above.

2. Chalmers Johnson, "Political Institutions and Economic Performance: The Government-Business Relationship in Japan, South Korea, and Taiwan," and Bruce Cumings, "The Origins and Development of the Northeast Asian Political Economy: Industrial Sectors, Product Cycles, and Political Consequences," both in *The Political Economy of the New Asian Industrialism*, ed. Frederic C. Deyo (Ithaca: Cornell University Press, 1987), 136–164 and 44–83; Robert Wade, *Governing the Market: Economic Theory and the Role of Government in East Asian Industrialization* (Princeton: Princeton University Press, 1990); World Bank, *The East Asian Miracle* (New York: Oxford University Press, 1993).

3. Council on Economic Planning and Development, *Taiwan Statistical Data Book, 1998* (Taipei: CEPD, 1998); National Statistical Office, *Major Statistics of Korean Economy, 1997.3* (Seoul: National Statistical Office, 1997).

4. Tun-jen Cheng, "Political Regimes and Development Strategies: South Korea and Taiwan," in *Manufacturing Miracles,* ed. Gary Gereffi and Donald L. Wyman (Princeton: Princeton University Press, 1990), 139–178; Byung-Nak Song, *The Rise of the Korean Economy,* 2nd ed. (New York: Oxford University Press, 1997).

5. Kozo Yamamura and Yasukichi Yasuba, eds., *The Political Economy of Japan,* vol. 1, *The Domestic Transformation* (Stanford: Stanford University Press, 1987); Fujimoto Takahiro, *Nōryoku kōchiku Kyōsō: Nihon no Jidōsha Sangyō wa Naze Tsuyoi no ka* [Competition on the Basis of Constructing Ca-

pabilities: Why the Japanese Auto Industry Is Strong] (Tokyo: Chūō Kōron Sha, 2003), esp. chap. 3, pp. 61–110.

6. Wade, *Governing the Market;* Alice H. Amsden and Chu Wan-wen, *Beyond Late Development: Taiwan's Upgrading Policies* (Cambridge: MIT Press, 2003).

7. Through the Park era, the proportion of national investment going to the public sector was not much lower in Korea than in Taiwan. Wade, *Governing the Market,* 176–178.

8. Alice H. Amsden, *Asia's Next Giant: South Korea and Late Industrialization* (New York: Oxford University Press, 1989), 291–314; Ha-Joon Chang, *The Political Economy of Industrial Policy* (New York: St. Martin's Press, 1994), esp. chap. 4; Linsu Kim, *Imitation to Innovation: The Dynamics of Korea's Technological Learning* (Boston: Harvard Business School Press, 1997).

9. Changrok Soh, *From Investment to Innovation? The Korean Political Economy and Changes in Industrial Competitiveness* (Seoul: Global Research Institute, Korea University, 1997); Mark L. Clifford, *Troubled Tiger: Businessmen, Bureaucrats, and Generals in South Korea* (Armonk, N.Y.: M. E. Sharpe, 1994).

10. Eun Mee Kim, *Big Business, Strong State* (Albany: State University of New York Press, 1997).

11. Amsden, *Asia's Next Giant,* 291; Soh, *From Investment to Innovation?,* 168–170.

12. Standard accounts of the development of the Japanese steel industry are Iida Ken'ichi, Ōhashi Shūji, and Kuroiwa Toshiro, eds., *Tekkō* [Steel] (Tokyo: Gendai Nihon Sangyō Hattatsushi Kenkyūkai, 1969); Tsūsho Sangyōshō, *Shōkō Seisakushi, Dai 17 Kan, Tekkōgyō* [A History of Commercial and Industrial Policy, vol. 17, The Iron and Steel Industry] (Tokyo: Shōkō Seisaku Kankōkai, 1970); Seiichiro Yonekura, *The Japanese Iron and Steel Industry, 1850–1990* (New York: St. Martin's, 1994).

13. Kent E. Calder, *Strategic Capitalism* (Princeton: Princeton University Press, 1993), 183–195.

14. Yonekura, *Japanese Iron and Steel Industry,* 226.

15. Leonard H. Lynn, *How Japan Innovates: A Comparison with the U.S. in the Case of Oxygen Steel Making* (Boulder: Westview, 1982).

16. Taiwanqu Gangtie Tongye Gonghui (TISIA), *Taiwan Gangtie 20 Nian* [Twenty Years of the Taiwan Iron and Steel Industry] (Taipei: Taiwanqu Gangtie Tongye Gonghui, 1983), 503–532; Diao Ping and Yao Shifu, eds., *Shida Jianshe yu Guojia Qiantu* [The Ten Major Construction Projects and the Future of the Country] (Taipei: Ganjiang Chubanshe [1975]).

17. Jingjiren Bianji Weiyuanhui, ed., *Caijing Juece Qiangren* [Strong Men of Economic and Financial Decision Making] (Taipei: Jingjiren Zazhishe, 1984), 22; Liu Yuzhen, *Tietou Fengyun: Zhao Yaodong Chuanqi* [Ironhead: The Story of Zhao Yaodong] (Taipei: Lianjing Chuban, 1995).

18. Caixun Zazhishe, ed., *Toushi Caijing Renmai* [A Penetrating View of Human Networks in Finance and Economics] (Taipei: Caixun Zazhishe, 1986), 142–163.

19. Gregory W. Noble, *Collective Action in East Asia: How Ruling Parties Shape Industrial Policy* (Ithaca: Cornell University Press, 1998), 90.

20. Amsden, *Asia's Next Giant*, 293–295. Wade notes, however, that Korea made use of many other state-owned enterprises, including Korea Electric Power and Korea Telecom.

21. See Chapter 11 above.

22. Joseph J. Innace and Abby Dress, *Igniting Steel: Korea's POSCO Lights the Way* (Huntington, N.Y.: Global Village Press, 1992), 14.

23. Ibid., 33.

24. Clifford, *Troubled Tiger*, 4, 68–75; Innace and Dress, *Igniting Steel*.

25. Nagano Shin'ichirō, "Sōgō izon no Kannichi kankei: hokō sōgō seitetsujo setsuritsu to paku te jun no yakuwari" (Interdependent Korean-Japanese relations: The establishment of the Pohang integrated steel mill and the role of Pak Tae-joon), *Tōyō Keizai Nippō*, April 24, 2009. http://www.toyo-keizai.co.jp/news/opinion/2009/post_902.php.

26. Amsden, *Asia's Next Giant*, 295n1. On textiles, personal communication from Byung-Kook Kim.

27. Innace and Dress, *Igniting Steel*, 39–46.

28. Ibid., 63–103.

29. Amsden, *Asia's Next Giant*, 297, 302; Soh, *From Investment to Innovation?*, 172–173.

30. Amsden, *Asia's Next Giant*, 306–309; Innace and Dress, *Igniting Steel*, 135–137.

31. Amsden, *Asia's Next Giant*, 297; Innace and Dress, *Igniting Steel*, p. 2, emphasizes that POSCO never lost money even during downturns in the cyclical steel business, but the data at pp. 248–249 show that POSCO's rate of return was very thin.

32. Amsden, *Asia's Next Giant*, 301.

33. Clifford, *Troubled Tiger*, 312.

34. Noble, *Collective Action*, 167, 235.

35. *Korea Times*, March 25, 2008; *Korea Herald*, January 6, 2010.

36. Ira C. Magaziner and Thomas M. Hout, *Japanese Industrial Policy* (London: Policy Studies Institute, 1980).

37. Calder, *Strategic Capitalism*.

38. John Jay Tate, *Driving Production Innovation Home: Guardian State Capitalism and the Competitiveness of the Japanese Automobile Industry* (Berkeley: BRIE, 1995).

39. Calder, *Strategic Capitalism*, 178–182.

40. Winified Ruigrok and John Jay Tate, "Public Testing and Research Centres in Japan: Control and Nurturing of Small and Medium-Sized Enterprises in the Automobile Industry," *Technology Analysis and Strategic Management* 8, no. 4 (December 1996): 381–406; David Friedman, *The Misunderstood Miracle: Industrial Development and Political Change in Japan* (Ithaca: Cornell University Press, 1988).

41. Sumimaru Odano and Saiful Islam, "Industrial Development and the Guidance Policy Finance: The Case of the Japanese Automobile Industry," *Asian*

Economic Journal 8, no. 3 (1994): 285–315. Calder, *Strategic Capitalism,* emphasizes that the Industrial Bank of Japan, rather than government banks, was the crucial early source of financing for auto firms, but he also demonstrates that IBJ was deeply influenced by MITI and the Ministry of Finance.

42. Yun-han Chu, "The State and the Development of the Automobile Industry in South Korea and Taiwan," in *The Role of the State in Taiwan's Development,* ed. Joel D. Aberbach, David Dollar, and Kenneth L. Sokoloff (Armonk, N.Y.: M. E. Sharpe, 1994), 125–169; Walter Arnold, "Bureaucratic Politics, State Capacity, and Taiwan's Automobile Industry Policy," *Modern China* 15, no. 2 (April 1989): 178–214; Jingjibu Jishuchu, *1999 Qi, Ji, Zixingche Chanye Xiankuang yu Qushi Fenxi* [An Analysis of Current Conditions and Trends in the Automobile, Motorcycle and Bicycle Industries, 1999] (Xinzhu: Gongye Jishu Yanjiuyuan Jijie Gongye Yanjiusuo, 1999).

43. Gregory W. Noble, "Trojan Horse and Boomerang: Two-Tiered Investment in the Asian Auto Complex," Berkeley Roundtable on the International Economy Working Paper, December 1996.

44. Zhanghua Shangye Yinhang Zhengxinshi, ed., *Taiwan Qiche Gongye zhi Xiankuang yu Zhanwang* (7) [The Taiwan Automobile Industry: Current Conditions and Future Prospects (7)] (Taipei: Zhanghua Shangye Yinhang Zhengxinshi, 1985).

45. Noble, "Trojan Horse."

46. Edward Cunningham, Teresa Lynch, and Eric Thun, "A Tale of Two Sectors: Diverging Paths in Taiwan's Automotive Industry," in *Global Taiwan: Building Competitive Strengths in a New International Economy,* ed. Suzanne Berger and Richard K. Lester (Armonk, N.Y.: M. E. Sharpe, 2005).

47. Chapter 10 above; Amsden, *Asia's Next Giant;* Michael McDermott, "The Development and Internationalization of the South Korean Motor Industry: The European Dimension," *Asia Pacific Business Review* 2, no. 2 (Winter 1995): 23–47; Myung-oc Woo, "Export Promotion in the New Global Division of Labor: The Case of the South Korean Automobile Industry," *Sociological Perspectives* 36, no. 4 (1993): 335–357; Richard F. Doner, "Limits of State Strength: Toward an Institutionalist View of Economic Development," *World Politics* 44, no. 3 (April 1992): 398–431; Clifford, *Troubled Tiger,* 253–262; Maruyama Yoshinari, ed., *Ajia no Jidōsha Sangyō,* rev. ed. [The Asian Automobile Industry] (Tokyo: Aki Shobō, 1997).

48. Chapter 10 above.

49. Clifford, *Troubled Tiger,* 254.

50. Chapter 9 above.

51. Donald Kirk, *Korean Dynasty: Hyundai and Chung Ju Yung* (Armonk, N.Y.: M. E. Sharpe, 1994), 124–136.

52. Chapter 10 above.

53. Unless otherwise stated, all figures on auto production in Korea are from McDermott, "Development and Internationalization," 29–30, and for Taiwan from Zhanghua Shangye Yinhang Zhengxinshi, ed., *Taiwan Qiche Gongye,* 11. Differing definitions of light trucks and ways of compiling statistics preclude exact comparison, but the figures given in the text are fairly comparable.

54. McDermott, "Development and Internationalization," 26.
55. Chapter 10 above.
56. Quoted in Clifford, *Troubled Tiger*, 256.
57. Amsden, *Asia's Next Giant*, 132.
58. Clifford, *Troubled Tiger*, 256–261.
59. McDermott, "Development and Internationalization," 29; Maruyama, *Ajia no Jidōsha Sangyō*, 118–119.
60. Maruyama, *Ajia no Jidōsha Sangyō*, 111–120.
61. Amsden, *Asia's Next Giant*, 175–176. Amsden may overstate Hyundai's independence. Four-fifths of Hyundai's license fees went to Mitsubishi Motors. Clifford, *Troubled Tiger*, 262n15.
62. Maruyama, *Ajia no Jidōsha Sangyō*, 132.
63. Doner, "Limits of State Strength," 410–411.
64. Amsden, *Asia's Next Giant*, 179–188; Maruyama, *Ajia no Jidōsha Sangyō* 121–134; McDermott, "Development and Internationalization," 41–45.
65. Maruyama, *Ajia no Jidōsha Sangyō*, 140–141.
66. McDermott, "Development and Internationalization," 33.
67. Noble, *Collective Action*.
68. Although most Korean exports came from large companies, the number of small companies relative to GDP and the proportion of workers employed in small companies were nearly as high as in Japan and Taiwan. It is true that the share of very large enterprises was somewhat larger than in Japan or Taiwan, but the average number of employees per firm was slightly smaller in Korea (14) than in Japan (16). Korea lacked not small firms but medium-sized ones. Song, *Rise of the Korean Economy*, 111–114.
69. Noble, *Collective Action*.
70. Amsden, *Asia's Next Giant*.
71. Gregory W. Noble and John Ravenhill, "The Good, the Bad and the Ugly? Korea, Taiwan and the Asian Financial Crisis," in *The Asian Financial Crisis and the Structure of Global Finance*, ed. Noble and Ravenhill (Cambridge: Cambridge University Press, 2000).
72. Clifford, *Troubled Tiger*; Soh, *From Investment to Innovation?*

Conclusion

1. O Wŏn-ch'ŏl, *Han'gukhyŏng kyŏngje kŏnsŏl: enjiniŏring ŏp'ŭroch'i* 3 [Korean-Style Economic Development: An Engineering Approach], vol. 3 (Seoul: Kia kyŏngje yŏn'guso, 1995), 167.
2. The quotation is from Cho Kap-che's biography of Park Chung Hee, *Nae mudŏm-e ch'im-ŭl paet-ŏra* [Spit on my grave], vols. 1–5 (Seoul: Chosun Ilbosa, 1999), and vols. 6–8 (Seoul: Chosun Ilbosa, 2001).
3. Yung Chul Park and Dong Won Kim, "Korea: Development and Structural Change of the Banking System," in *The Financial Development of Japan, Korea, and Taiwan: Growth, Repression, and Liberalization*, ed. Hugh T. Patrick and Yung Chul Park (New York: Oxford University Press, 1994), 214.
4. Tibor Scitovsky, "Economic Development in Taiwan and South Korea," in

Models of Development: A Comparative Study of Economic Growth in South Korea and Taiwan, ed. Lawrence J. Lau (San Francisco: ICS Press, 1990), 165.

5. Gerardo R. Ungson, Richard M. Steers, and Seung-Ho Park, *Korean Enterprise: The Quest for Globalization* (Cambridge, Mass.: Harvard Business School Press, 1997), 23–81.

6. See Chapter 7 above for an analysis of Park's regulatory policy.

7. Bella Balassa and John Williamson, *Adjusting to Success: Balance of Payments Policy in the East Asian NICs* (Washington, D.C.: Institute for International Economics, 1987).

8. Ibid. The state generously rescheduled and even wrote off 74 percent of the nonperforming loans, a large part of which were financed through three trillion won in special assistance from the central bank. See Yung Chul Park and Dong Won Kim, "Korea: Development and Structural Change of the Banking System," 209.

9. *Dong-A Ilbo,* August 22, 1984; and December 16, 1986.

10. Robert E. Bedeski, *The Transformation of South Korea: Reform and Reconstruction in the Sixth Republic under Roh Tae Woo, 1987–1992* (Seoul: Routledge, 1994), 86–88.

11. *Dong-A Ilbo,* May 9, 1990.

12. *Dong-A Ilbo,* September 27, 1980.

13. *Joongang Ilbo,* July 24, August 6, and October 28, 1991.

14. *Chosun Ilbo,* September 20, 1991; and *Dong-A Ilbo,* August 3, October 10, and October 21, 1992.

15. The Ministry of Industry, Trade and Resources (MTIR), "Taegyumo kiŏp chipdanŭi ŏpjong jŏnmunhwa yudo pang'an (A measure to induce sectoral specialization of large-scale business groups)," May 1993.

16. Financial Team, Korea Development Institute, *1998nyŏn kŭmyung pumun jŏngch'aek yŏn'gu charyo moŭmjip* [A collection of policy study materials on the financial sector in 1998] (Seoul: Korea Development Institute, 1999), 3–14.

17. International Monetary Fund (IMF), "Republic of Korea: Economic and Policy Developments," IMF Staff Country Report No. 00–11 (February 2000), 96, 99–101.

18. *Han'gyorae sinmun,* August 16, August 26, and November 1, 1999; August 13 and August 24, 2000; and May 20 and July 9, 2001. See also Dong Gull Lee, "The Restructuring of Daewoo," in Haggard, Lim, and Kim, eds., *Economic Crisis and Corporate Restructuring in Korea* (Cambridge: Cambridge University Press, 2003), 150–177.

19. Korea Chamber of Commerce, "Giŏp yuboyul hyŏnhwang'gwa sisajŏm" [The current situation of corporate retained earnings and its implications], July 4, 2007.

20. Son Uk and Yi Sang-je, "Gŭmyung sŏbisŭ sŏnjinhwarŭl wihan kwaje" [Policy issues for the advancement of the financial service sector] in Kim Ju-hun and Ch'a Mun-jung, eds., *Sŏbisŭ bumun-ŭi sŏnjinhwa-rŭl wihan chŏngch'aek kwaje* [The policy agendas for advancing the service sector], Policy Paper 07–04, Korea Development Institute (2007), 288, 293–297, 300.

21. For data, see Yang Sŏng-ch'ŏl, *Han'guk chŏngburon: yŏkdae chŏnggwŏn*

kowijik haengjŏng elitŭ yŏn'gu, 1948–1993 [A Theory of the Korean State: Analysis of Its High-Ranking Executive Elite, 1948–1993] (Seoul: Pakyŏngsa, 1994).

22. The list of *chaebol* groups was compiled by Eun-Mi Kim and Gil-Sung Park. See Chapter 9.

23. The smaller regions of Kangwŏn, Ch'ungch'ŏng, and Seoul each produced two top-ten *chaebol* at one time or another after 1972, while Kyŏnggi Province belatedly had its share of power and glory in 1979 with Ch'oe Chonghyŏn's highly successful SK Group.

24. The other industrial complexes were built in Kyŏnggi-Inch'on (1966), Kuro (1967), Kumi (1967), P'ohang (1973), Masan (1969), Yŏch'ŏn-Kwangyang (1973), and Ch'angwŏn(1973).

25. The Korea Industrial Complex Corp.

26. Michael Borrus, Dieter Ernst, and Stephan Haggard, *International Production Networks in Asia: Rivalry or Riches?* (London: Routledge, 2000); and Gary Gereffi and Michael Korzeniewicz, eds., *Commodity Chains and Global Capitalism* (New York: Praeger, 1994).

27. *Dong-A Ilbo*, September 10, 1979.

28. *New York Times*, September 16, 1979. Also see *Dong-A Ilbo*, September 19, 1979.

29. *Dong-A Ilbo*, October 4 and 6, 1979.

30. Cho Kap-che, *Yugo!* [The death of Park!] (Seoul: Han'gilsa, 1987), 1:242–319, 2:5–111.

31. *Dong-A Ilbo*, December 13, 1978.

32. See Byung-Kook Kim, "Electoral Politics and Economic Crisis, 1997–1998," in Larry Diamond and Kim, eds., *Consolidating Democracy in South Korea* (Boulder: Lynne Rienner, 2000), 181.

33. See Angelo Panebianco, *Political Parties: Organization and Power* (Cambridge: Cambridge University Press, 1988), 3–32.

34. Consult Pak Pyŏng-sŏk, "Chŏngch'i piri" [Political corruption], in Im Chŏngch'ŏl et al., *Han'guk sahoe-ŭi piri* [Corruption in Korean society] (Seoul: Seoul National University Press, 1994), 5–36, for an analysis of political corruption.

35. Consult former Democratic Republican Party chairman Chŏng Ku-yŏng's *Chŏng Ku-yŏng hoegorok: silp'aehan tojŏn* [The recollections of Chŏng Ku-yŏng: The failed challenge] (Seoul: JoongAng Ilbosa, 1987), 264.

36. *Dong-A Ilbo*, October 5, 1971.

37. See Kim Dae-jung napch'i sagŏn-ui chinsang kyumyŏng-ŭl wihan simin-ŭi moim [the Citizens' Forum to Find the Truth about the Kidnapping of Kim Dae-jung], *Kim Dae-jung napch'i sagŏn chinsang* [The True Story behind the Kidnapping of Kim Dae-jung] (Seoul: P'urŭn namu, 1995).

38. See Kim Ch'ung-sik, *Namsan-ŭi pujangdŭl* [The KCIA Directors] (Seoul: Dong-A Ilbosa, 1992), 2:280–281.

39. Juan J. Linz defines authoritarian regimes as "political systems with limited, not responsible, political pluralism, without elaborate and guiding ideology, but with distinctive mentalities, without extensive nor intensive political mobilization, except at some points in their development, and in which a leader

or occasionally a small group exercises power within formally ill-defined limits but actually quite predictable ones." See Linz, "An Authoritarian Regime: The Case of Spain," in Erik Allardt and Stein Rokkan, eds., *Mass Politics: Studies in Political Sociology* (New Press, 1970), 255.

40. See *Dong-A Ilbo*, July 8, 11–15, and 17, 1967.

41. *Dong-A Ilbo*, July 7 and 8, 1974.

42. *Dong-A Ilbo*, April 10, 1975.

43. Han'guk kidokkyo kyohoe hyŏpŭihoe [Korean Council of Christian Churches], *1970nyŏndae minjuhwa undong: kidokkyo undongŭl chungsimŭro I-V* [Democratization Movements of the 1970s: A Focus on Christian Movements, vols. 1–5] (Seoul: Korean Council of Christian Churches, 1987).

44. Consult former KCIA director Kim Hyŏng-uk's autobiography, Kim Hyŏng-uk and Pak Sa-wŏl, *Kim Hyŏng-uk hoegorok 2: Han'guk chungang chŏngbobu* [The recollections of Kim Hyŏng-uk, vol. 2, The Korea Central Intelligence Agency] (Seoul: Ach'im, 1985), 119.

45. Interview with Chŏng So-yŏng, who served as a secretary for macroeconomic policy with jurisdiction over the Economic Planning Board and the Ministry of Finance at Park's Blue House between 1963 and 1969 after assisting Park as an advisor during his military junta years.

46. See Kim Hyŏng-uk and Pak Sa-wŏl, *Kim Hyŏng-uk hoegorok 2* [The recollections of Kim Hyŏng-uk vol. 2], 13–15, 119–128, 231–240, and 273–314; and Cho Kap-che, *Nae mudŏm-e ch'im-ŭl paetŏra 6: maengho-nŭn kanda* [Spit on My Grave, vol. 6: The Tiger Corps Is Going to Vietnam] (Seoul: Chosun Ilbosa, 1999), 144–150.

47. See Chŏng Ku-yŏng, *Chŏng Ku-yŏng hoegorok: Silp'aehan tochŏn* [The recollections of Chŏng Ku-yŏng: The failed challenge], for his complex personal relationship with Park.

48. See Cho Kap-che, *Yugo!* [The Death of Park!], vols. 1 and 2; and Kim Youngsam, *Kim Young-sam Hoegorok 2: minjujuŭi-rŭl wihan na-ŭi t'ujaeng* [The recollections of Kim Young-sam, vol. 2: My struggle for democracy] (Seoul: Paeksan sŏdang, 2000), 106, 153–156.

49. See Cho Kap-che, *Yugo!* [The Death of Park!], 2:237–242, for the full text of Kim Chae-gyu's last testimony.

50. Chung-in Moon, "Changing Patterns of Business-Government Relations in South Korea," in *Business and Government in Industrializing Asia,* ed. Andrew MacIntyre (Ithaca: Cornell University Press, 1994), 142, 145; and Eun Mee Kim, *Big Business, Strong State: Collusion and Conflict in South Korean Development, 1960–1990* (Albany: State University of New York, 1997), 167–211.

51. The 386 Generation refers to South Korea's radical political activists. The number "3" refers to their age (30~39 years old, as of 2000), the number "8" to their years of college entrance (1980~1989), and the number "6" to their decade of birth (1961~1970).

52. Consult Cho Hŭi-yŏn, "Sahoe kusŏngch'e nonjaengŭi pansŏnggwa 90nyŏndae nonjaeng-ŭi ch'ulbaljŏm" [A critical review of ideological polemics on social community and a new beginning of debates for the 1990s], *Wŏlgan Sahoe P'yŏngron,* vol. 11, December 1992, 187.

Acknowledgments

This volume was conceived over a decade ago and grows out of an awareness by many scholars, Korean and Western, of how important Park Chung Hee and his modernization era were and how difficult it has been to get an objective scholarly evaluation about both. Park seized power by staging a military coup and he derailed South Korea's early efforts to build up a democratic polity. The Park era was so thoroughly criticized by many intellectuals that it has not been easy to get the distance to write an objective integrated history of its accomplishments and limitations. We believe this is the first volume to fill this gap in our knowledge.

Byung-Kook Kim conceived the project, brought in South Korean authors, raised the funds, organized seminars in Seoul and Boston for critical review, carried out a detailed editing of each paper to give it tighter integration throughout our four rounds of intensive editing, and wrote four chapters. This is really his book. Ezra F. Vogel was responsible for selecting Western participants, editing their chapters, and keeping the project on track.

For a variety of reasons, this book has required a longer gestation period than most edited volumes. We are thankful to the authors for their patience and for their willingness to adapt their writings to provide an integrated overview of the Park era. The publication in the end was timed for the fiftieth anniversary of the beginning of Park Chung Hee's politics of nation building.

Over the decade of editing this book, we have become indebted to many people. We would like to thank Arthur J. Choy, Seok Hyun Hong, Thomas C. Kang, Byung-Kook Kim, Byung-Pyo Kim, Sang Woo Kim, Jae-Kwan Lee, Min-Kyo Lee, Sang-Hoon Lee, Woong Yeul Lee, and Hyun Park for generous funding. We are greatly indebted to the analytic feedback of Charles Armstrong, Ed Baker, Victor

D. Cha, Chang Jip Choi, Yoon-Jae Chung, Young-Sun Ha, Stephen Haggard, Sung-han Kim, Chae-Jin Lee, Seok-soo Lee, David McCann, David Steinberg, Byung-Hoon Suh, Jin-Young Suh, and Meredith Woo-Cumings during the initial stage in our project. We are grateful to Jung-Hoon Lee, Jongrin Mo, and especially Chaibong Hahm, for valuable assistance in editing some of our chapters in 2003. Moreover, we were able to conclude this project only because of generous support from two institutions: the East Asia Institute, based in Seoul, and the Asia Center, Harvard University, housed in Cambridge. We are grateful to the chairman of the East Asia Institute, Hong Koo Lee, for his personal interest and inspiration. We also thank Jin-seok Bae, Hwee-seon Kim, Seung-Chae Kim, and So Yeong Park at the East Asia Institute for administrative support.

Two people, in particular, deserve our gratitude. Elizabeth Gilbert has been very patient and diligent in turning the chapters written by our South Korean scholars into articles accessible to a Western audience in natural idiomatic English, and has done an extraordinary job in pulling this together as a single volume. Without her skillful efforts over several years, this volume would never have been completed. We are also grateful to Ha-jeong Kim for her immensely valuable coordination of our project since it was launched over a decade ago, and for her supervision of much of the final checking and the creation of the Index of Persons.

Contributors

Chang Jae Baik, Professor of Political Science, Seoul National University

Jorge I. Domínguez, Professor of Government and Vice Provost for International Affairs in the Office of the Provost, Harvard University

Yong-Sup Han, Professor of Korea National Defense University

Sung Gul Hong, Professor of Public Administration, Kookmin University

Paul D. Hutchcroft, Professor, Department of Political and Social Change, and Director, School of International, Political, and Strategic Studies, College of Asia and the Pacific, The Australian National University

Hyug Baeg Im, Professor of Political Science and International Relations, Korea University

Byung-joon Jun holds a master's degree in political science from Yonsei University and currently works for SK Telecom

Byung-Kook Kim, Professor of Political Science and International Relations, Korea University

Eun Mee Kim, Professor, Graduate School of International Studies, Ewha Womans University

Hyung-A Kim, Professor of Pacific and Asian Studies, Australian National University

Joo-Hong Kim, Professor of Political Science and International Relations, University of Ulsan

Taehyun Kim, Professor, Graduate School of International Studies, Chung-Ang University

Yong-Jick Kim, Professor of Political Science and International Affairs, Sungshin University, and standing commissioner, Truth and Reconciliation Committee, Republic of Korea

Jung-Hoon Lee, Professor of International Relations, Graduate School of International Studies, Yonsei University

Min Yong Lee, Professor of Security Studies and Management, Korea Military Academy

Nae-Young Lee, Professor of Political Science and International Relations, Korea University

Young Jo Lee, Professor of Political Science, Graduate School of International Studies, Kyung Hee University

Seok-jin Lew, Professor of Political Science, Sogang University

Chung-in Moon, Professor of Political Science, Yonsei University

Gregory W. Noble, Professor of Politics and Administration, Institution of Social Science, University of Tokyo

Gil-Sung Park, Professor of Sociology, Korea University

Myung-Lim Park, Professor of Regional Studies, Yonsei University

Sang-young Rhyu, Professor, Graduate School of International Studies, Yonsei University

Ezra F. Vogel, Henry Ford II Research Professor Emeritus, Harvard University

Index